Case Studies in Finance
Managing for Corporate Value Creation

Second Edition

Robert F. Bruner
Darden Graduate School of Business
University of Virginia

IRWIN

Burr Ridge, Illinois
Boston, Massachusetts
Sydney, Australia

© RICHARD D. IRWIN, INC., 1990 and 1994

Publisher:	Michael W. Junior
Senior sponsoring editor:	James M. Keefe
Marketing manager:	Ron Bloecher
Project editor:	Ethel Shiell
Production manager:	Laurie Kersch
Cover designer:	Stuart Patterson
Art coordinator:	Heather Burbridge
Compositor:	Graphic World, Inc.
Typeface:	10/12 Times Roman
Printer:	R. R. Donnelley & Sons Company

Library of Congress Cataloging-in-Publication Data

Bruner, Robert F.
   Case studies in finance : managing for corporate value creation /
by Robert F. Bruner. — 2nd ed.
       p.   cm. — (The Irwin series in finance)
   ISBN 0-256-09464-0
   1. Corporations — Finance — Case studies.   2. International business enterprises — Finance — Case studies.   3. Management — Decision making--Case studies.   4. Women executives.   I. Title.   II. Series.
HG4015.5.B78   1993
658.15 — dc20   93–8383

THE IRWIN SERIES IN FINANCE

In Dedication to My Father,

Henry Pfeiffer Bruner

Ah, but a man's reach should exceed his grasp,
Or what's a heaven for?
. . .
Well, I fancy how he did it all,
Pouring his soul, with kings and popes to see,
Reaching, that heaven might so replenish him,
Above and through his art . . .

(Robert Browning, "Andrea del Sarto")

About the Author

Robert F. Bruner is presently Robert F. Vandell Research Professor of Business Administration at the Darden Graduate School of Business, University of Virginia. Published in such journals as *Financial Management, Journal of Accounting and Economics, Journal of Applied Corporate Finance, Journal of Financial Economics, Journal of Financial and Quantitative Analysis,* and *Journal of Money, Credit, and Banking,* his research has dealt mainly with mergers, restructurings, and corporate financing policies. Four graduating classes of Darden MBA students have recognized him for excellence in case teaching, as did a graduating class at INSEAD during a year's visit there. He was twice the recipient of *The First Wachovia Award for Faculty Excellence* in case writing. He has consulted for various industrial corporations and financial institutions.

Foreword to the Second Edition

by John W. Rosenblum
Dean, Darden Graduate Business School
University of Virginia

In recent years, several studies and reports have challenged management educators to adapt more promptly to the changing world. The environment of business has become global. Political and technological changes have created global financial markets. The work force at all levels increasingly reflects the cultural and demographic diversity of the national and world societies. Increased entry and success of women and minorities in management has changed the profile of decision makers. Technological change and complexity have become permanent attributes of managerial life. Individuals and organizations must continually learn new knowledge, skills, and attitudes.

The implications of these realities for students and faculty are inescapable. Significant investment is, and will continue to be, required in the development of new learning materials and methods. The problems and opportunities facing finance practitioners in the 1990s, for example, are different from those that preoccupied us in the 1980s.

With *Case Studies in Finance: Managing for Corporate Value Creation*, Professor Robert Bruner has responded to these pedagogic challenges in a way that will set the standard for efforts to come. Not satisfied to make minor modifications to the very successful first edition, Bob Bruner presents in this second edition 33 new field-based cases, many of which explore international financial issues and have women as the key decision makers. The statistics are impressive: 64 percent new material, 50 percent of the cases with an international setting or problem focus, and 33 percent with women decision makers.

The casebook has another important and less obvious attribute. It has been created by a master teacher. The cases are crafted in a way that engages faculty and students in exciting explorations of real business situations. Classroom discussions and management simulations based on these studies bring financial decision making alive. Reactions of Darden School faculty and students to this curriculum have been overwhelmingly positive.

My Darden colleagues and I are proud of Bob Bruner's accomplishments. We share his commitment to the creation of field-based, decision-oriented case material. We value his skills as a curriculum designer and leader of classroom discussions. We are pleased to have been able to support his efforts so that faculty and students around the world also can benefit from his energy and insights.

February 1993

Foreword to the First Edition

by John H. McArthur,
Dean, Harvard Business School

One should never declare oneself to be "objective" regarding the work of a former student. Let us admit a truth: The teacher's natural tendency is to lay claim to any flashes of genius in the student's later intellectual life—and, just as naturally, to deny responsibility for any shortcomings or disappointments over the course of that same life.

In that spirit, I'm happy to take fully vicarious responsibility for *Case Studies in Finance: Managing for Corporate Value Creation*. In the early 1970s, Robert F. Bruner was a student and a friend of mine in the MBA Program at the Harvard Business School, where he subsequently earned his doctorate. As he immersed himself ever more deeply in the rich and strange world that is corporate finance, Bob soon evidenced the mix of personal qualities that would come to serve him well: tenacity, patience, skepticism, iconoclasm, and good will.

These same qualities have directed the research behind the following cases. The case materials are, at once, rigorous and engaging. They meet the essential criteria for good cases—that is, they convey complexity without confusion; they initiate the questioning process, rather than end it; they convey multiple perspectives with clarity and force.

Collectively these cases describe a world greatly changed from the one that Bob first began to analyze in the 1970s. In the last decade and a half, we have had to invent an entirely new vocabulary just to keep up with the amazing changes in corporate finance and the world economy. Fifteen years ago, how many of us could have defined leveraged buyouts, swaps, floating-rate notes, convertible Eurobonds, exchangeable preferreds, junk bonds, currency-linked bonds, zero-coupon bonds, and the like.

For two reasons, therefore, those of us in business education are fortunate indeed to have a researcher of Bob Bruner's caliber involved in substantive and systematic case research. First, his efforts help explain our field to ourselves. More important, they provide a key point of entry for tomorrow's business practitioners. Finance (like all other fields of inquiry in business) can and must be brought to life for managers-in-training, and case research and teaching are absolutely vital tools in that effort. These tools must be kept sharp and up to date. Happily, *Case Studies in Finance* is both well honed and bracingly contemporary.

December 1989

Contents

PART III
The Cost of Capital

PART IV
Capital Budgeting and Resource Allocation

PART V
Management of Shareholders' Equity

PART VI
Management of Corporate Debt

PART VII
Analysis of Financing Tactics: Swaps, Options, and Foreign Currency

PART VIII
Evaluating Mergers, Buyouts, Restructurings, Projects, and Joint Ventures

PART IX
Setting Corporate Financial Strategy

Introduction

ORIENTATION OF THE BOOK

> *Without a vision, the people are lost.*
>
> Proverbs 29:18

A sound vision is the seed of all good efforts. My experience in teaching executives and degree students has taught me that clarity about goals and process is the first requirement for a successful course. Let me apply that lesson as I introduce you to this collection of 53 case studies: I believe the teaching and learning possibilities herein will unfold more vividly as you apprehend the vision motivating the selection of these cases.

The subtitle of the book remains *Managing for Corporate Value Creation*. In the 1980s, the objective of "creating value" won a prominent place in the pantheon of managerial virtues. Now, in the 1990s other virtues compete for managerial attention. Is creating value still relevant? Economics teaches us that value creation should be an enduring focus of concern because value is the foundation of survival and prosperity of both private and public enterprise. The focus on value also helps managers understand the impact of the firm on the world around it. These cases harness and exercise this economic view of the firm. It is the special province of finance to highlight value as a legitimate concern for managers—if finance teachers fail to do this, then who else will? This second edition reshapes, redirects, and reamplifies this perspective in six dimensions.

1 Normative Analysis

> *"What's new?" is an interesting and broadening eternal question, but one which if pursued exclusively, results only in an endless parade of trivia and fashion, the silt of tomorrow. I would like, instead, to be concerned with the question, "What is best?" a question which*

> *cuts deeply rather than broadly, a question whose answers tend to move the silt downstream. There are eras of human history in which the channels of thought have been too deeply cut and no change was possible, and nothing new ever happened, and "best" was a matter of dogma, but that is not the situation now. . . . Some channel deepening seems called for.*

> Robert Pirsig, *Zen and the Art of Motorcycle Maintenance*

A recurrent theme throughout this book is the question, "How can we do better?" This theme pushes beyond mere description or aimless exercise to an exploration of applied finance. The tools and concepts of modern finance permit us to estimate the extent to which a transaction or change in policies affects welfare and who may be impacted by that change. In most of the cases in this edition, a **valuation analysis** forms the basis for judging the appropriateness of some policy or transaction. The valuation problems cover a wide range of stocks, bonds, options, and real assets. Some of the cases permit the student to focus on **risk analysis:** for example, those concerning capital adequacy (Cases 26, 33, 51, 52, and 53); quality of earnings (Cases 4, 9, and 10); loan credit-worthiness (Cases 7, 11, and 12); default risk (Cases 31, 37, and 48); currency risk (Cases 35 and 36); basis risk (Cases 34 and 41); and underwriting risk (Cases 28, 40, and 45). Where risk is the focus, the underlying concerns are whether the firm is appropriately hedged and whether the price of the hedge is fair. Finally, the cases invite **allocational analysis:** Are the effects of a change in policy or transaction distributed in a way that makes sense? For instance, the allocation of risks and returns is essential to understanding several financial phenomena: leveraged buyouts, reorganizations, project financings, and joint ventures (Cases 46 through 50); why financial intermediaries exist (Cases 2, 27, and 39); and the great difficulties chief executive officers face in choosing among alternative financial policies (Cases 26, 32, 51, 52, and 53). My point in selecting case problems with significant normative aspects is to show students and managers that rigorous analysis can help firms improve decision making and/or avoid disastrous choices.

2 Linkage between the Firm and Capital Markets

> *Any player unaware of the fool in the market probably* is *the fool in the market.*

> Warren Buffet, money manager

> *It is not the employer who pays the wages—he only handles the money. It is the product that pays wages.*

> Henry Ford, industrialist

It is easy to focus business education *inwardly* on the firm and the manager. Doing so, however, ignores the crucial tie between the firm and the various markets in which it competes. A course in corporate finance should illuminate the relationship between the firm and the capital markets in at least four ways. First, it should describe the relationship, giving attention to the behavior of classes of investors (the cases on leveraged buyouts

help here: Cases 33, 46, and 47), and to the role and responsibilities of financial intermediaries (Cases 2, 7, 8, 9, 10, 11, 12, 24, 27, 28, 33, 36, 39, and 40). The purpose
of this description should be to help students understand Warren Buffet's **"players" in
the market,** and their motivations. Second, a course in corporate finance should build
a student's ability to derive practical implications from the interpretation of current **capital
market conditions.** Almost all of the cases in this edition present some information on
capital market conditions that are relevant to managerial decisions: most noteworthy are
cases that deal with market crashes (Cases 2 and 39); the demise of the merger and LBO
booms (Cases 33, 47, and 48); problems in currency translation (Cases 23, 35, 36, 43,
and 47) and anomalies in valuation (Cases 1, 4, 6, 28, and 51). Third, a complete survey
of corporate financial management as it relates to capital markets should consider **innovation in the design of securities.** Cases 33 to 41, 45 to 49, 52, and 53 invite students
to value and/or rationalize the use of exotic securities in support of a corporate financial
policy. And finally, a course in corporate finance should help students understand the
implications of the *transparency* of the firm to investors. Henry Ford was right: the
product and the customer pay the firm's dividends and interest—investors know this,
and **efficient markets** rapidly impound news about the company, its customers, suppliers,
and competitors into a firm's security prices (Case 2 explores market efficiency). If the
firm is basically a **nexus** (or crossroads) **of contracts,** then the analysis of contracts
among the firm and its investors can yield solid insights into the incentives, constraints,
threats, and opportunities under which managers operate: cases that illustrate this frame
of thinking deal with banking (see Cases 7 to 11); securities issuance (Cases 27, 28, 32,
35, and 37 to 41); restructuring (Cases 42 to 50); and major policy decisions (Cases 26,
and 51 to 53).

3 Contemporaneity

The future is a moving target.

Advertisement for IBM

If you think there was a lot of change in the 80s, wait until you see the 90s.

Jack Welch, CEO, General Electric

Students appreciate fresh cases. A case's proximity to students' own frames of experience
heightens their interest, energy, and learning. Half of all the cases in this edition are set
in the 1990s; only five cases are set before 1985. At the same time, the challenge for
teachers and students is to avoid undue investment in cases focusing on relatively ephem-
eral topics and to fasten instead onto cases posing enduring issues. This second edition
begins to adapt to two long-run changes that I believe will shape the business environment
for years to come.

   The first of these changes is the growing **globalization of business and finance.** In
this edition, half of the cases have a strong international element and/or are set outside
the United States. By and large, these cases illustrate that the tools and concepts of modern

finance can be transferred from one country to another and highlight practical adaptations that may be necessary. The cases also sensitize students to variations in business institutions, practices, and concerns outside the United States—Americans need to appreciate these differences. Certain cases (see Cases 8, 9, 18, 19, 44, and 50) shed light on the subtle influence of cultural setting on financial practices.

The second of the major changes this edition addresses is the growing representation of **women in management.** A third of the cases in the book and the instructors' manual feature women as decision makers and leaders. Cases such as these underscore the relevance of finance (and careers in finance) for a growing segment of students and managers.

4 The Administrative Point of View

> *The commander-in-chief is always in the midst of a series of shifting events, and so he can never at any moment consider the whole import of an event that is occurring. Moment by moment the event is imperceptibly shaping itself, and at every moment of this continuous, uninterrupted shaping of events, the commander-in-chief is in the midst of the most complex play of intrigues, worries, contingencies, authorities, projects, counsels, threats, and deceptions and is continually obliged to reply to innumerable questions addressed to him which constantly conflict with one another.*
>
> *An order to retreat must be given to the adjutant, at once, that instant. And the order to retreat carries us past the turn to the Kaluga Road. And after the adjutant comes, the commissary-general asks where the stores are to be taken and the chief of the hospitals asks where the wounded are to go, and a courier from Petersburg brings a letter from the sovereign which does not admit of the possibility of abandoning Moscow, and the commander-in-chief's rival, the man who is undermining him (and there are always not merely one, but several such) presents a new project diametrically opposed to that of turning to the Kaluga Road. . .*
>
> Nikolayevich Tolsoy, novelist (from *War and Peace*)

> *We have met the enemy, and he is us.*
>
> "Pogo," cartoon character

Case studies help illustrate the application of modern finance in a practical environment. As Tolstoy notes, the world is dynamic and messy. Information often is incomplete. Human grasp of facts and events is limited. Using models and frameworks may require heroic assumptions. And even if the theory points unambiguously toward some desirable outcome, there often remains a gap between analysis and implementation. Pogo tells us (among other things) that rational analysis does not necessarily culminate in rational action. Students and managers need to confront these problems: A course in corporate finance must illustrate the immense practicality of financial thinking in the messy world of bargaining problems (Cases 25, 44, and 50); corporate politics (Cases 20, 21, and 25); improper incentives (Cases 4 and 9), and mismatches between a leader's vision and corporate financial resources (Cases 9, 52, and 53).

5 Ethical Dilemmas

I was Snow White. But then I drifted.

Mae West, actress

The line separating good and evil passes not through States, nor between political parties either—but right through every human heart.

Aleksandr Solzhenitsyn, author

Students and managers increasingly show interest in business ethics. While a great deal has been written (and is being written) in this area, ethicists have yet to make the great leap into the functional areas, such as finance. We need cases that are not abstract, macroscopic, or cataclysmic, but that focus on the kind of ethical dilemmas students and managers are likely to encounter in their professional work. To expand on Mae West's metaphor, a course in corporate finance should touch on why "drift" occurs and what determines its speed and direction. Modern finance provides some helpful tools for the analysis of ethical dilemmas, and especially risks, penalties, the uses of incentives, and the costs of agency failure and moral hazard. When carefully applied, these tools can lend rigor to a discussion of ethical dilemmas. This edition affords opportunities to consider self-dealing in capital budgeting and in working capital management (see Case 20 and 9 respectively); the ethical dilemmas in the adoption of accounting policies (Case 4) and in negotiation (Case 25, 44, and 50); social activism (Case 5); and the ethics of greenmail (Case 1). All of these cases force the student to confront the relative importance of personal and corporate integrity in the resolution of ethics problems. Managers must understand the adverse consequences of poorly designed procedures, rules, and incentives. At the same time, individuals cannot escape personal responsibility for their own integrity and that of the corporation. As Solzhenitsyn would say, ethical failure originates not in the institutions of society, but in the individuals who comprise them. Thus, the task for teacher and students in finance must be to explore the role of individual choice in ethical dilemmas.

6 Growth in Judgment

Telling children, and then testing them on what they have been told inevitably has the effect of producing bench-bound learners whose motivation for learning is likely to be extrinsic to the task at hand—pleasing the teacher, getting into college, artificially maintaining self-esteem.

Jerome Bruner, child psychologist

The inexplicable is all around us. So is the incomprehensible. So is the unintelligible. Interviewing Babe Ruth in 1928, I put it to him "People come and ask what's your system for hitting home runs—that so?" "Yes," said the Babe, "and all I can tell 'em is I pick a good one and sock it. I get back to the dugout and they ask me what it was I hit and I tell 'em I don't know except it looked good."

Carl Sandburg, poet

It is much harder to ask the right question than to find the right answer; and even the right answer to the wrong question isn't worth much.

E. E. Morison, historian

Good judgment comes from experience. Experience comes from bad judgment.

Walter Wriston, banker

Experience, is for me, the highest authority . . . I have come to feel that the only learning which significantly influences behavior is self-discovered, self-appropriated learning. Such learning, . . . assimilated in experience, cannot be directly communicated to another.

Carl Rogers, psychologist

Professional education is nothing if it cannot culminate in decisions and action. The ultimate objective of case teaching in finance should be growth in judgment, rather than the accumulation of knowledge. Factual knowledge decays rapidly unless continually used. Deepened judgment lasts. Conveying knowledge is relatively easier than training judgment, but as Jerome Bruner points out can have unintended consequences. Training judgment is hard; some would say that judgment cannot be described (or taught), as witnessed by Babe Ruth's "it looked good." I believe, however, that good judgment *can* be learned. Morison suggests that an important characteristic of "breakthrough" thinkers (i.e., judges of important new technologies, discontinuities in the environment, and so on) is the ability to frame questions well, as opposed to answer those questions. Finance teachers must motivate their students by example and exhortation to question well. Wriston and Rogers suggest that another crucial element of training judgment is the student's personal engagement with the problem—a case course in finance should propel students into managers' shoes, and demand that recommendations be scrutinized by the class. I believe that judgment can be deepened through the study of cases that demand personal engagement, pose challenging dilemmas, and require decisions and specific action. I especially commend the following cases as meeting these criteria: 1, 8, 9, 10, 11, 20, 21, 24, 25, 26, 28, 32, 34, 41, 44, and 48 to 53.

PLAN OF THE BOOK

The cases may be taught in many different sequences. The sequence indicated by the table of contents corresponds to course designs used at Darden. The cases are clustered into concept modules, each with a particular orientation:

1. Setting Some Themes.   Disney (Case 1) and Peter Lynch (case 2) introduce basic concepts of **value creation** and **capital market efficiency** that reappear throughout a case course. The numerical analysis required is relatively light; the synthesis of many case facts is the main challenge.

2. Financial Analysis and Forecasting.   In this substantially expanded and updated section, students are introduced to the crucial skills of financial statement analysis, break-even analysis, ratio analysis, and financial statement forecasting (both by percent of sales and T-accounts). One case (The Body Shop, Case 5) takes the student step-by-step through preparation of forecasts, both by hand and with the aid of a computer-spreadsheet program. The analysis of **working capital management** is the main teaching vehicle in this sec-tion—problems include receivables management (Oracle Systems, Case 4; Bayern Brauerei, Case 9); seasonal variations in business (Sengupta Fibres, Case 8); and inventory problems (Merrill Electronics (A), Case 10). This section also lays the groundwork for understanding the firm's relationship with the capital markets: six of the cases involve **bank lending** and **credit analysis.**

3. Cost of Capital.   This module begins with the "Teletech" case (13), applying the risk-and-return paradigm to the evaluation of corporate and divisional performance. In "General Motors" (Case 14) and "The Boeing 777" (Case 15), the student must estimate capital costs for the firm, for business segments, and for a major project. In "Grand Metropolitan" (Case 16) the student must estimate the cost of capital for a multina-tional firm. The cases aim to exercise and solidify students' mastery of the **capital asset pricing model,** the **dividend-growth model,** and the **weighted average cost of capital** formula.

4. Capital Budgeting and Resource Allocation.   The focus of these cases is the evaluation of **individual investment opportunities** and the assessment of **entire capital budgets.** The first case (Investment Detective, Case 17) is a simple review of analytical techniques. "Dhahran Roads" (Case 18) offers an excellent introduction to the time value of money. The next several cases concern the evaluation of a plant automation project (Case 19, a go/no go decision); choices between plant renovation projects and mar-keting strategies (either/or decisions, Cases 20, 21, and 22); a lease-versus-buy decision (Case 24), and a major cross-border operational investment (Case 23). This module ends with the problem of setting the entire capital budget for a resource-constrained firm (Case 25).

5. Management of Shareholders' Equity.   This module seeks to develop practical principles about **dividend policy** and **common stock issuance** by drawing on concepts about dividend irrelevance, value conservation, signaling, investor clienteles, bonding, and agency costs. "Westboro Corporation" (Case 26) affords a rich survey of irrelevance, signaling, and clientele concerns in the context of a dividend decision. "Morgan Stanley" (Case 27) focuses on an American initial public stock offering and provides an interesting contrast with "British Aerospace" (Case 28) one of the more remarkable European rights offerings in recent years. These three cases explore the interface between the firm and the capital markets. "Morgan Stanley" lends useful insights into the workings of a bulge-bracket investment bank.

6. Management of Corporate Debt.   The problem of **setting target capital structures** is introduced in this module. Prominent issues are the use and creation of debt tax shields, the costs of financial distress, the role of industry economics and technology, the influence of corporate competitive strategy, and the trade-offs between debt policy, dividend policy, and investment goals. "Revco D.S." (Case 33) is a new part of this module and permits students to explore the definition and measurement of capital adequacy.

7. Analysis of Financing Tactics: Swaps, Options, and Foreign Currency.   While the preceding module six is concerned with setting debt targets, this module addresses a range of **tactics** a firm might use to pursue those targets, hedge risk, and exploit market opportunities. Included are domestic and international debt offerings, swaps of various types, recapitalizations, loan guarantees, warrants, and convertibles. With these cases, students will exercise techniques in securities valuation, including the use of option pricing theory. Three new cases in this module are "Merrill Electronics (B)" (Case 36), which deals with hedging foreign currency flows; "Bank of Tokyo" (Case 39), which considers warrant bond valuation; and "Syracuse Electric" (Case 41), an exercise in evaluating competing debt refinancing proposals.

8. Evaluating Mergers, Buyouts, Restructurings, Projects, and Joint Ventures.   This module focuses on **valuing the whole firm** (as opposed to valuing assets previously covered in module 4) "Brown-Forman" (Case 42), "Aguas Minerales" (Case 43), and "Gallery of Furs" (Case 44), are exercises in the valuation of companies. Next, several cases integrate **financing considerations** involved in mergers: "Rhône-Poulenc Rorer" (Case 45) explores financing with contingent payment securities; "Bumble Bee Seafoods" (Case 46) and "MediMedia" (Case 47) present leveraged buyouts with opportunities for analyzing senior debt, mezzanine debt, and equity investments. "Caledonian Newspapers" (Case 48) presents a case about **financial distress** and asks students to analyze competing proposals to reorganize the firm. "Euro Disneyland" (Case 49) and "GM-Euroslavia" (Case 50) invite the student to evaluate a **joint venture** and a **complex project financing,** respectively. Finally, the module contains two **simulated negotiation exercises** in combination with cases contained in the instructor's manual: "Gallery of Furs" (merger negotiation) and "GM-Euroslavia" (joint venture negotiation).

9. Setting Corporate Financial Strategy.   This module is new to the second edition and aims to give teachers and students **comprehensive problems in corporate financial policy and tactics.** The student must address three sets of questions: (1) What is the firm's financing requirement, and how does the chief executive officer's vision and strategy drive that requirement? (2) Are the firm's securities valued fairly in the capital markets? If not, why? And what should be done about this? (3) What should be the firm's financial policy? And what specific actions should be taken to meet the financing need? These cases are excellent vehicles for end-of-course classes, student term papers, and/or presentations by teams of students.

SUMMARY OF CHANGES FROM THE FIRST EDITION

The second edition represents a substantial change from the first edition:

- There are 33 **new cases,** or 62 percent of the total number of cases.
- Half of the cases are **set in the 1990s.**
- A **woman decision maker** is featured in 26 percent of all cases in the book or 33 percent of the cases in both the book and the instructor's manual.
- Half of the cases have a strong **international** aspect and/or are set outside of the United States.
- There is **significant expansion** of modules on "Financial Analysis and Forecasting" and "Capital Budgeting." More variety. Less complexity.
- A **revised section on mergers** gives less emphasis to highly leveraged transactions (though these are still represented here) and more emphasis to investing, restructuring, and venturing.
- There are two **new negotiation exercises.**
- There is a **new module** of cases on "Setting Corporate Financial Strategy": omnibus cases good for end-of-course classes, group presentations, and/or term papers.

ACKNOWLEDGMENTS

This book would not be possible without the contributions of many other people. Colleagues at Darden who have taught, contributed to, or commented on these cases are: Samuel E. Bodily, John Colley, Robert Conroy, James Dunstan, Kenneth Eades, Mark Eaker, Robert R. Fair, James Freeland, Sherwood Frey, Diana Harrington, Robert Harris, Mark Haskins, Charles Meiburg, Judson Reis, and William Sihler. I am grateful to the Darden School Foundation, the Citicorp Global Scholars Program, and INSEAD for generously supporting my casewriting efforts.

Colleagues at other schools whose work appears here include Anant Sundaram (Tuck), Herwig Langohr (INSEAD), Lee Remmers (INSEAD), Chris Muscarella (Penn State), and Michael Vetsuypens (Southern Methodist). I am delighted to give their excellent work exposure in this collection.

Colleagues at other schools provided worthy insights and encouragement. I am grateful to the following:

James Ang	*Florida State*	Kenneth Ferris	*Thunderbird*
Paul Asquith	*M.I.T*	Günter Franke	*Konstanz*
Michael Berry	*James Madison*	Dan Galai	*Jerusalem*
John Boquist	*Indiana*	Jim Gentry	*Illinois*
Kirt Butler	*Michigan State*	Philippe Haspeslagh	*INSEAD*
Jean Dermine	*INSEAD*	Pekka Hietala	*INSEAD*
Michael Dooley	*UVA Law*	Rocky Higgins	*Washington*
Peter Eisemann	*Georgia State*	Pierre Hillion	*INSEAD*
Thomas H. Eyssell	*Missouri*	Thomas Jackson	*UVA Law*

Pradeep Jalan	*Regina*	Richard Stapleton	*Lancaster*
Steven Kaplan	*Chicago*	Marti Subrahmanyam	*NYU*
Saul Levmore	*UVA Law*	Walter Torous	*UCLA*
Wilbur Lewellen	*Purdue*	Al Rappaport	*Northwestern*
Dennis Logue	*Dartmouth*	Allen Rappaport	*Northern Iowa*
Wesley Marple	*Northeastern*	Jay Ritter	*Michigan*
John Martin	*Texas*	Art Selander	*Southern Methodist*
Ronald Masulis	*Vanderbilt*	Dennis Sheehan	*Purdue*
John McConnell	*Purdue*	Nick Varaiya	*San Diego State*
Richard McEnally	*North Carolina*	Theo Vermaelen	*INSEAD*
Ed Moses	*Rollins*	Claude Viallet	*INSEAD*
Charles Moyer	*Wake Forest*	Ingo Walter	*NYU*
David Mullins	*Federal Reserve Board*	Peter Williamson	*Dartmouth*
Jack Parham	*Hillsdale*	Brent Wilson	*Brigham Young*
John Pringle	*North Carolina*	Betty Yobaccio	*Framingham State*
Luke Sparvero	*Texas*		

I also am grateful to the following practitioners (listed here with affiliated companies at the time of my work with them):

Norm Bartczak	*Brookline*	Marni Gislason Obernauer	*J.P. Morgan*
Bo Brookby	*First Wachovia*	Michael Pearson	*McKinsey*
W.L. Lyons Brown	*Brown-Forman*	Nancy Preis	*Kleinwort Benson*
Bliss Williams Browne	*First Chicago*	Joe Prendergast	*First Wachovia*
George Bruns	*Bank of Boston*	Christopher Reilly	*S.G. Warburg*
Ned Case	*General Motors*	Emilio Rottoli	*Glaxo*
Daniel Cohrs	*Marriott*	Barry Sabloff	*First Chicago*
David Crosby	*Johnson & Johnson*	Linda Scheuplein	*J.P. Morgan*
Jinx Dennett	*Bank of Boston*	Keith Shaughnessy	*Bank of Boston*
Ty Eggemeyer	*McKinsey*	Jack Sheehan	*Johnstown*
Geoffrey Elliott	*Morgan Stanley*	Betsy Silver	*Bank of Boston*
Catherine Friedman	*Morgan Stanley*	John Smetanka	*Security Pacific*
Ian Harvey	*Bank of Boston*	John Smith	*General Motors*
Christopher Howe	*Kleinwort Benson*	Rick Spangler	*First Wachovia*
Paul Hunn	*Manufacturers Hanover*	Martin Steinmeyer	*MediMedia*
James Gelly	*General Motors*	Stephanie Summers	*Lehman Brothers*
Ed Giera	*Kleinwort Benson*	Peter Thorpe	*Citicorp*
Thomas Jasper	*Salomon Brothers*	Katherine Updike	*Excelsior*
Mary Lou Kelley	*McKinsey*	Tom Verdoorn	*Land O'Lakes*
Andrew Kerr	*Devonshire Partners*	Frank Ward	*Corp. Performance*
Eric Linnes	*Kleinwort Benson*	David Wake Walker	*Kleinwort Benson*
Peter Lynch	*Fidelity Investments*	Ulrich Wiechmann	*UWINC*
Frank McTigue	*McTigue Associates*	Scott Williams	*McKinsey*
David Meyer	*J.P. Morgan*	Harry You	*Salomon Brothers*
Lin Morison	*Bank of Boston*		

Research assistants working under my direction have helped gather data and prepare drafts: Anne Campbell, Jerry Halpin, Peter Hennessy, Casey Opitz, Michael Schill, John Sherwood, Jane Sommers-Kelly, Thien Pham, Carla Stiassni, Larry Weatherford, and Steve Wilus. Valuable editorial assistance at Darden was provided by Bette Collins,

Stephen Smith, and Elaine Moran. Valuable production assistance at Darden was provided by Kathleen Collier, Dot Govoruhk, Pat Hall and, Bessie Truzy.

At Richard D. Irwin, Inc., Mike Junior (now publisher) served as both sponsoring editor and development editor—Mike recruited me into this casebook project years ago; Andrea Smith was editorial assistant on this project; Ethel Shiell was project editor; Heather Burbridge was the art coordinator. The patience and care of all these people is richly appreciated.

Of all the contributors, my wife, Barbara McTigue Bruner, and two sons, Jonathan and Alex, have endured some of the greatest sacrifices to see this book appear. As Milton said, "They also serve who only stand and wait." Development of this second edition would not have been possible without their fond patience.

All these acknowledgments notwithstanding, I am responsible for any errors that may remain and welcome comments and suggestions for enhancement. Please let me know of your experience with these cases, either through Irwin or at the address given below.

Robert F. Bruner
Robert F. Vandell Research Professor

Darden Graduate School of Business
University of Virginia
Post Office Box 6550
Charlottesville, Virginia 22906

Individual copies of all the Darden cases in this edition (and in the first edition) may be obtained promptly from Darden Educational Materials Services (804-982-2192). Proceeds from these case sales support case writing efforts. Please respect the copyrights on these materials.

Part I

Setting Some Themes

Case 1

Walt Disney Productions, June 1984

"One of the best examples of service through people is Walt Disney Productions. . . . How Disney looks upon people, internally and externally, handles them, communicates with them, rewards them, is in my view the basic foundation upon which its five decades of success stand."

Peters and Waterman, *In Search of Excellence*

"In Search of Excellence didn't simplify enough! In the private or public sector, in big business or small, we observe that there are only two ways to create and sustain superior performance over the long haul. First, take exceptional care of your customers via superior service and superior quality. Second, constantly innovate. That's it. There are no alternatives in achieving long-term performance. Financial control is vital but one does not sell financial control."

Peters and Austin, *A Passion for Excellence*

INTRODUCTION

Ron Miller, president and chief executive officer of Disney Productions, Inc., pondered the essence of his dilemma. For the past two and a half months, his company had been the subject of a takeover attempt by Saul Steinberg, a well-known raider. The attempt had started innocently enough, with the announcement of the purchase of 6.3 percent of Disney's outstanding common stock. In subsequent announcements, Steinberg's holdings rose to 12.1 percent. When Steinberg announced his intention of acquiring 25 percent of Disney, Miller undertook a series of evasive actions, including the purchase of Arvida

This case was prepared by Robert F. Bruner.
Copyright © 1985 by the Darden Graduate Business School Foundation, Charlottesville, VA.

Corporation for $200 million in common stock (3.33 million shares) and the attempted purchase of Gibson Greetings, Inc., for $310 million in stock. Just yesterday, June 11, 1984, Steinberg retaliated with a public tender offer for 49 percent of the company at $67.50 per share if Disney completed its acquisition of Gibson Greetings and at $72.50 per share without Gibson. Before the raid began, Disney stock was trading around $50 per share.

The senior executives at Disney were shocked at this turn of events. Consumers identified Disney with wholesome family entertainment more closely than they did any other corporation. The animated characters emerging from Disney were hallmarks of American culture. Millions of visitors delighted in the ingenuity of Disney theme parks, which business pundits cited as a model of excellence. The artistic creativity of Disney Productions was virtually a national resource. It was inconceivable to Miller that such an excellent company would be dismantled, or, for that matter, raided in the first place.

There seemed to be two possible responses to the tender offer. The first was to fight the offer in the courts and media. However, Steinberg had shown himself to be very determined, so even a successful outcome would be costly. The other alternative would be to offer to repurchase Steinberg's shares. In fact, Steinberg was a notorious "green-mailer," who had been paid $47 million by Quaker State Oil Company only that previous April. Steinberg was believed to own 4.2 million shares of Disney stock, which he had acquired at an average price of $63.25 per share. Miller wondered what an appropriate repurchase price would be.

BUSINESSES AND STRATEGY

The origins of Disney Productions were described in the 1982 annual report:

> In July 1923, a young cartoonist named Walt Disney arrived in Hollywood with drawing materials under his arm, $40 in his pocket, and hopes that he could get started in the animated film business. Before boarding the train he had known failure, disappointment, and even hunger. Waiting for him at Union Station in Los Angeles was his brother, Roy, who was to dedicate his life to helping make Walt's dreams come true. With a $500 loan, they started their film business, working at home late at night with their wives, Lilly and Edna, working alongside them around a kitchen table . . . struggling to keep a tiny studio going. There was no instant success for them in this era of silent pictures, and every dime was plowed back into keeping the company running. In 1928 came the first real break. While the movie industry was still turning its back to the possibilities of sound, Walt produced *Steamboat Willie*, the first cartoon with sound. It also introduced a new star. . . . Mickey Mouse. In the decades that followed, Walt became an extraordinary filmmaker, a motion picture innovater and pioneer. And the name "Walt Disney" became universally known as the symbol of the finest in family entertainment.[1]

In 1984, the company described itself as a "diversified international company engaged in family entertainment and community development." In fiscal 1983, Disney had sales of $1.3 billion on assets of $2.38 billion (see Exhibits 1 and 2). The business activities

---

[1]1982 annual report, Walt Disney Productions.

of the company are in four segments: theme parks, films, consumer products, and real estate development. The Disney strategy was to form these segments into interlocking pieces of a portfolio, each supporting the activities of another.

The entertainment and recreation segment included theme parks and resorts. For example, Disneyland Park consisted of seven principal areas or themes: Fantasyland, Adventureland, Frontierland, Tomorrowland, New Orleans Square, Main Street, and Bear Country. In each area were rides, attractions, restaurants, refreshment stands, and souvenir shops in keeping with the surrounding theme. Theme parks were located in Anaheim, California; Orlando, Florida; and Tokyo, Japan. A new theme park near Orlando (opened in October 1982), EPCOT (for Experimental Prototype Community of Tomorrow) introduced two new themes—Future World and World Showcase. Disneyland covered 344 acres in Anaheim and the Disney World complex in Orlando included 28,000 acres of land (twice the size of Manhattan Island), most of which was undeveloped. Even before the Arvida acquisition, analysts estimated Disney's raw land holdings to be worth $300–700 million. Disneyland was carried on the balance sheet at $20 million, although its replacement value was estimated to be $140 million. The company owned and operated hotels, consisting of 400 units of vacation villas and 5,163 rooms, in various locations. Management believed that its theme parks benefited substantially from its reputation in the entertainment business and from its other activities. There were 23 other major theme parks in the continental United States in 1984. Recently, theme parks in the South and Midwest had been sold for about two times operating income.

In film entertainment, the company produced films for release under its own label as well as the Touchstone label, a brand oriented toward an adult audience. The company's film library consisted of 25 full-length animated features in color, 123 full-length live-action features, 8 "true-life adventure" feature films, and over 500 other shorter films. Certain films proved to be an enduring source of cash, as indicated by the billings of *Snow White* over the years given in Exhibit 3. The company produced the television program "Wonderful World of Disney" from 1961 through 1981. The Disney Channel, a new venture into pay television, provided 19 daily hours of entertainment through cable system operators. Exhibit 4 provides an overview of the competitors in the cable programming services industry. Finally, the company marketed 114 films and cartoon titles to the home entertainment market, principally for use with video recorders. The company's studios included 44 acres in Burbank, California, and a ranch of 691 acres outside of Burbank.

Real estate or community development was conducted through the company's new subsidiary, Arvida Corporation, acquired on June 6, 1984. Whereas Arvida was not a factor in the performance predating the takeover bid, it now represented a significant asset in the valuation of the company. Arvida owned or controlled the development of 17,334 acres of land in Florida, Georgia, and California.

In the area of consumer products, the company licensed the name Walt Disney, its animated characters, literary properties, songs, and music to manufacturers, publishers, and retailers. Historically, the returns in the consumer products segment were quite high. For instance, in 1978 this segment gave a pretax return on assets of 179 percent.

Overall, Miller wrote in the 1983 annual report, "We expect our company to flourish because we have created unique value along with competitive and strategic advantage in the marketplace."

FINANCIAL PERFORMANCE

In contrast to the upbeat optimism of management, securities analysts and some journalists were less enthusiastic. The performance of Walt Disney Productions in the aggregate is given in Exhibits 5 and 6. Exhibit 7 disaggregates corporate performance by business segment.

The lukewarm financial appraisal was motivated by worsening performance in the film and theme park segments. In 1979, films accounted for 20 percent of pretax earnings and gave a pretax return on assets of 56 percent; in 1983, this segment lost $33 million. This disappointment was attributable to losses in the pay TV start-up operation, a $20 million write-off for a new-release film, *Something Wicked This Way Comes,* and cancellation of the "Wonderful World of Disney" on CBS, which caused a decline of $16 million in TV revenues. Losses in this segment were not surprising, analysts contended, because only 2 out of 10 films in general did better than break even. Indeed, the film entertainment industry showed highly volatile operating performance (see Exhibit 8). But, as the market shares presented in Exhibit 9 suggest, some competitors were better positioned to withstand industry volatility than others. Industry observers also noted the large latent values in the studios' film libraries (see Exhibit 10). Recent events in the industry were viewed as attempts to exploit these values: (1) Taft Broadcasting's purchase of QM Productions and Worldvision in 1979; (2) HBO's purchase of Filmways in 1982; and (3) purchase of Columbia Pictures by Coca-Cola in 1982.

The theme park performance was similarly lackluster. Disney's attendance growth had been low or zero over the preceding decade, though as recently as 1978 the entertainment and recreation segment had shown a pretax return on assets of 15.7 percent. For the industry in general, attendance over those 10 years had grown at about 5 percent annually, but the benefits of this growth were diluted by inflation and narrowing margins (see Exhibit 11). The debuts of Disney World and EPCOT Center had boosted attendance to a new level, but attendance dropped 8 percent in the final quarter of 1983 and another 19 percent in the first quarter of 1984. Analysts felt that, with 25 major theme parks in competition for an aging population (see Exhibit 12), demand was thoroughly saturated and park attendance would grow no more than 5 percent per year—one-third the rate of the 1970s. Indeed, a major question in analysts' minds was why Disney had chosen to grow the theme parks segment as aggressively as it had. The initial cost estimate of Disney World/EPCOT Center had been $600 million; six years later the cost had accumulated to $1.9 billion. One analyst commented, "The increment to the theme parks' operating earnings from Disney's . . . investment probably did not exceed $80 million before taxes. After charging itself with taxes, Disney is left with about $45 million. That represents less than a 4 percent return on EPCOT. If Disney had invested in Treasury bills it could have done better."[2]

Disney's stock price reflected this softened performance. As recently as April 1983, shares had traded at $84.38. Then, in November 1983, Disney announced a 17 percent

---

[2](No author given) "Problems in Walt Disney's Magic Kingdom," *Business Week,* March 12, 1984, p. 51. This estimate assumes an accrual-based investment of $1.125 billion; on a cash-based investment of $1.9 billion the after-tax return on EPCOT would have been 2.4 percent.

drop in quarterly earnings. In response, the share price dropped from $62.38 to $47.50. Richard Simon, an analyst at Goldman Sachs, wrote:

> Disney stock . . . has not been a growth vehicle for four years. We do not believe theme park earnings will grow rapidly and think that fiscal 1983's operating earnings of $197 million was a higher plateau achieved because of EPCOT; nor do we believe the consumer product line is a dynamic growth area. As we have stated in the past, a more positive investment stance must be based on a turn in the company's film business and pay TV channels, both extremely risky endeavors.[3]

Simon estimated the firm's asset value per share at about $75, and forecasted fiscal 1984 earnings per share to be $3.25; the current P/E was 15.

The stock price began to recover in January 1984, but for reasons unknown to the company. A newspaper column on the subject of this recovery is reproduced in Exhibit 13.

A QUESTION OF LEADERSHIP

Some analysts doubted that this declining performance was temporary and pointed to the lack of creative leadership after the death of Walt Disney in 1966. One former executive said, "If there were projects under discussion, people would say, 'Walt wouldn't do that'." And Dennis Forst, a securities analyst with Bateman Eichler, said, "Walt was a real genius. He was running the company 15 years after his death."[4]

Business Week noted:

> Change will not come easily at Disney, partially because so many of its key executives worked under the founder that a Walt Disney cult developed. . . . Until recently it appeared that new ventures were undertaken only if Walt had conceived them or if they seemed like projects he would have approved.[5]

THE REPURCHASE PROPOSAL

As Miller pondered the question of whether to repurchase Steinberg's holdings of Disney stock, he considered what price would be appropriate. (Exhibit 14 presents the time series of Disney's stock price over the past seven months.) He also wondered whether paying greenmail would be fair to other shareholders. And finally, he wondered whether, and if so, how, this episode should change the management policies of the company.[6]

---

[3]Richard P. Simon, "Walt Disney Productions," *Investment Research,* Goldman Sachs & Company, November 17, 1983, pp. 1–2.

[4]Tom Nicholson, "Saving the Magic Kingdom," *Newsweek,* October 4, 1984, p. 44.

[5](No author given), "Problems in Walt Disney's Magic Kingdom," *Business Week,* March 12, 1984, p. 50.

[6]Disney's beta was 0.90. In June 1984, the average yield to maturity of one-year Treasury bonds was 12.08 percent. The average difference between the return on the market portfolio and the risk-free rate was 8.6 percent.

EXHIBIT 1

**Consolidated Statement of Income
Capital Expenditures, Depreciation, and Assets
(dollar amounts in thousands, except per share data)**

Year Ended September 30	1983	1982	1981
Revenues:			
Entertainment and recreation	$1,031,202	$ 725,610	$ 691,811
Motion pictures	165,458	202,102	196,806
Consumer products and other	110,697	102,538	116,423
Total revenues	1,307,357	1,030,250	1,005,040
Costs and expenses of operations:			
Entertainment and recreation	834,324	592,965	562,337
Motion pictures	198,843	182,463	162,180
Consumer products and other	53,815	54,706	65,859
Total costs and expenses of operation	1,086,982	830,134	790,376
Operating income (loss) before corporate expenses:			
Entertainment and recreation	196,876	132,645	129,474
Motion pictures	(33,385)	19,639	34,626
Consumer products and other	56,882	47,832	50,564
Total operating income before corporate expenses	220,375	200,116	214,664
Corporate expenses (income):			
General and administrative	35,554	30,957	26,216
Design projects abandoned	7,295	5,147	4,598
Interest expense (income) − net	14,066	(14,781)	(33,130)
Total corporate expenses (income) ..	56,915	21,323	(2,316)
Income before taxes on income	163,460	178,793	216,980
Taxes on income	70,300	78,700	95,500
Net income	$ 93,160	$ 100,093	$ 121,480
Earnings per share	$2.70	$3.01	$3.72
Capital expenditures:			
Entertainment and recreation	$ 287,940	$ 645,632	$ 344,361
Motion pictures	1,845	2,794	4,040
Consumer products and other	222	66	277
Corporate	1,195	273	110
Depreciation expense:			
Entertainment and recreation	88,059	40,078	37,338
Motion pictures	1,643	1,517	1,200
Consumer products and other	135	118	155
Corporate	347	204	193
Identifiable assets:			
Entertainment and recreation	2,018,787	1,808,731	1,141,657
Motion pictures	180,201	146,337	157,106
Consumer products and other	37,381	34,129	39,239
Corporate	144,826	113,619	272,007

Source: 1983 annual report, Walt Disney Productions, pp. 29 and 41.

EXHIBIT 2

Consolidated Balance Sheet
(dollar amounts in thousands)

September 30	1983	1982
ASSETS		
Current Assets		
Cash	$ 18,055	$ 13,652
Accounts receivable, net of allowances	102,847	78,968
Income taxes refundable	70,000	41,000
Inventories	77,945	66,717
Film production costs	44,412	43,850
Prepaid expenses	19,843	18,152
Total current assets	333,102	262,339
Film Production Costs — Non-Current	82,598	64,217
Property, Plant and Equipment, at cost		
Entertainment attractions, buildings and equipment	2,251,297	1,916,617
Less accumulated depreciation	(504,365)	(419,944)
	1,746,932	1,496,673
Construction and design projects in progress		
Epcot Center	70,331	120,585
Other	37,859	39,601
Land	16,687	16,379
	1,871,809	1,673,238
Other Assets	93,686	103,022
	$ 2,381,195	$ 2,102,816
LIABILITIES AND STOCKHOLDERS EQUITY		
Current Liabilities		
Accounts payable, payroll and other accrued liabilities	$ 187,641	$ 210,753
Taxes on income	50,557	26,560
Total current liabilities	238,198	237,313
Long Term Borrowings, including commercial paper of $118,200 and $200,000	346,325	315,000
Other Long Term Liabilities and Non-Current Advances	110,874	94,739
Deferred Taxes on Income and Investment Credits	285,270	180,980
Commitments and Contingencies		
Stockholders Equity		
Preferred shares, no par		
Authorized — 5,000,000 shares, none issued		
Common shares, no par		
Authorized — 75,000,000 shares		
Issued and outstanding — 34,509,171 and 33,351,482 shares	661,934	588,250
Retained earnings	738,594	686,534
	1,400,528	1,274,784
	$ 2,381,195	$ 2,102,816

Source: 1983 annual report, Walt Disney Productions.

EXHIBIT 3 Annual Revenue from *Snow White*

Year	($ millions)
1937	$10.00
1944	4.00
1952	5.00
1958	6.50
1965	13.00
1967	23.00
1983	28.50

Source: Published by special permission of Donald Rosenthal, Buena Vista Pictures, Burbank, California.

EXHIBIT 4 Cable Programming Services, December 1983

Service	Systems	Subscribers
Basic		
ESPN	7,074*	28,500,000
WTBS	5,717	27,654,000
CBN Cable	3,900	23,000,000
CNN	4,186	22,626,000
USA	3,600	21,000,000
MTV	2,000	17,600,000
Nickelodeon	3,000	17,600,000
C-SPAN	1,200	16,000,000
Lifetime†	1,602	16,000,000
Cable Health	1,315	14,000,000
ARTS	1,936	12,500,000
Nashville Network	1,300	11,245,000
WGN	4,200	10,900,000
Satellite Program Network	460	10,440,000
Weather Channel	1,000	10,000,000
Daytime	734	10,000,000
MSN-Information Channel	521	8,685,000
CNN Headline	891	8,330,000
PTL Club	825	8,100,000
WOR	1,055	6,200,000
Black Entertainment TV	240	5,200,000
Learning Channel	474	3,913,000
Trinity Broadcast Network	290	3,350,000
National Jewish Network	165	3,200,000
Eternal Word TV Network	104	1,628,000
National Christian Network	108	1,434,353
Genesis Story Time (on CBN subcarrier)	1	6,000
Pay		
HBO	5,200	13,500,000
Showtime	2,900	4,750,000
Cinemax	2,000	2,700,000
Movie Channel	2,700	2,000,000
Playboy	320	577,000
Disney	1,136	531,000
HTN Plus	400	250,000
Bravo	101	155,000
Galavision/SIN	160	120,000
Spotlight‡	237	750,000
Pay-per-view		
PPV Associates	250	7,600,000
Don King Sports & Entertainment	9*	500,000

* Includes other pay-TV outlets.
† Combination of CHN and Daytime as of February 1, 1983.
‡ To be shut down January 31, 1984.

Source: "Broadcasting, December 12, 1983," in H. L. Vogel, *Entertainment Industry Economics* (Cambridge University Press, 1986), p. 195.

EXHIBIT 5

Selected Financial Data
(in thousands, except per share data)

	1983	1982	1981	1980	1979
Statement of Income Data					
Revenues (Page 46)	$ **1,307,357**	$ 1,030,250	$ 1,005,040	$ 914,505	$ 796,773
Operating income before					
corporate expenses	**220,375**	200,116	214,664	231,300	205,695
Corporate expenses	**42,849**	36,104	30,814	25,424	20,220
Interest expense (income) — net	**14,066**	(14,781)	(33,130)	(42,110)	(28,413)
Taxes on income	**70,300**	78,700	95,500	112,800	100,100
Net income	**93,160**	100,093	121,480	135,186	113,788
Balance Sheet Data					
Current assets	**333,102**	262,339	457,829	506,202	484,141
Property, plant and equipment —					
net of depreciation	**1,871,809**	1,673,238	1,069,369	762,546	648,447
Total assets	**2,381,195**	2,102,816	1,610,009	1,347,407	1,196,424
Current liabilities	**238,198**	237,313	181,573	145,291	119,768
Long term obligations, including					
commercial paper of $118,200 —					
1983 and $200,000 — 1982	**457,199**	409,739	171,886	30,429	18,616
Total liabilities and deferred					
credits	**980,667**	828,032	442,891	272,609	235,362
Total net assets (stockholders					
equity)	**1,400,528**	1,274,784	1,167,118	1,074,798	961,062
Statement of Changes in Financial					
Position Data					
Cash provided by operations	**337,356**	274,782	210,805	204,682	182,857
Cash dividends	**41,100**	39,742	32,406	23,280	15,496
Investment in property, plant					
and equipment	**333,738**	614,416	333,407	149,674	56,629
Investment in film production					
and programming	**83,750**	52,295	55,454	68,409	44,436
Per Share Data					
Net income (earnings)	$ **2.70**	$ 3.01	$ 3.72	$ 4.16	$ 3.51
Cash dividends	**1.20**	1.20	1.00	.72	.48
Stockholders equity	**40.58**	38.22	35.99	33.22	29.76
Average number of common and					
common equivalent shares					
outstanding during the year	**34,481**	33,225	32,629	32,513	32,426
Other Data					
Stockholders at close of year	**60,000**	61,000	60,000	62,000	65,000
Employees at close of year	**30,000**	28,000	25,000	24,000	21,000

Source: 1983 annual report, Walt Disney Productions.

EXHIBIT 6 Ratio Analysis by Year

Year	1965	1966	1967	1968	1969	1970	1971	1972	1973	1974
Pretax margin	20.24%	20.13%	17.31%	19.36%	21.91%	26.16%	27.63%	22.58%	22.12%	20.59%
× Asset turnover	1.41	1.25	1.08	0.97	0.74	0.66	0.46	0.60	0.60	0.60
= Pretax return on assets	28.53%	25.15%	18.73%	18.72%	16.12%	17.28%	12.69%	13.44%	13.22%	12.46%
× (1 − Tax rate)	0.51	0.53	0.55	0.49	0.49	0.50	0.55	0.54	0.56	0.55
= After-tax return on assets	14.59%	13.28%	10.38%	9.24%	7.84%	8.60%	6.99%	7.28%	7.42%	6.80%
/ Leverage (equity/assets)	0.61	0.64	0.66	0.59	0.59	0.72	0.70	0.70	0.75	0.74
= After-tax return on equity	24.05%	20.88%	15.78%	15.65%	13.36%	11.94%	9.96%	10.34%	9.88%	9.13%
Dividend payout rate	6.46%	6.22%	7.21%	9.62%	8.28%	7.65%	8.84%	6.84%	7.18%	7.21%
EPS	$0.63	$0.67	$0.59	$0.67	$0.79	$0.90	$1.00	$1.42	$1.64	$1.66
Beta	NA	NA	NA	NA	NA	NA	NA	NA	1.23	1.35
Rate on one-year T-bills	4.06%	5.07%	4.71%	5.45%	6.79%	6.49%	4.67%	4.77%	7.01%	7.71%

NA means not available.

Year	1975	1976	1977	1978	1979	1980	1981	1982	1983
Pretax margin	23.26%	24.01%	24.98%	25.57%	26.84%	27.12%	21.59%	17.35%	12.50%
× Asset turnover	0.68	0.70	0.69	0.72	0.70	0.72	0.68	0.55	0.58
= Pretax return on assets.......	15.18%	16.93%	17.12%	18.51%	18.77%	19.50%	14.67%	9.63%	9.63%
× (1 − Tax rate)	0.53	0.53	0.52	0.52	0.53	0.55	0.56	0.56	0.57
= After-tax return on assets.......	8.10%	9.01%	8.92%	9.61%	9.98%	10.63%	8.22%	5.39%	4.16%
/ Leverage (equity/assets)	0.77	0.79	0.80	0.80	0.80	0.80	0.76	0.66	0.60
= After-tax return on equity	10.54%	11.38%	11.20%	12.05%	12.49%	13.28%	10.84%	8.20%	6.96%
Dividend payout rate............	5.75%	4.90%	5.77%	10.44%	13.62%	17.22%	26.68%	39.71%	44.12%
EPS	$2.00	$2.41	$2.53	$3.04	$3.51	$4.16	$3.72	$3.01	$2.70
Beta	1.45	1.50	1.55	1.50	1.40	1.35	1.15	1.05	1.00
Rate on one-year T-bills	6.76%	5.88%	6.09%	8.34%	10.67%	12.05%	13.16%	11.10%	8.86%

Source: Annual reports, Walt Disney Productions, Value Line.

EXHIBIT 7

Other Financial Data
(in thousands)

	1983	1982	1981	1980	1979
ENTERTAINMENT AND RECREATION					
Walt Disney World					
Admissions and rides	$ 278,320	$ 153,504	$ 139,326	$ 130,144	$ 121,276
Merchandise sales	172,324	121,410	121,465	116,187	101,856
Food sales	178,791	121,329	114,951	106,404	95,203
Lodging	98,105	81,427	70,110	61,731	54,043
Disneyland					
Admissions and rides	102,619	98,273	92,065	87,066	75,758
Merchandise sales	72,300	76,684	79,146	72,140	60,235
Food sales	45,699	44,481	44,920	41,703	35,865
Participant fees,					
Walt Disney Travel Co.,					
Tokyo Disneyland royalties					
and other	83,044	28,502	29,828	28,005	26,843
Total revenues	$ 1,031,202	$ 725,610	$ 691,811	$ 643,380	$ 571,079
Theme Park Attendance					
Walt Disney World	22,712	12,560	13,221	13,783	13,792
Disneyland	9,980	10,421	11,343	11,522	10,760
Total	32,692	22,981	24,564	25,305	24,552
MOTION PICTURES					
Theatrical					
Domestic	$ 38,635	$ 55,408	$ 54,624	$ 63,350	$ 49,594
Foreign	43,825	64,525	76,279	78,314	57,288
Television					
Worldwide	27,992	44,420	43,672	19,736	27,903
Home Video and Non-Theatrical					
Worldwide	55,006	37,749	22,231	10,565	9,273
Total revenues	$ 165,458	$ 202,102	$ 196,806	$ 171,965	$ 144,058
CONSUMER PRODUCTS AND OTHER					
Character merchandising	$ 45,429	$ 35,912	$ 30,555	$ 29,631	$ 24,787
Publications	20,006	20,821	24,658	22,284	18,985
Records and music publishing	30,666	26,884	27,358	23,432	16,129
Educational media	10,269	15,468	21,148	21,908	19,967
Other	4,327	3,453	12,704	1,905	1,768
Total revenues	$ 110,697	$ 102,538	$ 116,423	$ 99,160	$ 81,636

Source: 1983 annual report, Walt Disney Productions.

EXHIBIT 8 Filmed Entertainment Industry Operating Performance, Major Theatrical Distributors, 1973–84*

Year	Revenues ($ million)	Operating Income ($ million)	Margin (%)	Film Inventory ($ million)	Invent./Rev.	Trade-weighted† Dollar Exchange-rate Index	Adjusted Operating Income†	Difference‡ ($ million)
1983	$5,140.9	$581.9	11.3%	$2,789	0.54	125.3	$464.3	$ − 117.6
1982	4,448.3	550.7	12.4	2,631	0.59	116.5	472.7	− 78.0
1981	3,932.5	330.3	8.4	1,741	0.44	103.3	319.9	− 10.4
1980	3,961.8	473.5	12.0	1,580	0.40	87.4	541.9	68.4
1979	3,630.2	643.3	17.7	1,043	0.29	88.1	730.4	87.1
1978	2,667.4	557.8	20.9	1,119	0.42	92.4	603.7	45.9
1977	2,217.8	394.1	17.8	857	0.39	103.4	381.3	− 12.8
1976	1,847.1	289.8	15.7	817	0.44	105.6	274.4	− 15.4
1975	1,733.6	323.5	18.7	721	0.42	98.5	328.4	4.9
1974	1,516.1	240.8	15.9	755	0.50	101.4	237.4	− 3.4
1973	1,222.2	75.5	6.2	761	0.62	99.1	76.2	0.7

* Includes fiscal-year data for Columbia Pictures, Disney, MCA, MGM/UA, Twentieth Century-Fox, Warner Communications, and Paramount after 1978.
† Because between 30 and 45 percent of gross rentals were generated outside of the domestic market, it is useful to adjust for changes in foreign currency exchange rates. Adjusted operating income reflects operating performance net of exchange rate fluctuations.
‡ Adjusted operating income less regular operating income.

Source: H. L. Vogel, *Entertainment Industry Economics* (Cambridge University Press, 1986), p. 46.

15

EXHIBIT 9   Film Industry Market Shares*

Year	20th Century-Fox	Warner Bros.	Paramount	Columbia	Universal	MGM/UA	Buena Vista (Disney)
1983	21%	17%	14%	14%	13%	10%	3%
1982	14	10	14	10	30	11	4
1981	13	18	15	13	14	9	4
1980	16	14	16	14	20	7	4
1979	9	20	15	11	15	15	4
1978	13	13	24	11	17	11	5
1977	20	14	10	12	12	18	6
1976	13	18	10	8	13	16	7
1975	14	9	11	13	25	11	6
1974	11	23	10	7	19	9	7
1973	19	16	9	7	10	11	7
1972	9	18	22	9	5	15	5
1971	12	9	17	10	5	7	8
1970	19	5	12	8	13	9	9

* Total domestic market shares do not add to 100 percent: residual amount accounted for by smaller distributors.

Source: H. L. Vogel, *Entertainment Industry Economics* (Cambridge University Press, 1986), p. 47.

EXHIBIT 10   Estimated Probable Minimum Library Values as of 1983

	Value ($ million)	Approximate Number of Titles
Columbia	500	1,800 features
Disney	275	25 animated, 125 live action, 500 shorts
MGM/UA Entertainment	950	4,600 features (2,200 MGM), 1,310 shorts, 1,080 cartoons
Paramount	275	700 features
20th Century-Fox	350	1,400 features
Universal	700	3,000 features, 12,500 TV episodes
Warner Bros.	450	1,600 features
Total	3,450	

Source: H. L. Vogel, *Entertainment Industry Economics* (Cambridge University Press, 1986), p. 61.

EXHIBIT 11   Revenue and Attendance Estimates for 35 U.S. Theme Parks

Year	Total Revenues ($ million)	Total Operating Income ($ million)	Margin (%)	Per Capita Revenues ($)	Per Capita Operating Income ($)	Consumer Price Deflator (1967 = 1.000)
1983	$1,793.2	$323.9	18.06%	$24.49	$4.42	.335
1982	1,414.9	249.0	17.60	23.30	4.10	.346
1981	1,396.4	260.8	18.68	22.00	4.11	.367
1980	1,205.1	221.6	18.39	19.42	3.57	.405
1979	1,070.7	213.3	19.92	17.43	3.47	.460
1978	951.9	203.4	21.37	15.48	3.31	.512
1977	790.7	168.0	21.25	14.28	3.03	.551
1976	698.5	149.4	21.39	13.49	2.89	.587
1975	537.6	106.8	19.87	11.79	2.34	.620
CAGR*	16.25%	14.88%		9.57%	8.27%	

* Compound annual growth rate, 1975–83 (percent).

Source: H. L. Vogel, *Entertainment Industry Economics* (Cambridge University Press, 1986), p. 341.

EXHIBIT 12   U.S. Population by Age Bracket: Components of Change and Trends by Life Stage, 1970–95

A.   Components of Population Change

Age	Percentage Distribution			
	1970	1980	1990*	1995*
Under 5	8.4%	7.2%	7.7%	7.2%
5–19	29.3	24.6	21.0	21.2
20–29	15.1	18.2	16.0	13.8
30–59	33.2	34.3	38.3	40.9
60 and over	14.0	15.7	17.0	16.9
Total	100.0	100.0	100.0	100.0

B.   Population Trends by Life Stage (millions)

Life Stage	1970	1980	1990*	1995*
0–14 children	57.9	51.3	54.6	56.7
15–24 young adults	36.5	42.7	35.5	34.1
25–34 peak family formation	25.3	37.6	43.5	40.5
35–44 family maturation ...	23.1	25.9	37.8	42.0
45–54 peak earning power	23.3	22.7	25.4	31.4
55–64 childless parents	18.7	21.8	21.1	21.0
65 and retirement	20.1	25.7	31.8	34.0
Total population	205.1	227.7	249.7	259.6

Source: U.S. Department of Commerce.

EXHIBIT 13

Disney's Recent Buoyancy Tied to Assets Value
by Some Who See a Ripeness for Takeover Bids
(The Wall Street Journal, *January 4, 1984*)
By Gary Putka

Walt Disney Productions has stopped being a Mickey Mouse stock lately, despite a lack of analyst enthusiasm for the shares or the company's fiscal 1984 earnings prospects. Instead, buyers have been attracted by Disney's considerable asset values. Some of them have raised the possibility that the company, once regarded as the quintessential American success story, may be ripe for a change of ownership.

Culminating a 44 percent drop in price from the 1983 high, Disney shares fell 11½ points to 47¼ on November 10 after a disappointing earnings announcement. Since then, however, the shares have risen to 52⅝ at yesterday's close, while the overall market has been about flat. Most recently, the shares gained on nine of the past 11 trading days, with volume considerably higher than the levels that preceded the November selling binge.

Disney says it knows of no reason for the market activity, except that it might represent a recovery from the "overreaction" that followed the earnings announcement, according to Michael Bagnall, chief financial officer. Asked about rumors that Disney's management might be exploring the possibility of taking the company, or part of it, private, he replies, "Absolutely not."

Mr. Bagnall says Disney also is unaware of any accumulation of its shares by a hostile party. An aggressor would have to overcome corporate bylaws that require approval by 80 percent of the shares for a change in ownership. Including a 4.2 percent holding by officers and directors, Disney employees and family members are believed to hold 15 percent to 20 percent of the 34.7 million shares.

So what's all the speculation about? Disney, according to merger speculators and others who've been buying the stock, has all the characteristics of a concern that can be bought through borrowing against its property. Its debt is relatively low; it has assets, such as Disneyland, which can be revalued upward to generate tax deductions for a prospective buyer, and its cash flow could turn significantly higher within a brief time. And even if these factors don't prompt a buyout, they significantly reduce the risk that the stock could go lower, says Michael Metz, market strategist at Oppenheimer.

Mr. Metz, who also manages money at Oppenhiemer, has been buying Disney shares for his clients recently. He argues that large amounts of pension fund and bank capital are eager to finance leveraged buyouts currently, and that Disney probably will be approached. "This company has one of the great American franchises, assets and the prospect of a dramatic upswing in cash flow." In addition, he says, institutional selling of the stock was "climactic" in early November, which may mean that those inclined to get out of Disney already have done so.

Disney's book value is about $40 a share, but the company owns considerable real estate and a film library, both carried on its books at substantially below market values. Land holdings include 28,000 acres in central Florida at its Disneyworld/Epcot Center complex, and another 1,340 acres in California, which includes Disneyland and filming facilities. Mr. Metz says that valuing the land is an impossible task since most of the Florida tract is undeveloped. But a recent report by Cyrus J. Lawrence analyst Peter Appert placed Disney's asset value at $64 to $99 a share.

Just how much Disney's cash flow might improve in its fiscal year, ending September 30, is debatable. But it is clear that a five-year spending spree to finance Epcot Center, its newest theme park, will peak in 1984. Mr. Bagnall says that "not much more than $100 million" remains to be spent on building at Epcot, on which Disney has spent $1.3 billion.

Accounting for tax changes and other adjustments that would be made in a leveraged buyout, Disney could improve its cash flow to $8 a share, says David Londoner, an analyst at Wertheim. That cash flow would more than support debt payments necessary to finance a buyout, but Mr. Londoner doesn't believe one will happen and isn't recommending the stock.

EXHIBIT 13 *(concluded)*

Disney's management isn't prone to make big borrowings for buyouts on anything else, Mr. Londoner notes. It borrowed only about a quarter of its Epcot needs, and currently has debt of about $330 million.

And in the absence of any kind of bid for the company. Mr. Londoner sees an unspectacular future. He figures Disney will make $3.10 a share in its current year, up from last year's $2.70. Attendance has been down at Disney's Florida complex since September, and Mr. Londoner says he's worried about the erosion of profit margins at the parks, which marked the disappointing earnings statement that hurt the stock.

Harold Vogel, who follows Disney for Merrill Lynch, rates the stock "three" on his firm's five-point rating system. Mr. Vogel says the main reason is the losses of the Disney pay TV channel and his belief that its profitability may be some time in coming.

EXHIBIT 14 Share Price of Walt Disney Productions

Date	Price	News
November 7, 1983	$62⅜	
November 10, 1983 ...	47½	Quarterly earnings
January 3, 1984	52⅝	
March 26, 1984	63⅞	Takeover rumors
April 9, 1984	67	Steinberg acquired 6.3%
April 18, 1984	62¼	Quarterly earnings
May 2, 1984	66	Steinberg has 12.1%
May 18, 1984	63	Disney to buy Arvida
June 7, 1984	65⅛	Disney to buy Gibson Greeting
June 11, 1984	54¼	Steinberg tender offer for 49.9%

Case 2

Peter Lynch and the Fidelity Magellan Fund

There is nothing flamboyant about him, nothing exotic, nothing larger-than-life. He is 43 years old, tall and thin, his hair completely white, with classic Irish features. The only thing that sets him apart is this: for 10 years now, he has been the best mutual fund manager alive. . . . "Around Fidelity," says one former marketing aide, "Peter Lynch is God." [1]

In March 1988, Peter Lynch, the manager of the Magellan Fund of Fidelity Management and Research Company, gave an interview in which he said, "My goal is to outperform the market over the long term by 5–6 percent annually."[2] This goal stood in stark contrast to the historical performance of equally ambitious and talented managers of other mutual funds. The goal also contrasted with the conventionally held view that it would be difficult to outperform the broad stock market averages because of increased volatility in the market.

The Magellan Fund was the largest equity mutual fund in the world, with nearly $7.7 billion in net assets after the stock market crash in October 1987. Fidelity Management Company, which provided management and advisory services to the fund's shareholders, was a privately held company, managing over 100 mutual funds. Fidelity's operating revenue in 1987 was $1.07 billion; operating profit was $80.7 million. Fidelity's assets under management at the end of 1987 were $75.3 billion. Wide acknowledgment placed Fidelity among the most innovative—and aggressive—mutual fund advisors in the industry.[3]

---

[1] Joseph Nocera, "The Ga-Ga Years," *Esquire,* February 1988, p. 87.
[2] "A Magellan Update with Fund Manager Peter Lynch," *Fidelity Investments,* March 1988.
[3] Christopher J. Chipello, "Fidelity Investments, Resigned to Drops in Profit, Growth, Remains Aggressive," *The Wall Street Journal,* Wednesday, May 18, 1988, p. 46.

This case was prepared by Robert F. Bruner.
Copyright © 1988 by the Darden Graduate Business School Foundation, Charlottesville, VA.

THE U.S. EQUITY MARKET

Institutional investors or "money managers" who managed pension funds and mutual funds on behalf of individual investors dominated the market for common stocks in the United States in the late 1980s. While statistics still revealed that households, life insurance companies, personal trusts (i.e., those managed by bank trust departments), and nonprofit institutions held the majority of shares of common stock (62.1 percent) the percentage had been declining in recent years (down from 69.7 percent in 1981). Growth in the percentage of equity held by pension funds and mutual funds offset this decline, as shown in Exhibit 1.

But the aggregate figures somewhat masked the rapid growth of mutual funds from 1981 to 1987. Over this period, assets in equities-oriented mutual funds grew from $37.4 billion to $210.1 billion. Moreover, the percent of individual investors who owned mutual fund shares rose from 15.8 percent to 30.3 percent between 1981 and 1985.

More importantly, the sheer dominance of money managers appeared not in assets held but in their trading muscle—their ability to move huge sums of money into and out of stocks on short notice. Accordingly, money managers were the principal price setters (or "lead steers") in the stock market. Approximately 85 percent of all trades on the New York Stock Exchange involved institutional investors.

The rising dominance of institutional investors resulted in the growth of trading volume, average trade size, and, especially, in the growth of block trading (i.e., individual trades of more than 10,000 shares), which was virtually nonexistent 20 years ago but now accounted for about half of the trading volume (see Exhibit 2). The surge in size and power of institutional investors coincided with a bull market in common stocks that emerged in August 1982 and ended with the crash in October 1987 (see Exhibit 3). The collapse of the bull market resulted from several cumulative developments: (1) rising interest rates; (2) trade and government budget deficits; (3) instability in foreign exchange markets; (4) threatened changes in merger regulation; and (5) the failure of market clearing systems to keep up with the heavy volume of transactions—all compounded by (6) panic selling by the institutional investors.

MUTUAL FUND INDUSTRY

Mutual funds served several economic functions for investors. First, they afforded the individual investor the opportunity to efficiently diversify his or her portfolio (i.e., own many different stocks) without having to invest the sizable amount of capital usually necessary to achieve efficiency. Efficiency also was reflected in the ability of mutual funds to exploit scale economies in trading and transactions costs, economies unavailable to the typical individual investor. Second, in theory, mutual funds provided the individual investor the professional expertise necessary to earn abnormal returns through successful securities analysis.

A third view was that the mutual fund industry provided:

an insulating layer between the individual investor and the painful vicissitudes of the marketplace. This service, after all, allows individuals to go about their daily lives without spending too much time on the aggravating subject of what to buy and sell and when, and it spares them the even greater aggravation of kicking themselves for making the wrong decision. . . . Thus, the money management industry is really selling "more peace of mind" and "less worry," though it rarely bothers to say so.[4]

At the end of 1987, there existed 1,389 mutual funds.[5] This total included many different kinds of funds, each pursuing a specific investment focus and categorized into several acknowledged segments in the industry: aggressive growth (i.e., capital appreciation-oriented), equity income, growth, growth and income, international, option, specialty, small company, balanced, and a variety of bond or fixed-income funds.[6]

Funds whose principal focus of investing was common stocks comprised the largest sector of the industry—890 funds. There were, in comparison, 40 balanced funds, and 428 fixed-income funds. In short, the mutual fund industry could be thought of as a predominantly equity-oriented industry.

The performance of a mutual fund could be evaluated in terms of its total returns to investors as calculated by:

Annual total return =

$$\frac{\text{Change in net asset value} + \text{Dividends} + \text{Capital gain distributions}}{\text{Net asset value (at the beginning of the year)}}$$

Exhibits 4 and 5 indicate how net asset value (NAV) and the change in NAV were calculated for Magellan. For instance, using the data in Exhibit 6, the annual total return for 1986 would be:

$$\text{Total return 1986} = \frac{(48.69 - 45.21) + .46 + 6.84}{45.21} = 23.74\%$$

It is worth noting that computing the annual total return in this manner *does* take into account annual management fees, and *does not* take into account front-end or back-end "loads."

Mutual fund advisors received compensation under various schemes that featured variations on two components:

Initial Payments.   Nearly three quarters of all mutual funds were sold under some kind of commission, sales fee, or "load." The load could be as large as 8.5 percent of the investor's principal. Back-end loads (i.e., redemption fees) also were possible.

---

[4]Contrarious, "Good News and Bad News," *Personal Investing* III, no. 16, August 26, 1987, p. 128.

[5]This estimate is based on the number of funds followed by Lipper Analytical Services, Inc. Excluded from this count are money market funds and short-term municipal funds, of which there were about 800.

[6]Aggressive growth funds seek to maximize capital gains. Current income is of little concern. Growth funds invest in more well-known companies with steadier track records. Growth and income funds invest in companies with longer track records that are expected to increase in value and provide a steady income stream. International funds invest in foreign companies. Option funds seek to maximize current returns by investing in dividend-paying stocks on which call options are traded. Balanced funds attempt to conserve principal while earning both current income and capital gains.

Annual Fees.   Annual management fees ranged from under 0.5 to 2.0 percent of fund assets. Some funds also charged a separate fee for marketing and promotion expenses, which could run up to 2 percent of assets.

The net effect of these payments on shareholder returns could be dramatic.[7] Another drag on returns to shareholders was the tendency of funds to keep 10 percent of assets in cash—5 percent to meet redemptions and 5 percent to meet unexpected bargains. In comparison, Magellan carried only 1.4 percent in cash before the stock market crash in October 1987, ultimately forcing Peter Lynch to dump $1 billion worth of shares in the market in order to meet unexpectedly high redemptions.

The number and types of mutual funds increased dramatically during the bull market (see Exhibit 7 for a summary of the growth of mutual fund assets). This reflected the increased liquidity in the market and the demand by investors for equity surrogates. But more importantly, it reflected the effort by mutual fund organizations to *segment the market* (i.e., to identify the specialized and changing needs of investors and to create products to meet those needs). One important result was a broader customer base for the mutual fund industry as well as deeper penetration of the total market for financial services.

Another important result of this development was that it added a degree of complexity to the marketplace that altered the investment behavior of some equity investors. In particular, this tended to encourage fund switching, especially from one type of fund to another within a family of funds. Such exchange activity increased from a few billion dollars in volume in 1980 to over $100 billion in 1986. This reflected the greater range of mutual funds from which to choose, the increased volatility in the market, and the increased fashionability of timing-oriented investment strategies. In short, as the bull market matured, mutual fund money became "hotter" (i.e., tended to turn over faster).

PERFORMANCE OF THE MUTUAL FUND INDUSTRY

Exhibit 8 reveals that the average return on 683 general equity funds over the 1-, 5-, and 10-year periods was below that of the Standard & Poor's 500 index of common stocks (S&P 500). In 1987, only one third of all equity mutual funds provided returns (before fees and expenses) greater than the S&P 500. This result was consistent with the performance of pension funds as well: over the period 1969 to 1984, pension funds, on average, underperformed the S&P 500 by one percentage point.[8] Exhibit 9 presents summary data on the highest performing funds in recent years.

The two most frequently used measures of performance were (1) the percentage annual growth rate of net asset value (i.e., total return on investment), and (2) the absolute dollar value today of an investment made at some time in the past. These measures were then compared to the performance of a benchmark portfolio, such as the S&P 500. However, academicians criticized these approaches because of their failure to adjust for the

---

[7]For instance, suppose that you invested $10,000 in a fund that would appreciate at 10 percent annually, and that you sold out after three years. Also suppose that the advisory firm charged annual fees of 2 percent and a redemption fee of 4 percent. The fees would cut pretax profit by 35 percent—from $3,310 to $2,162.

[8]Burton Malkiel, *A Random Walk Down Wall Street* (New York: W.W. Norton, 1985), p. 170.

riskiness of the mutual fund. For instance, it should be expected that a conservatively managed mutual fund would yield a lower return—precisely because it took fewer risks.

After adjusting for the riskiness of the fund, academic studies reported that mutual funds were able to perform up to the market on a gross returns basis; however, when expenses were factored in, they underperformed the market.[9] Some analysts attributed this to the average 1.3 percent expense ratio of mutual funds and the need to hold cash.[10]

Most mutual fund managers relied on some variation of two classic schools of securities analysis:

Technical Analysis. This involves the identification of profitable investment opportunities based on trends in stock prices, volume, market sentiment, Fibonacci numbers, and the like.

Fundamental Analysis. This approach relies on insights afforded by an analysis of the economic fundamentals of a company and its industry: demand and supply, costs, growth, prospects, and so on.

While variations on these approaches often produced supernormal returns in certain years, there was no guarantee that they would produce such returns consistently over time. Burton Malkiel, an academic researcher, concluded that a passive buy-and-hold strategy (of a large diversified portfolio) would do as well for the investor as the average mutual fund:

> While funds may have very good records for certain short time periods, there is generally no consistency to superior performance. The only dependable relationship in mutual fund performance is the tendency for funds assuming greater risks to earn, on average, a larger long-run rate of return.[11]

Many academicians expected this result. They argued that the stock market followed a "random walk," where the price movements of tomorrow are essentially uncorrelated with the price movement of today. In essence, this denied the possibility that there could be momentum in the movement of common stock prices. By this view, technical analysis was the modern-day equivalent of alchemy.

Fundamental analysis, too, had its academic detractors. They argued that capital markets are informationally efficient and that the insights available to any one fundamental analyst are bound to be available to all. Thus, they concluded that stock prices already impound all that is known about a company.

By implication, these academic theories were highly critical of the services provided by active mutual fund managers. Paul Samuelson, the Nobel Prize–winning economist said:

---

[9]For instance, Michael Jensen (1968) reported that gross risk-adjusted returns were − .4 percent and that net risk-adjusted returns (i.e., net of expenses) were − 1.1 percent. Main (1977) updated the study and found that for a sample of 70 mutual funds, net risk-adjusted returns were essentially zero.

[10]Jeffrey M. Laderman, "The Best Mutual Funds," *Business Week,* February 22, 1988, p. 64.

[11]Malkiel, *A Random Walk Down Wall Street,* p. 161.

Stock prices already have discounted in them an allowance for their future prospects. Hence . . . one stock [is] about as good or bad a buy as another. To [the] passive investor, chance alone would be as good a method of selection as anything else.[12]

Various popular tests of this thinking seemed to support it. For instance, *Forbes* magazine chose 28 stocks by throwing darts in June 1967 and invested $1,000 in each. By 1984, the $28,000 investment was worth $131,697.61 for a 9.5 percent compound rate of return. This beat the broad market averages and almost all mutual funds. *Forbes* concluded, "It would seem that a combination of luck and sloth beats brains."[13]

Yet the nagging problem remained that there were still *some* superstar money managers—like Peter Lynch—who, over long periods, way outperformed the market. In reply, Professor Burton Malkiel suggested[14] that beating the market was much like participating in a coin-tossing contest where those who consistently flip heads are the winners. At the first flip, half the contestants are eliminated. At the second flip, half of the surviving contestants are eliminated. And so on until on the seventh flip only eight contestants remain. To the naive observer, the ability to flip heads consistently looks like extraordinary skill. By analogy, Professor Malkiel suggested that the success of a few superstar portfolio managers could be explained as luck. Consistent with this view, the ranking of high-return equity funds (see Exhibit 9) displayed little consistency across performance measurement periods.

As might be expected, the community of money managers received the academic theories with great hostility. And even in the ranks of academicians, dissension appeared in the form of the "investment behaviorists" who suggested that greed, fear, and panic are much more significant factors in the setting of stock prices than the mainstream theory admits. For instance, the stock market crash of October 1987 seemed to many to be totally inconsistent with the view of markets as fundamentally rational and efficient. Professor Lawrence Summers of Harvard argued that the crash was a "clear gap with the theory. If anyone did seriously believe that price movements are determined by changes in information about economic fundamentals, they've got to be disabused of that notion by [the] 500-point drop."[15] Professor Robert Shiller of Yale said, "The efficient market hypothesis is the most remarkable error in the history of economic theory. This is just another nail in its coffin."[16]

FIDELITY MAGELLAN FUND

Exhibit 6 presents a summary of the Magellan Fund as it stood in late 1987 and of its performance over the previous 10 years. The balance sheet and operating statements of the fund are presented in Exhibits 4 and 5 respectively. The long-term performance results

---

[12]Paul Samuelson, quoted in Malkiel, *A Random Walk Down Wall Street*, p. 175.

[13]*Forbes,* summer 1984, cited in Malkiel, *A Random Walk Down Wall Street*, p. 164.

[14]Malkiel, *A Random Walk Down Wall Street*, pp. 167–68.

[15]B. Donnelly, "Efficient-Market Theorists Are Puzzled by Recent Gyrations in Stock Market," *The Wall Street Journal*, October 23, 1987, p. 7.

[16]Ibid.

suggested to at least one analyst that Magellan tended to outperform the market in bull markets and underperform the market in bear markets. This was attributable to Peter Lynch's conscious strategy of staying fully invested at all times, rather than attempting to time the extent of the market investments.

The other striking fact about Magellan's recent financial results was its sheer rate of growth. One analyst pointed out that:

> Because of its enormous size, Magellan can no longer beat the market the way it once could. Lynch himself advises people looking for big gains to try another fund. But they won't.[17]

In the fourth quarter of 1987, investors added approximately $96 billion to their savings. Thus, it was a particularly relevant question to decide whether these funds should be allocated to superstars like Peter Lynch.

---

[17]Nocera, "The Ga-Ga Years," p. 88.

EXHIBIT 1   Breakdown of Control of U.S. Equity (billions of dollars, except ratios)

	1981	1982	1983	1984
Total market value*	$1,504.9	$1,720.9	$2,021.9	$2,021.5
Amount controlled by pensions*	$266.3	$322.2	$403.2	$405.2
Percent of total	17.7	18.7	19.9	20.0
Amount controlled by households, personal trusts, and nonprofits*	$1,049.4	$1,175.0	$1,324.5	$1,320.6
Percent of total	69.7	68.3	65.5	65.3
Amount controlled by foreign sector	$64.4	$76.3	$96.4	$94.6
Percent of total	4.3	4.4	4.8	4.7
Amount controlled by mutual funds	$37.4	$49.4	$74.4	$80.6
Percent of total	2.5	2.9	3.7	4.0
Amount controlled by life insurance companies*	$47.7	$55.7	$64.9	$63.3
Percent of total	3.2	3.2	3.2	3.1

*Does not include mutual fund shares.

Source: Federal Reserve Board.

1985	1986:I	II	III	IV	1987:I	II
$2,584.3	$2,876.7	$3.068.4	$2,836.3	$2,948.0	$3,521.1	$3,623.7
$513.4	$593.4	$627.0	$580.6	$606.6	$711.0	$739.1
19.9	20.6	20.4	20.5	20.6	20.2	20.4
$1,687.0	$1,833.0	$1,955.1	$1,792.9	$1,844.8	$2,215.9	$2,251.7
65.3	63.7	63.7	63.2	62.6	62.9	62.1
$124.1	$143.0	$160.4	$155.7	$167.4	$209.4	$223.8
4.8	5.0	5.2	5.5	5.7	5.9	6.2
$113.7	$140.9	$150.8	$148.1	$161.2	$195.6	$210.1
4.4	4.9	4.9	5.2	5.5	5.6	5.8
$77.5	$83.8	$87.1	$84.3	$90.9	$101.8	$105.4
3.0	2.9	2.8	3.0	3.1	2.9	2.9

EXHIBIT 2 Growth of Block Trading, NYSE

	Total Block Trades	Percent of Total Share Volume
1965	2,171	3.1
1970	17,217	15.4
1975	34,420	16.6
1976	47,632	18.7
1977	54,275	22.4
1978	75,036	22.9
1979	97,509	26.5
1980	133,597	29.2
1981	145,564	31.8
1982	254,707	41.0
1983	363,415	45.6
1984	433,427	49.8
1985	539,039	51.7
1986	665,587	49.9

Source: NYSE Factbook.

EXHIBIT 3   U.S. Market: S&P 500 Index, January 1982 to November 1987

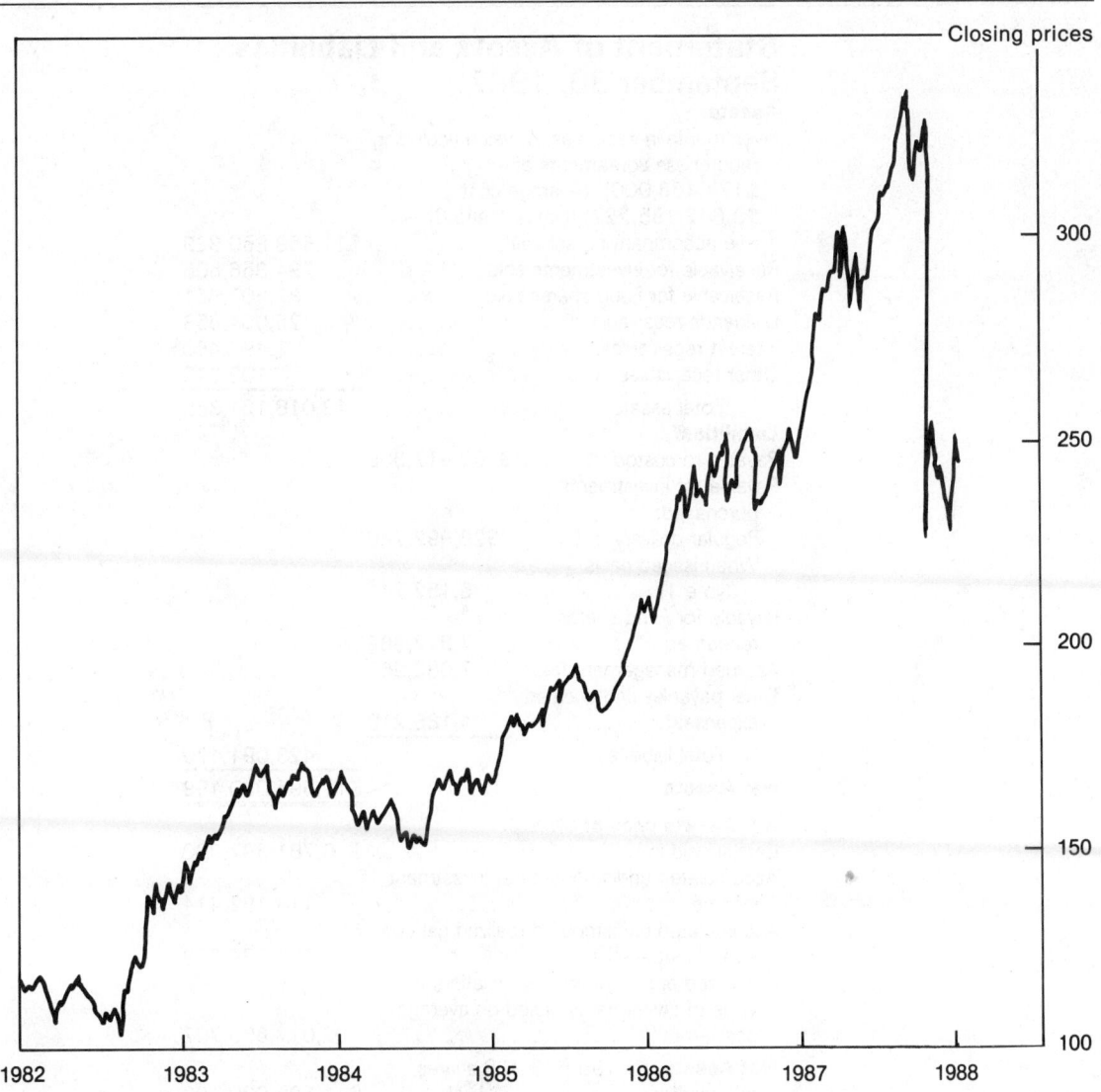

Source: U.S. Government Report on Market Mechanisms.

EXHIBIT 4

Statement of Assets and Liabilities
September 30, 1987

Assets:

Investments in securities, at value (including repurchase agreements of $174,166,000), (Average cost $9,642,195,222) (Notes 1 and 6)— See accompanying schedule	$11,659,850,929
Receivable for investments sold	294,356,506
Receivable for Fund shares sold	37,307,861
Dividends receivable	25,004,653
Interest receivable	1,497,480
Other receivables	103,940
Total assets	12,018,121,369

Liabilities:

Payable to custodian	$ 68,917,308	
Payable for investments purchased:		
Regular delivery	328,992,246	
When-issued basis (Note 1)	6,152,741	
Payable for Fund shares redeemed	7,812,689	
Accrued management fee .	7,030,967	
Other payables and accrued expenses	4,185,219	
Total liabilities		423,091,170
Net Assets		$11,595,030,199

Net Assets consist of:

Capital paid in	$ 8,781,397,800
Accumulated undistributed net investment income	114,192,414
Accumulated undistributed realized gain on investments—net	681,784,278
Unrealized appreciation (depreciation) in value of investments based on average cost—net	2,017,655,707
Net Assets, for 198,673,409 shares outstanding	$11,595,030,199
Net Asset Value and redemption price per share ($11,595,030,199 ÷ 198,673,409 shares)	$58.36
Offering price per share (100/97 of $58.36)	$60.16

Source: Six-month report, Magellan Fund.

EXHIBIT 5

Statement of Operations
Six Months Ended September 30, 1987

Investment Income:

Dividends:

Unaffiliated issuers	$106,352,900	
Affiliated issuers (Note 6)	3,811,274	$110,164,174
Interest		7,129,932
Total income		117,294,106

Expenses:

Management fee (Note 4)	40,724,990	
Transfer and shareholders' servicing agent (Note 4)	13,730,330	
Accounting (Note 4)	48,804	
Trustees' fees and expenses (Note 4)	74,922	
Custodian fees and expenses	696,502	
Reports to shareholders	511,867	
Audit	91,762	
Legal	139,259	
Registration fees	409,259	
Interest (Note 5)	48,232	
Miscellaneous	99,598	
Total expenses		56,575,525
Investment income—net		60,718,581

Realized and Unrealized Gain (Loss) on Investments (Note 3):

Realized gain (loss) on investments on basis of average cost—net:

Unaffiliated issuers	801,416,371	
Affiliated issuers (Note 6) . . .	30,117,285	
Realized gain (loss) on investments on basis of average cost—net		831,533,656
Increase in unrealized appreciation (depreciation)		64,305,483
Net gain (loss) on investments		895,839,139
Net increase (decrease) in net assets resulting from operations		$956,557,720

Source: Six-month report, Magellan Fund.

Appendix to Exhibits 4 and 5

PETER LYNCH AND THE FIDELITY MAGELLAN FUND

1. Significant Accounting Policies.   Fidelity Magellan Fund (the "Fund") is registered under the Investment Company Act of 1940, as amended, as an open-end, diversified management investment company established as a "Massachusetts business trust." The Declaration of Trust permits the Trustees to create an unlimited number of series, and with respect to each series, to issue an unlimited number of full and fractional shares of a single class. There is currently only one series. The following is a summary of significant accounting policies of the Fund.

Security Valuation.   Investments in securities traded on the New York Stock Exchange or the American Stock Exchange are valued at the last sale price, or, if no sale, at the closing bid price. Securities traded on any other exchange are valued in the same manner, or, if not so traded, on the basis of closing over-the-counter bid prices. Debt securities are valued in the same manner or, in some other manner, if, in the opinion of the Board of Trustees, such other manner would more accurately reflect the value of such securities. All other securities and other assets are appraised at their fair value as determined in good faith under consistently applied procedures established by and under the general supervision of the Board of Trustees. Short-term securities are valued at amortized cost which approximates current value.

*****

4. Management Fee and Other Transactions with Affiliates.   The Fund employs FMR to furnish investment advisory and other services to the Fund. Under FMR's Management Contract (the "Contract") with the Fund, approved by shareholders on March 31, 1987, and effective April 1, 1987, FMR acts as investment advisor and, subject to the supervision of the Board of Trustees, directs the investments of the Fund in accordance with its investment objective, policies, and limitations. FMR also provides the fund with all necessary office facilities and personnel for servicing the Fund's investments, and pays the salaries and fees of all officers of the Fund, of all Trustees who are "interested persons" of the Fund or FMR, and of all personnel of the Fund or FMR performing services relating to research, statistical and investment activities. In addition, FMR or its affiliates, subject to the supervision of the Board of Trustees, provide the management and administrative services necessary for the operation of the Fund. These services include providing facilities for maintaining the Fund's organization, supervising relations with custodians, transfer and pricing agents, accountants, underwriters, and other persons dealing with the Fund, preparing all general shareholder communications and conducting shareholder relations, maintaining the Fund's records and the registration of the Fund's shares under federal and state law, developing management and shareholder services for the Fund and furnishing reports, evaluations, and analyses on a variety of subjects to the Trustees.

For its services under the Contract, FMR receives a monthly management fee composed of a basic fee and a performance adjustment. The basic fee is composed of two elements: a group fee rate and an annual individual fund fee rate. The monthly group fee rate is based on the aggregate monthly average net assets of all of the registered investment companies having advisory and service or management contracts with FMR. The monthly group fee rate is the weighted average of a graduated series of annual rates ranging from 0.52 percent for average group net assets of $3 billion to 0.33 percent of average group net assets in excess of $48 billion. The annual individual fund fee rate is 0.30 percent. One twelfth of the annual basic fee rate is applied to the average net assets of the Fund for each month to arrive at the basic fee for that month.

FMR adopted the graduated group fee rate schedule in part in accordance with the settlement of the *Labaton* vs. *Fidelity Management Company et al*. litigation, approved by the United States District Court for the District of Massachusetts on April 7, 1986. Under the terms of the settlement, FMR will not seek an increase in fee rates paid by the Fund to FMR for a five-year period ending April 6, 1991.

The monthly basic fee is subject to an upward or downward adjustment based upon the comparative investment performance of the Fund and the Standard & Poor's Daily Stock Price Index of 500 Common Stocks over a 36-month period (the most recent month plus the previous 35 months). The performance adjustment is calculated by applying the performance adjustment rate (maximum annual rate $\pm$ 0.20 percent) to the average net assets of the Fund for the performance period giving the dollar amount which is added to or subtracted from the basic fee. The management fee for the six-month period ending September 30, 1987, amounted to $40,724,990 after an upward performance fee adjustment of $5,146,563 to the basic fee of $35,578,427. The total fee was equivalent to an annual rate of 0.7579 percent of the average net assets of the Fund.

Fidelity Service Co. ("Service"), an affiliate of FMR, is transfer and shareholders' servicing agent for the Fund, for which Service received fees of $11,172,598 for the six-month period ended September 30, 1987. In addition, Service was reimbursed $2,557,732 for out-of-pocket expenses incurred in the performance of such services. The Fund and Service also have an agreement under which Service determines the net asset value per share and maintains the portfolio and general accounting records of the Fund, for which Service received fees during the six-month period ended September 30, 1987, of $7,500 and out-of-pocket expenses of $41,304.

During the six-month period ended September 30, 1987, the Fund placed a portion of its portfolio transactions through an affiliate of FMR, Fidelity Brokerage Services, Inc., for which brokerage commissions of $1,875,068 were paid.

Fidelity Distributors Corporation, an affiliate of FMR and the general distributor of the Fund, received sales charges aggregating $39,225,960 on sales of shares of the Fund during the six-month period ended September 30, 1987.

The fees and expenses of the noninterested Trustees amounted to $74,922 for the six-month period ended September 30, 1987.

EXHIBIT 6

Fidelity Magellan

Objective	Load%	Yield%	Assets $mil	N.A.V.
Growth	3.0%	1.4%	11590	40.74

Fidelity Magellan Fund seeks capital appreciation. The fund invests primarily in common stock and securities convertible into common stock; up to 20% of its assets may be invested in debt securities of all types and quality. The fund looks for capital appreciation in the following areas: 1) domestic corporations operating primarily in the United States; 2) domestic corporations that have significant activities and interest outside the U.S.; and 3) foreign companies. There is no limitation on total foreign investment but no more than 40% of the fund's assets will be in companies operating exclusively in one foreign country.

Risk
Average
Rating
★★★★★
Buy

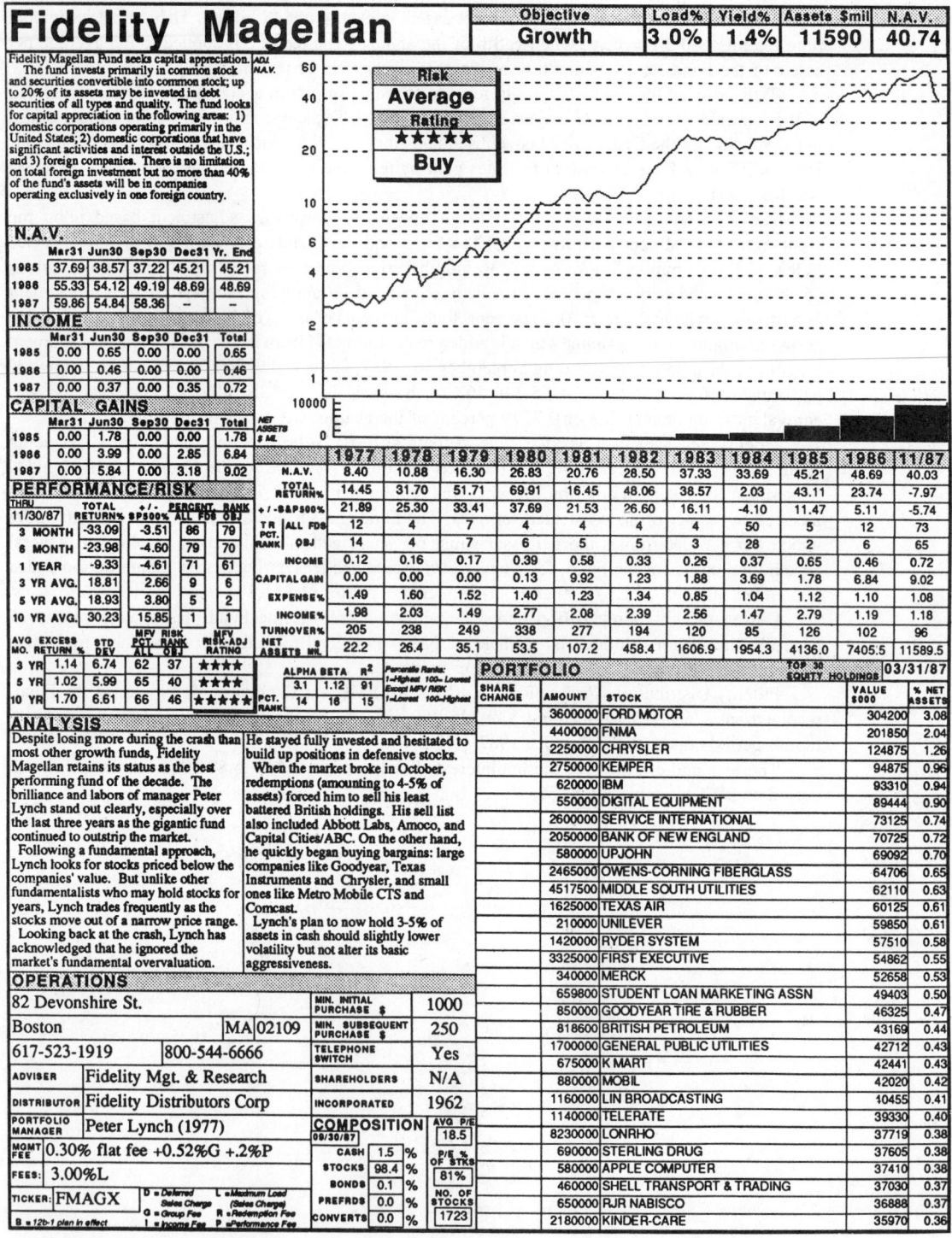

N.A.V.

	Mar31	Jun30	Sep30	Dec31	Yr. End
1985	37.69	38.57	37.22	45.21	45.21
1986	55.33	54.12	49.19	48.69	48.69
1987	59.86	54.84	58.36	--	--

INCOME

	Mar31	Jun30	Sep30	Dec31	Total
1985	0.00	0.65	0.00	0.00	0.65
1986	0.00	0.46	0.00	0.00	0.46
1987	0.00	0.37	0.00	0.35	0.72

CAPITAL GAINS

	Mar31	Jun30	Sep30	Dec31	Total
1985	0.00	1.78	0.00	0.00	1.78
1986	0.00	3.99	0.00	2.85	6.84
1987	0.00	5.84	0.00	3.18	9.02

PERFORMANCE/RISK

THRU 11/30/87	TOTAL RETURN%	+/- S&P500%	PERCENT RANK ALL FDS	RANK OBJ
3 MONTH	-33.09	-3.51	86	79
6 MONTH	-23.98	-4.60	79	70
1 YEAR	-9.33	-4.61	71	61
3 YR AVG.	18.81	2.66	9	6
5 YR AVG.	18.93	3.80	5	2
10 YR AVG.	30.23	15.85	1	1

	AVG EXCESS MO. RETURN %	STD DEV	MFV RISK PCT. RANK ALL OBJ	MFV RISK-ADJ RATING
3 YR	1.14	6.74	62	37	★★★★
5 YR	1.02	5.99	65	40	★★★★
10 YR	1.70	6.61	66	46	★★★★★

	ALPHA	BETA	R²
	3.1	1.12	91
PCT. RANK	14	16	15

Percentile Ranks:
1=Highest 100=Lowest
Except MFV RISK
1=Lowest 100=Highest

	1977	1978	1979	1980	1981	1982	1983	1984	1985	1986	11/87
N.A.V.	8.40	10.88	16.30	26.83	20.76	28.50	37.33	33.69	45.21	48.69	40.03
TOTAL RETURN%	14.45	31.70	51.71	69.91	16.45	48.06	38.57	2.03	45.21	23.74	-7.97
+/-S&P500%	21.89	25.30	33.41	37.69	21.53	26.60	16.11	-4.10	11.47	5.11	-5.74
TR PCT. RANK ALL FDS	12	4	7	4	4	4	4	50	5	12	73
TR PCT. RANK OBJ	14	4	7	6	5	5	3	28	2	6	65
INCOME	0.12	0.16	0.17	0.39	0.58	0.33	0.26	0.37	0.65	0.46	0.72
CAPITAL GAIN	0.00	0.00	0.00	0.13	9.92	1.23	1.88	3.69	1.78	6.84	9.02
EXPENSE%	1.49	1.60	1.52	1.40	1.23	1.34	0.85	1.04	1.12	1.10	1.08
INCOME%	1.98	2.03	1.49	2.77	2.08	2.39	2.56	1.47	2.79	1.19	1.18
TURNOVER%	205	238	249	338	277	194	120	85	126	102	96
NET ASSETS MIL.	22.2	26.4	35.1	53.5	107.2	458.4	1606.9	1954.3	4136.0	7405.5	11589.5

ANALYSIS

Despite losing more during the crash than most other growth funds, Fidelity Magellan retains its status as the best performing fund of the decade. The brilliance and labors of manager Peter Lynch stand out clearly, especially over the last three years as the gigantic fund continued to outstrip the market.

Following a fundamental approach, Lynch looks for stocks priced below the companies' value. But unlike other fundamentalists who may hold stocks for years, Lynch trades frequently as the stocks move out of a narrow price range.

Looking back at the crash, Lynch has acknowledged that he ignored the market's fundamental overvaluation.

He stayed fully invested and hesitated to build up positions in defensive stocks. When the market broke in October, redemptions (amounting to 4-5% of assets) forced him to sell his least battered British holdings. His sell list also included Abbott Labs, Amoco, and Capital Cities/ABC. On the other hand, he quickly began buying bargains: large companies like Goodyear, Texas Instruments and Chrysler, and small ones like Metro Mobile CTS and Comcast.

Lynch's plan to now hold 3-5% of assets in cash should slightly lower volatility but not alter its basic aggressiveness.

OPERATIONS

82 Devonshire St.

Boston MA 02109

617-523-1919   800-544-6666

ADVISER	Fidelity Mgt. & Research
DISTRIBUTOR	Fidelity Distributors Corp
PORTFOLIO MANAGER	Peter Lynch (1977)
MGMT FEE	0.30% flat fee +0.52%G +.2%P
FEES:	3.00%L
TICKER:	FMAGX

D = Deferred   L = Maximum Load Sales Charge   (Sales Charge)
G = Group Fee   R = Redemption Fee
B = 12b-1 plan in effect   I = Income Fee   P = Performance Fee

MIN. INITIAL PURCHASE $	1000
MIN. SUBSEQUENT PURCHASE $	250
TELEPHONE SWITCH	Yes
SHAREHOLDERS	N/A
INCORPORATED	1962

COMPOSITION 09/30/87

CASH	1.5	%
STOCKS	98.4	%
BONDS	0.1	%
PREFRDS	0.0	%
CONVERTS	0.0	%

AVG P/E 18.5
P/E % OF STKS 81%
NO. OF STOCKS 1723

PORTFOLIO

TOP 30 EQUITY HOLDINGS 03/31/87

SHARE CHANGE	AMOUNT	STOCK	VALUE $000	% NET ASSETS
	3600000	FORD MOTOR	304200	3.08
	4400000	FNMA	201850	2.04
	2250000	CHRYSLER	124875	1.26
	2750000	KEMPER	94875	0.96
	620000	IBM	93310	0.94
	550000	DIGITAL EQUIPMENT	89444	0.90
	2600000	SERVICE INTERNATIONAL	73125	0.74
	2050000	BANK OF NEW ENGLAND	70725	0.72
	580000	UPJOHN	69092	0.70
	2465000	OWENS-CORNING FIBERGLASS	64706	0.65
	4517500	MIDDLE SOUTH UTILITIES	62110	0.63
	1625000	TEXAS AIR	60125	0.61
	210000	UNILEVER	59850	0.61
	1420000	RYDER SYSTEM	57510	0.58
	3325000	FIRST EXECUTIVE	54862	0.55
	340000	MERCK	52658	0.53
	659800	STUDENT LOAN MARKETING ASSN	49403	0.50
	850000	GOODYEAR TIRE & RUBBER	46325	0.47
	818600	BRITISH PETROLEUM	43169	0.44
	1700000	GENERAL PUBLIC UTILITIES	42712	0.43
	675000	K MART	42441	0.43
	880000	MOBIL	42020	0.42
	1160000	LIN BROADCASTING	40455	0.41
	1140000	TELERATE	39330	0.40
	8230000	LONRHO	37719	0.38
	690000	STERLING DRUG	37605	0.38
	580000	APPLE COMPUTER	37410	0.38
	460000	SHELL TRANSPORT & TRADING	37030	0.37
	650000	RJR NABISCO	36888	0.37
	2180000	KINDER-CARE	35970	0.36

EXHIBIT 7   Total Assets of Mutual Funds (in billions of dollars)

Date	Total Assets All Types of Funds	Equity Funds[1]	Bond and Income Funds	Money Market	Short Term Municipal
End of year:					
1979.....................	$94.5	$32.5	$16.6	$45.2	$0.3
1980.....................	134.8	41.0	17.4	74.5	1.9
1981.....................	241.4	38.4	16.9	181.9	4.2
1982.....................	296.7	50.6	26.3	206.6	13.2
1983.....................	292.9	73.9	39.7	162.5	16.8
1984.....................	370.7	78.1	59.1	209.7	23.8
1985.....................	495.5	109.6	142.1	207.5	36.3
1986.....................	716.3	152.5	271.6	228.3	63.8
1987 end of month:					
January	766.0	174.3	290.1	232.5	69.1
February	796.3	188.5	302.2	235.6	70.1
March	811.6	196.9	310.3	234.2	70.2
April	803.5	200.8	301.7	235.4	65.6
May	805.3	203.3	297.4	237.5	67.2
June	818.4	212.0	304.9	234.8	66.7
July	837.2	224.1	306.9	239.2	67.0
August..................	848.4	234.3	304.9	242.7	66.5
September	827.3	233.4	287.6	241.4	64.9
October.................	774.1	179.1	277.3	255.0	62.7

*Equity funds include aggressive growth, growth, growth and income, precious metals, and international.

Source: *Report of the Presidential Task Force on Market Mechanisms,* U.S. Government Printing Office, January 1988, page IV–5.

EXHIBIT 8 Lipper—Mutual Fund Performance Analysis

TOTAL REINVESTED CUMULATIVE PERFORMANCE

12/31/87 T.N.A. ($ MILS)	NO. OF FUNDS	TYPE OF FUND	3/31/73 TO 3/31/88	3/31/78 TO 3/31/88	3/31/83 TO 3/31/88	3/31/87 TO 3/31/88	12/31/87 TO 3/31/88
17,085.2	153	CAPITAL APPRECIATION FUNDS	+ 490.86%	+ 389.05%	+ 49.74%	- 10.06%	+ 7.24%
49,742.2	245	GROWTH FUNDS	+ 414.14%	+ 369.91%	+ 64.32%	+ 9.62%	+ 7.50%
6,833.2	62	SMALL COMPANY GROWTH FUNDS	+ 552.08%	+ 376.65%	+ 50.77%	+ 12.50%	+ 14.05%
59,082.2	174	GROWTH & INCOME FUNDS	+ 426.38%	+ 334.88%	+ 86.96%	+ 6.29%	+ 6.78%
16,216.6	49	EQUITY INCOME FUNDS	+ 526.22%	+ 336.93%	+ 84.89%	+ 5.46%	+ 6.46%
-------	---						
148,959.4	683	GENERAL EQUITY FUNDS AVERAGE	+ 443.53%	+ 360.62%	+ 68.62%	+ 8.84%	+ 7.77%
593.9	8	HEALTH FUNDS	+ 0.00%	+ 0.00%	+ 59.73%	+ 16.14%	+ 9.37%
2,361.0	14	NATURAL RESOURCES FUNDS	+ 477.19%	+ 381.64%	+ 75.09%	+ 6.06%	+ 10.40%
2,184.1	26	SCIENCE & TECHNOLOGY FUNDS	+ 336.75%	+ 321.50%	+ 29.24%	+ 13.55%	+ 7.33%
2,255.6	10	UTILITY FUNDS	+ 310.27%	+ 222.68%	+ 104.81%	+ 5.83%	+ 5.15%
2,375.8	43	SPECIALTY FUNDS	+ 314.94%	+ 327.55%	+ 77.68%	+ 12.09%	+ 9.64%
10,548.1	33	GLOBAL FUNDS	+ 692.28%	+ 479.37%	+ 123.25%	+ 4.23%	+ 6.87%
7,519.8	55	INTERNATIONAL FUNDS	+ 424.62%	+ 447.02%	+ 209.50%	+ 7.39%	+ 9.04%
4,419.5	25	GOLD ORIENTED FUNDS	+ 349.10%	+ 452.36%	+ 15.63%	+ 15.62%	+ 7.63%
87.1	4	OPTION GROWTH FUNDS	+ 0.00%	+ 239.17%	+ 56.90%	+ 9.15%	+ 1.26%
6,251.6	20	OPTION INCOME FUNDS	+ 222.95%	+ 211.95%	+ 59.30%	+ 5.55%	+ 6.38%
-------	---						
187,555.9	921	ALL EQUITY FUNDS AVERAGE	+ 440.72%	+ 361.31%	+ 72.84%	+ 8.14%	+ 7.43%
3,850.6	26	CONVERTIBLE SECURITIES FUNDS	+ 482.30%	+ 294.57%	+ 66.42%	+ 8.02%	+ 7.62%
8,819.2	39	BALANCED FUNDS	+ 381.02%	+ 293.91%	+ 90.05%	+ 3.27%	+ 5.03%
2,750.9	19	INCOME FUNDS	+ 342.62%	+ 228.22%	+ 69.57%	+ 0.69%	+ 5.29%
2,429.1	25	WORLD INCOME FUNDS	+ 0.00%	+ 0.00%	+ 123.07%	+ 13.04%	+ 1.28%
174,330.6	416	FIXED INCOME FUNDS	+ 250.08%	+ 165.14%	+ 69.13%	+ 2.44%	+ 3.73%
=======	====						
379,536.3	1446	ALL FUNDS AVERAGE	+ 415.41%	+ 321.59%	+ 72.80%	+ 4.76%	+ 6.18%
	1446	ALL FUNDS-MEDIAN	+ 358.95%	+ 302.47%	+ 71.85%	+ 4.77%	+ 5.23%
		NO. OF FUNDS IN UNIVERSE WITH A % CHANGE	354	410	568	1273	1429

UNMANAGED INDICES WITHOUT DIVIDENDS CUMULATIVE PERFORMANCE

VALUE 3/31/88		3/31/73 TO 3/31/88	3/31/78 TO 3/31/88	3/31/83 TO 3/31/88	3/31/87 TO 3/31/88	12/31/87 TO 3/31/88
1,988.06	DOW JONES IND AVERAGE	+ 109.05%	+ 162.50%	+ 75.93%	- 13.74%	+ 2.54%
258.89	STANDARD & POORS 500	+ 132.15%	+ 190.20%	+ 69.25%	- 11.25%	+ 4.78%
300.39	STANDARD & POORS 400	+ 140.31%	+ 206.46%	+ 75.00%	- 10.47%	+ 5.08%
146.60	NYSE COMPOSITE	+ 146.06%	+ 199.08%	+ 66.53%	- 11.63%	+ 6.06%
296.43	ASE INDEX	+ 144.21%	+ 359.80%	+ 52.38%	- 10.89%	+ 13.86%

ESTIMATED REINVESTED UNMANAGED INDICES CUMULATIVE PERFORMANCE

VALUE 3/31/88		3/31/73 TO 3/31/88	3/31/78 TO 3/31/88	3/31/83 TO 3/31/88	3/31/87 TO 3/31/88	12/31/87 TO 3/31/88
1,988.06	* DOW JONES IND REINVESTED	+ 341.09%	+ 336.87%	+ 116.95%	- 10.86%	+ 3.46%
258.89	* S & P 500 REINVESTED	+ 356.81%	+ 361.78%	+ 105.99%	- 8.3%	+ 5.69%

VALUE 2/29/88		2/28/73 TO 2/29/88	2/28/78 TO 2/29/88	2/28/83 TO 2/29/88	2/28/87 TO 2/29/88	11/30/87 TO 2/29/88
116.00	CONSUMER PRICE INDEX	+ 170.21%	+ 84.45%	+ 18.52%	+ 3.92%	+ 0.49%

* THE METHOD OF CALCULATING TOTAL RETURN DATA ON INDICES UTILIZES ACTUAL DIVIDENDS ON X-DATES ACCUMULATED FOR THE QUARTER AND REINVESTED AT QUARTER END. THIS CALCULATION IS AT VARIANCE WITH SEC RELEASE 327 OF AUGUST 8, 1972 WHICH UTILIZES LATEST 12 MONTH DIVIDENDS. THE LATTER METHOD IS THE ONE USED BY STANDARD & POOR'S.

EXHIBIT 9 Returns on the Highest-Ranked Equity Funds over 1, 3, 5, and 10 Year Measurement Periods

1 YEAR

1 YEAR	OBJ	THRU 01/01/88					ANNUALIZED THRU 12/31/87		
		1 WK	4 WK	13 WK	26 WK	52 WK	3 YR	5 YR	10 YR
Oppenheim Gold	SP	0.09	13.74	13.17	18.80	68.15	30.89	--	--
G.T.-Japan	IS	1.03	10.07	-3.01	24.66	52.36	--	--	--
IDS Prec Metals	SP	0.65	0.85	-21.03	-5.22	50.30	--	--	--
Franklin Gold	SP	0.72	2.04	-21.45	-6.05	48.53	20.62	7.45	23.28
Lexington Gold	SP	1.78	3.70	-15.77	0.23	46.12	30.25	9.48	--
Van Eck Gold/Res	SP	0.35	-0.17	-25.78	-12.58	45.00	--	--	--
Colonial Adv Gold	SP	1.25	2.89	-20.09	-7.52	44.49	--	--	--
Oppenheim Prem In	OI	-0.42	17.57	11.90	16.35	43.70	19.84	15.45	13.99
Hutton-Prec Metal	SP	-0.11	-0.43	-17.39	-2.60	43.59	--	--	--
Keystone Metals	SP	1.00	3.07	-23.07	-6.91	39.94	21.52	--	--
Fidelity-Amer Gld	SP	-0.30	3.43	-18.56	-3.59	39.91	--	--	--
Vanguard-Gold	SP	1.19	-0.12	-21.16	-7.84	35.06	25.46	--	--
Nomura Pac Basin	IS	-0.11	7.65	-8.36	-1.78	34.77	--	--	--
Dreyfus Cap Value	GI	-0.60	2.99	-2.84	6.44	34.45	--	--	--
Fidelity-Metals	SP	0.53	2.21	-22.02	-8.47	34.13	17.81	--	4.04
Midas Gold Shares	SP	0.57	3.51	-22.71	-8.34	34.11	--	--	--
Intl Investors	SP	0.33	2.66	-20.35	-7.23	32.10	20.86	8.27	24.59
US New Prospector	SP	0.00	1.79	-27.85	-17.84	30.09	--	--	--
First Inv Intl	IS	-0.77	10.36	-19.07	-8.82	29.10	24.81	--	--
Bull & Bear Gold	SP	0.20	0.18	-23.84	-12.51	28.91	21.78	6.35	15.39
United Gold & Gov	SP	0.63	1.59	-25.31	-12.57	28.36	--	--	--
US Gold Shares	SP	1.96	1.42	-16.59	-8.33	28.26	9.90	-1.31	19.80
TR Price Intl Bd	IB	3.90	6.15	17.27	18.57	27.65	--	--	--
MerLyn Nat Res	SN	--	18.03	-21.54	-10.54	24.98	--	--	--
Templeton Foreign	IS	0.64	9.01	-18.01	-8.00	24.72	26.78	22.39	--
Mathers Fund	G	-1.37	16.24	-3.94	1.03	24.47	22.68	15.92	18.00
Mass Finl Intl-Bd	IB	2.55	4.81	17.55	14.72	24.31	27.62	16.65	--
Trustees Intl Eq	IS	0.01	10.03	-12.10	-4.98	24.06	37.87	--	--
US Prospector	SP	1.14	0.00	-29.92	-20.54	23.61	18.86	--	--
Industrial-Amer	G	-1.38	11.75	-14.95	-9.28	23.07	--	--	--

3 YEAR

3 YEAR	OBJ	THRU 01/01/88					ANNUALIZED THRU 12/31/87		
		1 WK	4 WK	13 WK	26 WK	52 WK	3 YR	5 YR	10 YR
Fidelity Overseas	IS	1.06	9.76	-17.32	-11.67	18.99	52.97	--	--
MerLyn Pacific	IS	1.28	6.49	-25.84	-17.14	13.37	41.22	32.31	24.47
Vanguard World-In	IS	0.37	12.62	-12.71	-3.32	12.78	39.93	31.15	--
Trustees Intl Eq	IS	0.01	10.03	-12.10	-4.98	24.06	37.87	--	--
Transatlantic Gr	IS	-0.15	9.56	-18.85	-11.61	9.59	36.66	23.78	16.28
TR Price Intl Stk	IS	-0.72	12.99	-17.24	-12.09	8.49	36.28	25.10	--
Paine Web Atlas	IS	-0.54	13.38	-22.14	-14.46	8.56	35.83	--	--
Putnam Intl Eqty	IS	-0.73	12.12	-20.06	-13.92	6.66	34.55	25.71	20.24
Financial-Pac Bas	IS	-0.38	9.39	-27.32	-21.15	9.71	34.01	--	--
Kemper Intl	IS	-0.24	13.38	-16.02	-9.63	6.85	33.75	22.73	--
PruBache Global	IS	-0.52	7.93	-21.60	-14.90	8.15	31.49	--	--
Keystone Intl	IS	-0.77	5.20	-17.87	-14.28	9.16	31.42	18.92	15.44
Scudder Intl	IS	-1.00	11.60	-23.53	-15.13	1.17	31.29	23.88	18.02
IDS International	IS	-0.38	6.59	-24.31	-19.37	0.05	31.00	--	--
Oppenheim Gold	SP	0.09	13.74	13.17	18.80	68.15	30.89	--	--
Lexington Gold	SP	1.78	3.70	-15.77	0.23	46.12	30.25	9.48	--
Alliance Intl	IS	0.50	12.51	-24.61	-15.97	-5.32	30.19	22.36	--
Loom-Say Cap Dev	G	-3.04	18.57	-25.14	-13.81	14.26	29.80	18.40	25.48
20th Cent Gltr	SC	-1.52	25.87	-28.27	-16.23	7.44	29.32	--	--
Oppenheim Global	IS	1.11	8.53	-32.93	-22.61	-4.31	28.25	15.83	19.28
United Intl Grth	IS	-1.12	6.85	-14.50	-9.07	16.59	28.24	21.41	20.02
Mass Finl Intl-Bd	IB	2.55	4.81	17.55	14.72	24.31	27.62	16.65	--
Templeton Foreign	IS	0.64	9.01	-18.01	-8.00	24.72	26.78	22.39	--
EuroPacific Grth	IS	0.26	11.52	-19.51	-11.91	7.40	26.78	--	--
Vanguard-Gold	SP	1.19	-0.12	-21.16	-7.84	35.06	25.46	--	--
First Inv Intl	IS	-0.77	10.36	-19.07	-8.82	29.10	24.81	--	--
Fidelity-Health	SH	-1.74	12.84	-29.46	-25.62	-2.67	24.54	16.87	--
New Perspective	IS	-0.70	10.24	-19.36	-10.49	12.84	24.49	18.97	20.56
Dean Wit World	IS	-0.71	9.42	-17.07	-10.37	5.54	24.44	--	--
G.T.-Pacific	IS	-1.12	11.53	-22.57	-15.55	3.20	24.13	20.54	14.96

EXHIBIT 9 *(concluded)*

5 YEAR	OBJ	THRU 01/01/88					ANNUALIZED THRU 12/31/87		
		1 WK	4 WK	13 WK	26 WK	52 WK	3 YR	5 YR	10 YR
MerLyn Pacific	IS	1.28	6.49	-25.84	-17.14	13.37	41.22	32.31	24.47
Vanguard World-In	IS	0.37	12.62	-12.71	-3.32	12.78	39.93	31.15	—
Putnam Intl Eqty	IS	-0.73	12.12	-20.06	-13.92	6.66	34.55	25.71	20.24
TR Price Intl Stk	IS	-0.72	12.99	-17.24	-12.09	8.49	36.28	25.10	—
Scudder Intl	IS	-1.00	11.60	-23.53	-15.13	1.17	31.29	23.88	18.02
Transatlantic Gr	IS	-0.15	9.56	-18.85	-11.61	9.59	36.66	23.78	16.28
Kemper Intl	IS	-0.24	13.38	-16.02	-9.63	6.85	33.75	22.73	—
Templeton Foreign	IS	0.64	9.01	-18.01	-8.00	24.72	26.78	22.39	—
Alliance Intl	IS	0.50	12.51	-24.61	-15.97	-5.32	30.19	22.36	—
United Intl Grth	IS	-1.12	6.85	-14.50	-9.07	16.59	28.24	21.41	20.02
Putnam OTC Emerg	SC	0.00	24.44	-24.80	-18.78	3.69	20.16	20.70	—
G.T.-Pacific	G	-1.12	11.53	-22.57	-15.55	3.20	24.13	20.54	14.96
Fidelity Magellan	G	-1.57	13.53	-26.30	-20.32	-0.59	21.37	20.38	30.92
Vanguard Hi Yd St	EI	-1.79	2.33	-16.72	-15.68	-5.95	14.73	20.32	19.36
PruBache Utility	SU	0.32	3.44	-11.77	-8.52	-10.12	17.50	20.30	—
Strong Tot Return	GI	-0.92	4.11	-14.34	-10.81	5.12	16.87	20.02	—
Mutual Shares	G	-0.67	6.20	-16.57	-11.67	5.54	16.26	19.95	19.89
Phoenix Growth	G	-1.48	13.63	-14.24	-8.60	9.71	20.62	19.95	20.26
United Income	EI	-1.63	9.47	-12.21	-9.64	5.92	20.63	19.62	15.63
Dodge & Cox Stock	GI	-1.94	11.51	-21.14	-13.07	10.62	22.33	19.50	17.70
Mutual Qual Inc	GI	-0.57	6.76	-16.60	-11.61	6.96	16.22	19.41	—
Federated Stock	GI	-1.13	9.27	-21.67	-17.10	0.11	16.81	19.40	—
Windsor Fund	GI	-1.68	7.34	-19.66	-18.15	-0.27	15.95	19.35	18.86
SoGen Intl Fund	IS	-0.55	6.16	-15.41	-7.37	12.25	23.23	19.25	19.65
New Perspective	IS	-0.70	10.24	-19.36	-10.49	12.84	24.49	18.97	20.56
Keystone Intl	IS	-0.77	5.20	-17.87	-14.28	9.16	31.42	18.92	15.44
Princor Cap Accum	G	-1.74	12.29	-24.30	-16.46	4.88	18.23	18.91	16.17
Sequoia Fund	G	0.34	5.72	-11.13	-8.36	6.67	15.86	18.58	19.28
Phoenix Stock	AG	-1.29	16.32	-26.17	-10.48	9.38	18.08	18.47	—
Guardian Park Ave	G	-1.01	13.81	-21.55	-15.14	2.14	17.17	18.41	18.68

10 YEAR	OBJ	THRU 01/01/88					ANNUALIZED THRU 12/31/87		
		1 WK	4 WK	13 WK	26 WK	52 WK	3 YR	5 YR	10 YR
Fidelity Magellan	G	-1.57	13.53	-26.30	-20.32	-0.59	21.37	20.38	30.92
Loom-Say Cap Dev	G	-3.04	18.57	-25.14	-13.81	14.26	29.60	18.40	25.48
20th Cent Growth	G	-1.84	17.77	-28.90	-18.88	11.19	21.51	14.92	24.67
Intl Investors	SP	0.33	2.66	-20.35	-7.23	32.10	20.86	8.27	24.59
MerLyn Pacific	IS	1.28	6.49	-25.84	-17.14	13.37	41.22	32.31	24.47
20th Cent Select	G	-2.16	13.19	-24.50	-17.34	4.09	19.47	15.43	24.31
New Eng Growth	G	-2.34	19.91	-24.07	-12.32	16.93	23.74	14.74	24.08
Weingarten Equity	G	-1.57	15.58	-19.91	-15.94	8.03	23.16	17.72	23.38
Franklin Gold	SP	0.72	2.04	-21.45	-6.05	48.53	20.62	7.45	23.28
Amer Cap Pace	G	-1.96	11.34	-28.23	-21.33	-0.11	11.31	10.36	22.23
Quasar Associates	AG	-1.14	20.24	-28.81	-21.65	-6.53	16.15	13.45	22.19
AMEV Growth	G	-0.14	17.99	-25.85	-23.36	-1.40	17.30	13.03	22.12
Lindner Fund	G	-0.54	5.21	-16.66	-9.20	8.16	13.99	15.78	21.98
Lehman Capital	G	0.48	22.53	-29.70	-18.67	0.75	12.58	13.63	21.65
United Vanguard	G	-1.50	16.31	-19.60	-11.59	7.39	16.41	13.13	21.55
Evergreen Fund	SC	-1.09	10.98	-22.46	-18.97	-4.22	14.04	14.03	21.18
IDS New	G	-1.91	15.13	-15.79	-11.39	13.87	23.18	16.46	20.62
New Perspective	IS	-0.70	10.24	-19.36	-10.49	12.84	24.49	18.97	20.56
Shearson Apprec	G	-1.89	10.07	-20.75	-14.26	5.49	19.87	16.63	20.53
AMEV Capital	G	-1.11	12.68	-19.66	-16.82	2.09	18.16	14.11	20.43
Nicholas Fund	G	-0.75	6.87	-17.47	-14.29	-1.77	12.85	14.36	20.40
New York Venture	G	-0.97	10.50	-19.48	-15.57	-2.88	17.83	16.08	20.36
Phoenix Growth	G	-1.48	13.63	-14.24	-8.60	9.71	20.62	19.95	20.26
Putnam Intl Eqty	IS	-0.73	12.12	-20.06	-13.92	6.66	34.55	25.71	20.24
Constellation Gr	AG	-0.58	25.10	-28.27	-24.89	0.90	19.35	12.41	20.23
Growth Fund Amer	G	-0.26	16.71	-20.71	-14.38	6.31	16.82	13.86	20.06
IDS Growth Fund	G	-0.90	15.43	-25.63	-25.02	-2.81	17.25	8.30	20.06
United Intl Grth	IS	-1.12	6.85	-14.50	-9.07	16.59	28.24	21.41	20.02
Mass Cap Develop	IS	-1.31	15.29	-26.17	-18.83	2.11	19.87	9.07	19.91
Tudor Fund	G	-1.60	18.75	-29.08	-22.29	-0.28	14.21	12.16	19.90

AG = Aggressive Growth
B = Balanced
CG = Corporate Bond - General
CG = Corporate Bond - High Quality

CV = Convertible Bond
CY = Corporate Bond - High Yield
EI = Equity-Income
G = Growth

CG = Government Bond - General
GM = Government Bond - Mortgage Backed
GT = Government Bond - Treasury
GI = Growth & Income

I = Income
B = International Bond
IS = International Stock
OI = Option - Income

S = Specialty
SC = Small Company
SF = Specialty - Financial
SH = Specialty - Health

SN = Specialty - Natural Resource
SP = Specialty - Precious Metals
ST = Specialty - Technology
SU = Specialty - Utilities

Dividend dates listed are ex-dates

Reprinted with verbal permission.

Part II

Financial Analysis and Forecasting

The Financial Detective

The financial statements of no two companies are alike. Industries differ, and each has a financial norm around which companies within the industry operate. An airline, for example, would naturally be expected to have high fixed assets (airplanes), while a consulting firm would not. A paper company would be expected to have a lower gross margin than an automobile manufacturer, because its product is more likely a commodity.

Similarly, companies within industries have different financial characteristics, in part, because of varied strategies. The following paragraphs describe two participants in each of a number of different industries. Their strategies and market niches provide clues to the financial condition and performance one would expect of them. The companies' common-sized financial statements and operating data, which have been put in a standardized format, are provided in Exhibit 1. It is up to you to match the financial data with the company descriptions.

HEALTH PRODUCTS

Of companies A and B, one manufactured pharmaceuticals and a variety of low-margin hospital supplies, and both product lines were marketed primarily through direct sales to doctors and hospitals. The firm had recently acquired a large hospital supply company and, therefore, had significant goodwill on its books. The other firm manufactured and nationally mass marketed a broad line of name-brand toiletries, non-prescription drugs, and consumer and baby-care products, through 165 decentralized subsidiaries.

This case was written by Casey S. Opitz under the direction of Robert F. Bruner.
Copyright © 1988 by the Darden Graduate Business School Foundation, Charlottesville, VA.

HOUSEHOLD APPLIANCES

The two home-appliance manufacturers are companies C and D. One focused on marketing high-quality washers, dryers, dishwashers, and refrigerators under its own name. The other company attempted to segment the market for the same products by selling under its own name and under three other brand names. The second firm had a contract to sell one brand solely as a private-label item through a large department store chain.

COMPUTERS

Companies E and F manufactured computers. One had a highly focused product line: supercomputer systems for scientific applications. Most of these computers were used for physical research, such as that related to weather, energy, and defense. Although the output of these units was relatively small, the price tag was the highest in the industry. The other firm manufactured large mainframe computers and had an emerging position in the supercomputer segment; it also developed and marketed related software and provided financial and insurance services as well. Computer and software sales were responsible for about two thirds of the company's revenues, and financial services for the remaining one third.

RETAILING

Companies G and H were two retailers with different market emphases. One company was a large, national chain of department stores that sold largely on credit everything from automotive equipment and services to clothing and household items, through its (primarily) leased properties. It also marketed its products through a catalog and provided a variety of financial services. Merchandise sales were responsible for about 60 percent of revenues, and insurance sales for about 32 percent. The other firm was a rapidly growing chain of discount department stores and wholesale clubs that owned a large portion of its outlets. As a discounter, it provided little or no credit to customers.

ELECTRONICS

Two electronics companies are shown as companies I and J. Both produced semiconductors, but one specialized in their manufacture and also produced small desktop and hand-held computing equipment. About half its electronic components were sold to the defense industry. The other firm was financially conservative. It specialized in radio and television equipment and made semiconductors as a secondary, but increasingly important, line of business (over 30 percent of revenues).

HOTELS

Companies K and L were both large hotel/motel chains. In addition, one company owned one of the largest food-service contractors in the country, a large chain of family restaurants, and a large chain of fast-food restaurants. This firm financed its hotels via off-balance-sheet limited partnerships. The company had significant assets in the form of food service and hotel management contracts. Hotel revenues accounted for about 40 percent of the total and contract services for about 45 percent. The other firm operated a worldwide chain of high-quality hotels and motels in addition to a smaller line of casinos.

NEWSPAPERS

Companies M and N owned newspapers. One had a large flagship newspaper that was sold around the country and around the world. Because the company was centered largely around one product, it had strong central controls. This company's second most important line of business was periodicals (16 percent of revenues). The other firm owned a number of small newspapers throughout the Midwest. Broadcasting was its secondary line of business and accounted for about 27 percent of total revenues. This company had a significant amount of goodwill stemming from acquisitions.

TRANSPORTATION

Of transportation companies O and P, one was a large national trucking and freight-forwarding company. The other was primarily a railroad, although 20 percent of its revenues were derived from real estate and exploitation of natural resources.

EXHIBIT 1   Common-Sized Financial Data

	Health Products		Appliances		Computers	
	"A"	"B"	"C"	"D"	"E"	"F"
Percentage of total assets:						
Cash & equivalents	11.3%	0.7%	1.8%	3.7%	15.4%	19.3%
Receivables	14.6	16.7	23.9	13.4	18.7	10.7
Inventory	17.8	16.7	30.5	25.8	22.7	21.4
Other current assets	6.3	2.0	4.9	2.8	9.1	0.6
Total current assets	50.0	36.1	61.1	45.7	65.9	52.0
Net property, plant, & equipment	34.4	23.3	31.0	32.3	23.1	42.2
Other assets	15.6	40.6	7.9	22.0	11.0	5.8
Total assets	100.0%	100.0%	100.0%	100.0%	100.0%	100.0%
Accounts payable	14.1%	15.1%	11.3%	12.1%	9.5%	2.1%
Other current liabilities	12.8	9.5	16.3	21.2	31.0	16.5
Total current liabilities	26.9	24.6	27.6	33.3	40.5	18.6
Long-term debt	11.2	21.5	16.5	6.8	14.6	12.0
Other liabilities	8.7	5.3	7.3	3.3	4.4	1.7
Total liabilities	46.8	51.4	51.4	43.4	59.5	32.3
Minority interest	0.0	0.0	0.0	2.7	0.8	0.0
Equity	53.2	48.6	48.6	53.9	39.7	67.7
Total liability & equity	100.0%	100.0%	100.0%	100.0%	100.0%	100.0%
Percentage of sales:						
Revenues	100.0%	100.0%	100.0%	100.0%	100.0%	100.0%
Cost of goods sold	36.9	64.0	72.8	79.3	69.7	35.7
Gross profit	63.1	36.0	27.2	20.7	30.3	64.3
SG&A (all operating expenses for H & O)	40.3	21.7	13.3	14.4	29.4	16.3
R&D expense	7.7	3.2	NAv.	NAv.	NAv.	15.8
Interest expense	1.4	3.4	0.6	0.6	1.9	1.3
Other expense (income)	−1.2	0.5	−0.4	−0.4	−2.7	0.0
Income before taxes	14.9	7.2	13.7	6.1	1.7	30.9
Taxes	4.5	1.9	5.7	1.5	1.1	9.5
Net income	10.4%	5.3%	8.0%	4.6%	0.6%	21.4%
Operating & condition ratios:						
Sales/assets	122%	82%	223%	173%	128%	76%
Return on assets	13	4	18	8	1	16
Return on equity	24	12	37	15	2	24
Quick ratio	96	71	93	51	84	162
Current ratio	186	147	221	137	163	280
Days sales outstanding	43	75	39	28	54	51
Receivables turnover (X)	8.41	4.87	9.33	12.92	6.81	7.09
Inventory turnover (X)	6.88	4.87	7.32	6.69	5.62	3.56
Long-term debt/equity	21%	44%	34%	13%	37%	18%
Market data:						
Dividend payout ratio	33%	49%	50%	43%	0%	0%
Price/earnings	17.9	22.1	13.5	13.5	32.0	21.5
Market/book value	4.44	2.09	5.16	1.91	1.21	5.05
Beta	1.05	1.10	1.05	1.15	1.25	1.40

	Retailing		Electronics		Hotel		Newspapers		Transportation	
	"G"	"H"	"I"	"J"	"K"	"L"	"M"	"N"	"O"	"P"
	0.2%	15.6%	5.8%	15.6%	14.1%	0.3%	8.5%	4.4%	1.8%	0.9%
	1.9	34.7	20.7	19.9	7.3	9.2	8.7	9.0	6.5	18.7
	51.7	5.5	17.1	17.4	NAv.	3.5	4.5	2.1	1.5	3.9
	2.8	0.0	7.3	7.3	NAv.	4.1	2.6	3.1	0.9	1.3
	56.6	55.8	50.9	60.2	23.1	17.1	24.3	18.6	10.7	24.8
	41.8	6.4	45.9	35.7	49.5	48.0	14.0	56.2	82.3	73.3
	1.6	37.8	3.2	4.1	27.4	34.9	61.7	25.2	7.0	1.9
	100.0%	100.0%	100.0%	100.0%	100.0%	100.0%	100.0%	100.0%	100.0%	100.0%
	21.4%	8.6%	10.3%	25.0%	8.9%	9.5%	5.4%	6.2%	12.0%	5.1%
	12.6	31.1	21.0	4.3	0.9	11.4	9.7	11.9	1.4	21.0
	34.0	39.7	31.3	29.3	9.8	20.9	15.1	18.1	13.4	26.1
	3.6	12.8	6.5	11.4	21.6	46.5	25.6	19.6	14.5	13.7
	18.4	29.4	5.7	6.5	14.3	17.5	7.9	14.1	27.4	17.7
	56.0	81.9	43.5	47.2	45.7	84.9	48.6	51.8	55.3	57.5
	0.0	0.0	0.0	0.0	0.0	0.0	0.0	0.0	0.4	0.0
	44.0	18.1	56.5	52.8	54.3	15.1	51.4	48.2	44.3	42.5
	100.0%	100.0%	100.0%	100.0%	100.0%	100.0%	100.0%	100.0%	100.0%	100.0%
	100.0%	100.0%	100.0%	100.0%	100.0%	100.0%	100.0%	100.0%	100.0%	100.0%
	77.0	NAv.	60.5	78.3	41.0	92.1	45.9	54.2	NAv.	82.4
	23.0	100.0	39.5	21.7	59.0	7.9	54.1	45.8	100.0	17.6
	16.3	97.1	24.7	17.8	33.8	1.1	28.6	28.6	86.1	7.6
	NAv.	NAv.	NAv.	NAv.	NAv.	NAv.	NAv.	NAv.	NAv.	NAv.
	0.7	NAv.	1.2	0.4	6.5	1.4	2.3	1.4	2.5	0.5
	−0.7	−1.1	7.4	−3.9	0.7	−0.7	−11.8	−0.1	0.0	5.8
	6.7	4.0	6.2	7.4	18.0	6.1	35.0	15.9	11.4	3.7
	2.8	0.6	1.6	1.9	4.4	2.7	14.4	6.4	4.5	1.4
	3.9%	3.4%	4.6%	5.5%	13.6%	3.4%	20.6%	9.5%	6.9%	2.3%
	311%	65%	126%	131%	55%	121%	73%	99%	46%	191%
	12	2	6	7	8	4	15	9	3	4
	28	12	10	18	14	28	29	19	7	11
	6	127	81	121	218	45	114	74	62	75
	167	141	162	206	236	82	161	103	80	95
	2	196	60	55	49	28	43	33	52	36
	166.37	1.86	6.09	6.60	7.52	5.41	8.48	11.01	7.08	10.18
	6.02	11.77	7.38	7.57	NAv.	13.21	16.24	47.28	30.97	49.22
	8%	70%	11%	22%	40%	308%	50%	41%	33%	32%
	11%	46%	27%	24%	21%	10%	33%	20%	42%	43%
	27.7	11.0	22.7	19.6	17.8	21.8	20.9	20.7	20.9	23.3
	8.02	1.11	2.15	2.43	2.53	5.13	4.58	3.98	1.52	2.42
	1.30	1.20	1.45	1.40	0.95	1.10	0.90	1.10	NAv.	1.30

Oracle Systems Corporation

The company has experienced phenomenal growth, having doubled in size, year after year, for most of its 13-year history. Lawrence J. Ellison is known for his almost fanatical aggressiveness and take-no-prisoners attitude regarding competitors. "It is not sufficient that I succeed; all others must fail," he once said, paraphrasing Genghis Khan. But now the picture could be changing.[1]

Until 1990, Oracle Systems Corporation had logged a nearly unparalleled record of sustained rapid growth: 118 percent compound annual sales growth from 1982 to 1989. Competitors, investors, and customers had searched the financial results of the company for clues to its success. These searches, however, tended to generate more questions than answers. Now, in the first half of 1990, the company had disclosed unsettling news that triggered a *66 percent drop* in the company's share price. About $2 billion in market value of equity simply vanished. This event renewed efforts of outsiders to understand the company: Was the company healthy? Had management made the right choices in running the company? Was management doing a good job? What represented the real source of value in this company? Investors also wondered what, exactly, was happening in the company that warranted such a dizzying drop in share price?

THE COMPANY

Oracle Systems Corporation was founded in 1979 by Lawrence J. Ellison to commercialize an innovative data-base management system (DBMS) that he had just developed for an American intelligence agency. The company produced a broad product line of systems,

---

[1] Quoted from Andrew Pollack, "Fast Growth Oracle Systems Confronts the First Downturn," *The New York Times,* September 10, 1990.

This case was prepared by Robert F. Bruner from public information with the assistance of Fadi Micaelian. Copyright © 1992 by the Darden Graduate Business School Foundation, Charlottesville, VA.

tools, and applications, which, by 1990, were portable across all major computing platforms, from personal computer to mainframe. Under Ellison's aggressive leadership, Oracle more than doubled its sales every year from 1980 to 1989; it became the fastest-growing software company in the world and, with sales of $971 million in the fiscal year (FY) ended May 31, 1990, was the dominant software producer in its specialty. Exhibits 1, 2, and 3 present the firm's income statements, balance sheets, and financial ratios for 1985–90.

An extremely aggressive business strategy distinguished Oracle from its peers. Outside observers cited four main elements to this strategy:

- **Sell aggressively.** Oracle distributed its products through a proprietary sales force and had 44 offices in the United States alone. This approach allowed close management and control of the field sales force. Sales representatives were given ambitious objectives each quarter. Typically, a quota almost doubled on a yearly basis, while the representative's territory often was reduced. The firm was particularly generous to representatives who achieved or exceeded their objectives. Those who fell short of their quotas were summarily fired. Sales representatives, perceived by some as arrogant and aggressive, often sold Oracle software that was not yet available in order to achieve their quotas. Outsiders attributed the company's marketing style to its founder.
- **Maintain technology and product leadership.** Oracle's current technological leadership benefited from an early lucky decision to use the SQL computer language. Eventually adopted by IBM, this language became the industry standard. Continued development efforts had widened the use of Oracle's software to virtually all types and brands of computer systems. Oracle was the first to offer networking capabilities with its data base, and Oracle had aggressively expanded its range of products.

To maintain its leadership, Oracle recruited aggressively from what it believed were the top five computer schools in the United States (Harvard, the Massachusetts Institute of Technology, Stanford, the University of California at Berkeley, and Carnegie–Mellon). Engineers in research and development enjoyed flexible work schedules, higher salaries than the industry average, sizable bonuses, and stock-purchase plans. In 1990, the company built a large headquarters complex in Belmont, California, that included the largest and most modern corporate gymnasium in northern California.

- **Diversify into related fields.** The company had expanded out of the production of software and into computer consulting services and then into the area of system integration. As the range of Oracle's product line expanded, these compatible services expanded as well.
- **Expand internationally.** Oracle had established subsidiaries and close exclusive distributors in more than 70 countries around the world. Oracle ranked among the top 50 U.S. exporters.

Oracle Systems went public on March 12, 1986, at an issue price of $2.00. Three years later, the share price peaked at $28.375.

THE SOFTWARE INDUSTRY

The broad business sector referred to as computing had, until the 1980s, been dominated by equipment manufacturers. With the advent of personal computers and the increasing competition among hardware vendors, however, the software vendors had become significant players in the computing sector. In the 1980s, customers increasingly made hardware decisions based on software availability. This trend drove the hardware manufacturers to integrate forward into software development, a step with comparatively low capital requirements.

By 1990, the DBMS segment of the software industry included three types of competitors: (1) hardware producers that had integrated forward (e.g., IBM, DEC), (2) specialized data-base vendors (e.g., Oracle, Ingres, Informix, Sybase, Ashton-Tate, Gupta Technologies) whose software could work on a variety of hardware platforms, and (3) many small software houses providing highly specialized DBMS products. One analyst estimated that the market demand for DBMS exceeded $10 billion.[2] The major buying segment of this market consisted of large corporations that had heterogeneous computing environments. Oracle permitted these firms to link their machines together and share the data. Exhibit 4 reveals that IBM and Oracle dominated the DBMS market. Oracle's revenues had grown faster than IBM's because of Oracle's multiple-platform operating ability.

DISCLOSURES IN MARCH 1990

On March 20, Oracle reported quarter earnings essentially unchanged from the same quarter a year earlier. The company attributed the zero growth results to the disallowal by auditors of about $15 million in sales. Many Oracle software contracts were sold on a trial basis, which raised questions about when revenue could be recognized.[3] For the

---

[2]S. M. Smith et al., "Oracle Systems," Donaldson, Lufkin and Jenrette, 1991.

[3]Accountants acknowledge that *when* revenue can be recognized is a matter of some judgment. Typically, revenues represent not only cash sales but also credit sales. The key point of judgment is when revenue has been earned, or "realized." Once it has been realized, it can be "recognized" in the income statement. Realization depends on *(a)* management's being able to *measure* the revenue (i.e., knowing with fair certainty how much revenue has been earned) and *(b)* the occurrence of a *critical event* at which there is fair certainty that the revenue-generating transaction will be completed. For instance, consider at which moment revenue should be recognized: the "hand-shake" deal, receipt of a formal order, shipment of the order, receipt of cash? The crucial phrase here is "fair certainty," and it is an important focus of the auditor's work. There are many revenue-recognition methods. Special industries (e.g., consulting, project management, contracting, mining and petroleum, land sales, franchising, and entertainment) have unique recognition techniques.

One prominent accounting textbook states:

A misconception about reported numbers is that they are exact or precise. In spite of the best efforts of managers and internal and external auditors, this is rarely if ever the case. There are many reasons for the lack of precision in accounting measures; some may be attributed to necessarily arbitrary cost allocations or alternative reporting procedures, while others may be a function of the intentional manipulation of reported accounting numbers. [E. R. Brownlee II, K. R. Ferris, and M. E. Haskins, *Corporate Financial Reporting* (Homewood, Ill.: Richard D. Irwin, 1990), pp. 80–81.]

first time, the auditors opined that some of these "sales" would never actually be realized. This surprise triggered rumors about declining product quality, increases in accounts receivable (and doubtful accounts), and reports of sales representatives leaving the company. Upon this revelation, the company's stock price plunged 31 percent from its all-time high of $28.375 per share (achieved just days before the announcement). Journalists reported the following comments by securities analysts:

> There is a credibility issue on the part of management . . . are these random and fragmentary items constrained to this one quarter, or are they symbolic of a longer-term problem? [David Readermann, analyst with Shearson Lehman Hutton]

> Management is stretching harder and harder to make their growth objectives. The disallowal of some sales by auditors tells you that the growth is not sustainable; that the business is just not there. [Rick Sherlund, analyst with Goldman Sachs]

> There is a lot of controversy still swirling around Oracle. Most people would consider the first bit of bad news a big red flag and stand clear. I'm still a big fan of the strategy and how well they've done to date. [Mark Findlay, analyst with Soundview Financial Group][4]

Following the announcement and price drop, 20 lawsuits were filed against Oracle. Essentially, these suits alleged fraud and misrepresentation. Investors vented more outrage when it was disclosed that six Oracle officers profited by selling 645,000 shares before the March earnings disclosure. The company denied any wrongdoing.

ANNOUNCEMENT IN SEPTEMBER 1990

On September 25, 1990, Oracle announced its first-ever quarterly loss, $36 million (versus a profit of $11.7 million for the same quarter a year earlier). Ellison told investors that the loss came mainly from a $45 million shortfall in U.S. sales, plus a $25 million write-down resulting from a restructuring of the firm. Oracle's U.S. finance department, which was responsible for the faulty third- and fourth-quarter 1990 financial statements, was merged into the corporate finance department to ensure strict accounting standards. The company also announced that 10 percent of its domestic work force (about 400 persons) would be laid off. Ellison said,

> Oracle is shifting its strategy to emphasize profitability and product quality, instead of market share and sales growth, to meet demands in the maturing market for database applications. . . . Implementation of the reorganization just took too long. Several managers responsible for the restructuring have been fired.[5]

Oracle also indicated that its revenue growth for the first fiscal quarter would be only 30 percent, rather than the 50 percent the company had projected. Finally, the company reduced its growth projections for the rest of the year from 50 percent to 25 percent.

---

[4]All quotations are from Lawrence M. Fisher, "Surprise Hurts Oracle Systems," *The New York Times,* April 5, 1990.

[5]Quoted from Reuters financial report, September 25, 1990.

At this September announcement, the company's stock price dropped to $8.125. One journalist commented,

> . . . investors had been becoming increasingly wary of Oracle, if only because it was inevitable that the company's breakneck growth would have to slow eventually. Some analysts have also said the company had angered customers in part by promising more product features than it could deliver in its rush for sales. . . . If the suspicions are correct, it would indicate that the company's problems run deeper . . . . But Oracle paints a rosier picture, saying it continues to gain market share. "As we adjust to a more conventional growth rate, our company will be stronger than ever," Mr. Ellison said. Some other providers of data-base software have also seen some softening of business.[6]

CONCLUSION

As about $3.5 billion in Oracle Systems' market value of equity evaporated between the end of February and the end of September 1990, analysts wondered whether this change in value was, in fact, associated with changes in financial performance in the recent past. The company's share-price performance had been outstanding (as shown in Exhibit 5). What had changed? What was the rate of change? Was the company *unhealthy?* For comparison purposes, Exhibit 6 gives financial ratios for a portfolio of other software companies, and Exhibit 7 presents comparative financial ratio information on the 11 leading producers of relational DBMSs.

---

[6]Andrew Pollack, "Fast-Growth Oracle Systems Confronts First Downturn," *The New York Times,* September 10, 1990.

EXHIBIT 1 Income Statements, 1984–90 (In Thousands Except Per Share Amounts)

	Fiscal Year Ended May 31							1990 Qtr. Ended	
	1984	1985	1986	1987	1988	1989	1990	Aug. 31	Feb. 28
Revenues:									
Licenses	$12,282	$21,902	$44,657	$101,264	$205,435	$417,825	$689,898		
Services	433	1,257	10,726	30,007	76,678	165,848	280,946		
Total revenues	12,715	23,159	55,383	131,271	282,113	583,673	970,844	$214,799	$245,561
Operating expenses:									
Sales and marketing	6,431	14,542	27,171	65,651	124,148	272,812	465,074		
Cost of services			5,644	18,661	51,241	100,987	160,426		
Research and development	2,009	3,886	7,478	9,949	25,708	52,570	88,291	20,615	21,685
General and admin.	1,673	1,989	4,248	8,603	17,121	34,344	67,258	230,187	174,673
Total operating expenses	10,113	20,417	44,541	102,864	218,218	460,713	781,049		
Operating income	2,602	2,742	10,842	28,407	63,895	122,960	189,795	(36,003)	49,203
Other income (expense)	(305)	(157)	(367)	(509)	1,084	(2,715)	(17,135)	7,516	5,342
Income before taxes	2,297	2,585	10,475	27,898	64,979	120,245	172,660		
Taxes	908	1,034	4,579	12,275	22,093	38,479	55,250	(14,796)	14,035
Net income	$ 1,389	$ 1,551	$ 5,896	$ 15,623	$ 42,886	$ 81,766	$117,410	(28,723)	29,826
Earnings per share	$0.11	$0.12	$0.11	$0.12	$0.32	$0.61	$0.86		
Number of shares outst.	12,340	12,770	54,864	125,028	132,950	135,066	136,826		

Source: Company annual reports.

51

EXHIBIT 2 Balance Sheets, 1985–90 (In Thousands)

	Fiscal Year Ended May 31						Aug. 31, 1990
	1985	1986	1987	1988	1989	1990	
Assets							
Current assets:							
Cash and cash equivalents	$ 599	$12,524	$ 37,557	$ 48,610	$ 49,393	$ 49,828	$ 50,198
Trade receivables	9,032	26,554	65,205	129,999	261,989	468,071	394,648
Other current assets	331	2,393	6,376	13,218	25,551	51,358	76,428
Total current assets	9,962	41,471	109,138	191,827	336,933	569,257	521,274
Property, net	4,491	14,152	26,896	47,554	94,455	171,945	203,887
Computer software develop.	0	0	4,818	6,920	13,942	33,396	41,707
Other assets	1,010	1,805	2,940	3,267	14,879	12,649	12,245
Total assets	$15,463	$57,428	$143,792	$249,568	$460,209	$787,247	$779,113
Liabilities and stockholders' equity							
Current liabilities:							
Notes payable	$ 694	$ 3,164	$ 5,196	$ 6,507	$ 23,334	$ 42,501	$ 34,970
Accounts payable	1,432	4,835	10,645	23,502	51,582	64,922	57,281
Accrued expenses	3,360	11,301	28,737	62,627	88,014	134,028	82,135
Customer advances	897	2,993	3,847	9,547	15,403	42,121	70,011
Total current liabilities	6,383	22,293	48,425	102,183	178,333	283,572	244,397
Long-term debt	1,373	5,641	9,025	5,363	39,208	94,065	165,643
Deferred income taxes	340	843	3,686	7,379	12,114	22,025	10,397
Stockholders' equity	7,367	28,651	82,656	134,643	230,554	387,585	358,676
Total liabilities and stockholders' equity	$15,463	$57,428	$143,792	$249,568	$460,209	$787,247	$779,113

Note: Accounts receivable (A/R) are net of these allowances for doubtful accounts:

		% of A/R	% of A/R (restated)
1987	$ 6,628,000	10.2%	
1988	$10,102,000	7.8	14.2%
1989	$16,829,000	6.4	
1990	$28,445,000	6.1	

The 1990 allowance for doubtful accounts was restated to $66,445,000.

Source: Company annual reports.

52

EXHIBIT 3   Analytical Financial Ratios, 1985–90

	Fiscal Year Ended May 31					
	1985	*1986*	*1987*	*1988*	*1989*	*1990*
Current ratio..........	1.56	1.86	2.25	1.88	1.89	2.01
Quick ratio	1.51	1.75	2.12	1.75	1.75	1.83
Debt/total assets	13.37%	15.33%	9.89%	4.76%	13.59%	17.35%
Days' sales outstanding	142	175	181	168	164	176
Debt/equity	0.28	0.31	0.17	0.09	0.27	0.35
Times interest earned..	17.46	29.54	55.81	58.94	45.29	11.08
Inventory turnover	69.97	23.14	20.59	21.34	22.84	18.90
Asset turnover	1.50	0.96	0.91	1.13	1.27	1.23
Operating profit margin	11.84%	19.58%	21.64%	22.65%	21.07%	19.55%
Net profit margin......	6.70%	10.65%	11.90%	15.20%	14.01%	12.09%
Return on total assets	10.03%	10.27%	10.86%	17.18%	17.77%	14.91%
Return on equity	21.05%	20.58%	18.90%	31.85%	35.47%	30.29%

Source: Company annual reports.

EXHIBIT 4   Percentage Shares of Market for Data-Base Management Systems Expected in 1991

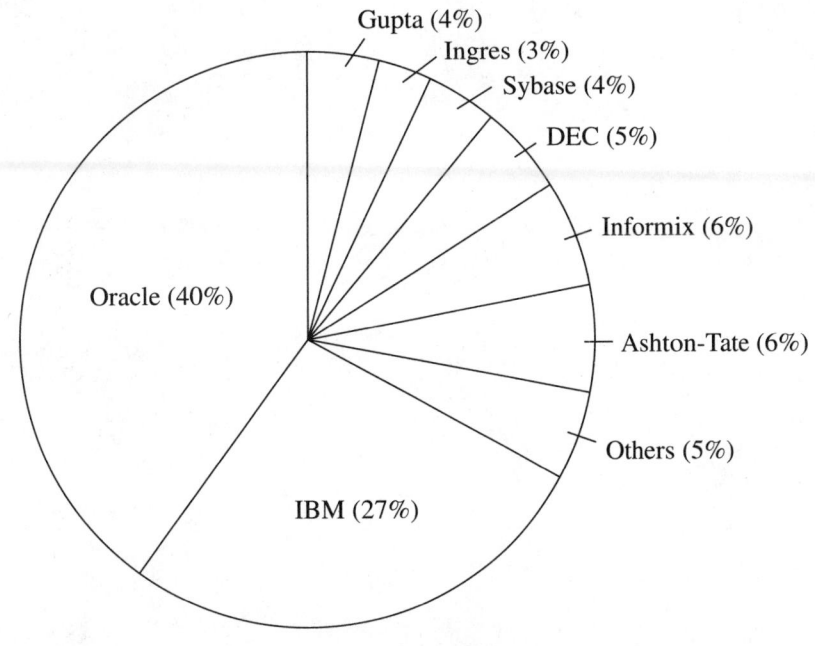

Source: Datamation.

EXHIBIT 5   Oracle Systems Month-End Share Prices, Adjusted for Stock Splits

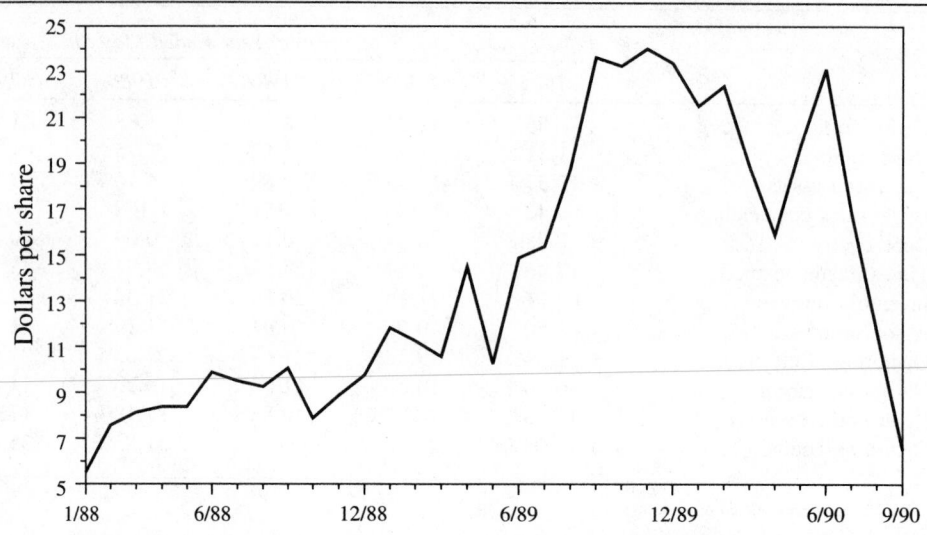

Source of data: Standard & Poor's Corporation.

EXHIBIT 6   Common-Sized Financial Statements of Computer-Software Producers' Averages, 1986–90 (In Percentages)

	1986	1987	1988	1989	1990
Income statement					
Sales.............................	100.0	100.0	100.0	100.0	100.0
Costs and expenses	80.6	79.9	79.0	78.9	82.3
Operating income	19.4	20.1	21.0	21.1	17.7
Depreciation.......................	6.1	6.1	5.9	5.3	5.2
Interest............................	1.0	1.1	0.8	1.0	1.1
Special items	0.9	−0.7	0.0	0.0	0.0
Income taxes	4.9	5.4	5.2	4.7	4.1
Net income........................	6.5	8.2	9.1	10.1	7.3
Common dividends	1.6	1.2	1.1	1.5	1.3
Balance sheet: Assets					
Cash and equivalents...............	28.8	24.2	20.1	17.2	19.2
Receivables	22.9	26.0	27.9	32.4	31.8
Inventories	1.3	1.7	1.7	1.7	1.5
Other current assets	6.1	4.3	3.3	3.7	3.5
Total current assets.................	59.2	56.2	53.0	55.0	55.9
Net property, plant, and equipment...	26.8	19.5	20.0	19.1	17.5
Intangibles	9.7	8.5	9.2	10.0	9.1
Other assets	4.3	15.9	17.7	15.8	17.5
Total assets.......................	100.0	100.0	100.0	100.0	100.0
Balance sheet: Liabilities and equity					
Notes payable	0.8	0.8	0.8	0.9	3.3
Current long-term debt	1.4	1.4	1.4	0.7	0.9
Accounts payable	3.3	3.8	3.8	4.5	3.9
Taxes payable	6.6	6.2	5.7	5.9	5.7
Accrued expenses..................	5.1	3.7	3.2	5.0	5.8
Other current liabs.	8.5	9.2	9.8	9.0	9.8
Total current liabs..................	25.7	24.6	24.6	26.1	29.4
Long-term debt	18.7	12.2	11.0	11.2	5.8
Deferred taxes	1.4	2.6	3.7	3.4	3.5
Investment tax credit	0.9	0.0	0.0	0.0	0.0
Other liabs.	2.4	2.3	1.8	1.9	1.7
Common stock	1.1	1.0	0.9	2.1	2.0
Capital surplus.....................	12.0	23.1	22.8	19.4	19.0
Retained earnings	38.6	37.6	41.0	43.9	46.6
Less treasury stock.................	−0.8	−3.3	−5.8	−8.0	−8.1
Total liabilities and equity	100.0	100.0	100.0	100.0	100.0

Note: The companies on which this exhibit is based include Autodesk, Automatic Data, Computer Associates, Computer Sciences, Lotus Development, Novell, Oracle, Shared Medical Systems, and Cullinet.

Source: Standard & Poor's Corporation.

EXHIBIT 7 Financial Ratios for Competitors in Data-Base Management Software

Ratio	Ask Computer (FY 6/90)	BMC Software (FY 3/90)	Borland Int'l. (FY 3/90)	Computer Assoc. (FY 3/90)	Informix Corp. (12/89)	Lotus Devel'p. (12/89)	Microsoft Corp. (FY 6/90)	Oracle Systems (FY 5/90)	Platinum Technol. (12/89)	Progress Software (11/89)	Software Publish. (FY 9/90)	Sybase, Inc. (12/89)
Business focus	DBMS	DBMS	Broad Line	Broad Line	DBMS	Broad Line	Broad Line	DBMS	DBMS	DBMS	Broad Line	DBMS
Previous four quarters' sales	$112 mm	$110 mm	$262 mm	$1.25 bn	$14.9 mm	$652 mm	$1.3 bn	$980 mm	$11.1 mm	$26.9 mm	$140 mm	$89 mm
Liquidity ratios												
Quick ratio	1.88	2.97	2.54	2.13	2.68	3.39	3.37	1.51	1.99	1.54	3.64	2.00
Current ratio	2.01	3.26	2.92	2.20	2.94	3.73	3.85	1.75	1.99	1.67	3.95	2.07
Sales/cash	0.35	1.66	8.79	11.32	5.76	2.02	2.63	18.39	12.93	3.61	1.78	3.43
Activity ratios												
Receiv. turnover	3.42	9.53	27.20	2.11	2.00	5.69	6.54	2.18	2.57	4.24	7.38	2.23
Days' sales out.	105	38	13.23	170	180	63	55	165	140	85	48.8	161
Inventory turn.	53.6	N.A.	290	49.16	27.46	24	21.3	N.A.	N.A.	46.23	73.4	N.A.
Days' inv. out.	6.67	N.A.	1.24	7.32	13.11	15	16.9	N.A.	N.A.	7.8	4.9	N.A.
Sales/net working capital	40.5	1.86	8.87	3.14	2.05	1.85	2.22	3.90	4.32	4.5	1.77	2.54
Sales/plant and equip.	20.18	4.64	18.63	3.90	6.68	3.55	3.64	5.33	37.7	9.62	11.83	4.79
Sales/curr. assets	2.03	1.29	5.78	1.72	1.35	1.36	1.64	1.68	2.15	1.80	1.32	1.31
Sales/assets	1.25	1.00	4.36	0.86	1.01	0.92	1.07	1.20	2.03	1.48	1.17	1.01
Sales/employees	220,028	205,396	649,407	180,348	122,570	198,583	210,017	134,546	N.A.	N.A.	214,033	105,385
Leverage ratios												
Liabilities/assets	0.32	0.34	0.38	0.32	0.48	0.54	0.17	0.56	0.48	0.54	0.25	0.49
Liabilities/capital	0.47	0.52	0.51	0.46	0.86	0.68	0.20	1.00	0.90	1.08	0.34	0.97
Liabilities/equity	0.47	0.52	0.61	0.47	0.93	1.17	0.20	1.27	33.47	1.15	0.34	0.97
Times int. earned	37.8	N.A.	N.A.	N.A.	N.A.	N.A.	N.A.	10.77	N.A.	31.66	N.A.	7.76
Total debt/equity	0.01	N.A.	0.19	0.03	N.A.	0.73	N.A.	0.30	N.A.	0.11	N.A.	N.A.
Assets/equity	1.47	1.52	1.61	1.47	1.93	2.17	1.20	2.27	1.90	2.15	1.34	1.97
Profitability ratios												
Net income/sales	0.02	0.19	−0.04	0.10	0.04	0.12	0.24	0.09	0.06	0.09	0.14	0.06
Net income/assets	0.03	0.19	−0.19	0.08	0.04	0.11	0.25	0.11	0.12	0.13	0.16	0.06
Net income/capital	0.04	0.29	−0.26	0.12	0.08	0.14	0.30	0.19	0.23	0.25	0.22	0.12
Net income/equity	0.04	0.29	−0.31	0.12	0.09	0.24	0.30	0.24	8.66	0.27	0.22	0.12

N.A. means not available.

Source: Disclosure Incorporated.

The Body Shop International PLC: An Introduction to Financial Modeling

Finance bored the pants off me; I fell asleep more times than not.[1]

Anita Roddick, *Founder and Managing Director, The Body Shop International*

Roddick, as self-righteous as she is ambitious, professes to be unconcerned [with financial results]. . . . "Our business is about two things: social change and action, and skin care," *she snaps. "Social change and action come first. You money-conscious people . . . just don't understand." Well, maybe we don't but we sure know this: Roddick is one hell of a promoter. . . . . She and her husband, Gordon, own shares worth not far from $300 million. Now that's social action.*[2]

In the late 1980s and early 1990s, The Body Shop International PLC was one of the fastest-growing manufacturer-retailers in the world. Focusing on the production and sales of naturally-based skin- and hair-care products, the company boasted 1,102 outlets spread across Europe, North America, and Japan. The Body Shop was headquartered in Britain. In the fiscal years ended February 28, 1991 and 1992, the sales of The Body Shop grew

---

[1]Anita Roddick, *Body and Soul* (London: Ebury Press, 1991), p. 105.
[2]Jean Sherman Chatzky, "Changing the World," *Forbes*, March 2, 1992, p. 87.

This case was written by Robert F. Bruner and Robert M. Conroy.
Copyright © 1993 by the Darden Graduate Business School Foundation, Charlottesville, VA. Revised July 1993.

by 37 and 28 percent, respectively. The dramatic success notwithstanding, some analysts worried that large retailers would successfully imitate the firm's products and merchandising format and that the decline in sales growth in 1992 was an early indication of future competition. In the face of these concerns, Anita Roddick lent iconoclastic leadership to the company and a deep commitment to quality natural products, customer satisfaction, and social activism. She seemed to disavow any interest in the financial performance of her firm.

Suppose that Ms. Roddick came to you in the spring of 1992 for assistance in near-term and long-range planning for The Body Shop. As a foundation for this work you will need to estimate The Body Shop's future earnings and financial needs. The challenge of this advisory work should not be underestimated: Anita Roddick is a talented manager with little taste for finance and financial jargon. Your projections must not only be technically correct; they must yield practical insights and be straightforward to understand. What you have to say, and how you say it, are equally important.

AN OVERVIEW OF FINANCIAL FORECASTING

In seeking to respond to Ms. Roddick's request, you can draw on at least two classical forecasting methods and a variety of hybrids that use some of each method. The two methods are:

T-Account Forecasting.   This method starts with a base year of financial statements (e.g., last year). Entries through double-entry bookkeeping determine how each account will change and what the resulting new balances will be. While exactly true to the mechanics of how funds flow through the firm, this method is cumbersome and may require a degree of forecast information unavailable to many analysts outside (and even inside) a firm.

Percent-of-Sales Forecasting.   This method starts with a forecast of sales and then estimates other financial statement accounts based on some presumed relationship between sales and that account. While simple to execute, this technique easily is misused. For instance, some naive analysts may assume that operational capacity can increase in fractional amounts with increases in sales—but can an airline company really buy only half a jumbo jet? Operational capacity usually increases in "lumps," rather than by smooth amounts. The lesson here is that, when you use this technique, you should scrutinize the percent-of-sales relationships for their reasonableness.

The most widely used approach is a hybrid of these two. For instance, T-accounts are used to estimate shareholders' equity and fixed assets. Percent-of-sales forecasting is used to estimate income statements, current assets, and current liabilities—because these latter items may credibly vary with sales. Other items will vary as a percentage of other accounts than sales: tax expense will usually be a percentage of pre-tax income; dividends will vary with after-tax income; and depreciation usually will vary with gross fixed assets.

A FORECAST WITH PENCIL AND PAPER

Prepare a pro forma (or projected) income statement and balance sheet for The Body Shop for 1993 (income statement for the entire year; balance sheet for year-end). All values should be in pounds sterling. Use the following assumptions as a guide:

Sales:	£191,673,000 (a 30 percent increase over 1992)
Cost of goods sold:	44 percent of sales
Distribution and administration (D&A) expense:	36 percent of sales
Interest expense:	10 percent of debt (about the current interest rate)
Profit before tax:	Sales − COGS − D&A − Interest
Tax:	35 percent of profit before tax (the going corporate tax rate in Britain)
Profit after tax:	Profit before tax − Tax
Dividends:	19 percent of profit after tax
Earnings retained:	Profit after tax − dividends
Current assets:	42 percent of sales
Fixed assets:	£58,657,000
Total assets:	Current assets + Fixed assets
Current liabilities:	35 percent of sales
Debt:	Total assets − Current liabilities − Shareholders' equity
Common equity:	£74,360,000 plus retentions to earnings

Income Statement.   Begin with sales, and use it to estimate COGS and D&A. For the time being, leave interest expense at zero since we do not yet know the amount of debt. Estimate profit before tax, tax expense, profit after tax, earnings to minority interests, dividends, and earnings retained.

Balance Sheet.   Estimate current assets (42 percent of sales) and add that to £58,657,000 to get an estimate for total assets. Next, estimate current liabilities (35 percent of sales), and common equity. Debt becomes the "plug" figure that makes the two sides of the balance sheet balance. This amount is your estimate of the external financing The Body Shop will need by year-end 1993. Estimate the plug by subtracting the amounts for current liabilities and common equity from total assets.

Iterate.   Initially, you entered an interest expense of zero on the income statement. But this cannot be correct if debt is outstanding. This is a classic problem in finance arising from the dependence of the income statement and balance sheet on each other: Interest expense is necessary to estimate retained earnings, which is necessary to estimate debt, which is necessary to estimate interest expense, which is necessary to estimate debt . . . let's call this the problem of "circularity." The way to deal with this problem is to insert your best estimate of interest expense in the income statement (using 10 percent times debt), then reestimate the plug figure, then reestimate interest expense, and so on. By *iterating* through the two statements four or five times, you will come to estimates of interest expense and debt that do not change very much further. Stop iterating when the changes get to be small.

A FORECAST WITH A SPREADSHEET MODEL

Fortunately, the tedium of iterating can be eliminated with the aid of a computer and spreadsheet software (such as Lotus, Excel, and Quattro Pro). The specific commands reviewed here relate to Lotus; the adaptation to other spreadsheet programs should be straightforward. Try the same forecast for The Body Shop using a computer spreadsheet.

Setup: Start with a clean spreadsheet. Set the recalculation mode to MANUAL so the model will iterate only when you press CALC [F9]. The commands here are /WGRM. Use the format in Exhibit 1 as a guide to plan your worksheet. To facilitate sensitivity analysis, it generally is best to place the "Input Data" at the top of the worksheet. You may wish to widen column A at this point. (Commands: /WCS. A width of 20 is usually enough.)

Viewing: You may find splitting the screen handy so that you can see the different sections of the worksheet simultaneously. Place the cursor at the point where you want to split and enter /WWH. The [F6] key will move your cursor to either side of the window. To clear the window, enter /WWC.

Saving: As you develop your model, be sure to save it onto a disk every 5 minutes or so just for insurance (/FS).

Format: Next, develop the income statement just as you did by pencil and paper. Use Exhibit 2 as a guide. Be sure to tie the cells to the proper percentage rate in the Input Data section. (It probably is best to "point" with the cursor the first several times.) The first time through, enter 0 for interest. We will return to it later.

Now do the balance sheet. Again, be sure to tie the balance sheet together by formulas. Don't forget to tie starting equity to earnings retained (see Exhibit 2 lines 13 and 25).

With the basic format laid out, go back and enter the formula to calculate interest as "interest rate times debt." Press the [F9] key and you should see the worksheet change. (In order to watch, split your worksheet again.) You should be able to press the [F9] key several more times until the numbers stop changing, which means the model has converged to a solution. You should have interest as exactly 10 percent of long-term liabilities and a balance sheet that balances.

Once you have seen how this works, you may want to have the model converge without having to press CALC several times. To do this, set the number of iterations you wish Lotus to perform by entering /WGRI and then a number. In this case, 4 or 5 should do.

Your Lotus 1-2-3 worksheet should look like Exhibit 3.

PROJECTING FARTHER

So far you have managed to project The Body Shop's financial statements through 1993. Now extend your projection to 1994 and 1995. A simple way to do this is to copy your model for the two additional years. It will be easiest to copy the entire range of your data by entering /C, and then pointing to the data. Press <Enter> and then move the cursor to the cell where you want the upper left-hand of the copy to begin. Press <Enter> again. Note that you will have to change the equity formula for 1994 and 1995. For 1994 it should take 1993's equity, +B35, and add 1994's additions to retained earnings. Also, you should make sales grow by compounding. To do this, multiply 1993's sales (+B17) times 1994's expected sales growth rate (say, 28 percent). As you enter these changes, you should see the effect ripple through your model.

WHEN DEBT IS NEGATIVE

Now modify the model to deal with the situation where the plug for debt is negative— this can happen routinely for firms with seasonal or cyclical sales patterns. Negative debt can be interpreted as excess cash. But this is an odd way to show cash; a nonfinancial manager (like Anita Roddick) might not appreciate this type of presentation. The solution is to add a line for "Excess Cash" on the assets side of the balance sheet, and then set up three new lines below the last entry in the balance sheet.

Name	*Formula*
Trial assets	Current assets + Fixed assets
Trial liabilities and equity	Current liabilities + Equity
Plug	Trial assets − Trial liabilities

Now, enter the formula for "Excess Cash": @IF(PLUG<0, −PLUG, 0). Instead of the word, "PLUG" you should use the cell address for the actual plug number. The formula for DEBT is @IF(PLUG>0, +PLUG,0). See Exhibit 4 for an example of how your spreadsheet should look. To see how these modifications really work, change your COGS/SALES assumption to 0.60 and press [F9].

With excess cash, you might want to add the interest you would draw on marketable securities. Add a new input, INTEREST ON MARKETABLE SECURITIES, and a new line to the income statement. Enter the formula to calculate the amount and fix the total formulas to account for the new line. (This is optional and not shown in Exhibit 5.)

An example of finished results appears in Exhibit 5.

EXPLORE SENSITIVITIES

After your model replicates the exhibit, you are ready to conduct a sensitivity analysis on the pro forma years by seeing how variations in the forecast assumptions will affect the financing requirements. Try the following variations one at a time (then, later, in combination).

- Suppose sales in 1993 will be £250 million.
- Suppose COGS runs at 55 percent of sales.
- Suppose dividends are increased to 50 percent of net income.
- Suppose that The Body Shop must double its manufacturing capacity by adding a new £60 million facility in 1993.
- Assume inventories run higher than expected (model this by increasing current assets to 55 percent of sales).
- Assume that accounts receivable collections improve so that current assets run at 40 percent of sales.
- Assume that Distribution and Administration expense increases faster than sales.

What happens to the "plug" value (i.e., debt) under these different circumstances? In general, which of the assumptions in the "Input Data" section of your spreadsheet seem to have the biggest effect on future borrowing needs?

The "Data Table" is an invaluable tool for conducting a sensitivity analysis. It automatically calculates debt (or whatever else you want to focus on) as it varies across different values for a particular assumption, such as growth rates. In Lotus 1-2-3 you can create a data table in a two-step process illustrated in the following example. Suppose that you want to estimate The Body Shop's debt required and excess cash generated at COGS/SALES ratios of .45, .55, .65, .66, .67, .70, and .75.

1. **Set up the table.** Move to a clean part of the spreadsheet and type the COGS/SALES ratios in a column. At the top of the next column to the right, enter the location value to be estimated, debt, or +B34. In the column next to that type the cell location for excess cash, +B28. Your data table should be formatted as in Exhibit 6.
2. **Set the program to iterate automatically.** Rather than pressing [F9] continually, tell the computer to do it for you. If you want it to iterate automatically five times, then type the following commands: /WGRI5.
3. **Enter the data table commands.** Type /DT1. The program will ask you to identify the range of the table; using the pointer, highlight the entire area of the table, starting from the northwest corner—the area to highlight is from C9 to E16. After you press <Enter> the program will ask you to specify where the COGS/SALES assumption is in your analysis; using the arrow keys, point to B5 (or else simply type it in). After you press <Enter> again, the computer will fill in the table. The result should look like Exhibit 7.

The data table in Exhibit 7 reveals that at COGS/SALES ratios higher than 66 percent, the firm will need to borrow. This should trigger questions in your mind about what might cause that to happen, such as a price war or a surge in materials costs. Your spreadsheet format can tell you about more sophisticated data table formats. No financial analyst can afford to ignore this valuable tool.

MS. RODDICK WANTS TO KNOW . . .

Now that you have completed a simplified forecast, please prepare a forecast based on the full range of accounts as actually reported by The Body Shop in 1992. Exhibit 8 presents the results for the past three years. Please forecast all of the accounts individually for the next three years: You will see many familiar accounts, as well as some unusual accounts like minority interests.[3] Also, please make "overdrafts" (i.e., short-term bank loans) the plug figure, and base interest expense (at 10 percent) on both the long-term liabilities and overdrafts. You should get a very different forecast of financing needs than was derived on the preceding pages of this note. The reason is that in the preceding example, overdrafts was bundled with all other current liabilities; therefore, interest on overdrafts was ignored. Use your knowledge about the basic mechanics of forecasting to generate this more detailed forecast.

The average expectation of securities analysts was that The Body Shop's revenues would grow at the rate of 28 percent per year over this period, though the growth estimates ranged from a high of 75 percent to a low of 10 percent. Please make other assumptions as needed. Prepare to report to Ms. Roddick your answers to the following questions:

- How did you derive your forecast? Why did you choose the "base case" assumptions that you did?
- Based on your pro forma projections, how much additional financing will The Body Shop need during this period?
- What are the three or four most important assumptions ("key drivers") in this forecast? What is the effect on financing need of varying each of these assumptions up or down from the base case? Intuitively, *why* are these assumptions so important?
- Why are your findings relevant to a senior general manager like Ms. Roddick? What are the implications of these findings for her? What action should she take based on your analysis?

In discussing your analysis with Ms. Roddick, do not permit yourself to get mired in the forecasting technicalities or financial jargon. Rather, focus your comments on your results; state them as simply and intuitively as you can. Do not be satisfied with simply presenting results. Link your findings to recommendations: key factors to manage; opportunities to enhance results; issues warranting careful analysis. Remember that Ms. Roddick plainly admits she finds finance boring; wherever possible, try to express your analysis in terms that she finds interesting: people, customers, quality natural products, and the health and dynamism of her business. Good luck!

---

[3]Minority interests arise where The Body Shop owns less than 100 percent of an asset (i.e., shares ownership with a minority owner) and yet consolidates 100 percent of the earnings and asset values into the financial statement. The minority interest entries in the income statement and balance sheet in effect adjust for The Body Shop's less than full ownership.

EXHIBIT 1   Format for Developing a Spreadsheet Model

	A	B
1		
2		
3	Input Data	
4	SALES	191,673
5	COGS/SALES	.44
6	D&A/SALES	.36
7	INTEREST RATE	.10
8	TAX RATE	.35
9	DIVIDENDS/NET PROFITS	.19
10	CURR. ASSETS/SALES	.42
11	CURR. LIABS./SALES	.35
12	FIXED ASSETS	58,657
13	STARTING EQUITY	74,360
14		
15	INCOME STATEMENT	1993
16		
17	SALES	
18	COGS	
19	D&A	
20	INTEREST EXPENSE (INCOME)	
21	PROFIT BEFORE TAX	
22	TAX	
23	PROFIT AFTER TAX	
24	DIVIDENDS	
25	EARNINGS RETAINED	
26		
27	BALANCE SHEET	
28		
29	CURRENT ASSETS	
30	FIXED ASSETS	
31	TOTAL ASSETS	
32		
33	CURRENT LIABILITIES	
34	DEBT	
35	EQUITY	
36	TOTAL LIAB. & NET WORTH	
37		
38		

EXHIBIT 2   Spreadsheet Formulas

	A	B
1		
2		
3	Input Data	
4	SALES	191,673
5	COGS/SALES	.44
6	D&A/SALES	.36
7	INTEREST RATE	.10
8	TAX RATE	.35
9	DIVIDENDS/NET PROFITS	.19
10	CURR. ASSETS/SALES	.42
11	CURR. LIABS./SALES	.35
12	FIXED ASSETS	58,657
13	STARTING EQUITY	74,360
14		
15	INCOME STATEMENT	1993
16		
17	SALES	+B4
18	COGS	+B5*B17
19	D&A	+B6*B17
20	INTEREST EXPENSE (INCOME)	+B7*B34
21	PROFIT BEFORE TAX	+B17-B18-B19-B20
22	TAX	+B21*B8
23	PROFIT AFTER TAX	+B21-B22
24	DIVIDENDS	+B9*B23
25	EARNINGS RETAINED	+B23-B24
26		
27	BALANCE SHEET	
28		
29	CURRENT ASSETS	+B10*B17
30	FIXED ASSETS	+B12
31	TOTAL ASSETS	+B29+B30
32		
33	CURRENT LIABILITIES	+B11*B17
34	DEBT	+B31-B33-B35
35	EQUITY	+B13+B25
36	TOTAL LIAB . & NET WORTH	+B33+B34+B35
37		
38		

EXHIBIT 3 Basic Forecasting Results for 1993

	A	B
1		
2		
3	Input Data	
4	SALES	191,673
5	COGS/SALES	.44
6	D&A/SALES	.36
7	INTEREST RATE	.10
8	TAX RATE	.35
9	DIVIDENDS/NET PROFITS	.19
10	CURR. ASSETS/SALES	.42
11	CURR. LIABS./SALES	.35
12	FIXED ASSETS	58,657
13	STARTING EQUITY	74,360
14		
15	INCOME STATEMENT	1993
16		
17	SALES	191,673
18	COGS	84,336
19	D&A	69,002
20	INTEREST EXPENSE (INCOME)	(2,372)
21	PROFIT BEFORE TAX	40,706
22	TAX	14,247
23	PROFIT AFTER TAX	26,459
24	DIVIDENDS	5,027
25	EARNINGS RETAINED	21,432
26		
27	BALANCE SHEET	
28		
29	CURRENT ASSETS	80,503
30	FIXED ASSETS	58,657
31	TOTAL ASSETS	139,160
32		
33	CURRENT LIABILITIES	67,086
34	DEBT	(23,718)
35	EQUITY	95,792
36	TOTAL LIAB. & NET WORTH	139,160
37		
38		

EXHIBIT 4   Adjusting to Reflect Excess Cash

	A	B
1		
2		
3	Input Data	
4	SALES	191,673
5	COGS/SALES	.44
6	D&A/SALES	.36
7	INTEREST RATE	.10
8	TAX RATE	.35
9	DIVIDENDS/NET PROFITS	.19
10	CURR. ASSETS/SALES	.42
11	CURR. LIABS./SALES	.35
12	FIXED ASSETS	58,657
13	STARTING EQUITY	74,360
14		
15	INCOME STATEMENT	1993
16		
17	SALES	191,673
18	COGS	84,336
19	D&A	69,002
20	INTEREST EXPENSE (INCOME)	+(B7*B34)-(B7*B28)
21	PROFIT BEFORE TAX	40,706
22	TAX	14,247
23	PROFIT AFTER TAX	26,459
24	DIVIDENDS	5,027
25	EARNINGS RETAINED	21,432
26		
27	BALANCE SHEET	
28	EXCESS CASH	@IF(B40<0,-B40,0)
29	CURRENT ASSETS W/O EX. CASH	80,503
30	FIXED ASSETS	58,657
31	TOTAL ASSETS	+B28+B29+B30
32		
33	CURRENT LIABILITIES	67,086
34	DEBT	@IF(B40>0,+B40,0)
35	EQUITY	95,792
36	TOTAL LIAB. & NET WORTH	+B33+B34+B35
37		
38	TRIAL ASSETS	+B29+B30
39	TRIAL LIABILITIES AND EQUITY	+B33+B35
40	PLUG: DEBT (EXCESS CASH)	+B38-B39
41		
42		
43		
44		
45		

EXHIBIT 5 Finished Results

	A	B
1		
2		
3	Input Data	
4	SALES	191,673
5	COGS/SALES	.44
6	D&A/SALES	.36
7	INTEREST RATE	.10
8	TAX RATE	.35
9	DIVIDENDS/NET PROFITS	.19
10	CURR. ASSETS/SALES	.42
11	CURR. LIABS./SALES	.35
12	FIXED ASSETS	58,657
13	STARTING EQUITY	74,360
14		
15	INCOME STATEMENT	1993
16		
17	SALES	191,673
18	COGS	84,336
19	D&A	69,002
20	INTEREST EXPENSE (INCOME)	(2,372)
21	PROFIT BEFORE TAX	40,706
22	TAX	14,247
23	PROFIT AFTER TAX	26,459
24	DIVIDENDS	5,027
25	EARNINGS RETAINED	21,432
26		
27	BALANCE SHEET	
28	EXCESS CASH	23,718
29	CURRENT ASSETS W/O EX. CASH	80,503
30	FIXED ASSETS	58,657
31	TOTAL ASSETS	162,877
32		
33	CURRENT LIABILITIES	67,086
34	DEBT	0
35	EQUITY	95,792
36	TOTAL LIAB. & NET WORTH	162,877
37		
38	TRIAL ASSETS	139,159
39	TRIAL LIABILITIES AND EQUITY	162,877
40	PLUG: DEBT (EXCESS CASH)	(23,718)
41		
42		
43		
44		
45		

EXHIBIT 6   Setup for a Data Table

	A	B	C	D	E
1					
2					
3	Input Data				
4	SALES	191,673	Sensitivity Analysis		
5	COGS/SALES	.44	Debt and Excess Cash		
6	D&A/SALES	.36	By COGS/SALES		
7	INTEREST RATE	.10			
8	TAX RATE	.35	COGS/SALES	DEBT	Ex.Cash
9	DIVIDENDS/NET PROFITS	.19		+B34	+B28
10	CURR. ASSETS/SALES	.42	.75		
11	CURR. LIABS./SALES	.35	.70		
12	FIXED ASSETS	58,657	.67		
13	STARTING EQUITY	74,360	.66		
14			.65		
15	INCOME STATEMENT	1993	.55		
16			.45		
17	SALES	191,673			
18	COGS	84,336			
19	D&A	69,002			
20	INTEREST EXPENSE (INCOME)	(2,372)			
21	PROFIT BEFORE TAX	40,706			
22	TAX	14,247			
23	PROFIT AFTER TAX	26,459			
24	DIVIDENDS	5,027			
25	EARNINGS RETAINED	21,432			
26					
27	BALANCE SHEET				
28	EXCESS CASH	23,718			
29	CURRENT ASSETS W/O EX. CASH	80,503			
30	FIXED ASSETS	58,657			
31	TOTAL ASSETS	162,877			
32					
33	CURRENT LIABILITIES	67,086			
34	DEBT	0			
35	EQUITY	95,792			
36	TOTAL LIAB. & NET WORTH	162,877			
37					
38	TRIAL ASSETS	139,159			
39	TRIAL LIABILITIES AND EQUITY	162,877			
40	PLUG: DEBT (EXCESS CASH)	(23,718)			
41					
42					
43					
44					
45					

EXHIBIT 7   A Finished Data Table

	A	B	C	D	E
1					
2					
3	Input Data				
4	SALES	191,673	Sensitivity Analysis		
5	COGS/SALES	.44	Debt and Excess Cash		
6	D&A/SALES	.36	By COGS/SALES		
7	INTEREST RATE	.10			
8	TAX RATE	.35	COGS/SALES	DEBT	Ex.Cash
9	DIVIDENDS/NET PROFITS	.19		+B34	+B28
10	CURR. ASSETS/SALES	.42	.75	9,305	0
11	CURR. LIABS./SALES	.35	.70	3,979	0
12	FIXED ASSETS	58,657	.67	783	0
13	STARTING EQUITY	74,360	.66	0	282
14			.65	0	1,348
15	INCOME STATEMENT	1993	.55	0	12,000
16			.45	0	22,653
17	SALES	191,673			
18	COGS	84,336			
19	D&A	69,002			
20	INTEREST EXPENSE (INCOME)	(2,372)			
21	PROFIT BEFORE TAX	40,706			
22	TAX	14,247			
23	PROFIT AFTER TAX	26,459			
24	DIVIDENDS	5,027			
25	EARNINGS RETAINED	21,432			
26					
27	BALANCE SHEET				
28	EXCESS CASH	23,718			
29	CURRENT ASSETS W/O EX. CASH	80,503			
30	FIXED ASSETS	58,657			
31	TOTAL ASSETS	162,877			
32					
33	CURRENT LIABILITIES	67,086			
34	DEBT	0			
35	EQUITY	95,792			
36	TOTAL LIAB. & NET WORTH	162,877			
37					
38	TRIAL ASSETS	139,159			
39	TRIAL LIABILITIES AND EQUITY	162,877			
40	PLUG: DEBT (EXCESS CASH)	(23,718)			
41					
42					
43					
44					
45					

EXHIBIT 8   Historical Financial Statements (in £ thousands)

	1990	1990	1991	1991	1992	1992
	£	% Sales	£	% Sales	£	% Sales
Income Statement						
Turnover.................	£84,480	100.0%	£115,599	100.0%	£147,441	100.0%
Cost of sales.............	36,831	43.6	50,393	43.6	68,210	46.3
Gross profit..............	47,649	56.4	65,206	56.4	79,231	53.7
Distribution exp.	19,767	23.4	27,494	23.8	32,021	21.7
Administrative exp........	11,008	13.0	15,725	13.6	19,335	13.1
Net interest expense	2,366	2.8	1,950	1.7	2,672	1.8
Profit before tax..........	14,508	17.2	20,037	17.3	25,203	17.1
Tax expense	5,519	6.5	7,311	6.3	8,688	5.9
Profit after tax	8,989	10.6	12,726	11.0	16,515	11.2
Minority interest	454	0.5	623	0.5	120	0.1
Ordinary dividends	1,558	1.8	2,261	2.0	2,995	2.0
Profit retained............	6,977	8.3	9,842	8.5	13,400	9.1
Assets						
Cash	239	0.3	344	0.3	483	0.3
Accounts receivable	9,358	11.1	18,298	15.8	26,485	18.0
Inventories...............	23,360	27.7	33,484	29.0	38,457	26.1
Other current assets.......	6,981	8.3	8,597	7.4	9,576	6.5
Net fixed assets	31,442	37.2	45,598	39.4	58,657	39.8
Total assets	71,380	84.5	106,321	92.0	133,658	90.7
Liabilities and Equity						
Accounts payable.........	8,577	10.2	9,307	8.1	10,112	6.9
Taxes payable............	5,351	6.3	7,002	6.1	6,157	4.2
Accruals.................	2,369	2.8	2,752	2.4	3,356	2.3
Overdrafts	19,404	23.0	12,708	11.0	29,748	20.2
Other current liabilities ...	2,722	3.2	4,374	3.8	4,687	3.2
Long-term liabilities	5,991	7.1	3,480	3.0	5,128	3.5
Minority interests.........	974	1.2	1,552	1.3	292	0.2
Shareholders' equity	25,992	30.8	65,149	56.4	74,178	50.3
Total liabs. & equity ...	71,380	84.5	106,324	92.0	133,658	90.7

Fiscal Year Ended February 28

Alfin Fragrances, Inc.

Alfin Fragrances, Inc., a U.S.-based importer and marketer of high-priced French perfumes, was introducing a line of skin creams called "Glycel" in February 1986. Designed to reduce wrinkles, Glycel was considered a breakthrough by many in the industry, because it worked at the cell level and, according to its codiscoverer, Dr. Christiaan Barnard, "can make older skin behave and look like younger skin."[1] The product would be demonstrated and sold at the best department stores, and Glycel was expected to yield sales of $30 million in fiscal 1987. Advance orders totaling $5 million had already been placed. Industry observers speculated on what Alfin's external funds needs would be as a result of that growth and whether those needs should be financed with debt or equity.

In fiscal 1985, Alfin's corporate sales were only $21 million. As shown in Exhibit 1, however, the company's stock price had risen from $19 to $67.25 per share over the past three months in anticipation of Glycel's success.

THE COSMETICS INDUSTRY

The cosmetics and toiletries industry was huge and consisted of at least 150 companies,[2] some of the more important of which are listed in Exhibit 2. Sales of all toiletries and cosmetics were growing at an average annual real rate of only 2 percent to 3 percent per year. Thus, the industry was marked by strong competition for brand loyalty and product proliferation; in order to maintain and increase sales in a market rife with product introductions and new twists on old themes, companies relied heavily on advertising. As shown in Exhibit 3, nine toiletries and cosmetics firms or firms with cosmetics divisions were among the top 80 advertisers in the United States in 1985. Bandwagon or "me too"

---

[1] *The Wall Street Journal,* May 29, 1986, p. 33.
[2] *Million Dollar Directory,* Dun & Bradstreet, Inc., 1987.

This case was prepared by Casey Opitz under the direction of Robert F. Bruner.
Copyright © 1988 by the Darden Graduate Business School Foundation, Charlottesville, VA.

production by many companies of another firm's newly introduced products also made trademark infringement suits a common business practice.

Cosmetic and soap stocks underperformed the market in December 1985, after leading it for five months, as shown in Exhibit 4. The stocks were expected to continue to underperform somewhat in the near future, especially if the market continued to strengthen. One analyst stated:

> The major problem of cosmetics and soap companies now is producing growth rates commensurate with the reinvestment rates of their highly profitable, but fully developed, basic business. A decision to buy a stock should hinge as much as anything on a company's plans and ability to increase its sales.[3]

As shown in Exhibit 5, earnings growth within the cosmetics industry mirrored that of the Standard & Poor's 400 over time, but growth fluctuated less radically in any given year. Dollar and unit sales for the entire industry were off in the first half of 1985, as shown in Exhibit 6—a reflection of lower consumer spending on nondurables and a general slimming of inventories by retailers. The industry was expected to do unusually well in 1986, however (see estimates in Exhibit 5), because product inventories were now low and increasing real personal income was providing consumers with more "loose change."

Although overall cosmetics sales growth was low, sales growth within the skin care products segment, defined primarily as antiaging creams and oils that reduce the harmful effects of the sun, was a different story. This $1.9 billion segment of the domestic cosmetics industry was almost twice as large in 1985 as it had been five years earlier.

Some 60 percent of all skin care product sales took place in department stores, where most top-of-the line products, with names like Creme Contour des Yeux, Bain de Soleil Under Eye Protector 15, and Eye Rescue Gel by Germaine Monteil, were sold at very high prices with the assistance of trained specialists:

> At as much as $20 to $50 an ounce, the most expensive creams have markups that can be "hundreds of times more costly than the ingredients," says H.K. Bhargava, a cosmetics researcher at the Massachusetts College of Pharmacy.[4]

Lower-priced Oil of Olay, Almay (made by Beatrice), Raintree, and Revlon products were sold successfully in drug stores, grocery stores, and discount stores.

THE COMPANY

Alfin Fragrances, Inc., was founded in 1976 to import and distribute French perfumes in the United States. By 1985, the company was operating through its distributors in 31 countries. Alfin sold its products only with the aid of specially trained demonstrators

---

[3]A.B. Longley, Donaldson, Lufkin, & Jenrette, "Personal and Household Products," *Industry Report,* January 13, 1986.

[4]*The Wall Street Journal,* May 29, 1986, p. 33.

through prestigious department and specialty stores, such as Saks-Fifth Avenue, Bergdorf Goodman, Bloomingdale's, Bonwit Teller, Lord & Taylor, Macy's, Marshall Field, and Neiman-Marcus. The company did little advertising, concentrating instead on long-term brand building at the high end of the market through direct customer contact at department stores.

Alfin held exclusive, worldwide manufacturing and distribution rights to a number of French and Italian designer fragrances. The company also owned 80 percent of an exclusive worldwide perfume venture with an American designer. Two fragrances—Ombre Rose ($150 per ounce) and Bal a Versaille—were considered classics; they provided steady sales and high margins. Ombre Rose had continued to set domestic and foreign sales records in 1985. Alfin was also the worldwide manufacturer and distributor of the Irma Shorell brand of skin care products. Through 1985, all but one of the company's products were made in either France, Italy, or Switzerland. Typically, a product would be introduced through about 100 stores and would eventually be sold through about 1,200 stores.

Almost all the members of Alfin's management had significant experience from other cosmetic companies. Chairman Irwin Alfin, aged 56 and holder of 22 percent of the company's stock, was a former Fuller Brush man, but also had been president of Chanel, Inc.; Max Factor, Inc.; and Halston Fragrances, Inc. He had held executive positions at Revlon, Inc.[5]

FINANCIAL PERFORMANCE AND BORROWINGS

Alfin's sales rose from $12 million in fiscal 1983 to $21 million in fiscal 1985. Over the same period, net income rose from $1.7 million to $4.3 million, and earnings per share doubled from $0.65 to $1.27. The company reinvested all earnings in 1984 and 1985. In the first fiscal quarter ended October 1985, however, sales, reflecting retailers' efforts to keep inventories down and buy selectively for the Christmas season, had been flat.

The company was leveraged at 13 percent debt to equity. In July 1983, Alfin financed the $1.4 million purchase of a distribution and administrative facility with a New Jersey Economic Development Authority mortgage loan at 75 percent of the floating prime lending rate; the rate could fluctuate between 7.5 percent and 14 percent. The prime rate since the second half of 1985 had been 9.5 percent. At the end of fiscal 1985, the long-term portion of the loan was $1.1 million, payable in monthly installments of $5,483 through July 1, 1993, at which time the remaining balance would be paid. Exhibits 7

---

[5]Sam Reich, Alfin's 53-year-old chief financial officer and owner of 21 percent of the company, had worked with Mr. Alfin at Revlon and was also the vice president of administration at Chanel. Mr. Alfin and Mr. Reich represented almost all insider ownership of the company. Alfin's senior vice presidents of sales, finance, and operations had significant experience at Coty, Cosmair, and Revlon. The company's vice president of sales for the Glycel line had helped Jacqueline Cochran launch the exclusive La Prairie line of skin creams in the United States.

and 8 show Alfin's income statements and balance sheets; Exhibit 9 presents the company's sources and uses statements.

Also in fiscal 1985, the company issued two noninterest-bearing notes at a 10 percent discount from the total face value of $1.6 million. Equal payments of $800,000 would be made at the ends of fiscal 1986 and 1987. Other debts contracted in 1985 were $65,000 payable on demand to the subsidiary of Designer Fragrances, Inc., at the prime lending rate and $408,000 of long-term debt payable to the subsidiary of Orinter S.A. at prime. The latter loan had no due date, because it was payable out of Orinter's profits.

License agreements with and trademarks of the Irma Shorell line of skin care products, the fragrances of Robert Piquet, and Glycel were also reflected on the balance sheet as a $4.5 million increase in total assets in fiscal year 1985.

GLYCEL

Glycel, a cell-regenerating skin cream, stemmed from research done by South African heart surgeon Christiaan Barnard, who had become interested in tissue regeneration to promote healing of transplanted organs. In 1981, Dr. Barnard was introduced to Dr. Rolf Schaefer, who owned a cosmetics lab near Basel, Switzerland, called Chemisches Institut Schaefer. As a result of their mutual interest in cell-regeneration research, Drs. Schaefer and Barnard began a joint venture that culminated in the development of Glycel.

Glycel contained glycosphingolipids (GSL), a substance discovered at about the turn of the century and found naturally in the body, but with age, in diminishing quantities. The product did not bring old cells back to life; it regenerated and repaired them. It did not eliminate wrinkles but reduced their appearance.

Arman Mattli, who owned a Swiss health spa and manufactured the La Prairie line of skin creams, began to develop and package Glycel, but he turned down the offer of exclusive rights to the product, stating that a new miracle skin cream was invented in Switzerland every year. Mr. Alfin had discussed the possibility of purchasing the worldwide rights to Glycel in 1984, before Mr. Mattli had turned down the offer. The estimate was that Mr. Alfin paid between $3 and $4 million plus a 4 percent royalty when he acquired the rights in July 1985. Total license agreements and trademarks for the year, as reflected on the balance sheet, were $4.5 million, including Glycel and Irma Shorell.

Dr. Barnard had wanted to develop Glycel into a drug, but Dr. Schaefer wanted to develop it into a cosmetic. The difference was a large one for Alfin: cosmetics did not require lengthy testing and approval by the Food and Drug Administration.

Glycel would be marketed at $75 per ounce or between $25 and $195 per kit. The five-product regimen would cost about $1,500 per year. Repeat sales would be critical to Alfin's success; but, given Alfin's traditional market niche and Glycel's unique history and quality, achieving repeat sales was of little concern.

Dr. Barnard agreed to participate in the advertising of the product, which Irwin Alfin planned to keep relatively subdued (not featuring "half-naked women, celebrities, and movie stars").

The firm's public relations officer stated;

"Our claims will be less than those by other cosmetics companies, simply because we have Dr. Barnard," . . . "It's not a wonder drug."[6]

SALES PROSPECTS

By the mid-1980s, the baby boom population was aging, and the large and growing upper-middle income group contained unprecedented numbers of two-income families. In addition, mounting news of the negative effects of the sun on skin was thought to be making a strong seller of any product that would help women minimize the effects of years of suntanning. One analyst estimated Alfin's total sales in 1986 would be $34 million, but this estimate assumed relatively modest growth. He also forecasted Alfin's future performance under more buoyant assumptions for its two principal business segments. The fragrance business was expected to realize 15 percent annual growth through product line extension and introduction of new fragrances. Fragrance sales in 1986 would be $26–$27 million; EPS would be $1.50–$1.60. As for the skin-care segment of Alfin:

> The company believes the Glycel line could possibly match last year's $21 million sales volume within 18–24 months as it expands to 1,200–1,500 stores. Should that occur, it could add at least $15–$20 million in sales and $1.00 to $1.20 per share. . . . This would bring total sales to $41–$47 million and earnings to $2.50–$2.80 per share.[7]

Of longer-term prospects, Ronald Koenig, chairman of Ladenburg, Thalman & Co., investment bankers for Alfin, said, "The American woman puts no price on beauty."[8] Mr. Koenig estimated that worldwide annual sales of Glycel would be $70 to $100 million. But there were some questions about how fast Alfin should expand Glycel's sales. If expansion were carried out rapidly, Alfin would be able to preempt competitors and possibly gain a greater market share. After all, it was likely that still more products that could make the same claims as Glycel would enter the market soon. On the other hand, very rapid expansion would consume capital; cost controls could also become sloppy.

FINANCIAL REQUIREMENTS

Analysts outside the company speculated about how Alfin would finance the unusual rate of sales growth Glycel was expected to have. The company seemed to be underleveraged, and debt would be cheaper than equity, especially given the current level of interest rates

---

[6]Both quotes from *Business Week*, January 13, 1986, p. 113.
[7]William F. Jelin, CFA, *Wall Street Transcript*, February 3, 1986, p. 81,011.
[8]"New Money in Old Wrinkles," *Dun's Business Monthly*, May 1986, p. 25.

(shown in Exhibit 10) and the expected rate of growth for the firm. On the other hand, the company had paid no cash dividends to date, although it had declared a 2-for-1 stock split payable on February 20, 1986. After the split, book value per share would be less than at any time in the company's history.

One analyst produced the cash-flow projections provided in Exhibit 11, based on the market's sales projections for the firm and on the assumption that Alfin issued equity to finance growth.

EXHIBIT 1   Stock Price Data, July 5, 1985, through February 14, 1986

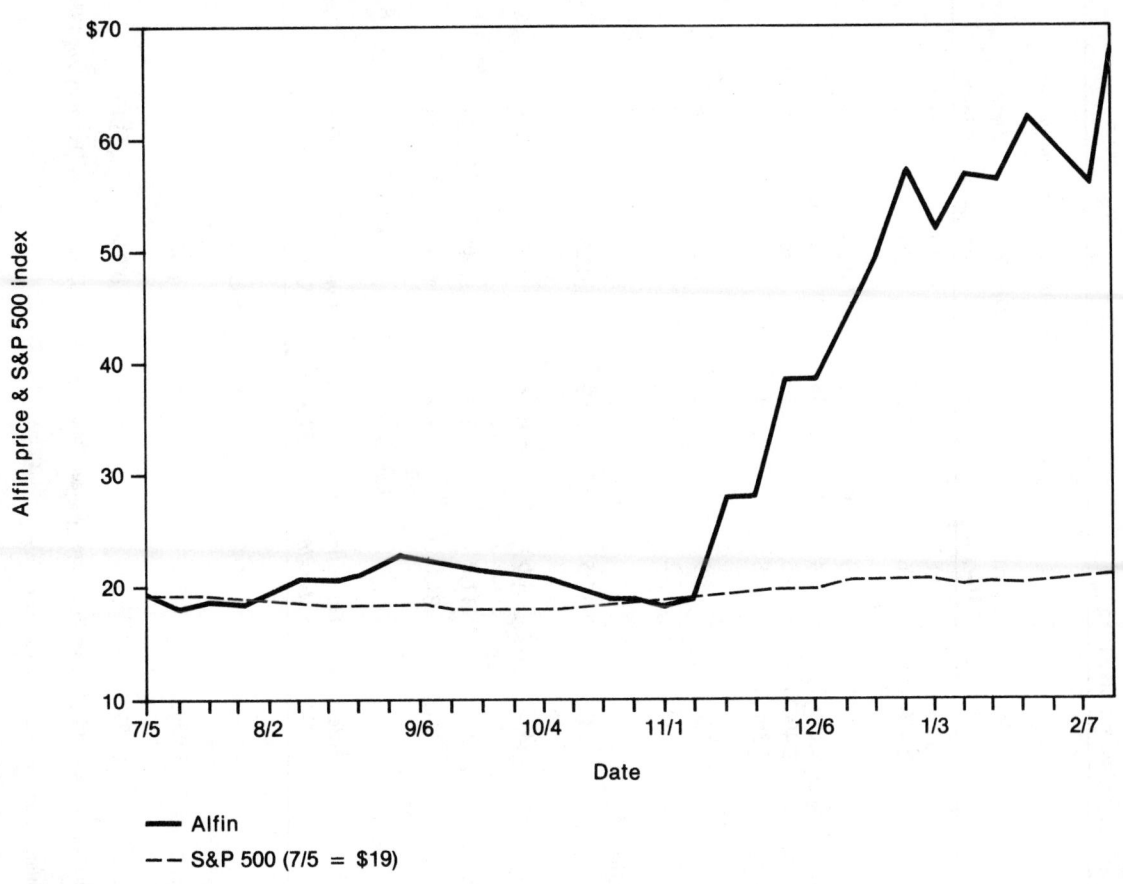

— Alfin
-- S&P 500 (7/5 = $19)

Source: *ISL Daily Stock Price Index.*

EXHIBIT 2 Comparative Industry Data, 1985*

Cosmetic/Toiletry Companies

	Sales ($ MM)	Operating Margin	EPS	Dividends/ Share	Debt/ Equity	Market/ Book	Price/ Earnings	Beta
Alberto Culver	$368.6	7.8%	$0.68	$0.19	43%	2.50	12.4	1.10
Avon	2,470.1	2.6	1.61	2.00	67	2.48	14.3	1.05
Carter-Wallace (Arid, Rise, Nair)	400.2	14.9	1.82	0.29	16	1.93	11.9	1.00
Chesebrough-Pond's	2,699.5	12.4	1.94	2.00	173	2.50	18.4	0.90
Gillette	2,400.0	19.5	1.30	0.65	49	2.48	11.9	0.90
Helene Curtis	360.8	7.8	2.44	0.00	44	1.48	7.8	1.10
Minnetonka (Calvin Klein)	124.4	6.9	0.27	0.00	5	3.37	14.6	1.40
Neutrogena	74.5	17.2	0.29	0.04	0	13.74	28.1	0.85
Noxell (Noxema, Cover Girl, Rain Tree)	382.1	17.5	0.82	0.25	0	4.14	15.4	0.95
Redken Labs	108.5	16.2	2.77	0.58	22	1.83	10.1	1.05
Revlon	345.1	4.6	–0.32	0.00	229	2.10	NMF	0.85
Richardson-Vick's (Oil of Olay)	1,223.6	11.0	3.01	1.48	34	1.82	14.0	NA
Alfin†	21.3	34.0	1.27	0.00	13	13.10	53.0	

Pharmaceutical Companies with Large Cosmetic Divisions

	Sales ($ MM)	Operating Margin	EPS	Dividends/ Share	Debt/ Equity	Market/ Book	Price/ Earnings	Beta
Eli Lilly (Elizabeth Arden)	$3,720.4	27.5%	$3.69	$1.60	10%	3.27	11.5	0.90
Pfizer (Coty)	4,024.5	25.1	3.44	1.48	11	3.14	13.5	1.05
Schering-Plough (Maybelline)	1,927.1	19.9	1.89	0.84	14	2.31	12.3	0.95

* December 31, except Alberto Culver (September 30), Carter-Wallace (March 31, 1986), Helene Curtis (February 28, 1986), Noxell, Redken Labs, Revlon, and Alfin (July 31).
† Alfin stock data calculated from February 1986 stock price.

Source: *Value Line Investment Survey.*

EXHIBIT 3   Cosmetic Company Advertising Budgets, Fiscal Year 1985

Rank of U.S. Firms	*Company*	*Advertising ($ MM)*
6	Beatrice	$684
31	American Cyanamid	266
48	Schering-Plough	169
50	Gillette	161
52	Chesebrough-Pond's	160
53	Pfizer	158
60	Revlon	147
68	Cosmair	122
80	Noxell	106

Source: *Advertising Age,* September 4, 1986, p. 1.

EXHIBIT 4   Monthly Cosmetic and Soap Stock Price Changes, Relative to S&P 400

	Cosmetic and Soap	*S&P 400*	*Spread*
1984:	5.6%	2.1%	3.5%
June	−3.1	−2.2	−0.9
July	6.3	10.9	−4.6
Aug.	1.0	−1.1	2.1
Sept.	2.0	−0.4	2.4
Oct.	1.3	−2.0	3.3
Nov.	0.9	1.9	−1.0
Dec.			
1985:	0.8	7.9	−7.1
Jan.	2.3	0.8	1.5
Feb.	−1.7	−0.5	−1.2
Mar.	0.9	−0.9	1.8
April	2.3	5.0	−2.7
May	3.3	1.0	2.3
June	1.6	0.3	1.3
July	0.9	−1.5	2.4
Aug.	−0.4	−3.6	3.2
Sept.	13.2	5.4	7.8
Oct.	5.4	5.8	−0.4
Nov.	3.3	4.3	−1.0
Dec.			

Source: A.B. Longley, "Cosmetics Mirror."

EXHIBIT 5   Comparative Annual Rates of Earnings Growth

	Cosmetics Industry	*All S&P 400 Companies*	*Cosmetics Growth Less S&P 400 Growth*
1982...........	8.4%	20.9%	(12.5%)
1983...........	6.2	11.9	(5.7)
1984...........	5.6	21.5	(15.9)
1985(E)........	4.0	(5.0)	9.0
1986(E)........	13.0	9.0	4.0
1975–84........	8.9	7.4	1.5
1980–84........	2.6	3.1	(0.5)
1982–86(E)	4.1	3.3	0.8

Source: A.B. Longley, "Cosmetics Mirror."

EXHIBIT 6   Public Cosmetic and Toiletries Companies, Growth of Domestic Sales

	Dollar Sales by Quarter			
	First	*Second*	*Third*	*Fourth*
1980	12.0%	5.5%	9.0%	9.7%
1981	13.9	13.0	8.4	6.0
1982	2.3	4.0	3.8	4.1
1983	5.0	8.9	3.3	5.7
1984	7.3	6.7	6.8	2.1
1985	−0.5	−2.5	0.6	N.Av.

	Unit Sales by Quarter			
	First	*Second*	*Third*	*Fourth*
1980	−0.9%	−15.1%	−10.7%	−9.8%
1981	−2.6	5.3	−0.8	−1.7
1982	−6.5	−5.7	−5.2	−1.6
1983	2.6	6.3	1.1	1.7
1984	5.9	4.1	3.5	−1.0
1985	−4.2	−6.2	−1.5	N.Av.

Source: A.B. Longley, "Cosmetics Mirror."

EXHIBIT 7   Consolidated Income Statement (dollars in thousands, except per share data)

	Fiscal Years Ended July 31		
	1983	1984	1985
Net sales	$11,911	$18,107	$21,297
Cost of goods sold	3,465	4,911	5,330
Gross profit	8,456	13,196	15,967
Selling, general, & administrative	5,513	7,539	8,722
Operating profit	2,943	5,657	7,245
Interest income, net	191	734	785
Other income, net	173	200	212
Minority interest in subsidiary loss	0	0	29
Earnings before taxes	3,306	6,591	8,272
Income taxes	1,652	3,207	3,994
Net income	$ 1,654	$ 3,384	$ 4,278
Earnings per share	$0.65	$1.08	$1.27

Source: Annual reports of Alfin Fragrances, Inc.

EXHIBIT 8 Consolidated Balance Sheets (dollars in thousands)

	As of July 31	
	1984	1985
Cash	$ 398	$ 257
Short-term investments..................	8,700	9,387
Accounts receivable, net	1,905	3,480
Inventory	2,900	5,023
Income taxes receivable.................	281	0
Prepaid expenses & other	61	154
Total current assets.................	14,245	18,300
Property & equipment	1,912	2,042
Less: depreciation....................	263	468
Net property & equipment	1,649	1,574
License agreement & trademarks	0	4,511
Other..................................	143	114
Total assets	$16,038	$24,498
Current portion of note & mortgage		
payable..............................	$ 158	$ 793
Accounts payable.......................	1,408	2,687
Commissions payable....................	852	234
Accrued expenses	705	329
Loan payable to minority interest	0	65
Taxes payable..........................	0	1,139
Total current liabilities	3,123	5,248
Mortgage and note payable..............	1,120	1,773
Long-term advance from minority interest	0	408
Minority interest	20	77
Total liabilities.....................	4,263	7,506
Common stock: $0.01 par,		
3,252,100 shares in 1984,		
3,309,684 shares in 1985	33	33
Additional paid-in capital	6,166	7,106
Retained earnings	5,576	9,854
Total shareholders' equity	11,775	16,993
Total liabilities & equity	$16,038	$24,498

Source: 1985 annual report, Alfin Fragrances, Inc.

EXHIBIT 9 Consolidated Statement of Changes in Working Capital (dollars in thousands)

	Fiscal Years Ended July 31		
	1983	*1984*	*1985*
Sources:			
Net income	$1,654	$3,384	$4,278
Depreciation & amortization	43	212	205
Funds from operations	1,697	3,596	4,483
Proceeds from sale of stock	0	6,174	940
Total sources	1,697	9,770	5,423
Uses:			
Purchases of property & equipment	1,452	315	130
Increase in other assets	36	82	4,481
Decrease (increase) in long-term debt & mortgage	(1,240)	135	(1,061)
Purchase of treasury stock	100	0	0
Dividend net of tax provision on subchapter S corporation	75	0	0
Other	0	(20)	(57)
Total uses	422	512	3,493
Net increase in working capital	$1,275	$9,257	$1,930

Source: Annual report, Alfin Fragrances, Inc.

EXHIBIT 10 Average Interest Rates and Yields

| | Treasuries | | | | | Moody's | | Prime |
| | Bills | | | Notes & Bonds | | | | Rate |
	3-Mo.	6-Mo.	1-Yr.	3-Yr.	10-Yr.	Aaa	Baa	Rate
1982	10.61	11.07	11.07	12.92	13.00	13.79	16.11	14.86
1983	8.61	8.73	8.87	10.45	11.10	12.04	13.55	10.79
1984	9.52	9.76	9.92	11.89	12.44	12.71	14.19	12.04
1985 Jan.	7.76	8.00	8.33	10.43	13.38	12.08	13.26	10.50
Feb.	8.27	8.39	8.56	10.55	11.51	12.13	13.23	10.50
March	8.52	8.90	9.06	11.05	11.86	12.56	13.69	10.50
April	7.95	8.23	8.44	10.49	11.44	12.23	13.51	10.50
May	7.48	7.65	7.85	9.75	10.85	11.72	13.15	10.00
June	6.95	7.09	7.27	9.05	10.16	10.94	12.40	9.50
July	7.08	7.20	7.31	9.18	10.31	10.97	12.43	9.50
Aug.	7.14	7.32	7.48	9.31	10.33	11.05	12.50	9.50
Sept.	7.10	7.27	7.50	9.37	10.37	11.07	12.48	9.50
Oct.	7.16	7.33	7.45	9.25	10.24	11.02	12.36	9.50
Nov.	7.24	7.30	7.33	8.88	9.78	10.55	11.99	9.50
Dec.	7.10	7.14	7.16	8.40	9.26	10.16	11.58	9.50
1986 Jan.	7.04	7.16	7.31	8.41	9.19	10.05	11.44	9.50
Feb.	7.03	7.11	7.19	8.10	8.70	9.67	11.11	9.50

Sources: *Federal Reserve Bulletin* and *Economic Report of the President*.

EXHIBIT 11   Alfin Fragrances—Cash Flow Projections[a] (dollars in thousands)

	For the Fiscal Year Ended July 31, 1986
Sales[b]	$34,000
Gross profits[c]	25,500
− Selling, general, & administrative[d]	15,300
+ Interest income[e]	770
− Interest expense[f]................	125
+ Other income	220
+ Minority interest	29
Profit before tax	11,094
Taxes (48%)	5,325
Profit after tax	5,769
+ Depreciation & amortization[g]	487
− Additions to working capital[h].....	7,785
− Capital expenditures[i]...........	500
− Debt amortization[j]	866
Residual cash flow	($2,895)

[a] Calculations of an independent analyst.
[b] Based on William Jelin's projections from the *Wall Street Transcript*.
[c] 75 percent of sales; compared with 71, 73, and 75 percent in 1983, 1984, and 1985, respectively.
[d] 45 percent of sales—3 to 4 percent higher than in the past two years to accommodate new product.
[e] Fiscal year-end 1985 cash and investments at 8 percent.
[f] Debt of: $1.1 million at 75 percent of 9.5 percent prime rate; $65,000 at prime rate; $408,000 at prime rate.
[g] Depreciation at 10 percent of property and equipment assumes $500,000 of capital expenditures. Amortization assumes cost of Glycel licensing agreement, estimated at $3.5 million, is amortized over 15 years.
[h] Assumes working capital equals 61 percent of sales (61 percent in 1985, 55 percent in 1984). Working capital is equal to current assets less current liabilities.
[i] High expenditures to accommodate Glycel.
[j] $800,000 payment on $1.6 million notes and $66,000 on New Jersey Economic Development Authority mortgage loan.

Case 7

Padgett Blank Book Company

Negotiations with Padgett Blank Book Company had been going on for almost a year, and Mr. Francis Libris hoped the time had come when they could be pushed to a mutually satisfactory conclusion. If not, Padgett might elect to seek another bank as its source of funds. Alternatively, Mr. Libris would be subject to criticism by his superiors for failing to deliver on his commitment to manage and structure the relationship properly. Mr. Libris was vice president of the Windsor Trust Company of New York, one of the largest banks in the United States. He was responsible for the East Midtown branch of the bank, to which Padgett's account was assigned because its small executive offices were on an upper floor of the same building in which the branch was located. It was a significant account for the branch and an important one to its profitability.

Padgett had borrowed relatively small amounts off and on from Windsor since it had first established an account with the bank in 1939. Even the acquisition of several small companies (for less than $1 million each) in the late 1970s and early 1980s did not require high levels of debt. The acquisition of a long-coveted competitor at an attractive price on short notice in early 1988 brought Padgett suddenly to the bank, asking for an additional $3.6 million loan. Combined with the $3.6 million already outstanding at the time, Windsor's total exposure could rise to $7.2 million, well in excess of the $5 million advised credit line that had been approved for the company. The request was granted nevertheless, under an internal guidance line of $8 million, and the rate was continued at prime. Mr. Libris had been working since then to structure the arrangement on a more orderly basis than on 90-day notes with no protective covenants.

This case was prepared by William W. Sihler from material written by Paul H. Hunn, vice president, Manufacturers Hanover Trust Company, whose cooperation is acknowledged with appreciation.
Copyright © 1989 by the Darden Graduate Business School Foundation, Charlottesville, VA.

It was now January 1989. Mr. Libris hoped to have the new terms worked out so they could be reflected on the financial statements for the 1989 fiscal year, which would end April 30. While he knew there was some possibility that a negotiation completed before the auditors finished their field work could be shown in the report, he preferred to have the arrangements made without this complication.

Mr. Libris wondered whether he should take a fresh look at the situation. He had originally attempted to persuade Padgett's management to finance part of the company's requirements in the form of long-term debt from a life insurance company. When the financial vice president declined this idea, Mr. Libris decided to see how the loan could be repaid to the bank within the period initially suggested by the credit committee. As time had gone on, he began to think that these constraints might not be appropriate to the situation and that a more creative solution might prove acceptable both to the credit committee and to Padgett's management. Because Mr. Libris knew he would have to get the approval of his superiors before he undertook a different initiative with Padgett's management, time was getting exceedingly short. He had to develop both the implications of the credit committee's original decision and of any alternatives which appeared to be superior.

PADGETT BLANK BOOK COMPANY

The Padgett Blank Book Company, a closely held, publicly traded (over-the-counter) company, manufactured a variety of stationery products, including notebooks, loose-leaf binders, forms, and filler paper for students and record-keeping purposes. The company was over 100 years old. Its ownership remained primarily with the descendants of the founders, now a large and widely spread group. Few family members were active in the company's management, however, and the major connection with most of the owners came in the form of the quarterly dividend check. A few members of the family depended on the dividends for the majority of their income. Most of the shareholders considered it just another investment—and an illiquid one at that, because the market for Padgett's stock was extremely thin. A significant payout was considered important by management.

Management, which was largely professional, appeared competent, responsible, and reasonably effective. Its expertise was largely in operations, which were carried on at a number of plants in the New England and mid Atlantic areas, and in marketing, which was controlled out of the executive office in New York. Management was not financially oriented, Mr. Libris had observed.

Padgett's customers were some 5,000 wholesalers and retailers in the United States and Canada. No single customer or small group of customers accounted for a substantial share of Padgett's sales. Terms were 2/10 net 30, but few customers took the discount, and many stretched payment for an additional 30 days. The business had a slight seasonal peak in the late summer when big back-to-school sales took place. Because the company attempted to maintain level production in order to reduce unit costs in the highly competitive market, a seasonal variation of about $2 million occurred in its borrowing pattern. The peak occurred in early fall.

A consolidation had been taking place in the business since the early 1970s, initially caused by the high inflation rate of that period which made it difficult for small firms to finance their current assets. Financial difficulties and inventory problems resulting from the subsequent mid-1970s recession further reduced the level of the competition. Changes in the tax rules effective in 1986 provided new impetus for the smaller companies to sell. Finally, the sharp drop in the stock market in October 1987 combined with a resurgence of paper price increases and shortages of supply had frightened some owners, such as those at Tri-State Tablet, enough that they put their firms on the market. It had not been possible to pass all the price increases through to the customers because of strong competition from Canadian and Scandinavian sources. In Padgett's case, the drop in the corporate tax rate helped compensate for smaller margins.

Many competitors had been acquired by national corporations with strong marketing skills and good financial resources. The response of Padgett's management had been to acquire smaller companies that fit into its product or marketing needs. The acquisition of its competitor, Tri-State Tablet Company, in April 1988 was the culmination of these efforts.

Padgett's financial statements for fiscal year 1988 had been given an unqualified opinion by the national CPA firm that audited them. Straight-line depreciation was used for reporting purposes, with accelerated depreciation used for taxes. Inventory had been valued on a lower of cost (FIFO) or market basis. Financial statements for the 1985–88 fiscal years are presented in Exhibits 1 and 2. Exhibit 3 is a standard computer spread used by Windsor's credit department to organize a company's financial statements for analysis.

PADGETT'S RELATIONSHIP WITH WINDSOR TRUST

Windsor Trust had historically been Padgett's only lending bank and was the only lending bank in early 1989. Among other benefits of this relationship, Padgett used Windsor Trust as the depository for its substantial New York state and federal tax payments. So far during the 1989 fiscal year, Padgett's average collected balance with Windsor had been $524,000. Affiliated companies and subsidiaries had balances that averaged $231,000. The loan balances outstanding had ranged from $3.3 to $7.2 million, with an average of $5.05 million. The loan had last been cleaned up for an extended period from March 31, 1985, to January 8, 1986.

Padgett maintained a small deposit relationship with the Phoenix Bank of Manhattan, a major bank that had long been soliciting a more important role in the company's financial arrangements. In addition, several out-of-town banks were used to service the various plant locations.

The speed with which the Tri-State Tablet acquisition had been made had not allowed for careful planning of the financial arrangements. Mr. Libris's superiors had been reluctant to double the loan to Padgett in the absence of a carefully structured repayment program as well as appropriate protective covenants. With Mr. Libris's assurance that these questions could be quickly resolved, the divisional senior vice president had authorized the loan and established a new temporary credit limit of $8 million. It had been expected, however, that the loan would be formally structured long before January 1989, which was a source of embarrassment to Mr. Libris. He knew he would also be embarrassed and his profit plan damaged if he should lose the account to Phoenix or if it were taken over completely by an insurance company.

Once the dust created by the acquisition had settled down, Mr. Libris met with John Ruhl, Padgett's financial vice president, to discuss the company's plans. Based on these conversations, Mr. Libris and Windsor's credit department prepared a preliminary financial forecast for Padgett's 1989-92 fiscal years. Summary figures from this forecast are presented in Exhibit 4.

Mr. Libris was distressed to note that, even under what he thought were assumptions which minimized the need for funds, Padgett would still have $4.4 million in short-term debt on the books at the end of the 1992 fiscal year. Assuming the company could generate about $1 million in "undedicated" cash each year thereafter, a total of eight years would be required to retire the debt. This was considerably longer than the typical bank five-year term loan a company of Padgett's size might expect. Windsor was willing to stretch to six years for important relationships, but a seven-year term loan would be considered a bit long for a company like Padgett, which did not enjoy the financial flexibility afforded firms having easy entry to the public capital markets.

Mr. Libris decided that a need of this duration appropriately called for insurance company financing. After he had met with officers of several companies, he wrote Mr. Ruhl to propose a 12–15 year loan and to quote terms an insurance company might offer. (Mr. Libris's letter is reproduced as Exhibit 5.) He also pointed out that Windsor might be able to structure an arrangement that would allow the bank to take the seasonal needs while the insurance company would take the long-term core requirements of $5 million.

Mr. Ruhl's response was emphatically negative. While he appreciated the information, he reported that management did not like the high fixed rates that were currently being charged. Furthermore, management did not like the idea of an elaborate set of covenants. Mr. Ruhl said he particularly disliked the type of covenant that could throw the company in default without management's explicit action. "Violation of a debt-capital ratio, for instance," explained Mr. Ruhl, "could occur as the result of an adverse year rather than anything we do. I don't mind agreeing not to borrow or pay dividends if certain conditions would result, but I just don't see agreeing to a lot of things which are out of my control. I can't see getting tied up in all these technicalities." Mr. Ruhl indicated that he did not see anything wrong with the present friendly and informal loan. "After all," he said, "if you don't like what we are doing—anything at all—you can call your entire loan at the end of any 90-day period. I don't see why that isn't better protection for you than fancy agreements."

In the months that followed this disappointing outcome, Mr. Libris met frequently with Mr. Ruhl in order to get a thorough understanding of the business. He planned to prepare a forecast of future needs that would accurately reflect Padgett management's thinking and his own insights into the company. By late in 1988, preliminary estimates for the 1989 fiscal year were becoming available so Mr. Libris could incorporate them into his forecasts. The forecasts, which were prepared showing the effects of 5 percent, 10 percent, and 15 percent growth in sales over the 1990–92 fiscal years, are included as Exhibit 6.

Mr. Ruhl thought that this effort was most helpful, although he noted that two last-minute changes should be incorporated in the planning. First, he expected to shift to LIFO inventory valuation for the 1989 fiscal year, which would result in a tax benefit of $500,000. Second, management had decided to dispose of a redundant warehouse, which had been part of the Tri-State acquisition. Management expected to receive $700,000 from the cash sale and tax refunds on the book loss.

ALTERNATIVES

Mr. Libris still thought that splitting the loan—maybe with the bank's own real estate department—had promise. For instance, Padgett owned outright a large, general-purpose warehouse. Its appraisal value of $3 million was in excess of the amount at which it was carried on the books. Although Mr. Libris was not an experienced real estate lending officer, he believed the property would be attractive collateral for a mortgage loan. Another alternative might be to wait until the loan had been partly retired and then invite another bank to share the remainder for the duration of the repayment. Part of the loan could be rotated between banks to allow each one a cleanup period of several months. Finally, he had discovered that Padgett's small Canadian operation was self-contained, with a negligible amount of intercompany transfers and charges. With net current assets of $1.8 to $2.0 million to offer as collateral and no direct debt, the Canadian subsidiary could probably raise $1.0 million from Canadian banks. The Canadian banks would require a "floating charge," a form of security agreement, against all current assets. He wondered whether there were any other alternative sources he should consider.

Although U.S. banking law and practice was not identical with Canadian and British practice with respect to "floating liens," asset-based finance might offer useful alternatives. It would be expensive to take effective security against Padgett's receivables because the company had so many customers and the average account was relatively small. A factoring arrangement might be suitable, in which Padgett could sell its accounts on a non-recourse basis to a commercial finance company. Windsor Bank itself did not operate a factoring function, however. It would be necessary to find one that had experience in the paper distribution business or the costs of the factoring, which were usually about 2 percent of accounts purchased, would be too high. On the other hand, if Padgett factored its accounts, it could eliminate its credit department and would have no bad debts.

Windsor could always grant credit against the security of the accounts receivable even though it was not monitoring the accounts as closely as a factor would. The loan would be limited to a percentage of receivables in order to provide some protection against losses. A security interest in the inventory could also be required, although the granting of this security could upset some major paper companies who were Padgett's sources of supply.

MONEY MARKET CONSIDERATION AND PRICING ASPECTS

Funds were readily available in the financial markets in January 1989, although the prime rate had risen rapidly during 1988 and now stood at 10.5 percent. The prime's low in recent years had been 7.5 percent from September 1986 to March 1987. By January 1988, prime had risen to 8.75 percent. Thirty-day commercial paper was currently yielding 9.30 percent, up from 8.82 percent the first week in December 1988. The Treasury yield curve was relatively flat, with one-year notes trading at 9.07 percent, five-year notes at 9.18 percent, 10-year bonds at 9.17 percent, and 30-year bonds at 9.0 percent.

These increases in the interest rates were an issue which Mr. Libris would have to address in preparing a proposal for Mr. Ruhl. First, should the loan (or loans) be priced at a fixed rate or at a floating rate? Fixed-rate loans were generally offered at a premium of .5 to 1 percent above the floating rate.

In adjusting the prime rate to the conditions of the borrower, Windsor bank officers often used what they termed a "risk premium" system. This approach added or subtracted 25 basis points (0.25 percent) to the price for such factors as the size of the company's sales (add points for small size and lack of access to public markets), purpose, term, escalating versus level payments, debt profile, liquidity posture, and (subtract points for) relationship benefits (e.g., balances, tax payments, and corporate trust). Of course, the final rate had to be checked against the market, which in Padgett's case was highly competitive as the result of Phoenix's interest.

Second, Mr. Libris was considering whether to offer Padgett a "cash cap" on the loan, if Mr. Ruhl decided to put a significant portion of it on a floating rate. A cash cap loan was one which established a maximum rate of interest due currently in cash as well as an index rate by which the total interest due would be determined. If the index rose above the cash cap rate, the difference between total interest and the cash cap amount due would be set up as a separate loan on the respective books. Interest on this loan would also be calculated under the index-cash cap arrangement. When the index interest rate again declined below the cash cap rate, the borrower would continue to pay at the cash cap rate, with the difference being used to amortize the separate "cash cap" loan. When that loan had been repaid, the interest rate would fall to the index level.

Because of the complications that had already been experienced and that were likely to arise in the course of completing the negotiations, Mr. Libris knew he had no more time to collect information. He had to work quickly toward a satisfactory resolution of the loan structure with Padgett's management.

EXHIBIT 1 Income Statements for the Fiscal Years Ended April 30, 1985–1988 (thousands of dollars)

	1985	1986	1987	1988
Net sales	$26,331	$27,219	$36,897	$41,308
Cost of goods sold	15,728	16,077	21,937	24,555
Depreciation and amortization.....	*	510	667	739
	10,603	10,632	14,293	16,014
General and administrative expense	5,814	5,087	7,139	7,821
Selling expense	†	1,878	2,603	3,147
Operating expenses	5,814	6,965	9,742	$10,968
Operating profit.................	4,789	3,667	4,551	5,046
Interest expense.................	—	32	220	379
Other expenses (income).........	83	(42)	(39)	(71)
Profit before taxes	4,706	3,677	4,370	4,738
Income taxes	2,702	1,893	2,216	2,132
Profit after taxes	$ 2,004	$ 1,784	$ 2,154	$ 2,606
Number of shares (000)...........	1,000	1,115	1,116	1,118
Earnings per share	$2.00	$1.60	$1.93	$2.33
Dividends per share	$1.00	$1.00	$1.00	$1.00

* Included in cost of goods sold in 1985.
† Included in general and administrative expenses in 1985.

EXHIBIT 2 Balance Sheets as of April 30, 1985–1988 (thousands of dollars)

	1985	*1986*	*1987*	*1988*
Assets				
Current assets:				
Cash and securities	$ 1,691	$ 266	$ 658	$ 834
Accounts receivable.........	4,734	5,542	6,350	7,754
Inventory	7,276	7,743	10,959	14,360
Prepayments and other	233	194	153	563
Total current assets	13,934	13,745	18,120	23,511
Property, plant, equipment.....	—	8,718	11,265	12,468
Less: Accumulated depreciation	—	3,384	4,912	5,209
Net property, plant, equipment	4,797	5,334	6,353	7,259
Other assets	59	257	386	224
Total assets..................	$18,790	$19,336	$24,859	$30,994
Liabilities and Owners' Equity				
Current liabilities:				
Short-term notes............	$ —	$ —	$ 3,118	$ 7,221
Accounts payable...........	1,127	1,619	2,158	1,958
Accruals	395	397	703	1,014
Other current liabilities......	271	251	418	824
Current portion, long-term debt.....................	615	117	51	52
Total current liabilities	2,408	2,384	6,448	11,069
Long-term debt	338	221	507	455
Deferred taxes	538	568	714	756
Other liabilities	136	126	116	151
Total liabilities	3,420	3,299	7,785	12,431
Owners' equity:				
Common stock	5,587	5,587	5,587	5,587
Retained earnings...........	9,783	10,450	11,487	12,976
Total owners' equity......	15,370	16,037	17,074	18,563
Total liabilities and net worth ..	$18,790	$19,336	$24,859	$30,994

EXHIBIT 3 Cash Flow and Ratio Analysis, Fiscal Years Ended April 30, 1985–1988 (dollar figures in thousands)

	1985	1986	1987	1988
Sources:				
Current assets				
Profit after taxes plus depn. and amort.*		$ 2,294	$ 2,821	$ 3,345
Deferred taxes		30	146	42
New long-term debt		—	337	—
New short-term debt		—	3,118	4,103
Accounts payable		492	539	(200)
Accruals		2	306	311
Other current liabilities		(20)	167	406
Other liabilities		(10)	(10)	35
Total sources		2,788	7,424	8,042
Uses:				
Dividends paid in cash		1,117	1,117	1,117
Capital expenditure		979	1,575	1,530
Repayment of long-term debt		615	117	51
Accounts receivable		808	808	1,404
Inventory		467	3,216	3,401
Prepayments and other current assets		(39)	(41)	410
Other assets		198	129	(162)
Intangibles*		68	111	115
Total uses		4,213	7,032	7,866
Change in cash and securities		(1,425)	392	176
Working capital	$11,526	$11,361	$11,672	$12,442
Profitability:				
Sales growth	NA%	3.4%	35.6%	12.0%
Gross profit margin	40.3	39.1	38.7	38.8
Operating expenses/sales	22.1	25.6	26.4	26.5
Pretax margin	17.9	13.5	11.8	11.5
After-tax margin	7.6	6.6	5.8	6.3
Return on average owners' equity	NA	11.4	13.0	14.6
Return on total assets	10.7	9.2	8.7	8.4
EBIT/total assets	25.0	19.2	18.5	16.5
Divided payout	50.2	62.6	51.9	42.9
Turnover:				
Receivables	5.6×	4.9×	5.8×	5.3×
Inventory	3.6	3.5	3.4	2.9
Accounts payable	23.4	16.8	17.1	21.1
Working capital	2.3	2.4	3.2	3.3
Fixed asset	5.5	5.1	5.8	5.7
Net worth	1.7	1.7	2.2	2.2
Leverage:				
Total debt/owners' equity	22.3%	20.6%	45.6%	67.0%
Long-term debt/owners' equity	2.2	1.4	2.9	2.4
Interest coverage	NA×	115.9×	20.9×	13.5×
Liquidity:				
Quick ratio	2.7×	2.4×	1.1×	0.8×
Current ratio	5.8	5.8	2.8	2.1

* Intangibles amortized as purchased.

EXHIBIT 4   Summary Figures from Preliminary Projection of Financial Position, Fiscal Years Ended April 30, 1989–1992 (millions of dollars)

	1989	1990	1991	1992
Net sales......................	$55.2	$60.7	$66.8	$73.5
Profit after taxes..............	3.3	3.6	4.2	4.8
Noncash charges..............	0.9	0.9	1.0	1.1
Cash generated from operations	4.2	4.5	5.2	5.9
Disposition of assets	0.2	—	—	—
Total sources...............	4.4	4.5	5.2	5.9
Dividends....................	1.1	1.1	1.1	1.1
Increase in working capital* ...	2.4	2.4	3.1	3.6
Capital expenditures	1.0	1.0	1.0	1.0
	4.5	4.5	5.2	5.7
* Including retirement of short-term debt:......................	0.7	0.2	0.8	1.1
Leaving a balance in short-term debt of	6.5	6.3	5.5	4.4

Assumptions:
1. 10 percent sales growth.
2. 6.0 to 6.5 percent after-tax margin.
3. Accounts receivable turnover 5.7 (17.5 percent of sales).
4. Inventory turnover 3.6 (27.8 percent of sales).
5. Accounts payable turnover 21.3 × (4.7 percent of sales).

EXHIBIT 5 Mr. Libris's Letter Outlining Proposed Term-Loan Agreement

May 15, 1988

Mr. John Ruhl
Vice President—Finance
Padgett Blank Book Company
New York, New York

Dear John:

Thank you for the opportunity last week to review the financial plans you have for Padgett. This letter sets forth our thoughts relating to the need for properly incorporating your bank loan into these plans.

Currently, Padgett has $6,853,000 outstanding in short term 90-day notes, and we understand that an additional $1.0–$1.5 million is likely to be borrowed to support new receivables of your new acquisition. This is in contrast with the circumstance of May, 1986 when we financed your previous acquisition, and our loan outstanding increased from $500,000 to $1,850,000. At that time, an anticipated restructuring of the loan was postponed until a clearer definition of longer term corporate cash need could be ascertained.

In late 1987, we expressed an interest in discussing with you a restructuring of the then loan outstanding so that legitimately long-term funds could be sourced on a proper long-term basis. Our subsequent conversations and cash flow study were complicated by the anticipated major acquisition and its impact.

Enclosed is a copy of our most recent Padgett forecast, the results of which we have jointly reviewed. On balance, our feeling is that the forecast may tend to understate the cash requirement in that it assumes moderate sales growth, the upholding of traditional margins, and tight control over capital expenditures and dividends. The forecast does seem to indicate a long-term need of at least $5 million, which cannot be properly funded through the bank on anything resembling a full payout term-loan basis.

Given what appears to be the clear nature of the need, it seems appropriate that financing discussions with an insurance company be initiated. This suggestion is rooted in our firm feeling that it is strategically unwise from the standpoint of the company, as well as that of the bank, to fulfill substantial long-term financial need through the continued use of 90-day notes.

On a confidential basis and without revealing your name, we have talked with three insurance companies within the last week. Discussions included the following generalized parameters for life insurance company lending:

Amount:	No problem.
Term:	12–15 years.
Rate:	Fixed, 9.5 percent minimum.
Payback:	Level payments desired but flexibility offered (e.g., three years of grace).
Prepayment:	All want protection designed to discourage it; however, there are provisions for prepayment without penalty if they were to turn you down for a requested increase in amount and you were able to obtain a commitment from another source.
Availability of money:	Good.

EXHIBIT 5 *(concluded)*

There is the possibility of bank participation in the first five years of an insurance company loan, but (as you can well understand) it is the lender taking the longest maturities who controls the negotiation of loan agreement covenants from the lenders' point of view. Inclusion of the Bank whose interest rates are geared to a floating prime rate offers a partial hedge, without guarantee, against known fixed interest cost. Bank pricing would probably look like the prime plus 0.25 percent for the first three years and prime plus 0.50 percent for years four and five. While an insurance company loan requires no deposit balances to be maintained, we would expect balances of 15 percent against the average loan outstanding. Each 5.00 percent balance increment is roughly equivalent to 0.25 percent in interest rate.

We all recognize the fact that interest rates are at a high level; however, the Economics Department of this Bank does not feel that long-term interest rates will see reduced levels in the foreseeable future. Financing demands on the capital markets are expected to continue strong, inflation psychology has become imbedded, and any advantage to be gained in avoiding the long-term market is, at best, marginal.

For any needs consistent with prudent bank lending, Windsor Trust stands ready to finance your business. Our desire to assist in every way we can is complete and sincere.

Sincerely,

Francis Libris
Vice President
Windsor Trust Company

EXHIBIT 6 Projected Financial Statements for 1990–1992 Fiscal Years Ending April 30, Assuming 5%, 10%, and 15% Sales Growth (dollar figures in millions except per share figures)

	1988 Actual	1989 Est.	5% Growth 1990	5% Growth 1991	5% Growth 1992	10% Growth 1990	10% Growth 1991	10% Growth 1992	15% Growth 1990	15% Growth 1991	15% Growth 1992
A. Income Statements											
Sales, net	$41.32	$57.80	$60.69	$63.72	$66.91	$63.58	$69.94	$76.93	$66.47	$76.44	$87.91
Cost of sales	24.56	36.08	37.27	38.86	40.81	39.05	42.65	46.93	40.82	46.61	53.61
Depn. & amort.	0.74	0.94	0.91	1.00	1.10	0.91	1.00	1.10	0.91	1.00	1.10
General & admin.	7.82	10.23	10.75	11.29	11.87	11.26	12.40	13.65	11.77	13.55	15.59
Selling expense	3.15	4.61	4.84	5.09	5.35	5.08	5.60	6.15	5.30	6.11	7.03
Operating profit	5.05	5.94	6.92	7.48	7.78	7.28	8.29	9.10	7.67	9.17	10.58
Interest expenses*	0.38	0.95	0.80	0.72	0.61	0.90	0.86	0.81	1.01	1.10	1.18
Other exp. (income)	(0.07)	(0.71)	0.07	0.07	0.07	0.07	0.07	0.07	0.07	0.07	0.07
Pretax earn.	4.74	5.70	6.05	6.69	7.10	6.31	7.36	8.22	6.59	8.00	9.33
After-tax earn.	$ 2.61	$ 3.42	$ 3.63	$ 4.01	$ 4.26	$ 3.79	$ 4.42	$ 4.93	$ 3.95	$ 4.80	$ 5.60
Earnings per share (1,118)	$ 2.33	$ 3.06	$ 3.25	$ 3.59	$ 3.81	$ 3.39	$ 3.95	$ 4.41	$ 3.54	$ 4.29	$ 5.01
Dividends per share	1.00	1.03	1.08	1.19	1.27	1.13	1.31	1.47	1.18	1.43	1.66
B. Balance Sheets											
Assets											
Cash, minimum	$ 0.83	$ 1.17	$ 1.23	$ 1.29	$ 1.36	$ 1.29	$ 1.42	$ 1.56	$ 1.35	$ 1.55	$ 1.78
Excess cash	—	—	0.01	0.73	1.24	—	—	—	—	—	—
Acc. receivable	7.75	10.12	10.62	11.15	11.71	11.13	12.24	13.46	11.63	13.38	15.38
Inventory	14.36	16.18	16.99	17.84	18.74	17.80	19.58	21.54	18.61	21.40	24.61
Prepayments, etc.	0.56	0.23	0.24	0.26	0.27	0.26	0.28	0.31	0.27	0.31	0.36
Total current assets	23.51	27.71	29.10	31.27	33.32	30.48	33.52	36.87	31.86	36.64	42.14
Plant & equipt.	12.47	13.27	14.27	15.27	16.27	14.27	15.27	16.27	14.27	15.27	16.27
Less: accum. depn.	5.21	6.04	6.95	7.95	9.05	6.95	7.95	9.05	6.95	7.95	9.05
Net plant & equipt.	7.26	7.23	7.32	7.32	7.22	7.32	7.32	7.22	7.32	7.32	7.22
Other	0.22	0.11	0.11	0.11	0.11	0.11	0.11	0.11	0.11	0.11	0.11
Total assets	$30.99	$35.05	$36.54	$38.71	$40.65	$37.91	$40.95	$44.20	$39.29	$44.07	$49.47

* Includes interest calculated on the cash deficit at 11 percent.
Figures may not add correctly because of rounding.

Liabilities and Owner's Equity

Short-term notes	$ 7.22	$ 7.45	$ 6.29	$ 5.50	$ 4.35	$ 6.29	$ 5.50	$ 4.35	$ 6.29	$ 5.50	$ 4.35
Acc. payable	1.96	2.72	2.85	3.00	3.14	2.99	3.29	3.62	3.12	3.59	4.13
Accruals	1.01	1.44	1.52	1.59	1.67	1.59	1.75	1.92	1.66	1.91	2.20
Other	0.82	1.15	1.21	1.33	1.40	1.27	1.39	1.53	1.33	1.61	1.85
Current portion, LTD	0.05	0.05	0.05	0.05	0.05	0.05	0.05	0.05	0.05	0.05	0.05
Total current liabilities	11.06	12.82	11.93	11.48	10.61	12.19	11.98	11.47	12.46	12.66	12.58
Long-term debt	0.46	0.40	0.35	0.30	0.25	0.35	0.30	0.25	0.35	0.30	0.25
Deferred taxes	0.76	0.80	0.80	0.80	0.80	0.80	0.80	0.80	0.80	0.80	0.80
Other	0.15	0.20	0.20	0.20	0.20	0.20	0.20	0.20	0.20	0.20	0.20
Cash deficit*	—	—	—	—	—	1.02	1.37	1.89	2.01	3.44	5.23
Total liabilities	12.43	14.22	13.28	12.78	11.86	14.56	14.65	14.61	15.82	17.40	19.06
Common stock	5.59	5.59	5.59	5.59	5.59	5.59	5.59	5.59	5.59	5.59	5.59
Retained earnings	12.98	15.98	17.67	20.34	23.18	17.76	20.71	24.00	17.88	21.09	24.82
Total owner's equity	18.56	20.83	23.25	25.93	28.77	23.35	26.30	29.59	23.47	26.68	30.41
Total liab. & owner's eq.	$30.99	$35.05	$36.53	$38.71	$40.63	$37.91	$40.95	$44.20	$39.29	$44.07	$49.47

C. Cash Flow Sources

After-tax earnings	$ 3.42	$ 3.63	$ 4.01	$ 4.26	$ 3.79	$ 4.42	$ 4.93	$ 3.95	$ 4.80	$ 5.59	
Noncash charges	0.94	0.91	1.00	1.10	0.91	1.00	1.10	0.91	1.10	1.10	
Funds from operations	4.36	4.54	5.01	5.36	4.70	5.42	6.03	4.86	5.80	6.69	
Deferred taxes	0.04	—	—	—	—	—	—	—	—	—	
Accounts payable	0.76	0.14	0.14	0.14	0.27	0.30	0.33	0.41	0.47	0.54	
Accruals	0.43	0.07	0.07	0.08	0.14	0.16	0.17	0.22	0.25	0.29	
Other and misc. curr. liab.	0.33	0.06	0.12	0.07	0.11	0.12	0.14	0.17	0.27	0.24	
Other liabilities	0.05	—	—	—	—	—	—	—	—	—	
Other assets	6.08	—	—	—	—	—	—	—	—	—	
Total sources	6.08	4.81	5.34	5.65	5.22	6.00	6.67	5.66	6.79	7.76	

* Includes interest calculated on the cash deficit at 11 percent.

EXHIBIT 6 (concluded)

	1988 Actual	1989 Est.	5% Growth 1990	5% Growth 1991	5% Growth 1992	10% Growth 1990	10% Growth 1991	10% Growth 1992	15% Growth 1990	15% Growth 1991	15% Growth 1992
Uses											
Dividends		1.16	1.21	1.34	1.42	1.26	1.47	1.64	1.31	1.59	1.86
Capital expenditures		0.80	1.00	1.00	1.00	1.00	1.00	1.00	1.00	1.00	1.00
S.T. debt		(0.23)	1.16	0.79	1.15	1.16	0.79	1.15	1.16	0.79	1.15
L.T. debt		0.05	0.05	0.05	0.05	0.05	0.05	0.05	0.05	0.05	0.05
Minimum cash		0.34	0.06	0.06	0.06	0.12	0.13	0.14	0.18	0.20	0.23
Accounts receivable		2.36	0.50	0.53	0.56	1.01	1.11	1.22	1.52	1.52	2.01
Inventory		1.82	0.81	0.85	0.89	1.62	1.78	1.96	2.43	2.79	3.21
Prepay & def. chg.		(0.33)	0.01	0.01	0.01	0.02	0.02	0.03	0.04	0.04	0.05
Intangibles		0.11	—	—	—	—	—	—	—	—	—
Total uses		6.08	4.80	4.63	5.14	6.24	6.35	7.19	7.69	8.20	9.56
Net cash flow		—	0.02	0.71	0.51	(1.01)	(0.27)	(0.51)	(2.03)	(1.41)	(1.80)
Cumulative		—	0.02	0.73	1.24	(1.01)	(1.28)	(1.79)	(2.02)	(3.43)	(5.23)
D. Analytical Ratios Profitability											
Sales growth	12.0%	39.9%	5.0%	5.0%	5.0%	10.0%	10.0%	10.0%	15.0%	15.0%	15.0%
E.P.S. growth	20.7	31.4	6.2	10.3	6.3	10.8	16.5	11.2	15.5	21.4	16.5
Gross profit margin	38.8	35.9	38.6	39.0	39.0	38.6	39.0	39.0	38.6	39.0	39.0
Operating exp./sales	26.5	25.7	25.7	25.7	25.3	25.7	25.7	25.7	25.7	25.7	25.7
Pretax margin	11.5	10.3	10.0	10.5	10.6	9.9	10.5	10.7	9.9	10.5	10.6
After-tax margin	6.3	5.9	6.0	6.3	6.4	6.0	6.3	6.4	5.9	6.3	6.4

Return on average											
owner's equity	14.6	17.4	16.5	16.3	15.6	17.1	17.8	17.6	17.9	19.1	19.6
Return on total assets	8.4	9.8	9.9	10.4	10.5	10.0	10.8	11.2	10.1	10.9	11.3
EBIT/total assets	16.5	19.0	18.7	19.1	19.0	19.0	20.1	20.4	19.4	20.7	21.2
Dividend payout	42.9	33.8	33.3	33.3	33.3	33.3	33.3	33.3	33.2	33.2	33.2
Turnover											
Receivables	5.3x	5.7x	5.7x	5.7x	5.7x	5.7x	5.7x	5.7x	5.7x	5.7x	5.7x
Inventory	2.9	3.6	3.6	3.6	3.6	3.6	3.6	3.6	3.6	3.6	3.6
Accounts payable	21.1	21.3	21.3	21.3	21.3	21.3	21.3	21.3	21.3	21.3	21.3
Working capital	3.3	3.6	3.5	3.2	2.9	3.5	3.3	3.0	3.4	3.2	3.0
Fixed asset	5.7	8.0	8.3	8.7	9.3	8.7	9.6	10.6	9.1	10.4	12.2
Net worth	2.2	2.8	2.6	2.4	2.3	2.7	2.6	2.6	2.8	2.9	2.9
Leverage											
Total debt/owners' equity	67.0%	68.3%	57.1%	49.3%	41.3%	62.3%	55.7%	49.3%	67.4%	65.2%	62.7%
Long-term debt/owners' equity	2.4	1.9	1.5	1.1	0.9	1.5	1.1	0.8	1.5	1.1	0.8
Interest coverage	13.5x	7.0x	8.7x	10.3x	12.6x	8.0x	9.6x	11.1x	7.5x	8.3x	8.9x
Liquidity											
Quick ratio	0.8x	1.0x	1.0x	1.1x	1.3x	1.0x	1.1x	1.3x	1.1x	1.2x	1.4x
Current ratio	2.1	2.2	2.4	2.7	3.1	2.5	2.8	3.2	2.6	2.9	3.3
Working capital	$12.44	$14.89	$19.40	$29.98	$29.55	$18.29	$21.46	$25.23	$19.40	$23.98	$29.55

Sengupta Fibres, Ltd.

Mrs. Sharma, the managing director and principal owner of Sengupta Fibres, Ltd., discovered the problem when she arrived at the parking lot of the company's plant at 10 A.M. one morning in early January 1990. Trucks filled with rolls of fiber yarns were being unloaded, but they had been loaded just the night before and had been ready to depart that morning. The fiber was intended for customers who had been badgering Mrs. Sharma to fill their orders in a timely fashion. The government tax inspector, who was stationed at the company's warehouse, would not clear the trucks for departure because the excise tax had not been paid. The tax inspector required a cash payment; but, in seeking to draw funds for the excise tax that morning, Mr. Ashoka, the bookkeeper, discovered that the company had overdrawn its bank account again—the third time in as many weeks. The truck drivers were independent contractors who refused to wait while the company and government settled their accounts. They cursed loudly as they unloaded the trucks.

Now this shipment would not leave for at least another two days, and angry customers would no doubt require an explanation. Moreover, before granting a loan with which to pay the excise tax, the branch manager of the All-India Bank & Trust Company had requested a meeting with Mrs. Sharma for the next day to discuss Sengupta's financial condition and plans for restoring the firm's liquidity.

Mrs. Sharma told Mr. Ashoka, "This cash problem is most vexing. I don't understand it. We're a very profitable enterprise, yet we seem to have to depend increasingly on the bank. Why do we need more loans just as our heavy selling season begins? We can't repeat this blunder."

This case was developed by Robert F. Bruner from a study written by Thien T. Pham. Names and figures have been disguised.

Copyright © 1990 by the Darden Graduate Business School Foundation, Charlottesville, VA. Revised February 1993.

COMPANY BACKGROUND

Sengupta Fibres, Ltd., was founded in 1962 to produce nylon fiber at its only plant, in Kota, India, about 100 kilometers south of New Delhi. By using new technology and domestic raw materials, the firm had developed a steady franchise among dozens of small local textile weavers. It supplied synthetic fiber yarns used in weaving colorful cloths for making saris, the traditional women's dress of India. On average, each sari required eight yards of cloth. An Indian woman typically would buy three saris per year. With a female population of over 500 million in India, the demand for saris would account for more than 12 billion yards of fabric. This demand currently was being supplied entirely from domestic textile mills that, in turn, filled their yarn requirements from suppliers, such as Sengupta Fibres.

SYNTHETIC-TEXTILE MARKET

The demand for synthetic textiles was characterized by stable year-to-year growth and predictable seasonal fluctuations. Unit demand increased with both population and national income. In addition, India's population celebrated hundreds of festivals each year, in deference to a host of deities, at which saris traditionally were worn. The most important festival, the Diwali celebration in mid-autumn, caused a seasonal peak in the demand for new saris, which, in turn, caused a seasonal peak in demand for nylon textiles in late summer and early fall. Thus, the seasonal demand for nylon yarn would peak in mid-summer. Unit growth in the industry was expected to be 15 percent per year.

Consumers purchased saris and textiles from cloth merchants located in villages around the country. A cloth merchant was an important local figure usually well known to area residents; the merchant generally granted credit to support consumer purchases. Merchants maintained relatively low levels of inventory and built stocks of goods only shortly in advance of and during the peak selling season.

Competition among suppliers (the many small textile-weaving mills) to these merchants was keen and was affected by price, service, and credit that the mills could grant to the merchants. The mills essentially produced to order, building their inventories of woven cloth shortly in advance of the peak selling season and keeping only maintenance stocks at other times of the year.

The yarn manufacturers competed for the business of the mills through responsive service and credit. The suppliers to the yarn manufacturers provided little or no trade credit. Being near the origin of the textile chain in India, the yarn manufacturers essentially banked the downstream activities of the industry.

PRODUCTION AND DISTRIBUTION SYSTEM

Thin profit margins had prompted Mrs. Sharma to adopt policies against overproduction and overstocking, which would require Sengupta to carry inventories through the slack selling season. She had adopted a plan of seasonal production, which meant that the yarn plant would operate at peak capacity for two months of the year and at modest levels the rest of the year. This policy imposed an annual ritual of hirings and layoffs.

To help ensure prompt service, Sengupta Fibres maintained two distribution ware-houses, but getting the finished yarn quickly from the factory in Kota to the customers was a challenge. The roads were narrow and mostly in poor repair. A truck could take 10 to 15 days to negotiate the trip between Calcutta and New Delhi, a distance of 700 miles. Except when they passed through cities, highways had only one lane. When two cars or trucks met, they had to slow down and squeeze past each other or else stop and wait for the traffic to pass. Journeys were slow and dangerous, and accidents frequent.

COMPANY PERFORMANCE

Sengupta Fibres had been consistently profitable. Moreover, sales had grown at an annual rate of 18 percent in 1988 and 1989. Gross sales were projected to reach 78.2 million rupees (Rs) in the fiscal year ended December 31, 1990 (see Exhibit 1).[1] Net profits reached Rs.2.6 million in 1989. Exhibits 2 and 3 present recent financial statements for the firm.

REASSESSMENT

After the episode in the parking lot, Mrs. Sharma and her bookkeeper went to her office to analyze the situation. She pushed aside the several items on her desk to which she had intended to devote the morning—a letter from a field sales manager requesting permission to grant favorable credit terms to a new customer (see Exhibit 4), a note from the transportation manager regarding possible railroad-based movement of goods (Exhibit 5), a proposal from the purchasing agent regarding the delivery lead times of certain supplies (Exhibit 6), and a proposal from the plant manager for a scheme of level annual production (Exhibit 7).

To prepare a forecast on a business-as-usual basis, Mrs. Sharma and Mr. Ashoka agreed on various parameters. Cost of goods sold would run at 75 percent of gross sales—a figure that was up from recent years because of increasing price competition. Operating expenses would be about 6 percent of sales—also up from recent years to include the addition of a quality-control department, two new sales agents, and three young nephews in whom she hoped to build an allegiance to the Sharma family business. The company's income tax rate was 30 percent and, although accrued monthly, was actually paid quarterly in March, June, September, and December. The excise tax (at 15 percent of sales) was different from the income tax and was collected at the factory gate as trucks left to make deliveries to customers and the regional warehouses. Mrs. Sharma proposed to pay dividends of Rs 450,000 per quarter to the 11 members of her extended family who held

---

[1]The rupee was at the time pegged to the U.S. dollar at the rate of 16 rupees per dollar.

the entire equity of the firm. For years, Sengupta had paid high dividends. The Sharma family believed that excess funds left in the firm were at greater risk than if the funds were returned to shareholders.

Mr. Ashoka observed that sales collections in any given month had been running steadily at the rate of 40 percent of the last month's sales plus 60 percent of the sales from the month before last. Raw materials purchased in any month represented on average 55 percent of the value of sales expected to be made in the following month. Wages and other expenses in a given month were equivalent to about 34 percent of purchases in that month. As a matter of policy, Mrs. Sharma wanted to see a cash balance of no less than Rs 640,000.

Sengupta Fibres had a line of credit from All-India Bank & Trust Company, where it also maintained its cash balances. All-India's short-term interest rate was currently 16 percent, but Mr. Ashoka was worried that inflation and interest rates might rise in the coming year. The seasonal line of credit had to be cleaned up for at least 30 days each year. The usual cleanup month had been October[2], but Sengupta Fibres had failed to make a full repayment at that time. Only after strong assurances by Mrs. Sharma that she would clean up the loan in November or December had the bank lending officer reluctantly agreed to waive the cleanup requirement in October. Unfortunately, Sengupta Fibres' credit needs did not abate as rapidly as expected in November and December, and, although his protests increased each month, the lending officer agreed to meet Sengupta's cash requirements with loans. Now he was refusing to extend any more seasonal credit until Mrs. Sharma presented a reasonable financial plan for the company that demonstrated its ability to clean up the loan by the end of 1990.

FINANCIAL FORECAST

Mr. Ashoka hurriedly developed a monthly forecast of financial statements using the current operating assumptions (see Exhibit 8). As an alternative way of looking at the forecasted funds flows, Mr. Ashoka also prepared a forecast of cash receipts and disbursements (Exhibit 9). The monthly T-accounts underlying the forecasts are given in Exhibit 10, and a summary of the forecast assumptions is in Exhibit 11.

Mr. Ashoka handed over the forecast to Mrs. Sharma with a graph showing projected sales and month-end debt outstanding (Exhibit 12). After studying the forecasts for a few moments, Mrs. Sharma expostulated,

This is worse than I expected. The numbers show that we can't repay All-India's loan by the end of December. The loan officer will not accept this forecast as a basis for more credit. We need a new plan, and fast. We need those loans in order to scale up for the most important part of our business season. Let's go over these assumptions in detail and look for any opportunities to improve our debt position.

---

[2]The selection of October as the loan clean-up month was imposed by the bank on the grounds of tradition. Seasonal loans of any type made by this bank were to be cleaned up in October. Mrs. Sharma had seen no reason previously to question the bank's tradition.

EXHIBIT 1   Summary of Monthly Sales (actual for 1989 and forecast for 1990, in rupees)

	1989	1990
January.........	1,341,600	1,744,080
February........	2,005,692	2,507,115
March..........	2,005,692	2,607,400
April..........	6,976,320	8,720,400
May	10,464,480	12,034,152
June	13,952,640	16,045,536
July...........	12,208,560	14,039,844
August	5,232,240	6,278,688
September......	3,488,160	4,360,200
October	2,964,936	3,854,417
November	2,616,120	3,400,956
December	2,092,896	2,616,120
Year	65,349,336	78,208,908

EXHIBIT 2   Historical and Forecasted Annual Income Statements (in rupees)

	1988	1989	1990 Forecast
Gross sales	55,546,936	65,349,336	78,208,907
Excise tax	8,332,040	9,802,400	11,731,336
Net sales	47,214,895	55,546,936	66,477,571
Cost of goods sold (COGS)......	38,327,385	46,398,029	58,353,036
Gross profits...................	8,887,510	9,148,907	8,124,535
Operating expenses.............	3,012,444	4,159,275	4,692,534
Interest expense................	910,000	1,240,000	1,214,259
Profit before tax................	4,965,066	3,749,632	2,217,741
Income tax	1,489,520	1,124,890	665,322
Net profit......................	3,475,546	2,624,742	1,552,419

EXHIBIT 3   Historical and Forecasted Year-End Balance Sheets (in rupees)

	1989	*1990 Forecast*
Cash	641,123	640,000
Accounts receivable	2,302,186	3,296,311
Inventories	1,076,000	1,287,529
Total current assets	4,019,309	5,223,840
Gross plant, property, and equipment (PP&E)	8,696,000	9,896,000
Accumulated depreciation	1,278,500	2,203,100
Net PP&E	7,417,500	7,692,900
Total assets	11,436,809	12,916,740
Accounts payable	654,234	654,234
Notes to bank	587,575	2,315,087
Accrued taxes	0	0
Total current liabilities	1,241,809	2,969,321
Owners' equity	10,195,000	9,947,419
Total liabilities and equity	11,436,809	12,916,740

EXHIBIT 4   Memo from Field Sales Manager

To: Mrs. G. Sharma
From: Mr. A. Bajpai

January 7, 1990

As you know, Pondicherry Textiles is considering us to be their prime yarn supplier for this year. Purchases would be in the neighborhood of Rs 4 million and are not reflected in our current sales forecast. Pondicherry would be one of our largest accounts. They have accepted our terms on price, but have asked for credit terms of 80 days, net. Without extending our credit terms, Pondicherry will not do business with us. We can expect that Pondicherry will purchase our yarn across the year in about the same pattern as our other customers.

If you approve this exception to our standard terms (45 days), the Pondicherry district sales office immediately will meet its quarterly sales quota. Please indicate your approval below.

Approved:

EXHIBIT 5   Memo from Transportation Manager

To: Mrs. G. Sharma
From: Mr. R. Sikh

January 2, 1990

I thought you might like to know that the government is considering a new express bulk-shipment scheme on railroad trunk lines between major cities. This raises an alternative mode of transportation on about 60 percent of our transportation needs (i.e., shipments between our plant and our two distribution warehouses). If this works the way the proposal indicates, it would reduce transit times by about three days on average. This scheme might permit us to reduce our finished-goods inventory. (I doubt that it will affect our raw materials or work-in-process inventory at all.)

EXHIBIT 6   Memo from Purchasing Agent

To: Mrs. G. Sharma
From: Mr. R. Mohan

January 5, 1990

Hibachi Chemicals of Yokohama has approached us with a proposal to supply us polyester pellets on a "just-in-time" basis from their plant in Majala (20 km away). These pellets account for 35 percent of our raw-material purchases. I am looking into the feasibility of this scheme—in particular, whether Hibachi can actually perform on this basis—and will report back in two weeks. If the proposal is feasible, it would reduce our inventory of pellets from 25 days outstanding to only 2 or 3 days.

EXHIBIT 7   Memo from Operations Manager

To: Mrs. G. Sharma
From: Mr. L. Gupta

January 7, 1990

You asked me to estimate the production efficiencies arising from a scheme of level annual production. In essence, there are significant advantages to be gained:

Gross profit margin would rise by 2 or 3 percent.

Seasonal hirings and layoffs would no longer be necessary, permitting us to cultivate a stronger work force and, perhaps, suppressing labor unrest. You will recall that the unions have indicated that reducing seasonal layoffs will be one of their major negotiating objectives this year.

Level production entails lower manufacturing risk. With the load spread throughout the year, we suffer less from equipment breakdowns and can match the routine maintenance better with the demand on the plant and equipment.

EXHIBIT 8   Monthly Forecast of Income Statements and Balance Sheets for 1990 (in rupees)

	January	February	March	April	May
Income Statements					
Gross sales	1,744,080	2,507,115	2,607,400	8,720,400	12,034,152
Excise taxes	261,612	376,067	391,110	1,308,060	1,805,123
Net sales	1,482,468	2,131,048	2,216,290	7,412,340	10,229,029
COGS	1,319,397	1,777,523	1,975,367	5,358,770	8,324,465
Gross profit	163,071	353,525	240,923	2,053,570	1,904,564
Operating expenses	391,045	391,045	391,045	391,045	391,045
Interest expense (income)[1]	1,590	10,551	27,826	103,591	186,245
Profit before taxes	(229,563)	(48,070)	(177,948)	1,558,934	1,327,275
Income taxes	(68,869)	(14,421)	(53,384)	467,680	398,183
Net profit	(160,694)	(33,649)	(124,564)	1,091,254	929,093
Balance Sheets					
Assets					
Cash[2]	640,000	640,000	640,000	640,000	640,000
Accounts receivable[3]	1,639,435	2,193,181	2,751,286	8,924,457	15,906,010
Inventories[4]	1,534,126	1,731,970	5,115,374	8,081,069	10,907,001
Total current assets	3,813,562	4,565,151	8,506,660	17,645,526	27,453,011
Net PP&E[5]	7,345,033	7,272,567	7,497,600	7,422,633	7,347,667
Total assets	11,158,595	11,837,718	16,004,260	25,068,159	34,800,678
Liabilities and Owners' Equity					
Accounts payable[6]	1,073,903	1,129,060	4,491,210	6,313,774	8,520,035
Note payable, bank[7]	119,255	791,291	2,086,957	7,769,359	13,968,341
Accrued taxes[8]	(68,869)	(83,290)	0	467,680	865,863
Total current liabilities	1,124,289	1,837,061	6,578,167	14,550,813	23,354,238
Shareholders' equity[9]	10,034,306	10,000,657	9,426,093	10,517,347	11,446,439
Total liabilities and equity	11,158,595	11,837,718	16,004,260	25,068,159	34,800,678

[1] Interest expense = Notes payable × 16 percent/12 months.
[2] See Exhibit 9.
[3] See panel 1, Exhibit 10.
[4] See panel 2, Exhibit 10.
[5] See panel 6, Exhibit 10.
[6] See panel 3, Exhibit 10.
[7] Plug figure.
[8] See panel 5, Exhibit 10.
[9] See panel 4, Exhibit 10.

June	July	August	September	October	November	December
16,045,536	14,039,844	6,278,688	4,360,200	3,854,417	3,400,956	2,616,120
2,406,830	2,105,977	941,803	654,030	578,163	510,143	392,418
13,638,706	11,933,867	5,336,885	3,706,170	3,276,254	2,890,813	2,223,702
11,150,398	10,799,896	6,156,196	3,649,691	3,015,253	2,671,268	2,154,811
2,488,308	1,133,971	(819,311)	56,479	261,001	219,544	68,891
391,045	391,045	391,045	391,045	391,045	391,045	391,045
279,824	272,871	151,113	67,817	45,742	36,222	30,868
1,817,439	470,055	(1,361,468)	(402,383)	(175,785)	(207,723)	(353,022)
545,232	141,017	(408,440)	(120,715)	(52,736)	(62,317)	(105,907)
1,272,207	329,039	(953,028)	(281,668)	(123,050)	(145,406)	(247,115)
640,000	640,000	640,000	640,000	640,000	640,000	640,000
21,905,645	22,306,783	13,342,212	6,767,030	5,110,154	4,353,224	3,296,311
10,556,500	5,912,799	3,406,295	2,771,857	2,427,872	1,911,415	1,287,529
33,102,144	28,859,583	17,388,507	10,178,887	8,178,026	6,904,639	5,223,840
7,570,200	7,492,733	7,415,267	7,635,300	7,555,333	7,475,367	7,692,900
40,672,344	36,352,316	24,803,773	17,814,187	15,733,360	14,380,005	12,916,740
7,416,904	3,148,268	2,093,100	1,814,919	1,565,516	1,133,856	654,234
20,986,794	20,465,345	11,333,439	5,086,278	3,430,639	2,716,667	2,315,087
0	141,017	(267,424)	0	(52,736)	(115,052)	0
28,403,698	23,754,630	13,159,116	6,901,197	4,943,420	3,735,471	2,969,321
12,268,647	12,597,686	11,644,658	10,912,990	10,789,940	10,644,534	9,947,419
40,672,344	36,352,316	24,803,773	17,814,187	15,733,360	14,380,005	12,916,740

EXHIBIT 9   Monthly Forecast of Schedule of Cash Receipts and Disbursements (in rupees)

	January	February	March	April	May
Assume: Sales	1,744,080	2,507,115	2,607,400	8,720,400	12,034,152
Purchases*	1,378,913	1,434,070	4,796,220	6,618,784	8,825,045
Debt outstanding	119,255	791,291	2,086,957	7,769,359	13,968,341
Receipts					
Accounts receivable collected	2,406,830	1,953,370	2,049,294	2,547,229	5,052,600
New borrowings (repayments)	(468,320)	672,036	1,295,666	5,682,402	6,198,982
Disbursements					
Accounts paid†	959,244	1,378,913	1,434,070	4,796,220	6,618,784
Capital expenditures	0	0	300,000	0	0
Interest payments	1,590	10,551	27,826	103,591	186,245
Excise tax paid	261,612	376,067	391,110	1,308,060	1,805,123
Operating expenses	391,045	391,045	391,045	391,045	391,045
Accrued income tax paid	0	0	(136,674)	0	0
Wages	326,143	468,831	487,584	1,630,715	2,250,386
Dividends	0	0	450,000	0	0
Subtotal: Disbursements	1,939,634	2,625,406	3,344,960	8,229,631	11,251,582
Receipts—Disbursements	(1,123)	0	0	0	0
Cumulative net cash flow	(1,123)	(1,123)	(1,123)	(1,123)	(1,123)
Beginning-of-period cash balance	641,123	640,000	640,000	640,000	640,000
End-of-period cash balance	640,000	640,000	640,000	640,000	640,000

* Equal to 55% of sales in period $(T + 1)$.
† Equal to purchases in period $(T - 1)$.

June	July	August	September	October	November	December
16,045,536	14,039,844	6,278,688	4,360,200	3,854,417	3,400,956	2,616,120
7,721,914	3,453,278	2,398,110	2,119,929	1,870,526	1,438,866	959,244
20,986,794	20,465,345	11,333,439	5,086,278	3,430,639	2,716,667	2,315,087
10,045,901	13,638,706	15,243,259	10,935,382	5,511,293	4,157,887	3,673,032
7,018,452	(521,448)	(9,131,906)	(6,247,161)	(1,655,639)	(713,972)	(401,581)
8,825,045	7,721,914	3,453,278	2,398,110	2,119,929	1,870,526	1,438,866
300,000	0	0	300,000	0	0	300,000
279,824	272,871	151,113	67,817	45,742	36,222	30,868
2,406,830	2,105,977	941,803	654,030	578,163	510,143	392,418
391,045	391,045	391,045	391,045	391,045	391,045	391,045
1,411,094	0	0	(388,139)	0	0	(220,959)
3,000,515	2,625,451	1,174,115	815,357	720,776	635,979	489,214
450,000	0	0	450,000	0	0	450,000
17,064,353	13,117,257	6,111,353	4,688,220	3,855,654	3,443,915	3,271,452
0	0	0	0	0	0	0
(1,123)	(1,123)	(1,123)	(1,123)	(1,123)	(1,123)	(1,123)
640,000	640,000	640,000	640,000	640,000	640,000	640,000
640,000	640,000	640,000	640,000	640,000	640,000	640,000

EXHIBIT 10   Forecasted T-Accounts Supporting Financial Statements (in rupees)

	January	*February*	*March*	*April*	*May*
1. Schedule of Accounts Receivable					
Beginning of period	2,302,186	1,639,435	2,193,181	2,751,286	8,924,457
Plus net sales	1,744,080	2,507,115	2,607,400	8,720,400	12,034,152
Less:					
Collections, last mo.*	837,158	697,632	1,002,846	1,042,960	3,488,160
Collections, month before last†	1,569,672	1,255,738	1,046,448	1,504,269	1,564,440
End of period	1,639,435	2,193,181	2,751,286	8,924,457	15,906,010
2. Schedule of Inventories					
Beginning of period	1,076,000	1,534,126	1,731,970	5,115,374	8,081,069
Plus purchases	1,378,913	1,434,070	4,796,220	6,618,784	8,825,045
Plus labor	326,143	468,831	487,584	1,630,715	2,250,386
Plus depreciation	72,467	72,467	74,967	74,967	74,967
Less shipments (COGS)	1,319,397	1,777,523	1,975,367	5,358,770	8,324,465
End of period	1,534,126	1,731,970	5,115,374	8,081,069	10,907,001
3. Schedule of Accounts Payable					
Beginning of period	654,234	1,073,903	1,129,060	4,491,210	6,313,774
+ Purchases‡	1,378,913	1,434,070	4,796,220	6,618,784	8,825,045
− Payments§	959,244	1,378,913	1,434,070	4,796,220	6,618,784
End of period	1,073,903	1,129,060	4,491,210	6,313,774	8,520,035
4. Schedule of Shareholders' Equity					
Beginning of period	10,195,000	10,034,306	10,000,657	9,426,093	10,517,347
Plus net income	(160,694)	(33,649)	(124,564)	1,091,254	929,093
Less dividends	0	0	450,000	0	0
End of period	10,034,306	10,000,657	9,426,093	10,517,347	11,446,439
5. Schedule of Accrued Taxes					
Beginning of period	0	(68,869)	(83,290)	0	467,680
Plus monthly tax exp. (30%)	(68,869)	(14,421)	(53,384)	467,680	398,183
Less quarterly tax payments	0	0	(136,674)	0	0
End of period	(68,869)	(83,290)	0	467,680	865,863
6. Schedule of PP&E					
Beginning gross PP&E	8,696,000	8,696,000	8,696,000	8,996,000	8,996,000
Plus capital expenditures	0	0	300,000	0	0
Ending gross PP&E	8,696,000	8,696,000	8,996,000	8,996,000	8,996,000
Monthly depreciation exp.	72,467	72,467	74,967	74,967	74,967
Less cumulative deprec.	1,350,967	1,423,433	1,498,400	1,573,367	1,648,333
Ending net PP&E	7,345,033	7,272,567	7,497,600	7,422,633	7,347,667

* 40% of sales in period (T − 1).
† 60% of sales in period (T − 2).
‡ Equal to 55% of sales in period (T + 1).
§ Equal to purchases in period (T − 1).

June	July	August	September	October	November	December
15,906,010	21,905,645	22,306,783	13,342,212	6,767,030	5,110,154	4,353,224
16,045,536	14,039,844	6,278,688	4,360,200	3,854,417	3,400,956	2,616,120
4,813,661	6,418,214	5,615,938	2,511,475	1,744,080	1,541,767	1,360,382
5,232,240	7,220,491	9,627,322	8,423,906	3,767,213	2,616,120	2,312,650
21,905,645	22,306,783	13,342,212	6,767,030	5,110,154	4,353,224	3,296,311
10,907,001	10,556,500	5,912,799	3,406,295	2,771,857	2,427,872	1,911,415
7,721,914	3,453,278	2,398,110	2,119,929	1,870,526	1,438,866	959,244
3,000,515	2,625,451	1,174,115	815,357	720,776	635,979	489,214
77,467	77,467	77,467	79,967	79,967	79,967	82,467
11,150,398	10,799,896	6,156,196	3,649,691	3,015,253	2,671,268	2,154,811
10,556,500	5,912,799	3,406,295	2,771,857	2,427,872	1,911,415	1,287,529
8,520,035	7,416,904	3,148,268	2,093,100	1,814,919	1,565,516	1,133,856
7,721,914	3,453,278	2,398,110	2,119,929	1,870,526	1,438,866	959,244
8,825,045	7,721,914	3,453,278	2,398,110	2,119,929	1,870,526	1,438,866
7,416,904	3,148,268	2,093,100	1,814,919	1,565,516	1,133,856	654,234
11,446,439	12,268,647	12,597,686	11,644,658	10,912,990	10,789,940	10,644,534
1,272,207	329,039	(953,028)	(281,668)	(123,050)	(145,406)	(247,115)
450,000	0	0	450,000	0	0	450,000
12,268,647	12,597,686	11,644,658	10,912,990	10,789,940	10,644,534	9,947,419
865,863	0	141,017	(267,424)	(0)	(52,736)	(115,052)
545,232	141,017	(408,440)	(120,715)	(52,736)	(62,317)	(105,907)
1,411,094	0	0	(388,139)	0	0	(220,959)
0	141,017	(267,424)	(0)	(52,736)	(115,052)	(0)
8,996,000	9,296,000	9,296,000	9,296,000	9,596,000	9,596,000	9,596,000
300,000	0	0	300,000	0	0	300,000
9,296,000	9,296,000	9,296,000	9,596,000	9,596,000	9,596,000	9,896,000
77,467	77,467	77,467	79,967	79,967	79,967	82,467
1,725,800	1,803,267	1,880,733	1,960,700	2,040,667	2,120,633	2,203,100
7,570,200	7,492,733	7,415,267	7,635,300	7,555,333	7,475,367	7,692,900

EXHIBIT 11   Forecast Assumptions

Ratio of:

Income tax/profit before tax.................	30 %
Excise tax/sales............................	15 %
This-month collections/last-month's sales	40 %
This-month collections/month-before-last	
month's sales	60 %
Purchases/next-month sales..................	55 %
Wages/purchases	34 %
Annual operating expenses/annual sales	6 %
Capital expenditures (every third month)	Rs 300,000
Interest rate on borrowings (and deposits)	16 %
Minimum cash balance	Rs 640,000
Depreciation/gross PP&E (per year)	10 %
(per month)	1 %
Dividends paid (every third month)	Rs 450,000

EXHIBIT 12   Forecast Sales and Debt by Month

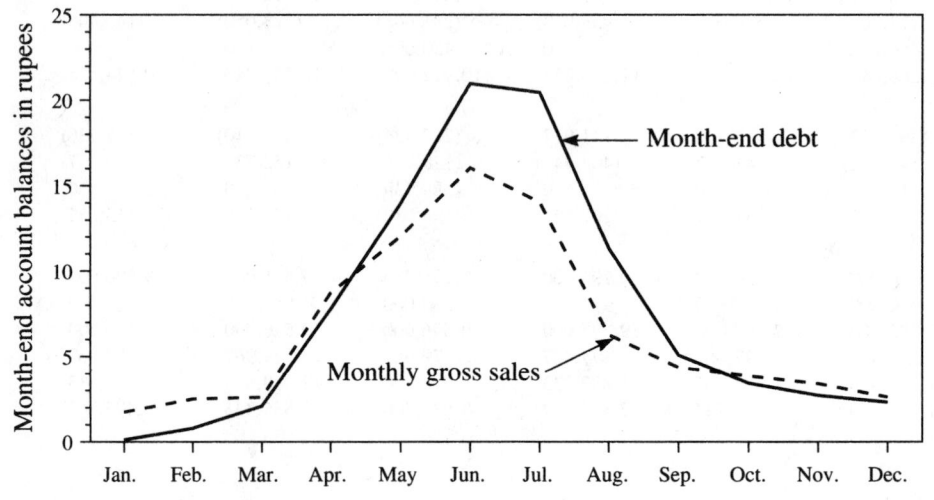

Bayern Brauerei

In early January 1993, Maria Ober arrived at Bayern Brauerei[1] to participate in her first meeting of the board of directors. She had recently joined the board at the behest of her uncle, the managing director of the company. August Ober had told her that the board could use her financial expertise in addressing some questions that would come up in the near future, but he would not be specific about the nature of those questions. The company was owned entirely by 16 uncles, aunts, and cousins in the Ober family. Maria had received an MBA degree from a well-known business school and had worked for the past six years as a commercial loan officer for a leading bank in Frankfurt, Germany. With the permission of the bank, she agreed to join the Bayern Brauerei board.

The agenda for the January meeting of the directors consisted of three items of business: (1) approval of the 1993 financial budget, (2) declaration of the quarterly dividend, and (3) approval of the compensation scheme for Max Leiter, the company's sales and marketing manager. Because she knew little about the company, Maria decided to visit it for a day before the first board meeting.

THE COMPANY

Bayern Brauerei produced two varieties of beer, dark and light, for which it had won quality awards consistently over the years. Its sales and profits in 1992 were DM102.3 million and DM2.6 million, respectively.[2] (See Exhibit 1 for historical and projected financial statements.) Founded in 1737, the Bayern Brauerei had been in the Ober family for 12 generations. An etching of Gustav Ober, the founder, graced the label of each bottle of beer.

---

[1] In English, Bayern Brauerei (BI-ern BROW-reye) means Bavarian Brewery.
[2] In January 1993, the deutsche mark could be exchanged for about US$0.63.

This case was prepared by Professor Robert F. Bruner.
Copyright © 1992 by the Darden Graduate Business School Foundation, Charlottesville, VA. Revised June 1993.

The company was located in a village just outside Munich, Germany. Its modern equipment was capable of producing 700,000 hectoliters of beer per year, and in 1992 the company sold 667,000 hectoliters. This equipment was acquired in 1987 following a fire that destroyed the old equipment.

Because of its efficiency improvements and slightly larger size, the new equipment increased the potential output of the brewery. This additional capacity remained unused, however, until late 1989. In that year, the Berlin Wall fell, and Germans were permitted to move freely between the eastern and western portions of Germany. August Ober envisioned a significant new market for high-quality beer in eastern Germany and resolved to penetrate that market. Accordingly, in 1990 he hired Max Leiter away from a major beer producer to rejuvenate the Bayern Brauerei sales staff and to move aggressively to position Bayern's beer in *die neuen Bundesländer* (the new federal states, *Länder*)[3] that joined with West Germany in the unification of 1990.

In early 1993, German consumers accounted for all of the company's sales, of which 81 percent were in western Germany (mainly the states of Baden and Bavaria) and 19 percent in the new federal states. Despite their relatively small portion of total sales, however, the eastern *Länder* had accounted for most of the unit growth in Bayern's sales over the past three years.

Bayern served its markets through a network of independent distributors. In western Germany, these distributors purchased Bayern's beer, stored it temporarily in their own refrigerated warehouses, and ultimately sold it to *their* customers at the retail end of the distribution chain (e.g., stores, restaurants, and hotels). Max Leiter had adopted a different distribution strategy with regard to the eastern *Länder*.

LUNCH WITH UNCLE AUGUST

After driving down from Frankfurt, Maria's visit began with a luncheon meeting with August Ober. Now age 57, August had worked at the brewery for his entire career. His experience had been largely on the production side of the brewery, where he had risen to the position of brewmaster before assuming general management of the company upon the retirement of his father. He said,

> Over the long history of this company, the Obers have had to be brewers, not marketers or finance people. As long as we made an excellent product, we always sold our output at the price we asked. Then, in 1989, I realized that we needed more than just production know-how. I wanted to enter the eastern Länder because it had traditionally been a good market for our beer

---

[3]Five new federal *Länder* emerged from the former German Democratic Republic, commonly known as East Germany. This region included an area of 106,000 square kilometers and a population of about 15.1 million. The region was dominated by Berlin, which added a population of about 3.4 million. Emigration from the eastern *Länder* was expected to reduce population slightly over the next few years. At the time of unification, manufacturing industry in this region was plagued by badly outdated premises, plant, and equipment. Shortly thereafter, industrial production and incomes fell dramatically as enterprises in the region closed their doors. In January 1993, the economic recovery of the eastern *Länder* was proving to be painfully slow.

before the partition in 1949. Returning to eastern Germany was, for me, reclaiming a lost market. Thus, I hired Max Leiter to lead this initiative.

I'm quite pleased with what Max has been able to accomplish. He has organized five distributorships, taken us from 0 to 211 customer accounts, and set up warehousing arrangements— in 30 months, and on a small budget! He really produces results. I am afraid I will have to pay him a lot more money next year, if I am to keep him. As it is, I paid him DM122,860 in 1992, consisting of a base salary of DM80,000 and an incentive payment of DM42,860, which is calculated as 0.5 percent of the annual sales increase. As you know from my letter to the board of directors, I am proposing increases in both his base salary (to DM95,000) and incentive payment (to 0.8 percent of the annual sales increase).

Max was very helpful in pulling together the financial plan for 1993 [see Exhibit 1]. It shows handsomely rising sales and profits! Also, he prepared various analytical presentations, including a sources and uses of funds statement [Exhibit 2] and a detailed ratio analysis [Exhibit 3]. One very helpful analysis was the breakeven chart[4] Max prepared [Exhibit 4]. It shows that, as we increase our volume above the breakeven volume, our profits rise disproportionately faster.

If we keep on this growth course, we'll exhaust our existing unused productive capacity by late 1993. The budget for 1993 calls for investment of DM8.8 million in new plant and equipment. Max has proposed that in 1994 we invest DM8.6 million in a state-of-the-art warehouse and distribution center in Berlin. He argues that we won't be able to sustain our growth in the eastern *Länder* without these major investments. I haven't even begun thinking about how we will finance all this growth. In recent years, we have depended more on short-term bank loans than we used to. I don't know whether we should continue to rely on them to the extent we have. Right now, we can borrow from our long-standing *Hausbank* at an 11 percent rate of interest.[5] Our banker asked me to meet with him next week to discuss our expansion plans; I'm guessing that he can't wait to get more of our business!

With the improved profits, I am proposing an increase in dividends for this quarter to a total of DM545,500, one fourth of the projected dividends to be paid in 1993. This should keep the Ober family happy. As you know, half of our family stockholders are retirees and rely on the dividend to help make ends meet. We have traditionally aimed for a 75 percent dividend payout from earnings each year, to serve our older relatives.

August Ober had been quite talkative during the meal, allowing Maria little opportunity to ask questions or offer her own opinions. She was disquieted by some of the statements she heard, however, and resolved to study the historical and forecasted financials in detail. Then, quite abruptly, Uncle August announced that lunch was done and he would take her to meet Max Leiter.

---

[4]This chart shows the relationship between revenues, costs, and volume of output. For instance, revenues are calculated as the volume of hectoliters of beer sold times the unit price of DM153.46 per hectoliter. Fixed costs (DM27.814 million) remain constant as unit output varies and are the sum of administration and selling expense plus depreciation. Variable costs are the sum of production costs, excise duties, and allowance for doubtful accounts, or DM102.29 per hectoliter. At any given level of output, total costs are the sum of variable and fixed costs. Profits or losses are illustrated as the difference between the revenue and total-cost lines, but note carefully that "profit" here is implicitly defined as earnings before interest and taxes (EBIT). This analysis identifies the breakeven volume, where revenues just equal total costs. Bayern Brauerei's breakeven volume was 540,600 hectoliters.

[5]In January 1993, the annual rate of return on short-term German government debt was 8.25 percent.

MEETING WITH MAX LEITER

After the introductory pleasantries, Maria asked Max to describe his marketing strategy and achievements in the eastern *Länder*. Max said,

Our beer almost sells itself; discount pricing and heavy advertising are unwarranted. The challenge is getting people to try it and getting it into a distribution pipeline, so that when the consumer wants to buy more, she can do so. But in 1990 and 1991, the beer distribution pipeline in eastern Germany was nonexistent. I had to go there and set up distributorships from nothing; there were willing entrepreneurs, but they had no capital. I provided the best financing I knew how, in the form of trade credit concessions. First, I extended credit to distributors in the East who could not bear the terms we customarily gave our distributors in western Germany. I relaxed the terms to these new distributors from 2 percent 10, net 40 to 2 percent 10, net 80.[6] Even on these terms, our distributors are asking for more time to pay; I plan to relax the payment deadline to 90 days. I am confident that we will collect on all of these receivables; my forecast assumes that bad debts as a percentage of accounts receivable will amount to only 2 percent.

These distributors are real entrepreneurs. They started with nothing but their brains. They have great ambitions and learn quickly. Some of them have gotten past due on their payments to us, but I suspect that they will catch up in due course. Virtually all the retailers and restauranteurs we supply are expanding and enhancing their shops, buying modern equipment, and restocking their own inventories—all without the support of big banks like yours in Frankfurt! Most of these retailers can't get bank credit; their "bootstrap" financing is ingenious and admirable. A little delay in payment is understandable.

I should add that the other parts of my marketing strategy involved field warehousing, to permit rapid response to market demand, and quite a lot of missionary activity, to see that our beer received the proper placement in stores and restaurants. My policy on field inventories has been to support the fragile distributor network by carrying a substantial part of the inventory on behalf of the distributor. This resulted in a sizable increase in inventory for the company in 1991 and 1992.

These new marketing policies have paid off handsomely in terms of our unit growth in the new federal states. Sales in the eastern *Länder* grew 47 percent in 1992—a rate of increase that I aim to sustain for the foreseeable future. Without my changes in credit and inventory policy, we would have realized only a small fraction of our current level of sales there. In 1993, I hope to establish five more distributors and place our beer in 100 more stores and restaurants.

Maria inquired about the signs of economic recession in Germany and the deep recession in the eastern *Länder*. Max seemed relatively unconcerned and said confidently that unit sales in the new federal states would rise significantly in 1993. At the close of their meeting, Maria asked for information on Bayern's credit customers. Max supplied several files from which she extracted the summary information in Exhibit 5.

---

[6]"2 percent 10, net 40" means that Bayern's customers can take a 2 percent discount if payment is made within 10 days of invoice, and that otherwise the full payment is due within 40 days.

CONCLUSION

After a lengthy dinner that evening, at which she met the other directors, Maria returned to the information she had gathered that day. She would need to form an opinion on the three matters coming before the board the next day (the financial plan, the dividend declaration, and the compensation plan for Max). She also wanted to study the company's reliance on debt financing. The other directors would be interested to know why, if the company was operating so profitably above its breakeven volume, it needed to borrow so aggressively? Maria also wondered about the wisdom of Bayern's aggressive penetration of the eastern *Länder*: did rapid sales growth necessarily pay off in terms of more profits or dividends? All this would take more study. She yawned and then poured herself a cup of coffee before returning to scrutinize the numbers.

EXHIBIT 1 Historical and Projected Income Statements and Balance Sheets (fiscal year ended December 31; all figures in DM thousands)

Historical and Projected Income Statements

		Actual			Projected	
	1989	1990	1991	1992	1993	1994
1. Sales: Western *Länder*	78,202	78,984	80,959	83,476	85,981	88,560
2. Sales: Eastern *Länder*	—	3,113	12,825	18,879	27,375	35,587
3. Net sales	78,202	82,097	93,784	102,356	113,355	124,147
Operating expenses						
4. Production costs and expenses	40,667	43,390	50,159	56,298	65,410	71,292
5. Admin. and selling expenses	15,734	15,967	18,663	20,164	21,000	24,000
6. Depreciation	4,550	5,439	7,367	7,650	7,650	8,530
7. Excise duties	11,526	11,174	11,734	11,949	12,211	12,566
8. Total operating expenses	(72,477)	(75,970)	(87,923)	(96,061)	(106,271)	(116,388)
9. Operating margin	5,725	6,127	5,861	6,294	7,084	7,759
10. Allowance for doubtful accounts	(9)	(6)	(28)	(19)	(188)	(46)
11. Interest expense	(841)	(778)	(2,260)	(2,085)	(2,421)	(2,711)
12. Earnings before taxes	4,884	5,349	3,574	4,191	4,476	5,002
13. Income taxes	(1,647)	(1,845)	(1,412)	(1,634)	(1,566)	(1,751)
14. Net earnings	3,237	3,504	2,162	2,557	2,909	3,251
15. Dividends to all common shares	2,428	2,628	1,622	1,917	2,182	2,439
16. Retention of earnings	809	876	541	639	727	813

EXHIBIT 1   *(concluded)*

Historical and Projected Balance Sheets

	Actual				Projected	
	1989	*1990*	*1991*	*1992*	*1993*	*1994*
Assets						
1. Cash	6,764	10,040	11,254	12,283	13,603	14,898
2. Accounts receivable:						
Western *Länder*	8,740	9,004	9,104	9,477	9,658	9,948
Eastern *Länder*	0	310	2,987	4,505	6,750	8,775
Allowance for doubtful accounts	(87)	(93)	(121)	(140)	(328)	(374)
3. Inventories	7,732	7,853	8,965	14,330	15,870	17,381
4. Total current assets	23,149	27,114	32,189	40,454	45,552	50,627
5. Investments and other assets	3,911	3,913	3,918	3,914	3,000	3,000
6. Gross property, plant, and equipment	73,667	73,667	76,500	76,500	85,300	93,933
7. Accumulated depreciation	(29,505)	(34,944)	(42,311)	(49,961)	(57,611)	(66,141)
8. Net property, plant, and equipment	44,162	38,723	34,189	26,539	27,689	27,792
9. Total assets	71,222	69,750	70,296	70,908	76,242	81,419
Liabilities and stockholders' equity						
10. Bank borrowings (short term)	3,765	7,166	7,633	7,884	12,785	17,267
11. Accounts payable	4,511	4,607	4,705	5,328	5,668	6,207
12. Other current liabilities	9,325	9,031	10,316	11,259	12,469	13,656
13. Total current liabilities	17,601	20,804	22,654	24,471	30,922	37,131
14. Long-term debt, bank borrowings	20,306	14,755	12,911	11,066	9,222	7,378
15. Stockholders' equity	33,315	34,191	34,732	35,371	36,098	36,911
16. Total liabilities and stockholders' equity	71,222	69,750	70,296	70,908	76,242	81,419

EXHIBIT 2 Sources and Uses of Funds Statements (fiscal year ending December 31; all figures in DM thousands)

	Actual			Projected	
	1990	*1991*	*1992*	*1993*	*1994*
Sources of Funds					
1. Net income	3,504	2,162	2,557	2,909	3,251
2. Increases in allowance for doubtful accounts	6	28	19	188	46
3. Depreciation	5,439	7,367	7,650	7,650	8,350
4. Increases in short-term debt	3,401	467	251	4,901	4,482
5. Increases in accounts payable	96	98	623	340	540
6. Increases in other current liabilities	(294)	1,286	943	1,210	1,187
7. Total sources of funds	12,152	11,408	12,042	17,198	18,036
Uses of Funds					
8. Dividend payments	2,628	1,622	1,917	2,182	2,439
9. Increases in cash balance	3,276	1,214	1,029	1,320	1,295
10. Increases in accts. receivable (W. Ger.)	264	100	373	181	290
11. Increases in accts. receivable (E. Ger.)	310	2,677	1,518	2,245	2,025
12. Increases in inventories	121	1,112	5,365	1,540	1,511
13. Increases in other assets	2	5	(4)	(914)	0
14. Reductions in long-term debt	5,551	1,844	1,844	1,844	1,844
15. Capital expenditures	0	2,834	0	8,800	8,633
16. Total uses of funds	12,152	11,408	12,042	17,198	18,036

EXHIBIT 3   Ratio Analyses of Historical and Projected Financial Statements (fiscal year ended December 31)

	Actual				Projected	
	1989	*1990*	*1991*	*1992*	*1993*	*1994*
Profitability		EXPAN ⟶				
1. Operating profit margin (%)	7.3	7.5	6.2	6.1	6.2	6.3
2. Average tax rate (%)	33.7	34.5	39.5	39.0	35.0	35.0
3. Return on sales (%)	4.1	4.3	2.3	2.5	2.6	2.6
4. Return on equity (%)	9.7	10.2	6.2	7.2	8.1	8.8
5. Return on net assets (%)	6.7	7.9	7.8	8.5	9.8	11.0
6. Return on assets (%)	4.5	5.0	3.1	3.6	3.8	4.0
Leverage						
7. Debt/equity ratio (%)	0.72	0.64	0.59	0.54	0.61	0.67
8. Debt/total capital (%)	41.9	39.1	37.2	34.9	37.9	40.0
9. EBIT/interest (×)	6.8	7.9	2.6	3.0	2.9	2.9
Asset Utilization						
10. Sales/assets	1.10	1.18	1.33	1.44	1.49	1.52
11. Sales growth rate (%)	4.0	5.0	14.2	9.1	10.7	9.5
12. Assets growth rate (%)	6.0	-2.1	0.8	0.9	7.5	6.8
Receivables growth rate (%):						
13. Germany	4.0	6.6	29.8	15.6	17.4	14.1
14. Western *Länder*	4.0	3.0	1.1	4.1	1.9	3.0
15. Eastern *Länder*	0.0	NMF	863.5	50.8	49.8	30.0
Days in receivables:						
16. Germany	40.8	41.4	47.1	49.9	52.8	55.0
17. Western *Länder*	40.8	41.6	41.0	41.4	41.0	41.0
18. Eastern *Länder*	NMF	36.3	85.0	87.1	90.0	90.0
19. Payables to sales (%)	5.8	5.6	5.0	5.2	5.0	5.0
20. Inventories to sales (%)	9.9	9.6	9.6	14.0	14.0	14.0
Liquidity						
21. Current ratio	1.32	1.30	1.42	1.65	1.47	1.36
22. Quick ratio	0.88	0.93	1.03	1.07	0.96	0.90

Notes: These financial ratios show the performance of the firm in four important areas:

Profitability is measured both in terms of *profit or expense margins* (lines 1–3) and as *investment returns* (lines 4–6). Investors will focus on the latter measures of profitability.

Leverage ratios measure the use of short-term and long-term debt financing by the firm. In general, higher usage of debt increases the risk of the firm. Higher ratios of debt to equity and to capital (lines 7 and 8) suggest higher financial risk. The ratio of EBIT to interest expense measures the ability of the firm to "cover" its interest payments; lower levels of this ratio suggest higher risk (line 9).

Asset-utilization ratios measure the efficiency of asset use. For instance, the sales-to-assets ratio (line 10) shows how many DM of sales are generated per DM of assets; a higher figure suggests more efficiency, and a lower figure suggests less efficiency. Over the long term differences in the growth rates of sales (line 11) and assets (line 12) can lead to production problems of over- or undercapacity. Days in receivables (lines 16–18) shows how many days it takes to collect the average credit sale; the longer it takes, the greater the investment in receivables.

Liquidity ratios measure the resources available to meet short-term financial commitments. The current ratio (line 21) is the ratio of all current assets to all current liabilities. The quick ratio (line 22) is the ratio of only cash and receivables (i.e., those assets that can be liquidated quickly) to all current liabilities.

EXHIBIT 4   Profit Breakeven Analysis

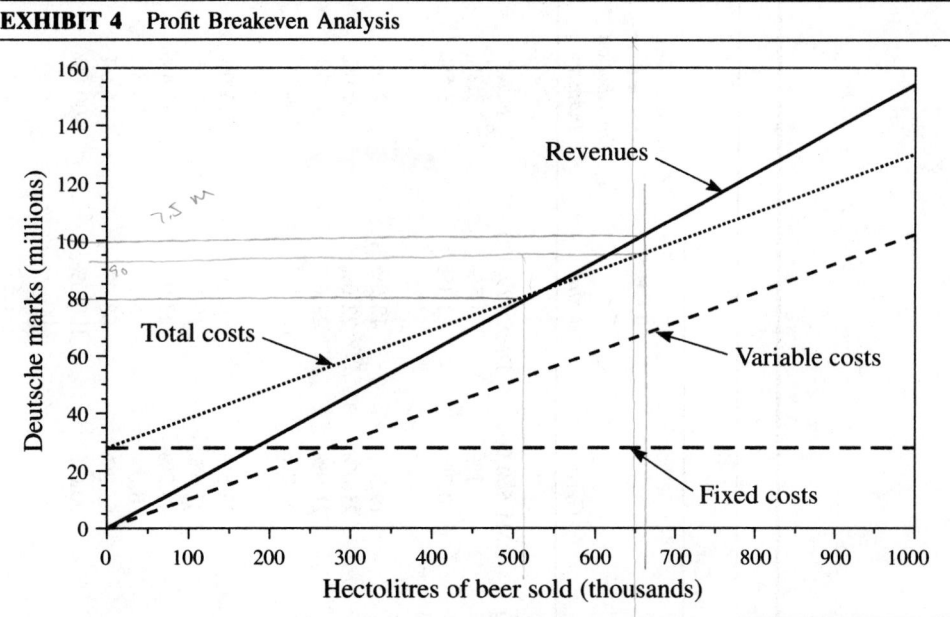

EXHIBIT 5 Selected Information on Bayern's Distributors in the Eastern *Länder*

Bayern Distributors by City

	Magdeburg	Chemnitz	Dresden	Gera	Berlin	Composite Ratios, German Beer-Distribution Industry
Income data:						
Net sales, 1992	DM4,500,00	DM3,600,000	DM3,100,000	DM1,500,000	DM6,179,000	N.A.
Operating profit/sales	1.8%	2.2%	3.0%	1.1%	3.5%	3.7%
Pretax profit/sales	1.7%	1.9%	2.3%	0.7%	3.1%	3.5%
Assets (as % of total):						
Trade receivables	12.9%	13.5%	16.5%	19.5%	13.0%	12.0%
Inventory	15.1%	19.0%	30.0%	25.0%	22.0%	31.0%
Fixed assets	33.1%	29.1%	25.0%	21.0%	28.0%	24.0%
Total	100.0%	100.0%	100.0%	100.0%	100.0%	100.0%
Liabilities:						
ST bank borrowings	0.1%	2.1%	1.5%	2.5%	4.0%	15.0%
Trade payables	29.2%	32.2%	28.7%	37.5%	19.0%	16.3%
Total curr. liabs.	35.0%	41.0%	33.2%	43.2%	27.0%	39.4%
LT debt	2.5%	0.0%	3.0%	0.0%	5.0%	16.0%
Net worth	32.5%	59.0%	63.8%	56.2%	68.0%	44.6%
Total	100.0%	100.0%	100.0%	100.0%	100.0%	100.0%
Ratios:						
Current ratio	1.1	1.2	1.1	.9	1.6	1.4
Days' sales outstanding	27.7	25.9	27.4	39.5	19.8	19.4
Sales/assets	2.0	1.9	2.2	1.8	2.4	2.3
Pretax profit/assets	2.9%	3.6%	5.1%	1.3%	7.4%	8.0%
Debt/equity	8.0%	3.6%	7.1%	4.4%	13.2%	69.5%

Case 10

Merrill Electronics Corporation (A)

In early July 1991, Patricia Merrill, the President and largest shareholder of Merrill Electronics, was preparing to evaluate her company's operating results for the first half of 1991. She was particularly interested in these results for two reasons: first, she wished to determine the effectiveness of the policies and efforts of the company's new general manager, Charles Brown; and, second, she was to meet with Brown later in the day to discuss the company's cash position and the renegotiation of the lines of credit with its banks.

Since its founding in 1950 by Thomas Merrill, Merrill Electronics had been a distributor for GEC,[1] a large manufacturer of electrical and electronics products for consumer and institutional markets. Over the years, in addition to the GEC products, the company had added noncompeting lines of electrical appliances, records, compact disks, and cassettes. In 1980, it began to broaden its product lines by importing Japanese consumer electronics. Four years later, it entered into an exclusive import agreement with the Goldstone Corporation of Taiwan, a major producer of television and other electronic equipment. These products were distributed to retail firms and dealers throughout a broad geographical area.

By the mid-1980s, Merrill had entered into the personal computer (PC) market, distributing both hardware and software products. It became the national distributor for Fuji Electronics, a major Japanese manufacturer of PCs and related products, in March 1989. This had proven to be a fast-growing market, accounting for close to half of total sales and even more of the profits during the latest six-month period; but at the same time, it

---

[1]Formerly the Global Electrical Company. In 1982, the company's name and logo had been changed to create a new image.

This case was prepared by Professor H. Lee Remmers at the European Institute of Business Administration (INSEAD), Fontainebleau, France.
Copyright H. L. Remmers, INSEAD, 1992.

was becoming more and more competitive. By 1991, price cutting had become rampant as mail order and discount houses entered the business.

Patricia Merrill had been working in the company for two years when her father, Thomas Merrill, died in January 1989. As the only family member with experience in the company, she succeeded him as president. Together with her mother, she controlled 75 percent of the share capital of the firm. The remaining shares were held by her father's brother and sister and their families. Although she herself received a salary from the company, Patricia Merrill's mother and the other shareholders in the family relied on dividends from the company for a portion of their income.

Twenty-nine at the time of her father's death, Patricia Merrill had been working in the company as his personal assistant and heir apparent. During that period, he had delegated relatively little responsibility to her. Anxious to prove herself in her newly assumed capacity, she set ambitious growth targets for the company and then began to try to recruit a seasoned operating manager to help achieve those objectives. When she reviewed the operating statements for the first half of 1990, generally regarded as a good year in the industry, she was convinced she needed help. That October, she was able to attract Charles Brown into the company as general manager by offering him a share of the profits in addition to salary. Brown had been the general sales manager of a distributor handling the products of a major GEC competitor. It was agreed by them that as general manager, Brown would have full authority to execute any changes he desired.

At the time of her father's death, Merrill had been troubled by the question of whether the family should retain its interest in the company or sell out. She had been aware of her father's concern over the steadily declining margins in the electrical distribution business in recent years, and, while the family enjoyed considerable wealth, she wondered whether they should not sell all or part of their shareholdings and invest the proceeds elsewhere. In fact, her uncle had been putting pressure on her to put the company up for sale ever since the death of her father.

At the end of 1990, her first year at the head of the company, Patricia Merrill had almost decided that they should sell out. In fact, she had told Brown at their first meeting that she might be interested in finding a buyer for the company because margins had fallen so drastically in recent years. She said,

> My father worked on an average gross margin of about 20 percent not many years ago. Nowadays, aside from the computer line and records, we don't average 14 percent any more. Television, which used to yield 15 percent, is now below 12 percent. The market for computers and software has become cutthroat, and margins have fallen drastically during the past year and a half. So how can we make money? My feeling is that, if this keeps up, the distribution business will soon disappear. That's why I feel we should get out of this business now.

Brown replied that he was certainly familiar with the declining margins problem, and that he had given it a great deal of thought. He was convinced, he said, that the answer lay in doing a high-volume business:

> I don't think we'll ever see average gross margins of 20 percent in the traditional lines of our business again, but I do think we can maintain the return on investment by building volume, adding new product lines and rationalizing or possibly dropping old ones, and controlling costs. It won't be easy, but I think it can be done.

Brown's confidence had been an important element in Merrill's decision to leave the family's money in the company, at least for the time being.

During his first few weeks with the company, Brown reviewed in detail the records of the operating and sales departments. He was particularly concerned with the market penetration achieved by the company's salesmen in 1990 in relation to the estimated market potential as supplied by GEC, Fuji, and certain other suppliers. He also was interested in the gross margin trends and in the earnings shown by product lines.

As a result of his review, and with the aid of the operations manager, Julian McNeil, and the sales manager, Michael Teresi, Brown developed a forecast of sales, gross margins, operating expenses, and earnings for the first six months of 1991 (see Exhibit 1). The forecast was submitted to Merrill in late December of 1990, along with the following memorandum:

To: Patricia Merrill
From: Charles Brown

Summary of sales, gross margin and operating earnings objectives, January 1 to June 30, 1991.

1. The budgeted sales increase of $4,565,000 over the first six months of this past year is based primarily on the distribution of Fuji personal computers and accessories, and further growth in GEC's Vortex line of white goods[2] which the company took on in late spring 1990. Sales of all other lines are also expected to increase. The primary emphasis in 1991 will be on adding volume to the PC Division while maintaining margins, and bringing white goods into a position where they will be a profitable addition to the company's existing lines of products.
2. The budgeted gross margins are in accordance with 1990 experience, except for television and VCRs where a slight increase is predicted. PC margins have been under pressure, but we believe that our figures are realistic. The gross margin percentages on new products are based on factory representatives' estimates.
3. The budgeted operating earnings percentages are expected to be above 1990 figures, since fixed costs will be spread over the greater volume that we expect to sell. In making these projections, we have included the cost of additional sales, office, service, and warehouse personnel to handle the planned increase in sales. We will continue to spend heavily on promotion and other investments to maintain a quality after-sales service.
4. Every effort will be made to speed up collection of accounts receivable and to obtain an overall inventory turnover of eight times in order to obtain the greatest use of the company's financial resources.

During the first six months of 1991, Brown began to put his plans into effect. Additional personnel were added to the staff, and, as the monthly sales reports were received, Merrill observed a substantial overall increase in sales in comparison with the same period in 1990.

---

[2]Clothes washers and dryers, dishwashers, refrigerators, and freezers.

With the increased volume, however, the company began to have difficulty meeting payments to suppliers while holding borrowing within the credit lines agreed with its banks.

During the last three months of 1990, the company had found it necessary to increase the overall bank credit line limit to $2.5 million to finance larger inventories and receivables. It was planned that the credit line should be partially, if not wholly, paid off during the first three months of 1991. However, sales in the first quarter of 1991 ran higher than had been anticipated, thus prolonging the company's need for borrowed funds. The problem was compounded by the arrival in February and March of large computer and software inventories; it worsened in May and June as white goods and small appliances moved more slowly than expected.

Accordingly, Merrill and Brown approached the company's banks in March and arranged for an increase in their credit lines to $3 million and for them to be extended to September 30, 1991. During the next three months, sales continued to expand, so in late June they made a further request to the banks for an extension of the $3 million limit to March 31, 1992. The request was turned down. However, the bankers told Merrill and Brown they would consider continuing the current line until December 31, 1991. But they would have to be presented with a realistic operating plan, including a cash flow forecast to show that the company could stay within the $3 million credit limit during the second half of the year, *and* reduce the amount of credit lines used to no more than $500,000 by December 31.

The chairman of the loan committee of the company's principal bank told Merrill and Brown that he believed part of the company's financial needs were long-term in nature and, therefore, should be supplied by an increase in equity or long-term capital. He insisted that, without an increase of capital from the shareholders, his bank would find it very difficult to extend its present credit line of $1.5 million beyond the end of December if the conditions outlined above (preceding paragraph) were not met.

At the beginning of the second week in July, Merrill received from McNeil, the operations manager, copies of the company's income statement and balance sheet for the six months ended June 30, 1991, together with his comments on sales, gross margins, and earnings. (See Exhibits 1, 2, 3 and 4.) For comparative purposes, McNeil also gave Merrill a set of selected financial and operating statistics drawn from a sample of other companies in the consumer electronics distribution industry (see Exhibit 5). On receipt of these reports, Merrill began to analyze the effectiveness of Brown's plans and operations during the first half of 1991.

She next turned her attention to the company's financial position, giving consideration to a number of alternative ways of meeting its cash needs during the second half of 1991. In assessing these needs, she bore in mind that both Fuji and GEC recently had sent reminders that the credit terms *"net 30 days"* meant just that (ie., that they were going to be enforced). This could take a number of forms: interest could be charged on past due payables, perhaps at considerably above market rates; much worse, the suppliers could stop shipping or ship only upon receipt of cash payment. Merrill also discussed with Brown, McNeil, and Teresi the expected sales targets for the company until the end of June 1991. Between them they agreed upon a sales forecast for the next 12 months (Exhibit 6).

Second, Merrill wondered to what extent the funds required for their ambitious sales program could be met internally—specifically, through a combination of reduced operating expenses, reduced inventory levels, improved collection of receivables, and, possibly, the dropping of one or more product lines.

Finally, she wondered whether—on the basis of Brown's performance to date and the long-term prospects of the business—the Merrill family might be justified in investing additional funds of their own in the company or, instead, begin to look for someone to buy them out sooner rather than later. Even if the family were to hold onto the company for now, investing additional capital if needed, she believed that, within the next three to five years, they should try to realize part of their investment by placing some their shares on the *over-the-counter* market. To keep peace in the family, one way or another she would have to give the other shareholders a way to realize part of their investment. And she was well aware that to go public would require a solid track record—strong, stable growth of sales revenues and earnings, and a sound financial position.

EXHIBIT 1   Budgeted versus Actual Performance January 1 to June 30, 1991

	Budgeted Amount	Percent of Sales	Actual Amount	Percent of Sales	Variance in Amount	Actual as Percent of Budget	Difference in Percent
			Net Sales				
PC products and services ...	$ 6,500,000	100.0%	$ 7,261,500	100.0%	$ +778,020	112%	
Records, CDs, cassettes	736,125	100.0	986,730	100.0	+250,605	134	
Television and VCR	3,289,425	100.0	3,153,765	100.0	−135,660	96	
HiFi and electronics	1,311,840	100.0	1,397,160	100.0	+85,320	107	
Vortex	2,520,000	100.0	2,546,670	100.0	+26,670	101	
Small appliances	863,560	100.0	956,535	100.0	+92,970	111	
Total sales	15,220,950		16,302,360		1,097,925	1.07	
			Gross Margin				
PC products & services.....	$ 1,718,120	26.5%	$ 1,724,600	23.7%	$ +6,480		−2.8
Records, CDs, cassettes	147,220	20.0	202,280	20.5	+55,060		+0.5
Television & VCR.........	332,240	10.1	352,365	11.1	+20,125		+1.0
HiFi & electronics........	204,650	15.6	205,095	14.7	+445		−0.9
Vortex	348,090	13.8	312,225	12.3	−35,865		−1.5
Small appliances	99,730	11.5	107,130	11.2	+7,400		−0.3
Total gross margin.......	2,850,050	18.7	2,903,695	17.8	53,645		−0.9
			Operating Expenses				
PC products & services.....	$ 1,170,000	18.0%	$ 1,430,520	19.7%	$ +260,520		+1.7
Records, CDs, cassettes	113,700	15.4	115,170	11.7	+1,470		−3.7
Television & VCR.........	250,000	7.6	253,380	8.0	+3,380		+0.4
HiFi & electronics........	177,110	13.5	168,285	12.0	−8,825		−1.5
Vortex	317,850	12.6	285,290	11.2	−32,560		−1.4
Small appliances	91,550	10.6	105,720	11.1	+14,170		+0.5
Total expenses..........	2,120,210	13.9	2,358,365	14.5	238,155		
			Earnings before Interest & Tax (EBIT)				
PC products & services.....	$ 548,120	8.5%	$ 294,080	4.1%	$ −254,040		−4.4
Records, CDs, cassettes	33,520	4.0	87,110	8.8	+53,590		+4.2
Television & VCR.........	82,230	2.5	98,985	3.1	+16,755		+0.6
HiFi & electronics........	27,540	2.1	36,810	2.6	+9,270		+0.5
Vortex	30,240	1.2	26,935	1.1	−3,305		−0.1
Small appliances	8,180	0.9	1,410	0.1	−6,770		−0.8
Total earnings before tax	729,830	4.8	545,330	3.4	−184,500		

EXHIBIT 2   Report of Operations— January 1 to June 30, 1991

To: Patricia Merrill, President
From: Julian McNeil, Operations Manager
Re: Report of operations for 6 months ending 30 June 1991

1. Summary results are shown for the first half of 1991 on the previous page (Exhibit 1).

2. Division Analysis

PC Products Division

Sales volume during the six months exceeded forecasts by over three quarters of a million dollars. The new Fuji 2500XEC laptop has been especially popular and accounted for close to 20 percent of the total—in spite of some teething problems discussed below. However, gross margins have been under considerable pressure from discounters, especially for software products. We are concerned that this will continue and very likely become even more severe during the next few months. Margins overall may fall to as low as 20 percent before stabilizing. In addition, since well over half of this division's products are purchased from Japanese suppliers, margins may also be affected by currency fluctuations. Finally, we are beginning to explore the possibility of starting a mail order operation with our own brand label—similar to Dell Computers.

Operating expenses also are running above those forecast. Part of this is due to problems with the color screens on the new F2500XEC laptop, but a number of other products have needed more service than planned. As our service and repair personnel become more experienced, expenses should be easier to control in this area. Inventories are still more than $500,000 over our target level, and competition will make it difficult to improve this situation much in the short term. There is some $200,000 in obsolete merchandise; we may be able to return some of this to our suppliers, but most will have to be sold off below cost.

Records Division

1991 should make history. Sales were especially strong in compact disks. Our most recent analysis of obsolete inventories indicates that we have approximately $30,000 to dispose of. We will probably have to sell this stock at below cost.

We are negotiating with another major producer and hope to add its label to our existing lines. This should have a favorable effect on revenues. On the other hand, margins continue to be under pressure from discounters.

Television & VCR Division

TV sales for the first six months are slightly below last year, although gross margin and operating earnings are ahead. On the negative side, ending June inventory is well above target and includes roughly $250,000 worth of older models. We will try to move these as fast as possible, but will probably mean discounting below cost.

According to GEC factory reports on television distributor sales to dealers, our market share in this area for the year to date is 14.7 percent. This compares to GEC's overall market share for 17.8 percent for this same period. In 1990, our market share was 15.2 percent, compared to the GEC national average of 16.9 percent. In 1989, we had 17.0 percent of the market in our area compared to the GEC national average of 16.5 percent. Fortunately, our market share for Fuji TVs is up from the same period a year ago.

VCR sales of the new Fuji and Goldstone lines as well as earnings are better than forecast, somewhat offsetting the currently weak TV market. We have had some servicing problems with the Goldstone VCRs, and, although the factory has promised help, repair expenses may rise.

EXHIBIT 2   *(continued)*

Hi Fi & Electronics Division

Sales for the first half of 1991 have exceeded 1990 by $225,000. Although gross margins have decreased slightly in percentage terms, our operating earnings have increased.

Factory reports of distributor sales of Hi Fi equipment to dealers show our market share for the first months of 1991 to be 19.4 percent. This compares to the GEC national average of 12.0 percent for the same period. In 1990, our market share was 18.2 percent, compared to the GEC national average of 11.8 percent. In 1989, the figures were 15.6 percent and 12.0 percent, respectively. Likewise, our market share for Fuji products is better than their overall national average.

Our order backlog amounts to more than $125,000. If business remains at or near the present level, this will be a banner year for this department. However, there are some orders in jeopardy because of slow delivery of merchandise from suppliers. Given this situation, our inventory target of 45 days may prove to be unrealistic.

Vortex Division

Because we took on the Vortex line in the middle of 1990, there are no comparable figures for the first half operation. We realize that this division has not done much more than break even for the first six months of 1991; however, in view of the promotional costs that we had (approximately $85,000) and some discounting, it may be considered satisfactory. Since most of these costs have been incurred, the balance of the year should be profitable.

Small Appliance Division

Sales in this division include portable air conditioners, small kitchen appliances, and lamps. Sales and gross margins are running ahead of last year, but increased expenses from repairs on defective merchandise has virtually wiped out operating earnings.

The principal challenge we are facing is excessively high inventories. With interest rates at current levels, carrying costs exceed operating earnings.

We need to follow closely this division's performance during the next months. If results cannot be improved substantially, we might be advised to phase it out and focus our attention on the more promising lines.

3. Accounts Receivable

Our receivables are in good condition with 91.25 percent current. Bad debt expense for the latest six months was $81,500, or 0.5 percent of total sales. This amount is based on past experience, but may be conservative. Our bad debt reserve is $191,410, of which about $120,000 will probably be written off when the final accounts for the year are prepared. The condition of our accounts receivable is shown by the following ageing schedule:

	June 18, 1991	*May 17, 1991*
Current	91.25%	93.05%
Past due:		
1 to 30 days	4.15	3.85
31 to 60 days	1.85	1.55
61 to 90 days	1.10	0.81
91 days and over	1.65	0.74

EXHIBIT 2   *(concluded)*

4. Inventories

Our inventories as at June 30, 1991, amounted to $5,591,470. They are up considerably from a year ago, primarily as a result of the addition of the new line of personal computers, obsolete merchandise in the PC and TV divisions, problems with TVs that were mentioned earlier, and the need to carry a relatively broader range of Vortex washers and dryers than was previously the case. Our inventory position by product line is as follows:

	Actual Inventory Level		Target Inventory Level	
Product Line	*Amount*	*In Days**	*Amount*	*In Days†*
PC products & services	$2,092,400	68	$1,526,000	50
Records, CDs, etc. . . .	255,365	58	193,560	45
Television, VCRs	1,319,945	75	739,600	50
Hi Fi, electronics	450,300	65	285,750	45
Vortex.	723,110	60	530,580	45
Small appliances	750,350	110	266,000	60
Total	$5,591,470	67	$3,541,490	49

* Based on anticipated sales volume (value at cost) for period July–October 1991.
† Based on our best estimates of optimum inventory levels taking into account expected cost of product, delivery lead-time from suppliers, diversity of products, sales forecasting uncertainties.

EXHIBIT 3   Income Statements

	6 Months to 30 June 1990		6 Months to 31 December 1990		6 Months to 30 June 1991	
Net sales	$10,654,900	100.0	$18,096,400	100.0	$16,302,360	100.0
Cost of sales.	8,939,610	83.9	15,020,010	83.0	13,398,665	82.2
Gross margin	1,715,290	16.1	3,076,390	17.0	2,903,695	17.8
Operating expenses:						
Direct selling	460,280	4.3	742,780	4.1	665,400	4.1
Advertising & promotion	119,680	1.1	231,300	1.3	205,200	1.3
After sales service	253,250	2.4	522,650	2.9	566,800	3.5
Warehouse & shipping	178,150	1.7	262,400	1.5	236,400	1.5
General administration	542,550	5.1	575,005	3.1	608,115	3.7
Depreciation.	44,175	0.4	54,590	0.3	76,450	0.5
Total expenses.	1,598,085	15.0	2,388,725	13.2	2,358,365	14.5
Operating earnings [EBIT]	117,205	1.1	687,665	3.8	545,330	3.4
Interest expense.	62,650	0.6	143,225	0.8	178,800	1.1
Earnings before taxes.	54,555	0.5	544,440	3.0	366,530	2.3
Corporate taxes	22,900	0.2	206,890	1.2	146,850	0.9
Earnings after taxes	31,655	0.3	337,550	1.9	219,680	1.4
Dividends paid.	20,000		50,000		50,000	

EXHIBIT 4   Balance Sheets (amounts in dollars)

	30 June 1990	*31 December 1990*	*30 June 1991*
Assets			
Current assets:			
Cash & bank	$ 58,900	$ 38,850	$ 35,220
Accounts receivable [net].........	2,841,100	4,826,600	4,166,180
Inventories	2,895,200	3,534,120	5,591,470
Other current assets	29,700	41,450	65,980
Total current assets	5,824,900	8,441,020	9,858,850
Fixed assets:			
Buildings & equipment [net]......	632,900	718,200	789,750
Goodwill.......................	100,000	100,000	100,000
Total	732,900	818,200	889,750
Total assets	$6,557,800	$9,259,220	$10,748,600
Capital & Liabilities			
Current liabilities:			
Short-term bank loans	$ 455,000	$2,050,000	$ 2,985,000
L T debt due in one year	80,000	80,000	80,000
Accounts payable *(domestic)*......	1,155,700	1,819,130	1,705,110
Accounts payable *(foreign)**	241,200	391,250	895,620
Accrued expenses................	171,980	217,370	251,720
Total current liabilities	2,103,880	4,557,750	5,917,450
Long-term debt	560,000	520,000	480,000
Capital stock.....................	1,000,000	1,000,000	1,000,000
Retained earnings	2,893,920	3,181,470	3,351,150
Owners' equity	3,893,920	4,181,470	4,351,150
Total capital & liabilities...........	$6,557,800	$9,259,220	$10,748,600

* Primarily yen denominated invoices.

EXHIBIT 5   Selected Financial & Operating Data—Electronics Equipment Distributors*

	Average—Lower Quartile	Median	Average—Upper Quartile
Current ratio......................	1.5	2.0	2.7
Acid-test ratio	0.6	1.0	1.3
Debt ratio[a].........................	41.2%	48.6%	55.1%
Asset turnover[b].....................	3.0	3.5	3.9
Collection period[c]	28 days	33 days	39 days
Payment period[d].....................	29 days	31 days	35 days
Inventory turnover[e]	7.5 times	8.6 times	9.2 times
Gross margin	12.7%	15.4%	18.0%
Operating expenses/sales	9.8%	12.2%	14.4%
Operating earnings [EBIT]/sales	2.9%	3.2%	3.6%
Earnings after tax [EAT]/sales	1.1%	1.3%	1.5%
Return on equity [ROE][f].............	4.7%	6.9%	9.5%

* Based on latest six-month results (January–June 1990).
[a] Total liabilities divided by total assets.
[b] Sales revenue for January–June 1991 divided by total assets for June 30, 1991 (annualized by multiplying by 2).
[c] Receivables on 30 June 1991 divided by sales revenue for January–June 1991 multiplied by 180 days.
[d] Payables on 30 June 1991 divided by purchases for January–June 1991 multiplied by 180 days.
[e] Inventories on 30 June 1991 divided by cost of sales for January–June 1991 (annualized by multiplying by 2).
[f] Earnings after tax for January–June 1991 divided by owners' equity for 30 June 1991 (annualized by multiplying by 2).

EXHIBIT 6   Sales Forecasts July 1991–June 1992 (thousands of dollars)

Product Line	July	Aug.	Sept.	Oct.	Nov.	Dec.	Jan.	Feb.	Mar.	Apr.	May	June
PC products ...	1,200	1,200	1,350	1,450	1,600	1,500	1,300	1,450	1,750	1,900	1,850	1,800
Records, etc. ..	150	175	290	450	570	240	170	230	250	280	300	270
TV & VCRs...	470	550	930	1,400	1,850	1,260	650	750	820	850	900	800
Hi-fi	210	250	400	630	800	640	225	325	345	360	350	320
Vortex.........	380	450	750	1,120	1,470	1,150	500	600	650	700	720	680
Appliances	135	170	275	420	550	450	180	240	250	270	280	250
Total........	2,545	2,795	3,995	5,470	6,840	5,240	3,025	3,595	4,065	4,360	4,400	4,120

Atlantic Southeast Airlines

Rick Spangler of Wachovia Bank and Trust sat at his desk the morning of March 7, 1985, preparing his recommendation on Wachovia's participation in a $19.2 million loan to Atlantic Southeast Airlines (ASA). The commuter carrier, based in Atlanta, sought the loan to fund 65 percent of the purchase price of six new 30-seat Embraer Brasilia airplanes. The day before, Wachovia had received an invitation to participate in $3 million of the credit from the agent bank for the financing, Lloyds Bank International. Wachovia had been exploring a relationship with ASA for two years; it now had a week to decide whether this loan was the way to begin.

THE COMMUTER AIRLINE INDUSTRY

The modern commuter airline industry began with the Airline Deregulation Act of 1978, which shifted responsibility for determining route structure, fares, and operating policies from the Civil Aeronautics Board, a federal agency, to the airlines themselves. One response to the act was that major airlines eliminated flights to and from smaller towns, a service that had been traditionally unprofitable. Demand for passenger air service still existed in those towns, however, and scores of commuter airlines were ready to meet it. Flying less-costly propeller-driven planes rather than jets, the commuter airlines could make money on routes that the major airlines had abandoned.

From 1978 to 1983, the number of passengers taking commuter airline flights had risen at an annual rate of 14 percent. The number of passengers was projected to grow from 26 million in 1984 to 40 million in 1990. The number of commuter carriers, however, had declined from 246 in 1981 to 196 in 1983 and was expected to fall to 100 by 1993. Mergers and acquisitions were expected to constitute part of the decline, although the elimination of weaker carriers was also anticipated.

This case is an adaptation of a supervised business study written by David Jarrett under the direction of Robert F. Bruner.

Industry observers had pinpointed six keys to survival in the commuter airline industry:

- Attaining a sustainable size.
- Attracting quality management.
- Building a fleet of modern aircraft.
- Maintaining a strong capital base.
- Establishing a well-defined market niche.
- Associating with a major carrier.

The last characteristic was felt to be crucial. The larger commuter airlines associated themselves with major carriers by working agreements through which they would schedule flights to and from the major carrier's hub at times that would allow passengers to make connections conveniently. The two airlines usually would have adjacent terminal facilities, and the commuter airline's flights would be scheduled under the major carrier's two-letter reservations designator. These arrangements provided a presence for major airlines in small markets and a source of ready demand for commuter airlines.

Demand for air travel was cyclical, lagging the business cycle by one to two quarters. Business travel was affected less by economic conditions than was personal travel. The commuter airlines were thought to be more susceptible to a recession than the major carriers, simply because many travelers could drive to a major airport, rather than take a connecting commuter flight.

Most companies in the industry were considered to be highly leveraged, with the average debt–equity ratio about 2.0. Only 21 commuter airlines were publicly owned, including ASA, and banks generally had been wary in extending funds because of the volatility of the industry. Many companies, thus, had been funded by venture capitalists.

ATLANTIC SOUTHEAST

ASA was founded in June 1979 by three former executives of Southern Airways, all of whom were still part of ASA management in 1985. The airline turned a profit in 1980, its first full year of operations, and improved its earnings each year afterward. In April 1983, it acquired Southeastern Airlines for 340,000 shares of stock, adding six planes and 64 percent more available seat-miles to its fleet. (Exhibits 1 through 3 present recent operating statistics and financial statements.)

In May 1984, ASA was the first regional carrier to enter a working agreement with Delta Airlines. Delta scheduled flights from Atlanta, its major hub, to destinations nationwide. The two airlines had a five-year agreement, cancelable by either party on six months' notice.

By March 1, 1985, ASA was flying to 22 cities from its Atlanta hub and to 6 cities from a second hub in Memphis which opened in December 1984, making it the 18th largest regional airline in the United States. ASA faced competition on 8 of its routes. (Exhibit 4 outlines the airline's route system.) The company thought 80 percent of its passengers were business fliers or military personnel.

Two events, one financial and the other operational, had threatened to cast ASA in an unfavorable light. In 1983 the company fell short of its earnings projections; it blamed the shortfall on a miscalculation of the investment tax credits it had available that year. The company changed external auditors the following year and took steps to improve its accounting department. Then on December 5, 1984, engines failed on three ASA planes in flight. Although engine failures were not uncommon, and all three planes landed safely, the coincidence was enough to prompt ASA to ground its entire fleet temporarily for inspection. It found no problems and returned the planes to service.

All in all, industry analysts were currently favorably impressed by the company. They felt the ASA management team knew its market well and had a strong business orientation, which was considered important in an industry where many companies were run by executives who liked airplanes but lacked business sense. (Exhibit 5 contains excerpts of five analysts' reports.) The quality of the nonunionized work force of 593 was considered to be another strength of the company. Although ASA employees worked for lower wages than employees of major airlines, morale was considered high and turnover was low.

Because a commuter airplane had a maximum flying time of about nine hours per day, ASA's growth increased its need for airplanes of the size, range, and cost efficiencies suitable for its route system. The airline both owned and leased aircraft; the current market rate for leased commuter airplanes of the type flown by ASA was estimated at about $45,000 per month. In March 1985 the ASA fleet included:

Airplane Model	Number of Seats	Number Owned	Number Leased
Dash 7	48	1	4
Bandeirante	19	4	9
Shorts 360	35	—	8

The Dash 7 was a four-engine propeller plane manufactured by de Havilland Aircraft of Canada. The complexity and high maintenance costs associated with a four-engine airplane made the Dash 7 less than ideal for ASA, however. The Shorts 360 (SD3-60), manufactured in Northern Ireland, had two engines and was better suited for commuter airline use. The Shorts 360s were held on operating leases of 10 years with an option to cancel on each anniversary of the lease, while five years was more typical for aircraft operating leases. The Bandeirante was an efficient and popular plane made by Embraer, the Brazilian company that was selling the Brasilias to ASA.

THE EMBRAER BRASILIA

Embraer was founded in 1969 as an enterprise controlled by the government of Brazil. While the government had reduced its equity position in the company to 6 percent by 1985, it still held most of the voting stock. The company's first plane, the Bandeirante, had been introduced in 1972, and, since then, more than 450 Bandeirantes had been sold. The plane remained popular through the mid-1980s, and production continued at a rate of four per month.

The Bandeirante attracted unwelcome public attention in December 1984, however, when a Bandeirante flown by Provincetown–Boston Airlines crashed near Jacksonville, Florida, killing all 13 people aboard. Rescuers found the tail section of the plane in two pieces, and the speculation was that a structural weakness in the tail had caused the crash. The Federal Aviation Administration was examining that possibility, although one industry insider said he expected there would be no evidence that the plane's design or construction was faulty. While the FAA did not ground other Bandeirantes flown by U.S. carriers, it did order them inspected. ASA inspected its Bandeirante aircraft, but found no structural problems and returned them to service.

The Brasilia, a successor to the Bandeirante, was one of the first airplanes manufactured specifically for the short-haul commuter market. It had 30 large seats, overhead luggage bins running the length of the plane, and a 5-foot 11-inch ceiling to allow passengers freedom of movement during a flight. The Brasilia flew faster than 300 miles per hour and could complete a 250-mile flight in only five minutes longer than a jet. The plane was believed to have the lowest operating costs on a passenger-mile basis of any commuter airplane. The standard purchase price was $5.2 million or $165,000 per seat, as opposed to $2 million or $105,000 per seat for the Bandeirante. ASA was to receive a 1 percent discount, increasing by 1 percent for each plane it ordered, up to 10 aircraft.

Because ASA planned to retire none of its existing planes, the purchase of six Brasilias in 1985 and four more in 1986 would add 300 seats to ASA's current capacity of 767 seats. The new planes would allow for expanded service on current routes and the addition of markets to ASA's route system. The airline had been limited by the speed and refueling needs of its current fleet in scheduling flights to more distant communities such as Myrtle Beach, South Carolina; Gulfport, Mississippi; Gainsville, Florida; and Roanoke, Virginia. Passengers on commuter flights expected to arrive at their destinations within an hour, and flying round-trip without refueling would significantly reduce operating expenses. The Brasilias speed and efficiency would allow ASA to meet these demands.

The six Brasilias to be shipped to ASA would be among the first planes manufactured for sale. Embraer had orders and options for 117 commuter Brasilias and an order from the Brazilian government for 26 Brasilias designed for military use.

ASA's COMPETITIVE ENVIRONMENT

Delta and Eastern Airlines, holding 90 percent market share between them, were the major carriers with the largest presence in the Atlanta market. (Exhibit 6 compares the recent performance of the two airlines.) In April 1984, Eastern entered a working agreement with Metro Airlines, a commuter airline founded in 1969. Before this agreement, Metro Airlines flights were concentrated around Houston and Dallas/Fort Worth. The Eastern alignment led Metro Airlines to add a hub in Atlanta, where it scheduled flights under the name of a wholly owned subsidiary, Metro Express. While Express offered just 24 flights per week initially, flights to and from Atlanta were expected to represent one third of Metro Airlines' capacity by 1986. Because of market expansion, it planned to purchase 21 additional aircraft by 1987 and lease a dozen more. (Exhibit 7 presents operating and financial data for Metro Airlines.)

Three other external forces could change ASA's competitive environment. The first was the possibility that other major carriers or discount carriers would compete vigorously in the Atlanta market, thereby forcing prices and margins down. Because ASA was closely linked to Delta, any decline in Delta's market share could reduce ASA's earnings. Second, a major carrier having difficulty establishing a working agreement with a commuter airline might file suit to break competitors' agreements as anticompetitive. Third, pressure might develop for tougher regulation of commuter airlines if profits on monopoly routes were felt to be excessive or safety was thought to be threatened in any way.

WACHOVIA BANK AND TRUST

Wachovia, based in Winston-Salem, was one of the nation's leading regional banks. "Wachovia has developed a strong culture leading to excellence in banking with avoidance of undue risk," one analyst had written. "The bank has embraced the most modern tools and technology . . . but it has avoided fad and fancy." This strategy of innovation within a conservative tradition had given Wachovia a return on equity of 19.1 percent in 1984, compared with an average of 13.1 percent for the 24 largest U.S. banks. Wachovia also had annual compound earnings growth of 18.6 percent from 1979 to 1984.

Wachovia had first contacted ASA in March 1983. While Wachovia had considered the commuter airline industry to carry a higher degree of risk than lending to the major carriers, it did lend to two major carriers and wanted to begin assessing a possible future relationship with ASA. The bank had been aware several months earlier of the company's intention to purchase six Brasilias, and the company was interested in having Wachovia as a participant in this loan. The bank also recognized that it could meet ASA's local banking needs at North Carolina terminals, where the airline scheduled flights, as well as offer other financial services to the company. Trust Company Bank in Atlanta was ASA's agent bank for operations. Continental Illinois had provided much of the financing for ASA's earlier airplane purchases.

The Loan Proposal

This loan would fund 65 percent of the purchase price of the six Brasilias to be delivered in 1985. Of the remainder, 20 percent was to be financed as supplier credit, and ASA was to pay 15 percent in cash as a down payment. In addition to Wachovia, Lloyds had invited Continental Illinois, First Chicago, Barclays Bank PLC, Canadian Imperial Bank of Commerce, and National Bank of Georgia to participate in the loan. During the first seven months of the loan, ASA would draw upon a revolving line of credit each time one of the six planes was delivered. Each participant bank would receive a fee of three-eighths of 1 percent on the unused portion of its commitment during this period. The balance outstanding on January 31, 1986, would convert to a 10-year term with semiannual repayments of principal. The loan was priced at LIBOR + 2.25 percent and included an agreement in which the manufacturer agreed to remarket the aircraft should it be repossessed from ASA. (The complete terms and covenants of the loan are described in Exhibit 8.) In 1984, three-month LIBOR rates had risen from 9.75 percent to 12.375 percent before settling back to 8.688 percent in December. In March 1985, it was 9.75 percent.

Interest payments were to come from two sources. Through an export subsidy program known as FINEX, the Brazilian government would pay the difference between 8 percent of principal, which ASA would pay, and the current rate on the loan. All interest payments would be denominated in dollars, eliminating any foreign-currency translation risk. The involvement of the Brazilian government, however, was a consideration for Wachovia, because the bank was trying to reduce its exposure in South America. Repayment of many U.S. loans had been delayed during a debt crisis in Brazil three years earlier, although interest and principal were repaid on schedule for all FINEX loans.

Because Wachovia was one of six participants in the credit, it could not easily ask Lloyds to change the terms or covenants negotiated with ASA. To help him in his analysis, Spangler had received from ASA projected financial statements (Exhibits 9 and 10) and operating projections (Exhibit 11) through 1989. While he believed the price of the loan was attractive, he wanted to assess whether the terms offered Wachovia enough protection to face the risks of lending long term—with South American exposure—to a company in a volatile industry buying an airplane that had never been commercially flown.

EXHIBIT 1 ASA Operating Statistics

	1980	1981	1982	1983	1984
Revenue passengers carried (thousands)	60	149	198	358	614
Available seat-miles* (millions)	10	37	68	141	210
Revenue passenger-miles† (millions)	5	16	25	53	98
Passenger load factor‡	46.5%	43.3%	37.6%	37.9%	46.7%
Break-even load factor§	45.9%	36.1%	33.1%	34.4%	35.7%
Average passenger trip length (miles)	80	107	128	148	160
Flights per week (end of period)	135	362	564	870	1,426

* Available seat-miles, a measure of capacity, refers to the number of miles passengers would fly on a carrier's route system if all seats were filled for all flights.
† Revenue passenger-miles, a measure of capacity utilization, refers to the number of miles passengers actually fly on a carrier's route system.
‡ Passenger load factor equals revenue passenger-miles divided by available seat-miles.
§ Break-even load factor is the load factor required for the contribution earned on all flights to meet all the airline's fixed costs.

EXHIBIT 2   ASA Income Statements (dollars in thousands, except per share data)

	1980	1981	1982	1983	1984
Operating revenues:					
Passenger	$2,350	$7,668	$12,018	$22,613	$41,817
Other	72	863	1,163	1,172	1,945
Operating revenues	2,422	8,531	13,181	23,785	43,762
Operating expenses:					
Flying operations	935	2,734	4,264	9,063	15,045
Maintenance	381	839	944	2,126	4,121
Aircraft, traffic service	348	943	1,528	3,058	4,587
Reservations/sales/advertising	205	632	1,172	2,217	4,013
General & administrative	294	801	1,200	2,265	3,226
Depreciation	114	515	1,106	1,693	1,859
Miscellaneous	27	88	69	63	173
Operating expenses	2,304	6,552	10,283	20,485	33,024
Operating income	118	1,979	2,898	3,300	10,738
Other (income) expenses:					
Interest income	0	(34)	(241)	(394)	(541)
Interest expense	86	586	1,555	1,524	1,126
Other (net)	2	1	2	(9)	(128)
Total expenses	88	553	1,316	1,121	457
Profit before tax	30	1,426	1,582	2,179	10,281
Net income taxes	7	202	100	375	4,981
Profit after tax	23	1,224	1,482	1,803	5,301
Loss carryforward benefit	7	112	0	0	0
Net income	$ 30	$1,335	$ 1,482	$ 1,803	$ 5,301
Earnings per share	$ 0.02	$ 0.88	$ 0.26	$ 0.23	$ 0.66
Shares outstanding (000)	1,524	1,524	5,650	7,935	6,883

Note: Figures may not add because of rounding.

EXHIBIT 3   ASA Balance Sheets (dollars in thousands)

	1981	*1982*	*1983*	*1984*
Cash & equivalents	$ 1,389	$4,586	$4,499	$10,975
Accounts receivable	1,024	1,375	2,821	5,352
Income tax refund receivable	0	66	0	0
Expendable parts (net)	56	226	471	556
Other current assets	71	105	185	591
Total current assets	2,540	6,358	7,976	17,473
Property & equipment:				
Flight equipment	6,395	15,579	16,915	17,496
Other property & equipment	181	348	916	2,300
Less depreciation	(821)	(1,961)	(3,800)	(4,813)
Total property & equipment	5,755	13,966	14,031	14,983
Intangible assets	26	16	4,301	4,265
Other assets	4,138	5,077	1,313	1,211
Total assets	$12,459	$25,417	$27,621	$37,932
Current long-term debt	$ 1,058	$ 1,036	$ 2,557	$ 1,455
Accounts payable	389	412	1,065	2,736
Air traffic liability	273	324	802	1,456
Accrued expenses	574	986	1,026	1,322
Income taxes payable	90	7	19	2,409
Total current liabilities	2,384	2,765	5,469	9,378
Long-term debt	4,610	10,703	8,795	7,340
Deferred income taxes	0	159	449	3,000
Notes payable	4,057	4,610	0	0
Total liabilities	$11,051	$18,236	$14,713	$19,718
Owners' equity:				
Preferred stock	150	0	0	0
Common stock	152	232	266	400
Capital in excess of par	0	4,415	8,304	8,177
Retained earnings	1,105	2,534	4,337	9,637
Total owners' equity	1,408	7,181	12,908	18,214
Total liabilities & equity	$12,459	$25,417	$27,621	$37,932

EXHIBIT 4 ASA Route System

Airport Served	Air Miles from Hub	Flights/Week
From Atlanta hub:		
Albany, Ga.	146	78
Anniston, Ala.	82	52
Asheville, N.C.	164	40
Athens, Ga.	67	49
Augusta, Ga.	143	28
Brunswick, Ga.	238	52
Columbus, Ga.	83	66
Dothan, Ala.	171	80
Fort Walton Beach, Fla.	250	54
Gadsden, Ala.	98	37
Golden Triangle, Miss.	241	52
Greenville/Spartanburg, S.C.	154	66
Huntsville, Ala.	151	94
Laurel/Hattiesburg, Miss.	308	26
Macon, Ga.	79	104
Meridian, Miss.	267	40
Montgomery, Ala.	147	26
Muscle Shoals, Ala.	198	40
Panama City, Fla.	247	64
Tri-Cities, Tenn.	227	52
Tuscaloosa, Ala.	186	52
Valdosta, Ga.	208	52
From Memphis hub:		
Golden Triangle, Miss.	136	38
Huntsville, Ala.	184	40
Laurel/Hattiesburg, Miss.	250	26
Meridian, Miss.	200	52
Muscle Shoals, Ala.	136	40
Tuscaloosa, Ala.	185	26

Note: Regular service was provided on all routes every weekday, with reduced service on weekends.

EXHIBIT 4 *(concluded)*

EXHIBIT 5   Analysts' Report

Robinson Humphrey/American Express, James D. Parker (December 1982): "ASA is forecast to continue to show rapid revenue growth . . . primarily through the addition of new markets . . . [and] from adding frequency of flights to cities already served by other airlines but where there are only a few flights per day. . . . Thus, very few significant markets are likely to open up in the foreseeable future as a result of major and regional airlines discontinuing service in those markets."

Blackstock & Co., Carol A. Robichaud (February 1984): "We recommend purchase of Atlantic Southeast's shares. . . . We anticipate revenue growth averaging 25 percent per year for the next three to five years as additional destinations are added to their hub-and-spoke system and existing routes are expanded."

Robinson Humphrey/American Express, James D. Parker (March 1984): "[The] profitability of ASA may be attributed largely to the following three factors: (1) rapid passenger traffic growth brought about primarily by moving quickly to fill voids in smaller markets . . . (2) an unusually high yield (revenue per passenger mile) made possible by limited competition on most of ASA's routes, and (3) management that was experienced.

First Boston Corp., Michael W. Derchin (May 1984): "During the first quarter of 1984, the two most profitable airlines under my coverage were regionals—Atlantic Southeast was number one with a 15.1 percent operating margin. . . ."

First Boston Corp., RoseAnn Tortora and Michael Derchin (February 1985): "We have been impressed by the company's strong management and its consistent profitability. On May 1, 1984, Atlantic Southeast became a member of Delta's commuter program, the Delta Connection, and its earnings momentum and visibility skyrocketed."

EXHIBIT 6   Financial and Operating Results for Delta and Eastern (dollars in millions)

	1981	*1982*	*1983*	*1984*
Delta Air Lines*:				
Revenues	$3,533	$3,617	$3,616	$4,263
Net profit	$21	($87)	$176	$260
Operating profit margin	11.2%	6.7%	2.7%	13.1%
Load factor	55.5%	53.8%	54.5%	51.2%
Long-term debt/net worth	0.19	0.35	1.22	0.64
Eastern Air Lines:				
Revenues	$3,727	$3,769	$3,942	$4,363
Net profit	($66)	($75)	($184)	($38)
Operating profit margin	4.8%	5.5%	4.7%	10.9%
Load factor	55.8%	56.7%	59.0%	56.9%
Long-term debt/net worth	3.41	4.84	7.32	7.04

* Delta's beta was 1.2. The 30-day Treasury bill rate was 7.77 percent.

EXHIBIT 7 Metro Airlines Performance Summary (dollars in thousands)

	Fiscal Year Ended April 30			6-Months Ended 10/84
	1982	*1983*	*1984*	
Operating revenue	$33,680	$35,279	$36,972	$24,375
Earnings before int., leases	$4,999	$4,345	$3,391	NA
Interest expense	$2,037	$1,387	$1,389	$627
Lease expense	$2,731	$2,734	$2,384	NA
Net income	$194	$133	$6	$2,507
Passengers	673	655	635	NA
Available seat-miles	175,692	193,410	204,066	NA
Revenue passenger-miles	79,709	88,984	97,141	NA
Load factor	45.4%	46.0%	47.6%	NA
Break-even load factor	45.2%	47.8%	48.3%	NA
Total assets	$23,110	$22,269	$24,021	$28,288
Debt/net worth	2.27	2.13	1.89	1.59
Current ratio	0.72	0.65	0.64	0.92
Cash flow from operations	$2,431	$2,740	$2,335	$4,974
Fixed-asset expenditures	$10,764	$954	$2,836	$2,703
Long-term debt increase (decrease)	$3,601	($1,803)	$250	$635

Markets

Subsidiary	States Served	Cities
Metroflight	Texas	11
	Oklahoma	6
	Arkansas	2
	Louisiana	2
Metro Express	Georgia	5
	Alabama	4
	FL, TN, NC	5

Long-term Debt Obligations

1985	$2,220
1986	$2,200
1987	$2,300

EXHIBIT 8   Terms and Covenants of Loan Proposal

Commitment from Wachovia: $3 million.

Maturity: Semiannual payments of $150,000 beginning March 31, 1986, with final maturity September 30, 1995.

Rate: LIBOR plus 2.25 (8 percent fixed from borrower with the remainder to be paid pursuant to the Brazilian FINEX program).

Commitment fee: Three-eighths of 1 percent on the unused portion of the loan.

Prepayment: Right to prepay a series of drafts with no penalty or premium at interest due date. Thirty days prior written notice must be given.

Collateral: First security interest in aircraft, engines, propellers, replacement parts, accessories, equipment, parts, appliances, appurtenances, log books, and manuals.

Principal Covenants

Financial statements: Annual statements within 90 days of year end, quarterly statements within 45 days. Included with statements will be an officer's certificate with covenant compliance computations.

Required ratios and balances:

	1985	1986	1987	1988	1989+
Long-term debt to tangible net worth	1.6	1.5	1.4	1.3	1.3
Total liabilities to tangible net worth	2.50	2.45	2.25	2.00	1.75
Current ratio	1.0	1.0	1.0	1.0	1.0
Fixed charge coverage ratio*	1.0	1.0	1.0	1.0	1.0
Minimum tangible net	$16.5MM	$19.0MM	$21.5MM	$24.0MM	$26.5MM

Insurance: Casualty and comprehensive insurance as well as insurance against confiscation, requisition, and seizure.

Disposition of assets: Limited to aggregate book value of $1 million.

Mergers: Permitted only with surviving corporations.

Dividends: Permitted up to 10 percent of earnings if earnings exceed $5 million.

Investments: None in excess of 5 percent of outstanding common stock allowed.

Other: Working agreement with Delta may not be voluntarily terminated.

* Defined as profit before tax plus depreciation divided by current maturity of long-term debt.

EXHIBIT 9   ASA Pro Forma Income Statements (dollars in thousands, except per share data)

	1985	*1986*	*1987*	*1988*	*1989*
Operating revenues:					
Passenger	$69,487	$92,622	$104,645	$109,195	$113,745
Other	2,085	2,779	3,139	3,276	3,412
Operating revenues	71,572	95,401	107,784	112,471	117,157
Operating expenses:					
Aircraft leases	9,080	9,650	9,800	9,800	9,800
Flying operations	17,853	23,550	24,792	24,792	24,792
Maintenance	7,862	10,108	11,718	12,834	13,950
Indirect expenses	22,187	29,574	33,413	34,866	36,319
Depreciation	2,443	4,907	5,600	5,600	5,600
Operating expenses	59,425	77,789	85,323	87,892	90,461
Operating income	12,147	17,612	22,461	24,579	26,696
Nonoperating expense	1,420	3,320	3,600	3,450	3,300
Profit before tax	10,727	14,292	18,861	21,129	23,396
Net income taxes	2,243	5,066	9,431	10,565	11,698
Net income	$ 8,484	$ 9,226	$ 9,430	$ 10,564	$ 11,698
Earnings per share	$2.12	$2.31	$2.36	$2.64	$2.93

EXHIBIT 10   ASA Pro Forma Balance Sheets (dollars in thousands)

	1985	1986	1987	1988	1989
Cash	$15,067	$ 27,540	$ 39,805	$ 53,050	$ 67,440
Accounts receivable	6,961	7,545	8,903	9,559	10,057
Expendable parts (net)	1,500	1,650	1,900	1,950	2,000
Other current assets	700	750	800	800	800
Total current assets	24,228	37,485	51,408	65,359	80,297
Property & equipment	50,996	71,796	71,796	71,796	71,796
Less depreciation	(7,256)	(12,163)	(17,763)	(23,363)	(28,963)
Total property & equipment	43,740	59,633	54,033	48,433	42,833
Deposits	1,140	0	0	0	0
Deferred charges	4,800	4,600	4,400	4,200	4,000
Total assets	$73,908	$101,718	$109,841	$117,992	$127,130
Current long-term debt	$ 4,020	$ 5,824	$ 5,867	$ 5,914	$ 5,964
Accounts payable	4,000	6,000	6,800	7,000	7,100
Air traffic liability	2,000	2,600	3,000	3,200	3,250
Accrued expenses	1,500	1,800	1,960	2,000	2,050
Other	650	700	750	750	750
Total current liab.	12,170	16,924	18,377	18,864	19,114
Long-term debt	29,800	39,050	33,200	27,300	21,400
Deferred income taxes	5,240	9,820	12,920	15,910	19,000
Total liabilities	47,210	65,794	64,497	62,074	59,514
Owners' equity:					
Common stock	400	400	400	400	400
Capital in excess of par	8,177	8,177	8,177	8,177	8,177
Retained earnings	18,121	27,347	36,777	47,341	59,039
Total owners' equity	26,698	35,924	45,354	55,918	67,616
Total liabilities & equity	$73,908	$101,718	$109,851	$117,992	$127,130

EXHIBIT 11   ASA Operating Statistics Forecast

	1985	1986	1987	1988	1989
Passengers*	1,018	1,323	1,474	1,538	1,602
Revenue passenger-miles†	175	238	265	277	288
Available passenger-miles†	406	541	577	577	577
Load factor	43.1%	44.0%	45.9%	48.0%	49.9%
Statistics by plane type					
Bandeirante:					
Departures	36,100	36,200	36,200	36,200	36,200
Hours in Flight	36,100	36,200	36,200	36,200	36,200
Miles*	6,047	5,792	5,792	5,792	5,792
Shorts 360:					
Departures	26,500	29,000	29,000	29,000	29,000
Hours in Flight	25,175	27,550	27,550	27,550	27,550
Miles*	3,889	4,060	4,060	4,060	4,060
Dash 7:					
Departures	15,700	16,500	16,500	16,500	16,500
Hours in Flight	17,270	18,150	18,150	18,150	18,150
Miles*	2,744	2,640	2,640	2,640	2,640
Brasilia:					
Departures	3,824	22,275	27,000	27,000	27,000
Hours in Flight	4,208	24,503	29,700	29,700	29,700
Miles*	956	5,569	6,750	6,750	6,750
Total fleet:					
Departures	82,124	103,975	108,700	108,700	108,700
Hours in Flight	82,753	106,403	111,600	111,600	111,600
Miles*	13,636	18,061	19,242	19,242	19,242
Passengers per departure	12.4	12.7	13.6	14.1	14.7
Speed (miles/hour)............	165	170	172	172	172
Average seats per mile	29.8	30	30	30	30
Length of haul (miles).........	172	180	180	180	180
Average fare	$68	$70	$71	$71	$71
Passenger yield	$0.397	$0.389	$0.395	$0.394	$0.395
Cost/available seat-mile	$0.150	$0.150	$0.154	$0.158	$0.162
Breakeven load factor	36.7%	37.4%	37.9%	39.0%	39.9%

* Thousands of units.
† Millions of units.

Case 12

The L. S. Starrett Company

INTRODUCTION

On October 12, 1984, Susan Craig, a lending officer in the New England region for Wachovia Bank and Trust, made a conference call with Jim Cook, a Wachovia national banking loan administration officer, to Douglas R. Starrett, the president of the L.S. Starrett Company. The 90-minute conversation yielded two lending opportunities for Wachovia. The first was a $12 million participation in an $18 million loan to Starrett's Employee Stock Ownership Plan (ESOP)[1] for the purchase of treasury stock. The second opportunity was a participation in a $15 million revolver/term loan that would ensure Starrett's liquidity as the firm planned to repurchase more than the number of shares that would be sold to the trust.

In just one year, Wachovia's relationship with Starrett, a manufacturer of precision hand tools and measuring instruments, had grown from no outstandings to a commitment for a $7.5 million industrial revenue bond (IRB), and, now, the possibility of the additional term commitments. Susan was comfortable with Starrett's ability to cover the existing IRB debt, but she was concerned about how the new debt would affect the company's financial position. Of additional concern was how much term debt she was willing to commit to a customer the bank had known for just over one year.

---

[1] Strictly speaking, the loan would be made to the Employee Stock Ownership *Trust*. The trust would be established by a plan approved by the U.S. Labor Department. For simplicity, practitioners use "ESOP" to refer to both the plan and the trust.

This case was written by Peter R. Hennessy and Robert F. Bruner.
Copyright © 1985 by the Darden Graduate Business School Foundation, Charlottesville, VA.

THE L.S. STARRETT COMPANY

Founded in 1880, the L.S. Starrett Company had flourished as a result of its operating philosophy, which emphasized quality products and concern for its employees.

The first Starrett tool, known as a combination square, combined a precision ground rule and a movable right angle. By 1984, the company's catalog included over 3,000 items in three product lines: measuring tools, precision instruments and granite surface plates, and saws. Hand measuring tools included such items as micrometers, steel rules, and combination squares, which were used by individual craftsmen. Precision instruments included vernier calipers, height and depth gauges, and measuring instruments, which were traditionally purchased by manufacturing companies for their employees' use.

Granite surface plates are level work areas, precision-ground for use by craftsmen whose tasks demanded that work surfaces be extremely flat. The instrument and measuring tool lines historically accounted for slightly less than two thirds of Starrett's total sales, with the balance being in saws and flat stock.

Starrett sold its products through industrial distributors in the United States and more than 100 foreign countries. The company's offices and primary manufacturing facility were located in Athol, Massachusetts, with additional manufacturing plants in Cleveland, Ohio, and Mt. Airy, North Carolina. In 1984, the firm built a new facility in Mt. Airy to improve the handling of that location's existing production and to meet future expansion needs for the entire company.

In 1958, the firm had established manufacturing facilities in Scotland and Brazil, which were used to supply foreign markets, rather than to serve as an import source for the United States. In FY (fiscal year) 1984, 25 percent of sales and 30 percent of operating profits were generated outside of the United States and Canada.

The conservatively managed company had avoided using debt for its domestic operations and chose instead to fund its growth internally. Starrett's debts in the last 10 years were primarily obligations of the two foreign operating subsidiaries. Outstanding debt at year-end peaked in FY 1980 at $3.5 million, or 8.8 percent of equity. Since 1981, though, Starrett had had no outstanding debt at year-end. "If you're not in debt," commented Doug Starrett, "you're not in trouble. Some people would argue, the higher the leverage the better. I would disagree. The flexibility is too important."

Prior to 1984, debt was used extensively only once, to block an unfriendly takeover attempt. During the 1950s, a corporate raider had accumulated roughly a third of the company's stock before management became aware of the plan and arranged with a regional insurance company for a 10-year loan to buy back the shares. The loan was repaid in less than five years. More recently, the company decided to fund plant construction at its Mt. Airy facility through an industrial revenue bond, not because it was unable to cover the expenditure internally but because the tax-exempt financing was shown to create value for the company's shareholders.

Even though the company was traded on the New York Stock Exchange, over half the outstanding shares were held by existing or former employees. As a result, the stock was thinly traded, which caused the stock price to vary widely when large blocks were bought or sold.

Since the 1950s, the company had encouraged employee ownership. In 1984, about 70 percent of current employees were stockholders through the voluntary payroll deduction plan or the employee stock purchase plan. Management felt that the high degree of worker ownership and the company's concern for the employees were responsible for the absence of unions. The proposed Employee Stock Ownership Plan would shift a portion of future pension contributions away from traditional pension investments into the purchase of company shares for the benefit of the employees.

Of the company's five executive officers, Doug Starrett, 64, was the dominant force in directing the company. Two officers—Bill Oleson, 57, treasurer, and John Grant, 61, director of research and development—had announced their forthcoming departure in 1984. The remaining officers were George Webber, 63, who managed the Webber Gage Division, and Charles Morrow, 49, who acted as sales manager.

INDUSTRY

The precision instrument and measuring tool business was highly concentrated among three manufacturers, while the saw and flat stock industry had numerous competitors. Despite increased foreign competition, Starrett remained the market leader and the only remaining domestic manufacturer in the instrument and tool sectors. Mitutoyo, a Japanese firm, had expanded its market share in the United States through aggressive pricing, abetted by favorable exchange rates and less concern over earnings. Starrett was considered to be priced between the Japanese manufacturer on the low end and Brown & Sharpe, the third main competitor, on the high end. Brown & Sharpe, which was based in the United States, had recently begun to manufacture its precision tool line abroad because of labor difficulties.

While price was a factor in the instrument and tool industry competition, the ability to deliver a high-quality product that would remain accurate over many years was much more important. Instrument and tool quality was so important because it had a direct bearing on the quality of the user's final product.

The industry was mildly seasonal and highly cyclical, and it lagged the general economy by one to two quarters. Sales in the summer months reflected the general slowdown in manufacturing industries. Cyclicality and the lag were explained by the composition of the industry's customer base, which was dominated by manufacturing. Sales were made predominantly to the metal manufacturing industry (65 percent); but other important markets included the automobile, aerospace, and building industries. Sales were handled exclusively through industrial distributors, who normally carried products from the three major manufacturers.

Industry demand was expected to increase as domestic manufacturers placed a greater emphasis on retooling plants to increase efficiency and improve quality. Competition for this business was likely to increase, also; the Japanese manufacturers, for example, were positioning themselves for a larger share of the instrument and tool business. Recent product innovations were dominated by electronics, which meant there was a greater emphasis on research and development. Product obsolescence was minimal, as products tended to evolve, rather than be replaced with revolutionary new models.

FINANCIAL CONDITION

The strength of the dollar and the decline of American manufacturing had reduced Starrett's domestic margins and market share in 1983 and 1984. The strong dollar not only made Starrett's products less attractive in the export market but also gave a significant advantage to the Japanese tool manufacturers in the U.S. market.

Despite the lower margins, Starrett remained highly profitable and in extremely strong financial condition. (See Exhibits 1, 2, 3, and 4.) Cash and marketable securities at the end of the first quarter of FY 1985 amounted to $22.9 million, or 1.3 times total liabilities. Even though sales dropped in 1982 and 1983, management decided to continue normal production levels to minimize layoffs of skilled workers. Inventories thus increased by 36 percent, from 199 days at FYE 1982 to 271 days at FYE 1983. While the higher inventory levels increased working capital needs, they also allowed Starrett to take advantage of the recovery in 1984. Starrett expected sales in FY 1985 to approach the record levels achieved in FY 1981 and then grow at a slightly lower rate. (See Exhibit 5 for pro forma income statements and Exhibit 6 for pro forma balance sheets.)

Since the company had no outstanding debentures or commercial paper, no debt ratings were available. Value Line, prior to the time of the proposed ESOP and repurchase transactions, listed a beta for Starrett of 0.65, which reflected no actual or anticipated debt. The prevailing risk-free rate of return was assumed to be 11.56 percent and the market premium for holding stocks was 8.30 percent.

WACHOVIA

Wachovia Bank and Trust, which was consistently rated as one of the best managed and most profitable banks in the United States, was known for its conservative lending policies, high degree of capitalization, and superior loan portfolio.

While many competing institutions focused on increasing asset size and market share, Wachovia had concentrated on maintaining the quality of its loan portfolio and improving its already strong earnings record. Bank officials emphasized the need to know the character of a firm's management. Interaction between the senior management of the bank and that of a borrower was encouraged as exposure to a company increased.

THE OPPORTUNITY

Starrett management had initiated the idea of an ESOP purchase and tender offer to enhance employee ownership and to give them a decisive voice in the firm. Management felt there were numerous shareholders who, due to age or financial commitments, were preparing to sell their holdings. Rather than risk allowing the shares to fall into the hands of anyone interested in a hostile takeover, management decided to repurchase the shares. The fact that the company was extremely liquid, employed no debt, and had an impressive earnings record even during major economic downturns made it susceptible to a takeover attempt. As Doug Starrett commented, "Cash or no cash, people would be interested in us for our operating record. Our main objective in establishing the trust was to enhance employee ownership."

Recent tax law changes made the ESOP transaction quite attractive for the company and the bank. The company was allowed to use existing pension contributions to repay the principal and debt associated with the purchase of stock by the trust. The principal and interest payments for Starrett would both be considered pretax expenses; interest income for the bank would be 50 percent tax-free. In addition, dividends that were paid to the ESOP would be considered tax-deductible. The debt assumed by the ESOP, however, would have to be shown on Starrett's balance sheet, with the offset being a reduction in equity (accomplished by an increase in a contra-equity account). As the ESOP retired the debt through pension contributions from the parent, Starrett's owners' equity would increase (through a reduction of the contra account). (See Exhibits 7 and 8 for a description of the accounting treatment for Starrett and the ESOP.)

In the course of their conversation with Doug Starrett, Susan and Jim learned that the company was interested in having the ESOP purchase 600,000 shares from Starrett, while the company would repurchase a like number of shares in the open market at around $30 per share, which reflected a $2.875 premium over the current market price of $27.125. For planning purposes, management assumed that without the ESOP, pension expense would average $1.8 million per year for the 1985–89 time period. The firm's pension expense for 1984, 1983, and 1982 had amounted to $1.4 million, $2.06 million, and $2.2 million, respectively, which meant that the interest expense and principal reduction on the 10-year term loan with equal amortization would greatly exceed recent pension contributions, even when dividends for the ESOP shares were considered. The ESOP loan interest rate would be set at 85 percent of prime, or about 11.5 percent.

Starrett had reserved the right to increase the repurchase to 800,000 shares. However, a weak public response to the tender offer might result in fewer than 600,000 shares being repurchased. Proceeds to fund the repurchase would come from the $18 million received from the ESOP stock purchase, as well as from idle cash and marketable securities.

The two-year revolver/five-year term loan was being arranged to ensure liquidity and flexibility for the company. The interest rate on the revolver term loan would be set at prime. The loan would require 3 percent compensating balances and a commitment fee of .25 percent. The revolver could easily be drawn on if the company had the opportunity to repurchase all 800,000 shares, or if management decided to increase the tender price to increase the response or fend off hostile bidders. The funds also might be used if an attractive acquisition arose for Starrett. Susan understood that Starrett was considering two possible acquisitions that would require roughly $10 million. At the same time, the commitment could easily go unused, given the $22.9 million the company had in cash and short-term investments at the end of September 1984.

The credit decision facing Susan had certainly become more complicated than the one she had faced earlier in 1984 when she committed the bank to the $7.5 million IRB, which was scheduled to close in December. Covenants established for the 15-year IRB included:

- Current ratio greater than 2.5.
- Total liabilities less than 80 percent of tangible net worth.
- Net working capital greater than $45 million.
- Tangible net worth greater than $70 million.

Given the possible changes in Starrett's financial structure, Susan needed to determine whether the ESOP loan should be made and, if so, how much she would be willing to lend. In addition, she would need to decide how much of the revolver she would be willing to commit to and what adjustments to make to the existing covenants. Susan was well aware of the bank's concern about committing to term debt, especially to customers that were relatively new to the bank.

The relationship had grown so quickly that Susan was not as familiar with company management as she would have liked to have been. While she had visited Starrett's headquarters on several occasions to meet with the treasurer, she had met with Doug Starrett only once before the October 12 conference call. The limited contact with company officials and the recent departures of two of its executives had also left Susan uncertain about managerial succession.

The concern was warranted: The bank could have almost half of its house limit committed, all in term debt, if the loans were approved. An additional issue was whether the bank was financing the purchase of a fairly priced security. The complexity of the situation made Susan realize that the opportunity deserved a thorough analysis before responding to the lead bank, which wanted an initial indication the following day.

EXHIBIT 1 Ten-Year Historical Financial Data for the Years Ended June 30 (in millions except where noted)

	1975	1976	1977	1978	1979	1980	1981	1982	1983	1984
Sales ($)	55.7	58.2	66.6	76.8	92.9	110.3	122.5	112.7	88.5	105.8
Net income ($).....	5.8	6.0	5.7	7.9	10.8	12.1	13.8	11.3	6.2	8.6
Earnings										
per share ($)	$1.49	$1.52	$1.45	$2.02	$2.83	$3.13	$3.52	$2.92	$1.61	$2.27
Dividends										
per share ($)	$0.50*	$0.53*	$0.59*	$0.65*	$0.71*	$0.89*	$1.00*	$1.05*	$1.00	$1.00
Payout ratio	33.6%	34.9%	40.7%	32.2%	25.1%	28.4%	28.4%	36.0%	62.1%	44.1%
Average annual P/E	5.4	6.0	7.5	5.9	4.7	4.9	6.7	8.3	15.4	11.7
Stock price† ($):										
High	$9.62	$11.50	$12.25	$14.75	$16.50	$25.87	$35.25	$30.25	$31.75	$30.37
Low	$7.12	$8.37	$9.82	$11.50	$11.87	$12.87	$21.00	$18.75	$24.25	$23.62
Working capital ...	25.8	28.9	30.5	34.6	39.4	47.9	55.1	58.6	59.2	59.8
Current ratio	3.18	3.59	3.23	2.88	2.92	3.31	4.11	4.38	5.09	4.46
Long-term debt	0.1	0.3	0.2	0.8	0.1	—	—	—	—	—
Net worth	35.7	40.0	43.0	46.8	54.9	63.7	72.2	77.4	77.5	79.2
Cash & short-term										
investment	1.5	6.6	8.1	8.6	8.9	13.5	14.5	19.6	16.6	22.1

* Reflects annual dividend payment plus an extra dividend payment in June quarter of: '75, 13¢; '76, 3¢; '77, 3¢; '78, 5¢; '79, 5¢; '80, 15¢; '81, 10¢; '82, 5¢.
† Calendar year.

EXHIBIT 2   Historical Income Statements

	Year Ended June 30 *(in millions except for per share data)*		
	1982	*1983*	*1984*
Net sales	$112.7	$88.5	$105.8
Cost of sales	68.0	54.4	63.2
Gross profit	44.7	34.1	42.6
Selling, general, & administrative expenses	23.1	19.9	23.2
Depreciation expense	2.8	3.0	3.5
Operating profit	18.8	11.2	15.9
Interest income	2.9	1.9	2.2
Interest expense	.2	.3	.1
Profit before tax	21.5	12.8	18.0
Income tax	10.2	6.6	9.4
Net income	11.3	6.2	8.6
Earnings per share ($)	2.92	1.61	2.27
Dividends per share ($)	1.05	1.00	1.00

EXHIBIT 3 Consolidated Balance Sheets (in millions)

	Year Ended June 30		
	1982	*1983*	*1984*
Cash & short-term investments	$19.6	$16.6	$22.1
Accounts receivable (net)	17.5	12.6	17.3
Inventories	37.5	40.9	34.2
Other	1.3	3.6	3.5
Total current assets	75.9	73.7	77.1
Land	1.0	1.0	1.0
Plant & equipment	38.7	40.0	41.8
Accumulated depreciation	18.1	20.4	22.5
Net plant & equipment	20.6	20.6	20.3
Other assets	0.5	0.3	0.3
Total assets	$98.0	$94.6	$97.7
Notes payable	$ 0.0	$ 0.0	$ 0.0
Accounts payable	7.2	6.8	7.2
Accrued salaries & wages	4.4	2.4	3.8
Accrued taxes	4.5	3.8	5.4
Employee deposits for stock purchase plan	1.2	1.5	0.9
Total current liabilities	17.3	14.5	17.3
Long-term debt	0.0	0.0	0.0
Deferred income taxes	3.3	2.6	1.2
Total liabilities	20.6	17.1	18.5
Common stock	4.6	4.6	4.7
Paid in capital	7.4	7.8	9.1
Retained earnings	67.5	67.9	69.4
Treasury stock*	(.7)	(.8)	(1.0)
Foreign currency translation	(1.4)	(2.0)	(3.0)
Total stockholders' equity	77.4	77.5	79.2
Total liabilities & equity	$98.0	$94.6	$97.7
Shares outstanding at year-end (000)	3,847	3,794	3,744

*At year-end 1984, there were 1 million shares in treasury.

EXHIBIT 4   First Quarter Financial Statements (in millions)

	3 Months Ended Sept. 30	
	1983	*1984*
Income statement:		
Net sales	$22.6	$26.9
Costs, expenses, and interest	19.7	21.7
Profit before tax	2.9	5.2
Income tax	1.4	2.3
Net income	$ 1.5	$ 2.9
Earnings per share	$ 0.38	$ 0.77
Balance sheet:		
Assets		
Cash and short-term investments	$15.5	$22.9
Other current assets	54.0	52.4
Total current assets	69.5	75.3
Property, plant, and equipment and other assets	21.6	21.3
Total assets	$91.1	$96.6
Liabilities and Stockholders' Equity		
Accounts payable and other current liabilities	$ 8.2	$11.6
Accrued taxes	4.2	5.3
Total current liabilities	12.4	16.9
LTD	0.0	0.0
Deferred taxes	2.0	0.4
Total liabilities	14.4	17.3
Stockholders' equity	76.7	79.3
Total liabilities and stockholders' equity	$91.1	$96.6

EXHIBIT 5 The L.S. Starrett Company Pro Forma Income Statements (no ESOP/no repurchase) (in millions) for the Year Ended June 30

	1985	1986	1987	1988	1989
Sales	$120.7	$132.7	$146.0	$160.6	$176.7
CGS & other operating expenses	100.8	110.8	121.9	134.1	147.5
Operating profit*	19.9	21.9	24.1	26.5	29.2
Interest income†	2.7	3.0	3.3	3.7	4.0
Interest expense‡	0.3	0.6	0.6	0.6	0.6
Profit before tax	22.3	24.3	26.8	29.6	32.6
Taxes§	11.1	12.2	13.4	14.8	16.3
Net income	$ 11.2	$ 12.1	$ 13.4	$ 14.8	$ 16.3
EPS ($)	$2.98	$3.24	$3.57	$3.94	$4.35
Dividends	$1.00	$1.05	$1.16	$1.28	$1.41

Pro formas are based on company projections for FY 1985 and historical patterns for years 1986 through 1989.

* Operating margin: 16.5 percent (includes pension expense at no ESOP levels of $1.8 million per year).

† Interest income: Estimated averaged 5-year rate, 11 percent.

‡ Interest expense: Estimated average prime for five-year period, 13.5 percent; IRB at 63 percent of prime; ESOP would be priced at 85 percent of prime.

§ Tax rate: 50 percent.

Dividend policy: Dividend will be the higher of $1 or 32.4 percent of profit.

Pension contributions: Under the proposed ESOP, pension contributions would be replaced by payments to the trust for five to eight years.

EXHIBIT 6 The L.S. Starrett Company Pro Forma Balance Sheets (no ESOT/no repurchase) (in millions) for the Year Ended June 30

	1985	1986	1987	1988	1989
Assets					
Cash	$ 1.5	$ 1.5	$ 1.5	$ 1.5	$ 1.5
Short-term investments*	24.9	27.3	30.1	33.4	36.6
Inventory†	43.7	48.0	52.8	58.1	63.9
Other current assets‡	20.9	23.0	25.3	27.8	30.6
Current assets	91.0	99.8	109.7	120.8	132.6
Net fixed assets and other§	25.7	26.7	27.7	28.7	29.7
Total assets	$116.7	$126.5	$137.4	$149.5	$162.3
Liabilities					
Notes payable	—	—	—	—	—
Current liabilities‖	$ 21.5	$ 23.6	$ 26.0	$ 28.6	$ 31.4
Current portion of long-term debt: IRB	—	—	—	0.6	0.6
Total current liabilities	21.5	23.6	26.0	29.2	32.0
Long-term debt: IRB	7.5	7.5	7.5	6.9	6.3
Deferred income tax	1.5	1.5	1.5	1.5	1.5
Total liabilities	30.5	32.6	35.0	37.6	39.8
Common stock	4.7	4.7	4.7	4.7	4.7
Paid-in capital	9.1	9.1	9.1	9.1	9.1
Retained earnings	76.8	85.0	94.0	104.0	115.1
Less: Treasury stock	1.0	1.0	1.0	1.0	1.0
Foreign currency translation	(3.4)	(3.9)	(4.4)	(4.9)	(5.4)
Total stockholders' equity	86.2	93.9	102.4	111.9	122.5
Total liabilities and equity	$116.7	$126.5	$137.4	$149.5	$162.3

Assumptions:
Pro formas based on projected sales and historical relationships between sales and balance sheet items.
* Short-term investments: Investments from prior year + Excess cash flow + interest income from current year.
† Inventory: Historical [inventory/sales] ratio * Expected sales = 0.362 * projected sales.
‡ Other current assets: Historical relationship [(Accounts Receivable + Prepaid Expenses)/Sales] = 0.173 * projected sales.
§ Net fixed assets: Capital expenditures exceed depreciation by $5.1 million in 1985; $1 million thereafter. Includes other assets of $0.350 million.
‖ Current liabilities (excluding debt): Historical relationship [(Accounts payable + Taxes payable + Accrued expenses)/Sales] = 0.178 * projected sales.

EXHIBIT 7   Accounting for Employee Stock Ownership Trust and Repurchase

Transactions on L.S. Starrett's Books

Cash (A)		Long-Term Debt (L)		Additional Paid-In Capital	
(a) 18,000,000	18,000,000 *(c)*	*(e)* 1,800,000	18,000,000 *(b)*	*(c)* 17,400,000	17,400,000 *(e)*
	3,866,000 *(d)*				

Treasury Stock (COE)		Retained Earnings (OE)		Deferred Compensation Expense	
(c) 600,000	600,000 *(a)*	*(d)* 3,866,000		*(b)* 18,000,000	1,800,000 *(e)*

Description of transactions:

  a. Cash (A)   inc 18,000,000
      Treasury Stock (COE)   dec   600,000
      Paid-In Capital and/or Retained Earnings (COE)   inc 17,400,000
  Starrett sells 600,000 shares of treasury stock to ESO for $30 a share.

  b. Deferred Compensation Expense (COE)   inc 18,000,000
      Long-Term Debt (L)   inc 18,000,000
  To reflect debt guaranteed by parent, offset by a reduction in equity.

  c. Treasury Stock (COE)   inc   600,000
      Paid-In Capital and/or Retained Earnings (OE)   dec 17,400,000
      Cash (A)   dec 18,000,000
  Repurchase 600,000 shares @ $30 a share.

To account for Starrett's pension payments at close of first year:
  Assume level amortization over 10 years.
    Interest expense   = $18.0 mm 0.85 (13.5%) = $2.06 mm
    Principal payment =   1.8 mm
                             $3.86 mm total required funding

  d. Retained Earnings (pension expense) (OE)   dec 3,866,000
      Cash (A)   dec 3,866,000
  Pension expense for year 1.*

  e. Long-Term Debt (L)   dec 1,800,000
      Treasury Stock (COE)   dec 1,800,000
  To reflect reduction in ESOP debt by Starrett, the offset being an increase in equity.

*Includes both current and prepaid amount.

EXHIBIT 8   Accounting for Employee Stock Ownership Plan

Transactions on the Books of the Employee Stock Ownership Plan

Cash		Investment in Starrett (A)	
(a) 18,000,000	18,000,000 *(b)*	*(b)* 18,000,000	
(c) 3,866,000	3,866,000 *(d)*		

Long-Term Debt (L)		Retained Earnings (OE)	
(d) 1,800,000	18,000,000 *(a)*	*(d)* 2,066,000	3,866,000 *(c)*

Description of transactions:

  a. Cash (A)   inc 18,000,000
      Long-Term Debt (L)   inc 18,000,000
  ESOP uses debt to raise cash to purchase 600,000 shares @ $30 a share.

  b. Investment in Starrett (A)   inc 18,000,000
      Cash (A)   dec 18,000,000
  ESOP purchases shares from Starrett.*

At the end of the year the ESOP receives a pension payment to cover interest and principal due.

  c. Cash (A)   inc   3,866,000
      Retained Earnings (pension contribution) (OE)   inc 3,866,000
  ESOP receives pension contribution.

  d. Retained Earnings (interest expense) (OE)   dec 2,066,000
    Long-Term Debt (L)   dec 1,800,000
      Cash (A)   dec 3,866,000
  ESOP pays interest expense and reduces principal.

*May include both current and prepaid accounts.

Part III

The Cost of Capital

Teletech Corporation

In May 1988, Jim Barrymore, Teletech's vice president of finance, was concerned with a number of issues that had been recently raised about the company's capital-budgeting policies and procedures. His task was to develop new methods of capital budgeting that might be more appropriate to the firm.

Teletech was a high-technology company with two prominent operating divisions—telecommunications and computer software and workstations.[1] The company's overall sales totaled $2 billion, three quarters of which were contributed by the telecommunications division.

Top management had determined an overall corporate hurdle rate based on a moving average of the firm's estimated historical average cost of capital over the previous 10 years. In April 1988, the hurdle rate was 13 percent. The company applied this rate as a minimum return-on-investment criterion for both operating divisions.

In evaluating an investment opportunity, an operating unit would discount cash inflows and outflows at the hurdle rate. Projects with present value ratios greater than 1 (present value of inflows divided by present value of outflows) were given further consideration. A number of projects could not be evaluated exclusively on economic grounds (e.g., safety modifications and security systems), and some projects with inadequate net present value (NPV) ratios were submitted and approved. Most projects, however, were justified on economic grounds. Riskier projects might not be approved even if their present value ratio, based on expected value calculations, was above 1. While there were no firm guidelines, management tended to use an NPV ratio of 1 only for very low-risk projects. Moderate-risk projects tended to be evaluated against a standard of a 1.2 present value ratio, and high-risk projects usually required a ratio of 1.5. These guidelines were applied arbitrarily because of different views on risk.

---

[1] The firm also had three other comparatively small and inconsequential divisions.

This case is dedicated to the memory of Darden Professor Robert F. Vandell, the author of an antecedent case and researcher on the cost of capital of corporations. The case was prepared by Casey Opitz, research assistant, under the direction of Robert F. Bruner.

Copyright © 1988 by the Darden Graduate Business School Foundation, Charlottesville, VA.

THE DIVISIONS

A financial summary of Teletech's two main divisions is provided in Exhibit 1. Comparative industry data are provided in Exhibit 2. Telecommunications was the company's core business and was its only business until 1983, when the company entered the burgeoning software and computer workstations markets. In addition to providing telephone service to more than 1.8 million customer lines in several markets throughout the Southwest, the telecommunications division also operated seven cellular communications systems in the same region. An integral and growing segment of the telecommunications division's business was designing, installing, and maintaining systems that integrated data and voice communications. This segment served a customer base of 750,000 telephones and 60,000 computers. In 1987, division revenues amounted to $1.5 billion on identifiable assets of $3.0 billion.

The explosive growth in the microcomputer market and the increased use of telephone lines to connect home- and office-based computers with mainframes brought home to Teletech the potential value of entering the computer industry. The company entered the market in 1983, when Teletech acquired an upstart company consisting of 75 employees that developed network systems software and manufactured computer workstations. Over the past five years, using Teletech's capital base, borrowing ability, and distribution network to catapult growth, the division increased its sales from $8.5 million in the Southwest to $538 million nationwide.

Both divisions were virtually autonomous and, by 1987, both were borrowing funds for their own use. Now, as the computer software and workstation division burgeoned, it required still more infusions of capital.

HURDLE RATES

The weighted-average cost calculation Teletech had always used was backward looking. It was calculated by averaging the past 10 years' annual weighted average costs (WACC), and then "massaging" the result into a round percentage. All of these annual WACCs were based on historical capital mixes and costs. Mr. Barrymore wondered whether he should be projecting future capital mixes and their related costs in determining an appropriate hurdle rate. For instance, according to the data he had gathered regarding the company's weighted-average cost of capital over time, given in Exhibit 3, new debt funds might cost about 10.13 percent (6.08 percent after tax). But the figure Teletech used as its hurdle rate, 13 percent, still reflected some financings in the early 1980s when borrowing rates were in the 17 percent range.

Mr. Barrymore thought the marginal cost of capital would be more appropriate to use but, by definition, the present hurdle rate used an average of the rates used in the past. Related to this question was how far in the future to project. Forecasting market prices for common equities for six months was problematic enough, let alone trying to anticipate what these prices might become in several years. Capital costs could be affected drastically, because the company was borrowing a greater percentage of its total capital to cover the growing needs of the computer software and workstation division, and because the stock price increasingly reflected the growing importance of and expectations about that division. (Since 1983, Teletech's average beta[2] had risen from 0.75 to 1.00, reflecting market expectations for the new division.) He was uncertain what sort of planning horizon was appropriate, especially given the firm's current circumstances.

When the present value ratio was adopted for evaluating projects, management was completely satisfied with the intellectual relevance of a hurdle rate as an expression of the opportunity cost of money. While the notion that the average cost of capital represented this opportunity cost had been debated, and its measurement was never considered wholly scientific, it had been accepted. Circumstances had changed, however. No longer was the company in one line of business. Instead, it was now essentially both a utility and a high-technology, high-growth firm. Mr. Barrymore wondered what the relevant notion of hurdle rates should be under such circumstances.

Recently one of his assistants, Jessica England, had raised a question about how the hurdle rate should be used. Five years earlier, in recognition of the effects of inflation, Teletech had adjusted its methods of present value calculations. In effect, future cash flows were adjusted to reflect the effects of inflation. Estimates of the rates of inflation for various items (such as labor costs, prices, construction costs) were supplied by the firm's economics department and plugged into future cash flows. The net cash flows in future years were then deflated by an estimate of the cost of living index in order to convert them to current terms. The common dollar cash flows were then discounted at the hurdle rate to determine the NPV ratio for the project. Ms. England argued that the last step was wrong. The cost of capital had fallen to reflect investors' views of inflation. If this was so, the double step of deflating the value of future cash flows and discounting at a hurdle rate, reflecting inflation expectations, overcompensated for inflation.

Mr. Barrymore believed that Ms. England was right in part, but he doubted that money costs fully considered inflation expectations. This doubt was troublesome, for considering inflationary effects was certainly appropriate in evaluating investment opportunities, yet a procedure that dealt with them incorrectly would only increase confusion and misinformation. To the extent that inflation did, in fact, influence money costs, it also meant that capital would remain expensive or could become more costly.

Even if the appropriate hurdle rate was clear cut, how the rate should be used within the company in evaluating projects was not. Given the different natures of the two businesses and the risks each one faced, differences of opinion arose at the division-management level over the appropriateness of measuring all projects against the corporate hurdle rate of 13 percent. The chief protagonist of multiple rates was Ralph Aragon, president of the telecommunications division, who presented his views as follows:

> Each phase of our business is different, must compete differently, and must draw on capital differently. Until recently, telecommunications was a regulated industry, and the return on our total capital is highly certain, given the stable nature of the industry.

---

[2]Beta is the covariance of a stock's price with changes in the market average. If a stock swings with the market, but more widely, it will have a beta greater than 1.0; if the swing is less volatile, the beta will be less than 1.0.

Given the recognized safety of the investment, many telecommunications companies can raise large quantities of capital from the debt markets. In projects comparable to the ones we would consider, 75 percent of the necessary capital is raised in the debt markets at interest rates reflecting AA quality, on average. Moreover, I estimate that our cost of equity is only 14 percent as compared to 20 percent for computer software. If we make these changes, notice what they would do to our capital costs (using 1987 data):

	Weight	Cost	Weighted Cost
Debt	75%	6.08%	4.56%
Equity	25	14.00	3.50
Total			8.06%

Especially at today's relatively low capital costs, telecommunications projects yield favorable present value ratios. I contrast this with the computer software and workstation division where, although sales and profitability are strong, risks are high. Independent companies are financed by higher yield debt and more equity with higher expected total returns. In my book, their hurdle rate should reflect these higher cost of funds.

There is another subtlety. In 1988, our corporate tax rate is 34 percent, but heavier write-offs for R&D in the computer software and workstation division will potentially yield a lower divisional tax rate of, say, 25 percent. This is the case, despite the division's higher tax rate in recent years, due to the elimination of investment tax credits. The firm's marginal interest costs before taxes are about 10.1 percent. At 34 percent, this means the after-tax cost of interest is only 6.67 percent for telecommunications, compared to a possible 7.58 percent for computer software and workstations.

In short, I believe that we are really rationing equity funds. We should be seeking a constant rate of return on equity. Those of us who benefit from lower risk, and hence can trade on our equity more extensively, should not be penalized.

Implicit in Mr. Aragon's argument, as Mr. Barrymore understood it, was that, if each division in the company had a different hurdle rate, the costs of the various forms of capital would remain the same (except perhaps for the tax element). However, the mix of capital used would change in the calculation. Low-risk operations would use leverage more extensively, while the high-risk divisions would have little or no debt funds. Thus, lower-risk divisions would have lower hurdle rates.

Mr. Aragon's views were supported by several others within Teletech; opposition was just as strong, however, particularly within the computer software and workstation division. Fred Alegra, division manager, expressed his opinion as follows:

All money is green. We should be putting our money where the returns are best. A single hurdle rate may deprive an underprofitable division of investments in order to channel more funds into a more profitable division, but isn't that the aim of the process?

In reality, we don't finance each division separately. The corporation raises capital based on its overall prospects and record. The diversification of the company probably helps keep our capital costs down and enables us to borrow more in total than the sum of the capabilities of the divisions separately. As a result, developing separate hurdle rates is both unrealistic and misleading. All our stockholders want is for us to invest our funds wisely in order to increase the value of their stock. This happens when we pick the most promising projects, irrespective of their source.

Several years ago, we installed probability calculations in our project evaluations in order to determine the expected value of projects. I thought the purpose of this calculation was to take risk and uncertainties fully into account. Multiple hurdle rates will only confuse things by adding a second dimension to our risk appraisals in a way that will obscure the meaning of the basic calculation.

Mr. Aragon countered these arguments as follows:

In deciding how much to loan us, lenders will consider the composition of risks. If money flows into safer investments, over time their willingness to lend us funds will tend to increase. While multiple hurdle rates may not reflect capital-structure changes on a day-to-day basis, over time they will reflect prospects more realistically.

Our stockholders are just as concerned with risk. If they perceive our business as being more risky than other companies, they will not pay as high a price for our earnings. Perhaps this is why our price/earnings ratio is below the industry average most of the time.

Probability calculations that lead to measures of the expected value of the return of projects measure average prospects. They do not consider the dispersion around the expected value. Projects with high dispersion should be less attractive.

It is not a question of whether we adjust for risk—we already do. We look for higher present value ratios before we fund riskier projects. The only question in my mind is whether we make these adjustments systematically or not. If we attribute a capital structure to a division or, for that matter, to a project, so that the rate of return on equity represents equivalent risks, then we are in a position to pick the projects with the best returns on imputed equity.

At the moment, as I understand it, our real problem is an inadequate and very costly supply of equity funds. If we are really rationing equity capital, then we should be striving for the best returns on equity for the risk. Multiple hurdle rates achieve this objective.

As he listened to these arguments, presented over the course of several months, Mr. Barrymore became increasingly concerned with some related considerations. First, the corporate strategy directed the company toward integrating the two divisions. One effect of using multiple hurdle rates would be to make justifying high-technology research and application proposals more difficult, since the required rate of return would be increased. Perhaps, he thought, multiple hurdle rates were the right idea, but the notion that they should be based on capital costs, rather than strategic considerations, was wrong. On the other hand, perhaps multiple rates based on capital costs should be used, but in allocating funds, higher NPV ratios should be used for screening projects in areas that were strategically less important. In Mr. Barrymore's mind, theory was certainly not clear on how to achieve strategic objectives when allocating capital.

Second, when the present value ratio had replaced the discounted rate of return as the primary economic screening tool, it had been adopted because it was considered an ideal tool for the economic rationing of capital, which was now a material problem for Teletech. Using a single measure of the cost of money (the hurdle rate or discount factor) made the present value-ratio results consistent, at least in economic terms. If Teletech adopted multiple rates for discounting cash flows, Mr. Barrymore was afraid the calculation would lose its meaning. A present value ratio of 1.2 : 1 would not mean the same thing among divisions. To him, a screening criterion had to be consistent and understandable, or its usefulness would decrease.

In addition, Mr. Barrymore was concerned with the problem of attributing capital structures to divisions. In the computer software and workstation division, a major software development project might be financed by debt, but this financing was feasible only because the corporation guaranteed the debt. Such projects were considered highly risky — perhaps at best warranting only a minimal debt structure. Also, Mr. Barrymore considered the debt-capacity decision difficult enough to make for the corporation as a whole, let alone for each division. Judgments could only be very crude.

In further discussions with those in the organization about the use of multiple hurdle rates, Mr. Barrymore ran across two predominant trains of thought. One argument held that the investment decision should never be mixed with the financing decision. A firm should decide what its investments should be and then how to finance them most efficiently. Adding leverage to a present value calculation would distort the results. Use of multiple hurdle rates was simply a way of mixing financing with investment analysis. This argument also held that a single rate left the risk decision clear cut: management could simply adjust its standard (demanded present value ratio) as risks increased.

The contrasting line of reasoning noted that the weighted-average cost of capital tended to represent an average market reaction to a mixture of risks. Lower-than-average-risk projects should probably be accepted even though they did not meet a weighted-average criterion. Higher-than-normal-risk projects should provide a return premium. While the multiple-hurdle-rate system was a crude way of achieving this end, at least it was a step in the right direction. Moreover, some argued that Teletech's objective should be to maximize return on equity funds, and, because equity funds were and would remain a comparatively scarce resource, a multiple-rate system would tend to maximize returns to stockholders better than a single-rate system.

Mr. Barrymore had one further factor to consider. A recently concluded study that reviewed the actual results against forecasts for new investments made 5 to 10 years ago produced disturbing results. Although the methodology might have been debatable, the results seemed consistent with his hunch: the real returns on projects, according to the study, were about three percentage points less than originally forecast, on average.

CONCLUSION

Mr. Barrymore could not realistically hope that all the issues before him would be resolved systematically anytime soon. However, he did want to institute a pragmatic system of appropriate hurdle rates (or one rate) that would facilitate judgments in the changing circumstances Teletech faced.

The capital-budgeting process for 1989 would begin with the submission of plans and expenditure proposals by division managers in September 1988. Some business segments within the two divisions already had begun to make preliminary plans. If any changes were to be made in this coming year's budgeting analysis, the announcements would have to be made soon.

EXHIBIT 1   Divisional Financial Data for the Years Ended December 31 (dollars in millions)

Telecommunications Division

	1986	1987
Revenues	$1,370	$1,476
Operating income	315	360
Earnings before interest & taxes	289	338
Interest expense	93	104
Interest income	16	17
Income taxes	103	85
Net income	$ 109	$ 166
Identifiable assets	$2,879	$3,014
Long-term debt	952	985
Net identifiable assets	$ 885	$ 962

Computer Software and Workstation Division

	1986	1987
Revenues	$210	$538
Operating income	20	68
Earnings before interest & taxes	20	68
Interest expense	2	1
Interest income	2	2
Income taxes	9	24
Net income	$ 11	$ 45
Identifiable assets	$329	$524
Long-term debt	4	12
Net identifiable assets	$256	$292

EXHIBIT 2 Comparative Industry Data, 1987

	P/E Ratio	Payout Ratio	Dividend Yield	ROE	Debt/Total Capital	Beta
Telecommunications Services Industry						
Altel	10.6	49.8%	5.4%	15.3%	47.5%	0.90
Ameritech	10.5	60.2	5.1	15.6	36.9	0.85
AT&T	14.9	63.8	4.3	14.1	33.3	0.85
Bell Atlantic	11.2	61.4	5.5	14.2	37.3	0.80
BellSouth	11.4	63.6	5.6	13.9	34.5	0.95
Comm. Sat.	15.2	62.2	4.1	6.9	39.0	0.90
MCI	25.9	0.0	0.0	6.3	19.8	1.20
NYNEX	10.9	59.4	5.4	13.9	39.8	0.85
Pacific Telesis	12.4	74.2	6.0	12.0	40.2	0.90
Computer Software and Peripherals Industry						
AGS Computers ..	15.3	0.0%	0.0%	13.3%	30.5%	1.55
Ashton-Tate	14.1	0.0	0.0	24.1	3.0	1.55
Computer Sciences	19.7	0.0	0.0	13.0	20.9	1.25
Lotus	17.8	0.0	0.0	35.6	12.9	1.55
Microsoft	39.7	0.0	0.0	32.7	0.8	NA
Teletech	12.5	51.2	4.1	14.8	44.3	1.00

EXHIBIT 3   Weighted-Average Cost of Capital

	After-Tax Cost of Debt	Cost of Equity	Percent of Capital		Weighted-Average Cost
			Debt	Equity	
1981–1	9.31%	19.12%	54.5%	45.5%	13.77%
2	9.31	19.47	54.8	45.2	13.90
3	10.93	21.32	55.1	44.9	15.60
4	9.40	19.72	55.2	44.8	14.02
1982–1	9.68	19.86	55.8	44.2	14.18
2	9.89	20.30	56.9	43.1	14.38
3	8.42	18.34	57.5	42.5	12.63
4	7.13	16.54	57.4	42.6	11.14
1983–1	7.10	17.51	47.3	52.7	12.59
2	7.39	17.85	47.1	52.9	12.92
3	7.84	18.65	46.8	53.2	13.59
4	7.88	18.83	46.3	53.7	13.76
1984–1	8.15	19.82	45.8	54.2	14.48
2	9.11	20.56	46.5	53.5	15.23
3	8.60	19.52	46.3	53.7	14.47
4	7.54	18.50	45.7	54.3	13.49
1985–1	7.83	18.86	45.2	54.8	13.87
2	6.63	17.16	44.6	55.4	12.46
3	6.82	17.37	44.1	55.9	12.72
4	6.24	16.26	44.0	56.0	11.85
1986–1	5.58	14.78	43.7	56.3	10.76
2	5.65	14.80	47.5	52.5	10.45
3	5.17	14.35	46.3	53.7	10.10
4	5.06	14.11	45.6	54.4	9.98
1987–1	5.15	14.25	44.2	55.8	10.23
2	5.89	15.40	44.0	56.0	11.22
3	6.40	16.42	43.8	56.2	12.03
4	6.08	15.99	44.3	55.7	11.60

General Motors Corporation, 1988

In mid-April 1988, some observers were arguing that General Motors had misallocated its capital over the previous few years, and contended that GM's core business, automobile manufacturing, was the main arena of value destruction within the company. Among the automotive hands within the company, the criticism was apostasy. To long-time employees, GM was the virtual embodiment of the automobile industry, and to question GM's continuing investment in its automotive division was to challenge its very corporate identity.

The debate over GM's performance focused on two specific topics. First, both the company's defenders as well as its critics wished to establish the soundness of GM's continued massive investment in its core automotive business, an investment which totaled roughly $40 billion in the 1980s alone for tooling, facilities, and product design. In order to assess this investment correctly, it would be necessary to determine the appropriate cost of capital for General Motors Corporation as a whole and also for GM's major nonautomotive operating divisions. Second, in the spring of 1988, there were those who suspected that GM was attempting to overcome shortcomings in its automotive performance by shifting profits to other divisions, such as its financing subsidiary, General Motors Acceptance Corporation (GMAC), and its consolidated data-processing services division, Electronic Data Systems (EDS).

THE COMPANY

In 1988 General Motors was composed of three major consolidated entities and one major unconsolidated operation, GMAC. The three consolidated divisions were, in order of revenues, the automotive operation (identified as GMC in this discussion to distinguish

This case was written by Casey S. Opitz under the direction of Robert F. Bruner.

Copyright © 1988 by the Darden Graduate Business School Foundation, Charlottesville, VA. Revised August 1990.

the corporation's automotive activities from the performance of GM, the consolidated corporate entity), the aerospace and electronics operation, General Motors Hughes Electronics (GMHE), and Electronic Data Systems (EDS). GMC had 31 major operating divisions, including its North American nameplates Chevrolet, Pontiac, Oldsmobile, Buick, Cadillac, and GMC Truck. GMHE had two divisions, Hughes Aircraft Company and Delco Electronics Corporation.

As shown in Exhibits 1 and 2, in 1987, consolidated GM revenues totaled over $100 billion on an $87 billion asset base, excluding GMAC's unconsolidated gross assets of $98.5 billion. GMC's worldwide automotive business accounted for over 90 percent of consolidated revenues, as befitted the largest vehicle manufacturer in the world. But, in 1987, due to intense competition and, according to some, boring "look-alike" cars with poor maintenance records, GMC sold 9.5 percent fewer cars than in 1986 and its share of the domestic market had declined from 40.3 percent in 1985 to 34.7 percent in 1987 as unit sales declined from 9.3 million in 1985 to 7.8 million in 1987 (over the same period, both Ford and Chrysler increased unit sales).

To recover this loss, GMC was planning to introduce 11 new models and 21 vehicles with major redesigns in 1988 and 1989. The company also planned to improve profits through a cost-cutting program to run through 1990. Since mid-1986, salaried positions had declined by 36,000, and cost reductions totaling $3.7 billion were implemented in 1987.

Analysts expected GM sales to increase 5 percent in 1988 and 3 percent in 1989.[1] Over the same period, earnings per share were projected to increase 7 percent, then decline 25 percent to $8. Return on equity was expected to remain at 11.5 percent, then decline to 8.0 percent. Dividends were expected to stay constant, taking the payout ratio to 47 percent and subsequently to 63 percent. Capital expenditures were forecasted to remain weak.

Electronic Data Systems designed and operated large data-processing and communications systems. The division was primarily involved with benefits administration, engineering and manufacturing technologies, and business information systems. In 1987, two thirds of its revenues were from GMC, as shown in Exhibit 3. The division was acquired in October 1984 for $2.5 billion through an offer to exchange each share of EDS common stock for either $44.00 in cash or $35.20 in cash plus two tenths of a share of Class E common stock plus a Contingent Note.[2] In June 1985, the Class E shares underwent a two-for-one stock split. In December 1986, GM paid Ross Perot, the founder of EDS, $750 million for his 11.8 million Class E shares, his outstanding Contingent Notes, and certain contractual tax obligations assumed by GM at the time of the acquisition. In 1987, the stock price of E shares ranged between $24 and $51. As established at the time of the initial exchange, each Class E share was worth one fourth of a vote (post-split) at the GM annual meeting or on other GM issues submitted to stockholders.

---

[1] *Value Line Investment Survey,* June 24, 1988.

[2] Each Contingent Note was payable no later than seven years after the acquisition and guaranteed, in effect, that GM would pay the holder the difference between $62.50 (post-split) and the then market price of the Class E stock.

EDS's revenues, including business with GM, increased from $3.4 to $4.4 billion between 1985 and 1987, and the percentage growth from customers outside GM increased 47 percent over the same two-year period. Returns on sales increased from 5.5 to 7.3 percent, and EDS's retained earnings doubled in the same period. Earnings per share rose from $1.57 in 1985 to $2.65 in 1987, and dividends per share rose from $0.20 to $0.52. Some equity analysts regarded EDS's non-GM business as a "growth company" with the potential to achieve annual growth in revenue of 20 percent through 1993.

Although 1987 was a slow year for EDS, analysts[3] expected revenues, excluding the interest income, to increase to $4.7 billion in 1988. Earnings per share were expected to rise 17 percent to $3.10, and dividends were projected to grow 31 percent to $0.68. However, return on equity was forecasted to fall about 3 percentage points to 28 percent. Capital spending was expected to rise from $346 million in 1987 to $500 million in 1988.

Hughes Aircraft Company, a manufacturer of navigation, avionics, and communications systems for military and aviation applications, was acquired from the Howard Hughes Medical Institute by GM on December 31, 1985, for $2.7 billion in cash, 50 million shares (100 million shares after the March 1988 stock split) of Class H common stock, and a guarantee to pay the Howard Hughes Medical Institute on December 31, 1989, the amount by which the market value of the Class H stock was below $30 (post-split), up to $20 per share, for each share the Institute still held. GM also issued 15 million shares to owners of GM common stock (properly called "$1⅔ par value common stock" but popularly referred to as "GM common stock") as a dividend in January 1986. As established at the time of the acquisition, each Class H share was worth one fourth of a vote (post-split) in corporate matters.

At the time of its acquisition of Hughes Aircraft Company, GM merged its Delco Electronics division with Hughes to form GMHE, although both Delco and Hughes were operated largely as independent companies. Delco produced automotive electronics, including car radios and stereos, electronic controls, and microprocessors for automotive applications. GM's long-run strategy for GMHE was to apply technology developed by Hughes to evolving automotive electronics and control systems requirements. As shown in Exhibit 3, GMC provided about one third of GMHE's revenues.

In 1986, GMHE's revenues increased 9.9 percent, then held steady at roughly $10.5 billion in 1987 while net income margin rose from 4.3 percent to 5.0 percent as cost of goods sold fell. Earnings per share increased 37 percent to $1.67 between 1985 and 1987.

Value Line analysts projected revenues would increase to $12 billion over the next two years, but return on equity was forecasted to remain steady at 9.5 percent. Capital spending at GMHE was expected to rise from $468 million in 1987 to $760 million in both 1988 and 1989:

> Hughes' aerospace and defense unit should continue to grow despite cutbacks in military spending. Priority is increasingly being given to upgrade existing weapons systems and extend their applications. That's right up Hughes' alley. . . . Prospects at Delco Electronics are improving. . . . With the electronic content in automobiles continuing to rise, albeit at a slower pace

---

[3]*Value Line Investment Survey,* June 17, 1988.

than in recent years, sales and earnings for the division probably will advance about 5 percent in 1988 and about 9 percent in 1989.[4]

General Motors Acceptance Corporation, an unconsolidated company wholly owned by GM, was one of the largest financial institutions in the world. Exhibit 3 provides financial data on GMAC. Through 1987, GMAC was accounted for by the single-line equity method, although accounting standards required that it be fully consolidated by the end of 1988; this change would not affect net income or equity, but GM assets and liabilities as reported on the parent company's financial statements would increase.

Three quarters of GMAC's financing revenues came from retail (car buyer) financing, primarily of GMC's cars and trucks, and 9 percent resulted from lease financing. GMAC's financing receivables grew at an average annual rate of almost 16 percent throughout the 1980s, stalling only during the economic recession of 1982 and 1983, when wholesale (car dealer inventory) financing actually declined.

Although GMAC had focused its attention on its core business of financing the sale of GM vehicles to dealers, fleets, and retail buyers, it had expanded cautiously into other businesses. Through the purchase of Colonial Mortgage Group and the servicing portfolio and servicing facilities of Norwest Mortgage in 1985, GMAC became a large originator and servicer of mortgages (originations were $5.1 billion in 1987 and the servicing portfolio totaled $24.5 billion). In this business, the company acquired mortgages through its Colonial offices or from other financial institutions, held them for 60 to 90 days, and then sold mortgage packages to large investors but retained the collection and payment process as a fee-based business.

GMAC's net income varied considerably between 1983 and 1987, as substantial increases in gross revenues were matched or even exceeded by interest expense, operating costs, or loss provisions. Part of the variability of GMAC's earnings was due to its strategic decision to finance not only short-term floating-rate wholesale receivables but also to a great extent intermediate-term, fixed-rate retail receivables with a huge ($33.3 billion outstanding at 12/31/87) commercial paper program. Consequently GMAC's profitability was exposed to rapid changes in short-term interest rates.

Comparative industry data for each of GM's four major divisions are provided in Exhibit 4.

SALES INCENTIVE: LOW-COST AUTOMOBILE LOANS

In late August of 1986, GM responded to stagnant growth in automobile unit sales by offering consumer loans at the unprecedented interest rate of 2.9 percent for retail contracts, with a term of 24 months along with other, less spectacular below-market-rate financing choices for longer-term retail contracts. The other U.S. automobile manufacturers quickly followed suit. At the time, the open-market interest rate on four-year retail

---

[4]*Value Line Investment Survey,* July 15, 1988.

new-automobile loans was about 10 percent. GMAC acquired $47.0 billion of new-car and truck retail and wholesale financing (3.7 million units) in 1986, compared with $33.2 billion and 2.6 million units in 1985, although it was estimated that only a relatively small proportion of these assets represented 2.9 percent retail contracts. The figures fell back to $34.1 billion and 2.4 million units in 1987, which caused net retail financing to increase by $13.4 billion in 1986 and $2.4 billion in 1987.

Analysts wondered why GM chose to offer concessionary financing terms, rather than simply to cut the prices of its automobiles. Although some marketing professionals defended the move by explaining that low-interest financing lowered car buyers' monthly payments more effectively than the alternative of cash rebates as a sales incentive (and this was important, because the average car buyer worried about the monthly payment more than the car's selling price), some financial observers speculated that GM sought to disguise the performance of its automotive division by sharing its results with GMAC. Under the special rate financing programs offered by GM, most notably in 1986, an interest rate differential was paid to GMAC by GM's car groups for each vehicle financed by GMAC at a below-market rate. These payments, although received in cash, were included in unearned income by GMAC and were recognized as income over the life of the retail contract. (In contrast, the payments represented selling expense to the automotive business in the year the vehicle was sold.) These payments from GMC to GMAC constituted 7 percent of GMAC gross revenues in 1987, 11 percent in 1986, and 3 percent in 1985. The effect of these programs was to reduce GMC's earnings in the initial year and to boost GMAC's earnings over the life of the retail contract. GM filed a consolidated tax return, which included GMAC's earnings.

Other analysts speculated that GMC's cost of capital may have been higher than that of GMAC, because GMC had a huge capital investment and, therefore, was inherently riskier. As a result, the present value of losses taken at GMC would be smaller than if they were taken at GMAC.

THE COST OF CAPITAL

Because much of the criticism of GM was based on its performance against an assumed cost of funds, attention turned to estimating the cost of capital for GM and its main business units GMC, GMHE, EDS, and GMAC. A variety of tools for estimating the return investors required were available to analysts.

Weighted-average cost of capital was defined as the proportion of debt in the capital structure times the after-tax cost of debt, plus the proportion of equity in the capital structure times the cost of equity. Data on GM's consolidated debt are provided in Exhibit 5. In 1988, the company's bonds were rated Aa3 by Moody's and AA − by Standard & Poor's.

On the other side of the coin, techniques for measuring the average cost of equity, as broken down for General Motors in Exhibits 6 and 7, were more varied than those for measuring debt costs. The alternative methods are described in the appendix to this case.

Exhibits 8, 9, 10 and 11 contain data relevant to the calculation of equity costs using the estimation approaches given in the appendix. The following data, also derivable from the exhibits, are necessary for the calculations as well:

- Projected earnings/common share = $10.75.
- 1987 average price/earnings ratio = 5.2.
- Projected dividends/share = $5.00.
- Expected return on equity = 10.7 percent.

Exhibit 12 provides general U.S. economic data and forecasts.

CONCLUSION

From the data provided on GM, a stock analyst, individual investor, or corporate financial officer could attempt to derive at least five different corporate hurdle rates, depending on how they valued the cost of debt. In addition, it would be necessary to determine whether the same hurdle rates should apply to all divisions. Was it fair to assume that the cost of equity was the same for each division? Was it fair to assume that the cost of debt was the same for each? A breakdown of cost of debt by division was not available; if debt costs should be different by division, what should the cost of capital be for each? What should be the expected impact of relative stock price volatility? And how would divisional growth, and divisional dividends, affect the cost of capital? What was the effect of preferred and preference stock?

Finally, had General Motors really misallocated capital, and, if so, what financial decision should have driven its choice to avail itself of or avoid the use of low-interest loans and intercompany transfers in 1986 and 1987?

Appendix

COST OF EQUITY

Formulas for estimating the cost of equity, include the following:

The **earnings capitalization approach** holds that the cost of equity is that rate at which expected earnings must be capitalized to yield the present stock price. The formula is:

$$K_e = \frac{\text{Expected earnings/share}}{\text{Present stock price}}$$

When using this formula, analysts often simply invert the price/earnings ratio.

The **constant dividend-growth model** recognizes that investors receive returns from two sources: (1) current income in the form of a stock's dividend yield (dividend/stock price) and (2) capital gains from the growth rate *(g)* in the stock price. The formula is:

$$K_e = \frac{\text{Expected dividends}}{\text{Present stock price}} + \text{Expected long-term growth rate } (g)$$

where:

Growth rate $= (1 - \text{Payout ratio}) \times \text{Expected return on equity.}$

Risk premium assumes that investors require some return on risky stock yields over the cost of a risk-free security, such as Treasury bills:

$K_e =$ Current risk-free rate of return $+$ (Historical average return on equity $-$ Historical average risk-free return)

The **capital asset pricing model (CAPM)** builds on the risk-premium approach but takes into account the volatility of the stock in question. It uses the stock's beta (the covariance of the stock's price with average market price changes) as a measure of risk to raise or lower the size of the risk premium. The formula is:

$K_e =$ Current risk-free rate of return $+$ [Beta $\times$ (Return on market portfolio $-$ Risk-free return)]

The result is called the *risk-adjusted discount rate*.

EXHIBIT 1 Consolidated Income Statements (dollars in millions, except per share data)

	For the Years Ended December 31			
	1984	*1985*	*1986*	*1987*
Net revenues:				
Manufactured goods	$83,699.7	$95,268.4	$101,506.9	$100,118.5
Computer services	190.2	1,103.3	1,306.8	1,663.4
Total revenues	83,889.9	96,371.7	102,813.7	101,781.9
Cost of sales	70,217.9	81,654.6	89,198.3	87,204.4
SG&A	4,003.0	4,294.2	5,590.8	5,896.1
Depreciation	2,663.2	2,777.9	3,499.2	3,417.5
Amortization	2,305.8	3,430.6	3,094.1	2,694.5
Operating income	4,700.0	4,214.4	1,430.9	2,569.4
Interest income*	1,713.5	1,299.2	983.1	1,066.7
Capitalized interest	23.3	52.6	183.3	97.5
Interest expense†	932.5	944.9	1,137.0	1,728.2
Income before taxes	5,504.3	4,621.3	1,460.3	2,005.4
Income taxes (credit)	1,805.1	1,630.3	(300.3)	(59.9)
Income after taxes	3,699.2	2,991.0	1,760.6	2,065.3
Equity in earnings of unconsolidated subs. (primarily GMAC)	817.3	1,008.0	1,184.1	1,485.6
Net income	$4,516.5	$3,999.0	$2,944.7	$3,550.9
Preferred & preference dividends	$12.5	$11.6	$10.8	$13.7
Earnings available to common stockholders	$4,504.0	$3,987.4	$2,933.9	$3,537.2
Earning on:				
$1⅔ par common‡	4,498.3	3,883.6	2,607.7	3,178.9
Class E common§	5.7	103.8	136.2	139.1
Class H common‖	—	—	190.0	219.2
Earnings/share on:				
$1⅔ par common‡	$14.27	$12.28	$8.21	$10.06
Class E common§	0.16	1.57	2.13	2.65
Class H common‖	—	—	1.48	1.67
Stock prices:				
$1⅔ par common‡—high	$82.8	$85.0	$88.6	$94.1
—low	61.0	64.3	65.9	50.0
Class E common§—high	23.8	46.8	49.6	51.0
—low	18.3	20.8	24.8	24.0
Class H common‖—high	—	25.0	24.8	25.3
—low	—	19.0	16.3	19.5

* Includes in 1986 and 1987 dealer inventory financing previously received by GMAC.

† Includes interest paid to GMAC of $84 million in 1986 and $741 million in 1987 on an intercompany loan related to dealer financing.

‡ $1⅔ par value common stock was the stock of General Motors Corporation. Each share was entitled to one vote.

§ Class E stock was that of EDS acquired by GM in October 1984. Each share was entitled to one-fourth vote.

‖ Class H stock was that of GMHE acquired by GM in December 1985. Each share was entitled to one-fourth of a vote.

EXHIBIT 2 Consolidated Balance Sheets (dollars in millions)

	December 31			
	1984	*1985*	*1986*	*1987*
Cash & equivalents	$8,567.4	$5,114.4	$4,018.8	$4,706.4
Receivables	7,357.9	7,282.0	11,304.3	22,194.1
Net inventories	7,359.7	9,723.5	8,825.7	9,695.7
Prepaid expenses	428.3	2,136.1	2,619.6	3,175.3
Total current assests ...	23,713.3	24,256.0	26,768.4	39,771.5
Equity in net assets of unconsolidated subs. (primarily GMAC)	4,603.0	5,718.5	7,232.3	7,977.0
Other investments	2,488.6	3,260.0	2,498.7	2,446.6
Gross PP&E	41,051.3	48,978.0	58,034.4	63,016.4
Less depreciation	(21,649.8)	(24,325.0)	(27,658.0)	(30,976.0)
Net PP&E	19,401.5	24,653.0	30,376.4	32,040.4
Net intangible assets	1,938.5	5,945.3	5,717.2	5,186.4
Total assets	$52,144.9	$63,832.8	$72,593.0	$87,421.9
Accounts payable	$4,743.5	$7,322.2	6,368.0	$7,087.8
Loans payable	3,086.0	2,655.2	2,730.1	2,878.7
Taxes payable	618.9	243.1	333.1	376.0
Accruals & other	8,988.2	12,078.0	13,416.9	15,185.7
Total current liab.	17,436.6	22,298.5	22,848.1	25,528.2
Long-term debt	2,417.4	2,500.2	4,007.3	3,949.3
Payable to GMAC	300.0	300.0	5,500.0	13,981.0
Capitalized leases	355.5	367.0	318.0	364.1
Other liabilities	5,671.9	6,879.8	6,991.7	8,229.4
Deferred credits	1,749.2	1,962.6	2,249.9	2,144.8
Preferred stocks	255.6	250.7	234.4	234.4
Preference stocks	529.2	531.4	—	2.0
Common stocks:				
$1⅔ par	2.9	6.6	532.3	521.1
Class E	—	6.6	5.4	5.2
Class H	—	—	6.6	6.5
Capital surplus	3,347.8	6,667.8	6,332.6	6,764.6
Retained earnings	20,796.6	22,606.6	23,888.7	25,771.7
Currency translation	(717.8)	(545.0)	(322.0)	(80.4)
Total equity	24,214.3	29,524.7	30,678.0	33,225.1
Total liab. & equity	$52,144.9	$63,832.8	$72,593.0	$87,421.9

Note: Excludes assets, liabilities, and equity of the unconsolidated finance subsidiary GMAC.

EXHIBIT 3   Summary Financial Statements (dollars in millions, except per share data)

	For the Year Ended December 31, 1987		
	EDS	*GMHE*	*GMAC§*
Revenues:			
GMC & affiliates	$2,883.3	$3,134.4	
Other customers	1,440.5	7,273.2	
Interest & other	112.1	73.4	
Total revenue	4,435.9	10,481.0	$13,400.7
Cost & expenses	3,905.8	9,581.8	11,024.3
Earnings before taxes ...	530.1	899.2	2,376.4
Income taxes	207.0	669.9	923.2
Net income	323.1	521.1	1,453.2
Adjustments to exclude effects of purchase accouting*		148.8	
Adjusted net income	323.1	669.9	1,453.2
Available net income†	$139.1	$219.2	$1,453.2
Average Class E or H shares outstanding (millions)‡	52.6	130.8	21.7
Stock price—high‡	$51.0	$25.3	NA
—low‡	24.0	19.5	NA
Earnings per share‡	$2.65	$1.67	$67.12
Dividends per share‡	$0.52	$0.36	$41.57
Long-term debt	$529.4	$168.4	$30,869.4
Equity	1,053.5	7,071.4	6,975.2
Average interest rate	8.8%	8.8%	7.7%

* GMHE: amortization of intangibles arising from Hughes acquisition.

† Net income multiplied by a fraction, the numerator of which was the weighted-average number of shares of Class E or H common stock outstanding (i.e., held by individuals or institutions other than GM) and the denominator of which was currently 121.9 million shares of Class E and 400 million post-split for Class H. GMHE excludes purchase accounting adjustment.

‡ Adjusted to reflect the two-for-one stock split in the form of a 100 percent stock dividend distributed on June 10, 1985, for EDS, and March 10, 1988, for GMHE. GMAC based on 21.65 million shares held by GM.

§ GMAC assets totaled $98.5 billion and short-term debt $50.9 billion.

EXHIBIT 4   Comparative Industry Data, 1987

	ROE	P/E Ratio	Yield	Payout Ratio	Debt/ Equity	Beta	Projected Percentage Average Rate of Growth for Five Years	
							Dividends	Earnings
Automotive								
Chrysler	19.8%	5.8	2.9%	16.9%	51.3%	1.45	18.5	3.0
Ford	25.0	4.9	4.0	19.3	9.5	1.20	26.5	12.0
Honda	13.6	12.3	1.0	12.2	21.7	1.00	10.5	9.0
Mack trucks	0.8	NMF	0.0	0.0	14.2	1.05	NMF	NMF
Navistar	12.2	20.7	0.0	0.0	29.7	1.25	NIL	23.5
GM (corporate)	10.7	5.2	7.1	49.7	55.1	0.95	3.0	5.5
Computer Services								
Auto Data Proc.	15.1%	22.8	1.0%	22.7%	23.5%	1.15	18.5	21.5
Bolt Beranek	16.8	28.4	0.3	7.6	104.9	1.25	7.0	27.5
Computer Sciences ..	11.3	19.2	0.0	0.0	30.9	1.25	NIL	21.5
ISC Systems	6.5	26.5	0.0	0.0	20.2	1.40	NIL	8.0
National Data	17.3	18.0	2.0	36.7	17.9	1.00	5.5	17.5
EDS	30.7	14.8	1.3	19.6	50.3	1.15*	22.5	18.0
Aerospace/Defense								
Boeing	9.6%	15.2	3.0%	45.2%	5.1%	0.95	11.0	15.0
General Dynamics ...	22.3	7.8	1.5	11.9	26.7	1.00	3.0	2.5
Grumman	3.5	NMF	3.8	149.3	83.5	1.00	7.0	14.5
Lockheed	20.9	7.4	2.6	19.6	42.5	1.25	20.0	8.0
McDonnell Douglas	9.9	9.8	3.3	31.9	25.9	1.00	11.5	13.0
GMHE	9.5	13.7	1.6	21.6	2.4	0.65*	12.0	10.0
Financial Service								
Beneficial Cp	12.2%	10.1	3.8%	55.0%	890.10%	1.20	7.0	10.5
Green Tree Accept ..	16.4	14.5	2.0	35.0	733.33	1.10	NIL	17.5
Household Int'l	19.8	9.5	3.7	38.0	614.30	1.15	8.5	19.0
Ryder System	13.2	15.4	1.5	24.0	203.00	1.25	11.0	13.0
Xtra Corp	5.2	17.2	2.4	43.0	244.80	.95	4.0	24.5
GMAC†	20.8	NA	NA	61.9	442.60	NA	NA	NA

*Prior to its acquisition, EDS's beta was 1.10; Hughes was owned by Howard Hughes Medical Institute and, therefore, had no beta before its acquisition.
†GMAC's ROE, payout, and debt/equity were actual figures.

Source: *Value Line Investment Survey.*

EXHIBIT 5   Long-Term Debt Outstanding (dollars in millions)

	Coupon Rate	Maturity	Amount Outstanding December 31	
			1986	1987
U.S. dollars	8.13%–14.70%	1989–2016	$2,618.0	$2,239.2
Other currencies	3.90%–14.40%	1989–2017	1,477.8	1,786.4
Total			4,095.8	4,025.6
Less unamortized discount (principally on $500 million of 14.7% notes due 1991)			88.5	76.3
Total			$4,007.3	$3,949.3

Maturities*	
1988	$321.1
1989	265.1
1990	217.5
1991	1,319.1
1992	220.0

* At December 31, 1987, the current portion of long-term debt was $401.4 million.

EXHIBIT 6   Statement of Equity Position, 1987 (dollars in millions)

	December 31, 1987
Preferred stock, $5 series at $100 per share	$153.0
Shares outstanding	1,530,194
$3.75 series at $100 per share	$81.4
Shares outstanding	814,100
Preference stock, $0.10 par value E series	$1.0
Shares outstanding	9,786,918
H series	$1.0
Shares outstanding	9,786,918
Common stock, $1⅔ par value..................	$521.1
Shares outstanding	312,654,018
Class E common, $0.10 par value	$5.2
Shares outstanding	51,601,687
Class H common, $0.10 par value	$6.5
Shares outstanding	65,434,936
Total capital stock at 12/31/87	$769.2
Capital surplus at 12/31/87	6,764.6
Retained earnings at 12/31/87	25,771.7
Net income in 1987	3,550.9
Dividends in 1987:	
Preferred, $5.00	7.7
Preferred, $3.75	3.0
Preference E, $0.13	1.3
Preference H, $0.18	1.7
$1⅔, $5.00/share	1,579.6
Class E common	27.4
Class H common	47.2
Total cash dividends in 1987	1,667.9
Retained earnings in 1987	1,883.0
Accumulated currency translation at 12/31/87	(80.4)
Total equity at 12/31/87	$33,225.1

EXHIBIT 7   Comparative Stock Price Data

	General Motors			Ford	Chrysler	S&P 500
	Common	Class E	Class H			
1984 High	$82.750	$23.750	—	$17.250	$ 9.250	$166.39
Low	61.000	18.250	—	11.000	15.000	151.08
1985 High	85.000	46.750	$25.000	19.750	20.875	207.26
Low	64.250	20.750	19.000	13.375	13.250	171.61
1986 High	88.625	49.625	24.750	31.750	31.375	248.61
Low	65.875	24.750	16.250	17.875	18.125	208.19
1987 High	94.125	51.000	25.325	56.375	48.000	329.36
Low	50.000	24.000	19.500	28.500	19.625	240.96
Feb 17, 88	69.000	36.875	53.125	44.500	25.750	259.21
2/18	67.500	36.875	53.625	42.250	24.875	257.91
2/19	69.125	37.625	54.000	44.750	25.125	261.61
2/22	70.625	38.500	53.875	44.250	25.500	265.64
2/23	70.125	38.500	55.500	44.500	25.000	265.02
2/24	70.000	39.750	56.125	45.125	24.875	264.43
2/25	68.625	40.000	57.000	44.250	24.625	261.58
2/26	69.125	39.625	56.375	44.250	24.625	262.46
2/29	72.250	40.125	57.000	45.125	25.125	267.82
3/1	71.125	41.500	56.500	45.500	24.500	267.22
3/2	71.125	41.750	56.375	45.875	24.875	267.98
3/3	70.750	41.875	56.250	46.000	24.375	267.88
3/4	71.500	42.500	56.500	46.000	24.750	267.30
3/7	72.000	43.000	56.500	46.000	24.500	267.38
3/8	72.750	42.875	29.375*	45.750	25.125	269.43
3/9	72.500	43.625	30.125	45.125	25.125†	269.06
3/10	70.250	42.375	29.625	43.375	24.250	263.84
3/11	71.750	41.500	30.000	44.375	24.500	264.94
3/14	71.750	41.875	31.000	44.250	24.375	266.37
3/15	71.750	41.750	32.500	44.000	24.250	266.13
3/16	73.750	42.125	33.000	44.125	24.250	268.65
3/17	73.500	42.750	34.250	44.625	24.750	271.22
3/18	72.000	42.250	35.375	44.750	24.625	271.12
3/21	72.000	41.625	36.625	44.125	24.000	268.74
3/22	72.250	41.000	37.125	43.750	24.375	268.84
3/23	72.375	40.125	39.500	43.750	24.375	268.91
3/24	71.000	39.250	36.875	43.125	24.125	263.35
3/25	69.250	39.250	34.125	42.000	23.750	258.51
3/28	69.500	38.375	33.750	42.250	23.375	258.06
3/29	70.875	38.125	34.000	42.500	23.625	260.07
3/30	71.250	38.500	34.125	43.625	23.500	258.07
3/31	71.375	38.500	34.250	42.875	23.500	258.89

* Two-for-one stock split.
† Dividend of $0.25.

Sources: *ISL Daily Stock Price Index* and *Value Line Investment Survey.*

EXHIBIT 8 Quarterly Stock-Performance Data

	Corporate			Electronic Data Systems*		
	EPS	P/E	Yield	EPS	P/E	Yield
1984—1	$5.11	3.2	1.6%	$0.30		
2	5.09	3.1	2.0	0.31		
3	1.31	15.3	1.6	0.32	15.6	0.5%
4	2.71	7.3	1.6	0.33	13.6	0.0
1985—1	3.32	5.4	1.7	0.32	25.0	0.1
2	3.58	5.0	1.7	0.35	28.6	0.1
3	1.53	11.1	1.8	0.43	19.8	0.1
4	3.85	4.9	1.6	0.47	21.3	0.1
1986—1	3.52	6.0	1.5	0.46	23.9	0.2
2	2.92	6.5	1.6	0.51	22.5	0.2
3	0.80	21.3	1.8	0.58	13.8	0.3
4	0.97	18.0	1.8	0.58	10.3	0.4
1987—1	2.62	8.1	1.5	0.53	12.3	0.5
2	2.80	7.6	1.5	0.59	17.8	0.3
3	2.28	9.3	1.5	0.68	15.4	0.3
4	2.36	6.4	2.1	0.85	9.4	0.4
1988—1E	3.11	5.6	1.8	0.73	12.3	0.5
2E	4.20	4.8	1.6	0.75	13.3	0.4
3E	0.75			0.80		
4E	2.69			0.82		
1991–93E	14.00	10.0	4.3	4.50	15.0	1.5

	GM Hughes Electronics*			GMAC†
	EPS	P/E	Yield	EPS‡
1984—1				
2				
3				
4				$36.24
1985—1				
2				
3				
4				47.16
1986—1	$0.39	14.1	0.3%	
2	0.43	12.8	0.3	
3	0.41	12.2	0.4	
4	0.26	21.2	0.3	54.74
1987—1	0.44	12.5	0.4	
2	0.44	13.6	0.4	
3	0.43	13.4	0.4	
4	0.36	16.7	0.4	67.12
1988—1E	0.45	17.8	0.3	
2E	0.45	17.8	0.3	
3E	0.50			
4E	0.40			54.75
1991–93E	2.60	14.0	2.3	

* Based on average EDS or GMHE shares outstanding.
† P/E and yield data unavailable for GMAC.
‡ Based on GMAC's 21.65 million outstanding shares.

Source: *Value Line Investment Survey.*

EXHIBIT 9   Bond and Preferred Stock Yields and Prime Lending Rate

	U.S. Government		AA Industrial	Prime	6-month Commercial Paper
	3-month	*30-year*			
1982 High	13.48%	14.22%	15.13%	17.00%	14.27%
Low	7.71	10.54	10.96	11.50	8.50
1983 High	9.34	11.88	12.62	11.50	9.68
Low	7.86	10.48	10.72	10.50	8.15
1984 High	10.47	13.44	14.13	13.00	11.34
Low	8.06	11.52	11.73	11.00	8.55
1985 High	8.52	11.81	12.43	10.75	9.23
Low	6.95	9.54	10.13	9.50	7.38
1986 High	7.07	9.54	10.41	9.50	7.62
Low	5.18	7.27	9.18	7.50	5.61
1987 High	6.40	9.61	11.09	9.00	7.96
Low	5.43	7.39	8.89	7.50	5.76
1987 Apr	5.64	8.25	9.43	7.75	6.50
May	5.66	8.78	9.93	8.25	7.04
Jun	5.67	8.57	9.77	8.25	7.00
Jul	5.69	8.64	9.71	8.25	6.72
Aug	6.04	8.97	9.95	8.25	6.81
Sep	6.40	9.59	10.62	8.75	7.55
Oct	6.13	9.61	10.70	9.25	7.96
Nov	5.69	8.95	10.07	9.00	7.17
Dec	5.77	9.12	10.13	8.75	7.49
1988 Jan	5.81	8.83	9.89	8.75	6.92
Feb	5.66	8.43	9.44	8.50	6.58
Mar	5.70	8.63	9.66	8.50	6.64
Apr	5.91	8.95	9.80	8.50	6.92

Preferred Stock Yields
(end of period)

	$3.75	*$5.00*	*Rating*
1982	10.2%	10.5%	AA+
1983	10.8	10.8	AA+
1984	10.1	10.3	AA+
1985	9.0	9.2	AA+
1986	7.2	6.9	AA
1987	8.7	8.9	AA
1988 Mar	8.2	8.3	AA−

Sources: *Moody's Bond Guide; Economic Report of the President; Federal Reserve Bulletin; Standard & Poor's Stock Guide.*

EXHIBIT 10   Average Returns on Securities, 1926–1987

	Arithmetic	Geometric
Common stock	12.1%	10.0%
T-bills	3.5	3.5
Long-term Treasuries	4.7	4.4

Source: *Stocks, Bonds, Bills, and Inflation*, 1987 Yearbook, Ibbotson Associates, Chicago, p. 25.

EXHIBIT 11   Treasury-Yield Data

	Historical* April 10, 1987	Current* April 11, 1988	Projected Average†	
			1988	1990–92
3 Months	5.21%	6.17%	5.80%	5.50%
6 Months	6.21	6.36		
Years—1	6.59	7.03		
2	6.91	7.05		
3	7.26	7.73		
4	7.47	7.99		
5	7.62	8.13		
6	7.74	8.27		
7	7.77	8.42		
8	7.88	8.55		
10	8.01	8.57		
14	8.20	8.89		
20	8.32	8.94		
30	8.20	8.80	8.50	7.50

* *The Wall Street Journal*
† *Value Line Investment Survey*

EXHIBIT 12   U.S. Economic Data and Forecasts

	1986	1987	Projected 1988
Real GNP growth	2.9%	2.9%	2.0%
Change in GNP deflator	2.6	3.0	3.3
Consumer price index	1.9	3.7	4.2
3-month Treasury bill	6.0	5.8	5.9
High-grade corporate bond	9.2	9.7	10.2
Change in personal consumption expend.	4.2	1.8	1.8
Net corporate profits (bill. $)	$126.9	$137.4	$138.3
Business failures per 10,000	120.0	102.0	NA

Sources: *Economic Report of the President;* and *Economic Outlook USA*, Spring 1988, p. 20.

Case 15

The Boeing 777

The Boeing 777 will set a new standard for aircraft around the world. With the introduction of the 777, we will be able to offer our airline customers a complete family of Boeing airplanes that meets any seating requirement from approximately 100 to 500 passengers. We believe the 777 will allow us to offer the right product for the changing market requirements of the 1990s and beyond.[1]

Shrontz says his mission is raising Boeing's return on equity from the recent average of about 12 percent. Although Boeing makes money while its main competitors don't, Shrontz isn't satisfied. "We've got to enhance our earnings," he says.[2]

It takes a lot of courage to launch an industrial program in this uncertain economic environment.[3]

In October 1990, Frank Shrontz officially announced the launch of the latest addition to the Boeing family, the 777. This plane would fit in a market niche of medium-to-large passenger airframes and would carry 350 to 390 passengers up to 7,600 nautical miles (14,000 kilometers; for instance, from Sydney to Tokyo or Los Angeles to Frankfurt). The first planes were expected to be delivered in May 1995 to United Airlines, which had announced firm orders for the 777 on October 15, 1990. No other orders had as yet been received.

---

[1]Frank Shrontz, chief executive officer, The Boeing Company, October 29, 1990.

[2]Dorin Jones Yang, "To Frank Shrontz, the Blue Yonder Is Anything but Wild," *Business Week*, July 9, 1990, p. 49.

[3]A quotation of Howard A. Rubel, airline industry analyst, with C. J. Lawrence, Morgan Grenfell, Inc., in "It's Fat and Snazzy—And Worth Billions to Boeing," *Business Week*, October 29, 1990, p. 32.

This case was prepared by Dena Gollish, Henrik Clausen, Niels Koggersbol, Peter Christey, and Professor Robert F. Bruner. The financial support of the Citicorp Global Scholars Program is gratefully acknowledged.

Copyright © 1992 by the Darden Graduate Business School Foundation, Charlottesville, VA, and INSEAD, Fontainebleau, France.

Industry analysts had mixed views on Boeing's decision to go ahead with the 777. Pessimists noted that Airbus Industrie and McDonnell Douglas both already had announced aircraft targeted for this niche and had sizable head starts on firm orders. This competition, they believed, would drive down prices for the aircraft. Furthermore, research-and-development expenditures on the 777—estimated at $4 billion to $5 billion— would be more than twice as high as for the 757 and 767 projects. If this new product failed, the financial loss would substantially deplete Boeing's book value of equity. Finally, Iraq's invasion of Kuwait and the ensuing international crisis had led to a sharp decline in airline travel. Political and economic conditions seemed to have turned against the project.

Optimists believed that the 777 would outperform its competitors and gain at least Boeing's historical 54 percent market share. Boeing believed that air travel would double by the year 2005, creating a large demand for new capacity. Moreover, the aging of large passenger aircraft would mean a replacement demand of 640 new units. Some analysts also pointed to the expected high growth rate on the routes targeted by the 777, resulting particularly from growth in the Asian market. In addition, many analysts believed that Boeing's R&D spending on the 777 could be used to develop other aircraft (e.g., a new derivative of the 747) at a much reduced cost. Finally, the 777 offered airlines the most flexibility in designing the interior of the aircraft and the best cost efficiency of all its competitors.

In October 1990, perhaps the prime question was whether the Boeing 777 project remained a sensible investment for Boeing. Two and one-half years had elapsed since

Share Prices, Compared to S & P 500

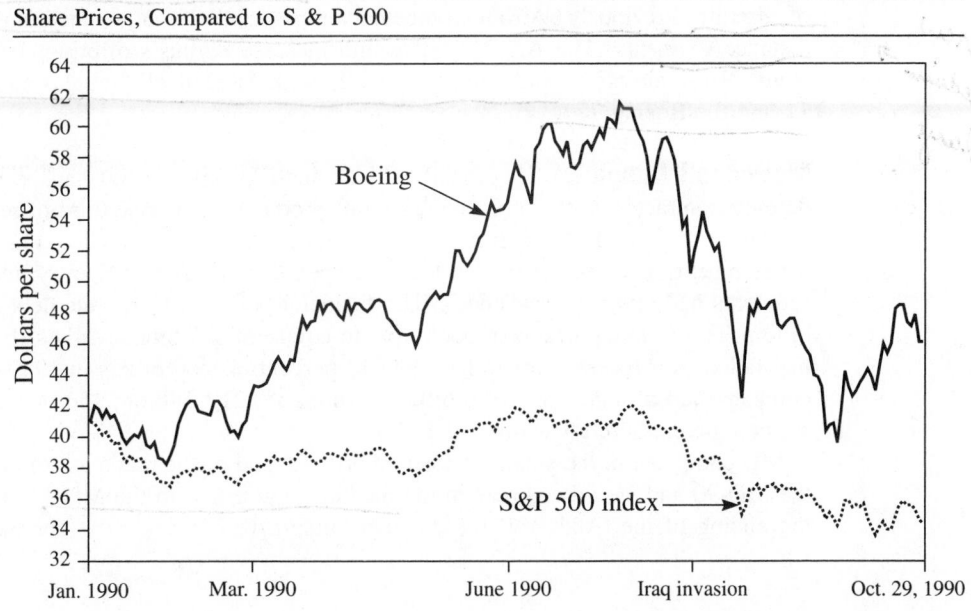

the start of the preliminary design effort. Political and economic conditions had worsened. *Value Line* noted:

> Boeing stock has been pummeled since Iraq's invasion of Kuwait [see graph of share prices], reflecting, we think, the surge in the cost of petroleum and jet fuel, which has sent airline fares rising and weakened global economies. As a result, passenger counts are under pressure and many investors are concerned that the boom in airliner demand will dissipate.[4]

Was the recent slump in Boeing's share price a result strictly of the Gulf Crisis, or was the stock market giving an advance signal of its evaluation of the Boeing 777? The advance orders for competitors' aircraft models to be launched in this segment had proved that demand existed for a new generation of aircraft, but would the new model be profitable at any level of demand? Finally and most importantly, would the Boeing 777 project serve Frank Shrontz's ultimate mission of improving Boeing's return on equity?

COMMERCIAL AIRCRAFT INDUSTRY

Only three companies built large airframes in 1990. These three had 90 percent of the total world market: Boeing (53 percent), Airbus Industrie (18 percent), and McDonnell Douglas (19 percent). Boeing was by far the largest player, not only in terms of current aircraft deliveries but also in terms of revenues, earnings, and aircraft orders.

Airbus Industrie.   Established 20 years earlier, Airbus had moved into second place in the world aircraft market, although it had yet to turn a profit. With the introduction of the A330 and A340 models in 1992–93, Airbus claimed it would have a full family of aircraft. Previously, Airbus competed mainly in the small-to-medium payload and distance segments. The A330/A340 would increase Airbus's offerings on both dimensions. These aircraft would compete directly with McDonnell Douglas's proposed MD-11 and the Boeing 777.

McDonnell Douglas.   Historically, McDonnell Douglas (MD) had been primarily a defense contractor, with commercial aircraft producing only one third of revenues. Consequently, the company's commercial-jet product range was limited and had shown little development. The decline in U.S. defense spending and Airbus's entry into key market segments had severely weakened MD's financial position. Corporate debt stood at $4.9 billion (representing a ratio of book debt to equity of 1.5 times). MD's share of market had fallen over recent years to less than 13 percent of total orders in 1989. In 1989, the company had revenues of $14.6 billion, profits of $219 million, and outstanding orders for commercial aircraft worth $21 billion.

MD competed in the small-payload, short-haul end of the market with the MD-80 and the MD-90 and would compete in the medium segment with the MD-11. In response to the ending of the Cold War, the company planned to increase the commercial-aircraft

---

[4]*Value Line Investment Survey,* October 12, 1990.

portion of sales from current levels of 36 to 50 percent over the next few years. To meet these goals, it was developing another new aircraft, the MD-12X, to compete with Boeing's 747-400. This project would cost $4 billion to $5 billion.

The Boeing Company.   Boeing was the world's leading manufacturer of commercial-jet aircraft. Half of its aircraft sales were to airlines within the United States. Boeing's estimated sales for 1990 were $27 billion (compared with $20 billion in 1989), and profits were expected to be approximately $1.4 billion (up from $675 million in 1989). The company had a record-breaking order backlog of $97 billion, enough to keep its plants operating at full capacity over the next three years.

Boeing had two principal business segments: commercial aircraft and defense (the latter included space and missile products). Exhibit 1 gives a breakdown by segment for sales, assets, and profits for 1987–89. The commercial-aircraft segment produced and sold four main airframes (the 737, 747, 757, and 767) and numerous derivatives of them. Boeing's defense segment was the main contractor on numerous military transportation projects and major missile systems. While the defense division had recorded losses in the most recent years, it provided valuable support to the commercial-aircraft group through the manufacturing of parts and the design and manufacture of electronic systems. Analysts also believed there were significant technology transfers from defense R&D to the commercial-aircraft segment.

Boeing possessed a remarkably strong balance sheet, with book value of debt making up only 4 percent of total capital. Exhibit 2 presents Boeing's balance sheets, and Exhibit 3 presents income statements for 1988 and 1989. Analysts were predicting that Boeing would increase the debt ratio to 14 percent over the next year or so because of future financing needs. Nevertheless, the company had historically shown an aversion to debt financing. Therefore, analysts believed that, in the long run, Boeing's debt capitalization would remain quite low.

DEMAND FOR COMMERCIAL AIRCRAFT

In 1989, world commercial-aircraft revenues exceeded $25 billion; total jet aircraft delivered were 398; orders outstanding were valued at $165 billion. While overall airline traffic was expected to increase by 5.2 percent per year over the next 15 years, traffic in Asia was forecasted to grow at a rate of 10.6 percent a year. At the 5.2 percent overall rate of increase, new aircraft sales would aggregate $615 billion by 2005.

The growth in aircraft demand was a function of increases in passenger air traffic, which in turn was a function of economic growth. Air traffic was highly sensitive to variations in consumer and business confidence. In the brief time since Iraq had invaded Kuwait, fuel prices had risen, passenger air traffic had declined, the inflow of aircraft orders had stopped, and several airlines had canceled existing orders. While the long-term association between economic growth and aircraft orders tended to be quite stable, the health of the commercial airlines tended to be a major determinant of aircraft orders in the short term; airlines could postpone purchases for a year or two, creating havoc in the finances of the aircraft manufacturers.

The demand for aircraft could be segmented along two dimensions: seating capacity and range in nautical miles. As Exhibit 4 reveals, the three major producers of aircraft covered the entire range. Commercial aircraft varied in price from approximately $35 million for Boeing's 737 to $145 million for the 747-400. Boeing produced 21 of the 737s per month, although many models of aircraft had production rates of 5 to 7 per year.

Despite the high up-front costs and the fact that most market segments could support only one model of aircraft, the major manufacturers tried to compete across all segments, partly because of the gains expected from derivative aircraft that could be developed to serve selected subsegments or new major segments. Derivatives had design and many parts in common with the original aircraft and, thus, could be developed and manufactured relatively inexpensively. These derivatives expanded a model's market, extended its lifetime, and led to economies of scale and experience. Incremental development costs of stretching an aircraft design were believed to be usually less than 25 percent of the original cost. Other factors that led the manufacturers to develop a broad range of aircraft included image issues (being a major player), time-based competition (each company trying to pre-empt the others in a particular segment), and pressure from major customers to fill a market niche.

Boeing was particularly adept at exploiting the advantages of aircraft derivatives. Its 707, 727, 737, and 757 models had similar fuselage shapes, which reduced design costs and allowed them all to be built using common production facilities. These basic shapes also were stretched and shortened into several different models to fill numerous product niches. In addition to development work on the 777, Boeing also was expected to begin working on a super jumbo jet (600+ passengers).

AIRCRAFT DEVELOPMENT AND LIFE CYCLE

Any individual airframe was characterized by huge outlays (for research, development, and tooling) and a long life cycle. The average new airplane in the early 1990s would cost over $4 billion to bring to production and might require 12 to 20 years before breaking even. Substantial negative cash flows would accumulate before an airframe product line broke even. Because of the financial strains a new product line might create, each new airframe was a "bet the ranch" proposition for the aircraft manufacturers. Over time, survival in the industry depended on introducing successful products and having the financial "deep pockets" with which to survive the cash-flow trough. Most analysts concluded, in fact, that few airframes ever yielded positive cumulative cash flows—but the few financial successes were spectacular.

Boeing aircraft tended to follow predictable sales patterns across their lives. Deliveries tended to rise to a peak during the first few years of availability and then decline moderately until a new version of the aircraft (a derivative) was introduced. This pattern was followed by one or more additional cycles of decline and new introduction. Exhibit 5 illustrates these cycles for four of Boeing's aircraft over their first 20 years of delivery.

THE 777

Boeing had been working on a new, revolutionary aircraft since 1988. The aircraft would be the largest and longest haul twin-bodied jet and (according to Boeing) the most flexible and cost-efficient plane ever. The aircraft's most unique feature would be a folding wing tip, which would enable it to fit into the smaller slots in airport terminals. The 777 also would be the first jet to use fly-by-wire technology, an advanced flying system already used on Airbus turbo-prop planes.

Analysts estimated that R&D expense on the 777 had amounted to hundreds of millions of dollars in the 1980s and $200 million in 1990 alone. The new aircraft created a revolution in Boeing's design and manufacturing processes. In terms of the design process, two features were unique:

- **Up-front involvement of the airlines.**   Boeing had asked six of its major customers to play active roles in designing the new aircraft in order to ensure that the aircraft would meet customer needs and, Boeing hoped, give it a competitive advantage over the A330/A340 and MD-11.
- **Use of "current engineering."**   That is, having 400 or so project engineers work side by side with the aircraft's designers. Until this development, designers worked independently, sent the plans over to the engineers, and then continued to make improvements. Each subsequent change cost upward of $10,000, and hundreds of such changes were made. With the 777, Boeing intended to get the details right before production started. The change in the relationship between design and production was organizational (i.e., the two groups would talk to each other before production began) and technological. Through an advanced CAD/CAM (computer-aided design and manufacturing) system, Boeing engineers could fully simulate production of the aircraft. The bugs could be found and eliminated before the aircraft went into production. Boeing hoped this design/production approach would save as much as 20 percent of the 777's estimated $4 billion to $5 billion development cost.   .8 → 1.0 B in Savings   average $4 B

Despite the many innovations, analysts believed that the R&D costs for the 777 would be higher than for any other plane to date. One analyst forecasted that the R&D expenditures would aggregate to $4.467 billion.[5] In addition to R&D, Boeing would incur major capital expenditures to double the size of the manufacturing facility in Renton, Washington, where the 747 and 767 aircraft were produced. A new facility would be built to produce the major wing components and advanced composite tailplanes. Analysts estimated that these facilities would cost nearly $1.5 billion. Boeing also planned to build a special laboratory for integrating and testing aircraft systems; the 777 and other aircraft would make use of this facility. The company also would increase its spending on employee training to focus on the CAD system used on the 777. Engineers would receive over 350,000 hours of training on this system. Some analysts predicted that all of these

---

[5]George Shapiro, Salomon Brothers.

new facilities and training programs would increase Boeing expenditures by $2.5 billion over the next few years.

With these large initial outlays, Boeing would need significant revenues to make the 777 program a success. The company expected each aircraft to sell for $130 million on average. Several analysts, however, believed that the A330/A340 and MD-11 would put downward pressure on this price, forcing Boeing to price the 777 at $100 million.

The 777 was targeted to the fastest-growing market segment in terms of passenger seats and distance. This segment serviced medium- and long-haul routes. Boeing estimated that, over the next 15 years, two thirds of aircraft sales by value would be in this market segment. If the company maintained its market share of approximately 50 percent, it would achieve unit sales of 1,000 aircraft in the 777's first 10 years of production. Production costs would begin at high levels and rapidly fall as the product moved down the learning curve. Boeing executives believed that the 777 would have a life span of 30 to 40 years.

FINANCIAL FORECAST AND ANALYSIS

Exhibit 6 contains a forecast of free cash flows from the Boeing 777 project, based on the casewriters' analyses and drawing on numerous assumptions of securities analysts in their published commentaries on the 777 project. The appendix to this exhibit discusses these forecast assumptions in detail. The primary implication of the forecast is that the internal rate of return (IRR) in the base case would be 19 percent.

Numerous sensitivity analyses of the IRR could be made. One important question was the impact of variations in aircraft prices. Another key assumption was the size of demand in the first 10 years. If the recession in the early 1990s were particularly long or severe, planes sold could fall well short of the estimate of 1,000. On the other hand, a resumption of prolonged economic growth could trigger higher sales, not only to replace aging planes but also to expand overall capacity. The IRRs associated with different unit prices and unit sales volumes in the first 10 years are given in Exhibit 7.

A key determinant of the attractiveness of the 777 project was Boeing's cost of capital. As Exhibit 8 reveals, relatively minor variations in discount rates produced rather large variations in project payback on a discounted-cash-flow (DCF) basis. If the cash flows were undiscounted, the payback would occur in the 10th year. At the other extreme, if cash flows were subject to a 20 percent discount rate, payback would never occur.

COST OF CAPITAL

Boeing's weighted-average cost of capital (WACC) could be estimated using the well-known formula:

$$WACC = [i \times (1 - t) \times W_d] + (K_e \times W_e)$$

where:

i = pretax cost of debt capital,

t = marginal tax rate,

W_d = proportion of debt in a market-value capital structure,

K_e = cost of equity capital, and

W_e = proportion of equity in a market-value capital structure.

Exhibit 9 gives information about Boeing and comparable companies to use in the WACC equation. Exhibit 10 depicts five-year stock-price performance relative to the Standard & Poor's (S&P) 500 Index. Boeing had faced a relatively low effective tax rate in the past; but, because of changes in tax and accounting regulations, its marginal effective tax rate was expected to rise to 34 percent in the future. In October 1990, the yield on long-term U.S. Treasury bonds was 8.82 percent, and the 64-year geometric average equity-market risk premium was 5.6 percent. At a recent stock price of $43 per share, Boeing's dividend yield was 2.5 percent. *Value Line* forecasted Boeing's dividends to grow at the rate of 17 percent over the next five years.

Analysts had pointed out that Boeing actually consisted of two separate businesses, the relatively more stable and (in the midst of the Gulf War crisis) thriving defense business and the more volatile commercial-aircraft business. Thus, the question arose of whether one should estimate *Boeing's* cost of capital to serve as the benchmark required rate of return. Would a required return on a portfolio of these two businesses be appropriate for evaluating the 777 project? If necessary, how might it be possible to isolate a required return for commercial aircraft?

CONCLUSION

Within the aircraft-manufacturing industry, the magnitude of risk posed by the launching of a major new jet aircraft was accepted as a matter of course. One observer said,

> Sustained success demands a willingness to gamble regularly, even though the effects of guessing wrong may be fatal. . . . The business of making and selling commercial airliners is not for the diffident or faint of heart. It is remarkably difficult and, by anyone's standard, intensely competitive. There are a few industries that consume as much or more capital; certain others rely as heavily on quantities of highly skilled personnel; probably no other is involved with as many advanced technologies.[6]

Other observers worried that the technical challenges might obscure the commercial considerations: "The mystery behind this business isn't building an airplane that flies and is safe. It's building an airplane that is salable and profitable."[7]

---

[6]John Newhouse, *The Sporty Game* (New York: Knopf, 1982), p. 92.

[7]A quotation of Wolfgang Demisch of UBS Securities, Inc., in "How Boeing Does It," *Business Week*, July 9, 1990, p. 50.

Frank Shrontz had indicated that his primary mission during his tenure as CEO of Boeing would be to raise the firm's return on equity. Given that the 777 would be the major new product introduction for Boeing in the 1990s, the prime question was whether it would help Shrontz pursue his objective.

EXHIBIT 1   Revenues, Operating Profits, and Identifiable Assets by Segment for the Boeing Company

	1987	1988	1989
Revenues:			
Commercial aircraft	$ 9,827	$11,369	$14,305
Defense and other	5,986	5,971	6,318
Total	15,813	17,340	20,623
Operating profit:			
Commercial aircraft	352	585	1,165
Defense and other	306	235	(243)
Total	658	820	922
Identifiable assets:			
Commercial aircraft	5,170	4,558	6,675
Defense and other	7,396	8,050	6,603
Total	12,566	12,608	13,278

Source: The Boeing Company annual reports.

EXHIBIT 2   Boeing Balance Sheets (dollars in millions)

	1988	1989
Assets		
Cash	$ 3,544	$ 1,863
Other current assets	5,017	6,797
Total current assets	8,561	8,660
Customer financing	1,039	822
Net property, plant, and equipment	2,703	3,481
Investments	305	315
Total assets	$12,608	$13,278
Liabilities and Stockholders' Equity		
Accounts payable	$ 4,697	$ 4,932
Current portion of long-term debt	7	5
Other current liabilities	697	291
Total current liabilities	6,705	6,673
Long-term debt*	251	275
Deferred taxes	205	174
Deferred investment credit	43	25
Stockholders' equity:†		
Common shares	1,341	1,736
Retained earnings	4,137	4,452
Treasury stock	(74)	(57)
Total stockholders' equity	5,404	6,131
Total liabilities and stockholders' equity	$12,608	$13,278

* Boeing's long-term debt consisted entirely of two issues: $250 million of 8.375% notes due December 31, 1996, and $37 million of long-term notes payable believed to bear floating rates of interest and currently costing 9.31%. The market value of the first bond issue was $234.5 million, found by valuing the issue at a discount rate of 9.73%, the average yield to maturity of AA-rated debt with five years to maturity. Because the notes payable yielded a floating rate, their market value equaled book value. Thus, the total market value of the two debt issues was estimated to be $271.5 million.

† In October 1990, Boeing had 346,436,214 common shares outstanding. At a trading price of $43 per share, Boeing's market value of equity was $14,896.76 million.

Source: The Boeing Company annual report, 1989.

EXHIBIT 3 Boeing Income Statements (in millions except per share data)

	1988	1989
Revenues	$16,962	$20,276
Cost and expenses	16,514	19,695
Earnings from operations	448	581
Other income (interest)	378	347
Interest expense	(6)	(6)
Profit before taxes	820	922
Taxes*	206	247
Effect of change in method of accounting for taxes		298
Net earnings	$ 614	$ 973
Earnings per share	$2.68	$4.23
Cash dividend per share	$1.0333	$1.11666

* Boeing's marginal tax rate was 35 percent

Source: The Boeing Company annual report, 1989.

EXHIBIT 4   Competitive Positioning of Major Jet Aircraft

Boeing and Competitors: Product Range

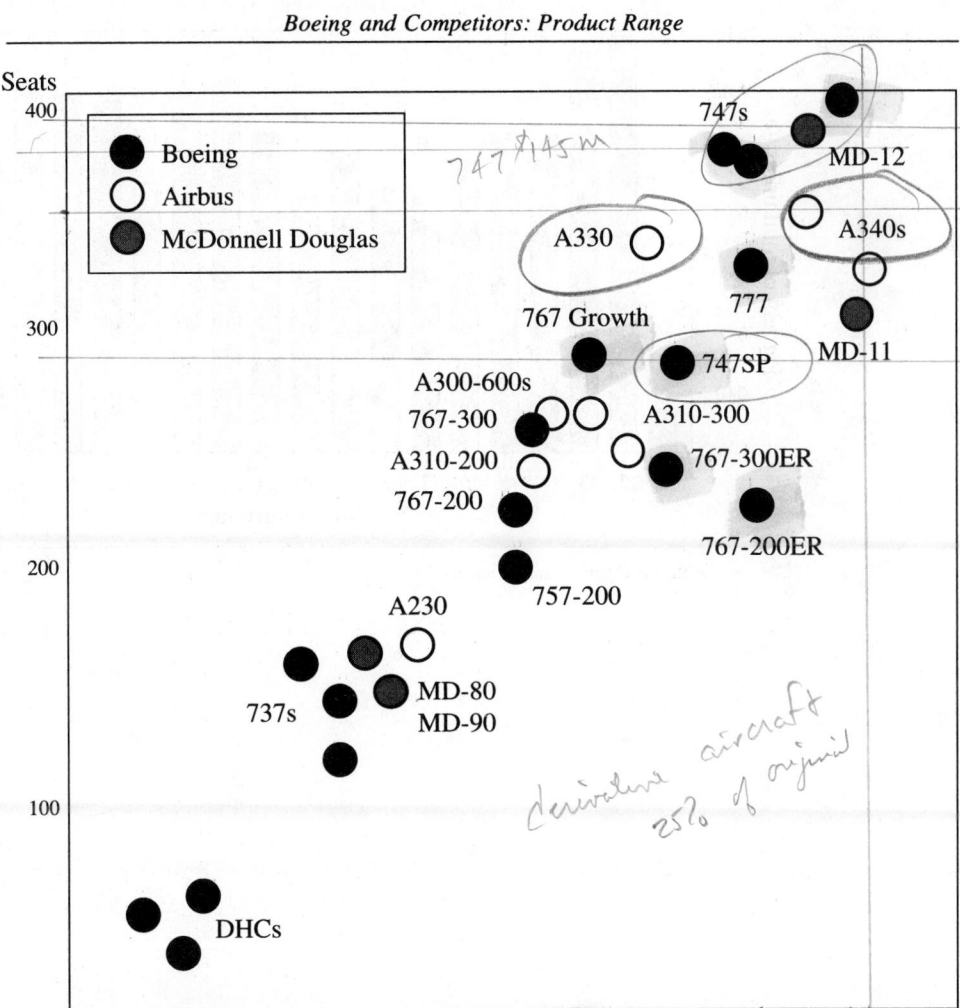

EXHIBIT 5 Airframe Life Cycle of Unit Sales Averaged across the Boeing 707, 727, 737, and 747

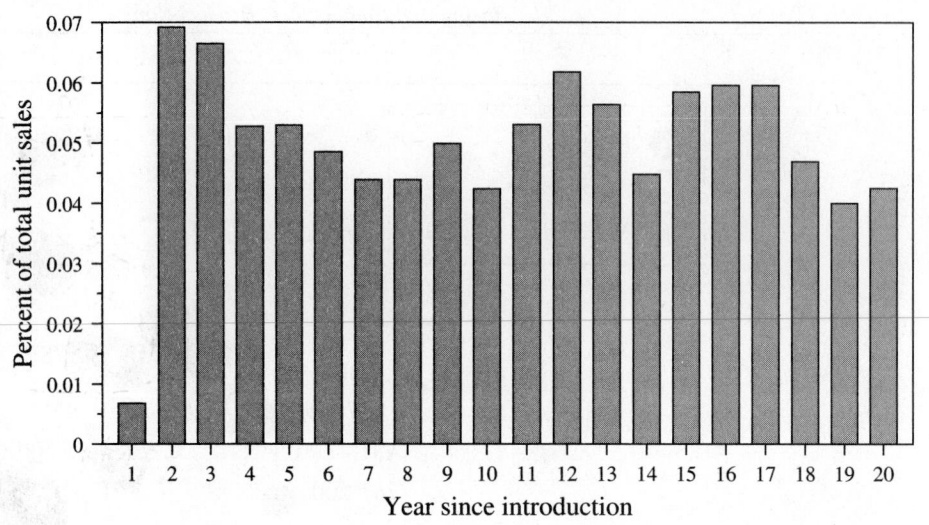

Source: The Boeing Company annual reports.

EXHIBIT 6   Forecast of Boeing 777 Free Cash Flows

Assumptions

Price per plane	130
Working-capital requirement (WCR) as % of sales	9.8%
General, selling, and administrative (GS&A) expense (% of sales)	4.0%
R&D expense (% of sales)	3.0% (excluding 1990–95)
Capital expenditure (% of sales)	0.1% (excluding 1990–94 and years before introduction of derivatives)
Depreciation	Double-digit accelerated method
Total no. of planes yrs. 1–10	1,000
Total no. of planes yrs. 11–20	1,000
Inflation	3.0%
Marginal effective tax rate	34.0%

	1990	1991	1992	1993	1994	1995
Revenues						
Number of planes delivered						14
Price per plane						$ 130.00
Total revenues						1,847.55
Cost of goods sold						1,662.79
Gross profit						184.75
Depreciation				$ 116.40	$ 124.76	112.28
GS&A expense						73.90
Operating profit (before R&D)	0.00	(40.00)	(96.00)	(116.40)	(124.76)	(1.43)
R&D expense	142.00	865.00	1,340.00	1,240.00	840.00	240.00
Pretax profit	(142.00)	(905.00)	(1,436.00)	(1,356.40)	(964.76)	(241.43)
Taxes (or tax credit)	(48.28)	(307.70)	(488.24)	(461.18)	(328.02)	(82.09)
After-tax profit	(93.72)	(597.30)	(947.76)	(895.22)	(636.74)	(159.34)
Capital expenditure	0.00	400.00	600.00	300.00	200.00	1.85
Depreciation add-back	40.00	96.00	116.40	124.76	112.28	181.06
Change in WCR						
Annual free cash flow	$ (93.72)	$(957.30)	$(1,451.76)	$(1,078.82)	$(711.98)	$(229.97)

209

EXHIBIT 6 *(continued)*

	1996	1997	1998	1999	2000	2001	2002
Revenues							
Planes delivered	145	140	111	111	102	92	92
Price per plane	$ 133.90	$ 137.92	$ 142.05	$ 146.32	$ 150.71	$ 155.23	$ 159.88
Total revenues	19,418.96	19,244.23	15,737.95	16,257.35	15,333.42	14,289.29	14,717.97
Cost of goods sold	16,506.12	15,202.94	12,275.60	12,518.16	11,653.40	10,859.86	11,038.48
Gross profit	2,912.84	4,041.29	3,462.35	3,739.19	3,680.02	3,429.43	3,679.49
Depreciation	101.06	90.95	82.72	77.75	75.63	75.00	75.00
GS&A expense	776.76	769.77	629.52	650.29	613.34	571.57	588.72
Operating profit (before R&D)	2,035.03	3,180.57	2,750.11	3,011.14	2,991.06	2,782.86	3,015.77
R&D expense	582.57	577.33	472.14	487.72	460.00	428.68	441.54
Pretax profit	1,452.46	2,603.24	2,277.97	2,523.42	2,531.05	2,354.18	2,574.23
Taxes (or tax credit)	493.84	885.10	774.51	857.96	860.56	800.42	875.24
After-tax profit	958.62	1,718.14	1,503.46	1,665.46	1,670.49	1,553.76	1,698.99
Capital expenditure	19.42	19.24	15.74	16.26	15.33	14.29	14.72
Depreciation add-back	101.06	90.95	82.72	77.75	75.63	75.00	75.00
Change in WCR	1,722.00	(17.12)	(343.62)	50.90	(90.54)	(102.33)	42.01
Annual free cash flow	$ (681.74)	$ 1,806.97	$ 1,914.06	$ 1,676.05	$ 1,821.34	$ 1,716.79	$ 1,717.27

	2003	2004	2005	2006	2007	2008	2009
Revenues							
Planes delivered	105	89	111	130	118	94	123
Price per plane	$ 164.68	$ 169.62	$ 174.71	$ 179.95	$ 185.35	$ 190.91	$ 196.64
Total revenues	17,233.97	15,066.42	19,468.56	23,307.53	21,911.40	17,944.00	24,103.23
Cost of goods sold	12,925.47	11,299.82	16,548.27	18,879.10	17,310.01	13,996.32	20,487.75
Gross profit	4,308.49	3,766.61	2,920.28	4,428.43	4,601.39	3,947.68	3,615.49
Depreciation	99.46	121.48	116.83	112.65	100.20	129.20	96.99
GS&A expense	689.36	602.66	778.74	932.30	876.46	717.76	964.13
Operating profit	3,519.67	3,042.47	2,024.71	3,383.48	3,624.73	3,100.72	2,554.37
R&D expense	517.02	451.99	584.06	699.23	657.34	538.32	723.10
Pretax profit	3,002.65	2,590.47	1,440.65	2,684.25	2,967.39	2,562.40	1,831.27
Taxes (or tax credit)	1,020.90	880.76	489.82	912.65	1,008.91	871.22	622.63
After-tax profit	1,981.75	1,709.71	950.83	1,771.61	1,958.48	1,691.19	1,208.64
Capital expenditure	244.64	244.64	19.47	23.31	21.91	567.22	24.10
Depreciation add-back	99.46	121.48	116.83	112.65	100.20	129.20	96.99
Change in WCR	246.57	(212.42)	431.41	376.22	(136.82)	(388.81)	603.60
Annual free cash flow	$ 1,590.00	$ 1,798.97	$ 616.79	$ 1,484.73	$ 2,173.59	$ 1,641.97	$ 677.92

EXHIBIT 6 *(concluded)*

	2010	2011	2012	2013	2014	2015	2016
Revenues							
Planes delivered	125	125	98	84	89	89	89
Price per plane	$ 202.54	$ 208.61	$ 214.87	$ 221.32	$ 227.96	$ 234.79	$ 241.84
Total revenues	25,316.97	26,076.48	21,133.07	18,550.25	20,321.64	20,931.29	21,559.23
Cost of goods sold	20,506.75	20,600.42	16,483.79	14,283.69	15,444.45	15,907.78	16,385.01
Gross profit	4,810.22	5,476.06	4,649.27	4,266.56	4,877.19	5,023.51	5,174.21
Depreciation	76.84	65.81	61.68	57.96	54.61	52.83	52.83
GS&A expense	1,012.68	1,043.06	845.32	742.01	812.87	837.25	862.37
Operating profit	3,720.71	4,367.19	3,742.27	3,466.59	4,009.72	4,133.43	4,259.02
R&D expense	759.51	782.29	633.99	556.51	609.65	627.94	646.78
Pretax profit	2,961.20	3,584.89	3,108.28	2,910.08	3,400.07	3,505.49	3,612.24
Taxes (or tax credit)	1,006.81	1,218.86	1,056.82	989.43	1,156.02	1,191.87	1,228.16
After-tax profit	1,954.39	2,366.03	2,051.46	1,920.65	2,244.05	2,313.63	2,384.08
Capital expenditure	25.32	26.08	21.13	18.55	20.32	20.93	21.56
Depreciation add-back ...	76.84	65.81	61.68	57.96	54.61	52.83	52.83
Change in WCR	118.95	74.43	(484.45)	(253.12)	173.60	59.75	61.54
Annual free cash flow ..	$ 1,886.97	$ 2,331.34	$ 2,576.47	$ 2,213.18	$ 2,104.74	$ 2,285.77	$ 2,353.81

	2017	2018	2019	2020	2021	2022	2023	2024
Revenues								
Planes delivered	89	89	89	89	89	89	89	89
Price per plane	$ 249.09	$ 256.57	$ 264.26	$ 272.19	$ 280.36	$ 288.77	$ 297.43	$ 306.35
Total revenues	22,206.00	22,872.18	23,558.35	24,265.10	24,993.05	25,742.85	26,515.13	27,310.58
Cost of goods sold	16,876.56	17,382.86	17,904.35	18,441.48	18,994.72	19,564.56	20,151.50	20,756.04
Gross profit	5,329.44	5,489.32	5,654.00	5,823.62	5,998.33	6,178.28	6,363.63	6,554.54
Depreciation	52.83	52.83	47.52	35.28	28.36	28.36	28.36	16.05
GS&A expense	888.24	914.89	942.33	970.60	999.72	1,029.71	1,060.61	1,092.42
Operating profit	4,388.38	4,521.61	4,664.15	4,817.74	4,970.25	5,120.21	5,274.67	5,446.07
R&D expense	666.18	686.17	706.75	727.95	749.79	772.29	795.45	819.32
Pretax profit	3,722.20	3,835.45	3,957.40	4,089.78	4,220.46	4,347.92	4,479.21	4,626.75
Taxes (or tax credit)	1,265.55	1,304.05	1,345.52	1,390.53	1,434.96	1,478.29	1,522.93	1,573.09
After-tax profit	2,456.65	2,531.39	2,611.89	2,699.26	2,785.50	2,869.63	2,956.28	3,053.65
Capital expenditure	22.21	22.87	23.56	24.27	24.99	25.74	26.52	27.31
Depreciation add-back ...	52.83	52.83	47.52	35.28	28.36	28.36	28.36	16.05
Change in WCR	63.38	65.29	67.24	69.26	71.34	73.48	75.68	77.95
Annual free cash flow ..	$ 2,423.88	$ 2,496.06	$ 2,568.60	$ 2,641.01	$ 2,717.53	$ 2,798.77	$ 2,882.44	$ 2,964.44

EXHIBIT 6   Appendix: Discussion of Assumptions Underlying the Estimation of Cash Flows

---

Revenue Estimation

In order to project revenues for the project, several assumptions were made about market size, market share, units per year, initial 777 price, the rate of price increases, and introduction of derivatives.

Market size: Boeing estimated that, from 1990 to 2005, the total aircraft market would be worth approximately $615 billion.[1] The company predicted that two thirds of this market would be in the aircraft segment in which the 777 would compete.[2] Because the 777 would not be available until 1995, this forecast uses a total market base from 1995 to 2005, estimated as two thirds of the 1990–2005 number (i.e., $410 billion). If the 777 segment had two thirds of this market, it would have a market of $275 billion. The $130 million per aircraft (Boeing's estimate for the 777 price tag) would translate into a market size of over 2,000 planes during the 777's first 10 years of production. The replacement market alone was expected to demand 670 aircraft,[3] and this market was supposed to be the fastest growing in the aircraft industry.

Market share: If Boeing maintained its historical 50+ percent market share, its absolute share of the market between 1995 and 2005 would accumulate to $135 billion. With the 777s expected to sell for approximately $130 million each, the figures translate into a projection of 1,000 units during the 777's first 10 years of production.

Units per year: The number of units sold per year is based on historical trends for other Boeing aircraft for the first 10 years of their lives. The percentage distributions estimated from these other aircraft are then applied to the total 10-year figure (i.e., 1,000 aircraft) to yield annual unit sales. Units per year for years 21 to 30 are estimated to be the same as year 20 to reflect an average of two possibilities: (1) another derivative aircraft is introduced, resulting in higher unit sales, and (2) no new derivatives are introduced and the plane's sales decline.

Initial price: Boeing estimated that the 777 would sell for $130 million—the high end of the aircraft market; analysts' estimates ranged between $100 and $130 million. The forecast presented here assumes a price of $130 million.

Rate of price increases: Aircraft prices are assumed to increase at the rate of inflation. Inflation is assumed to be 3 percent annually for the next 35 years.

Introduction of derivatives: Based on historical trends from other Boeing aircraft, the forecast assumes that Boeing will introduce a derivative plane after 10 years and again after 15 years of 777 production. These moves would lead to temporary increases in sales in the following years.

Expense Estimation

Cost of goods sold: Based on gross-profit-margin experience from other Boeing aircraft models, the forecast assumes that gross profit begins at 10 percent of sales and reaches 25 percent when the company has produced 500 units. Gross profit margin remains at this level until a derivative model is introduced, when the profit margin falls to 15 percent and then recommences the improvement to 25 percent at a faster rate.

General, selling, and administrative expense: Boeing's ratio of GS&A to sales has run historically at about 4 percent. In certain years, the ratio has been as low as 2 percent and, in others, as high as 5 percent.

Depreciation: Boeing depreciated its assets on an accelerated basis. The forecast uses double-declining depreciation with a 20-year asset life and 0 salvage value as the base.

---

[1] McDonnell Douglas estimates are significantly higher, but Boeing estimates are used here to be consistent with the expectations of Boeing executives.

[2] "It's Fat and Snazzy," *Business Week*, October 29, 1990, p. 32.

[3] Lawrence Harris, "The Boeing Company, Attractive for Value-Oriented Accounts," Kemper Securities Group, Inc., December 26, 1991.

EXHIBIT 6 *(concluded)*

Research and development: The forecast uses an analyst's[4] estimate of up-front R&D expenses of $4.467 billion. The cash flows exclude $200 million that Boeing spent on the project in early 1990, on the principle that the expenditures prior to October 1990 are sunk costs. After this period, annual R&D expense is esti- mated to be 3 percent of sales, a figure that draws on various analysts' assumptions and historical levels of R&D spending. The forecast assumes that this level of expenditure is sufficient to enable Boeing to introduce two 777 derivatives, in 2005 and 2009. This forecast does not assume Boeing's belief that its development- process innovations will reduce the cost of development by 20 percent.

Tax expense: Boeing has historically had a low marginal effective tax rate. Analysts believed this rate would increase in the future, however, to about 30 percent. The forecast reflects this expectation.

Other Adjustments to Cash Flow

Capital expenditures: The forecast assumes total capital expenditures of $1.5 billion for the original version of the 777 and future capital expenditures for the two derivatives at 25 percent of the original but increased at the rate of inflation. One might use a higher estimate, $2.5 billion, but it is believed to include facilities and systems not incremental to this project.

Working-capital requirement: The forecast assumes the past five-year average of the Boeing Company ratio of working capital to sales—9.8 percent.

[4] George Shapiro, Salomon Brothers.

EXHIBIT 7 Sensitivity Analysis of Project IRRs by Price, Volume, GS&A, and R&D Expenses

Unit Volume (first 10 years)	*Unit Price (millions)*			
	$100	*$110*	*$120*	*$130*
700	13.9%	14.8%	15.5%	16.3%
800	14.7	15.5	16.4	17.2
900	15.4	16.3	17.2	18.0
1,000	16.1	17.1	18.0	18.9
1,100	16.9	17.9	18.9	19.8
1,200	17.6	18.6	19.7	20.6

GS&A/Sales	*R&D Expense/Sales*				
	1.0%	*2.0%*	*3.0%*	*4.0%*	*5.0%*
1.0%	23.5%	22.7%	21.8%	20.9%	19.9%
2.0	22.6	21.8	20.8	19.9	19.0
3.0	21.7	20.8	19.9	18.9	17.9
4.0	20.8	19.9	18.9	17.9	16.9
5.0	19.9	18.9	17.9	16.9	15.8
6.0	18.9	17.9	16.9	15.8	14.7
7.0	17.9	16.8	15.8	14.7	13.5

Source: Casewriter's analysis.

EXHIBIT 8 DCF Break-Even by Different WACCs

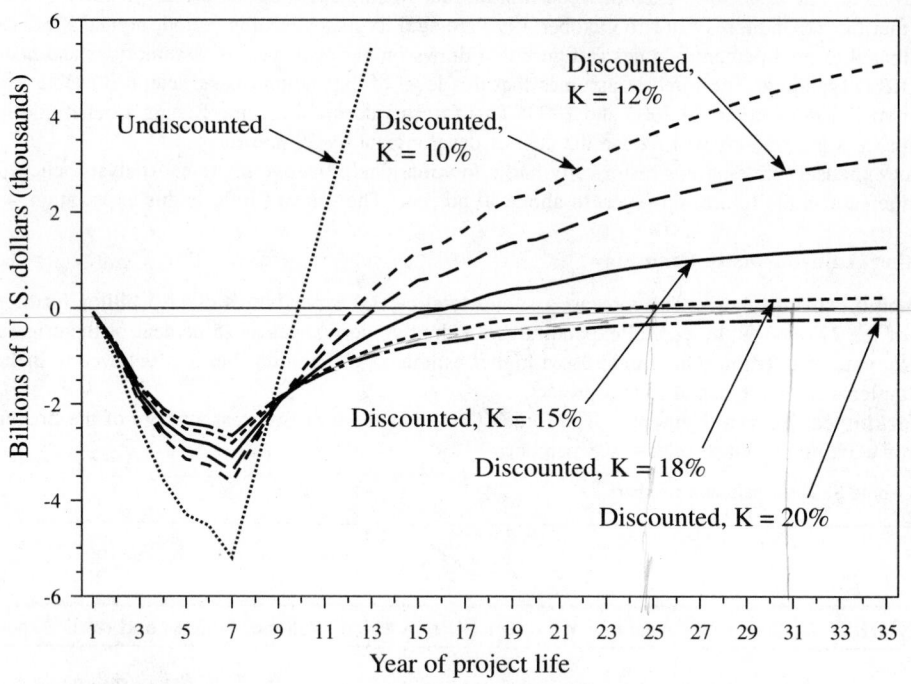

Cumulative Project Cash Flows (undiscounted and discounted)

EXHIBIT 9 Information on Comparable Companies (specially calculated betas estimated from *daily* stock returns and market returns over the periods indicated)

	Boeing	Grumman	Northrop	Lockheed	McDonnell Douglas
Percentage of revenues derived from defense and U.S. space program ..	26%	87%	89%	85%	66%
Estimated betas					
1. Statistical services:					
Value Line*	1.00	0.95	1.00	1.10	0.85
Datastream†	1.06	0.53	0.94	0.97	0.51
2. Calculated against the S&P 500 Index:					
58 months	0.81	0.80	0.74	0.87	0.60
12 months	1.37	0.73	0.72	0.69	0.63
60 days	1.65	0.68	0.50	0.52	0.64
3. Calculated against the NYSE Composite Index:					
58 months	0.87	0.86	0.79	0.95	0.66
12 months	1.51	0.80	0.77	0.75	0.71
60 days	1.79	0.73	0.53	0.57	0.71
Market-value debt/equity ratio	0.018	1.756	1.288	1.182	2.714

* Value Line betas are calculated from a regression analysis between the weekly percentage changes in the price of a stock and the weekly percentage changes in the New York Stock Exchange Composite Index. The beta is calculated over the last five years of data.
† Datastream betas are calculated from a regression analysis between weekly adjusted prices of the stock and Datastream's own composite index. The betas are calculated over a four-year-period.

EXHIBIT 10   Daily Boeing Stock Prices Compared with the S&P 500 Index, January 1, 1986, to October 29, 1990

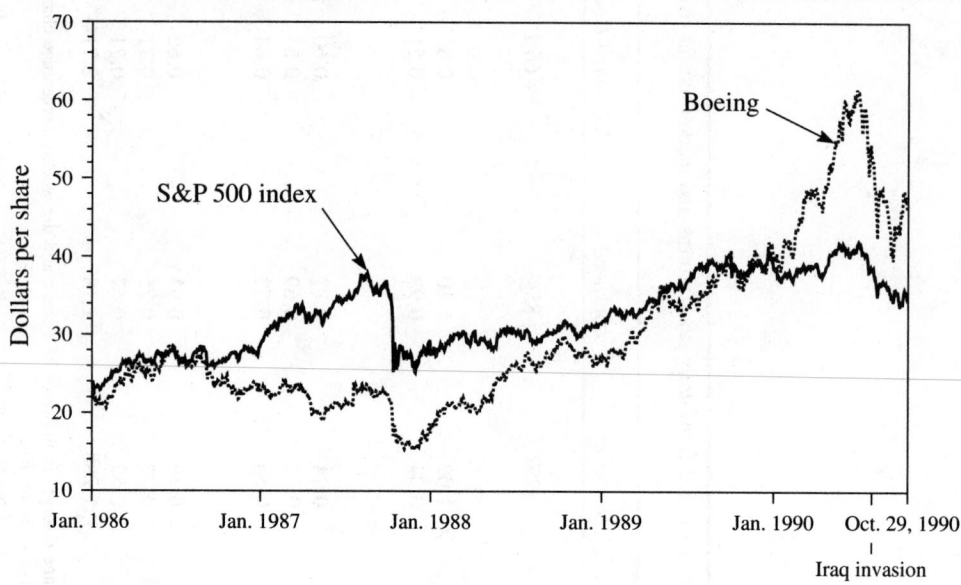

Source: Datastream.

Case 16

Grand Metropolitan PLC

Grand Metropolitan PLC is the world's largest wine and spirits seller, and the only one analysts expect will show volume gains this year. Its Burger King hamburger chain, the world's second biggest, has just completed a turnaround. So why is the price of GrandMet shares in New York, compared with its earnings, 10% below the average price/earnings ratio of the companies in the Standard & Poor's 500 index? And more important, why have rumors surfaced that GrandMet, valued at more than $14 billion in the stock market, may be a takeover target?[1]

It is our goal to build on GrandMet's strengths and continue to create sustainable competitive advantage in our businesses, which is the bedrock of shareholder value and wealth.[2]

By April 1992, senior managers of Grand Metropolitan PLC could look back on a flurry of financial activity. GrandMet had just acquired Cinzano, the Italian vermouth and wines company, for £100 million. In the United States, GrandMet was negotiating a joint venture in which it would receive £39.5 million in exchange for the U.S. flour-milling business it had acquired when it bought Pillsbury in 1989. In 1991, the group sold off about £800 million in businesses in its effort to focus on core activities: food, drink, retailing.

In spite of the world recession, Grand Metropolitan beat market forecasts in 1991 with a 4.8 percent increase in pretax profits, which brought the group to a record £963 million. This success was accomplished in what chairman Sir Allen Sheppard believed was "one of the toughest years in Grand Metropolitan's history." Sheppard emphasized that the positive results demonstrated the validity of GrandMet's strategic intent to focus on its

---

[1]Peter Waldman, "Sir Allen Cools the Pace at Grand Met," *European Wall Street Journal*, October 8, 1991.
[2]"1990 Annual Report to Shareholders," Grand Metropolitan PLC.

This case was prepared by Philippe Demigne, Jean-Christophe Donck, Bertrand George, and Michael Levy with Professor Robert F. Bruner. The financial support of the Citicorp Global Scholars Program is gratefully acknowledged.

Copyright © 1992 by the Darden Graduate Business School Foundation, Charlottesville, VA, and INSEAD, Fontainebleau, France. Revised February 1993.

core businesses. While conceding that "1992 will be another tough year," he reiterated the company's goal "to constantly improve on rather than match previous achievements." The 1991 annual report carried the slogan " . . . adding value" imprinted under the company name. Achieving the goal, however, might mean selling off some of the group's poorly performing businesses, such as Pearle Vision. Furthermore, in the previous year, rumors had circulated that GrandMet might be a takeover target.

THE COMPANY

With a total 1991 turnover (sales) of £8.75 billion, Grand Metropolitan ranked among Britain's 10 largest companies. It currently acted as a pure holding company for a group of business units that were widely diversified both geographically and in terms of products. Exhibit 1 presents a summary and description of GrandMet's three major operating sectors: foods (30 percent of 1991 trading profit), drinks (46 percent), and retailing (24 percent). The brands it owned and managed ranked among the best known worldwide: Green Giant, Haagen-Dazs, Alpo, and Pillsbury in foods; Smirnoff, Bailey's, J&B, and Cinzano in drinks; Burger King and Pearle Vision in retailing. Geographically, 51 percent of GrandMet's 1991 turnover was generated in the United States, 34 percent came from the United Kingdom, and 10 percent from continental Europe.

Exhibit 2 gives GrandMet's historical financial performance broken down by operating sector and by geographical region. Exhibit 3 summarizes the group's consolidated balance sheets and income statements for the past five years.

GrandMet was founded in the late 1940s as the Washington Group, a chain of hotels established by Sir Maxwell Joseph. With the acquisition of the Mount Royal Hotel in 1957, the company changed its name to Mount Royal, Ltd., to reflect the fact that, with 712 rooms, this new acquisition was much larger than the group's existing hotels. In 1961, the company was listed on the London stock exchange and, in 1962, the group changed its name to Grand Metropolitan Hotels.

The 1960s saw the first in a series of acquisitions that would move GrandMet into nonhotel businesses. In 1966, the group bought Levy & Franks, owners of the Chef and Brewer pub and restaurant chain. By 1969, GrandMet had expanded into dairy products with the acquisition of Express Dairy (£32 million). During the 1970s, its most important purchases included the Mecca gaming establishments (bought for £33 million, sold in 1985 for £95 million) and Watney (£435 million), the owner of International Distillers and Vintners, which would form the core of GrandMet's drinks division.

GrandMet's pace of acquisition and divestiture accelerated during the 1980s. Its major acquisitions during this decade included the Liggett Group (owner of Alpo pet food, bought for $450 million), Intercontinental Hotels (bought for $500 million, sold in 1988 for $2 billion), Pearle Optical ($385 million), Heublein (U.S. wines and spirits company and owner of Smirnoff vodka, bought for $1.2 billion), and finally, Pillsbury (owner of Burger King and Haagen-Dazs, bought for £3.3 billion).

The 1990s started with a flurry of divestitures, as close to £800 million in businesses were sold off. By 1992, GrandMet had divested all of its hotels, breweries, gaming establishments, soft-drink bottling plants, fitness products, and all food brands that were judged not to have international branding potential. The result was a group focused on a "core competence": the management of international brands in food, drinks, and retailing. Exhibit 4 summarizes the transactions that GrandMet undertook from 1960 through 1992.

FINANCIAL STRATEGY

In an analysts' briefing given by GrandMet in December 1991, Ian Martin, group managing director and chief operating officer, stated that the group's positive financial results "demonstrate the effectiveness of our operational principles, which can be simplified down to just seven words: build brands, cut costs, develop products, all within the framework of total quality."[3] At this same briefing, David Nash, financial director, outlined the financial strategy that supported these operational principles: capitalize brand value, increase interest coverage, dispose of products that do not provide an adequate return.

Brand Valuation

In 1988, GrandMet was the first U.K. company to begin the practice of assessing the value of recently acquired brands and then capitalizing that value on the balance sheet. As shown in Exhibit 3, the value of the brands (principally, Smirnoff, Pillsbury, Green Giant, and Burger King), consolidated under the label "Intangible assets," constituted 40 percent of 1991 fixed assets and 27 percent of the company's 1991 total assets.

Interest Coverage and Debt Policy

Senior management was committed to reducing GrandMet's financial gearing (leverage) and noted in announcing the results for 1991 that the ratio of debt/capital had fallen by 9 percentage points in the last year and that the firm's interest-coverage ratio had risen from 4.8 times to 6.6. Exhibit 5 shows the historical evolution of GrandMet's debt structure in terms of its maturity profile and currency profile.

Invest in Projects Meeting Growth Criteria

At the December 1991 analysts' briefing, CEO Sheppard outlined GrandMet's investment policy as follows: "In addition to Brewing, we have continued to exit those businesses whose future potential earnings do not meet our growth criteria. . . . All these decisions were driven by a thorough analysis of income growth prospects."[4] As Exhibits 2 and 3

---

[3]GrandMet preliminary-results briefing, December 5, 1991.
[4]Ibid.

indicate, during the 1987–91 fiscal years, GrandMet had generated a compound growth rate in pretax profits of 20.5 percent per year. Implicit in Sheppard's statement was the assumption that only those investments that would not jeopardize this growth trend would be undertaken.

GROUP COST OF CAPITAL

Were GrandMet's financial objectives consistent with the creation of value? To approach this question, analysts often used the discounted cash flows of any project as a measure of value creation. This method required knowledge of the opportunity cost of capital for investments of similar risk. One commonly used discount rate was the weighted-average cost of capital (WACC), defined as:

$$WACC = (1 - T)i(D/V) + K_e(E/V)$$

where T is the corporate tax rate, i is the pretax cost of debt, D is the market value of debt, E is the market value of equity, K_e is the cost of equity, and V is the market value of the firm's assets $(V = D + E)$.

In basic terms, the WACC blends the requirements of the different providers of capital — bondholders and shareholders. A separate WACC could be calculated for each of the three operating sectors as well as for the entire company.

Capital-Structure Weights

Exhibit 6 gives the book-value and market-value weightings for the company's capital structure.

Cost of Debt and Preferred Stock

Exhibit 7 estimates the weighted-average pretax cost of debt for GrandMet in both pounds sterling and U.S. dollars. The 1990 annual report stated,

> The group interest expense is arranged centrally and is not attributable to individual activities or geographical areas. . . . The group has arranged interest rate swaps which have the effect of fixing the rate of interest at an average of 8.6 percent on U.S. dollar and Deutschemark borrowings totalling £616 million. . . . In addition, the interest rate on borrowings of £1,070 million has been capped for 1 year by the purchase of interest rate caps at a rate of 9 percent. The interest rates shown . . . are those contracted on the underlying borrowings before taking into account any interest rate protection.

The firm noted that most of the commercial-paper borrowings were classified as "mid-term" (i.e., longer in maturity than one year but shorter than long term), because the firm intended to roll over the maturing commercial paper indefinitely.

The statutory maximum corporate income tax rate prevailing in the United Kingdom in 1992 was 35 percent. In the United States, it was 34 percent.

Exhibit 7 also presents the cost of preferred stock (calculated as the annual dividend divided by the market value of the stock) and the cost of convertible debt. Convertible debt was recognized to be a hybrid, a mixture of "straight" debt and equity. Therefore, the cost of the convertible debt, 9.75 percent, was estimated[5] as an average of the cost of equity and cost of debt, weighted by proportions implicit in the convertible; that is, 9.75 percent was not simply the yield on the bond portion of the convertible.

Cost of Equity

Several methods could be used for estimating the cost of equity. One approach was based on the theory that the current stock price was simply the discounted flow of future dividends. In this model, the after-tax cost of equity (K_e) could be approximated by

$$K_e = DIV/P + g$$

where *DIV* is the current dividend per share, *P* is the current share price, and *g* is the expected growth rate of dividends to infinity.

Another approach was based on the capital asset pricing model. This model explicitly sets required returns by considering the risk of the investment, where risk is defined with respect to a fully diversified portfolio. This model leads to the following expression for the expected after-tax cost of equity:

$$K_e = R_f + \beta(R_m - R_f)$$

where R_f is the risk-free rate (typically a government-bond rate), β is beta,[6] and $R_m - R_f$ is the stock market risk premium.

Exhibit 8 gives information for GrandMet relevant to measuring cost of equity, and Exhibit 9 presents the financial-market conditions in the United States and United Kingdom in April 1992. Which risk-free rate should one use—the U.S. rate (because half the company's revenues were dollar denominated) or the U.K. rate? How should the decision maker decide on which maturity to use (2 years, 10 years)? What did "risk free" really mean? The same questions arose in the case of the market risk premiums. Should the decision maker use the historical long-term geometric averages or short-term ones? With which market(s) should the decision maker be concerned?

---

[5]By the casewriters.

[6]In technical terms, *beta* is the normalized covariance of the asset's return with respect to the market return— basically, a measure of how the company's returns vary with respect to overall market fluctuations. A company with a beta of 1.0 experiences as much volatility as a broad portfolio of stocks, and it varies synchronously with the market. A company with a beta of less than 1.0 is less risky than the market portfolio. A beta greater than 1.0 indicates greater risk than the market portfolio.

The most recent Risk Measurement Service report from the London Business School reported that GrandMet had a beta of 1.14 with respect to the London stock market.[7] *Value Line*, however, the U.S. investment information service, had estimated GrandMet's beta at 0.8 with respect to the New York stock exchange.[8] What might account for the difference between these two numbers?

BUSINESS-SEGMENT CAPITAL-COST ESTIMATION

How should one estimate the cost of equity for each of GrandMet's individual sectors? Should each segment have a different risk-free rate based on different project lifetimes? How should one determine the beta for each sector? Finally, how should one determine the weights necessary to combine the business segments into an overall WACC for GrandMet? Should one base the weighting factor on revenues, profits, or some other measure?

The decision maker knew that he could examine the capital structures of comparable companies to facilitate the evaluation GrandMet's gearing in each of its segments. Therefore, he collected the information in Exhibit 8 on various companies that competed with GrandMet in each of its operating sectors. Would the fact that this information reflected only book values dramatically affect the estimation of overall cost of capital? Which tax rate should he use, the U.S. marginal rate, the U.K. marginal rate, or some effective rate?

COST OF CAPITAL AND CURRENCY

In evaluating GrandMet's performance, analysts wondered whether the cost of capital should be the same in London as in New York. If differences among local capital markets (such as those induced by country risk) existed, one might be able to diversify the

---

[7]Risk Measurement Services (RMS) estimated betas using five years of *monthly* returns. The returns included dividends and capital gains or losses. RMS noted, "Betas may change because the company changes. For example, if a company becomes more highly geared, the beta of its shares will increase. Similarly, if it acquires a less risky firm, the beta of the shares after the merger will be lower than before. You may find it helpful to bear this in mind when interpreting the estimates." (London Business School, "Your Questions Answered," *Risk Measurement Services*, October 1991, pp. 63–65.)

[8]*Value Line* estimated its betas by regressing *weekly* percentage changes in the price of a stock against the weekly percentage changes in the New York Stock Exchange Composite Index over a period of five years. *Value Line* noted, "There has been a tendency over the years for high Beta stocks to become lower and for low Beta stocks to become higher. This tendency can be measured by studying the Betas of stocks in consecutive five-year intervals. The Betas published in The Value Line Investment Survey are adjusted for this tendency and hence are likely to be a better predictor of future Betas than those based exclusively on the experience of the past five years." ("How to Use the Value Line Investment Survey: A Subscriber's Guide," *Value Line Investment Survey*, 1985, p. 57.)

differences away by holding a portfolio of international investments. Using this kind of assumption could free an analyst to work with local costs of capital.

The assumption of purchasing-power parity implied the following relationship between home and foreign local costs of capital:

$$Local\ K = (1 + Home\ K) \left\{ \frac{1 + Local\ inflation\ rate}{1 + Home\ inflation\ rate} \right\} - 1$$

This equation implies that real risk-free rates, equity risk premia, and betas are constant across countries. Little evidence either to prove or refute such an assertion existed, although in competitive world capital markets, arbitrage activity would tend to drive the three elements into equilibrium. Using home capital costs to discount cash flows translated into home currencies would be a conservative response to these uncertainties.

CONCLUSION

Analysts noted with interest the circulation of rumors that the company might be the target of a takeover attempt. Had the company performed that badly? Were all segments of the group's business portfolio performing equally well? Might one or two of them be targeted for aggressive restructuring? The decision maker decided to compare the returns on net assets in Exhibit 2 against the segment WACCs.

EXHIBIT 1   Grand Metropolitan PLC

Food *Trading Profit £300 m (30%)*	*Drinks* *Trading Profit £454 m (46%)*	*Retailing* *Trading Profit £ 236 m (24%)*
Pillsbury Brands (U.S.) Baked goods (biscuits, sweet foods, pizzas); fresh, frozen, and canned vegetables; milled flour and processed food. Brands included Pillsbury, Janos, Green Giant, Totino's.	**International Distillers and Vintners (worldwide)** Production and distribution of wines and spirits. Owned brands included Smirnoff vodka, J&B Rare Scotch whisky, Bailey's Irish Cream liqueur, Malibu liqueur, Croft Original sherry, La Plat d'Or wines, Metaxa Greek brandy, Popov vodka, Gilbey's gin, Bombay Dry gin, Cinzano vermouth, Ouzo 12, Inglenook, Almaden, and Beaulieu California wines.	**Grand Metropolitan Retailing (U.K.)** Management and operation of one small restaurant chain, Old Orleans, and around 1,540 managed pubs, both unbranded and under the Chef & Brewer, Clifton Inns, and Country Carvery brand names.
Pillsbury Food Group (Europe) Prepared meals; baked goods (cookies, cakes, gateaux, pies, savoury pastries); savoury products (meat pies, sausages, burgers, and buns). Brands included Erasco, Jokish, Peter's, Hofmann Menu, Fleur de Lys, Memory Lane, Kaysens, Brossard, Goldstein, Jus-rol, Bélin Surgelés, Vinchon Jeanette.		**Pearle, Inc. (U.S., Europe, Far East)** Retailing of eye-care products/ services with over 1,100 stores. Brands included Pearle Vision.
Häagen-Dazs (U.S., Europe, Far East) Premium ice cream.	Agency brands included Grand Marnier liqueur, Cointreau, Jose Cuervo Tequila, Absolut vodka, Jack Daniel's bourbon.	**Burger King (worldwide)** Chain of 6,400 franchised hamburger restaurants in 41 countries.
Alpo Pet Food (U.S.) Cat and dog food. Brands included Alpo, Jim Dandy, Blue Mountain.	*Note:* This division also previously included Grand Metropolitan Brewing, with owned and licensed beer brands including Webster's, Watney, Foster's, Carlsberg, Budweiser, Holsten. This segment was sold to Courage in February 1991 as part of a pubs-for-breweries swap transaction (Inntrepreneur Estates).	
GrandMet Foodservice (U.S.) Food goods for bakery and catering sectors.		

Property Interests

Grand Metropolitan Estates (U.K.)
Property management and development.

Inntrepreneur Estates (U.K.)
50% joint venture with Courage responsible for licensed estate of 7,350 tenanted pubs.

EXHIBIT 2 GrandMet's Distribution of Turnover, Profits, and Assets by Segment and Region

	Absolute Performance					As a Percentage of Totals				
	1991	1990	1989	1988	1987	1991	1990	1989	1988	1987
Drinks										
Turnover	2,425	3,000	2,784	2,581	2,178	32%	33%	36%	47%	46%
Operating profit	454	473	389	316	257	46	45	45	55	53
Net assets	1,536	1,623	1,626	1,479	1,504	26	26	26	40	49
Operating margin	18.7%	15.8%	14.0%	12.2%	11.8%					
RONA*	19.2%	18.9%	15.6%	13.9%	11.1%					
Food										
Turnover	3,026	3,506	2,872	1,253	1,047	40	39	37	23	22
Operating profit	300	309	245	84	69	30	29	28	15	14
Net assets	1,997	1,763	2,468	310	260	34	29	39	8	9
Operating margin	9.9%	8.8%	8.5%	6.7%	6.6%					
RONA	9.8%	11.4%	6.5%	17.6%	17.3%					
Retailing										
Turnover	2,051	2,531	2,040	1,671	1,467	27	28	27	30	31
Operating profit	236	278	230	179	160	24	26	27	31	33
Net assets	2,332	2,785	2,266	1,898	1,290	40	45	36	51	42
Operating margin	11.5%	11.0%	11.3%	10.7%	10.9%					
RONA	6.6%	6.5%	6.6%	6.1%	8.1%					

*Return on net assets is computed as EBIAT (earnings before interest and after taxes) divided by net assets (total assets less current liabilities). A benchmark against which to compare RONA is the weighted-average cost of capital.

EXHIBIT 2 (concluded)

	Absolute Performance					As a Percentage of Totals				
	1991	1990	1989	1988	1987	1991	1990	1989	1988	1987
U.K. and Ireland										
Turnover	3,559	2,940	3,685	4,688	3,836	62	34	39	50	64
Operating profit	331	385	451	424	364	58	36	42	44	56
Net assets	1,945	1,816	2,500	2,626	2,700	62	30	40	41	64
Continental Europe										
Turnover	214	862	661	471	221	4	10	7	5	4
Operating profit	36	104	81	66	46	6	10	7	7	7
Net assets	335	557	427	330	384	11	9	7	5	9
United States										
Turnover	1,720	4,433	4,537	3,720	1,758	30	51	48	40	29
Operating profit	185	517	475	395	218	32	48	44	41	33
Net assets	759	3,466	3,149	3,314	1,034	24	57	50	51	25
Rest of America										
Turnover	58	216	216	174	54	1	2	2	2	1
Operating profit	13	20	21	20	14	2	2	2	2	2
Net assets	61	128	148	145	50	2	2	2	2	1
Rest of world										
Turnover	155	297	295	265	160	3	3	3	3	3
Operating profit	6	45	54	62	12	1	4	5	6	2
Net assets	24	86	91	68	22	1	1	1	1	1

Source: Annual reports of Grand Metropolitan PLC.

EXHIBIT 3   Historical Financial Statements (in £ millions)

	1991	1990	1989	1988	1987
Balance sheet					
Total assets	£9,187	£9,420	£9,570	£5,846	£4,577
Fixed assets:					
Intangible assets	2,464	2,317	2,652	588	0
Tangible assets	2,764	3,756	3,839	3,279	2,725
Investments	851	214	144	206	177
Total fixed assets	6,079	6,287	6,635	4,074	2,902
Current assets:					
Stocks	1,286	1,349	1,269	761	734
Debtors	1,561	1,541	1,451	874	828
Cash at bank and in hand	261	243	215	138	113
Total current assets	3,108	3,133	2,935	1,772	1,675
Creditors (less than one year):					
Borrowings	(157)	(206)	(362)	(187)	(330)
Other creditors	(2,135)	(2,343)	(2,316)	(1,301)	(1,166)
Total current liabilities	(2,292)	(2,549)	(2,678)	(1,488)	(1,496)
Current assets − Current liabilities	816	584	257	284	179
Total assets − Current liabilities	6,895	6,871	6,892	4,358	3,081
Creditors (greater than one year):					
Borrowings	(2,703)	(2,925)	(3,494)	(702)	(1,142)
Other creditors	(169)	(191)	(231)	(163)	(103)
Total noncurrent liabilities	(2,872)	(3,116)	(3,725)	(865)	(1,245)
Provisions	(569)	(328)	(325)	(55)	(70)
Total assets − Total liabilities	3,454	3,427	2,842	3,438	1,765
Capital and reserves:					
Capital	515	508	506	443	441
Reserves	2,907	2,893	2,304	2,964	1,296
Minority interests	32	26	32	31	28
Total equity	3,454	3,427	2,842	3,438	1,765
Profit-and-Loss Account					
Turnover	8,748	9,394	9,298	6,029	5,706
Cost of sales	(7,473)	(8,119)	(8,159)	(5,262)	(5,016)
Depreciation	(204)	(216)	(190)	(125)	(126)
Trading profit	1,071	1,059	949	642	564
Income of related companies	10	23	18	12	8
Other income	18	79	80	39	14
Net interest	(171)	(239)	(280)	(93)	(120)
Exceptional items	35	(3)	(35)	(25)	(9)
Pretax profit	963	919	732	576	456
Taxation	(298)	(279)	(216)	(155)	(120)
Net income	665	640	516	421	336
Minority interests	(7)	(6)	(8)	(8)	(2)
Extraordinary items	(226)	435	560	290	128
Dividends payable	(218)	(198)	(167)	(129)	(104)
Retained earnings	214	871	901	574	358

Source: Annual reports of Grand Metropolitan PLC.

EXHIBIT 4 Acquisitions and Divestitures

	Acquisitions	Divestitures
1960s and 1970s	**1966** Levy & Franks: pub and restaurant chain **1967** Bateman & Midland Catering: contract catering **1969** Express Dairy: distribution of milk products **1970** Berni Inns: hotels in U.K.; Mecca: gaming, betting, and amusement centers **1971** Truman Hanbury Buxton: brewing, pubs, and hotels **1972** Watney (incl. IDV): brewing, distribution of wines and spirits	
1980s	**1980** Liggett Group (U.S.): cigarettes, wines and spirits, soft-drink bottling, fitness products, pet food (Alpo) **1981** Intercontinental Hotels: worldwide luxury hotel chain **1983** Childrens' World (U.S.): early education services **1985** Cinzano (25%): drinks; Quality Care (U.S.): home health care; Pearle Optical (U.S.): world's largest eye-care products retailing **1986** G. Ruddle & Co.: brewer **1987** Heublein (U.S.): wines and spirits; Almaden Vineyards (U.S.): wines; Saccone & Speed and-Roberts & Cooper: wines and spirits; Dairy Produce Packers: dairy products; Martell (10%): cognac; two pet-food manufacturers (U.S.)	**1984** CC Soft Drinks: soft-drink manufacturer **1985** Express Dairy (northern area): milk/dairy products; Pinkerton Tobacco (U.S.): chewing tobacco (Liggett); L&M do Brasil: tobacco leaf (Liggett); Mecca Leisure: bingo halls/amusement centers **1986** Dryborough & Co. (U.K.), Stern Brauerei (D), Brouwerij Maes (B): brewing; Liggett Group (U.S.): cigarettes **1987** Compass Group: contract and other services; Childrens' World (U.S.): child care products; Quality Care (U.S.): home health-care products; Diversified Products (U.S.): fitness products (Liggett); McGuinness Distillers: Canadian spirits

1988 Vision Express and Eye & Tech (U.S.): optical superstores; Kaysens: frozen desserts; Peter's Savoury Products: meat and pastry products; William Hill Org.: retail betting; Wienerwald/Spaghetti Factory: German and Swiss restaurants

1989 The Pillsbury Company (U.S.): international food group: Burger King, Green Giant, Haagen-Dazs; Metaxa: Greek brandy; Ouzo-Kaloyannis (30%): Greek spirits; Brent Walker: pubs; UB Restaurants: Wimpy, Pizzaland, and Pizza Perfect fast-food chains

1990s

1990 Remy Martin-Cointreau (20%): joint-venture spirits/liqueurs; Anglo Espanola de Distribucion: Spanish wines and spirits distributor; Jus-rol: food manufacturer

1991 Belin Surgelés (France): frozen cakes and pastries; Inntrepreneur Estates (50%) joint venture with Courage: management company for all Courage and 3,570 GrandMet pubs under pubs-for-breweries swap

1992 Cinzano: remaining 75%

1988 Hotel Meurice (F); Atlantic Soft Drink Co./Pepsi-Cola San Joaquin Bottling Co. (U.S.); Intercontinental Hotels

1989 Steak & Ale/Bennigans (U.S.): restaurant chain; London Clubs: London casino business; Van De Kamp's: branded frozen foods; Bumble Bee: branded seafood; William Hill: retail betting

1990 Berni Inns: family restaurant chain

1991 Pizzaland/Pastificio: pizza/pasta restaurant chains; Perfect Pizza: take-away/delivery pizza chain; Watney Truman, Ruddles Brewery, Samuel Webster and Wilsons: breweries; 4 Pillsbury flour mills (U.S.); 3,570 managed and tenanted pubs to Inntrepreneur Estates; The Dominic Group: off-license chain; Express Dairy: liquid milk products; Eden Vale: chilled products

Source: Annual reports of Grand Metropolitan PLC and IBCA report, "Grand Metropolitan" (October 1991).

EXHIBIT 5   Debt Profile

	1991	1990	1989	1988	1987
Debt maturity:					
Current	5%	7%	9%	21%	22%
1 to 2 years	2	58	11	19	25
2 to 5 years	77	30	69	14	28
Over 5 years	16%	5%	11%	46%	25%
Debt currency:					
U.S. dollar	77%	79%	11%	8%	11%
Pound sterling	18	15	9	47	33
Deutsche mark (DM) ..	2	1	1	0	0
Multicurrency	0	0	77	34	47
Various	3%	5%	3%	10%	8%

Market value of equity (as of April 15, 1992):

Common shares prices	£9.48 per share
Shares outstanding	1,005,896,041
Market value of equity	£9,535,894,468

Sources: Annual reports of Grand Metropolitan PLC and *The Wall Street Journal*.

EXHIBIT 6 Summary of Percentage Weights of the Various Classes of Capital

| | £ Outstandings | | £ Weights* | | US$ Outstandings | | US$ Weights | |
	Book	Market	Book	Market	Book	Market	Book	Market
Column number	(1)	(2)	(3)	(4)	(5)	(6)	(7)	(8)
Specified debts†	1,777.4	1,794.8	33.0%	15.6%	3,107	3,137	33.0%	15.6%
Unspecified debts‡ ..	87.0	87.0	1.6	0.8	152	152	1.6	0.8
Convertible debt	52.0	63.0	1.0	0.5	91	110	1.0	0.5
Preferred stock	12.2	6.3	0.2	0.1	21	11	0.2	0.1
Common stock	3,454.0	9,535.9	64.2	83.0	6,038	16,669	64.2	83.0
Total capital	5,382.6	11,487.1	100.0%	100.0%	9,409	20,079	100.0%	100.0%

* The £ weights are calculated by dividing the £ outstanding in each class of capital by the total amount of £ capital. The US$ weights are estimated the same way.

† The balance sheet listed eight separate classes of debt capital to which costs could be attributed: bank loans, commercial paper, guaranteed notes, guaranteed debentures, debenture stock, and bonds.

‡ The balance sheet listed £87 million of debt outstanding without citing a specific cost. Presumably, this debt consisted of a number of small issues. One way to treat those issues in cost-of-capital estimation is to assume that their average cost is equal to a weighted-average cost of all the other specified debt securities.

233

EXHIBIT 7 Estimation of Average Costs of Debt and Preferred Stock

	Currency	Yield on Book Value	Yield on Market Value	£ Yields Book Value	£ Yields Market Value	US$ Yields Book Value	US$ Yields Market Value
Bank loans and overdrafts	£	9.54%	9.54%	9.54%	9.54%	7.86%	7.86%
Commercial paper	US$	5.93	5.93	7.58	7.58	5.93	5.93
Guaranteed notes 1996	US$	8.13	7.97	9.81	9.65	8.13	7.97
Guaranteed notes 2001	US$	8.63	7.87	10.32	9.55	8.63	7.87
Guaranteed debentures 2011	US$	9.00	8.02	10.70	9.70	9.00	8.02
Commercial paper	£	10.80	10.80	10.80	0.80	9.10	9.10
Debenture stock 2008	£	12.13	11.15	12.13	11.15	10.40	9.44
Bonds 1992	DM	6.63	8.57	6.93	8.88	5.29	7.21
Weighted-average cost of debt		7.15	7.13	8.69	8.63	7.03	6.96
Subord. convert. bonds 2002	£	6.25	9.75	6.25	9.75	4.62	8.07
Preferred stock issues							
4.75%	£	4.75	10.05	4.75	10.05	3.14	8.36
6.25%	£	6.25	10.15	6.25	10.15	4.62	8.46
5.00%	£	5.00	10.35	5.00	10.35	3.39	8.66
Weighted-average cost of pfd.		5.31%	10.27%	5.31%	10.27%	3.76%	8.57%

Note: The weighted-average costs are based on the following estimated weightings:

	Securities Outstanding*	Book Value		Book % Weights		Outstdg.	Market Value		Market % Weights	
		£	US$	£	US$		£	US$	£	US$
Bank loans and overdrafts	£280	280	489	15.8	15.8	280	280	489	15.6	15.6
Commercial paper	$1,696	970	1,696	54.6	54.6	$1696	970	1,696	54.1	54.1
Guaranteed notes 1996	$170	97	170	5.5	5.5	$171	98	171	5.5	5.5
Guaranteed notes 2001	$170	97	170	5.5	5.5	$178	102	178	5.7	5.7
Guaranteed debentures 2011 ...	$169	97	169	5.4	5.4	$185	106	185	5.9	5.9
Commercial paper	£139	139	243	7.8	7.8	£139	139	243	7.7	7.7
Debenture stock 2008	£50	50	87	2.8	2.8	£54	54	94	3.0	3.0
Bonds 1992	DM137	47	82	2.6	2.6	DM136	46	80	2.6	2.6
Total specified debts		1,777	3,107	100.0	100.0		1,795	$3,137	100.0	100.0
Various unspecified debts	£87	87	152			£63	63	110		
Subord. convert. bonds 2002 ..	£52	52	91							
Preferred stock issues:										
4.75%	£1.2	1.2	2.1	9.8	9.8	£0.56	0.56	1.0	9.0	9.0
6.25%	£3.3	3.3	5.8	27.0	27.0	2.03	2.03	3.5	32.1	32.1
5.00%	£7.7	7.7	13.5	63.1	63.1	3.72	3.72	6.5	58.9	58.9
Total preferred stock	£12.2	12.2	21.3	100.0	100.0	£6.31	6.31	11.0	100.0	100.0

* Currencies were translated to U.S. dollars or pounds sterling at the following rates of exchange prevailing in mid-April 1992: Dollar/Pound = 1.748; DM/Pound = 2.917; DM/Dollar = 1.669.

EXHIBIT 8 Information on Comparable Companies

	Sales (in US$ m)	Dividend Yield	Price-Earnings Ratio	Interest Coverage	Debt to Capital Book Value	Debt to Capital Market Value	Debt to Equity Book Value	Debt to Equity Market Value	Avg. Tax Rate	Beta	Expected Growth Rate in: Sales	Expected Growth Rate in: Dividends
Grand Metropolitan	15,222	3.4%	13.3	6.6	35%	17%	55%	21%	31%	1.14UK 0.80US	6.5%	12.0%
Restaurant/retailing:												
Forte (U.K.)	4,600	5.7	14.1	2.4	27%	30%	36%	42%	16%	1.18	12.3%	10.6%
McDonald's	6,695	0.8	17.3	4.0	42	2	72	2	34	0.95	12.0	13.5
Luby's	328	3.5	14.2	nil	1	0	1	0	34	0.90	10.0	9.0
National Pizza		0.0	16.9	3.3	49	37	96	58	36	1.00	15.5	0.0
TCBY Enterprises	129	3.9	26.8	7.8	14	3	16	3	35	1.25	9.0	23.0
Wendy's Int'l	1,060	2.0	20.7	5.9	33	23	49	30	34	1.15	6.0	0.0
Average	2,186	2.7	18.3	3.9	28%	16%	45%	23%	31%	1.07	10.8%	9.4%
Food processing:												
Argyll Group (U.K.)	7,830	4.3	13.5	12.9	32	14	47	16	28	0.72	19.8	18.3
Assoc. Brit. Foods (U.K.)	6,110	3.2	9.6	8.3	19	19	23	23	32	0.47	2.3	14.9
Borden	7,235	3.6	14.1	3.9	43	20	75	25	36	1.15	5.5	9.5
Cadbury-Schweppes (U.K.)	5,475	3.6	17.4	3.8	38	17	62	21	28	0.83	10.9	14.3
Campbell Soup	6,204	1.8	21.1	5.9	30	8	43	9	40	1.00	7.5	15.5
CPC International	6,189	2.7	15.3	6.5	38	12	61	14	40	1.10	8.5	12.5
Dean Foods	2,158	1.9	16.1	9.5	26	10	35	12	42	0.90	8.0	7.0
Dreyer's Grand Ice Cream	355	0.7	31.6	4.2	31	22	45	28	40	1.05	16.5	0.0
Flowers Industries	825	4.1	20.0	5.2	35	14	54	16	40	0.85	5.5	6.5
General Mills	7,153	2.3	23.3	8.4	39	6	64	6	39	1.00	11.0	15.0

Heinz	6,800	2.8	19.4	7.6	10	2	11	2	38	1.00	8.5	11.0
Michael Foods	455	1.3	14.7	4.1	35	26	54	36	36	1.15	9.5	19.0
Quaker Oats	5,491	2.8	17.8	5.6	40	13	67	15	43	0.90	9.0	11.5
Ralston Purina	7,375	2.2	15.8	4.1	70	18	233	23	40	0.90	9.5	11.0
Sara Lee	12,831	1.9	22.0	6.6	29	6	41	7	36	1.00	7.0	13.5
Tate & Lyle (U.K.)	5,680	3.7	10.1	3.1	52	32	110	47	29	1.10	14.7	14.3
Tesco (U.K.)	11,050	3.3	13.2	4.0	19	10	23	11	32	0.73	13.6	22.8
Unilever (NL and U.K.)	42,250	3.2	15.1	4.6	22	31	28	44	35	0.86	8.5	9.5
United Biscuits (U.K.)	4,225	5.0	13.7	8.5	32	14	48	16	33	0.88	6.1	12.2
Universal Foods	834	2.6	14.7	7.2	34	13	52	15	37	0.90	9.0	12.5
Average	$7,326	2.9%	16.9	6.2	34%	15%	59%	19%	36%	0.92	9.5%	12.5%
Drinks:												
Allied Lyons (U.K.)	8,940	4.1%	23.4	2.3	43%	30%	75%	44%	29%	0.97	9.2%	14.6%
Anheuser-Busch	10,996	2.0	15.7	8.2	38	15	61	18	38	1.00	7.0	12.0
Bass (U.K.)	7,630	4.8	10.6	4.3	29	38	40	62	26	0.77	10.1	16.5
Brown-Forman	1,250	2.8	14.7	23.5	14	4	16	4	35	1.20	9.5	11.5
Coors	1,917	2.3	15.2	10.3	13	10	15	11	39	0.85	5.0	0.0
Guinness (U.K.)	6,110	2.5	15.9	4.7	31	18	44	22	28	1.01	24.2	21.1
Labatt (Canada)	4,400	3.0	14.3	2.9	33	28	49	38	34	0.75	2.0	6.5
Molson (Canada)	2,500	2.1	13.9	3.3	45	37	82	59	34	0.75	5.0	13.0
Scottish & Newcastle (U.K.)	2,398	5.0	13.5	5.8	23	20	31	25	33	0.59	19.3	16.5
Seagram (Canada)	5,000	1.7	17.2	3.1	29	26	41	35	22	1.10	5.0	12.0
Whitbread (U.K.)	3,585	5.2	10.7	5.6	15	15	17	17	24	0.70	6.1	15.9
Average	4,975	3.2%	15.0	6.7	28%	22%	43%	30%	31%	0.88	9.3%	12.7%

Notes:

U.S. and Canadian companies: 1991 and expected annual growth rates until 1997.
U.K. companies: 1990 and average annual growth rates of the last five years.

EXHIBIT 8 *(concluded)*

Restaurant:

Forte (U.K.)	Active in contract catering and hotel- and motel-chain management.
Luby's Cafeteria (U.S.) ..	Operates a chain of cafeterias.
McDonald's (U.S.)	Licenses and operates a fast-food hamburger chain.
National Pizza (U.S.)	Largest franchisee of PepsiCo's Pizza Hut chain.
TCBY Enterprises (U.S.) ...	Largest franchisor of soft-frozen yogurt stores.
Wendy's Int'l (U.S.)	Licenses and operates a chain of quick-service hamburger restaurants.

Food processing:

Argyll Group (U.K.)	One of the leading food retailers in the United Kingdom.
Assoc. British Foods (U.K.)	Operator of grocery stores, retail bakeries, beauty shops.
Borden (U.S.)	Diversified producer of packaged food (dairy, snacks, pasta, popcorn, jams, potato chips) and adhesives (Elmer's Cement, Crazy Glue).
Cadbury-Schweppes (U.K.)	Manufacturer of bottled and canned soft drinks, candy and other confectionary products, food preparations.
Campbell Soup (U.S.)	A leading manufacturer of canned soups, spaghetti, fruit and vegetable juices, frozen foods, salads, bakery products, olives, pickles.
CPC International (U.S.)	A leading producer of grocery products (soups, mayonnaise, peanut butter, pasta, baked goods) and a large corn refiner (corn syrups, dextrose, starches).
Dean Foods (U.S.)	Manufactures, distributes dairy products (fluid milk, ice cream, cheeses) and processes canned and frozen vegetables, sauces, powdered drinks, and creamers.
Dreyer's Grand (U.S.) ...	Manufacturer and distributor of premium ice cream products.
Flowers Ind. (U.S.)	Producer of bakery and snack-food goods.
General Mills (U.S.)	Processes and markets consumer foods (cereals, flour, seafood, yogurt) and operates restaurants.

Heinz (U.S.) .... Manufactures soups, ketchup, baby foods, cat food, frozen potatoes.

Michael Foods (U.S.) .... Producer and distributor of egg and egg products, frozen potato products, ice cream products, refrigerator-case products.

Quaker Oats (U.S.) .... Produces foods (cereals, breakfast products, beverages) and pet foods, owns Fisher-Price toys.

Ralston Purina (U.S.) ..... World's largest producer of dry dog and cat foods and dry-cell batteries.

Sara Lee (U.S.) .... Diversified, international, packaged consumer goods (Hanes, Dim), with operations in coffee, specialty meats, frozen baked goods, and food-services distribution.

Tate & Lyle (U.K.) .... Producer and distributor of sugar products, beverages, food products.

Tesco (U.K.) .... One of the leading food retailers in the United Kingdom.

Unilever (N.L. and U.K.) . One of the world's largest producers and marketers of branded and packaged consumer goods.

United Biscuits (U.K.) .... Maker of biscuits, cookies and crackers, snack foods, frozen foods and owner/operator of fast-food restaurant chain.

Universal Foods (U.S.) ... International manufacturer and marketer of value-added food products and ingredients for food processing, baking, foodservice and retail markets.

Drinks:

Allied Lyons (U.K.) ...... Active in beer and retailing, wines, spirits, eating and drinking places.

Anheuser-Busch (U.S.) ... Largest U.S. brewer, also active in baked and snack goods, frozen foods, theme parks.

Bass (U.K.) .... Active in malt beverages, amusement and recreation, hotels and motels, soft drinks.

Brown-Forman (U.S.) .... A leading wine and spirits producer and importer, producer of fine china, crystal, and luggage.

Coors (U.S.) .... U.S. brewer.

Guinness (U.K.) .... Active in malt beverages, wines, brandy spirits, liquors.

Labatt (CN) .... One of Canada's leading brewers, also active in foods, dairy products, fruit juices.

Molson (CN) .... Engaged in brewing, cleaning and sanitizing, and retail merchandising.

Scottish & Newcastle (U.K.) .... Active in malt beverages, wine and liquor stores, hotels and motels, soft drinks.

Seagram (CN) .... One of the world's largest wine and spirits distillers/producers.

Whitbread (U.K.) .... Maker of malt beverages, operator of hotels and motels, bottler of soft drinks, active in recreation.

Sources: *Value Line; Risk Measurement Services*, January–March 1992 (London Business School); Compact Disclosure (Digital Library System, Inc.); casewriters' estimates.

EXHIBIT 9   Capital-Market Conditions, April 1992

U.K. Gilt and U.S. Treasury Bond Yields (April 8, 1992)

Term	U.K. Gilts, Yield to Maturity	U.S. Treasuries, Yield to Maturity
1	10.50%	4.45%
2	20.40	5.29
3	10.30	5.95
5	10.00	6.82
10	9.80	7.45
15	9.60	7.59
20	9.60%	7.83%

Foreign Exchange Rates

$$\$/\pounds = 1.748$$
$$DM/\pounds = 2.917$$
$$DM/\$ = 1.669$$

Long-Term Expected Rates of Inflation:

United Kingdom	4.3% annually
United States	2.7% annually
Germany	4.0% annually

Equity Market Risk Premium

Market	Estimated Current Premium	Geometric Mean Historical Premium	Arithmetic Mean Historical Premium
London	3.9%	4.1%	6.9%
New York	2.7%	5.6%	8.4%

Sources: *Financial Times; The Wall Street Journal,* OECD *Economic Outlook,* June 1992; Banque Degroof, Belgium.

Part IV

Capital Budgeting and Resource Allocation

The Investment Detective

The essence of capital budgeting and resource allocation is a search for good investments in which to place the firm's capital. The process can be simple when viewed in purely mechanical terms, but a number of subtle issues can obscure the best investment choices. The capital-budgeting analyst is, therefore, necessarily a detective who must winnow good evidence from bad.

Much of the challenge is knowing what quantitative analysis to generate in the first place. Suppose you are a new capital-budgeting analyst for a company considering investments in the eight projects listed in Exhibit 1. The chief financial officer of your company has asked you to rank the projects and recommend which the company should accept.

In this assignment, only the quantitative considerations are relevant. No other project characteristics are deciding factors in the selection, except that management has determined that projects 7 and 8 are mutually exclusive.

All the projects require the same initial investment, $2 million. Moreover, all are believed to be of the same risk class. The weighted-average cost of capital of the firm has never been estimated. In the past, analysts have simply assumed that 10 percent was an appropriate discount rate (although recently certain officers of the company have asserted that the discount rate should be much higher).

To stimulate your analysis, consider the following questions:

1. Can you rank the projects simply by inspecting the cash flows?
2. What criteria might you use to rank the projects? Which quantitative ranking methods are better? Why?
3. What is the ranking you found by using quantitative methods? Does this ranking differ from the ranking obtained by simple inspection of the cash flows?
4. What kinds of real investment projects have cash flows similar to those in the Exhibit?

This case was prepared by Robert F. Bruner, drawing from an antecedent case prepared under the direction of Gordon Donaldson.

EXHIBIT 1 Project Free Cash Flows (in $ thousands)

Project Number	1	2	3	4	5	6	7	8
Initial investment	($2,000)	($2,000)	($2,000)	($2,000)	($2,000)	($2,000)	($2,000)	($2,000)
Year 1	$ 330	$1,666		$ 160	280	$2,200*	$1,200	($ 350)
2	330	334*		200	280		900*	(60)
3	330	165		350	280		300	60
4	330			395	280		90	350
5	330			432	280		70	700
6	330			440*	280			1,200
7	330*			442	280*			2,400*
8	1,000			444	280			
9				446	280			
10				448	280			
11				450	280			
12				451	280			
13				451	280			
14				452	280			
15			$10,000*	(2,000)	280			
Sum of cash flow benefits	$3,310	$2,165	$10,000	$3,561	$4,200	$2,200	$2,560	$4,300
Excess of cash flow over initial investment	$1,310	$ 165	$ 8,000	$1,561	$2,200	$ 200	$ 560	$2,300

*Indicates year in which payback is accomplished.

Dhahran Roads (A)

Hassan Malik, the financial manager of SADE, a Bahraini civil engineering company, reread the recently received fax. He was delighted that the nearly endless conversations with the Transportation Ministry of the municipality of Dhahran in eastern Saudi Arabia were finally coming to a close.

SADE had been selected as the prime contractor for an SR 168 million[1] project that involved the reconstruction and upgrading of the highway network linking the several terminals of the Dhahran airport and connecting the entire complex with the city. The Dhahran Roads project was indicative of projects on which SADE had established its international reputation for being a leading construction contractor. The total cost of the project was estimated to be SR 146 million, so the SR 168 million value provided only a 15 percent return, which was, unfortunately, below the 18 percent hurdle rate required by SADE for projects of this nature. On the other hand, the less-than-desired returns seemed a small cost to pay to maintain a steady flow of new projects during these slow economic times.

The fax requested from Malik a response to the project proposal within a week. The wording of the contract would then be finalized in the subsequent weeks, and the contract signed by mid-January 1993.

---

[1]The unit of currency in Saudi Arabia was the Saudi riyal (SR). In 1992, the exchange rate was approximately SR 1 = US\$ 0.27.

This case was prepared by Michel Schlosser, the Swedish Management Institute (IFL), and Sherwood C. Frey, Jr., the Darden Graduate School of Business Administration, as a basis for class discussion, rather than to illustrate either effective or ineffective handling of an administrative situation. Versions of the case also appear in *Corporate Finance: A Model Building Approach* by Michel Schlosser (N.Y.: Prentice Hall), and *Cases in Quantitative Business Analysis* by Bodily, Carraway, Frey, and Pfeifer (Homewood, Ill.: Richard D. Irwin).

THE PROJECT

The terms of the proposed contract contained several provisions:

- The ministry would advance to SADE at the signing of the contract 15 percent of the total value.
- If work progressed on schedule, SADE could bill the Ministry as milestones were reached in accordance with the following schedule:

1993	SR 11,000,000
1994	SR 43,000,000
1995	SR 48,000,000
1996	SR 39,000,000
1997	SR 27,000,000

- The ministry would pay 80 percent of each bill received. Payment, of course, would be subject to a satisfactory inspection of the site by the ministry. The 20 percent deduction would be withheld for *(a)* the recovery of the advance payment (15 percent) and *(b)* the accumulation of a retention fund (5 percent).
- Half of the retention would be reimbursed at the time of completion (end of 1997). The second half would be repaid at the end of 1998, provided the roads did not show any flaws in their first year of use.

During the past several months, the SADE engineering department had inspected the site, confirmed the surveys, and reviewed the drawings that had been provided by the ministry. In the opinion of the vice president of engineering, the project presented "no unusual challenges." It was similar to several SADE projects in other countries that were now nearly complete and that had moved ahead without difficulty.

For SADE to proceed, equipment would have to be ordered immediately so it would be available in the fourth quarter of 1993 when earth-moving would commence. The cost of the equipment would be SR 38 million with payment due upon delivery. At the end of the project, the equipment would have no salvage value. The engineering department estimated that the cost of completing the project (not including the equipment) would be SR 108 million. SR 7 million would be expended in 1993 for preliminary site work. The project would then proceed at estimated costs of SR 28 million, SR 31 million, SR 25 million, and SR 17 million for the subsequent years.

The project would be managed by one of SADE's experienced project managers, Harold Smithers. Smithers had just completed a major waterworks project in East Africa and was noted for strong engineering skills and tight cost control.

Although the contract would be denominated in Saudi riyals, the foreign exchange exposure would be minimal since the Bahraini dinar was pegged to the Saudi riyal. In addition, Saudi Arabian and Bahraini tax laws would not require SADE to pay taxes on the profits of this contract.

Vesuvio Fonderia S.p.A.

In November 1992, Angela Lombardi, managing director of Vesuvio Fonderia S.p.A.,[1] was considering the purchase of a Bond-O-Matic automated molding machine. This machine would prepare the sand molds into which molten iron was poured to obtain iron castings. The Bond-O-Matic would replace an older machine and would offer improvements in quality and some additional capacity for expansion. Similar molding-machine proposals had been rejected by the board of directors for economic reasons on three previous occasions, however, most recently in 1990. Therefore, and given the size of the proposed expenditure, about 1.5 billion lira,[2] Lombardi was seeking a careful estimate of the project's costs and benefits.

THE COMPANY

Vesuvio Fonderia specialized in the production of precision metal castings for use in automotive, aerospace, and construction equipment. The company had acquired a reputation for quality products, particularly for safety parts (i.e., parts where failure would result in loss of control for the operator). Products included crankshafts, transmissions, brake calipers, axles, wheels, and various steering-assembly parts. Customers were original-equipment manufacturers (OEMs), mainly in Europe. OEMs were growing to be especially demanding of product quality, and Vesuvio's response had reduced the reject rate of its castings by the OEMs to 70 parts per 1 million.

This record had won the company coveted quality awards from BMW, Ferrari, and Peugeot and had resulted in strategic alliances with those firms: Vesuvio and the OEMs

---

[1]S.p.A. indicates a public corporation.

[2]In November 1992, the exchange rate of the Italian lira to the U.S. dollar was about 1,300:1.

This case was prepared by Robert F. Bruner from field research and public information and draws elements from an antecedent case written by Brandt Allen. The author gratefully acknowledges the financial support of the Citicorp Global Scholars Program.

exchanged technical personnel and design tasks; in addition, the OEMs shared confidential market-demand information with Vesuvio, which increased the precision of Vesuvio's production scheduling. In certain instances, the OEMs had provided cheap loans to Vesuvio to support capital expansion. Finally, Vesuvio received relatively long-term supply contracts from the OEMs and had a preferential position for bidding on new contracts.

Vesuvio, located in Naples, Italy, had been founded in 1912 by Angela Lombardi's great-grandfather, Benito Lombardi, a naval engineer, to produce castings for the armaments industry. In the 1920s and 1930s, the company expanded its customer base into the automotive industry. Although the company barely avoided financial collapse in the late 1940s, Benito Lombardi predicted a postwar demand for precision metal casting and positioned the company to meet it. From that time, Vesuvio Fonderia grew slowly but steadily; its sales for calendar-year 1992 were expected to be 230 billion lira. It was listed for trading on the Milan stock exchange in 1991, but the Lombardi family owned 55 percent of the common shares of stock outstanding. (The company's beta was 1.25.[3])

The company's traditional hurdle rate of return on capital deployed was 12 percent. (This rate had not been reviewed since 1984.) In addition, company policy sought payback of an entire investment within five years. At the time of the case, the market value of the company's capital was 33 percent debt and 67 percent equity. The debt consisted entirely of short-term loans from Banco Nazionale del Ercolano, bearing an interest rate of 16 percent. The company's effective tax rate was about 46 percent, which reflected the combination of national and local corporate income tax rates.

Angela Lombardi, age 57, had assumed executive responsibility for the company 20 years earlier upon the death of her father. She held a doctorate in metallurgy and was the matriarch of an extended family. Only a son and a niece worked at Vesuvio Fonderia, however. Over the years, the Lombardi family had sought to earn a rate of return on its equity investment of about 18 percent.

THE BOND-O-MATIC MOLDING MACHINE

Sand molds used to make castings were prepared in a semiautomated process in 1992. Workers stamped impressions in a mixture of sand and adhesive under heat and high pressure. The process was relatively labor intensive, required training and retraining to obtain consistency in mold quality, and demanded some heavy lifting from workers. Indeed, medical claims for back injuries in the molding shop had doubled since 1982 as the mix of Vesuvio's casting products shifted toward heavy items. (Items averaged 20 kilograms in 1992.)

The new molding machine would replace six semiautomated stamping machines that, together, had originally cost 700 million lira. Depreciation of 220 million already had

---

[3]The 10-year rate of return on Italian government bonds was 14.25 percent. Angela Lombardi assumed that the equity risk premium would be 5.6 percent.

been charged against this original cost; total depreciation on these machines had been averaging 80 million lira yearly. Vesuvio's management believed that these semiautomated machines would need to be replaced after six years. Lombardi had received an offer of 250 million lira for the six machines.

The current six machines required 12 workers per shift[4] (24 in total) at 13,000 lira per worker per hour, plus the equivalent of 3 maintenance workers, each of whom was paid 14,000 lira per hour, plus maintenance supplies of 5 million lira per year. Lombardi assumed that the semiautomated machines, if kept, would continue to consume electrical power at the rate of 21.6 million lira per year.

The Bond-O-Matic molding machine was produced by a company in Allentown, Pennsylvania. Vesuvio Fonderia had received a firm offering price of 1.25 billion lira from the Allentown firm. The estimate for modifications to the plant, including wiring for the machine's power supply, was 250 million lira. Allowing for shipping, installation, and testing, the total cost of the Bond-O-Matic machine was expected to be 1.502 billion lira, all of which would be capitalized and depreciated for tax purposes over eight years. (Lombardi assumed that, at a high and steady rate of machine utilization, the Bond-O-Matic would need to be replaced after the eighth year.)

The new machine would require two skilled operators (one per shift), each receiving 20,000 lira per hour (including benefits), and contract maintenance of 90 million lira per year and would incur power costs of 40 million yearly. In addition, the automatic machine was expected to save at least 10 million lira yearly through improved labor efficiency.

With the current machines, over 30 percent of the foundry floor space was needed for the wide galleries the machines required; raw materials and in-process inventories had to be staged near each machine to smooth the work flow. With the automated machine, almost half of this space would be freed for other purposes (although at present there was no need for new space).

Certain aspects of the Bond-O-Matic purchase decision were difficult to quantify. First, Lombardi was not sure whether the tough collective-bargaining agreement her company had with the employees' union would allow her to lay off the 24 operators of the semiautomated machines. Reassigning the workers to other jobs might be easier, but the only positions needing to be filled were those of janitors, who were paid 6,000 lira per hour. The extent of any labor savings would depend on negotiations with the union. Second, Angela believed that the Bond-O-Matic would result in even higher levels of product quality and lower scrap rates than the company was now boasting. In light of the ever-increasing competition, this outcome might prove to be of enormous, but currently unquantifiable, competitive importance. Finally, the Bond-O-Matic had a theoretical maximum capacity that was 30 percent higher than the six semiautomated machines, but these machines were operating at only 90 percent of capacity, and Lombardi was not sure when added capacity would be needed. The latest economic news suggested that the economies of Europe were slipping into recession.

---

[4]The foundry was operating two shifts per day. The foundry did not operate on weekends or holidays. At maximum, the foundry would produce for 210 days per year.

Empirical Chemicals, Ltd. (A): The Merseyside Project

Late one afternoon in January 1992, Jim Hawkins told Frances Trelawney, "No one seems satisfied with the analysis so far, but the suggested changes could kill the project. If solid projects like this can't swim past the corporate piranhas, the company will never modernize."

Trelawney was plant manager of Empirical Chemicals' Merseyside Works in Liverpool, England. Her controller, Jim Hawkins, was discussing a capital project she wanted to propose to senior management. The project consisted of a £7 million expenditure to renovate and rationalize the polypropylene production line at the Merseyside plant in order to make up for deferred maintenance and exploit opportunities to achieve increased production efficiency.

Empirical Chemicals was under pressure from investors to improve its financial performance as a result of both the worldwide recession in the chemicals industry and the accumulation of the firm's common shares by a well-known corporate raider, William Lord Bones. Earnings per share had fallen to £4.55 at the end of 1991 from £12.75 at the end of 1990. Trelawney thus believed that the time was ripe to obtain funding from corporate headquarters for a modernization program for the Merseyside Works—at least she had believed so until Hawkins presented her with several questions that only recently had surfaced.

This case was written by Professor Robert F. Bruner as the basis for classroom discussion, rather than to illustrate effective or ineffective handling of an administrative situation. Facts and figures have been disguised. The author wishes to acknowledge the helpful comments of Dr. Frank H. McTigue and the financial support the Citicorp Global Scholars Program. Copyright © 1992 by the Darden Graduate Business School Foundation, Charlottesville, VA.

EMPIRICAL CHEMICALS AND POLYPROPYLENE

Empirical Chemicals (EC), a major competitor in the worldwide chemicals industry, was a leading producer of polypropylene, a polymer used in an extremely wide variety of products (ranging from medical products to packaging film, carpet fibers, and automobile components) and known for its strength and malleability. Polypropylene was essentially priced as a commodity.

The production of polypropylene pellets at Merseyside began with propylene, a refined gas received in tank cars. Propylene was purchased from four refineries in England that produced it in the course of refining crude oil into gasoline. In the first stage of the production process, polymerization, the propylene gas was combined with a diluent (or solvent) in a large pressure vessel. In a catalytic reaction, polypropylene precipitated to the bottom of the tank and then was concentrated in a centrifuge.

The second stage of the production process compounded the basic polypropylene with stabilizers, modifiers, fillers, and pigments to achieve the desired attributes for a particular customer. The finished plastic was extruded into pellets for shipment to the customer.

The Merseyside production process was old, semicontinuous at best, and, therefore, higher in labor content than competitors' newer plants. The Merseyside plant was constructed in 1967.

EC produced polypropylene at Merseyside and in Rotterdam, Holland. The two plants were of identical scale, age, and design. The managers of both plants reported to Trevor Livesey, executive vice president and manager of the Intermediate Chemicals Group (ICG) of EC. The company positioned itself as a supplier to customers in Europe and the Middle East. The strategic-analysis staff estimated that, in addition to numerous small producers, seven major competitors manufactured polypropylene in EC's market region. Their plants operated at various cost levels. Exhibit 1 presents a comparison of plant sizes and indexed costs.

THE PROPOSED CAPITAL PROGRAM

Trelawney had assumed responsibility for the Merseyside Works only 12 months previously, following a rapid rise from an entry position of shift engineer eight years before. When she assumed responsibility, she undertook a detailed review of the operations and discovered significant opportunities for improvement in polypropylene production. Some of these opportunities stemmed from the deferral of maintenance over the preceding five years. In an effort to enhance the operating results of the works, the previous manager had limited capital expenditures to only the most essential. Now, what had been routine and deferrable was becoming essential. Other opportunities stemmed from correcting the antiquated plant design in ways that would save energy and improve the process flow: (1) relocating and modernizing tank-car unloading areas, which would enable the process flow to be streamlined; (2) renovating the polymerization tank to achieve higher pressures and, thus, greater throughput; and (3) renovating the compounding plant to increase extrusion throughput and obtain energy savings.

Trelawney proposed the expenditure of £7 million on this program. The entire polymerization line would need to be shut down for 60 days, however, and, because the

Rotterdam plant was operating near capacity, Merseyside's customers would buy from competitors. Hawkins believed the lost custom would not be permanent. The benefits would be a lower energy requirement[1] as well as a 7 percent greater manufacturing throughput. In addition, the project was expected to improve gross margin (before depreciation and energy savings) from 11.5 percent to 13.1 percent. The engineering group at Merseyside was highly confident that the efficiencies would be realized.

Merseyside currently produced 135,000 metric tons of polypropylene pellets per year. Currently, the price of polypropylene averaged £611 per ton for EC's product mix. The tax rate required in capital-expenditure analyses was 35 percent. Hawkins discovered that any plant facilities to be replaced had been completely depreciated. New assets could be depreciated on an accelerated basis[2] over 15 years, the expected life of the assets. The increased throughput would necessitate a one-time increase of work-in-process inventory equal in value to 5.7 percent of cost of goods. Hawkins included in the first year of his forecast "preliminary engineering costs" of £500,000, which had been spent over the preceding nine months on efficiency and design studies of the renovation. Finally, the corporate manual stipulated that overhead costs be reflected in project analyses at the rate of 3.5 percent times the book value of assets acquired in the project, per year.[3]

Hawkins had produced the discounted-cash-flow summary given in Exhibit 2. It suggested that the capital program would easily hurdle EC's required return of 10 percent for engineering projects.

CONCERNS OF THE TRANSPORT DIVISION

EC owned the tank cars with which Merseyside received propylene gas from four petroleum refineries in England. The Transport Division, a cost center, oversaw the movement of all raw, intermediate, and finished materials throughout the company and was responsible for managing the tank cars. Because of the project's increased throughput,

---

[1]Hawkins characterized the energy savings as a percentage of sales and assumed that the savings would be equal to 1 percent of sales in the first 5 years and 0.5 percent in years 6–10. Thereafter, without added aggressive "green" spending, the energy efficiency of the plant would revert to its old level, and the savings would be 0. He believed that the decision to make further environmentally oriented investments was a separate choice (and one that should be made much later) and, therefore, that to include such benefits (of a presumably later investment decision) in the project being considered today would be inappropriate.

[2]The company's capital-expenditure manual suggested the use of double-declining-balance depreciation, even though other, more aggressive procedures might be permitted by the tax code. The reason for this policy was to discourage jockeying for corporate approvals based on tax provisions that could apply differently for different projects and divisions. Prior to senior-management approval, the controller's staff would present an independent analysis of special tax effects that might apply. Division managers, however, were discouraged from relying heavily on these effects.

[3]The corporate policy manual stated that:

new projects should be able to sustain a reasonable proportion of corporate overhead expense. Projects which are so marginal as to be unable to sustain these expenses and also meet the other criteria of investment attractiveness should not be undertaken. Thus, all new capital projects should reflect an annual pretax charge amounting to 3.5 percent of the value of the initial asset investment for the project.

Transport would have to increase its allocation of tank cars to Merseyside. Currently, the Transport Division could make this allocation out of excess capacity, although doing so would accelerate from 1996 to 1994 the need to purchase new rolling stock to support anticipated growth of the firm in other areas. The purchase would cost £2 million. The rolling stock would have a depreciable life of 10 years, but, with proper maintenance, the cars could operate much longer.

A memorandum from the controller of the Transport Division suggested that the cost of these tank cars should be included in the initial outlay of Merseyside's capital program. In response, Hawkins told Trelawney,

> The Transport Division isn't paying one pence of actual cash because of what we're doing at Merseyside. In fact, we're doing the company a favor in using its excess capacity. Even *if* an allocation has to be made somewhere, it should go on the Transport Division's books. The way we've always evaluated projects in this company has been with the philosophy of "every tub on its own bottom"—every division has to fend for itself. The Transport Division isn't part of our own Intermediate Chemicals Group, so they should carry the allocation of rolling stock.

Accordingly, Hawkins had not reflected any charge for the use of excess rolling stock in his preliminary DCF analysis given in Exhibit 2.

The Transport Division and Intermediate Chemicals Group reported to separate executive vice presidents, who, themselves, reported to the chairman and chief executive officer of the company. The executive VPs received an annual incentive bonus pegged to the performance of their divisions.

CONCERNS OF THE ICG SALES AND MARKETING DEPARTMENT

Hawkins' analysis had led to questions from the director of sales. In a recent meeting, the director told Hawkins,

> Your analysis assumes that we can sell the added output and, thus, obtain the full efficiencies from the project, but as you know, the market for polypropylene is extremely competitive. To move the added volume, we will have to shift capacity away from Rotterdam toward Merseyside. Is this really a gain for EC? Why spend money just so one plant can cannibalize another?

The vice president of marketing was less skeptical. He said that, with lower costs at Merseyside, EC might be able to take business from the plants of competitors such as Saone-Poulet or Vaysol. In the current severe recession, competitors would fight hard to keep customers, but, sooner or later, the market would revive, and it would be reasonable to assume that any lost business volume would return at that time.

Hawkins had listened to both the director and vice president and chose to reflect no charge for a loss of business at Rotterdam in his preliminary analysis of the Merseyside project. He told Trelawney,

> Cannibalization really isn't a cash flow; there is no check written in this instance. Anyway, if the company starts burdening its cost-reduction projects with fictitious charges like this, we'll never maintain our cost competitiveness. A cannibalization charge is rubbish!

CONCERNS OF THE ASSISTANT PLANT MANAGER

Harry Mulvaney, the assistant plant manager and direct subordinate of Trelawney, proposed an unusual modification to Hawkins' analysis during a late-afternoon meeting with Hawkins and Trelawney. Over the past few months, Mulvaney had been absorbed with the development of a proposal to modernize a separate and independent part of the Merseyside Works, the production line for ethylene–propylene–copolymer rubber (EPC). This product, a variety of synthetic rubber, had been pioneered by Empirical Chemicals in the early 1960s and was sold in bulk to European tire manufacturers. Despite hopes that this oxidation-resistant rubber would dominate the market in synthetics, in fact, EPC remained a relatively small product in the European chemical industry. Empirical, the largest supplier of EPC, produced the entire volume at Merseyside. EPC had been only marginally profitable to Empirical because of entry by competitors, the development of competing synthetic rubber compounds, and the slump in tire sales over the past five years.

Mulvaney had proposed a renovation of the EPC production line for a cost of £1 million. The renovation would give Empirical the lowest EPC cost base in the world and improve cash flows by £25,000 ad infinitum. Even so, at current prices and volumes, the net present value (NPV) of this project was −£750,000. Mulvaney and the EPC product manager had argued strenuously to the executive committee of the company that the negative NPV ignored strategic advantages from the project and increases in volume and prices when the recession ended. Nevertheless, the executive committee had rejected the project, mainly on economic grounds.

In a hushed voice, Mulvaney said to Trelawney and Hawkins,

Why don't you include the EPC project as part of the polypropylene line renovations? The positive NPV of the poly renovations can easily sustain the negative NPV of the EPC project. This is an extremely important project to the company, but the bigwigs up at corporate won't see the light. If we invest now, we'll be ready to cream the market when the recession ends. If we don't invest now, you can expect that we will have to exit the business altogether in three years. Do you look forward to more layoffs? Do you want to manage a shrinking plant? Recall that our annual bonuses are pegged to the size of this operation. Also remember that in the last 20 years no one from corporate has monitored renovation projects once the investment decision was made.

EVALUATING CAPITAL-EXPENDITURE PROPOSALS AT EMPIRICAL CHEMICALS

In submitting a project for senior-management approval, the proposers had to identify it as belonging to one of four possible categories: (1) new product or market, (2) product or market extension, (3) engineering efficiency, or (4) safety or environment. The first three categories of proposals were subject to a system of four performance "hurdles," of which at least three had to be met for the proposal to be considered.

1. Impact on earnings per share. The corporate target growth rate in EPS was 15 percent per year. The contribution to net income from contemplated projects had to be positive. This criterion was calculated as the average annual EPS contribution of the project over its entire economic life, with the number of outstanding shares at the most recent fiscal year end used as the basis for the calculation. (At FYE 1991, Empirical Chemicals had 92,891,240 shares outstanding.)

2. Payback. This criterion was defined as the number of years necessary for free cash flow of the project to amortize the initial project outlay completely. For engineering-efficiency projects, the maximum payback period was six years.

3. Discounted cash flow. DCF was defined as the present value of future cash flows of the project (at the hurdle rate of 10 percent for engineering-efficiency proposals), less the initial investment outlay. This net present value of free cash flows had to be positive.

4. Internal rate of return. IRR was defined as being that discount rate at which the present value of future free cash flows just equaled the initial outlay—in other words, the rate at which the NPV was 0. The IRR of engineering-efficiency projects had to be greater than 10 percent.

CONCLUSION

Trelawney wanted to review Hawkins' analysis in detail and settle the questions surrounding the tank cars and potential loss of business volume at Rotterdam. As Hawkins' analysis now stood, the Merseyside project met all four investment criteria:

1.	Average annual addition to EPS	= £0.012
2.	Payback period	= 4.38 years
3.	Net present value	= £4.57 million
4.	Internal rate of return	= 20.13 percent

Trelawney was concerned that further tinkering might seriously weaken the attractiveness of the project.

EXHIBIT 1   Comparative Information on Seven Largest Polypropylene Plants in Europe

	Plant Location	Age	Plant Annual Output (metric tons)	Production Cost per ton (indexed to low-cost producer)
CBTG A.G.	Saarbrün	1981	200,000	1.00
Empirical Chem.	Liverpool	1967	135,000	1.09
Empirical Chem.	Rotterdam	1967	135,000	1.09
Hosche A.G.	Hamburg	1977	200,000	1.02
Montecassino SpA	Genoa	1961	90,000	1.11
Saone-Poulet S.A.	Marseille	1972	145,000	1.07
Vaysol S.A.	Antwerp	1976	160,000	1.06
Next 10 largest plants			450,000	1.19

EXHIBIT 2   Hawkins' Preliminary DCF Analysis: Merseyside Project (all financial quantities in £ millions)

Annual output (metric tons)	135,000	Output gain/original output	7.0
Price/ton (pounds sterling)	611	Gross margin (ex. deprec.)	13.1%
Old gross margin	11.5%	Tax rate	35.0%
Investment outlay (mill.)	7	Depreciable life (years)	15
Discount rate	10.0%	Salvage value	0
Overhead/investment	3.5%	Months downtime, construction	2
Work-in-process inventory/cost of goods sold	5.7%	Preliminary engineering costs	0.5
After-tax scrap proceeds	0		

	1 1992	2 1993	3 1994	4 1995	5 1996	6 1997
1. Estimate of incremental gross profit:						
New output	144,450	144,450	144,450	144,450	144,450	144,450
Lost output, construction	(22,500)	—	—	—	—	—
New sales (£ m)	74.51	88.26	88.26	88.26	88.26	88.26
New gross margin	14.1%	14.1%	14.1%	14.1%	14.1%	13.6%
New gross profit	10.51	12.44	12.44	12.44	12.44	12.00
Old output	135,000	135,000	135,000	135,000	135,000	135,000
Old sales	82.49	82.49	82.49	82.49	82.49	82.49
Old gross profit	9.49	9.49	9.49	9.49	9.49	9.49
Incremental gross profit	1.02	2.96	2.96	2.96	2.96	2.52
2. Estimate of incremental depreciation:						
New depreciation	0.93	0.81	0.70	0.61	0.53	0.46
3. Overhead	0.25	0.25	0.25	0.25	0.25	0.25
4. Preliminary engineering costs	0.50	—	—	—	—	—
5. Pretax incremental profit	−0.66	1.90	2.01	2.11	2.19	1.82
6. Tax expense	−0.23	0.67	0.70	0.74	0.77	0.64
7. After-tax profit	−0.43	1.24	1.31	1.37	1.42	1.18
8. Cash-flow adjustments:						
Less capital expend. −7.00						
Add back depreciation	0.93	0.81	0.70	0.61	0.53	0.46
Less added WIP inventory	−0.28	0.00	0.00	0.00	0.00	0.00
After-tax scrap proceeds	—	—	—	—	—	—
9. Free cash flow −7.00	0.22	2.05	2.01	1.98	1.95	1.64

DCF of the Merseyside project = £ 4.57 million
IRR of the Merseyside project = 20.13%

Energy saving/sales	Yrs. 1–5	Yrs. 6–10	Yrs. 10+
	1.0%	0.5%	0.0%

7	8	9	10	11	12	13	14	15
1998	1999	2000	2001	2002	2003	2004	2005	2006
144,450	144,450	144,450	144,450	144,450	144,450	144,450	144,450	144,450
—	—	—	—	—	—	—	—	—
88.26	88.26	88.26	88.26	88.26	88.26	88.26	88.26	88.26
13.6%	13.6%	13.6%	13.6%	13.1%	13.1%	13.1%	13.1%	13.1%
12.00	12.00	12.00	12.00	11.56	11.56	11.56	11.56	11.56
135,000	135,000	135,000	135,000	135,000	135,000	135,000	135,000	135,000
82.49	82.49	82.49	82.49	82.49	82.49	82.49	82.49	82.49
9.49	9.49	9.49	9.49	9.49	9.49	9.49	9.49	9.49
2.52	2.52	2.52	2.52	2.08	2.08	2.08	2.08	2.08
0.40	0.34	0.30	0.26	0.22	0.19	0.17	0.15	0.13
0.25	0.25	0.25	0.25	0.25	0.25	0.25	0.25	0.25
—	—	—	—	—	—	—	—	—
1.88	1.93	1.98	2.01	1.61	1.64	1.66	1.69	1.71
0.66	0.68	0.69	0.71	0.56	0.57	0.58	0.59	0.60
1.22	1.25	1.28	1.31	1.05	1.06	1.08	1.10	1.11
0.40	0.34	0.30	0.26	0.22	0.19	0.17	0.15	0.13
0.00	0.00	0.00	0.00	0.00	0.00	0.00	0.00	0.00
—	—	—	—	—	—	—	—	—
1.62	1.60	1.58	1.57	1.27	1.26	1.25	1.24	1.23

Empirical Chemicals, Ltd. (B): Merseyside and Rotterdam Projects

Trevor Livesey, executive vice president of the Intermediate Chemicals Group (ICG) of Empirical Chemicals (EC), met with his financial analyst, Karen Cooper, to review two mutually exclusive capital-expenditure proposals. The firm's capital budget would be submitted for approval to the board of directors early in February 1992, and any projects proposed by Livesey for the ICG had to be forwarded soon to the chief executive officer of EC for his review. Plant managers in Liverpool and Rotterdam independently had submitted expenditure proposals, each of which would expand the polypropylene output of their respective plants by 7 percent.[1] EC's strategic-analysis staff argued strenuously that a companywide increase in polypropylene output of 7 percent made no sense, but half that amount did. Thus, Livesey decided he could not accept *both* projects; he could sponsor only one for approval by the board.

Corporate policy was to evaluate projects based on four criteria: (1) net present value (NPV), computed at the appropriate cost of capital, (2) internal rate of return (IRR), (3) payback, and (4) growth in earnings per share. In addition, the board of directors was receptive to "strategic factors"—considerations that might be difficult to quantify. The

---

[1]Background information on Empirical Chemicals and the polypropylene business is given in "Empirical Chemicals (A): The Merseyside Project" (UVA-F-1020).

This case was written by Professor Robert F. Bruner as the basis for classroom discussion, rather than to illustrate effective or ineffective handling of an administrative situation. Facts and figures have been disguised. The author wishes to acknowledge the helpful comments of Dr. Frank H. McTigue and the financial support of the Citicorp Global Scholars Program.

manager of the Rotterdam plant, Johan Silver, argued vociferously that his project easily hurdled all the relevant quantitative standards, and that it had important strategic benefits. Indeed, Silver had interjected these points in two recent meetings with senior management and at a cocktail reception for the board of directors. Livesey expected to review the proposal from Frances Trelawney, manager of the Liverpool plant, at this meeting with Cooper, but he suspected that neither proposal dominated the other on all four criteria. Livesey's choice would apparently not be straightforward.

THE PROPOSAL FROM MERSEYSIDE, LIVERPOOL

The project for the Merseyside plant entailed the enhancement of existing facilities and production process. Based on the type of project and the engineering studies, the potential benefits of the project were fairly certain [see "Empirical Chemicals (A)" for a detailed discussion of this project]. To date, Trelawney, manager of the Merseyside Works, had limited her discussions about the project to conversations with Livesey and Cooper. Cooper had raised various exploratory questions about the project and had presented preliminary analyses of it to managers in marketing and transportation for their comments. Separately, she had approached EC's environmental adviser about the likelihood of further environmental investment at Merseyside.[2] The revised analysis emerging from these discussions would be the focus of discussion with Cooper in the forthcoming meeting.

Cooper had indicated that Trelawney's final memo on the project was short, only three pages and one exhibit. Trevor wondered whether this memo would satisfy his remaining questions.

THE ROTTERDAM PROJECT

Johan Silver's proposal consisted of a 90-page document replete with detailed schematics, engineering comments, strategic analyses, and financial projections. The basic discounted-cash-flow (DCF) analysis is presented in Exhibit 1 and shows that the project had an NPV of £9.12 million and an IRR of 17.87 percent; accounting for a "worst-case" scenario, in which erosion of Merseyside's volume by undertaking the Rotterdam project, the NPV was £8.03 million and the IRR about 17.3 percent.

In essence, Silver's proposal called for the expenditure of £8 million spread over three years (and having a present value of about £7 million) to convert the plant's polymerization line from batch to continuous-flow technology and to install sophisticated state-of-the-art process controls throughout the polymerization and compounding operations. The heart of the new system would be an analog computer driven by advanced software written by

---

[2] The environmental adviser indicated that the trend in the United Kingdom and European Community made the likelihood of further environmental investment at Merseyside a virtual certainty. For this reason, Livesey had advised Trelawney to include energy savings over the entire life of the Merseyside project.

a team of engineering professors at an institute in Japan. The three-year-old process-control technology had been used on a smaller polypropylene production facility in Japan and had produced significant improvements in cost and output. Other major producers were known to be evaluating this system for use in their plants.

Silver explained that installing the sophisticated new system would not be feasible without also obtaining a continuous source of supply of propylene gas. He proposed to obtain this gas by pipeline from one refinery five kilometers away (rather than by railroad tank cars sourced from three refineries). EC had an option to purchase a pipeline and its right-of-way for £3 million; then, for relatively little cost, the pipeline could be extended to the Rotterdam plant and the refinery at the other end. The option had been purchased several years earlier. A consultant had informed Silver that to purchase a right-of-way at today's prices and to lay a comparable pipeline would cost approximately £6 million. The consultant also forecasted that in 15 years the value of the right-of-way would be £35 million.[3] This option was to expire in six months.

Some senior EC executives believed firmly that, if the Rotterdam project were not undertaken, the option on the right-of-way should be allowed to expire unexercised. The reasoning was summarized by Henry Digbee, chairman of the executive committee:

> Our business is chemicals, not land speculation. Simply buying the right-of-way with an intention of reselling it for a profit takes us beyond our expertise. Who knows when we could sell it, and for how much? How distracting would this little side venture be for Johan Silver?

Younger members of senior management were more willing to consider a potential investment arbitrage on the right-of-way.

Silver expected to realize benefits (such as increased output and gross margin) of this investment gradually over time as the new technology was installed and shaken down and as learning-curve effects were realized. He advocated a phased investment program (as opposed to all at once) to minimize disruption to plant operations and to allow the new technology to be calibrated and fine-tuned.

Given the complexity of the technology and the extent to which it would permeate the plant, the system would be very expensive to dismantle. Practically, there would be no going back once the decision had been made to install the new controls. Silver's project would represent an irrevocable commitment to the analog technology at the Rotterdam plant.

Livesey recalled that the "strategic factors" to which Silver referred had to do with the obvious cost and output improvements expected from the new system, as well as from an advantage from being the first major European producer to implement the new technology. Being the first to implement the technology probably meant a head start in moving

---

[3]The right-of-way had several alternate commercial uses. Most prominently, the Dutch government had expressed an interest in using the right-of-way for a new high-speed railroad line. However, the planning for this line had barely begun, which suggested that land-acquisition efforts were years away. Moreover, government budget deficits threatened the timely implementation of the rail project. Another potential user was Medusa Communications, an international telecommunications company that was looking for pathways along which to bury its new optical-fiber cables. Power companies and other chemical companies or refiners might also be interested in acquiring the right-of-way.

down the learning curve toward reducing costs as the organization became familiar with the technology. Silver argued,

> The Japanese, and now the Americans, exploit the learning-curve phenomenon aggressively. Fortunately, they aren't major players in European polypropylene, at least for now. This is a once-in-a-generation opportunity for EC to leapfrog its competition through the exploitation of new technology.

In an oblique reference to the Merseyside proposal, Silver went on to say,

> There are two alternatives to implementation of the analog process-control technology. One is a series of myopic enhancements to existing facilities; but this is nothing more than sticking one's head in the sand, for it leaves us at the mercy of our competitors who *are* making choices for the long term. The other alternative is to exit the polypropylene business; but this amounts to walking away from the considerable know-how we've accumulated in this business and from what is basically a valuable activity. Our commitment to analog controls makes the right choice at the right time.

The analog process-control system seemed to be the most advanced on the market. There were rumors, however, that an engineering design team at Glüßingen University in Germany was testing a radically different process-control technology—based on lasers, spectral chromatography, and digital computing—and that it was outperforming the Japanese system on cost reduction and output improvement by a factor of 1.1:1. If these rumors were true, such a system might become commercially available within five years.

Livesey wondered how to take the potential new technology into account in making his decision. Even if he recommended the Merseyside project and no better technology emerged, the new controls could be installed later at Merseyside. Cooper had suggested that the flexibility to change technologies under the Merseyside project represented essentially two mutually exclusive call options (one each on the German and Japanese systems).[4]

CONCLUSION

Trevor Livesey wanted to give this choice careful thought, because the plant managers at Merseyside and Rotterdam seemed to have so much invested in their own proposals. He wished that the capital-budgeting criteria would give a straightforward indication about the relative attractiveness of the two mutually exclusive projects. He wondered by what rational analytical process he could extricate himself from the ambiguities of the present measures of investment attractiveness. Moreover, he wished he had a way to evaluate the primary technological difference between the two proposals: the Rotterdam project firmly committed EC to the new process technology; the Merseyside project did not, but it retained the flexibility to allow the technology in the future.

---

[4]Using Monte Carlo simulation, she had estimated that the cash returns from both the German and Japanese technologies had standard deviations of 8 percent and that the correlation of the two returns was predictably high: 80 percent. The risk-free rate of return was about 7.5 percent. The German digital-based process-control system would emerge in the next five years or not emerge at all.

EXHIBIT 1 Johan Silver's DCF Analysis

Assumptions Used in the DCF Analysis

Annual output (metric tons)	135,000
Output gain per year/prior year	0.8%
Maximum possible output	144,450
Price/ton (pounds sterling)	611
Rate of growth in gross margin per year . .	0.40%
Maximum possible gross margin	16.0%
Old gross margin	11.5%
Tax rate	35.0%
Setup and labor savings/sales (year 1)	0.0%

	1 1992	2 1993	3 1994	4 1995	5 1996	6 1997
1. Estimate of incremental gross profit:						
New output	136,080	137,169	138,266	139,372	140,487	141,611
Lost output, construction	(45,360)	(34,292)	(11,522)	0	0	
New sales (millions)	55.43	83.81	84.48	85.16	85.84	86.52
New gross margin	11.5%	11.6%	11.8%	12.0%	12.2%	12.5%
New gross profit	6.40	9.75	9.95	10.19	10.48	10.82
Old output	135,000	135,000	135,000	135,000	135,000	135,000
Old sales	82.49	82.49	82.49	82.49	82.49	82.49
Old gross profit	9.49	9.49	9.49	9.49	9.49	9.49
Incremental gross profit	−3.09	0.27	0.46	0.71	0.99	1.33
2. Estimate of incremental depreciation:						
Year 1 outlays	0.27	0.23	0.20	0.17	0.15	0.13
Year 2 outlays		0.21	0.18	0.16	0.13	0.12
Year 3 outlays			0.15	0.13	0.11	0.09
Total, new depreciation	0.27	0.45	0.54	0.46	0.40	0.34
3. Overhead	0	0	0	0	0	0
4. Pretax incremental profit	−3.35	−0.18	−0.07	0.24	0.60	1.00
5. Tax expense	−1.17	−0.06	−0.03	0.09	0.21	0.35
6. After-tax profit	−2.18	−0.11	−0.05	0.16	0.39	0.65
7. Cash-flow adjustments:						
Add back depreciation	0.27	0.45	0.54	0.46	0.40	0.34
Less added WIP inventory	−0.81	0.22	0.44	0.23	0.02	0.02
Capital spending 3	2	1.5	1			
Terminal value, land	—	—	—	—	—	—
8. Free cash flow . . . . −3	−3.10	−1.39	−0.95	0.39	0.76	0.97

DCF of Rotterdam project = £9.12 million
IRR of Rotterdam project = 17.87%

Adjustment for possible erosion in Merseyside volume:						
Lost Merseyside output	0	0	0	4,372	5,487	6,611
Lost Merseyside revenue	0	0	0	2.67	3.4	4.0
Lost Merseyside gross profits	0	0	0	0.31	0.4	0.5
Lost gross profits after taxes	0	0	0	0.20	0.3	0.3
Change in Merseyside inventory	0	0	0	0.08	0.1	0.1
Total effect on free cash flow	0	0	0	−0.12	-0.15	−0.18

DCF of erosion at Merseyside = −£1.09 million
DCF of Rotterdam project
adjusted for possible
erosion at Merseyside   = £8.03 million

Assumptions Used in the DCF Analysis

Discount rate	10.0%
Depreciable life (years)	15
Overhead/investment	3.5%
Salvage value	0
Work-in-process (WIP) inventory/sales ...	3.0%
Terminal value of right-of-way	£35 million

	Initial	1992	1993	1994
Investment outlay (millions)	3	2	1.5	1
Months downtime, construction		4	3	1

7	8	9	10	11	12	13	14	15
1998	1999	2000	2001	2002	2003	2004	2005	2006
142,744	143,886	144,450	144,450	144,450	144,450	144,450	144,450	144,450
87.22	87.91	88.26	88.26	88.26	88.26	88.26	88.26	88.26
12.9%	13.3%	13.8%	14.3%	15.0%	15.7%	16.0%	16.0%	16.0%
11.22	11.67	12.15	12.64	13.21	13.86	14.12	14.12	14.12
135,000	135,000	135,000	135,000	135,000	135,000	135,000	135,000	135,000
82.49	82.49	82.49	82.49	82.49	82.49	82.49	82.49	82.49
9.49	9.49	9.49	9.49	9.49	9.49	9.49	9.49	9.49
1.73	2.19	2.66	3.16	3.72	4.37	4.64	4.64	4.64
0.11	0.10	0.08	0.07	0.06	0.06	0.05	0.04	0.04
0.10	0.08	0.07	0.06	0.05	0.05	0.04	0.03	0.03
0.08	0.07	0.06	0.05	0.04	0.03	0.03	0.02	0.02
0.29	0.25	0.21	0.18	0.16	0.14	0.12	0.10	0.09
0	0	0	0	0	0	0	0	0
1.44	1.94	2.45	2.97	3.57	4.24	4.52	4.54	4.55
0.50	0.68	0.86	1.04	1.25	1.48	1.58	1.59	1.59
0.94	1.26	1.59	1.93	2.32	2.75	2.94	2.95	2.96
0.29	0.25	0.21	0.18	0.16	0.14	0.12	0.10	0.09
0.02	0.02	0.01	0.00	0.00	0.00	0.00	0.00	0.17
—	—	—	—	—	—	—	—	35
1.21	1.49	1.79	2.12	2.48	2.89	3.05	3.05	38.22
7,744	8,886	9,450	9,450	9,450	9,450	9,450	9,450	9,450
4.7	5.4	5.8	5.8	5.8	5.8	5.8	5.8	5.8
0.5	0.6	0.7	0.7	0.7	0.7	0.7	0.7	0.7
0.4	0.4	0.4	0.4	0.4	0.4	0.4	0.4	0.4
0.1	0.2	0.2	0.2	0.2	0.2	0.2	0.2	0.2
−0.21	−0.24	−0.26	−0.26	−0.26	−0.26	−0.26	−0.26	−0.26

Case 22

Glaxo Italia S.p.A.: The Zinnat Marketing Decision

The laws of the marketplace now apply as much to pharmaceuticals as to consumer electronics: once armed with a new product, a company must establish its market share as quickly as possible, before rival firms produce competitive brands. . . . In the past, drugs brought in good profits for a decade or more.

Ernest Mario, *Chief Executive Officer of Glaxo Holdings PLC*[1]

In September 1990, the laws of the pharmaceutical marketplace prompted Emilio Rottoli, financial controller of Glaxo Italia S.p.A.,[2] to evaluate competing strategies for the launch of a promising new product in Italy. Zinnat was a new formula of oral antibiotic. After a research-and-development cost of more than 200 billion Italian lira,[3] the product represented a significant innovation in its market segment. However, the huge quantity of competing antibiotics and antihistaminics made success of the product launch unpredictable.

---

[1]Quoted in *The Economist,* September 6, 1990.

[2]Societa per Azioni; literally, a business under share ownership, like a public corporation in the United States. Also, PLC means a public limited company.

[3]On September 14, 1990, one U.S. dollar could purchase 1,165 lira.

This case was prepared from field interviews and public information by Matteo Davoli, Giuseppe Geneletti, Marco Ghiotto, Diogo Rezende, and Professor Robert F. Bruner. The cooperation of Emilio Rottoli and Glaxo Italia S.p.A. is gratefully acknowledged. The financial support of the Citicorp Global Scholars Program is also gratefully acknowledged.

Glaxo's general approach to launching a new product called for rapid and massive distribution into the target market in order to capture a large market share quickly, but Mr. Rottoli had decided to evaluate two competing strategies for selling Zinnat:

- **Comarketing** distribution, under which Glaxo would permit another pharmaceutical company to make and market the same product but under a different brand name. Glaxo would receive a fee from the comarketer, plus profits on the sales of certain ingredients to that firm. This arrangement would sacrifice some market share for Glaxo's own brand, Zinnat. Glaxo had used comarketing arrangements to promote other products.

    The major market for Glaxo's best selling product, Zantac, an antiulcer drug, was developed under a comarketing agreement with Hoffmann-La Roche, whose sales teams organized the introduction of the product among doctors in the United States. The tremendous success of this initiative had built up an appetite (and an expertise) within the company for such arrangements.

- **Direct sales,** under which Glaxo's own sales force would be the sole channel of distribution. This approach would permit the company to exploit the potential gains from its new product most fully. Under this approach, demands on Glaxo's sales organization would be greater than in comarketing, however, and market penetration for the product would take longer.

The choice between the two approaches would hinge not only on financial criteria (such as payback and internal rate of return) but also on qualitative factors such as the potential strength of the brand, uncertainties about the future regulation of a possible over-the-counter (OTC) product, the need to generate cash in the short term to sustain a large R&D budget, uncertainties about the rate of technological change in the pharmaceutical industry and the development of products competitive to Zinnat, potential price wars, and the peculiar aspects of the Italian market.

GLAXO HOLDINGS PLC

Glaxo Italia S.p.A. was a wholly owned operating company of Glaxo Holdings PLC, headquartered in London. Glaxo Holdings was the world's second largest pharmaceutical company in terms of sales, which totaled £2,894 million in the fiscal year ending June 30, 1990, and were expected to grow to £3.4 billion in 1991.[4] The company's growth had been phenomenal: £1 invested in the company in 1979 was worth £85 in 1990, approximately a 50 percent annual compound rate of growth in value (see Exhibit 1). Glaxo's shares were listed for trading in London, New York (as American Depositary Receipts), Tokyo, and Paris. With an equity market value of $23 billion, the company had the distinction of being the largest capitalization stock traded on the London stock market and the 26th largest traded in the United States.

Glaxo was a leader in products for the relief of peptic ulcers and of asthma and was a major supplier of antibiotics and of treatments for skin disorders. For several reasons,

---

[4]On September 14, 1990, £1 = 2,212 Italian lira and US$1.898.

many of Glaxo's new drugs eventually achieved dominant market positions. First, Glaxo focused its research on unmet medical needs. Second, the company always coupled its R&D strategy with a fast track record in new-drug approval time. Third, Glaxo had built up one of the world's biggest sales forces for drugs, 9,500 representatives. Fourth, its marketing machine went into action early in a product's life. While the new drug was being developed, Glaxo held costly symposiums to which it invited opinion leaders who knew about the disease the drug was designed to treat. The idea was to build and gauge market potential. Once a drug was presented to regulators for approval, the marketers used public-relations firms to work out ways to create demand. Doctors were flooded with medical literature and given guidelines on how to diagnose the disease. Medical authorities were persuaded of the economic savings from the product introduction. Almost immediately after a drug had been launched, Glaxo established small studies to monitor the performance of the drug in a normal population to spot any new adverse effect. Doctors were paid for their contributions to these studies.

GLAXO ITALIA S.P.A.

Glaxo Italia S.p.A. was the oldest Glaxo subsidiary. Exhibit 2 reveals that the subsidiary had the third largest market share in the highly fragmented Italian pharmaceutical market. Based in Verona (in the northeastern part of the country and the town of Shakespeare's *Romeo and Juliet*), Glaxo Italia had manufacturing facilities producing most of Glaxo Holdings' products. The company work force was about 2,000 people, 400 of whom were involved in research.

Glaxo Holdings granted unusual autonomy to its operating subsidiaries, including discretion over product positioning, the choice of promotional mix, the timing of line extensions, and resource allocation to various products. Glaxo Italia's objectives were to achieve a turnover[5] of 2 trillion lira, which would represent 9 percent of the market, with a 50 percent profit margin, by the turn of the century. To achieve these challenging goals, the company was rapidly expanding its sales force and had invested heavily in new research facilities (156 billion lira), which was one of the five most important R&D centers for Glaxo Holdings. Last but not least, Glaxo Holdings had selected Italy as the site for the Glaxo Management School.

As shown in Exhibit 3, this expansion strategy was expected to dampen profitability in the short term; but, within five years, the heavy investment and debt-based financing were forecasted to pay off in a sevenfold growth of profits. Glaxo Italia sales in 1991 were expected to be 719 billion lira, which included 183 billion lira of sales by licensees and comarketers. The total would represent 6.2 percent of the pharmaceutical market (3.8 percent through direct sales only). Exhibit 4 reveals that a quarter of these sales would derive from licensees in comarketing agreements; Exhibit 5 indicates that continued sales growth depended significantly on new products and sales by licensees.

---

[5]"Turnover" is equivalent to sales revenue.

ZINNAT

The Zinnat oral antibiotic offered a new competitive remedy to current drugs for influenza-like feverish diseases. Zinnat's launch would be a major opportunity and challenge for the company to support and expand its presence in the antibiotic segment. The product would be introduced in two formulations: (1) a package of 12 pills of 250 milligrams each with a retail price of 34,400 Italian lira (ITL) and (2) a 2.5-g. syrup with a retail price of 29,880 ITL. The manufacturer's price was 61 percent of the retail price. Gross margin was 53 percent of the manufacturer's price. The cost of goods sold consisted mainly of the costs of raw materials, local production, bottling, and fees. The raw material was sold to Glaxo Italia S.p.A. and any co-marketers from Glaxo Holdings at a transfer price of 1,566 ITL/gram. Glaxo Italia would pay an additional 4 percent of this price for customs fees, transportation, and the like. The transfer price consisted of variable costs (20 percent) and the product's share of R&D expenses incurred (80 percent). Glaxo Italia and any co-marketers had to anticipate a 20 percent cost for local production and marketing.

THE ETHICAL AND OTC PHARMACEUTICAL MARKETS

Glaxo planned to introduce Zinnat solely into the ethical-drug market, although at some point in the future, Zinnat might convert into an OTC drug. (When a drug was prescribed over a long time, it could develop a strong brand image.) These two main segments of the market were significantly different.

In the ethical-drug market, a doctor's prescription was necessary to obtain the product; therefore, the doctor was the "gate keeper" to the end user and was the target of marketing efforts by the manufacturers.

Italian doctors were renowned in Europe for their interest in new drugs. As a result, the average life cycle of ethical drugs tended to be shorter in Italy than elsewhere. Glaxo managers believed that aggressive use of sales force marketing (both direct and comarketed) would have a strong effect on Zinnat's market share.

OTCs, by definition, could be purchased directly from retailers (usually, but not necessarily, pharmacies). No patents applied in the case of OTCs, and all OTCs were branded. In most countries, OTCs could be directly advertised to the public, while ethical drugs were subjected to government regulations that allowed them to be advertised only in media targeted to the medical profession.

In general, manufacturers decided whether a drug they were developing fit the ethical or the OTC market, but a final decision was made by national drug-control authorities. OTC drugs usually were established remedies for minor illnesses, such as coughs, colds, and flu or preventive preparations, such as vitamins and tonics. For a new drug to be launched straight into the OTC market was extremely rare.

Ethical drugs, however, might be sold over the counter when their patents expired. This conversion could occur when an ethical drug, after a number of years on the market, was found not to have significant side effects and its potency for other conditions than those for which it was prescribed was limited. When government regulators were satisfied that a drug's side effects and potency were limited, they would permit the drug to be sold without a prescription.

Marketers at Glaxo believed that OTC marketing would increase for several reasons: (1) tighter control of national health-service budgets was leading to increasing incentives for self-medication; (2) patients were becoming more and more able to take on active roles as consumers; (3) liberalization in national drug-approval agencies had increased the number of products in this market (e.g., in Denmark, H2 antagonists,[6] such as Zantac, had been permitted to go OTC since 1989).

Antibiotics, because of their consumption patterns and intrinsic characteristics, were one product category that might experience movement into the OTC market early in their life cycles. Glaxo Holdings wanted to enter this segment first, however, because of its large share of revenues. But Glaxo Holdings considered itself an ethical-drug company and was structured accordingly (substantial R&D facilities and investments, marketing and distribution organizations centered on sales representatives, rather than on advertising or brand management). One Glaxo Holdings executive was quoted as saying that "strong brand images were not our area. OTC was a different sort of business."[7] But the company was prepared to adapt.

THE POLICY OF RAPID PRODUCT LAUNCH: THE ROLE OF COMARKETING

Glaxo's strategy of rapid market penetration for new products sought to create several advantages: (1) the "snow-ball" effect of word-of-mouth advertising within the medical community; (2) economies of scale and scope (the introduction costs, such as presentations to doctors and hospitals, conferences, advertising, were relatively fixed) could be gained if the costs were spread across the largest possible volume; and (3) raised barriers to entry (preemption of market space). Rapid penetration also served the fundamental need to generate positive cash flows in the shortest possible time to finance investments in R&D for future products. Glaxo Holdings' new products that reached the launch phase were, in fact, extremely profitable, with internal rates of return generally greater than 200 percent. In the pharmaceutical industry, 1 R&D project in 10 became a commercialized new product; thus, new-product development in a growing company, such as Glaxo, required significant investment.

Glaxo Italia possessed two direct sales-force teams (called *lines*) employing about 320 sales representatives each. In comarketing agreements, Glaxo would pursue rapid market penetration by adding the sales efforts of the comarketer as each marketed its own brands of the same product.[8] With comarketing, Glaxo anticipated various benefits: volumes would be higher and reached in shorter times than when marketing alone. In addition,

---

[6]H2 antagonists (also called *H2 blockers*) block the histamine receptor (H2) in the body and, thus, reduce the production of gastric acids believed to cause stomach ulcers.

[7]In the *Financial Times*, November 8, 1989.

[8]Another classic joint marketing arrangement included codetailing (same product, same brand name).

establishing close ties with other firms could provide additional lobbying leverage in regulatory environments where the registration process for new products was particularly slow and bureaucratic. The comarketer could benefit in two ways. First, that firm's sales force could carry more products and, thereby, make each sales call more productive. Second, a broader product line might help keep the sales force productive during any trough in the firm's business cycle.

On the other hand, the presence of a distribution partner had several disadvantages. First, Glaxo had to increase its sales force and marketing efforts to compete against the comarketer's products. Second, the comarketer, which was also a pharmaceutical company in 90 percent of the cases, might be tempted to reformulate the product (and, thus, side-step licensing fees) if it proved to be successful. Comarketing strategies also were vulnerable to price wars and litigation over allocation of resources and territories, and risked saturation of the doctors' attention.

INNOVATION AND PATENT LIFE

Patent life was an important influence on the Zinnat marketing decision. A shortening of effective patent life could reduce the period during which protected profits on a drug could be made. The total patent life in the United States was 17 years, whereas in Europe it was 20 years. Patent life was taken up by (1) the time required to develop the specific application after the new compound had been developed, (2) the time necessary for registration, (3) the time required to introduce the product, and (4) the remaining (so-called effective) patent life.

Exhibit 6 shows how effective patent life fell from 13 to 5 years between 1965 and 1985. As Sir Peter Girolami, chairman of Glaxo, had recently said,

> Medicines which are now emerging from the development pipeline are more complex and more powerful than their predecessors; this inevitably complicates the necessary process of satisfying regulatory authorities.

While patent life had shortened, R&D expenditures were constantly increasing. One widely accepted estimate of the average cost to discover and bring a major new drug to the market was US$100 million. The implication of these high costs was that large revenues had to be generated to pay for them. According to one study of The Wellcome Foundation, to achieve an adequate return on an R&D expenditure of US$100 million, a drug had to reach peak annual sales of over US$200 million and total sales revenues of 11 times the R&D spent.[9] Mr. Rottoli estimated that a delay of just one week in development time represented a loss in terms of revenues of US$1-US$2 million. At the same time, the reduction in effective patent life led to a quicker significant drop in sales revenues when the price had to be reduced to face competition from the generic product. Comarketing could increase the risk of competition when a patent expired, because the comarketer

---

[9]Trevor M. Jones, "Improving the Development Process," paper presented at the World Pharmaceutical Conference, London, March 1990.

might be prepared to manufacture the product in house. To manufacture Zinnat, for instance, the comarketer would have to pay a licensing fee and would be required to purchase some ingredients from Glaxo Holdings. Without the protection of a patent, the fee and the supply arrangement would disappear.

FINANCIAL CRITERIA

Glaxo Italia used two main criteria as the basis for evaluating decisions about sales strategies: payback and internal rate of return (IRR).

- **Payback.** Any new product launched had to have a payback period of less than three years. This period reflected the company's strategic emphasis on rapid market penetration. The use of the payback criterion was justified on two grounds. First, given the extended industry practice of "cross-subsidization" among products, senior managers needed to know when a new product would start to generate cash surpluses that could be used to finance new R&D projects. Payback helped focus managers' attention on the cash-flow breakeven. Second, uncertainty about the time at which competitors could launch a similar product made it relevant to know how much time was necessary to recover the additional investment to market the product.
- **IRR.** The more desirable strategy would have the higher IRR. The minimum required IRR in Italy was a firm's cost of debt there (12.5 percent in September 1990).[10] Exhibit 7 contains information on current capital-market conditions.

When asked if an appropriate discount rate should take into account the cost of equity capital as well as the cost of debt, Mr. Rottoli answered:

Investors expect to get higher returns? Well, if I produce good returns, they'll get them. If I don't, they won't! To begin with, let's start from zero cash and a new project on the way. At this point in time, the firm, hypothetically, can borrow money from a bank at, say, 12.5 percent; that represents the cost of debt. After this initial cost is entirely paid back from the project cash flows, what is left to the shareholders is the project net IRR (net of financial charges). Thus we do not fix any a priori target for shareholders' returns, be they based on market averages or historical trends or even future forecasts. It is sufficient for the net IRR to be greater than zero to justify the investment. It then falls to the investors to accept the expected rate of return on the project or to reject it. However, the net IRR is still clearly higher than what the shareholders will ultimately get from the business. I mean, we need yet to include and subtract all the fixed and structural costs necessary to run the business before getting to the investors' payoff. These are basically the reasons why I tend to consider discounted cash flow based on the project WACC [weighted-average cost of capital] premature at this stage.

Referring to the choice of costs and cash flows included in the forecast, Mr. Rottoli said,

Only manufacturing and promotional cost are considered relevant. The remaining items—such as G&A [general and administrative], historical and future R&D (at local and group level),

---

[10]Glaxo Holdings' pretax cost of debt in the United Kingdom was 12 percent. Its book value of debt amounted to £420 million. Its market value of equity was £12,193 million.

medical testing cost, real financial charges, taxes—are not taken into account.[11] Not at all! We are really interested in evaluating the marginal profitability between direct sales and comarketing. Therefore, all of those items being shared by the two alternatives end up complicating the measures while not dramatically improving the final decision.

FINANCIAL PROJECTIONS

To evaluate the strategic choice between direct sales and comarketing, Mr. Rottoli had prepared a financial model as presented in Exhibits 8, 9, and 10. Assumptions underlying the model are summarized in Exhibit 8. Aspects of the forecast that required some judgment were the following:

- **Product mix.**   In the first year, the model assumed this mix: 85 percent pills and 15 percent syrup. From the second year on, the mix was assumed to be 80 percent pills and 20 percent syrup. The licensee was assumed to weight the product mix differently: 40 percent pills and 60 percent syrup.
- **Promotional costs.**   These costs included (1) the cost of drug samples given to doctors and clinics, (2) the cost of medical promotions (trials to hospitals, clinics, and local health-care units), (3) the cost of seminars, congresses, and social promotions (one-hour short conferences plus dinners held by technical/scientific sales reps), and (4) the cost of training the sales force.
- **Sales force.**   Zinnat was assigned principally to the sales force termed *Line 1*. In the first year only, sales force Line 2 would support the launch. The cost of the direct sales force was calculated according to the estimated percentage time to be spent on the specific product. The cost per salesperson increased by 12 percent each year on average. The sales force in Line 1 was supposed to grow from 320 to 440 reps within three years, but Mr. Rottoli wrestled with the question of whether this increased sales-force promotional time was a marginal item or just a reallocation of corporate resources that would be needed anyway. He said,

It was an eternal source of discussion between me and Mr. [Giuseppe] Ferrari, the sales V.P. I told him that as long as new employees were hired for new-product promotional support, the sales structure was an incremental expense of this product launch. Mr. Ferrari argued that the sales force supported the company as a whole and that, therefore, the cost of new sales recruits should not be included in the forecast.

The financial forecasts in Exhibits 8, 9, and 10 charge Zinnat for the percent of actual sales force time that the product is assumed to command.

- **Group profit on parent-subsidiary transfer of raw materials.**   This figure was the profit that Glaxo Holdings PLC (the parent) made on the sales of raw materials to Glaxo Italia (the subsidiary). Glaxo explained that this profit was a means of reimbursing the

---

[11]Glaxo Italia's marginal tax rate was 47 percent. Glaxo Holdings' marginal tax rate in the United Kingdom was 29 percent.

parent for R&D expenses. The raw material could be directly processed by Glaxo Italia or possibly resold to the comarketer.

- **Capital generated and interest.**   Glaxo Holdings viewed the product launch as having a cash flow (or "flow of capital generated") equal to the product margin less the working-capital requirement (equivalent to two months of sales). The interest inflow or outflow was equal to the interest rate multiplied by the arithmetic average of the capital generated in the current year and the previous year. The interest rate used by Glaxo was 12.5 percent, close to the risk-free rate. It also reflected the company's approximate present cost of debt.

The initial phase of a project was somewhat similar to an entrepreneur venturing upon a new business. Initial exposure for a new-product launch was burdened by interest expenses at the stated rate until the early outlays were recovered. From then on, the business's profits would be "loaned" to new emerging projects at the same stated rate, according to the following logic: "One line generates cash, while another—internally—absorbs part of it," as Mr. Rottoli said. The capital employed then turned from a use (−) to a generation of cash (+). Investors expected higher returns from a project, however, than from purchasing securities on the market.

- **Time horizon.**   Although the product life cycle of pharmaceutical products was typically between 10 and 20 years, the forecast was carried out to only 6 years. Product managers and marketing directors found extending a forecast beyond six years difficult, but they generally acknowledged that the product was mostly successful in its first six years of life. From the seventh year on, the product's market share usually declined. Mr. Rottoli estimated that a reasonable rate of decline would be 5 percent per year.[12] He wondered, however, whether the rate of decline and/or the cash flows beyond the forecast horizon mattered.

CONCLUSION

The data in the forecasts Mr. Rottoli was holding (Exhibits 8, 9, and 10) suggested he should undoubtedly recommend that the company go forward with comarketing instead of direct sales:

	Direct Sales	*Comarketing*
IRR	204%	1,469%
Payback	2.5 years	2.5 years

---

[12]That is, share of market in year 2 would be 95 percent of the share of market in year 1.

He wondered, however, whether these base-case results adequately captured the richness of the problem. For instance, how robust was the preference for comarketing to such considerations as these:

- In the direct-sales scenario, a 20–30 percent decrease in sales force and promotional effort to sell the same amount of final goods was possible in the absence of competitors with the same product but different brand. Alternatively, if the sales force and promotional effort were not reduced, the sales were likely to be higher in the absence of a comarketer. What combinations of sales force and promotional cost would leave Glaxo indifferent between the two marketing strategies?
- Taking Mr. Ferrari's argument, suppose the cost of the field sales force were not incremental to the Zinnat launch.
- The combined action of two firms would allow reaching the maximum market share in 12 months, whereas the effort of only one firm required 36 months in the forecast. How significant was the benefit of the incremental speed?
- After the product proved itself in the marketplace, a comarketer might defect to its own brand; thus, direct selling could have a distinctly different set of cash flows beyond year 6. In addition, the appearance or nonappearance of newer products could affect the more distant cash flows. What should be done about cash flows beyond the five-year forecast horizon?

On top of these concerns, Mr. Rottoli wondered if the forecasting system with which he was endowed captured the best insights. Glaxo had delivered abundant value to shareholders. Would the current financial evaluation of the Zinnat marketing decision promote that value? Were IRR and payback the best decision criteria? Was he missing any relevant cash flows?

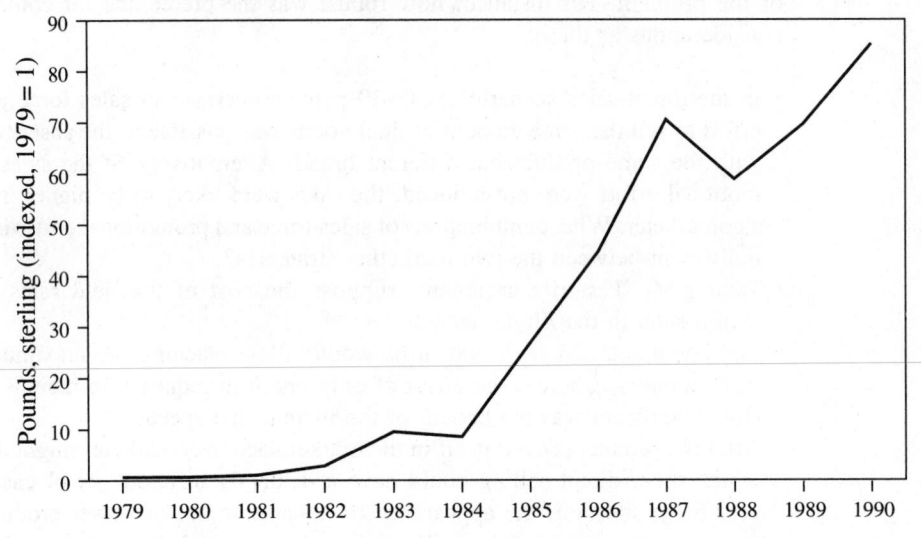

EXHIBIT 2   Shares of Pharmaceutical Market, Italy, 1990

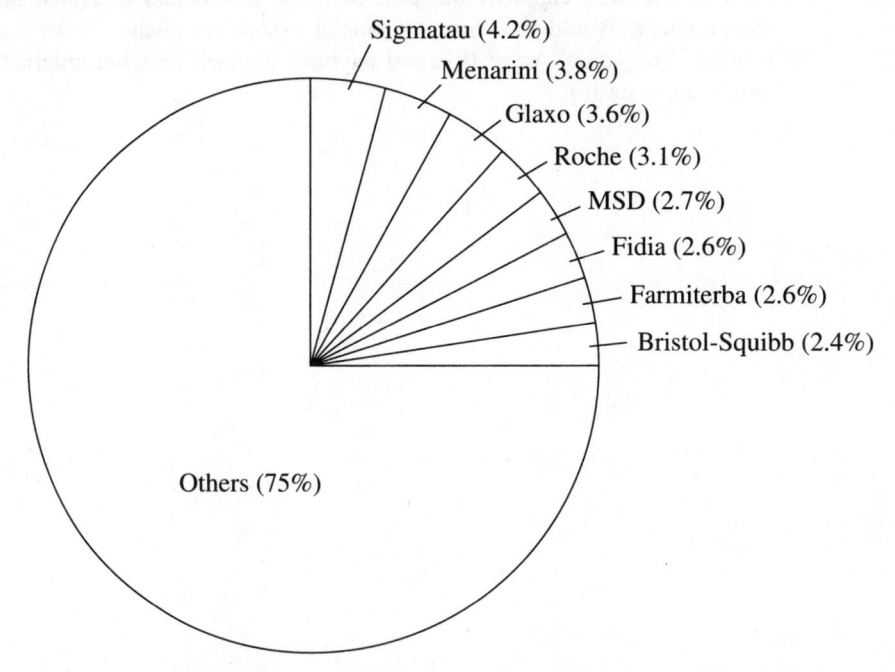

Source: Glaxo marketing department.

EXHIBIT 3   Glaxo Italia S.p.A., Financial Performance, Historical and Projected, 1989–1995

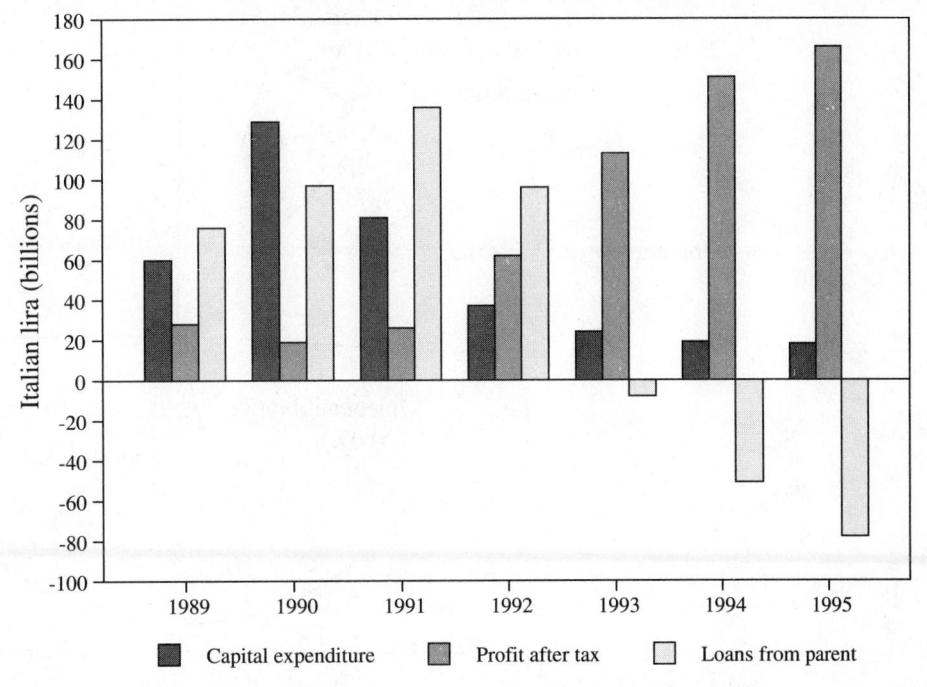

Source: Glaxo Italia S.p.A.

EXHIBIT 4 Glaxo Italia Product Portfolio, 1991 (projected revenues, 720 billion ITL)

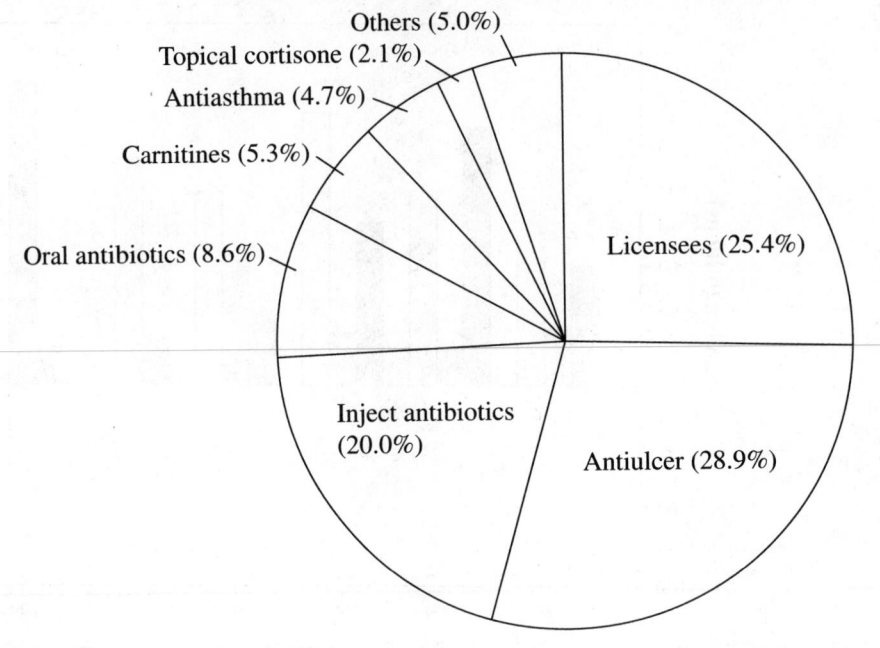

Source: Glaxo Italia S.p.A.

EXHIBIT 5   Sales Composition, Historical and Projected, 1989–1995

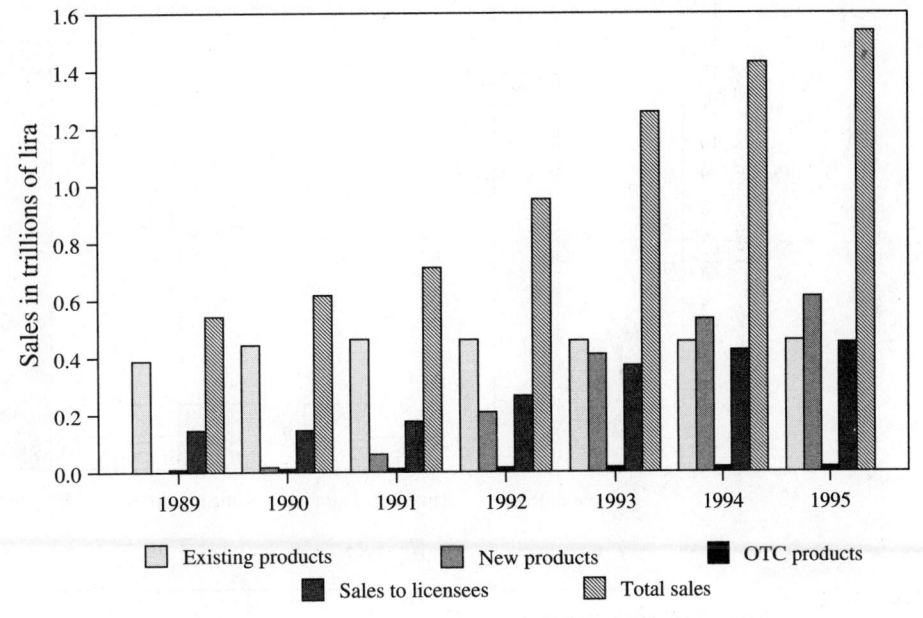

Source: Glaxo Italia S.p.A.

EXHIBIT 6   Effective Patent Life of Drugs in EC, 1965 and 1985

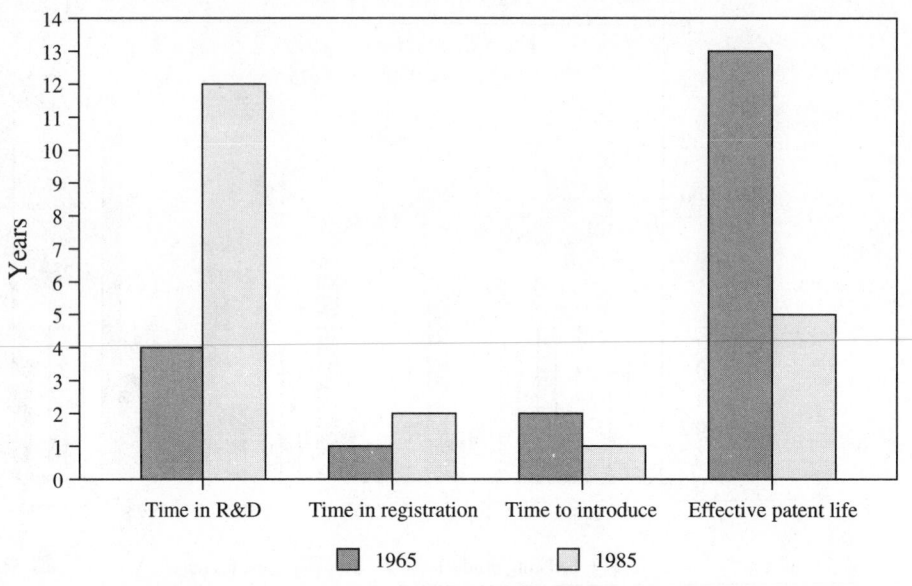

Source: Economist Intelligence Unit, 1989.

EXHIBIT 7   Capital-Market Conditions, September 1990

Yield on Long-Term Government Bonds

	United Kingdom	Italy
June	11.01%	11.32%
September	11.32%	11.60%
Expected inflation rate	5%	4%

	Price-Earnings Ratio	Share Price (US$)	Beta
Glaxo Holdings PLC	15.6%	$30	0.90
Bristol Myers-Squibb	18.5	66	1.00
Eli Lilly	17.6	77	1.10
Pfizer	16.1	81	1.05
Rhône-Poulenc Rorer	7.5	9⅜	1.05
Schering Plough Corp.	17.5	16	1.15
Equity market risk premium (64-year geometric mean)	5.6%		

Sources: *Financial Times, Risk Measurement Services, Value Line Investment Survey.*

EXHIBIT 8 Forecast Assumptions

	Product Mix					
	First Year (%)	Later Years (%)	Retail Price (ITL)	Raw Matls. (grams)	Mfr. Price (ITL)	Raw Mtl. Cost (ITL)
Glaxo: pills	85%	80%	34,400	3	20,984	1,566
Glaxo: syrup	15	20	29,880	2.5	18,227	1,566
Comarketer: pills ...	40	40				
Comarketer: syrup ...	60	60				
Tax rate, Italy	47.0					
Tax rate, United Kingdom ...	29.0					
Expected inflation, Italy ...	4.0					
Expected inflation, United Kingdom ..	5.0					

	1990	1991	1992	1993	1994	1995	1996
Market forecast .... (millions of units)	0	52	47	47	45	46	47
Per unit:							
Cost of raw materials	1,566	1,566	1,566	1,566	1,566	1,566	1,566
Retail price, pills	34,400	34,400	34,400	34,400	34,400	34,400	34,400
Retail price, syrup	29,880	29,880	29,880	29,880	29,880	29,880	29,880
Sales force:							
Sales force 1 (number of reps) ...		320	350	400	400	400	440
% time on Zinnat (direct)		26%	33%	24%	21%	23%	23%
% time on Zinnat (licensing)		26%	33%	24%	21%	23%	23%
Sales force 2 (number of reps) ...		320					
% time on Zinnat (direct)		18%					
% time on Zinnat (licensing)		18%					
Cost per sales rep (ITL millions)		105.0	117.6	131.7	147.5	165.2	185.0
Interest rate	0.125						

Sources: Company analysis and casewriters' analysis.

EXHIBIT 9 Financial Forecast: Direct Sales (all figures in ITL billions)

	1990	1991	1992	1993	1994	1995	1996
Market share	0.0%	3.1%	7.0%	7.1%	7.1%	7.1%	6.8%
Quantities:							
Volumes (000)		912	2,560	2,711	2,764	2,889	2,862
Samples (000)		710	700	600	400	400	350
Revenues	0	18.76	52.27	55.36	56.45	59.00	58.43
Gross margin (a)		9.9	27.7	29.3	29.9	31.3	31.0
Gross margin/revenues		53%	53%	53%	53%	53%	53%
Cost of samples		3.3	3.5	3.0	2.0	2.0	1.8
Med. promotion	0.2	0.2	0.5	0.6	0.6	0.6	
Mkt. promotion	0.2	2.6	3.7	3.3	1.7	1.8	1.8
Sales rep. prom.		0.7	0.3	0.3	0.9	0.9	0.9
Total promotion cost (b)	0.4	6.7	7.9	7.2	5.2	5.3	4.4
Total sales force cost:							
Line 1 (c)		8.7	13.6	12.6	12.4	15.2	18.7
Line 2 (d)		5.9					
Total marketing cost							
(e = b + c + d)	0.4	21.3	21.5	19.8	17.6	20.5	23.2
Marketing margin (f = a − e)	-0.4	-11.4	6.2	9.5	12.3	10.7	7.8
Group profit on transfer (g)	0.0	7.1	14.2	14.4	13.8	14.3	14.0
Interest (h)	0.0	-0.5	-0.1	2.4	6.0	10.2	14.6
Product margin (i = f + g + h)	-0.4	-4.8	20.3	26.3	32.1	35.2	36.4
Investment in working capital (j)	0.0	3.1	5.6	0.5	0.2	0.4	-0.1
Capital generated (k = i − j)	-0.4	-7.9	14.7	25.8	31.9	34.8	36.5
Cumulative capital generated	-0.4	-8.3	6.3	32.2	64.1	98.9	135.4
IRR on capital employed	204%						
Payback period	2.5 years						

Sources: Company analysis and casewriters' analysis.

EXHIBIT 10 Financial Forecast: Comarketing (all figures in ITL billions)

	1990	1991	1992	1993	1994	1995	1996
Market share	0.0%	5.2%	10.4%	10.4%	10.1%	9.6%	9.2%
Quantities:							
Volumes (000s)		912	2,560	2,711	2,764	2,889	2,862
Samples (000s)		710	700	600	400	400	350
Licensees (000s)	200	1,099	1,583	1,540	1,337	1,158	1,133
Direct sales	0	18.8	52.3	55.4	56.4	59.0	58.4
Sales to licensees	1.1	6.0	8.6	8.4	7.3	6.3	6.2
Total revenues	1.1	24.8	60.9	63.7	63.7	65.3	64.6
Gross margin (a)	0.0	9.7	27.4	29.0	29.6	31.0	30.7
Gross margin/direct sales		53%	53%	53%	53%	53%	53%
Gross margin/tot. revs.	0%	39%	45%	46%	46%	47%	48%
Cost of samples	0.2	3.3	3.5	3.0	2.1	2.1	1.9
Med. promotion	0.2	0.2	0.5	0.6	0.6	0.6	
Mkt. promotion		2.6	3.7	3.3	1.7	1.8	1.8
Sales rep. prom.		0.7	0.3	0.3	0.9	0.9	0.9
Total promotion cost (b)	0.4	6.7	7.9	7.2	5.3	5.4	4.5
Total sales-force cost							
Line 1 (c)		8.7	13.6	12.6	12.4	15.2	18.7
Line 2 (d)		5.9					
Total marketing cost (e = b + c + d)	0.4	21.3	21.5	19.8	17.7	20.6	23.3
Marketing margin (f = a − e)	-0.4	-11.6	5.8	9.2	11.9	10.4	7.5
Group profit on product transfer (g)	0.8	11.0	19.7	19.7	18.3	18.1	17.6
Interest (h)	0.0	-0.3	0.7	4.0	8.4	13.4	18.8
Product margin (i = f + g + h)	0.4	-0.9	26.2	32.8	38.6	41.8	43.9
Investment in working capital (j)	0.2	4.1	6.0	0.3	0.0	0.3	-0.1
Capital generated (k = i − j)	0.2	-5.0	20.1	32.5	38.6	41.6	44.0
Cumulative capital generated	0.2	-4.8	15.4	47.9	86.5	128.1	172.0
IRR on capital employed	1,469%						
Payback period	2.5 years						

Sources: Company analysis and casewriters' analysis.

281

Case 23

Marriott Corporation: Frankfurt and Dusseldorf

Frankfurt ist die finanzielle Drehscheibe in Deutschland . . . die wichtigste Stadt in Europa nach 1992.

Die Internationale Automobile Show wird dieses Jahr wohl wieder alle Besucherrekorde brechen.

Jetzt hat die Deutsche Bank schon Banca d'America in Italien, ich wuesste gerne mal gerne wann die die restlichen Banken in Europa auch noch ueberhehmen![1]

Amid the noise of clattering dishes and lively dinner conversations, Nick Ward sat in Weinhaus Bruckenkellar, finishing his bratwurst and sauerkraut and watching the September sun set on the Main River. An international hotel developer for Marriott Corporation, Ward had been looking for a suitable hotel site in Frankfurt for the past seven years. He knew the city well, a modern industrial city steeped in rich Germanic culture, and appreciated the difficulty of finding a suitable piece of real estate for a hotel development.

Through the window, Ward could see the most impressive building in the city, the Kiwi Grand Hotel. Four weeks earlier, in August 1988, a tremendous opportunity had developed for Marriott to take over Kiwi's hotels in Frankfurt and in Dusseldorf. Ward envisioned a big red Marriott sign on the Kiwi lighting up the Frankfurt skyline. "What

---

[1]"Frankfurt is the financial engine of Germany . . . the most important city on the continent in 1992."

"The International Motor Show is expected to draw a record-breaking crowd this year."

"Now that Deutsche Bank has acquired Bank of America in Italy, I suppose they will buy the rest of the banks in Europe!"

This case was written by Camille E. Humphries, with the cooperation of B. Wendell Ward and other executives at Marriott Corporation, and under the supervision of Professor Robert F. Bruner. All financial and market data about the project have been disguised.

Copyright © 1989 by the Darden Graduate Business School Foundation, Charlottesville, VA. Rev. 2/93.

a coup that would be," Ward thought—a prime location in Frankfurt's central business district, one of the few remaining Gothic buildings in the city; taking a competitor out of the market.

The financial analysis of the Kiwi opportunity had indicated, however, that the deal did not achieve Marriott's economic objectives. Ward wrestled with the question of whether to establish a strategic presence in Frankfurt with a deal structure that fell short of Marriott's standards for maximizing shareholder value.

Last May, Nick had received a call from British Royal Investment Bank about Kiwi's hotel sites in Frankfurt and in Dusseldorf. Nick could hardly believe the offer. Kiwi was searching for another hotel company to assume the leases, and Marriott was the first choice. Marriott was not particularly interested in entering the Dusseldorf market, but the overriding strength of the Frankfurt property made the proposal attractive. Exhibit 1 describes the hotel properties.

Nick presented the deal to Michael Dearing, director of financial planning at Marriott, but the resulting valuation was not what Nick had hoped. Mike remarked, "On a 30-year basis, the net present value is negative. If we go by the numbers alone, Nick, the deal simply does not achieve Marriott's targeted rate of return for hotel properties." On the other hand, John Dasburg, executive vice president and head of Marriott's Lodging Division, had said during the International Division's annual strategic-planning meeting, "Nick, in light of the strategic significance of Frankfurt in 1992 and Marriott's targeted growth objectives in the German market, establishing a hotel in Frankfurt in 1989 is a top priority for the corporation."

MARRIOTT CORPORATION

Founded by J. Willard Marriott in 1927, the Marriott Corporation began as a small root-beer stand in Washington, D.C. From a 62-year history of uncompromising attention to customer service and savvy financial management, Marriott had earned a reputation as a world leader in the hospitality business, with principal segments in lodging, contract services, and restaurants. In 1988, the Lodging Division generated sales of $3.1 billion and operating income of $298 million. The Contract Services and Restaurant divisions produced revenues of $3.3 billion and $1 billion and operating income of $180 million and $94 million, respectively (see Exhibit 2).

In a public announcement proclaiming Marriott's intention to achieve better than a 20 percent return on shareholders' equity in the coming decade, chairman J. W. Marriott, Jr., initiated dramatic changes in the company in 1980. The subsequent restructuring stripped away the company's need to use its own capital and set a precedent for the industry. Marriott sold its hotel properties but retained long-term contracts to manage them. For the nine years between 1980 and 1988, the company earned an average return on equity in excess of 20 percent, thereby gaining an enviable position among *Fortune*'s Top Nine of the Service 500 companies.[2]

---

[2]C. William Pollard and Kenneth T. Wessner, "Stars of the Service 500," *Fortune*, June 5, 1989.

Marriott's operating strength, combined with changing demographic trends and favorable tax laws, fueled the company's success in the 1980s. A consistent winner in industry surveys, Marriott was able to achieve annual room-rate increases at a premium over the annual rate of inflation while maintaining occupancy rates well above industry averages.

As a result of the rapid growth of hotel development during the 1980s, abundant supply and intense competition characterized the outlook for the U.S. lodging industry in 1988. Maintaining its goal of 15–20 percent annual growth in earnings per share, Marriott was divesting slow-growth businesses and investing in areas offering high-growth potential.

Marriott focused particular attention on international hotel development, because of the less-intense competition and greater growth potential in foreign markets than in the United States. In 1988, the European hotel industry was highly fragmented, with low chain dominance. Existing hotel properties were typically old and not properly maintained. Overall, the environment for the hotel industry was similar to U.S. industry conditions in the 1960s. Thus, from a strategic standpoint, Marriott's management recognized an opportunity to expand aggressively in the European market. The values of European hotels, however, often were driven by anticipated real estate appreciation. Basing hotel valuations on operating cash flows, Marriott's management questioned the reliance on real estate appreciation. Marriott's short-term strategy focused on aggressive expansion in "gateway" cities and in a few chosen countries. Marriott targeted West Germany in particular for an aggressive growth strategy. In an effort to establish a strong presence in Germany, Marriott was developing hotels in Munich and Hamburg, to be opened in 1988.

FRANKFURT

Located on the banks of the Main River in the center of Germany, Frankfurt was in 1988 the transportation hub and the financial capital of the European Continent. Frankfurt had the second largest airport in Europe, as well as a network of railroads and highways connecting the city with all parts of Western Europe. With three major harbor areas, the city had a river and canal system providing access to the North Sea.

Frankfurt was ranked fourth in the world after New York, London, and Tokyo as a financial center. Home of the Bundesbank (the Central Bank of the Federal Republic of Germany), the city had over 370 commercial and investment banks, including approximately 230 foreign banks. The European Economic Community's reduction of trade and financial barriers in 1992 was expected to increase the level of banking and commercial activity in the city dramatically.

Trade shows and industry were vital to Frankfurt's economy. The International Automobile Show, the International Book Show, and other world-class exhibitions drew as many as 2.5 million visitors to the city for 80 to 105 event days each year. The city had over 2,400 manufacturing facilities.

Site Review

The location of the Kiwi Grand Hotel offered strong visibility, close proximity to demand generators, and quality use of the surrounding land area. Located in the middle of the central business district, the hotel was across the street from the Deutsche Bank headquarters. Moreover, future developments were expected to enhance the desirability of the site. Deutschland Properties and Kredit Bank had recently signed an agreement to build a 55-story office tower within four miles of the Kiwi Grand. The building, which would be the tallest in continental Europe, would be part of a three-tower office complex of 1.5 million square feet. The offices in the towers were expected to be the most expensive in Frankfurt.

Market Demand

Five hotels (including the Kiwi) with a total of 2,561 rooms were the primary competitive supply in the central business district area. Exhibit 3 presents a summary of the supply and demand for daily rooms and competitive characteristics in this district. In the first quarter of 1988, the primary hotels in the central business district achieved an average occupancy rate of 59.4 percent and a composite average daily rate (ADR)[3] of deutsche marks (DM) 182—both down slightly from the comparable period of 1987. In 1987, occupancy showed only a modest increase from the 1986 level, but the ADR increased 10 percent. The ADR for the major competitors had grown at a compound annual rate of 4.7 percent since 1982, compared with a 2.6 percent compound annual rate of inflation. During 1987, total demand could be segmented as follows: 56 percent commercial transient, 20 percent group or fair related, 12 percent pleasure, and 12 percent airline demand. Exhibit 4 summarizes the hotel competition in Frankfurt.

DUSSELDORF

Dusseldorf was located in the Rhine–Westphalia region of northwestern Germany. The city had a strong commercial base, primarily in the industries of chemicals, textiles, iron, and steel. A convention center under construction was to be be completed in 1989 and was expected to attract significant regional conferences.

Located in the heart of the central business district, the Kiwi in Dusseldorf was the leading commercial hotel in the city. The hotel's primary competitors were two other commercial hotels with a combined total of 372 rooms. The Kiwi had good facilities and would not require any substantial refurbishment to become a Marriott product.

---

[3]ADR is the average room rate paid per night during the year. The ADR is calculated by dividing total room revenues by total occupied room nights for the year. Because different types of customers pay different rates, the ADR varies according to the proportional customer mix during the year.

Kiwi and Buren

In 1975, Kiwi signed a 30-year lease on a 950-room hotel property in Frankfurt, which became the Kiwi Grand. A strong, successful cruise-line company based in New Zealand, Kiwi had opened three hotels in New Zealand and the two hotels in Germany in the 1970s. The German hotels had been marginally profitable in the past but had incurred operating losses in 1986 and 1987. The landlord at that time was a passive owner, who took no particular interest in Kiwi's Frankfurt operations. Kiwi operated only two hotels in Europe, in Frankfurt and Dusseldorf. In May 1988, after undergoing a leveraged buyout and under pressure to maximize cash flow and to divest unrelated businesses, Kiwi's management made a public announcement of its intention to divest hotel operations and commissioned British Royal Investment Bank to find another hotel company to assume its leases in Germany. The transfer of the Dusseldorf lease posed no problem, because that contract included the right of transfer without the landlord's approval.

In July 1988, shortly after Kiwi's announcement of withdrawing from Germany, the original owner sold the Frankfurt property to Buren, a German real estate investment trust owned by shareholders and managed by Kredit Bank. Kiwi hoped that the new landlord would remain disinterested in the operations of the property, thus allowing Kiwi to find a new tenant and extricate itself from the lease without any additional cost. To Kiwi's dismay, however, Buren asserted that Kiwi had not fulfilled its contractual agreement to maintain the building as a first-class international hotel and demanded that Kiwi make a DM 40 million payment to cover DM 28.8 million in leasehold improvements and DM 11.2 million in structural repairs. Kiwi maintained that it would be in full compliance of the lease agreement with only a DM 8 million expenditure. Deadlocked in a hostile stalemate, Kiwi hoped to find another hotel company to assume the lease and fund the renovation.

History of the Deal

Nick Ward, from his prior experience in overseas investment banking, understood the unique market opportunities as well as the complex cultural factors in international deals. With primary responsibility for Marriott's international hotel development, Nick had negotiated real estate purchases and leases in a variety of foreign markets, including Paris, Istanbul, and Warsaw. His pursuit of the property had seemingly paid off: based on Marriott's desire to enter the market and strong operating reputation, Kiwi saw Marriott as a desirable tenant to assume the lease. Ward believed that the Kiwi, a top-flight "billboard" property located in the central business district, would be ideal for Marriott.

After meeting with both Kiwi and Buren, Ward believed the two parties simply did not understand each other. In explaining the deal to Mike Dearing, Nick said,

> Buren's attitudes reflect typical Germanic values. Their style is hands-on, forceful, straightforward, and unyielding in their assertion that Kiwi must uphold what Buren defined to be their full obligation under the contract. Buren insists on the restoration of the building to its first-class

international hotel standard. It's the German Gestalt, Mike—that uncompromising dedication to precision and quality.

Nick had executed a three-month exclusivity agreement with Kiwi, whereby Kiwi agreed to engage in lease negotiations only with Marriott. In order for Marriott to take over the hotels, Nick had to resolve the conflict between Buren and Kiwi, and the negotiations were delicate. In the event that he was unsuccessful, a lengthy legal battle in the German courts was likely to ensue, and Buren could find a new tenant, thereby preempting Marriott's exclusive position as the prospective tenant. Sterling Hotel Corporation, a major U.S. competitor trying to capture the lead among American hotel chains in Europe, had negotiated a backup contract on the Frankfurt property with Buren. Because the landlord had the final authority to accept or reject the transfer of the lease, Nick had to maintain a favorable relationship with Buren. Marriott's relationship with Kiwi was also critical, because Kiwi had the legal right to propose the new tenant. Knowing that a breakdown in the relationship with either party would result in Marriott's loss of a valuable opportunity, Nick stayed in close contact with both Buren and Kiwi and renewed the exclusivity agreement with Buren during the negotiations.

Terms of the Proposed Transaction

After four months of negotiations, Marriott and Kiwi had a proposal for Buren. The terms of the deal were as follows:

1. Marriott would take over leasehold interests in both Frankfurt and Dusseldorf with no cash payment to Buren.
2. Marriott would undertake a DM 28.8 million leasehold-improvement program to bring the Frankfurt hotel up to international standards. Nick thought that Buren would agree to pay for the structural repairs.
3. Marriott would make fixed annual payments to Buren of DM 10 million, in addition to a percentage of revenues. The percentage payments were as follows:

January 1989–December 1991	2.0% of annual revenue
January 1992–December 1994	2.5% of annual revenue
January 1995 and thereafter	3.5% of annual revenue

The initial lease would expire in 2004, with one or two 10-year renewal options, under the same terms, for a total lease-occupancy term of 50 years. If both renewal options were exercised, the total remaining term of the lease would be 36 years. Marriott, however, considered the economic life of a hotel property to be 30 years, so the Frankfurt hotel was evaluated on a 30-year horizon.

4. Marriott would make a fixed annual payment of DM 1.0 million to the landlord of the Dusseldorf property. The lease on the Dusseldorf property would extend through 2008.

In what was expected to be the final round of negotiations, the deal blew up. Buren's lawyers informed Marriott and Kiwi that an operating lease, such as the one currently in effect, was not legally enforceable in Germany beyond 30 years. Thus, only 16 years of the lease remained. The hotel's return simply did not meet Marriott's standards on a 16-year basis.

MARRIOTT'S VALUATION

Marriott's cash-flow forecasts for the two hotels are given in Exhibits 5 and 6. Future DM/$ exchange rates are given in Exhibit 7. A discounted cash flow valuation of the two hotels is given in Exhibit 8.

1. Hotel valuations were based on a 30-year time horizon, the projected economic life of a hotel property. If a hotel lease was less than 30 years, the valuation was based on the actual life of the lease.

2. Total Revenues were composed of Room, Food, and Beverage and Other revenues. Room Revenues were a function of occupancy levels and room rates. As Ward said, "Hotel managers live and die by small variations in occupancy rates. Given 950 rooms and 365 days per year, a 1 percent change in occupancy means a lot." The projected 1989 ADRs for the Frankfurt and Dusseldorf properties were estimated as follows:

Customer Room Rate Categories	Frankfurt		Dusseldorf	
	Market Mix	*1989 ADR*	*Market Mix*	*1989 ADR*
Regular rate.....	20.6%	DM 244	15.0%	DM 160
Corporate rate ...	25.6	195	17.5	137
Special	16.0	164	17.5	120
Group	26.6	144	15.1	117
Air crew	11.2	120	10.8	83
Conference......	0%	0	24.2%	64
Average		DM 178		DM 130

The room rates were expected to grow faster than inflation because of the strength of Marriott's reputation and the relatively tight lodging supply in Germany. The occupancy level was expected to increase over a three-year time horizon as Marriott built operating strength and a strong reputation in the market.

3. Rooms Department Profit was the gross margin on Room Revenue. Food and Beverage and Other Department Profits were similarly derived by subtracting the respective variable costs from the revenues. The increasing trend in the Total Department Profit Margin reflected expected efficiencies and a shift toward a relative increase in the more profitable room revenues. Based on Marriott's historical performance, the percentage profit margins were expected to stabilize in year three.

4. SG&A Expense included depreciation, maintenance, utilities, and insurance.
5. Marriott Central Office Expense was the management fee paid to Marriott. This fee, which was a constant percentage of total revenues, covered expenses that Marriott incurred in managing the hotel property.
6. Net House Profit was the total pretax cash flow to total capital, before rent and tax expense. Net House Profit was analogous to free cash flow before rent expense. Ward believed that Marriott would repatriate cash flows to the United States, rather than reinvest them in Germany.
7. Land rent was the annual lease payment to be paid to Buren. It was composed of a base annual payment and a supplemental payment tied to revenues.
8. The tax rate assumed was 60 percent, the maximum statutory German income tax rate.
9. The Dusseldorf hotel was expected to generate tax credits because of the hotel's projected operating losses. Marriott's four hotels in Germany were owned by one subsidiary, which consolidated the earnings of the properties. Marriott expected to generate income on the other German hotels. Thus, the Dusseldorf tax credit was valuable for shielding income from the profitable properties.

Inflation and foreign exchange rate projections for the United States and West Germany that were available to Ward are outlined in Exhibit 7. Marriott's Treasury Group forecasted future exchange rates for the deutsche mark based on the relationship between the expected inflation rates for the United States and West Germany. Because Marriott used a U.S. cost of capital, the cash flows were converted to U.S. dollars and multiplied by a country-risk adjustment factor for valuation. The net present value (NPV) could then be converted to deutsche marks at the current spot rate.

Ward remembered his conversation with Dearing about the use of different discount rates in the DCF analysis.

Nick

When I was in B school, Mike, we used one discount rate for net cash flow. Since the discount rate is effectively a blending of the different discount rates for the various line items, why complicate the analysis with different discount rates and net present values?

Mike

The purpose, Nick, is to help you negotiate more effectively. We break out the net present values of separate line items to illustrate the relative importance of the components in the value of the deal. Consider, for example, the negotiation for rent payments. Minimum rent is a specified contractual expense and is, therefore, a certain cash-flow item, with a relatively low discount rate. Supplemental rent is variable, because it is a percentage of revenues, and revenues show a significant amount of variability. Supplemental rent is, therefore, discounted at a higher discount rate because of the higher degree of uncertainty of the cash flow. For a given dollar amount of rent based on future expected revenues, minimum rent is effectively more expensive than supplemental rent.

Nick

That makes sense. Focusing on relevant discount rates and NPVs will help me to negotiate a deal with the highest possible value to Marriott. But how do you determine the correct discount rate for each line item?

Mike

The 6.5 percent discount rate for the base-rent payment is equivalent to the after-tax cost of debt, since lease payments are as certain as debt. The risk premium included in the 11 percent discount rate for net house profit is based on the historical variability of cash flows for comparable hotels, as measured by their betas.

Nick

So the different discount rates capture the relevant degrees of risk for the various sources of cash flow. But Mike, do the discount rates reflect a U.S. cost of capital or a German cost of capital? If I remember correctly from my finance classes in B school, the cost of capital captures the systematic risk of the local economy. So would you use a U.S. cost of capital because Marriott is a U.S. company or a German cost of capital because the hotel is in Germany?

Mike

We use a U.S. cost of capital, Nick. Our shareholders are U.S. investors, and the U.S. cost of capital accurately reflects their alternative investment opportunities. To capture the political, or sovereign, risk of doing business in Germany, we multiply each cash-flow item by a risk-adjustment factor. The combination of the U.S. cost of capital and the risk-adjustment factor, therefore, encompasses all the relevant risks for the investor.

Nick

How are the country-risk adjustment factors determined?

Mike

Using country-risk analysis, we determine the country's risk-adjustment factor based on political and sovereign risk, which is the risk associated with tax-law changes and expropriation. The system is based on the assumption of a risk factor of 1.0 for the United States, which corresponds to the U.S. cost of capital. Countries with a greater degree of political risk have a risk factor below 1.0, and countries with a lower degree of political risk have a factor more than 1.0. For instance, Switzerland's risk factor is 1.05, and Mexico's risk factor is 0.85. Germany's risk factor of 0.99 reflects the country's stable economic and political system.

Nick

If we convert the cash flows to dollars before multiplying by the discount factor, why don't we just project the cash-flow statements in dollars instead of deutsche marks?

Mike

The projections must be in deutsche marks for the accurate calculation of tax expense. The German taxes are based on pretax income in deutsche marks. Because the exchange rate changes over time as a function of the relative U.S. and German inflation rates, calculating the tax expense on U.S. dollar amounts would not produce the correct tax expense.

Nick thought about the time horizons assumed in the analysis. The Dusseldorf hotel was valued over a 20-year time horizon, corresponding to the life of that lease. As noted, Marriott had assumed that, with the renewal options, the Frankfurt lease would expire in 36 years, in the year 2025; but as Buren's lawyers had pointed out, the contract was not legally enforceable because the lease term exceeded 30 years. The lease, therefore, would legally expire according to the original 30-year term, in 2004.

In spite of the misunderstandings, the cultural conflicts between Kiwi and Buren, and the economic problems, Ward believed the deal was still compelling because the alternative of no deal was the worst outcome for all three parties. Marriott's management had made the strategic decision to enter the Frankfurt market, and no alternative sites were available. Kiwi was losing money in Germany and had made the announcement that it was pulling out of Europe. Buren would benefit from a tenant that would properly maintain the building and would receive a higher level of rental income if the new tenant generated stronger revenues. Nick thought, there had to be a deal that works. He thought about options to restructure the deal:

1. *Terms of the leases:* Reduce annual lease payments, extend the terms of the lease or alter the mix of minimum rent and rent supplement. Buren should recognize the value of extending the lease contract with a tenant as desirable as Marriott.
2. *Cost of renovations:* Marriott could ask that Kiwi pay part of the renovation expense. Kiwi's management had made a strategic decision and a public announcement that the company was divesting its hotel operations. Perhaps it would be willing to pay to get out of a losing situation.

Nick decided that he should examine and test the key value drivers in the pro formas. "Mike and I should revisit our operating assumptions," he thought. "Maybe the hotel managers should swallow hard and step up to the plate for the larger strategic objectives."

EXHIBIT 1   Description of Hotels

	Frankfurt	*Dusseldorf*
Structure	24 stories	6 stories
Types of guest rooms (number of units):		
Queen beds	600	130
Oversized twin beds	200	50
Studio suites	75	20
Executive suites	75	0
Total	950	200
Food and beverage facilities (number of seats):		
Casual restaurant	200	90
Specialty restaurant	130	50
Cocktail lounge	150	60
Total	480	200
Meeting spaces	Grand ballroom. Ballroom foyer. 7 Meeting rooms.	Grand ballroom. 3 Meeting rooms.
Other facilities	Gift shop. Laundry. Boutique. Health club.	Gift shop. Laundry. Boutique. Whirlpool.

Source: Company documents.

EXHIBIT 2   Marriott Corporation 1988 Financial Performance (in millions of U.S. dollars except per share figures)

Sales:

Lodging:

Rooms	$1,815
Food and beverage	997
Other	3,140
Contract services	3,252
Restaurants	978
Total sales	$7,370

Operating expenses:

Lodging	$2,842
Contract services	3,072
Restaurants	884
Total operating expenses	$6,798

Operating income:

Lodging	$ 298
Contract services	180
Restaurants	94
Total operating income	$ 572

Corporate expenses	$ 93
Interest expense	136
Interest income	40
Income before income taxes	383
Provision for income taxes	151
Net income	$ 232
Earnings per share	$1.95

Source: Company annual report.

EXHIBIT 3 Historical and Projected Supply and Demand Analysis, Frankfurt

	1985	1986	1987	1988	1989	1990	1991	1992	1993	Compound Annual Projected Growth (1987–1993)
Average daily rooms sold	2,639	2,416	2,489	2,564	2,692	2,800	2,912	2,999	3,089	
Demand growth		−8.5%	3.0%	3.0%	5.0%	4.0%	4.0%	3.0%	3.0%	3.7%
Average daily rooms available	3,655	3,655	3,655	3,655	3,905	4,288	4,288	4,538	4,788	
Additions				250	383		250	250		
Total				3,905	4,288	4,288	4,538	4,788	4,788	
Supply growth				6.8%	9.8%	0.0%	5.8%	5.5%	0.0%	4.6%
Composite market occupancy	72.2%	66.1%	68.1%	65.7%	62.8%	65.3%	64.2%	62.6%	64.5%	

293

EXHIBIT 4 Competitor and Market Segment Analysis, Frankfurt

Property	No. of Rooms	1985		1986		1987		Year to Date through March			
								1987		1988	
		Occ.	Rate	Occ.	Rate	Occ.	Rate	Occ.	Rate	Occ.	Rate
Primary:											
Habsburg Hof	376	67.3%	230	63.7%	239	68.1%	254	67.2%	258	61.9%	269
Goethe Gasthof	161	61.5	207	57.2	201	55.8	211	61.8	228	56.5	229
English Imperial Hotel	278	69.7	174	59.6	169	55.9	182	61.0	187	58.3	184
Volks Hof	796	79.6	160	70.7	158	74.0	163	67.4	176	69.1	180
Kiwi Grand	950	60.9	13	63.2	138	58.3	157	55.6	187	55.9	170
Subtotal	2,561	69.9%	170	64.9%	171	65.5%	183	62.7%	198	61.8%	196
Secondary:											
Hotel Europa	820	86.3%	185	75.3%	180	81.7%	178	76.5%	187	81.3%	181
Deutsche Hof	323	85.4	130	79.1	130	82.4	132	77.7	144	78.1	148
Schweizerisch Hof	310	65.7	170	62.0	173	64.1	189	57.7	183	62.4	197
Subtotal	1,453	83.1%	169	73.4%	168	77.7%	176	67.7%	189	67.7%	188

Property	Quality Level	Year Opened	1987 Market Segmentation				Meeting Space		1988 Quoted Prices (DM)	
			Business	Fair	Pleasure	Airline Crew	No. of Rooms	No. of People	Single	Double
Primary:										
Habsburg Hof	H	1910	85%	10%	5%	0	18	20–400	180–379	270–420
Goethe Gasthof	H	1960	85	15	0	0	12	30–200	156–420	274–468
English Imperial Hotel	M	1895/1980	75	15	10	0	13	20–300	255–304	295–412
Volks Hof	M	1950	55	15	20	10%	9	30–450	230–356	258–398
Kiwi Grand	L	1963/1978	35	30	10	25	5	20–300	230–376	240–400
Subtotal			57%	19%	12%	12%				
Secondary:										
Hotel Europa	M	1978	20%	20	10%	50%	9	30–1200	185–375	199–425
Deutsche Hof	M	1959	30	20	15	25	14	20–350	170–356	190–400
Schweizerisch Hof	H	1951	70	20	10	0	7	20–400	210–395	220–425

EXHIBIT 5   Cash Flow Forecast, Frankfurt (in DM expressed in thousands)

	1989	1989 Ratios	1990	1990 Ratios	1991	1991 Ratios
Assumptions:						
Number rooms	950					
Average occupancy	60%		64%		67%	
Average room rate (DM)	178.00		194.73		202.52	
Average daily % change	—		9.4%		4.0%	
SG&A expense	30%		30%		30%	
Marriott central office fee	3.0%					
Tax rate	60%					
Fixed annual rent payment	10,000					
Buren rent supplement	2.0%		2.0%		2.0%	
Country risk adjustment factor	0.99					
Capital investment (DM)	28,800					
Revenue:						
Rooms	37,033	65.0%	43,215	70.0%	47,050	75.0%
Food & beverage	10,255	18.0%	9,878	16.0%	9,410	15.0%
Other	9,686	17.0%	8,643	14.0%	6,273	10.0%
Total revenue	56,974	100.0%	61,736	100.0%	62,734	100.0%
Departmental profits:						
Rooms	25,553	69.0%	31,547	73.0%	37,170	79.0%
Food & beverage	1,128	11.0%	1,284	13.0%	1,553	16.5%
Other	2,228	23.0%	2,074	24.0%	1,506	24.0%
Total department profits	28,908		34,905	56.5%	40,228	64.1%
Administrative expenses:						
SG&A	17,092	30.0%	18,521	30.0%	18,820	30.0%
Marriott Central Office	1,709	3.0%	1,852	3.0%	1,882	3.0%
Total other expenses	18,801	33.0%	20,373	33.0%	20,702	33.0%
Earnings before interest, rent,						
& tax	10,107	17.7%	14,533	23.5%	19,526	31.1%
Tax expense	6,064	60.0%	8,720	60.0%	11,716	60.0%
Earnings before interest and rent						
and after taxes	4,043	7.1%	5,813	9.4%	7,810	12.5%
Depreciation	1,400	2.5%	1800	2.9%	1700	2.7%
Capital expenditure	1,250	2.2%	1700	2.8%	1800	2.9%
Net house profit after taxes, or free cash flow before rent						
expense	4,193		5,913		7,710	
Rent expense:						
Minimum rent	10,000	17.6%	10,000	16.2%	10,000	15.9%
After-tax minimum rent	4,000	7.0%	4,000	6.5%	4,000	6.4%
Rent supplement	1,139	2.0%	1,235	2.0%	1,255	2.0%
After-tax rent supplement	456	0.8%	494	0.8%	502	0.8%

1992	1993	1994	1995	1996	1997	1998	1999
210.62	219.05	227.81	236.92	244.03	251.35	258.89	266.66
4.0%	4.0%	4.0%	4.0%	3.0%	3.0%	3.0%	3.0%
30%	30%	30%	30%	30%	30%	30%	30%
2.5%	2.5%	2.5%	3.5%	3.5%	3.5%	3.5%	3.5%
48,932	50,890	52,925	55,042	56,693	58,394	60,146	61,950
9,786	10,178	10,585	11,008	11,339	11,679	12,029	12,390
6,524	6,785	7,057	7,339	7,559	7,786	8,019	8,260
65,243	67,853	70,567	73,390	75,591	77,859	80,195	82,601
38,656	40,203	41,811	43,483	44,788	46,131	47,515	48,941
1,615	1,679	1,747	1,816	1,871	1,927	1,985	2,044
1,566	1,628	1,694	1,761	1,814	1,869	1,925	1,982
41,837	43,511	45,251	47,061	48,473	49,927	51,425	52,968
19,573	20,356	21,170	22,017	22,677	23,358	24,058	24,780
1,957	2,036	2,117	2,202	2,268	2,336	2,406	2,478
21,530	22,391	23,287	24,219	24,945	25,693	26,464	27,258
20,307	21,119	21,964	22,842	23,528	24,234	24,961	25,709
12,184	12,671	13,178	13,705	14,117	14,540	14,976	15,426
8,123	8,448	8,786	9,137	9,411	9,693	9,984	10,284
1700	2200	2100	1950	1930	1920	1900	1900
1900	2200	2000	2000	2000	2000	2000	2000
7,923	8,448	8,886	9,087	9,341	961	9,884	10,184
10,000	10,000	10,000	10,000	10,000	10,000	10,000	10,000
4,000	4,000	4,000	4,000	4,000	4,000	4,000	4,000
1,631	1,696	1,764	2,569	2,646	2,725	2,807	2,891
652	679	706	1,027	1,058	1,090	1,123	1,156

EXHIBIT 5   *(concluded)*

	2000	2001	2002	2003	2004	2005	2006	2007
Assumptions:								
Number rooms								
Average occupancy								
Average room rate (DM)	274.66	282.90	291.38	300.12	309.13	318.40	327.95	337.79
Average daily % change	3.0%	3.0%	3.0%	3.0%	3.0%	3.0%	3.0%	3.0%
SG&A expense	30%	30%	30%	30%	30%	30%	30%	30%
Marriott central office fee								
Tax rate								
Fixed annual rent payment								
Buren rent supplement	3.5%	3.5%	3.5%	3.5%	3.5%	3.5%	3.5%	3.5%
Country risk adjustment factor								
Capital investment (DM)								
Revenue:								
Rooms	63,809	65,723	67,695	69,726	71,818	73,972	76,191	78,477
Food & beverage	12,762	13,145	13,539	13,945	14,364	14,794	15,238	15,695
Other	8,508	8,763	9,026	9,297	9,576	9,863	10,159	10,464
Total revenue	85,079	87,631	90,260	92,968	95,757	98,629	101,588	104,636
Departmental profits:								
Rooms	50,409	51,921	53,479	55,083	56,736	58,438	60,191	61,997
Food & beverage	2,106	2,169	2,234	2,301	2,370	2,441	2,514	2,590
Other	2,042	2,103	2,166	2,231	2,298	2,376	2,438	2,511
Total department profits	54,557	56,193	57,879	59,616	61,404	63,246	65,143	67,098
Administrative expenses:								
SG&A	25,524	26,289	27,078	27,890	28,727	29,589	30,476	31,391
Marriott central office	2,552	2,629	2,708	2,789	2,873	2,959	3,048	3,139
Total other expenses	28,076	28,918	29,786	30,679	31,600	32,548	33,524	34,530
Earnings before interest, rent, & taxes	26,481	27,275	28,093	28,936	29,804	30,698	31,619	32,568
Tax expense	15,888	16,365	16,856	17,362	17,883	18,419	18,972	19,541
Earnings before interest and rent and after taxes	10,592	10,910	11,237	11,574	11,922	12,279	12,648	13,027
Depreciation	1900	1900	1900	1900	1900	1900	1900	1900
Capital expenditure	2000	2000	2000	2000	2000	2000	2000	2000
Net house profit after taxes, or free cash flow before rent expense	10,492	10,810	11,137	11,474	11,822	12,179	12,548	12,927
Rent expense:								
Minimum rent	10,000	10,000	10,000	10,000	10,000	10,000	10,000	10,000
After-tax minimum rent	4,000	4,000	4,000	4,000	4,000	4,000	4,000	4,000
rent supplement	2,978	3,067	3,159	3,254	3,351	3,452	3,556	3,662
After-tax rent supplement	1,191	1,227	1,264	1,302				

Source: Company documents and casewriter's analysis.

2008	2009	2010	2011	2012	2013	2014	2015	2016	2017	2018
347.93	358.36	369.12	380.19	391.59	403.34	415.44	427.91	440.74	453.97	467.58
3.0%	3.0%	3.0%	3.0%	3.0%	3.0%	3.0%	3.0%	3.0%	3.0%	3.0%
30%	30%	30%	30%	30%	30%	30%	30%	30%	30%	30%
3.5%	3.5%	3.5%	3.5%	3.5%	3.5%	3.5%	3.5%	3.5%	3.5%	3.5%
80,831	83,256	85,754	88,326	90,976	93,706	96,517	99,412	102,395	105,466	108,630
16,166	16,651	17,151	17,665	18,195	18,741	19,303	19,882	20,479	21,093	21,726
10,777	11,101	11,434	11,777	12,130	12,494	12,869	13,255	13,653	14,062	14,484
107,775	111,008	114,338	117,769	121,302	124,941	128,689	132,550	136,526	140,622	144,841
63,857	65,772	67,746	69,778	71,871	74,027	76,248	78,536	80,892	83,318	85,818
2,667	2,747	2,830	2,915	3,002	3,092	3,185	3,281	3,379	3,480	3,585
2,587	2,664	2,744	2,826	2,911	2,999	3,089	3,181	3,277	3,375	3,476
69,111	71,184	73,320	75,519	77,785	80,118	82,522	84,997	87,547	90,174	92,879
32,332	33,302	34,302	35,331	36,391	37,482	38,607	39,765	40,958	42,187	43,452
3,233	3,330	3,430	3,533	3,639	3,748	3,861	3,976	4,096	4,219	4,345
35,566	36,633	37,732	38,864	40,030	41,230	42,467	43,741	45,054	46,405	47,797
33,545	34,551	35,588	36,655	37,755	38,888	40,054	41,256	42,494	43,769	45,082
20,127	20,731	21,353	21,993	22,653	23,333	24,033	24,754	25,496	26,261	27,049
13,418	13,821	14,235	14,662	15,102	15,555	16,022	16,502	16,998	17,507	18,033
1900	1900	1900	1900	1900	1900	1900	1900	1900	1900	1900
2000	2000	2000	2000	2000	2000	2000	2000	2000	2000	2000
13,318	13,721	14,135	14,562	15,002	15,455	15,922	16,402	16,898	17,407	17,933
10,000	10,000	10,000	10,000	10,000	10,000	10,000	10,000	10,000	10,000	10,00
4,000	4,000	4,000	4,000	4,000	4,000	4,000	4,000	4,000	4,000	4,000
3,772	3,885	4,002	4,122	4,246	4,373	4,504	4,639	4,778	4,922	5,069

EXHIBIT 6 Cash Flow Forecast, Dusseldorf (DM in thousands)

	1989	1989 Ratios	1990	1990 Ratios	1991
Assumptions:					
Number rooms	200				
Average occupancy	65%		67%		68%
Average room rate (DM)	130		134.55		139.26
Average daily % change	—		3.5%		3.5%
SG&A expense	30%		30%		30%
Marriott central office fee	3.0%				
Tax rate	60%				
Annual rent payment (DM)	1,000				
Country risk adjustment factor	0.99				
Revenue:					
Rooms	6,169	55.0%	6,581	57.0%	6,913
Food & beverage	4,598	41.0%	4,618	40.0%	4,378
Other	561	5.0%	346	430%	230
Total revenue	11,215	100.0%	11,545	100.0%	11,521
Departmental profits:					
Rooms	3,886	63.0%	4,212	64.0%	4,424
Food & beverage	460	10.0%	531	11.5%	503
Other	90	16.0%	59	17.0%	41
Total department profits	4,436	39.6%	4,802	41.6%	4,969
Administrative expenses:					
SG&A	3,365	30.0%	3,464	30.0%	3,456
Marriott central office fee	336	3.0%	346	3.0%	346
Total other expenses	3,701	33.0%	3,810	33.0%	3,802
Inc. before rent, int., and tax exp.	735	6.6%	992	8.6%	1,167
Tax expense	441	3.9%	595	5.2%	700
Income before rent & interest after tax expense	294	2.6%	397	3.4%	467
Depreciation	320	2.9%	360	3.1%	470
Capital expenditure	440	3.9%	530	4.6%	550
Net house profit after taxes, or free cash flow before rent expense	174	1.6%	227	2.0%	387
Land rent	1,000	8.9%	1,000	8.7%	1,000
Land rent after taxes	400		400		400
Land rent tax shield	600		600		600

1991 Ratios	1992	1993	1994	1995	1996	1997	1998	1999
	143.44	147.74	151.43	155.22	159.10	162.28	165.53	168.84
	3.0%	3.0%	2.5%	2.5%	2.5%	2.0%	2.0%	2.0%
60.0%	7,120	7,334	7,517	7,705	7,898	8,056	8,217	8,381
38.0%	4,509	4,645	4,761	4,880	5,002	5,102	5,204	5,308
2.0%	237	244	251	257	263	269	274	279
100.0%	11,867	12,223	12,529	12,842	13,163	13,426	13,695	13,969
65.0%	4,628	4,767	4,886	5,008	5,134	5,236	5,341	5,448
11.5%	519	534	548	561	575	587	598	610
18.0%	43	44	45	46	47	48	49	50
43.1%	5,189	5,345	5,479	5,616	5,756	5,871	5,989	6,108
30.0%	3,560	3,667	3,759	3,853	3,949	4,028	4,108	4,191
3.0%	356	367	376	385	395	403	411	419
33.0%	3,916	4,034	4,134	4,238	4,344	4,431	4,519	4,610
10.1%	1,273	1,312	1,344	1,378	1,412	1,441	1,469	1,499
6.1%	764	787	807	827	847	864	882	899
4.1%	509	525	538	551	565	576	588	600
4.1%	520	530	530	530	530	530	530	530
4.8%	580	580	580	580	580	580	580	580
3.4%	449	475	488	501	515	526	538	550
8.7%	1,000	1,000	1,000	1,000	1,000	1,000	1,000	1,000
	400	400	400	400	400	400	400	400
	600	600	600	600	600	600	600	600

EXHIBIT 6 *(concluded)*

	2000	2001	2002	2003	2004	2005	2006	2007	2008
Assumptions:									
Number rooms									
Average occupancy	171.37	173.94	176.55	178.32	180.10	181.90	183.72	185.56	187.41
Average room rate (DM) ...	1.5%	1.5%	1.5%	1.0%	1.0%	1.0%	1.0%	1.0%	1.0%
Average daily % change									
SG&A expense									
Marriott central office fee ...									
Tax rate									
Annual rent payment (DM) ...									
Country risk adjustment factor ...									
Revenue:									
Rooms	8,507	8,634	8,764	8,852	8,940	9,030	9,120	9,211	9,303
Food & beverage	5,388	5,468	5,551	5,606	5,662	5,719	5,776	5,834	5,892
Other	284	288	292	295	298	301	304	307	310
Total revenue	14,178	14,391	14,607	14,753	14,900	15,049	15,200	15,352	15,505
Departmental profits:									
Rooms	5,529	5,612	5,697	5,754	5,811	5,869	5,928	5,987	6,047
Food & beverage	620	629	638	645	651	658	664	671	678

302

	51	52	53	53	54	54	55	55	56
Other									
Total department profits	6,200	6,293	6,387	6,451	6,516	6,581	6,647	6,713	6,780
Administrative expenses:									
SG&A	4,253	4,317	4,382	4,426	4,470	4,515	4,560	4,606	4,652
Marriott central office fee	425	432	438	443	447	451	456	461	465
Total other expenses	4,679	4,749	4,820	4,868	4,917	4,966	5,016	5,066	5,117
Inc. before rent, int., and tax exp. ...	1,521	1,544	1,567	1,583	1,599	1,615	1,631	1,647	1,664
Tax expense	913	926	940	950	959	969	979	988	
Income before rent & interest after tax expense	609	618	627	633	640	646	652	659	665
Depreciation	530	530	530	530	530	530	530	530	530
Capital expenditure	580	580	580	580	580	580	580	580	580
Net house profit after taxes, or free cash flow before rent expense	559	568	577	583	590	596	602	609	615
Land rent	1,000	1,000	1,000	1,000	1,000	1,000	1,000	1,000	1,000
Land rent after taxes	400	400	400	400	400	400	400	400	400
Land rent tax shield	600	600	600	600	600	600	600	600	600

Source: Company documents and casewriter's analysis.

EXHIBIT 7 Financial and Foreign Exchange Market Data

Financial Market Data

Forward Rates (per US$)	Price
30-Day forward	1.8717
90-Day forward	1.8615
180-Day forward	1.8468

Marriott's beta: 1.1

Year	U.S. Inflation (%)	German Inflation (%)	Foreign Exchange Rate (DM/$)
1985*	3.50%	2.20%	2.94
1986*	2.00	−0.20	2.17
1987*	3.00	1.50	1.80
1988	3.50	0.20	1.77
1989	4.30	2.00	1.73
1990	4.30	2.20	1.69
1991	4.80	2.20	1.65
1992	4.80	2.20	1.61
1993	4.80	2.20	1.57
1994	4.80	2.20	1.53
1995	4.80	2.20	1.49
1996	4.80	2.20	1.45
1997	4.80	2.20	1.42
1998	4.80	2.20	1.38
1999	4.80	2.20	1.35
2000	4.80	2.20	1.32
2001	4.80	2.20	1.28
2002	4.80	2.20	1.25
2003	4.80	2.20	1.22
2004	4.80	2.20	1.19
2005	4.80	2.20	1.16
2006	4.80	2.20	1.13
2007	4.80	2.20	1.10
2008	4.80	2.20	1.08
2009	4.80	2.20	1.05
2010	4.80	2.20	1.02
2011	4.80	2.20	1.00
2012	4.80	2.20	0.97
2013	4.80	2.20	0.95
2014	4.80	2.20	0.93
2015	4.80	2.20	0.90
2016	4.80	2.20	0.88
2017	4.80	2.20	0.86
2018	4.80	2.20	0.84

*Actual median results for the year. All other figures are forecasts.

Sources: Company documents; *Value Line,* September 9, 1988; *The Wall Street Journal,* September 1, 1988.

EXHIBIT 8 Summary of Discounted Cash Flow Analysis (US$ expressed in thousands)

Year	Exchange Rate	Country Risk Factor	Frankfurt Hotel				Dusseldorf Hotel	
			FCF Before Rent*	Minimum Rent*	Rent Supplement*	Capital Investmt.*	FCF Before Rent†	Rent Payment
1988	1.77	0	0	0				
1989	1.73	0.99	$ 2,405	$2,294	$ 261	(16,315)	$100	$229
1990	1.69	0.99	3,461	2,341	289		133	234
1991	1.65	0.99	4,627	2,401	301		232	240
1992	1.61	0.99	4,876	2,462	402		277	246
1993	1.57	0.99	5,331	2,524	428		300	252
1994	1.53	0.99	5,750	2,589	457		316	259
1995	1.49	0.99	6,030	2,654	682		333	265
1996	1.45	0.99	6,356	2,722	720		350	272
1997	1.42	0.99	6,708	2,791	761		367	279
1998	1.38	0.99	7,073	2,862	803		385	286
1999	1.35	0.99	7,472	2,935	849		403	293
2000	1.32	0.99	7,895	3,010	896		420	301
2001	1.28	0.99	8,341	3,086	947		438	309
2002	1.25	0.99	8,812	3,165	1,000		456	316
2003	1.22	0.99	9,309	3,245	1,056		473	325

* US$ value of DM flows obtained from Exhibit 5, adjusted for country risk factor.
† US$ value of DM flows obtained from Exhibit 6, adjusted for country risk factor.

Source: Company documents and casewriter's analysis.

EXHIBIT 8 (concluded)

			Frankfurt Hotel				Dusseldorf Hotel	
Year	Exchange Rate	Country Risk Factor	FCF Before Rent*	Minimum Rent*	Rent Supplement*	Capital Investmt.*	FCF Before Rent†	Rent Payment
2004	1.19	0.99	9,835	3,328	1,115		490	333
2005	1.16	0.99	10,390	3,412	1,178		508	341
2006	1.13	0.99	10,977	3,499	1,244		527	350
2007	1.10	0.99	11,597	3,588	1,314		546	359
2008	1.08	0.99	12,251	3,680	1,388		$566	$368
2009	1.05	0.99	12,943	3,773	1,466			
2010	1.02	0.99	13,673	3,869	1,548			
2011	1.00	0.99	14,444	3,968	1,635			
2012	0.97	0.99	15,259	4,069	1,727			
2013	0.95	0.99	16,120	4,172	1,824			
2014	0.93	0.99	17,029	4,278	1,927			
2015	0.90	0.99	17,990	4,387	2,035			
2016	0.88	0.99	19,004	4,499	2,150			
2017	0.86	0.99	20,076	4,613	2,270			
2018	0.84	0.99	$21,208	$4,730	$2,398			
Discount rate			11.0%	6.5%	8.0%	11.0%	11.0%	6.5%
Present value (Aug. 1988)			$56,428	$(37,967)	$(8,739)	$(16,315)	$2,332	$(2,970)

	Both Hotels	Frankfurt Only	Dusseldorf Only
Net present value	$(7,231)	$(6,593)	$(638)

* US$ value of DM flows obtained from Exhibit 5, adjusted for country risk factor.
† US$ value of DM flows obtained from Exhibit 6, adjusted for country risk factor.

Primus Automation Division

In early 1991, Tom Baumann, an analyst in the marketing and sales group of the Factory Automation Division of Primus Corporation had to recommend to the division sales manager, Jim Feldman, the terms on which Primus Automation Division would lease one of its advanced systems to Avantjet Corporation, a manufacturer of corporate jet aircraft. Tom considered a choice among four sets of lease terms.

The problem of analyzing and setting lease terms was relatively new to Tom and had arisen only a month earlier, when Avantjet informed Tom and Jim that their pending purchase of the factory automation system had been put on indefinite hold. Avantjet's CEO had just ordered a moratorium on any capital expenditures that might negatively affect the income statement and balance sheet in 1991. Tom was not completely surprised by Avantjet's decision; just recently *The Wall Street Journal* had singled out Avantjet's declining stock price and worsening balance sheet as an example of the deteriorating condition of manufacturers in the economic recession.

Only three months before, Tom and Jim had won an apparent competition among Primus's leading competitors, Faulhaber Gmbh, a German company, and Honshu Heavy Industries of Japan. Tom feared that Avantjet's temporizing would give these two competitors an opportunity to renew their selling efforts to Avantjet.

Jim Feldman challenged Tom to find a way to make the sale: "Help me salvage this deal or we won't make our sales budget for the year. Also, given the steep competition, we might lose the customer altogether on future sales." Tom explored a range of creative financing terms, such as leasing, that might resolve Avantjet's reluctance to proceed. He concluded that structuring the transaction as a lease might save the deal. Now, choosing the annual lease payment remained the only detail to be settled before returning to Avantjet with a proposal.

This case was prepared by Robert Hengelbrok under the supervision of Professor Robert Bruner. Names, places, and figures have been disguised.

PRIMUS AUTOMATION DIVISION

Primus Automation, a division of a large, worldwide manufacturing and services firm, was an innovative producer of world-class factory automation products and services, with operations in the United States, Europe, and Asia. Primus's products included programmable controllers, numerical controls, industrial computers, manufacturing software, factory automation systems, and data communication networks.

The business environment had changed dramatically over the past year. Slower economic growth coupled with increasing competition for market share was forecasted for the next few years. Still, a recent resurgence in the U.S. manufacturing base—due to the weakened dollar driving up U.S. exports—was spurring factory automation. Cross-continental industry alliances and an accelerated rate of new-product introduction had heightened industry rivalries.

Primus Automation's objectives were to maintain leadership market share, to grow sales by 15 percent a year, and to achieve net income and working capital turnover targets. These objectives were to be realized by providing the most responsive customer service, obtaining a strong share position in high-volume growing segments, and offering leading technology products based on industry standards.

Meeting these objectives required stimulating demand by creating new incentives for purchasing automation equipment. Many unsophisticated users of automation equipment in the United States needed to be educated in analyzing capital expenditures, tax incentives, and alternative methods for acquiring the needed equipment. Division executives had discussed various asset-financing approaches as means of assisting placement of their systems.

ASSET-FINANCING APPROACHES

Tom reviewed for the division executives the variety of ways a firm might acquire the use of a Primus Automated Factory System. First, a customer could purchase the system with cash or borrow funds either unsecured or through a mortgage collateralized by the equipment. Second, a firm could acquire equipment through a conditional sale where title would pass on the completion of the final installment payment. Third, the customer might rent short term or rent with an option to own. Finally, one could lease the equipment one of two ways. A cancellable operating lease would carry a term less than the economic life of the property. A noncancellable financial capital lease would cover the entire economic life of the property.

Capital versus Operating Lease

Tom reviewed his notes on the rules defining the two types of leases. To be classified as an operating lease under Financial Accounting Standard Board (FASB) *Statement No. 13* guidelines, the lease had to meet the following four criteria:

A. Ownership of the asset could not transfer after the lease term.
B. The lease could not have a bargain-purchase option; the lessee had to pay the fair market value for the property at the end of the lease.
C. The lease term could not exceed 75 percent of the economic life of the property.
D. The present value of the lease payments over the lease term could not exceed 90 percent of the fair market value of the leased property at the beginning of the lease.

If classified as an operating lease, the lease payments would be treated as an ordinary expense, deductible from taxable income. The leased property would not appear on the lessee's balance sheet and, after the lease term, would revert to the lessor.

If the lease met none of the four conditions, it would be classified as a capital lease. In this case, the lessee would be required to depreciate the equipment by showing an asset and liability on the balance sheet. The lessee could not deduct the lease payment from income taxes. At the end of the lease, the lessee retained ownership and bore the risk of early changes in the asset's value.

LEASING INDUSTRY

Tom Baumann had learned that leasing as a form of financing had expanded dramatically over the last 15 years, to an estimated $135 billion of newly leased assets in 1991. The compound annual growth rate for 1978–1986 was over 18 percent, much greater than the growth in equipment purchases for the same period. Figure 1 shows the growth in

FIGURE 1   Annual Volume of New Lease Commitments in the United States

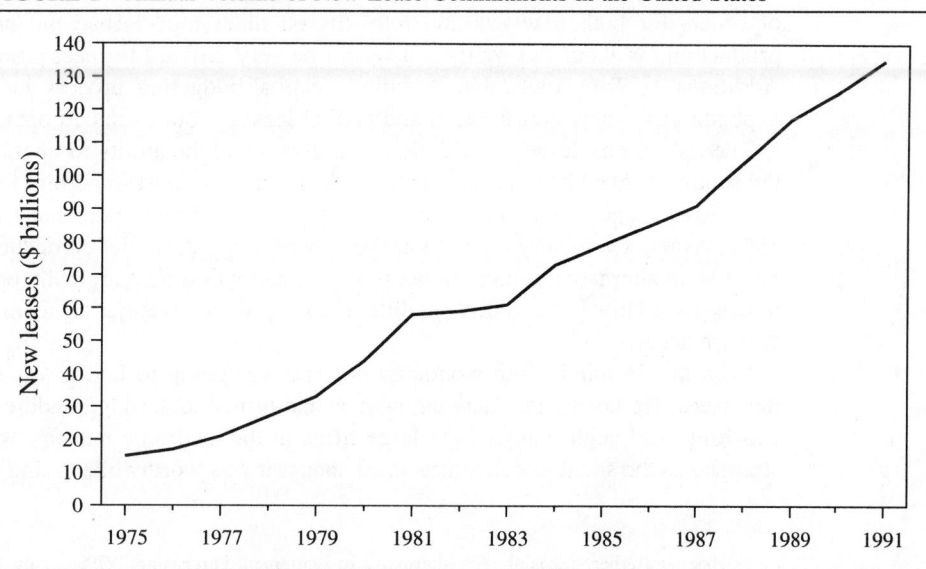

Sources: American Association of Equipment Elssors, and casewriter's estimates.

annual leasing volume since 1975. Eight out of ten companies currently leased some portion of their equipment.[1] Primus Automation's senior management felt this area offered an avenue for new sales growth because none of their competitors were offering leasing.

Primus Automation had never offered leasing before and was unfamiliar with the actual workings of leasing arrangements. Fortunately, Primus's Equipment Finance Division of the parent company had extensive leasing expertise and assisted Tom in his research. As he dug out some of the information the division had sent him, Tom realized that this was the first application of his efforts and he wanted to make sure he understood all of leasing's nuances.

TAX REFORM

The Tax Reform Act of 1986 (TRA '86) made substantial changes in a company's ability to benefit from large capital expenditures. TRA '86 lowered the corporate tax rates, removed the investment tax credit (ITC), implemented an alternative minimum tax (AMT), and added a mid-quarter depreciation requirement when more than 40 percent of equipment purchased in a year was put in service in the last quarter. These provisions meant that companies were finding it more difficult to justify capital expenditures.

AVANTJET

Tom had heard that Avantjet's vice president of operations was determined to get an automation system to cut costs and accelerate Avantjet's production line. A large backlog of orders for both new jets and retro-fits on older models had put new demands on production. Without this system, it would be very difficult to meet promised deliveries. Additionally, Tom knew that Avantjet's capital-budgeting process included all major expenditures—new construction and capital leases—but excluded operating leases.

The risk of obsolescence with this technology and the ability to upgrade equipment in the future weighed heavily in Avantjet's decision. The most important factor overall was cash flow, because Avantjet wanted to avoid any additional unplanned expenditures for 1991. Avantjet was very capital intensive, with large depreciation deductions that might put it in an alternative minimum tax position, and was only marginally profitable because it was so highly leveraged. (Exhibits 1 and 2 show Avantjet's income statement and balance sheet.)

With this in mind, Tom wondered how he was going to find a way to resolve all of the issues. He knew that many companies had turned to leasing to address some of these concerns. Although many of the large firms in the air-frame industry were not as cash-strapped as the small and medium-sized shops, it was worthwhile to find out what classes

---

[1]Michael Hofferber, "Leasing: An Alternative to Equipment Purchasing," *Office,* July 1988, pp. 85–87.

of customers would benefit financially from leasing. Tom surmised that tax rates and cost-of-capital disparities between the lessor and lessee might be critical drivers in any lease arrangement.

PRIMUS'S COMPETITORS

Several months earlier, when Avantjet was reviewing system proposals from Primus, Honshu, and Faulhaber, Tom and Jim learned from Avantjet that all three systems were roughly equivalent, but that they differed in terms of pricing. The following table summarizes what Avantjet communicated about pricing:

System Manufacturer	Purchase Price of System if Avantjet Were to Buy	Quoted Annual Lease Expense and Assumed Residual Market Value for 5-Year Operating Lease
Faulhaber Gmbh	US$759,000	$170,000, 15%
Honshu Heavy Industries	US$737,000	$163,000, 24%
Primus Automation Division	US$715,000	Not previously quoted

Tom had learned from industry newsletters that foreign manufacturers sometimes exploited their allegedly lower costs of capital as a competitive weapon in designing financing terms for their customers. Tom wondered whether this was apparent in the lease terms proposed by Faulhaber and Honshu, and he planned to estimate the effective lease costs under their respective proposals.

PRIMUS'S LEASE PROPOSAL

The particular deal Jim Feldman had called him about was a proposal for nearly $715,000 of factory automation equipment. This system would enable Avantjet to operate a group of workstations from a central control site while gaining valuable feedback and planning capabilities.

Realizing that he had to find out more about Avantjet's motives for delaying the project, Tom quizzed Jim about Avantjet's performance and requirements. Jim told Tom that Avantjet's last CEO had been replaced by a senior executive from outside the firm who was more concerned with the bottom line and the balance sheet than making capital expenditures that had long paybacks.

With this in mind, Tom began to assess this particular deal. The price of the total package was $715,000. Primus might be able to offer Avantjet some discount off the price to encourage it to rethink its decision. Another possibility was offering either delayed or progress billing. Jim also had mentioned that the project could be scaled back if necessary to bring it under some maximum dollar amount.

Tom assumed that Avantjet's primary alternative was to borrow the purchase price of the equipment on a five-year interest-bearing term loan payable in equal annual amounts of $188,615 due at the *end* of each year. The leasing division quoted Tom a five-year operating lease with equal annual payments that varied depending on Avantjet's actual tax rate and cost of debt, due at the *beginning* of each year. At the end of the lease term, renewal was subject to negotiation between the two parties. Factory automation equipment was classified as technological equipment with a five-year life. Five-year MACRS depreciation rates based on the full value of the property were:

Income Tax Depreciation Rate Schedule	
Year	Percentage
1	20.00%
2	32.00
3	19.20
4	11.52
5	11.52
6	5.76

To structure this as an operating lease, the leasing division required a 11.2729 percent residual guarantee from Tom's division. Tom did not know how risky this was. Because his division was trying to move into leasing to bolster sales, he figured that it might be willing to assume some of the risk of the value of the equipment declining substantially in five years. Primus Automation also might have to assist the leasing division in re-marketing the equipment to another user if a new lease was not signed when the original lease expired. (Exhibit 3 lists the various price and leasing terms.)

To analyze leasing scenarios, Tom created a leasing model (Exhibits 4 and 5) computing the net present value and the internal rate of return of cash flows to get a better understanding of which alternative would be least costly to Avantjet. The scenario with the lowest present value would be the cheapest financing alternative. The internal rate of return represented the effective cost of the lease financing. If this rate was below the after-tax cost of capital, then leasing would be the more attractive method of financing.

Although Tom guessed that Avantjet had about the same borrowing cost as Primus (about 10 percent), he suspected that Avantjet was in a lower tax bracket. Tom decided to run some sensitivity analyses with a zero marginal tax rate. With such a low tax rate, Avantjet could not fully exploit the tax savings on interest and depreciation.

Small and medium-sized customers probably paid higher interest rates than Primus and could save money if Primus financed the equipment and passed on some of the financing savings to them. Leasing terms might be adjusted to exchange tax benefits for lower lease rates. Tom's analysis used the after-tax cost of debt as the discount rate, but Tom thought he might want to use a higher discount rate, perhaps the weighted-average cost of capital, based on the greater risk involved with leasing high technology equipment.

Finally, a sensitivity analysis based on various discount and tax rates might help to determine under what circumstances a customer might want to lease. Sample calculations for four lease rates that Primus might offer different customers are presented in Exhibit 6. With a variety of options and scenarios in hand to propose to Avantjet depending on actual tax and hurdle rates, Tom felt that Primus had a better chance of resurrecting this deal and meeting its sales goals for 1991. Moreover, this experience would assist Primus in offering lease proposals to other customers in the future.

EXHIBIT 1   Avantjet Statement of Income (in thousands)

	1990	1989	1988
Sales	$576,327	$575,477	$432,522
Other income	9,985	6,976	9,677
Gross income	$586,312	$582,453	$442,199
Cost of goods sold	$425,076	423,443	325,016
SG&A	43,624	36,215	35,632
R&D	13,773	12,873	9,064
Interest	84,062	87,259	27,002
Total expenses	$566,535	$559,791	$396,714
Income before taxes	$ 19,777	$ 22,662	$ 45,485
Taxes	9,690	11,105	22,288
Net income	$ 10,087	$ 11,557	$ 23,197

Source: Company records.

EXHIBIT 2 Avantjet Balance Sheet (in thousands)

	1990	1989
Assets		
Current assets:		
Cash and temporary investments	$ 19,918	$ 27,263
Accounts receivable	37,791	37,307
Inventories	310,180	323,101
Prepaid expenses	13,928	13,362
Total current assets	$ 381,817	$ 401,033
Property, plant, and equipment:		
Land	$ 2,245	$ 2,245
Buildings	30,654	30,229
Machinery and equipment	26,932	21,244
Furniture and fixtures	1,683	1,520
Construction in progress	1,668	885
	63,182	56,123
Less accumulated depreciation	12,634	8,267
Net PP&E	50,548	47,856
Other assets	640,369	648,339
Total assets	$1,072,734	$1,097,228

	1990	1989
Liabilities and Stockholders' Equity		
Current liabilities:		
Long-term debt	$ 592	$ 563
Accounts payable	42,355	38,760
Notes payable	4,750	5,764
Accrued compensation, interest, and other liabilities	39,627	43,855
Deposits and progress payments	146,964	160,946
Total current liabilities	234,288	249,888
Long-term notes payable to banks	646,633	671,225
Deferred income taxes	42,661	41,498
Total	689,294	712,723
Common stockholders' equity:		
Common stock	3,385	3,027
Capital in excess of par value	74,081	69,770
Retained earnings	72,017	62,156
Less common stock in treasury	(331)	(336)
Total stockholders' equity	149,152	134,617
Total liabilities and stockholders' equity	$1,072,734	$1,097,228

Source: Company records.

EXHIBIT 3   Terms under Hypothetical Leasing and Buy-and-Borrow Strategies

Loan payment: • 5-year term loan • Payments in arrears Equipment cost	$715,000
Cash down payment	0
Loan amount	$715,000
Annual percentage rate	10.00%
Annual term	5
Annual loan payment	$188,615
Lease: • 5-year net lease • Payments in advance	
Lease payment 1	$155,040
Lease payment 2	$161,718
Lease payment 3	$162,350
Lease payment 4	$164,760
Both methods	
Residual value	11.2729%
Investment tax credit	0%
Depreciation	5-year MACRS

EXHIBIT 4 Sample Calculation of the Present Value of Cash Outflows: Scenario I, Lease Payment 2 ($161,718)

Year	Payment of Interest after Tax	Principal Payment	5-Year MACRS Deprec. Rates	Depreciation before Tax	Tax Savings Associated with Depreciation	Less Residual Value after Tax	Loan Cash Outflows	After-Tax Lease 2 Outflows
0							0	$106,734
1	$ 47,190	$117,115	20.00%	$143,000	$ (48,620)		$115,685	106,734
2	39,460	128,827	32.00	228,800	(77,792)		90,495	106,734
3	30,958	141,709	19.20	137,280	(46,675)		125,992	106,734
4	21,605	155,880	11.52	82,368	(28,005)		149,480	106,734
5	11,317	171,468	11.52	82,368	(28,005)	$(67,199)*	87,581	0
Sum	$150,530	$715,000	94.24%	$673,816	$(229,097)	$(67,199)	569,233	533,669
NPV							$471,551	$471,553

Note: Columns may not total exactly because of rounding.
*The residual value after tax is equal to the sales proceeds of the equipment (calculated as the cost of the equipment times residual percentage) less tax expense (calculated as the tax rate times the difference between sale proceeds and book value at the time of sale).

EXHIBIT 5   Sample Calculation of the Internal Rate of Return: Scenario I, Lease Payment 2 ($161,718)

Year	Lease Payment 2 after Tax	Forgone Tax Savings Associated with Depreciation	Forgone Residual Value after Tax	Initial Purchase Price Saved		Less Incremental Cash Flows
0	$(106,734)			$715,000		$ 608,266
1	(106,734)	$ (48,620)				(155,354)
2	(106,734)	(77,792)				(184,526)
3	(106,734)	(46,675)				(153,409)
4	(106,734)	(28,005)				(134,739)
5	0	(28,005)	$(67,199)			(95,204)
Sum	$(533,668)	$(229,097)	$(67,199)	$715,000		$(114,966)
IRR						6.6%

EXHIBIT 6   Summary Table of the Net Present Value and Internal Rate of Return for Four Tax and Cost-of-Capital Scenarios

Scenario	I	II	III	IV
Effective tax rate	34%	34%	0%	0%
Pretax cost of debt	10.00%	14.00%	10.00%	14.00%
After-tax cost of debt	6.60%	9.24%	10.00%	14.00%
NPV of borrow-and-buy	$471,552	$488,634	$664,953	$673,138
IRR of borrow-and-buy	6.60%	9.24%	10.00%	14.00%
NPV of lease payment 1	$452,081			
IRR of lease	5.32%			
Lease advantage over borrowing	$19,471			
NPV of lease payment 2	$471,553			
IRR of lease	6.60%			
Lease advantage over borrowing	$(2)			
NPV of lease payment 3	$473,396			
IRR of lease	6.72%			
Lease advantage over borrowing	$(1,844)			
NPV of lease payment 4	$480,423			
IRR of lease	7.19%			
Lease advantage over borrowing	$(8,871)			
Faulhaber Gmbh: • IRR of lease • Lease advantage over borrowing				
Honshu Heavy Industries: • IRR of lease • Lease advantage over borrowing				

Pan-Europa Foods S.A.

In early January 1993, the senior-management committee of Pan-Europa Foods was to meet to draw up the firm's capital budget for the new year. Up for consideration were 11 major projects that totaled over (European Currency Unit) ECU208 million. Unfortunately, the board of directors had imposed a spending limit of only ECU80 million; even so, investment at that rate would represent a major increase in the firm's asset base of ECU656 million. Thus, the challenge for the senior managers of Pan-Europa was to allocate funds among a range of compelling projects: new-product introduction, acquisition, market expansion, efficiency improvements, preventive maintenance, safety, and pollution control.

THE COMPANY

Pan-Europa Foods, headquartered in Brussels, Belgium, was a multinational producer of high-quality ice cream, yogurt, bottled water, and fruit juices. Its products were sold throughout Scandinavia, Britain, Belgium, the Netherlands, Luxembourg, western Germany, and northern France. (See Exhibit 1 for a map of the company's marketing region.)

The company was founded in 1924 by Theo Verdin, a Belgian farmer, as an offshoot of his dairy business. Through keen attention to product development, and shrewd marketing, the business grew steadily over the years. The company went public in 1979 and by 1993 was listed for trading on the London, Frankfurt, and Brussels exchanges. In 1992, Pan-Europa had sales of almost ECU1.1 billion.

Ice cream accounted for 60 percent of the company's revenues; yogurt, which was introduced in 1982, contributed about 20 percent. The remaining 20 percent of sales was divided equally between bottled water and fruit juices. Pan-Europa's flagship brand name

This case was prepared by Professor Robert F. Bruner and draws certain elements from an antecedent case by him.

Copyright © 1993 by the Darden Graduate Business School Foundation, Charlottesville, VA. Revised June 1993.

was "Rolly," which was represented by a fat dancing bear in farmers' clothing. Ice cream, the company's leading product, had a loyal base of customers who sought out its high butterfat content, large chunks of chocolate, fruit, nuts, and wide range of original flavors.

Pan-Europa sales had been static since 1990 (see Exhibit 2), which management attributed to low population growth in northern Europe and market saturation in some areas. Outside observers, however, faulted recent failures in new-product introductions. Most members of management wanted to expand the company's market presence and introduce more new products to boost sales. These managers hoped that increased market presence and sales would improve the company's market value. Pan-Europa's stock was currently at eight times earnings, just below book value. This price-earnings ratio was below the trading multiples of comparable companies, but it gave little value to the company's brands.

RESOURCE ALLOCATION

The capital budget at Pan-Europa was prepared annually by a committee of senior managers who then presented it for approval by the board of directors. The committee consisted of five managing directors, the *président directeur-général* (PDG), and the finance director. Typically, the PDG solicited investment proposals from the managing directors. The proposals included a brief project description, a financial analysis, and a discussion of strategic or other qualitative considerations.

As a matter of policy, investment proposals at Pan-Europa were subjected to two financial tests, payback and internal rate of return (IRR). The tests, or hurdles, had been established in 1991 by the management committee and varied according to the type of project:

Type of Project	Minimum Acceptable IRR	Maximum Acceptable Payback Years
1. New product or new markets	12%	6 years
2. Product or market extension	10%	5 years
3. Efficiency improvements	8%	4 years
4. Safety or environmental	No test	No test

In January 1993, the estimated weighted-average cost of capital (WACC) for Pan-Europa was 10.5 percent.

In describing the capital-budgeting process, the finance director, Trudi Lauf, said,

We use the sliding scale of IRR tests as a way of recognizing differences in risk among the various types of projects. Where the company takes more risk, we should earn more return. The payback test signals that we are not prepared to wait for long to achieve that return.

OWNERSHIP AND THE SENTIMENT OF CREDITORS AND INVESTORS

Pan-Europa's 12-member board of directors included three members of the Verdin family, four members of management, and five outside directors who were prominent managers or public figures in northern Europe. Members of the Verdin family, combined, owned 20 percent of Pan-Europa's shares outstanding, and company executives, combined, owned 10 percent of the shares. Venus Asset Management, a mutual-fund management company in London, held 12 percent. Banque du Bruges et des Pays Bas held 9 percent and had one representative on the board of directors. The remaining 49 percent of the firm's shares were widely held. The firm's shares traded in London, Brussels, and Frankfurt.

At a debt-to-equity ratio of 125 percent, Pan-Europa was leveraged much more highly than its peers in the European consumer-foods industry. Management had relied on debt financing significantly in the past few years to sustain the firm's capital spending and dividends during a period of price wars initiated by Pan-Europa. Now, with the price wars finished, Pan-Europa's bankers (led by Banque du Bruges) strongly urged an aggressive program of debt reduction. In any event, the bankers were not prepared to finance increases in leverage beyond the current level. The president of Banque du Bruges had remarked at a recent board meeting,

> Restoring some strength to the right-hand side of the balance sheet should now be a first priority. Any expansion of assets should be financed from the cash flow after debt amortization until the debt ratio returns to a more prudent level. If there are crucial investments that cannot be funded this way, then we should cut the dividend!

At a price-to-earnings ratio of eight times, shares of Pan-Europa common stock were priced below the average multiples of peer companies and the average multiples of all companies on the exchanges where Pan-Europa was traded. This was attributable to the recent price wars, which had suppressed the company's profitability, and to the well-known recent failure of the company to seize significant market share with a new product line of flavored mineral water. Since January 1992, all of the major securities houses had been issuing "sell" recommendations to investors in Pan-Europa shares. Venus Asset Management in London quietly had accumulated shares during this period, however, in the expectation of a turnaround in the firm's performance. At the most recent board meeting, the senior managing director of Venus gave a presentation in which he said,

> Cutting the dividend is unthinkable, as it would signal a lack of faith in your own future. Selling new shares of stock at this depressed price level is also unthinkable, as it would impose unacceptable dilution on your current shareholders. Your equity investors expect an improvement in performance. If that improvement is not forthcoming, or worse, if investors' hopes are dashed, your shares might fall into the hands of raiders like Carlo de Benedetti or the Flick brothers.[1]

At the conclusion of the most recent meeting of the directors, the board voted unanimously to limit capital spending in 1993 to ECU80 million.

---

[1] De Benedetti of Milan and the Flick brothers of Munich were leaders of prominent hostile-takeover attempts at the time.

MEMBERS OF THE SENIOR MANAGEMENT COMMITTEE

The capital budget would be prepared by seven senior managers of Pan-Europa. For consideration, each project had to be sponsored by one of the managers present. Usually the decision process included a period of discussion followed by a vote on two to four alternative capital budgets. The various executives were well known to each other:

Wilhelmina Verdin (Belgian), PDG, age 57. Granddaughter of the founder and spokesperson on the board of directors for the Verdin family's interests. Worked for the company her entire career, with significant experience in brand management. Elected "European Marketer of the Year" in 1982 for successfully introducing low-fat yogurt and ice cream, the first major roll-out of this type of product. Eager to position the company for long-term growth but cautious in the wake of recent difficulties.

Trudi Lauf (Swiss), finance director, age 51. Hired from Nestlé in 1982 to modernize financial controls and systems. Had been a vocal proponent of reducing leverage on the balance sheet. Also had voiced the concerns and frustrations of stockholders.

Heinz Klink (German), managing director for distribution, age 49. Oversaw the transportation, warehousing, and order-fulfillment activities in the company. Spoilage, transport costs, stock-outs, and control systems were perennial challenges.

Maarten Leyden (Dutch), managing director for production and purchasing, age 59. Managed production operations at the company's 14 plants. Engineer by training. Tough negotiator, especially with unions and suppliers. A fanatic about production-cost control. Had voiced doubts about the sincerity of creditors' and investors' commitment to the firm.

Marco Ponti (Italian), managing director for sales, age 45. Oversaw the field sales force of 250 representatives and planned changes in geographical sales coverage. The most vocal proponent of rapid expansion on the senior-management committee. Saw several opportunities for ways to improve geographical positioning. Hired from Unilever in 1985 to revitalize the sales organization, which he successfully accomplished.

Fabienne Morin (French), managing director for marketing, age 41. Responsible for marketing research, new-product development, advertising, and, in general, brand management. The primary advocate of the recent price war, which, although financially difficult, realized solid gains in market share. Perceived a "window of opportunity" for product and market expansion and tended to support growth-oriented projects.

Nigel Humbolt (British), managing director for strategic planning, age 47. Hired two years previously from a well-known consulting firm to set up a strategic-planning staff for Pan-Europa. Known for asking difficult and challenging questions about Pan-Europa's core business, its maturity, and profitability. Supported initiatives

THE EXPENDITURE PROPOSALS

The forthcoming meeting would entertain the following proposals:

Project	Expenditure (ECU millions)	Sponsoring Manager
1. Replacement and expansion of the truck fleet	22	Klink, distribution
2. A new plant	30	Leyden, production
3. Expansion of a plant	10	Leyden, production
4. Development and introduction of new artificially sweetened yogurt and ice cream	15	Morin, marketing
5. Plant automation and conveyer systems	14	Leyden, production
6. Effluent water treatment at four plants	4	Leyden, production
7. Market expansion eastward	20	Ponti, sales
8. Market expansion southward	20	Ponti, sales
9. Development and roll-out of snack foods	18	Morin, marketing
10. Networked, computer-based inventory-control system for warehouses and field representatives	15	Klink, distribution
11. Acquisition of a leading schnapps brand and associated facilities	40	Humbolt, strategic planning
Total	208	

aimed at growth and market share. Had presented the most aggressive proposals in 1992, none of which were accepted. Becoming frustrated with what he perceived to be his lack of influence in the organization.

1. Replacement and expansion of the truck fleet.   Heinz Klink proposed to purchase 100 new refrigerated tractor-trailer trucks, 50 each in 1993 and 1994. By doing so, the company could sell 60 old, fully depreciated trucks over the two years for a total of ECU1.2 million. The purchase would expand the fleet by 40 trucks within two years. Each of the new trailers would be larger than the old trailers and afford a 15 percent increase in cubic meters of goods hauled on each trip. The new tractors would also be more fuel and maintenance efficient. The increase in number of trucks would permit more flexible scheduling and more efficient routing and servicing of the fleet than at present and would cut delivery times and, therefore, possibly inventories. It also would allow more frequent deliveries to the company's major markets, which would reduce the loss of sales caused by stock-outs. Finally, expanding the fleet would support geographical expansion over the long term.

As shown in Exhibit 3, the total net investment in trucks of ECU20 million and the increase in working capital to support added maintenance, fuel, payroll, and inventories of ECU2 million was expected to yield total cost savings and added sales potential of ECU7.7 million over the next seven years. The resulting IRR was estimated to be 7.8 percent, marginally below the minimum 8.0 percent required return on efficiency projects. Some of the managers wondered if this project would be more properly classified as "efficiency" than as "expansion."

2. A new plant.   Maarten Leyden noted that Pan-Europa's yogurt and ice-cream sales in the southeastern region of the company's market were about to exceed the capacity of its Melun, France, manufacturing and packaging plant. At present, some of the demand was being met by shipments from the company's newest, most efficient facility, located in Strasbourg, France. Shipping costs over that distance were high, however, and some sales undoubtedly were being lost when the marketing effort could not be supported by delivery. Leyden proposed that a new manufacturing and packaging plant be built in Dijon, France, just at the current southern edge of Pan-Europa's marketing region, to take the burden off the Melun and Strasbourg plants.

The cost of this plant would be ECU25 million and would entail ECU5 million for working capital. The ECU14 million worth of equipment would be amortized over 7 years, and the plant over 10 years. Through an increase in sales and depreciation, and the decrease in delivery costs, the plant was expected to yield after-tax cash flows totaling ECU23.75 million and an IRR of 11.3 percent over the next 10 years. This project would be classified as a market extension.

3. Expansion of a plant.   In addition to the need for greater production capacity in Pan-Europa's southeastern region, its Nuremberg, Germany, plant had reached full capacity. This situation made the scheduling of routine equipment maintenance difficult, which, in turn, created production-scheduling and deadline problems. This plant was one of two highly automated facilities that produced Pan-Europa's entire line of bottled water, mineral water, and fruit juices. The Nuremberg plant supplied central and western Europe. (The other plant, near Copenhagen, supplied Pan-Europa's northern European markets.)

The Nuremberg plant's capacity could be expanded by 20 percent for ECU10 million. The equipment (ECU7 million) would be depreciated over 7 years, and the plant over 10 years. The increased capacity was expected to result in additional production of up to ECU1.5 million per year, yielding an IRR of 11.2 percent. This project would be classified as a market extension.

4. Development and introduction of new artificially sweetened yogurt and ice cream.   Fabienne Morin noted that recent developments in the synthesis of artificial sweeteners were showing promise of significant cost savings to food and beverage producers as well as stimulating growing demand for low-calorie products. The challenge was to create the right flavor to complement or enhance the other ingredients. For ice-cream manufacturers, the difficulty lay in creating a balance that would result in the same flavor as was obtained when using natural sweeteners; artificial sweeteners, of course, might create a superior taste.

ECU15 million would be needed to commercialize a yogurt line that had received promising results in laboratory tests. This cost included acquiring specialized production facilities, working capital, and the cost of the initial product introduction. The overall IRR was estimated to be 17.3 percent.

Morin stressed that the proposal, although highly uncertain in terms of actual results, could be viewed as a means of protecting present market share, because other high-quality ice-cream producers carrying out the same research might introduce these products; if the Rolly brand did not carry an artificially sweetened line and its competitors did, the Rolly brand might suffer. Morin also noted the parallels between innovating with artificial sweeteners and the company's past success in introducing low-fat products. This project would be classed in the new-product category of investments.

5. Plant automation and conveyer systems. Maarten Leyden also requested ECU14 million to increase automation of the production lines at six of the company's older plants. The result would be improved through speed and reduced accidents, spillage, and production tie-ups. The last two plants the company had built included conveyer systems that eliminated the need for any heavy lifting by employees. The systems reduced the chance of injury by employees; at the six older plants, the company had sustained an average of 75 missed worker-days per year per plant in the last two years because of muscle injuries sustained in heavy lifting. At an average hourly wage of ECU14.00 per hour, over ECU150,000 per year thus was lost, and the possibility always existed of more serious injuries and lawsuits. Overall cost savings and depreciation totaling ECU2.75 million per year for the project were expected to yield an IRR of 8.7 percent. This project would be classed in the efficiency category.

6. Effluent water treatment at four plants. Pan-Europa preprocessed a variety of fresh fruits at its Melun and Strasbourg plants. One of the first stages of processing involved cleaning the fruit to remove dirt and pesticides. The dirty water was simply sent down the drain and into the Seine or Rhine rivers. Recent European Community directives called for any waste water containing even slight traces of poisonous chemicals to be treated at the sources and gave companies four years to comply. As an environmentally oriented project, this proposal fell outside the normal financial tests of project attractiveness. Leyden noted, however, that the water-treatment equipment could be purchased today for ECU4 million; he speculated that the same equipment would cost ECU10 million in four years when immediate conversion became mandatory. In the intervening time, the company would run the risks that European Community regulators would shorten the compliance time or that the company's pollution record would become public and impair the image of the company in the eyes of the consumer. This project would be classed in the environmental category.

7 and 8. Market expansions eastward and southward. Marco Ponti recommended that the company expand its market eastward to include eastern Germany, Poland, Czechoslovakia, and Austria and/or southward to include southern France, Switzerland, Italy, and Spain. He believed the time was right to expand sales of ice cream, and perhaps yogurt, geographically. In theory, the company could sustain expansions in both directions simultaneously, but practically, Ponti doubted that the sales and distribution organizations could sustain both expansions at once.

Each alternative geographical expansion had its benefits and risks. If the company expanded eastward, it could reach a large population with a great appetite for frozen dairy products, but it would also face more competition from local and regional ice-cream manufacturers. Moreover, consumers in eastern Germany, Poland, and Czechoslovakia did not have the purchasing power that consumers did to the south. The eastward expansion would have to be supplied from plants in Nuremberg, Strasbourg, and Hamburg.

Looking southward, the tables were turned: more purchasing power and less competition—but also a smaller consumer appetite for ice cream and yogurt. A southward expansion would require building consumer demand for premium-quality yogurt and ice cream. If neither of the plant proposals (i.e., proposals 2 and 3) were accepted, then the southward expansion would need to be supplied from plants in Melun, Strasbourg, and Rouen.

The initial cost of either proposal was ECU20 million of working capital. The bulk of this project's costs was expected to involve the financing of distributorships, but, over the 10-year forecast period, the distributors would gradually take over the burden of carrying receivables and inventory. Both expansion proposals assumed the rental of suitable warehouse and distribution facilities. The after-tax cash flows were expected to total ECU37.5 million for eastward expansion and ECU32.5 million for southward expansion.

Marco Ponti pointed out that eastward expansion meant a higher possible IRR but that moving southward was a less risky proposition. The projected IRRs were 21.4 percent and 18.8 percent for eastern and southern expansion, respectively. These projects would be classed in the market-extension category.

9. Development and roll-out of snack foods. Fabienne Morin suggested that the company use the excess capacity at its Antwerp spice- and nut-processing facility to produce a line of dried fruits to be test-marketed in Belgium, Britain, and the Netherlands. She noted the strength of the Rolly brand in those countries and the success of other food and beverage companies that had expanded into snack-food production. She argued that Pan-Europa's reputation for wholesome, quality products would be enhanced by a line of dried fruits and that name association with the new product would probably even lead to increased sales of the company's other products among health-conscious consumers.

Equipment and working-capital investments were expected to total ECU15 million and ECU 3 million, respectively, for this project. The equipment would be depreciated over seven years. Assuming the test market was successful, cash flows from the project would be able to support further plant expansions in other strategic locations. The IRR was expected to be 20.5 percent, well above the required return of 12 percent for new-product projects.

10. Networked, computer-based inventory-control system for warehouses and field representatives. Heinz Klink had pressed unsuccessfully for three years for a state-of-the-art computer-based inventory-control system that would link field sales representatives, distributors, drivers, warehouses, and even possibly retailers. The benefits of such a system would be shortening delays in ordering and order processing, better control of inventory, reduction of spoilage, and faster recognition of changes in demand at the customer level. Klink was reluctant to quantify these benefits, because they could range between modest and quite large amounts. This year, for the first time, he presented a cash-flow forecast, however, that reflected an initial outlay of ECU12 million for the system, followed by ECU3 million in the next year for ancillary equipment. The inflows reflected depreciation tax shields, tax credits, cost reductions in warehousing, and reduced inventory. He forecasted these benefits to last for only three years. Even so, the project's IRR was estimated to be 16.2 percent. This project would be classed in the efficiency category of proposals.

11. Acquisition of a leading schnapps brand and associated facilities.   Nigel Humbolt had advocated making diversifying acquisitions in an effort to move beyond the company's mature core business but doing so in a way that exploited the company's skills in brand management. He had explored six possible related industries, in the general field of consumer packaged goods, and determined that cordials and liqueurs offered unusual opportunities for real growth and, at the same time, market protection through branding. He had identified four small producers of well-established brands of liqueurs as acquisition candidates. Following exploratory talks with each, he had determined that only one company could be purchased in the near future, namely, the leading private European manufacturer of schnapps, located in Munich.

The proposal was expensive: ECU15 million to buy the company and ECU25 million to renovate the company's facilities completely while simultaneously expanding distribution to new geographical markets.[2] The expected returns were high: after-tax cash flows were projected to be ECU134 million, yielding an IRR of 28.7 percent. This project would be classed in the new-product category of proposals.

CONCLUSION

Each member of the management committee was expected to come to the meeting prepared to present and defend a proposal for the allocation of Pan-Europa's capital budget of ECU80 million. Exhibit 3 summarizes the various projects in terms of their free cash flows and the investment-performance criteria.

---

[2]Exhibit 3 shows negative cash flows amounting to only ECU35 million. The difference between this amount and the ECU40 million requested is a positive operating cash flow of ECU5 million in year 1 expected from the normal course of business.

EXHIBIT 1   Nations Where Pan-Europa Competed

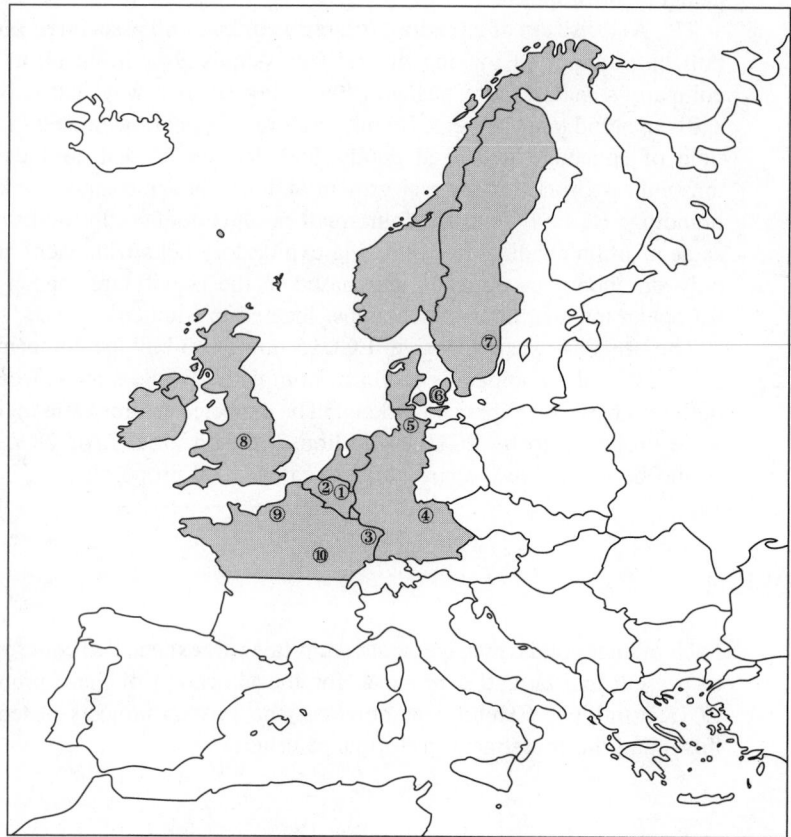

Note: The shaded area in this map reveals the principal distribution region of Pan-Europa's products. Important facilities are indicated by the following figures:

1. Headquarters, Brussels, Belgium.
2. Plant, Antwerp, Belgium.
3. Plant, Strasbourg, France.
4. Plant, Nuremberg, Germany.
5. Plant, Hamburg, Germany.
6. Plant, Copenhagen, Denmark.
7. Plant, Svald, Sweden.
8. Plant, Nelly-on-Mersey, England.
9. Plant, Caen, France.
10. Plant, Melun, France.

EXHIBIT 2   Summary of Financial Results (all values in ECU millions except per share amounts)

	Fiscal Year Ending December 31		
	1990	1991	1992
Gross sales	1,076	1,072	1,074
Net income	51	49	37
Earnings per share	0.75	0.72	0.54
Dividends	20	20	20
Total assets	477	580	656
Shareholders' equity (book value)	182	206	235
Shareholders' equity (market value)	453	400	229

EXHIBIT 3   Free Cash Flows and Analysis of Proposed Projects[1] (all values in ECU millions)

	(1) Expand Truck Fleet[3]	(2) New Plant	(3) Expanded Plant	(4) Artificial Sweetener
Investment:				
Property	20.00	25.00	10.00	15.00
Working capital	2.00	5.00		
Year				
0	(11.40)	(30.00)	(10.00)	(5.00)
1	(7.90)	2.00	1.25	(5.00)
2	3.00	5.00	1.50	(5.00)
3	3.50	5.50	1.75	3.00
4	4.00	6.00	2.00	3.00
5	4.50	6.25	2.25	4.00
6	5.00	6.50	2.50	4.50
7	7.00	6.75	1.50	5.00
8		5.00	1.50	5.50
9		5.25	1.50	6.00
10		5.50	1.50	6.50
Undiscounted sum	7.70	23.75	7.25	22.50
Payback (years)	6	6	6	7
Maximum payback accepted	4	5	5	6
Internal rate of return	7.8%	11.3%	11.2%	17.3%
Minimum ROR accepted	8.0%	10.0%	10.0%	12.0%
Net present value at corp. WACC (10.6%)	(1.92)	0.99	0.28	5.21
NPV at min. ROR	(0.13)	1.87	0.55	3.88
Equivalent annuity[2]	(0.02)	0.30	0.09	0.69

[1] The effluent treatment program is not included in this exhibit.

[2] The equivalent annuity of a project is that level annual payment over 10 years that yields a net present value equal to the NPV at the minimum required rate of return for that project. Annuity corrects for differences in duration among various projects. For instance, project 5 lasts only seven years and has an NPV of 0.32 million; a 7-year stream of annual cash flows of 0.06 million, discounted at 8.0 percent (the required rate of return) also yields an NPV of 0.32 million. In ranking projects on the basis of equivalent annuity, bigger annuities create more investor wealth than smaller annuities.

[3] 11 million spent initially and at the end of year 1.

[4] Free cash flow = incremental profit or cost savings after taxes + depreciation − investment in fixed assets and working capital.

[5] Franchisees would gradually take over the burden of carrying receivables and inventory.

[6] 15 million would be spent in the first year, 20 million in the second, and 5 million in the third.

(5) Automation and Conveyer Systems	(7) Eastward Expansion[5]	(8) Southward Expansion[5]	(9) Snack Foods	(10) Inventory-Control System	(11) Strategic Acquisition[6]
14.00			15.00	15.00	30.00
	20.00	20.00	3.00		10.00

Expected Free Cash Flows[4]

(5) Automation and Conveyer Systems	(7) Eastward Expansion[5]	(8) Southward Expansion[5]	(9) Snack Foods	(10) Inventory-Control System	(11) Strategic Acquisition[6]
(14.00)	(20.00)	(20.00)	(18.00)	(12.00)	(15.00)
2.75	3.50	3.00	3.00	5.50	(20.00)
2.75	4.00	3.50	4.00	5.50	5.00
2.75	4.50	4.00	4.50	5.00	9.00
2.75	5.00	4.50	5.00		11.00
2.75	5.50	5.00	5.00		13.00
2.75	6.00	5.50	5.00		15.00
2.75	6.50	6.00	5.00		17.00
	7.00	6.50	5.00		19.00
	7.50	7.00	5.00		21.00
	8.00	7.50	5.00		59.00
5.25	37.50	32.50	28.50	4.00	134.00
6	5	6	5	3	5
4	6	6	6	4	6
8.7%	21.4%	18.8%	20.5%	16.2%	28.7%
8.0%	12.0%	12.0%	12.0%	8.0%	12.0%
(0.87)	11.99	9.00	8.95	1.16	47.97
0.32	9.90	7.08	7.31	1.78	41.43
0.06	1.75	1.25	1.29	0.69	7.33

Part V

Management of Shareholders' Equity

Westboro Corporation

Late in the summer of 1992, Linda Kent, the newly appointed chief financial officer of Westboro Corporation, found herself the judge of a corporatewide debate over dividend policy. In the past few years, the company, with traditionally strong earnings and predictable dividend growth, had faltered. It had undergone two extensive restructuring programs, but both were accompanied by net issues. For three years in a row, dividends had exceeded earnings; then, in 1990, dividends were decreased to a level below earnings. Despite extraordinary losses in 1991, the board of directors had declared a small dividend. For the first two quarters of 1992, the board had declared no dividend, although in a special letter to shareholders the board had committed itself to resuming the dividend as early as possible—ideally, in 1992. Now, Linda Kent had to recommend to the board a dividend decision for the third quarter of 1992.

Overall, management's view was that Westboro was a resurgent company that demonstrated great potential for growth and profitability. The restructurings had revitalized the company's operating divisions, and a new product promised to make its predecessors' and competitors' products obsolete. Many within the company viewed 1992 as the dawning of a new era that, in spite of the company's recent performance, would turn Westboro into a growth stock. The company had no Moody's or Standard & Poor's rating because it had no bonds outstanding, but *Value Line* rated it an 'A' company.[1]

Out of this combination of a troubled past and a bright future arose Ms. Kent's dilemma. Did the market view Westboro as a "loser," as a blue-chip stock, or as a potential growth stock? How, if at all, could Westboro affect that perception? Did the company's investors expect capital growth or steady dividends? And, if those questions could be answered, what were the implications for Westboro's future dividend policy?

---

[1] *Value Line's* financial-strength ratings, from A ++ to C, were a measure of a company's ability to withstand adverse business conditions and were based on leverage, liquidity, business risk, company size, and stock-price variability, as well as analysts' judgments.

This case was written by Robert F. Bruner and draws features from an antecedent case by him.

THE COMPANY

Westboro Corporation was founded in 1923 in San Francisco, California, by two mechanical engineers, Francis Westing and Linus Peterboro. The two had gone to school together and were disenchanted with their positions and prospects as mechanics at a local bicycle manufacturer.

In its early years, Westboro had designed and manufactured a number of machinery parts, including metal presses, dies, and molds. In the 1940s, the company's large manufacturing plant was dedicated to the production of tank and armored vehicle parts and miscellaneous equipment for the war effort, including riveters and welders. After the war, the company concentrated on the production of industrial presses and molds, for plastics as well as metals. By 1975, the company had developed the reputation of being an innovative producer of industrial machinery and machine tools.

In the late 1970s, Westboro entered the new field of computer-aided design and computer-aided manufacturing (CAD/CAM). Working with a small software company, it developed a line of presses that would manufacture metal parts by responding to computer commands. Westboro merged the software company into its operations and, over the next several years, perfected the CAM equipment. At the same time, it developed a superior line of CAD software and equipment that would allow an engineer to design a part to exacting specifications on a computer. The design then could be entered into the company's CAM equipment, and the parts would be manufactured without the use of blueprints or human interference. By year-end 1991, CAD/CAM equipment and software were responsible for about 45 percent of sales; presses, dies, and molds for 40 percent; and miscellaneous machine tools for 15 percent.

Most press and mold companies were small local or regional firms with limited clientele. For this reason, Westboro stood out as a true industry leader. Within the CAD/CAM industry, however, a number of larger firms, including General Electric, Hewlett-Packard, and Digital Equipment, competed for dominance of the growing market.

Throughout the 1980s, Westboro helped set the standard for CAD/CAM, but the aggressive entry of large foreign firms into CAD/CAM and the rise of the dollar dampened sales. Moreover, Westboro fell behind some of its competition in the development of user-friendly software and in the integration of design and manufacturing. As a result, revenues declined from a high of $607 million in 1985 to $504 million in 1991.

To combat the decline in revenues and to improve weak profit margins, Westboro took a two-pronged approach. First, it devoted a greater share of its research and development budget to CAD/CAM in an effort to reestablish leadership in the field. Second, the company underwent two massive restructurings. In 1989, it sold two unprofitable lines of business with revenues of $31 million, sold two plants, eliminated five leased facilities, and reduced personnel. Restructuring costs totaled $44 million. Then, in 1991, the company began a second round of restructuring by altering its manufacturing strategy, refocusing its sales and marketing approach, and adopting administrative procedures that allowed for a further reduction in staff and facilities. The total cost of the operational restructuring in 1991 was $60 million.

The company's recent income statements and balance sheets are provided in Exhibits 1 and 2. Although the two restructurings resulted in losses totaling $135 million in 1989 and 1991, by 1992 they and the increased emphasis on CAD/CAM research appeared to have launched a turnaround. Not only was the company leaner than it had been in years, but also the CAD/CAM research led to the development of a system that Westboro management believed was destined to redefine the industry. Known as the Artificial Workforce, the system was an array of advanced control hardware, software, and applications that could distribute information throughout a plant.

Essentially, the Artificial Workforce allowed an engineer to design a part on the CAD and input the data into a CAM that could control the mixing of chemicals or the molding of parts from any number of different materials on different machines. The system also could assemble and can, box, or shrink-wrap the finished product. Thus, no matter how intricate, a product could be designed and manufactured and packaged solely by computer.

In 1991, Westboro had developed applications of the product for the plastics, food-processing, and pulp-and-paper industries and, in 1992, was developing applications for the oil- and gas-refining and chemicals industries.

By October 1991, when the first system was shipped, Westboro had received orders for the Artificial Workforce totaling $75 million; by year end, the backlog totaled $100 million. The future of the product looked bright. Several securities analysts were optimistic about the product's impact on the company. The following comments paraphrase their thoughts:

> Artificial Workforce products have compelling advantages over competing entries and will enable Westboro to increase its share of a market that, ignoring periodic growth spurts, will expand at a real annual rate of about 5 percent over the next several years.

> The company is producing the Artificial Workforce in a new automated facility which, when in full swing, will help restore margins to levels not seen for years.

> The important question now is how quickly Westboro will be able to ship in volume. Manufacturing foul-ups and missing components have delayed production growth through May 1992, about six months beyond the original target date. And start-up costs, which were a significant factor in last year's deficits, have continued to penalize earnings. Our estimates assume that production will proceed smoothly from now on and that it will approach the optimum level by year's end.

Westboro management expected domestic revenues from the Artificial Workforce series to total $90 million in 1992 and $150 million in 1993. Thereafter, growth in sales would depend on the development of more system applications and the creation of system improvements and add-on features. International sales through Westboro's offices in Frankfort, London, Paris, Hong Kong, and Tokyo were expected to provide additional revenues of between $50 million and $75 million beginning in 1993. Currently, international sales accounted for about 15 percent of total corporate revenues.

Two factors that could affect sales were of some concern to Westboro. First, although the company had successfully patented several of the processes used by the Artificial Workforce system, management had received hints through industry observers that two strong competitors were developing comparative products and probably would introduce them within the next 12 months. Second, sales of molds, presses, machine tools, and CAD/CAM equipment and software were highly cyclical, and predictions about the strength of the U.S. economy were mixed. The economy had been weak for almost two years. As shown in Exhibit 3, the projected indicators were sending mixed messages. Domestic real GNP was expected to grow at 3.2 and 2.8 percent in the next two years. On the other hand, capital spending on industrial durable equipment was expected to increase dramatically over the next two years, at 7.5 and 8.7 percent.

CORPORATE GOALS

A number of corporate objectives had grown out of the restructurings and recent technological advances. First and foremost, management wanted and expected the firm to grow at an average annual compound rate of 15 percent. A great deal of corporate planning had been devoted to that goal over the past three years and, indeed, second-quarter financial data suggested that Westboro would achieve revenues of about $580 million in 1992, as shown in Exhibit 1. If Westboro achieved a 15 percent compound rate of growth through 1996, the company would about double in size to $1 billion in sales and $60 million in net income.

To achieve this growth goal, Westboro management proposed a strategy relying on three key points:

1. Derive at least two thirds of its sales and profits from CAD/CAM and peripheral products on the cutting edge of the industry technology. (The remaining third would stem from the company's traditional line of presses and molds.)

2. Derive at least one third of its sales and profits from markets outside the United States and Canada, based on new field sales offices to be established throughout the world.

3. Derive about half of the new products through internal research. The rest would come through the acquisition of technology via joint ventures and cash acquisitions of small software companies.

Westboro management had always had an aversion to debt. It believed that small amounts of debt, primarily to meet working-capital needs, had their place, but that anything beyond a 40 percent debt-to-equity ratio was, in the oft-quoted words of Linus Peterboro, "unthinkable, indicative of sloppy management, and flirting with trouble." Senior management was aware that equity was typically more costly than debt but took great satisfaction in the company "doing it on its own." Westboro's highest debt-to-capital ratio in the past 25 years—28 percent—occurred in 1991, and was also the subject of frequent conversations among senior managers.

Although 11 members of the Westing and Peterboro families owned 30 percent of the company's stock and three were on the board of directors, management placed the interests of the public shareholders first. (Shareholder data are provided in Exhibit 4.) Reginald Peterboro, son of the co-founder and chairman of the board, sought to maximize the growth in the market value of the company's stock over time.

At the age of 63, Mr. Peterboro was actively involved in all aspects of the company's growth and future. He was conversant with a range of technical details of Westboro's products and was especially interested in finding ways to improve the company's domestic market share. His retirement was no more than seven years in the future, and he wanted to leave a legacy of corporate financial strength and technological achievement. The Artificial Workforce, a project he had taken under his wing four years earlier, was beginning to bear fruit. He now wanted to ensure that the firm would also soon be able to pay a dividend.

Mr. Peterboro took particular pride in selecting and developing young managers with promise. Ms. Kent, who had a bachelor's degree in electrical engineering and had been a systems analyst for Intel for several years, had been hired in 1982 fresh out of a well-known graduate business school and was offered the position of chief financial officer in 1991.

DIVIDEND POLICY

Westboro's dividend and stock-price histories are presented in Exhibit 5. Prior to 1986, both earnings and dividends per share had grown at a relatively steady pace, but the recession in the early 1980s and the restructurings took their toll on earnings. As a consequence, dividends were pared back in 1990 to $0.25 per share—the lowest dividend since 1977. In 1991, the board of directors declared a payout of $0.25 per share despite reporting the largest per-share earnings loss in the firm's history and, in effect, borrowing to pay the dividend. In the first two quarters of 1992, the directors had not declared a dividend. However, in a special letter to shareholders, the directors declared their intention to continue the annual payout later in 1992.

In August 1992, Paul Flowers, Westboro's treasurer, submitted a memo to the finance committee recommending that the company announce on September 15 its intention of declaring a quarterly cash dividend of 20 cents a share. September 15 was the date the board would have to announce a third-quarter dividend. Mr. Flowers argued that there was undoubtedly some anticipation of such an announcement in the current stock price of $32 per share. In his memo, Mr. Flowers backed his recommendation by stating that

> recent increases in orders and expected increases in sales justify higher dividends. Although the proposed dividend is somewhat higher than historic increases in payments, the market surely is expecting a payment of this magnitude and cash flow forecasts indicate that all necessary funds could be derived from retained earnings and moderate borrowings.

Ms. Kent noted that, if a 20-cent dividend were paid in the fourth quarter as well, the cash dividend would yield a payout ratio of 41 percent on expected 1992 profits of $12 million and earnings per share of 97 cents. This ratio was well above the 1980's average of 27 percent. She was uncomfortable with the notion of increasing the dividend so dramatically, even if doing so was financially justifiable.

A conversation between Ms. Kent and one of Westboro's investment bankers supported Mr. Flowers' argument, however. The investment banker suggested that the market might be expecting a strong dividend in order to bring the payout back in line with the 52 percent average within the electrical industrial equipment industry and/or with the 68 percent average in the machine tool industry.

Other investment bankers disagreed with this argument for different reasons. Some wondered whether the market still considered Westboro to be a traditional electrical equipment manufacturer or whether it was now viewed as a more technologically advanced CAD/CAM company. The latter would imply that the market was expecting strong capital appreciation but, perhaps, little in the way of dividends. Others cited Westboro's recent performance problems. One "questioned the wisdom of ignoring the financial statements in favor of acting like a blue chip." Was a high dividend in the long-term interests of the company and its stockholders, or would the strategy backfire and make investors skittish?

Mr. Flowers countered his argument by highlighting the importance of sending a strong signal to shareholders:

A 40 percent dividend payout would tell the markets that the company has conquered its problems and that management is confident of future earnings. After all, no responsible management would increase dividends if doing so would clearly be detrimental to the well-being of the firm.

Mr. Flowers also dealt with the question of whether a growth company—or any firm— should pay dividends if doing so necessitated borrowing:

Historically, Westboro has borrowed very little, maintaining a long-term debt level of about $20 million throughout the late 1970s and 1980s, compared with equity that increased from $135 million to a high of $322 million. Over the same period, dividends were increased steadily from $1.8 million to $12.8 million. More recently, when dividends were decreased, so was the level of debt to the year-end 1991 $6 million. Borrowing and paying dividends is not inconsistent with the company's record, nor is it inconsistent with the records of most firms.

Several newer members of the board and younger members of management agreed with Mr. Flowers. They cited a number of financial experts, who held that strong price/ earnings ratios were tied to an expression of management's confidence in the company and to payout ratios in keeping with the firm's growth rate. No definitive work on the issue was cited, but it was generally believed that a growth rate in the range of 10 to 20 percent should accompany a payout of 30 to 50 percent.

Others on the board and within management—most notably members of the Westing and Peterboro families—disagreed with Mr. Flowers' reasoning. Judy Campbell, a member of the board and chair of the board's finance committee, wanted to know the objectives of the present public shareholders owning Westboro stock—dividends or capital appreciation. She said,

Over the past five years, earnings have been weak and dividends have been reduced. Under those circumstances, it is difficult to ascertain why someone would hold or purchase the stock. In 1991, when the Artificial Workforce hit the market, the price of our stock increased from $24 to almost $40 per share, its highest level in two years. Are shareholders anticipating the reappearance of dividends or are they expecting us to move cautiously, taking advantage of the current lack of dividends to plow earnings back into further development and market expansion and renew our equity base?

As Linda Kent went over the issues in her mind, she realized that a number of questions had to be answered before she could make an intelligent dividend recommendation to the board. She then asked her assistant, Bud Valdosta, to poll the finance staff and solicit the opinions of several investment bankers. Mr. Valdosta's follow-up memo stated:

In response to your questions about company shareholders and dividend policy, a summary follows:

1. Why do current stockholders own shares of Westboro?

Three answers seem possible. First, they may have been anticipating extremely strong capital appreciation in light of the Artificial Workforce. Most of the investment bankers I spoke with thought this was unlikely, however, because super-growth companies generally grow at between 25 and 35 percent annually. They admitted, though, that if shareholders do consider Westboro to be a super-growth company, a high dividend could send the signal that the company expects low growth.

Second, shareholders could expect the company to return to its historic state of moderate growth and solid earnings combined with predictable dividends. Third, they may be looking forward to a higher rate of growth combined with an appropriate level of dividends. This view is held by most of the Peterboros and Westings. Exhibit 6 presents comparative information on companies in three industries: CAD/CAM, machine tools, and electrical industrial equipment.

2. Why should Westboro pay dividends at all?

All of the investment bankers with whom I spoke said that most research links dividends to high price/earnings ratios among low- to moderate-growth companies. Certainly, unless the market considers Westboro a high-growth company, some dividend seems appropriate. (See Exhibit 7.)

3. How much can the company distribute and still achieve a 15 percent compounded rate of growth?

Implicit in this question is the issue of whether Westboro could financially justify paying any dividend at all. If Westboro performs as expected in 1992 and 1993, it will earn about $12 million and $27 million, respectively. At 40 cents a share, dividends would total $4.9 million each year, allowing a total of $29.2 million to be reinvested. This would bring net worth to $217.6 million, up from $188.4 million in 1991. Debt, always low, is at its lowest point in years. Capital expenditures have averaged $25 million annually over the past three years, but are budgeted to be $35 million in 1992 and, tentatively, $40 million in 1993.

The question is whether the company wishes to increase its debt in order to grow at 15 percent a year. If dividends are reduced to zero, reinvested earnings should total $39 million over the next two years. Capital expenditures totaling $75 million and an increase in working capital would require about $27 million of new debt; if $9.8 million of dividends are paid over that period, debt would have to increase by almost $37 million. In the first case, the debt/equity ratio in 1993 would be 35.4 percent ($27 million of new debt and $53.4 million of old debt [$5.8 million is long term and $47.6 million is short term, although effectively permanent] and $227.4 million of equity); if the proposed dividends are paid, debt/equity would be 41.5 percent ($90.2 million/$217.6 million).

4. To what extent is stock price related to dividends? To capital appreciation expectations?

Conjecture and opinion play a large role in answering these questions. Comparative industry data [given in Exhibits 6 and 7] may assist in an effort to gain a foothold on this question. Most investment bankers believe that a dividend that does not restrict growth would enhance market value; also, Company staff generally suggested that, all else being equal, a firm with a high payout should have a higher price/earnings multiple.

To test the feasibility of a 40 percent dividend payout rate, Linda Kent developed the projected sources and uses of cash provided in Exhibit 8. She took the boldest approach by assuming that the company would grow at a 15 percent compound rate, that operating margins would improve over the next few years to historical levels, and that the firm would pay a dividend of 40 percent of earnings every year.

CONCLUSION

Ms. Kent was caught in a difficult position. Members of the board and of management disagreed on the very nature of Westboro's future. Some managers saw the company as entering a new stage of rapid growth and thought that a large (or in the minds of some, any) dividend would be inappropriate. Others believed that it was important to make a firm gesture to the public—that management believed Westboro had turned the corner and was about to return to the levels of growth and profitability seen in the 1970s. This action only could be accomplished through a dividend. As Ms. Kent wrestled with the different points of view, she wondered whether management might be representative of the company's shareholders. Did the majority of the public shareholders own the stock for the same reason, or were their reasons just as diverse as those of management?

EXHIBIT 1   Consolidated Income Statements (dollars in thousands except per share data)

| | For the Years Ended December 31 | | | |
	1989	1990	1991	Projected 1992
Net sales	$572,175	$543,986	$504,425	$580,000
Cost of sales	360,498	334,305	332,586	366,500
Gross profit	211,677	209,681	171,839	213,500
Research and development	51,785	47,030	50,278	51,500
Selling, general, and administrative	153,314	149,089	154,005	141,000
Restructuring costs	43,632	0	59,607	0
Operating profit (loss)	(37,054)	13,562	(92,051)	21,000
Other income (expense)	(3,000)	710	(2,305)	(2,800)
Income (loss) before taxes	(40,054)	14,272	(94,356)	18,200
Income taxes (benefit)	827	5,610	(500)	6,188
Net income (loss)	$(40,881)	$ 8,662	$(93,856)	$ 12,012
Earnings (loss) per share	$(3.31)	$0.70	$(7.62)	$0.97
Dividends per share	$0.78	$0.25	$0.25	$0.40*

* Per Paul Flower's recommendation.

EXHIBIT 2   Consolidated Balance Sheets (dollars in thousands)

	December 31		
	1990	1991	Projected 1992
Cash and equivalents	$ 9,278	$ 14,820	$ 17,110
Accounts receivable	139,027	124,824	145,000
Inventories	153,561	135,925	145,000
Prepaid expenses	9,506	8,677	10,000
Other	14,789	13,809	14,000
Total current assests	326,161	298,055	331,110
Property, plant, and equipment	218,402	239,227	274,000
Less depreciation	111,609	122,324	137,000
Net property, plant, and equipment ...	106,793	116,903	137,000
Intangible assets	6,286	1,399	1,000
Other assets	10,482	11,792	12,000
Total assets	$449,722	$428,149	$481,110
Bank loans	$ 22,797	$ 47,563	$ 50,000
Accounts payable	24,299	22,826	25,000
Current portion of long-term debt	200	100	1,000
Accruals and other	86,249	107,734	122,000
Total current liabilities	133,545	178,223	198,000
Deferred taxes	11,324	9,179	11,000
Long-term debt	6,000	5,850	20,000
Deferred pension costs	29,860	42,886	47,000
Other liabilities	1,545	3,629	5,000
Common stock, $1 par value	12,570	12,570	12,570
Capital in excess of par	71,916	71,938	71,938
Cumulative translation adjustment	(4,377)	13,472	18,000
Retained earnings	194,332	97,398	104,598
Less treasury stock at cost: 1990—256,151; 1991—255,506 ..	(6,993)	(6,996)	(6,996)
Total shareholders' equity	267,448	188,382	200,110
Total liabilities and equity	$449,722	$428,149	$481,110

EXHIBIT 3   Economic Indicators and Projections

	1989	1990	1991	June 1992	Projected 1993	1994
3-month Treasury bill rate						
(at auction)	8.12%	7.51%	5.37%	3.43%	3.51%	4.52%
30-year Treasury bond rate	8.45	8.61	8.14	7.67	7.68	8.00
AAA corporate bond rate	9.26	9.32	8.77	8.14	8.16	8.39
Change in:						
Real gross national product ...	2.5	0.8	−1.2	2.0	3.2	2.8
Producer price index	4.8	6.0	0.01	1.7	0.3	1.1
Industrial durable equipment						
purchases	7.8	−2.6	−9.1	−1.6	7.5	8.7
Price deflator	3.6	4.7	4.1	2.3	2.5	3.1
Consumer spending	6.9%	6.4%	3.7%	5.3%	6.2%	6.5%

Sources: *U.S. Economic Outlook*, WEFA Group, January 1993; *Federal Reserve Bulletin*, June 1992; *Value Line Investment Survey*, July 17, 1992.

EXHIBIT 4   Stockholder Comparative Data,* 1981 and 1991 (thousands of shares)

	1981		1991	
	Shares	*Percentage*	*Shares*	*Percentage*
Founders' families	1,540	13	11,540	13
Other officers' families	2,483	20	2,063	17
Insurance companies	1,546	13	786	6
Employees and families	987	8	1,588	13
Public investors	5,614	46	6,337	51
Total	12,170	100	12,314	100

* Adjusted for 3-for-2 stock split in January 1982 and 50 percent stock divident in June 1986.

EXHIBIT 5 Per Share Financial and Stock Data*

	Sales/ Share	EPS	Dividends per Share	Cash Flow/ Share	Stock Price			Average P/E	Payout Ratio	Average Yield	Shares Out (millions)
					High	Low	Average				
1976	$14.62	$0.45	$0.18	$0.98	$20.50	$ 9.75	$14.58	32.4	40%	1.2%	10.25
1977	16.11	0.74	0.22	1.30	21.25	10.25	14.95	20.2	30	1.5	10.31
1978	22.40	0.90	0.27	1.44	21.38	8.25	13.59	15.1	30	2.0	10.62
1979	25.81	1.60	0.31	2.06	18.63	10.25	13.44	8.4	19	2.3	11.83
1980	27.37	2.31	0.40	2.85	22.63	12.25	18.48	8.0	17	2.2	11.97
1981	30.26	2.61	0.57	3.27	24.00	18.13	21.44	8.1	22	2.7	12.17
1982	31.87	2.63	0.72	3.36	26.88	18.38	22.88	8.7	27	3.2	12.42
1983	37.97	2.71	0.82	3.62	29.63	19.63	24.39	9.0	30	3.4	12.42
1984	40.97	2.58	0.87	3.64	40.00	20.25	29.67	11.5	34	2.9	12.43
1985	48.56	3.60	0.93	4.84	41.25	27.50	34.20	9.5	26	2.7	12.50
1986	43.88	2.81	1.04	4.28	39.00	21.50	32.03	11.4	37	3.2	12.35
1987	43.16	0.65	1.04	2.24	47.50	29.75	37.05	57.0	160	2.8	12.35
1988	41.76	0.35	1.04	2.01	40.50	27.00	31.47	89.9	297	3.3	12.35
1989	46.32	-3.31	0.78	2.88	30.75	22.13	26.45	N.M.F.	N.M.F.	2.9	12.35
1990	44.18	0.70	0.25	2.00	31.88	22.50	27.20	88.2	36%	1.0	12.31
1991	$40.96	-$7.62	$0.25	-$0.98	$39.88	$18.38	$29.15	N.M.F.	N.M.F.	0.9%	12.31

Note: N.M.F. means not a meaningful figure.
* Adjusted for 3-for-2 stock split in January 1982 and 50 percent stock dividend in June 1986.

EXHIBIT 6 Comparative Industry Data (as of December 31, 1991)

	Sales (millions)	Annual Growth Rate of Cash Flow		Current Payout Ratio	Current Dividend Yield	Debt/ Equity	Insider Ownership	P/E Ratio
		Last 10 Years	Next 3–5 Years					
Westboro	$ 504	−1.5%	+15%	Nil	Nil	28%	30%	N.M.F.
CAD/CAM Companies (software and hardware)								
Autodesk	285	41.5¹	10	20%	1.3%	0	10	22
GM-EDS	7,028	27	9.5	27	1.2	11	Nil	24
Digital Equip.	13,911	13	10.0	Nil	Nil	1	3.5	N.M.F.
Intergraph	1,195	32.5	5.5	Nil	Nil	2	28	13
Mentor Graphics	400	16.0¹	16.0	>100	1.2	20	27	N.M.F.
SCI Systems	1,129	24.5	9.5	Nil	Nil	100	7.6	22
Sun Microsystems	3,221	57.9	29.5	Nil	Nil	25	3.7	12
Gerber Scientific	250	14.5	5.5	59	1.7	3	13.7	39
Hewlett-Packard	14,494	14.0	12.5	16	1.0	3	18.1	16
Electrical Industrial Equipment Manufacturers								
Emerson Electric	7,427	9.0	10.0	47	2.7	14	0.9	18
General Electric	43,089	10.0	10.0	41	3.0	15	0.7	14
General Signal	1,616	3.5	7.0	54	2.8	50	6.6	17
Honeywell	6,193	3.5	8.5	33	2.4	33	0.6	16
Measurex	254	11.5	12.5	86	1.9	1	4.0	16
Machine Tool Manufacturers								
Acme-Cleveland	184	−10.5	8.0	91	5.3	14	3.4	30
Cincinnati Milacron	754	−5.5	15.5	>100	2.3	100	10.3	33
Giddings & Lewis	327	N.M.F.	N.A.	13	1.3	50	1.2	21
Monarch	$ 106.6	−16.0%	14.0%	68%	2.0%	1%	2.1%	32

Note: N.M.F. means not a meaningful figure because of recent reported losses. N.A. means not available. And > means greater than.
* Last 5 years only.

Source: *Value Line Investment Survey.*

EXHIBIT 7 Selected Healthy Companies with High- and Zero-Dividend Payouts (as of December 31, 1991)

	Industry	Expected Return on Total Capital (next 3–5 years)	Expected Growth Rate of Dividends (next 3–5 years)	Current Dividend Payout	Current Dividend Yield	Expected Growth Rate of Sales (next 3–5 years)	Current P/E Ratio
High-Payout Companies							
BRE Properties	Real estate inv.	13.5%	3.0%	125%	7.7%	8.0%	12.1
Federal Realty	Real estate inv.	10.0	9.0	500	7.2	7.0	52.5
Idaho Power	Electric power	8.5	1.5	118	7.2	+3.0	16.1
Sierra Pacific	Electric power	7.5	0	103	8.0	−0.5	13.7
Halliburton	Oilfield services	14.5	6.5	97	3.4	9.0	39.7
Consolidated	National gas	10.5	5.5	97	4.0	7.5	21.1
Sonat	Gas transmission	8.5	0	110	4.7	+4.0	20.0
Pacific Enterprises	Gas utility	8.0	0	125	15.2	−11.0	10.3
Zero-Payout Companies							
Oracle systems	Software	20.0	0	0	0	15.0	37.2
Novell	Software	22.5	0	0	0	25.0	33.9
King World Productions	TV shows	19.0	0	0	0	9.5	10.4
Harley-Davidson	Motorcycles	15.5	0	0	0	10.5	24.1
Duty Free International	Retail	16.5	0	0	0	31.0	28.9
50-Off Stores	Retail	18.5	0	0	0	24.0	24.3
Lands' End	Retail	19.5	0	0	0	16.5	17.8
Cabletron	Network systems	21.0	0	0	0	32.5	22.2
Cisco Systems	Network systems	23.0	0	0	0	34.0	30.3

Source: *Value Line Investment Survey.*

EXHIBIT 8 Projected Sources and Uses Statement, Assuming a 40 Percent Payout Ratio* (dollars in millions)

	1992	1993	1994	1995	1996	1997	1998	Total, 1992–98
Sales	$580	$667	$767	$882	$1,015	$1,167	$1,342	
Sources of cash:								
Net income	12	27	38	49	61	65	107	$358
Depreciation	15	17	20	23	27	31	35	168
Total	27	44	58	72	88	96	142	526
Uses of cash:								
Capital expenditure ...	35	40	45	50	55	60	65	350
Working capital	13	10	10	10	10	10	10	73
Total	48	50	55	60	65	70	75	423
Excess cash (borrowings needed)* ...	(21)	(6)	3	12	23	26	67	103
Dividend†	5	11	15	19	24	26	43	143
Excess cash (borrowings needed) after dividend* ...	$(26)	$(17)	$(12)	$(7)	$(1)	$0	$24	$(40)

* This analysis ignores the effects of borrowing on interest and amortization. It includes all increases in long-term liabilities and equity items, other than retained earnings.

† Dividend calculated as 40 percent of net income.

Morgan Stanley Group, Inc.: Initial Public Offering

On February 14, 1986, the investment bank of Morgan Stanley & Company issued a preliminary prospectus for the sale of 4,500,000 shares of its own common stock to the public at a price estimated to be between $42 and $46 per share. This move signaled a new era in the firm's history, as heretofore Morgan Stanley had been organized as a "partnership"[1] consisting of 111 managing directors and 143 principals. The offering raised numerous questions: Why had Morgan Stanley chosen to go public, rather than sell to a large and well-capitalized buyer? Why did Morgan Stanley need external capital at all? Also, was the offering price range appropriate? And finally, how would the firm preserve an entrepreneurial spirit as a public corporation? Answers to some of these questions were believed to be rooted in the evolving character of the investment banking business.

---

[1]Actually, the firm was organized as a corporation, rather than a partnership, but it loosely resembled a partnership in that the shareholders consisted of employees—managing directors (voting shareholders) and principals (nonvoting shareholders). Furthermore, the internal management style was collegial, the organization structure was relatively flat, and major decisions were based on consensus. The firm also guaranteed the repurchase of shares at book value. On this last point, one should note that managing directors and principals had been allowed to purchase holdings of the company's relatively small common share capital providing a pro rata credit on earnings retained in the firm. The longer one stayed with the firm, the greater the buildup of retained earnings, so partners near retirement could in some cases have attributable book value higher than new partners with the same common stock ownership. But the real issue facing the firm was that the bigger it grew, and the higher its book value, the greater the liability it faced to redeem shares of outgoing partners in an era when *permanence* of capital, as well as size, was critical. Redemptions of stock had amounted to $32.9 million, $30.2 million, and $15.8 million in 1985, 1984, and 1983, respectively.

This case was written by Robert F. Bruner.
Copyright © 1986 by the Darden Graduate Business School Foundation, Charlottesville, VA.

SECURITIES INDUSTRY

Morgan Stanley competed with an array of firms providing underwriting, financial advice, distribution, and trading/market-making functions. Exhibit 1 provides general financial information on major domestic investment banks; but, in addition, Morgan Stanley regarded itself as an international securities firm and included in its realm of competitors merchant banks (e.g., S. G. Warburg & Company), universal banks (e.g., Deutschebank), the London investment banking subsidiaries of U.S. money center banks, and large Japanese financial services firms (e.g., Nomura Securities).

Several trends were changing the competitive structure of the securities industry. Exhibit 2 suggests the magnitude and avenues of change. The trends included increasing concentration of competition, technological change in information support systems, rising demand for a highly specialized work force, innovation in the design of financial securities, the advent of globalized trading and underwriting, intermarket trading (e.g., between futures, options, and stocks), and quasi-merchant banking activities. Of special significance was the introduction of Rule 415 in 1982, which allowed corporations to keep registration statements "on the shelf" and quickly (i.e., in two days) issue securities. This rule was credited with eroding investment banking relationships and motivating issuers to seek bids for underwriting business. More recently, investment bankers had begun to bid for the entire underwriting issue in "bought deals" that were then sold directly to investors and distributed to other firms. The new levels of competition in underwriting required more capital.

The trends affected the various firms differently. Retail firms were forced to become more price competitive. Investment banks found their business becoming more complex and capital-intensive. Full-line firms (both retail and investment banks) found themselves pressed both ways. Firms with more strategic focus performed better than others. Between 1980 and 1985, the full-line firms averaged 11.68 percent return on equity, while the investment banking firms averaged 25.17 percent.

Consistent with this changing competitive environment, in 1986 newspapers reported changes in the following firms in the industry:

- *Kidder, Peabody & Co.* agreed to sell 80 percent of its stock to General Electric for about $600 million, or 2.6 times book value. Management believed that the best way to improve the company's competitive position on Wall Street was to "leapfrog" many of its rivals by selling a controlling interest to a cash-rich corporation. An executive said, "This is about competitive positioning for the 1990s; Kidder is going to be in the top three in this business." The combination would mesh Kidder's advisory and trading services with GE Financial Services' extensive business in leasing, leveraged-buyout financing, and lending. GE also intended to inject $180 million in additional capital into the firm. Kidder's president had acknowledged that the firm had passed up certain transactions, such as financing leveraged buyouts, because of lack of capital. The remaining 20 percent of the firm's stock would be distributed to Kidder, Peabody shareholders.
- *Dillon, Read & Co.* agreed to sell to Travelers Corporation for $157.5 million, or about three times book value. Travelers was one of the nation's largest diversified

insurers and announced that Dillon, Read would manage an "important part" of the insurer's equity portfolio. A journalist commented, "The rapid growth of rival securities firms, coupled with the liberalization of underwriting practices, left Dillon, Read less able to compete with Wall Street's investment banks."

- *Goldman, Sachs & Co.* sold a 12.5 percent interest in its annual profits to Sumitomo Bank, Ltd., of Japan in return for a capital investment of $500 million. Sumitomo was one of the world's largest commercial banks, with assets of $173 billion. Goldman's capital was $1.3 billion. Analysts believed that this combination illustrated the growing internationalization of securities markets and the need for greater amounts of capital to finance larger trading positions and investment banking activities. Under the agreement, Sumitomo's interest would be nonvoting and Goldman, Sachs would remain a partnership.

The stock market in early 1986 was buoyant, as indicated by the capital-market information presented in Exhibit 3. Indeed, this period had turned out to be one of the more attractive market "windows" in which to take a company public. The yield to maturity on 30-year U.S. government Treasury bonds was 7.96 percent. In commenting on investment prospects in the securities brokerage industry, *Value Line* (February 14, 1986) wrote:

> Brokerage stocks have outperformed the market recently. . . . Part of the story is takeover rumors, which briefly drove Merrill Lynch to new highs. Another reason for bullishness is the prospect of higher earnings.

MORGAN STANLEY

Morgan Stanley's current strategy consisted of three initiatives: (1) to position itself as a full-service investment bank, (2) to cover the entire globe as an integrated financial system, and (3) to introduce new information technologies into its organization.

Full Service

The move to full-service investment banking began in 1970. Before then, Morgan Stanley stuck closely to its strategy of wholesale investment banking. The firm was reluctantly spun off by J. P. Morgan & Company in 1935 to comply with the Glass-Steagall Act of 1933, which required the separation of commercial and investment banking activities. For a long time, its strategy was to be the lead manager in corporate securities underwritings and private placements—dealing almost exclusively with issuers of securities.

In 1970, Morgan employed 300 people, of which only 6 were traders, and the firm earned $3 million on capital of $12 million. By February 1986, there were 3,850 employees. This massive expansion occurred in two phases.

The first phase, between 1973 and 1977, focused on building a distribution capability and the mastery of additional securities. Much of the growth was in corporate bond sales and trading (entered in 1971), equity sales and trading (1973), a London operation and asset management (1975), government bonds (1976) and high-net-worth individuals (1977). The second phase, between 1982 and 1985, emphasized trading and positioning activities and the expansion into related markets: money markets, commercial paper, commodities and fixed-income research (1982), tax-exempt bonds and foreign exchange (1983), and mortgage-backed and high-yield bonds (1984).

This steady expansion was not without its difficulties.[2] Rapid growth in a period of intensifying competition narrowed the firm's pretax margins (on revenues net of interest expenses) from 28.5 percent in 1981 to 20.5 percent in 1985. Also, the firm continued to move slowly in establishing regional offices; by early 1986, there were offices in Chicago, San Francisco, and Los Angeles, in addition to New York.

Globalization and Information

The second strategic thrust, toward a global, integrated financial system, began in about 1980. The firm had long served as advisors to governments and sought to increase its client base overseas; by early 1985, 20 percent of Morgan Stanley's employees were overseas, including 525 in London and 220 in Tokyo. Morgan Stanley had achieved significant penetration in corporate finance in the United Kingdom, Scandinavia, and Japan, with some business in France and Italy as well. In sales and trading, its London convertible securities operation was very strong; it was also the leader in the trading of American Depository Receipts. Morgan Stanley was one of only three American firms allowed to trade on the Tokyo Stock Exchange. Geoffrey Elliott, managing director, commented: "Everywhere we do business overseas, the local regulators want capital on-site. They won't allow U.S. firms to double-leverage their capital base in the United States. This requires us to dedicate new capital to these new markets."

The final strategic thrust concerned the development of state-of-the-art management information systems. Although the company was reticent about discussing its Trade Analysis and Processing System in public, it was believed to feature (1) global communication, (2) real-time access, (3) sophisticated statistical functions, and (4) extensive data bases and data-retrieval facilities. Such a system was neither inexpensive nor straightforward to develop.

---

[2] In 1985, the firm curtailed for two months its trading of mortgage-backed securities in order to move to self-clearing of those securities and, thus, avoid backlog and clearing problems that were becoming an industrywide issue in the face of rapid growth. Also, in 1984, the firm underwrote a debt securities offering for Oxoco, Inc., a petroleum company. During the offering, oil stocks crashed, leaving Morgan with an unsold inventory of $18 million. A few months later, Oxoco suspended interest and dividend payments and then entered bankruptcy proceedings. The inventory was written off.

Performance

By early 1986, Morgan ranked among the top half-dozen competitors in almost all areas in which it chose to compete. As Exhibit 4 indicates, however, the firm no longer was incontestably dominant in underwritings. If the domestic and international market shares are combined, Morgan Stanley's share drops from 11.6 percent in 1982 to 5.6 percent in 1985. In municipal finance, the firm's market share was small (2.6 percent), largely because of late entry (1983).

However, the firm remained strong in equity underwritings, on which the spread could be triple that of a debt underwriting. It was perceived in the marketplace as being especially competent at big and complicated equity deals. Another special strength was in mergers and acquisitions, which provided $200 million or 22 percent of net revenues in 1985.

In sales and trading, the firm's position was strong but not dominant. Commissions had risen dramatically in recent years, as had equity principal transactions. However, the firm's retail effort remained relatively small, and it appeared to take smaller risks in positioning and trading.

Management anticipated returns on equity in the future consistent with the 30 percent-plus returns historically enjoyed by the firm. An analyst at Brown Brothers Harriman & Company, however, forecast ROE of 22.4 percent for 1986 and 20.3 percent for 1987. An analyst at Paine Webber feared that, although 1985 was a record year for Morgan Stanley, its compensation and benefits may have been unsustainably low at 47.1 percent of net revenues (as opposed to 51.4 percent and 54.1 percent in the previous two years).

Expected Future Capital Requirements

Management of Morgan Stanley asserted that the firm had no immediate need for new capital; but Geoffrey Elliott allowed that, in recent years, the growth in the firm's volume of business had consistently exceeded forecasts. He also recognized that there might be unpredictable needs for equity arising from rapid change in the industry, for acquisitions, and for the temporary commitment of large amounts of capital in support of the firm's activities in mergers and acquisitions, junk-bond financings, and leveraged buyouts.

Various regulations required Morgan Stanley to maintain at least minimum levels of net capital relative to "aggregate debit items." Net capital was defined as net worth (assets less liabilities) (1) plus subordinated debt, (2) less the value of assets not readily convertible into cash, and (3) less a "haircut," or deductions on the value of securities to reflect the possibility of a market decline prior to disposition. Aggregate debit items were assets that have as their source transactions with customers. If net capital were to fall below 2 percent of aggregate debit items, the firm could be suspended from trading, expelled from the exchanges, and liquidated. Below 5 percent, the firm would be prohibited from paying dividends, redeeming stock, or expanding its business. At December 31, 1985, Morgan Stanley had net capital of $128 million, or $102 million in excess of the 2 percent rule and $65 million in excess of the 5 percent rule.

Goals

Elliott said that the goal of market dominance was subordinate to realizing superior returns on equity: "We won't chase volume for volume's sake. We want to be among the leaders in all the businesses we choose to be in, but we will not lose money in order to get to the top of the league tables."

Another objective was to develop a financing program for the firm's expansion, which would provide some or all of the following features: (1) new capital, not merely a rearranged balance sheet; (2) improved financial flexibility; (3) continued control by significant employees; (4) suitable financial incentives for employees; and (5) improved financial standing and permanence of capital.

Decision to Go Public

The offering was the result of a strategic plan prepared nine months earlier that explored and rejected a range of alternatives, including (1) selling 25 percent of the firm to a passive investor, (2) selling the entire firm to a large institution, and (3) becoming a minority player in a joint venture. Elliott said, "Selling the firm was unthinkable. The public offering was the only alternative which preserved all our options."

Management described this public offering as the start of a third phase of growth: enlarging and making permanent the firm's capital, allowing a fuller response to perceived high-return trading opportunities, and broadening funding sources (including commercial paper).

Two further considerations influenced the design of the offering. The first was to demonstrate that no insiders were using the offering to bail out of the firm. The second was to preserve the economic incentives for employees below the level of principal.

Recapitalization Prior to Public Offering

In late 1985, the company undertook a major restructuring of its various classes of equity, which involved an exchange of old common and preferred for new common and preferred. Changes in terms of number of shares and dollar amounts are summarized in Exhibit 5.

While the exchange ratios in this restructuring were not made public, Exhibit 5 suggests a 1:1 exchange of $8 cumulative senior preferred stock into $8 cumulative convertible preferred stock. Noncumulative preferred stock and old common stock were exchanged for new common stock.

The convertible preferred stock had voting privileges (one vote per share), was convertible into 2.5 shares of common stock (which was equivalent to a conversion price of $40), and could be redeemed at the company's option for $108 per share in 1987, declining to $100 in 1997 and thereafter.

THE PRELIMINARY PROSPECTUS

The "red herring" prospectus offered 4.5 million shares at a price expected to be between $42 and $46 per share. After the offering, there would be 24,201,714 shares of common stock, with approximately 81 percent of shares owned by managing directors and principals of the firm, which would allow them to elect all of the directors. An agreement among the managing directors and principals would prevent any of them from selling their shares within two years after the registration date, except in the instances of disability or death. Thereafter, only certain percentages of each person's stockholdings could be disposed of

EXHIBIT 1   Selected Financial Information on Certain U.S. Financial Services Firms

	1985 (millions of dollars)			Forecast		
	Total Capital	Total Equity	Net Capital*	LTD/ TC	Revenue Growth	Net Profit Margin
Merrill Lynch	$6,063	$2,341	$801	58%	11.5%	6.2%
Shearson Lehman ..	2,741	1,237	431	—	—	—
Salomon	2,599	1,931	789	50	5.0	3.0
Dean Witter	1,590	940	136	—	—	—
Prudential-Bache ...	—	—	462	—	—	—
Goldman Sachs	1,300	—	783	—	—	—
E. F. Hutton	1,143	810	208	31	12.0	5.0
First Boston	1,042	704	385	25	15.5	17.6
Drexel Burnham	—	—	222	—	—	—
Paine Webber	873	578	167	40	9.0	4.4
Bear Stearns	836	617	309	—	19.6§	—
Morgan Stanley	726	553‖	128	—	28.4§	—

Notes: All forecast data obtained from *Value Line Report*, February 14, 1986.

Forecasts are based on a three-year horizon, 1986–1989.

Data on capital positions obtained from S. G. Liss, "Security Brokers—The Convoluted Issue of Capital," Salomon Brothers, April 11, 1986.

* "Net Capital" is determined for regulatory purposes as aggregate debit items at market value less liabilities.

† Percentage of shares owned directly or beneficially by directors and senior employees.

‡ Obtained from Morgan Stanley memo dated February 20, 1986.

§ Growth in net revenues, 1981–1985.

‖ Includes additional capital (approximately $240 million) from initial public offering.

each year. If a person departed to work for a competing firm, Morgan Stanley would have the right to purchase his or her shares at book value. Finally, the Stockholders' Agreement provided that employee-stockholders would be bound to vote their shares as deemed by a majority of the employee-stockholders.

The prospectus provided some insight into the stockholdings and compensation of Morgan Stanley's senior management, which is summarized in Exhibit 6. The prospectus also provided selected historical income statements (see Exhibit 7) and the latest balance sheet (see Exhibit 8).

	Forecast				*1985*	
Percent Principal Transactions	*Percent Investment Banking*	*Return on Equity*	*Price- Earnings Ratio*		*Beta*	*Percent Insider Ownership†*
12.0%	13.0%	18.5%	11×		1.90	1.0%
—						
47.8	7.0	18.5	12		1.95	2.6
—	—	—	—		—	—
—	—	—	—		—	100.0
8.0	10.0	18.5	10		2.00	7.5
37.8‡	38.8‡	19.5	11		1.40	4.5
—	—	—	—		—	100.0
18.0	16.0	17.5	11		1.95	6.1
17.6‡	18.3‡	—	—		1.30‡	—
27.5‡	46.6‡	—	—		—	81.0‖

EXHIBIT 2 Equity Underwriting Syndicate Positions: 1971 versus 1978 and Status in 1986

1971	1978	Ownership Status 1986
	Special Bracket:	
Dillon, Read & Co., Inc.		
The First Boston Corp.	The First Boston Corp.	Publicly held
Kuhn, Loeb & Co.	—	
Merrill Lynch, Pierce, Fenner & Smith, Inc.	—	
Morgan Stanley & Co., Inc.	Merrill Lynch, Pierce, Fenner & Smith, Inc.	Publicly held
Salomon Brothers	Morgan Stanley & Co., Inc.	Publicly held
	Salomon Brothers	Publicly held
	Goldman Sachs & Co.	Interest sold to Sumitomo
	Major Bracket:	
Blyth & Co., Inc.	Bache, Halsey Stuart Shields, Inc.	Owned by Prudential
Drexel, Harriman, Ripley, Inc.	Blyth, Eastman Dillon & Co., Inc.	Owned by Paine Webber
DuPont, Glore, Forgan, Inc.	Dillon, Read & Co., Inc.	Owned by Travelers Insurance
Eastman Dillon, Union Securities & Co.	Donaldson, Lufkin & Jenrette Securities Corp.	Owned by Equitable Insurance
Goldman, Sachs & Co.	Drexel Burnham Lambert, Inc.	Closely held
Halsey, Stuart & Co., Inc.	E. F. Hutton & Company, Inc.	Publicly held
Hornblower & Weeks—Hemphill, Noyes	Kidder, Peabody & Co., Inc.	Owned by General Electric
Kidder, Peabody & Co., Inc.	Lazard Freres & Co.	Closely held
Lazard Freres & Co.	Lehman Brothers Kuhn Loeb, Inc.	Owned by Shearson/American Express
Lehman Brothers, Inc.	Loeb Rhoades, Hornblower & Co.	Dissolved
Loeb, Rhoades & Co.	Paine, Webber, Jackson & Curtis, Inc.	Publicly held
Paine, Webber, Jackson & Curtis	Smith Barney, Harris Upham & Co., Inc.	Closely held
Smith, Barney & Co., Inc.	Warburg Paribas Becker, Inc.	Acquired by Merrill Lynch
Stone & Webster Securities Corp.	Wertheim & Co., Inc.	Closely held
Wertheim & Co.	Dean Witter Reynolds, Inc.	Owned by Sears Roebuck
White, Weld & Co.		
Dean Witter & Co., Inc.		
	Major Out of Order:	
Bache & Co., Inc.	Bear, Stearns & Co.	Publicly held
Paribas Corp.	L. F. Rothschild, Unterberg, Towbin	Publicly held
	Shearson Hayden Stone, Inc.	Owned by American Express

Mezzanine Bracket:

Oppenheimer & Co., Inc.	Closely held
Thomson McKinnon Securities, Inc.	Closely held

Submajor Bracket:

Ladenburg Thalmann & Co., Inc.	Closely held
Moseley, Hallgarten & Estabrook, Inc.	Closely held

Bear, Stearns & Co.
A.G. Becker & Co., Inc.
CBWL-Hayden, Stone, Inc.
Clark, Dodge & Co., Inc.
Dominick & Dominick, Inc.
Equitable Securities, Morton & Co., Inc.
Hallgarten & Co.
Harris, Upham & Co., Inc.
E.F. Hutton & Co.
W.E. Hutton & Co.
Ladenburg, Thalmann & Co.
F.S. Moseley & Co.
John Nuveen & Co. (Inc.)
R.W. Pressprich & Co., Inc.
Reynolds & Co.
L.F. Rothschild & Co.
Shearson, Hammill & Co., Inc.
Shields & Co.
F.S. Smithers & Co., Inc.
Spencer Trask & Co., Inc.
G.W. Walker & Co.
Walston & Co., Inc.
Wood, Struthers & Winthrop, Inc.

Source of 1971 and 1978 rankings: S. L. Hayes III, "The Transformation of Investment Banking," *Harvard Business Review*, January–February 1979, p. 165.

EXHIBIT 3 Recent Capital-Market Conditions

| | Common Stock Prices | | Daily Trading Volume, NYSE (millions of shares) | Returns | | | | Domestic Stock, Bond, and Preferred New Issues ($ billions) |
	S&P 500	NYSE Finance Index		90-Day Treasury Bills (%)	AAA Bonds (%)	30-Year Treasury Bonds (%)	
1983*	$160.41	$ 95.34	85.4	8.63%	12.04%	11.18%	$ 96.1
1984*	160.46	89.28	91.1	9.58	12.71	12.39	82.2
1985*	186.84	114.21	109.2	7.48	11.37	10.79	142.5
1985 (Dec.)	207.26	128.86	133.4	7.07	10.16	9.97	N.A.
1986:							
January	208.19	132.36	130.9	7.04	10.05	9.45	N.A.
February	219.37	142.13	152.6	7.03	9.67	8.93	N.A.
March 1	225.17	146.23	160.7	6.96	9.64	7.96	280.0†

* Yearly averages.   Source: *Federal Reserve Bulletin.*

† Annualized volume in the first quarter of 1986.   Source: *Investment Dealer's Digest.*

EXHIBIT 4 Market Share of Leading Underwriters (in percent)

	1980	1981	1982	1983	1984	1985
Salomon	9.5%	10.1%	12.8%	12.6%	30.9%	17.1%
First Boston	9.1	8.6	9.8	8.4	10.2	13.7
Merrill	13.6	13.6	14.5	13.3	10.4	14.2
Goldman	7.7	9.7	10.4	10.6	11.5	10.4
Drexel	2.0	2.8	3.2	6.7	7.5	9.5
Morgan	12.3	13.1	11.9	6.1	3.4	6.8
Shearson/Lehman	9.0	7.5	7.4	8.6	5.4	7.1
Kidder	5.7	4.2	3.7	3.3	2.3	2.9
Paine Webber	5.7	3.7	4.3	3.1	1.4	2.2
Smith Barney	2.7	1.1	1.8	1.5	0.5	1.6
Top 5	53.5	53.1	59.4	53.5	70.5	64.9
Top 10	77.3	74.4	79.8	74.2	83.5	85.5

Note: Although the source of this table does not indicate how it was developed, it appears to give full credit for each underwriting to the lead firm. Obviously, this practice skews the underwriting shares toward the lead underwriters. The alternative approaches would be to give equal credit to all members of an underwriting syndicate and/or give some bonus credit to the lead. Furthermore, the table masks differences in shares of various submarkets (e.g., equity versus debt offerings, domestic versus Euromarket, etc.).

Source: "Capital Markets Firms" by Rodney Schwartz, Paine Webber, April 18, 1986.

EXHIBIT 5 Changes in Stockholders' Equity Resulting from the Recapitalization (dollar values in thousands)

	Before Recapitalization	Adjustment	After Recapitalization
$8 Cumulative Senior Preferred Stock ($100 par):			
In shares	119,261	(119,261)	—
In dollars	$11,926	($11,926)	—
Non-Cumulative Preferred Stock ($100 par):			
In shares	1,956,677	(1,956,677)	—
In dollars	$195,668	($195,668)	—
Old Common Stock ($1 par):			
In shares	2,685,010	(2,685,010)	—
In dollars	$2,685	($2,685)	—
$8 Cumulative Convertible Preferred Stock ($100 par):			
In shares	—	119,261	119,261
In dollars	—	$11,926	$11,926
New Common Stock ($1 par):			
In shares	—	19,701,715	19,701,715
In dollars	—	$19,702	$19,702

Source: Preliminary prospectus, February 14, 1986.

EXHIBIT 6 Compensation and Share Ownership by Key Officers of Morgan Stanley

	1985 Cash Compensation	Share Ownership (February 14, 1986)	
		Number	Percent of Total
S. Parker Gilbert, chairman	1,500,000	772,113	3.9%
Richard B. Fisher, president	1,450,000	729,574	3.7
Lewis W. Bernard, managing director	1,375,000	673,521	3.4
Robert F. Greenhill, managing director	1,375,000	710,275	3.6
Ned R. Sachs, secretary	400,000	N.A.	N.A.
Total shares outstanding	19,701,715		

Source: Preliminary prospectus dated February 14, 1986.

EXHIBIT 7 Income Statement (in thousands of dollars, except per share amounts)

	Year Ended December 31				
	1981	*1982*	*1983*	*1984*	*1985*
Revenues:					
Investment banking	$159,284	$172,863	$212,247	$ 266,870	$ 423,515
Principal transactions	45,485	75,091	78,385	121,703	243,040
Commissions	76,662	95,994	131,133	130,129	154,360
Interest and dividends	345,248	362,647	415,005	794,858	937,995
Asset management	8,939	16,342	21,315	25,241	34,825
Other	1,396	2,481	1,466	1,683	1,167
Total revenues	637,014	725,418	859,551	1,340,484	1,794,902
Expenses:					
Interest	323,156	335,510	390,867	747,957	900,216
Employee compensation and benefits	145,857	191,442	253,747	304,504	421,473
Occupancy and equipment rental	24,040	32,619	38,177	51,658	79,092
Brokerage, clearing, and exchange fees	10,222	13,874	22,818	31,472	45,480
Communications	12,000	15,860	20,146	28,815	39,159
Business development	11,074	12,434	17,756	25,452	35,725
Professional services	9,136	9,828	10,247	14,499	29,529
Other	11,993	21,126	19,634	30,393	60,938
Total expenses	547,478	632,693	773,392	1,234,750	1,611,612
Income before income taxes	89,536	92,725	86,159	105,734	183,290
Income taxes	41,642	42,072	35,003	44,526	77,440
Net income	$ 47,894	$ 50,653	$ 51,156	$ 61,208	$ 105,850
Pro forma net income per share*	—	—	—	—	$5.32

* Gives effect to the recapitalization as if it had occurred on January 1, 1985.

Source: Preliminary prospectus, February 14, 1986.

EXHIBIT 8 Balance Sheet (in thousands of dollars)

	December 31, 1985
Assets	
Cash and interest-bearing equivalents	$ 173,353
Cash and securities deposited with clearing organizations or segregated in compliance with federal regulations	27,337
Securities and commodities owned:	
U.S. government and agency	1,751,121
Certificates of deposit and bankers' acceptances	435,541
Corporate debt	1,629,918
Corporate equities	776,046
State and municipal	347,586
Commodities	74,451
Securities purchased under agreements to resell	5,732,855
Receivables from brokers, dealers, and clearing organizations	3,416,026
Receivables from customers	998,134
Fees and other receivables	262,808
Net office furniture, equipment, and leasehold improvements.	83,276
Other assets	85,655
Total assets	$15,794,107

EXHIBIT 8   *(concluded)*

	December 31, 1985
Liabilities and Stockholders' Equity	
Short-term borrowings	$ 1,810,315
Securities and commodities sold, not yet purchased:	
U.S. government and agency	1,406,788
Corporate debt	262,353
Corporate equities	626,879
State and municipal	755
Commodities	229,009
Securities sold under agreements to repurchase	6,950,067
Payables to brokers, dealers, and clearing organizations	2,261,472
Payables to customers	1,028,283
Accrued compensation and benefits	199,424
Other liabilities	346,819
Notes payable	256,491
Subordinated liabilities	101,471
Total liabilities	15,480,126
Commitments and contingencies	
Stockholders' equity:	
$8 Cumulative Convertible Preferred Stock, stated value $100; authorized, 120,000 shares; issued and outstanding, 119,261 shares	11,926
Preferred stock, no par value; authorized, 15,000,000 shares; none issued	—
Common stock, $1 par value; authorized, 200,000,000 shares; issued and outstanding, 19,701,715 shares	19,702
Retained earnings	281,815
Cumulative translation adjustment	538
Total stockholders' equity	313,981
Total liabilities and stockholders' equity	$15,794,107

Source: Preliminary prospectus, February 14, 1986.

Case 28

British Aerospace PLC (A)

In the summer of 1991, Sir Roland Smith, chairman of the board of directors of British Aerospace (BAe), concluded that the company required £432 million in additional equity. This capital would be used to finance export sales, to continue the delivery of products already financed by customer advances, to fund ongoing restructuring and rationalization of the firm, and to rebuild the firm's equity base. In January 1991, Sir Roland had told securities analysts that he expected BAe's pre-tax profit for the year would total £300 million. In late August, however, there was troubling news than the recession in Britain was imposing a significantly greater strain on the company's performance and finances than had been expected. Results for the first six months ending in June 1991 showed a pre-tax profit of £86 million, off from £146 million in the first half of 1990. BAe's financial staff estimated that pre-tax profits for the year would drop to −£85 million.

In these circumstances, should BAe go to the market immediately, just as news of the first-half results were being absorbed by the financial community? Or should it wait a few months and risk a rights offering of shares under the darker cloud of the full-year results? The financial results and a sale of new shares would depress the share price from the 565-pence level prevailing in late August. If the company moved quickly, before it had to report first-half results in early September, it might exploit the high current price. Although capital market conditions were improving, BAe could not predict how soon it would be able to return to the market at August's 565-pence share price once it released first-half results. On the other hand, a rights offering of shares would require the firm to forecast near-term financial performance, which also might depress share prices. If the firm did proceed soon with a rights offering, what should its terms be? Specifically, where should BAe set the exercise price of each right, and how many rights should be issued per share of outstanding stock?

This case was prepared by Professor Robert F. Bruner.

Copyright © 1993 by the University of Virginia Darden School Foundation, Charlottesville, VA. Revised May 1993.

THE COMPANY

British Aerospace was among the largest industrial firms in the United Kingdom (U.K.), with 1990 sales and net income of £10.54 billion and £278 million, respectively. Its principal business sectors consisted of (1) defense systems, (2) commercial aircraft, (3) the Rover automobile group, and (4) property and construction. Exhibit 1 presents the contributions of each of these sectors to the firm's total annual sales and profits in recent years.

Defense Systems.   The company was a significant competitor in the defense-systems market: it led all Western European defense contractors, and it ranked third, after McDonnell Douglas and General Dynamics, among all defense contractors in the industrialized countries. BAe's products included military airframes, missiles, ammunition, explosives, and guns. The company declared that its objective was to "consolidate its position as one of the world's leading defense contractors as the industry restructures." Given the decline of the Soviet bloc from 1989 to 1991, it appeared that the defense-systems industry would enter a period of reduced demand and major rationalization. Although the demand for defense products was dropping in August 1991, BAe's management believed that demand would recover to previous levels by the year 2000. Outside analysts were especially interested in the "Al Yamamah" defense construction program for Saudi Arabia, for which BAe was the prime contractor. This program supplied defense systems, construction services, training, and support to the Saudi government. As of August 1991, BAe's gross revenues from this program exceeded £8.3 billion. BAe's management believed that sales from the contract would amount to £2 billion per year to the year 2000.

Commercial Aircraft.   BAe participated in Airbus Industrie and produced original commercial aircraft and executive jets. Airbus was a consortium venture between BAe, Aerospatiale of France, Deutsche Airbus of Germany, and CASA of Spain. BAe designed and manufactured wings for the various Airbus models. Airbus was expected to grow and introduce new models over the next few years, which suggested that BAe would have to make significant commitments of working capital to the project.

Although demand for regional commercial aircraft was expected to grow, competition was expected to be particularly keen. Analysts believed that no manufacturers would earn a satisfactory return on capital employed in this sector; consequently, they expected the regional aircraft industry to undertake a substantial program of rationalization. BAe intended to participate in this rationalization and to introduce new models in conjunction with partners. The executive-jet segment was growing well and provided a satisfactory return on capital.

The Rover Automobile Group.   BAe produced and sold automobiles under the Rover, Land Rover, MG, and Sterling marques. BAe acquired Rover in August 1988, in what most observers agreed was a distress sale. Rover had been operating unprofitably for years prior to 1988. Since the acquisition, BAe had focused on improving profitability in the Rover group. This had entailed emphasizing export sales, repositioning Rover's car products toward the upper quartile of its respective market sectors, raising prices, changing the management process and working practices, and collaborating closely with Honda in product engineering and manufacturing. BAe expected that continued product enhancement and expansion would require capital expenditures greater than £350 per year over the next three years. Even with declining demand for automobiles in late 1990, management believed that the Rover group would be self-financing over the next three years.

Property and Construction.   BAe entered this sector in 1987 when it acquired Ballast Nedham, an engineering and construction firm. In 1989, BAe also acquired Arlington, a developer of industrial parks. BAe offered three reasons for its entry into this sector: (1) the defense-systems sector required construction capability; (2) BAe's own restructuring would create surplus land and industrial facilities that BAe would want to sell or develop; and (3) complete infrastructure projects generally were viewed as an important industrial growth segment. The recession in real estate that began in 1990 was gaining in severity, however, and depressing the financial performance of this sector of BAe's business.

PAST FINANCIAL PERFORMANCE AND ANALYSTS' EXPECTATIONS

In late 1990, securities analysts openly acknowledged the business and financial challenges facing BAe: one analyst cited BAe as "one of the last really inefficient U.K. manufacturing companies." Nevertheless, he also issued a "buy" recommendation at 526 pence per share, arguing:

> there is obviously a lot wrong with British Aerospace. The company is, however, aggressively coming to terms with its difficulties through a radical programme of restructuring that will improve trading margins. The buy case rests upon defense profits stabilizing on a much reduced cost base, upon which recovery in motors, aerospace, and property can build. With growth in telecommunications and asset sales reducing debt, these could double profits on a five-year view. . . . 1991 will be a particularly strong year for BAe.[1]

Other analysts echoed this view. Their forecasts of financial performance for the year ending December 31, 1991, projected pre-tax profits at about £465 million, earnings per share at about 110 pence, and a dividend per share at 27.5 pence. These forecasts were, in part, an extrapolation of favorable historical trends in the company

---

[1]P. Compton, "British Aerospace—Company Report," UBS Phillips & Drew Global Research Group, December 5, 1990.

(see Exhibit 1). They also were founded on expectations of a robust market for automobiles, a strong recovery in property, and large exports under the Al Yamamah program.

RESULTS FOR FIRST-HALF 1991 AND FUTURE FINANCING REQUIREMENTS

Exhibit 1 presents the financial results for the first half of 1991, which Sir Roland would soon be obliged to report to investors. The figures showed that pre-tax income had fallen to £86 million, compared with £146 million for the same period a year earlier. Even worse, BAe analysts projected that, although the pre-tax income for the full year would be no greater than £150 million, it would be offset by £235 million in extraordinary restructuring charges. Thus, Sir Roland's staff projected that pre-tax earnings would be −£85 million *at best*. These results would be a stunning reversal of the historical trend and of the expectations of securities analysts.

The earnings decline was due to softening of business in the commercial aircraft and property sectors of the firm's activities. The defense sector remained robust, although growth in orders under the Al Yamamah program had not yet materialized. The Rover group had been saddled with £45 million in extraordinary expenses arising from its withdrawal from the North American automobile market.

Against this backdrop, management sought to raise £432 million in new common equity. The cash position of the firm had deteriorated sharply in the first half of 1991, because of heavy capital expenditures and seasonal buildup of working capital in the Rover group; reductions in customer advances as deliveries continued under the Al Yamamah program; and extraordinary rationalization expenses. The firm's net cash balance (cash less short-term debt) had declined from £711 million outstanding at the end of 1990 to −£120 million by the end of the first half of 1991. BAe's financial staff believed that net cash would return to a positive balance of £100 million by the end of 1991, although this would be well below prior years' balances (see Exhibit 1).

Exhibit 2 presents the prevailing price trends for BAe shares. BAe shares had enjoyed a surge in value in February 1991, along with the rest of the stock market, upon the conclusion of the Gulf War. Since then, the share value had subsided somewhat. At a level of 565 pence, shares were trading at a multiple of 5.8 times 1990 earnings per share (compared with a market-average multiple of 13.9 times 1990 earnings per share), and at a substantial discount from the 1990 book value per share of 845 pence. One analyst argued that the book value understated the true breakup of the firm, because it ignored future cash flows from the Al Yamamah program, the intangible values in the Rover group's brand names, and potential gains in more than 6,000 acres of developable land.[2]

---

[2]Ibid.

RIGHTS-OFFERING METHOD OF ISSUING COMMON STOCK

In Britain, as in the rest of the European Community,[3] securities regulations required public companies to first offer new shares of common stock to existing shareholders. Shareholders retained the right (but not the obligation) to purchase shares offered to them; in other words, shareholders had "preemptive rights" over newly issued shares. The prevailing method of selling common stock was called a *rights offering of shares*. In a typical rights offering, existing shareholders were offered the opportunity to buy new shares in proportion to their current holdings; the exercise price was fixed at some discount to prevailing market prices; and the option to buy lasted for a limited time, such as 30–50 days. The task for the shareholder was to decide whether to (1) exercise the rights, (2) sell the rights to someone else, or (3) do nothing and allow the rights to expire worthless. If the shareholder exercised the rights, his or her percentage interest in the company would remain unchanged; but if the rights were sold or allowed to expire, the shareholder's interest would be *diluted* to the extent of new shares issued.

The primary task for the issuing company was to design the rights issue to promote its success. Three elements needed to be decided:

- *Proportion of new shares to current holdings:* The right typically entitled the shareholder to purchase a specified number of new shares in proportion to the number of shares he or she currently held. For instance, a two-for-five rights issue meant that two new shares were offered for every five shares already owned.
- *The price discount:* Most rights offerings discounted the shares by 12 to 20 percent from prevailing prices. It was commonly believed that shares were discounted as an incentive to investors to buy the shares. Some analysts argued that the price at which shares were to be issued was irrelevant, because any discount affected the number of shares to be issued, which, in turn, affected the dilution of preexisting shares. Thus, discount and dilution might offset each other. Exhibit 3 illustrates the theoretical effect of a rights offering by BAe on its share price and market value of equity. The exhibit reveals that, if the shareholder failed to exercise or sell the rights, he or she would sustain a loss in value, and that loss would grow with increases in the rights ratio or the price discount, or both.
- *Underwriting:* In theory, companies had no need of an intermediary for the share issue, because they would be selling shares to their own shareholders. An intermediary would, however, insure that the company would receive the desired amount of proceeds in the

---

[3]The rights offering, a preemptive offering of shares to existing shareholders, was the predominant method of share issuance outside the United States. The technique preferred in the United States was the "general cash offer," or "bought deal," where an underwriter would buy the shares from the issuing company and resell them to *any* interested investor. Some evidence suggested that rights offerings were about as costly as general cash offers to the issuer. Rights offerings differed from general cash offers mainly in that (1) in a rights offering, the price of the new shares was theoretically irrelevant and (2) rights offerings protected existing investors against involuntary dilution.

issue: a firm underwriting commitment was essentially a put option that enabled the issuer to sell its shares to the underwriter in the event that its own shareholders did not exercise their rights. The typical fee for a standby commitment was 1.25 percent of the gross proceeds of the issue. Sir Roland wondered whether this would be a fair fee in BAe's case.[4]

CONCLUSION

The decisions about the timing and terms of the share rights offering seemed to depend on the financial information that the firm would soon release. How would the stock market respond to this information? Was there a way to frame the information to best advantage? Raising £432 million from existing shareholders meant a significant addition to the book value of the firm's equity and an even larger addition to its market value. Sir Roland Smith would, however, need to proceed cautiously in taking any action.

---

[4]The commitment would need to be outstanding for 30 to 50 days. BAe's sigma, or volatility, was 0.36; its beta was 1.08. Short-term British government Treasury bills were yielding 10.07 percent at the end of August 1991. BAe's dividend yield was about 5 percent. The stock price currently was 565 pence. The exercise price of the standby commitment would be the same as the exercise price of the shareholder right.

EXHIBIT 1 Historical, Projected, and Expected Financial Performance (values expressed in £ millions except per share amounts, which are in pence, and shares outstanding, which are in millions)

	1988	1989	1990 Actual	1991 Projected	1992 Projected	1st Half 1990 Actual	1st Half 1991 Actual
Revenues:							
Defense	3,000	3,800	4,423	5,500	5,000	2,055	1,918
Aircraft	978	1,525	1,560	1,950	2,300	687	910
Rover	1,179	3,430	3,785	4,000	4,000	1,863	1,863
Property	409	547	577	570	800	269	315
Other	80	100	195	155	165	−88	−120
Total	5,646	9,402	10,540	12,175	12,265	4,786	4,886
Operating profit:							
Defense	315	300	486	460	420	177	273
Aircraft	−9	19	35	20	20	12	−33
Rover	52	64	55	80	120	33	−45
Property	18	58	9	20	60	9	15
Intercompany	−34	0	N.A.	10	11	3	5
Total	342	441	585	590	631	234	213
Interest expense	−40	−103	−138	−90	−90	−45	−100
Exceptional items	−40	−5	−71	−35	−35	−43	−27
Pre-tax profit	236	333	376	465	506	146	86
Tax rate (%)	34	28	26	28	28	28	31
Minority interest	0	−26	−18	−42	−45	−3	15
EPS (p)	62	83	98.2	112	123	35.6	24.7
DPS (p)	20.6	22.7	28.7	27.5	31	10.5	13.8
Net cash	215	1,142	711	600	500	576	−120
Book value/share(p)	860	826	845	1,000	1,050	821	1,678
Shares outstanding	—	—	299.89	—	—	294.94	238.8

N.A. means not available.

Sources: Company annual reports and "British Aerospace—Company Report," UBS Phillips & Drew, December 5, 1990.

EXHIBIT 2   British Aerospace Prices per Share versus London Stock Market Index
(FTSE100)*

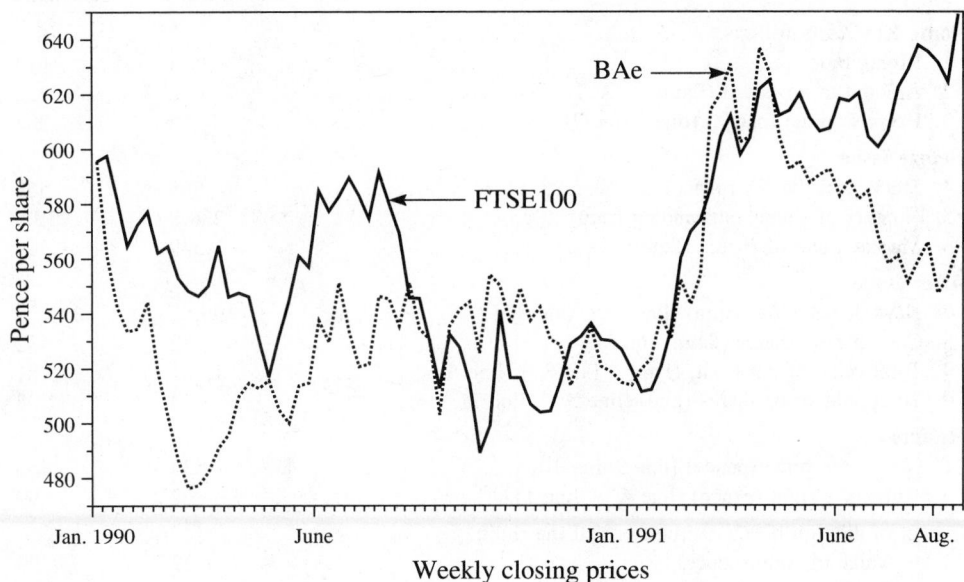

Weekly closing prices

* For the sake of comparison, the FTSE100 has been indexed to the British Aerospace share price at
January 1, 1990.

Source of price data: Datastream, Inc.

EXHIBIT 3   Example of a Rights Offering, Using Values for BAe, Summer 1991

	Scenario 1	Scenario 2	Scenario 3
Some Key Assumptions			
1. Rights ratio	2:5	3:5	4:5
2. Amount to be raised (£mm)	432	432	432
3. Exercise price (pence) [line 2/line 7]	452	302	226
Before Issue			
4. Stock price before (pence)	565	565	565
5. Number of shares outstanding (mm)	238.8	238.8	238.8
6. Market value of shares (£mm)	1,349	1,349	1,349
After Issue			
7. New shares added (mm) [line 1 × line 5]	95.52	143.28	191.04
8. Cost of new shares (£mm) [line 2]	432	432	432
9. Total value of outst. sh. (£mm) [line 8 + line 6]	1,781	1,781	1,781
10. Total number of shares (mm) [line 5 + line 7]	334.32	382.08	429.84
Results			
11. New share price (pence) [line 9/line 10]	533	466	414
12. Value of a right (pence) [line 4 − line 11]	32	99	151
Impact of dilution if you exercise or sell the right:			
13. + Value of right (pence)	32	99	151
14. − Decline in stock price (pence)	(32)	(99)	(151)
15. = Dilution in value (pence)	0	0	0
Dilution in value if you do not exercise or sell the right:			
16. + Value of right (pence)	0	0	0
17. − Decline in stock price (pence)	(32)	(99)	(151)
18. = Dilution in value (pence)	(32)	(99)	(151)

Comment: The amount to be raised (line 2) is assumed to remain constant across different rights offering deals. Thus, the rights ratio (line 1) and the exercise price (line 3) are interdependent. The *ex post* share price (line 11) declines as more shares are issued. The value of the right (line 12) rises as the exercise price (line 3) declines, consistent with option pricing theory. Lines 13–15 reveal the hypothesized value neutrality of rights offerings. Lines 16–18 reveal the consequences for the unwitting.

Source: Casewriter's analysis.

Part VI

Management of Corporate Debt

An Introduction to Debt Policy and Value

Many factors determine how much debt a firm takes on. Chief among them ought to be the effect of the debt on the value of the firm. Does borrowing create value? If so, for whom? If not, then why do so many executives concern themselves with leverage?

If leverage affects value, then it should cause changes in either the discount rate of the firm (i.e., its weighted-average cost of capital) or the cash flows of the firm.

1. Please fill in the following:

	0% Debt/ 100% Equity	25% Debt/ 75% Equity	50% Debt/ 50% Equity
Book value of debt	0	$2,500	$5,000
Book value of equity	$10,000	$7,500	$5,000
Market value of debt	0	$2,500	$5,000
Market value of equity	$10,000	$8,350	$6,700
Pretax cost of debt	0.07	0.07	0.07
After-tax cost of debt	0.0462	0.0462	0.0462
Market value weights of:			
Debt	0.0	_____	_____
Equity	1.0	_____	_____
Unlevered beta	0.8	0.8	0.8

(continued)

This case was written by Robert F. Bruner.
Copyright © 1989 by the Darden Graduate Business School Sponsors, Charlottesville, VA.

	0% Debt/ 100% Equity	25% Debt/ 75% Equity	50% Debt/ 50% Equity
Risk-free rate	0.07	0.07	0.07
Market premium	0.086	0.086	0.086
Cost of equity			
Weighted-average cost of capital			
EBIT	$2,103	$2,103	$2,103
− Taxes (@ 34%)			
EBIAT			
+ Depreciation	$500	$500	$500
− Capital exp.	($500)	($500)	($500)
Free cash flow			
Value of assets (FCF/WACC)			

Why does the value of assets change? Where, specifically, do the changes occur?

2. In finance, as in accounting, the two sides of the balance sheet must be equal. In the previous problem, we valued the asset side of the balance sheet. To value the other side, we must value the debt and the equity, and then add them together.

	0% Debt/ 100% Debt	25% Debt/ 75% Debt	50% Debt/ 50% Debt
Cash flow to creditors:			
Interest	0	$175	$350
Pretax cost of debt	0.07	0.07	0.07
Value of debt:			
(CF/r_d)			
Cash flow to shareholders:			
EBIT	$2,103	$2,103	$2,103
− Interest		($175)	($350)
Pretax profit			
Taxes (@ 34%)			
Net income			
+ Depreciation	$500	$500	$500
− Capital exp.	($500)	($500)	($500)
− Debt amortiz.	0	0	0
Residual cash flow			
Cost of equity			
Value of equity (CF/r_e)			
Value of equity plus value of debt			

As the firm levers up, how does the increase in value get apportioned between creditors and shareholders?

3. In the preceding problem, we divided the value of all assets between two classes of investors—creditors and shareholders. This process tells us where the change in value is *going,* but it sheds little light on where the change is *coming from.* Let's divide the free cash flows of the firm into *pure business flows* and cash flows resulting from *financing effects.* Now, an axiom in finance is that you should discount cash flows at a rate consistent with the risk of those cash flows. Pure business flows should be discounted at the unlevered cost of equity (i.e., the cost of capital for the unlevered firm). Financing flows should be discounted at the rate of return required by the providers of debt.

	0% Debt/ 100% Equity	25% Debt/ 75% Equity	50% Debt/ 50% Equity
Pure business cash flows:			
EBIT	$2,103	$2,103	$2,103
Taxes (@ 34%)	($715)	($715)	($715)
EBIAT	$1,388	$1,388	$1,388
+Depreciation	$500	$500	$500
−Capital exp.	($500)	($500)	$500
Cash flow	$1,388	$1,388	$1,388
Unlevered beta	0.8	0.8	0.8
Risk-free rate	0.07	0.07	0.07
Market premium	0.086	0.086	0.086
Unlevered WACC	————	————	————
Value of pure business flows: (CF/unlevered WACC)	————	————	————
Financing cash flows:			
Interest	————	————	————
Tax reduction	————	————	————
Pretax cost of debt	0.07	0.07	0.07
Value of financing effect: (Tax reduction/pretax cost of debt)	————	————	————
Total value (sum of values of pure business flows and financing effects)	————	————	————

The first three problems illustrate one of the most important theories in finance. This theory, developed by two professors, Franco Modigliani and Merton Miller, revolutionized the way we think about capital-structure policies. The M&M theory says:

$$\begin{array}{ccccccc}
\text{Value of} & = & \text{Value of} & + & \text{Value of} & = & \text{Value of} & + & \text{Value of} \\
\text{assets} & & \text{debt} & & \text{equity} & & \text{unlevered} & & \text{debt tax} \\
& & & & & & \text{firm} & & \text{shields}^1
\end{array}$$

$$\begin{array}{ccc}
\wedge & \wedge & \wedge \\
\text{Problem 1} & \text{Problem 2} & \text{Problem 3}
\end{array}$$

4. What remains to be seen, however, is whether shareholders are better or worse off with more leverage. Problem 2 does not tell us, because there we computed total value of equity, and shareholders care about value *per share*. Ordinarily, total value will be a good proxy for what is happening to the price per share; but in the case of a relevering firm, that may not be true. Implicitly we assumed that, as our firm in problems 1–3 levered up, it was repurchasing stock on the open market (you will note that EBIT did not change, so management was clearly not investing the proceeds from the loans in cash-generating assets). We held EBIT constant so we could see clearly the effect of financial changes without getting them mixed up in the effects of investments. The point is that, as the firm borrows and repurchases shares, the total value of equity may decline, but the price per share may *rise*.

Now, solving for the price per share may seem impossible, because we are dealing with two unknowns—share price and change in the number of shares:

$$\text{Share price} = \frac{\text{Total market value of equity}}{(\text{Original shares} - \text{Repurchased shares})}$$

But, by rewriting the equation, we can put it in a form that can be solved:

$$\text{Share price} = \frac{\text{Total market value of equity} + \text{Cash paid out}}{\text{Number of original shares}}$$

Referring to the results of problem 2, let's assume that all the new debt is equal to the cash paid to repurchase shares. Please complete the following table:

	0% Debt/ 100% Equity	25% Debt/ 75% Equity	50% Debt/ 50% Equity
Total market value of equity	_____	_____	_____
Cash paid out	_____	_____	_____
No. original shares	1,000	1,000	1,000
Total value per share	_____	_____	_____

---

[1]Debt tax shields can be valued by discounting the future annual tax savings at the pretax cost of debt. For debt that is assumed to be outstanding in perpetuity, the tax saving is the tax rate, t, times the interest payment, $r \times B$. The present value of this perpetual savings is $trB/r = tB$.

5. In this set of problems, is leverage good for shareholders? Why? Is levering/unlevering the firm something shareholders can do for themselves? In what sense should shareholders pay a premium for shares of levered companies?

6. From a macroeconomic point of view, is society better off if firms use more than zero debt (up to some prudent limit)?

7. As a way of illustrating the usefulness of the M&M theory and consolidating your grasp of the mechanics, consider the following case and complete the work sheet. On March 3, 1988, Beazer PLC. (a British construction company), and Shearson Lehman Hutton, Inc. (an investment banking firm), commenced a hostile tender offer to purchase all the outstanding stock of Koppers Company, Inc. (a producer of construction materials, chemicals, and building products).

Originally, the raiders offered $45 per share; subsequently, the offer was raised to $56, and then finally $61 per share. The Koppers board generally asserted that the offers were inadequate and its management was reviewing the possibility of major recapitalization.

To test the valuation effects of the recapitalization alternative, assume that Koppers could borrow a maximum of $1,738,095,000 at a pretax cost of debt of 10.5 percent and that the aggregate amount of debt will remain constant in perpetuity. The amount of new borrowings will be equal to $1,737,922,591 ($1,738,095,000 − $172,409). Also, assume that the proceeds of the new debt would be paid as an extraordinary dividend to shareholders. Exhibit 1 presents Koppers' book- and market-value balance sheets assuming the capital structure before recapitalization. Please complete the work sheet for the recapitalization alternative.

EXHIBIT 1   Koppers Company, Inc.

	Before Recapitalization	*After Recapitalization*
Book-Value Balance Sheets:		
Net working capital	$ 212,453	_____
Fixed assets	601,446	_____
Total assets	813,899	_____
Long-term debt	172,409	_____
Deferred taxes, etc.	195,616	_____
Preferred stock	15,000	_____
Common equity	430,874	_____
Total capital	813,899	_____
Market-Value Balance Sheets:		
Net working capital	$ 212,453	_____
Fixed assets	1,618,081	_____
PV debt tax shield	58,619	_____
Total assets	1,889,153	_____
Long-term debt	172,409	_____
Deferred taxes, etc.	0	_____
Preferred stock	15,000	_____
Common equity	1,701,744	_____
Total capital	$1,889,153	_____
Number of shares	28,128	_____
Price per share	$60.50	_____
Value to Public Shareholders:		
Cash received	0	_____
Value of shares	$1,701,744	_____
Total	1,701,744	_____
Total per share	60.50	_____

Tonka Corporation

Tonka Corporation, the fifth largest toy company in the United States, had two of the most successful years in its history in 1985 and 1986. The company's sales of $293 million and profitability of $22 million were unprecedented; Tonka also had issued more than 1 million shares of common stock in December 1986 and had retired its long-term debt in January 1987, both of which contributed to its low leverage and high liquidity.

Becoming and remaining financially sound was a difficult task in the toy industry, because of the typically short life spans and "hit or miss" nature of most products. Now, in February 1987, Tonka's management was undergoing a capital-structure policy review in an effort to determine whether the company could use its financial resources more efficiently and yet remain conservative.

THE TOY INDUSTRY

Over the past several years, a trend toward consolidation was evident within the toy industry. In 1983, the top five toy companies in the United States were responsible for 32.7 percent of total sales; by 1986, that figure had risen to an estimated 44.2 percent. In 1984, Hasbro, Inc., acquired Milton Bradley, and, in 1985, it acquired certain assets of another toy company, Child Guidance. In 1986 alone, Coleco Industries had acquired two other companies (including Selchow & Righter, the producer of Scrabble and of the blockbuster board game of 1984, Trivial Pursuit), the product line of another company, and the North American subsidiary of Tomy Kogyo, a toy company that specialized in high-technology applications. The results of these consolidations are shown in Exhibit 1.

Of the approximately 800 toy companies in the United States, only the largest were able to minimize sales and profit volatility through diversification. Even they were not

---

This case was written by Casey S. Opitz under the direction of Robert F. Bruner.
Copyright © 1988 by the Darden Graduate Business School Foundation, Charlottesville, VA.

always successful, however, as shown in Exhibits 2 and 3. Each company's fortunes rose and fell with the success or failure of its latest products, and even the biggest hits tended to have life cycles of only one or two years. In 1984, Coleco's sales, for example, rose from $597 million to $775 million, then declined to $501 million in 1986. Kenner Parker's sales rose from $539 million in 1983 to $648 million in 1984, before falling back to $503 million in 1986. Mattel's sales rose rapidly for two years and then stabilized for two years at about $1.06 billion. Tonka's sales, however, grew rapidly for four straight years.

Exhibit 4 provides a breakdown of total industry sales by product type. With the exception of games and puzzles, plush toys, and infant and preschool toys, estimated 1986 sales by category were flat or down by as much as 25 percent, as was the case with action figures, dolls, and electronic games. As a result, overall industry sales were down $27 million in 1986. Within each segment, the basic and technology-enhanced toys did well, and industry analysts expected retailers to limit inventory risk in 1987 by concentrating on those types.

Regarding the strength of the toy industry as it moved into 1987, a December 1986 report stated:

> Aggregate industry shipments remain flat. . . . The industry has essentially been unable to offset this softening with any meaningful new or exciting category of products.[1]

The toy industry also was susceptible to changes in demographics, in seasons, and in the economy. By early 1987, the factors that contributed to toy company sales were sending mixed messages. According to an August 1986 industry report:

> Demographic trends are increasing demand for toy products. A rising number of births is creating more toy recipients for the next 10 years. Also, an increasing percentage of births (over 40 percent) is now firstborn children, and more dollars (estimates as high as 45 percent more) are generally spent on firstborns. Finally, an expanding population of grandparents due to divorce and the increasing number of two-income families are resulting in more buyers with more money to spend on toys.[2]

As shown in Exhibit 5, the U.S. economy had just experienced its fourth straight year of economic growth. Growth of real gross national product was down, but so were unemployment and interest rates, and real per capita disposable income rose 2 percent in 1986.

THE COMPANY

Tonka Corporation was best known for its traditional line of sturdy metal toy trucks, bulldozers, backhoes, and construction vehicles, which were responsible for about $70 million of corporate sales in recent years. Over the past several years, however, the

---

[1] Steven Eisenberg, Bear, Stearns & Company, "Toy Industry Review," December 1986, p. 1.

[2] Keith J. DeVore and Stephen M. Carnes, "Piper, Jaffray & Hopwood Research Update," August 1986, p. 2.

company had diversified into other products, including dolls and other toys that would be more appealing to girls. One of Tonka's greatest successes over the past two years had been GoBots—small vehicles that could be changed into action figures; they competed directly with Hasbro's Transformers, which generally outsold them. GoBots contributed $132 million to sales in 1985; but, in 1986, even though 41 new characters were introduced, including large Super GoBots, and even though 33 episodes were added to the Saturday morning cartoon, *Challenge of the GoBots*, only $25 million worth were sold—a signal of the end of the product's life cycle. The company closed out the GoBots product line later in the year.

Even more successful for Tonka had been its line of Pound Puppies, which contributed $34 million to corporate sales in 1985 and $156 million (53 percent of sales) in 1986. Pound Puppies were plush toys with broad age appeal across genders. In addition, Tonka introduced Puppy Newborns, Super Pound Puppies, and Pound Purries in 1986, as well as such accessories as a doghouse, dog dish, and clothing.

As a result of its recent successes, built on its relatively nonvolatile sales of toy trucks, Tonka's revenues rose from $81 million in 1982 to $293 million in 1986. (Exhibit 6 gives the last three years' income statements.) Between 1982 and 1986, earnings per share rose from −$0.12 to $3.04, despite the stock offering of 1.1 million shares in December 1986. Between 1984 and 1986, return on assets rose from 6.9 to 14.1 percent, and return on average equity increased from 16.7 to 28.8 percent. Exhibit 7 provides information on Tonka's stock price during this growth period.

Tonka's consolidated balance sheets for 1985 and 1986 (Exhibit 8) indicated a rising current ratio (from 1.66 to 2.52). This liquidity stemmed not only from the company's strong sales but also from the December 1986 stock offering, which netted $22 million, or $20.27 per share. Exhibit 9 details the company's debt structure, which totaled $8.1 million and $8.2 million for the past two years.

COMPANY PROSPECTS

Stephen Shank, Tonka's president and chief executive officer, stated the greatest challenge facing the company:

> First, Tonka's performance is still too dependent on the success of a single line of products—be it GoBots in 1985 or Pound Puppies in 1986. The challenge is to expand our base of stable toys.[3]

Tonka reviewed between 3,000 and 4,000 new toy ideas each year. For 1987, the company's hopes were pinned on Pound Puppies, its traditional line of trucks, and the nine other toy lines described in the appendix. (See Exhibit 10 for current and projected Tonka sales by product line.) The company's objective was to increase the number of product lines to the point were no single toy would account for more than 25 percent of sales.

---

[3]Tonka Corporation 1986 annual report, p. 4.

One industry analyst stated, however:

After reviewing the company's 1987 line, we can find nothing particularly distinctive or exciting of a breakthrough nature that would dramatically enhance the company's industry presence or market share.[4]

As another challenge, Mr. Shank also said:

we have the need and the opportunity to build our sales base internationally, where Tonka's market share is much smaller than in the United States.[5]

The estimated $5 billion developed-country toy market was witnessing increased penetration by U.S. companies, except in Japan. In most markets, non-U.S. companies tended to be smaller and, therefore, had fewer strong brands and weaker marketing programs than U.S. companies. Exhibit 11 provides information on Tonka's domestic and international operations. The decline in international revenues and the resulting $100,000 operating loss (which led to a $1 million net loss) were primarily caused by a sharp decline in GoBot sales in Canada. Total sales in the United Kingdom and Australia improved in 1986. Management stated that Tonka's objective for its international business in 1987 was:

to achieve significant sales growth and a return to profitability. For the longer term, our goal is to build international sales to 30 percent of consolidated revenues compared with 11 percent in 1986. Our strategy is to continue to strengthen Tonka's position in its existing international markets, primarily Canada, the United Kingdom, and Australia, and to enter other major markets.[6]

In 1986, Tonka began to introduce other products in addition to its traditional line of trucks internationally, and it planned to make most of its toys available in its large international markets in 1987. The company also had just agreed to become the exclusive distributor in Australia and New Zealand for Bandai Company, Ltd., Japan's leading toy company.

CONCLUSION

Tonka's management wanted to determine what the possible financial results of different degrees of leverage might be. Exhibit 12 provides pro forma financial summaries for Tonka in 1986 under alternative capital structures. The exhibit assumes debt-to-total capital ratios of 20 percent, 40 percent, and 60 percent, which reflects the range of leverage for the major toy companies in 1986, as shown in Exhibit 2. It also assumes that the recapitalizations would have been achieved through stock repurchases. Revenues, cost of debt, and payout ratios are assumed to be the same as Tonka's actual 1986 results.

---

[4]Eisenberg, "Toy Industry Review," p. 8.
[5]1986 annual report, p. 4.
[6]Ibid., p. 8.

As part of its review, Tonka's management also studied the interest rate data provided in Exhibit 13. Management was trying to determine whether the company could use its financial resources more efficiently than at present; but in light of the cyclical and seasonal nature of the business and the company's dependence on strong toy introductions, it wanted Tonka to remain conservative.

Appendix

SALES PROSPECTS FOR 1987

Pound Puppies and Pound Purries, the company's line of plush toys, were to be supported by continued airing of an ABC-TV show and a feature-length movie, *Dog Days of Summer,* later in 1987. This product line was the company's strongest in 1986.

Keypers were plastic and plush characters for girls aged 4 to 10, based on a collection of greeting cards. Plastic Keypers had a hidden storage compartment and a large plastic key. Plush Keypers were more like handbags. They were introduced in the second quarter of 1986 and had good initial sales ($10 million, estimated).

Bathing Beauties and Hollywoods were for girls aged three and up. They both had hair that changed color either in warm water or by touch. Bathing Beauties, introduced in the third quarter of 1986, were 14-inch baby dolls, and newer Hollywoods were 5 inches long and had a modern, trendy appearance.

Love Me Tender was designed to be a girl's first doll. It was soft and frilly, to appeal to girls aged 18 months and older.

Aurora was a line of fashion dolls with shiny metallic or crystal-like bodies, long brightly colored hair, and gem-like eyes.

Maple Town was composed of a broad line of poseable vinyl miniature animal characters and play sets for children aged four to seven. Its introduction in Japan had been successful, and its sales in the United States were to be supported by a 52-part syndicated "Maple Town" TV show that would begin airing later in 1987.

SuperNaturals were the first action figures that used holographic technology (mirrors) to create three-dimensional images on the surface of photographic film. They were designed to appeal to boys five years and older.

Spiral Zone characters were futuristic action figures with accessories based on a military theme. The line was to be introduced through a 65-part syndicated TV show in the fall of 1987. Spiral Zone targeted boys aged 7 to 11.

Rock Lords, based on the GoBots theme, were rocks that sprouted heads (sometimes more than one), legs, and arms to become action figures. The toys were to be introduced through a movie, *GoBots: Battle of the Rock Lords,* to be released at Easter 1987; a comic book to be released at the same time; and 13 episodes of the "Challenge of the GoBots" TV series. Revenue estimates in 1986 were between $20 and $30 million.

Tonka Trucks had been the company's longest success. The company was estimated to hold about 75 percent of the mature, preschool toy truck market. Tonka began to raise the operation's gross margins in 1985. In 1986, it introduced a new line for even younger children: My First Tonka.

Steel Monsters, based on the Tonka Truck line, were designed to appeal to boys aged five to nine. They were similar in construction to the traditional line of trucks, but, with names like Assassin and Executioner, they looked like vehicles from the post-apocalyptic *Mad Max* movies. Revenue estimates in 1986 were between $10 and $20 million.

EXHIBIT 1   Percentage of Industry Sales by Company (dollars in millions)

	1982	*1983*	*1984*	*1985*	*Est. 1986*
Coleco Industries	7.8%	9.4%	10.2%	9.2%	6.0%
Hasbro, Inc.	2.1	3.5	9.4	14.7	16.1
Kenner Parker Toys*	NA	8.5	8.5	7.6	6.0
Mattel, Inc.†	21.1	9.9	11.6	12.5	12.6
Tonka Corporation	1.2	1.4	1.8	2.9	3.5
Subtotal for 5 largest toy companies	32.2%	32.7%	41.6%	46.9%	44.2%

* Kenner Parker was a wholly owned subsidiary of General Mills until November 1985.
† In 1982, Mattel sales included revenues from Ringling Brothers, Barnum & Bailey Circus.

Sources: Steven Eisenberg, Bear, Stearns & Company, "Toy Industry Review," December 1986, p. 1; and *Value Line Investment Survey.*

EXHIBIT 2 Comparative Financial Data, 1986 (dollars in millions, except per share data and stock prices)

	Coleco	Hasbro	Kenner Parker*	Mattel	Tonka
Sales	$500.7	$1,344.7	$502.8	$1,058.7	$293.4
Net income	(111.3)	99.2	16.0	(1.0)	22.3
Current assets	393.5	601.5	329.1	587.5	134.6
Current liabilities	287.7	272.4	109.0	252.5	53.5
Long-term debt	307.9	125.0	99.6	297.5	8.2
Net worth	(7.7)	580.3	199.7	152.4	96.3
Return on sales	NMF	7.4%	3.2%	NMF	7.6%
Return on equity	NMF	17.1	8.0	NMF	23.2
Earnings per share	($6.52)	$1.71	$1.22	($0.20)	$3.04
Dividends per share	0.00	0.09	0.00	0.00	0.07
Average P/E	NMF	14.0	16.8	NMF	8.1
Beta	1.30	1.15	N.A.†	1.20	1.10
Stock price range:					
High	$20.5	$30.9	$24.0	$15.5	$32.3
Low	8.3	16.6	15.1	7.8	15.9
Book value	$(0.5)	$10.4	$17.1	$ 2.5	$12.6

Note: NMF means not a meaningful figure.
* Current assets and current liabilities as of 3/29/87.
† Insufficient data were available to calculate a beta, because Kenner Parker had been a wholly owned subsidiary of General Mills until November 1985.

Source: *Value Line Investment Survey.*

EXHIBIT 3 Toy Industry—Company Sales (dollars in millions)

	1982	1983	1984	1985	1986
Coleco	$ 510.4	$596.5	$774.9	$ 776.0	$ 500.7
Hasbro	137.9	225.4	719.0	1,233.4	1,344.7
Kenner Parker	NA	539.3	648.1	638.3	502.8
Mattel	1,341.9	633.4	880.9	1,050.9	1,058.7
Tonka	81.1	87.8	139.0	244.4	293.4

Source: *Value Line Investment Survey.*

EXHIBIT 4   Toy Industry—Sales by Category (dollars in millions)

	1982	1983	1984	1985	Est. 1986
Action figures/dolls	$ 882	$1,036	$2,316	$3,000	$2,300
Electronic games	2,605	2,397	1,094	800	600
Games/puzzles	617	514	1,043	1,100	1,300
Cars, boats, planes, trains	752	707	789	800	850
Infant/preschool	459	508	715	900	1,000
Plush animals	281	300	544	800	1,300
Sports/outdoor	348	328	419	400	423
Arts/crafts/models	353	326	391	350	300
Riding toys	232	255	285	250	300
Total	$6,529	$6,371	$7,596	$8,400	$8,373

Source: Eisenberg, "Toy Industry Review," p. 1.

EXHIBIT 5   Summary U.S. Economic Data, 1980–1986

	Real GNP Growth	Per Capita Annualized Disposable Personal Income (1982 $)	Unemployment Rate*	Change in Consumer Price Index	Average Prime Lending Rate*	Net Merchandise Exports ($ in MM)
1980	−0.2%	$ 9,722	7.1%	13.5%	15.27%	($25,480)
1981	1.9	9,769	7.6	10.4	18.87	(27,978)
1982	−2.5	9,725	9.7	6.1	14.86	(36,444)
1983	3.6	9,930	9.6	3.2	10.79	(67,080)
1984	6.8	10,419	7.5	4.3	12.04	(112,522)
1985	3.0	10,622	7.2	3.6	9.93	(122,148)
1986	2.9	10,947	7.0	1.9	8.33	(144,339)
1986—Q1	5.4	10,842	7.1	(0.4)	9.00	(34,978)
Q2	0.6	11,024	7.1	0.3	8.50	(33,651)
Q3	1.4	10,968	7.0	0.5	7.50	(37,115)
Q4	1.5	10,956	6.7	0.6	7.50	(38,595)

* Quarterly figures are end of period.

Source: "Economic Report of the President."

EXHIBIT 6   Consolidated Income Statements (dollars in millions, except per share data)

	Fiscal Year		
	1984	1985	1986
Net revenues	$139.0	$244.4	$293.4
Cost of goods sold	93.9	131.9	159.3
Gross profit	45.1	112.5	134.1
Advertising expense	13.8	40.2	45.7
Selling, general, and administrative	19.4	29.9	43.1
Other expenses (income)	−1.9	2.6	1.2
Interest expense, net	5.5	3.6	3.8
Earnings before income taxes	8.3	36.2	40.3
Income taxes	3.3	16.7	18.0
Net earnings	$ 5.0	$ 19.5	$ 22.3
Net earnings per average share	$0.78	$2.99	$3.04
Shares outstanding (millions)	6.46	6.56	7.67

Source: Annual reports.

EXHIBIT 7   Common Stock Prices,* 1985–1986

	Tonka	S&P 500
1985 Jan	$21.250	179.63
Feb	29.750	181.18
Mar	15.750	180.66
Apr	18.750	179.83
May	20.375	189.55
June	21.750	191.85
July	29.750	190.92
Aug	26.875	188.63
Sept	22.750	182.08
Oct	23.500	189.82
Nov	28.625	202.54
Dec	27.500	211.28
1986 Jan	29.125	208.19
Feb	27.625	219.37
Mar	33.750	232.33
Apr	22.125	237.97
May	25.250	238.46
June	28.000	245.30
July	28.325	240.18
Aug	29.625	245.00
Sept	24.875	238.27
Oct	26.625	237.36
Nov	26.625	245.09
Dec†	19.875	248.61
1987 Jan: 2	20.500	246.45
9	21.325	258.73
16	21.625	266.28
23	22.625	270.10
30	23.000	274.08
Feb: 6	24.500	280.04

* Adjusted for 2-for-1 stock split July 15, 1985.
† 1.1 million share stock offering.

Source: *ISL Daily Stock Price Index.*

EXHIBIT 8 Consolidated Balance Sheets (dollars in millions)

	December 28, 1985	January 3, 1987
Cash and short-term investments	$ 22.9	$ 44.8
Accounts receivable, net	44.1	58.4
Inventories	25.7	20.8
Prepaid items	6.0	5.8
Other current assets	4.5	4.8
Total current assets	103.2	134.6
Property, plant, and equipment	53.0	56.5
Less: Accumulated depreciation	(33.1)	(34.1)
Net property, plant, and equipment	19.9	22.4
Other assets	0.2	1.6
Total assets	$123.3	$158.6
Accounts payable	$ 21.4	$ 17.6
Accrued liabilities	34.7	23.5
Current portion long-term debt	0.1	7.9
Other current liabilities	6.0	4.5
Total current liabilities	62.2	53.5
Long-term debt	8.1	8.2
Other liabilities	1.7	0.6
Total liabilities	72.0	62.3
Common equity	4.3	5.1
Additional paid-in capital	3.0	25.3
Retained earnings	46.4	68.2
Cumulative translation adjustments	(2.4)	−2.3
Total stockholders' equity	51.3	96.3
Total liabilities and equity	$123.3	$158.6

Source: 1987 annual report.

EXHIBIT 9   Debt Structure (dollars in millions)

	December 28, 1985	*January 3, 1987*
Bank term loan—interest due on a current basis 12.1%, due January 5, 1987	$ 7.8	$ 7.8
Revolving-credit agreement	—	8.0
Other notes	0.2	0.1
Total notes	8.0	15.9
Capital lease obligations	0.2	0.2
Total debt	8.2	16.1
Less amounts due within 1 year included in current portion of long-term debt	−0.1	−7.9
Total long-term debt	$ 8.1	$ 8.2

In January 1986, Tonka established a $20 million revolving-credit and term-loan facility. The company had the option of converting borrowings under the facility into term borrowings of up to five years at a time prior to December 31, 1987. The $8 million outstanding carried an average interest rate of 7.5 percent.

In 1986, Tonka had seasonal credit lines that allowed the company to borrow from $32.6 million to $80.3 million. At this time the company had $46.3 million of credit lines available.

Interest expense on all debt was $4.3 million in 1986 and $4.3 million in 1985.

Source: 1987 annual report.

EXHIBIT 10   Company Sales by Product (dollars in millions)

	1984	1985	1986E	1987E
Trucks	$ 73.7	$ 68.4	$ 73.0	$ 75.0
GoBots	52.8	132.0	25.0	10.0
Pound Pets	0.0	34.2	130.0	100.0
Rock Lords			30.0	15.0
Steel Monsters			10.0	15.0
Legions of Power			10.0	15.0
Keypers			12.0	20.0
Bathing Beauties and Hollywoods			10.0	30.0
Other*	13.0	9.8	15.0	90.0
Total	$139.5	$244.4	$315.0†	$370.0

* Includes licensing fees and incremental international sales in truck line.
† Actual sales in 1986 were $293.4 million.

Source: Keith J. DeVore and Stephen M. Carnes, "Piper, Jaffray & Hopwood Research Report," August 1986.

EXHIBIT 11   Summary of World Operations (millions of dollars)

	Fiscal Year		
	1984	*1985*	*1986*
Net revenues:			
United States	$117.2	$216.2	$265.5
International	25.8	33.4	32.0
Transfers	−4.0	−5.2	−4.1
Total net revenues	139.0	244.4	293.4
Operating profits:			
United States	10.6	39.4	45.4
International	1.3	3.0	−0.1
Total operating profits ...	11.9	42.4	45.3
Other	1.9	−2.6	−1.3
Interest, net	−5.5	−3.6	−3.7
Earnings before taxes	$ 8.3	$ 36.2	$ 40.3
Assets:			
United States	$ 57.2	$106.2	$141.7
International	14.9	17.1	16.9
Total assets	$ 72.1	$123.3	$158.6
Liabilities:			
United States	$ 34.4	$ 64.0	$ 54.8
International	5.8	8.0	7.6
Total liabilities	$ 40.2	$ 72.0	$ 62.4

Source: Annual reports.

EXHIBIT 12   Pro Forma Capitalization Changes, 1986 (dollars in millions, except per share data)

	Jan. 3, 1987 Actual	Debt/Total Capital 20%	Debt/Total Capital 40%	Debt/Total Capital 60%
EBIT	$ 44.1	$ 44.1	$ 44.1	$ 44.1
Interest expense—net (Note 1)	3.8	4.4	6.5	8.7
Earnings before taxes	40.3	39.7	37.6	35.4
Income taxes (45%)	18.0	17.9	16.9	16.0
Net income	$ 22.3	$ 21.9	$ 20.7	$ 19.5
Dividends (millions) (2)	$ 0.50	$ 0.49	$ 0.46	$ 0.44
Shares outstanding (millions)	7.67	7.38	6.37	5.47
Earnings per share (3)	$ 2.91	$ 2.96	$ 3.25	$ 3.56
Dividends per share (2,3)	$ 0.07	$ 0.07	$ 0.07	$ 0.07
Book value:				
Net working capital	$ 89.0	$ 89.0	$ 89.0	$ 89.0
Long-term assets	24.0	24.0	24.0	24.0
Total assets (4)	$113.0	$113.0	$113.0	$113.0
Debt (5)	16.7	22.7	45.2	67.8
Equity	96.3	90.3	67.8	45.2
Total capital	$113.0	$113.0	$113.0	$113.0
Market value:				
Net working capital	$ 89.0	$89.0	$89.0	$89.0
Long-term assets	75.7	75.7	75.7	75.7
PV of debt tax shield (45%)	7.5	10.2	20.4	30.5
Total assets	$172.2	$174.9	$185.0	$195.2
Debt (6)	16.7	22.7	45.2	67.8
Equity	155.5	152.2	139.8	127.4
Market value of capital	$172.2	$174.9	$185.0	$195.2
Price per share (7)	$20.27	$20.62	$21.94	$23.27
Shares repurchased (millions)	0.00	0.29	1.30	2.20

Assumes: (1) Interest expense of 9.5 percent on new debt + $3.8 million net interest on old debt (January 1986 prime lending rate).
(2) Dividends of 2.24 percent of earnings (actual 1986 rate).
(3) No dividends paid or earnings per share calculated on treasury stock.
(4) Total assets remain constant.
(5) The debt balance as of January 3, 1987, includes the $16.1 million of total debt indicated in Exhibit 9, plus $0.6 million of "other liabilities" indicated in Exhibit 8. The analyst assumed the other liabilities were fixed-interest obligations.
(6) Assumes market values of debt equal book values.
(7) Stock repurchase prices based on maintaining actual end-of-year 1986 company market value of net assets.

Source: Casewriter estimates.

EXHIBIT 13 Interest Rates and Yields

	Treasuries					Moody's		Prime Lending
	Bills		Notes & Bonds					
	3-Mo.	1-Yr.	3-Yr.	10-Yr.	20-Yr.	Aaa	Baa	
1982	10.61	11.07	12.92	13.00	12.92	13.79	16.11	14.86
1983	8.61	8.80	10.45	11.10	11.34	12.04	13.55	10.79
1984	9.52	9.92	11.89	12.44	12.48	12.71	14.19	12.04
1985	7.48	7.81	9.64	10.62	10.97	11.37	12.72	9.93
1986 Jan	7.04	7.31	8.41	9.19	9.59	10.05	11.44	9.50•
Feb	7.06	7.11	8.10	8.70	9.08	9.67	11.11	9.50
Mar	6.56	6.59	7.30	7.78	8.09	9.00	10.50	9.00
Apr	6.06	6.06	6.86	7.30	7.50	8.79	10.19	8.50
May	6.15	6.25	7.27	7.71	7.81	9.08	10.29	8.50
June	6.21	6.32	7.41	7.80	7.69	9.13	10.34	8.50
July	5.83	5.90	6.86	7.30	7.29	8.88	10.16	8.00
Aug	5.53	5.60	6.49	7.17	7.28	8.72	10.18	7.50
Sept	5.21	5.45	6.62	7.45	7.56	8.89	10.20	7.50
Oct	5.18	5.41	6.56	7.43	7.61	8.86	10.24	7.50
Nov	5.35	5.48	6.46	7.25	7.42	8.68	10.07	7.50
Dec	5.53	5.55	6.43	7.11	7.28	8.49	9.97	7.50
1987 Jan	5.43	5.46	6.41	7.08	7.25	8.36	9.72	7.50

Source: *Federal Reserve Bulletin.*

$$20 \quad \begin{array}{l} 20.62 \\ 20.75 \end{array}$$

$$\begin{array}{l} \times \\ 40 \end{array} \quad 21.99$$

$$\frac{20}{40-x} = \frac{1.32}{1.19}$$

$$20 = 1.11(40-x)$$

Coleco Industries, Inc.

Coleco's chief financial officer, Paul Meyer, had to devise a capital-restructuring plan to put the company back on its feet. Just a couple of years earlier, Coleco could not make its smash-hit Cabbage Patch Kids fast enough to keep up with demand. Now, March 1988, the Cabbage Patch craze was spent, and Coleco had not come up with any new blockbuster products. The company's annual sales were two thirds of what they had been only two years earlier, which resulted in losses that contributed to its negative equity position of $84 million.

Coleco's capital position was precarious, and impatient creditors were wary of lending any more to the firm, which was going into default on its loans.[1] In its present condition, new equity from outsiders was virtually out of the question. As shown in Exhibit 1, the company's stock price had ranged between $22.25 and $8.125 from 1984 through 1986 (when the company had a loss of $111 million). As losses continued to mount, the stock price fell to its year-end 1987 price of $3.625. By March 1988, following announcement of an annual loss of $105 million, the stock reached a low of $2.50 per share. The issue with which Mr. Meyer and the rest of Coleco's board had to wrestle was how to restructure the company's capital in a way that would satisfy its creditors without diluting the stock any further than was necessary.

THE TOY INDUSTRY

Toy companies depended on several factors for success: the economy, demographic changes, seasonality, and successful product introductions on a regular basis. In the mid-1980s, the first two factors tended to favor toy manufacturers. In 1988, the economy was

---

[1] Coleco announced that it might miss interest payments of $10 million due on debentures on April 1, 1988, and another $4 million due on May 1. The company also was not in compliance with most of the covenants for its $30 million revolving-credit facility.

This case was written by Casey S. Opitz under the direction of Robert F. Bruner.
Copyright © 1988 by the Darden Graduate Business School Foundation, Charlottesville, VA.

entering its sixth year of overall strength, and unemployment and interest rates were at their lowest in years. Demographics also were favorable; birth rates were increasing, and over 40 percent were of firstborn children. The expanding population of grandparents and two-income families led to more potential buyers. The Christmas season tended to be the most important for toy manufacturers. To reduce seasonality, the larger toy companies were spending more on advertising throughout the year, and retailers tended to devote more shelf space to those manufacturers.

The last factor, successful product introductions, was perhaps the most important. Of the approximately 800 toy companies in the United States, only the largest were able to minimize sales and profit volatility through diversification, but, as shown in Exhibits 2 and 3, even they were not always successful. Each company's fortunes rose and fell with the strength of its new products, and even the biggest hits tended to have product lives of only one or two years.

In an attempt to reduce volatility through diversification, the toy industry had begun to consolidate. In 1984, Hasbro acquired Milton Bradley, and in 1985 it acquired certain assets of another toy company, Child Guidance. In 1987, Tonka acquired Kenner Parker Toys, which, prior to November 1985, had been a wholly owned subsidiary of General Mills. In 1986 alone, Coleco had acquired two companies (including Selchow & Righter,[2] the producer of Scrabble and of the blockbuster board game of 1984, Trivial Pursuit), the product line of another company, and the North American subsidiary of Tomy Kogyo, a toy company that specialized in high-technology applications.

Sales for the entire toy industry remained flat in 1987 as a result of lack of exciting new toy introductions. Basic and technology-enhanced toys did well, so retailers were attempting to reduce their risks by concentrating on those toys.

THE COMPANY

Coleco Industries, headquartered in West Hartford, Connecticut, was the third largest toy manufacturer in the United States. In addition to Cabbage Patch Kids, its line of toys included plush Alf dolls and puppets based on the television show character ($75 million in sales in 1987), Couch Potato Pals (plush potatoes with which to sit on the sofa and watch TV), and playsets based on TV programs, "The Flintstones," "Sesame Street," and "Sylvanian Families." But sales were weak. One analyst called Coleco the "high-wire act of the toy industry," citing its recovery from disaster on two previous occasions.[3] The first was the introduction of ColecoVision in response to the failure of the Telstar video game in the late 1970s. The second was the introduction of Cabbage Patch Kids

---

[2]Coleco acquired Selchow & Righter for $60 million, but Trivial Pursuit had just peaked, with sales of $300 million in 1984. By the end of 1987, its annual sales were $15 million. The prospects for increasing the company's sales based on its current product line were limited.

[3]This, and following quote, from Joseph Pereira, "Coleco Is Looking for Lettuce as Cabbage Patch Wilts," *The Wall Street Journal*, March 18, 1988, p. 4.

in response to the failure of Adam, Coleco's home computer product. Observers were skeptical of Coleco's ability to recover a third time:

> Can Coleco come up with a winner to revive it a third time? The outlook isn't promising. Coleco had high hopes for Rambo, the boys' action figure based on the Sylvester Stallone movie character, but it flopped. So did Wrinkles, a plush animal made by a company that Coleco bought. And Starcom, a space-age action figure, appears to be burning out.

Exhibit 4 details Coleco's sales by product and an analyst's estimates for 1988.

FINANCIAL PERFORMANCE

Coleco's financial statements are provided in Exhibits 5 and 6. As late as December 1987, industry analysts were projecting minimal losses for the company, but as shown in Exhibit 7, fourth-quarter 1987 losses totaled $99 million, as the negative effects of the October 19 stock market crash dampened Christmas sales and the ensuing corporate retrenchment program created write-offs.[4]

The company's problems were compounded by the financial constraints it operated under, which disrupted production. Coleco estimated that fourth-quarter shipments were at least $15 million less than they would have been had adequate working-capital financing been available.

At year-end 1987, Coleco had $460 million of debt outstanding on an equity base of negative $84 million. The company had lines of credit totaling $189.9 million, including a $150 million line with a group of foreign banks that allowed the company to borrow against receivables, and a $30 million revolving-credit line with Connecticut National Bank and National Bank of Canada that allowed it to borrow against receivables and inventory. The revolver's credit agreement contained various covenants regarding maintenance of working capital, net worth, and pretax income, ratio of debt to net worth, restrictions on unsecured indebtedness, and a prohibition of payment of cash dividends. Coleco was not in compliance with most of these restrictions, but the creditor banks had amended the agreement "to eliminate the violations at that date and to take into consideration the projected financial condition of the Company at the end of the first quarter of 1988," according to the company's annual report.

Coleco generally borrowed as much as it could under these lines throughout 1987 at interest rates averaging 9.5 percent, as shown in Exhibit 8. The $150 million credit agreement was set to expire on April 15, 1988, but the company was negotiating with a

---

[4]The company reported that, "More than 40 percent of the fourth quarter loss was attributable to reserves established and charges taken related to cost reduction efforts, modifying the company's distribution channels and contracting certain product lines to assure greater operating efficiency." Staff was reduced by 300 people, or by almost 25 percent, between November 1987 and March 1988. These reductions were expected to eliminate $70 million from operating costs in 1988.

group of foreign banks to extend the agreement for one year for $135 million. The $30 million credit was to expire on May 1, 1988, and renewal negotiations for it were also underway with a group of domestic banks.[5] As shown in Exhibit 8, the company also had $10.8 million of mortgage and equipment term loans at rates up to 2.5 percent over prime.

As shown in Exhibit 1, in March 1988, the 11.125 percent and 14.375 percent debentures traded around prices of $27.00 and $34.25, respectively.[6] Coleco also had $80 million in convertible subordinated debentures outstanding. The 11 percent convertibles were issued at a maturity value of $55 million and had a conversion price of $13.75 per common share. If remaining debentures outstanding were to be converted, the company would have to issue 3.54 million shares of stock. Coleco could terminate the convertibility of the debentures if the value of the company's stock exceeded 150 percent of the conversion price for 20 straight days. These debentures traded around a price of $38 in March 1988.

The 6.5 percent convertibles were issued at a maturity value of $44.48 million and had a yield to maturity at the date of issue of 10.4 percent; interest was payable in Swiss francs. The conversion price was $17.125 per common share. If remaining debentures were to be converted, Coleco would have to issue 1.72 million shares. The company could redeem the debentures if the stock price were over $20.55 for 25 days. These debentures were not widely traded in the first quarter of 1988.

In February 1987, MCA, Inc., a motion picture company, bought $20 million of the company's preferred stock (22,223 shares) that would convert to 2.2 million shares of common stock on January 1, 1995. MCA had sued Coleco over its use of the name Donkey Kong for one of its games, because MCA held the rights to the King Kong movies; Coleco had then countersued in an attempt to recoup royalties it already had paid MCA. The stock acquisition resolved the dispute, and MCA agreed not to purchase any more stock in the company for eight years without Coleco's approval.

The investment made MCA one of the largest equity investors and legally an "insider" (23 percent of common) in the company; Coleco chairman Arnold Greenberg owned 16 percent. Insiders owned a total of 25.3 percent, and holders of 5 percent or more owned a total of 41.2 percent. Mr. Greenberg's brother, Leonard, a private investor not directly associated with the company, owned 9.7 percent. Institutions owned 11.4 percent.

In August 1987, Coleco issued 644,295 shares of common stock worth $6 million as final payment of a 1985 settlement related to an Adam computer lawsuit against the company and several officers. In October 1987, the company's shareholders increased the number of authorized preferred shares from 300,000 to 12 million.

---

[5]"Coleco's 4th-Period Loss Is $98.8 Million; Toy Maker May Miss Interest Payment," *The Wall Street Journal,* March 15, 1988, p. 10.

[6]According to a company analyst, based on monthly data for the previous two years, the annual volatility of the 11.125 percent debenture was 41.1 percent; the annual volatility of the 14.375 percent debt was 43.1 percent. Weekly data for the past seven months suggested that the annual volatility of Coleco's common stock was 64.7 percent.

ALTERNATIVES

Mr. Meyer sifted through this financial information in an effort to find some means of satisfying management, creditors, and shareholders. Should the company continue with business as usual, in the hope that one or more of its products would do well? He wondered whether liquidation was an alternative, especially given the numbers and classes of creditors (as shown in Exhibit 9); it would certainly get to be a very messy process. Also, it had been suggested that the company might be able to merge with another firm; Mr. Meyer wondered whether there might be some latent value in the company's assets. Alternatively, Coleco could issue more equity, but the market price would have to be right. Finally, the company could financially restructure. This would involve the renegotiation of debts, either through a debt/equity swap or the issuance of common stock or warrants. This also would mean that the old shareholders' shares would be badly diluted. Bankruptcy could be a part of either the liquidation or restructuring option. Relevant interest rate data are provided in Exhibits 10 and 11. Coleco's debt was rated CCC+ by Standard & Poor's.

EXHIBIT 1   Stock and Bond Price Data

	Stock Price				Closing Bond Prices		S&P Long-Term Govt.
	High	*Low*	*Close*	*S&P 500*	*11.125%*	*14.375%*	*Bond Index*
1984	$22.250	$ 9.625	$12.125	167.24	—	$ 90.125	40.29
1985	21.500	10.125	16.000	211.28	—	101.875	48.93
1986	20.500	8.125	8.375	242.17	$81.875	100.875	58.04
1987 Apr	11.625	10.000	10.375	288.36	82.000	99.500	60.69
May	10.750	9.875	10.500	290.10	77.750	96.500	51.55
June	11.625	10.250	10.625	304.00	76.000	95.000	52.42
July	11.000	9.750	9.750	318.66	94.000	95.000	51.89
Aug	10.375	9.125	9.375	329.80	75.625	98.625	50.40
Sept	10.250	8.500	9.125	321.83	76.125	96.000	47.39
Oct	9.125	4.250	5.500	251.79	72.000	94.375	47.17
Nov	6.000	4.375	4.625	230.30	55.250	68.875	50.31
Dec	4.625	3.625	3.875	247.08	50.000	63.500	49.89
1988 Jan	4.250	3.125	3.500	257.07	41.500	50.000	51.28
Feb	3.500	2.625	3.000	267.82	41.750	54.125	53.67
March 14			2.500	266.37	27.000	34.250	52.50

Sources: Datext; *Moody's Bond Record; Standard & Poor's Bond Guide;* and *Standard & Poor's Statistical Service.*

EXHIBIT 2   Comparative Financial Data, 1987 (dollars in millions, except per share data)

	Coleco	Hasbro*	Mattel	Tonka
Sales	$504.5	$1,345.1	$1,020.1	$382.6
Net income	(105.4)	48.2	(114.6)	(7.5)
Current assets	334.8	692.6	546.4	324.3
Current liabilities	311.4	303.9	322.6	234.9
Long-term debt	304.9	127.1	226.2	526.2
Net worth	(84.9)	641.5	104.5	95.8
Return on sales	NMF	3.6%	NMF	NMF
Return on equity	NMF	7.5%	NMF	NMF
Earnings per share	($6.08)	$0.82	$2.41	($0.97)
Dividends per share	0.00	0.09	0.00	0.06
Average P/E	NMF	25.4	NMF	NMF
Beta	1.35	1.15	1.20	1.10
Stock price range:				
High	$12.6	$26.5	$15.9	$25.0
Low	3.6	10.0	6.4	7.4
Book value	$(4.8)	$11.4	$2.2	$12.4

* *Value Line* estimates.
Note: NMF means not a meaningful figure.

Sources: *Value Line Investment Survey,* annual reports.

EXHIBIT 3   Selected Toy Company Sales (dollars in millions)

	1982	1983	1984	1985	1986	1987
Coleco	$ 510.4	$596.5	$774.9	$ 776.0	$ 500.7	$ 504.5
Hasbro*	137.9	225.4	719.0	1,233.4	1,344.7	1,345.1
Kenner Parker†	NA	539.3	648.1	638.3	502.8	NA
Mattel‡	1,341.9	633.4	880.9	1,050.9	1,058.7	1,020.1
Tonka†	81.1	87.8	139.0	244.4	293.4	382.6

* Hasbro acquired Milton Bradley in 1984.
† Tonka acquired Kenner Parker in October 1987.
‡ Mattel sold Ringling Brothers, Barnum & Bailey Circus combined shows in 1982. Figure for 1982 includes Ringling revenues.

Source: *Value Line Investment Survey.*

EXHIBIT 4   Sales and Estimates by Product (dollars in millions)

	1983	1984	1985	1986	1987E	1988E
Cabbage Patch	$ 67	$540	$600	$230	$125	$125
Electronics	404	100	56	5		
Pools, furniture, ride-ons	125	135	90	70	75	80
Sectaurs			30	10		
Furskins				60	15	
Wrinkles				25	10	
Rambo				30	10	
Play/learn				25	30	35
Lakeside				10	15	15
Selchow & Righter				35	40	45
Total	$596	$775	$776	$500	$320	$300
U.S. Space Force					40	20
Alf					75	50
Tomy preschool					40	40
Flintstone Kids					10	15
Aurora car racing					10	10
Ride-ons, Tomy					30	30
Sylvanian Families					30	20
Tomy, other					15	15
Total					$570	$500
New products, 1988						$125

Source: Oppenheimer & Co., Inc., Toy Industry Report, November 27, 1987.

EXHIBIT 5 Consolidated Income Statements (dollars in thousands, except per share data)

	For the Years Ended December 31							
	1980	1981	1982	1983	1984	1985	1986	1987
Sales	$162,907	$178,031	$510,380	$596,498	$774,860	$776,002	$500,658	$504,483
Cost of goods sold	97,595	115,172	279,840	403,793	504,650	407,458	320,565	325,535
SG&A	38,539	44,925	135,386	197,959	201,598	249,297	254,970	224,742
Interest expense	3,672	4,470	9,707	19,595	39,188	26,435	42,747	59,557
Loss from disposition of Adam					118,602			
Earnings (loss) before taxes and extraordinary credit	23,101	13,464	85,447	(24,849)	(89,178)	92,812	(117,624)	(105,351)
Income tax (benefit)	10,064	5,753	40,551	(17,416)	(9,360)	28,597	(6,375)	
Earnings (loss) after tax and before extraordinary credit	13,037	7,711	44,896	(7,433)	(79,818)	64,215	(111,249)	(105,351)
Extraordinary credit from use of tax loss carryforwards	3,612					18,700		
Net earnings (loss)	$ 16,649	$ 7,711	$ 44,896	($ 7,433)	($ 79,818)	$ 82,915	($111,249)	($105,351)
Per share results:								
Primary earnings	$2.33	$1.01	$2.90	($0.48)	($4.95)	$5.00	($6.52)	($6.08)
Fully diluted earnings	$2.33	$1.01	$2.90	($0.48)	($4.95)	$4.05	($6.52)	($6.08)
Number of shares (000)	7,515	7,649	15,298	16,014	16,155	16,998	17,140	17,802

Source: annual reports.

EXHIBIT 6 Consolidated Balance Sheets, at December 31 (dollars in thousands)

	1980	1981	1982	1983	1984	1985	1986	1987
Cash & equivalents	$11,765	$ 7,749	$ 52,474	$ 5,931	$ 1,506	$110,734	$ 82,483	$ 34,633
Accounts receivable, net	13,766	21,236	107,803	158,022	206,712	100,314	161,481	196,684
Inventories	29,933	42,629	69,149	164,664	86,474	40,672	78,662	67,486
Other	2,742	3,502	21,489	78,473	30,716	53,893	70,851	36,039
Total current assets	58,206	75,116	250,915	407,090	325,408	305,613	393,477	334,842
Property, net	16,869	20,340	31,893	58,183	49,947	49,912	63,910	60,377
Other assets	4,142	3,939	3,057	12,259	13,649	42,016	134,003	140,338
Total assets	$79,217	$99,395	$285,865	$477,532	$389,004	$397,541	$591,390	$535,557
Current long-term debt	$ 1,044	$ 1,194	$ 3,604	$ 3,669	$ 5,087	$ 5,784	$ 10,320	$ 10,023
Notes payable	7,689	19,130	64,388	166,420	106,047	35,382	115,588	142,114
Accounts payable	13,079	13,628	53,316	81,385	86,358	77,129	51,704	74,501
Other				47,839	46,606		110,108	84,774
Total current liabilities	21,812	33,952	121,308	299,313	244,098	118,295	287,720	311,412

Senior long-term debt	9,585	16,388	21,670	28,594	26,485	16,604	17,075	17,499
Deferred liabilities	3,523	3,420	27,002	700	10,028	3,075	901	723
Subordinated debentures	215,359	213,722	52,445	52,359	52,287	52,225		
Convert. subord. debent.	79,949	77,804	75,777	52,751				
Total liabilities	619,828	599,054	295,189	378,502	388,113	193,212	51,928	40,034
Preferred stock; 22,224 shares	22							7,515
Common stock	17,802	17,140	16,998	16,155	16,014	15,298	7,649	
Common stock subscribed		11	157	416				
Capital in excess of par value	48,642	23,284	22,222	13,241	10,035	6,427	12,942	12,503
Retained earnings (deficit)	(150,737)	(48,099)	62,975	(19,310)	63,370	70,928	26,876	19,165
Total equity (deficit)	(84,271)	(7,664)	102,352	10,502	89,419	92,653	47,467	39,183
Total liabilities & equity	$535,557	$591,390	$397,541	$389,004	$477,532	$285,865	$99,395	$79,217

Source: Annual reports.

EXHIBIT 7   Quarterly Financial Performance (dollars in thousands)

	Sales	Gross Profit (Loss)	Net Earnings (Loss)	Earnings/Share
1986 1	$113,418	$ 61,934	$ 5,738	$0.34
2	127,778	53,655	1,058	0.06
3	185,715	66,337	(7,473)	(0.44)
4	73,747	(1,833)	(110,572)	(6.48)
Year	500,658	180,093	(111,249)	(6.52)
1987 1	124,470	47,629	(8,899)	(0.52)
2	146,069	64,836	752	0.04
3	164,978	78,992	1,554	0.09
4	68,966	(12,509)	(98,758)	(5.69)
Year	504,483	178,948	(105,351)	(6.08)

Source: Annual reports.

EXHIBIT 8 Liquidity and Long-Term Debt* (dollars in thousands)

Lines of Credit

	1986	1987
Average amount outstanding	$ 33,886	$ 89,737
Maximum amount outstanding	100,803	170,733
Average effective interest rate	8.8%	9.5%
Effective year-end interest rate	8.4%	9.7%

Senior Long-Term Debt

	1986	1987	Amortization of Senior Debt	
11% term loan due 1988	$ 5,929	$ 2,879	1988	$8,881
Mortgage, building, and equipment loans			1989	1,779
due through 1998	14,070	10,786	1990	764
Capitalized lease obligations	6,709	5,943	1991	433
	26,708	19,608	1992	283
Current portion	(10,320)	(10,023)		
Senior long-term debt	$ 16,388	$ 9,585		

Subordinated Debentures

	1986	1987	Sinking Fund Payments on Sub. Debentures	
11.125% subordinated debentures due			1992	$ 0
2001	$161,177	$162,696	1993	6,050
			1994	6,050
			1995	6,050
14.375% subordinated debentures due			1996	33,605
2002	52,545	52,663	1997	33,605
Subordinated debentures	$213,722	$215,359		

Convertible Subordinated Debentures

	1986	1987	Conversion Value of Sub. Debentures
11% convertible subordinated debentures			
due 1989	$ 47,487	$ 47,948	3.54 MM shares
6.5% convertible subordinated debentures due 1993	30,317	32,001	1.72 MM shares
Convertible subordinated debentures	$ 77,804	$ 79,949	

* In addition, Coleco had to make lease payments of between $4.4 million and $5.9 million a year between 1988 and 1992.

Source: Annual reports.

EXHIBIT 9 Creditors

Secured Debt

Largest Creditors	Approximate Amount
Connecticut National Bank and National Bank of Canada	$30 million
Credit Suisse de National, Banque Indo Suez, and 3 others	$68 million

Unsecured Debt Securities
($295.3 million; 650 holders)

Trustee	Securities
Midlantic National Bank	11% and 6.5% convertible subordinated; $77.9 million
U.S. Trust	14⅜% and 11⅛% subordinated; $215.4 million

Other Liabilities
($135.2 million; 1,200+ creditors)

Largest Creditors	Approximate Amount
Kader Industries (Hong Kong)	$4.0 million
Applied Electronics	3.4
Original Appalachian Artworks (Cabbage Patch creator)	2.5
Sunshine Garment (Hong Kong)	2.3
Kam Toys (Hong Kong)	1.9
Basel Jacobs (advertising)	1.8
Barry & Lloyd	1.6
Concorde Express	1.5
Wah Shing Toys (Hong Kong)	1.3
Texas Instruments	1.1
Rapid Industries Plastics	1.1
McLaren, Morris, & Todd, Ltd (Canada)	1.0
Admerex International	1.0
Jet Speed	0.9
Children's T.V. Workshop	0.8
1st America Bank of New York	0.8
Perfekta Enterprises (Hong Kong)	0.8
D & E Packaging	0.8
Scott Lancaster Mills (Los Angeles)	0.7
Rand Whitney Container Corp.	0.7

Source: Gary Jacobson, Kidder Peabody.

EXHIBIT 10   Interest Rates and Yields

| | Treasuries | | | | Moody's | | | 3-Month LIBOR on |
| | Bills | | Notes & Bonds | | | | Prime | U.S. $ |
	3-Mo.	1-Yr.	3-Yr.	10-Yr.	Aaa	Baa	Lending	Deposits
1982	10.61	11.07	12.92	13.00	13.79	16.11	14.86	13.29
1983	8.61	8.80	10.45	11.10	12.04	13.55	10.79	9.72
1984	9.52	9.92	11.89	12.44	12.71	14.19	12.04	10.94
1985	7.48	7.81	9.64	10.62	11.37	12.72	9.93	8.40
1986	5.98	6.08	7.06	7.68	9.02	10.39	8.33	8.86
1987 Jan	5.43	5.46	6.41	7.08	8.36	9.72	7.50	6.21
Feb	5.59	5.63	6.56	7.25	8.38	9.65	7.50	6.43
March	5.59	5.68	6.58	7.25	8.36	9.61	7.50	6.49
April	5.64	6.09	7.32	8.02	8.85	10.04	7.75	6.87
May	5.66	6.52	8.02	8.61	9.33	10.51	8.00	7.35
June	5.67	6.35	7.82	8.40	9.32	10.52	8.25	7.23
July	5.69	6.24	7.74	8.45	9.42	10.61	8.25	7.00
Aug	6.04	6.54	8.03	8.76	9.67	10.80	8.25	7.04
Sept	6.40	7.11	8.67	9.42	10.18	11.31	8.75	7.63
Oct	6.13	7.05	8.75	9.52	10.52	11.62	9.25	8.39
Nov	5.69	6.50	7.99	8.86	10.01	11.23	9.00	7.53
Dec	5.77	6.69	8.13	8.99	10.11	11.29	8.75	7.98
1988 Jan	5.81	6.52	7.87	8.67	9.88	11.07	8.75	7.26
Feb	5.66	6.21	7.38	8.21	9.40	10.62	8.50	6.84

Sources: *Federal Reserve Bulletin, International Financial Statistics,* and "Economic Report of the President."

EXHIBIT 11 Selected Bond Yields

Company	Rating*	Form of Debt	Coupon	Mat. Date	Current Yield	Yield to Maturity
Champion Int'l	BBB	Notes	8.625	1996	9.02	9.41
Chrysler Corp.	BBB−	Sinking fund debent.	10.950	2017	10.53	10.50
Chrysler Fin.	BBB−	Subordinated notes	9.300	1994	9.49	9.72
Great Amer. Comm.	CCC+	Senior sub. debent.	14.375	1999	13.82	13.67
Great Amer. Comm.	CCC	Sen. sub. sf. nts.	9.000	1993	10.59	13.08
Harcourt Brace J. ...	CCC+	Senior sub. debent.	13.750	1999	12.73	12.42
Hutton, E. F.	BBB−	Notes	8.500	1991	8.59	8.86
Interlogic Trace	CCC+	Subordinated debent.	11.990	1996	16.89	19.05
Maxus Energy	BBB−	Notes	10.500	1995	10.47	10.45
McCrory Corp.	CCC−	Senior subord. notes	15.750	1991	17.03	18.85
McCrory Corp.	CCC−	Sen. sf. debent.	7.750	1995	12.86	17.42
Occidental	BBB	Senior debentures	11.750	2011	11.11	11.05
S'mark	CCC+	Senior subord. notes	13.250	1994	20.54	—
TWA	CCC	Sub. sf. debent.	5.000	1994	7.35	12.99
Western Union	CCC−	Sinking fund debent.	8.100	1998	15.88	19.08

* According to *Standard & Poor's Bond Guide,* "Debt rated BBB is regarded as having an adequate capacity to pay interest and repay principal . . . adverse economic conditions or changing circumstances are more likely to lead to a weakened capacity to pay interest and repay principal. . . . Debt rated . . . CCC . . . is regarded, on balance, as predominantly speculative with respect to capacity to pay interest and repay principal. . . ."

Source: *Standard & Poor's Bond Guide,* March 1988.

Johnstown Corporation

In March 1988, Jack Sheehan sat in a comfortable chair in the living room of his Georgetown, Washington, D.C., home telling, almost like he would a war story, the history of the small steel mill he owned. The initial years of Johnstown Corporation, the former Johnstown Works of U.S. Steel Corporation, had been one battle after another—negotiating wage concessions with workers, searching for new customers during the six-month U.S. Steel strike (at a time when sales to U.S. Steel accounted for nearly one half the company's total sales), and arguing with local bankers over the acceptability (as part of loan guarantees) of receivables due from integrated steel producers facing possible bankruptcy.

Now, after six profitable quarters, the company was preparing to add the first injection of long-term private capital into its financial structure since its incorporation in 1984. The issue Jack Sheehan faced in the spring of 1988 was what source of capital to pursue. The company's size—revenues were below $35 million—definitely limited options, but Mr. Sheehan, as majority shareholder and chairman of Johnstown Corporation's board of directors, wanted to consider all the options available at the time.

He had engaged Bill Stiles, an independent financial consultant, to investigate a private placement of 10-year senior notes with warrants. Mr. Stiles's initial report stated that Johnstown Corporation could raise its required $7.5 million at 13 percent. (Additional terms of the placement are discussed later in the case.) Another option Mr. Sheehan was interested in evaluating was an initial public offering of Johnstown Corporation's stock through a regional investment bank. Or perhaps now was the time to sell the entire company to another firm.

Robert F. Bruner adapted this case from a supervised business study written by Renee Weaver under the direction of William W. Sihler.

THE COMPANY

History.   Just two days after Christmas 1983, U.S. Steel announced the closing of some 50 unprofitable units, among which was the Johnstown, Pennsylvania, plant, operated by U.S. Steel since 1901. In April 1984, Jack Sheehan, a Johnstown native, Harvard Business School graduate, and successful small business entrepreneur, was introduced by Johnstown civic leaders to an investment group made up of three members of the plant's top management. After reviewing the situation, Mr. Sheehan agreed to commit the necessary capital, time, and managerial expertise to make the mill a viable source of employment in Johnstown. The plant began operating as Johnstown Corporation in July 1984.

Taking advantage of existing facilities and a well-trained labor force that operated at one half the cost of operation under U.S. Steel management, Johnstown management positioned the company as a niche player in the industry. Along with obtaining a defendable position as a specialty steel producer, the company also was committed to providing employment in the depressed western Pennsylvania area in which the plant was located. A portion of the company's initial debt came with employment-target covenants in exchange for below-market interest rates.

Product Lines and Sales.   Johnstown Corporation sold a variety of cast and fabricated steel products to over 35 steel and other heavy industry customers. The percentage of sales in each major product category for the years 1985–88 is shown in Exhibit 1. Six product managers located in Johnstown oversaw each of six product categories: rolling mill rolls, steel castings, fabrications, mill liners, continuous caster rolls, and batch annealing diffuser bases. The company employed five outside salesmen located in Philadelphia, Pittsburgh, Birmingham (Alabama), and Chicago on straight salary. An independent sales representative serviced seven rolling mill accounts in Pennsylvania, West Virginia, Ohio, Kentucky, and Canada.

The vast majority of the company's sales were to integrated steel producers (USX and Bethlehem Steel together accounted for 65 percent in 1985, 49 percent in 1986, and 42 percent of sales in 1987) and mini-mills. These buyers were very different types of customers. The integrated producers tended to multi-source orders, which made them less price-sensitive consumers than the mini-mills; they also tended to place more value on their long-standing supplier relationshps. Mini-mills tended to be price sensitive, and, though they relied on a single supplier, they were more likely to consider purchasing from foreign suppliers.

The company's chief product was rolling mill rolls, which accounted for nearly half of net sales in 1987. The company produced steel rolls for use in the formation of hot- and cold-rolled steel products. The company estimated its margins on steel rollers at 32 percent. The company ranked itself second, with a 17 percent share, in the $35 million mini-mill roll market.

Continuous caster rolls were used to channel molten steel as it was cooled during the casting process. Repair and remachining of rolls was required on a regular basis. Johnstown Corporation provided this refurbishment, in addition to preparation of new rolls, to its customers who did not have the in-house capability to refurbish rolls. Company officials estimated margins on continuous cast rolls at 12 percent. The market for new rolls was approximately $25 million in 1987, so Johnstown's sales gave it about a 13 percent share.

Johnstown Corporation produced both machined (finished) and nonmachined (rough) steel castings in a variety of sizes from 3,000 to 100,000 pounds for a diverse group of customers, including steel makers, cement producers, shipbuilders, automotive manufacturers, extrusion-press operators, and rock and coal crushers. The company estimated the total potential slag pot portion of the castings market at $5 million and its share in the manufacture of small pots (those under 60,000 lbs.) to be 80 percent. Margins on rough castings were approximately 18 percent; margins on finished castings fell to just 2 percent.

Mill liner is a rolled steel liner plate and lift bar used in industrial grinding machines for grinding cement, pulverizing coal, and grinding high-silica sand for glass production. Johnstown Corporation produced mill liners from purchased parts at margins of 40 percent.

Facilities and Operations. All of Johnstown Corporation's production took place at the company's sole facility in Johnstown. The plant housed two electric furnaces, used to melt scrap metal for production (for a total melting capacity of 67 tons). All melting and pouring was done from 5 P.M. to 9 A.M. weekdays, or on weekends, to minimize energy costs. This practice saved an estimated $50,000 in monthly electricity costs. Factory overhead accounted for 63 percent of Johnstown Corporation's costs of goods sold.

Plant equipment and facilities had been well maintained under U.S. Steel ownership, with capital spending totaling over $25 million from 1967–81. Capital spending by Johnstown Corporation totaled $3 million from 1984 to March 1988, with additional spending planned from a portion of the long-term capital to be raised.

Johnstown Corporation relied on one primary source, located in Toledo, Ohio, for the scrap metal used in its production of rolls and castings. Exhibit 2 lists scrap prices during the recent year. Within the structure of Johnstown Corporation's costs, direct materials including scrap accounted for 26 percent of the cost of goods sold in 1987.

The company's plant operated seven days a week on three shifts, as of the end of 1987, with an hourly work force of 408. The unionized work force, 40 percent semiskilled and 60 percent skilled, earned an average hourly wage of $11, including $3 in benefits, during 1987. In addition to wages, employees participated in a profit-sharing plan that distributed 25 percent of quarterly profits to hourly and administrative personnel on a quarterly basis. Direct labor, not including profit sharing, accounted for 11 percent of Johnstown Corporation's cost of goods sold in 1987. Employees had the opportunity to purchase company stock and held 17 percent of outstanding shares at the end of 1987. The hourly work force was represented by two jointly selected employees on the corporate board of directors. All hourly employees were represented by the United Steelworkers of America under a contract that expired in June 1989.

The company also operated with 118 administrative employees, and a new CEO, Charles Slater, was appointed in May 1987 to replace Jack Sheehan. Other members of senior management under U.S. Steel ownership held the same positions now, with the exception of the former company president, who had resigned in February 1988. Top management held 25 percent of company stock; Mr. Sheehan, as chairman of the board, held 58 percent of the outstanding stock at the end of 1987.

THE STEEL INDUSTRY IN 1988

In 1987, the U.S. steel industry enjoyed its first profitable year since 1981. Several factors accounted for this turnaround in the industry. First, capacity cutbacks and modernization programs of the past half decade paid off; the industry reached 80 percent capacity in 1987, with utilization for high-demand items near 100 percent. In addition, the weaker U.S. dollar of 1987 resulted in decreased steel imports. Finally, less pricing competition allowed all U.S. producers to benefit from rising prices.

Forecasts for 1988 and the next three to five years were favorable, but contingent on producers continuing their recent efforts to remain competitive in the industry. Domestic steel shipments were estimated to be 70 million tons, slightly below 1987's figure, because of cutbacks in inventories, rather than lower consumption. Imports were expected to continue their decline from the 1987 level of 20 million tons to less than 19 million tons in 1988.

The favorable outlook for the near future depended on continued rationalization of the industry to reduce capacity by as much as another 20 percent. This pruning was expected to occur within plants, rather than through closing entire mills as had occurred in the past. Growth in mini-mills was also expected to stabilize, with these strong new competitors maintaining their share of industry capacity at 17 percent.

JOHNSTOWN CORPORATION'S OUTLOOK

Johnstown Corporation's revenues and earnings had grown since the company began operations in July 1984. The company's balance sheets and income statements for this period are provided in Exhibits 3 and 4. Management predicted continued growth into the 1990s, with different product lines growing at different rates. Annualized rates of growth from 1987 to 1993 were projected by product line as follows:

Product Line	1987 Sales (in millions)	1987–1993 Projected Growth Rate (%)
Rolling mill rolls	$16.0	13.9%
Castings	9.0	1.4
Slag pots.............	1.4	19.6
Mill liners	1.6	14.5
Continuous caster rolls	3.3	5.7
Fabricated and other ..	3.5	6.8
Total	$34.8	10.3%

In addition to continuing to serve present customers, Mr. Sheehan had expressed an interest in seeing the company pursue clients outside the United States, but no action to investigate such markets had yet been taken.

JOHNSTOWN CORPORATION'S FINANCING ALTERNATIVES

Management was seeking $7.5 million in long-term capital for three different purposes in early 1988: (1) An amount of $4.8 million would be used to pay down the company's present working-capital line of credit; (2) $975,000 would repay subordinated notes to top management; and (3) the remaining $1,725,000 would be used for capital improvements and general purposes. The company would retain its recently negotiated $7 million working-capital line of credit with Mellon Bank of Pittsburgh. This line, at 2 percent above prime, was secured with a maximum of 80 percent of the company's receivables less than 90 days old and up to 40 percent of inventory.

The private placement of 10-year notes recommended by Mr. Stiles would have the terms set forth in Exhibit 5. The fee associated with issuing the placement through Mr. Stiles would be $52,000. The company would have to offer warrants with the debt, because all assets of the company were under liens of other loans. Exhibit 6 lists the amount of these loans and describes the conditions of Johnstown Corporation's present debt structure.

A second option that Mr. Sheehan thought deserved consideration was an initial public offering (IPO) of the company's stock. While the 233,000 shares of stock currently outstanding were not presently traded, employees had been offered a chance to invest three times since the company's inception at prices based on book value as follows:

December 1985:	35,480 shares at $3/share
January 1986:	14,220 shares at $4/share
December 1987:	44,235 shares at $9/share

In addition to stock purchased by employees, options to purchase stock had been granted to certain members of top management over the past three years. These transactions included:

March 1987:	20,250 options at $1/share
April 1987:	11,250 options at $4/share
September 1987:	37,500 options at $9/share
September 25, 1987:	1,945 options at $3/share

Fees associated with an IPO were expected to be about 8 percent, but they could be minimized if a "best effort" placement was selected, rather than a guaranteed underwriting. Public trading of the stock would have implications for the shares held by employees, top management, and Mr. Sheehan himself. For instance, Mr. Sheehan wanted to see the issue open at a price at least slightly higher than the $9 employees had most recently paid for their shares of Johnstown Corporation. For this reason, he had concluded that the size of the issue would have to be determined after a market value had been placed on the company.

The IPO market had been tested a few times since the stock market crash of October 1987. By spring 1988, the stock market was making a slow but steady comeback, and the market for IPOs was following this same recovery route. The success of IPOs during this period depended a great deal on the quality of the offering; issues in more stable and mature industries that appealed to the institutional investor were faring better than high-technology issues. The first large-scale offering after the crash was sold in late January 1988. This spin-off of a subsidiary involved in a commodity fertilizer business brought $22 a share on 11 million shares, which surpassed expectations of $17 to $20 a share set for the issue prior to the October crash. In contrast was a software vendor's first issue that had been planned for the end of November 1987. The company had expected to issue $7.5 million in equity, but it was forced to look elsewhere for funds when it could not locate another underwriter after its first banker withdrew.

Johnstown Corporation recently had entertained the idea of selling out to another concern, although no specific price had been set for the company at that time. This option could be considered again, this time as a means of obtaining funds or as a means of issuing stock to the public.

To assist him in placing a value on Johnstown Corporation, Mr. Sheehan had obtained average valuation multiples for mini-mills from a recent investment report of Oppenheimer & Company: 1.5 times book value, 6 times cash flow, 21 times 1987 earnings, and 18 times estimated 1988 earnings. Mr. Sheehan had also gathered information on several publicly held steel producers that were somewhat similar to Johnstown Corporation. This information is contained in Exhibit 7. Interest rates over the past few years are provided in Exhibits 8 and 9. Based on his own experience with leveraged buy-outs, Mr. Sheehan believed that a potential LBO purchaser might place a value on the company's equity by using a multiple of 4 times EBIT and then subtracting total debt.

Mr. Sheehan realized that, as chairman of the board, he could easily rely on someone else to explore the various options that might be available to Johnstown Corporation. As the key framer of the company's success so far, however, he had an interest in seeing the board select the alternative that would best assure a continuation of that financial and employment success. With much information in front of him and all of his knowledge of Johnstown Corporation in his head, Jack Sheehan sat down to determine which long-term financing option he would support.

EXHIBIT 1   Percent of Company Sales by Product Line*

	1985	1986	1987	1988†	Recent Profit Margins
Rolls	40%	46%	46%	68%	32%
Castings	29	27	29	20	18 rough, 2 finished
Continuous caster rolls	4	6	9	6	12
Mill liners	8	5	5	2	40
Staves	0	3	1	1	
Other products	17	8	5	4	80 small pots
Services	2	4	4	0	
Total	100%	100%	100%	100%	

* Columns may not add to 100 because of rounding.
† 1988 percentages based on bookings as of February 1988.

EXHIBIT 2   Scrap Prices of No. 1 Dealer Bundles (price per ton delivered from Pittsburgh)

Date of Estimate	Price Range	Date of Estimate	Price Range
12/86	$ 96–97	7/87	$115–116
1/87	99–100	8/87	119–120
2/87	104–105	9/87	131–132
3/87	98–99	10/87	159–160
4/87	93–94	11/87	159–160
5/87	103–104	12/87	144–145
6/87	114–115	1/88	139–140

Source: *Iron Age.*

EXHIBIT 3   Balance Sheets (dollars in thousands)

	As of December 31		
	1985	*1986*	*1987*
Cash	$ 119	$ 0	$ 245
Accounts receivable	3,077	3,845	6,846
Inventories	5,186	4,786	4,682
Other current assets	865	168	381
Total current assets	9,247	8,799	12,154
Property, plant, and equipment ...	13,938	14,054	14,210
Other	193	187	116
Total assets	$23,378	$23,040	$26,480
Working-capital notes payable	$ 4,650	$ 4,998	$ 4,821
Current portion long-term debt	1,706	1,171	1,335
Accounts payable	3,313	3,048	4,663
Other current liabilities	804	1,993	2,315
Total current liabilities	10,473	11,210	13,134
Long-term debt	11,804	8,847	8,467
Deferred taxes and leases	312	1,258	1,282
Total liabilities	22,589	21,315	22,883
Common stock (par = $1/sh)	210	202	233
Additional paid-in capital	71	114	191
Retained earnings	508	1,409	3,173
Total owners' equity	789	1,725	3,597
Total liabilities and equity	$23,378	$23,040	$26,480

EXHIBIT 4   Johnstown Corporation Income Statements (dollars in thousands, except per share data)

	For the Years Ended December 31		
	1985	*1986**	*1987*
Revenues	$25,084	$26,605	$34,836
Cost of goods sold (including depreciation)†	18,138	21,784	27,654
Selling, general, and administrative	3,598	3,767	3,959
Interest	1,586	1,461	1,098
Profit sharing	445	142	537
Profit before tax	1,317	(549)	1,588
Tax provision (benefit)	577	(285)	4
Income (loss) before extraordinary item	740	(264)	1,584
Extraordinary item‡	265	1,165	179
Net income	$ 1,005	$ 901	$ 1,763
Earnings per share	$4.79	$4.46	$7.57

* Company loss in 1986 was attributed to sales lost as a result of a six-month strike against USX, a major account for Johnstown.

† COGS includes depreciation of $736,000 in 1985, $876,000 in 1986, and $935,000 in 1987.

‡ Extraordinary income resulted from refunding of debt, net of applicable income taxes in 1986 and 1987. Redemption of income taxes due to net operating loss carryovers resulted in extraordinary income in 1985.

EXHIBIT 5   Summary of Terms of Proposed Private Placement

Amount: $7,500,000.

Issue: Senior notes with warrants.

Maturity: 10 years due 1998.

Takedown: Second quarter 1988.

Interest Rate: 13% per annum, payable semiannually

Amortization: Interest only for the first six years. Mandatory level annual principal repayments starting at the end of the seventh year of $1,875,000 annually.

Optimal Redemption: None for the first six years. Callable thereafter at the following redemption prices as a whole or in part:

Year 7	108%
Year 8	105%
Year 9	103%
Year 10	100% (no premium)

Warrants: The notes will be accompanied by a 10-year nondetachable warrant entitling the holder to purchase 40,000 shares of common stock at an exercise price of $1 per share. The warrant shares will be subject to antidilution provisions and be adjusted for stock splits, stock dividends, recapitalizations, mergers, and the sale of stock, issuance of options, or securities or warrants convertible or issuable into common stock, all at a price in excess of $1 per share.

     The number of warrant shares will be adjusted on a one-time basis based on the average of net operating income for the years 1988 and 1989. Such adjustment will occur in the first quarter of 1990.

Net Operating Income	Number of Shares	Percent of Ownership
$6,000,000 or greater	40,000	15.0%
5,999,999–5,000,000	47,725	17.5
4,999,999–4,000,000	56,250	20.0
3,999,999–3,000,000	65,325	22.5
less than 3,000,000	75,000	25.0

EXHIBIT 5 *(concluded)*

	Net operating income will be defined as stated in the company's audited financials, before interest, provision for income taxes, and profit sharing, and will conform with generally accepted definitions of operating income.
Optional Put:	The warrant shares can be put to the company, starting at the end of the sixth year, by the holder of the warrant at a price per share equivalent to the then "appraised market value per share." Such value shall be calculated by taking operating income before taxes, interest, and profit sharing for the latest four quarters, plus cash and marketable securities, less short-term and long-term debt and multiplying the sum by six. This sum will be divided by fully diluted shares outstanding to arrive at an "appraised market value per share." The warrant holder may not put in excess of 25% of his warrant shares to the company in any one year.
Call Option:	Starting at the end of the seventh year, the company may call the warrants, as a whole or in part, at a price per share equivalent to the then "appraised market value per share." Such valuation will follow the same technique used in the put option, except the multiple will be seven times.
Registration Rights:	The warrant shares will be subject to one free right of registration after the company's initial public offering and unlimited rights to piggyback other public offerings of the stock, subject to consent of underwriters.
Restrictive Covenants on the Notes:	To be negotiated.

Source: William F. Stiles, second draft of Private Placement Memorandum.

EXHIBIT 6   Details of Significant Debt Components, as of December 31, 1986

Lender	Amount	Interest Rate	Maturity	Terms	Liens
U.S.N.B.[a] No. 1	$ 862,000	Bank prime plus 1%	3/1/2000	$4,167/month plus interest	First mortgage on real estate
P.I.D.A.[b]	$ 863,000	4.5%	3/1/2000	$7,650/month plus interest	Second mortgage on real estate
City[c]	$4,000,000	3% through 1989; 10% for balance of term	2/27/2000	Monthly interest only through 1989; $158,581/ qtr. + 1% gross sales over $30 million/yr. after 1989	Fourth mortgage on real estate
U.S.N.B.[a] No. 2	$1,974,000	Bank prime plus 1%	3/1/2000	Interest for preceding month plus a principal amount, which is total principal balance/240	Third mortgage on real estate
Shareholders	$ 975,000	Bank prime plus 1%	None	Subordinated to other obligations; no principal payments during subordination period	Unsecured

[a] United States National Bank of Johnstown.
[b] Pennsylvania Industrial Development Authority.
[c] City of Johnstown (via United States Urban Development Action Grant).

EXHIBIT 6   *(concluded)*

Interest Payments[f]	Yearly Debt Service					
	1988	*1989*	*1990*	*1991*	*1992*	*1993*
U.S.N.B.[d]	$ 77	$ 73	$ 68	$ 64	$ 59	$ 54
P.I.D.A	37	33	28	24	20	16
City of Johnstown	120	120	400	377	351	323
U.S.N.B.[d]	178	169	161	153	145	138
Shareholders[e]	90	90	90	90	90	90
Total	$ 502	$ 485	$ 747	$ 708	$ 665	$ 621
Principal Payments	*1988*	*1989*	*1990*	*1991*	*1992*	*1993*
U.S.N.B.	$ 50	$ 50	$ 50	$ 50	$ 50	$ 50
P.I.D.A.	92	92	92	92	92	92
City of Johnstown	0	0	234	257	283	311
U.S.N.B.	99	94	89	85	80	76
Shareholders	0	0	0	0	0	0
Total	$ 241	$ 236	$ 465	$ 484	$ 505	$ 529
Loan Balance at End of Year	*1988*	*1989*	*1990*	*1991*	*1992*	*1993*
U.S.N.B.	$ 812	$ 762	$ 712	$ 662	$ 612	$ 562
P.I.D.A.	771	679	587	495	403	311
City of Johnstown	4,000	4,000	3,766	3,509	3,226	2,915
U.S.N.B.	1,875	1,781	1,692	1,607	1,527	1,451
Shareholders	975	975	975	975	975	975
Total	$8,433	$8,197	$7,732	$7,248	$6,743	$6,214

[d] Loans at prime + 1% charged at 9.25% over life of loan. This rate was average prime rate, November 1985–November 1987.
[e] Assumed no principal payments on shareholder loan.
[f] Interest computed on average outstanding loan balance during year.

EXHIBIT 7 Selected 1986 Data on General Steel Producers

Description of Business

Florida Steel (FLS):	Production and fabrication of steel reinforcing and merchant bars. Principal customers: building, road, and bridge contractors; municipal, county, and state agencies; concrete manufacturers; railroad, utility, and industrial companies. Marketing areas: Florida, Southeast, Midwest, and South Central states, and the Caribbean. Directors owned 3 percent of stock.
General Refractories (GRX):	Made and distributed furnace lining materials (69% of sales), mainly to the (GRX) steel industry. Produced filter media, filters, oil control products. Mined a variety of ores and clays (14 percent). Insiders controlled about 55 percent of stock.
Northwestern Steel & Wire Company (NSW):	Produced carbon steel products exclusively by the electric furnace method. Steel scrap was a major raw material. Made 75 percent of sales in Midwest to steel service centers, fabricators, and hardware jobbers. Main markets: agriculture and construction. Dillon family owned about 45 percent of stock.
Nucor Corporation (NUE):	Manufactured steel and steel joists (held 30 percent of market for joists). Major markets: construction, energy, rail, agriculture.
Proler International Corporation (PS):	Leading processor of ferrous scrap (75 percent of sales) and nonferrous scrap (10 percent). Proler family held about 25 percent of stock; Tiger group about 15 percent.

*Operating Information**	FLS	GRX	NSW	NUE	PS
Sales	$381.0	$362.8	$397.4	$755.2	$117.1
Oper. margin	55.6	11.7	26.0	144.9	(1.1)
Net income	16.9	7.5	10.3	46.4	(5.1)
Oper. margin/sales	14.6%	3.2%	6.5%	19.2%	(0.9%)
Net income/sales	4.4	2.1	2.6	6.1	(4.4%)
LTD/capital	40%	56%	22%	12%	32%
Total debt/capital	57%	88%	40%	33%	11%
Payout ratio (3-yr. avg.)	27%	0%	15%†	12%	55%‡
Dividend yield	3.0%	0%	3.3%	1.0%	2.9%
P/E ratio	9.5	15.9	11.3	15.0	7.3
Beta§	1.35	1.10	1.05	1.25	.90
Stock range	$44½–18¼	$20¼–13½	$24¼–11⅛	$49½–29½	$54–31¾
Close 4/8/88	$32¾	$18⅝	$19½	$42½	$55

5-Year Annualized per Share Growth Projections					
Sales	10%		9%	10%	5%
Earnings	17%			12%	
Dividends	14%			12%	8%

* All operating information for most recent fiscal year as of March 1988 and in millions of dollars. Other information current as of March 1988 unless noted.
† Payout based on 1987 only. No dividends paid previously.
‡ Payout and P/E based on 1984 and 1985 only due to net income loss in 1986.
§ An analyst informed Mr. Sheehan that he believed Johnstown would have a beta of 1.30.

Sources: *Value Line* reports and company annual reports.

EXHIBIT 8   Selected Interest Rates: January 1985–November 1987

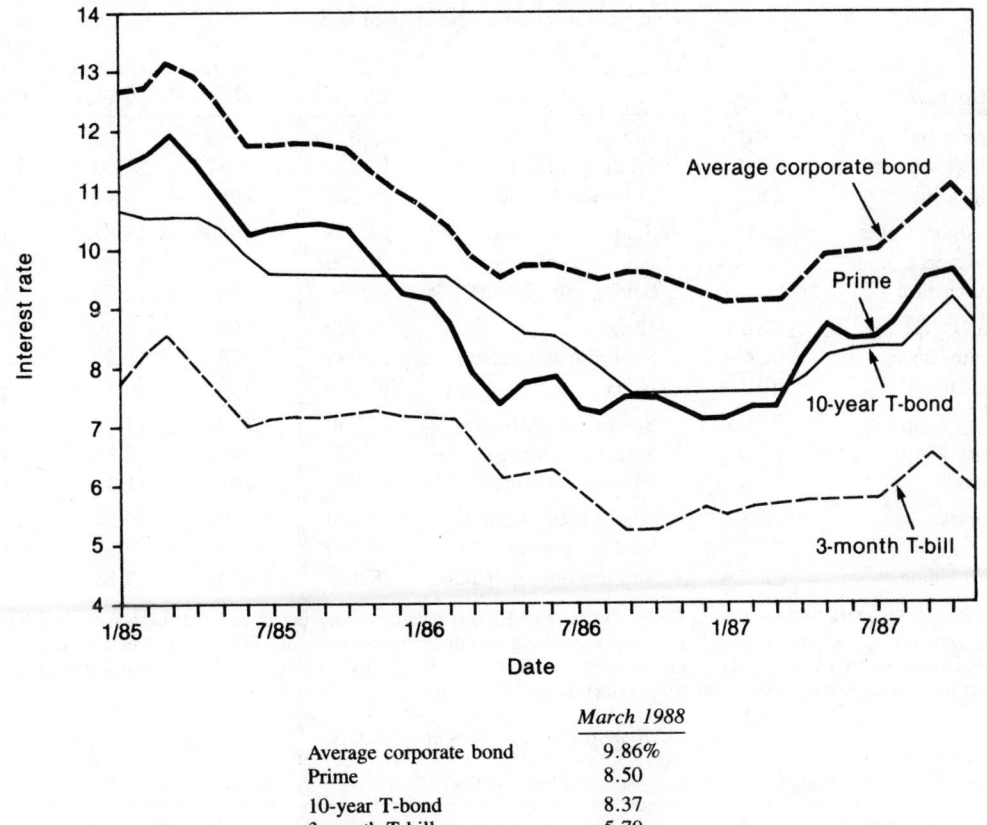

	March 1988
Average corporate bond	9.86%
Prime	8.50
10-year T-bond	8.37
3-month T-bill	5.70

EXHIBIT 9   Johnstown Corporation

Current Yields on Selected Debt Issues

Company	Rating*	Form of Debt	Coupon	Mat. Date	Current Yield	Yield to Maturity
Champion Int'l	BBB	Notes	8.625%	1996	9.02%	9.41%
Chrysler Corp.	BBB −	Sinking fund debent.	10.950	2017	10.53	10.50
Chrysler Fin.	BBB −	Subordinated notes	9.300	1994	9.49	9.72
Great Amer. Comm.	CCC +	Senior sub. debent.	14.375	1999	13.82	13.67
Great Amer. Comm.	CCC	Sen. sub. sf. nts.	9.000	1993	10.59	13.08
Harcourt Brace J.	CCC +	Senior sub. debent.	13.750	1999	12.73	12.42
Hutton, E. F.	BBB −	Notes	8.500	1991	8.59	8.86
Interlogic Trace	CCC +	Subordinated debent.	11.990	1996	16.89	19.05
Maxus Energy	BBB −	Notes	10.500	1995	10.47	10.45
McCrory Corp.	CCC −	Senior subord. notes	15.750	1991	17.03	18.85
McCrory Corp.	CCC −	Sen. sf. debent.	7.750	1995	12.86	17.42
Occidental	BBB	Senior debentures	11.750	2011	11.11	11.05
Southmark	CCC +	Senior subord. notes	13.250	1994	20.54	—
TWA	CCC	Sub. sf. debent.	5.000	1994	7.35	12.99
Western Union	CCC −	Sinking fund debent.	8.100	1998	15.88	19.08

* According to *Standard & Poor's Bond Guide:* "Debt rated BBB is regarded as having an adequate capacity to pay interest and repay principal . . . adverse economic conditions or changing circumstances are more likely to lead to a weakened capacity to pay interest and repay principal. . . . Debt rated . . . CCC . . . is regarded, on balance, as predominantly speculative with respect to capacity to pay interest and repay principal. . . ."

Recent Private-Placement Yields

	Company	Form of Debt	Maturity Date	Coupon
January	Meditrust	Fixed-rate notes	1992	10.25%
	Goer Manufacturing	Sr. notes	1997	11.03
	Intercraft	Sr. notes	1997	11.40
February	Energas	Sr. notes	2002	11.20
	Energas	Sr. notes	1989	8.94
	Vemco	Sub. secured notes	1997	11.50
March	Luz Solar	Sec. nonrecourse notes	2006	12.22
	Service Merchandise	Sec. notes	1995	10.80
	Strick Lease	Sr. sec. notes	1998	10.75
	WTD Industries	Sr. notes	1997	10.20

Sources: *Standard & Poor's Bond Guide*, March 1988, and *Investment Dealer's Digest*, various issues.

Revco D.S., Inc.: Assessing Capital Adequacy

Anac[1] regards the acquisition of Revco as an attractive investment opportunity because it believes that Revco's future business prospects are favorable on the basis of projections of future operations, and that Revco, as a private company with a substantially higher debt-to-equity ratio than it would be likely to have as a public company, will realize a greater percentage return on equity and will achieve a more rapid percentage growth in its net worth. . . . An equity investment in [Revco] following the merger will involve substantial risk for several reasons.[2]

In December 1986, the management of Revco D.S. and a group of investors took the company private in a leveraged buyout (LBO).[3] Revco was the operator of the largest chain of discount drugstores in the United States. The buyers paid a 48 percent premium for the shares, compared to the price in January 1986, before the announcement of plans for the buyout. In addition to the large acquisition premium, this buyout arrested the attention of investors and analysts because of its unusual financing terms. Goldman Sachs, advising the board of directors, had declared that the purchase price was "fair." Salomon Brothers, advising the buyout group, had designed the transaction and employed its considerable bond-trading muscle to promote it—indeed, this was Salomon's first major "done deal" acting simultaneously as buyout advisor, underwriter, and merchant banker. On the other hand, Moody's and Standard & Poor's, the bond rating agencies, declared Revco's LBO to have a "negative outlook" and downgraded their ratings of Revco's public bonds to "speculative" categories. Analysts noted that debt repayment in the first few years depended

---

[1]Anac was a "shell company" owned by Revco managers and some outside investors. Anac bought Revco. But to gain certain tax advantages, Anac actually was merged into Revco, leaving Revco the surviving entity.

[2]*Proxy Statement,* Revco D.S., Inc., November 14, 1986, p. 16.

[3]In a typical leveraged buyout, managers and investors would buy the entire common stock of a company mainly using borrowed funds, the repayment of which would come from the operating cash flow of the company or asset sales, or both.

This case was written by Professor Robert F. Bruner.

significantly on asset sales, an especially uncertain source of cash. More important, the operating performance of the firm had been declining over recent quarters.

What could account for the unusual capital structure employed in this deal? Would the high degree of leverage set a new trend for the financing of buyouts in the retail sector? Was the financing appropriate for Revco? The leveraged buyout of Revco raised questions about the adequacy of equity capital in this and other buyouts. What proportion of equity was sufficient? In general, when was a firm "adequately capitalized"?

THE COMPANY

In 1986, Revco was the nation's largest discount drugstore chain, operating 2,049 stores in 30 states. Fiscal 1986 sales were $2.7 billion with after-tax profits of $56.9 million. Revco was formed in 1956 and utilized the marketing concept of "everyday, low prices," a concept still in use in 1986. Strip centers in small cities were the primary location of Revco stores, with approximately 70 percent of the company's stores located in cities with a population of less than 25,000. Over the previous five years, the number of stores had grown at an annual compound rate of 6.24 percent, from 1,514 stores in 1981. The average cost of opening a new store was approximately $300,000, with inventory comprising approximately $200,000 of this total.[4]

COMPETITION

Revco competed with health maintenance organizations, hospital pharmacies, mail-order organizations, discount drugstores, combination food-and-drug stores, mass merchandisers, and the rapidly emerging "deep discount" drugstores. Deep discounters were large "super" drug stores relying on volume to compensate for the unusually low prices they charged. Consequently, deep discount drugstores were located primarily in cities with populations over 250,000 and were not seen as a major threat to Revco. The drugstore industry exhibited little cyclicality, since most sales were necessity items and few substitute products existed.

ORIGIN AND TERMS OF THE BUYOUT

Since April 1984, chief executive officer and chairman of the board Sidney Dworkin had been concerned with possible takeover threats, following a series of highly publicized mishaps at Revco.[5] Revco's common stock price had not recovered from the negative impact of these adversities. Rumors of an impending hostile takeover attempt on Revco had ebbed through the financial community in 1984, 1985, and 1986. On March 11,

---

[4]Casewriter's estimate based on interviews of industry executives.

[5]The mishaps included a sudden product liability disclosed in April 1984; the hasty and unfortunate purchase of Odd Lot Trading, Inc.; disclosures of purchasing irregularities later in 1984 associated with Sidney Dworkin's two sons, who were also employees at Revco; and open disputes among senior managers.

1986, Dworkin struck first by submitting a buyout proposal to Revco's board of directors. He later raised the offer price to a cash payment of $38.50 per share. The board accepted the offer on August 15. The buyout closed on December 29, 1986.

The buyout would require nearly $1.5 billion, to be placed through the issuance of nine different classes of securities, the bulk of them being debt and preferred stock. The sources and uses of funds in this transaction were as follows:

Sources	Dollars (thousands)
Bank term loan (Rate = Prime rate + 1.75% or 9.25%, due 1992)[1]	$ 455,000
Senior subordinated notes (rate 13.125%, due 1994)[2]	400,000
Subordinated notes (rate 13.3%, due 1996)[3]	210,000
Units:[4]	
Junior subordinated notes (rate 13.3%, due 2001)	91,145
Common stock (375,000 shares)	2,605
Stock puts (on 375,000 shares)	93,750
Convertible preferred stock (rate 12%, due 2001)[5]	85,000
Exchangeable preferred stock (dividend 15.25%, due 2002)[6]	130,020
Junior preferred stock (dividend 17.62%, due 2002)[7]	30,098
Common stock[8]	34,276
Cash of Revco	10,655
Total sources	1,448,799
Uses:	
Purchase of Revco common stock	1,253,315
Repayment of debt	117,484
Fees and expenses[9]	78,000
Total uses	1,448,799

[1] The senior debt had a first claim on all the assets of the firm. Principal payments over the fiscal years 1987 to 1992 were to be (in $ millions) 45, 142.5, 117.5, 50, 60, and 40, respectively. The interest rate would decrease by 0.25 percent once $255 million in principal payments and various divestitures had occurred. Exhibit 4, which projects results on a fiscal year basis, is consistent with this amortization schedule. But Exhibit 7 presents this amortization on a calendar year basis and thus uses amortization payments appropriate for calendar years. The reason for shifting to calendar years in Exhibit 7 was to permit estimation of coverage ratios for the three whole years following the buyout.

[2] The senior subordinated notes required sinking-fund payments of $200 million in both 1993 and 1994.

[3] The subordinated notes required $105 million in sinking-fund payments, to be made in both 1995 and 1996.

[4] These units were bundles of junior subordinated debt, common stock and stock puts. The puts entitled the holder to require Revco to repurchase the common stock in 1993 at a fair market value determined by an independent appraiser. The junior subordinated notes required sinking fund payments of $18.75 million in each year from 1997 to 2001.

[5] The convertible preferred stock was convertible, at the option of the investor, into common stock of Revco. If not converted, the preferred stock was to be redeemed by Revco in 2001. Dividends on this security were to be paid in cash.

[6] For the first five years, dividends on the exchangeable preferred stock were to be "paid in kind" or in more shares of exchangeable preferred stock. Revco had to redeem this issue in equal amounts over the five years from 1997 to 2001. Revco retained the option to force investors to exchange their preferred stock for subordinated debt yielding 15.25 percent and due 2001.

[7] Dividends on this issue were cumulative and payable only upon retirement of the issue in 2002. The entire issue was purchased by Salomon Brothers and certain common stockholders.

[8] Management owned 60 percent of the shares on a fully diluted basis, either directly or through a mutual trust. New York Life Insurance Company was the next largest investor, with 25 percent. Salomon Brothers held 9.4 percent.

[9] The fees included underwriting commissions of $31,150,000, investment banking advisory fees of $16,100,000, bank commitment fees of $14,800,000, and legal and accounting fees of $10,300,000.

Salomon Brothers, the buyout group's investment banker and a part-equity owner, had lined up the required financing from a variety of sources.

MANAGEMENT OF NEW REVCO

Once the LBO was completed, Sidney Dworkin became chairman of the board and chief executive officer of the "new" Revco, the same positions he had held at Revco D. S. As in the old entity, Dworkin did not control a majority of the outstanding shares of stock; he owned about 15.4 percent. However, these shares were subject to a voting trust of which he was a member. Apparently, Mr. Dworkin would have more control in the new Revco than he had had at Revco D. S., where his ownership percentage was only 2.32 percent. Dworkin received $29.6 million for the stock and stock options that he held in the "old" Revco. He invested about $8 million in the new Revco.

STRATEGY AND RESTRUCTURING PLANS

If the merger had occurred on June 2, 1985, earnings before depreciation, amortization, interest, and income taxes would have been $161.8 million for the year ended May 31, 1986, just sufficient to cover proforma interest expense of $155 million. Revco managers believed that the company's results since the beginning of fiscal 1985 were not indicative of future prospects and that Revco's performance in 1987 and beyond would be more in line with pre-1985 results. Nevertheless, because the interest-coverage ratio would be very low, management adopted a program to increase the margin of safety. Elements of the program included the following:

Focus on Drugstore Business.   Management planned to divest virtually all of Revco's nondrugstore businesses plus 100 drugstores, thus permitting management to concentrate on expanding its drugstore operations and improving drugstore gross margins and profitability. Management had earmarked $230 million in assets for sale by the end of June 1987 and had, in principle, reached agreements to sell $89 million of those assets by the time the company went private. At least four months would be needed to consummate these agreements. First, management devised a divestiture program to dispose of all the nondrugstore subsidiaries. The credit agreement with the major banks called for Revco to make principal payments in 1987, 1988, and 1989, that would reduce the term loan to $150 million from $455 million. Of the $305 million in payments, $255 million were expected to occur through the divestiture program. Duff & Phelps had been engaged to value Revco's seven subsidiaries, and an analysis dated October 17, 1986, estimated the aggregate market value of these subsidiaries at $224.5 million. Book value of these subsidiaries was $178 million.

Expand.   Future expansion plans included opening or acquiring approximately 100 stores per year over the subsequent five years. This expansion would be financed by working capital from operations. Most of this expansion was to be in small communities. Management believed that Revco's presence in prime locations in these small markets discouraged entry by other large drugstore chains. In addition, the small size of the market tended to bar entry for deep discount stores, which generally required a larger population base to support profitable operations.

Reduce Capital Expenditures.   Because approximately 75 percent of all Revco drugstores either were new or had been remodeled since the beginning of fiscal 1981, management believed that Revco's program of remodeling its existing stores could be implemented each year within a modest budget.

Reduce Inventory and Selling Expense.   As part of its efforts to increase Revco's profitability, management implemented an inventory-reduction program, which was to be substantially completed by the end of fiscal 1987. Assuming a ratio of inventory-to-sales consistent with past experience, management anticipated that inventory levels would be reduced by approximately $129 million from the levels that otherwise would exist. In addition, management initiated a program designed to reduce selling, general, and administrative expenses by approximately $24 million during 1987 from the levels that otherwise would have existed.

Maintain Current Marketing Strategy.   Management would continue to build on two of Revco's fundamental strengths: its many convenient locations and its "everyday low prices" pricing strategy. Dworkin believed that these two strengths would continue to frame consumers' perceptions of Revco as a convenience drugstore, selling quality products at low prices at all times.

Increase Sales of Nonprescription Items.   Revco's merchandising and marketing strategy was to maintain its strong prescription sales as the company increased sales of and improved margins on nonprescription items. This would entail rearranging store layouts to draw the customer through aisles of nonprescription items as the customer proceeded to the drug counter. Nonprescription merchandise would include lawn furniture, kitchen appliances, small consumer electronic items, and the like.

OUTLOOK

Sales for the stub period (from the closing on December 26, 1986, to the next fiscal year end, May 31, 1987) were expected to be about $990 million, resulting in an operating profit of about $47 million. This would leave an operating profit of $147 million for the 1987 fiscal year ending May 31, modestly higher than for 1986's operating profit of $141.4 million.

In making their assessments of the transaction, outside analysts considered historical financial performance (Exhibits 1 and 2), projected financial performance (Exhibits 3 and 4), information on comparable companies (Exhibit 5), and current capital market rates and indices (Exhibit 6). Analysis identified a number of key assumptions:

Growth Rate of Sales per Store.   The forecast assumed 6 percent annual growth in sales per store, reflecting an anticipated 5 percent inflation rate and a 1 percent real growth rate. Analysts wondered about the appropriateness of the real-growth-rate assumption, especially given the very low (or even negative) population growth rates in small communities.

Cost of Goods Sold(COGS)/Sales.   The forecast assumed Revco's five-year historical average, 73 percent. Analysts compared Revco with other drug retailers, whose COGS/sales ratio averaged 71 percent (see Exhibit 5). Acknowledging the difficulty of achieving a 1 percentage point improvement in this ratio (especially with a policy of discount pricing), analysts wondered whether Dworkin could realize some economies following the buyout.

Selling, General, and Administrative Expenses/Sales.   The forecast assumed Revco's five-year historical average of 20.8 percent, as opposed to an industry average of 23.6 percent. Analysts also wondered whether economies were possible in this area.

Timing of Asset Sales.   Consistent with Dworkin's plan (and bankers' expectations), the forecast assumed the sale of $230 million in assets in 1988. However, any softening in the acquisitions market might delay the sale until 1989 or even 1990.

Timing and Volume of New Store Openings.   The forecast assumed that Revco would open 100 new stores each year for the next five years and then would stop expanding as the target market became saturated. Some analysts questioned Dworkin's ambitious store-opening plans, especially in light of Revco's high leverage. Dworkin countered that the next five years offered a temporary window to gain dominance in certain markets, and that the cash-flow growth afforded by this expansion would assist in the amortization of debt and boost returns to the equity investors.

COMPARATIVE ANALYSIS

Analysts considered the experience of another major drugstore retailer, Jack Eckerd Corporation, which had been taken private in an LBO in April 1986. In most respects the two companies were quite similar: Eckerd had been taken private, however, at a multiple of only 21.3 times, compared with Revco's 24.8 times earnings. Eckerd also was financed at a debt/equity[6] ratio of 11.5 times, compared with Revco's 37.6 times.

Exhibit 7 presents a forecast of how well Revco and Eckerd could cover their financial obligations in the next three years, the period over which analysts perceived the greatest

---

[6]This "debt/equity" ratio is measured as the sum of all long- and short-term debt plus preferred stock, divided by common equity.

possible risk of default. For each company, the financial obligations included interest expense, principal payments, and preferred stock dividend payments. The "coverage" of these obligations was estimated as a multiple, compared with earnings before interest and taxes (EBIT); and "cash flow," which consisted of earnings before interest, taxes, depreciation, and amortization (EBITDA) plus the receipts from any asset sales less capital expenditures. (Additions to net working capital are ignored in this calculation. Ordinarily they should be included. Their exclusion biases upward the estimated coverage ratios.)

Analysts acknowledged, however, that comparative figures, such as those in Exhibit 7, were *point estimates* and, thus, ignored the uncertainty surrounding key assumptions. Revco's financial obligations[7] were well known at the time of the buyout. Thus, the uncertainty about Revco's comparative standing versus Jack Eckerd and other firms devolved from forecast uncertainty about the following points:

- **Interest rates:** Revco's senior debt bore interest that floated at 1.75 percent above prime rate,[8] currently at 7.50 percent.
- **Asset sales:** Revco had to sell assets to meet its principal payments. One could give Revco the benefit of the doubt and assume that all $230 million actually would be realized. But analysts were uncertain about the *timing*[9] of that realization. By comparison, Jack Eckerd would try to sell $72 million in assets.
- **Capital expenditures:** Capital expenditures could be assumed to be driven by Revco's goal of opening 100 stores per year at an investment of $100,000 per store. Depreciation could be approximated at $20 million for 1987, and thereafter scaled according to the percentage net change of the difference between asset sales and capital expenditures. By contrast, Jack Eckerd envisioned opening no new stores in the foreseeable future. Eckerd's depreciation was forecasted to be $123 million, a much higher figure than Revco's, because Eckerd tended to own, rather than lease, its stores.
- **Growth:** Salomon Brothers contemplated a sales-growth rate at no lower than 8 percent; it presented forecasts to commercial bankers that assumed growth at 12 percent. Goldman Sachs, the advisor to Revco's outside directors, determined that a 12 percent growth rate assumption was "too aggressive." Analysts assumed sales growth at mature stores to be equal to the rate of inflation.[10] In addition, the net growth from opening new stores would yield an annual corporate growth rate of 9 percent.

---

[7]It would be necessary to focus only on *cash* payments and to ignore noncash obligations, such as payment-in-kind (PIK) preferred dividends.

[8]Over the period 1974–1986 the mean and standard deviation for the prime rate had been 11.00 percent and 3.60 percent, respectively. This rate was normally distributed.

[9]One could assume that Revco and Eckerd would divest the target assets entirely over the first two years. Asset sales in 1987 would be uniformly distributed over 25 to 75 percent of the $230 million. Asset sales in 1988 would be the balance necessary to bring the total sales up to the targeted amount.

[10]A time series of historical inflation rates over the 13 years preceding the Revco LBO revealed that inflation had a normal distribution, with a mean and standard deviation of 7.00 percent and 3.90 percent, respectively. Analysts assumed a current mean inflation rate of 5 percent, although U.S. Treasury bills had yielded slightly less than 6 percent since June 1986.

- **EBIT margin:** From 1974 to 1986, Revco's mean EBIT margin was 6.62 percent (standard deviation was 1.32 percent). The mean and standard deviation for Jack Eckerd Corporation were 8.11 and 1.42 percent, respectively; a sample of peer companies over the same period indicated that the mean and standard deviation were 5.15 and 1.25 percent, respectively. Salomon Brothers assumed an EBIT margin of 8 percent. Goldman Sachs opined that this assumption was "a bit aggressive." Only once over the past 13 years did Revco reach that level, in 1984; thereafter, Revco's EBIT margin fell to 3.50 and 4.84 percent. Sales growth and EBIT margin depended in part on the rate at which Revco planned to open new stores—analysts challenged the wisdom of this strategy, noting that 70 percent of Revco's stores that had been open for less than one year lost money; the figure dropped to 48 percent for stores that had been open from one to two years.

Analysts were unable to decide whether to assume any covariance between growth and margins and generally assumed that each year was an independent draw (i.e., that there was no serial covariance in the forecast assumptions).

CAPITAL ADEQUACY

Leveraged buyouts were very difficult to evaluate. Typically, the prospective returns to creditors and investors were quite high, but were they high enough to compensate for the risk involved? Ultimately, the decision of whether to invest or lend in these deals hinged on some judgment about the likelihood that the buyout firm would *survive* a period of arduous financial demand. This judgment necessarily entailed some analysis of the adequacy of the firm's capitalization.

The adequacy of Revco's capitalization after the LBO could be judged in several ways. First, one could test whether, at the time that Revco went private, the market value of Revco's assets was greater than the value of Revco's liabilities. This was the classic test of bankrupt firms. If assets were worth less than the face value of liabilities, the creditors would be handed ownership of the firm; but those who used this approach confronted a number of challenging valuation questions. Most important, this valuation approach said nothing about the adequacy of capitalization where assets were worth a little more than the face value of liabilities. The key question, how much debt could or should the firm carry, was poorly answered by the bankruptcy test.

A second approach would be to compare Revco's capitalization ratios (e.g., debt/equity) with those of other firms that had gone private in leveraged buyouts and with peer firms. In response to this suggestion, one scholar wrote:

> . . . widely used rules of thumb which evaluate debt capacity in terms of some percentage of balance sheet values or in terms of income statement ratios can be seriously misleading and even dangerous to corporate solvency . . . debt policy in general and debt capacity in particular cannot be prescribed for the individual company by outsiders or by generalized standards; rather, they

can and should be determined by management in terms of individual corporate circumstances and objectives and on the basis of observed behavior of cash flows.[11]

To focus on "the observed behavior of cash flows" meant asking this question: Under the existing capital structure, how likely was Revco to default on servicing its liabilities? If the probability of default were high, one might judge that Revco was too dependent on debt financing and should alter the mix away from debt and toward equity. If the probability of default were extremely low, this analysis would suggest that Revco could bear additional debt.

---

[11]Gordon Donaldson, "New Framework for Corporate Debt Policy," *Harvard Business Review,* September–October 1978, p. 150.

EXHIBIT 1   Historical Income Statements

Income Statements
1982–1986
(dollars in thousands)

	5/31/82	5/31/83	5/31/84	5/31/85	5/31/86
Net sales	$1,554,656	$1,792,756	$2,227,510	$2,395,640	$2,743,178
Cost of goods sold	1,135,335	1,306,887	1,602,150	1,794,734	2,018,149
Warehousing, sales, & administration	321,237	359,629	447,777	519,781	563,248
Operating profit	98,084	126,240	177,583	81,125	125,343
Interest expense	10,500	5,729	6,402	14,796	28,989
Interest income	2,404	2,159	3,363	1,777	(350)
Earnings before tax	89,988	122,670	174,544	68,106	96,004
Taxes	40,350	56,200	81,133	29,200	44,700
Net income	$ 49,638	$ 66,470	$ 93,411	$ 38,906	$ 51,304
Memo: Depreciation and amortization	$ 17,268	$ 19,021	$ 22,534	$ 28,250	$ 36,438

Source: Revco annual reports.

EXHIBIT 2   Historical Balance Sheets

Balance Sheets
1982–1986
(dollars in thousands)

	5/31/82	*5/31/83*	*5/31/84*	*5/31/85*	*5/31/86*
Assets					
Cash	$ 26,948	$ 51,205	$ 18,591	$ 8,152	$ 45,074
Accounts receivable	30,506	41,089	53,680	75,429	68,534
Inventory	276,372	316,990	471,871	491,583	501,956
Prepaids	10,835	15,225	18,617	26,271	24,022
Total current assets	344,661	424,509	562,759	601,435	639,586
Land	32,584	34,926	41,960	58,131	62,929
Equipment	103,858	117,350	148,960	185,135	223,328
Lease	59,045	63,139	73,798	88,656	105,388
Construction in progress	3,860	2,638	6,382	12,668	36,386
Less: depreciation and amortization					
	(58,637)	(69,058)	(83,553)	(101,738)	(126,684)
Net PP&E	140,710	148,995	187,547	242,852	301,347
Other assets	15,513	24,358	26,910	30,685	46,021
Total assets	500,884	597,862	777,216	874,972	986,954
Liabilities and Stockholders' Equity					
Short-term debt	0	0	50,908	120,939	0
Current LTD	2,973	3,523	3,576	4,117	4,490
A/P, trade	89,571	100,410	141,814	144,769	155,179
A/P, other	10,235	10,370	17,151	21,452	21,904
Accruals	16,484	20,491	17,814	18,998	22,705
Other accruals	12,490	17,900	22,989	27,216	42,861
Current taxes	10,457	17,620	14,165	7,706	6,442
Total current liabilities	142,210	170,314	268,417	345,197	253,581
Long-term debt	66,169	42,818	39,408	44,781	304,885
Deferred taxes	7,362	12,535	22,265	27,640	35,958
Common stock	20,484	32,121	36,593	36,641	36,743
Additional paid-in capital	14,556	40,920	38,638	39,194	41,764
Retained earnings	250,103	299,154	371,895	381,519	411,729
Treasury stock at cost					(97,706)
Total stockholders' equity	285,143	372,195	447,126	457,354	392,530
Total liabilities and equity ...	500,884	597,862	777,216	874,972	986,954

Source: Revco annual reports.

EXHIBIT 3 Forecast Income Statements

Common Assumptions in Financial Forecast
(dollars in thousands)

Cost of goods sold/sales	73.00%	Interest, cash balance	6.00%
Selling, general, and administrative		Days trade payables	30
expenses/sales	20.80%	Other payables (days)	5
Inventories/sales	20.00%	Depreciation/gross FA	5.00%
Minimum cash balance	$50,000	Tax rate	36.00%
Goodwill amortization	$14,056	Cost of opening each new store	$100,000
Growth rate of store sales:		New store openings/year	100
Mature stores	6.00%	Year assets divested	1988
New stores	6.00%		
Interest, working-capital debt	9.25%		

	1987	1988	1989	1990	1991	1992	1993	1994
Mature-store sales	$1,074	$1,138	$1,206	$1,279	$1,355	$1,437	$1,523	$1,614
New-store sales	$ 965	$1,023	$1,084	$1,149	$1,218	$1,291	$1,369	$1,451
New stores	97	100	100	100	100	100	0	0
Old stores, beginning of year	2,031	2,051	2,151	2,251	2,351	2,451	2,551	2,551
Divestitures	0	77	0	0	0	0	0	0

Pro Forma Income Statement

	Actual FY 1986	Expected Stub Period* 12/26/86 –5/30/87	Pro Forma* FY 1987	1998
Sales	$2,743,178	$ 991,184	$2,317,381	$2,436,143
Cost of sales	(2,018,149)	(733,344)	(1,720,525)	(1,778,385)
Gross profit	725,029	257,840	596,856	657,759
Selling, general, & administrative expense	(563,248)	(190,540)	(449,931)	(506,718)
Depreciation	(36,438)	(20,131)	(62,318)	(10,530)
Amortization of leaseholds		0	0	(8,043)
Amortization of other assets		0	0	
Operating profit	125,343	47,169	84,607	127,420
Interest, working-capital debt				288
Accrued-interest expense	(28,989)	(64,682)	(152,064)	(145,983)
Interest income	2,465	2,030	2,930	2,989
Extraordinary items	(2,815)	0	(5,018)	0
Pretax earnings	96,004	(15,483)	(69,545)	(15,286)
Income taxes	(44,700)	(1,555)	0	0
Amortization of goodwill		(5,892)	(5,892)	(14,056)
Net income	$ 51,304	$ (22,930)	$ (75,437)	$ (29,342)
Less: Dividends on:				
Convertible preferred stock		$ (5,149)	$ (5,149)	$ (10,200)
Exchangeable preferred stock†		(16,244)	(16,244)	(34,036)
Junior preferred stock‡		(2,214)	(2,214)	(5,693)
Old Revco common stock	$ (26,724)			
Additions to retained earnings	24,580	(46,537)	(99,044)	(79,271)

* The buyout was consummated on December 26,1986. For the sake of comparison, statements are presented for both the entire fiscal year and the stub period (i.e., from December 26 to May 30, 1987).

† For the first five years, the exchangeable preferred stock would accrue additional shares at the rate of 15.25 percent per year. These shares were to be valued at the liquidation value of $25 per share. Dividends during the stub period actually accrued through the end of the second quarter because as of May 30 the firm was liable for the dividend of the entire quarter.

‡ Stub period dividends on the junior preferred stock were calculated at the simple dividend rate of 17.62 percent, calculated over the 155 days from the date of issue, December 26, 1986, to fiscal year end.

Note: columns may not exactly foot because of rounding in the forecast model.

Sources: SEC filings, historical financial ratios, and casewriters' estimates.

(dollars in thousands)

	1989	1990	1991	1992	1993	1994
			Projected (Fiscal Years Ending May 30)			
	$2,702,930	$2,992,962	$3,308,066	$3,650,209	$3,884,612	$4,117,689
	(1,973,139)	(2,184,862)	(2,414,889)	(2,664,653)	(2,835,767)	(3,005,913)
	729,791	808,100	893,178	985,556	1,048,845	1,111,776
	(562,210)	(622,536)	(688,078)	(759,243)	(807,999)	(856,479)
	(11,030)	(11,530)	(12,030)	(12,530)	(12,970)	(13,352)
	(8,043)	(8,043)	(8,043)	(8,043)	(8,043)	(8,043)
	(5,048)	(5,048)	(5,048)	(5,048)	(5,048)	(5,048)
	143,460	160,942	179,979	200,692	214,784	228,854
	(7,707)	(18,811)	(24,090)	(27,411)	(29,895)	(32,378)
	(135,346)	(127,599)	(121,124)	(116,499)	(114,649)	(101,524)
	3,000	3,000	3,000	3,000	3,000	3,000
	0	0	0	0	0	0
	3,408	17,532	37,764	59,781	73,241	97,951
	0	0	0	(4,987)	(26,367)	(35,263)
	(14,056)	(14,056)	(14,056)	(14,056)	(14,056)	(14,056)
	$ (10,648)	$ 3,476	$ 23,709	$ 40,739	$ 32,818	$ 48,633
	$ (10,200)	$ (10,200)	$ (10,200)	$ (10,200)	$ (10,200)	$ (10,200)
	(41,956)	(51,719)	(63,754)	(78,623)	(63,494)	(63,494)
	(5,693)	(5,693)	(5,693)	(5,693	(5,693)	(5,693)
	(68,497)	(64,136)	(55,939)	(53,778)	(46,569)	(30,754)

EXHIBIT 4   Forecast Balance Sheets

				Pro Forma Balance Sheets	
	Actual May 31 1986	*Leveraged Buyout Adjustments*	*LBO Pro Forma 1986*	*Operating and Restructuring Pro Forma Adjustments May-to-May*	*1987*
Assets					
Current assets:					
Cash[1]	$ 45,074	$ (10,655)	$ 34,419	$ 15,213	$ 49,632
Acct's receivable	68,534	(2,565)	65,969	46,884	112,853
Inventories[2,3]	501,956	81,000	582,956	(129,207)	453,749
Prepaid expenses	24,022	0	24,022	(4,560)	19,462
Assets to be divested[4]	0	0	0	230,819	230,819
Total current assets	639,586	67,780	707,366	159,149	866,515
Plant, property, & equipment:					
Land, improvements, etc.	62,929	NAv	NAv	NAv	48,862
Equipment & fixtures	223,328	NAv	NAv	NAv	120,373
Leasehold improvements	105,388	NAv	NAv	NAv	36,315
Construction in progress	36,386	NAv	NAv	NAv	46
Gross PP&E	428,031	NAv	NAv	NAv	205,596
Accumulated depreciation	(126,684)	NAv	NAv	NAv	(8,388)
Net PP&E[2]	301,347	54,000	355,347	(158,139)	197,208
Leasehold interests[2]		194,000	194,000	(33,133)	160,867
Other assets[2]	32,521	57,400	89,921	11,040	100,961
Goodwill	13,500	519,027	532,527	29,709	562,236
Total assets	$986,954	$ 892,207	$1,879,161	$ 8,626	$1,887,787

[1] Reduction of cash as part of the LBO financing.
[2] LBO write-up of asset values by allocating purchase premium across relevant assets.
[3] 1987 result of inventory reduction program.
[4] 1987 initiation of asset divestment program.
Note: columns may not exactly foot because of rounding in the forecast model.

(dollars in thousands)

	Projected (Fiscal Years Ending May 30)						
1988	*1989*	*1990*	*1991*	*1992*	*1993*	*1994*
$ 50,000	$ 50,000	$ 50,000	$ 50,000	$ 50,000	$ 50,000	$ 50,000
118,637	131,629	145,753	161,098	177,760	189,175	200,525
495,144	540,498	589,804	643,371	701,536	741,384	781,007
20,459	22,700	25,136	27,782	30,655	32,624	34,581
0	0	0	0	0	0	0
684,240	744,827	810,692	882,251	959,951	1,013,183	1,066,114
51,239	53,615	55,992	58,368	60,745	60,745	60,745
126,228	132,083	137,937	143,792	149,647	155,502	161,357
38,081	39,848	41,614	43,380	45,147	46,913	48,679
48	50	53	55	57	59	62
215,596	225,596	235,596	245,596	255,596	263,219	270,843
(18,918)	(29,948)	(41,477)	(53,507)	(66,037)	(79,007)	(92,359)
196,678	195,648	194,119	192,089	189,559	184,212	178,484
152,824	144,780	136,737	128,694	120,650	112,607	104,564
95,913	90,865	85,817	80,769	75,721	70,673	65,625
548,180	534,124	520,068	506,012	491,956	477,901	463,845
$1,677,835	$1,710,245	$1,747,433	$1,789,815	$1,837,837	$1,858,575	$1,878,631

EXHIBIT 4   *(concluded)*

Pro Forma Balance Sheets

	Actual May 31 1986	*Leveraged Buyout Adjustments*	*LBO Pro Forma 1986*	*Operating and Restructuring Pro Forma Adjustments May-to-May*	*1987*
Liabilities & Stockholders' Equity					
Current liabilities:					
Working capital loan	0	0	0	0	0
Current portion LTD[5]	$ 4,490	$ 130,091	$ 134,581	$ 9,560	$ 144,141
Trade accounts payable	155,179		155,179	(13,603)	141,576
Other accounts payable	21,904		21,904	(1,756)	20,148
Accrued salaries	22,705		22,705	1,975	24,680
Other accrued liabilities	42,861		42,861	33,533	76,394
Taxes payable	6,442		6,442	(2,089)	4,353
Restructuring reserve	0		0	29,238	29,238
Total current liabilities	253,581	130,091	383,672	56,858	440,530
Long-term debt[6]	304,885	908,570	1,213,455	(58,597)	1,154,858
Restructuring reserve			0	38,596	38,596
Deferred income taxes	35,958	(35,958)	0	0	0
Stockholders' equity:					
Convertible preferred stock[7] ...	0	85,000	85,000	0	85,000
Exchangeable preferred stock[7]	0	130,020	130,020	16,244	146,264
Junior preferred stock[7]	0	30,098	30,098	2,214	32,312
Total preferred stock	0	245,118	245,118	18,458	263,576
Common Stock[8]		2,605	2,605	(60)	2,545
Common held by management investors[9]	10,158	10,158	(92)	10,066	10,066
Revco common stock	36,743	(36,743)	0	0	0
Holding common stock	0	35	35	0	35
Additional paid-in capital	41,764	(17,646)	24,118	(24,118)	0
Retained earnings	411,729	(411,729)	0	(22,419)	(22,419)
	490,236	(453,320)	36,916	(46,689)	(9,773)
Less treasury stock	97,706	(97,706)	0	0	0
Total stockholders' equity	392,530	(355,614)	36,916	(46,689)	(9,773)
Total liabilities & equity	$986,954	$ 892,207	$1,879,161	$ 8,626	$1,887,787

NAv means not available.

[5] LBO reflects repayment of $2,049 of current installments and addition of the current portion of term loan of $132,500.

[6] Long Term Debt includes noncurrent portion of term loan, senior sub. notes, sub. notes, and junior sub. notes (all totalling $1,023,645), less repayments of $115,075.

[7] Reflects initial issuance of these securities in LBO.

[8] Reflects a portion of the purchase price of the Units allocated to the common stock and common stock puts and recorded as a discount on the Junior Subordinated Notes.

[9] Reflects issuance of common stock in the surviving firm to the managers. This is to distinguish these shares from common shares sold in units and from common shares arising from the conversion of debt.

[10] Over the first five years after the LBO, the number of exchangeable preferred shares will compound from 7.88 to 16.654 million. Also, accounting rules for redeemable preferred stock require that the par value accrete from the initial offering price of $16.50 to the redemption price of $25.00 over the period until redemption or exchange becomes possible.

Note: columns may not exactly foot because of rounding in the forecast model.

Sources: SEC filings, historical financial ratios, and casewriters' estimates.

(dollars in thousands)

| | | | *Projected (Fiscal Years Ending May 30)* | | | |
1988	1989	1990	1991	1992	1993	1994
$ (6,229)	$ 172,861	$ 233,873	$ 287,002	$ 305,674	$ 340,697	$ 359,374
117,500	50,000	60,000	40,000	0	0	200,000
146,169	162,176	179,578	198,484	219,013	233,077	247,061
24,361	27,029	29,930	33,081	36,502	38,846	41,177
25,510	28,304	31,341	34,640	38,223	40,678	43,118
80,309	89,104	98,665	109,053	120,332	128,059	135,742
0	0	0	0	0	0	0
38,596	0	0	0	0	0	0
426,216	529,474	633,386	702,260	719,743	781,357	1,026,473
1,037,358	987,358	927,358	887,358	887,358	887,358	687,358
0	0	0	0	0	0	0
0	0	0	0	0	0	0
85,000	85,000	85,000	85,000	85,000	85,000	85,000
180,300	222,255	273,974	337,728	416,351	416,351	416,351
38,005	43,699	49,392	55,085	60,779	66,472	72,166
303,305	350,954	408,366	477,813	562,130	567,823	573,517
2,545	2,545	2,545	2,545	2,545	2,545	2,545
10,066	10,066	10,066	10,066	10,066	10,066	
0	0	0	0	0	0	0
35	35	35	35	35	35	35
0	0	0	0	0	0	0
(101,690)	(170,187)	(234,324)	(290,262)	(344,040)	(390,609)	(421,362)
(89,044)	(157,541)	(221,678)	(277,616)	(331,394)	(377,963)	(408,716)
0	0	0	0	0	0	0
(89,044)	(157,541)	(221,678)	(277,616)	(331,394)	(377,963)	(408,716)
$1,677,835	$1,710,245	$1,747,433	$1,789,815	$1,837,837	$1,858,575	$1,878,631

EXHIBIT 5   Drugstore Industry Financial Data (latest fiscal year)

	Sales ($mm)	Expected 5-Year Growth Rate	Net Profit Margin	Number of Stores	Stock Price (Hi/lo)	Book Value Per Share
Big B	175.4	17.5%	2.3%	135	$ 20/10.8	5.22
Eckerd*	2,508.5	NAv	2.3	1,688	32.9/20	14.49
Fay's Drug ...	445.1	9.5	0.6	154	13/8	4.3
Long's Drug ..	1,480.8	12.0	2.5	208	31.8/21.6	13.33
Perry Drug.....	521.6	10.0	1.8	367	18.8/10.8	7.79
Rite Aid	1,564.1	18.0	4.3	1,485	33.5/21.5	9.65
Thrifty	1,404.9	NAv	2.3	641	25.4/18.1	6.86
Walgreen	3,161.9	15.5%	3.0%	1,087	$30.3/21.5	7.83

* The figures for Jack Eckerd Corporation reflect performance for the last full fiscal year preceding Eckerd's leveraged buyout. NAv means not available.

Source: *Value Line Investment Survey.*

EXHIBIT 6   Capital-Market Information (for December 1986)

U.S. Treasury bills:
   3 months 5.49%
   6 months 5.60%

U.S. Treasury notes:
   1 year 5.87%
   2 years 6.27%
   3 years 6.43%
   5 years 6.67%
   7 years 6.97%
  10 years 7.11%

U.S. Treasury bonds:
  20 years 7.28%
  30 years 7.37%

Sources: Federal Reserve *Bulletin* and *Value Line.*

Debt/ Equity Ratio	E.P.S.	P/E Ratio	Annual Dividend	Beta	Days Inventory Outstanding	Cost of Goods-to-Sales
0.22	0.61	25.4	0.00	1.00	123	70.3%
0.18	1.55	17.7	1.02	1.00	100	72.2
0.96	0.20	52.5	0.20	1.00	71	76.2
0.00	1.74	16.0	0.70	0.85	54	75.9
1.27	0.97	13.7	0.19	1.10	133	68.3
0.35	1.65	15.9	0.52	1.15	105	70.7
1.13	1.60	12.7	0.58	1.10	100	71.9
0.12	1.53	15.8	0.44	1.10	76	69.3%

Corporate bonds (Moody's):

Aaa 6.29%

Baa 7.25%

Commercial paper—6 months 5.88%

Prime rate 7.50%

Federal Reserve discount rate 5.50%

Federal funds rate 6.91%

Standard & Poor's 500 Index 248.61

Median price-earnings ratio .... 11.0×

Expected dividend yield, 12 months 3.6%

Expected values for retailers
  (next 12 months):

  P/E   15×

  Dividend yield   1.5%

EXHIBIT 7   Comparative Forecast of Coverage Ratios

Key Simulation Assumptions:			*Revco Drug Stores*	
		Mean	*Standard Deviation*	
EBIT		6.60%	1.32%	
Same store growth rate (inflation)		5.00%	3.90%	
Realization percentage		100.00%	20.00%	
Divestment assumptions:		*$ Assets Divested*	*Realization Percentage*	*Divestment in 1987*
	1987	50.00%	100.00%	$115,000
	1988	25.00%	100.00%	
	1989	12.50%	100.00%	
Divestment target	$230,000			

Common Assumptions in Financial Forecast

	Mean	*Std. Dev.*			
			Stores to be divested		77
			Cost of opening		
Gross margin, old stores	6.60%	1.32%	Each new store	$100,000	
Gross margin, new stores	6.60%	1.32%	New stores/year	100	
Growth rate of store sales . . .			Assets 1987	$115,000	$115,000
			divested		
Mature stores	5.00%	3.90%	1988	$57,500	
New stores	5.00%	3.90%	1989	28,750	
Prime rate + 1.75%	9.25%	3.60%	Total assets divested	$201,250	

Year	*1986*	*1987*	*1988*	*1989*	*1990*
Gross margin, old stores		6.60%	6.60%	6.60%	6.60%
Gross margin, new stores		6.60%	6.60%	6.60%	6.60%
Growth rate, old stores		5.00%	5.00%	5.00%	5.00%
Growth rate, new stores		5.00%	5.00%	5.00%	5.00%
Inflation rate		5.00%	5.00%	5.00%	5.00%
Prime + 1.75%		9.25%	9.25%	9.25%	9.25%
Mature store sales	$1,015	$1,066	$1,119	$1,175	$1,234
New store sales	$945	$992	$1,042	$1,094	$1,149
New stores	95	97	100	100	100
Old stores (BOP)	1936	2031	2090	2170	2261
Divestitures		39	19	10	10

Key Simulation Assumptions:		Jack Eckerd Corporation		
			Standard	
Gross margin		Mean	Deviation	
Same store growth rate		5.00%	3.90%	

Divestment assumptions		% Assets Divested	Realization Percentage	Divestment in 1987
	1987	50.00%	100.00%	$36,000
	1988	25.00%	100.00%	
	1989	12.50%	100.00%	
Divestment target		$72,000		

Common Assumptions in Financial Forecast

	Mean	Std. Dev.		Cost of opening		
Gross margin, old	8.11%	1.42%		Each new store		$100,000
Gross margin, new	8.11%	1.42%		New stores/year		
						100
Growth rate of store sales				Assets divested	1987	$36,000
Mature stores	5.00%	3.90%			1988	$18,000
New stores	5.00%	3.90%			1989	$9,000
Prime rate − revo	10.25%	3.60%		Total assets divested		$63,000
(prime was about 9% in April 1986)						

Year	1986	1987	1988	1989	1990
Gross margin, old stores		8.11%	8.11%	8.11%	8.11%
Gross margin, new stores		8.11%	8.11%	8.11%	8.11%
Growth rate, old stores		5.00%	5.00%	5.00%	5.00%
Growth rate, new stores		5.00%	5.00%	5.00%	5.00%
Inflation rate		5.00%	5.00%	5.00%	5.00%
Prime + 1.75%		10.25%	10.25%	10.25%	10.25%
Mature store sls.	$1,520	$1,596	$1,676	$1,760	$1,848
New store sales	$0	$0	$0	$0	$0
New stores	0	0	0	0	0
Old stores, (BOP)	1729	1729	1729	1729	1729
Divestitures		0	0	0	0

EXHIBIT 7   *(concluded)*

Revco D.S. Forecast of EBIT and Cash Flow
(Calendar years ending December 31, $ in thousands)
Projected

	Actual 1986	1987	1988	1989	1990	
Sales	$2,743,178	$2,222,585	$2,422,359	$2,648,887	$2,892,830	
EBIT, old stores		$142,860	$154,323	$168,301	$184,075	
EBIT, new stores		$6,352	$6,876	$7,220	$7,581	
Total EBIT	**$149,211,909**	**$149,212**	**$161,199**	**$175,521**	**$191,656**	
Old depreciation		$33,701	$34,720	$36,156	$37,781	
New depreciation		$1,019	$1,436	$1,625	($40,964)	
Outlay for new stores		($10,185)	($11,025)	($11,576)	($12,155)	
Asset sales		$115,000	$115,000	$0	$0	
Total CF available to service obligations		**$288,747**	**$301,331**	**$201,726**	**$176,318**	
	Shortfall	($8,843)	($4,003)	($7,001)		
Cash obligations to be covered ...	Term balance	$455,000	$322,500	$170,000	$100,000	
Change in long portion LTD		$132,500	$152,500	$70,000	$60,000	
Interest expense-fixed rate		$112,802	$112,802	$112,802	$112,802	
Interest expense-floating		$42,088	$29,831	$15,725	$9,250	
Conv. pfd dividend		$10,200	$10,200	$10,200	$10,000	
Total obligations to be covered		**$297,590**	**$305,334**	**$208,727**	**$192,252**	
						1987–90 Cumulative
Coverage ratio: EBIT		**50.14%**	**52.79%**	**84.09%**	**99.69%**	**67.50%**
Coverage ratio: Total CF		**97.03%**	**98.69%**	**96.65%**	**91.71%**	**96.44%**

	Actual 1986	*Jack Eckerd Corporation Forecast of EBIT and Cash Flow* *(Calendar years ending December 31, $ in thousands)* *Projected*				
		1987	*1988*	*1989*	*1990*	
Sales	$2,628,660	$2,760,093	$2,898,098	$3,043,003	$3,195,153	
EBIT, old stores		$223,844	$235,036	$246,788	$259,127	
EBIT, new stores		$0	$0	$0	$0	
Total EBIT		**$223,844**	**$235,036**	**$246,788**	**$259,127**	
Depreciation		$32,020	$32,020	$32,020	$32,020	
Outlay for new stores		$0	$0	$0	$0	
Asset sales		$36,000	$36,000	$0	$0	
Total CF available to service obligations		**$291,864**	**$303,056**	**$278,808**	**$291,147**	
		$690,000	**$595,000**	**$395,000**	**$95,000**	
Cash obligations to be covered	$0	95,000	200,000	300,000	400,000	
Paydown of revolver		$95,000	$105,000	$100,000	$100,000	
Interest expense (Revolver & SubDeb) . . .		$118,719	$108,981	$88,481	$58,444	
Pfd dividend		$10,875	$10,875	$10,875	$10,875	
Total obligations to be covered		**$224,594**	**$224,856**	**$199,356**	**$169,319**	
						1987–90 Cumulative
Coverage ratio: EBIT		**99.67%**	**104.53%**	**123.79%**	**153.04%**	**108.76%**
Coverage ratio: Total CF		**129.95%**	**134.78%**	**139.85%**	**171.95%**	**134.67%**

Analysis of Financing Tactics: Swaps, Options, and Foreign Currency

Merit Marine Corporation

January 1985 started with an opportunity for Ginny Shields, a relationship manager for Omni Bank, N.A., and Jeff Finch, a member of the bank's corporate finance department, to expand the bank's reputation for providing financial advisory services to existing credit customers. Ms. Shields, who had moved to Omni Bank's regional office in Miami two months earlier, had identified the need to restructure the balance sheet (shown in Exhibit 1, with debt components in Exhibit 2) of Merit Marine Corporation, the Florida distributor of Olympus brand marine products. Omni Bank was a large money center financial institution.

Prior to phoning Jeff Finch in New York, Ginny had concluded that Merit was in need of long-term, fixed-rate financing to reduce the firm's interest-rate sensitivity and to match its funding sources better with its level of fixed assets. Merit's inability to obtain reasonably priced fixed-rate debt for $27 million in capital expenditures incurred between 1980 and 1983 had left the company relying on two-year, variable-rate financing.

Ginny's conversation with Jeff Finch concentrated on the prospects for restructuring Merit's balance sheet through the use of a private placement or an interest-rate swap, or both. Jeff initially was skeptical of the market's receptiveness to an offering of Merit securities because of the firm's size and recent performance (see earnings statements in Exhibit 3), yet he agreed to meet with Ginny on his upcoming trip to Miami.

COMPANY BACKGROUND

Located in Tampa, Florida, Merit Marine Corporation had been the exclusive Florida distributor of Olympus brand commercial and recreational marine products since January 1976, when John Merit, the company's president, had acquired the assets of the Olympus

This case was written by Peter R. Hennessy, research assistant, under the direction of Robert F. Bruner.

Copyright © 1985 by the Darden Graduate Business School Foundation, Charlottesville, VA. Revised July 1993.

Florida franchise. In 1985, the company was closely held by John Merit and some relatives. John Merit himself held a majority of the common shares. Merit distributed Olympus products to independent marinas across the state and, in addition to the distribution function, ran one of the state's largest marinas at its headquarters in Tampa.

Since 1948, Olympus had been considered the premier manufacturer of engines and steering mechanisms for boats ranging from pleasure crafts to large cabin cruisers. Olympus products accounted for 90 percent of Merit's sales in 1984, with remaining revenues generated from sales and service provided at the firm's Sunshine Marina. (Exhibit 4 gives the distribution of Merit's sales.)

Merit's sales of Olympus products to marinas across the state were concentrated in three product lines: drive trains, which included engines and steering mechanisms; Olympia recreational boats; and Olympus replacement parts. Olympus differentiated itself by stressing quality throughout the manufacturing process and by providing the highest level of service in the industry. Through its unique distribution network, Olympus guaranteed marinas one-day delivery of replacement parts. The formula had been successful: Olympus controlled over one quarter of the $5 billion marine products market in the United States.

The previous owner of the Florida franchise, Alex Stalworth, had operated the franchise since Olympus's inception in 1948. Prior to selling the franchise, Mr. Stalworth had been hesitant to make the substantial investment necessary to serve the booming recreational and commercial boating market in Florida. As a result, beginning in 1977, Merit found it necessary to make substantial investments in new fixed assets for the company, climaxing in 1982 with a $14 million addition to the warehouse and the service center. While the investment had been substantial, the new capacity would allow Merit to more than double sales. With the new facility in place, Merit anticipated that capital expenditures over the next several years would be approximately $3 million a year.

Sales for Merit Marine, which had increased at an annual rate of 16 percent between 1977 and 1981, dropped sharply in 1982 and 1983, as shown in Exhibit 4. The decline was a function of a severe recession, high interest rates, and oil prices. The subsequent economic recovery and the decline in oil prices brought a stronger market for Olympus's products in Florida, which allowed Merit's 1984 sales to increase 30 percent to $120 million.

INDUSTRY INFORMATION

Total marine product sales were expected to decline by as much as 5 percent in 1985. However, the Florida market was expected to increase by 5 percent annually for the next several years. The recreational market, which accounted for most sales of Olympus outboard engines and Olympia boats, was highly seasonal and cyclical. Sales of stern-drive and sea-drive engines, which were used primarily for larger recreational and commercial boats, were less seasonal and slightly less cyclical.

The outboard engine market was concentrated among three major manufacturers— Outboard Marine Corporation (Johnson and Evinrude), Brunswick (Mercury), and Olympus. Japanese manufacturers, such as Yamaha, were just beginning to market outboard engines in the United States. Olympus competed against Volvo, Mercury, and Chrysler in the stern-drive and sea-drive markets. Olympia boats, on the other hand, faced a much more fragmented market: over 20 national and regional manufacturers competed for the recreational boat dollar.

BANKING RELATIONSHIPS

John Merit's relationship with Omni Bank began in 1967, when he joined Olympus's treasury office at the firm's headquarters in Zion, Illinois. When the distributorship became available in Florida in 1976, Mr. Merit, with the help of some family financial support, purchased the franchise from Mr. Stalworth. Omni Bank, along with Sun Coast Bank in Orlando and Ybor National Bank in Tampa, had met Merit Marine's credit needs since the company was purchased in 1976. Mr. Merit had remained loyal to the bank group over the years, but he insisted on the most attractive rates possible.

While both Omni Bank and Sun Coast had $25 million credit commitments to Merit Marine as of January 1985, neither considered itself Merit's lead bank. (Merit's credit relationships are detailed in Exhibit 5.) At year-end 1984, Merit was fully utilizing the $25.0 million revolver and had $12.7 million of the $40.0 million line of credit outstanding. John Merit had intimated that lead-bank status would go to the bank that offered the most attractive rates. Being the lead bank in the credit group would become more significant in the future, as Merit planned to displace current bank debt with below-market-rate financing offered by Olympus Credit Corporation to qualified dealers.

SOURCES OF FUNDING

Beginning in the spring of 1984, Olympus Credit Corporation had made available to Olympus distributors $10 million in guaranteed, short-term, floating-rate debt at the A1-P1 commercial paper rate plus 50 basis points. Olympus then announced in December that qualified distributors would be eligible for up to $20 million in commercial paper-based financing, beginning in April of 1985. The prospect of having an additional $10 million in outstandings displaced concerned Ginny Shields and heightened her determination to gain lead-bank status.

Omni Bank had priced the $25 million commitment to Merit to achieve a target spread of 110 basis points over the bank's cost of funds. The Merit relationship produced a net contribution of $279,000 in 1983 and $305,000 in the first 11 months of 1984. The contribution for 1984 included earned interest on average deposits of $1.37 million and interest income on average outstanding debt of $14.5 million.

Omni Bank's loan agreement called for Merit Marine to keep compensating balances with the bank based on the total amount of credit committed to the company. To attempt to gain lead-bank status, Ginny Shields, in December 1984, lowered the compensating-balance agreement from 5.0 percent to 2.5 percent of the total credit commitment. Next Ms. Shields positioned Omni bank to act as Merit's financial advisor with the help of the bank's corporate finance department. It was apparent that Merit needed long-term, fixed-rate funding; accomplishment of this task, however, was easier said than done. Ms.

Shields had recalled a memo (shown as Exhibit 6) that had recently been distributed to relationship managers describing the profile of a private-placement candidate. She realized that Merit would be a borderline case. Merit had been unsuccessful in arranging a reasonably priced mortgage in 1982. Since then, the bank had been unable to provide long-term, fixed-rate financing at an acceptable rate, because of Merit's questionable creditworthiness and the prevailing interest rate environment. (Exhibits 7 and 8 show historic rates and spreads.)

Ginny thought that, while Merit did not need additional debt, the firm did need to limit its exposure to fluctuations in interest rates by fixing the interest rate on $10 to $15 million in debt. After discussions with John Merit, it was evident that a rate in excess of 12 percent would be unacceptable.

ALTERNATIVES

On January 8, 1985, Jeff Finch and Ginny Shields visited with John Merit in Tampa. The three discussed Merit Marine's funding needs and the possibility of fixing interest payments through an interest-rate swap or a private placement, or both.

Jeff was uncertain whether institutional investors would be interested in privately placed debt of Merit's quality; however, he suggested this alternative and pointed out that, under present market conditions, the shorter the maturity, the lower the interest rate. Jeff then introduced the concept of an interest-rate swap as a means of effectively fixing interest payments on existing floating-rate debt. Merit initially was unreceptive to the swap alternative, mainly because of a lack of understanding of the offer. Upon returning to New York, Jeff requested the right to approach a small number of private investors to see how receptive the market might be to Merit's debt. After speaking with institutional investors, he concluded that three alternatives existed to help restructure Merit's capital base.

The first proposal was to fix the interest payments on $10 million in existing debt for three years using an interest-rate swap funded with the commercial paper-based debt supplied by Olympus Credit Corporation. If additional interest payments needed to be fixed in the future, a subsequent swap could be arranged, since additional commercial paper-based debt would be available to Merit in April 1985. Omni Bank would arrange with Merit to swap interest payments on $10 million of the commercial paper-based, floating-rate debt, which cost Merit the A1-P1 paper rate plus 50 basis points. The bank would pay Merit the six-month London Interbank Lending Rate (LIBOR) and, in return, Merit would pay a fixed rate equal to the current three-year Treasury note rate plus 108 basis points. Historical six-month LIBOR was 102 basis points higher than the 30-day, A1-P1 commercial paper rate. Merit's effective interest rate under this proposal would vary to the extent that the spread between LIBOR and the commerical paper rate was different from the historical spread of 102 basis points. A larger spread would lower Merit's effective interest rate, while a smaller spread would increase the overall rate. Omni Bank's compensation in the transaction would amount to approximately 25 basis points per year. The bank's compensation, which was included in the 108 basis point spread, was higher than normal, because the rate Omni Bank could offer

Merit through an interest-rate swap was at least 3 percent lower than bank-funded, fixed-rate debt.

The second alternative considered was a $10 million, three-year private placement at a fixed rate of 12 percent. The debt would be placed with an insurance company that had an appetite for high-yielding, noninvestment-grade bonds. The 12 percent coupon represented a 125 basis-point premium over an A-rated private placement and a 75 basis-point premium over a BBB placement. Interest would be paid quarterly and the principal would be repaid at the end of three years. Since the institutional investor would be matching the transaction with similar term liabilities, there would be no option for Merit to prepay the commitment. This option would leave the commerical paper debt available to support working-capital needs and would allow Merit to enter into an interest-rate swap if additional interest payments needed to be fixed.

The final alternative combined the same private placement as in the second alternative with a 10-year, $15 million, adjustable-rate private placement with a three-year option to fix for a term of three years. If the option to fix were exercised, the remaining term of the loan would be three years from the date of exercise. The principal on the second placement would also be repaid in full upon maturity. The variable-rate note would be set at the 91-day Treasury rate plus 200 basis points, while the rate if Merit chose to fix would be 122 percent of three-year Treasuries. The variable-rate note could not be repaid prior to June 30, 1986. Between June 30, 1986 and March 31, 1988, there would be no prepayment penalty, while prepayment after March 31, 1988, would incur a 5 percent penalty. If Merit exercised the fixed-rate option, no prepayment would be allowed during the three-year period. Omni Bank's compensation on the private-placement package would be 1.0 percent of the first $10 million and 0.5 percent of any additional debt placed.

In making a recommendation to Merit, Jeff Finch had to consider a number of issues. First, Merit Marine could look forward to the possibility of very strong cash flow over the next several years, because of low level of planned capital expenditures and a likelihood of increased sales. In addition, Merit had been concentrating on speeding receivables and reducing the level of inventory carried. Jeff knew that if too much of Merit's debt was fixed for too long a period, the firm would incur a prepayment penalty if cash flow was sufficient to reduce outstanding long-term debt.

A second issue that concerned Jeff involved the permanence of the commercial paper-based, floating-rate debt. If those funds became unavailable during the life of the swap, Merit would have to fund the swap with prime-based debt and would incur the additional interest expense between the prime rate and the commercial paper rate plus 50 basis points.

While the rate structure at three years met the 12 percent level that Mr. Merit set as his threshold, Jeff was concerned whether the three-year term was appropriate for the company or whether a longer maturity was needed.

While Jeff considered these alternatives, Ginny Shields was faced with a dilemma regarding the profitability of the relationship. She wondered whether her initiative to position Omni Bank as Merit's financial advisor might move the bank into the lead position in a credit group that had no outstandings. If Jeff were to place the $10 to $25 million in institutional debt, Merit would reduce its bank debt by a like amount; as a result, Omni Bank would stand to lose $10 million in outstandings. The decision to pursue the private-placement option would be a function of whether Ginny believed Merit's condition was evident enough that, if Omni Bank did not fix the firm's interest payments, another institution would. In such a case, Omni Bank would not only lose the interest income from the debt that would be assumed by another lender but also would lose the fees that would have been generated from a swap or private placement. One incentive for Ginny to provide corporate finance services in this situation was the fact that her division would be credited with a shadow profit equal to 60 percent of the fee generated by the corporate finance department.

EXHIBIT 1   Consolidated Balance Sheet for the Years Ended December 31 (in thousands)

	1980	1981	1982	1983	1984
Assets:					
Cash	$ 8,385	$ 3,997	$ 3,635	$ 3,692	$ 4,127
Net receivables	27,068	27,414	16,175	22,100	26,435
Inventories	33,877	27,059	22,094	25,201	21,347
Net rental equipment	25,335	21,672	16,510	27,604	28,976
Prepaid expenses	64	88	17	85	108
Total current assets	94,729	80,230	58,431	78,682	80,993
Investments	117	0	0	0	0
Net PP & E	6,125	7,503	20,969	24,565	23,204
Other assets	406	301	132	867	579
Total assets	$101,377	$88,034	$79,532	$104,114	$104,776
Liabilities:					
Notes payable	$ 66,143	$27,738	$36,877	$ 35,879	$ 31,122
Current portion LTD	691	20,107	195	97	101
Accounts payable	3,847	2,918	4,973	4,480	4,558
Accrued expenses	3,491	3,116	2,160	3,027	2,824
Dividends payable	0	78	77	77	77
Deferred income	0	0	0	0	170
Taxes payable	495	834	964	698	2,788
Total current liabilities	74,667	54,791	45,246	44,258	41,640
Long-term debt	2,158	3,665	3,503	28,398	28,083
Deferred income taxes	0	0	477	981	1,994
Total liabilities	76,825	58,456	49,226	73,637	71,717
Stockholders' equity:					
Preferred stock	0	1,290	1,290	1,290	1,290
Common stock	1,000	1,000	1,000	1,000	1,000
Additional paid-in capital	8,178	12,487	12,487	12,487	12,487
Treasury stock	0	(1,367)	(1,367)	(1,367)	(1,367)
Retained earnings	15,374	16,168	16,896	17,067	19,649
Total stockholders' equity	24,552	29,578	30,306	30,477	33,059
Total liabilities and equity	$101,377	$88,034	$79,532	$104,114	$104,776

EXHIBIT 2 Debt Components

Year	(1) Total Short-Term Debt (Cols. 2+3)	(2) Floating Rate	(3) Noninterest Bearing	(4) Total Long-Term Debt (Cols. 5+6 or Cols. 7+8)	(5) Floating Rate	(6) Fixed Rate	(7) Current Portion Long-Term Debt	(8) Long-Term Portion	(9) Total Debt (Cols. 1+4)
1984	31,122	22,589*	8,533	28,184	27,263	921	101	28,083	59,306*
1983	35,879	15,200	20,679	28,495	26,468	2,027	97	28,398	64,374
1982	36,877	30,706	6,171	3,698	2,196	1,502	195	3,503	40,575
1981	27,738	27,221	517	23,772	22,713	1,385	20,107	3,665	51,510
1980	66,143	64,859	1,284	2,849	1,693	1,156	691	2,158	68,992

* Includes $9,866,000 in commercial paper-based debt from Olympus Credit Corp.

Maturing portion of long-term debt and notes payable are as follows:

Year	Amount
1985	31,223
1986	25,595
1987	195
1988	317
1989	308

EXHIBIT 3   Consolidated Statement of Earnings for the Years Ended December 31 (in thousands)

	1980	*1981*	*1982*	*1983*	*1984*
Net sales	$129,891	$130,012	$89,112	$85,492	$120,472
Cost of sales	101,869	101,292*	66,748*	64,590*	94,999*
Gross profit	28,022	28,720	22,364	20,902	25,473
Selling, general & administrative	19,353	22,662	19,630	19,505	18,860
Operating profit	8,669	6,058	2,734	1,397	6,613
Int. income & earned discount	5,158	6,712	4,537	3,144	5,007
Interest (expense)	(9,102)	(11,042)	(5,413)	(4,066)	(6,493)
Other, net (expense)	(361)	(723)	(403)	(874)	(92)
Profit before taxes	4,364	1,005	1,455	(399)	5,035
Income taxes	2,280	114	650	(647)	2,376
Net earnings	$ 2,084	$ 891	$ 805	$ 248	$ 2,659

* Liquidation of LIFO layers caused cost of goods sold to be lower by the following amounts: '81, $474,000; '82, $417,000; '83, $344,000; '84, $358,000.

EXHIBIT 4   Distribution of Sales for the Years Ended December 31 (in thousands)

	1980	*1981*	*1982*	*1983*	*1984*
Total sales	$129,891	$130,012	$89,112	$85,492	$120,472
Olympus products	118,201	119,611	75,745	74,378	108,425
Drive train	52,009	56,217	32,570	30,495	45,538
Olympia boats	28,368	27,511	16,664	17,107	29,275
Replacement parts	37,824	35,883	26,511	26,776	33,612
Merit Marina	11,690	10,401	13,367	11,114	12,047
Sales:					
Boats & accessories	3,858	3,224	3,876	3,223	3,614
Gas	4,676	4,264	5,079	4,112	4,698
Service	3,156	2,912	4,411	3,779	3,735

EXHIBIT 5   Banking Relationships

Total available short-term and long-term notes payable to banks and Olympus Credit Corporation aggregated $75,000,000 at December 31, 1985.

Compensating balance agreement on bank lines amounted to 5%.

Revolving Credit Agreement

		$25,000,000
Consisting of:		
Sun Coast Bank, N.A.	$10,000,000	
Omni Bank	$10,000,000	
Ybor National Bank	$ 5,000,000	

Rate: prime

Average usage: 90%

Borrowing base: 75% of qualified current assets plus $15.0 million for headquarters until mortgaged.

Maturity: December 31, 1986, or 13 months from demand.

Covenants:	Working capital	$28.0 million
	Current ratio	1.5 : 1.0
	Total liabilities to net worth	3.0 : 1.0
	Tangible net worth	$27.0 million

Unsecured Lines of Credit

Total:		$40,000,000
Consisting of:		
Sun Coast Bank, N.A.	$15,000,000	
Omni Bank	$15,000,000	
Ybor National Bank	$10,000,000	

Rate: prime

Purpose: finance inventory and receivables.

EXHIBIT 6

To: Relationship Managers

From: Capital Markets Division

Subject: *Private Placement* Candidate Profile

The purpose of this profile is to provide the Relationship Managers with a brief description of the conditions under which a given company may or may not be a likely candidate for a private placement.

A. *Is There a Need?*
   1. The need to restructure the balance sheet in some way.
      a. Interest-rate risk management.
      b. Match funding.
   2. The identification of a significant cash need in the future.
      a. Impending refinancing.
      b. Capital expenditures.
      c. Merger or acquisition financing.
      d. Improving quality of financing.

B. *Can a Private Placement Be Done?—Minimum Financial Criteria*
   1. Sales greater than $75 million.
   2. Tangible equity greater than $25 million.
   3. Long-term debt/capital less than 50 percent.
   4. No losses in last three years.
   5. Pretax interest coverage greater than 1.2 ×.

C. *Can the Bank Get the Deal?*
   1. What is the bank's relationship with the client?
   2. Is there a competing party trying to get the same business?

EXHIBIT 7   Rate Structure (as of January 23, 1985)

Maturity	Treasuries	LIBOR Swaps[1]	A-Rated Private Placements[1]	Baa-Rated Private Placements[2]	Ba-Rated Private Placements[2]
3	10.10	T + 108	T + 70	T + 95	T + 120
5	10.61	T + 80	T + 75	T + 100	T + 125
7	10.88	T + 65	T + 80	T + 105	T + 130
10	11.00	T + 60	T + 90	T + 115	T + 140

31-Day Commercial Paper (A1-P1)	6-Month LIBOR	Prime Rate (CRB)[3]
8.01	8.75	10.50

10-year average prime rate = 11.71% (std. dev. = 4.32%)
Average spreads:

> LIBOR over A1-P1 commercial paper = 1.02%[4]
> Prime rate over LIBOR = 1.465%[4]
> Prime rate over 91-day Treasury bills = 3.849% (std. dev. = 1.681%)[5]

[1] Spreads are disguised from actual quoted rates. Relative differences between options are valid.
[2] Nonquoted rate. Reflects average premium paid for less than A-rated private placements. Actual rates would be on negotiated basis.
[3] Corporate borrowing rate—approximates prime rate.
[4] Average spread between 1/79–11/84.
[5] Average spread between 1/80–12/84.

EXHIBIT 8 Interest Rates

	Prime*	91-Day T-Bills	1-Month Commercial Paper	10-Year T-Notes	30-Year T-Notes
1985:					
January 23	10.50	7.69	8.01	11.00	11.45
1984:					
January	11.00	8.93	9.23	11.67	11.75
February	11.00	9.03	9.35	11.84	11.95
March	11.50	9.44	9.81	12.32	12.38
April	12.00	9.69	10.17	12.63	12.65
May	12.50	9.90	10.38	13.41	13.43
June	13.00	9.94	10.82	13.56	13.44
July	13.00	10.13	11.06	13.36	13.21
August	13.00	10.49	11.19	12.72	12.54
September	13.00	10.41	11.11	12.52	12.29
October	12.75	9.97	10.05	12.16	11.98
November	12.00	8.79	9.01	11.57	11.56
December	11.25	8.16	8.39	11.50	11.52
1983:					
July	10.50	9.12	9.15	11.38	11.40
August	11.00	9.39	9.41	11.85	11.82
September	11.00	9.05	9.19	11.65	11.63
October	11.00	8.71	9.03	11.54	11.58
November	11.00	8.71	9.10	11.69	11.75
December	11.00	8.96	9.56	11.83	11.88

* Average for 10 money center banks; weekly close in 1985; monthly average in 1984 and 1983.

Source: *Federal Reserve Bulletin* (vols. 69–71).

EXHIBIT 9 External Funds Requirements (in thousands)

	1983	1984
Net sales	$85,492	$120,472
Sources of funds:		
Net income	248	2,659
Depreciation	1,388	1,650
Deferred taxes	504	672
Total	2,140	4,981
Uses of funds:		
Net capital expenditures	4,984	289
Cash dividends (preferred stock)	77	77
Reduction in long-term debt	105	315
Increase in net working capital	21,239	4,929
Increase in other assets	735	(289)
Total	27,140	5,321
External funds required	25,000	340
Capitalization:		
Short-term debt	35,879	31,122
Long-term debt	28,495	28,184
Total debt	64,374	59,306
Shareholders' equity	30,477	33,059
Total	94,851	92,365
Short-term debt/capitalization	37.8%	33.7%
Total debt/capitalization	67.9%	64.2%
Net working capital/sales	40.3%	32.4%

EXHIBIT 10 Pro Forma Assumptions

	1985	1986	1987	1988
Change in net sales	5%	5%	5%	5%
Net income/sales	2.4%	2.4%	2.4%	2.4%
Depreciation expense (000)	$1,700	$1,734	$1,847	$1,755
Increase in deferred taxes (000)	1,022	805	704	592
Dividends	77	77	77	77
Increase in other assets (000)	300	300	300	300
Capital expenditures (000)	3,000	3,000	3,000	3,000
Net working capital/sales	0.31	0.30	0.29	0.28

EXHIBIT 11 Account Profitability

Type	Amount ($mm)	Usage	Rate	Ginny Shields's Division				Omni Bank			
				1985 Income (thousands)	1985 ROA	1986 Income (thousands)	1986 ROA	1985 Income (thousands)	1985 ROA	1986 Income (thousands)	1986 ROA
Scenario 1 (no change in revolver, 2.5% compensating balance, $2.0mm LOC)											
Revolver	$10.0	$10.0	1.1%	$110		$110					
Line of credit (LOC)	$12.0	$2.0	1.1%	22		22					
Compensating balance	$22.0	2.5%	10.0%	55		55					
Total				$187	1.56%	$187	1.56%	$187	1.56%	$187	1.56%
Scenario 2 ($25 million private placement, 2.5% compensating balance, $2.0mm LOC)											
Revolver											
Fees—private placement	0.175		60.0%	105							
Line of credit (LOC)	$12.0	$2.0	1.1%	22		22					
Compensating balance	$12.0	2.5%	10.0%	30		30					
Total				$157	7.85%	$ 52	2.6%	$227	11.35%	$ 52	2.6%
Scenario 3 ($10 million private placement, 2.5% compensating balance, $2.0mm LOC)											
Revolver	$6.0	$6.0	1.1%	66		66					
Fees—private placement	0.1		60.0%	60							
Line of credit (LOC)	$12.0	$2.0	1.1%	22		22					
Compensating balance	$18.0	2.5%	10.0%	45		45					
Total				$193	2.41%	$133	1.66%	$233	2.91%	$133	1.66%
Scenario 4 ($10 million swap, 2.5% compensating balance, $2.0mm LOC)											
Revolver	$10.0	$10.0	1.1%	110		110					
Fees—swap	10.0		0.250%	25		25					
Line of credit (LOC)	$12.0	$2.0	1.1%	22		22					
Compensating balance	$22.0	2.5%	10.0%	55		55					
Total				$212	1.77%	$212	1.77%	$212	1.77%	$212	1.77%
Scenario 5 (no change and revolver is displaced by private mortgage)											
Revolver											
Line of credit (LOC)	$12.0	$2.0	1.1%	22		22					
Compensating balance	$12.0	2.5%	10.0%	30		30					
Total				$ 52	2.6%	$ 52	2.6%	$ 52	2.6%	$ 52	2.6%

Emerson Electric Company

W. F. Bousquette, Emerson Electric Company's chief financial officer, was developing a plan for his company's financings in the spring of 1987. He was considering a range of financing tactics, including three possible two-year debt issues. Management wanted to raise $65 million to finance general corporate activities. The Aaa-rated company could issue a domestic bond with a coupon rate of 8.65 percent, a Swiss Eurobond with a 4.58 percent coupon rate, or a New Zealand Eurobond with a coupon of 18.55 percent. The relative attractiveness of each of the issues would depend on expectations about the three countries' economies and Emerson Electric's international net asset and economic exposures.

THE COMPANY

Emerson Electric Company was founded in 1890. By 1986, it had 50 operating divisions that manufactured a broad range of electrical and electronic products and systems. The company had 185 subsidiaries in 27 countries. Seven subsidiaries were in Switzerland and one was in New Zealand.

Emerson Electric's sales had almost reached the $5 billion mark. Over the past three years, the company's international sales, including exports, had risen from $883 million to $1.1 billion. Over the same period, the company changed its strategy from exporting to offshore production; the number of offshore plants increased from 50 in 1981 to 82 in 1986. Reflecting this trend, as shown in Exhibit 1, total foreign assets increased from $458 million to $813 million between 1984 and 1986; net foreign assets increased commensurately, from $220 million to $376 million. Sales of products manufactured by foreign subsidiaries rose from $539 million to $861 million. Corporate management believed Asia was the best source of future sales growth.

This case was written by Casey S. Opitz under the direction of Robert F. Bruner.
Copyright © 1988 by the Darden Graduate Business School Foundation, Charlottesville, VA.

PREVIOUS FOREIGN FINANCING

The company's prior long-term foreign financing had been limited; as shown in Exhibit 2, it now had two $100 million Eurodollar notes outstanding.

Emerson Electric made a practice of borrowing short term in the local currencies where it had operations needing temporary funding. In 1986, its foreign subsidiaries had credit facilities totaling $220 million.

ECONOMIC REVIEWS

United States

The United States had experienced its fourth straight year of economic growth in 1986, as shown in Exhibit 3. (The case appendix provides a glossary of economic terms.) Gross national product was increasing, while unemployment, inflation, and interest rates were at their lowest levels in years. Only two negative indicators continued to darken the horizon: the government deficit and the trade deficit. The dollar, however, which had increased in value over several years through mid-1985 and had contributed to the trade deficit, was weakening against other world currencies.

Projected economic growth for the next two years was fairly steady. Three economists at the University of Michigan were forecasting the indicators summarized in Exhibit 4. Real gross national product (GNP) was expected to increase by 3.4 percent and 3.2 percent in 1987 and 1988, and prices as measured by the GNP deflator were expected to increase by 3.2 percent and 4.1 percent. As a result of slower growth in government spending, the federal deficit was expected to decline to about $150 billion by the end of 1988. This decrease was expected to lower Treasury bill rates to less than 5 percent. Regarding the trade deficit, one economist[1] suggested that real economic growth would have to be accompanied by a dramatic increase in exports on the order of $30–$40 billion, even though this would still leave the United States with a trade deficit of over $100 billion. But such an increase seemed unlikely, given that the dollar's exchange rate had declined over two years earlier and an improvement in trade had not yet occurred. Perhaps there would be more serious structural barriers (such as deepening poverty in developing countries or the emergence of major new agricultural exporters), which prevented a turnaround in the U.S. trade deficit.

Overall, a fairly stagnant economy was expected. Consumer sentiment—which had bottomed out in 1980, peaked in early 1984, and stabilized over the succeeding two years—was beginning to show some signs of deterioration. Consumers did not foresee a recession in the near future, but they also did not expect any positive changes for the economy.

---

[1]Paul W. McCracken, "Foreign Trade Improvement to Boost the Economy," *Economic Outlook USA,* Survey Research Center, University of Michigan, fourth quarter 1986, pp. 12-13.

Switzerland

Switzerland's economy continued to demonstrate why it had long been considered the epitome of stability. Real gross domestic product (GDP) grew between 2 and 3 percent as inflation ranged between 0.7 and 3.4 percent. The country ran a constant merchandise trade deficit; but its service industry, most notably banking, created a current account surplus of between $4.5 and $6.0 billion. Foreign portfolio investment added to the positive current account balance to create a positive balance of payments as foreign investors placed more money in Switzerland (as they did in the United States) than domestic investors placed offshore.

The federal government was comparatively small, because most political power was held at the canton (provincial) level; federal revenues and expenditures were only about 10 percent of GDP, compared with 19 percent for the United States. Although the effect of the government's fiscal policies was not as great as in the United States, the Swiss government surplus in 1986 had decreased the competition for Swiss francs and contributed to the recent decline in interest rates.

The Swiss government had been adept at controlling the growth of the monetary base, and, in a recent attempt to improve the government's ability to control the money supply through monetary policy, the Swiss National Bank persuaded other central banks to agree that there should be no Swiss franc bond issues outside the country. Within Switzerland, only domiciled banks could issue the bonds, and the government collected a 0.3 percent stamp tax on them. It was this tax that was largely responsible for the Eurobond market moving from Switzerland to London.

According to a recent report, Swiss franc securities issued in the country by foreigners in 1985 amounted to 9 percent of the $166 billion of international debt issued that year. That figure put Swiss francs in third place behind Eurodollars and the combined Euro-currency market as a source of funds.[2] In 1986, over $23 billion in Swiss franc bonds were issued, compared with $15 billion in 1985. United States dollar bond issues totaled $124 billion in 1986.[3]

The few banks that did issue bonds were known for their ability to place them, either with their depositors or their investment clients. Commission charges for the placements, however, were high.

There were some disturbing signs about the country's long-term financial strength, particularly regarding its future as a leading financial center:

> The whirlwind of innovation that is sweeping through the world capital markets, born of deregulation and new communications technology, is bringing disturbing eddies to . . . Zurich's financial market. With round-the-clock trading centered on New York, Tokyo, and London, there is an increasing tendency for Switzerland to be seen as a backwater. The Swiss are trailing behind the Americans, the Japanese, and the British . . . in their ability to invent and adapt new financial instruments.[4]

---

[2]"Moneymen Feel the Squeeze," *The Economist*, September 6, 1986, supplement, p. 8.
[3]*World Financial Markets*, April 1987, p. 16.
[4]*The Economist*, p. 9.

Also, the Swiss labor force was shrinking, which raised some questions about the economy's ability to grow at its historical average of 2 percent a year. The country had used foreign workers as a safety valve, bringing in more during expansions and forcing them to leave when jobs were scarce. But the current shortage of labor was expected to dampen the expansions of Switzerland's economy. Forecasts for the Swiss economy are provided in Exhibit 5.

New Zealand

> There is both pessimism and optimism in New Zealand today. Both make sense. On the one hand, the country is in recession, and the recession is likely to get worse; inflation is high and certain to go higher. On the other hand, the country has been taking a series of dramatic economic measures which . . . may well put the economy in better shape than it has been for 20 years.[5]

In the 1950s, New Zealanders enjoyed what may have been the highest standard of living in the world, based on the country's agricultural commodity exports to the United Kingdom. In 1968, 94 percent of the country's exports were commodities, and 39 percent went to Great Britain. This reliance on a single market and type of export led to complacency, however, and, in 1973, when the oil embargo took place and Great Britain joined the European Economic Community, the New Zealand economy was hit by a double shock. As energy costs rose from NZ$80 million in 1972 to NZ$1.5 billion in 1984, exports fell. Then the collapse of world commodity prices in the 1980s added a third shock to the economy. As recently as 1980, providers of syndicated loans had ranked New Zealand as number 1; by 1985, it had dropped to number 15.

Sir Robert Muldoon was New Zealand's prime minister and finance minister throughout the decline. Rather than combat the economic blows with long-term policies, he had instituted controls. By the early 1980s, controls had been placed on prices, wages, interest rates, exchange rates, and imports. When the price freeze was lifted in February 1984, inflation rose from 6.1 percent to 15.5 percent in one year. Federal government expenditures reached 41 percent of GDP in 1983–84, in sharp contrast to the United States (19 percent) and Switzerland (10 percent).

When David Lange of the Labour Party succeeded Sir Robert as prime minister in July 1984 and a separate finance minister was installed, the country faced a number of economic problems:

- Artificially supported terms of trade.
- Large balance-of-payments deficits.
- A rapidly growing money supply and high inflation.
- High unemployment.
- A highly regulated economy.

---

[5]"No More Free Lunches," *Euromoney,* September 9, 1986, supplement, p. 1.

In July 1984, the government eliminated all interest-rate controls and began to pay the market rate for its own borrowings. In December 1984, exchange controls were eliminated; and, in May 1985, the New Zealand dollar began to float freely. Unexpectedly, the currency strengthened instead of collapsing—a reflection of the world capital markets' approval of the new government policies.

In October 1986, a number of tax changes went into effect that put a ceiling of 48 percent, down from 66 percent, on corporate and personal income taxes. In the long run, this move was expected to boost the economy, but it was also expected to increase inflation in the near term. Most forecasters were projecting a rate of inflation for the year ended March 1987 of about 15 percent. The lowest projection was 8 percent. The change in the tax structure and a number of additional costs led the finance minister to project a deficit of NZ$2.45 billion for the same period.

In 1986, the country continued to rely on agricultural products for 50 percent of its export revenues; the argument was that, with 3 million people, it did not have the population base to support an industrial economy. Although continued high inflation relative to its trading partners and a stronger currency would act as brakes to higher exports, there were some bright spots. For example, the foreign exchange generated by tourism had increased since 1980 by 200 percent to NZ$1 billion. Between 1980 and 1985, tourism rose from the seventh to the fifth most important source of foreign exchange. Thus, overall, in spite of the strengthening currency, most forecasters expected the balance-of-payments deficit for the year ending March 1987 to fall to about $630 million—about half its previous level. Forecasts for the "Kiwi" economy are provided in Exhibit 5.

The demand for New Zealand dollar debt had expanded dramatically. The two-year-old market in NZ$–Eurobonds was at NZ$2 billion. In 1986, total New Zealand bond issues were $8.1 billion. International bond mutual funds, which had committed themselves to investing specific percentages of debt in given currencies, had "discovered" the Pacific Basin and debt in given currencies, and were eager to invest in Kiwi debt, but the supply from quality New Zealand-based companies was limited. As a result, offshore companies like Emerson might be able to issue NZ$ debt to these mutual funds on relatively favorable terms.

CONCLUSION

As he considered the economic forecasts for the three countries, Mr. Bousquette also studied the interest-rate and exchange-rate data provided in Exhibit 6 and the forward-rate data given in Exhibit 7. Swiss rates were low, and New Zealand rates were high, compared with those in the United States, but future inflation and exchange rates would affect the real cost of borrowing in any of the currencies. Mr. Bousquette had to decide whether he agreed with the general market expectations.

Appendix

DEFINITIONS OF ECONOMIC TERMS

Consumer price index (CPI) A measure of inflation based on the cost of a standard "basket" of goods.

Current account balance The merchandise trade balance (see below) plus the value of service exports minus service imports, plus net unrequited transfers (grants and gifts).

Direct foreign investment Physical assets acquired offshore.

Eurobond Bonds issued in the unregulated Eurobond market, a market for debt beyond the country in whose issue the currency is dominated.

Fiscal policy Governmental control of an economy exercised through spending and taxation.

Foreign portfolio investment Financial assets acquired offshore.

Government debt Accumulated government deficit.

Government deficit Annual government expenditures less government receipts.

Merchandise trade balance The value of exports minus imports over a specific period, generally a year.

Monetary policy Governmental control of an ecomony exercised through manipulation of the money supply.

Real gross national product (GNP) The total value of goods and services produced in a country in a fiscal year, less the effect of inflation. **GDP (gross domestic product)** is GNP less income from property owned abroad.

EXHIBIT 1   Emerson Worldwide Sales, Profits, and Assets (dollars in millions)

	1984	1985	1986
Sales to unaffiliated customers:			
United States	$3,816	$3,951	$4,092
Foreign	539	698	861
Eliminations	—	—	—
Total sales	$4,355	$4,649	$4,953
Earnings before taxes:			
United States	$ 590	$ 610	$ 607
Foreign	64	90	111
Eliminations	2	(6)	(3)
Total earnings	$ 656	$ 694	$ 715
Total assets:			
United States	$2,746	$2,715	$3,034
Foreign	458	609	813
Eliminations	(71)	(67)	(78)
Total assets	$3,133	$3,257	$3,769
Net assets:			
United States	$1,788	$1,938	$2,006
Foreign	220	291	376
Eliminations	(4)	(7)	(8)
Total net assets	$2,004	$2,222	$2,374

Source: Annual reports.

EXHIBIT 2   Emerson Long-Term Debt Summary (dollars in millions)

	1985	1986
9⅝% Eurodollar notes due 1995	—	$100.0
7⅞% Eurodollar notes due 1998	—	100.0
Notes payable in installments through 2004 at a weighted-average interest rate of 7.3% at September 30, 1986	$ 31.9	48.5
Lease obligations payable in installments through 2014 at a weighted-average interest rate of 7.0% at September 30, 1986	88.1	81.2
Other	8.3	7.8
Total	128.3	337.5
Less current maturities	13.7	9.2
Total debt	$114.6	$328.3

Note: The company partially hedged its foreign-currency net asset exposure by converting its $100 million 7⅞ percent Eurodollar notes through financial swaps into fixed-rate foreign-currency obligations due 1998. The foreign obligations were denominated in yen, deutsche marks, and Swiss francs, with a weighted-average foreign-currency interest rate of 5.86 percent as of December 31, 1986.

Source: Annual reports.

EXHIBIT 3   Comparative Financial Data (all in millions of U.S. dollars, except as noted)

	1982	1983	1984	1985	1986
Real GNP growth:					
United States	−2.5%	3.6%	6.4%	2.7%	3.6%
Switzerland (GDP)	−1.1	0.6	2.0	3.8	2.7
New Zealand	3.1	0.1	6.6	1.5	NA
Change in CPI:					
United States	6.1%	3.2%	4.3%	3.5%	2.0%
Switzerland	5.6	3.0	2.9	3.4	0.7
New Zealand	16.2	7.4	6.1	15.5	13.2
Merchandise trade balance:					
United States	($36,450)	($67,080)	($112,510)	($122,150)	($144,340)
Switzerland	(2,107)	(5,394)	(2,616)	(1,561)	(4,844)
New Zealand	(220)	345	(247)	81	224
Current account balance:					
United States	($8,640)	($46,280)	($107,090)	($116,430)	($141,460)
Switzerland	3,928	1,209	4,597	6,039	4,537
New Zealand	(1,612)	(968)	(1,748)	(1,265)	(1,294)
Direct foreign investment:					
United States	$16,160	$11,580	$22,570	$1,760	($3,000)
Switzerland	—	151	(362)	(3,305)	384
New Zealand	(79)	46	102	94	101
Foreign portfolio investment:					
United States	($880)	$4,730	$28,760	$64,430	$77,020
Switzerland	(1,248)	(3,987)	(2,876)	(1,104)	1,401
New Zealand	—	—	—	—	—
Government surplus (deficit):					
United States (bil $)	($126)	($203)	($178)	($212)	($213)
Switzerland (MM SF)	901	(1,446)	(889)	(490)	1,813
New Zealand (MM NZ$)	(2,389)	(3,209)	(3,234)	(2,086)	NA
Government debt:					
United States (bil $)	$988	$1,175	$1,373	$1,599	$1,819
Switzerland (MM SF)	24,968	25,249	27,745	29,266	28,228
New Zealand (MM NZ$)*	10,728	13,670	16,266	17,026	NA

* Period ending April 1, following year.

Source: *International Financial Statistics.*

EXHIBIT 4   Economic Forecasts—United States (dollars in billions)

	1987	1988
Change in real GNP	3.4%	3.2%
Inflation (GNP deflator)	3.2%	4.1%
Unemployment	6.9%	6.7%
Net exports	($137)	($172)
Government deficit	$160	$150
3-Month Treasury bill rate	4.6%	4.7%

Source: *Economic Outlook USA*, Survey Research Center, University of Michigan, fourth quarter 1986, pp. 9–11.

EXHIBIT 5   Economic Forecasts

Switzerland
(millions of Swiss francs)

	1987	1988
Change in real GNP	2.0%	2.8%
Inflation	1.5%	2.5%
Unemployment	NA	NA
Net exports	($4,979)	($4,905)
Government deficit	NA	NA
Domestic government bond rate	4.0%	4.0%

New Zealand*
(millions of New Zealand dollars)

	1987/88	1988/89
Change in real GNP	−1.0%	1.0%
Inflation	15.0%	6.5%
Unemployment	NA	NA
Net exports	$2,000	$2,000
Government deficit	$2,450	NA
5-year government bond rate	15.0%	12.0%
90-day bank bill rate	18.0%	15.0%

* Fiscal year ending April 1.

Sources: *Business Europe; Business Asia;* "No More Free Lunches," *Euromoney,* September 9, 1986, supplement, p. 1.

EXHIBIT 6 Comparative Interest Rates

	1983 Dec	1984 Dec	1985 Dec	1986 Nov	1986 Dec	1987 Jan	1987 Feb	1987 Mar
Domestic government bonds:								
United States	12.00%	11.61%	9.49%	7.69%	7.79%	7.17%	7.62%	7.90%
Switzerland	4.53	4.60	4.42	4.07	4.05	3.93	4.01	4.11
New Zealand	10.50	16.90	17.00	16.00	15.85	16.20	16.80	16.20
Prime lending rate:								
United States	11.00%	10.75%	9.50%	7.50%	7.50%	7.50%	7.50%	7.50%
Switzerland	6.00	6.00	6.00	5.75	5.75	5.25	5.25	5.25
New Zealand	11.00	14.00	21.00	18.50	18.50	24.00	25.00	27.00
Money market rates (short-term):								
United States	9.89%	8.34%	8.01%	5.96%	8.04%	6.97%	6.24%	6.70%
Switzerland	3.88	5.00	4.75	4.00	4.50	3.75	4.00	3.87
New Zealand	11.75	15.00	20.00	16.50	24.25	23.60	25.15	25.60
Exchange rate—currency/U.S. dollar:								*Mar 17*
Swiss franc	2.180	2.585	2.077	1.647	1.624	1.522	1.538	1.530
New Zealand dollar	1.528	2.094	2.006	1.932	1.910	1.840	1.791	1.762

Sources: *World Financial Markets; International Financial Statistics.*

EXHIBIT 7   Forward Rates

Days	SF / US$*	NZ$ / US$†
30	1.527	1.789
90	1.520	1.843
180	1.510	1.905
360	1.470	1.992
540	1.440	2.079
720	1.410	2.166

* Researcher's estimates after 180 days.
† Researcher's estimates after 360 days.

Sources: *The Wall Street Journal* and Bank of New Zealand.

Merrill Electronics Corporation (B)

Patricia Merrill, president and majority shareholder of Merrill Electronics, was pleased with her company's results over the past year (see Exhibits 1, 2, and 3). Sales had increased by over 40 percent and profits by more than 50 percent, compared to the previous year, in line with her ambitious growth objectives for the company. A number of operational improvements had been implemented with considerable success in reducing the working capital and cash needs of the firm. Also, she had secured additional long-term financing and an increase in the company's credit line. Although continued growth would require some additional investment in new computer and office equipment and in other fixed assets, she expected this could be largely financed out of cash flow—if margins held up and working capital could be kept under control.

Since its founding in 1950 by Thomas Merrill, Merrill Electronics had been a distributor for GEC,[1] a large manufacturer of electrical and electronics products for consumer and institutional markets. Over the years, in addition to the GEC products, the company had added noncompeting lines of electrical appliances, records, compact disks, and cassettes. In 1980, it began to broaden its product lines by importing Japanese consumer electronics. Four years later, it entered into an exclusive import agreement with the Goldstone Corporation of Taiwan, a major producer of television and other electronic equipment. These products were distributed to retail firms and dealers throughout a broad geographical area.

By the mid-1980s, Merrill had entered into the personal computer (PC) market, distributing both hardware and software products. It became the national distributor for Fuji

---

[1]Formerly the Global Electrical Company. In 1982, the company's name and logo had been changed to create a new image.

This case was prepared by Professor H. Lee Remmers at the European Institute of Business Administration (INSEAD), Fontainebleau, France.

Copyright © H. L. Remmers, INSEAD, 1992.

Electronics, a major Japanese manufacturer of PCs and related products, in March 1989. This had proven to be a fast-growing market, accounting for close to half of total sales and even more of the profits during the latest six-month period; but at the same time, it was becoming more and more competitive. By 1991, price cutting had become rampant as mail order and discount houses entered the business.

Patricia Merrill had been working in the company for two years when her father, Thomas Merrill, died in the spring of 1989. As the only family member with experience in the company, she succeeded him as president. Together with her mother, she controlled 75 percent of the share capital of the firm. The remaining shares were held by her father's brother and sister and their families.

During that first week of July 1992, she had been taking advantage of the relative calm that usually marked that time of the year. This was when they took the semiannual inventory, tended to various small problems that had been pushed aside during the past two or three months, and thought about the future.

One of the things that had been bothering her for some time was the volatility of the yen. About half of the equipment sold in the PC, TV & VCR, and hi-fi product lines were imported from Japanese suppliers. From a volume of about $12 million in the year ending in June 1991, yen-denominated purchases had exceeded $20 million during the past 12 months. With the growing volume expected in the PC product line, Merrill foresaw yen purchases from Fuji Electronics, Merrill's principal supplier, and other Japanese manufacturers to increase substantially in the future.

Typical of most Japanese exporters, Merrill's suppliers insisted on invoicing in yen. On average, once an order was placed the Japanese suppliers shipped by airfreight within 60 days. Payment terms were 30 days from the end of the delivery month; hence, the ¥225 million value of goods delivered in June 1992 would be paid at the end of July. With few exceptions, the yen spot price on the last day of the month in which the order was placed was used for the invoice. This meant that Merrill had on average a 90-day yen currency exposure for each order. Concerned about the potential impact from a varying exchange rate on the dollar cost of these purchases, Merrill had asked her general manager, Charles Brown, to gather some data on the monthly volume of purchases from Japanese suppliers as well as the yen/dollar exchange rates and interest rates over the past year. These appear on Exhibits 4 and 5.

The data gathered by Brown stunned Patricia Merrill. The effect of the yen's continual appreciation against the dollar between July and December 1991 meant that purchases during that period had cost Merrill over $370,000 more than if the exchange rate had been stable. Put another way, pre-tax profits were over 30 percent lower. Although Brown explained that a similar analysis performed on the January–June period in both 1991 and 1992 showed "gains" due to a weakening yen, Merrill decided that they could no longer leave a major element of cost hostage to uncertain market conditions. She immediately got on the phone to her banker and arranged a meeting for that same afternoon.

Listening to Merrill and Brown's story, their banker agreed that Merrill did face significant currency risk, observing that the cost impact of a strong yen was amounting to more than the interest it was paying on loans. Further, he reminded them that, since Merrill Electronics imported a higher portion of its products from Japan than other distributors competing in the market, its profit margins were much more sensitive to the value of the yen than theirs were. He explained there were several ways of dealing with their problem.

First, Merrill could continue as before, buying yen on the spot market each time payments to the Japanese suppliers were made. If the ¥580[2] million worth of goods on order or already invoiced at the end of June were to be settled at the current spot rate of ¥124.60,[3] Merrill would suffer higher purchase costs of about $225,000—compared to the dollar costs that would have been incurred at the spot rates when the orders were placed. On the other hand, if the yen weakened in the future, Merrill would benefit from lower dollar costs for the goods imported. The banker cautioned that neither he, nor anyone else for that matter, could guess what the yen would do during the next few months. He showed Merrill and Brown some news commentary on the currency markets (Exhibit 6) and other evidence that the dollar was undervalued in terms of its relative purchasing power (see Exhibit 7), but he stressed that the various market uncertainties were such as to make predictions highly risky.

Second, there were other alternatives: (1) "lock-in" today an exchange rate that would be close to the current spot rate or (2) enter into an option contract that would set the upper limit on the cost of yen but allow Merrill to take advantage of a cheaper yen, if that should occur over the next few months. Since foreign currency was something that Merrill and Brown had never given much thought to before, the banker decided to go over the basic issues with them. To help them follow, he handed them a copy of the currency markets quotations page from *The Wall Street Journal* (Exhibit 8).

To "lock-in" an exchange rate, the banker explained, meant that the future price of a foreign currency—*the future spot rate*—would in effect be set today. This type of hedge insured that, whatever the future spot rate might turn out to be, the *effective* price paid for yen would still be what was agreed today. There were three ways to lock-in an exchange rate: a forward contract, a money market transaction, and a currency futures contract. Each of these carried precisely defined terms with regard to price, maturity, and certain other performance measures. Any changes in the terms of the contract, such as lengthening its maturity, would have to be negotiated and agreed with the counterparty, possibly resulting in additional cost.

The **forward contract hedge** would be an arrangement in which Merrill would buy from the bank a specified quantity of yen to be delivered at a specified date in the future. The exchange rate would be fixed at the outset. At ¥124.95, a 90-day forward contract was at present slightly cheaper than the spot rate. If this hedge was used, Merrill would receive yen from the bank on the agreed date, pay the bank the amount of dollars at the forward exchange rate set earlier, and then use the yen to pay the Japanese suppliers.

The **money market hedge** was also an arrangement with the bank. Merrill would buy yen today on the spot market and place it in a yen time deposit or some other yen asset until needed to pay the suppliers. The purchase of yen would be financed in dollars by

---

[2]The goods were worth $4.43 million at the spot rates prevailing when the orders were placed.

[3]¥124.60 per dollar ($0.8026 per 100 yen) was the spot rate on July 8, 1992, for transactions of at least $1 million equivalent. Merrill Electronics usually bought yen from its bankers at from 1 to 2% less favorable rates since most transactions were under $250,000.

a short-term loan or by using cash reserves if they were available. The cost of this hedge would be the difference between the interest paid on the dollar loan and that received from the yen deposit. The banker reminded them that Merrill could borrow dollars at 25 *basis points*[4] over the current *prime* rate (6 percent), and earn 4.3125 percent on a 3-month Euroyen time deposit.

The **yen futures hedge** was provided by an instrument traced on the International Monetary Market (IMM) exchange in Chicago.[5] As protection against loss from currency fluctuations, this hedge was very similar to the forward contract provided by the bank. Merrill would *buy* a sufficient number of futures to create the hedge. It then could wait until the futures contracts came to maturity and take delivery of the yen. Alternatively, if Merrill decided the hedge was no longer needed, but the futures contracts had not yet come to maturity, they could be *sold*. If a rise in the value of the yen meant it cost more dollars to settle the purchase account with the Japanese suppliers, it also meant that the futures would be sold at a profit, thereby providing an offset. However, the mechanics of futures contracts differ considerably from forwards. The contracts are made through a member of the futures exchange, usually a broker. Currency futures come in standard sizes (¥12.5 million), and standard maturity dates (the third Wednesday of March, June, September, December). They are revalued daily *(marked-to-market)* with any profit or loss immediately settled between broker and client. To trade on the futures market, the client must open and maintain a margin account with the broker. At present, this is a minimum of $1,500 per contract. In addition, the broker will charge a small commission.

The **currency option contract** was available from either banks or exchanges. Option contracts give the *right but not the obligation* to buy **(a call)** or to sell **(a put)** currency or some other asset within a specified period and at a predetermined price.

Bank or OTC[6] options can be tailored to meet the clients precise needs for maturity, amount, or currency. They are usually "European"-type options (i.e., they may only be exercised at expiration). Most bank options are on spot currency. Merrill's banker pointed out that, besides dealing in call and put options, he also could offer them *synthetic* instruments. These were combinations of calls, puts, and sometimes forward contracts, which were designed to meet particular risk/return objectives of a client.

Like futures, exchange traded options have standardized maturities and amounts. The expiration dates are similar to those for futures: March, June, September, and December. In addition, the American exchanges offer some "near-by" expiration dates. For example, at the beginning of July, contracts were offered for July and August expiration as well as for the September standard month. Only a few major currencies are available. Most are priced in U.S. dollars, including those traded on European or Asian exchanges. They are typically so-called American-type options (i.e., they may be exercised at any time before expiration). Those traded on the Philadelphia exchange are on spot currency. Chicago's IMM and London's Liffe contracts are on currency futures. To buy an option

---

[4]A basis point is 1/100 of a percent (i.e., 0.0001). Basis points generally are used in pricing loans and certain other financial instruments.

[5]Currency futures are also traded on exchanges in London (LIFFE), Singapore (SIMEX), Sidney, and elsewhere in the world.

[6]OTC: over the counter.

on an exchange, the full premium[7] must be paid in advance. To sell (or write) an option requires a specified margin to be maintained with the broker.

There was yet another aspect to Merrill Electronic's currency management problem. The company imported goods from its Japanese suppliers on a continuous basis throughout the year. If Merrill did decide to hedge these purchases, should it be done when the orders were placed, when the purchase invoice was actually received, or periodically for a longer period of 6 to 12 months based on operating plans and budgets?

The banker concluded his exposé by stressing there was no "correct" hedging approach. It depended on the particular needs and financial position of the company and on the attitudes of its management and shareholders toward risk. The efficiency of the hedge would only be known *ex post*—after the supplier was paid. In the case of Merrill's currency problem, if the yen strengthened, locking in the rate would have been the correct decision. If yen weakened, either no hedge or an option hedge would have produced the best results.

The banker's explanation of the various hedging methods left Merrill and Brown somewhat bewildered. As they were leaving, they told their banker that they would need a few days to decide what they wanted to do. On their way back to the office, Merrill told Brown that she was convinced that they should begin to actively manage their currency position. There was simply too much money at risk to allow things to continue as they had during the past several months. The problem was how should they go about it?

Not wanting to let the matter drag any longer, Patricia Merrill asked Brown to prepare a brief report on how their company's currency risk should be managed. In particular, she asked him to set out the relative advantages in terms of cost and risk for each of the alternatives that had been described to them by the banker. To provide a practical example, he could use the ¥225 million (rounded off) exposure arising from the goods that were being ordered during July and which would be due for payment in October, 90 days from then. She suggested he use the July 8 market rates, which they had picked up at the bank (Exhibit 1), and assume that the suppliers would be paid and the hedges lifted on October 8. She also asked if he would give some thought to *when and under what circumstances* any currency hedging should be done.

---

[7]The LIFFE exchange uses a margin system similar to that for futures trading. Hence, a specified minimum margin is maintained with the broker, rather than paying a cash premium up-front.

EXHIBIT 1   Currency and Other Financial Market Data, July 8, 1992

Spot yen: 124.60 to 124.70 ($0.008019 to $0.008026)
90-Day forward yen: 124.95 to 125.10 ($0.007994 to $0.008003)

90-Day Euroyen interest rates: 4.3125 to 4.4375% p.a.
90-Day Eurodollar interest rates: 3.3750 to 3.5000% p.a.
Merrill short-term borrowing rate: prime (6.00%) + 25 basis points

September yen futures (IMM): $0.8046; December yen futures (IMM): $0.8036

October yen call options (IMM): $0.8000 strike to $0.0170 per 100 yen

---

EXHIBIT 2

Comparative Income Statements
(dollars in thousands)

	Actual Year Ending 30 June 1991	Pro Forma Year Ending 30 June 1992
Sales revenue	$34,398	$50,118
Cost of goods sold	28,419	41,866
Gross margin	$ 5,979	$ 8,252
Variable expenses	$ 2,100	$ 3,060
Fixed expenses	2,516	3,245
Depreciation	131	180
Operating earnings (EBIT)	1,232	1,767
Interest expense	322	340
Earnings before taxes	910	1,427
Income taxes	354	562
Earnings after taxes	556	865

EXHIBIT 3

Comparative Balance Sheets
(dollars in thousands)

	Actual June 30, 1991	Pro Forma June 30, 1992
Assets		
Current assets:		
Cash & deposits	$ 35	$ 45
Prepaid expenses	66	75
Accounts receivable	4,166	5,312
Inventories	5,591	4,530
Total current assets	9,858	9,962
Fixed assets (net)	790	1,031
Goodwill	100	100
Total assets	$10,748	$11,093
Capital & Liabilities		
Current liabilities:		
Bank credit	$ 2,985	$ 853
Mortgage—current	80	80
Accrued expenses	252	561
Accounts payable:		
Domestic	1,705	1,452
Foreign (yen)*	896	1,784
Total	5,918	4,650
Mortgage loan	480	400
Subordinated loan	—	250
Capital stock	1,000	1,500
Retained earnings	3,351	4,213
Owners' equity	4,351	5,713
Total capital & liabilities	$10,749	$11,093

* Dollar value of ¥224.8 million order at spot rate on June 30 (¥126 = $).

EXHIBIT 4

Actual Purchases from Japanese Suppliers (July 1991–June 1992)

Purchase Amount ¥ million	Order Date	¥ / $ Spot	Delivery & Invoice Date	Payment Date	¥ / $ Spot	Gain/Loss in $000s
210.2	Jul 91	138	Sept 91	Oct 91	131	− 81.4
244.1	Aug 91	137	Oct 91	Nov 91	130	− 95.9
327.8	Sept 91	133	Nov 91	Dec 91	125	− 157.7
274.3	Oct 91	131	Dec 91	Jan 92	125	− 100.5
156.0	Nov 91	130	Jan 92	Feb 92	127	− 28.3
192.5	Dec 91	125	Feb 92	Mar 92	133	+ 92.6
186.3	Jan 92	125	Mar 92	Apr 92	133	+ 89.6
216.5	Feb 92	127	Apr 92	May 92	130	+ 39.3
229.4	Mar 92	133	May 92	Jun 92	128	− 67.4
224.8	Apr 92	133	Jun 92	Jul 92	?	?
195.0	May 92	130	Jul 92	Aug 92	?	?
159.4	Jun 92	128	Aug 92	Sept 92	?	?

Forecasted Purchases from Japanese Suppliers (July–October 1992)

225.3	Jul 92	?	Sept 92	Oct 92	?	?
325.0	Aug 92	?	Oct 92	Nov 92	?	?
395.0	Sept 92	?	Nov 92	Dec 92	?	?
385.0	Oct 92	?	Dec 92	Jan 93	?	?

EXHIBIT 5

Yen–Dollar Spot Rates, January 1990–July 1992

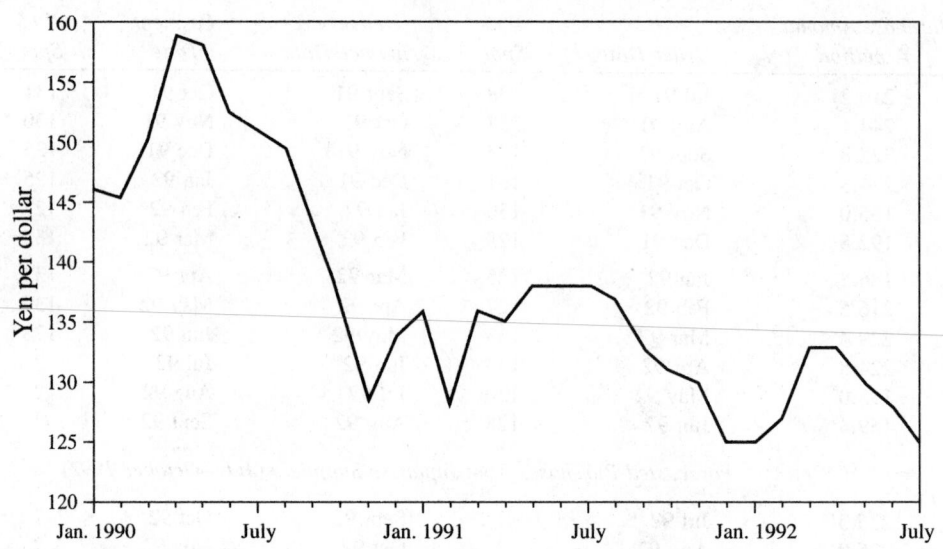

Euroyen Interest Rates, January 1990–July 1992

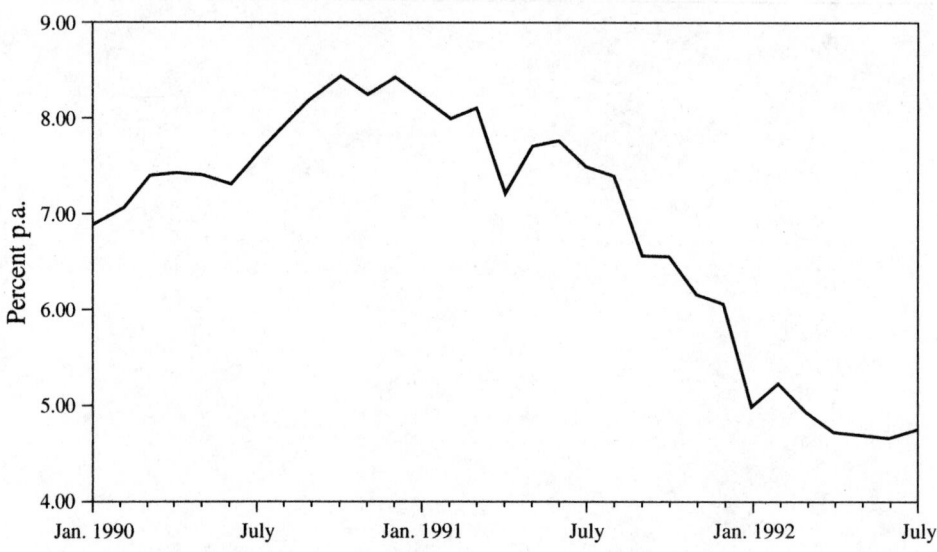

Source: Reprinted with permission of the *International Herald Tribune*, Paris (various issues).

EXHIBIT 6

DOLLAR FALLS ON MARK; SELL-OFF IS STEMMED*

CURRENCY MARKETS

By Charlene Lee
AP–Dow Jones News Service

NEW YORK—The dollar declined against the mark on Wednesday, but rose from its lows on frantic short-covering after Treasury Secretary Nicholas Brady said the United States isn't actively "seeking to depreciate the dollar."

Mr. Brady, speaking in Munich after the conclusion of the annual economic summit of the Group of Seven most industrialized nations, backed away from remarks made in a television interview aired in the United States late on Tuesday.

In that interview, Mr. Brady said he wasn't bothered by the dollar's fall below 1.5000 marks or its proximity to the historical low of 1.4425 marks. Those comments opened the floodgates to a dollar sell-off, sending the currency to a new 1992 low of 1.4770 marks early on Wednesday.

In late New York trading, the dollar was quoted at 1.4885 marks, down from 1.4900 marks late Tuesday in New York. The U.S. currency also was changing hands at 124.70 yen, up from 124.10 yen. Sterling fell to $1.9300 from $1.9340.

During the session, the U.S. unit also set new lows for the year at 1.3291 Swiss francs and $1.9430 to the pound.

"I think what happened was Mr. Brady didn't realize what effect he would have on the market," said Joseph Cambria, foreign exchange manager in New York for Banque Paribas. "It was some sort of damage control," he added, referring to Mr. Brady's statements on Wednesday clarifying his remarks in the interview.

The Treasury Secretary's back-pedaling triggered a flurry of short-covering and helped the currency rally to a session high of 1.5010 marks. Nevertheless, the U.S. unit's rally was greeted by heavy selling interest as dealers took the opportunity to establish fresh short positions at the higher levels and forced the dollar back down.

Traders noted that Mr. Brady's comments and the G-7's final communique did little to change bearish sentiment toward the U.S. currency. And they likely won't deter the market from testing the dollar's all-time low in the coming weeks.

"I think this trend is still intact for the dollar to go down. It's been around for several weeks, and there's

nothing to change that," Mr. Cambria said.

Observers said this year's G-7 communique was more significant for what it didn't say, rather than its actual contents. The statement, issued around midday in Europe, indicated to the currency market that "all around, things are pretty much status quo" in the United States, Germany, Japan, Britain, France, Canada, and Italy, said Peter Iversen, a trader for Shawmut Bank of Boston NA. Those seven countries make up the G-7.

Unlike G-7 statements issued in January and April, the latest contained no specific reference to the yen. In its previous statements, the G-7 frowned upon the yen's weakness, calling it an undesirable factor in the global economy.

Traders and analysts said the lack of a strongly unified call by the G-7 for a stronger yen was somewhat surprising, especially after Japan on Wednesday released figures that continued to show a ballooning trade surplus. A stronger yen would, in theory, help shrink that surplus by making Japanese goods more expensive abroad while making imports more attractive to Japanese consumers.

The absence of a reference to the yen in the communique weakened the yen against the

---

EXHIBIT 6   *(continued)*

---

dollar and mark, and left many observers wondering whether the Bank of Japan has any room to ease monetary policy.

Late in New York, the mark changed hands at 83.78 yen, well above 83.29 yen on Tuesday. During the session the mark set a new 1992 peak of 83.91 yen.

With the economic summit now concluded, traders said the market's attention will return to the U.S. economy and today's release of the weekly jobless claims and money supply reports. Market watchers said participants will be paying close attention to jobless claims data in the next several weeks in the wake of the surprisingly bleak June employment report.

According to an average of estimates from economists surveyed by Dow Jones Capital Markets Report, initial claims for state unemployment benefits are seen falling 4,000 to 416,000 in the week ended June 27. The market isn't expected to regard the jobless claims figure favorably until the total drops below 400,000.

The closely watched M2 aggregate of money supply is expected to contract by $4 billion in the week ended June 29 after failing by $10.6 billion the previous week. The M2 growth rate is currently running at 1.3 percent from the fourth quarter 1991 base, well below the Fed's targeted range of 2.5 to 6.5 percent. M2 consists of cash and all private deposits except very large ones left for a specified time. It also includes certain short-term assets, such as the amounts held in money-market mutual funds.

Also on Wednesday, the Canadian dollar firmed after a breakthrough in constitutional reform talks late Tuesday. The Canadian government and 9 of the country's 10 provinces agreed on major constitutional changes aimed at keeping Quebec in Canada.

The agreement would constitutionally recognize French-speaking Quebec as a distinct society. It also would provide for a senate with equal representation for all provinces.

"I think this agreement more than anything, just limits the weakness, rather than providing strength" to the Canadian currency, said Dave Glowacki, a senior trader for National Bank of Detroit.

Late in New York, the U.S. dollar was quoted at C$1.1916, down from C$1.1948 a day earlier.

European Trading

The dollar was bolstered in European trading earlier Wednesday after U.S. Treasury Secretary Nicholas Brady said the G-7 and United States aren't encouraging a weaker currency. But it slipped again in late trading.

The currency fetched 1.4965 marks late Wednesday, off from 1.4985 marks late Tuesday. The dollar also was trading at 124.80 yen, up from 124.45 yen a day earlier.

EXHIBIT 6   *(concluded)*

FUTURE OF DOLLAR DARKENS†

FURTHER FALLS SEEN AS UNIT TUMBLES

By Erik Ipsen
International Herald Tribune

LONDON—The dollar suffered another bruising day against the Deutschemark on Wednesday, as hopes for a pickup in the U.S. economy continued to recede.

"The latest figures all suggest yet another false dawn for the American recovery," said Jane Edwards, senior international economist at Lehman Brothers International.

With no growth spurt in America to boost or even to stabilize interest rates, and with no sign from Germany that it will cut its interest rates, the huge gap between the two is proving irresistible. "If interest rates are 3 percent in the United States and 10 percent in Europe, it is easy to see where I'd like to have my money," said Steven Bell, chief economist with Morgan Grenfell.

In late London trading, the dollar declined to 1.4950 Deutsche marks from Tuesday's close of 1.4990, after meeting a 17-month low during the day of 1.4760 DM. But it edged up to 124.675 yen, from 124.305 yen.

In New York, the currency was also weaker against the mark, closing at 1.4897 DM, down from 1.4903 DM. But it was slightly higher against

other major currencies, gaining to 124.78 yen from 124.05, to 5.0165 French francs from 5.0160, and to 1.3425 Swiss francs from 1.3406. The British pound stood at $1.9277, down from the previous day's $1.9332.

Most foreign exchange traders think that the dollar will soon test its all-time low of 1.4460 DM, set in February 1991. With the interest rate gap widely expected to persist well into next year, the dollar looks like it's in for a long, hard slog. In fact, some economists argue that the only reason that the American currency has not fallen even further and faster is that it has already fallen too far. "The dollar is greatly undervalued if you look at purchasing power parity," said David Twynam, a currency trader with Swiss Bank Corporation.

Many economists calculate that on the basis of purchasing power parity, the dollar ought to be worth around 2 DM. American tourists stepping off planes from Manchester to Madrid will note almost instantly that their currency has seen far better days.

Nonetheless, most economists argue that a further drop in the currency is desirable.

Calling it fairly "benign," Mr. Bell said "it helps the two key countries—the United States and Germany—with their No. 1 problems."

For the Americans, a lower dollar should give the econ-

omy a boost, he said. By making its exports less expensive it will boost U.S. competitiveness and sales in international markets. For the Germans, the fact that basic commodities, such as oil, are priced in dollars means that the cheaper dollar will help to keep inflation under control.

Political uncertainties in the United States will test the benevolent decline theories in coming weeks.

Many currency traders fear that the Federal Reserve Board will cut interest rates in the early autumn in one last stab at setting the economy on its feet again before the November election. "Politicians will be concerned with getting the economy moving not the fate of the dollar," said Ms. Edwards.

Against the yen, the outlook for the dollar is a bit cloudier. With Japanese overnight interest rates currently around 4.75 percent versus 3.30 percent in the United States, the gap is not overpowering.

Not all observers said they felt the Japanese were keen to do whatever they could to maintain a strong yen and thus reduce their politically embarrassing current-account surplus. "By cutting interest rates and stimulating domestic demand the Japanese will be able to tackle their current-account problem," said Ifty Islam, a currency strategist with Barclays de Zoete Wedd.

†Reprinted with permission of the International Herald Tribune, Paris.

EXHIBIT 7 Value of the U.S. Dollar

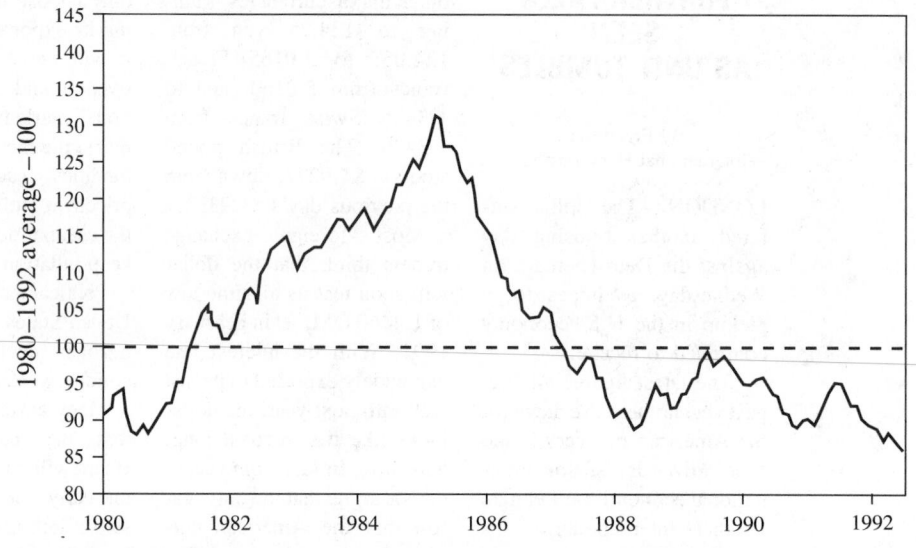

Source: World Financial Markets, Morgan Guaranty Trust Company.

The index number 100 represents the average value of the dollar in 1980–1982 as measured against the currencies of the 40 principal U.S. trading partners, each weighted by its relative importance.

The Hamburger Standard

Big Mac Prices

Country	Prices* in Local Currency	Implied PPP† of the Dollar	Actual Exchange Rate 10/4/92	Percent Over(+) or Under(−) Valuation of Dollar
Argentina	Peso3.30	1.51	0.99	−34
Australia	A$2.54	1.16	1.31	+13
Belgium	BFr108	49.32	33.55	−32
Brazil	Cr3,800	1,735	2,153	+24
Britain	£1.74	0.79	0.57	−28
Canada	C$2.76	1.26	1.19	−6
China	Yuan6.30	2.88	5.44	+89
Denmark	DKr27.25	12.44	6.32	−49
France	FFr18.10	8.26	5.55	−33
Germany	DM4.50	2.05	1.64	−20
Holland	Fl5.35	2.44	1.84	−24

EXHIBIT 7 *(concluded)*

Country	Prices* in Local Currency	Implied PPP† of the Dollar	Actual Exchange Rate 10/4/92	Percent Over(+) or Under(−) Valuation of Dollar
Hong Kong	HK$8.90	4.06	7.73	+91
Hungary	Forint133	60.73	79.70	+31
Ireland	I£1.45	0.66	0.61	−8
Italy	Lire4,100	1,872	1,233	−34
Japan	Y380	174	133	−24
Russia	Ruble58	26.48	98.95†	+273
Singapore	S$4.75	2.17	1.65	−24
S. Korea	Won2,300	1,050	778	−26
Spain	Ptas315	144	102	−29
Sweden	SKr25.50	11.64	5.93	−49
United States††	$2.19	—	—	—
Venezuela	Bs170	77.63	60.63	−22

Source: McDonald's *prices may vary locally, **Purchasing-power parity local price divided by dollar price, †Market rate, ††New York, Chicago, San Francisco and Atlanta.

The *Economist's* Big Mac index was first launched in 1986 as a ready reckoner to whether currencies are at their "correct" exchange rate. It is time for our annual update.

The case for munching our way around the globe on Big Macs is based on the theory of purchasing-power parity. This argues that the exchange rate between two currencies is in equilibrium when it equalizes the prices of an identical basket of goods and services in both countries. Advocates of PPP argue that in the long run currencies tend to move towards their PPP.

The Big Mac PPP is the exchange rate that leaves hamburgers costing the same in each country. Comparing the current exchange rate with its PPP gives a measure of whether a currency is under- or overvalued.

For example, the average price of a Big Mac in four American cities is $2.19. In Japan our Big Mac watcher had to fork out ¥380 ($2.86) for the same gastronomic delight. Dividing the yen price by the dollar price gives a Big Mac PPP of $1 = ¥174. On April 10 the actual dollar exchange rate was ¥133, which implies that on PPP grounds the dollar is 24 percent undervalued against the yen.

Some readers find the Big Mac index hard to digest. To be sure, hamburgers are primitive predictors of exchange rates. Local price differences may be distorted by taxes, property costs, or trade barriers. Nevertheless, the Big Mac can provide a rough and ready guide to how currencies might move over the long term. Experts who calculate PPPs by more sophisticated means come up with results that are not radically different. Indeed, many of them suggest that the dollar is even more undervalued than the hamburger standard indicates.

Note: Excerpts are from *The Economist,* April 18, 1992. © 1992 The Economist Newspaper Group, Inc.

EXHIBIT 8

Currency and Options Markets

CURRENCY TRADING

Tuesday, July 7, 1992

EXCHANGE RATES

The New York foreign exchange selling rates below apply to trading among banks in amounts of $1 million and more, as quoted at 3 p.m. Eastern time by Bankers Trust Co., Telerate and other sources. Retail transactions provide fewer units of foreign currency per dollar.

Country	U.S.$ equiv. Tues.	Mon.	Currency per U.S.$ Tues.	Mon.
Argentina(Peso)	1.01	1.01	.99	.99
Australia(dollar)	.7422	.744	1.3473	1.3435
Austria(Schilling)	.09531	.09398	10.49	10.64
Bahrain(Dinar)	2.6522	2.6522	.3771	.3771
Belgium(Franc)	.03258	.03214	30.69	31.11
Brazil(Cruzeiro)	.00029	.00029	3460.21	3430.00
Britian(Pound)	1.9325	1.9115	.5175	.5231
30-Day Forward	1.9213	1.9001	.5205	.5263
90-Day Forward	1.9016	1.8815	.5259	.5315
180-Day Forward	1.8734	1.8543	.5338	.5393
Canada(Dollar)	.8361	.8331	1.1960	1.2004
30-Day Forward	.8345	.8316	1.1983	1.2025
90-Day Forward	.8321	.8291	1.2018	1.2061
180-Day Forward	.8294	.8262	1.2057	1.2104
Czechosolvakia(Koruna)				
Commercialrate	.0368372	.0368732	27.1200	27.1200
Chile(peso)	.002895	.002895	345.40	345.47
China(Renminbi)	.182815	.182815	5.4700	5.4700
Columbia(Peso)	.001722	.001722	580.64	580.64
Denmark(Krone)	.1745	.1721	5.7315	5.8100
Ecuador(Sucre)				
Floatingrate	.000717	.000717	1394.00	1394.00
Finland(Markka)	.24606	.24284	4.0640	4.1180
France(Franc)	.19928	.19641	5.0180	5.0915
30-Day Forward	.19811	.19523	5.0478	5.1222
90-Day Forward	.19598	.19319	5.1026	5.1762
180-Day Forward	.19292	.19026	5.1835	5.2560
Germany(Mark)	.6709	.6616	1.4905	1.5115
30-Day Forward	.6672	.6579	1.4987	1.5200
90-Day Forward	.6605	.6514	1.5140	1.5351
180-Day Forward	.6508	.6422	1.5365	1.5572
Greece(Drachma)	.005488	.005423	182.20	184.40
Hong Kong(Dollar)	.12932	.12932	7.7325	7.7330
Hungary(Forint)	.0130293	.0130582	76.7500	76.5800
India(Rupee)	.03550	.03550	28.17	28.17
Indonesia(Rupiah)	.0004921	.0004921	2032.02	2032.02
Ireland(Punt)	1.7892	1.7641	.5589	.5669
Isreal(Shekel)	.4164	.4194	2.4013	2.3846
Italy(Lira)	.0008877	.0008741	1126.53	1143.98
Japan(Yen)	.008058	.008045	124.10	124.30
30-Day Forward	.008050	.008037	124.22	124.42
90-Day Forward	.008040	.008027	124.38	124.58
180-Day Forward	.008035	.008022	124.45	124.65
Jordan(Dinar)	1.5207	1.5207	.6576	.6576
Kuwait(Dinar)	3.4614	3.4614	.2889	.2889
Lebanon(Pound)	.000587	.000587	1705.00	1705.00
Malaysia(Ringgit)	.4002	.3998	2.4987	2.5010
Malta(Lira)	3.3058	3.3058	.3025	.3025
Mexico(Peso)				
Floatingrate	.0003210	.0003210	3115.75	3115.75
Netherland(Guilder)	.5951	.5870	1.6803	1.7037
New Zealand(doolar)	.5437	.5445	1.8392	1.8365
Norway(Krone)	.1711	.1688	5.8430	5.9255
Pakistan(Rupee)	.0400	.0400	25.00	25.00
Peru(New Sol)	.8752	.8752	1.14	1.14
Philippines(Peso)	.04008	.04008	24.95	24.95
Poland(Zioty)	.00007741	.00007741	12918.01	12918.00
Portugal(Escodo)	.007997	.007909	125.05	126.44
Saudi Arabia(Riyal)	.26738	.26738	3.7400	3.7400
Singapore(Dollar)	.6198	.6203	1.6135	1.6120
South Africa(Rand)				
Commercialrate	.3637	.3625	2.7493	2.7583
Financialrate	.2558	.2525	3.9100	3.9600
South Korea(Won)	.0012721	.0012721	786.10	786.10
Spain(Peseta)	.010614	.010468	94.21	95.53
Sweden(Krona)	.1856	.1830	5.3885	5.4635
Switzerland(Franc)	.7460	.7386	1.3405	1.3540
30-Day Forward	.7423	.7349	1.3472	1.3608
90-Day Forward	.7357	.7285	1.3592	1.3727

Country	U.S.$ equiv. Tues.	Mon.	Currency per U.S.$ Tues.	Mon.
180-Day Forward	.7267	.7192	1.3771	1.3904
Taiwan(Dollar)	.041186	.041152	24.28	24.30
Thailand(Baht)	.03954	.03954	25.29	25.29
Turkey(Lira)	.0001466	.0001461	6820.03	6843.00
United Arab(Dirham)	.2723	.2723	3.6725	3.6725
Uruguay(New Peso)				
Financial	.000316	.000316	3160.01	3160.01
Venezuela(Bolivar)				
Floatingrate	.01522	.01523	65.70	65.65
SDR	1.44632	1.43898	.69494	.69494
ECU	1.37280	1.35490		

Special Drawing Rights (SDR) are based on exchange rates for the U.S., German, British, French and Japanese currencies. Source: International Monetary Fund.

European Currency Unit (ECU) is based on a basket of community currencies.

ECU VALUES

The value of one ECU in terms of other currencies as reported by the European Community Commission.

Currency	Tue.	Prev.	Currency	Tue.	Prev.
Belg Fr	42.153	42.148	D-Mark	2.0475	2.0476
Guilder	2.3082	2.3080	Pound Stg.	0.7097	0.7080
Dan Kr	7.8740	7.8706	French Fr.	6.8909	6.8972
It Lira (100)	1547.0	1549.7	Irish Pound	0.7680	0.7678
Gr Drachma	250.37	249.86	Sp Peseta	129.38	129.39
Por Escuda	171.57	171.10	U.S. Dollar	1.3693	1.3520
Swiss Franc	1.8362	1.8353	Swed Kr.	7.4030	7.4032
Nor Kr	8.0240	8.0268	Can Dollar	1.6386	1.6217
Aus Sch	14.410	14.412	Fin-Mark	5.5839	5.5810
Aust Dollar	1.8404	1.8160	Nz Dollar	2.5138	2.4853
Malt Pound	0.4104	0.4125	Tur Lira	9471.4	9339.7
Yen	169.52	168.26			

TRADE-WEIGHTED VALUES

Morgan Guaranty Trust Co.'s trade-weighted currency statistics show a currency's percentage rates against average market rates in the period 1980-82. The statistics show the devaluation or upvaluation of each currency against 15 other currencies, weighed by each country's 1980 bilateral trade patterns.

Currency	Tue	Prev	Currency	Tue	Prev
Dollar	−18.2	−17.9	Sterling	−18.9	−19.1
D Mark	+26.3	+26.1	Fr Franc	−10.8	−11.1
Sw Franc	+16.5	+16.9	Lire	−19.6	−19.8
Yen	+77.9	+78.3	Nor Krone	−15.5	−15.7
Can Dir	−3.2	−3.4			

OPTIONS

PHILADELPHIA EXCHANGE

Option & Underlying	Strike Price	Calls-Last Jul	Aug	Sep	Puts-Last Jul	Aug	Sep
50,000 Australian Dollars-cents per unit.							
ADollr	73	r	r	r	r	r	0.43
74.43	74	r	r	0.93	r	r	0.77
74.43	76	r	r	0.22	r	r	r
31,250 British Pounds-European Style.							
BPound	180	r	r	r	r	r	0.60
191.13	182½	9.60	r	8.35	r	r	r
191.13	187½	r	4.98	r	r	r	r
191.13	190	r	3.40	r	r	r	r
191.13	192½	r	r	r	r	3.60	s
191.13	195	r	r	r	r	5.18	s
191.13	197½	r	0.82	r	r	r	r
31,250 British Pounds-cents per unit.							
BPound	177½	r	r	r	r	r	0.34
191.13	185	r	r	6.98	r	0.76	1.61
191.13	187½	r	5.30	r	r	1.38	2.60

Option & Underlying	Strike Price	Calls-Last Jul	Aug	Sep	Puts-Last Jul	Aug	Sep
191.13	190	2.78	3.60	r	8.30	2.32	r
191.13	192½	1.16	r	3.05	0.90	r	4.85
191.13	195	0.28	r	r	2.65	r	r
191.13	197½	r	r	1.30	r	6.75	r
50,000 Canadian Dollar-cents per unit.							
CDollr	81	2.59	r	r	r	r	r
83.29	83½	0.15	0.37	r	r	r	r
83.29	84	r	0.15	0.26	r	r	r
83.29	85	0.02	r	r	r	r	r
250,000 French Francs-10ths of a cent per unit.							
FFranc	19¾	r	r	r	r	r	4.90
250,000 French Francs-European Style.							
FFanc	19¾	1.50	r	r	r	r	r
1,000,000 German/Mark-Japanese Yen cross.							
GMk-Yn	82	r	r	r	r	0.10	r
82.22	83	0.25	r	r	r	0.36	r
62,500 German Marks-European Style.							
DMark	61	r	r	5.05	r	r	r
66.14	62½	r	3.55	3.39	r	r	r
66.14	63	r	3.12	2.99	r	r	r
66.14	63½	r	2.68	2.58	r	r	r
66.14	64½	r	2.16	r	r	r	r
66.14	65	r	r	r	r	r	1.12
66.14	66	r	1.16	r	0.20	r	r
66.14	67	0.30	r	r	r	r	r
66.14	67½	r	r	r	r	1.75	r
66.14	68	r	r	r	r	2.03	r
66.14	69	r	0.24	r	r	2.81	r
66.14	70	r	0.13	r	r	r	r
62,500 German Marks-cents per unit.							
DMark	62	4.40	r	4.72	r	r	0.21
66.14	62½	r	r	r	r	r	0.25
66.14	63	3.73	3.31	3.30	r	0.14	r
66.14	63½	r	2.83	2.84	0.01	0.20	r
66.14	64	2.75	r	2.93	0.02	0.31	r
66.14	64½	2.26	2.08	r	r	0.37	r
66.14	65	r	r	0.96	0.34	0.51	r
66.14	65½	r	r	r	r	0.12	1.07
66.14	66	0.81	1.23	1.51	0.15	0.87	1.27
66.14	67	0.32	0.76	1.00	0.60	r	r
66.14	67½	0.15	0.57	0.54	0.86	r	r
66.14	68	0.10	0.44	0.65	r	1.96	r
66.14	68½	0.27	r	r	r	r	r
66.14	69	r	r	r	r	r	3.35
6,250,000 Japanese Yen-100ths of a cent per unit.							
JYen	78	r	r	r	r	0.21	r
80.45	78½	r	r	r	r	0.33	r
80.45	79	r	r	r	r	0.04	r
80.45	80	0.60	r	r	r	0.18	1.03
80.45	80½	0.30	0.96	1.19	0.45	1.06	1.40
80.45	81	0.16	0.73	r	r	r	r
80.45	82	r	0.75	r	r	r	r
6,250,000 Japanese Yen-European Style.							
JYen	79½	r	1.56	s	r	0.54	s
80.45	81	r	0.78	r	r	r	r
62,5000 Swiss Francs-European Style.							
SFranc	66	r	r	r	r	r	0.06
73.85	71	r	r	s	r	0.28	r
73.85	72½	1.65	r	s	r	r	r
73.85	75	r	0.70	r	r	r	r
62,500 Swiss Francs-cents per unit.							
SFranc	69	r	5.50	r	r	r	r
73.85	71	r	3.30	3.27	r	0.32	r
73.85	71½	r	r	r	r	r	0.69
73.85	72	r	2.54	r	r	0.50	0.87
73.85	72½	r	r	s	r	0.63	s
73.85	73	r	r	r	r	r	1.24
73.85	74	0.65	r	r	0.47	r	r
73.85	74½	0.39	r	0.94	r	r	r
73.85	75	0.32	0.56	1.25	r	r	r
73.85	75½	r	r	r	r	1.14	r
73.85	76	r	0.56	r	r	r	r
Total Call Vol 29.658					Call Open int 247,571		
Total Put Vol 39,477					Put Open int 539,131		

EXHIBIT 8   *(continued)*

*Futures and Options Markets**

Currency

	Open	High	Low	Settle		Change	Lifetime High	Lifetime Low	Open Interest
Japan Yen (IMM)—12.5 million yen; $ per yen (.00)									
Sept	.8030	.8067	.8000	.8046	+	.0017	.8090	.7265	52,191
Dec	.8057	.8057	.7987	.8036	+	.0017	.8070	.7410	3,065
Mr93	....	....	....	.8036	+	.0016	.8050	.7445	2,140
Est vol 21,071, vol Mon 15,533; open int 57,396, + 1,938									
Deutschemark (IMM)—125,000 marks; $ per mark									
Sept	.6528	.6641	.6503	.6639	+	.0102	.6641	.5685	65,860
Dec	.6513	.6549	.6490	.6543	+	.0101	.6549	.5645	6,110
Mr93	.6440	.6465	.6425	.6459	+	.0100	.6465	.5724	760
Est vol 52,713; vol Mon 36,981; open int 72,740, +7,996									
Canadian dollar (IMM)—100,000 dirs.; $ per Can $									
Sept	.8325	.8338	.8322	.8337	+	.0038	.8774	.8191	21,240
Dec	.8291	.8300	.8291	.8303	+	.0038	.8740	.8130	992
Mr93	....	....	....	.8274	+	.0038	.8712	.8115	237
Est vol 2,869; vol Mon 2,261; open int 22,506, − 125									
British Pound (IMM)—62,500 pds.; $ per pound									
Sept	1.9072	1.9110	1.8986	1.9104	+	.0222	1.9110	1.6490	27,347
Dec	1.8770	1.8830	1.8704	1.8820	+	.0218	1.8830	1.6280	832
Mr93	1.8550	1.8570	1.8550	1.8570	+	.0212	1.8570	1.7620	138
Est vol 12,856; vol Mon 9,751; open int 28,317, − 532									
Swiss Franc (IMM)—125,000 francs; $ per franc									
Sept	.7377	.7394	.7327	.7391	+	.0081	.7394	.6335	29,871
Dec	.7280	.7300	.7230	.7295	+	.0078	.7300	.6280	685
Est vol 21,460; vol Mon 14,092; open int 30,619, − 946									
Australian Dollar (IMM)—100,000 dirs.; $ per A$									
Sept	.7401	.7415	.7392	.7394	−	.0015	.7610	.7388	1,814
Est vol 132; vol Mon 675; open int 1,928, +272.									
U.S. Dollar Index (FINEX)—1,000 times USDX									
Sept	84.24	84.33	83.13	83.14	−	1.07	94.20	83.13	4,410
Dec	85.50	84.86	84.75	84.44	−	1.02	94.93	84.75	416
Est vol 3,750; vol Mon 1,734; open int 4,827, +162.									
The index: High 83.24; Low 82.15; Close 82.15—.98									

Currency Futures Contracts

**The Wall Street Journal Europe*, Wednesday, July 8, 1992.

EXHIBIT 8 *(continued)*

Futures and Options Markets*

Currency

Japanese Yen (IMM)
12,500,000 yen; cents per 100 yen

Strike Price	Calls—Settle			Puts—Settle		
	Aug	Sep	Oct	Aug	Sep	Oct
7900	1.54	1.85	....	0.40	0.71	....
7950	1.21	1.54	....	0.57	0.90	....
8000	0.94	1.27	1.52	0.80	1.13	1.49
8050	0.70	1.04	....	1.06	1.40	....
8100	0.52	0.84	....	1.38	1.40	....
8150	0.38	0.68	....	....	....	....

Est. vol. 3,903;
Tues vol. 1,500 calls; 4,026 puts
Op. int. Tues 21,013 calls; 27,607 puts

Deutschemark (IMM)
125,000 marks; cents per mark

Strike Price	Calls—Settle			Puts—Settle		
	Aug	Sep	Oct	Aug	Sep	Oct
6550	1.56	1.86	....	0.59	0.89	....
6600	1.26	1.58	1.18	0.79	1.11	....
6650	0.99	1.30	....	1.02	1.33	....
6700	0.77	1.09	....	1.30	1.62	....
6750	0.58	0.89	....	....	....	....
6800	0.43	0.73	....	....	2.26	....

Est. vol. 38,873;
Tues vol. 11,288 calls; 165,250 puts
Op. int. Tues 124,636 calls; 153, 736 puts

Canadian Dollar (IMM)
100,000 Can.$, cents per Can.$

Strike Price	Calls—Settle			Puts—Settle		
	Aug	Sep	Oct	Aug	Sep	Oct
8250	....	1.32	....	0.07	0.19	....
8300	0.78	0.94	....	0.15	0.31	....
8350	0.45	0.63	....	0.32	0.50	....
8400	0.23	0.40	....	0.60	0.77	....
8450	0.10	0.24	....	0.97	....	....
8500	0.03	0.12	....	....	1.48	....

Est. vol. 833;
Tues vol. 422 calls; 516 puts
Op. int. Tues 7,635 calls; 7,884 puts

The Wall Street Journal Europe, Wednesday, July 8, 1992.

EXHIBIT 8   *(concluded)*

Futures and Options Markets*

Currency

British Pound (IMM)
62,500 pounds; cents per pound

	Calls—Settle			Puts—Settle		
Strike Price	*Aug*	*Sep*	*Oct*	*Aug*	*Sep*	*Oct*
1850	6.50	7.16	....	0.78	1.50	....
1875	4.64	5.46	4.72	1.40	2.28	....
1900	3.12	4.04	....	2.38	3.32	....
1925	1.96	2.88	....	3.70	4.64	....
1950	1.16	1.98	....	5.40	....	....
1975	0.66	1.30	....	7.36	....	....

Est. vol. 2,236;
Tues vol. 540 calls; 797 puts
Op. int. Tues 12,107 calls; 10,292 puts

Swiss Franc (IMM)
125,000 francs; cents per franc

	Calls—Settle			Puts—Settle		
Strike Price	*Aug*	*Sep*	*Oct*	*Aug*	*Sep*	*Oct*
7300	1.66	2.01	....	0.75	1.10	....
7350	1.36	1.72	....	0.95	1.31	....
7400	1.11	1.47	....	1.20	1.56	....
7450	0.89	1.25	....	1.48	....	....
7500	0.70	1.05	....	....	....	....
7550	0.55	....	....	....	....	....

Est. vol. 2,668;
Tues vol. 4,667 calls; 1,774 puts
Op. int. Tues 15,615 calls; 19,724 puts

Mark/Yen Cross Rate (CME)
125,000 marks; yen per mark

	Calls—Settle			Puts—Settle		
Strike Price	*Aug*	*Sep*	*Oct*	*Aug*	*Sep*	*Oct*
8200	1.40	1.69	....	....	0.78	....
8250	....	....	....	....	....	....
8300	0.83	1.15	....	....	....	....
8350	0.63	....	....	....	....	....
8400	0.47	0.76	....	....	....	....
8450	....	....	....	....	....	....

Est. vol. 32;
Tues vol. 60 calls; 0 puts
Op. int. Tues 1,602 calls; 1,373 puts

Currency Futures Options Contracts

*The Wall Street Journal Europe, Wednesday, July 8, 1992.

Chrysler's Warrants: September 1983

> We quietly asked the government to surrender the warrants to us at little or no cost. What a mistake! There was a huge uproar over our request. . . . I was furious. . . . Their attitude was "Screw Chrysler, let's get every cent we can."[1]
>
> Lee Iacocca

> There is no justification for forgoing one penny. Any profit the government could earn would be a reasonable reward for taking on the risk of saving Chrysler.[2]
>
> Rep. William S. Green

At the bottom of its financial distress in 1980, Chrysler Corporation arranged with the U.S. government for guarantees of Chrysler's debt up to $1.5 billion in return for cash fees and common stock warrants.[3] The fees, to be paid annually, would be equal to 1 percent of the loans guaranteed. The warrants were for 14.4 million shares exercisable at $13 per share until 1990. The government also had a first lien on Chrysler's assets, which were estimated to have a liquidation value of $2.5 billion. Participating banks

---

[1]Lee Iacocca, *Iacocca* (New York: Bantam Books, 1984), p. 283.

[2]"The Kicker," *The New Yorker*, January 7, 1985, p. 56.

[3]Numerous arguments were advanced in favor of providing assistance: (1) the impact on the federal budget of a Chrysler failure would be greater than the cost of assistance. Budget impacts were expected in unemployment benefits, trade adjustment assistance payments, other social programs, and reduced tax revenues. (2) A Chrysler failure would disproportionately affect a city and region that already had substantial economic problems. (3) Failure would lead to either greater monopoly power by surviving U.S. firms or to worsening balance of payments as foreign producers captured increased U.S. market share. (4) Chrysler's output of its popular small cars was 300,000 units in 1979 and 1980; this would expand to 1 million units in the near future.

This case was written by Robert F. Bruner.

were also given warrants on the same terms for 13.286 million shares. During the period when the loan guarantee was negotiated, the price of Chrysler's shares was about $7.50. (See Exhibit 1 for a history of Chrysler's share price during the period of the guarantee negotiations.)

Eventually, only $1.2 billion of the guarantee was used. In June 1980, $500 million in notes were issued at 10.35 percent. Another $300 million were issued at 11.40 percent. And in February 1981, $400 million were issued at 14.90 percent.

By the summer of 1983, Chrysler was plainly recovering. Exhibit 2 presents the share-price history during the period of recovery. In the spring, an offering of 26 million new shares at $16.625 was sold out within an hour, and, in the following weeks, the price per share rose to $35. Then on July 13, Lee Iacocca, the chief executive officer, presented a check repaying the guaranteed loans in their entirety.

CHRYSLER'S REQUEST

In the context of this recovery, Chrysler asked the government to return its warrants at no cost to Chrysler. On May 6, Gerald Greenwald, Chrysler's vice-chairman, argued that, in view of the rapid recovery, the terms of the guarantee had been too onerous. The government had not "paid a nickel" for the loans, he said, "At some point, you have to define what the term 'usury' means." Lee Iacocca added,

> These warrants were a sword hanging over our head. At any point over the next seven years, the government—or anyone else who owned the warrants—could demand that we issue an extra 14.4 million shares of Chrysler stock at bargain-basement prices. . . . When you consider that the government's money was never at risk in the first place—they had a lien on everything we owned, which was worth far more than $1.2 billion—that kind of profit was almost indecent.[4]

Chrysler initially had borrowed only $1.2 billion on its $1.5 billion line of credit for a term of up to 10 years, and repaid the debt after 3 years. The cash costs associated with this debt included $404 million in interest, $33 million in administrative fees to the federal government, and $67 million in fees to investment bankers and lawyers. Mr. Iacocca viewed the potential dilution from the exercise of the warrants as an additional cost to shareholders. Chrysler had a total of 68.5 million shares outstanding.

During the 1930s' depression, the federal government had bought preferred stock of large commercial banks in order to improve their financial stability; but in the long history of government loan guarantees, there were no examples of equity kickers. At the time Chrysler requested the loan guarantees, government loan guarantees of $409 billion were currently outstanding. In general, the government's loan losses had been quite small; the most notable loss was related to the bankruptcy of the Penn Central railroad, which eventually required $3 billion in cash assistance in order to maintain operations.

---

[4]Iacocca, p. 283.

Frederick Zuckerman, the treasurer of Chrysler said,

> In May of 1980, Chrysler had a poker hand full of deuces and the government had one full of face cards. We *had* to give the warrants. In 1983, there was a philosophical issue as to whether or not it was right for the government to be profiting so enormously. Remember, it hadn't put up any money—only guaranteed loans made by others.[5]

REACTION TO THE REQUEST

G. William Miller, Secretary of the Treasury at the time the loan guarantee was approved, wrote to the Chrysler Loan Guarantee Board urging the members not to return the warrants as "a matter of grave public concern and an ill-advised precedent."

In reacting to the news of Chrysler's request, Representative William Green said,

> The equity kicker that Congress insisted on is entirely consistent with the high risk. There is no reason for surrendering a penny of it. It wasn't a windfall. I didn't notice Mr. Iacocca offering to give back his options on Chrysler stock.[6]

Mr. Iacocca owned 1,000 common shares and held options for 320,000 shares exercisable at prices ranging from $9.88 to $11.02.

John Albertine, president of the American Business Conference, said that the request bordered on "disgrace." Kenneth McLean, staff director of the Senate Banking Committee, called the proposal "outrageous." And David Healey, an auto industry analyst with Drexel Burnham Lambert, said, "They're trying to change the score of the game after it's over."

Only Representative Stewart McKinney saw merit in the request. He argued that Chrysler had paid $33 million in fees to the government "—a hefty price. And having the government make a windfall is a little bit absurd."

The Loan Guarantee Board rejected Chrysler's initial request as well as a subsequent offer of $218 million for the warrants Chrysler made in July 1983. Instead, the board proposed to sell the warrants to the highest bidder in a sealed-bid auction in September 1983.

DECISION

With the prospect of an open auction for the warrants, Chrysler executives faced the likelihood of paying a competitive price. Mr. Iacocca assigned Robert S. Miller, Chrysler's executive vice president of finance, the task of making a winning bid. But, said Mr. Miller, "He told me that if the bid was a penny too low or more than a dollar too high not to come home." Mr. Miller was reminded that, in July, Shearson/American Express

---

[5]"The Kicker," p. 56.
[6]Ibid, p. 456.

had offered $20.10 per warrant. How should Chrysler's bid be determined? Moreover, was that price at all consistent with the risks the government had run? In fact, had the government been overpaid?

Historical information was available that might assist in valuing the warrants. Exhibit 3 presents certain definitions about the information, and Exhibit 4 calculates the standard deviation of the log-normalized return on Chrysler's common stock in July and August 1983. Exhibits 5 through 8 calculate the standard deviation over various time periods when the loan guarantee was being negotiated. Exhibit 9 presents the long-term volatilities of selected companies. During this entire period, Chrysler paid no dividends on its common stock. This historical look affords a check on the estimates at the time of the case.

Chrysler had other warrants outstanding that could provide another benchmark in the valuation. These other warrants (for 5 million shares) had been issued in connection with preferred stock. They could be exercised at $13 per share any time until June 15, 1985. Chrysler retained the option to shorten the life of the warrants, however, which it exercised in the summer of 1983. The new expiration date would be December 1, 1983. Exhibit 10 presents historical information relevant to the value of these warrants.

Exhibit 11 calculates the standard deviation of log-normalized returns on two issues of Chrysler's debt that were trading on the New York Exchange at the time the loan guarantees were negotiated. These issues were *(a)* the $100 million sinking fund debentures (8.875s) of 1995 and *(b)* the $200 million sinking fund debentures (8.5s) of 1998. The return is an average of the daily trading returns of the bonds weighted by par value. This information might provide a foundation for evaluating the loan guarantee itself.

Exhibit 12 presents interest rates on selected debt instruments over the 1979–83 period. And Exhibit 13 presents the yields to maturity on selected corporate bonds as of May 12, 1980, the date the loan guarantee was signed.

EXHIBIT 1   Chrysler Stock Price, August 1979–August 1980

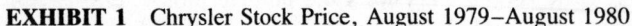

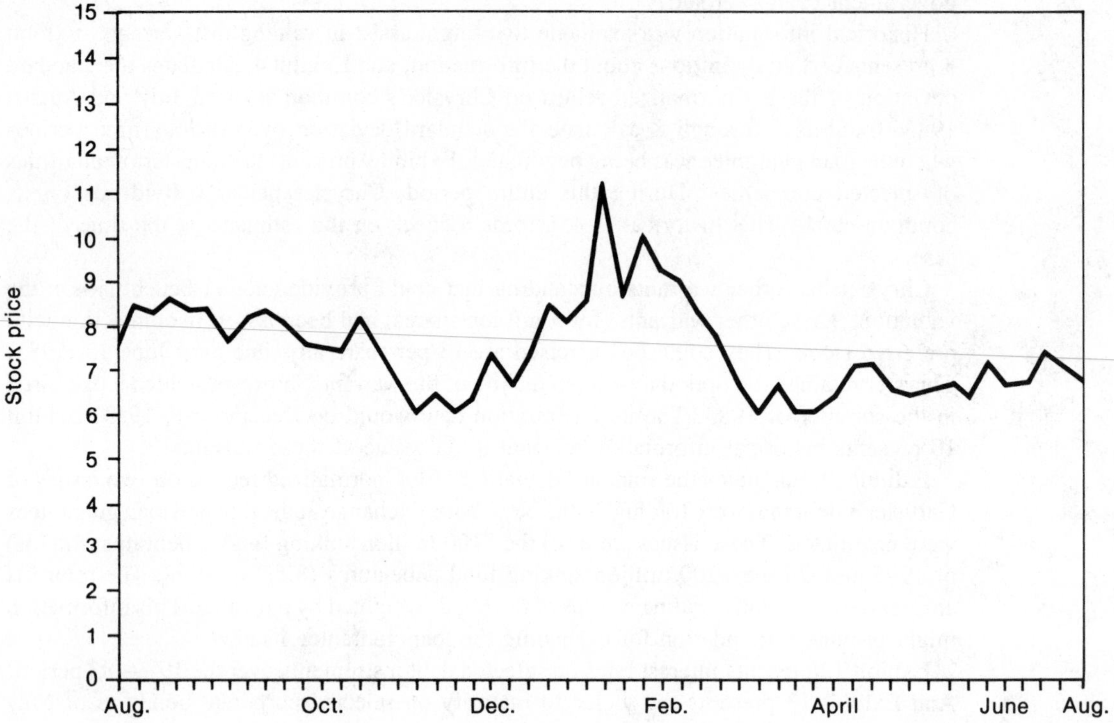

EXHIBIT 2   Chrysler Stock Price, August 1980–September 1983

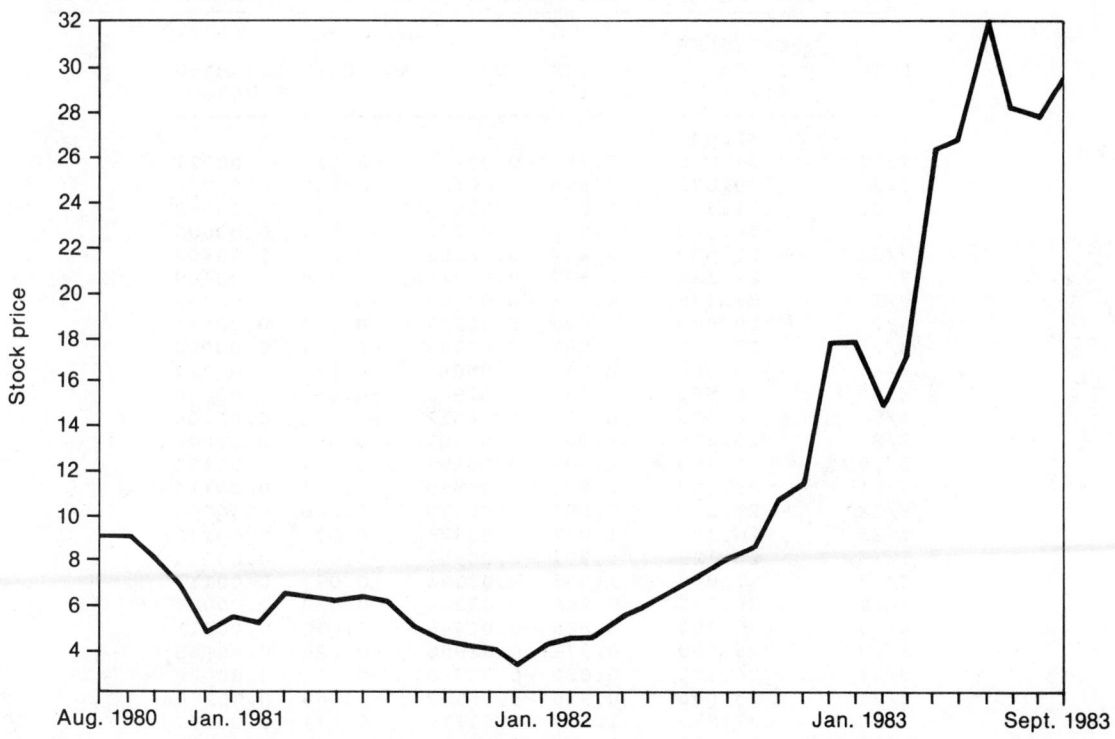

EXHIBIT 3   Definition of Components of Exhibits 4 through 8

Sj = Stock price.

Rj = Price relatives, calculated as today's closing stock price divided by yesterday's closing stock price.

Log Rj = Log to base of daily price relatives. This corrects for the possibility that the distribution of price relatives does not have a normal distribution.

U = Mean of Log Rj.

Log Rj-U = Deviation of price relatives from mean.

Sigma = Standard deviation of log-normalized daily price relatives annualized.

EXHIBIT 4 Calculation of Standard Deviation of Daily Percentage Changes in Stock Price, September 1, 1983 (date bids for the government's Chrysler warrants were due)

DATE	CHRYSLER STOCK PRICE	Rj=Sj/ Sj-1	LOG Rj	LOG Rj-U	LOG Rj-U SQUARED
7/21/83	32.000				
7/22	31.000	0.969	-0.03175	-0.028	0.00077
7/25	30.875	0.996	-0.00404	0.000	0.00000
7/26	31.375	1.016	0.01606	0.020	0.00040
7/27	30.500	0.972	-0.02828	-0.024	0.00000
7/28	28.500	0.934	-0.06782	-0.064	0.00407
7/29	28.125	0.987	-0.01325	-0.009	0.00009
8/1	27.375	0.973	-0.02703	-0.023	0.00053
8/2	28.000	1.023	0.02257	0.027	0.00071
8/3	27.625	0.987	-0.01348	-0.009	0.00009
8/4	26.000	0.941	-0.06062	-0.057	0.00321
8/5	25.500	0.981	-0.01942	-0.015	0.00000
8/8	24.375	0.956	-0.04512	-0.041	0.00169
8/9	25.625	1.051	0.05001	0.054	0.00000
8/10	26.750	1.044	0.04297	0.047	0.00221
8/11	25.750	0.963	-0.03810	-0.034	0.00116
8/12	25.500	0.990	-0.00976	-0.006	0.00003
8/15	26.375	1.034	0.03374	0.038	0.00142
8/16	26.125	0.991	-0.00952	-0.006	0.00003
8/17	27.000	1.033	0.03294	0.037	0.00137
8/18	26.125	0.968	-0.03294	-0.029	0.00084
8/19	25.750	0.986	-0.01446	-0.010	0.00011
8/22	25.000	0.971	-0.02956	-0.026	0.00065
8/23	24.500	0.980	-0.02020	-0.016	0.00026
8/24	23.000	0.939	-0.06318	-0.059	0.00350
8/25	23.875	1.038	0.03734	0.041	0.00171
8/26	26.000	1.089	0.08526	0.089	0.00797
8/29	26.000	1.000	0.00000	0.004	0.00002
8/30	26.375	1.014	0.01432	0.018	0.00034
8/31	27.750	1.052	0.05082	0.000	0.00000
9/1/83	28.375	1.023	0.02227	0.026	0.00069

$$SUM= -0.12023 \qquad SUM= 0.03386$$
$$U= -0.00401$$

SIGMA= (SUM OF LOG Rj-U SQUARED/30)*(30/29)=   0.001167
        TO CONVERT TO ANNUAL VARIANCE: * 365 OR   0.426159
        ANNUAL VOLATILITY=SQUARE ROOT OR   0.652808

EXHIBIT 5   Calculation of Standard Deviation of Daily Percentage Changes in Stock Price, September 14, 1979 (first date of loan guarantee bill with equity kicker drawn up at Treasury)

DATE	CHRYSLER STOCK PRICE Sj	Rj=Sj/ Sj-1	LOG Rj	LOG Rj-U	LOG Rj-U SQUARED
8/2/79	7.875				
8/3	7.625	0.968	-0.03226	0.000	0.00000
8/6	7.500	0.984	-0.01653	-0.017	0.00027
8/7	7.750	1.033	0.03279	0.000	0.00000
8/8	7.750	1.000	0.00000	0.000	0.00000
8/9	8.750	1.129	0.12136	0.121	0.01473
8/10	8.625	0.986	-0.01439	-0.014	0.00021
8/13	8.500	0.986	-0.01460	-0.015	0.00021
8/14	8.375	0.985	-0.01482	-0.015	0.00022
8/15	8.500	1.015	0.01482	0.000	0.00000
8/16	8.500	1.000	0.00000	0.000	0.00000
8/17	8.375	0.985	-0.01482	-0.015	0.00022
8/20	8.375	1.000	0.00000	0.000	0.00000
8/21	8.500	1.015	0.01482	0.000	0.00000
8/22	8.625	1.015	0.01460	0.015	0.00021
8/23	8.750	1.014	0.01439	0.000	0.00000
8/24	8.750	1.000	0.00000	0.000	0.00000
8/27	8.625	0.986	-0.01439	-0.014	0.00021
8/28	8.625	1.000	0.00000	0.000	0.00000
8/29	8.500	0.986	-0.01460	0.000	0.00000
8/30	8.375	0.985	-0.01482	-0.015	0.00022
8/31	8.500	1.015	0.01482	0.000	0.00000
9/4	8.500	1.000	0.00000	0.000	0.00000
9/5	8.375	0.985	-0.01482	-0.015	0.00022
9/6	8.625	1.030	0.02941	0.029	0.00087
9/7	8.500	0.986	-0.01460	-0.015	0.00021
9/10	8.000	0.941	-0.06062	-0.061	0.00368
9/11	7.750	0.969	-0.03175	0.000	0.00000
9/12	7.750	1.000	0.00000	0.000	0.00000
9/13	7.875	1.016	0.01600	0.016	0.00026
9/14/79	7.875	1.000	0.00000	0.000	0.00000

| | | SUM= | 0.00000 | SUM= | 0.02173 |
| | | U= | 0.00000 | | |

SIGMA=   (SUM OF LOG Rj-U SQUARED/30)*(30/29)=   0.000749
         TO CONVERT TO ANNUAL VARIANCE: * 365 OR   0.273493
         ANNUAL VOLATILITY=SQUARE ROOT OR   0.522965

EXHIBIT 6   Calculation of Standard Deviation of Daily Percentage Changes in Stock Price, January 7, 1980 (President signs the loan guarantee bill with no equity kicker)

DATE	CHRYSLER STOCK PRICE	Rj=Sj/ Sj-1	LOG Rj	LOG Rj-U	LOG Rj-U SQUARED
11/21/79	6.375				
11/23	6.000	0.941	-0.06062	-0.066	0.00436
11/26	6.000	1.000	0.00000	-0.005	0.00003
11/27	5.875	0.979	-0.02105	-0.026	0.00070
11/28	5.750	0.979	-0.02151	-0.027	0.00072
11/29	6.000	1.043	0.04256	0.037	0.00138
11/30	6.500	1.083	0.08004	0.075	0.00557
12/3	6.250	0.962	-0.03922	-0.045	0.00199
12/4	6.250	1.000	0.00000	-0.005	0.00003
12/5	6.000	0.960	-0.04082	-0.046	0.00214
12/6	6.000	1.000	0.00000	-0.005	0.00003
12/7	6.000	1.000	0.00000	-0.005	0.00003
12/10	6.000	1.000	0.00000	-0.005	0.00003
12/11	6.000	1.000	0.00000	-0.005	0.00003
12/12	6.000	1.000	0.00000	-0.005	0.00003
12/13	6.000	1.000	0.00000	-0.005	0.00003
12/14	6.375	1.063	0.06062	0.055	0.00305
12/17	6.625	1.039	0.03847	0.033	0.00109
12/18	6.500	0.981	-0.01905	-0.024	0.00060
12/19	7.375	1.135	0.12629	0.121	0.01461
12/20	7.375	1.000	0.00000	-0.005	0.00003
12/21	7.375	1.000	0.00000	-0.005	0.00003
12/24	7.750	1.051	0.04960	0.044	0.00195
12/26	7.625	0.984	-0.01626	-0.022	0.00047
12/27	7.250	0.951	-0.05043	-0.056	0.00312
12/28	6.750	0.931	-0.07146	-0.077	0.00591
12/31/79	6.750	1.000	0.00000	-0.005	0.00003
1/2/80	6.750	1.000	0.00000	-0.005	0.00003
1/3	7.000	1.037	0.03637	0.031	0.00096
1/4	7.375	1.054	0.05219	0.047	0.00219
1/7	7.500	1.017	0.01681	0.011	0.00013

$$
\begin{aligned}
\text{SUM} &= 0.16252 & \text{SUM} &= 0.05129 \\
\text{U} &= 0.00542 &&
\end{aligned}
$$

SIGMA=   (SUM OF LOG Rj-U SQUARED/30)*(30/29)=   0.001768
         TO CONVERT TO ANNUAL VARIANCE: * 365 OR   0.645594
         ANNUAL VOLATILITY=SQUARE ROOT OR   0.803489

EXHIBIT 7   Calculation of Standard Deviation of Daily Percentage Changes in Stock Price, April 8, 1980 (Chrysler and the Treasury negotiate; warrants proposed)

DATE	CHRYSLER STOCK PRICE	Rj=Sj/ Sj-1	LOG Rj	LOG Rj-U	LOG Rj-U SQUARED
2/25/80	8.875				
2/26	8.625	0.972	-0.02857	-0.019	0.00035
2/27	8.625	1.000	0.00000	0.010	0.00009
2/28	8.625	1.000	0.00000	0.010	0.00009
2/29	9.000	1.043	0.04256	0.052	0.00274
3/3	8.875	0.986	-0.01399	-0.004	0.00002
3/4	8.625	0.972	-0.02857	-0.019	0.00035
3/5	8.625	1.000	0.00000	0.010	0.00009
3/6	8.250	0.957	-0.04445	-0.035	0.00120
3/7	8.250	1.000	0.00000	0.010	0.00009
3/10	8.000	0.970	-0.03077	-0.021	0.00044
3/11	8.250	1.031	0.03077	0.041	0.00164
3/12	8.000	0.970	-0.03077	-0.021	0.00044
3/13	8.000	1.000	0.00000	0.010	0.00009
3/14	7.750	0.969	-0.03175	-0.022	0.00048
3/17	7.500	0.968	-0.03279	-0.023	0.00053
3/18	7.125	0.950	-0.05129	-0.042	0.00173
3/19	7.125	1.000	0.00000	0.010	0.00009
3/20	6.750	0.947	-0.05407	-0.044	0.00196
3/21	6.750	1.000	0.00000	0.010	0.00009
3/24	6.375	0.944	-0.05716	-0.047	0.00225
3/25	6.250	0.980	-0.01980	-0.010	0.00010
3/26	6.375	1.020	0.01980	0.030	0.00087
3/27	6.000	0.941	-0.06062	-0.051	0.00259
3/28	6.000	1.000	0.00000	0.010	0.00009
3/31	6.125	1.021	0.02062	0.030	0.00092
4/1	6.250	1.020	0.02020	0.030	0.00000
4/2	6.375	1.020	0.01980	0.030	0.00087
4/3	6.750	1.059	0.05716	0.067	0.00448
4/7	6.625	0.981	-0.01869	-0.009	0.00008
4/8/80	6.625	1.000	0.00000	0.010	0.00009

```
                              SUM= -0.29239      SUM=   0.02492
                              U=   -0.00975
```

```
SIGMA=    (SUM OF LOG Rj-U SQUARED/30)*(30/29)=        0.000859
          TO CONVERT TO ANNUAL VARIANCE: * 365 OR      0.313596
          ANNUAL VOLATILITY=SQUARE ROOT OR             0.559996
                                                       ---------
```

EXHIBIT 8   Calculation of Standard Deviation of Daily Percentage Changes in Stock Price, May 12, 1980 (government signs guarantee including warrants)

DATE	CHRYSLER STOCK PRICE	Rj=Sj/ Sj-1	LOG Rj	LOG Rj-U	LOG Rj-U SQUARED
3/28	6.000				
3/31	6.125	1.021	0.02062	0.021	0.00043
4/1	6.250	1.020	0.02020	0.020	0.00041
4/2	6.375	1.020	0.01980	0.020	0.00039
4/3	6.875	1.078	0.07551	0.076	0.00570
4/7	6.625	0.964	-0.03704	-0.037	0.00137
4/8	6.625	1.000	0.00000	0.000	0.00000
4/9	6.500	0.981	-0.01905	-0.019	0.00036
4/10	6.500	1.000	0.00000	0.000	0.00000
4/11	6.000	0.923	-0.08004	-0.080	0.00641
4/14	5.750	0.958	-0.04256	-0.043	0.00181
4/15	5.625	0.978	-0.02198	-0.022	0.00048
4/16	5.500	0.978	-0.02247	-0.022	0.00051
4/17	6.250	1.136	0.12783	0.128	0.01634
4/18	6.000	0.960	-0.04082	-0.041	0.00167
4/21	5.625	0.938	-0.06454	-0.065	0.00417
4/22	5.875	1.044	0.04349	0.043	0.00189
4/23	5.875	1.000	0.00000	0.000	0.00000
4/24	6.125	1.043	0.04167	0.042	0.00174
4/25	6.375	1.041	0.04001	0.040	0.00160
4/28	6.875	1.078	0.07551	0.076	0.00570
4/29	7.250	1.055	0.05311	0.053	0.00282
4/30	7.125	0.983	-0.01739	-0.017	0.00030
5/1	7.000	0.982	-0.01770	-0.018	0.00031
5/2	7.000	1.000	0.00000	0.000	0.00000
5/5	6.750	0.964	-0.03637	-0.036	0.00132
5/6	6.625	0.981	-0.01869	-0.019	0.00035
5/7	7.250	1.094	0.09015	0.090	0.00813
5/8	6.625	0.914	-0.09015	-0.090	0.00813
5/9	7.125	1.075	0.07276	0.073	0.00529
5/12	7.500	1.053	0.05129	0.051	0.00263

```
                         SUM=  0.22314    SUM=  0.08026
                           U=  0.00744
```

```
SIGMA=    (SUM OF LOG Rj-U SQUARED/30)*(30/29)=           0.002767
          TO CONVERT TO ANNUAL VARIANCE: * 365 OR         1.010145
          ANNUAL VOLATILITY=SQUARE ROOT OR                1.005060
                                                          --------
```

EXHIBIT 9   Historical Volatility of Selected Companies

Name	Industry	Historical Volatility (1/1/80 to 1/1/84)
Caterpillar Tractor	machinery (construction and mining)	0.27
John Deere	agricultural equipment	0.29
Firestone Tire ...	tire and rubber	0.33
Ford Motor	autos and trucks	0.36
General Motors ..	autos and trucks	0.28
Goodyear Tire ...	tire and rubber	0.29
Winnebago	recreational vehicles	0.68

Source: J. C. Cox and M. Rubinstein, *Options Markets* (New York: Prentice-Hall, 1985), pp. 346–58.

EXHIBIT 10   Chrysler's Publicly Traded Warrants

	Price of Warrant	Time in Warrant (years)	Stock Price	Exercise Price
(1) September 14, 1979	$2.875	5.75	$7.875	$13
(2) January 7, 1980	2.750	5.42	7.500	13
(3) April 8, 1980	3.000	5.17	6.625	13
(4) May 12, 1980	3.630	5.00	7.500	13
(5) September 1, 1983	16.380	0.25	28.375	13

EXHIBIT 11 Calculation of Standard Deviation of Daily Percentage Changes in Bond Price: Using Weighted Average of Chrysler Bonds: 100 Million of 8⅞% Bonds of 95 and 200 Million of 8% Bonds of 98: as of May 12, 1980 (government signs guarantee including warrants)

DATE	WEIGHTED AVG. BOND PRICE	Rj=Sj/ Sj-1	LOG Rj	LOG Rj-U	LOG Rj-U SQUARED
3/28	31.268				
3/31	35.434	1.133	0.12509	0.112	0.01259
4/1	35.640	1.006	0.00580	-0.007	0.00005
4/2	37.001	1.038	0.03748	0.025	0.00060
4/3	37.950	1.026	0.02532	0.012	0.00015
4/7	38.899	1.025	0.02469	0.012	0.00014
4/8	39.270	1.010	0.00950	-0.003	0.00001
4/9	40.260	1.025	0.02490	0.012	0.00014
4/10	41.333	1.027	0.02629	0.013	0.00018
4/11	38.693	0.936	-0.06600	-0.079	0.00622
4/14	34.485	0.891	-0.11512	-0.128	0.01639
4/15	35.764	1.037	0.03641	0.024	0.00055
4/16	38.198	1.068	0.06584	0.053	0.00280
4/17	40.590	1.063	0.06075	0.048	0.00229
4/18	40.920	1.008	0.00810	-0.005	0.00002
4/21	37.538	0.917	-0.08628	-0.099	0.00984
4/22	36.300	0.967	-0.03352	-0.046	0.00215
4/23	37.496	1.033	0.03242	0.020	0.00038
4/24	39.435	1.052	0.05041	0.038	0.00141
4/25	39.518	1.002	0.00209	-0.011	0.00012
4/28	40.219	1.018	0.01759	0.005	0.00002
4/29	44.220	1.099	0.09484	0.082	0.00672
4/30	45.788	1.035	0.03483	0.022	0.00048
5/1	45.581	0.995	-0.00451	-0.017	0.00030
5/2	45.375	0.995	-0.00454	-0.017	0.00030
5/5	46.695	1.029	0.02868	0.016	0.00025
5/6	45.293	0.970	-0.03050	-0.043	0.00188
5/7	47.190	1.042	0.04104	0.028	0.00079
5/8	41.993	0.890	-0.11669	-0.130	0.01679
5/9	42.900	1.022	0.02138	0.008	0.00007
5/12	46.035	1.073	0.07053	0.058	0.00332

| | | SUM= | 0.38682 | SUM= | 0.08698 |
| | | U= | 0.01289 | | |

```
SIGMA=   (SUM OF LOG Rj-U SQUARED/30)*(30/29)=          0.002999
         TO CONVERT TO ANNUAL VARIANCE: * 365 OR        1.094799
         ANNUAL VOLATILITY=SQUARE ROOT OR               1.046326
                                                        --------
```

EXHIBIT 12 Yields to Maturity on Selected Debt Instruments

	Debt of the U.S. Treasury				*AAA Bonds, Moody's Average*	*BAA Bonds, Moody's Average*
	90-Day T-Bill	*1-Year T-Bond*	*5-Year T-Bond*	*10-Year T-Bond*		
September 14, 1979	11.42%	10.79%	9.25%	9.27%	9.42%	10.48%
January 7, 1980	12.31	11.67	10.49	10.63	10.88	12.29
April 8, 1980	15.70	14.60	12.45	11.03	12.95	14.75
May 12, 1980	9.34	9.34	9.83	10.52	10.93	13.20
September 1, 1983	9.59	10.48	11.92*	11.94	12.54	13.65

* On September 1, 1983, the yield on a 7-year Treasury bond was 0.1193.

EXHIBIT 13 Yield to Maturity of Selected Corporate Bonds on May 12, 1980

	Percent Yield
Selected CCC issues:	
McCrory Corp. deb. 10.5s '85	15.310%
McCrory Corp. deb. 7.5s '94	15.850
LTV Corp. sub. s.f. deb. 5.0s '88	15.360
Fedders Corp. sub. s.f. deb. 8.875s '94	16.300
Allegheny Beverage, sub. deb. 10.0s '97	16.820
Selected Chrysler issues:	
S.f. deb. 8⅞s '95	19.480%
S.f. deb. 8s '98	18.700
Chrysler financial notes 8⅞s '84	20.800
Chrysler financial notes 9s '86	21.450
Chrysler financial sub. deb. 7⅜s '86	23.360

Flowers Industries, Inc. (Abridged)

In early March 1985, Marty Wood, senior vice president and chief financial officer of Flowers Industries, Inc., knew that changes taking place in the food industry could present important opportunities for the company. Anticipating these opportunities, Mr. Wood had proposed that Flowers issue $50 million in long-term securities. Among the alternatives considered were a common stock issue, a straight debt issue, and an issue of convertible subordinated debentures.

The Flowers management team felt that the convertibles offered a unique opportunity for prudently leveraging the company's balance sheet at a time when it did not immediately require the capital and, therefore, was able to retain significant control over the process. As Mr. Wood stated, "The best time to go to market is when you don't need the capital, so you can walk away if the terms are not acceptable. Plus we were at an all-time high on the stock, and the conversion premium added to that multiple."

THE COMPANY

Flowers Industries, Inc., headquartered in Thomasville, Georgia, produced a variety of branded baked foods, snack foods, and convenience foods. Founded in 1919, the company grew to be a Fortune 500 company and, in 1985, operated 36 profit centers in 14 states of the U.S. Sun Belt. The company's philosophy was summed up by former chairman, Langdon S. Flowers: "We don't want to be the biggest food company; we simply want to be the most profitable."

This case was written by Stephanie M. Summers under the direction of Robert F. Bruner.

Copyright © 1989 by the Darden Graduate Business School Foundation, Charlottesville, VA. Revised May 1993.

Flowers was one of the nation's largest wholesale baking companies. With fiscal 1984 sales of $603.0 million, it was smaller only than Continental Baking (acquired by Ralston Purina in 1984), which Drexel Burnham Lambert estimated had sales approximating $1,599.5 million in 1984; Campbell Taggart (acquired by Anheuser-Busch in 1982), which Drexel estimated had sales of $1,050.0 million in 1984; and Interstate Bakeries (an independent, publicly owned company), which posted sales of $685.6 million in 1984. The Flowers market area was concentrated in the Southeast—the nation's fastest-growing region—with some penetration in the midwestern and southwestern markets.

Flowers operated in two business segments: baked foods (bread, cakes, pies, and cookies), which accounted for 87 percent of the company's sales, and convenience foods (frozen vegetables, fruits and cobblers, and food ingredients), which accounted for 13 percent of sales.

OPERATIONS

The company's operational goals were to be least-cost producer in the markets it served, to distribute its products efficiently, to expand its product line, and to increase its market share and geographic penetration through acquisitions. A key to its operational efficiency was the company's unique "reciprocal baking" production system. With reciprocal baking, each plant performed long and efficient production runs, minimizing downtime for production changeovers, and produced only one or two products, which were then hauled between production facilities in 500 company-owned tractor-trailer rigs. In this way, Flowers was not only the least-cost producer of bread in the Atlanta market, for example, but in all the markets served by the Atlanta plant. The reciprocal baking system did incur high distribution costs, but the lower product costs more than offset these distribution costs. Through acquisitions, Flowers had established a network of highly automated plants, each located within 300 miles of other Flowers locations. This strategic clustering of its production plants facilitated reciprocal baking by minimizing shipping distances between plants.

In an industry where the rest of its competitors were approximately 100 percent unionized, the Flowers work force was 76 percent nonunion by contract, with 96 percent of the company's employees covered by Flowers' benefit programs versus union-sponsored plans. Among the benefit programs administered by Flowers was the pension fund, which was overfunded by $33 million. The company believed that it enjoyed greater flexibility in managing its operations for productivity than its heavily unionized competitors.

GROWTH GOALS

Flowers maintained a growth goal of 15 percent for earnings per share in the face of industry growth of only 1 percent. Possible avenues for future growth included new products and increased market penetration, but acquisitions were the primary focus of the company's growth plans. While the company pursued all of these alternatives, it did not have the resources at its disposal for new-product development on the scale necessary to achieve its growth goals, nor could it compete on a marketing-dollar basis with the other major players in the industry to steal share in currently mature markets. Additionally, Flowers did not want to gain share through price cutting, especially at this time, when industrywide price cutting was affecting margins. Continental Baking, prior to its acquisition by Ralston, was the big price cutter in the industry, and industry analysts had predicted that Ralston's profitability criteria would demand more stable pricing on Continental's part. A similar pressure was expected to be exerted on Campbell Taggart by its parent, Anheuser-Busch. Most analysts were expecting prices to firm at this time, and Flowers, as least-cost producer, would benefit most under this scenario.

GROWTH BY ACQUISITION

A significant portion of Flowers Industries' sales growth came from acquisitions. The Flowers management team pursued an opportunistic acquisition strategy: the company was committed to making good acquisitions for long-term growth when they were available. In making acquisitions, the company was willing to endure short-term earnings pressure to achieve long-term growth.

The company looked to acquire underperforming, often unprofitable, small food companies that provided immediate capacity and customers, if not earnings, at favorable prices. The company was able to improve productivity in turnaround acquisitions by automating the facilities and integrating the newly acquired operations into its reciprocal baking system. Many of the company's acquisitions were small operations using short, inefficient production runs to produce a full product line in a single plant. When integrated into the reciprocal baking system, acquired plants were able to use longer, more efficient production runs, allowing the company to achieve significant purchasing and cost efficiencies of scale. In this way, Flowers generated profits from previously unprofitable facilities. Acquisition activity tended to increase in tough market environments, when small operations were most hurt by their relative inefficiency.

Improving acquired turnaround situations had been a more profitable means of expansion for Flowers than building its own capacity, because of the relatively low investment needed to acquire underperforming operations. The company's acquisition strategy focused on limiting the size of individual acquisitions to avoid "betting the company on one roll of the dice," as Mr. Wood phrased it.

Flowers had invested over $28 million in acquisitions over the previous three years and Mr. Wood expected that the company would at least maintain its current acquisition pace. With the company's operations scattered throughout the Sun Belt, management believed there were still plenty of growth-by-acquisition opportunities. In fact, Flowers' management had looked at a number of these the preceding year, turning down acquisitions with combined sales volume exceeding $1 billion, because they either did not fit operationally or management decided they could not achieve the company's profitability goals.

The company had always financed acquisitions on the basis of balance-sheet requirements at the time of each transaction. Management did not have a pool of funds set aside to be used for acquisitions. Typically, Flowers would issue notes that carried a moratorium of at least two years on principal repayment to a company's previous owner. Flowers used this lag in principal repayment to improve the operations of the newly acquired facility. Of the major acquisitions made in the prior four years, five were in the snack food division, as shown in the following table:

Date	Company	Revenues
1/04/84	Sunbeam Cookie Co., Abilene, TX	$ 5.6 million
12/08/83	Jack's Cookie Co., Tampa, FL United Biscuit Co. of America, Grand Rapids, MI	$14.2 million (combined)
11/21/83	Vann's Baking Corp., Memphis, TN	$ 4.0 million
06/03/83	Griffin Pie Co., London, KY	$27.0 million
07/23/82	Jack's Cookie Co., Charlotte, NC	$28.0 million
12/01/81	Purity Baking Company, Charleston, WV	$30.0 million
	Betsy Ross, Bluefield, WV	$25.0 million

Because Flowers acquired underperforming operations, the company's sales usually were boosted before earnings experienced material gains. Sales and earnings growth in any given year were generally not related: sales gains came from current acquisitions (as well as from new products, population growth, etc.) while earnings growth stemmed from improved productivity in previously acquired plants. Approximately 50–60 percent of the company's sales growth was external, from acquisitions, while virtually 100 percent of earnings growth was developed internally.

THE BAKING INDUSTRY

The baking industry was characterized by low growth. Annual compound revenue growth averaged 3 percent during the 1974–1984 period while profits dropped, with earnings per share decreasing an average of 6 percent per year for the industry as a whole over the same period. This compared with 8 percent compound revenue growth and 6 percent earnings growth for the Standard & Poor's 500 Index. Flowers achieved a compound annual growth rate of 17 percent in both sales and earnings per share for the same period.

FLOWERS' FINANCIAL RECORD

Flowers' stated goals for financial performance were 15 percent compound growth of fully diluted earnings per share, 20 percent return on beginning shareholders' equity, and 15 percent return on invested capital. Exhibits 1 and 2 provide recent financial statements. The company's long-term debt carried an average interest cost of 9 percent, which compared with the current prime rate of 10.5 percent.

Flowers was known among Wall Street food-industry analysts as the most profitable U.S. baking company in terms of profit margins. The company's pretax profit margin of 6.6 percent compared with an industry average of 4.1 percent. Based on information available from publicly traded baking companies, Flowers' return on equity of 18.4 percent compared with an industry average of 9.1 percent, and the company's 9.0 percent return on assets compared with an industry average of approximately 3 percent.[1] Exhibit 3 provides data on the company's financial position and results versus those of the baking industry. Flowers' stock had a beta of 0.70. The company had no antitakeover provisions in place. The Flowers family and management owned 30 percent of the common shares outstanding; institutional investors owned 20 percent.

Wall Street analysts estimated that the company would earn $1.15 per share in fiscal 1985 and $1.35 per share in fiscal 1986.

FINANCING OPPORTUNITIES

Mr. Wood believed the company should consider raising approximately $50 million in anticipation of continued acquisition opportunities in the industry and ongoing capital expenditures required to maintain its least-cost-producer advantage. Mr. Wood was also interested in exchanging the $5 million of bank term debt on the balance sheet for longer-term financing, which would not require continued annual cash outflows for principal repayment. Flowers' growing business offered many investment opportunities to put its operating cash flow to work. He also thought the company should have the financial flexibility to move quickly should attractive acquisition opportunities arise in the future. Exhibit 4 provides historical cash-flow information. Exhibit 5 gives an internal-cash-flow forecast Mr. Wood had developed to project funds available should significant acquisition opportunities arise in the future.

He knew that the company's stock, trading at an all-time high of 20 times earnings, was selling at a substantial premium to the market and to its historical trading multiples; in his career with the company, Mr. Wood had seen the stock trade as low as 4 times earnings in the early 1970s.

Several Wall Street analysts had written in January that the stock, trading at a 60 percent premium to the S&P 400 based on 1985 estimates, was fully valued. Exhibit 6 provides

---

[1]According to the 1984 *Fortune* magazine listing of the 500 largest publicly held corporations in the United States, Flowers ranked 23rd for total returns to investors in 1983 (86.9 percent) and 26th for the 10-year average total return to investors (32.2 percent).

historical information regarding the stock's performance versus the S&P Food Index. Mr. Wood wondered how the valuation of the company's stock relative to the market would affect demand for a common stock offering. He thought the company should be making use of its equity to capitalize on the market's recognition of the company's performance, but he knew that significant dilution to current shareholders would have a negative impact on the company's return to shareholders.

A public issue of long-term bonds was another possibility. He suspected that the company would garner a BBB − rating from Standard & Poor's for a bond issue of about $50 million. Yields on Aaa corporate bonds were 11.89 percent, and corporate Baa bonds were yielding 13.12 percent. Mr. Wood expected that, if the company were to issue straight debt with a 20-year maturity, the coupon would be approximately 13.8 percent.

He had recently noticed that a lot of companies were issuing equity-linked debt, and he wondered if this option might be appropriate for the company. An issue of convertible bonds would allow the company to borrow funds at a lower rate than required with straight debt, because the convertible bondholder had the option to convert the bond into a fixed number of shares of the underlying common stock at a premium to the current trading price.[2] With the stock trading at an all-time high, he liked the idea of being able, in effect, to issue equity at a substantial premium. One offering that particularly caught his attention was the recent issue by Citizens and Southern Bank of Atlanta. C&S issued $25 million of convertible subordinated debt at 8.75 percent, convertible into common stock at a 20 percent premium.

Mr. Wood had been watching convertible bond issues and thought his company should be able to sell its equity at a 20 percent premium through this method. He had noticed that several recent convertible debt issues had coupons ranging from 7.25 percent to 9.75 percent. An executive of one of these issuers explained that convertibles were cheap: the interest costs were low enough relative to the cost of straight debt to offset the dilutive impact of the convertible feature on earnings per share. The shares optioned by the convertible holders were included in the calculation of fully diluted earnings per share, while the related interest charged was added back to net income to avoid, in effect, double counting the cost of capital.

Mr. Wood suspected that the real underlying cost of convertibles was higher than initially indicated by the lower coupon. He knew that convertibles were especially attractive if conversion did not occur, because the company would be able to borrow at less than the going rate without diluting common shareholdings. He had every reason to expect, however, that the company would continue its performance in the future, and that the stock, therefore, would appreciate. Mr. Wood wondered if the company would be better to wait and issue stock at the higher values he expected in the future, especially since the company did not require the funds for immediate use.

---

[2]The number of shares of common stock received per convertible bond is determined by applying a premium to the current price of the common stock. For example, if Company X's common stock traded at $10 per share, and Company X issued bonds convertible at $12 per share (a 20 percent premium) the bondholder would receive 83.3 shares of stock for the bond upon conversion ($1,000 per bond/$12 per share) by applying the face value of the bond toward purchase of common stock.

THE PROPOSED OFFERING

The company's investment bankers proposed a structure for the offering as outlined in Exhibit 7. The Flowers senior management team had questions about this proposal. Given the long life of the conversion option, the members wanted to make sure that they did not sell the company's equity at too low a price. An important uncertainty was the effect these variables would have on the price received for the bonds. They looked at some recent convertible offerings to gauge investor preferences. Exhibit 8 summarizes recent offerings and results.

The prior two years had seen a significant increase in the issuance of convertible securities over historical levels. In 1982, 73 issues worth $3.6 billion came to market, which grew to 151 new issues worth $9.4 billion in 1983. An additional $4 billion of convertible securities were issued (in 80 issues) in 1984, bringing the par value of total convertibles outstanding to some $50 billion. Market observers reported that the appeal of convertibles came from their lower volatility and better current income when compared with common stocks, together with the participation in potential upward movements in the underlying stock.

Since the beginning of 1985, the markets had remained volatile. Bond market weakness triggered some selling in the stock market. Interest rates, however, had increased over the previous week, as seen in Exhibit 9. On Friday, March 1, the company's common stock had traded between $20.25 and $19.75, closing the day at $19.75.

The structure proposed by the investment bankers was, Mr. Wood believed, within the range of other recent convertible structures. He knew that investment bankers often looked at the premium and payback (also known as "years to break-even") on comparable convertibles outstanding to value new issues. Exhibit 10 provides data on comparable convertible issues in the market at that time, and Exhibit 11 provides data on BBB − straight debt comparables of various maturities.

Mr. Wood knew that a convertible bond could be thought of as a bond and warrant package and so could be valued as a straight bond plus a call option on the common stock. He had heard that options were a play on the volatility of the underlying instrument, measured in terms of the standard deviation of a stock's daily prices, as shown in Exhibit 12. Volatility, therefore, could be used as a surrogate for an estimate of future stock prices in option valuation: stocks with higher volatility, by definition, had a greater probability of reaching a given strike price than stocks with lower volatility.

While this concept was too simplistic to incorporate fully the many variables involved in a convertible bond, Mr. Wood thought it would be useful to value the convertible bond as a package of straight debt plus call options in order to set a bounding value. He wondered if this bond would accurately reflect the true value of the convertible, whether it would be able to capture fully the interaction between the straight debt component and the option portion of the convertible.

EXHIBIT 1 Consolidated Statement of Income (amounts in thousands, except per share data)

	For the Year Ended		
	June 30, 1984	*July 2, 1983*	*July 3, 1982*
Sales	$602,995	$522,254	$461,062
Other income	3,481	2,225	3,000
Total	606,476	524,479	464,062
Cost of goods sold	323,621	272,351	246,004
Selling, delivery, and administrative expenses	220,711	196,697	170,839
Depreciation and amortization	16,795	14,862	12,859
Interest	5,184	5,367	5,345
Total	566,311	489,277	435,047
Income before income taxes	40,165	35,202	29,015
Federal and state income taxes	18,025	15,988	12,730
Net income	$ 22,140	$ 19,214	$ 16,285
Per share:			
Primary	$0.94	$0.83	$0.77
Fully diluted	$0.94	$0.83	$0.71

Source: Flowers Industries Form 8-K, February 27, 1985.

EXHIBIT 2 Balance Sheet

Assets

	June 30 1984	July 2 1983
Current assets:		
Cash and temporary investments	$ 23,699	$ 21,187
Accounts receivable	41,505	34,932
Inventories	28,289	27,011
Prepaid expenses	1,443	1,575
Total current assets	94,936	84,705
Property, plant, & equipment, at cost, less accumulated depreciation	154,654	136,774
Other assets and deferred charges:		
Property held for sale	1,693	1,437
Investments, at cost	757	1,331
Unamortized loan cost	566	525
Construction funds held by trustees	4,035	2,188
Miscellaneous	772	560
Total other assets	7,823	6,041
Cost in excess of net tangible assets	5,502	5,660
Total assets	$262,915	$233,180

Liabilities & Stockholders' Equity

	June 30 1984	July 2 1983
Current liabilities:		
Long-term debt	$ 4,125	$ 3,895
Accounts payable	29,898	24,879
Accrued taxes other than income taxes	3,054	2,813
Income taxes	2,699	5,674
Accrued compensation, interest, and other liabilities	25,623	21,459
Total current liabilities	65,399	58,720
Long-term notes payable	30,131	28,363
Industrial revenue bonds	27,263	20,030
Deferred income taxes	12,115	9,951
Redeemable preferred stock	1,349	1,821
Total liabilities	136,257	118,885
Common stockholders' equity:		
Common stock—$0.625 par value, authorized 30,000,000 shares, issued 23,606,612	14,754	14,754
Capital in excess of par value	10,502	10,502
Retained earnings	104,442	90,015
Less—Common stock in treasury, 412,304 and 273,045 shares, respectively	(3,040)	(976)
Total stockholders' equity	126,658	114,295
Total liabilities and stockholders' equity	$262,915	$233,180

EXHIBIT 3   Comparative Analysis, 1984

	Baking Industry	Flowers
Assets		
Cash & equivalents	8.3%	9.0%
Accounts & notes receivable	18.6	15.8
Inventory	12.9	10.8
All other current	1.9	0.5
Total current assets	41.7	36.1
Fixed assets	48.8	58.8
Intangibles	1.5	2.1
All other noncurrent	8.0	2.9
Total assets	100.0%	100.0%
Liabilities & Net Worth		
Short-term notes payable	4.4%	0.0%
Current maturities long-term debt	4.8	1.6
Accounts & notes payable	15.8	11.4
Accrued expenses	7.3	11.9
All other current	2.3	0.0
Total current liabilities	34.6	24.9
Long-term debt	24.7	22.3
All other noncurrent	2.9	4.6
Total liabilities	62.2	51.8
Net worth	37.8	48.0
Total liabilities & net worth	100.0%	100.0%
Income data:		
Net sales	100.0%	100.0%
Cost of sales	61.0	53.9
Gross profit	39.0	46.1
Operating expenses	33.8	36.4
Operating profit	5.2	9.7
All other expenses (net)	1.1	3.6
Profit before taxes	4.1	6.6

Source: Robert Morris Associates annual statement ratios.

EXHIBIT 4 Historical Cash Flow

	1984	1983	1982
Net income	$22,140	$19,214	$16,285
Depreciation & amortization	16,795	14,862	12,859
Deferred taxes	2,164	2,452	758
Other	94	152	121
Cash flow from operations	41,193	36,680	30,023
Changes in working capital	1,087	(1,814)	3,336
Cash internally generated	42,280	34,866	33,359
Capital expenditures*	(29,716)	(23,807)	(24,409)
	12,564	11,059	8,950
Dividends paid	(7,705)	(6,337)	(4,771)
	4,859	4,722	4,179
Acquisitions	(7,611)	(7,388)	(13,426)
	(2,752)	(2,666)	(9,247)
Financing activities	5,264	3,694	3,973
Net change in cash and short-term investments	$ 2,512	$ 1,028	($ 5,274)

* Net of disposals.

EXHIBIT 5 Cash-Flow Projections

Assumptions:

Tax rate	45.0%	Working capital % sales	5.0%
Sales & EBIT growth	15.0%	Deferred taxes growth	15.0%
(conservative to use 15% sales growth for cash-flow projection)		Depreciation % sales	2.8%
Changes in PPE (% sales)	5.0%	Dividend growth per quarter	$0.005
(assumes half of sales growth is from acquisitions)		Shares outstanding (000)	23,607
Acquisition $ growth	15.0%		

	1984 Actual	1985E	1986E	1987E	1988E	1989E
Sales	$602,995	$693,444	$797,461	$917,080	$1,054,642	$1,212,838
Working capital	29,537	34,672	39,873	45,854	52,732	60,642
EBIT	45,349	52,151	59,974	68,970	79,316	91,213
Old interest	5,184	5,184	5,184	5,184	5,184	5,184
Profit before taxes	40,165	46,967	54,790	63,786	74,132	86,029
Taxes @ 45%	18,025	21,135	24,656	28,704	33,359	38,713
Net income	22,140	25,832	30,135	35,082	40,772	47,316
Depreciation	16,795	19,416	22,329	25,678	29,530	33,959
Deferred taxes	2,164	2,489	2,862	3,291	3,785	4,353
Cash flow from operations	41,099	47,737	55,325	64,052	74,087	85,128
Changes in working capital	(3,552)	(5,135)	(5,201)	(5,981)	(6,878)	(7,910)
Total	37,547	42,602	50,124	58,071	67,209	77,718
Dividends	(7,705)	(9,207)	(11,095)	(12,984)	(14,872)	(16,761)
Total	29,842	33,395	39,029	45,087	52,337	60,957
Changes in PP&E	(29,716)	(34,672)	(39,873)	(45,854)	(52,732)	(60,642)
Preacquisition cash flow	126	(1,227)	(884)	(767)	(395)	315
Acquisitions	(7,611)	(8,753)	(10,066)	(11,575)	(13,312)	(15,308)
Prefinancing cash flow	($7,485)	($10,030)	($10,909)	($12,342)	($13,707)	($14,993)

Dividend Projections

1984 (Actual)	$0.326	7,705
Q1	0.090	
Q2	0.095	
Q3	0.100	
Q4	0.105	
FY1985	0.390	9,207
Q1	0.110	
Q2	0.115	
Q3	0.120	
Q4	0.125	
FY1986	0.470	11,095
Q1	0.130	
Q2	0.135	
Q3	0.140	
Q4	0.145	
FY1987	0.550	12,984
Q1	0.150	
Q2	0.155	
Q3	0.160	
Q4	0.165	
FY1988	0.630	14,872
Q1	0.170	
Q2	0.175	
Q3	0.180	
Q4	0.185	
FY1989	0.710	16,761

EXHIBIT 6 Stock Price History

	1978	1979	1980	1981	1982	1983
Price:						
High	$5.00	$3.92	$5.00	$5.67	$10.17	$14.17
Low	2.75	3.17	4.25	3.67	4.50	9.33
P/E:						
High	12.5×	8.5×	9.3×	9.1×	14.3×	17.0×
Low	6.9	6.9	5.4	5.9	6.3	11.2
Flowers' P/E as % S&P Food Index:						
High P/E	137%	110%	93%	97%	123%	137%
Low P/E	95	105	78	79	76	114
Average P/E	120	108	88	87	104	127
Earnings	5	4	5	6	8	8

Source: "Flowers Industries," Bonnie Rivers, J. C. Bradford & Company, January 16, 1984. Adjusted for subsequent 3-for-2 stock split.

EXHIBIT 7   Convertible Offering Structure Proposed by Merrill Lynch

---

Interest rate: 8.25 percent.

Maturity: 2005.

Conversion: Convertible at any time prior to maturity into shares of the company's common stock at a conversion price of $24, subject to adjustment in certain events, such as a common stock dividend or stock split.

Redemption premium: Redeemable at any time on or after March 1, 1987, or earlier if the closing price of the common stock equals or exceeds 140 percent of the conversion price during at least 20 out of 30 consecutive trading days ending within five days prior to notice of redemption.

   Redeemable at declining prices (see below) until March 1, 1995, and thereafter at par. Redemption price will include accrued interest to the redemption date. Any debentures called for redemption that are not converted into common stock on or before the redemption date are subject to purchase at the redemption price by one or more investment bankers or other purchasers, who may agree with the Company to purchase such Debentures and convert them into the Company's common stock.

Sinking fund: Annual sinking fund payments begin March 1, 1995, and will total 7.5 percent of the principal amount of Debentures issued. Sinking fund payments are calculated to retire 75 percent of the debt from the issue prior to maturity.

Over-allotment option (Green Shoe):   The underwriters will have the option to purchase from the Company up to an additional $7,500,000 in principal of Debentures at the Price to Public, less the Underwriting Discount, to cover any over-allotments.

Redemption Premiums for Convertible Debentures

Year	Percentage (of par)	Year	Percentage (of par)
1985	108.250%	1990	104.125%
1986	107.425	1991	103.300
1987	106.600	1992	102.475
1988	105.775	1993	101.650
1989	104.950	1994	100.825

[see preceding Redemption text] and thereafter at 100% of the principal amount, in each case together with accrued interest to the date fixed for redemption.

EXHIBIT 8 Recent Public Offerings of Convertible Debentures

Date Company	Amount ($ in millions)	Coupon (%)	Description	Maturity	Conversion Premium (%)	Yrs. Call Protection	Rating
11/84:							
Communications Industries	$ 50	9.00%	convertible debs	2009	18.70%	3	Ba2/BB –
Wachovia Corporation	100	8.75	convertible sub debs	2009	23.40	2	Aa2/AA
12/84:							
Computervision Corporation ...	100	8.00	convertible sub debs	2009	21.62	2	/BB –
2/85:							
Johnstown American	35	9.75	convertible sub debs	1995	14.80	2	B2/B –
Texas Air Corporation	30	10.00	exchangeable sub debs*	2005	10.00	2	Caa/CCC
Citizens & Southern Bank	25	8.75	convertible sub notes	2010	20.30	3	/A –
H.J. Heinz Company	41	7.25	convertible sub debs	2015	30.00	3	Aa3/A +
Bay Banks, Inc.	30	8.75	convertible sub debs	2010	22.00	3	Baa/
CooperVision	200	8.63	convertible sub debs	2005	22.00	2	Ba2/BB –

* Exchangeable into Continental Airlines Stock.

EXHIBIT 9   Money Market Rates

	Latest Week (%)	Week Ago (%)
Federal funds	8.63%	8.04%
Commercial paper	8.50	8.70
New Treasury bills, 3-month	8.22	8.46
Certificates of deposit, 3-month	8.70	8.85
U.S. governments (1994–1999)	11.29	11.62
New Aa industrials	12.38	12.75
New Aaa utilities	12.50	12.88

Figures cited are as of February 20, 1985.

Source: *Business Week*, March 4, 1985.

EXHIBIT 10 Convertible Debt Comparables, BBB-Rated Companies

	Shares Received per Bond	Conversion Price per Share	Dividend Income per Bond	Yield to Maturity (%)	Current Stock Price
Alaska Airlines 2003	55.17	$18.125	$ 7.72	7.31%	$19.13
Crown Zellerbach 2009	24.84	40.250	24.84	9.04	32.38
Fischbach 2005	27.78	36.000	27.78	8.35	36.50
Internat'l Lease Finance 2003	64.52	15.500	Nil	8.28	16.00
Keystone International 2005	49.31	20.280	23.67	8.19	18.00
Leggett & Platt 2001	48.66	20.550	23.36	7.17	20.88
M/A-Communications 2006	27.40	36.500	6.03	9.41	20.38
Moran Energy 2008	57.01	17.540	22.80	11.11	10.63
Paine Webber 2008	18.89	52.940	11.33	8.97	38.50
Protective Corporation 2006	82.85	12.070	51.37	4.34	21.63
Research-Cottrell 2006	58.82	17.000	18.82	8.38	19.75
SRI Corporation 2008	47.06	21.250	32.00	8.85	17.50
Tidewater, Inc. 2005	15.50	64.500	13.95	12.90	18.25
Flowers Industries 2005‡	41.67	24.000	16.25	8.25	20.00

All issues cited are sinking fund debentures outstanding in February 1985 with similar call protection. Yields to maturity are as of February 1.

* Income differential defined as interest income paid by convertible less the annual dividend income that would be received by converting into the underlying common stock.

† Assumes dividend of underlying security remains constant.

‡ As outlined by Merrill Lynch representatives.

Source: *Standard & Poor's Bond Guide*, February 1985.

Current Yield on Stock	Current Convert Price	Current Yield on Convert (%)	Income Spread*	Per Share Income Spread	Conversion Premium per Share	Years to Breakeven†
0.73%	$1,170	7.69%	$82.25	$1.49	($ 1.00)	−0.67
3.09	1,020	9.07	67.67	2.72	7.88	2.89
2.74	1,014	8.38	57.17	2.06	(0.50)	−0.24
0.00	1,090	8.49	92.54	1.43	(0.50)	−0.35
2.67	1,030	8.25	61.31	1.24	2.28	1.83
2.30	1,090	7.45	57.85	1.19	(0.32)	−0.27
1.08	985	9.39	86.46	3.16	16.13	5.11
3.76	805	10.80	64.14	1.13	6.92	6.15
1.56	930	8.87	71.16	3.77	14.44	3.83
2.87	1,791	5.58	48.58	0.59	(9.56)	−16.29
1.62	1,210	8.68	86.21	1.47	(2.75)	−1.88
3.89	990	8.84	55.52	1.18	3.75	3.18
4.93	630	12.30	63.54	4.10	46.25	11.28
1.95	1,000	8.25	71.25	1.71	4.00	2.34

EXHIBIT 11 Straight Debt and Treasury Comparables, BBB-Rated Companies

Maturity		Yield to Maturity (%)
	20-Year Maturities	
2008 ...	Home Group	14.36%
2005 ...	Dayton Power & Light	13.40
2005 ...	Jim Walter Corporation	13.10
2003 ...	Northwest Industries	14.34
	15-Year Maturities	
2000 ...	Armco Steel	14.06
2000 ...	Carter Hawley Hale	13.09
2000 ...	Inland Steel	13.52
1999 ...	Integrated Resources	14.57
1999 ...	Paine Webber	13.14
	10-Year Maturities	
1995 ...	Armco Steel	12.69
1995 ...	Carter Hawley Hale	13.54
1995 ...	Inland Steel	13.01
1995 ...	Montgomery Ward Credit	13.78
1995 ...	National Steel	13.36
	5-Year Maturities	
1991 ...	CP National	13.20
1990 ...	Fremont General	13.67
1990 ...	Montgomery Ward Credit	12.30
1989 ...	Inland Steel	12.27
1989 ...	National Steel Corp.	12.96

All issues cited are sinking fund debentures outstanding in February 1985. Yields to maturity cited are as of 2/85.

Source: *Standard & Poor's Bond Guide*, February 1985.

Government Bonds			
Maturity	Yield (%)	Maturity	Yield (%)
1987 ...	10.05%	1993	11.28%
1988 ...	10.50	1994	11.34
1989 ...	10.80	1995	11.28
1990 ...	11.02	1996	11.33
1991 ...	11.25	2001	11.52
1992 ...	11.38	2005	11.57

Source: *Barron's*, February 17, 1985.

EXHIBIT 12 Worksheet for Estimating Volatility

Flowers Industries, Inc., Daily Stock Prices

Day	Stock Price, S_j	Price Relatives, $R_j = S_j/S_j - 1$	Log R_j	Log $R_j -$ Mean	(Log $R_j -$ Mean)/2
0	$17.125	—	—	—	—
1	17.250	1.007	0.003	0.001002	0.000001
2	17.000	0.986	−0.006	−0.00849	0.000072
3	17.375	1.022	0.009	0.007320	0.000053
4	17.375	1.000	0.000	−0.00215	0.000004
5	17.500	1.007	0.003	0.000957	0.000000
6	18.000	1.029	0.012	0.010078	0.000101
7	18.375	1.021	0.009	0.006798	0.000046
8	18.500	1.007	0.003	0.000788	0.000000
9	18.750	1.014	0.006	0.003673	0.000013
10	18.500	0.987	−0.006	−0.00798	0.000063
11	18.125	0.980	−0.009	−0.01104	0.000122
12	18.250	1.007	0.003	0.000828	0.000000
13	18.375	1.007	0.003	0.000808	0.000000
14	18.250	0.993	−0.003	−0.00512	0.000026
15	18.250	1.000	0.000	−0.00215	0.000004
16	18.000	0.986	−0.006	−0.00814	0.000066
17	17.875	0.993	−0.003	−0.00518	0.000026
18	18.000	1.007	0.003	0.000870	0.000000
19	18.250	1.014	0.006	0.003834	0.000014
20	19.000	1.041	0.017	0.015334	0.000235
21	19.875	1.046	0.020	0.017397	0.000302
22	19.875	1.000	0.000	−0.00215	0.000004
23	19.125	0.962	−0.017	−0.01886	0.000355
24	19.750	1.033	0.014	0.011809	0.000139
25	20.125	1.019	0.008	0.006012	0.000036
26	20.625	1.025	0.011	0.008502	0.000072
27	20.250	0.982	−0.008	−0.01012	0.000102
28	20.375	1.006	0.003	0.000516	0.000000
29	20.625	1.012	0.005	0.003140	0.000009
30	19.875	0.964	−0.016	−0.01824	0.000332

Estimate of daily variance	$(0.00212/30) \star (30/29) =$	0.000076
Estimate of annual variance	$(0.000076) \star 365 =$	0.027848
Estimate of annual volatility	$(0.027848)\hat{}(1/2) =$	0.166877

Exhibit covers 30 days prior to February 28, 1985.

Estimated Volatilities of Other Food Processing Companies (%)

American Brands	21%
General Foods	21
Beatrice	24
Ralston Purina	29
Dart & Kraft	20

Bank of Tokyo

In October 1990, Tasuku Takagaki, recently appointed president of the Bank of Tokyo (BOT), wrestled with the first major challenge of his presidency: achieving a capital structure for the bank that would meet the capital-adequacy standards set by the Bank for International Settlements. BIS required that all banks engaged in international banking maintain a 7.25 percent capital/asset ratio by the end of the fiscal year 1991. The standards were imposed on all banks by governmental agreement in 1988 and would be in effect at the end of BOT's current fiscal year, March 1991. Failure to meet the standards would trigger restrictions in BOT's ability to engage in international banking activities. The massive paper losses incurred by the Bank of Tokyo, however, primarily a result of the downturn in the stock market, had dropped its ratio from a solid 8.0 percent in March 1990 to 6.8 percent by the semiannual book closing in September 1990.

To conform to the BIS standards, Mr. Takagaki could respond in one or more of the following ways:

Limit asset growth, the denominator of the capital/assets ratio, by restraining lending activity. Mr. Takagaki preferred increasing BOT's capital, the numerator, through a new issue so as not to restrain growth.

Issue ¥60 billion of common stock: Common stock was the purest form of capital from the BIS's standpoint and would contribute significantly to the perception of solidity. However, Mr. Takagaki questioned whether the time was right to sell shares. The year 1990 had been characterized as the year of the "bursting of the bubble economy" in the Japanese financial industry. By October 1990, the Nikkei 225 index (leading shares on the Tokyo stock exchange) had plunged 48 percent from its all-time high reached on the last day of 1989. As its current share price

This case was prepared by Michael J. Schill and Professor Robert F. Bruner.

Copyright © 1992 by the Darden Graduate Business School Foundation, Charlottesville, VA, and INSEAD, Fontainebleau, France. Revised May 1993.

of ¥1,050, BOT would need to sell 57.142 million shares. With 1,993,933,000 shares outstanding, the old shareholders' interest in BOT would be diluted 2.8 percent.

Issue ¥60 billion of convertible subordinated bonds: Equity-linked bonds had been a favorite form of financing for Japanese firms since the mid-1980s. The conventional view was that they permitted shares to be sold at a higher price than prevailed at present, and carried a lower coupon rate. Some observers were skeptical of these benefits and pointed to difficulties issuers had encountered when their bonds did not convert. Because of the equity-market downturn, Mr. Takagaki was worried that the demand for such issues was limited. He speculated, however, that being the first bank to float securities in the current capital markets might help maximize the value of the issue. The financial staff of the bank was studying a possible issue of five-year notes convertible at 2.5 percent over the current stock price of ¥1,050. The coupon rate and bond price had yet to be determined.

Mr. Takagaki wondered what the cost of the funds obtained from this convertible would be and how it would compare with the cost of common stock, which even at the current depressed prices had a low dividend yield. Should he consider other possible terms? How did the convertible bond compare with an issue of warrant bonds, an extremely popular form of financing for Japanese companies? What were the strengths and weaknesses of convertibles versus bonds with warrants? Were any other advantages and disadvantages associated with a convertible-bond issue that he should take into account?

Whatever he decided, Mr. Takagaki wished to move quickly. The capital markets were still unsettled: the Nikkei fell 40 percent in September. On October 1, 1990, the Nikkei index briefly fell below the psychological barrier of 20,000 and then recovered. The apparent stability of the Nikkei in the few weeks that followed gave financial planners some breathing room, but the underlying weaknesses in the market had not subsided.

JAPANESE BANKING INDUSTRY

The Japanese banks steadily built their global presence throughout the post-World War II era. By 1970, 4 Japanese banks ranked in the world's top 20 banks, based on total assets in dollars. By 1980, the Japanese banks boasted 6 in the world's top 20. Over the course of the 1980s, Japanese banks suddenly emerged as the world's dominant financial leaders in terms of global mass and resources. By the end of the decade, Japan's largest banks had achieved a spectacular compound growth rate of over 17 percent and represented 8 of the largest 10 banks in the world, as shown in Exhibit 1. Observers attributed much of this record to six factors:

Growth in the manufacturing sector: A major share of the banking sector growth could be linked to the dramatic global success of the Japanese manufacturing sector. Japanese banks followed their clients around the world as Americans and Europeans did more business with Japanese firms.

Appreciation of the yen: A portion of the shift in size resulted from decisions made in New York City's Plaza Hotel in 1985. A meeting of the Group of Seven (G-7)[1] finance ministers made an accord collectively to reduce the value of the U.S. dollar in foreign exchange markets. The results of the actions vaulted the yen from an average dollar exchange rate of ¥239 in 1985 to ¥128 in 1988. This appreciation of the yen was an important factor in the ability of Japanese banks to make large dollar-denominated investments in real estate and company acquisitions.

Advantageous cost of capital: From 1980 to February 1987, the Bank of Japan, Japan's central bank, consistently lowered Japan's discount rate, from 9.0 percent to 2.5 percent. The banks were able to use these comparatively low interest rates to raise inexpensive capital. Moreover, interest-rate regulation allowed banks to pay very low interest on bank deposits.

Bullish stock market: Two structural factors linked Japanese lending capacity directly to changes in the stock market. First, because of the significant cross-ownership within Japanese *keiretsu* relationships, banks maintained large investments in equity securities. The second factor was the BIS agreement to Japanese demands that a bank be allowed to recognize a portion of unrealized gains on stock holdings in the bank's capital calculation. Consequently, when large securities holdings increased in value, Japanese banks were able to generate loans backed by the unrealized gains applied to their capital base. Exhibit 2 shows the rise of the Nikkei versus the other major world markets over the late 1980s. This bull market generated vast capital gains, which then could be leveraged to create loans at the ratio of over 12 to 1.

Appreciating real estate values: The Japanese philosophy was that the price of real estate would never decrease. This traditional belief had long convinced most Japanese that land ownership provided a riskless asset. Moreover, in step with the cash generated during the prosperous 1980s, land prices soared. Banks loaned against land values; lenders then used the cash to invest further in the rising stock market and real estate market; the increase in the land value provided more backing for further lending; and the speculative cycle continued. Although the U.S. land area was 25 times larger than Japan in 1990, the Japanese total land value of ¥20 trillion was 4 times the total U.S. land value. By March 31, 1990, Japanese property-backed loans had increased to 23 percent of the city banks' (Tokyo financial-center banks') total loans.[2]

Deregulation of the Japanese financial system: Even though the banking and securities businesses were separated by law in Japan (as in the United States), Japanese banks had gained experience in universal banking in foreign markets beyond the Ministry of Finance's control. The MOF was studying reforms to abolish the barriers between commercial banks, trust banks, and securities houses, moreover, and the proposed reforms were expected by 1993.

---

[1] The Group of Seven nations were the United States, Canada, Japan, France, Britain, Germany, and Italy.

[2] David Lake, *Japanese Capital—How Corporations Tap the World's Largest Liquidity Pool*, Special Report no. P333 (London: The Economist Intelligence Unit; Business International Limited; February 1992).

CRASH OF THE JAPANESE STOCK MARKET

While the Nikkei average was approaching 40,000 during the latter part of 1989, underlying macroeconomic factors were undermining the buoyancy of the market. The Bank of Japan already had demonstrated its concern over rising inflation through back-to-back discount-rate hikes, from 2.50 to 3.75 percent, in May and October 1989. The increases in interest rates were particularly damaging to the banks because of the deregulation of interest rates previously mentioned. Even though banks were increasingly required to pay higher market rates on deposits, the banks maintained their low lending rates to hold or gain market share, even at near 0 percent spreads.[3]

In early December 1989, Yasushi Mieno was asked to assume the position of governor of the Bank of Japan, and he communicated his determination to shrink the speculative bubble in the stock market. Within one week of his appointment, he announced the third increase of the discount rate, to 4.25 percent. The repeated, unexpected discount-rate increases stunned short-term lenders, who reacted immediately with higher yields. The bond-market yields remained unchanged.

The interest-rate instability was accompanied by political instability created by worry that the long-ruling Liberal Democratic Party would lose its majority in the February 1990 elections. In the early months of 1990, the market remained jittery in anticipation of the election and of further expected hikes in the discount rate; bond yields finally increased to meet the short-term rates.

When the election votes were counted on February 18, the Liberal Democratic Party had achieved a landslide victory in the House of Representatives and managed better than expected in the lower house. Analysts expected the results to send the yen and the Nikkei up. The appreciation of the yen never materialized, however, and, when the Tokyo stock market closed February 19, the Nikkei was down. Within one week, the Nikkei dropped 5,000 points—a 14 percent drop from its peak level. A month later, governor Mieno upped the discount rate another full 100 basis points; the market continued in a downward spiral through April. A rebound in the early summer brought the Nikkei back to a steady 32,000.

Hopes that the market would make a quick recovery were dashed in August with the invasion of Kuwait by Iraq. The resulting global bear market had a doubling impact in Tokyo as the Bank of Japan raised the discount rate again on August 30 to 6 percent. To make matters worse, Daiwa Securities was found guilty of compensating losses incurred by preferred clients. The Sumitomo Bank chairman, Ichiro Isoda, accepted responsibility for illegal speculative lending activities by both a local branch and through direct support of a speculative real estate client, and announced his resignation. On October 1, 1990, the Nikkei dropped below 20,000, 48 percent below its peak eight months previously. This drop represented a paper-value loss of ¥300 trillion,[4] or 70 percent of Japan's 1990 gross domestic product.

---

[3]A lending "spread" was the difference between the interest rate charged by the bank to its customer and the bank's own cost of funds.

[4]Christopher Wood, "A Survey of Japanese Finance," *The Economist*, December 8, 1990.

CAPITAL ADEQUACY: BIS CAPITAL RATIOS

In July 1988, the Banking Regulations and Supervisory Practices committee of the Bank for International Settlements in Basle, Switzerland, adopted a set of capital-adequacy guidelines to reduce the sources of competitive inequality in the international banking industry. The original framework was devised jointly by the banking authorities in the United Kingdom and United States in January 1987. Banking regulators from each of the Group of Ten (G-10), as well as Luxembourg and Switzerland, having reviewed and approved the proposal, had the measure ratified within their home countries.

The regulation required all banks involved in international transactions to exceed a minimum capital-to-asset ratio, based on two different estimates of capital and a risk-adjusted asset calculation.[5] Exhibit 3 displays the comparative BIS ratios for the major Japanese banks.

Although the BIS could not enforce restrictions on the international banking activities of banks that were unable to meet the requirement, banks were compelled to clear the hurdles to maintain goodwill within the banking community. In 1987, as the proposal was first being considered, Japanese banks awoke to the important impact the BIS regulations would have on their financing. Based on prior-year financial statements, the average capital ratio of Japanese banks, 2.70 percent, was far below the 7.25 percent required rate. The Japanese banks pleaded that they were as stable as banks that met the requirement because of their operations, the Japanese interbank support, and the Bank of Japan's protection. The Ministry of Finance refused the Japanese bank arguments and demanded full adherence to the BIS guideline. By December 1988, the MOF had set a new capital-ratio requirement in line with BIS regulation.

The BIS believed that its regulation created much more equitable competition in the international banking industry than in the past. The existence of an international standard promoted better regulatory and commercial monitoring of banks' soundness. The emphasis on Tier 1 capital required banking operations to focus on profitability, rather than on volume. The risk-adjustment calculation discouraged excessive high-risk lending and off-balance-sheet exposure.

---

[5]The BIS required capital to back assets only in proportion to their relative risk. Tests of capital adequacy required calculating three quantities. **Tier 1 ("core") capital** was defined as retained earnings, common stock, qualifying noncumulative perpetual preferred stock, and minority interests, *less* goodwill. **Tier 2 ("supplementary") capital** included preferred stock, hybrid capital instruments, subordinated debt, and 45 percent of unrealized gains on marketable securities. Tier 2 capital was restricted to a maximum of 100 percent of Tier 1 capital. **Risk-adjusted assets:** all bank assets were assigned to one of four risk categories. Then the sum of each category was assigned a risk rating. For example, cash was assigned to the least-risky category and received a risk weighting of 0 percent, meaning that none of the cash balance was required to be backed by capital. Loans to private corporations were assigned to the most-risky category; their full value had to be backed by capital. Moreover, off-balance-sheet items that also increased claims on the bank's capital were added to the BIS asset calculation.

The BIS regulation required banks to meet two standards, to be phased in over two years. By March 1991, the minimum acceptable capital ratios would be 3.25 percent Tier 1 capital to risk-adjusted assets and 7.25 percent Tiers 1 and 2 capital to risk-adjusted assets. In March 1993, the respective minimum ratios would rise to 4 and 8 percent.

Faced with grossly deficient capital ratios in the late 1980s, the Japanese banks had two alternatives to prepare for the 1991 deadline. First, they could reduce their asset bases by slowing lending activities or by selling their large investments in the ownership of client companies (through *keiretsu* cross-ownership patterns). Second, the banks could raise Tier 1 capital through common equity issues or Tier 2 capital through issues of common stock, preferred stock, or subordinated debt.

The near trebling of the Nikkei 225 from 13,083 (end of 1985) to 38,916 (end of 1989) provided Japanese banks with the opportunity to raise all the required capital. Over the course of these three years, the 13 city banks issued ¥6 trillion in equity and equity-related financing.[6] In addition, Tier 2 capital was automatically increased through the ballooning of unrealized capital gains on the banks' security holdings. By March 1990, one year ahead of schedule, almost all of the banks were well above the 7.25 percent requirement.

The collapse of the Tokyo stock market reversed both effects; unrealized gains shrunk, and investor demand for new securities issues ebbed. In April 1990, the Ministry of Finance froze all new issues of both equity and debt to avoid further depression of the equity market. (The MOF was particularly worried that large life insurance companies would dump their equity holdings in search of the new subordinated debt issues.)

In June the ban on subordinated issues was eased. Over the summer, Japanese banks issued ¥2 trillion of subordinated debt at an uncomfortable 8.4 percent. Contrary to the spirit of the BIS regulations, however, many of these new issues were completed by subtle agreements between the banks and buyers. The banks loaned the necessary funds to their clients to allow them to purchase the banks' debt issue.

Nevertheless, by September 1990, all of the city banks except Kyowa Bank were still below the 7.25 percent ratio. The deficiency came primarily from the requirement that 50 percent of the total capital come from Tier 1 capital. Additional subordinated debt was effective only at increasing Tier 2 capital. After further decline of the Nikkei in September, the Ministry of Finance, believing that the market had reached bottom at 24,000, lifted the restriction on equity issues. Exhibit 3 shows the September 1990 status of the city banks' capital ratios.

BANK OF TOKYO

Founded in 1946 as the successor to the Yokahama Specie Bank, the Bank of Tokyo was granted the exclusive right to specialize in international finance. The bank used this opportunity to build Japan's most extensive international network, with over 250 overseas offices. Although the Ministry of Finance later had granted foreign exchange licenses to the other city banks, the BOT continued to maintain Japan's largest share of foreign exchange volume. The BOT also acted as the agent for all government or government-guaranteed bonds.

---

[6]Wood, "A Survey of Japanese Finance."

The BOT considered itself a "global service banker." It made a concerted effort to meet international-client needs through the most extensive network and internationally seasoned staff of any Japanese bank. The success of this strategy was seen in its profits, 70 percent of which were generated beyond Japanese shores. The BOT was also the largest lender among Japanese banks to debtor nations. Exhibit 4 provides peer comparisons for the BOT.

The company's president, Tasuku Takagaki, had joined the BOT at age 25 after receiving a degree at Tokyo University. By 1963, he was assistant manager at the New York agency and later became general manager of the International Investment Division and resident director for Europe. After six years as director of the head office, Mr. Takagaki was asked to assume the bank's presidency in June 1990.[7]

The BOT was different from the other 12 city banks in five key areas: (1) The majority of the firm's profits were generated abroad. (2) The BOT did not maintain a strong retail banking effort in Japan; in fact, the bank had offices in California three times the number it had in Japan. (3) Because of its unique access to the debenture issue market, the BOT maintained a much smaller portion of its assets in loans than the other banks did. (4) The bank derived its income mostly from fees and commissions and bond and foreign exchange trading, rather than from interest income. (5) The bank belonged to no *keiretsu* group and thus, was free to do business with any of them.

Some believed that the BOT would not be competitive in the long run. Critics cited the BOT's inability to penetrate the large, lucrative Japanese retail banking market. In effect, while the BOT's competitors were beginning to squeeze it in the international market, the BOT had not successfully established itself in Japan. Furthermore, the BOT's high exposure to LDC debt[8] was almost twice the amount of any other bank. Nevertheless, even though Moody's had twice lowered the BOT's debt rating (from AAA to Aa2), the BOT still had a rating higher than almost any large American bank.

Rumors of a possible merger of the BOT with a bank with a stronger domestic business had spread throughout the financial community. The Industrial Bank of Japan and Mitsubishi Bank were most often cited as potential merger candidates.

Exhibit 5 summarizes the BOT's issues of financial securities over the recent years. It reveals a strong appetite for Euromarket financings and a shift toward issuing hybrid bonds in the 1987–89 period.

MARKET DIRECTION

Mr. Takagaki was particularly concerned over the future direction of the stock market. A quick recovery would heal most of the bank's current wounds. Continued decline at the pace endured in 1990 would spell disaster.

Japanese equity had long been trading at extraordinary multiples of earnings relative

---

[7]*International Who's Who 1991–92*, 55th ed. (Europa Publications, Ltd.)

[8]LDC debt, loans to less-developed countries, was viewed as being riskier than sovereign or commercial loans to the industrially developed countries. In 1990, BOT's LDC loans outstanding amounted to ¥ 57 billion.

to other world markets. In the late 1980s, price/earnings (P/E) ratios had averaged over 60 times. By late 1990, the ratio had fallen to nearly 30 times but was still well above the U.S. average of 14 times. Although the shares of over 50 U.S. companies were listed for trading in Tokyo, they continued to be priced at American P/E levels,[9] and observers wondered whether the pricing disparity did not presage further declines in Japanese share prices.

One analyst at Nikko Securities countered that the causes of the P/E discrepancies were embedded in the accounting and economic structure of Japanese industry. By adjusting for such factors is depreciation rates, interlocking ownerships, and consolidations, he demonstrated a decrease in Japanse P/E ratios to match the levels observed in other markets.[10] Furthermore, this analyst studied all the other Japanese stock market declines of over 30 percent and concluded that a stock market upturn would begin only when Japanese fiscal and monetary policy eased.[11]

THE USE OF EQUITY-LINKED SECURITIES

In the late 1980s, Japanese companies issued large volumes of Eurodollar convertible bonds or bonds with attached warrants in London. Given the already low interest rates on the bonds and the spectacular returns expected from the convertible portions of the issues arising from the increase in stock prices, investors were willing to accept very low coupon rates on the bonds. The payment exposure then could be swapped from a fixed-rate liability to a floating rate and from dollars into yen, which resulted in zero-to-negative cost of funds.

If the BOT were to issue convertible bonds now, the issue would be the first such issue in several months, well after the tail end of what had been a surge in convertibles and warrant bonds. The use of convertible-bond financing had dramatically dominated the volumes of straight corporate bonds issued, as the graph in Exhibit 6 indicates. Similarly, the new-issue volume in warrant bonds had grown from insignificant in 1985 to US$70 billion in 1989. The bull market in warrant bonds peaked in March 1989 when three companies issued equity warrant packages of $1.5 billion each.

Both convertible bonds and warrant bonds would result in the release of new shares by the issuer. Although nominally both consisted of a call option and a straight bond, there were significant differences between the two:

> **Convertible bonds** offered the option of exchanging the bond for shares at some conversion ratio, or conversion price. The option component and bond component were inseparable in these securities.

---

[9]Ted Fikre, "Equity Carve-Outs in Tokyo," *Federal Reserve Board of New York Quarterly Review,* Winter 1991, p. 60.

[10]H. Takahashi, "The Sense of Overpricing on the Japanese Stock Market Gradually Subsides," *Nikko Monthly Report,* The Nikko Research Center, Ltd., October 25, 1990.

[11]H. Takahashi, "The Point at Which Stock Prices Will Bottom Out in the Correctional Phase," *Nikko Monthly Report,* The Nikko Research Center, Ltd., February 25, 1991.

Warrant bonds offered the option of buying shares at a certain exercise price either by paying in cash or, in certain instances, by exchanging bonds. In these cases, the warrants were *detachable* and could be traded (and held) separately from the bonds. The theory behind these bonds was that they permitted the investor to enjoy fixed bond income and a capital gain simultaneously; the two returns were not mutually exclusive. Even though the bulk of these Japanese bonds[12] was issued in the Euromarkets, 70 to 80 percent of the warrants found their way into the hands of Japanese institutions and individuals.[13] Typically, the warrants were issued with an exercise price very close to the prevailing share price (usually only 2.5 percent higher) at the time of issue.

The allure these hybrid securities had for issuers lay in the belief that they represented a cheaper source of financing than either subordinated bonds or common stocks. If the issuer performed poorly, the option would not be exercised and the issuer would enjoy a lower-than-normal coupon rate. If the issuer performed well, the options would be exercised and the shares sold—at a higher price than prevailing when the bonds were issued.

Some observers believed that these hybrid securities offered remarkably low costs of funds, especially those issued near the peak of the stock market cycle. In April 1989, Nomura Securities revealed that, taking into account currency-swap factors, the average current cost of funds issued would be 0.3 percent (which compared with 1.8 percent for an issue denominated in yen terms).[14] The lowest recorded coupon for a Japanese warrant bond was 0.875 percent in a June 1987 five-year issue by Tokyo Corporation. After swapping the proceeds, Tokyo realized a negative cost of funds (i.e., Tokyo was paid to issue the package). Coupon rates on convertible bonds could be even lower: in 1989, the Bank of Tokyo issued Swiss franc convertible notes with a coupon rate of 25 basis points. One journal commented, "At coupon levels up to 3 percent, Japanese issuers [of hybrid securities] are able to swap into yen funds at effectively no cost."[15]

Other analysts were not sure about this logic and questioned whether the advocates were making fair comparisons. Moreover, the advocates usually ignored the potential implications of a stock market slump; one market-maker estimated that 80 percent of the

---

[12]The issuance of convertibles and warrant bonds in the Euromarkets never gained great favor among corporations domiciled in other countries. In America and Britain, issuers had to account for dilution resulting from exercise of the warrants and, therefore, were discouraged from relying on hybrids; Japanese companies were not subject to such rules. In efficient markets, the presence or absence of reporting requirements regarding warrant dilution should be immaterial, but some observers believed that these rules have a material effect in the unregulated Euromarkets. (See, for instance, "Japan's Warrant Hangover," *The Economist*, September 8, 1990, p. 95.)

[13]Richard Downes and Chris Elven, *Japanese Equity Warrants: A Clear and Comprehensive Guide* (London: Eurostudy Publishing, 1990), p. 23.

[14]The examples of Nomura Securities and Tokyo Corporation ignore the implicit cost of the option and focus wholly on the cost of the bond component.

[15]Quoted by Downes and Elven, *Japanese Equity Warrants*, p. 27, from *International Insider*, August 3, 1987.

warrants issued in warrant-bond deals were out of the money in early September 1990.[16] The implications were that investors would not exercise the warrants and, thus, not provide the cash with which the issuer could repay the bonds.

Similarly, regarding convertible bonds, one journal commented:

> Japan's banks were forbidden from issuing warrants by the Ministry of Finance. Instead they resorted to the next best thing: convertible bonds, which give investors the right to convert their loans into shares. The party may have been slightly different to the warrant issuers' one; the morning after looks almost as painful. Japan's 12 commercial city banks have issued some ¥ 2 trillion ($14 billion) of convertible bonds since 1987. Most of the bonds are denominated in Swiss francs and most will mature during the financial year beginning April 1991. The share prices of the banks have fallen so far below their conversion prices that it looks as if the banks will probably have to pay most of the money back. Finding ¥ 2 trillion will not be easy.[17]

One approach to valuing hybrid securities such as convertibles and warrant bonds was to estimate the value of the components (bond and option) separately and then sum the component values. Exhibit 7 presents estimates of volatility on BOT common stock. Exhibit 8 gives information on current yields to maturity of "straight" and convertible bonds issued by Japanese corporations. Exhibit 9 presents a summary of equity-investment information for the Bank of Tokyo and a forecast of performance. The BOT was currently paying dividends at the rate of ¥ 8 per year, to give a dividend yield of about 0.8 percent.

CONCLUSION

The BOT needed to raise roughly ¥ 60 billion by March to conform to the BIS regulations. Typically, the par value of each Japanese yen bond was ¥ 100,000. Reflecting on the success of the convertible-bond issues of the BOT and other firms, Mr. Takagaki wondered whether the current low level of the stock market might be an ideal time for a new five-year convertible-bond issue.

---

[16]The market value of these warrants outstanding in September 1990 was $140 billion. Figures are taken from "Japan's Warrant Hangover," *The Economist*, September 8, 1990, p. 95.

[17]"More Trouble," *The Economist*, September 8, 1990, p. 96.

EXHIBIT 1   World's 20 Largest Banks in 1990 (dollars in millions)

Bank	Assets	Capital	Capital/Assets	Pretax Profits	Profits/Assets
1. Dai-Ichi Kangyo Bank	$455,069	$14,350	3.2%	$2,136	0.5%
2. Mitsui Taiyo Kobe Bank	420,539	11,402	2.7	1,478	0.4
3. Sumitomo Bank	415,384	14,476	3.5	2,611	0.6
4. Fuji Bank	408,954	12,782	3.1	2,201	0.5
5. Sanwa Bank	398,674	12,407	3.1	2,276	0.6
6. Mitsubishi Bank	395,765	11,571	2.9	1,916	0.5
7. Industrial Bank of Japan	289,759	9,177	3.2	1,130	0.4
8. Crédit Agricole	273,204	11,784	4.3	1,428	0.5
9. Banque Nationale de Paris	261,269	7,065	2.7	1,036	0.4
10. Tokai Bank	256,951	7,313	2.8	750	0.3
11. Barclays Bank	246,025	11,051	4.5	1,334	0.5
12. Crédit Lyonnais	237,897	6,339	2.7	1,060	0.4
13. Deutsche Bank	229,787	9,615	4.2	2,364	1.0
14. Citicorp	227,084	7,317	3.2	1,538	0.7
15. Bank of Tokyo	**226,119**	**6,608**	**2.9**	**1,150**	**0.5**
16. National Westminster Bank	224,058	10,732	4.8	779	0.3
17. ABN-Amro Bank	208,882	8,011	3.8	1,147	0.5
18. Long-Term Credit Bank of Japan	196,527	7,266	3.7	825	0.4
19. Groupe des Caisses d'Epargne	172,307	5,843	3.4	707	0.4
20. Union Bank of Switzerland	167,079	12,495	7.5	1,072	0.6

Source: *The Banker*. Data on Japanese institutions are as of March 1990; other data are as of December 1989.

EXHIBIT 2   Changes in the Stock Market Indexes of Major Countries

	1985	1989	October 31, 1990	1985–89 Compound Annual Growth Rate	1989–90 Compound Annual Growth Rate
Japan (Nikkei 225)	13,083	38,916	25,194	31%	−41%
United States (Dow Jones 30)	1,541	2,732	2,422	15	−13
United Kingdom (FT 100)	1,414	2,399	2,050	14	−17
Germany (FAZ)	626	741	622	4	−19

EXHIBIT 3   BIS Total Capital Ratios for Selected Japanese Banks

Bank	March 1990	Sept. 1990
Kyowa	8.8	7.5
Sanwa	8.5	7.2
Daiwa	8.4	7.1
Sumitomo	8.4	7.1
Mitsubishi	8.4	7.1
Saitama	8.3	7.1
Fuji	8.3	7.1
Hokkaido Takushoku	8.3	7.1
Dai-Ichi Kangyo	8.3	7.1
Long-Term Credit Bank	8.2	7.0
Bank of Tokyo	**8.0**	**6.8**
Industrial Bank of Japan	7.8	6.6
Tokai	7.8	6.6
Nippon Credit	7.3	6.2
Mitsui Taiyo Kobe	7.1	6.0

Source: James Capel, Inc., quoted in Christopher Wood, "A Survey of Japanese Finance," *The Economist,* December 8, 1990.

EXHIBIT 4   Information on Comparable Companies, 1990

Bank	Mkt. Value/ Book Value	International Profits/ Total Profits	International Profit Margin	Operating Return on Assets	Costs as Percentage of Operating Revenues	Costs as Percentage of Assets
Dai-Ichi Kangyo	2.0	20.0%	0.4%	—	—	—
Mitsui Taiyo Kobe	1.6	14.8	0.5	—	—	—
Sumitomo	2.0	32.6	0.8	—	—	—
Fuji	2.0	23.3	0.6	—	—	—
Mitsubishi	1.8	27.2	0.6	—	—	—
Sanwa	1.8	27.4	0.7	—	—	—
Bank of Tokyo ..	**2.3**	**56.0**	**1.0**	**0.39**	**58.9**	**0.39**
Composite average of other city banks	—	—	—	0.24	64.7	0.60

Sources: "Japanese Equity Research—City Banks," Salomon Brothers, March 5, 1992. Data in the three right-hand columns are as of March 1990; the rest of the data are as of September 1990.

EXHIBIT 5   History of Security Issuance

Year	Currency,* Amount	Rate and Type of Security
1985	C$ 75m	10⅞s Eurobonds, 7 yr.
	US$ 100m	11¼s Eurobonds, 10 yr.
	C$ 75m	10⅞s Eurobonds, 10 yr.
	US$ 100m	10⅜s Eurobonds, 10 yr.
	C$ 60m	11s Eurobonds, 10 yr.
	US$ 100m	Guaranteed floating-rate Euronotes, 12 yr.
1986	C$ 70m	10½s Eurobonds, 10 yr.
	US$ 100m	8⅜s guaranteed Eurobonds, 10 yr.
	US$ 100m	Zero-coupon guaranteed Eurobonds, 5 yr.
	Yen 15bn	6⅛s Eurobonds, 7 yr.
	US$ 50m	8¼s guaranteed deferred-coupon Eurobond, 5 yr.
	US$ 100m	7⅝s guaranteed Eurobonds, 7 yr.
	Yen 20bn	8½s Eurobonds, 7 yr.
	US$ 120m	8s Eurobonds, 7 yr.
1987	ItL 50bn	10¼s guaranteed Euronotes, 5 yr.
	DM 100m	5¾s guaranteed Eurobonds, 6 yr.
	US$ 100m	1¾s convertible Eurobonds, 15 yr.
	SFr 100m	8¾/¾s convertible Swiss notes, 5 yr.
	FFr 400m	Floating-rate Euronotes, 5 yr.
	ECU 70m	8⅛s guaranteed Eurobonds, 5 yr.
1988	C$ 120m	8½s guaranteed Eurobonds, 6 yr.
1989	US$ 100m	3⅜s convertible Eurobonds, 15 yr.
	SFr 200m	0¼s convertible Swiss notes, 5 yr.
	SFr 300m	0¼s convertible Swiss notes, 5 yr.
1990 (to Oct.)	US$ 225m	9s guaranteed Luxembourg bonds, 10 yr.
	DM 150m	0¼s floating/fixed-rate dual-coupon Eurobond, 6 yr.
	US$ 800m	Guaranteed subordinated floating-rate Euronotes, 10 yr.

* C$ = Canadian dollar; ItL = Italian lira; SFr = Swiss franc; FFr = French franc; ECU = European currency unit; DM = German mark.

Source: *Moody's Global Ratings*, Moody's Investor Services, April 1991.

EXHIBIT 6   Issuance of Japanese Corporate Bonds, by Year

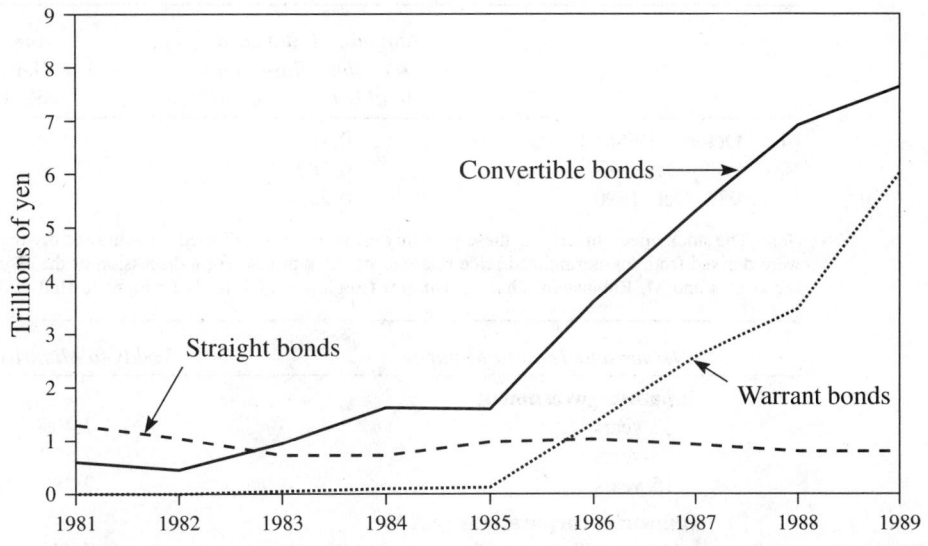

Sources: Data obtained from Bond Underwriters Association of Japan and Richard Downes and Chris Elven, *Japanese Equity Warrants* (London: Eurostudy Publishing, 1990).

EXHIBIT 7 Estimated Standard Deviation of Equity Returns and Selected Prevailing Interest Rates

	Annualized Standard Deviations Based on Monthly Observations	*Annualized Standard Deviations Based on Weekly Observations*
May–October 1990	0.1272	0.1717
Nov. 1989–Oct. 1990	0.1824	0.1427
Jan. 1987–Oct. 1990	0.2234	0.1345

Note: The stock prices underlying these volatility estimates were adjusted for splits and dividends. The estimates were derived from log-normalized price relatives of stock prices. For a discussion of the estimation procedure, see J. Cox and M. Rubinstein, *Options Markets* (Englewood Cliffs, N.J.: Prentice Hall, 1985), pp. 255–58.

Issuer and Term to Maturity	*Yields to Maturity (%)*
Japanese government	
3 years	7.40%
5 years	7.55
15 years	7.38
Industrial corporations (AAA)	
Average "long-term"	7.44
Financial institutions	
Average "long-term"	7.14

Sources of stock-price data: Datastream, Inc. (weekly data), and Global Disclosure, Investext (monthly data).
Source of interest-rate data: Tokyo Stock Exchange Factbook (Tokyo, 1991).
Source of estimated volatilities: Casewriters' analysis.

EXHIBIT 8   Comparable Bond Issues

Bond Issuer	Matures	Coupon (%)	Conversion Price	Current Bond Price	Yield to Maturity (%)
U.S. dollar convertible bonds:					
Fuji Bank	31 Mar 95	1.2%	2,971	79.3	6.9%
Fuji Bank	30 Sep 92	1.0	2,971	89.3	7.2
Dai-Ichi Kangyo Bank	30 Sep 92	1.0	2,966	89.0	7.4
Dai-Ichi Kangyo Bank	29 Sep 92	1.1	2,966	78.0	6.5
Mitsubishi Bank	30 Sep 92	1.1	2,867	89.2	7.4
Mitsubishi Bank	29 Sep 95	1.2	2,867	78.0	6.6
Sumitomo Bank	30 Sep 92	1.0	3,261	89.0	7.4
Sumitomo Bank	30 Sep 92	1.1	3,261	80.3	7.1
U.S. dollar "straight" bonds:					
Bank of Tokyo	1995	10.4	(Not applicable)	103.3	9.53
Bank of Tokyo	1999	10.8		101.5	9.28
Bank of Tokyo	1995	11.3		106.3	9.50
Bank of Tokyo	1993	7.6		96.3	9.14
Bank of Tokyo	1993	8.0		97.1	9.10
Bank of Tokyo	1996	8.4		95.5	9.45
Bank of Tokyo	2000	9.0		91.8	10.32
Industrial Bank of Japan	1995	11.5		107.8	9.30
Industrial Bank of Japan	1995	10.9		105.3	9.29
Industrial Bank of Japan	1995	10.5		104.3	9.30
Industrial Bank of Japan	1993	9.5		101.0	9.10
Industrial Bank of Japan	1997	7.9		91.9	9.60
Industrial Bank of Japan	2004	9.4		96.0	9.91
Sumitomo Bank	1993	9.4		100.8	0.07

Sources: *International Herald Tribune* and *Financial Times*.

EXHIBIT 9

BANK OF TOKYO

8313
東京銀行

Only foreign exchange specialized bank with worldwide network. Formerly Yokohama Shokin Bank. Issues bank debentures in Japan, and racks up 70% of gross profit from international operations. Issued high-coupon bonds, first ever issued by Japanese bank. Lending to debtor nations largest among Japanese banks.

Outlook: Domestic fund management profit reaching projected mark, although profit margin sagging in 2nd half. Covering loss from credits to Mexico with gains on securities sold. Net operating profit outlook may be revised slightly downward due to extra appropriation for bad-debt reserves. In Mar '91 term, suspended payment of interest on credits by debtor nations hurting, but domestic profit margin picking up. Small-lot discount bonds with currency option winning consumer's favor.

Income (¥mil)	Current Revenues	Net Oper. Profit	Current Profit	Net Profit	Earnings per sh	Dividend per sh	Equity per sh
Mar '86	1,133,517	–	71,919	39,126	¥22.0	¥6.5	¥203.3
Mar '87	1,020,690	–	81,969	47,125	26.6	7	222.8
Mar '88	1,116,006	–	88,068	51,061	28.5	7	255.9
Mar '89	1,443,715	–	102,294	59,237	30.9	7.5	318.5
Mar '90*	1,900,000	76,000	98,000	54,000	27.1	8	
•Sep '89	954,997	42,443	49,432	32,684	16.5	4	374.7
•Sep '90*	1,100,000	40,000	47,000	31,000	15.6	4	
□Mar '88	1,344,812	–	92,361	47,321	26.4		273.1
□Mar '89	1,734,095	–	121,825	60,691	31.7		334.5
□Mar '90*	2,250,000	–	119,500	56,000	28.1		

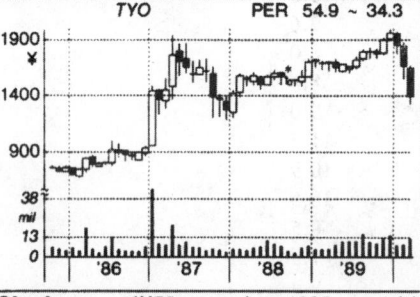

TYO　　　PER 54.9 ~ 34.3

Funds Breakdown (Sep '89, %)

Time Deposits	56
Deposits at Notice	4
Bonds	21
Other Deposits	19

Prices	High	Low	G/L(%)
~'86	999 ('86)	37 ('50)	
'87	1940 (Apr)	954 (Jan)	33.1
'88	1730 (Dec)	1200 (Jan)	36.0
'89	1990 (Dec)	1600 (Jun)	14.6
#'90	1970 (Jan)	1320 (Mar)	(-)29.1

Finance (000shs)

Apr '88 CB ¥20bil(¥1640.8)	
May'88 Pub 60(¥1554)	1,852,415
Nov '88 100:3 Gratis	1,913,110
Mar '89 CB $100mil(¥1772.9)	
Mar '89 CB SFr200mil(¥1772.9)	
Mar '89 CB SFr300mil(¥1772.9)	
May'89 Pub 60(¥1622)	1,975,519

Stocks (¥50 par value, 1000 per unit)
Shares Out.(Feb 28 '90 000shs) 1,993,933
No. of Shareholders(Sep 30 '89) 25,823

Major Holders(%)		**Foreign Owners**	1.3
Meiji Life Ins.	5.7	Mitsubishi Trust	1.6
Nippon Life Ins.	5.4	Tokio M.& F.Ins.	1.5
Dai-ichi Life Ins.	5.2	Nippon Steel	1.5
Taiyo Life Ins.	2.7	Norinchukin Bank	1.4
Mitsubishi Corp.	2.0	Mitsui Trust	1.3

Loans Breakdown (Sep '89, %)

To Small Firms, etc.	33
To Consumers	1

Financial Data(¥mil)	•Sep '89	□Mar '89
Total Assets	29,610,697	29,525,748
Cash & Due	7,140,844	6,519,506
Investment Securities	3,042,260	2,895,421
Loans & Bills Disc.	11,874,245	12,998,303
Deposit Certificates	1,571,014	1,850,344
Call & Borrowed	4,041,522	3,958,590
Capital Stock	225,140	171,380
Capital Surplus	143,520	89,767
Shareholders' Equity	742,169	640,370
Equity Ratio(%)	2.5	2.2
Funds Available	20,088,360	20,019,209

Highest in Current Profit(¥mil)
　　　　　　Mar '89　　102,294

No.of Branch Offices: 82
Exchanges: TYO, OSA
Underwriters: Yamaichi, Nomura, Daiwa, Nikko, Sanyo, Kokusai, Dainana
Est: Dec 1946　**Listed:** May 1949
Employees (Age) 8,019(36)
Chairman: Yusuke Kashiwagi
President: Minoru Inoue
Overseas Offices ⇨ See P. 1321
U.S.A., U.K., Hong Kong

Principal Office **Tel:** 03–245–1111
1–3–2, Nihonbashi-Hongokucho, Chuo-ku, Tokyo 103 **Telex:** 22220 **Fax:** 03–279–3926

Source: Japan Company Handbook, First Section (Tokyo: Toyo Keizai, Inc.), Summer 1990.

British Petroleum Company, Ltd. (1987 Stock Offering)

With the world's economic health said to be hanging in the balance, Britain announced that it would proceed with its offering of British Petroleum Co. shares. . . . Never has a single stock offering so galvanized the attention of Wall Street, world capital markets, and investors.

The Wall Street Journal, October 30, 1987

With these ominous words, the investment community was informed that the British government would not rescind its record $12.5 billion offering of British Petroleum Company, Ltd. (BP) shares in the aftermath of the unprecedented stock market crash of October 1987. The BP offering represented the largest equity offering in history. Not only did the British government sell its 1.735 billion shares of BP worth over $10 billion, but BP itself simultaneously sold new shares worth over $2.5 billion. The largest previous U.S. stock offering was Consolidated Railroad's offering of about $1.65 billion in March 1987. The largest previous worldwide stock offering was in 1984 when British Telecom (the British government-owned communications company) raised $4.76 billion.

COMPANY BACKGROUND

Based upon 1986 sales figures, British Petroleum was the world's seventh largest industrial company and the third largest oil company. It was Europe's second largest company, exceeded in size only by the Royal Dutch Shell Group. BP was formed in 1909.

The British Petroleum Company was engaged in all aspects of the petroleum industry, including exploration, production, transportation, processing, and marketing of crude oil,

---

petroleum products, and natural gas. BP had pioneered the discovery and development of oil and gas in several important oil-producing areas. In 1965, BP discovered the first commercial natural gas field under the North Sea. Reserves of crude oil were discovered in the Prudhoe Bay area of Alaska during 1967 and, in the next year, BP entered the U.S. market by purchasing certain marketing and refining assets formerly owned by Sinclair Oil and Atlantic Richfield. BP had refining interests in Europe, the Middle East, Africa, Australasia, Canada, and the United States. Its marketing and distribution network covered most of Europe and Africa, Australasia and parts of Asia, Canada, and the United States. BP had proved developed reserves of over 4.7 billion barrels of oil and 14.2 billion cubic feet of natural gas as of year-end 1986.

In addition to its oil and gas activities, the company also made chemicals, plastics, and household cleaning, household care, and personal care products. It operated tankers carrying cargoes for third parties, developed mineral properties, mined coal, produced hybrid breeds of various livestock, bred plants and seeds, made animal feed and consumer products, and provided computer processing, engineering, and other consulting services. Operations were greatly expanded in the United States when BP obtained partial ownership of Standard Oil of Ohio.

The Standard Oil Acquisition

British Petroleum first acquired a shareholding in Standard Oil of Ohio (Sohio) in 1970 in exchange for BP's interests in the Prudhoe Bay field in Alaska. Sohio was one of the 25 largest companies in the United States and, by 1986, BP had a 55 percent interest in Standard Oil. While Sohio's operating results were 100 percent consolidated with BP's in the group financial statements, BP only received dividends on shares it owned. Thus, to control Sohio's cash flows fully, BP proposed a complete takeover. In April 1987, BP offered $7.9 billion for the remaining 45 percent of Sohio that it didn't already own. By mid-May, BP was in control of 95 percent of the shares of Sohio, and Sohio was merged into BP on June 29, 1987. The acquisition placed considerable strain on the financial resources of BP, resulting in a negative net working-capital position for the company and helping precipitate the equity offering of October 1987. (See Exhibits 1, 2, and 3.)

History of Ownership

The British government acquired a 67 percent ownership in British Petroleum in 1914. In 1977, the percentage of BP ordinary capital held by the British government and the Bank of England was reduced from 68.3 percent to 51 percent as a result of public offers for the sale of shares in the United Kingdom and North America.

Shares were sold again in 1979 and 1983. At the beginning of 1987, only about 32 percent of all BP shares were government owned. As part of its denationalization program, Margaret Thatcher's Conservative Government decided in 1987 to sell the government's remaining equity stake in British Petroleum.

THE BP STOCK OFFERING

The Underwriting Process

Firms that wish to raise equity capital typically use investment bankers to manage the issuing process. Investment bankers are financial intermediaries who specialize in selling new securities to investors. Among other ways, they generate revenues from the difference between the price at which they acquire the securities from the firm and the price at which the securities are sold to investors (this is known as the underwriting commission).

Underwriting is the process whereby the investment banker purchases the issue from the firm at a given price (the public offer price less the underwriting commission) and then resells it to investors. In a "firm commitment" underwriting contract, the investment banker bears the risk that the issue will not sell out at the offer price. If the underwriter cannot sell all the securities at the agreed-upon offering price, he or she may have to lower the price on the unsold shares. In any case, the issuer receives the full amount of the proceeds less the underwriting commission, and all risk is transferred to the underwriter. On large issues, several investment banks often join together in a syndicate to spread the risk among all the participants and to help sell the issue. In a "best efforts" contract, on the other hand, the investment banker does not act as an underwriter but merely sells as many securities as he or she can for a fee. The issuer bears the risk of holding any unsold shares.

The Securities and Exchange Commission requires public disclosure of various aspects of the offering for any firm intending to sell securities in the United States. Once the basic characteristics of an offering have been established, a registration statement is filed with the SEC and a preliminary prospectus is issued. The preliminary prospectus usually contains all relevant facts concerning the company and the issue except for the actual price of the securities.

The final price for the securities to be sold is not usually set until after the SEC registration procedure has been completed. If a firm is issuing new equity and its shares are currently traded in the stock market, the offering price of the new shares usually will be somewhat lower than the market price at the end of the registration period. However, the final price will depend upon how stable the market has been recently and is a matter of negotiation between the seller and the investment banker. Once the offer price is set, the underwriter accepts the risk that the market price may change between the date the offering price is set and the time the issue is sold. This time period is typically less than two days for most U.S. offerings. In the case of the BP offering, however, this period lasted two weeks (from October 15, 1987, when the offer price was set, to October 30, 1987, the actual date of the issue) because the offering was primarily conducted in England and not in the United States.

History and Terms of the BP Offering

On March 18, 1987, after the close of the London and New York stock exchanges, the British government announced that it planned to sell its remaining 31.7 percent stake in British Petroleum. The government still owned 1.735 billion shares of BP worth over

$12 billion. As recently as September 1983, the British government had sold 7 percent of BP for about $900 million.

On July 21, 1987, British Petroleum announced that it would raise £1.5 billion ($2.4 billion) with the offering of new stock in conjunction with the British government sale. BP wanted to raise equity to retire some of the debt issued in May 1987 to finance the $8 billion purchase of the remaining 45 percent of Standard Oil shares it didn't already own. Under the terms of the unusual combined offering, the British government would pay £1.5 billion to BP for the shares, and the new shares, along with the British government-owned shares, would then be offered immediately to the public. At that time, 93 percent of BP shares were held in Britain and 6 percent in the United States, yet 60 percent of BP's recorded assets were in the United States because of the acquisition of Standard Oil.

In an effort to increase U.S. ownership, the British government announced on August 20, 1987, that over 20 percent of the BP shares would be allocated to foreign investors. This percentage would rise to nearly 50 percent by the time of the offering. On August 30, it was announced that the sale would take the form of two concurrent offerings: a "fixed-price" offer for existing BP stockholders and British individuals, and an "international" offer for British institutions and foreigners. The fixed-price offer would be executed at a predetermined fixed-offer price per share. The international offer would have a floor equal to the price in the fixed-price offer but could sell for a higher price if the underwriters were willing to bid higher prices for the shares.

More terms of the offering became available on September 17, when it was announced that the offer price would be at a discount to the current market value and that it would be payable to the British government in three installments. The installment-payment method had been used in previous government sales of stock and was intended to make the offering more appealing to first-time investors. On September 28, a preliminary SEC filing revealed that Goldman Sachs would be the U.S. managing underwriter for 46,250,000 (the number would change by the final prospectus) installment-payment American Depository Shares (ADSs), each representing 12 installment-payment ordinary shares.[1]

The final terms of the firm-commitment underwriting agreement were determined on Thursday, October 15, 1987. The offering date was set for October 30, 1987. The price for both the fixed-price offer and the international offer was set at £3.30 (a 6 percent discount to the previous day's closing price of £3.51) payable in three installments.[2] £1.20 was due immediately upon sale, £1.05 was due on August 30, 1988, and £1.05 was due on April 27, 1989.[3] The final offering consisted of a total of 2.194 billion shares of BP. The offer was allocated almost evenly between the domestic and international

---

[1]Technically, only American Depository Receipts (ADRs) trade on the New York Stock Exchange. Each ADR represents ADSs on deposit at Morgan Guaranty Trust Company of New York. Each ADS represents 12 ordinary shares held by the London office of Morgan Guaranty Trust Company (the custodian).

[2]This price ignores the time value of money. The true price was less than £3.30 given the proposed payment schedule for installment-payment shares. The underwriting commission was about £0.035 per share.

[3]The purchasers of the shares and not the underwriters were responsible for paying the second and third installments to the British Treasury in pounds sterling.

investors (Exhibit 4). The U.S. underwriters were allocated about 22 percent of the shares being sold by the British government. (Exhibit 5 lists the U.S. underwriters and the number of shares they committed to purchase.) For reasons that have not been publicly revealed, only four underwriters were included in the U.S. syndicate.[4]

THE STOCK MARKET CRASH

The day following the underwriting agreement, the Dow Jones Industrial Average (DJIA) fell by more than 100 points. On the following Monday, October 19, 1987, the stock market suffered its largest decline in history. The DJIA dropped 508 points, or 22.6 percent. The stock markets throughout the rest of the world reacted similarly. On the London Stock Exchange, the price of BP shares dropped from £3.48 on October 15 to £2.83 on October 20—far below the £3.30 price agreed to by the underwriters. On the NYSE the price of BP ADRs declined from $69.125 to $57.500 over the same five-day period.

As the offering date (October 30) drew closer, it became clear that the underwriters of the BP issue faced substantial losses as a result of the drop in BP price. On October 26, the U.K. underwriters asked for a postponement or cancellation of the offering because of the losses faced by local and foreign underwriters. The U.S. underwriters faced potential losses of almost $555 million.[5] The individual British underwriters' losses, however, were unlikely to be as large as the U.S. firms. Unlike the U.S. firms, the U.K. institutions had spread their risk among hundreds of subunderwriters. On October 28, U.S. Treasury Secretary James Baker interceded on behalf of the U.S. underwriters and told U.K. Chancellor of the Exchequer Nigel Lawson that the offering could damage U.S. capital markets. Wood Gundy, the lead Canadian underwriter, anticipated huge losses should the offering proceed, and Canadian Finance Minister Michael Wilson asked the British government to withdraw the offering.

The day before the offering, the rhetoric reached new heights. One Wall Street money manager was quoted as saying: "We helped the British during the Falklands war, and we can't even get them to stop the underwriting." (*The Wall Street Journal*, October 30, 1987). On the other hand, a former U.K. Treasury official said: "You've got to watch the Colonials. There's a feeling that Americans cheat in these circumstances." (*The Wall Street Journal*, October 30, 1987.) Some British bankers believed that the American investment banks should stand by their client, as Lloyds of London did after the 1906 San Francisco earthquake. The U.S. underwriters were finding that earlier indications of interest to purchase the BP ADRs were evaporating. Portfolio managers were backing

---

[4]This number is relatively small compared to the number of underwriters usually involved in large equity offerings. It also should be noted that underwriting agreements often have an escape clause that provides for the contract to be voided if the price of the security falls below some predetermined figure. No escape clause was included in the BP underwriting agreement.

[5]On October 26, BP shares closed at £2.65. (£3.30 − £2.65) × (505.8 million shares) = £328.8 million, or approximately $555 million given the then current exchange rate of $1.688/£.

off from previous commitments to purchase the shares at the offer price. The widespread belief was: "There is absolutely no market for this stuff in the United States." (*The Wall Street Journal*, October 30, 1987.)

THE REPURCHASE PLAN

On October 29, 1987, after the close of both the London and New York markets, the Chancellor of the Exchequer announced that the offering would proceed as planned. He also announced that the Bank of England agreed to buy for £0.70 any and all partly paid BP shares that would begin trading the following day.[6] The offer to re-purchase shares would expire on January 6, 1988. Anyone who owned partly paid BP shares (including the underwriters) could sell them at any time to the Bank of England for £0.70 regardless of the prevailing market price. Those who sold their shares to the Bank of England would be relieved of their obligation to pay the second and third installments. This repurchase plan was intended to be a safety mechanism that would provide the underwriters with an upper bound to their losses. Thus, the British government, while not completely bailing out the underwriters, agreed to support the price of the issue temporarily.

NOTE ON THE VALUATION OF PUT OPTIONS

Put options are contracts between two parties, whereby one party (the "buyer" or "holder" of the put) has the right, but not the obligation, to sell a specified number of shares to the other party (the "writer" of the put) at a specified price (the "strike" price or "exercise" price), at, or before, the maturity date. The put holder will pay a certain amount of money at issue to the writer of the put for this right. The put holder will exercise this right only if the market value of the underlying shares has fallen below the strike price. The profit, if any, at exercise to the holder, of course, represents an equivalent loss to the writer of the put. Put options are familiar financial instruments to speculators, arbitrageurs, and hedgers, and are widely traded on organized exchanges.

Finance theory provides us with a method to value put options. This method is known as *the Black and Scholes formula*. The Black-Scholes formula depends on five key input variables: the current price of the stock, the exercise price, the time to maturity, the level of interest rates, and the volatility of the stock. A detailed discussion of this formula is beyond the scope of this note, but the essential properties of the model are easily explained. (The interested reader may refer to most investment texts or to any standard option-pricing book.) Other things equal, a put option will be more valuable (*a*) the lower the current stock price (hence increasing the profit resulting from the difference between the

---

[6]Recall that the underwriters were committed to pay £1.20 (less underwriting commissions) for these shares.

exercise price and the stock price), (*b*) the higher the exercise price (for a similar reason as in (*a*)), and (*c*) the more volatile the underlying stock (and hence the higher the likelihood that the stock price will decline below the strike price).

The Black-Scholes put formula is formally defined as:

$$P = Kr^{-t}N(y + \sigma\sqrt{t}) - SN(y)$$

where $y = \dfrac{\ln(Kr^{-t}/S)}{\sigma\sqrt{t}} - \dfrac{1}{2}\sigma\sqrt{t}$

$$
\begin{aligned}
P &= \text{value of the put option} \\
K &= \text{exercise price} \\
S &= \text{current stock price} \\
r &= \text{one plus the risk-free interest rate} \\
t &= \text{time to maturity} \\
\sigma &= \text{volatility of the stock} \\
N(y) &= \text{cumulative normal probability density function (i.e., the probability}
\end{aligned}
$$
that a normally distributed random variable will be less than or equal to y)

EXHIBIT 1 Group Income Statements for Years Ending December 31, 1984–86, and for Six Months Ending June 30, 1987 (in £ million)

	1984	1985	1986	1987
Turnover	£37,933	£40,986	£27,171	£ 13,673
Replacement cost of sales	27,952	29,944	20,260	10,396
Production taxes	2,935	2,786	633	441
Gross profit	7,046	8,256	6,248	2,836
Distribution and administrative expense	2,867	3,223	3,361	1,641
Exploration expenditure written off	903	1,394	1,042	241
Total	3,276	3,639	1,845	981
Other income	625	799	786	409
Replacement cost operating profit	3,901	4,438	2,631	1,390
Realized inventory holding loss (gain)	(121)	249	1,173	246
Historical cost operating profit	4,022	4,189	1,458	1,636
Interest expense	567	576	500	255
Profit before taxation	3,455	3,613	958	1,381
Taxation	1,426	1,382	42	409
Profit after taxation	2,029	2,231	916	972
Minority shareholders' interest	627	633	99	197
Profit before extraordinary items	1,402	1,598	817	775
Extraordinary items	(298)	(929)	(318)	—
Profit for period	1,104	669	499	775
Distribution to shareholders	548	622	642	248
Retained profit/(deficit) for the period	556	47	(143)	527

Source: BP annual reports for 1986 and 1987 and Form 6-K dated September 23, 1987.

EXHIBIT 2   Group Balance Sheets at December 31, 1984–86, and June 30, 1987 (in £ million)

	1984	1985	1986	1987
Fixed assets:				
Intangible assets	£ 1,852	£ 1,295	£ 1,035	£ 1,074
Tangible assets	17,803	15,590	15,418	16,716
Investments	1,583	1,351	1,428	1,416
Total fixed assets	21,238	18,236	17,881	19,206
Current assets:				
Stocks (inventory)	5,097	4,163	2,899	2,997
Debtors	5,564	5,617	5,066	4,357
Investments	1,114	1,286	1,347	728
Cash at bank	1,201	919	1,182	401
Total current assets	12,976	11,985	10,494	8,483
Creditors—due within one year:				
Finance debt	2,217	1,328	1,210	2,621
Other creditors	7,837	7,328	5,966	6,189
Total creditors	10,054	8,656	7,176	8,810
Net current assets	2,922	3,329	3,318	(327)
Total assets	34,214	30,221	28,375	27,689
Total assets less current liabilities	24,160	21,565	21,199	18,879
Creditors—due after one year:				
Finance debt	4,841	3,802	3,862	4,052
Other debt	2,467	1,953	1,558	1,618
Provision for liabilities and charges:				
Deferred taxation	469	408	428	2,392
Other provisions	475	2,118	1,923	
Net assets	15,908	13,284	13,428	10,817
Minority shareholders' interest	4,365	3,376	3,456	660
BP shareholders' interest	11,543	9,908	9,972	10,157
Represented by:				
Capital shares	468	469	470	1,388
Paid-in surplus	913	926	940	38
Reserves	10,162	8,513	8,562	8,731
	11,543	9,908	9,972	10,157
Group reserves:				
Group reserves at January 1	8,264	10,162	8,513	8,562
Exchange adjustments	1,349	(1,688)	188	(371)
Retained profit/(deficit) for the period	556	47	(143)	527
Other movements	(7)	(8)	4	13
Group reserves at end of period	10,162	8,513	8,562	8,731

Source: BP annual reports for 1986 and 1987 and Form 6-K dated September 23, 1987.

EXHIBIT 3 Group Sources and Application of Funds Statements for Years Ended December 31, 1984–86 and Six Months Ended June 30, 1987 (in £ millions)

	1984	*1985*	*1986*	*1987*
Profit after taxation	£ 2,029	£ 2,231	£ 916	£ 972
Extraordinary items	(298)	(929)	(318)	—
Items not involving the movement of funds	2,680	4,231	3,630	1,108
Working-capital movements	580	83	591	997
Other movements	743	454	(358)	184
Funds generated from operations	5,734	6,070	4,461	3,261
Capital expenditures	3,610	3,875	3,303	1,363
Acquisitions	205	523	484	—
Standard Oil share purchase	418	—	—	4,672
Dividends paid:				
BP shareholders	493	585	623	516
Minority shareholders	223	229	202	
Funds generated or (required)	785	858	(151)	(3,290)
Financial movements:				
Shares Issued	(7)	(14)	(15)	(16)
Changes in external financing:				
BP	(134)	204	(288)	(1,934)
Standard Oil	(317)	565	(62)	
External funding—decrease (increase)	(458)	755	(365)	(1,950)
Changes in liquid resources (decrease) increase	1,243	103	214	(1,340)
	785	858	(151)	(3,290)

Source: BP annual reports for 1986 and 1987 and Form 6-K dated September 23, 1987.

EXHIBIT 4   Distribution of Shares in BP Offering (in millions of ordinary shares)

Fixed-price offer:

U.K. public offer	780	
Shareholder offer	314	
Total fixed-price offer		1,094

International offer:

United States*	480	
United Kingdom	250	
Japan	160	
Europe	105	
Canada*	105	
Total international offer		1,100
Total offering		2,194†

* Represented by Installment Payment American Depository Shares. Each ADS represents 12 ordinary shares.
† Includes 459 million new shares issued by BP to the British government at a price of £3.30 to raise £1.5 billion in new funds for BP. The 1,735 million other shares were previously owned by the British government. There were a total of 5.503 billion BP shares outstanding prior to the offering. After the offering there would be 5.962 billion shares outstanding.

Source: BP offering prospectus dated October 30, 1987.

EXHIBIT 5   Distribution of BP Shares among U.S. Underwriters

Underwriter	Number of Installment-Payment Ordinary Shares Purchased	Number of Installment-Payment American Depository Shares to Be Sold
Goldman Sachs & Co.	144,720,000	12,060,000
Morgan Stanley & Co., Inc.	120,360,000	10,030,000
Salomon Brothers, Inc.	120,360,000	10,030,000
Shearson Lehman Brothers, Inc.	120,360,000	10,030,000
	505,800,000*	42,150,000†

* Four hundred and eighty million shares are from the British government holdings. The remaining 25.8 million shares represent new shares sold by BP.
† Each American Depository Share represents 12 ordinary shares.

Source: BP offering prospectus dated October 30, 1987.

EXHIBIT 6   Selected Data on U.S. Underwriters

	Morgan Stanley	Salomon Brothers	Shearson Lehman Brothers
1986 sales ($000)	2,463,484	6,789,000	6,748,000
1986 net income ($000)	201,250	516,000	341,000
Total assets on 12/31/86 ($000)	29,190,361	78,164,000	53,911,000
Total debt to equity on 12/31/86	0.68	0.36	2.09
Beta	0.39	0.86	0.77
Shares outstanding on 10/30/87 (000)	24,864	152,000	86,729

Note: Goldman Sachs & Company is privately held.

Sources: Disclosure CD data base and casewriter calculations.

EXHIBIT 7 Daily Stock Prices and Exchange Rates for October 1987

Date	Morgan Stanley* (in $)	Salomon Brothers* (in $)	Shearson Lehman* (in $)	BP Ordinary Shares† (in £)	S&P 500 Index*	Exchange Rate‡ ($/£)
10/01/87	$81.500	$37.000	$28.000	£3.75	327.33	1.6135
10/02/87	85.375	37.000	27.625	3.74	328.07	1.6215
10/05/87	85.250	36.250	27.250	3.75	328.08	1.6230
10/06/87	83.750	35.125	26.625	3.71	319.22	1.6320
10/07/87	84.000	34.875	27.250	3.68	318.54	1.6400
10/08/87	83.750	34.625	26.000	3.66	314.16	1.6425
10/09/87	84.250	34.500	26.375	3.62	311.07	1.6490
10/12/87	83.250	34.875	25.875	3.61	309.39	1.6545
10/13/87	83.000	34.875	26.125	3.61	314.52	1.6460
10/14/87	81.250	34.375	25.125	3.50	305.23	1.6540
10/15/87	79.875	32.625	24.500	3.48	298.08	1.6645
10/16/87	76.500	30.750	24.500	3.48	282.70	1.6645
10/19/87	64.500	28.500	20.125	3.14	224.84	1.6810
10/20/87	55.500	22.000	17.000	2.83	236.83	1.6540
10/21/87	60.750	25.000	18.500	2.95	258.39	1.6555
10/22/87	58.250	23.700	17.000	2.82	248.25	1.6525
10/23/87	58.750	21.000	15.750	2.85	248.22	1.6780
10/26/87	52.000	19.250	13.750	2.65	227.67	1.6880
10/27/87	52.000	19.250	14.375	2.58	233.19	1.6955
10/28/87	46.750	17.875	13.875	2.52	233.28	1.7085
10/29/87	49.000	18.875	14.750	2.58	243.68	1.7230
10/30/87	53.375	20.000	15.750	2.65	251.79	1.7220

* New York Stock Exchange closing prices.
† The London Stock Exchange closing bid prices.
‡ Bank of England noon rate.

Sources: *The Wall Street Journal* and *The Times* (of London).

EXHIBIT 8   Term Structure of United Kingdom Interest Rates (October 1987)

Time to Maturity (in months)	Approximate Annualized Yield (in percent)
3	9.250%
6	9.250
12	9.250
18	9.250
24	9.375
36	9.500

Source: *Financial Times* (of London).

Case 41

Syracuse Electric, Inc.

In April 1988, Amelia Hornblower retired from her position as chief financial officer (CFO) of Syracuse Electric, a leading manufacturer of a wide range of commodity-type electrical components, defense and aerospace electronic equipment, and consumer appliances. Amelia, the youngest of the Hornblower sisters who founded the firm in 1948, was the last to relinquish an operating position. In place of the Hornblower sisters emerged a younger generation of well-trained managers, including Susan Chen, who became the company's CFO when Amelia retired.

In her first action as CFO, Ms. Chen solicited advisory financial studies from three large investment banks—Carlyle Savoy, Ltd.; Danbury, Brickhouse, & Company; Steinworth, Vader, Inc.—and a large commercial bank, Hudson Guaranty. She specifically requested that each of them review Syracuse's current financial structure and recommend a structure of long-term financing that would minimize Syracuse's cost of debt and preferred stock yet be consistent with management's other goals. Exhibit 1 presents the letter containing the advisory request. If Syracuse's management accepted any of the proposals, the winning firm would be awarded the position of lead advisor and underwriter to execute the recommendation.

THE COMPANY

Syracuse Electric, Inc., competed in the electrical equipment industry. The firm's mix of business included commodity-type electrical components and generators (about 40 percent of sales and cash flow); consumer appliances and equipment (about 25 percent); defense electronics and avionics (20 percent); and a finance subsidiary that not only supported leases and credit sales of Syracuse's own products but also invested in commercial paper and securities of other companies (15 percent).

This case was developed by Robert F. Bruner at the Darden Graduate School of Business Administration. Copyright © 1993 by the University of Virginia Darden School Foundation, Charlottesville, VA.

Economic indicators and forecasts important to the electrical equipment industry are provided in Exhibit 2, and comparative industry data are given in Exhibit 3. In the early 1980s, weak markets, excess capacity, and import competition caused domestic electrical equipment companies' growth to stagnate. To encourage growth and maintain profitability, companies were forced to cut costs—most notably, labor costs—and dedicate assets to faster-growing business segments tangentially related to their industry, including electronics, medical products, and waste disposal. This strategy was beginning to pay off by the mid- to late-1980s. Profits in the electrical equipment industry were especially strong; average operating margins improved from 12.6 percent in 1986 to 13.0 percent in 1987, and, despite a 3.5 percent increase in average taxes, the average net profit margin only fell from 6.4 percent to 5.5 percent in 1987.[1] Ms. Chen thought that there would be modest growth in nonresidential construction over the short term but that the increase would be followed by two years of decline. In addition, she expected foreign demand and replacement orders by utilities to begin to fade by mid-1988.

As shown in Exhibits 4 and 5, annual sales in 1987 were over $1.6 billion and assets totaled $1.4 billion. In the fourth quarter of 1985, management began to restructure the company by divesting a number of nonstrategic lines of business. As a result, the company realized a charge to earnings of $72 million before tax and $44 million after tax. The operations that were divested had sales in 1985 of $162 million and operating losses of $13.3 million. The divested businesses' total assets were $137 million.

In an effort to contain costs, Syracuse decreased labor from 22,312 employees in 1985 to 19,126 by year-end 1987. Management also limited capital expenditures to $34 million in 1987—half their 1985 level. In every division but one, capital expenditures were less than depreciation over the past two years.

In April 1988, the company's board was considering funneling funds toward a radar detection and screening project expected to require $75 million in capital and working-capital investments over the next five years ($15 million per year). Preliminary test results suggested that the project could improve radar detection accuracy by 50 percent; if this were true, Syracuse could corner the market for a number of years. If the project was indeed a success, heavy demand would require additional capital expenditures of between $25 and $40 million over a three-year period and $10 million in working capital each year thereafter. If the project took longer to develop, further cash inflows would be necessary.

CAPITAL POSITION

In April 1988, Syracuse Electric had a debt-to-equity ratio of 50 percent. The company had no bonds outstanding, but Ms. Chen guessed that the firm would be rated BBB. Management's plan had been to repurchase stock on a gradual basis when the price was low. But after the stock market crash of October 19, 1987, when the company's stock

---

[1] *Value Line Investment Survey*, May 6, 1988, p. 1001.

lost nearly 30 percent of its value, Syracuse repurchased $292 million worth of stock at between $33.25 and $40.00 per share. Until now, Syracuse had been relatively unsophisticated in its use of the capital markets; $350 million of its long-term debt consisted of bank financing through a number of domestic sources at the floating prime lending rate. The current position of the debt totaled $10.2 million. The remaining $12.7 million of long-term debt was an industrial revenue bond due in 2004 at 7.625 percent; no principal payments were due prior to maturity.

Syracuse also had working capital facilities totaling $136 million. Of this total, the company had about $4.8 million outstanding. Average outstanding working capital credit facilities in 1986 and 1987 were $5.6 million and $3.0 million, respectively. The average interest rate in 1987 was 11 percent, down from 13 percent in 1986. On December 31, 1987, the weighted-average interest rate on the amount outstanding was 8 percent. Syracuse paid a commitment fee of one eighth of 1 percent on the unused portion of the facilities.

Syracuse had authorized 10 million shares of cumulative preferred stock but had issued none to date. The company had issued 29.6 million shares of common stock as of December 1987.

Although none of the Hornblower family was now part of company management, the family still owned 35 percent of the firm, and Amelia Hornblower came to the office on a weekly basis "just to look things over." The family style had been highly conservative, as reflected by the company's almost exclusive use of bank credit. Although current management wanted to take advantage of Syracuse's strong financial condition and name to improve the company's cost of capital, it knew it would have to move cautiously to avoid alienating the Hornblower family.

THE ALTERNATIVES

Ms. Chen examined the suggested debt stuctures provided by the four potential financial advisors. To determine the best alternative, she wanted to determine their relative costs and durations.

Carlyle Savoy, Ltd., suggested that Syracuse replace $100 million of bank debt with the following structure:

- $10 million of term bank debt for five years, fixed at 9.5 percent,
- $30 million of senior, secured, fixed-rate debt for 10 years at 9.5 percent with a sinking fund,
- $40 million of 15-year junior debentures with a sinking fund fixed at 11 percent,
- $20 million of perpetual preferred stock redeemable in 10 years, providing a fixed yield of 10.25 percent.

The proposed amortization schedule and a complete analysis of the pre- and after-tax internal rate of return and duration for this debt structure are provided in Exhibits 6 and 7. The forecast of cash flows consistent with the proposal is given in Exhibit 8.

Danbury, Brickhouse, & Company recommended that the firm issue:

- $10 million of commercial paper fixed at 7 percent,
- $30 million of 20-year senior subordinated debentures with no sinking fund, fixed at 10 percent,
- $60 million of 30-year junior 11.5 percent coupon bonds with no sinking fund.

The analysis of this debt structure is given in Exhibit 9. The associated financial forecast is given in Exhibit 10.

Steinworth, Vader, Inc., thought it best that Syracuse issue the following debt:

- $30 million of commercial paper at 6.9 percent,
- $25 million of three-year secured notes with equal annual amortization and an interest rate fixed at 9.5 percent,
- $45 million of subordinated debentures with a sinking fund for seven years at 12 percent.

The duration analysis is given in Exhibit 11. The associated forecast is given in Exhibit 12.

Hudson Guaranty recommended the following fixed-rate structure:

- $60 million of senior revolving notes for three years at 9 percent,
- $30 million of privately placed subordinated debentures with a 10-year bullet payment at 10 percent,
- $10 million of privately placed preferred stock callable in 15 years yielding 12 percent.

The analysis of this debt structure is provided in Exhibit 13. The cash flow forecast is given in Exhibit 14.

Exhibit 15 provides historical data on bond and preferred stock yields, and Exhibit 16 gives Treasury yields and BB- and B-rated bond data. Yields on both corporate bonds and preferred stocks rose steadily throughout most of 1987, but in November began to decline as investors took their money out of the stock market and invested in debentures and preferred stock.

EVALUATION OF THE PROPOSALS

Ms. Chen wondered what the best package of securities should be, given the company's debt-service capacity and current interest rates. She wanted to ensure that, the faster the amortization and the shorter the duration, the lower the cost of the debt; she also wanted to compare the costs of the four proposals. She was not certain that shorter amortization and duration were necessarily better for the firm, however. Nor was she certain that the indicative interest rates were accurate for Syracuse or that the market would accept Syracuse's debt with yields equivalent to BBB or BB rates of return. To aid her analysis, she reviewed the latest Standard & Poor's ratings criteria, reproduced in Exhibit 17.

As she thought about the maturity structures of the alternatives, it occurred to Ms. Chen that assets also had lives and durations. Ms. Chen doubted that it was possible to measure accurately the asset duration for an industrial firm. But she speculated aloud as follows:

> In thinking about asset duration, you need to be careful to define the "asset" in question—we need to keep in mind assets that accountants don't capture, such as brand names, patents, unusual market franchises, and managerial know-how. Our finance subsidiary assets are mainly financial securities of one sort or another. It's not that hard to measure their duration; its about two years. Our defense electronics and avionics business is mainly built on "assets," such as government contracts; these typically run for 10 to 15 years, but I'll guess that the duration of assets in that sector is only about 10 years. Our consumer-appliance business is significantly comprised of assets, such as brand names and patents—these "wear out" over time. We turn over the designs of the entire product line within a 10-year cycle. I'll guess that the duration of assets in the consumer sector is eight years. Finally, our commodity electronics business has relatively low design turnover, but here our leadership in various products is know-how that produces cost advantages. Given the stability of product demand, technology, and know-how, I'll guess that the asset duration in the commodity electronics business is quite long, say 20 years. An average of these sector durations, weighted by proportion of business, would be 12 to 13 years.

Ms. Chen wondered whether "matching" asset and liability lives and durations would be beneficial.

Although Chen's initial goal was to obtain the most cost-effective financing package, she also sought to maintain operating and financial flexibility. To Ms. Chen, financial flexibility meant the ability to adapt to capital structure of the firm to changing market conditions, either through refundings of fixed-income securities or through new issues of debt or equity. From an operating perspective, Ms. Chen did not want to adopt a financial restructuring plan that might constrain capital spending in general or development of the radar detection-and-screening project in particular.

EXHIBIT 1 Letter from Susan Chen to the Investment and Commercial Banks

Dear _____:

In preparing a financing plan for the company, we invite a recommendation on the specific structure of fixed-income securities we should sell this year and then carry for the medium to long term. Toward this end, we are enclosing a confidential forecast of operating cash flows which you should use as a basis for your recommendations. Please assume this forecast is certain; we know of the many risks in our business and choose to deal with them in other ways. Our main interest is in your recommendation of a structure of fixed-income securities which minimizes the cost of the securities.

The other parameters of the situation are the following:

1. You should consider that we want to refinance $100 million (of about $350 million total) in bank debt this year; this financing will entail no operational changes in the firm.

2. We will entertain a structure of senior debt, subordinated debt, and preferred stock. Because we wish to preserve some ability to issue new senior debt in the future, no more than 50 percent of the fixed-income securities should consist of senior debt.

3. We assume that the senior debt would be rated BBB, the subordinated debt BB, and the preferred stock BB. We would like to have your independent confirmation of this assumption.

4. All of the securities should have a fixed coupon, in view of the current economic climate, we wish to shed floating-rate debt.

5. Terms of the issues should be relatively long, 10–15 years.

6. I will entertain any reasonable amortization schedule, but will assume that the more aggressive the amortization, the lower the cost.

You should know that we have invited [three other firms] to submit recommendations, and we will give the mandate for execution to the firm whose recommendations we accept. Naturally, we will reimburse all out-of-pocket expenses.

I look forward to receiving your proposal.

Sincerely,

Susan Chen
Chief Financial Officer

Assumptions to Be Used in Financial Projections by Financial Advisors (dollars in millions)

	1988	1989	1990	1991	1992	1993	1994	1995	1996	1997
Assumptions Varying by Year										
Earnings before interest & taxes	$135	$139	$151	$161	$178	$189	$214	$228	$255	$270
Depreciation	56	63	64	65	67	69	71	72	74	76
Capital expenditures: routine	35	38	42	47	52	57	63	69	77	85
Capital expenditures: radar project (not in routine category)	0	15	15	15	15	15	13	13	13	10
Additions to working capital	(4)	16	24	37	29	38	48	48	48	48
Amortization of old debt	10	40	40	40	40	40	40	0	0	0
Remaining balance on old debt	240	200	160	120	80	40	0	0	0	0
Dividends on common stock	52	52	54	54	56	56	59	59	64	64

Assumptions Common to All Years

Corporate tax rate = 34%
Average shares outstanding = 27,200,000
Interest rate on cash surpluses = 8%
Interest rate on new borrowings from banks = 9%
Target debt/equity ratio (over the long term) = 50%

EXHIBIT 2 Economic Indicators and Forecasts

	1982	1983	1984	1985	1986	1987	1988E
Real GNP growth	2.5%	3.6%	6.8%	3.0%	2.9%	2.9%	2.0%
Change in CPI	3.9%	3.8%	4.0%	3.8%	1.1%	4.4%	4.2%
Change in producer price index	3.7%	0.6%	1.7%	1.8%	-2.3%	2.2%	
3-Month Treasury bill interest rate	10.7%	8.6%	9.6%	7.5%	6.0%	5.8%	5.9%
Unemployment	9.5%	9.5%	7.4%	7.1%	6.9%	6.1%	6.2%
Housing starts*	$1,072	$1,713	$1,756	$1,745	$1,807	$1,634	$1,565
Nonresidential construction†	$108.2	$102.0	$117.1	$133.2	$129.4	$126.0	
Real trade-weighted dollar	$111.7	$117.3	$128.5	$132.0	$103.0	$ 90.6	

* Thousands of units.
† Billions of dollars.

Sources: *Economic Report of the President*; *Economic Outlook, USA*, Spring 1988, p. 20.

EXHIBIT 3   Comparative Financial Data—1987

	Sales ($ mm)	Operating Margin	Net Margin	Equity ($ mm)	Debt/ Equity	Average Price/ Earnings
Cooper Industries	$ 3,586	14.9%	4.9%	$ 1,592	55.5%	16.6
Dynamics Corp.	121	2.7	3.1	90	21.5	26.1
Emerson Electric	6,170	18.4	7.6	2,703	20.5	16.9
Federal Signal	318	10.0	4.7	103	20.2	12.9
Foxboro	504	N.M.F.	−7.7	188	3.1	N.M.F.
General Electric	39,315	13.3	5.4	16,480	27.3	22.6
Honeywell	6,679	12.6	3.8	2,245	30.2	12.6
Hubbell	581	17.9	10.8	357	2.3	14.8
Johnson Controls	2,677	10.3	3.4	770	25.7	14.7
RTE Corp.	348	10.2	4.7	102	36.7	13.5
Square D	1,484	18.5	7.4	680	18.8	13.9
Westinghouse	10,679	11.8	6.9	3,577	23.2	12.0
Syracuse	**$ 1,603**	**6.0%**	**4.2%**	**$ 674**	**49.7%**	**17.9**

N.M.F. means not a meaningful figure.

Source: *Value Line Investment Survey.*

EXHIBIT 4 Consolidated Income Statements (dollars in thousands except per share data)

For the Year Ended December 31

	1982	1983	1984	1985	1986	1987
Net sales	$1,622,136	$1,574,948	$1,786,883	$1,800,878	$1,583,368	$1,603,026
Cost of goods sold	1,110,422	1,097,143	1,240,037	1,278,648	1,114,564	1,151,503
SG&A	322,278	326,335	362,562	372,703	348,656	356,022
Restructuring provision	0	0	0	72,000	0	0
Operating income	189,436	151,470	184,284	77,527	120,148	95,501
Interest income	13,975	11,815	11,605	11,706	9,422	9,384
Interest expense	(10,902)	(8,473)	(7,434)	(9,044)	(12,023)	(11,406)
Earnings before taxes	192,509	154,812	188,455	80,189	117,547	93,479
Income taxes	84,734	65,114	79,945	30,922	42,925	26,524
Net income	$107,775	$89,698	$108,510	$49,267	$74,622	$66,955
Earnings/share	$3.85	$3.16	$3.80	$1.72	$2.60	$2.37
Dividends/share	$1.68	$1.68	$1.71	$1.80	$1.80	$1.80
Common stock prices:						
High	$47.000	$52.375	$54.000	$53.875	$54.250	$61.250
Low	$28.000	$40.500	$39.625	$37.000	$39.250	$33.250
Average shares outstanding (000)	28,013	28,414	28,568	28,706	28,730	27,183

EXHIBIT 5   Consolidated Balance Sheets (dollars in thousands)

	Year-end December 31	
	1986	*1987*
Cash & equivalents	$113,416	$ 82,215
Short-term investments	10,318	13,060
Accounts receivable—net	296,305	330,816
Contracts in progress	66,640	49,951
Inventories	360,382	343,064
Prepaid expenses	40,197	47,928
Total current assets	887,258	867,034
Property, plant, & equipment	630,281	626,442
Less depreciation & amortization	284,724	315,795
Net property, plant, & equipment	345,557	310,647
Intangibles—net	180,827	165,079
Other assets	44,464	53,923
Total assets	$1,458,106	$1,396,683
Short-term debt & current portion of long-term debt	$ 8,379	$ 15,034
Accounts payable	94,786	105,825
Accrued expenses	154,261	133,022
Income taxes	93,559	81,092
Total current liabilities	350,985	334,973
Long-term debt	124,270	335,060
Other liabilities	55,497	52,816
Total liabilities	530,752	722,849
Common stock	40,527	40,692
Additional paid-in capital	229,227	236,818
Retained earnings	712,323	730,286
Cumulative translation adjustments	(25,247)	(12,662)
Total	956,830	995,134
Treasury stock, at cost	(29,476)	(321,300)
Total shareholders' equity	927,354	673,834
Total liabilities & equity	$1,458,106	$1,396,683

EXHIBIT 6 Carlyle Savoy, Ltd. — Proposed Debt-Amortization Schedule with Pre-tax Interest Expense
(dollars in millions)

Year	(t) Years Hence	$10 Million Bank Debt			t*PV	$30 Million Senior Secured & Sinking Fund		
		Interest	Principal	Total		Interest	Principal	Total
1988	0.0	0.00	0.00	−10.00	0.00	0.00	0.00	−30.00
1988	0.5	0.48	1.00	1.48	0.70	1.43	1.50	2.93
1989	1.0	0.43	1.00	1.43	1.30	1.35	1.50	2.85
1989	1.5	0.38	1.00	1.38	1.80	1.28	1.50	2.78
1990	2.0	0.33	1.00	1.33	2.21	1.21	1.50	2.71
1990	2.5	0.29	1.00	1.29	2.55	1.14	1.50	2.64
1991	3.0	0.24	1.00	1.24	2.81	1.07	1.50	2.57
1991	3.5	0.19	1.00	1.19	3.01	1.00	1.50	2.50
1992	4.0	0.14	1.00	1.14	3.15	0.93	1.50	2.43
1992	4.5	0.10	1.00	1.10	3.25	0.86	1.50	2.36
1993	5.0	0.05	1.00	1.05	3.29	0.78	1.50	2.28
1993	5.5					0.71	1.50	2.21
1994	6.0					0.64	1.50	2.14
1994	6.5					0.57	1.50	2.07
1995	7.0					0.50	1.50	2.00
1995	7.5					0.43	1.50	1.93
1996	8.0					0.36	1.50	1.86
1996	8.5					0.29	1.50	1.79
1997	9.0					0.21	1.50	1.71
1997	9.5					0.14	1.50	1.64
1998	10.0					0.07	1.50	1.57
1998	10.5							
1999	11.0							
1999	11.5							
2000	12.0							
2000	12.5							
2001	13.0							
2001	13.5							
2002	14.0							
2002	14.5							
2003	15.0							
Total payment		2.61	10.00		2.61	14.96		30.00
Semiannual yield			4.75%					4.75%
Annual yield†			9.73%					9.73%
Duration (years)			2.41					4.01
Weighted average annual yield‡			10.51%					
Weighted average annual duration‡			4.72					

*Assumes preferred stock is called in 10th year.
†Annual yield was calculated as $(1 + \text{semiannual})^2 − 1$.
‡Weighted average annual yield and duration were calculated by weighting each by the dollar amount of the security.

t*PV	$40 Million Junior Debentures & Sinking Fund			t*PV	$20 Million Perpetual Preferred*			t*PV
	Interest	Principal	Total		Dividend	Principal	Total	
0.00	0.00	0.00	−40.00	0.00	0.00	0.00	−20.00	0.00
1.40	2.20	1.33	3.53	1.67	1.03	0.00	1.03	0.49
2.60	2.13	1.33	3.46	3.11	1.03	0.00	1.03	0.93
3.63	2.05	1.33	3.39	4.33	1.03	0.00	1.03	1.32
4.50	1.98	1.33	3.31	5.35	1.03	0.00	1.03	1.68
5.23	1.91	1.33	3.24	6.20	1.03	0.00	1.03	2.00
5.83	1.83	1.33	3.17	6.89	1.03	0.00	1.03	2.28
6.32	1.76	1.33	3.09	7.44	1.03	0.00	1.03	2.53
6.70	1.69	1.33	3.02	7.87	1.03	0.00	1.03	2.75
6.98	1.61	1.33	2.95	8.19	1.03	0.00	1.03	2.94
7.18	1.54	1.33	2.87	8.41	1.03	0.00	1.03	3.11
7.30	1.47	1.33	2.80	8.55	1.03	0.00	1.03	3.25
7.36	1.39	1.33	2.73	8.61	1.03	0.00	1.03	3.38
7.36	1.32	1.33	2.65	8.60	1.03	0.00	1.03	3.48
7.31	1.25	1.33	2.58	8.53	1.03	0.00	1.03	3.56
7.21	1.17	1.33	2.51	8.42	1.03	0.00	1.03	3.63
7.07	1.10	1.33	2.43	8.27	1.03	0.00	1.03	3.69
6.89	1.03	1.33	2.36	8.07	1.03	0.00	1.03	3.73
6.69	0.95	1.33	2.29	7.85	1.03	0.00	1.03	3.75
6.46	0.88	1.33	2.21	7.60	1.03	0.00	1.03	3.77
6.21	0.81	1.33	2.14	7.33	1.03	20.00	21.03	77.38
	0.73	1.33	2.07	7.05				
	0.66	1.33	1.99	6.75				
	0.59	1.33	1.92	6.44				
	0.51	1.33	1.85	6.13				
	0.44	1.33	1.77	5.81				
	0.37	1.33	1.70	5.49				
	0.29	1.33	1.63	5.17				
	0.22	1.33	1.55	4.86				
	0.15	1.33	1.48	4.54				
	0.07	1.33	1.41	4.23				
14.96		34.10	40.00	34.10		20.50	20.00	20.50
			5.50%				5.13%	
			11.30%				10.51%	
			4.94				6.48	

EXHIBIT 7 Carlyle Savoy, Ltd.—Proposed Debt Amortization Schedule Assuming After-tax Interest Expense (dollars in millions)

Year	(t) Years Hence	$10 Million Bank Debt			t*PV	$30 Million Senior Secured & Sinking Fund		
		Interest	Principal	Total		Interest	Principal	Total
1988	0.0	0.00	0.00	−10.00	0.00	0.00	0.00	−30.00
1988	0.5	0.31	1.00	1.31	0.64	0.94	1.50	2.44
1989	1.0	0.28	1.00	1.28	1.21	0.89	1.50	2.39
1989	1.5	0.25	1.00	1.25	1.71	0.85	1.50	2.35
1990	2.0	0.22	1.00	1.22	2.16	0.80	1.50	2.30
1990	2.5	0.19	1.00	1.19	2.55	0.75	1.50	2.25
1991	3.0	0.16	1.00	1.16	2.88	0.71	1.50	2.21
1991	3.5	0.13	1.00	1.13	3.17	0.66	1.50	2.16
1992	4.0	0.09	1.00	1.09	3.42	0.61	1.50	2.11
1992	4.5	0.06	1.00	1.06	3.62	0.56	1.50	2.06
1993	5.0	0.03	1.00	1.03	3.79	0.52	1.50	2.02
1993	5.5					0.47	1.50	1.97
1994	6.0					0.42	1.50	1.92
1994	6.5					0.38	1.50	1.88
1995	7.0					0.33	1.50	1.83
1995	7.5					0.28	1.50	1.78
1996	8.0					0.24	1.50	1.74
1996	8.5					0.19	1.50	1.69
1997	9.0					0.14	1.50	1.64
1997	9.5					0.09	1.50	1.59
1998	10.0					0.07	1.50	1.55
1998	10.5							
1999	11.0							
1999	11.5							
2000	12.0							
2000	12.5							
2001	13.0							
2001	13.5							
2002	14.0							
2002	14.5							
2003	15.0							
Total payment		1.72	10.00	1.72		9.88	30.00	9.88
Semiannual yield				3.14%				3.14%
Annual yield†				6.37%				6.37%
Duration (years)				2.51				4.36
Weighted average annual yield‡				7.61%				
Weighted average annual duration‡				5.12				

*Assumes preferred stock is called in 10th year.
†Annual yield was calculated as $(1 + \text{semiannual})^2 - 1$.
‡Weighted average annual yield and duration were calculated by weighing each by the dollar amount of the security.

$t*PV$	$40 Million Junior Debentures & Sinking Fund			$t*PV$	$20 Million Perpetual Preferred*			$t*PV$
	Interest	Principal	Total		Dividend	Principal	Total	
0.00	0.00	0.00	−40.00	0.00	0.00	0.00	−20.00	0.00
1.18	1.45	1.33	2.79	1.34	1.03	0.00	1.03	0.49
2.25	1.40	1.33	2.74	2.55	1.03	0.00	1.03	0.93
3.21	1.36	1.33	2.69	3.62	1.03	0.00	1.03	1.32
4.06	1.31	1.33	2.64	4.58	1.03	0.00	1.03	1.68
4.83	1.26	1.33	2.59	5.42	1.03	0.00	1.03	2.00
5.50	1.21	1.33	2.54	6.16	1.03	0.00	1.03	2.28
6.09	1.16	1.33	2.49	6.80	1.03	0.00	1.03	2.53
6.60	1.11	1.33	2.45	7.36	1.03	0.00	1.03	2.75
7.04	1.06	1.33	2.40	7.83	1.03	0.00	1.03	2.94
7.41	1.02	1.33	2.35	8.22	1.03	0.00	1.03	3.11
7.72	0.97	1.33	2.30	8.55	1.03	0.00	1.03	3.25
7.97	0.92	1.33	2.25	8.81	1.03	0.00	1.03	3.38
8.16	0.87	1.33	2.20	9.01	1.03	0.00	1.03	3.48
8.31	0.82	1.33	2.16	9.16	1.03	0.00	1.03	3.56
8.41	0.77	1.33	2.11	9.26	1.03	0.00	1.03	3.63
8.47	0.73	1.33	2.06	9.31	1.03	0.00	1.03	3.69
8.49	0.68	1.33	2.01	9.32	1.03	0.00	1.03	3.73
8.47	0.63	1.33	1.96	9.30	1.03	0.00	1.03	3.75
8.42	0.58	1.33	1.91	9.24	1.03	0.00	1.03	3.77
8.34	0.53	1.33	1.87	9.14	1.03	20.00	21.03	77.38
	0.48	1.33	1.82	9.02				
	0.44	1.33	1.77	8.88				
	0.39	1.33	1.72	8.71				
	0.34	1.33	1.67	8.53				
	0.29	1.33	1.62	8.32				
	0.24	1.33	1.58	8.10				
	0.19	1.33	1.53	7.87				
	0.15	1.33	1.48	7.63				
	0.10	1.33	1.43	7.37				
	0.05	1.33	1.38	7.11				
	22.51	40.00	22.51		20.50	20.50	20.50	
			3.63%				5.13%	
			7.39%				10.51%	
			5.66				6.48	

EXHIBIT 8 Carlyle Savoy, Ltd., Proposal—Projected Cash Flows (dollars in millions)

	1988	1989	1990	1991	1992	1993	1994	1995	1996	1997
Earnings before interest & taxes	$135	$139	$151	$161	$178	$189	$214	$228	$255	$270
Net interest (income):*										
Old debt & interest income	13	9	5	2	(2)	(5)	(9)	(9)	(9)	(9)
$10 mm bank debt	1	1	1	0	0	0	0	0	0	0
$30 mm senior secured	1	3	2	2	2	2	1	1	1	0
$40 mm junior debenture	2	4	4	4	3	3	3	2	2	2
Pre-tax profit	118	122	139	153	·175	189	219	234	261	277
Taxes (34%)	40	41	47	52	60	64	74	80	89	94
After-tax profit	78	81	92	101	115	125	145	154	172	183
Preferred dividends†	1	2	2	2	2	2	2	2	2	2
Earnings available to common shares	77	79	90	99	113	123	143	152	170	181
Plus depreciation	56	63	64	65	67	69	71	72	74	76
Less capital expenditures	35	38	42	47	52	57	63	69	77	85
Less capital expenditures for radar project	0	15	15	15	15	15	13	13	13	10
Less additions to working capital	(4)	16	24	37	29	38	48	48	48	48
Less amortization of or sinking fund payment on:										
Old debt	10	40	40	40	40	40	40	0	0	
$10 mm bank debt	1	2	2	2	2	1	0			
$30 mm senior secured	2	3	3	3	3	3	3	3	3	3
$40 mm junior debentures	1	3	3	3	3	3	3	3	3	3
Residual cash flow to equity holders	88	25	25	17	36	35	44	88	100	108
Common dividends	52	52	54	54	56	56	59	59	64	64
Remaining balance on:										
Old debt	240	200	160	120	80	40	0	0	0	0
$10 mm bank debt	9	7	5	3	1	0	0	0	0	0
$30 mm senior secured	29	26	23	20	17	14	11	8	5	2
$40 mm junior debentures	39	36	33	31	28	25	23	20	17	15
Callable preferred	20	20	20	20	20	20	20	20	20	20

* Interest on old bank debt between 9 and 12%; 7.625% on industrial revenue bond; and $10 million interest income. Assumes 9.5% on new bank debt, 9.5% on senior secured, and 11% on junior debentures.
† Assumes yield on preferred of 10.25%.

EXHIBIT 9 Danbury, Brickhouse, & Company—Proposed Debt-Amortization Schedule Pre-tax (dollars in millions)

Year	(t) Years Hence	$10 Million Commercial Paper				$30 Million Senior Debentures				$60 Million Junior Debentures			
		Interest	Principal	Total	t*PV	Interest	Principal	Total	t*PV	Interest	Principal	Total	t*PV
1988	0.0	0.00	0.00	−10.00	0.00	0.00	0.00	−30.00	0.00	0.00	0.00	−60.00	0.00
1988	0.5	0.35	10.00	10.35	5.00	1.50	0.00	1.50	0.71	3.45	0.00	3.45	1.63
1989	1.0					1.50	0.00	1.50	1.36	3.45	0.00	3.45	3.09
1989	1.5					1.50	0.00	1.50	1.94	3.45	0.00	3.45	4.38
1990	2.0					1.50	0.00	1.50	2.47	3.45	0.00	3.45	5.52
1990	2.5					1.50	0.00	1.50	2.94	3.45	0.00	3.45	6.52
1991	3.0					1.50	0.00	1.50	3.36	3.45	0.00	3.45	7.40
1991	3.5					1.50	0.00	1.50	3.73	3.45	0.00	3.45	8.16
1992	4.0					1.50	0.00	1.50	4.06	3.45	0.00	3.45	8.82
1992	4.5					1.50	0.00	1.50	4.35	3.45	0.00	3.45	9.39
1993	5.0					1.50	0.00	1.50	4.60	3.45	0.00	3.45	9.86
1993	5.5					1.50	0.00	1.50	4.82	3.45	0.00	3.45	10.26
1994	6.0					1.50	0.00	1.50	5.01	3.45	0.00	3.45	10.58
1994	6.5					1.50	0.00	1.50	5.17	3.45	0.00	3.45	10.84
1995	7.0					1.50	0.00	1.50	5.30	3.45	0.00	3.45	11.04
1995	7.5					1.50	0.00	1.50	5.41	3.45	0.00	3.45	11.19
1996	8.0					1.50	0.00	1.50	5.50	3.45	0.00	3.45	11.28
1996	8.5					1.50	0.00	1.50	5.56	3.45	0.00	3.45	11.34
1997	9.0					1.50	0.00	1.50	5.61	3.45	0.00	3.45	11.35
1997	9.5					1.50	0.00	1.50	5.64	3.45	0.00	3.45	11.33
1998	10.0					1.50	0.00	1.50	5.65	3.45	0.00	3.45	11.28
1998	10.5					1.50	0.00	1.50	5.65	3.45	0.00	3.45	11.20
1999	11.0					1.50	0.00	1.50	5.64	3.45	0.00	3.45	11.09
1999	11.5					1.50	0.00	1.50	5.62	3.45	0.00	3.45	10.97
2000	12.0					1.50	0.00	1.50	5.58	3.45	0.00	3.45	10.82
2000	12.5					1.50	0.00	1.50	5.54	3.45	0.00	3.45	10.66
2001	13.0					1.50	0.00	1.50	5.48	3.45	0.00	3.45	10.48
2001	13.5					1.50	0.00	1.50	5.42	3.45	0.00	3.45	10.29
2002	14.0					1.50	0.00	1.50	5.36	3.45	0.00	3.45	10.09
2002	14.5					1.50	0.00	1.50	5.28	3.45	0.00	3.45	9.89
2003	15.0					1.50	0.00	1.50	5.21	3.45	0.00	3.45	9.67
2003	15.5					1.50	0.00	1.50	5.12	3.45	0.00	3.45	9.45
2004	16.0					1.50	0.00	1.50	5.04	3.45	0.00	3.45	9.23
2004	16.5					1.50	0.00	1.50	4.95	3.45	0.00	3.45	9.00
2005	17.0					1.50	0.00	1.50	4.85	3.45	0.00	3.45	8.76

EXHIBIT 9 (continued) Danbury, Brickhouse, & Company—Proposed Debt-Authorization Schedule Pre-tax (dollars in millions)

Year	(t) Years Hence	$10 Million Commercial Paper				$30 Million Senior Debentures				$60 Million Junior Debentures			
		Interest	Principal	Total	t*PV	Interest	Principal	Total	t*PV	Interest	Principal	Total	t*PV
2005	17.5					1.50	0.00	1.50	4.76	3.45	0.00	3.45	8.53
2006	18.0					1.50	0.00	1.50	4.66	3.45	0.00	3.45	8.30
2006	18.5					1.50	0.00	1.50	4.56	3.45	0.00	3.45	8.07
2007	19.0					1.50	0.00	1.50	4.46	3.45	0.00	3.45	7.83
2007	19.5					1.50	0.00	1.50	4.36	3.45	0.00	3.45	7.60
2008	20.0					1.50	30.00	31.50	89.49	3.45	0.00	3.45	7.37
2008	20.5									3.45	0.00	3.45	7.15
2009	21.0									3.45	0.00	3.45	6.92
2009	21.5									3.45	0.00	3.45	6.70
2010	22.0									3.45	0.00	3.45	6.48
2010	22.5									3.45	0.00	3.45	6.27
2011	23.0									3.45	0.00	3.45	6.06
2011	23.5									3.45	0.00	3.45	5.86
2012	24.0									3.45	0.00	3.45	5.66
2012	24.5									3.45	0.00	3.45	5.46
2013	25.0									3.45	0.00	3.45	5.27
2013	25.5									3.45	0.00	3.45	5.08
2014	26.0									3.45	0.00	3.45	4.90
2014	26.5									3.45	0.00	3.45	4.72
2015	27.0									3.45	0.00	3.45	4.55
2015	27.5									3.45	0.00	3.45	4.38
2016	28.0									3.45	0.00	3.45	4.22
2016	28.5									3.45	0.00	3.45	4.06
2017	29.0									3.45	0.00	3.45	3.91
2017	29.5									3.45	0.00	3.45	3.76
2018	30.0									3.45	60.00	63.45	66.49
Total payment		$0.35	$10.00	$ 0.35	—	$60.00	$30.00	$ 60.00		$207.00	$60.00	$207.00	
Semiannual yield				3.50%				5.00%				5.75%	
Annual yield*				7.12%				10.25%				11.83%	
Duration (years)				0.50				9.01				8.87	

Weighted average annual yield† 10.89%

Weighted average annual duration† 8.08

* Annual yield was calculated as $(1 + \text{semiannual})^2 - 1$.

† Weighted average annual yield and duration were calculated by weighing each by the dollar amount of the security.

EXHIBIT 9 (continued) Danbury, Brickhouse After-Tax Debt Amortization Schedule

Year	(t) Years Hence	$10 Million Commercial Paper Interest	Principal	Total	t*PV	$30 Million Senior Debentures Interest	Principal	Total	t*PV	$60 Million Junior Debentures Interest	Principal	Total	t*PV
1988	0.0	0.00	0.00	-10.00	0.00	0.00	0.00	-30.00	0.00	0.00	0.00	-60.00	0.00
1988	0.5	0.23	10.00	10.23	5.00	0.99	0.00	0.99	0.48	2.28	0.00	2.28	1.10
1989	1.0					0.99	0.00	0.99	0.93	2.28	0.00	2.28	2.11
1989	1.5					0.99	0.00	0.99	1.35	2.28	0.00	2.28	3.05
1990	2.0					0.99	0.00	0.99	1.74	2.28	0.00	2.28	3.92
1990	2.5					0.99	0.00	0.99	2.10	2.28	0.00	2.28	4.73
1991	3.0					0.99	0.00	0.99	2.44	2.28	0.00	2.28	5.46
1991	3.5					0.99	0.00	0.99	2.76	2.28	0.00	2.28	6.14
1992	4.0					0.99	0.00	0.99	3.05	2.28	0.00	2.28	6.76
1992	4.5					0.99	0.00	0.99	3.33	2.28	0.00	2.28	7.33
1993	5.0					0.99	0.00	0.99	3.58	2.28	0.00	2.28	7.84
1993	5.5					0.99	0.00	0.99	3.81	2.28	0.00	2.28	8.31
1994	6.0					0.99	0.00	0.99	4.02	2.28	0.00	2.28	8.74
1994	6.5					0.99	0.00	0.99	4.22	2.28	0.00	2.28	9.12
1995	7.0					0.99	0.00	0.99	4.40	2.28	0.00	2.28	9.46
1995	7.5					0.99	0.00	0.99	4.56	2.28	0.00	2.28	9.77
1996	8.0					0.99	0.00	0.99	4.71	2.28	0.00	2.28	10.04
1996	8.5					0.99	0.00	0.99	4.85	2.28	0.00	2.28	10.28
1997	9.0					0.99	0.00	0.99	4.97	2.28	0.00	2.28	10.48
1997	9.5					0.99	0.00	0.99	5.08	2.28	0.00	2.28	10.66
1998	10.0					0.99	0.00	0.99	5.17	2.28	0.00	2.28	10.81
1998	10.5					0.99	0.00	0.99	5.26	2.28	0.00	2.28	10.94
1999	11.0					0.99	0.00	0.99	5.33	2.28	0.00	2.28	11.04
1999	11.5					0.99	0.00	0.99	5.40	2.28	0.00	2.28	11.12
2000	12.0					0.99	0.00	0.99	5.45	2.28	0.00	2.28	11.18
2000	12.5					0.99	0.00	0.99	5.50	2.28	0.00	2.28	11.22
2001	13.0					0.99	0.00	0.99	5.53	2.28	0.00	2.28	11.24
2001	13.5					0.99	0.00	0.99	5.56	2.28	0.00	2.28	11.24
2002	14.0					0.99	0.00	0.99	5.58	2.28	0.00	2.28	11.23
2002	14.5					0.99	0.00	0.99	5.60	2.28	0.00	2.28	11.21
2003	15.0					0.99	0.00	0.99	5.61	2.28	0.00	2.28	11.17
2003	15.5					0.99	0.00	0.99	5.61	2.28	0.00	2.28	11.12
2004	16.0					0.99	0.00	0.99	5.60	2.28	0.00	2.28	11.06
2004	16.5					0.99	0.00	0.99	5.60	2.28	0.00	2.28	10.99
2005	17.0					0.99	0.00	0.99	5.58	2.28	0.00	2.28	10.91
2005	17.5					0.99	0.00	0.99	5.56	2.28	0.00	2.28	10.82
2006	18.0					0.99	0.00	0.99	5.54	2.28	0.00	2.28	10.72

EXHIBIT 9 (*concluded*)   Danbury, Brickhouse After-Tax Debt Amortization Schedule

	(t)	$10 Million Commercial Paper				$30 Million Senior Debentures				$60 Million Junior Debentures			
Year	Years Hence	Interest	Principal	Total	t*PV	Interest	Principal	Total	t*PV	Interest	Principal	Total	t*PV
2006	18.5					0.99	0.00	0.99	5.51	2.28	0.00	2.28	10.62
2007	19.0					0.99	0.00	0.99	5.48	2.28	0.00	2.28	10.51
2007	19.5					0.99	0.00	0.99	5.44	2.28	0.00	2.28	10.39
2008	20.0					0.99	30.00	30.99	169.14	2.28	0.00	2.28	10.26
2008	20.5									2.28	0.00	2.28	10.14
2009	21.0									2.28	0.00	2.28	10.00
2009	21.5									2.28	0.00	2.28	9.87
2010	22.0									2.28	0.00	2.28	9.73
2010	22.5									2.28	0.00	2.28	9.59
2011	23.0									2.28	0.00	2.28	9.44
2011	23.5									2.28	0.00	2.28	9.29
2012	24.0									2.28	0.00	2.28	9.14
2012	24.5									2.28	0.00	2.28	8.99
2013	25.0									2.28	0.00	2.28	8.84
2013	25.5									2.28	0.00	2.28	8.69
2014	26.0									2.28	0.00	2.28	8.53
2014	26.5									2.28	0.00	2.28	8.38
2015	27.0									2.28	0.00	2.28	8.23
2015	27.5									2.28	0.00	2.28	8.07
2016	28.0									2.28	0.00	2.28	7.92
2016	28.5									2.28	0.00	2.28	7.77
2017	29.0									2.28	0.00	2.28	7.61
2017	29.5									2.28	0.00	2.28	7.46
2018	30.0									2.28	60.00	2.28	
Total payment		**$0.23**	**$10.00**	**$ 0.35**		**$ 9.60**	**$30.00**	**$ 39.60**		**$136.62**	**$60.00**	**$136.62**	**199.92**
Semiannual yield				2.30%				3.30%				3.80%	
Annual yield*				4.65%				6.71%				7.73%	
Duration (years)				0.50				11.38				12.21	
Weighted average annual yield†								7.12%					
Weighted average annual duration†								10.79					

* Annual yield was calculated as $(1 + \text{semiannual})^2 - 1$.

† Weighted average annual yield and duration were calculated by weighing each by the dollar amount of the security.

EXHIBIT 10 Danbury, Brickhouse, & Company Proposal—Projected Cash Flows (dollars in millions)

	1988	1989	1990	1991	1992	1993	1994	1995	1996	1997
Earnings before interest & taxes	$135	$139	$151	$161	$178	$189	$214	$228	$255	$270
Net interest (income):*										
Old debt & interest income	13	13	9	5	2	(2)	(5)	(9)	(9)	(9)
$10 mm commercial paper	0	0	0	0	0	0	0	0	0	0
$30 mm senior debentures	2	3	3	3	3	3	3	3	3	3
$60 mm junior 0-coupon	3	7	7	7	7	7	7	7	7	7
Pre-tax profit	117	116	132	146	166	181	209	227	254	269
Taxes (34%)	40	39	45	50	56	62	71	77	86	91
After-tax profit	77	77	87	96	110	119	138	150	168	178
Preferred dividends†	0	0	0	0	0	0	0	0	0	0
Earnings available to common shares	77	77	87	96	110	119	138	150	168	178
Plus depreciation	56	63	64	65	67	69	71	72	74	76
Less capital expenditures	35	38	42	47	52	57	63	69	77	85
Less capital expenditures for radar project	0	15	15	15	15	15	13	13	13	10
Less additions to working capital	(4)	16	24	37	29	38	48	48	48	48
Less amortization of or sinking fund payment on:										
Old debt	10	40	40	40	40	40	40	0	0	0
$10 mm commercial paper	10	0	0	0	0	0	0	0	0	0
$30 mm senior debentures	0	0	0	0	0	0	0	0	0	0
$60 mm junior 0-coupon	0	0	0	0	0	0	0	0	0	0
Residual cash flow to equity holders	82	31	30	22	41	38	45	92	104	111
Common dividends	52	52	54	54	56	56	59	59	64	64
Remaining balance on:										
Old debt	240	200	160	120	80	40	0	0	0	0
$10 mm commercial paper	0	0	0	0	0	0	0	0	0	0
$30 mm senior debentures	30	30	30	30	30	30	30	30	30	30
$60 mm junior 0-coupon	40	40	40	40	40	40	40	40	40	40
Callable preferred	0	0	0	0	0	0	0	0	0	0

*Interest on old bank debt between 9 and 12%; 7.625% on industrial revenue bond; and $10 million interest income. Assumes 7% on commercial paper, 10% on senior subordinated, and 11.5% on junior debt.

EXHIBIT 11 Steinworth, Vader, Inc.—Proposed Debt-Amortization Schedule Pre-tax (dollars in millions)

Year	(t) Years Hence	$30 Million Commercial Paper				$25 Million Notes				$45 Million Subord. Debent. & Sink. Fund			
		Interest	Principal	Total	t*PV	Interest	Principal	Total	t*PV	Interest	Principal	Total	t*PV
1988	0.0	0.00	0.00	−30.00	0.00	0.00	0.00	−25.00	0.00	0.00	0.00	−45.00	0.00
1988	0.5	1.04	30.00	31.04	15.00	1.19	4.17	5.35	2.56	2.70	3.21	5.91	2.79
1989	1.0				0.00	0.99	4.17	5.16	4.70	2.51	3.21	5.72	5.09
1989	1.5				0.00	0.79	4.17	4.96	6.47	2.31	3.21	5.53	6.96
1990	2.0				0.00	0.59	4.17	4.76	7.91	2.12	3.21	5.34	8.45
1990	2.5				0.00	0.40	4.17	4.56	9.04	1.93	3.21	5.14	9.61
1991	3.0				0.00	0.20	4.17	4.36	9.91	1.74	3.21	4.95	10.47
1991	3.5				0.00				0.00	1.54	3.21	4.76	11.07
1992	4.0				0.00				0.00	1.35	3.21	4.56	11.45
1992	4.5				0.00				0.00	1.16	3.21	4.37	11.64
1993	5.0				0.00				0.00	0.96	3.21	4.18	11.67
1993	5.5				0.00				0.00	0.77	3.21	3.99	11.55
1994	6.0				0.00				0.00	0.58	3.21	3.79	11.31
1994	6.5				0.00				0.00	0.39	3.21	3.60	10.97
1995	7.0				0.00				0.00	0.19	3.21	3.41	10.55
Total payment		1.04	30.00	$ 1.04		4.16	25.00	4.16		20.25	45.00	20.25	
Semiannual yield		3.45%				4.75%				6.00%			
Annual yield*		7.05%				9.72%				12.36%			
Duration		0.50				1.62				2.97			

Weighted average annual yield† 10.10%

Weighted average annual duration† 1.89

EXHIBIT 11 (concluded) Steinworth, Vader, Inc.—Proposed Debt-Amortization Schedule After-Tax

(t) Years Hence	Year	$30 Million Commercial Paper				$25 Million Notes				$45 Million Subord. Debent. & Sink. Fund			
		Interest	Principal	Total	t*PV	Interest	Principal	Total	t*PV	Interest	Principal	Total	t*PV
0.0	1988	0.00	0.00	−30.00	0.00	0.00	0.00	−25.00	0.00	0.00	0.00	−45.00	0.00
0.5	1988	0.68	30.00	30.68	15.00	0.78	4.17	4.95	2.40	1.78	3.21	5.00	2.40
1.0	1989				0.00	0.65	4.17	4.82	4.53	1.65	3.21	4.87	4.51
1.5	1989				0.00	0.52	4.17	4.69	6.41	1.53	3.21	4.74	6.33
2.0	1990				0.00	0.39	4.17	4.56	8.06	1.40	3.21	4.61	7.90
2.5	1990				0.00	0.26	4.17	4.43	9.49	1.27	3.21	4.49	9.24
3.0	1991				0.00	0.13	4.17	4.30	10.71	1.15	3.21	4.36	10.36
3.5	1991				0.00				0.00	1.02	3.21	4.23	11.29
4.0	1992				0.00				0.00	0.89	3.21	4.11	12.04
4.5	1992				0.00				0.00	0.76	3.21	3.98	12.62
5.0	1993				0.00				0.00	0.64	3.21	3.85	13.06
5.5	1993				0.00				0.00	0.51	3.21	3.72	13.36
6.0	1994				0.00				0.00	0.38	3.21	3.60	13.54
6.5	1994				0.00				0.00	0.25	3.21	3.47	13.61
7.0	1995				0.00				0.00	0.13	3.21	3.34	13.58
Total payment		1.69	30.00	1.04	0.00	2.74	25.00	2.74		13.36	45.00	13.37	
Semiannual yield		2.28%				3.13%				3.96%			
Annual yield*		4.61%				6.37%				8.08%			
Duration		0.50				1.66				3.20			

Weighted average annual yield† 6.61%
Weighted average annual duration† 2.00

* Annual yield was calculated as (1 + semiannual)^2 − 1.
† Weighted average annual yield and duration were calculated by weighing each by the dollar amount of the security.

EXHIBIT 12 Steinworth, Vader, Inc., Proposal—Projected Cash Flows (dollars in millions)

	1988	1989	1990	1991	1992	1993	1994	1995	1996	1997
Earnings before interest & taxes	$135	$139	$151	$161	$178	$189	$214	$228	$255	$270
Net interest (income):*										
Old debt & interest income	13	13	11	10	5	(0)	(5)	(9)	(9)	(9)
$30 mm commercial paper	1	0	0	0	0	0	0	0	0	0
$25 mm notes	1	2	1	0	0	0	0	0	0	0
$45 subordinated debentures	3	5	4	3	3	2	1	0	0	0
Pre-tax profit	117	119	135	147	170	187	217	237	264	279
Taxes (34%)	40	41	46	50	58	64	74	80	90	95
After-tax profit	77	79	89	97	112	124	144	156	174	184
Preferred dividends	0	0	0	0	0	0	0	0	0	0
Earnings available to common shares	77	79	89	97	112	124	144	156	174	184
Plus depreciation	56	63	64	65	67	69	71	72	74	76
Less capital expenditures	35	38	42	47	52	57	63	69	77	85
Less capital expenditures for radar project	0	15	15	15	15	15	13	13	13	10
Less additions to working capital	(4)	16	24	37	29	38	48	48	48	48
Less amortization of or sinking fund payment on:										
Old debt	10	40	40	40	40	40	40	0	0	0
$30 mm commercial paper	30	0	0	0	0	0	0	0	0	0
$25 mm notes	4	8	8	4	0	0	0	0	0	0
$45 subordinated debentures	3	6	6	6	6	6	6	3	0	0
Residual cash flow to equity holders	55	18	17	12	37	36	44	95	110	117
Common dividends	52	52	54	54	56	56	59	59	64	64
Remaining balance on:										
Old debt	240	200	160	120	80	40	0	0	0	0
$30 mm commercial paper	0	0	0	0	0	0	0	0	0	0
$25 mm notes	21	12	4	0	0	0	0	0	0	0
$45 subord. debentures	42	35	29	23	16	10	3	3	0	0
Callable preferred	0	0	0	0	0	0	0	0	0	0

*Interest on old bank debt between 9 and 12%; 7.625% on industrial revenue bonds; and $10 million interest income. Assumes 6.9% on commercial paper, 9.5% on secured notes, and 12% on subordinated debentures.

EXHIBIT 13 Hudson Guaranty—Proposed Debt-Amortization Schedule Pre-tax (dollars in millions)

		$60 Million Senior Revolving Notes				$30 Million Subord. Debentures				$10 Million Callable Debent. & Sink. Fund*			
Year	(t) Years Hence	Interest	Principal	Total	t*PV	Interest	Principal	Total	t*PV	Interest	Principal	Total	t*PV
1988	0.0	0.00	0.00	−60.00	0.00	0.00	0.00	−30.00	0.00	0.00	0.00	−10.00	0.00
1988	0.5	2.70	10.00	12.70	6.08	1.50	0.00	1.50	0.71	0.60	0.00	0.60	0.28
1989	1.0	2.25	0.00	12.25	11.22	1.50	0.00	1.50	1.36	0.60	0.00	0.60	0.53
1989	1.5	1.80	0.00	11.80	15.51	1.50	0.00	1.50	1.94	0.60	0.00	0.60	0.76
1990	2.0	1.35	0.00	11.35	19.04	1.50	0.00	1.50	2.47	0.60	0.00	0.60	0.95
1990	2.5	0.90	0.00	10.90	21.87	1.50	0.00	1.50	2.94	0.60	0.00	0.60	1.12
1991	3.0	0.45	10.00	10.45	24.07	1.50	0.00	1.50	3.36	0.60	0.00	0.60	1.27
1991	3.5					1.50	0.00	1.50	3.73	0.60	0.00	0.60	1.40
1992	4.0					1.50	0.00	1.50	4.06	0.60	0.00	0.60	1.51
1992	4.5					1.50	0.00	1.50	4.35	0.60	0.00	0.60	1.60
1993	5.0					1.50	0.00	1.50	4.60	0.60	0.00	0.60	1.68
1993	5.5					1.50	0.00	1.50	4.82	0.60	0.00	0.60	1.74
1994	6.0					1.50	0.00	1.50	5.01	0.60	0.00	0.60	1.79
1994	6.5					1.50	0.00	1.50	5.17	0.60	0.00	0.60	1.83
1995	7.0					1.50	0.00	1.50	5.30	0.60	0.00	0.60	1.86
1995	7.5					1.50	0.00	1.50	5.41	0.60	0.00	0.60	1.88
1996	8.0					1.50	0.00	1.50	5.50	0.60	0.00	0.60	1.89
1996	8.5					1.50	0.00	1.50	5.56	0.60	0.00	0.60	1.89
1997	9.0					1.50	0.00	1.50	5.61	0.60	0.00	0.60	1.89
1997	9.5					1.50	0.00	1.50	5.64	0.60	0.00	0.60	1.88
1998	10.0					1.50	0.00	1.50	118.72	0.60	0.00	0.60	1.87
1998	10.5					1.50	0.00	1.50		0.60	0.00	0.60	1.85
1999	11.0					1.50	0.00	1.50		0.60	0.00	0.60	1.83
1999	11.5					1.50	0.00	1.50		0.60	0.00	0.60	1.81
2000	12.0					1.50	0.00	1.50		0.60	0.00	0.60	1.78
2000	12.5					1.50	0.00	1.50		0.60	0.00	0.60	1.75
2001	13.0					1.50	0.00	1.50		0.60	0.00	0.60	1.71
2001	13.5					1.50	0.00	1.50		0.60	0.00	0.60	1.68
2002	14.0					1.50	0.00	1.50		0.60	0.00	0.60	1.64
2002	14.5					1.50	0.00	1.50		0.60	0.00	0.60	1.61
2003	15.0		10.00	10.45		1.50	30.00	31.50		0.60	10.00	10.60	27.68
Total payment		9.45	60.00	9.45	—	30.00	30.00	30.00	—	18.00	10.00	18.00	—
Semiannual yield				4.50%				5.00%				6.00%	
Annual yield†				9.20%				10.25%				12.36%	
Duration				1.63				6.54				7.30	
Weighted average annual yield‡				9.83%									
Weighted average annual duration‡				3.67									

*Assumes preferred stock called in year 15.
†Annual yield was calculated as (1 + semiannual)^2 − 1.
‡Weighted average annual yield and duration were calculated by weighing each by the dollar amount of the security.

EXHIBIT 13 (concluded) Hudson Guaranty—Proposed Debt-Amortization Schedule After-Tax

Year	(t) Years Hence	$60 Million Senior Revolving Notes — Interest	Principal	Total	r*PV	$30 Million Subord. Debentures — Interest	Principal	Total	r*PV	$10 Million Callable Debent. & Sink. Fund* — Interest	Principal	Total	r*PV
1988	0.0	0.00	0.00	−60.00	0.00	0.00	0.00	−30.00	0.00	0.00	0.00	−10.00	0.00
1988	0.5	1.78	10.00	11.78	5.72	0.99	0.00	0.99	0.48	0.60	0.00	0.60	0.28
1989	1.0	1.49	10.00	11.49	10.83	0.99	0.00	0.99	0.93	0.60	0.00	0.60	0.53
1989	1.5	1.19	10.00	11.19	15.37	0.99	0.00	0.99	1.35	0.60	0.00	0.60	0.76
1990	2.0	0.89	10.00	10.89	19.38	0.99	0.00	0.99	1.74	0.60	0.00	0.60	0.95
1990	2.5	0.59	10.00	10.59	22.88	0.99	0.00	0.99	2.10	0.60	0.00	0.60	1.12
1991	3.0	0.30	10.00	10.30	25.92	0.99	0.00	0.99	2.44	0.60	0.00	0.60	1.27
1991	3.5					0.99	0.00	0.99	2.76	0.60	0.00	0.60	1.40
1992	4.0					0.99	0.00	0.99	3.05	0.60	0.00	0.60	1.51
1992	4.5					0.99	0.00	0.99	3.33	0.60	0.00	0.60	1.60
1993	5.0					0.99	0.00	0.99	3.58	0.60	0.00	0.60	1.68
1993	5.5					0.99	0.00	0.99	3.81	0.60	0.00	0.60	1.74
1994	6.0					0.99	0.00	0.99	4.02	0.60	0.00	0.60	1.79
1994	6.5					0.99	0.00	0.99	4.22	0.60	0.00	0.60	1.83
1995	7.0					0.99	0.00	0.99	4.40	0.60	0.00	0.60	1.86
1995	7.5					0.99	0.00	0.99	4.56	0.60	0.00	0.60	1.88
1996	8.0					0.99	0.00	0.99	4.71	0.60	0.00	0.60	1.89
1996	8.5					0.99	0.00	0.99	4.85	0.60	0.00	0.60	1.89
1997	9.0					0.99	0.00	0.99	4.97	0.60	0.00	0.60	1.89
1997	9.5					0.99	0.00	0.99	5.08	0.60	0.00	0.60	1.88
1998	10.0					0.99	30.00	30.99	161.89	0.60	0.00	0.60	1.87
1998	10.5									0.60	0.00	0.60	1.85
1999	11.0									0.60	0.00	0.60	1.83
1999	11.5									0.60	0.00	0.60	1.81
2000	12.0									0.60	0.00	0.60	1.78
2000	12.5									0.60	0.00	0.60	1.75
2001	13.0									0.60	0.00	0.60	1.71
2001	13.5									0.60	0.00	0.60	1.68
2002	14.0									0.60	0.00	0.60	1.64
2002	14.5									0.60	0.00	0.60	1.61
2003	15.0									0.60	10.00	10.60	27.68
Total payment		6.24	60.00	6.24		19.80	30.00	19.80		18.00	10.00	18.00	27.68
Semiannual yield		2.97%				3.30%				6.00%			
Annual yield†		6.03%				6.71%				12.36%			
Duration		1.67				7.48				7.30			

Weighted average annual yield‡   6.87%

Weighted average annual duration‡   3.97

586

EXHIBIT 14 Hudson Guaranty Proposal—Projected Cash Flows (dollars in millions)

	1988	1989	1990	1991	1992	1993	1994	1995	1996	1997
Earnings before interest & taxes	$135	$139	$151	$161	$178	$189	$214	$228	$255	$270
Net interest (income):*										
Old debt & interest income	13	13	11	10	5	(0)	(5)	(9)	(9)	(9)
$60 mm bank debt	3	4	2	0	0	0	0	0	0	0
$30 mm subordinated debentures	2	3	3	3	3	3	3	3	3	3
Pre-tax profit	117	119	135	148	170	186	216	234	261	276
Taxes (34%)	40	40	46	50	58	63	73	80	89	94
After-tax profit	77	79	90	96	112	123	143	154	172	182
Preferred dividends†	1	1	1	1	1	1	1	1	1	1
Earnings available to common shares	76	78	89	95	111	122	142	153	171	181
Plus depreciation	56	63	64	65	67	69	71	72	74	76
Less capital expenditures	35	38	42	47	52	57	63	69	77	85
Less capital expenditures for radar project	0	15	15	15	15	15	13	13	13	10
Less additions to working capital	(4)	16	24	37	29	38	48	48	48	48
Less amortization of or sinking fund payment on:										
Old debt	10	40	40	40	40	40	40	0	0	0
$60 mm bank debt	10	20	20	10	0	0	0	0	0	0
$30 mm subordinated debentures	0	0	0	0	0	0	0	0	0	0
Residual cash flow to equity holders	81	12	12	11	42	40	48	95	107	114
Common dividends	52	52	54	54	56	56	59	59	64	64
Remaining balance on:										
Old debt	240	200	160	120	80	40	0	0	0	0
$60 mm bank debt	50	30	10	0	0	0	0	0	0	0
$30 mm subordinated debentures	30	30	30	30	30	30	30	30	30	30
Callable preferred	10	10	10	10	10	10	10	10	10	10

*Interest on old bank debt between 9 and 12%; 7.625% on industrial revenue bond; and $10 million interest income. Assumes 9% on bank debt, and 10% on subordinated debentures.
† Assumes yield on preferred of 12.0%.

587

EXHIBIT 15 Bond and Preferred Stock Yields and Prime Lending Rate

	Industrial Bonds				U.S. Government		Prime	6-Month Commercial Paper
	AAA	AA	A	BBB	Long-Term	Short-Term		
1982 High	14.76%	15.13%	15.57%	17.03%	14.32%	14.57%	17.00%	14.27%
Low	10.55	10.96	11.75	13.28	10.18	9.57	11.50	8.50
1983 High	12.38	12.62	12.94	13.67	11.99	11.26	11.50	9.68
Low	10.51	10.72	11.07	11.68	10.18	9.21	10.50	8.15
1984 High	13.66	14.13	14.42	15.12	13.89	13.22	13.00	11.34
Low	11.40	11.73	12.06	12.78	11.25	10.19	11.00	8.55
1985 High	12.00	12.43	12.50	13.19	11.84	10.82	10.75	9.23
Low	9.50	10.13	10.20	11.13	9.24	8.11	9.50	7.38
1986 High	9.80	10.41	10.58	11.26	9.51	8.44	9.50	7.62
Low	8.50	9.18	8.99	9.81	7.23	6.27	7.50	5.61
1987 High	10.74	11.09	11.48	12.06	10.30	8.90	9.00	7.96
Low	8.37	8.89	8.83	9.52	7.57	6.26	7.50	5.76
1987 Apr	8.80	9.43	9.33	9.94	8.36	6.97	7.75	6.50
May	9.29	9.93	9.84	10.43	8.92	7.68	8.25	7.04
Jun	9.31	9.77	9.86	10.36	8.76	7.46	8.25	7.00

Jul	9.31	9.71	9.91	10.44	8.86	7.28	8.25	6.72
Aug	9.67	9.95	10.24	10.64	9.14	7.51	8.25	6.81
Sep	10.26	10.62	10.88	11.35	9.78	8.14	8.75	7.55
Oct	10.41	10.70	11.14	11.70	9.80	8.23	9.25	7.96
Nov	9.71	10.07	10.69	11.22	9.16	7.45	9.00	7.17
Dec	9.75	10.13	10.89	11.34	9.24	7.58	8.75	7.49
1988 Jan	9.49	9.89	10.54	11.03	8.97	7.59	8.75	6.92
Feb	9.09	9.44	9.96	10.59	8.53	7.34	8.50	6.58
Mar	9.29	9.66	10.14	10.73	8.74	7.41	8.50	6.64
Apr	9.52%	9.80%	10.24%	10.67%	8.97%	7.67%	8.50%	6.92%

Public Utility Preferred

	AA	A	BAA
1982	11.63%	12.20%	13.26%
1983	12.18	12.61	13.34
1984	12.25	12.97	13.71
1985	10.00	10.28	11.09
1986	7.98	8.64	9.27
1987	9.35	10.24	10.45
1988 Apr	9.20%	9.87%	10.02%

Sources: Moody's Bond Guide; Economic Report of the President; Federal Reserve Bulletin.

EXHIBIT 16   Treasury Yields and Duration, and BB- and B-Rated Bond Yields

Treasury Yields and Duration, April 11, 1988

Maturity Date	Yield	Duration (years)
1988 May	5.97%	0.08
1988 Oct	6.36	0.50
1989 Apr	7.03	0.97
1990 Apr	7.50	1.89
1991 Apr	7.73	2.73
1992 Apr	7.99	3.50
1993 Apr	8.13	4.21
1994 Apr	8.27	4.85
1995 May	8.42	5.43
1996 May	8.55	5.95
1998 May	8.57	6.91
2002 May	8.89	8.27
2008 May	8.94%	9.65

BB- and B-Rated Bond Yields

Firm	Issue	Maturity	Rating	Yield to Maturity 12/87	Yield to Maturity 4/88
AMC Entertainment	Sen. sub. Deb.	2000	B	15.32%	13.60%
Bally's Grand	Mortgage notes	1996	BB	12.99	11.89
Charter Medical	Debentures	2007	BB	13.72	10.00
Clark Equipment	Notes	1993	BB	14.03	13.09
FMC Corp.	Sub. debentures	2001	B	12.50	12.50
Harnischfeger	Notes	1994	BB	12.88	12.50
Harnischfeger	Sub. debentures	2004	B	13.36	15.76
Heritage Communications	Notes	1998	BB	12.38	12.13
Heritage Communications	Sub. debentures	2001	B	13.18	11.75
Orion Pictures	Sub. sink fund deb.	1998	B	15.02	12.56
Seafirst Corp.	Sink Fund Deb.	2001	BB	12.28	9.30
Turner Broadcasting	0-Coupon senior note	1992	B	13.12%	13.85%

Sources: *The Wall Street Journal, Standard & Poor's Bond Guide, Moody's Bond Guide*, and analyst's duration model.

EXHIBIT 17 Standard & Poor's Bond-Ratings Criteria for Industrial Corporations, Three-Year (1984–1986) Medians

	AAA	AA	A	BBB	BB	B	CCC
Pre-tax interest coverage (×)	12.63	9.06	5.24	3.19	2.49	1.83	0.22
Pre-tax interest coverage, including rents (×)	7.39	4.62	3.02	2.32	1.83	1.54	0.52
Funds from operations/ long-term debt (%)	226.67	124.00	67.51	46.05	28.94	19.43	12.26
Funds from operations/ total debt (%)	135.22	90.32	54.63	40.45	24.64	16.43	10.19
Pre-tax return on permanent capital employed (%)	24.80	21.38	18.16	13.30	12.75	11.40	1.40
Operating income/sales (%)	20.63	14.85	12.21	10.91	11.44	10.55	7.09
Long-term debt/capital (%)	11.31	17.67	26.85	31.61	43.10	53.15	64.71
Total debt/capital including short-term debt (%)	18.59	24.11	31.52	34.81	45.77	55.67	67.10
Total debt/capital including short-term & 8 times rent (%)	30.39	35.40	46.14	48.18	58.24	65.78	71.07
Total liabilities/tangible equity & minority interest	78.89	107.26	118.28	146.11	188.22	224.97	379.66

AAA: Debt rated AAA has the highest rating assigned by S&P. Capacity to pay interest and repay principal is extremely strong.

AA: Debt rated AA has a very strong capacity to pay interest and repay principal and differs from the higher-rated issues only in small degree.

A: Debt rated A has a strong capacity to pay interest and repay principal, although it is somewhat more susceptible to the adverse effects of changes in circumstances and economic conditions than debt in higher-rated categories.

BBB: Debt rated BBB is regarded as having an adequate capacity to pay interest and repay principal. Whereas it normally exhibits adequate protection parameters, adverse economic conditions or changing circumstances are more likely to lead to a weakened capacity to pay interest and repay principal for debt in this category than in higher-rated categories.

BB, B, CCC, CC, C: Debt rated BBB, B, CCC, CC, and C is regarded, on balance, as predominantly speculative with respect to capacity to pay interest and repay principal in accordance with the terms of the obligation. BB indicates the lowest degree of speculation and C the highest degree of speculation. While such debt will likely have some quality and protective characteristics, these are outweighed by large uncertainties or major risk exposure to adverse conditions.

Sources: *Standard & Poor's Creditweek*, September 7, 1987, p. 15; *Standard & Poor's Bond Guide*.

Part VIII

Evaluating Mergers, Buyouts, Restructurings, Projects, and Joint Ventures

Brown-Forman Distillers Corporation

In early July 1978, W. L. Lyons Brown, Jr., president and chief executive officer of Brown-Forman Distillers Corporation, faced an important acquisition decision. The principal owners of Southern Comfort Corporation had approached Mr. Brown in May with an offer to sell the company at a price of $94.6 million. In preparing his response, Mr. Brown was evaluating the reasonableness of the asking price and the likely effects of the acquisition on Brown-Forman's share price.

As a leading producer, marketer, and importer of wines and distilled spirits (including the well-known Jack Daniel's brand), Brown-Forman ($457 million net sales*) was the fifth largest distiller in the United States, after National Distillers ($586 million*), Seagram ($2,018 million*), Heublein ($839 million*), and Hiram Walker ($875 million*). How Mr. Brown had chosen to position Brown-Forman among its competitors would affect the appraisal of Southern Comfort.

BROWN-FORMAN: FINANCIAL GOALS AND PERFORMANCE

In 1977, Brown-Forman's management adopted new long-range financial goals regarding (1) hurdle rates for investment, (2) size of the capital budget through 1980, (3) target capital structure, and (4) dividend payout. The primary objective of these goals was to "increase the value of the stockholders' investment."[1]

---

*These are net sales from the wine and distilled spirits business lines only.
[1]1978 annual report, p. 3.

This case was written by Robert F. Bruner.
Copyright © 1983 by the Darden Graduate Business School Foundation, Charlottesville, VA.

The dividend payout ratio (all dividends paid divided by net income) was targeted at a range of 30 percent to 35 percent. Planned investment during the 1978–80 period included $86 million for advertising and promotion, $39 million in barreled whiskey inventory, and $19 million in new plant and equipment. Regarding capital structure, the ratio of total debt to total tangible capital,[2] 26.6 percent at the end of 1977, was viewed as offering "considerable flexibility in financing investment opportunities with either debt or equity."[3] Finally, the target hurdle rate, calculated as the return on total capital employed,[4] was set at 14 percent for new capital projects in the distilling industry and 12 percent for investments in projects already in place.

The 1977 annual report declared:

> While we are pleased with our 1977 results, in order to improve our return on total capital employed, we will be selective in pursuing new capital projects and will concentrate our efforts on improving the profitability of our present business. Management will actively pursue investments in new capital projects that have an anticipated return of at least 14 percent after taxes on the capital employed. At the same time we will continue our efforts to expand the most profitable operations of the company. With respect to other areas of our business, your management is taking steps through price increases and closer attention to asset management to improve profitability. If the returns of these operations do not attain a higher level, management will consider channelling the capital supporting them into more profitable projects, products and acquisitions.

Exhibit 1 compares the expected financial performance of Brown-Forman to its largest competitors. The target hurdle rate contrasted with the company's longer-term historical performance. However, the company had a relatively larger profit margin, higher growth rates, and stronger balance sheet than its major competitors. The 1978 annual report noted:

> The Company's balance sheet is strong due to continued close attention to asset management. Our low debt/equity ratio and the excellent financial performance in recent years places the Company in a favorable position to assume higher levels of debt to finance acquisitions and other investment opportunities.

Value Line[5] identified Brown-Forman as the "premier liquor company in the United States," and noted that the firm's major brands continued to grow despite a flat industry growth trend. The company was expected to earn $2.40 per share in 1978, and to add another 15 percent to earnings per share (EPS) in 1979.

---

[2]Total tangible capital was defined as the sum of all interest-bearing debt, deferred income taxes, preferred equity, and common equity less intangible assets.

[3]1977 annual report, p. 15.

[4]*Return* was defined as the sum of net income (excluding extraordinary items), the after-tax cost of interest, the increase in deferred income taxes, and the amortization of intangible assets during the year. *Average total capital employed* was defined as the sum of all interest-bearing debt, deferred income taxes, and preferred and common equity averaged at year-end.

[5]*Value Line*, April 14, 1978, p. 350.

Brown-Forman's income statement and balance sheet for the year ended April 30, 1978, are given in Exhibits 2 and 3. In 1978, two classes of stock existed for the company: Class A stock had exclusive voting rights and was listed on the American Stock Exchange, while Class B common had no voting rights but also was listed. The Brown family held 74 percent of the Class A stock and 40 percent of the Class B. The family also provided some of the senior officers and directors of the company.

BROWN-FORMAN: PRODUCT/MARKET STRATEGY AND PERFORMANCE

"The production of distilled spirits is a relatively straightforward task. It is marketing skill that is critically important to the survival and growth of firms in this industry," said William Street, senior vice president.

Mr. Brown succinctly stated Brown-Forman's product/market strategy in a presentation to the New York Society of Security Analysts on June 29, 1978:

The company's marketing philosophy is to produce and sell high-quality products which retail at prices generally at the upper end of the price scale within whatever category the product is sold. The company is a strong believer in heavy advertising support in order to build brands which have long life cycles with generally higher margins than are found on brands whose consumer appeal is based on price and shorter life cycles.

Brown-Forman's product line included many well-known brands, which were categorized into three groups (see Exhibit 4).

Outside observers suggested that Brown-Forman's special competence was in building brand franchises. For example, the company purchased the Canadian Mist Brand from Barton Brands, Inc., in 1971, "Because we had no significant brand in the Canadian whiskey market and perceived significant growth in that market," said Mr. Brown. By 1978, it was Brown-Forman's largest brand and grew 11.5 percent during 1977 versus 3.1 percent for all Canadian whiskies. A second example would be the company's investment in the Bolla and Cella brand Italian wines. But the preeminent example of the firm's ability to build premium brand franchises was Jack Daniel's Tennessee whiskey. Mr. Brown said:

Jack Daniel's compounded annual growth rate over the last five years has been between 10 and 15 percent, and yet we know from tests in certain markets where we've allowed free supply both this year and last that the growth has jumped to between 25 percent and 40 percent. I believe we can state without equivocation that Jack Daniel's has the strongest and most loyal consumer franchise of any product in the industry. What are the reasons for this phenomenal success? Number one, it has been our long-term marketing philosophy that top quality deserves the highest price, and over many years Jack Daniel's has been the highest priced American whiskey of any significant volume on the market. The brand is probably the only one which by policy has never granted quantity discounts of any kind. The fact that there has been a supply shortage from time to time has added to the mystique surrounding the label and no doubt has been a factor contributing to long-term sales growth. . . . Jack Daniel's is a unique product. . . . Our advertising over the years has emphasized the character of the distillery and the whiskey it produces. . . . Finally, the most exciting thing for us for the long term is the big increase in demand, which is on the top of the normal 10–15 percent compounded annual growth, is coming primarily from the youth market. . . . The corporation sees a very healthy, long life cycle ahead for this brand.

A new marketing thrust on the Jack Daniel's brand had been to increase penetration of foreign marketing. This would require an expanded marketing organization overseas.

Whereas skillful branding and product positioning could improve the sales performance of a particular product or product group, another factor, product-line mix, also would affect the sales growth of the company in the long run. Exhibit 5 suggests how demand for distilled spirits changed over the past 10 years. Regarding the near future, *Value Line* expected sluggish industry growth overall, although "mystique" brands such as Jack Daniel's would continue to grow:

> The spirits companies are beset with a number of problems. While the shift to non-whiskies is firmly entrenched, the white goods (vodka, gin, rum, and tequila) aren't as profitable. . . . Since the overall liquor market hasn't gotten significantly larger, sales penetration by any one product type has come at the expense of another category.
>
> . . . Retail liquor prices have advanced about 15 percent over the last decade while the consumer price index rose 75 percent. Plainly, the industry has been reluctant to raise prices and has preferred to absorb cost increases because of the sluggish volume.[6]

SOUTHERN COMFORT

The object of Brown-Forman's acquisition interest was Southern Comfort Corporation (Consolidated) and Caligrapo, Inc., producers of Southern Comfort, a unique liqueur. By industry definition, a liqueur is a distilled spirit that contains more than 2.5 percent sugar by volume. Generally, a liqueur is produced by adding a syrup or concentrate to an alcohol base. The concentrate gives the liqueur its distinctive flavor. Southern Comfort's concentrate was mixed by a secret formula owned by Caligrapo Inc. Caligrapo sold the concentrate to Southern Comfort, which purchased alcohol and mixed, bottled, and marketed the liqueur. Southern Comfort employed 22 salesmen; its sales in 1978 were about $64 million (see Exhibits 6 and 7).

Southern Comfort was owned by the estate of Francis E. Fowler, Jr., while Caligrapo was owned directly by his heirs, principally his sons, Francis G. Fowler III, and Philip F. Fowler. Francis E. Fowler, Jr., had owned Southern Comfort for many years until his death in 1975.[7] His sons managed the St. Louis company largely from California, where they and their father had chosen to live in recent years. Despite absentee management, the company was regarded as well run and efficient. Plant visits by Brown-Forman employees revealed modern equipment.

---

[6]*Value Line*, April 14, 1978, p. 350.

[7]Following the death of Francis E. Fowler, Jr., an independent appraisal in 1977 deemed the fair market value of the common stock of Southern Comfort to be $120 per share for estate and inheritance tax purposes.

Southern Comfort had enjoyed above-average growth in shipments (see Exhibit 8), which was consistent with the general rise in the consumption of liqueurs shown in Exhibit 5, but surprising in view of the fact market surveys revealed that over half of Southern Comfort's consumers viewed it as a whiskey. Thus, compared to the slow growth of whiskey as a class, Southern Comfort's performance was arresting. It was attributed in part to rock and roll singer Janis Joplin, who drank Southern Comfort on stage during her performances. Southern Comfort had a strong franchise in the youth market (21–34 years old) and among heavy drinkers. Also, strengthened channels of foreign distribution accounted for growth in export sales. Among marketing professionals, it was considered a very strong brand. Southern Comfort had never been sold at a discount by its manufacturer. Its performance notwithstanding, Mr. Brown felt that the brand had not been aggressively marketed.

Through an intermediary, the Fowler brothers had approached Brown-Forman to solicit its interest in buying Southern Comfort Corporation and Caligrapo, Inc., for $94.6 million. Subsequently, Brown-Forman learned that, in recent years, two other major distillers had entertained the possible acquisition of Southern Comfort and had rejected it at that price. At the time of approaching Brown-Forman, the Fowlers were discussing the acquisition with no other potential buyers. They seemed sincerely interested in selling to Brown-Forman, primarily because of a perceived fit of Southern Comfort with the Brown-Forman product line. Also, Brown-Forman resembled Southern Comfort in broad outline: a family-run business with a southern heritage and a record of superior performance.

The Fowlers indicated a willingness to accept cash for the two companies. Through an intermediary, they also suggested two other features of the acquisition. First, Southern Comfort Corporation owned some real property unrelated to the operations of the company. The Fowlers offered to repurchase that property, after the acquisition, at book value, about $5.9 million. Second, they proposed that the acquisition be consummated after January 1979, when they expected Congress to lower the tax rate on capital gains.

Mr. Brown contemplated financing $20 million of the purchase price with cash and financing the balance with bank debt. He estimated that up to $70 million could be borrowed at a nominal rate of 8.75 percent repayable over seven years semiannually starting the following year. The company would be required to maintain an average compensating balancing of 7 percent on the amount borrowed.

Because the proposed transaction would be taxable to the Fowlers, Brown-Forman could write up the value of the assets to the purchase price paid. Brown-Forman's finance department estimated that the purchase price could be allocated as follows:

$55.0 million	Intangible assets (amortized over 40 years)
12.2	Property, plant, and equipment (depreciated over 20 years)
27.4	Current assets
$94.6	Asking price

Fundamentally, however, the attractiveness of the acquisition would rely on the strength of the cash flow from operations. A small team of executives developed a series of revenue, cost, and volume assumptions, which are summarized in Exhibit 9. The recent price history of Brown-Forman's common stock is given in Exhibit 10.

Cost of Eq = $K_{RF} + (K_m - K_{RF})\beta$

= 8% + (5.72%)(1.1)

= 14.2%

$D/E = 25\%$

$D = 20\%$ $E_q = 80\%$

$D+E = 1.0$

$.25+1 = \frac{1}{E}$

$E = \frac{1}{1.25}$

$\frac{1}{E} = \frac{8}{5}$

$E = \frac{5}{5/4}$

WACC = $(wd)(Debt)(1-T) + (W_{Eq})(\frac{Cost}{Eq})$

= $(.20)(.09)(1-.48) + (.80)(14.2\%)$

= 12.4%

$8.75\% = 9.4\%$

.85

7% comp. bd. rq.

cost = $\frac{8}{d out}$

d out ?

EXHIBIT 1   Comparative Financial Data, 1978

	American Distilling	Brown-Forman	Heublein	National Distillers	Publicker Industries	Seagram	Hiram Walker
Beta	1.41	1.10	1.71	0.79	1.63	1.04	0.65
Marginal tax rate	0.30	0.50	0.49	0.47	0.40	0.46	0.50
Debt/equity	1.14	0.247	0.55	0.34	0.84	0.53	0.20
(Debt − Cash) ÷ Total capital	0.50	0.11	0.28	0.16	0.44	0.32	0.12
Assets/equity	2.46	1.37	2.16	1.65	2.04	1.76	1.43
Sales/assets	1.66	1.46	1.80	1.35	1.49	1.22	1.04
Profit/sales	0.012	0.073	0.035	0.052	0.005	0.038	0.069
Price/earnings	9.4	8.2	9.6	6.5	nmf	8.8	7.7
Dividend yield at 4/14/78	nil	0.043	0.056	0.08	nil	0.042	0.062
Self-sustaining growth rate	0.049	0.102	0.053	0.079	0.015	0.041	0.054
1978 expected sales growth	0.02	0.09	0.06	0.08	0.04	0.07	0.06
Market value ÷ Book value	0.46	1.26	1.53	0.79	0.63	0.75	0.77

Notes: (1) The long-term geometric mean risk premium (calculated as the difference between the return on the market portfolio and the long-term return on government bonds) was 5.7 percent. The arithmetic risk premium was 8.7 percent. (2) The yield to maturity of 10-year U.S. Treasury bonds (a proxy for the ex ante risk-free rate) was 8 percent. The yield on 90-day U.S. Treasury bills was 7.08 percent.

nmf = not meaningful

Source of market premium: R. G. Ibbotson and R. A. Sinquefield, *Stocks, Bonds, Bills, and Inflation: The Past (1926–1978) and the Future (1978–2000)* (Charlottesville: Financial Analysts Research Foundation, 1977), Exhibit 28.

Source of financial ratios: *Value Line*, 4/14/78.

Source of betas: "Security Risk Evaluation," Merrill Lynch Pierce Fenner & Smith, Inc., April 1978.

EXHIBIT 2   Consolidated Statement of Income (expressed in thousands, except per share amounts)

	Years Ended April 30	
	1978	1977
Net sales	$457,071	$396,176
Cost of sales	310,539	274,733
Gross profit	146,532	121,443
Selling, advertising, administrative, and general expenses	76,395	69,714
Other income (expense):		
Write-off of intangible asset	(2,300)	—
Miscellaneous, net	1,314	1,760
Earnings before interest and taxes	69,151	53,489
Interest expense	5,804	6,249
Income before taxes	63,347	47,240
Taxes on income	32,100	23,500
Net income	$ 31,247	$ 23,740
Earnings per common share	$ 2.45	$ 1.85

Source: 1978 annual report.

EXHIBIT 3   Consolidated Balance Sheet (expressed in thousands)

	April 30	
	1978	*1977*
Assets		
Cash	$ 8,875	$ 9,354
Short-term money market investments	20,797	36,171
Accounts receivable, trade	59,759	40,446
Inventories	167,142	148,794
Other current assets	1,030	1,380
Total current assets	257,603	236,145
Investments in associated companies	6,554	6,494
Property, plant, and equipment, at cost:	81,010	74,229
Less accumulated depreciation	41,709	38,384
Net property, plant, and equipment	39,301	35,845
Other assets	6,360	4,716
Goodwill, franchises, brands, and trademarks	18,787	21,671
Total assets	$328,605	$304,871
Liabilities and Stockholders' Equity		
Current portion of long-term debt	$ 5,000	$ 5,000
Accounts payable and accrued expenses	39,361	32,213
Accrued taxes	11,475	6,659
Deferred income taxes	1,650	2,759
Total current liabilities	57,486	46,631
9.3% Serial notes, less current portion, $5,000 due each September 1, 1979–1988	50,000	60,000
Deferred income taxes	2,894	1,226
Total liabilities	110,380	107,857
Stockholders' equity:		
Capital stock:		
Preferred 40¢ cumulative, 1,177,948 shares authorized and outstanding	11,779	11,779
Class A common stock, voting, issued shares, 4,020,634	1,206	1,206
Class B common stock, nonvoting, issued shares, 8,888,105	2,667	2,667
Capital surplus	91,146	91,146
Retained earnings	115,349	94,138
Less common treasury stock, at cost (Class A, 61,742 shares; Class B, 261,377 shares)	(3,922)	(3,922)
Total stockholders' equity	218,225	197,014
Total liabilities and stockholders' equity	$328,605	$304,871

Source: 1978 annual report.

EXHIBIT 4   Product Line Information

Share of Market	American Spirits (53% Brown-Forman Sales)	Percent Sales Growth 1977	1977 Industry Sales Growth
NA	Jack Daniel's Tennessee Whiskey	NA	NA
3%	Old Forester Bottled in Bond Bourbon Whisky	+4.4%	−2.9%
	Old Forester Kentucky Straight Bourbon Whisky		−2.9%
7.2%	Early Times Kentucky Straight Bourbon Whisky	+2.0%	−2.9%
	Imported Spirits (24% Brown-Forman Sales)		
10.5%	Canadian Mist Canadian Whisky	+11.5%	+3.1
NA	Ambassador Scotch Whiskies	NA	+0.2
NA	Usher's Green Stripe Scotch Whisky	NA	+0.2
NA	Pepe Lopez Tequila	NA	NA
NA	Old Bushmills Irish Whisky	NA	NA
NA	Martell Cognacs	NA	NA
	Wines & Specialties (23% Brown-Forman Sales)		
4.6%	Bolla Italian Wines	+32.5%	+37%
3.3%	Cella Italian Wines	+77%	+37%
NA	Cruse French Wines	NA	NA
NA	Veuve Clicquot French Champagnes	NA	NA
NA	Noilly Prat Vermouths	NA	NA
NA	Anheuser German Wines	NA	NA
3.2%	Korbel California Champagnes	+11%	NA
6.1%	Korbel California Brandy		+15.2*
NA	Bols Liqueurs and Brandies	NA	+9.0%

* Five-year percent increase 1971–76.

Sources: Company estimates; and *Liquor Handbook* (New York: Gavin-Johnson Associates, 1982), p. 74.

EXHIBIT 5   Consumption Changes by Types of Distilled Spirit

	Case Shipments	
Product Type	*1966–1971 Percent Change*	*1971–1976 Percent Change*
Total distilled spirits	+ 22.2	+ 9.8
American whiskies	− 4.6	− 21.9
Blends	− 7.3	− 29.2
Straights	+ 0.9	− 14.7
Bonds	− 29.1	− 36.4
Other	− 26.2	+ 106.7
Scotch	+ 54.5	+ 8.2
Canadian	+ 70.6	+ 31.5
Gin	+ 18.9	+ 4.3
Rum	+ 77.1	+ 43.2
Brandy	+ 41.3	+ 15.2
Cordials, liqueurs	+ 44.1	+ 45.5
Vodka	+ 51.6	+ 55.1
Prepared cocktails	+ 30.3	+ 116.5
Other	+ 328.9	+ 97.7

Source: *Liquor Handbook* (New York: Gavin-Johnson Associates, 1982), pp. 44, 74.

EXHIBIT 6   Income Statement of Southern Comfort Corporation and Subsidiary (for the years
ended December 31)

	1977	1976
Net sales	$64,183,392	$57,308,426
Cost of sales	45,814,353	40,909,265
Gross profit	$18,369,039	$16,399,161
Selling, administrative, and general expenses	10,193,517	9,446,120
Income from operations	$ 8,175,522	$ 6,953,041
Other income (expense):		
Royalties on Canadian sales	$ 355,940	$ 329,804
Interest	(62,283)	(186,210)
Rental property, net	111,329	(141,457)
Other, net	2,466	(5,237)
	$ 407,452	$ (3,100)
Income before income taxes	$ 8,582,974	$ 6,949,941
Provision for income taxes	4,211,512	3,453,400
Net income	$ 4,371,462	$ 3,496,541
Earnings per common share	$79.95	$59.67

Source: Annual report.

EXHIBIT 7   Southern Comfort Corporation and Subsidiary, Consolidated Balance Sheets—
December 31

	1977	1976
Assets		
Current assets:		
Cash	$ 1,341,190	$ 750,108
Accounts receivable	$12,118,758	$12,305,064
Inventories	$ 7,365,841	$ 6,554,342
Prepaid expenses	$ 35,952	$ 59,218
Total current assets	$20,861,741	$19,668,732
Property, at cost:	$ 5,556,624	$ 4,933,708
Less: Accumulated depreciation	2,439,268	2,105,195
	$ 3,117,356	$ 2,828,513
Investment in rental property, less accumulated depreciation of $171,996 and $106,878	$ 1,614,633	$ 1,673,585
Total property, net	$ 4,731,989	$ 4,502,098
Display silver, at cost	$ 152,297	$ 152,297
Total assets	$25,746,027	$24,323,127
Liabilities and Stockholders' Equity		
Current liabilities:		
Notes payable to bank, unsecured	$ —	$ 2,350,000
Current portion of long-term notes payable	62,067	858,461
Federal spirits and rectification taxes payable	7,096,549	4,933,465
Accounts payable and accrued expenses	1,076,973	1,489,093
Dividends payable	8,343	8,493
Income taxes	738,279	572,571
Total current liabilities	$ 8,982,211	$10,212,083
Long-term notes payable, less current portion	$ 35,827	$ 1,297,894
Deferred compensation payable, less current portion	$ —	$ 51,200
Stockholders' equity:		
Preferred stock, no par redeemable at $10, $.50 cumulative outstanding 33,374 and 33,974 shares	$ 166,870	$ 169,870
Common stock, $1 par, authorized 170,000 shares, issued 120,000 shares	120,000	120,000
Retained earnings	23,363,049	19,011,274
	$23,649,919	$19,301,144
Less: Treasury stock, at cost, 66,214 and 65,437 common shares	6,921,930	6,539,194
Total stockholders' equity	$16,727,989	$12,761,950
Total liabilities and stockholders' equity	$25,746,027	$24,323,127

Source: Annual report.

EXHIBIT 8   Historical Data—Case Shipments of Southern Comfort Corporation

Calendar Years	U.S. Domestic	Export	Canada	Total
1958	109,347	2,380	5,635	117,362
1959	123,928	2,528	6,000	132,456
1960	145,667	2,621	6,707	154,995
1961	149,998	2,778	7,166	159,942
1962	168,063	3,409	7,505	178,977
1963	182,220	4,746	8,225	195,191
1964	210,331	5,569	9,600	225,500
1965	269,687	9,662	12,540	291,889
1966	332,719	8,937	15,518	357,174
1967	381,457	12,253	18,408	412,118
1968	443,993	16,024	19,484	479,501
1969	524,171	15,945	23,334	563,450
1970	541,832	20,784	26,923	589,539
1971	617,201	39,031	36,129	692,361
1972	684,115	61,184	48,478	793,777
1973	716,798	190,678	61,828	969,304
1974	829,341	232,795	70,407	1,132,543
1975	850,778	289,123	85,141	1,125,042
1976	904,993	291,185	95,070	1,291,248
1977	1,047,896	303,916	111,566	1,463,378
20-Year compound growth	11.9%	27.44%	16%	13.45%
5-Year compound growth	8.8%	37.8%	18.2%	13%

Source: Southern Comfort Corporation records.

EXHIBIT 9 Assumptions Used in Southern Comfort Cash Flow Forecast (in dollars except for case volumes (in units) and expenses (in $000))

	1978	1979	1980	1981	1982	1983	1984	1985	1986	1987	1988
Profit per case											
U.S. domestic revenue	$49.62	$50.62	$51.42	$52.42	$52.92	$53.92	$54.92	$55.92	$56.92	$57.92	$58.92
Cost of goods	33.52	34.10	34.75	35.41	36.14	36.93	37.78	38.70	39.70	40.77	41.93
Advertising	4.07	4.01	3.80	3.68	3.83	3.89	3.92	3.97	3.33	3.18	3.37
Selling:											
Regular	0.55	0.58	0.59	0.60	0.61	0.62	0.63	0.63	0.65	0.67	0.70
Transition	0.71	0.34	0.15								
Export:											
Revenue	19.21	20.32	21.50	22.55	23.21	23.80	25.16	26.15	27.15	28.15	29.15
		7.08 and increases at 8% annually thereafter.									
Cost of goods	1.44	1.38	1.37	1.37	1.37	1.36	1.37	1.37	1.37	1.37	1.37
Brokerage	2.75	2.76	2.75	2.85	2.72	2.69	2.68	2.67	2.67	2.67	2.67
Selling exp.	0.05	0.05	0.05	0.06	0.06	0.06	0.06	0.06	0.07	0.07	0.08
Canada:											
Royalty	3.48	3.48	3.48	3.48	3.48	3.48	4.00	4.00	4.00	4.00	4.00
Concentrate profit	1.55	1.55	1.55	1.55	1.55	1.55	1.55	1.55	1.55	1.55	1.55
Case volumes (in thousands)											
U.S.	1,140	1,225	1,315	1,410	1,510	1,615	1,725	1,835	1,923	1,984	2,015
Export	325	350	380	405	425	445	463	480	490	500	500
Canada	115	125	138	150	160	170	180	190	200	210	220
Corporate level*											
G&A expense	$1,665	$1,800	$1,944	$2,100	$2,268	$2,449	$2,645	$2,857	$3,086	$3,332	$3,599
Transition	430	380	180								
Settlements		400	400	400	400						
Interest expense†	113	122	132	142	154	166	179	194	209	226	244

* For forecasting purposes, it could be expected that investment to maintain plant and equipment would just be offset by depreciation expense. But there would be some additional investment in working capital as sales grew.

† On seasonal borrowings for working-capital financing. Analysts at Brown-Forman viewed this item as virtually an operating expense and considered including it in their forecast of free cash flows.

Source: Brown-Forman Distillers Corporation estimates.

EXHIBIT 10 Stock Price Data

	Brown-Forman		
	Class A	*Class B*	*S&P 500 Index*
1/3/78	19.875	20.00	93.82
2/1/78	19.75	19.375	89.93
3/1/78	20.50	20.50	87.19
4/3/78	21.875	21.25	88.46
5/1/78	23.50	23.75	97.67
6/1/78	24.75	24.875	97.35
6/2/78	24.875	25.00	98.14
6/9/78	25.625	26.375	99.93
6/16/78	26.375	27.00	97.42
6/23/78	26.00	26.50	95.85
6/30/78	25.625	24.875	95.53

Source: *ISL Daily Stock Price Record*, Standard & Poor's Corporation.

Aguas Minerales S.A. and Cadbury Schweppes PLC.

In February 1992, the mergers and acquisitions team of the Latin American department of Bankers Trust ("the Bankers Trust team") received the telephone call from Cadbury Schweppes PLC: Bankers Trust was awarded the role of sole advisor in its attempt to fully or partially acquire Mexico's Aguas Minerales S.A. (AMSA). AMSA is the wholly owned mineral water subsidiary of Mexico City-based Fomento Economico Mexicano S.A. (FEMSA), a producer of beer, mineral water, and other beverages.

This would be one of the largest acquisitions of a Mexican business by an overseas company. The country setting and the fact that Cadbury Schweppes currently competes with FEMSA's soft-drink business unit led the Bankers Trust team to conclude that valuation would not be easy.

FEMSA'S BACKGROUND

FEMSA was founded in 1890 by Isaac Garza and his brother-in-law, Francisco Sada, as the Cuauhtemoc Brewery in northeast Mexico. During the first quarter of this century, they expanded to other regions by opening new plants. During World War II, Garza, Sada, and their heirs began manufacturing steel to ensure an adequate supply of bottle caps. Around that time, they also expanded into financial services by acquiring Banca Serfin, the oldest bank in Mexico. In the 1970s, the brewery operation and Banca Serfin were spun off into a new group of family-owned companies called Valores Industriales S. A. (VISA). This group was led by Eugenio Garza.

In the second half of the 1970s, Garza, like many Mexican industrialists, got into financial trouble. During the boom years of the 1970s and early 1980s, credit was cheap

---

This case was developed by Pedro Beroy (T' 92) and Associate Professor Anant K. Sundaram of the Amos Tuck School, as a basis for class discussion. The Amos Tuck School, © 1992.

and VISA borrowed freely to diversify; it expanded into soft drinks and mineral water, as well as into unrelated fields like hotels, animal feed, and automotive parts. When the price of oil declined in 1982, so did VISA's businesses, which by then had accumulated over $1 billion in debt.

On top of all this, President Lopez Portillo's administration nationalized Banca Serfin. Desperate to raise cash, Garza sold VISA's hotels and other businesses unrelated to its core beverage and packaging businesses. In the reorganization of VISA's capital structure, Garza included World Bank's International Finance Corporation, Mexico's state-owned development bank NAFINSA, and Citicorp as new lenders.

In 1988, VISA undertook a debt-for-equity restructuring. The restructuring eliminated three quarters of VISA's $1.7 billion debt and gave its new creditors approximately 20 percent of the equity in a newly created, publicly traded beverage and packaging company called Fomento Economico Mexicano S.A., or FEMSA. VISA retained 60 percent of FEMSA and 20 percent of the shares traded on Mexico's stock exchange (Bolsa de Mexico). Grupo Proa, a private holding company (51 percent owned by Garza's family), owned around 80 percent of VISA (Garza's share is currently worth $550 million). The remaining 20 percent trades on Mexico's Bolsa. Grupo Proa also owns 60 percent of the insurance group, Valores de Monterrey S.A. or Vamsa (Garza's share in this is currently worth $200 million). The rest of the shares are publicly traded (see Exhibit 1).

By 1990, FEMSA was Mexico's fifth-largest company, with 1990 revenues exceeding $1.7 billion and net income in excess of $120 million. It was the nation's largest beverage company and the 13th-largest brewery in the world. This rapid growth was achieved through the acquisition of additional beer (Superior, Dos Equis, and Sol), soft drink, and mineral water brands. FEMSA acquired the Mexico City and southeastern Mexico Coca-Cola franchises and the flagship mineral water brands, Penafiel, Aguas de Tehuacan, and Balseca. FEMSA had a leadership position in all the segments it competed: 51 percent share of the brewery market; 59 percent of the soft-drink market; and 80 percent share of the flavored and unflavored mineral water market (see Exhibit 2).

In October 1991, VISA acquired 51 percent of Bancomer, the second-largest bank in Mexico with $28 billion in assets, for $2.6 billion (three times book value). The acquisition was financed with new stock issues worth $1 billion, debt worth $1 billion, and cash. To help finance Bancomer's acquisition, FEMSA announced that it would sell interests in its beverage operations.

FEMSA looked for investors with international beverage experience that could form a joint venture with it, provide marketing and operational expertise, and contribute significant potential for added shareholder value. In any event, the first divestiture—it was not clear whether it should be a full or partial divestiture—would be FEMSA's mineral water business, AMSA.

AMSA

AMSA bottled and franchised five brands: Penafiel, Balseca, Etiqueta Azul, Catemaco, and Extra Poma. Penafiel was the largest-selling mineral water brand in Mexico. Balseca was a strong regional brand in southeastern Mexico, and Etiqueta Azul was a discounted regional brand primarily sold through FEMSA's Coca-Cola bottling division. In 1991, Aguas Minerales made a pre-tax profit of $24.4 million (pesos 73.1 billion), on sales of $161.6 million (pesos 484.4 billion). AMSA was considered by industry experts to be a well-managed, operationally (rather than financially) driven company.

AMSA's product line included a portfolio of flavored and unflavored mineral waters positioned as "sourced from famous wells, intrinsically pure, and of high quality." The business owned five bottling plants with natural springs. In the Mexican mineral water industry, as opposed to the U.K. or France, waters are not required to be source-dependent. The law permits it to be sourced with high-quality water from wells anywhere in Mexico.

THE SOFT-DRINK MARKET

In 1991, the Mexican carbonated soft-drink market was one of the largest in the world, with annual sales of 2.8 billion gallons (at a price of approximately $1.07 per gallon). Mexico's per capita consumption was 34 gallons per person per year, which was more than half as much as in the United Kingdom. Colas represented 60 percent of total carbonates and flavored drinks accounted for the rest. Coca-Cola and Pepsi had a 47 percent share and 17 percent share, respectively, of total carbonates. The market had grown at 9 percent per year from 1987 to 1990 and had a forecasted growth of 6 percent per year (including the population growth of 2 percent per year). This indicated per capita consumption growth of 4 percent per year until the year 2000.

The bottled water market was underdeveloped, in comparison to other segments of the carbonates markets, representing only 5 percent of total soft drinks (142 million gallons). However, this market segment has been growing at nearly 12 percent per year since 1985.

Historically, prices for carbonated soft drinks in Mexico have been lower than world prices, and, despite the large volume, both franchisers and bottlers experienced marginal profitability. However, there were significant price increases in the last three years.

THE BANKERS TRUST TEAM'S FINANCIAL VALUATION ASSUMPTIONS

As a first step, the Bankers Trust team drew up an estimated base-case income statement and balance sheet for AMSA for financial year 1991 (Exhibit 5).

From a 1991 base, the team assumed sales (volume) growth of 9 percent per year through 1995, 5 percent per year from 1996 to 2000, and 2 percent per year thereafter. The team supported these assumptions with the following arguments:

Advertising: Since 1989, AMSA had supported its 80 percent market share of carbonated waters with national television advertising. In the past, no other Mexican water brand could afford such an investment.

New products and packaging: AMSA introduced Penafiel Light in 1990, and the Bankers Trust team believed that this flavored mineral water could grow without cannibalizing the rest of the product portfolio. The team believed that plastic bottles would become a key factor in the Mexican carbonated soft-drink industry, and it saw that significant capital expenditures behind this packaging of Penafiel represented a major portion of the projected growth rate of 9 percent.

Pricing: Since 1988, Mexico's inflation had declined in part due to "el Pacto," an annual agreement among government, business, and labor. Price increases at the consumer and retail levels were authorized nationally, and transportation services and energy were subsidized. In 1992, the Salinas' administration was expected to lower the IVA tax (value added tax) from 15 percent to 10 percent, which could support a net 4.6 percent price increase.

The Bankers Trust team expected revenues to increase by an achievable price increase. The valuation presumed a 28 percent increase in mineral water prices through December 1992. Assuming a small negative impact on next year's volume, it would increase overall revenues. During the longer term, Garza assumed price growth roughly in line with inflation.

If the North American Free Trade Agreement (NAFTA) came to fruition, it was expected to close the gap between U.S. and Mexican consumer prices, mainly in the beverage and cigarette industries (see Exhibit 6).

Capital expenditures: Between 1992 and 1996, the casewriters estimate that new capital expenditures would equal approximately 8 percent of sales. Thereafter, capital expenditures are expected to be at the same level as depreciation.

Currency: Given the considerable presence (and long-term plans) that Cadbury Schweppes had in the United States, it would not be inappropriate to undertake the valuation in US$. Data on projected inflation and exchange rates for Mexico are provided in Exhibits 7 and 8.

Tax rates: Corporate tax rate calculations are complicated in Mexico. There are two basic tax rates, consisting of a regular tax rate of 35 percent, and a "profit-sharing tax rate" of 10 percent. Moreover, the Mexican government required firms to set up a pension plan from 1992, whereby AMSA would have to set aside 10 percent of the pre-tax income; however, this amount would be tax deductible. In addition to this, there is a "net asset tax" rate of 2 percent that is based on a complicated inflation-adjustment formula, involving revaluation of fixed and current assets.

The Bankers Trust team estimated the net result of these tax rules to be approximately 20 percent of the post-pension plan income per year until 1995 and approximately 30 percent per year thereafter.

MEXICO'S ECONOMIC RECOVERY

The severe economic setbacks of the 1980s—Mexico's *"lost decade"*—shocked it into abandoning the statism, populism, and protectionism that had crippled its economy since colonial times. Mexico's economic style of the 1980s was to build infant industries protected with high tariffs (to achieve self-sufficiency), to discourage foreign investment seen as "imperialist," to disregard "experts," to allow fiscal deficits to grow, to nationalize near-bankrupt firms where jobs were at risk, and to borrow heavily from the only-too-willing foreign banks.

The cycle ended in August 1982. The administration of President Jose Lopez Portillo proposed a moratorium on the $19.5 billion of principal payments due in 1982 and 1983. His successor, Miguel de la Madrid, had little choice but to embark on a politically costly process of reform.

On December 1, 1988, Carlos Salinas de Gortari took office. He led the current Mexican economic recovery and built closer ties to the United States. The reforms established by the Salinas administration were characterized by drastic restructuring of its external debt under the Brady Plan, entering into international trade agreements (joining GATT and negotiating NAFTA with the United States and Canada), an aggressive privatization program, and support for Mexico's emerging private capital markets.

The consequence of the structural changes was an overall improvement in most economic indicators. In May 1989, the Salinas government unveiled its national development plan (Plan Nacional de Desarrollo) for 1989–94. The plan had two principal goals: (1) gradual increase in GDP growth from 1.5 percent in 1989 to 6 percent in 1994; and (2) gradual decrease in inflation rates to 9 percent by 1994 (see Exhibit 7). In addition to fiscal restraint, it was hoped that monetary and exchange rate policies would produce stable real interest rates and exchange rates (see Exhibit 8).

The renewed confidence in the Mexican economy meant that Mexican companies could now access international capital markets. Lowered inflation rates and nominal interest rates led to a narrowing of the spreads between Eurobonds issued by Mexican companies and United States treasuries of similar maturity—the average spread, reflecting country risk, was about 250 basis points (see Exhibit 9).

Mexican companies accessed equity financing not only through the domestic stock exchange (Bolsa de Mexico) and through American Depository Receipts (ADRs). By 1991, the P/E gap between United States and Mexican companies had narrowed considerably (Exhibit 10).

Mexican companies continue to raise capital by issuing debt in the Mexican market. The recent economic reforms had decreased the cost of borrowing (see Exhibit 11).

CADBURY SCHWEPPES PLC

Cadbury Schweppes PLC and its subsidiaries comprise an international group of companies engaged in the manufacturing, marketing, and distribution of branded confectionery and beverage products. Cadbury Schweppes was formed in 1969 through a merger of Cadbury Group Limited and Schweppes Limited. Cadbury originally was formed in 1831 as a family enterprise to produce cocoa and drinking chocolate. The Schweppes business was established by Jacob Schweppe in the late 18th century and was incorporated with the name Schweppes Limited in 1897.

In 1991, Cadbury Schweppes' net sales were $5.6 billion (£3.2 billion, at the current exchange rate of $1.75/£), and operating income was $644 million (£362.5 million; Exhibit 12). The company employed over 35,000 people and its products were sold in more than 140 countries. Its brands included the well-known Schweppes and Canada Dry lines of carbonated beverages. Other brands included Sunkist carbonated drinks, the Crush line of carbonated orange and other fruit flavors, Hires Root Beer, Sundrop, Pure Spring, and Old Colony carbonates. In the UK, a joint venture between Cadbury Schweppes (51 percent) and the Coca-Cola Company (49 percent) bottled, canned, and distributed Coca-Cola and Cadbury's soft drinks.

Cadbury Schweppes' subsidiary, Cadbury Beverages International, manufactured, bottled, and marketed its soft drinks in Europe. The subsidiary aimed to expand its market share in North and South America in both beverages and confections, through joint ventures and acquisitions (see Exhibit 13 for their recent past acquisitions).

Since the early 1980s, Cadbury Beverages International had achieved a healthy presence in Mexico's beverage market with its popular Orange Crush soda and its Canada Dry soft drinks. Acquiring AMSA would reinforce its Mexican presence and would be consistent with its growth strategy. AMSA's sales volume was larger than Cadbury Beverages International's businesses in France, Spain, or Australia.

POTENTIAL SYNERGIES

The acquisition provided an opportunity for synergies through a shared distribution system. The key success factor in Mexico was aggressive distribution. With 30 percent of the population living in rural areas and with low levels of car ownership even in urban areas, supermarkets played only a small role in soft-drink distribution. Therefore, the main channel was the small grocery store and the street vendors. Despite an area equal to one third of the United States, distribution channels were more dispersed and consumers more expensive to reach.

Orange Crush represented 77 percent of Cadbury Beverages International's 1991 volume in Mexico. The current Crush bottler network covered around 128,000 outlets out of Mexico's total 810,000 soft-drink outlets. This network covered around 19 percent of the Mexican population. AMSA's brands were distributed through the same outlets and had 50 percent penetration. The company expected to increase its Orange Crush penetration up to AMSA's levels by 1996. The current market size for carbonated soft drinks is approximately 2.8 billion gallons, at an average price of $1.07 per gallon, and the casewriters' estimate of Cadbury Scweppes' current sales is approximately 50 million gallons. Further, the casewriters estimate that the net income margin in this business would be approximately 6 percent.

CONSIDERATIONS IN FINANCING THE ACQUISITION

Cadbury Beverages International was undecided about how to finance the proposed acquisition. Issuing stock in the London Stock Exchange could have a dilution effect—and unknown signaling effects. The company was worried about the softness of the stock market following the news of the Labour Party's five-point lead in the polls in March 19. On March 18, 1992, Cadbury's shares closed at 443p. on the London Stock Exchange.

On the other hand, a stock issue in the United States or London could attract investors looking to diversify their equity interests into the booming Mexican market (during the period 1985–1990, the correlation coefficient between total returns on an index of Mexican stocks and the returns on the S&P 500 was 0.46, on an exchange rate adjusted basis).

The company recently had undertaken a leveraged recapitalization to defend itself against a possible unfriendly takeover by Philip Morris, and, as a result, its net debt is expected to rise from $592 million (£333 million) to about $782 million (£440 million).

Finally, given its past experience with debt, FEMSA would be averse to any additional debt on its balance sheet—this would be a consideration if the divestiture was partial and if Cadbury Beverages International wished to enter a joint venture agreement with FEMSA.

THE BANKERS TRUST TEAM'S FINAL CONCERNS

Assessing the appropriate cost of equity for the acquisition presented something of a problem, since AMSA is not a publicly traded company. Firms in lines of business similar to that of AMSA in the United States had betas that ranged from 0.9 to 1.1. The question that troubled Bankers Trust was whether the cost of capital for AMSA should reflect an appropriate premium for country risk—after all, the bond markets reflected such a premium, so why not equity markets?

Cadbury's management was concerned about the possibility of new competition and about AMSA's source-water quality. AMSA's biggest competitive risk would be that Coca-Cola decided to launch its own mineral water brand in Mexico. Although Coca-Cola was inexperienced in the mineral water market, the passage of NAFTA could be a factor.

Cadbury Beverages International analyzed AMSA's source waters at each of the well locations and confirmed that the water quality was acceptable.

Another major concern in selling AMSA to Cadbury was that FEMSA and Cadbury Beverages International competed in the soft-drink business—this acquisition could help Cadbury Beverages International strengthen its brands in Mexico by cannibalizing FEMSA's sales.

Bankers Trust also was concerned that completion of the deal was subject to certain commercial and regulatory conditions in Mexico (and Mexican government approvals). Mexico's foreign investment law allows 100 percent ownership of qualifying investments by foreign firms without prior authorization from the Foreign Investment Commission, but only if the investment does not exceed $100 million.

EXHIBIT 1 FEMSA's Ownership Structure

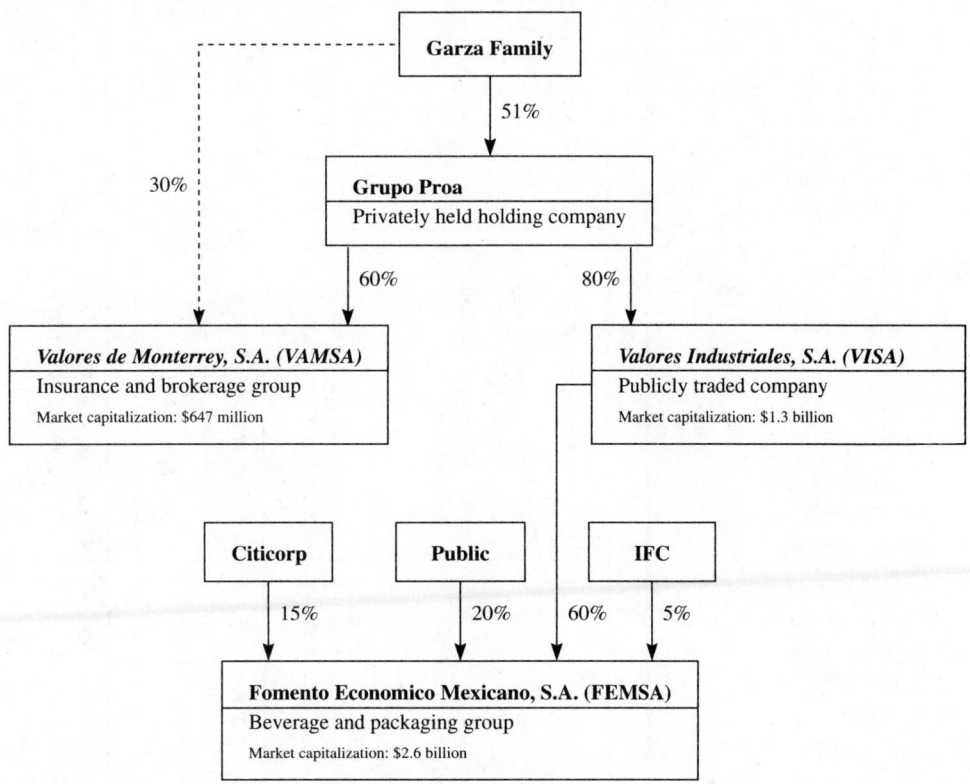

Source: C. Poole, "The Resurrection of Don Eugenio," *Forbes*, February 17, 1992.

EXHIBIT 2 FEMSA's Business Segments

	Activity	Main Companies	Main Products	Assets	Sales	Employ.
Beer Division	Beer	Cerveceria Cuauhtemoc Cerveceria Moctezuma Carta Blanca de Occidente Servicios Industriales y Comerciales Codicome del Centro Codicome del Sureste	Carta Blanca, Superior, Tecate, XX Lager, Bohemia, Sol, Indio, and Heineken Beers	3,141	2,037	19,213
	Convenience Stores	Cadena Comercial (Oxxo Stores)	Retailing of Convenience Products	84	317	867
	Marketing Supports	Vendo de Mexico, Anuncios y Servicios, Fomento Comercial, Distribucion y Comer de Hielo y Gas	Ice, Coolers, and Panoramic Advertising	32	50	500
Soft-Drink Division	Cola and Flavoured Soft Drinks	Industria Embotelladora de Mexico Embotelladora de Tlalnepantla Embotelladora del Istmo Refrescos de Oaxaca Embotelladora Sin Rival Distribuidora de Bebidas del Valle de Mexico Distribuidora Surena	Coca Cola, Diet Coke, Sprite, Fanta, and Sin Rival Soft Drinks	424	529	5,605

Division	Subdivision	Company	Products			
Mineral Waters Division	Mineral Waters	Manantiales Penafiel Extractora y Embotelladora de Aguas Minerales Productos Balseca Compania Exportadora de Aguas Minerales	Penafiel, Balseca, Etiqueta Azul, Extra Poma, and Dietafiel Mineral Waters	257	198	3,727
Packaging Division	Metallic Packaging	Fabricas Monterrey Partes Industriales Mecanicas	Beverage Cans, Foodstuff Cans, Crown Caps, and Caps	407	361	1,889
	Glass	Silices de Veracruz	Glass Bottles and Silicious Sand	105	60	527
	Flexible Packaging	Grafo Regia	Labels, Laminations and Wrappers for Cigarettes, Soaps, Chewing Gum, Snacks, and Milk	155	87	581
	Cardboard and Paper	Corrugados Tehuacan Celulosa y Papel de Xalapa	Corrugated Cardboard Boxes and Paper	25	44	379
	Plastics	Plasticos Tecnicos Mexicanos	Soft Drink Cases, Coolers, Containers, and Chairs	51	32	366
	Chemical Products	Quimiproductos	Detergents, Lubricants, and Adhesives	10	17	146

Note: All financial data is provided in billions of 1988's pesos.

EXHIBIT 3   FEMSA and Subsidiaries' Financial Statements (A)

**Consolidated Income Statement
For the years ended December 31
(amounts in billions of pesos)**

	1989	*1990*
Net sales	4,522	4,783
Other operating revenue	67	79
Total revenues	4,589	4,862
Cost of sales	(2,881)	(2,984)
Gross profit	1,708	1,878
Operating expenses:		
Administrative	(556)	(622)
Selling	(746)	(811)
Total operating expenses	(1,302)	(1,433)
Income from operations	406	445
Integral cost of financing:		
Interest, net	(235)	(231)
Foreign exchange loss, net	(133)	(68)
Gain on monetary position	212	278
Total cost of financing	(156)	(21)
Other expenses, net	(47)	(55)
Income before income tax, tax on assets,	203	369
employee profit sharing, and extraordinary credits		
Income tax, tax on assets, and employee profit sharing	(74)	(177)
Extraordinary credit derived from utilization of tax loss carryforward	24	112
Extraordinary income due to debt prepayment and other	135	39
Net income for the year	288	343

Source: FEMSA annual report.

EXHIBIT 4 FEMSA and Subsidiaries' Financial Statements (B)

Consolidated Balance Sheet
At December 31
(in billions of pesos)

Assets	1989	1990
Current assets:		
Cash and marketable securities	221	105
Accounts receivable:		
Notes	16	19
Trade	239	290
Other	39	47
Total accounts receivable	294	356
Inventories:		
Finished products and in process	150	174
Raw materials and supplies	608	708
Total inventories	758	882
Prepaid expenses	26	27
Total current assets	1,299	1,370
Investments and other assets:		
Shares and securities	26	8
Long-term notes	0	0
Other assets	1	0
Total investments and other assets	27	8
Property, plant, and equipment:		
Land	413	437
Buildings, machinery and equipment, net	4,606	4,874
Construction in progress	127	136
Total property, plant, and equipment	5,147	5,447
Deferred charges, net	38	52
Total assets	6,511	6,877

Liabilities and Shareholders' Equity	1989	1990
Current liabilities:		
Bank loans	82	185
Notes payable	3	5
Current maturities of long-term debt	0	68
Accrued interest	22	16
Suppliers	202	291
Accrued taxes	117	107
Accounts payable, accrued expenses and other liabilities	80	115
Total current liabilities	506	787
Long-term liabilities:		
Bank loans and debentures	1,042	879
Notes payable	20	10
Current maturities of long-term debt	0	(68)
Total long-term liabilities	1,062	821
Seniority premium and other liabilities	32	31
Stockholders' equity:		
Minority interest in consolidated subsidiaries	8	10
Majority interest:		
Capital stock	253	253
Additional paid-in-capital	2,995	2,995
Retained earnings	989	1,277
Net income for the year	288	343
Holding gain on nonmonetary assets	378	360
Total majority interest	4,903	5,228
Total stockholders' equity	4,911	5,238
Total liabilities and stockholders' equity	6,511	6,877

Source: FEMSA annual report.

621

EXHIBIT 5   AMSA—Base Case (1991) Estimated Income Statement and Balance Sheet

Estimated Income Statement (all figures in US$ mn)		*Estimated Balance Sheet (all figures in US$ mn)*	
Cases sold (000s)	54,202	Surplus cash	8.00
Annual growth (%)	*5.04*	Cash for operations	3.50
Sales	**161.60**	Accnts receivable—trade	6.60
Variable manufacturing cost	40.90	Inventories	6.00
Variable selling cost	42.80	Prepaids	2.00
Total variable cost	**83.70**	Accnts receivable—nontrade	21.00
Gross Margin	77.90	**Total current assets**	**47.00**
Gross margin/sales (%)	*48.20*	PPE	113.50
Marketing cost	8.30	Deferred tax assets	
Production salaries	4.90	Other assets	
Production—other	8.30	**Total assets**	**160.60**
Selling and dist'n salaries	7.90	Short-term debt	2.00
Selling and dist'n—other	7.60	Payables—trade	4.00
Admin salaries	7.20	Affiliated creditors	4.00
Admin—other	5.00	Payables—nontrade	8.00
Depreciation	4.30	Tax payable	5.30
Total Fixed Cost	**53.50**	**Total current liabilities**	**23.30**
Operating profit/sales (%)	*15.10*	**Long-term debt**	**36.30**
Interest expense	0.00	Common stock and paid-in capital	67.30
Interest income	0.00	Preferred stock	0.00
Pre-tax income	**24.40**	Retained earnings	33.70
Employee profit sharing*	0.00	Treasury stock	0.00
Taxable income	**24.40**	**Total equity**	**101.00**
Effective tax rate (%)	*45.00*	**Total liabilities and equity**	**160.60**
Income taxes	11.00		
Net income	**13.40**		

* Will be 10% of PTI from 1992.

EXHIBIT 6   Consumer Prices (in U.S. cents) in the United States and Mexico

Industry	Price in Mexico	U.S. Price
Cigarettes	59	200
Beer	32	58
Soft drinks	16	50
Mineral water	19	70

Source: Bankers Trust Company, March 1992.

EXHIBIT 7   Mexico's GDP and Inflation Rates

	Real GDP Growth/Yr. (%)	Inflation/Yr. (%)
1960–1970	5.5%	5%
1970–1976	6.2	13
1977–1982	6.0	42
1983–1988	−1.0	92
1989–1991	2.9–3.5%	20–25%
1992–1996 est.	5.3–6.0%	9–15%

Source: The *Economist* Intelligence Unit.

EXHIBIT 8 Mexico's Exchange-Rate Analysis (note 1)

	1985	1986	1987	1988	1989	1990	1991	1992	1993	1994	1995	1996
Exchange rate (note 2)	371	923	2200	2320	2683	2948						
Exchange rate (note 3)	256	611	1378	2272	2474	2831						
Projected (note 4)							3025	3136	3210	3277	3339	3403

Note 1: All exchange rates in peso/US$.
2: End of period. Source: International Finance Corporation.
3: Average of period. Source: International Finance Corporation.
4: Average of period. Source: VISA.

EXHIBIT 9   Major Eurobonds Issued by the Mexican Government

Eurobond	Due Date	BP Spread (note 1)
2008 Aztec	31-Mar-08	406
Par bonds	31-Dec-19	277
Discount bonds	31-Dec-19	367
MYRA	16-Nov-06	461
Banobras 10.75%	16-Aug-96	282
BNCE 9.875%	24-Jun-96	208
NAFINSA 11.75%	02-Aug-85	276
NAFINSA 10%	14-May-96	217
NAFINSA 10.625%	22-Nov-01	259
Pemex 10%	15-Mar-93	222
Pemex 11.625%	25-Oct-93	193
Pemex 17.75%	01-Jun-94	265
Pemex 10.25%	06-Oct-98	209

Note 1: Basis points over U.S. T-bonds of same maturity; the current U.S. T-bill rate is 6%, and yield on long-term U.S. government bonds is 7.9%.

Source: Bankers Trust Company, March 1992.

EXHIBIT 10   P/E Comparison between Mexican and U.S. Firms

Industry	Mexican Company	P/E	International Equivalent	P/E
Packaged goods	Bimbo	21	Gerber Products	21
	Tablex	16	CPC	17
Retailing	Cifra	21	Kmart	12
	Commercial	17	Sears	13
Paper	Kimberly Clark	14	Kimberly Clark	15
Cement	Cemex	13	LaFarge	11
	Tilomex	15	Holderbank	12
Container	Vitro	13	Ball Corp.	17

Source: Banker Trust Company, March 1992.

EXHIBIT 11   Cost of Debt for Mexican Companies

Company	Due Date	Yield to Maturity (%)
Apasco 10.25%	11-Dec-96	9.86%
Barton 12%	20-Sep-93	8.29
Cemex 9.41%	21-May-96	10.00
Dynaworld 10.5%	17-Jan-96	9.88
Novum 12%	27-Sep-93	9.97

Source: Bankers Trust Company, March 1992.

EXHIBIT 12 Cadbury Schweppes and Subsidiaries' Financial Statements

Consolidated Statements of Income
For the 52 weeks ended December 30, 1989, December 29, 1990, and December 28, 1991
(in millions except for share data)

	1989	1990	1991
Net sales	£2,777	£3,146	£3,232
Cost of sales	(£1,597)	(£1,738)	(£1,736)
Gross margin	£1,180	£1,408	£1,496
SG&A	(£906)	(£1,705)	(£1,130)
Other operating income (expense)	£0	£1	(£4)
Operating income	£274	£334	£363
Equity in earnings of associated companies	£3	£3	£11
Net interest espense	(£31)	(£57)	(£57)
Inc. before taxes, M.I., and exir. items (note 1)	£246	£280	£316
Taxes on income	(£70)	(£78)	(£88)
Inc. before M.I. and extraordinary items	£176	£202	£228
Minority interest	(£17)	(£22)	(£25)
Income before extraordinary items	£159	£179	£203
Extraordinary items net of tax	£14	£0	£0
Preference dividends	£0	(£3)	(£9)
Net income for ordinary shareholders	£173	£176	£194
Earnings per ordinary share	£27	£25	£28

Sources: SEC; Cadbury Schweppes annual report, May 1, 1992.
Note 1: Income before taxes, minority interest, and extraordinary items.

Consolidated Balance Sheet
At December 29, 1990, and December 28, 1991
(in millions)

	1990	1991
Assets		
Current assets:		
Cash	£63	£85
Investments at cost	£118	£262
Acc. receivable and prepayments	£554	£579
Inventories	£328	£332
Total current assets	£1,063	£1,258
Long-term investments	£17	£34
Trademarks	£304	£308
Property, plant, and equipment (net)	£979	£1,054
Total assets	£2,362	£2,655
Liabilities, Minority Interest, and Shareholders' Equity		
Current liabilities:		
Short-term borrowing and current portion of L.T. debt:		
Bank loans and overdrafts	£60	£72
Capital leases and others	£76	£66
Income taxes	£78	£95
Acc. payable and accrued interest:		
Trade creditors	£272	£275
Accruals and deferred income	£255	£275
Other taxes and social security costs	£66	£83
Customer deposits	£50	£33
Dividends proposed	£61	£67
Other payable	£44	£66
Total current liabilities	£962	£1,033
Long-term debt, less current portion	£408	£542
Restructuring provisions	£83	£27
Deferred tax	(£4)	(£1)
Other long-term liabilities	£29	£65
Total liabilities	£1,479	£1,666
Minority interests	£116	£112
Shareholders' equity:		
Preference shares	£0	£0
Ordinary shares	£174	£176
Premiums in excess of par values	£382	£394
Revaluation surplus	£96	£100
Retained earnings	£116	£207
Total shareholders' equity	£768	£877
Total liabilities, minority interest, and S.E.	£2,362	£2,655

EXHIBIT 13 Major Cross-Border Acquisitions by Cadbury Beverages International

Year	Country	Company or Brands	Comments
1987	Australia	Beatrice Australia	
1987	United States	Taylor Food Products	Owns "Red Cheek" apple juice
1988	France	Chocolat Poulain SA	Confectionary manufacturer
1989	United Kingdom	Basset Foods PLC	Sugar, confectionery
1989	Spain	Chocolates Hueso SA	Chocolate, sugar, confectionery
1989	Canada	ED Smith & Sons, Ltd.	
1990	Belgium & Luxembourg	N.V. Gibeco	The Gini franchise
1990	France	Oasis, Atoll & Bali	Noncola soft-drink business of Source Perrier
1991	Germany & Austria	Apollinaris Brunnen AG	Mineral water

Source: Cadbury Schweppes annual report, 1992.

Case 44

Gallery of Furs, Inc.: Fur-Industry Merger Exercise

In August 1989, Sally Browning, president and chief executive officer of Gallery of Furs, Inc., faced a dilemma that many senior executives would find daunting: how to dismember her firm, which had been hemorrhaging cash for the past 18 months. A bloc of dissident common stockholders had accumulated enough shares to elect two directors to Gallery of Furs' board and was now insisting that the company's assets be deployed to maximize shareholder value. Such a deployment could mean only one thing: the sale or liquidation of the firm's Fur Retailing Division, which was a chain of fur-garment stores and the larger of Gallery's two operating divisions. Under pressure from the dissidents, Browning would need to recommend to the board a method of deployment, a target sale price, and a timetable for execution. The main choices appeared to be the following:

- **Targeted and negotiated sale:** potential buyers were large direct competitors, such as Adams, Inc., and the new Finnish owners of Potemkin Furs. Also, a vertically integrated foreign firm, Jindo Corporation, had been expanding aggressively in the United States and might be interested in Gallery of Furs' stores. Finally, a Canadian fur-garment producer, Groupe Lessard, Ltd., was thought to be considering the acquisition of retail outlets in the United States.
- **Auction sale:** the directors would publicly announce a desire to sell certain assets and would invite any and all bidders to participate.

This case was prepared by Robert F. Bruner with the assistance of Salomon Brothers, Inc., and Jindo Corporation. Identities and information have been disguised for companies and persons other than Jindo and Salomon.

Copyright © 1991 by the Darden Graduate Business School Foundation, Charlottesville, VA. Revised August 1993.

FUR-GARMENT RETAILERS

THE INDUSTRY

Whether measured internationally or within specific countries, the fur-garment retailing industry was highly fragmented, with no individual firm accounting for more than 4 percent of worldwide sales. Indeed, most furriers were privately held, single-store operations targeted toward the high-price, high-quality segment of the market. A fur coat could vary in price from $500 for rabbit to $250,000 for Russian lynx belly, although a typical mink coat would cost between $8,000 and $15,000.

The annual worldwide retail trade in fur garments was estimated to be $6.5 billion for 1989.[1] Sales in the United States for 1989 were forecasted to range between $2.5 and $1.5 billion. Actual U.S. fur-garment sales for 1986 and 1987 each were about $1.8 billion.

The uncertainty about the actual size of the market arose from the current turmoil in the industry. First, the evidence was that industry sales had receded dramatically from their peak in 1987. Second, furriers were consolidating or leaving the industry at a fast rate.

Sales in 1988 were off 35 percent from 1987, and the preliminary figures for the first half of 1989 suggested continuing decline. The decline in demand had forced many retailers to liquidate their inventories at deep discounts from original ticket prices. As a result, profit margins had deteriorated across the entire industry. Also, inventory values had contracted, which triggered mandatory loan repayments, because many furriers' working-capital lines were set as a percentage of inventory.

The financial decline of the industry was attributed to several causes. First was the stock market crash of October 1987, which triggered a recession in sales of many luxury products but particularly of fur garments in the New York area. This recession, in turn, set in process the cycle of aggressive discounting and operating losses. Second, pelt prices had fallen, which caused unrealized inventory losses and the contraction of borrowing-base loans. Third, animal-rights activists claimed to have depressed the demand for fur garments by aggressive agitation against the purchase of these items. These activists had been especially prominent in Europe in 1986 and 1987. In 1988, New York City saw sizable marches, leafleting, picketing of furriers, and harassment of fur-coat wearers. In addition, several smoke-bomb attacks on stores and bomb threats had occurred. Fourth, retailers themselves were reluctant to admit to any permanent change in the buying patterns of the public, other than to say that the winters of 1988 and 1989 had been warmer than usual.

The turmoil in 1987 and 1988 had begun a process of shake-out in the fur-garment retailing industry around the world. In 1988, over 20 furriers went out of business in London alone. The third-largest fur-garment retailer in the United States, Potemkin Furs in Chicago, founded by Nikolas Potemkin, had been bought out by a group of Finnish pelt producers. Gallery of Furs, Inc., the second-largest U.S. fur-garment retailer, was

---

[1] *Financial Times*, April 15, 1989, p. 47.

being pursued by a prominent raider. Despite the shake-out, the market was seeing aggressive new entrants from Asia who had a material cost advantage because of low labor costs and new technology. Moreover, while demand was falling in the United States and Europe, new and rapidly growing markets were emerging in Brazil and Argentina.

Adams, Inc.

Reporting total revenues of $296 million, Adams' 1989 annual report proclaimed the company to be the "world's largest retail furrier." Adams operated 56 specialty stores, 30 full-line fur salons, 18 fur and apparel stores, and 144 leased fur salons in 22 major department store chains throughout the United States, all of which targeted the above-average quality/mid-price segment of the market. The company also operated eight other stores specializing in affordable furs and leathers. Adams was headquartered in New York City.

Adams was founded by the father of the current chairman, David Garabedian, who owned a block of 40 percent of common shares of the company, out of 20 million shares outstanding.

In all discussions about management and control of the company, the Garabedians drew on the counsel of Hyman Sokolof, a lawyer with a large New York law firm who had advised the Garabedian family in their business dealings for many years. He was known to be a tough negotiator.

Like other fur-garment retailers, Adams' financial peformance had worsened in recent years with the decline in demand. Sales and profits both declined over the 1987–89 period. Exhibit 1 presents the highlights of Adams' recent financial performance. Of the three major fur retailers, Adams' balance sheet was the strongest, however, showing an ample cash balance and unused debt capacity.

Exhibit 2 summarizes the stock-price performances of Adams and other firms in the industry. In the April–June 1989 period, Adams' stock price varied btween $5 and $6. The company's book value of equity was $156.5 million at FYE (fiscal year end) 1989; its market value of equity on August 1 was $117.5 million.

In its annual report of February 1989, management outlined various initiatives it would take in the future to enhance the performance of the firm. These included (1) sharpening the merchandising focus of its apparel lines to "better serve the 25- to 50-year-old working woman, offering a mixture of career and casual clothing"; (2) opening two new stores in the New York area, where consistently good sales performance invited continued expansion; (3) expanding the Arctic Fantasy stores in New York and other cities; (4) enlarging a distribution center to support a new direct-mail sales effort; and (5) an agreement to lease new fur salons in six deparmtent store chains. The annual report included these comments:

> Despite our poor sales performance, our overall financial condition is sound. . . . We mentioned a year ago that changes were being made in the organization of the fur division in order to separate buying, merchandising, and overall inventory management from retail store operations and sales promotion. Unfortunately, we did not complete this transaction. . . . In addition to

reductions that resulted from these recent management changes, we expect to further reduce expenses in all areas in the coming year. These include payroll, benefits, advertising, travel, and the planned closing of certain poorly performing locations. . . . Although the last two years have been difficult, we are committed to the long-term prosperity of the fur industry. We have taken steps to improve our performance in management and overall cost structure in the coming years.

For the quarter and six months that would end on August 26, sales and profits would apparently be down from the same period a year earlier. While the growth in new company-owned stores was a positive factor in Adams' performance, profit margins were expected to fall because of higher operating costs and price markdowns necessitated by the continued decline of fur prices.

Potemkin Furs, Inc.

The third-largest fur-garment retailer in the United States was Potemkin Furs, Inc., which had 18 stores, all concentrated in the Pacific Northwest region of the United States. The firm had been in business over 30 years. Exhibit 3 presents a summary of Potemkin's financial performance in recent years.

The firm had gone public in an initial offering of stock in March 1987 at $9.625 per share. In the first quarter of fiscal 1989 (ending June 30), the firm's stock had traded in a range between $2.190 and $0.375. The dramatic deterioration in the firm's fortunes was attributed to the industrywide factors discussed previously.

Before August 1989, the company's equity was substantially controlled by the founding brothers, Daniel and David Potemkin, as well as by the firm's chief financial officer, Ernest Kuttner. All officers and directors as a group held 83 percent of the firm's equity. As a reflection of the firm's deteriorating financial condition, management announced in April 1989 that it had been in preliminary discussions with a foreign fur manufacturer concerning the sale of a majority stock interest in Potemkin. Then in July 1989, Potemkin agreed to sell a 60 percent interest for $4 million at $0.31 per share to a company formed by major Finnish-based fur manufacturers. Erno Kikkonen, one of the Finnish investors, said, "I don't think fur prices can go any lower, because it would be uneconomical to make coats. . . . We feel this is an enormous opportunity, and I expect to make a great deal of money."

Industry observers generally believed that the acquisition of Potemkin by the Finnish manufacturers would not be their last. How soon the Finnish group reentered the market would depend on opportunity.

Gallery of Furs, Inc.

Gallery of Furs, with total revenues for the year ended June 30, 1989, of $211.5 million, was the second-largest retailer of fur garments in the United States. Exhibit 4 presents the highlights of Gallery's recent financial performance.

In mid-1989, Gallery of Furs' business came from two segments. One was the Cesare

Augusto Division, which retailed high-quality leather garments under its own brand name at "affordable prices" and which was showing excellent growth in sales and profits. Cesare Augusto accounted for a small fraction of Gallery of Furs' total business.

The second segment was the Fur Retailing Division, which consisted of 24 Gallery of Furs fur-garment stores and 24 Aurora Borealis fur salons in upscale department stores concentrated mainly in Chicago and the upper Midwest region of the United Staes. The Fur Retailing Division recently had consolidated all of its stores under these two stores names, after changing the names of the stores, and the company, from "Berman the Fur Man." The founder of the company, Al Berman, had a reputation for revolutionizing the fur business by aggressive pricing and innovative target marketing. Berman appeared in folksy advertisements that emphasized the affordability of the firm's furs. In one memorable ad, Berman crooned "Doreen, come in out of the cold." The Fur Retailing Division emphasized medium-priced furs and targeted the young working woman.

In 1988, the firm undertook a strategic shift toward upgrading its image and pricing. The intention was to exit the low-price segment of the market and penetrate the mid-price segment. Sally Browning was hired from Yvette LaMour, Inc., a cosmetics company, to direct the firm's new marketing efforts. Stores were refurbished and repositioned. The advertising budget was boosted, as was the investment in inventory. Glamor was emphasized over affordability.

The timing of this strategic shift was unfortunate. Some critics asserted that these changes confused the firm's customers and led to the subsequent deterioration in financial performance. Others observed that the contraction in demand hit the mid-price segment the hardest; anybody competing there would have been hurt.

By October 1988, conditions had worsened. Berman was removed by the board from day-to-day management of the firm, and Browning was appointed president and CEO. In her president's letter in the annual report of August 1989, Browning committed herself to a continuation of the mid-market strategy, but with an emphasis on cost cutting. The specific actions she mentioned were: (1) implementation of a better inventory-control system to improve inventory turnover and reduce inventory markdowns; (2) reducing corporate overhead; (3) improving store operating efficiency with such devices as a computerized fur-storage retrieval system and hand-held scanners for inventory tracking and control; (4) installation of a new financial-planning and management-information system to provide more information on a timely basis; (5) additional training of sales people to raise the level of customer service; (6) expansion of lines of accessories and outerwear; (7) a new, unified advertising and promotion campaign; and (8) no expansion of the number of stores in 1990.

Browning's corrective actions notwithstanding, the deterioration of Gallery of Furs' performance attracted the attention of investors looking for possible turnaround speculations. In March, June, and July, stock market observers saw unusual activity in the firm's shares. Then on July 31, Poseidon Partners notified the firm that it had purchased 14.97 percent of Gallery of Furs' shares. Within three more days, the percentage had increased to 25.61 percent. Exhibit 5 presents a summary of Poseidon's purchases of Gallery of Furs' shares and their approximate prices.

Poseidon Partners was an investment group, like Coniston Partners and Carlyle Group, that sought to invest in shareholder-value-creating opportunities involving a possible change of control and management of a firm. In 1989 alone, Poseidon had taken sizable investment positions in Fluco Chemicals, Pfschitzer Gas Transmission, and Lacoon Cables and was rumored to be taking a position in Alumo/Canadian. The Fluco situation was resolved by a "white knight" buyer who purchased all public shares—as well as Poseidon's—at a large premium. Poseidon made a $50 million cash profit on the Fluco investment in the space of a few months.

David Aufhauser, the spokesman for Poseidon, demanded two seats on the board of directors for the Poseidon group and said,

> We . . . would like to get positions on the board and help with input on the future of the company. We've left all our options open: we could buy or sell or increase our position. . . . We believe this is an undervalued stock.

Contemporaneous with Poseidon's stock purchases, Al Berman sold nearly 2 million shares, retaining only 2,000.

By mid-August, the trends that had appeared more than a year ago seemed to be worsening. Sales for the first quarter probably would show an increase from last year, but much of this growth was due to the successful Cesare Augusto Division, which more than offset a decrease in the firm's retail fur sales. Sales by stores open in the comparable first quarter period (ending September 2) were likely to be down by about 35 percent. Sales were especially weak in the Chicago area. On a cash flow basis, *all* of Gallery of Furs' stores were currently showing negative cash flows.

Similarly, the forecast for the first half (which would end on December 2) was for a modest increase in sales (from $91 to $96 million)—largely attributable to the Cesare Augusto Division—and a dramatic worsening in net income (from −$1.57 to −$2.68 million).

Sally Browning was contemplating closing some stores for refurbishing and cutting costs in the face of softness in the industry. Browning said:

> We will continue to review our assets to assure that they are used or deployed in a manner consistent with our goals of optimizing shareholder values. Additionally, while we have not yet identified a specific acquisition or business, we intend to actively explore a program to diversify our business.

Although *any* asset sale would be viewed favorably by Gallery of Furs' board of directors (and Poseidon), as a practical matter, only the Fur Retailing Division was the focus of Browning's attention. Gallery of Furs' other main divisions, Cesare Augusto, was profitable and growing and would be a good foundation for ongoing diversification efforts. While Browning was willing to entertain offers for both business segments, her main interest was in selling the Fur Retailing Division. A sale of the division would be a sale of assets, not of stock. The book value of assets of this divisiion at FYE 1989 was $44 million.

Exhibit 6 presents Sally Browning's forecast of the Fur Retailing Division's income statement. Exhibits 7 and 8 present the forecasted balance sheets and residual cash flows, respectively. In the balance sheet forecasts, negative debt could be interpreted as additional cash balances or as cumulative repayment of existing debt. Exhibit 9 summarizes the forecast assumptions underlying Lessard's forecasts.

Value Line estimated that, from 1988 to 1992, sales would grow at a compound rate of 12.5 percent, cash flow from operations at 23.5 percent, and net income at 23.5 percent. Also, *Value Line* estimated that Gallery's stock price would range between $9 and $6 per share in the 1992–94 period.

FUR-GARMENT MANUFACTURERS

Sally Browning assessed two firms as being possible acquirers of U.S. retailers: Jindo Corporation, a Korean producer, and Groupe Lessard, Ltd., a Canadian producer. The loose-knit Finnish group of producers that had bought Potemkin would probably not reenter the market soon.

Jindo Corporation

In mid-1989, Jindo Corporation consisted of two business segments: (1) a transportation equipment division that produced containers, container chassis, and trailers, which accounted for about 60 percent of sales; and (2) a fur-garment division, which accounted for about 40 percent of sales. Jindo was headquartered in Seoul, South Korea.

Jindo claimed a 3 percent share of the world market in fur garments and was believed to be the largest fur-garment manufacturer in the world, with annual capacity for 400,000 garments. Also 50 percent of Jindo's fur garments were exported, with the major overseas market being the United States, which accounted for 58 percent of division exports.

Jindo was integrated vertically from the purchasing of skins through dressing, tanning, and garment manufacture to retailing. Jindo has integrated forward into retailing in the mid-1980s, and it began integrating backward into mink farming, with a possible output of skins at 2 million per year, in 1987. While Jindo would remain the biggest buyer of skins in the world, its emergence as a breeder would put pressure on other breeders and fur dealers.

Exhibit 10 presents a summary of Jindo's financial performance for the past four years. Much of the growth in sales and profits were fueled by the recovery in the international marine transportation industry. The appreciation of the yen was also an important factor behind Jindo's sales growth, because the movement of the yen triggered the bankruptcy of some Japanese container manufacturers. Jindo was not expected to be badly affected by the Korean won's appreciation, because most of its raw materials, such as aluminum and raw furs, were imported. Growth in the fur segment, about 10 percent annually, reflected Jindo's global retail expansion, offset by declining demand.

At the end of July 1989, Jindo's share price was about 20,000 won, which reflected a price/earnings ratio of about 17 times and represented a fourfold gain in price since 1988, when Jindo stock was issued at 5,000 won (the Korean government required that

Korean stock be issued at par value of 5,000 won no matter what). Exhibit 11 gives information on the won/US$ exchange rate.

The three brothers who founded Jindo, Young Jin Kim, Young Do Kim, and Young Won Kim, had more than an absolute majority of shares outstanding. At a price of 20,000 won, the Kim brothers' stake was valued at about US$39 million.

Jindo aimed at the low-price end of the fur-coat market, where customers would pay less than $2,000 per item, a segment that Jindo had largely to itself. The target customer was predominantly a first-time fur buyer.

To achieve production economies, Jindo did not seek to match the quality of its high-price competitors. There were no silk linings, the furs were a bit coarse, the styling rudimentary. Yet one industry expert claimed, "Jindo's $2,000 furs look like $4,000 furs. Obviously their wholesale costs are less. They've got the magic price point where 60 percent of the dollars are done in the real world."[2]

Costs were kept down by using Korean labor, where hourly wages were only US$1.25, and self-sourcing through vertical integration provided additional cost advantages. Finally, Jindo carefully channeled its sales through stores in tourist shopping districts and avoided countries with high import duties and complicated distribution systems, such as Japan.

Groupe Lessard, Ltd.

Groupe Lessard originated as a cooperative of Canadian fur-pelt producers. The cooperative incorporated in 1981 under the strong leadership of the brothers Pierre and Henri Lessard, the eighth generation of French-Canadian Lessards to be involved in the fur industry. The firm invested aggressively in farming and production facilities and, by 1989, was the largest pelt producer, garment maker, and exporter in Canada, accounting for 2.5 percent of worldwide fur-garment production. Based on unit sales, the firm distributed its output as follows: 10 percent to Canada, 5 percent to the United Kingdom, 35 percent to France and the Benelux countries, 35 percent to the United States, and 15 percent to other countries. The firm was headquartered in Chicoutimi, Quebec.

Groupe Lessard had made its name in the production of high-quality fur garments warranting premium prices. In seeking to expand output, however, the firm had experimented with low-price-range garment lines using slightly coarser furs and simpler linings. Until the current difficulties in the industry, this new line of garments had attracted ample demand, particularly among first-time buyers.

Groupe Lessard currently had no U.S. retail presence. The firm was a publicly-owned corporation whose shares were traded on the Toronto Stock Exchange. However, 80 percent of the shares outstanding were concentrated in the holdings of officers and key investors. Exhibit 12 presents a summary of recent financial performance of Groupe Lessard.

---

[2]Howard Davidowitz, an industry consultant, quoted in J. A. Trachtenburg and A. Tanzer, "Moving the Mink," *Forbes*, April 18, 1988, p. 86.

ANALYSIS AND NEGOTIATION

SALLY BROWNING'S DILEMMA

The choice of whom to deal with (Adams, the Lessards, or Jindo), and how (auction or negotiation) would probably vastly influence the desirability of the asset sale and Sally Browning's tenure in office. Given the firm's worsening cash position, time was of the essence; yet it seemed self-defeating to create a "fire sale" atmosphere. There were many considerations which would drive Sally Browning's decision.

Potential Synergies.   The value of Gallery of Furs would be affected by potential economies arising from the combination of a manufacturer and a large retailer. Potentially 85–90 percent of a retailer's annual **fur-apparel purchases** could be supplied by a manufacturer. One might assume a 12 percent margin on manufacturing.

By integrating forward from manufacturing to retailing, a firm should be able to **reduce inventory** at the retail level, thus providing more cash for running the business. These reductions would arise from more careful planning and advance ordering.

Other synergies might be obtained from **consolidating head-office operations** or otherwise redundant activities, such as data processing, reporting, auditing, finance, and administration.

The forecasts of the Fur Retailing Division's financial performance do not reflect the effect of any possible synergies.

Valuation.   The valuation of fur retailers raised various unusual issues that could influence negotiations. The first was whether the retailer's **leases were assignable** to the buyer. Each lease was negotiated separately with the property owner; hence, the assignability of the lease had to be considered on a store-by-store basis. If a lease was not assignable, the property owner could raise the rent to current market levels, which in competitive commercial markets might mean a rent boost of 20–50 percent, depending on the age of the lease (i.e., the time since the rental payment was last negotiated). This issue was material to a buyer, because about one fifth of selling, general, and administrative expense was attributable to store leases. Browning reviewed the leases and determined that *only one* of her 22 store leases was assignable. One solution to this uncertainty would be to adjust the purchase price after the closing through a contigency provision. In any event, the leases could not be assigned prior to closing.

The second valuation issue concerned the **value of the store brand name.** Gallery of Furs had spent $7.6 million on brand advertising in 1988—an expenditure to help build store brands and consumer franchises at particular store locations.

Finally, the value of the retailer's **infrastructure** would have to be assessed. For instance, a strong management-information system or credit system could represent a significant focus of past investment for the retailer. As Gallery of Furs' recent annual report indicated, the firm intended to upgrade significantly its management-information systems; in practical terms, the existing MIS was worthless.

Much of Browning's strategic decision would be driven by what the fur-garment retail operation was worth. Exhibit 13 presents data on recent acquisitions in the U.S. retailing industry. Exhibit 14 provides a summary of current capital-market conditions in the United States.

Exchange of Information.   At the start of negotiations, a **confidentiality agreement** providing for the exhange of information with the target company would need to be structured. Usually such an agreement guaranteed that the bidder would observe a "stand-still" (i.e., not purchase shares in the target company) and would specify the length of the standstill and the kinds of information to be provided by the target, the use of that information, the process for gathering that information (whether in batch or by sequential requests), and the disposal of that information in the event of a failure to reach a merger agreement.

Disclosure.   A review of the constraints on Jindo imposed by **U.S. laws and regulations** would be needed. For instance, regulations dictated under what circumstances the news of a merger negotiation had to be announced to the public and what information had to be given. The same U.S. laws and regulations would bind directors of U.S. companies to certain standards of fairness and objectivity and to being properly informed prior to agreeing to any acquisition.

In short, the sale of Gallery of Furs' Fur Retailing Division would require careful planning, in-depth analysis and research, and artful negotiation.

EXHIBIT 1   Summary of Financial Performance for Adams, Inc. (in millions of U.S. dollars)

	FY Ending February	
	1987	1988
Sales	$296.0	$295.5
Gross profit	97.4	102.3
Operating profit	(4.3)	2.8
Pretax profit	(13.3)	(5.3)
Net profit	(7.6)	(3.4)
Assets	156.5	172.1
Liabilities	60.3	68.3
Shareholders' equity	96.2	103.8

EXHIBIT 2   Share Prices and Beta Information for Major American Fur Retailers

	Adams, Inc. (listed OTC*)	Gallery of Furs, Inc. (listed AMEX†)	Potemkin Furs, Inc. (listed OTC)	Standard & Poor's 500 Index
January–March 1989				
High	$5.50	$2.125	$0.56	273.81
Low	4.125	2.625	0.36	298.33
April–June 1989				
High	5.50	2.875	2.19	329.19
Low	4.50	2.25	0.375	294.62
July 3, 1989	5.50	2.625	1.33	319.23
July 14, 1989	5.125	2.625	1.30	331.35
August 1, 1989	$5.875	$4.25	$0.45	343.75
Beta	1.15	1.25	N.Av.‡	1.0

	Betas for Other Specialty Retailers		
	Burlington Coat	1.35	
	CML Group	1.25	
	Clothestime	1.55	
	Dress Barn	1.55	
	Ross Stores	1.40	
	Syms Corp.	1.20	

* OTC = over the counter.
† AMEX = American Stock Exchange.
‡ N.Av. = not available.

EXHIBIT 3   Summary of Recent Financial Performance, Potemkin Furs, Inc. (in millions of U.S. dollars)

	FY Ending June	
	1988	*1989*
Sales	$65.8	$48.6
Gross profit	29.1	24.3
SG&A	34.6	30.1
Net profit	(3.4)	(9.6)
Earnings per share	N.Av.*	N.Av.*
Assets	50.8	32.3
Liabilities	43.6	31.2
Shareholders' equity	7.2	1.1

* N.Av. = not available.

EXHIBIT 4   Summary of Recent Financial Performance, Gallery of Furs, Inc. (in millions of U.S. dollars except as noted)

	FY Ending June	
	1988	*1989*
Sales	$219.24	$211.48
Gross profit	87.44	96.08
SG&A	104.17	106.36
Operating profit	(16.73)	(10.28)
Net profit	(8.57)	(5.88)
Earnings per share (U.S. dollars)	(0.68)	(0.46)
Assets	114.50	122.40
Liabilities	39.35	52.80
Shareholders' equity	75.15	69.60
Shares outstanding (millions)	12.603	12.78

EXHIBIT 5   Summary of Poseidon Partners' Share Purchases of Gallery of Furs' Stock, 1989

Day	Additional Shares of Gallery of Furs Purchased by Poseidon	Share Prices of Purchase	Resulting Equity Interest (%)
July 31	1,880,000	$3.00–$3.25	14.97%
August 1	231,300	3.358	16.81
August 2	851,300	4.1667	23.59
August 3	253,500	4.4914	25.61

EXHIBIT 6   Forecasted Income Statements, Gallery of Furs, Inc., Fur Retailing Division
(U.S. dollars in thousands)

	Historical Data			Estimates	
	1987	*1988*	*1989*	*1990*	*1991*
Sales	$153,890	$166,700	$149,600	$149,600	$149,600
COGS (excl. depr.)	72,280	96,162	74,598	73,304	73,304
Gross profit	81,610	70,538	75,002	76,296	76,296
SG&A expense	51,006	58,804	58,840	58,793	53,856
EBDIAT	30,604	11,734	16,162	17,503	22,440
Depreciation and amortization	2,884	6,424	7,838	7,779	7,779
Operating profit	27,720	5,310	8,324	9,724	14,661
Other expenses (income)	9,626	14,332	16,276	9,425	9,425
EBIT	18,094	(9,022)	(7,952)	299	5,236
Interest expense at 11.0%	NA	NA	NA	2,127	1,900
Interest income at 8.0%	NA	NA	NA	180	239
Net interest expense	(2,654)	(338)	888	1,948	1,660
Pretax income	20,748	(8,684)	(8,840)	1,648	3,576
Income taxes at 40.0%	8,299	(3,474)	(3,536)	(659)	1,430
Net income	$ 12,449	$ (5,210)	(5,304)	(989)	2,145
Dividends (equity infusions)			$ 5,304	$ 989	0
Change in equity			0	0	$ 2,145
Gross margin	53.0%	42.3%	50.1%	51.0%	51.0%
Operating margin	18.0	3.2	5.6	6.5	9.8
EBIT margin	11.8	−5.4	−5.3	0.2	3.5
Net margin	8.1%	−3.1%	−3.5%	−0.7%	1.4%

				Estimates			
1992	*1993*	*1994*	*1995*	*1996*	*1997*	*1998*	*1999*
$157,080	$164,934	$173,181	$181,840	$990,932	$200,478	$210,502	$221,027
76,969	80,818	84,859	89,101	93,557	98,234	103,146	108,303
80,111	84,116	88,322	92,738	97,375	102,244	107,356	112,724
56,549	59,376	62,345	65,462	68,735	72,172	75,781	79,570
23,562	24,740	25,977	27,276	28,640	30,072	31,575	33,154
8,168	8,577	9,005	9,456	9,928	10,425	10,946	11,493
15,394	16,164	16,972	17,820	18,711	19,647	20,629	21,661
9,896	10,391	10,910	11,546	12,029	12,630	13,262	13,925
5,498	5,773	6,061	6,364	6,683	7,017	7,368	7,736
1,748	1.758	1,770	1,782	1,794	1,808	1,822	1,836
245	258	270	284	298	313	329	345
1,502	1,501	1,499	1,498	1,496	1,495	1,493	1,491
3,996	4,272	4,562	4,867	5,186	5,522	5,875	6,245
1,598	1,709	1,825	1.947	2,075	2,209	2,350	2,498
2,397	2,563	2,737	2,920	3,112	3,313	3,525	3,747
0	0	0	0	0	0	0	0
$ 2,397	$ 2,563	$ 2,737	$ 2,920	$ 3,112	$ 3,113	$ 3,525	$ 3,747
51.0%	51.0%	51.0%	51.0%	51.0%	51.0%	51.0%	51.0%
9.8	9.8	9.8	9.8	9.8	9.8	9.8	9.8
3.5	3.5	3.5	3.5	3.5	3.5	3.5	3.5
1.5%	1.6%	1.6%	1.6%	1.6%	1.7%	1.7%	1.7%

EXHIBIT 7   Forecasted Balance Sheets, Gallery of Furs, Inc., Fur Retailing Division
(U.S. dollars in thousands)

	Historical Data		Estimates	
	1988	*1989*	*1990*	*1991*
Assets				
Cash	$ 1,222	$ 1,496	$ 2,992	$ 2,992
Net working capital	9,612	4,010	4,010	2,514
Net property, plant, and equipment	36,500	38,170	39,367	39,367
Other assets	786	382	382	382
Goodwill	0	0	0	0
Total assets	$48,120	$44,058	$46,751	$45,255
Liabilities and Equity				
Other liabilities	0	402	402	402
Deferred taxes	0	0	0	0
Long-term debt and capital leases	15,788	19,974	18,700	15,839
Added debt			3,966	3,186
Existing preferred stock	0	0	0	0
Common equity	32,332	23,682	23,682	25,827
Total liabilities and equity	$48,120	$44,058	$46,751	$45,255
Equity total assets	67.2%	53.8%	50.7%	57.1%
Change in total assets	—	−8.4%	6.1%	−3.2%

			Estimates				
1992	*1993*	*1994*	*1995*	*1996*	*1997*	*1998*	*1999*
$ 3,142	$ 3,299	$ 3,464	$ 3,637	$ 3,819	$ 4,010	$ 4,210	$ 4,421
2,640	2,772	2,910	3,056	3,209	3,369	3,537	3,714
39,367	39,367	39,367	39,367	39,367	39,367	39,367	39,367
382	382	382	382	382	382	382	382
0	0	0	0	0	0	0	0
$45,530	$45,819	$46,123	$46,441	$46,776	$47,127	$47,496	$47,884
402	402	402	402	402	402	402	402
0	0	0	0	0	0	0	0
15,936	16,037	16,143	16,254	16,372	16,495	16,624	16,759
968	(1,407)	(3,947)	(6,660)	(9,554)	(12,639)	(15,924)	(19,420)
0	0	0	0	0	0	0	0
28,225	30,788	33,525	36,445	39,557	42,870	46,395	50,142
$45,530	$45,819	$46,123	$46,441	$46,776	$47,127	$47,496	$47,884
62.0%	67.2%	72.7%	78.5%	84.6%	91.0%	97.7%	104.7%
0.6%	0.6%	0.7%	0.7%	0.7%	0.8%	0.8%	0.8%

EXHIBIT 8   Forecasted Free Cash Flows, Gallery of Furs, Inc., Fur Retailing Division
(U.S. dollars in thousands)

	Historical Data			Estimates	
	1987	*1988*	*1989*	*1990*	*1991*
EBIT after taxes	10,856	(5,413)	(4,771)	180	3,142
Depreciation			7,838	7,779	7,779
Amortization of goodwill					
(40 years)			0	0	0
Deferred taxes			0	0	0
Total operating sources			3,067	7,959	10,921
Additions to cash balance			274	1,496	0
Capital expenditures			9,508	8,976	7,779
Change in non-cash net working					
capital			(5,602)	0	(1,496)
Change in other assets/liabilities			806	0	0
Total uses			4,986	10,472	6,283
Free cash flow			(1,919)	(2,513)	4,638

				Estimates			
1992	*1993*	*1994*	*1995*	*1996*	*1997*	*1998*	*1999*
3,299	3,464	3,637	3,819	4,010	4,210	4,421	4,642
8,168	8,577	9,005	9,456	9,928	10,425	10,946	11,493
0	0	0	0	0	0	0	0
0	0	0	0	0	0	0	0
11,467	12,040	12,642	13,274	13,938	14,635	15,367	16,135
150	157	165	173	182	191	200	211
8,168	8,577	9,005	9,456	9,928	10,425	10,946	11,493
126	132	139	146	153	160	168	177
0	0	0	0	0	0	0	0
8,443	8,866	9,309	9,774	10,263	10,776	11,315	11,881
3,023	3,175	3,333	3,500	3,675	3,859	4,052	4,254

EXHIBIT 9   Forecasted Assumptions, Gallery of Furs, Inc., Fur Retailing Division

	Historical Data			Estimates	
	1987	*1988*	*1989*	*1990*	*1991*
Operating Assumptions					
Annual sales growth	—	8.3%	−10.3%	0.0%	0.0%
COGS (excl. depr.)/sales	47.0%	57.7%	49.9%	49.0%	49.0%
SG&A expenses/sales	33.1%	35.3%	39.3%	39.3%	36.0%
Other expense (income)/sales	6.3%	8.6%	10.9%	6.3%	6.3%
Depreciation (U.S. dollars in thousands)	2,884	6,424	7,838	7,779	7,779
Depreciation/sales	1.9%	3.9%	5.2%	5.2%	5.2%
Depreciation/capital expenditures	28.8%	39.5%	82.4%	86.7%	100.0%
Noncash net working capital (U.S. dollars in thousands)		19,612	4,010	4,010	2,514
Noncash net working capital/sales ...		5.8%	2.7%	2.7%	1.7%
Cash/sales		0.7%	1.0%	2.0%	2.0%
Capital expenditures (U.S. dollars in thousands)	10,012	16,278	9,508	8,976	7,779
Capital expenditures/sales	6.5%	9.8%	6.4%	6.0%	5.2%
Deferred taxes/tax provision	0.0%	0.0%	0.0%	0.0%	0.0%
Change in other assets/sales			−51.4%	0.0%	0.0%
Change in other liabilities/sales			N.M.	0.0%	0.0%
Long-term debt and leases/assets		32.8%	45.3%	40.0%	35.0%

			Estimates				
1992	*1993*	*1994*	*1995*	*1996*	*1997*	*1998*	*1999*
5.0%	5.0%	5.0%	5.0%	5.0%	5.0%	5.0%	5.0%
49.0%	49.0%	49.0%	49.0%	49.0%	49.0%	49.0%	49.0%
36.0%	36.0%	36.0%	36.0%	36.0%	36.0%	36.0%	36.0%
6.3%	6.3%	6.3%	6.3%	6.3%	6.3%	6.3%	6.3%
8,168	8,577	9,005	9,456	9,928	10,425	10,946	11,493
5.2%	5.2%	5.2%	5.2%	5.2%	5.2%	5.2%	5.2%
100.0%	100.0%	100.0%	100.0%	100.0%	100.0%	100.0%	100.0%
2,640	2,772	2,010	3,056	3,209	3,369	3,537	3,714
1.7%	1.7%	1.7%	1.7%	1.7%	1.7%	1.7%	1.7%
2.0%	2.0%	2.0%	2.0%	2.0%	2.0%	2.0%	2.0%
8,168	8,577	9,005	9,456	9,928	10,425	10,946	11,493
5.2%	5.2%	5.2%	5.2%	5.2%	5.2%	5.2%	5.2%
0.0%	0.0%	0.0%	0.0%	0.0%	0.0%	0.0%	0.0%
0.0%	0.0%	0.0%	0.0%	0.0%	0.0%	0.0%	0.0%
0.0%	0.0%	0.0%	0.0%	0.0%	0.0%	0.0%	0.0%
35.0%	35.0%	35.0%	35.0%	35.0%	35.0%	35.0%	35.0%

EXHIBIT 10   Jindo Corporation, Summary of Financial Performance (in billions of won except as noted)

	FY Ending December			
	1985	*1986*	*1987*	*1988*
Sales	120.5	145.0	180.5	217.6
Percent change	+11.5	+20.4	+24.4	+20.6
Gross profit	13.0	17.4	19.9	20.0
Operating profit	5.1	6.8	6.4	3.4
Ordinary profit	2.0	2.8	4.3	3.6
Pretax profit	1.9	2.8	4.6	—
Net profit	1.4	2.1	3.1	4.1
Percent change	+1,861.1	+49.8	+46.3	+32.3
Ordinary profit to sales (%)	1.7	1.9	2.4	1.7
Net profit to sales (%)	1.2	1.4	1.7	1.9
Assets	60.4	71.8	108.8	139.5
Liabilities	53.2	62.5	93.0	81.7
Shareholders' equity	7.3	9.3	15.8	—
Paid-in capital	5.9	5.9	10.0	22.5
Retained earnings	1.4	3.4	5.8	9.5
Net profit to shareholders' equity (%)	19.2	22.6	19.6	7.1
Net profit to total sales (%)	2.3	2.9	2.8	2.9
Per share:				
Net income (W)		1,807	2,152	1,374
Net assets (W)		7,834	7,562	2,381
Cash flow (W)		3,897	4,160	2,218
Dividend (W) ord.		0	900	750
pfd.		—	—	800
Dividend ord.		0.0	4.9	3.3
Yield (%) pfd.		—	—	3.6
P/E (times) ord.		—	2.4–8.4	11.7–21.3
pfd.		—	—	11.3–16.5
P/B (times) ord.		—	.7–2.4	1.3–2.3
pfd.		—	—	1.2–1.8

EXHIBIT 11   Gallery of Furs, Inc., Historical Spot Exchange Rates and Related Economic Information

Date		Won/US$	Can$/US$
January	1988	791.31	1.29
November	1988	696.08	1.22
December	1988	687.89	1.20
January	1989	685.28	1.19
February	1989	680.28	1.19
March	1989	675.68	1.20
April	1989	672.10	1.19
May	1989	669.75	1.19
June	1989	669.43	1.19
July	1989	669.83	1.19
August 1,	1989	670.14	1.18
		Korea	*Canada*
Expected inflation rate for 1989		6.0%	5.10%
Prime lending rate		15.7%	13.50%
Government long-term bond yield		15.6%	9.72%

EXHIBIT 12 Summary of Financial Performance for Groupe Lessard, Ltd. (in millions of Canadian dollars except per share amounts)

	FY Ending December	
	1987	*1988*
Sales	105.65	125.6
Gross profit	11.65	11.71
Operating profit	3.75	1.99
Pretax profit	2.69	3.57
Net profit	1.81	2.40
Ordinary profit to sales (%)	2.4	1.7
Net profit to sales (%)	1.7	1.9
Assets	63.68	81.65
Liabilities	54.43	47.82
Shareholders' equity	9.25	33.83
Net profit to shareholders' equity (%)	19.6	7.1
Net profit to total sales (%)	2.8	2.9
Per share:		
Net income	$ 1.81	$ 2.40
Net assets	63.68	81.65
Dividend	$ 0.90	$ 1.20
Price/earnings (P/E) ratio (%)	8.4	21.3

EXHIBIT 13 Comparative Information on Recent Selected Merger and Acquisition Transactions in the U.S. Specialty Retail Industry

Date Announced (Closing)	Acquiring Company/ Acquired Company	Total Value (U.S. $ in millions)	Premium to Market[1]	Offer Price/ Book Value[2]	Offer Price/ EPS[3]	Firm Value/ Sales[4]	Firm Value/ EBDIAT[4]
10/16/89 (11/17/89)	Kmart Corporation/Pace Membership Warehouse, Inc.	$319.5	26.0%	271.8%	35.0×	20.9%	15.6×
07/10/89 (09/04/89)	Investor Group/General Nutrition, Inc.	364.9	43.8	362.3	19.1	97.7	7.8
01/17/89 (05/05/89)	Shamrock Holdings of CA, Inc./ Sound Warehouse, Inc.	133.9	128.0	331.2	28.8	68.4	6.0
12/14/88 (06/05/89)	Investor Group/Gump's, Inc.	36.5	N.Av.	N.Av.	14.0	N.Av.	N.Av.
02/09/88 (08/26/88)	Investor Group/The Musicland Group, Inc.	410.4	70.4	350.9	17.5	80.1	8.0
12/22/87 (02/25/88)	Adler & Shaykin/Wherehouse Entertainment, Inc.	119.4	43.6%	248.0%	46.9×	84.8%	8.1×
11/28/86 (12/28/86)	Barnes & Noble Bookstores, Inc./ B. Dalton	261.0	N.Av.	211.1%	N.Av.	51.3%	11.1×
07/09/85 (06/27/86)	Wm. Smith Canada Ltd./Classic Bookshops Ltd.	6.9	N.Av.	N.Av.	N.Av.	N.Av.	N.Av.

[1] Stock price taken approximately one month prior to announcement date.
[2] Based on latest available data.
[3] Earnings per share for trailing 12 months ending with the last quarter prior to announcement.
[4] Firm Value represents total value plus book value of total debt, preferred stock, and minority interest less cash. Sales and EBDIAT for trailing 12 months ending with the last quarter prior to announcement date.

EXHIBIT 13 *(concluded)*

Date Announced (Closing)	Acquiring Company/ Acquired Company	Total Value (U.S. $ in millions)	Premium to Market[1]	Offer Price/ Book Value[2]	Offer Price/ EPS[3]	Firm Value/ Sales[4]	Firm Value/ EBDIAT[4]
07/20/84 (08/09/84)	Kmart Corporation/Walden Book Co.	295.00	N.Av.	N.Av.	N.M.[5]	70.6	N.Av.
12/14/88 (06/05/89)	Investor Group/ Gump's, Inc.	36.5	N.Av.	N.Av.	14.0×	65.3×	N.Av.
08/09/89 (pending)	Investor Group/ Michele Stores, Inc.	131.3	31.5%	942.8%	23.4	79.9×	8.8×
07/10/89 (09/04/89)	Investor Group/ General Nutrition, Inc.	364.9	43.8%	342.3%	19.1×	97.7×	7.0×
	Average		63.4%	295.5%	26.9×	67.7%	9.4
	Median		43.8	301.5	24.0	70.6	8.1
	High		120.0	362.3	46.9	97.7	15.6
	Low		26.0%	211.1%	14.0×	20.9%	6.0×

[1] Stock price taken approximately one month prior to announcement date.
[2] Based on latest available data.
[3] Earnings per share for trailing 12 months ending with the last quarter prior to announcement.
[4] Firm Value represents total value plus book value of total debt, preferred stock, and minority interest less cash. Sales and EBDIAT for trailing 12 months ending with the last quarter prior to announcement date.
[5] Not meaningful.
N.Av. means not available.

Source: Salomon Brothers, Inc.

EXHIBIT 14   Indicators of Economic Condition, United States, August 1989

	Return (%)
90-day Treasury-bill rate	7.71%
1-year Treasury-note rate	7.73
10-year Treasury-bond rate	7.82
30-year Treasury-bond rate	7.91
Eurodollar deposit rate	8.48
12-Month LIBOR (London Interbank Borrowing Rate)	8.875
T-bill vs. Eurodollar futures spread	1.09
AAA-rated corporate-bond rate	8.81
A-rated corporate-bond rate	9.34
Inflation (last 12 months)	4.7
Equity risk premium 1926–88:	
Arithmetic average (stocks—bills)	8.4
Geometric average (stocks—bonds)	5.6

Case 45

Rhône-Poulenc Rorer, Inc.

The interest with which industry analysts, the financial community, and our shareholders have responded to RPR has been encouraging. As evidenced in the strong performance of our stock during 1990 and the attendant decline in the CVR since issuance of the security by Rhône-Poulenc S.A. in August, many among our key audiences have moved from curiosity to confidence in RPR's ability to fulfill its ambitious sales and earnings goals for the future.

Company, *1990 annual report*

. . . leadership requires, first, critical mass in order to compete effectively in research and marketing; second, a global presence to leverage these investments; and third, advantageous partnerships.

Company, *1989 annual report*

Désormais, le succès dépend de notre talent et non plus de nos moyens . . . [1]

Igor Landau

In August 1991, a year had elapsed since the $3.2 billion merger that created a major multinational pharmaceutical company, Rhône-Poulenc Rorer (RPR). The merger, noted for its size, novel terms, and ambitiousness, provoked considerable comment and some skepticism about the projected synergies. Now, a year later, the company had shown rapid post-merger integration and initial synergy gains. The skeptics were not completely muzzled, however; some doubted that the growth and cost savings could be sustained.

The expected performance of RPR was of crucial importance to at least one shareholder of the company—Rhône-Poulenc S.A., the seventh-largest chemical manufacturer in the

---

[1]"Henceforth, success depends more on our talents than financing . . . ," a quotation of Igor Landau, president of the Health Sector at Rhône-Poulenc S.A. in Isabelle Chaperon, "Affairs a Suivre," *La Vie Francaise,* June 7, 1991.

This case was prepared by Robert F. Bruner, as the basis for classroom discussion, while he was a Citicorp Global Scholar and visiting professor at INSEAD in Fontainebleau, France.

Copyright © 1992 by Darden Graduate Business School Foundation, Charlottesville, VA.

world, which owned 68 percent of RPR's shares. In the merger, Rhône-Poulenc gave the minority shareholders a "contingent value right" (CVR) that, in effect, promised to pay them on July 31, 1993, any shortfall between $49.13 and the then prevailing stock price. At year-end 1990, Rhône-Poulenc carried this contingent liability on its balance sheet at 4.96 billion French francs (about US$ 827 million). On August 1, RPR's shares closed at $45.75 and the CVRs closed at $2.50.

THE COMPANY

Rhône-Poulenc Rorer, Inc. (RPR), was created on July 31, 1990, in a merger between Rorer Group, Inc., and the Human Pharmaceutical Business (HPB) of Rhône-Poulenc S.A. As Exhibit 1 indicates, RPR reported sales of $2.9 billion for 1990; but if sales were annualized to include a full year of HPB's operations, RPR's sales would rise to $3.6 billion, ranking it as the 13th-largest pharmaceutical firm in the world. (See Exhibits 2 and 3 for comparisons of RPR with its key competitors.) Contenders in the field were numerous, and even the largest firms did not account for more than a 5 percent share of the market.

Worldwide pharmaceutical sales were estimated to be $145 billion, having risen at a rate of 13 percent a year in recent years. The growth rate in worldwide pharmaceutical sales was expected to slow, however, to 9 percent per year.[2] The largest markets were in the United States and Japan, which represented, respectively, sales of $44.5 and $31.3 billion in 1989.

RPR's mission statement dedicated the company to becoming the best pharmaceutical company in the world. This statement had been revised somewhat from a version published in the 1988 annual report (see Exhibit 4 for the comparison). The company defined its products according to three categories. *Strategic products* involved those that already enjoyed a broad international market or were expected to do so. The merger positioned RPR as the leading seller in Europe of over-the-counter (OTC) drugs, with sales of $280 million (see Exhibit 5). These products were earmarked for heavy investment in marketing and were expected to grow at 19.2 percent per year through 1994. (One analyst assumed only 17.2 percent growth, because of the maturity of the Maalox brand.[3]) *Specialty items* were defined as products with clearly defined regional markets, or limited sales potential, because of either maturity or the narrowness of the market. These products were expected to grow at about 8.5 percent per year. Finally, RPR estimated that *new products* to be rolled out in the near future would produce sales of $715 million in 1994. Given the uncertainties associated with introducing these products, however, one outside analyst expected only $422 million.[4]

---

[2]P. Chandarana, "Company Report—Rhône-Poulenc Rorer," Elysées Bourse, October 2, 1990.

[3]Chandarana, "Company Report," noted that *Informations Médicales et Statistiques* predicted demand for antacids sold OTC to rise 6.3 percent per year by the year 2000, compared with a 1.3 percent annual fall in sales for prescription antacids. Also, competitors were known to be increasing their marketing efforts to sell OTC antacids.

[4]Chandarana, "Company Report."

In its 1988 annual report, Rorer's chief executive officer, Robert Cawthorn, had celebrated this firm's sales level, clearing $1 billion for the first time, and reaffirmed the goal of producing growth in earnings of 15 percent or better. An important component of this growth strategy had been a program of acquisitions, because sales growth in the company's existing product lines was characterized as "mature." One observer described the Rorer strategy as "playing offense in an effort to remain independent."[5]

Rhône-Poulenc S.A. (RP), the diversified chemicals manufacturer, owned 68 percent of RPR shares. In turn, the French government owned 100 percent of RP's voting common stock. RP had been nationalized in 1982 and had since struggled to modernize and attain its goal of a ranking among the five largest chemicals producers worldwide. With the French government under its own budgetary pressures, RP's growth had been financed internally and through an increasingly sophisticated series of financings in the corporate capital markets. As yet, RP had not met its stated goals. Analysts expected that RP would be privatized in 1993 after the next general assembly elections in France, when the conservatives were expected to be returned to power.

Following the merger, Rorer's Robert Cawthorn continued as RPR's CEO, although the firm did assign a new chief financial officer and executive in charge of European operations and marketing. (These individuals are profiled in Exhibit 6.) The new senior executives came from Rhône-Poulenc. Outside observers believed that RP would slowly take over the company. Cawthorn, however, considered RPR to be a freestanding pharmaceutical operation with its own mission statement and Rhône-Poulenc S.A. to be merely an important shareholder.[6]

Some observers questioned RPR's claim to cultural integration and independence. The skeptics pointed to the predominantly American management team, an American-style mission statement, and a waning effort on the part of the American executives to learn French.

THE MERGER

Takeover rumors concerning Rorer had first appeared in the late 1980s, as the firm's relatively low cash balance and rising level of debt seemed to be handicapping its strategy of growth by acquisition. The final confirmation of this constraint surfaced in 1989, when Rorer bid for and lost the opportunity to take over the pharmaceutical business of A. H. Robins. Rorer thus surprised analysts with its announcement of a merger with the Human Pharmaceutical Business of Rhône-Poulenc. Later, the news emerged that several companies had expressed an interest in acquiring Rorer, including Hoffman-La Roche, Ciba-Geigy, Sandoz, Yamanouchi, Monsanto, and Du Pont.

The $3.2 billion combination with Rhône-Poulenc coincided with a wave of mergers in the pharmaceutical industry, including Merrill-Dow buying Marion Laboratories, the $2.1 billion acquisition of Genentech by Hoffman-La Roche, SmithKline and Beecham, Bristol-Myers and Squibb, and major joint ventures between Sanofi and Sterling Drug

---

[5]Janet Novak, "Please Pass the Maalox," *Forbes,* August 7, 1988.
[6]Mike Ward, "RPR Takes the Global Stage," *Financial Times,* July 23, 1991.

and between Du Pont and Merck. One observer commented, "Early evidence shows that the few mega-mergers that have been completed have been a stunning success, and we anticipate further duplication."[7]

Prior to the RPR combination, Rhône-Poulenc's Human Pharmaceutical Business had virtually no position in the United States and Japan, although it was strong in some European Community markets. Moreover, its channels of distribution were not fully utilized. Rorer, on the other hand, lacked a position in Europe and the channels with which to access the market. After the combination, the company ranked among the top three in Europe and had improved its position in the United States. One goal of the company was to rank in the top 10 pharmaceutical companies worldwide.

The merger was consummated in a three-stage transaction, by which Rhône-Poulenc obtained 68 percent of Rorer's common stock (91.6 million shares), which was enough to permit Rhône-Poulenc to consolidate Rorer's results for financial reporting.[8] First, Rhône-Poulenc would tender for 50.1 percent (43.2 million shares) of Rorer's common stock for $36.50 cash per share. (Rhône-Poulenc, by borrowing the funds to finance the tender offer, increased its debt/capital ratio to 45 percent, well above competitors' capitalizations of 20–30 percent.)

Second, Rorer assumed $265 million of RP debt (guaranteed by RP), made a $20 million cash payment to RP, and issued 48.4 million new common shares to RP in exchange for RP's HPB division.[9] Observers believed that Rorer's bylaws would require at least 85 percent of all shares be voted in favor of the issuance of new shares and, more generally, of this entire transaction.

Third, Rhône-Poulenc issued the 41.8 million CVRs to the remaining minority shareholders in Rorer. A CVR entitled the holder to the right at the end of three years, July 31, 1993 (or four years, at RP's option), to a cash payment of US$49.13 (or $53.06 if the payment was made at the end of four years) reduced by the higher of the value of the RPR share at that date or $26.00. Thus, if the value of the RPR share exceeded $49.13 (or $53.06), there would be no payment. The maximum amount of RP's liability on December 31, 1990, was FF4,960 million (FF5,165 million at the date of the issuance of the rights).[10]

The total market value of the rights on December 31, 1990, was FF844 million (FF1,306 million at the date of their issuance). The maximum amount of RP's liability at the date of issuance was hedged. Any changes in the value of the CVRs resulting from fluctuations in exchange rates, as well as the amortization of the cost of the hedge, were recorded

---

[7]Alan Archer, "Alliances Offer a Model," *Financial Times,* July 23, 1991.

[8]RPR split its common shares 2:1 on May 17, 1991. To avoid unnecessary confusion, all share numbers and prices reported in this case are given on a post-split basis. Actually, the acquisition terms involved half the number of shares and twice the share price reported here.

[9]The transfer of RP's health sector excluded RP's business units in veterinary products, serums, and vaccines and the firm's minority interest in a French pharmaceutical concern, Roussel-Uclaf.

[10]In general, the disclosure of contingent liabilities by a firm depended on whether the likelihood of realizing the liability was probable, possible, or remote. If the probability of realization was less than 50 percent, accounting conventions required that the liability be disclosed in the footnotes to the financial statements. The accounting rules contained no prescribed way, however, to estimate the magnitude of contingent liabilities.

directly into the consolidated equity of RP. The CVRs were quoted on the American Stock Exchange and traded independently of the shares of RPR, which were listed on the New York Stock Exchange (NYSE).

Rorer and Rhône-Poulenc jointly announced that they believed that the package of CVR and minority share in RPR was worth $36.50 and, thus, equal to the price at which RP was tendering for shares of RPR. Rorer investors responded favorably to the announcement of an agreement in principle to merge. During the week of the announcement (January 12–19, 1990), Rorer shares increased by $7.313 over the *ex ante* share price of $24.625, or 28 percent (net of the changes in the Standard & Poor's 500 Index over the week). This gain equaled about $632 million in new value. Meanwhile, RP's nonvoting common shares, traded on the Paris Bourse and the NYSE, lost 4.4 percent net of market during the announcement week, or about $175 million.

On April 7, 1990, Warren Buffet, an American investor with an unusually successful money-management record, announced that he had acquired 8 million shares of Rorer (5.8 percent of the total) at an average price of $32.85. As of March 31, 1991, RPR's 8,175 minority common stockholders were dominated by large institutional investors, including 30 mutual funds (2.1 million shares), 61 investment advisors (22.1 million shares), 36 banks (2.77 million shares), and 8 insurance companies (4.4 million shares). The institutions accounted for 23 percent of the 137.4 million shares outstanding and 71 percent of the 44 million shares not held by RP.

CVRs AND CONTINGENT PAYMENTS IN ACQUISITIONS

Contingent payments tended to appear in acquisitions involving a large potential difference between the target transaction prices of buyers and sellers or when the sellers were seeking some protection for the remaining minority shareholders against unfair treatment by the acquirer. Acquisitions in the pharmaceutical industry featured some of the most innovative forms of these contingent-payment schemes; Exhibit 7 summarizes the terms of three other contingent deals and compares them with the RPR terms.

CVRs have been used as merger vehicles since 1985, although they did not gain widespread recognition until used in 1989 in the takeover of Marion Laboratories by Merrill-Dow, the pharmaceutical subsidiary of Dow Chemical. The creation of Rhône-Poulenc Rorer was modeled on the Marion/Merrill-Dow deal.

On September 13, 1991, Dow Chemical stunned the markets by announcing that it would redeem for cash the contingent value rights on Marion Merrill shares that were soon to mature. Analysts estimated that the payment per CVR would be about $10. Marion Merrill's share price plunged $8.125 to $29.50 on the announcement; the CVRs rose $4.875 to trade at $11.00. The announcement deflated investor expectations that Dow Chemical would extend the life of the CVRs for another year and make a bid for the 32 percent of Marion Merrill that it did not already own. Analysts pointed out that Marion Merrill's growth appeared to be slowing because of its failure to find new "blockbuster" drug products in the face of several imminent patent expirations. Indeed, analysts expected that Marion Merrill would not be able to market any new products for several years. Thus, they speculated for Dow to redeem the rights now would be cheaper than to delay and redeem them in a year and cheaper than buying the remaining shares. Analysts also pointed out that Dow's earnings were under pressure. Dow's share price closed up $0.25 on September 13.

THE OUTLOOK

CEO Cawthorn implemented an aggressive post-merger integration process at RPR that rationalized the merging manufacturing operations, reorganized the R&D function to heighten collaboration and foster the exchange of ideas, and sold nonstrategic assets.[11] The successful post-merger integration permitted RPR to report that synergies and asset sales projected for 1990 were achieved. In its merger prospectus, the company had projected sales and earnings through 1994 (see Exhibit 8), and the results for 1990 and the first two quarters of 1991 were indeed consistent with these projections. Earnings and dividends per share for RPR showed the following trends:

	1988	1989	1990	1991 Quarter 1	1991 Quarter 2
Earnings per share (EPS)	$0.965	$1.215	$0.01	$0.39	$0.50
EPS (before restructuring charges)			1.26		
Dividends per share	$0.40	$0.41	$0.42	$0.105	$0.11
Return on equity	13.8%	14.7%	20.8%	—	—

Observers worried, however, about the sustainability of RPR's record. First, the cost of new-product development in the industry was rising—from an average $125 million per product in 1987 to $230 million in 1990. Industry R&D expenditures had been rising 15 percent per year since 1985, yet the number of new drug applications worldwide had fallen at the rate of 10 percent per year (also since 1985). Second, analysts predicted that governments would get tougher on the cost of drugs in an effort to slow down rapidly rising health costs. As a result, demand for drugs might shift from prescription remedies to OTC products. Other strategic risks included patent expiration and competition from low-priced generic drug manufacturers and decreasing product life cycles. On the positive side, analysts noted that computers and biotechnology were aiding new-product development, that the world population was aging, and that RPR was marketing harder than it had, which would boost the payback from its more aggressive R&D spending.

The following table summarizes comments by securities analysts about RPR in early 1991.

---

[11]RPR retained First Boston and Shearson Lehman to assist in the sale of certain assets. Asset sales were managed according to two key objectives: (1) to sell only if the net present value of future cash flows from retaining the assets would be less than the NPV of selling the assets and (2) to achieve earnings neutrality in the future.

Analyst and Date	Expectations for RPR	Comments
J.P. Riccardo, Bear, Stearns & Co. May 10, 1991 Stock price = $41.00	EPS 1991e $2.33 1992e $3.08 Gross margins will improve from 62.8% to 68% of sales.	"The company may struggle to achieve its sales target of $4,050 million in 1991. . . . While we remain concerned over the outlook for 1992, we believe that the Cawthorn-led team will pull off the right strategic moves to insure RPR's stated goals through 1994. On that basis, we would rate the stock a long-term buy."
R.C. Carryl, Value Line August 9, 1991 Stock price = $46.00	1991e $2.25 1992e $2.40	"Rhône-Poulenc Rorer appears to be entering a period of sustainable double-digit earnings growth . . . reflecting the shuttering of redundant facilities, a reduction in the employee head-count, and the cross-selling of each other's products. . . . Despite the positive long-term earnings outlook, investors looking for a drug stock would do well to consider other opportunities . . . RPR's margin remains well below that of its industry counterparts, primarily reflecting a higher cost of goods sold/sales ratio. Furthermore, with overseas operations accounting for a whopping 75–80% of its total business, the drug maker's income stream is far more sensitive to foreign currency exchange swings than any of its peers. Investors skeptical of RPR's growth prospects might want to consider the contingent value rights (CVRs) which guarantee a cash payment."
Jami Rubin, Smith Barney February 12, 1991 Stock price = $37.50	1991e $2.15 1992e $3.15	"We rate Rhône-Poulenc Rorer a BUY. Because of its dramatic profit margin expansion potential, [it] is expected to be the fastest-growing company in our universe—30% per year compared with 16% per year for our eight-company drug composite. . . . Few major Wall Street brokers actively follow the company; therefore, these strong fundamentals are not efficiently reflected in the stock price, in our opinion. . . . RPR's explosive EPS growth reflects dramatic margin expansion . . . RPR could trade around $46 per share in 12–18 months."
S. Weisbrod, Merrill Lynch February 26, 1991 Stock price = $40.50	1991e $1.95 1992e $2.90	"We recommend purchase . . . by long-term investors. We think the stock is fully valued near term . . . the dramatic margin expansion gives us more confidence in our 1992 and 1993 projections."
P. Chandarana, Elysées Bourse October 2, 1990 Stock price = $30.50	1991e $2.25	"A possible long-term buy, but risks on earnings growth and dollar. . . . Our own more conservative projections call for sales to advance 12% a year and net 32%. . . . trading at $30.50, the stock has little upward potential . . . investors could take an interest with an eye on the long term."
Zack's Earnings Estimates March 30, 1991	Average over Eight Analysts 1991e $2.75 1992e $3.63 EPS growth rate next 5 years 21.1% Industry EPS growth 14.2%	

RPR's estimated beta was 1.1. The sigma (standard deviation of returns) on RPR shares was about 0.18 (see Exhibit 9) and compared with an average of 0.27 for 12 pharmaceutical companies.[12]

On August 28, 1990, an analyst for Bear Sterns had recommended that investors buy CVRs and RPR common shares at a ratio of 1.4 to 1. At the time, the CVRs were trading at $6.56 and RPR common at $31.50. In March 1991, he recommended that the ratio be adjusted to 1.8 CVRs per 1 share of RPR common; by then the stock price had risen to $40.625. He said:

> You will not lose money (from today's prices) unless RPR EPS falls below $2.50 per share at the CVR expiration in 1993; if RPR does not fall lower than $15 per share, your return will be greater than 10 percent to the CVR expiration.[13]

Exhibit 10 graphs the price movements of RPR's common shares and CVRs after the merger, and Exhibit 11 gives information regarding current capital-market conditions. Over the previous 18 months, the price/earnings ratio of the S&P 500 Index had varied between 18.07 and 14.21; the P/E ratio at the last market peak (August 25, 1987) was 16.3 times and at the last market trough (August 12, 1982) was 7.6 times.

---

[12]Exhibit 8 estimates sigma over the prior 31 weekly closing prices. If sigma were estimated over the prior 52 weeks, its value would be 0.1875. Estimated over the 79 weeks since RPR shares began trading, the sigma was 0.266.

[13]B. Cohen, Bear Sterns & Co., "Rhône-Poulenc Rorer, Research Highlights," March 15, 1991.

EXHIBIT 1 RPR Selected Financial Data (dollars in thousands)

	1988	1989	1990
Net sales	$1,041,612	$1,182,152	$2,917,364
Cost of products sold	377,750	428,626	1,075,992
R&D expenses	103,952	121,806	350,178
Net interest	39,608	41,608	137,801
Restructuring costs	0	9,981	289,256
(Gain) loss on asset sales	7,065	(30,870)	(78,835)
Gain on contract termination fee		(19,949)	
Other expense	11,890	28,828	35,474
Income taxes	33,299	38,848	9,542
Minority interest			6,343
Net income	61,841	86,467	989
Capital expenditures:			
New headquarters	10,835	29,308	92,073
Other	59,942	82,107	124,785
Depreciation	56,494	63,817	144,693
Working capital	312,403	436,922	391,391
Property, plant, and equipment	395,651	488,167	1,930,702
Total assets	1,388,012	1,791,716	4,084,982
Long-term debt	564,599	882,525	1,634,352
Shareholders' equity	$ 414,171	$ 439,944	$ 693,454
Employees	8,394	8,527	23,454
Sales per employee	132	140	150

Source: Company 1990 annual report.

EXHIBIT 2   Data on Leading Pharmaceutical Companies

	Home Country	*1990 Sales ($m)*	*1990/91 Growth (%)*
Merck	U.S.	$6,425	9.4%
Bristol-Myers Squibb	U.S.	5,980	8.0
Glaxo	U.K.	5,286	9.2
SmithKline Beecham	U.K.	5,001	0.0
Hoechst	Ger.	4,628	18.2
Ciba-Geigy	Switz.	4,592	11.7
Johnson & Johnson	U.S.	4,200	12.4
American Home Products	U.S.	4,022	−3.0
Sandoz	Switz.	4,005	8.7
Eli Lilly & Co.	U.S.	3,720	16.8
Bayer	Ger.	3,720	8.3
Pfizer	U.S.	3,684	10.7
Rhône-Poulenc Rorer	**U.S./France**	**3,613**	**7.4**
Hoffman-La Roche	Switz.	3,471	19.6
Takeda	Japan	2,670	−23.9
Schering-Plough	U.S.	2,652	6.4
ICI	U.K.	2,474	8.6
Marion/Merrill-Dow	U.S.	2,438	3.0
Upjohn	U.S.	2,420	3.8
Wellcome	U.K.	2,260	15.5

Source: Alan Archer, "Alliances Offer a Model," *Financial Times*, July 23, 1991. Sales reported in the article were given in pounds sterling and have been converted here to dollars at the rate of 1.78 to the pound.

EXHIBIT 3 Information on Comparable Firms in the Pharmaceutical Industry

	P/E Ratio	Beta	Long-Term Sigma	Expected Growth of		Debt/Equity	Expected Dividend-Payout Ratio
				Sales	Profits		
American Home Products	15.0%	1.00	0.25	7%	10.5%	0.124	55%
Bristol-Myers Squibb	21.0	1.00	0.29	11	15.0	0.042	56
Eli Lilly & Co.	16.3	1.10	0.23	16	19.5	0.053	41
Marion/Merrill-Dow	17.6	N.A.	N.A.	13	16.0	0.111	43
Merck	23.5	1.00	0.23	14	17.5	0.031	42
Pfizer	22.5	1.05	0.28	13	14.0	0.031	47
Rhône-Poulenc Rorer	**20.4**	**1.00**	**0.176**	**15**	**27.5**	**2.00**	**20***
Schering-Plough	18.0	1.10	N.A.	11	17.5	0.087	41
Upjohn	15.8	1.05	0.25	9	12.5	0.299	41
Warner-Lambert	16.9	1.10	0.31	12	17.0	0.220	42

* RPR's quarterly dividend had been raised to $0.11 per share at the June 30 payment date, up from $0.105 per share.

N.A. means not available.

Source: *Value Line Investment Survey*, August 9, 1991. The sigma for RPR was obtained from Exhibit 8 of this case. Sigmas on other firms were obtained from J. Cox and M. Rubinstein, *Options Markets* (Englewood Cliffs, N.J.: Prentice Hall, 1985), pp. 346–58.

EXHIBIT 4   RPR Mission Statement

Mission Statement, 1990 Annual Report	*Mission Statement, 1988 Annual Report*

Our Mission is to become the BEST pharmaceutical company in the world by dedicating our resources, our talents, and our energies to help improve human health and the quality of life of people throughout the world.

Being the best means:

- Being the BEST at satisfying the needs of everyone we serve, patients, health-care professionals, employees, communities, governments and shareholders;
- Being BETTER AND FASTER than our competitors at discovering and bringing to market important new medicines in selected therapeutic areas;
- Operating with the HIGHEST professional and ethical standards in all our activities, building on the Rhône-Poulenc and Rorer heritage of integrity;
- Being seen as the BEST place to work, attracting and retaining talented people at all levels by creating an environment that encourages them to develop their potential to the full;
- Generating consistently BETTER results than our competitors, through innovation and a total commitment to quality in everything we do.

The Rorer Mission

To improve human health while maximizing shareholder value by becoming a world-class pharmaceutical company, able to compete effectively with any other company in selected therapeutic areas in the major developed markets of the world.

The Rorer Credo

We believe:

- That customer satisfaction is our first responsibility. To provide value for the people who benefit from our products and services, we must emphasize quality and integrity in everything we do.
- That we must treat each other fairly, with trust and respect, in an environment that fosters involvement, open communication, and teamwork.
- That we must continually adapt and renew our business. We must encourage and reward innovation, experimentation, and change.
- That we are responsible to the communities in which we work and live. We will actively support civic improvement, better health, and education.

Source: Company annual reports.

EXHIBIT 5   Data on OTC Drug Sales

A.   World Drug Sales (in $ billions)

	Prescription	OTC	Total
1990	$120	$25	$145
1986	90	20	110

B.   OTC Drug Sales in Europe by Company (in $ millions)

	Country of Headquarters	1990 Sales
Rhône-Poulenc Rorer	**U.S./France**	**$280**
Bayer	Germany	210
Sanofi	France	180
SmithKline Beecham	U.K.	170
Procter & Gamble	U.S.	170
Boeringer Ingelheim	Germany	150
Boots	U.K.	150
American Home Products	U.S.	140
Nicholas Laboratories	U.S.	120
Warner-Lambert	U.S.	110
Sterling Drug	U.S.	100
Hoffman-La Roche	Switzerland	100

Source: Clive Cookson, "Roche Deal Puts Fizz in Drugs Race," *Financial Times*, June 4, 1991.

EXHIBIT 6 Profiles of Senior RPR Executives

Robert E. Cawthorn (age 55)

Chairman, president, and CEO. Joined Rorer in 1982 as executive vice president (EVP) and president of its international pharmaceutical subsidiary. President from February 1984; CEO from May 1985. Chairman from May 1986.

Jean-Jacques Bertrand (age 51)

EVP and group president [specifically in charge of Europe, Africa, the Middle East, South America, and Asia (excluding Japan and Korea)]. Served as president, Worldwide Pharmaceutical Operations of Rhône-Poulenc Santé from 1987 to 1990. From 1985 to 1987, served as president of various RP pharmaceutical operations.

Ralph H. Thurman (age 41)

EVP and group president, North America, Japan/Korea, Australia/New Zealand, and Worldwide Industrial Operations. Vice president, Personnel from 1985 to 1987. Senior vice president (SVP), Organization and Administration in 1988. EVP and president of U.S. subsidiary in 1989.

Gilles D. Brisson (age 39)

SVP, Corporate Development. 1989–90 area vice president of Northern Europe for Rhône-Poulenc. 1987–89 deputy SVP of Worldwide Pharmaceutical Operations of Rhône-Poulenc Santé. 1983–87 general manager of Theraplix.

Patrick Langlois (age 45)

SVP and chief financial officer. 1988–90 SVP, Corporate Finance and Acquisitions of Rhône-Poulenc. 1975–86 director of International Financings of Rhône-Poulenc and finance director.

Source: Company merger proxy statement, 1990.

EXHIBIT 7 Landmark Acquisition Payment Structures in the Pharmaceutical/Biotechnology Industries

Deal	Eli Lilly and Company Buys 100% of Equity in Hybritech, Inc.	Rhône-Poulenc Acquires 68% of Equity in Rorer Group, Inc.	Dow Chemical Acquires 67% of Equity in Marion Laboratories	Roche Holding, Ltd., Acquires 60% of Equity in Genentech
Date of closing	February 1986	July 1990	July 1989	February 1990
Total estimated payment (US$)	$412.8 million	$1,600 million	$5,700 million	$1,295 million
General structure	One-stage exchange per each Hybritech share: (1) $22.00 cash or par value of 10-yr. conv. notes paying 6.75%. Conversion price $66.31 per share.	Three-stage transaction: (1) Cash tender offer for 50.1% of stock in Rorer. At $36.50 for 43.2 million shares, the initial cash outlay is $1,577 million.	Two-stage transaction: (1) Dow acquires 38.9% of Marion through a cash tender offer at $38 per share.	Two-step transaction: (1) Roche purchases a 20% interest in Genentech through the purchase of newly issued shares at $22 per share.

	(2) 1.4 warrants to buy Lilly common stock at $75.98 per share. (3) One contingent-payment unit (CPU) paying up to $22.00 in dividends over 10 years.	(2) RP transfers its worldwide HPB to Rorer. Rorer pays RP $20 million and assumes $265 million of RP debt. Rorer issues 48.4 million new common shares to RP. (3) RP issues 41.8 million CVRs (for terms of payment, see text of case).	(2) Dow contributes its pharmaceutical subsidiary, Merrill-Dow, and 92 million CVRs in exchange for new Marion shares.	(2) All non-Roche common shares are exchanged for $18 cash and ½ share of redeemable common stock. Following the transaction, public shareholders will own 40% of voting stock; Roche will own 60%.
Contingent terms	Annual dividend of CPU equal to: $$[6\% \text{ of sales} + 20\% \text{ of gross profits} - (\$11 \text{ million} * (1.35)^t)]$$ divided by number of Hybritech shares. t = years since 1986. Sales and gross profits are for Hybritech.	CVR entitles holders to receive from RP the amount by which $98.26 a share exceeds either a $52.00 floor price or the average market value of Rorer's share price 60 days before the rights' maturity date of July 31, 1993. Maximum payout $46.26 per share. RP has the right to extend maturity of CVRs for an additional year to July 31, 1994. In that event, the ceiling rises from $98.26 to $106.12. Maximum payout increased to $54.12.	Similar to RP CVR: a "put" spread guarantees shareholder returns within a predetermined range of stock prices through 1992.	Redeemable common stock entitles Roche to redeem the shares at predetermined prices until June 1995. Thereafter, these shares will automatically convert into an equal number of regular common shares. Redemption price starts at $38.00 at closing and rises $1.25 per quarter to the maximum of $60 per share in April–June 1995.

EXHIBIT 8   Five-Year Projected Financial Performance Forecasted by RPR* (dollars in millions except per share data)

	1990	1991	1992	1993	1994
Revenues	$2,533	$4,053	$4,657	$5,276	$5,906
Interest expense, net	100	176	168	137	107
Depreciation	131	165	173	186	197
Restructuring costs	218	—	—	—	—
Income before tax	37	497	599	906	1,125
Net income	7	328	462	600	743
Earnings per share	0.065	2.43	3.42	4.45	5.50
Cash	184	135	95	95	95
Total assets	3,731	3,855	3,968	4,141	4,341
Debt (including current portion)	2,021	1,812	1,505	1,158	774
Stockholders' equity	640	902	1,225	1,615	2,061
Capital expenditures	$ 173	$ 208	$ 150	$ 157	$ 176
Ratio of debt to debt plus equity	76%	67%	55%	42%	27%
Pretax interest-expense coverage, excluding restructuring costs	3.4×	3.7×	5.0×	7.3×	10.8×

* The financial projections . . . were developed by the managements of Rhône-Poulenc and Rorer Group, Inc., over a period of several months. The projections . . . represent the "base" case in the view of senior management of both Rhône-Poulenc and Rorer Group, Inc. There are numerous assumptions and attendant uncertainties with respect to these projections which are set forth in more detail below.

The 1990 data assume that the transactions are completed on June 30, 1990, and that the combined accounts include 12 months of results for Rorer Group, Inc., and 6 months of results for the Human Pharmaceutical Business as well as interest on the debt incurred in the restructuring from June 30, 1990. The projections also assume provisions of $218 million (before taxes) in 1990 for one-time costs related to the transactions.

The financial projections reflect substantial benefits anticipated from the combination and assume, among other factors: (1) increases in sales of existing products and introduction of new products, receipt of regulatory approvals required for new products within the planned timeframes, and achievement of marketing plans for both new and existing products; (2) reduction of sales in certain markets from overlapping products; (3) some disruption in sales from the business combination together with declines over time on products which will be less actively marketed by the combined company than previously; (4) exclusion of sales increases which may result from increased marketing emphasis on certain core products by the combined sales force; (5) price increases on existing products of both companies throughout the period on a basis generally consistent with historical experience; (6) improvement in operating margins, particularly in the first three years after the transactions, which improvement is expected to result from the consolidation of manufacturing operations, sales forces, marketing, distribution, and administrative functions, and research and development activities.

Source: Rorer Group, Inc., merger proxy statement, 1990.

EXHIBIT 9 Estimation of RPR Stock-Price Volatility across 31 Weeks, January 1991 to August 1991

	Weekly Closing Stock Prices*	Price Relative	Log of Price Relative	Squared Error of Log of Price Relative
Jan. 11	$34.69			
	33.75	0.973	−0.027	0.0012
	34.00	1.007	0.007	0.0000
	34.56	1.016	0.016	0.0001
	35.00	1.013	0.013	0.0000
	36.13	1.032	0.032	0.0006
	38.79	1.074	0.071	0.0041
	39.56	1.022	0.022	0.0002
	40.75	1.030	0.030	0.0005
	40.69	0.999	−0.001	0.0001
	41.44	1.018	0.018	0.0001
	40.44	0.976	−0.024	0.0010
	40.50	1.001	0.001	0.0000
	39.31	0.971	−0.030	0.0014
	39.75	1.011	0.011	0.0000
	39.44	0.992	−0.008	0.0002
	39.56	1.003	−0.003	0.0000
	39.38	0.995	−0.005	0.0001
	41.99	1.066	0.064	0.0033
	41.25	0.985	−0.015	0.0005
	41.19	0.999	−0.001	0.0001
	41.13	0.999	−0.001	0.0001
	41.88	1.018	0.018	0.0001
	42.00	1.003	−.003	0.0000
	42.50	1.012	0.012	0.0000
	41.50	0.976	−0.024	0.0010
	41.63	1.003	0.003	0.0000
	41.75	1.003	0.003	0.0000
	42.38	1.015	0.015	0.0001
	41.50	0.979	−0.021	0.0008
	43.38	1.045	0.044	0.0014
Aug. 2	$45.75	1.055	0.053	0.0021
	Sum		0.304	0.017998
	Average		0.010	0.000599

Number of price relatives: 30
Number of stock prices: 31
Adjusted weekly variance: 0.000620
Annual variance: 0.032
Annual std. deviation: 0.180 = Sigma or volatility

Comment: In this table, stock prices are converted into price relatives (which are simply the ratio of today's price to yesterday's price). Then the price relatives are transformed into logarithmic values (in order to normalize the distribution). In the right-hand column, the squared deviations of the logarithmic values are computed from their mean value (0.010). The weekly variance is computed by dividing the sum of the right-hand column (.018) by the number of price relatives (30) and then multiplying by a correction factor (30/29) to adjust for sampling bias. The annual variance is obtained by multiplying the weekly variance by 52. The standard deviation is the square root of annual variance. For a more detailed discussion of this estimation procedure, see J. Cox and M. Rubinstein, *Options Markets* (Englewood Cliffs, N.J.: Prentice-Hall, 1985), pp. 255–58.
* These stock prices include dividend payments as of ex dividend dates.

Source of stock prices: Datastream, Inc.

EXHIBIT 10   Graph of Prices of RPR Common Stock and CVRs since July 1990 (all values indexed to 1.00 from first day of trading)

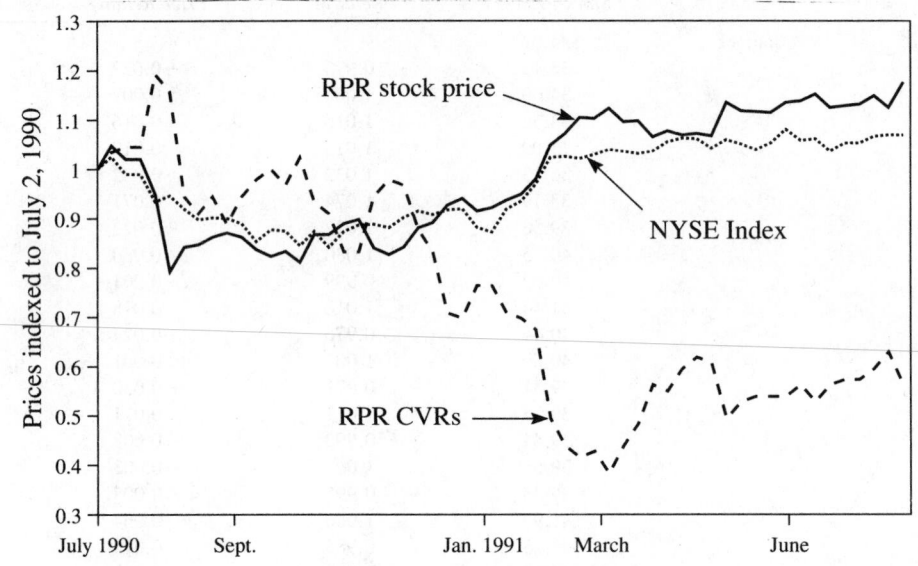

	Security Prices	
	July 2, 1990	*August 1, 1991*
RPR common stock	$ 36.88	$ 45.75
RPR CVRs	5.56	2.50
Standard & Poor's Index	$196.23	$210.99

Source: Datastream, Inc.

EXHIBIT 11   Current Capital-Market Conditions, Early August 1991

	August 9, 1991	*July 26, 1990*
Equity-market multiples		
Median price/earnings ratio	15.2×	13.3×
Median dividend yield	3.0%	3.7%
Equity-market indexes		
Dow-Jones Industrial Average	3,017.67	2,920.79
S&P 500 Index	380.96	365.91
NASDAQ* OTC Composite Index	504.15	455.43
Change in equity-market indexes over past 12 months (%)		
Dow-Jones Industrial Average	+5.3	+10.8
S&P 500 Index	+10.1	+4.1
NASDAQ OTC Composite Index	+17.6	−1.6
U.S. Treasury yield curve (yields by maturity, %)		
3-month bills	5.69	7.83
6-month bills	5.89	7.85
1-year notes	6.17	7.90
2-year notes	6.85	8.09
3-year notes	7.09	8.20
5-year notes	7.74	8.26
10-year bonds	8.16	8.47
30-year bonds	8.35	8.53
Benchmark corporate costs of funds (%)		
Prime rate	8.5	10.0
Aaa corporate bond rate	8.9	9.3
Other bond rates:		
A-rated corporates (25 yrs.)	9.6	9.67
A-rated financials (10 yrs.)	9.15	N.A.
Preferred stocks, dividend yield:		
A-rated utilities	8.99	N.A.
A-rated financials	9.37	N.A.

* National Association of Securities Dealers.
N.A. means not available.

Source: *Value Line Investment Survey,* August 9, 1991, and August 3, 1990.

Bumble Bee Seafoods, Inc.

The simple but catchy jingle, "Yum-Yum-Bumble Bee, Bumble Bee Tuna," had been stuck in Keith Shaughnessy's mind ever since his recent trip to New York City in February 1985. While there, Mr. Shaughnessy, a lending officer with the First National Bank of Boston (the Bank), had been approached by the First Boston Corporation (First Boston) to help finance a $60 million, management-led leveraged buyout of Bumble Bee Seafoods from its cash-starved, financially troubled parent, Castle & Cooke, Inc.

Having helped First Boston finance a leveraged buyout in 1984, Mr. Shaughnessy felt confident that the proposed transaction warranted serious consideration. As the deal was initially outlined, the Bank would not be the sole creditor; Castle & Cooke had agreed to take back $15 million in junior subordinated notes. In addition, First Boston was seeking an institutional investor to purchase $7 million in senior subordinated debt that included an opportunity to acquire a 20 percent equity interest in the new company for an additional $1 million. The remaining $2.3 million in equity would be divided between the management team and First Boston.

The proposed structure appeared unusual to Keith Shaughnessy because the junior subordinated note would amortize at the same time as the senior bank debt and before the senior subordinated note. First Boston had estimated that the Bank's initial exposure would be approximately $60 million, consisting of $40 million in revolving term debt and $20 million in short-term working-capital lines. Mr. Shaughnessy had to decide not only whether to pursue the transaction for the Bank but also whether the proposed structure provided the Bank a sufficient level of return. In addition, he was interested in evaluating the attractiveness of the senior subordinated debt and equity package that First Boston planned to place. The proposal would have to be acted on quickly; Castle & Cooke, whose solvency at the time was questionable, had already initiated merger negotiations with the David H. Murdock-controlled Flexi-Van Corporation.

This case was written by Peter R. Hennessy under the direction of Robert F. Bruner.
Copyright © 1985 by the Darden Graduate Business School Foundation, Charlottesville, VA.

THE TUNA INDUSTRY

In 1983, sales of canned tuna in the United States totaled $1.4 billion. Retail sales accounted for $1.1 billion of this total, while the remaining $0.3 billion was sold in the institutional market. Annual tuna consumption was expected to increase only at the rate of population growth, roughly 2 percent.

The three varieties of tuna used most frequently for canning were skipjack, yellowfin, and albacore. Skipjack and yellowfin were considered lightmeat tuna; albacore was the only variety of whitemeat tuna. Lightmeat tuna had evolved into a commodity item, but whitemeat tuna was still perceived as a differentiated good. Because the supply of albacore tuna was static and the fish were difficult to catch, whitemeat tuna sold for a 50 to 60 percent premium over lightmeat tuna.

Traditionally, tuna had been packed in oil, but since 1970, the share of tuna packed in water had grown, and in 1983, sales of such tuna accounted for 57 percent of industry sales (see Exhibit 1). Imported tuna packed in water incurred a maximum tariff of 12.5 percent (versus 35.0 percent for imported oil-packed tuna). Future volume growth in whitemeat tuna was not expected to increase because of the supply limitations. Tuna consumption was highly sensitive to changes both in its own price and in the prices of substitute products, such as red meat and chicken.

The manufacturing and distribution functions for the retail tuna industry were highly concentrated, with the top three companies accounting for over 70 percent of industry retail sales. Star-Kist, a division of H. J. Heinz, was the industry leader in 1984 with 32 percent of all retail sales. Chicken-of-the-Sea, a division of Ralston Purina, accounted for 24 percent of the market, and Bumble Bee had 15 percent. (See Exhibit 2 for historical market-share levels.) The remaining 29 percent of the market consisted of smaller regional manufacturers, such as C.H.B. Foods, private-label producers, and more recently, Japanese imports. In 1984, foreign converting facilities supplied approximately 28 percent of retail canned tuna through sourcing contracts with U.S.-based manufacturers like Bumble Bee and Chicken-of-the-Sea. Direct sales of Japanese branded tuna, such as Mitsubishi's Three-Diamond brand, were less important.

The strategies of the three industry leaders had changed significantly in the last four years, including a move away from vertical integration, which had locked the producers into expensive domestic canning operations, company-owned fishing fleets, and domestic sourcing contracts. More recent trends were toward using conversion facilities in areas with lower labor costs than the continental United States and outright sourcing of finished canned tuna from such countries as Thailand, Japan, and the Philippines. As a result of expansion in foreign fishing and conversion capacity, cheaper raw materials, and lower labor costs, foreign-sourced lightmeat tuna prices were $100 a ton less than U.S.-caught tuna. The structural change the industry was undergoing resulted in losses or marginal profits for Bumble Bee, Chicken-of-the-Sea, and Star-Kist during the early 1980s.

Star-Kist was not only the leader in terms of market share; the firm also was the most profitable of the three major manufacturers and the only firm with an international market presence. As a result of competitive global sourcing, Star-Kist, through 1984, was considered the low-cost provider in terms of total tuna sold. Chicken-of-the-Sea's recent performance had suffered from declining market share, bloated inventories, and increased costs. During 1984, industry sources had mentioned that Ralston Purina was contemplating selling the Chicken-of-the-Sea operation because of its poor performance.

Bumble Bee had successfully marketed itself as a quality leader rather than a price leader. As a result, Bumble Bee could price its whitemeat tuna at a 6 to 8 percent premium over other branded whitemeat tuna. While Bumble Bee ranked third in terms of tuna sales, its products were well positioned. As shown in Exhibit 1, Bumble Bee sold a higher proportion of whitemeat tuna and water-packed tuna than its competitors.

BUMBLE BEE SEAFOODS

Bumble Bee manufactured and/or distributed canned tuna, salmon, and tuna-based pet food. While tuna sales accounted for 80 percent of Bumble Bee's revenues, the remaining product lines were themselves visible consumer products. In fact, in 1983, Castle & Cooke rejected an $11 million offer made by a major marketer of dog food for the trademark to Bumble Bee's Figaro brand pet food line.

In 1984, Bumble Bee led the industry in sales of whitemeat tuna with a 30 percent share (as shown in Exhibit 2). Furthermore, because Bumble Bee's sales were highly regionalized, it had captured more than a 30 percent share in its primary markets. Even though Bumble Bee was distributed in over 20 major metropolitan areas, 70 percent of its whitemeat tuna sales were concentrated in four markets. (See Exhibit 3 for the distribution of Bumble Bee's whitemeat market share.)

Bumble Bee's dominance of the whitemeat market stemmed from its low-cost sourcing and conversion of albacore. The company maintained long-term supply contracts for albacore tuna, which were then processed in its canning facility in Puerto Rico. Following the proposed buyout, Bumble Bee planned to modify its domestic lightmeat purchasing in favor of sourcing its lightmeat tuna from Thailand. The new sourcing, which management estimated would provide a saving of $3 a case, would allow Bumble Bee finally to be a competitive provider of lightmeat tuna. The managers anticipated that growth in Bumble Bee's market share would come principally from expansion of lightmeat sales in its traditional markets and in new markets.

CASTLE & COOKE

Bumble Bee's parent, Castle & Cooke, was best known for its consumer products, such as Dole pineapple and bananas and A&W root beer. In addition to consumer products, Castle & Cooke had vast land holdings in Hawaii that were significantly undervalued on its books. Between July 1982 and December 1984, Castle & Cooke reported net losses of $190 million. Continuing operations accounted for $78 million of the losses; the remaining $112 million were attributable to discontinued operations. By the spring of 1985, Castle & Cooke was experiencing significant cash-flow problems, which culminated with the company's attempt to restructure $255 million of its total debt, $468 million. In early 1984, the managers of Castle & Cooke decided to divest Bumble Bee, because the tuna operation did not fit with the company's overall strategy. It approached the senior manager of the division and invited a possible management buyout. Later an investment banking firm (Kidder Peabody) was retained to market the business outside. The majority of the firms that bid on Bumble Bee were competing tuna manufacturers; and when none of the bids exceeded Bumble Bee's net book value, Castle & Cooke concentrated its efforts on the management group.

In an attempt to alleviate its tight cash-flow position, Castle & Cooke in early 1985 had entered into the merger negotiations with Flexi-Van, a transportation-equipment leasing company. The merger, valued at $600 million, would give Castle & Cooke additional debt capacity to ease its cash crisis and also would help thwart an apparent attempt by Minneapolis investor Irwin L. Jacobs to take control of Castle & Cooke.

THE BANK OF BOSTON

As early as the 1950s, the Bank of Boston had been involved in financing highly leveraged transactions (which have more recently been termed leveraged buyouts). In 1984, the Bank, in conjunction with First Boston, provided debt for the $200 million leveraged buyout of the Amerace Corporation, a manufacturer of industrial and consumer products and components. Following the Amerace transaction, First Boston considered the Bank its lead source of debt financing for leveraged buyouts.

The economic incentives for lending in this growing market were dramatic. The debt regularly provided a 300 basis-point spread over the Bank's cost of funds, as well as lucrative up-front fees and the opportunity to finance the new company's continuing working-capital needs.

With significant experience in lending straight senior debt, the Bank's managers were interested in examining whether the Bank's venture-capital subsidiary should take an equity position in some of the more attractive transactions. Such an investment position would require the Bank to consider the increased risk incurred in being an equity investor and to determine whether the potential return was sufficient to compensate it for the risk.

BUMBLE BEE MANAGEMENT STRATEGY

The four principals involved in the Bumble Bee buyout were young but experienced, with over 50 years of cumulative experience in the tuna industry. The current management team had been assembled in 1982 during the worst downturn in the history of both Bumble Bee and the U.S. tuna industry. In its first 12 months, the team reduced losses by 75 percent, and, in 1984, it generated Bumble Bee's first operating profit since 1980. (See Exhibit 4 for a description of the management team.)

The attractiveness of the buyout relied on the buying management's insistence that it only purchase certain assets. Exhibit 5 gives Bumble Bee historical balance sheets and a projected balance sheet for the new company following the buyout. With the exception of $1.9 million in organizational expenses, which are included in noncurrent assets, the assets shown in the right-hand column of Exhibit 5 were the only assets management expected to purchase from Castle & Cooke. Just as important as the assets being purchased were the assets and obligations that Bumble Bee would not inherit—namely, two outdated manufacturing facilities and idle tuna boats that had contributed to the division's problems over the past three years.

Bumble Bee's poor performance had stemmed from Castle & Cooke's decision to expand capacity, to enter into long-term procurement contracts, and to purchase the largest tuna boat fleet in the industry. To make matters worse, these actions were taken in a period characterized by overcapacity and stable demand. The effort to expand Bumble Bee's penetration left the company with excess inventory in areas where the company commanded little market share. Industrywide recalls in 1982–83 also contributed to Bumble Bee's losses during the period.

The management involved in the buyout had initiated cost-cutting measures beginning in 1982. The effort to gain national market share was abandoned in favor of retrenching in traditional markets. In addition, management closed the San Diego cannery and retired a portion of the fishing fleet. While these actions resulted in lower overhead, the cost of discontinuing the operations caused Bumble Bee to lose money in 1983. The lower overhead and improved production efficiencies did, however, enable Bumble Bee to generate $7 million in earnings before interest and taxes in fiscal year 1984. (See Exhibit 6 for historical income statements.) For the assets that were difficult to sell, Castle & Cooke took $27 million in write-downs for fiscal years 1984 and 1985. As shown in the pro forma income statements and balance sheets given in Exhibits 7 and 8, management anticipated that the improved performance would continue.

The proposed new managers estimated that $9.6 million in annual savings would be realized from three specific areas. The absence of the Hawaiian cannery would reduce annual overhead by $3.0 million, and the lower cost lightmeat tuna from new sources would save the company roughly $3.6 million a year. From marketing studies, management determined that advertising had little effect on tuna purchasers in the short term. As a result, they estimated that Bumble Bee's marketing budget could be cut in half, to $3 million, without losing significant market share.

With the exception of the canning facility in Puerto Rico, which under the proposed plan Bumble Bee would lease from Castle & Cooke for five years with an option to buy, the company would be out of the canning business. The streamlined Bumble Bee would primarily be a sourcing and distribution operation positioned as the overall low-cost provider in the tuna business.

THE TRANSACTION

The debt financing for the buyout, described in Exhibit 9, held several concerns for Mr. Shaughnessy. First, because the new company would not be purchasing existing trade receivables, the Bank would have to rely solely on raw material and finished goods inventory for security. As set forth in Exhibit 5, those assets were estimated to have a value of $55 million at the time of the closing. Assuming a 50 percent advance ratio on inventory and 75 percent on receivables, the Bank would lack coverage for approximately $12 million of the $40 million revolver. Mr. Shaughnessy wondered whether, in case of liquidation, the shortfall could be made up by the sale of the trademarks.

The effort to source lightmeat tuna from foreign manufacturers added additional risks, including interruptions in supplies or possible protectionist legislation that would make foreign-sourced tuna uneconomical. The managers believed, however, that if the threats materialized, plant capacity in Puerto Rico could be expanded to supply the U.S. market with domestically manufactured lightmeat tuna.

Mr. Shaughnessy's final concern involved the status of the debt and the preferential tax treatment under Section 936 of the Internal Revenue Code.[1] During early 1985, Congress began considering a major overhaul of the existing tax system. Under certain Treasury Department proposals, Section 936 would be eliminated. In such a case, the lower effective interest rate would revert to levels charged on domestic loans, and the expected income tax rate would increase. Not only would higher interest and tax rates affect Bumble Bee's ability to repay its debt but the changes would also have an impact on the value of the company to potential investors. (To aid in the valuation process, Exhibit 10 gives information for several other companies that were involved in consumer canned goods.)

Keith Shaughnessy realized that he had a great deal of ground to cover before he could give officials at First Boston a reply to their request for financing.

---

[1] Under Section 936, U.S. companies operating in Puerto Rico were exempt from U.S. taxes on their Puerto Rican-sourced income. Bumble Bee had separately negotiated a partial Puerto Rican tax exemption on all income and property taxes for 15 years. Profits generated by Section 936 companies were subject to an additional 10 percent tax if profits were repatriated to a U.S. parent. The penalty for repatriated income caused banks operating in Puerto Rico to have excess deposits from Section 936 companies, which allowed the banks to offer loans to Section 936 companies at rates below those offered in the United States. In Bumble Bee's case, its Section 936 debt was expected to be priced 4 percent lower than its domestic borrowing rate.

EXHIBIT 1   Product Mix (as a percentage of sales)

	Bumble Bee		*Industry*
Whitemeat	43%		20%
Lightmeat	57		80
Water packed	58		57
Oil packed	42		43

	1972	*1977*	*1983*
Water packed	17%	19%	57%
Oil packed	83	81	43
Total case volume (in thousands)	21,854	27,776	28,220

Source: First Boston Corporation.

EXHIBIT 2   Brand Shares of Retail Market

	Bumble Bee (%)	Star-Kist (%)	Chicken-of-the-Sea (%)	All Others (%)
Whitemeat:				
1984 ...	30%	26%	15%	29%
1983 ...	26	27	14	33
1982 ...	26	28	18	28
Lightmeat:				
1984 ...	9	34	24	33
1983 ...	10	33	24	33
1982 ...	10	31	24	35
Total share:				
1984 ...	15	32	24	29
1983 ...	13	33	25	29
1982 ...	16	31	27	26

Source: First Boston Corporation.

EXHIBIT 3   Bumble Bee Share of Whitemeat Market

	1983	1984	1985	Percent of Bumble Bee's Whitemeat Sales in 1985
New York City	35.7%	37.6%	45.4%	46.8%
Boston	22.3	20.6	28.6	10.6
Miami	51.0	53.8	59.6	6.8
Hartford	43.8	47.2	52.3	5.8
Baltimore/Washington	54.5	51.1	53.8	4.3
Other markets	—	—	—	25.7
				100.0%

Source: First Boston Corporation.

EXHIBIT 4   Description of Managers

Patrick W. Rose (43), President

Rose joined Castle & Cooke in 1982 following 15 years with Ralston Purina's Van Camp Seafoods division, which included Chicken-of-the-Sea brand tuna. Rose's final position before joining Castle & Cooke was vice president of marketing, where he was responsible for marketing, sales, distribution, and production planning for the Van Camp division. He would serve as president and CEO of the new company.

James T. McCarthy (42), Vice President, Resources and Development

After service as a lieutenant commander in the U.S. Navy, McCarthy joined Bumble Bee in 1973. Over the last 12 years, he has been responsible for production, resourcing, financial management, and fleet operations. In his new position he was to be responsible for securing supplies of competitively priced raw materials, finished goods manufactured by others, and business development.

Ernest W. Peterson (47), Vice President, Production

Peterson came to Bumble Bee after 20 years with Van Camp Seafoods, where his responsibilities included production, research and development, quality assurance, and industry and government affairs. While with Van Camp, Peterson gained recognition for fish-processing advancements, and since joining Bumble Bee, he had been instrumental in increasing the firm's operational efficiency. He would become vice president of operations for the company.

Harley K. Branson (42), Vice President and General Counsel

After spending five years as divisional counsel at Van Camp Seafoods, Branson joined Bumble Bee in the same capacity in 1983. While with Van Camp, he handled the legal matters related to marine construction programs, joint ventures in Mexico, Ecuador, and Ghana, and Eurodollar and domestic credit facilities for the division's global activities. Prior to joining Van Camp, Branson spent 10 years in private practice. He would serve as vice president/general counsel for the new company.

EXHIBIT 5   Bumble Bee Historical and Projected Balance Sheets (dollars in thousands)

	For the Year Ended June 30			Pro Forma for New Company, March 1985
	1982	1983	1984	
Assets:				
Cash	$ (75)	$ 8	$ 122	$ 0
Trade receivables	9,668	13,932	15,565	0
Other receivables	14,945	14,152	3,980	1,054
Inventories	90,744	59,927	63,884	54,876
Prepaid expenses	4,130	4,417	3,196	4,017
Total current assets	119,412	92,436	86,747	59,947
Minority interests	717	659	235	0
Land	768	588	588	0
Property, plant, & equipment	35,994	19,420	15,231	570
Noncurrent receivables	5,155	9,446	9,274	0
Other assets	84	116	404	1,983
Total assets	$162,130	$122,665	$112,479	$62,500
Liabilities:				
Notes payable	—	428	477	0
Current portion LTD	1,050	1,050	1,050	0
Taxes payable	(15,404)	(14,604)	5,080	0
Other payables & accruals	9,840	9,189	20,752	0
Intercompany payables	116,596	78,408	60,191	0
Total current liabilities	110,182	74,471	87,550	0
Long-term debt	4,580	3,530	2,480	59,200*
Deferred taxes	14,125	26,140	24,404	0
Other deferrals	685	6,136	6,154	0
Minority interest	3,774	1,698	(700)	0
Total liabilities	133,346	111,975	119,888	59,200
Equity	28,784	10,690	(7,409)	3,300
Total liabilities & owners' equity ..	$162,130	$122,665	$112,479	$62,500

* Long-term debt would consist of (in 000): U.S. line of credit, $27,165; Puerto Rican line of credit, $10,035; senior subordinated notes, $7,000; and junior subordinated notes, $15,000.

Source: First Boston Corporation.

EXHIBIT 6   Historical Income Statements (dollars in thousands)

	Year Ended June			Seven Months Ended
	1982	*1983*	*1984**	*1/26/85*
Sales	$208,030	$190,190	$214,807	$131,479
Cost of sales	198,550	168,110	184,302	112,294
Gross profit	9,480	22,080	30,505	19,185
Distribution	420	2,210	2,931	1,623
Selling & marketing	17,730	15,310	14,130	7,677
General & administrative	8,660	7,620	8,861	5,339
Operating income†	(17,330)	(3,060)	4,583	4,546
Other income	1,080	(2,910)	2,684	578
Profit before taxes	(16,250)	(5,970)	7,267	5,124
Depreciation	5,370	4,110	2,531	—

* Before extraordinary reserves, write-offs, and write-downs.

† Operating income contains no capital charge or provision for interest expense on intercompany payables.

Source: First Boston Corporation.

EXHIBIT 7   Pro Forma Balance Sheets (dollars in millions)

	For the Year Ended June 30							
	1985	*1986*	*1987*	*1988*	*1989*	*1990*	*1991*	*1992*
Cash	$ 0.0	$ 0.0	$ 0.0	$ 0.0	$ 0.0	$ 0.0	$ 0.0	$ 2.4
Other receivables	1.1	1.1	1.1	1.1	1.1	1.1	1.1	1.1
Accounts receivable	0.0	10.9	11.0	10.9	10.9	11.7	11.7	11.7
Inventory	54.9	56.6	57.4	56.6	56.8	61.2	61.2	61.2
Other current assets	4.0	4.0	4.0	4.0	4.0	4.0	4.0	4.0
Total current assets	60.0	72.6	73.5	72.6	72.8	78.0	78.0	80.4
Plant, property, & equipment	0.5	1.3	1.8	2.2	2.6	2.9	3.1	3.3
Other assets	2.0	2.0	2.0	2.0	2.0	2.0	2.0	2.0
Total assets	$62.5	$75.9	$77.3	$76.8	$77.4	$82.9	$83.1	$85.7
Accruals & payables	$ 0.0	$ 9.6	$ 9.7	$ 9.6	$ 9.6	$10.4	$10.4	$10.4
Current portion LTD	3.0	2.0	2.5	2.5	5.0	0.0	0.0	0.0
Total current liabilities	3.0	11.6	12.2	12.1	14.6	10.4	10.4	10.4
Debt: Sr. bank	37.2	38.6	35.8	30.8	25.3	23.4	11.4	0.0
Sr. sub. notes	7.0	7.0	7.0	7.0	7.0	7.0	7.0	7.0
Jr. sub. notes	12.0	10.0	7.5	5.0	0.0	0.0	0.0	0.0
Total liabilities	59.2	67.2	62.5	54.9	46.9	40.8	28.7	17.4
Equity	3.3	3.3	3.3	3.3	3.3	3.3	3.3	3.3
Retained earnings	0.0	5.4	11.5	18.6	27.2	38.8	51.1	65.0
Total liabilities & owners' equity	$62.5	$75.9	$77.3	$76.8	$77.4	$82.9	$83.1	$85.7
Capital expenditures		$1.0	$1.0	$1.0	$1.0	$1.0	$1.0	$1.0
Depreciation		$0.3	$0.5	$0.6	$0.6	$0.7	$0.8	$0.8

Source First National Bank of Boston.

EXHIBIT 8   Pro Forma Income Statements (dollars in millions)

	For the Year Ended June 30						
	1986	1987	1988	1989	1990	1991	1992
Sales	$208.9	$211.9	$208.7	$209.5	$225.7	$225.7	$225.7
Cost of goods sold	170.5	172.2	169.0	168.9	181.0	181.0	181.0
Gross profit	38.4	39.6	39.7	40.6	44.7	44.7	44.7
Distribution	5.0	5.1	5.0	5.0	5.4	5.4	5.4
Selling	10.2	10.4	10.2	10.3	11.1	11.1	11.1
General & administrative	8.6	8.7	8.6	8.6	9.3	9.3	9.3
Operating income	14.6	15.5	15.9	16.8	19.0	19.0	19.0
Interest expense	8.4	8.2	7.6	6.6	5.4	4.5	2.5
Profit before taxes	6.2	7.3	8.2	10.2	13.6	14.5	16.4
Income taxes	0.9	1.1	1.2	1.5	2.0	2.2	2.5
Net income	$ 5.3	$ 6.2	$ 7.0	$ 8.7	$ 11.6	$ 12.3	$ 14.0
Assumed interest rates:							
U.S. bank debt	16.0%						
Puerto Rican bank debt	12.0%						

Source: First National Bank of Boston.

EXHIBIT 9   Proposed Debt Structure

Senior Secured Bank Debt

Amount: $40 million—reducing revolver inclusive of $10 million in Section 936 debt;
$10 million—line of credit facility for seasonal procurement needs;
$10 million—1-year working-capital facility for build-up of receivables.

Rate: Base + 1.5% (domestic); 936 debt cost + 3% (Puerto Rican debt).
Commitment fee: 0.5%.
Closing fee: $500,000.

Maturity: 7 years

Amortization: End of June: 1987, $3mm; 1988, $4mm; 1989, $7mm; 1990, $3mm; 1991, $12mm; 1992, $10mm.

Covenants	Interest Coverage	Tangible Net Worth	Minimum Working Capital	Total Liabilities less Subordinated Debt/ Subordinated Debt plus Equity
closing—12/27/85	1.33:1	$ 3.3mm	$47.0mm	4.0:1
12/27/85— 6/27/86	1.33:1	4.5mm	47.0mm	4.0:1
6/28/86—12/26/86	1.5:1	6.25mm	47.0mm	3.0:1
12/27/86— 1/1/88	1.7:1	9.5mm	47.0mm	2.5:1
1/2/88—12/30/88	2.0:1	16.0mm	47.0mm	2.0:1
12/31/88—12/29/89	2.0:1	23.0mm	47.0mm	2.0:1
12/30/89—	2.0:1	31.0mm	47.0mm	2.0:1

Subordinated debt only includes the junior subordinated note.
Security: All assets, including trademarks.

Senior Subordinated Notes (Institutional Investor)

Amount: $7 million.
Rate: 16%.
Maturity: 15 years.
Amortization: 20% of face amount in years 11 through 15.
Security: Inventory and receivables, no trademarks.

Junior Subordinated Notes (Castle & Cooke)

Amount: $15 millon.
Rate: 12%.
Maturity: 5 years.
Amortization: End of: 6 months, $1.5mm; 12 months, $1.5mm; 18 months, $2.0mm; 3 years, $2.5mm; 4 years, $2.5mm; 5 years, $5.0mm.
Security: Trademarks, Puerto Rican cannery leasehold, inventory, and receivables.
Subordination: Subordinated to principal and interest payments of senior bank debt and interest payments of senior subordinated notes.

Source: First National Bank of Boston.

EXHIBIT 10   Comparable Consumer Products Companies

	Campbell Soup	Ralston Purina	Castle & Cooke	H. J. Heinz	C.H.B. Foods
5-Year average (1980–84):					
ROE	14.2%	18.7%	3.0%	19.5%	8.5%
ROA	5.1%	4.2%	0.8%	5.6%	1.2%
5-Year average annual growth rate:					
Sales	10.2%	1.6%	.9%	7.3%	5.6%
Profits	7.6%	15.4%	NMF	12.7%	−4.2%
1984 Performance:					
ROE	15.2%	26.3%	NMF	21.2%	7.1%
ROS	5.2%	5.3%	NMF	6.3%	1.2%
Expected growth rates (1985–88);					
Sales	9.7%	12.6%	7.0%	10.1%	—
Profits	14.1%	11.1%	NMF	11.0%	—
Average ROE	17.0%	32.0%	12.0%	19.0%	—
Beta, levered	0.70	0.85	0.75	0.75	—
Long-term debt (in millions)	$283	$897	$660	$273	$11
Equity (in millions)	$1,259	$862	$460	$1,247	$48
Price/earnings	11.0×	12.2×	NMF	13.0×	12.0×
Market value/book value	179.3%	363.6%	124.2%	289.7%	84.7%

$$\text{Risk-free rate} = \text{Long-term Treasury rate} - 1\%$$
$$= 11.47\% - 1.1\%$$
$$= 10.37\%$$

$$\text{Market rate} = \text{Risk-free rate} + \text{average difference between return on equities and risk-free rate}$$
$$= 10.37 + 8.6\%$$
$$= 18.97\%$$

NMF means Not a meaningful figure.

Source (for beta information and capital structure): *Value Line Investment Survey*, vol. 40.

EXHIBIT 11   Sample of Interest Rates, February 1985

	Yield to Maturity (%)
U.S. Treasury 30-year Bonds	11.47%
Moody's AAA Industrial Bonds	12.13
Moody's BAA Industrial Bonds	13.51
Allegheny International (BB+) SF Deb 9s '95	14.48
Allis Chalmers (B+) SF Deb 6.10s '90	14.43
American Sign & Indicator (B−) Sub SF Deb 15s 2001	16.17
Athlone Industries (B) Sub SF Deb 11s '93	15.79
LaBarge, Inc. (B−) Sub Deb 14 ½s 2008	15.80
Prime rate	10.50

Case 47

MediMedia International, Ltd.

We had a clear vision that we could do much better on our own than as part of a bureaucracy. The demotivating factors of a big operation paralyze activity. We saw opportunities for revenue growth, cost savings, and asset management—all things that required people to take extra initiative at the local level. Across 25 countries this is quite a challenge: we wanted to be able to act locally under a common global understanding. Accordingly, we re-created the sense of partnership, the feeling that "it is our company" by inviting all the key managers in as equity investors. Raising the equity completely internally was not the hard part; indeed, the equity offering was oversubscribed by $2 million.

Dr. Martin Steinmeyer, *chairman and chief executive officer of MediMedia*

As Martin Steinmeyer later recounted, the major challenges in the buyout had to do with negotiating the transaction and arranging the debt financing. Buyout negotiations had been ongoing since February 1990. Now, in February 1991, the leveraged buyout (LBO) department of Kleinwort Benson, Ltd. (KB), in London, in collaboration with Berliner Handels und Frankfurter Bank (BHF) in Frankfurt, was circulating a confidential memorandum soliciting senior-debt financing for a management buyout. The total funds required, $70.13 million, would be raised in part with debt denominated in European currency units (ECUs), the first time a buyout would be so financed. Was this structure appropriate? Could the debt financing be arranged? Was the purchase price sensible? What were the risks and potential returns to the various players in the deal: the senior creditors, Dun & Bradstreet (the seller and source of a vendor note), KB and BHF (mezzanine investors and financial advisors to management), and management (who were to provide the entire source of equity capital)?

This case was prepared by Robert F. Bruner and draws on field interviews and company documents. The cooperation of MediMedia International, Ltd., and Kleinwort Benson is gratefully acknowledged.

THE COMPANY

The target of the buyout bid, MediMedia International, Ltd., had a corporate office in London and published medical journals and distributed promotional supplies primarily for prescribing doctors. MediMedia's business included 30 largely autonomous operations in 25 countries, producing more than 70 products. Table 1 presents a breakdown of revenues by global region and reveals that over two thirds of MediMedia's business was in Europe. Most of the firm's products afforded pharmaceutical companies the opportunity to promote their prescription drugs to prescribers.

MediMedia occupied a leading position in almost all of the local markets in which it operated. No other pharmaceutical promotional companies operated on as wide a scale as MediMedia. Almost all of the company's products were exclusive to a specific geographical market; even where products were produced in one country and sold in another, they were tailored to local conditions and regulations.

MediMedia had four principal medical product groups: medical journals, drug directories, office media (such as prescription pads and other medical stationery), and custom media (such as single-sponsored publications, educational videos, and training services). Directories and office media represented the most stable products in terms of both revenue and margins, whereas several journal markets had recently experienced not only reduced growth in display advertising expenditures but also structural changes favoring certain types of journals over others. Competition, modest in office media and directories, was quite intense in journals.

The principal source of revenue from journals was the sale of display advertising to pharmaceutical companies. On the other hand, directories, office media, and custom media generated a substantial portion of their income from line fees, sponsorship and sale of products, and subscriptions from doctors, pharmacists, and veterinarians. Pharmaceutical companies used directories and office media to advertise and promote brand awareness of essential products in daily use. Journals and custom media tended to benefit from new-product launches.

MediMedia maintained its own editorial staff, many of whom had medical or pharmaceutical training. The staff was responsible for writing or commissioning journal articles and maintaining the data bases for the various directories. On some products, the production process extended to photocomposition or even typesetting, but MediMedia was not a printing company. Virtually all physical production and distribution were performed by external suppliers or contractors.

TABLE 1 MediMedia International Revenue by Region, 1990 (in US$ millions)

Europe	$ 77.5
U.S.A.	17.5
Asia/Oceania	11.8
Other	5.0
Interco.	(0.9)
Total	$110.9

Given the importance of government regulation in the drug industry (especially on promotional activities), MediMedia's national markets tended to behave independently. Few global trends existed, other than the expectation that the world pharmaceutical industry would continue to grow and to spend a fairly constant proportion of sales on marketing and promotional activities. However, MediMedia management identified five trends that warranted careful attention:

- Pharmaceutical advertisers were fine-tuning the targeting of advertising promotion to maximize the value of advertising spending. This strategy would tend to favor customized media, special editions of drug directories, and prescription pads.
- Pharmaceutical companies were concentrating advertising expenditures in the early stage of a product's life cycle. This focus would favor targeted and customized or educational media.
- European Community (EC) members as well as countries in other regions were considering proposals to extend patent lives for ethical drugs.
- Some markets were tending to favor high-frequency journals, often in tabloid format.
- The globalization of product sales was an ongoing trend.

Advertising-based journals were clearly less favored by the above factors, and the journal market in some countries already had been adversely affected. Where expenditures on journals had been reduced, however, the resulting detriment tended to be to the marginal players, rather than across the board. MediMedia management had responded to these threats with higher publication frequency and increased circulation, coupled with some switches to tabloid formats.

HISTORICAL PERFORMANCE

The businesses that were to form the MediMedia International group hitherto had been structured, for management purposes, as a distinct subgroup of companies within Dun & Bradstreet. Accordingly, historical financial information existed on a pro forma, stand-alone basis only down to the operating-profit level, below which the business accounts were distorted by such items as goodwill amortization. Operating performance for the four years ended 1990 is summarized in Exhibit 1.

During the fiscal year ended November 30, 1990, the group's total revenue amounted to $111.0 million and its operating profit to $8.9 million. During the period 1987–90, the group's revenue grew at a compound annual rate of 7.8 percent and gross profit at 5.2 percent. Revenue from drug directories, journals, and office media together accounted for 83.4 percent of total revenue and had grown each year from 1987 to 1990. Sales in Europe accounted for 73 percent of the group's revenue, with France being the largest single contributor (37 percent of revenue and 30 percent of operating profit). No single product in any country accounted for a material portion of the group's total revenue or gross profit.

Printing and production, which accounted for half of the group's direct costs, were largely variable in nature and consisted principally of paper and third-party printing. The other half, while not completely variable, could be controlled by skillful management of the editing and production processes. Editorial costs accounted for about 17 percent of direct costs and were largely fixed, although some free-lancers were used. Sales costs had a significant variable element, because a proportion of the sales staff's remuneration was in the form of commissions and bonuses. Distribution costs were substantially variable, because the group had no in-house distribution capabilities.

The slight decline of gross-margin percentages over the past three years generally was due to product reformating and enhancement efforts in the journal segment. These efforts reflected the highly competitive nature of the journal sector, the significant costs incurred by the group to reposition and relaunch several major titles in response to market trends, and internal restructuring. Gross margins on office media were constant throughout the period.

The group's principal tangible assets were two French freehold properties in central Paris with a net book value of US$3.5 million. Management estimated the current market value of the properties to be US$10.8 million; the buildings were expected to be the only tangible security available to lenders. Intangibles consisted of deferred software costs and, following the acquisition, goodwill in the form of intellectual-property rights. Trade debt consisted of high-quality receivables from international pharmaceutical companies. Work-in-progress inventory was generally small. Current liabilities consisted mainly of amounts due suppliers and deferred income liabilities with respect to subscription amounts received in advance of delivery.

ORIGINS OF THE BUYOUT PROPOSAL

MediMedia was to be carved out of the IMS International unit of Dun & Bradstreet (D&B), which had acquired IMS International in May 1988. At the time, IMS consisted of two businesses, market research and communications. D&B, interested in only the market research segment of IMS, would have quickly sold the communications business; but because the acquisition had been completed by means of a tax-free exchange of stock and had been accounted for as a "pooling of interests," D&B was prohibited for two years from making any significant disposals from IMS under United States Securities and Exchange Commission regulations. Martin Steinmeyer commented:

> We expressed a desire to buy these businesses at the time when D&B bought IMS. D&B demurred because of the two-year waiting period. Toward the end of the period, D&B hired S.G. Warburg & Company to advise them on the sale of the medical publishing businesses. Five other bidders emerged—three others willing to pay much more than we. Among the potentially interested buyers was Elsevier (in Holland), who were themselves publishers of specialized journals and magazines. D&B called our offer ridiculous and told us to give up hope of buying the business. But we insisted that our offer remain on the table. Ultimately, the other bidders withdrew. Maybe they did not want to bid against the people on whom they would have to rely to make the acquisition succeed.

To raise the debt financing, management approached BHF (which had known Dr. Steinmeyer for many years) and KB to co-manage the deal. Exhibit 2 summarizes the principal hurdles faced by KB and BHF in structuring the financing for the acquisition.

TABLE 2   Sources and Uses of Funds (ECU securities translated at ECU1 = US$1.388)

Sources	US$ Millions
Existing liabilities	1.13
Senior debt	32.00
Mezzanine debt	15.00
Vendor note	11.00
Equity	11.00
Total sources	70.13
Uses	
Purchase price	65.80
Decr. net working capital	(4.47)
Interest on purch. price	1.30
Cost and expenses	7.50
Total uses	70.13

The sources and uses of funds are given in Table 2. Exhibits 3, 4, and 5 give the detailed terms for the senior debt, mezzanine debt, and vendor note, respectively. Almost half of the debt financing, or $29 million, would be denominated in ECU.[1] Following the freeing up of capital movements within the European Community, many observers believed the ECU would play a larger role in financial services. Indeed, by February 1991, a robust secondary market in ECU-denominated corporate bonds had formed. Until this time, however, no leveraged buyout had been funded in whole or part with the ECU.

The development of the buyout proposal for MediMedia occurred in a declining market for buyouts. The peak in buyouts had occurred in 1989 (see Exhibit 6); since then, the volume and average size of buyouts had dropped dramatically, as had the degree of financial leverage, or gearing, in such deals. To a large extent, this trend was coincident with a softening in capital-market conditions over the 1988–91 period. The European leveraged buyout market was dominated by U.K. deals in terms of both transaction volume and value.

----

[1]The European currency unit (ECU) was created in 1979 as part of the founding of the European Monetary System. In value the ECU equaled a "basket" of 12 European national currencies, weighted as follows: Belgian franc, 7.6 percent; Luxembourg franc, 0.3 percent; Danish kroner, 2.45 percent; German mark, 30.1 percent; Spanish peseta, 5.3 percent; French franc, 19.0 percent; Irish pound, 1.1 percent; Italian lira, 10.15 percent; Dutch florin, 9.4 percent; U.K. pound, 13 percent; Greek drachma, 0.8 percent; and Portuguese escudo, 0.8 percent. The ECU could be valued in US$ terms by translating each constituent currency into dollars at the prevailing exchange rate, multiplying by the weights, and summing. The easier approach would be to consult the published exchange rates given in financial newspapers. Although not used as legal tender, ECUs were recognized as foreign currency in all EC countries and were used in bond issues, bank deposits, and checks. In 1988, ECU-denominated bond issues accounted for 5.5 percent of all international bond issues and ranked sixth among all global currencies.

MANAGEMENT

MediMedia was expected to employ 537 persons at closing. Of these, 52 managers proposed to contribute the $11 million in equity necessary to consummate the buyout. Several managers were keen to participate in the auction themselves, because they had significant net worth from the profits they realized when they sold their publications to the group. After closing, 11 million shares would be outstanding; on a fully diluted basis, the total would rise to 12.94 million shares.

The board was to consist of four managers, plus two nonexecutive directors. Dr. Steinmeyer (German, age 55) would be the president and chairman of the board of MediMedia. He was president of IMS International's Communications Division and had personally founded some of the business units subsequently acquired by IMS International and then by D&B. Dr. Steinmeyer, who would be based in Germany, also would be responsible for group operations in Germany, Austria, Switzerland, and the United States.

Mr. Gerard Lashermes (French, age 47), to be based in Brussels, would be the chief operating officer and the director responsible for group operations in France, Belgium, Italy, Spain, and Portugal. He had joined the staff of Les Ordonnances Médicales de France (OMF) in 1968 and become its managing director and co-owner in 1972. OMF was acquired by the MediMedia group in 1976.

Mr. David Bromilow (British, age 48) would be manager of MediMedia's operations in the Australasia/Asia region and would be based in Bangkok. Qualified as a chartered accountant, he had joined IMS International in 1972 and served in the finance department until 1987, when he assumed his present operational responsibility in Bangkok.

Mr. Paul Keane (British, age 46) would be the chief financial officer, based in London. He had served as financial controller of the IMS International Communications Division since 1987 and was a chartered accountant. Prior to IMS, he had worked for various firms in auditing, merchant banking, and corporate planning.

DUN & BRADSTREET

D&B, the seller of the businesses that would form MediMedia, was a major purveyor of business information. It sold credit reports on more than 9 million businesses, published the Yellow Pages telephone directories, published bond ratings through its Moody's Investors Services subsidiary, and measured television audiences through its A. C. Nielsen subsidiary. D&B had been thrown on the defensive in late 1990 by charges that its Credit Services unit (which sold credit reports on companies) had engaged in systematic sales churning. In addition, its A. C. Nielsen subsidiary was being squeezed by price competition and rising costs. *Value Line* expected D&B's earnings to decline by 10 percent, but believed the company was in "rock-solid" financial shape.

THE FINANCIAL ADVISORS

Kleinwort Benson, Ltd., was one of the major international merchant banks in the city of London and had acted as senior lender, mezzanine lender, equity investor, and corporate advisor to investors in over 100 buyouts. Its European Mezzanine Fund[2] (formed in a partnership among KB and other major institutional investors) had committed resources available to it in excess of £80 million. The fund aimed to place amounts between £3 million and £20 million with Western European borrowers that had cash flow, strong market share, high barriers to entry, strong management, the absence of cyclicality, and low capital intensity.

BHF was headquartered in Frankfurt and provided a full range of corporate-banking and investment-banking services. At the end of 1990, its total assets were (deutsche marks) DM38.8 billion. BHF's shares were listed for trading on all regional stock exchanges in Germany as well as on exchanges in Basle and Zurich.

MEDIMEDIA'S BUSINESS PLAN AND FINANCIAL FORECAST

The financial forecast for the period 1991–98 (see Exhibits 7, 8, and 9) suggested that the outstanding debt under the senior term loan facility could be repaid in full within six years. The figures for 1991 were extracted from management's annual budget for D&B and reflected a consolidation of local operating units' own projections. The figures for 1992 also were based on local operating-unit estimates (the projections for 1993 and beyond had no detailed recourse to local operating units). An important feature of the projections was that they assumed no asset sales, acquisitions, capital expenditure cutbacks, or cost-reduction programs.

---

[2]A promotional brochure published by Kleinwort Benson explained mezzanine debt as follows:

[It] is a form of capital that comes between equity and debt. In essence, it fills the gap between the amount of senior debt which can be advanced against the security of a company's assets and its cash flow, and the limited amount of equity normally available. Mezzanine finance is generally subordinated to senior debt. It will typically have a junior pledge of security or be unsecured. Therefore, mezzanine providers look almost exclusively towards the cash flow generated by the business (although sometimes they also consider asset sales) in order to assess the likelihood of repayment. To compensate for the lack of security and the greater risk of nonpayment should the investee company encounter difficulty, mezzanine debt typically receives a higher rate of interest than a traditional bank loan. Specifically, the interest rate is often in the range of standard money market rates (LIBOR in the U.K.) plus 3 to 5%. There is also usually a further payment to the mezzanine provider after 3 or 5 years related to the increase in the value of the company over that period. This final payment can be made by issuing warrants which are convertible into ordinary shares in the company. Typically, the Fund would expect the mezzanine finance that it provides to have a 6 to 9 year nominal maturity but realistic prospects for refinancing or repayment from other sources within 3 to 5 years, if the business is as successful as planned. . . . An institutional investor would usually expect an internal rate of return (IRR) of over 40% for providing equity capital in an MBO, whereas a mezzanine lender would aim for an IRR of between 20% and 30%, depending on interest rates and the risks inherent in the transaction. The use of mezzanine finance reduces the amounts required of senior debt and equity. This results in a safer senior loan in terms of better asset coverage and a larger capital base. It is, therefore, easier to raise senior debt and, since mezzanine can improve the return on investment, it becomes easier to raise equity capital.

Revenue in 1991 was expected to grow at 21 percent; this forecast was significantly influenced by the weakening of the U.S. dollar against those European currencies that accounted for over two thirds of the group's revenues. At constant rates, revenue growth would be 11 percent. Growth in 1991 was expected to be achieved through a combination of price increases (to keep pace with inflation), new products, increased publication frequency, and the publication of certain biannual products.

The modest improvement in gross margins projected for 1991 was believed to be conservative, because of the absence of substantial one-time costs for restructuring, relaunches, and redundancies taken to direct costs during 1990. Management forecasted no other significant margin improvements, although it expected improved performance from several products.

Management assumed no improvement in working-capital control in 1991 and only a modest improvement in 1992. Historically, there had been little incentive to speed cash collection, although management believed there was considerable room for improvement.

The projections assumed a 30 percent effective tax rate, even though the marginal corporate tax rate throughout most of the European Community and the United States was about 35 percent. This lower rate reflected efforts to create a tax-efficient corporate structure by channeling earnings away from high-tax jurisdictions and debt toward those countries.

Exhibit 10 presents information on publishing and information services companies. Given MediMedia's peculiar market niche, no single company could be a perfect comparison; but the multiples and aggregate information could give a financial analyst a sense of comparative financial performance.

Exhibits 11, 12, and 13 summarize information on capital-market conditions in dollars, pounds, and ECUs. KB analysts assumed, for the sake of their financial analyses (see projections in Exhibits 7, 8, and 9), that the ECU London Interbank Offering Rate (LIBOR) would be 10 percent and the dollar LIBOR would be 6.75 percent for the duration of the forecast period.

CONCLUSION

This proposed transaction was structured around the classic model for the leveraged buyout: the financing structure involved the aggressive use of debt, arrayed across several tiers of the capital structure; management also expected to service the debt from the strong cash flow of the business, its growth, and hoped-for operating economies; finally, the layer of mezzanine debt included warrants, giving those investors a play on MediMedia's equity. Observers wondered how large the gains from improved operating performance and debt financing would be in this instance, and how the new wealth thus created would be parlayed among the various participants in the transaction.

More important, were the prospective returns sufficient to attract lenders and investors? Kleinwort Benson had noted that mezzanine investors looked for internal rates of return of between 20 and 30 percent, and that institutional-equity investors looked for internal rates of return of over 40 percent. To generalize about target rates of return for bank lenders was difficult, although most banks had difficulty producing returns of more than

1 percent on their entire loan portfolios. For highly leveraged transactions, some banks looked for internal rates of return of more than 2 percent on loans.[3] MediMedia's *marginal* tax rate was especially difficult to estimate, although outside observers believed 35 percent would be appropriate.[4]

The transaction also offered some unusual twists: (1) a significant part of the debt was denominated in ECUs, (2) the managers of the new company would be the sole providers of the equity capital—no outside equity investors would help consummate the deal, and (3) the structure included a vendor note that appeared to carry an extraordinarily low coupon. Observers wondered what motivated these unusual features, and how, if at all, they might contribute to the success of the transaction.

---

[3]The 1 and 2 percent benchmarks assumed that the internal rate of return was calculated as *net* of funding costs and of the bank's taxes on profits from the loan. Observers estimated that 35 percent would be an appropriate marginal tax rate for a bank lender. Also, a bank's cost of funds was typically 200 basis points (two percentage points) *below* LIBOR.

[4]MediMedia generated profits in countries that applied maximum marginal rates on taxes ranging from 60 percent (Germany) to 0 percent in certain tax havens. The prevailing maximum statutory tax rates in the United States, Britain, and France were about 35 percent. Assuming that increasing European integration would result in some equalization of tax rates there, a marginal rate of 35 percent became a focal point for analysts.

EXHIBIT 1   Historical Operating Performance, 1987–1990

	1987	1988 (11 Months Only)	1989	1990
Revenue	$89,387	$87,819	$97,772	$110,897
Costs	(76,874)	(77,666)	(85,201)	(98,466)
Local operating profit	12,513	10,153	12,521	12,431
Central costs	(3,953)	(2,523)	(2,984)	(3,525)
Operating profit	8,560	7,630	9,537	8,906
Local operating profit margin (%)	14.0	11.6	12.8	11.2
Operating profit margin (%)	9.6	8.7	9.8	8.0

Source: Offering memorandum.

EXHIBIT 2   Prominent Issues in Approaching the Buyout

1. **Price.**   It is crucial to determine the appropriate purchase consideration for the target company. This is done using several different methods, the most common of which are: (1) comparable transactions in the industry; (2) discounted cash flow. In a more general sense financiers seek to answer the question, "How much debt can the company prudently service given its industry, competitive position, growth potential, and other factors?"

2. **Capital Structure.**   Once the purchase price is determined, the question becomes how the buyout should be financed. That is, what proportion of the total capital should be equity, mezzanine (if applicable), or bank loans (senior debt). This decision is made on the basis of a variety of factors but must accommodate both the need for a decent return on the equity and mezzanine layers and the need for an amount of senior debt that banks are likely to provide.

3. **Identity of the Financiers.**   As the issues of capital structure are resolved, the lead debt arranger for the transaction must have a firm idea on which specific financial institution can be counted upon to finance the deal. The "target list" of senior and mezzanine lenders and equity providers (the latter is not applicable in this case) is drawn up by a combination of people from the LBO unit and the financing desk (bank syndications group) based on knowledge of the deal and the market.

4. **Deal Timetable.**   The various parties involved in an LBO often are driven by external constraints. These constraints need to be known and a realistic timetable designed, within those limits.

5. **Due Diligence.**   This term traditionally refers to the process of researching and investigating the target company, its competitive position, and the industry. With regard to the company, the emphasis is on the accounting and a legal examination of all relevant ledgers, books, contracts, and documents. The purpose of this examination is to determine the *historical* status and performance of the company: this forms the basis of a view on the likely *projected* performance of the business. The most time-consuming part of this process is undoubtedly the accountants' investigative report, usually called a "Long Form Report."

6. **Legal and Tax Structure.**   Apart from the capital structure, parties in an LBO must decide how the new company will be organized, because organizational decisions will have a decisive impact on whether the financing can be arranged in a satisfactory form and whether an inappropriately high level of tax can be avoided. The advice of legal and tax counsel is necessary.

Source: Internal memorandum, Kleinwort Benson.

EXHIBIT 3   Proposed Terms, Senior Revolving and Term Debt

Borrowers: New holding companies in the Netherlands, Hong Kong, Switzerland, Germany, and France, as well as Les Editions du Médecin Généraliste S.A.

Guarantors: MediMedia (the ultimate parent), the regional holding companies, and Les Editions du Médecin Généraliste S.A., jointly and severally.

Purpose: To finance the acquisition, and pay the fees, costs, and expenses relating thereto.

Currency: The senior term loan facility will be divided into two tranches, A and B. Tranche A drawings will be denominated in ECUs, and tranche B drawings will be denominated in U.S. dollars. Advances under the revolving loan facility may be in U.S. dollars and other freely convertible foreign currencies.

Amounts: The senior term loan facility aggregate drawings under tranche A: ECU 10,090,000. Aggregate drawings under tranche B: US$18,000,000. Revolving loan facility amount is US$4,000,000, or the equivalent in other currencies.

Agent: BHF-Bank, Frankfurt.

Lead Managers: Kleinwort Benson, Ltd., and BHF-Bank.

Repayment: Revolving loan facility must be repaid in full no later than the seventh anniversary of the senior facilities agreement.

Senior term loan installments:

	Tranche A	*Tranche B*
30 November 1991	0	US$2,000,000
30 November 1992	0	US$4,000,000
30 November 1993	ECU 1,550,000	US$1,850,000
30 November 1994	ECU 1,800,000	US$2,000,000
30 November 1995	ECU 2,150,000	US$2,500,000
30 November 1996	ECU 2,525,000	US$3,000,000
30 November 1997	The balance	The balance

EXHIBIT 3 *(concluded)*

The facilities will be automatically repayable in full upon the occurrence of (1) a flotation or listing of MediMedia's share capital, (2) any material change in control, or (3) any event that would give rise to mandatory prepayment of the subordinated vendor note.

Prepayment: All prepayments shall be applied against scheduled repayment installments in inverse order of maturity. Drawings prepaid may not be reborrowed.

Voluntary prepayment: Permissible, subject to a prepayment fee equal to 2.5 percent of any amounts repaid in year 1 and 1.5 percent of any amounts prepaid in year 2.

Mandatory prepayment: Excess cash flow shall be applied in prepayment of outstanding principal. Excess cash flow shall mean (1) amounts received by way of rebate of the purchase consideration, (2) amounts received from asset disposals, (3) proceeds of any money-raising activities, and (4) cash generated for financing, less net interest accrued and scheduled principal payments.

Interest rate: For both the revolving loan facility and the senior term loan facility, 2.25 percent over LIBOR for the relevant currency and period.

Commitment fee: For the revolving loan facility, 0.5 percent per year on the unused portion of the facility.

Financial covenants included:

EBIT/Total interest expense	Minimum 2×.
EBIT/Senior debt interest expense	Minimum 3×.
Cash generated for financing/Total interest expense	Minimum 1.2×.

General covenants:

Negative pledge by MediMedia and all companies in the group.
No payment of dividends or other distributions to investors.
No share repurchase or redemption of shares.
No change in the fiscal-year end.
No acquisitions or formations of subsidiaries.
No asset disposals.
No additional borrowings.

Security: A first charge over all the assets, including goodwill and other intangible assets, group revenue, and equity in subsidiaries.

Governing law: English law.

Source: Kleinwort Benson memorandum.

EXHIBIT 4   Proposed Terms, Mezzanine Debt

Mezzanine Debt: ECU 10,810,000, Subordinated Secured Term Loan

---

Borrowers: New regional holding companies in the Netherlands, Hong Kong, and Switzerland.

Guarantors: MediMedia International (the ultimate parent company) and the regional holding companies, jointly and severally.

Repayment: One installment, due 30 November 1998. Repayment and prepayment provisions similar to senior debt facilities. Prepayment is not permitted while senior debt is outstanding.

Interest: 3.25 percent per annum over LIBOR.

Warrants: To subscribe for ordinary shares in MediMedia equivalent to 15 percent of its fully diluted ordinary share capital (or 1.94 million shares). Exercisable at any time for a nominal consideration (i.e., $0.01 per share) either in whole or in part at the option of the warrantholders. After the seventh anniversary of the financing, the warrantholders may put shares acquired through exercise of the warrants to MediMedia at a price per share equal to 7 times earnings per fully diluted share. There will be 12.94 million shares on a fully diluted basis.

Financial and general covenants: Similar to the senior debt facility.

Participants: Agent: Kleinwort Benson, Ltd. Lead managers: Kleinwort Benson, Ltd., and BHF. Investors: Kleinwort Benson European Mezzanine Fund L.P. and BHF.

Source: Offering memorandum.

EXHIBIT 5   Proposed Terms, Subordinated Vendor Note

Subordinated Vendor Note: US$11 Million Junior Subordinated Debt

---

Issuer: Regional holding companies of MediMedia in the Netherlands, Hong Kong, and Switzerland.

Guarantors: MediMedia and its regional holding companies, jointly and severally.

Holder: Dun & Bradstreet Group.

Final Maturity: 10 years from the issuance date.

Interest: Years 1 and 2: fixed rate equal to 0.52 percent per year over the average yield of 9- and 10-year U.S. treasury bonds. During the first two years, interest will be paid by means of noninterest-bearing deferred notes, payable at final maturity of the subordinated vendor note.

Years 3-10: cash interest of 0.52 percent over the interpolated yield on the two U.S. Treasury bonds whose final maturities are, at the subordinated note's interest reset date, nearest to the final maturity of the subordinated vendor notes. Interest that cannot be paid in cash after year 2 will be satisfied by another issue of notes carrying same terms.

Mandatory prepayment: After satisfaction of the senior and mezzanine loans, prepayment must occur upon: (1) sale or disposal of all the assets; (2) sale of share capital; (3) listing of share capital; (4) merger or consolidation of MediMedia.

Security: Ranking junior to senior and mezzanine loans. Otherwise, security interest is similar to those facilities.

Subordination: Repayments of principal on these notes may not be made unless the senior and mezzanine loans have been fully discharged.

Profit participation: The noteholder will be entitled to share in gains arising from disposals made by, or flotation of, the MediMedia group while the notes are outstanding. The noteholder's share will be equal to 25 percent of the gain if sold in the first year, 20 percent if in the second, 15 percent in the third, and 10 percent each year thereafter until maturity of the loan. No amounts may be paid in cash until the senior and mezzanine loans have been fully discharged.

Source: Offering memorandum.

EXHIBIT 6 Volume of Deals, and Total Value Paid in U.K. Leveraged Buyouts, by Year

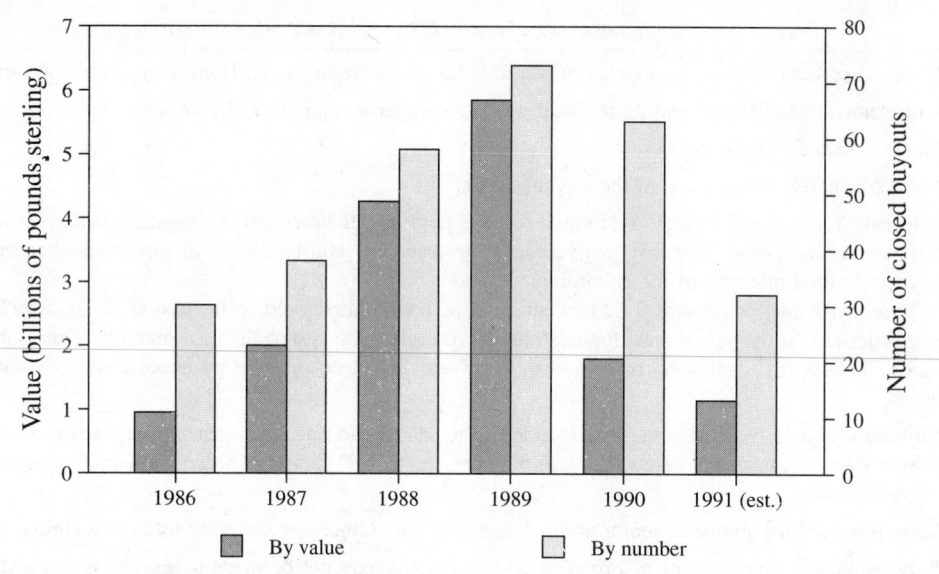

Sources: Kleinwort Benson and KMPG Corporate Finance.

EXHIBIT 7 Forecasted Profits and Cash Flows, 1991–98, Fiscal Years Ending November 30 (US$ millions)

	Historical				Projected						
	1988	1989	1990	1991	1992	1993	1994	1995	1996	1997	1998
EBIT	7.60	9.50	8.90	11.42	14.60	16.89	18.25	19.71	21.29	23.00	24.85
Less interest on:											
Existing debt	N.Av.	N.Av.	N.Av.	1.00	0.03	0.03	0.03	0.03	0.03	0.03	0.04
Working cap. revolver	N.Av.	N.Av.	N.Av.	0.17	0.17	0.17	0.17	0.17	0.17	0.17	0.17
Senior term loan	N.Av.	N.Av.	N.Av.	1.69	3.20	2.83	2.83	1.87	1.25	0.52	0.00
Mezzanine loan	N.Av.	N.Av.	N.Av.	0.99	1.99	1.99	1.99	1.99	1.99	1.99	1.99
Junior sub. debt	N.Av.	N.Av.	N.Av.	0.47	0.94	0.94	0.94	0.94	0.94	0.94	0.94
Total interest expense	N.Av.	N.Av.	N.Av.	(4.32)	(6.33)	(5.96)	(5.51)	(5.00)	(4.38)	(3.65)	(3.14)
Interest income	N.Av.	N.Av.	N.Av.	0.32	0	0.13	0.25	0.38	0.55	0.74	1.06
Tax expense	N.Av.	N.Av.	N.Av.	(1.82)	(2.53)	(3.38)	(3.95)	(4.58)	(5.29)	(6.08)	(6.89)
Net income	N.Av.	N.Av.	N.Av.	5.60	5.74	7.68	9.04	10.51	12.17	14.01	15.88
Depreciation	0	1.30	2.00	1.90	1.98	2.01	2.11	2.22	2.22	2.22	2.22
Incrs. deferred taxes	(0.10)	0	0.70	(0.25)	(0.19)	(0.20)	(0.20)	0	0	0	0
Capital expenditures	0	0	0	(2.69)	(1.40)	(2.64)	(2.77)	(2.91)	(2.91)	(2.91)	(2.91)
Decrs. accts. recvbl.	1.80	0.70	(6.40)	(0.02)	(2.24)	(2.73)	(2.95)	(3.19)	(3.44)	(3.72)	(4.02)
Decrs. inventories	0.30	0	(1.20)	0.17	(0.23)	(0.32)	(0.40)	(0.43)	(0.46)	(0.50)	(0.54)
Decrs. prepaid expense	0	(1.20)	(0.80)	0.40	(0.12)	(0.14)	(0.15)	(0.16)	(0.18)	(0.19)	(0.21)
Incrs. accts. payable	0.50	0.80	(10.80)	0.18	0.80	1.15	1.41	1.52	1.64	1.77	1.91
Incrs. taxes payable	0	0	1.30	0.45	0.57	0	0	0	0	0	0
Incrs. accrued liabs.	0	0	11.30	(1.33)	0.70	0.85	0.92	0.99	1.07	1.16	1.25
Noncash interest exp.	0	0	0	0.47	0.94	0.47	0	0	0	0	0
Cash avail. for debt repayment	N.Av.	N.Av.	N.Av.	4.88	6.55	6.13	7.01	8.55	10.11	11.84	13.58
Scheduled debt repayments											
Senior term	N.Av.	N.Av.	N.Av.	2.00	4.00	4.00	4.50	5.50	6.50	5.50	0
Mezzanine	N.Av.	N.Av.	N.Av.	0	0	0	0	0	0	0	15.00
Junior sub.	N.Av.	N.Av.	N.Av.	0	0	0	0	0	0	0	0
Total	N.Av.	N.Av.	N.Av.	2.00	4.00	4.00	4.50	5.50	6.50	5.50	15.00
Revolver repayment	N.Av.	N.Av.	N.Av.	(1.70)	0	0	0	0	0	0	0
Residual cash flow (Addition to cash balance)	10.10	11.10	5.00	4.58	2.55	2.13	2.51	3.05	3.61	6.34	(1.42)

Source: Offering memorandum.

EXHIBIT 8   Historical and Forecasted Net Assets and Capital Structure, 1991–98 (US$ millions)

	Pre-Closing Nov. 1990	Changes	Pro Forma Nov. 1990	1991	1992	1993	1994	1995	1996	1997	1998
Net Assets											
Net working capital	$11.04	$ (4.47)	$ 6.57	$11.30	$14.37	$17.69	$21.37	$25.69	$30.67	$ 38.49	$ 38.68
Gross PPE	7.71		7.71	10.40	11.80	14.44	17.21	20.12	23.03	25.94	28.85
Accumulated depreciation	0		0	1.90	3.88	5.89	8.00	10.22	12.44	14.66	16.88
Net PP&E	7.71		7.71	8.50	7.92	8.55	9.21	9.90	10.59	11.28	11.97
Other LTA	2.42		2.42	2.42	2.42	2.42	2.42	2.42	2.42	2.42	2.42
Goodwill	0	45.93	45.93	45.93	45.93	45.93	45.93	45.93	45.93	45.93	45.93
Transaction costs	0	7.50	7.50	7.50	7.50	7.50	7.50	7.50	7.50	7.50	7.50
Total net asset	21.17	48.96	70.13	75.65	78.14	82.09	86.43	91.44	97.11	105.62	106.50
Capital structure:											
Existing debt	0.29		0.29	0.29	0.29	0.29	0.29	0.29	0.29	0.29	0.29
Revolver	0	0	0	1.70	1.70	1.70	1.70	1.70	1.70	1.70	1.70
Senior term debt	0	32.00	32.00	30	26.00	22.00	17.50	12.00	5.50	0	0
Mezzanine debt	0	15.00	15.00	15.00	15.00	15.00	15.00	15.00	15.00	15.00	0
Junior subordinated debt	0	11.00	11.00	11.47	12.41	12.88	12.88	12.88	12.88	12.88	12.88
Total debt	0.29	58.00	58.29	58.46	55.40	51.87	47.37	41.87	35.37	29.87	14.87
Deferred tax	0.84		0.84	0.59	0.40	0.20	0	0	0	0	0
Equity	32.33	(21.33)	11.00	16.60	22.34	30.02	39.06	49.57	61.74	75.75	91.63
Total capital	33.46	48.96	70.13	75.65	78.14	82.09	86.43	91.44	97.11	105.62	106.50
Ending debt/equity (×)	0.01	36.67	4.92	3.40	2.44	1.72	1.21	0.84	0.57	0.39	0.16
Avg. debt/equity (×)				4.16	2.92	2.08	1.46	1.03	0.71	0.48	0.28
EBIT/interest (×)				2.6	2.3	2.8	3.3	3.9	4.9	6.3	7.9
EBIT/interest & principal (×)				2.5	1.4	1.7	1.8	1.9	2.0	2.5	1.4

Source: Offering memorandum.

EXHIBIT 9 Forecast of Free Cash Flows and Tax Savings from Debt (US$ in millions)

	1991	1992	1993	1994	1995	1996	1997	1998
Free Cash Flow Forecast								
EBIT	$11.42	$14.60	$16.89	$18.25	$19.71	$21.29	$23.00	$ 24.85
Taxes	−4.00	−5.11	−5.91	−6.39	−6.90	−7.45	−8.05	−8.70
EBIAT	7.42	9.49	10.98	11.86	12.81	13.84	14.95	16.15
Cash flow adjustments:								
+ Depreciation	1.90	1.98	2.01	2.11	2.22	2.22	2.22	2.22
+ Increase in deferred taxes	−0.25	−0.19	−0.20	−0.20	0	0	0	0
− Capital expenditures	−2.69	−1.40	−2.64	−2.77	−2.91	−2.91	−2.91	−2.91
+ Decrease in accounts receivable	−0.02	−2.24	−2.73	−2.95	−3.19	−3.44	−3.72	−4.02
+ Decrease in inventories	0.17	−0.23	−0.32	−0.40	−0.43	−0.46	−0.50	−0.54
+ Decrease in prepaid expenses	0.40	−0.12	−0.14	−0.15	−0.16	−0.18	−0.19	−0.21
+ Increase in accounts payable	0.18	0.80	1.15	1.41	1.52	1.64	1.77	1.91
+ Increase in taxes payable	0.45	0.57	0	0	0	0	0	0
+ Increase in accrued liabilities	−1.33	0.70	0.85	0.92	0.99	1.07	1.16	1.25
− Investment								
Free cash flow	6.23	9.36	8.96	9.83	10.85	11.78	12.78	13.85

	1991	1992	1993	1994	1995	1996	1997	1998
Forecast of Annual Debt Tax Shields								
Interest expense	4.32	6.33	5.96	5.51	5.00	4.38	3.65	3.14
− Interest income	(0.32)	0	(0.13)	(0.25)	(0.38)	(0.55)	(0.74)	(1.06)
− Interest not paid in cash	(0.47)	(0.94)	(0.47)	0	0	0	0	0
Net deductible interest expenses	3.53	5.39	5.36	5.26	4.62	3.83	2.91	2.08
Annual tax reduction	1.24	1.89	1.88	1.84	1.62	1.34	1.02	0.73

Source: Casewriter analysis, drawing on offering memorandum.

EXHIBIT 10 Information on Comparable Companies

	Beta	Volatility or Sigma	Book Value Debt/Equity Ratio	Market Value Debt/Equity Ratio	Last Year Operating Margin	P/E Ratio	Expected Dividend Yield	Expected Five Year Growth Rate of	
								Revenues	Divs.
Axel Springer Verlag AG (Germany) Publishes newspapers, specialty magazines, books, and market research data reports.	N.Av.	N.Av.	0.362	N.Av.	2.7%	N.Av.	N.Av.	N.Av.	N.Av.
Commerce Clearing House (U.S.) Publishes looseleaf reports, periodicals, and books on current developments in tax and business law. Foreign operations account for 13 percent of revenues.	0.70	0.35	0.075	0.028	13.5	21.3	2.3%	7.5%	4.0%
Dun & Bradstreet (U.S.) Sells credit information, "Yellow Pages," and financial ratings.	1.10	0.20	0.120	0.030	22.0	16.5	3.1	8.5	8.0
Elsevier N.V. (Netherlands) Publishes newspapers, consumer magazines, trade books, scholarly journals, and scientific and medical journals.	1.05	0.30	0.030	0.005	18.9	19.0	4.0	N.Av.	N.Av.
EMAP PLC (U.K.) Publishes consumer magazines, business magazines, and newspapers, and holds trade shows. Owns 13 radio stations.	1.03	0.32	0.061	0.021	12.3	11.1	N.Av.	N.Av.	N.Av.
Euromoney Publications PLC (U.K.) Publishes international financial news, information and analyses through magazines, surveys, books, directories, data bases, conferences, and seminars.	1.05	0.23	0.037	0.010	19.0	15.5	4.5	N.Av.	N.Av.

Company									
Havas S.A. (France) Sells local media, directories, international multimedia, tour services, advertising, and consulting.	1.10	N.Av.	0.283	0.059	3.7	23.6	1.0	N.Av.	N.Av.
Houghton Mifflin Co. (U.S.) Publishes textbooks and materials for colleges and schools.	1.20	0.20	0.250	0.176	17.0	18.3	2.1	9.5	9.5
International Thomson Organization Specialized publisher for professional groups (39% of revenues), publisher of regional newspapers in U.K. (21%), and operator of leisure travel business (40%).	1.15	0.45	0.950	0.300	15.6	16.0	3.4	N.Av.	N.Av.
McGraw-Hill Inc. (U.S.) Publishes textbooks, technical, and popular books, business and industrial periodicals (e.g., *Business Week, Aviation Week,* etc.). Owns 4 TV stations.	1.20	0.20	0.500	0.249	19.5	15.3	2.7	6.5	6.5
Meredith Corp. (U.S.) Publishes *Better Homes and Gardens, Ladies Home Journal, Country Home, Metropolitan Home, Successful Farming,* plus books on cooking and hobbies. Owns 7 TV stations. Insiders control 59 percent of shareholder votes.	1.20	0.65	0.294	0.200	3.0	27.0	1.9%	7.0%	6.5%
Pearson PLC (U.K.) Publishes newspapers and magazines (*The Economist*) holds interests in entertainment, oil services, and investment banking.	1.00	0.30	0.570	0.250	16.0	14.0	N.Av.	N.Av.	N.Av.
Reed International PLC (U.K.) Principal activities are publishing and business information.	1.33	0.37	0.618	0.400	15.7%	11.3	N.Av.	N.Av.	N.Av.

Sources: *Value Line Investment Survey,* March 8, 1991; *Moody's International Corporate Manual,* 1991; Risk Measurement Services, January 1991; and casewriter estimates.

Yields on U.S. Treasury Debt Securities

1-month	6.37%	4-years	7.41%
3-months	6.18	5-years	7.58
6-months	6.27	7-years	7.82
1-year	6.37	8-years	7.87
2-years	7.00	10-years	7.92
3-years	7.22%	30-years	8.08%

Yields on 10-Year Debt of Other Governments

United Kingdom	9.97%
Japan	8.06
Germany	8.29
France	8.97
Netherlands	8.56%

Yields on High-Grade U.S. Corporate Bonds

1–3 years	8.13%
5–10 years	8.66
15+ years	9.20%

Bank Lending Rates

U.S. prime rate	9.00%
U.K. base lending rate	13.50
LIBOR (US$)	6.75%

Interest Rate Trends

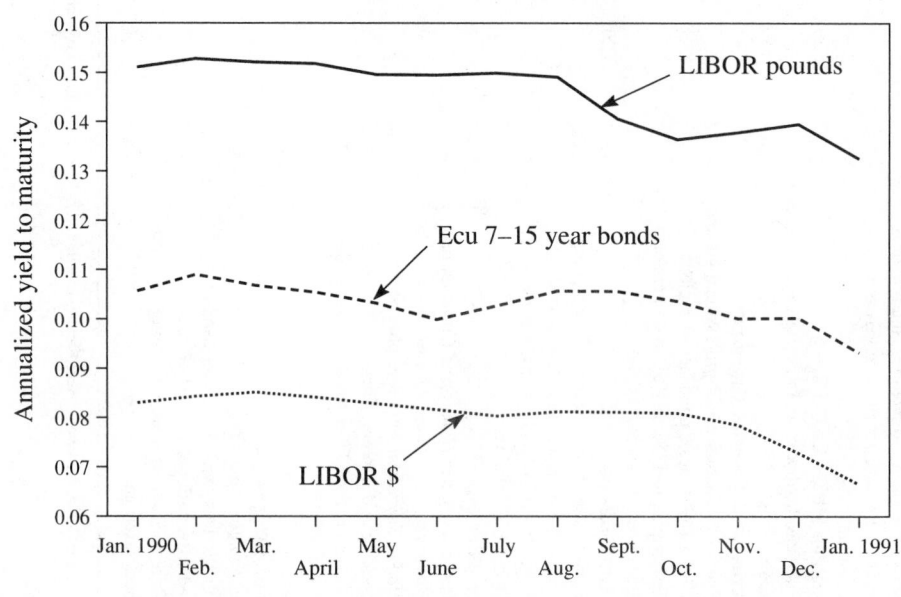

Sources: *Financial Times,* February 26, 1991; and OECD *Financial Indicators,* March 1991 and June 1990.

EXHIBIT 12   Current Equity Capital Market Conditions as of Late February, 1991

	Dividend Yield	*P/E Ratio*
FTSE 500 (London)	4.91%	11.49 ×
S&P 500 (New York)	2.19	17.77
Dow Jones Industrials	3.44	N.Av.

Equity Market Trends
Major World Equity Markets

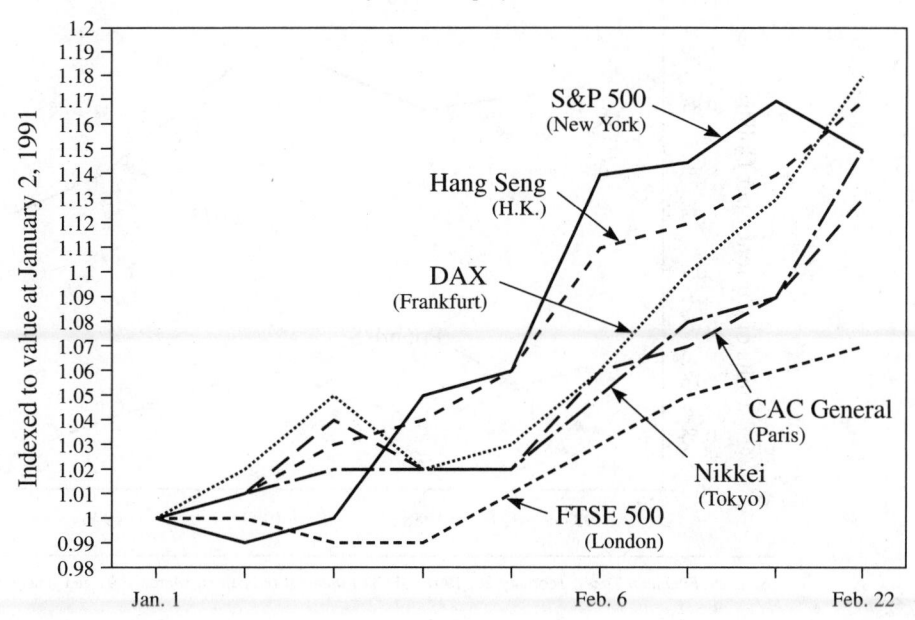

Source: *Financial Times*.

EXHIBIT 13   Current Foreign Exchange Market Conditions as of Late February, 1991

	Spot	*1-Month Forward*	*3-Month Forward*
US$/ECU	1.3535	+0.31	+0.91
US$/£	1.92225	+0.98	+2.76

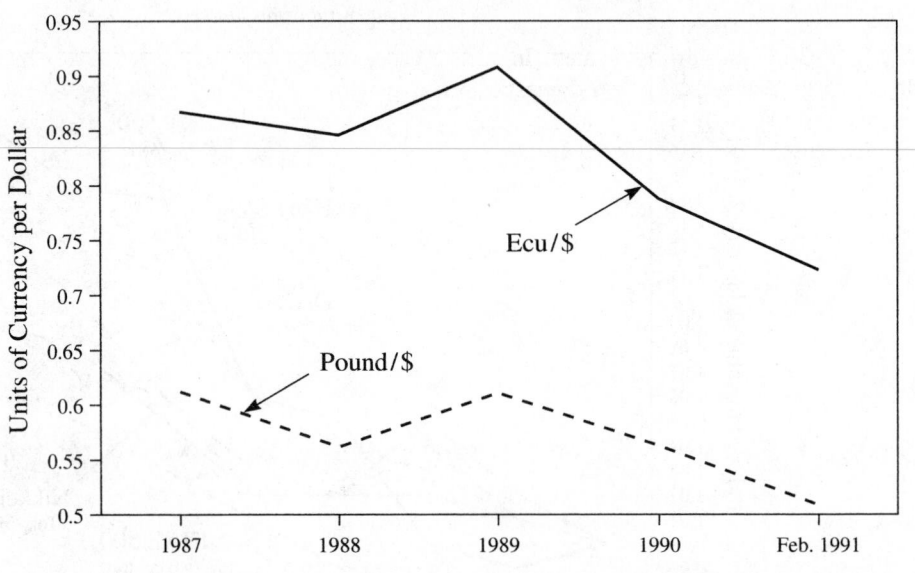

Trends in Foreign Exchange Rates
(Last Four Years)

Sources: *Financial Times,* February 26, 1991; OECD *Financial Indicators,* March 1991 and June 1990.

Case 48

Caledonian Newspapers, Ltd. (Abridged)

The buyout was difficult from the word "go." First, our due diligence was a massive hurry-up, because the seller was anxious to close. The deal closed on June 30, 1989, three weeks after a venture capitalist brought it to us. We had to close the financing on a demand basis, because the lawyers couldn't get the documentation done in time. The documentation took longer because, just before the closing, we all discovered that, in its haste, the venture capitalist had negotiated one deal with us and another deal with management. It took three more months of negotiation to align everybody's participation.

Second, a month after closing, a difficulty in understanding the operations of the company led to a warranty claim against the seller involving a dispute on some of the terms of sale. The negotiations with the seller delayed the entire program of layoffs, which were crucial to meeting the financial projections. The old financial forecasts were irrelevant. We had to approach it as if the deal were starting over.

Third, a year after closing [the summer of 1990] advertising revenue in the entire regional newspaper industry went into free fall. . . .

With these words, Ian Stirling recounted the unexpected difficulties with his debtor, Caledonian Newspapers, Ltd., which had been taken private in June 1989. Stirling was a vice president at the London branch of Eagle American Bank (EAB), which originally had financed the acquisition with the expectation of realizing high returns on the loan, both from high interest rates and from exercising a warrant for 9 percent of the shares of the company. Over the 18 months following the buyout, the company had fallen far short of its plan and its covenants, and two cash infusions were required to keep it solvent. Now, in December 1990, the company was nearly insolvent again: just a few days

---

This case was prepared by Robert F. Bruner while he was a visiting professor at INSEAD, in Fontainebleau, France. The case draws extensively on interviews with and memoranda of a financial institution that chooses to remain unidentified. Names and numerous facts have been disguised.

previously, Stirling had recommended that his bank write off one half the value of the loan, £1.25 million. He wanted to devise a plan of action that would put Caledonian on a sound financial basis permanently (permitting repayment of the loan) or at least terminate the bank's losses on the credit. He was contemplating two alternative courses of action:

- Restructure the company's capital in a way that would make available enough cash for the company to survive through some combination of new equity investment and debt rescheduling or forgiveness. Two separate proposals recently had been put forward.
- Liquidate the company. Because Caledonian was in default of its loan agreement, EAB could force an immediate sale of the business by demanding repayment of its £2.5 million loan in full.

To pursue the best course would require careful analysis of Caledonian, not only from a creditor's point of view but also from an equityholder's. In addition, any analysis would have to take place fast: Stirling estimated that Caledonian's cash would run out completely in less than two months.

CALEDONIAN NEWSPAPERS

Caledonian published two newspapers, the *Glasgow News Clarion* (a morning daily except Sunday) and *The Sunday Leader* (circulation, 27,000). The *Glasgow News Clarion*, with a record of over 250 years of uninterrupted publication, was the English-speaking world's oldest daily newspaper. Published in Glasgow, its circulation, covering the whole of Scotland, had been declining gradually, since it peaked at 49,000 in 1963 to its current 39,000. In recent years, circulation had been relatively stable, because existing readers were extremely loyal.

The newspaper market in Glasgow was dominated by three local daily publications: Caledonian's *News Clarion* and two competitors, the *Glasgow Telegraph* and *Scots News*. The *Glasgow Telegraph* held 34 percent of circulation in Glasgow and Scotland at large. The *Scots News* held 10 percent, and the *News Clarion*'s market share was 8 percent. Various "national" daily newspapers published in Edinburgh and England accounted for 48 percent of circulation. Like the *News Clarion*, the *Scots News* was a morning paper; the *Glasgow Telegraph* was published in the evening.

Caledonian's head office and plant were leased. Production equipment was up to date. Text was keyed directly by journalists; production employees set advertisements and made up the pages. Caledonian operated a rotary press that, although nearly 40 years old, provided a reasonable level of printing quality but at a level below the quality provided by the web offset press in use at the *Glasgow Telegraph* and other national newspapers from England. Caledonian handled its own distribution through a fleet of 69 vehicles. The retailer margin on sales of Caledonian newspapers was in line with U.K. standards, 30 percent of cover price.

THE MANAGEMENT BUY-IN[1]

Caledonian Newspapers had been owned by the Rutherglen family since 1796 and was currently run by Captain William Rutherglen (age 64), who wanted to retire. With no "heir apparent" in the family, Rutherglen, as noted previously, had sought to sell the company to a large U.K. publisher. The price had been set at £3.8 million. Rutherglen was somewhat dismayed by the sudden failure of this deal and quickly had set out to close a deal with another purchaser. The management buy-in team negotiated a price of £3.25 million; subsequently, other offers had been made to Rutherglen in excess of £4.00 million, but he had agreed to honor his deal with the original buy-in team so long as the agreed time schedule was met.

John Dumbarton, an executive with years of experience in turning around regional daily newspapers, led the management buy-in team. Dumbarton had decided that reducing payroll costs was the key to improved profit margins at Caledonian. He targeted a work-force reduction of 67 employees, which yielded annual savings of £767,000. The total one-time cost of these redundancies, £400,000, would be paid back in 9 to 18 months. New typesetting technology permitted the staff to be reduced without affecting the quality of the newspaper.

In addition to the program of cost reductions, Dumbarton developed an unusual proposal for increasing advertising revenue by issuing a free newspaper in Glasgow, essentially a clone of the *News Clarion* but under a different title, while continuing to sell the *News Clarion* outside Glasgow. This move would permit Caledonian to climb to circulation parity with the *Glasgow Telegraph* and compete more effectively for advertisers. More than 45 percent of advertising revenue in Scotland originated in Glasgow.

The acquisition was to involve £300,000 of equity financing to be provided by the new management team and £1,200,000 by Emergent Ventures (EV), a large U.S. venture-capital company with which Eagle American Bank had participated in many profitable deals. The acquisition was an asset purchase with sources and uses of funds as follows:

	Sources *(£ 000s)*		*Uses* *(£ 000s)*
Bank debt (EAB)	2,500		
Conv. preferred stock (EV)	900	Acquisition price	3,250
Common stock: EV	300		
Common stock: Management	300	Redundancies & working capital	750
Total	4,000	Total	4,000

---

[1]"Buy-in" was a term used by Ian Stirling and was synonymous with "buyout" as used in the United States.

Emergent Ventures' preferred stock would be convertible into common shares.

On a fully diluted basis, management and EV would control, respectively, 18.2 and 72.8 percent of the common shares.[2] The preferred stock would receive a 9 percent dividend if cash were available. EAB would provide a £2.50 million, six-year, revolving/term loan to finance £1.75 million of the purchase price and £750,000 toward restructuring costs and working-capital requirements for the first 12 months. Exhibit 1 details the terms of the loan agreement.

The sale transaction was so structured that Caledonian could occupy the leasehold premises rent free for two years and would pay £60,000 annually thereafter. Caledonian also had an option to buy the property at any time during the next three years exercisable at £900,000. Stirling learned from an outsider familiar with the property that the land had considerable potential and could be worth £2 million within two years. He did not include this possibility in his projections but believed that the potential property values provided some credit support in the event of liquidation.

Stirling's analysis of the deal, which suggested a "base-case" after-tax return on assets to the bank of 3 to 4.5 percent, reflected the benefits of fees, expected warrant conversion, high and rising interest rates, and the bank's ability to fund the loan through an interest-rate swap at an all-in cost of 11 percent. Over the previous four years, Eagle American Bank had realized after-tax returns on its entire loan portfolio of about 1 percent. On its portfolio of loans in highly leveraged transactions, EAB had realized returns of just over 2 percent. In addition, Stirling expected that participation in the deal would encourage Emergent Ventures to present other business opportunities to the bank.

THE SECOND- AND THIRD-ROUND FINANCINGS

Although the buyout nominally occurred in June 1989, the new management team was not free to begin its restructuring until January 1990 when the warranty settlement with Rutherglen, the seller, was agreed. Accordingly, a new business plan dated January 1990 was formulated.

Stirling continued:

> In the first three months of 1990, the company started to underperform. Indeed, the company missed an interest payment, and management asked us to forgive interest. We were unhappy with that and told them that, if they needed more money, to raise it themselves. In March 1990, management and Emergent Ventures agreed to invest another £390,000 in total. EAB also invested £14,000 to avoid dilution of its warrant equity interest. At the time, we were still fairly bullish on the company's prospects. By the spring, Dumbarton, in fact, was back

---

[2]EV's £900,000 investment in convertible preferred stock would be exercisable into 54.6 percent of the fully diluted shares outstanding. EV's £300,000 investment in common equity would, like management's £300,000 investment, claim 18.2 percent of the shares on a fully diluted basis. EAB's warrants would be exercisable into the remaining 9 percent of shares on a fully diluted basis.

on schedule with the program of redundancies: 40 had been completed. There were 27 more redundancies under the original program to go (at a cost of £160,000). Dumbarton had identified opportunities for 12 more redundancies beyond that to be incurred over 12 months, at a total cost of £257,000 and an annual saving of £15,000 per position.

By May 1990, it was apparent that the company would need more money. At that time, the U.K. recession was really beginning to bite. Advertising spending had dropped dramatically. Regional newspapers were hit badly. Even though the company was making the promised cost savings, these savings were chased by the declining revenue. EAB decided not to put any more money up. Emergent Ventures told management that they would put more money up, but if so, it was "good-bye management." Emergent Ventures invited management to put more money in.

John Dumbarton went to Sir Max Ealing,[3] a personal acquaintance of John's and a senior figure in the U.K. publishing industry. Dumbarton persuaded Ealing to invest £350,000 for 20 percent of the common stock of the company. All the former equity investors got diluted; EAB's interest upon exercise of the warrants would be 7.2 percent. The deal was closed in June 1990. Everyone thought this round had done it.

August 1990 was Armageddon for regional newspapers. Advertising revenues fell through the floor. There were several big business failures in the industry. By November 1990, the company was broke again. The money Ealing had invested was gone. There were no buyers for the company. We thought it was going to fail any day. This was a novel experience for Ealing. In November, Emergent Ventures went to Ealing with a new plan for restructuring [presented later] and said, "Put in another £250,000 in support of our plan, or you'll get diluted." He thought Emergent Ventures was taking the wrong approach and told them to go away; shortly thereafter, he put forward his own restructuring proposal [presented later].

At that point, a few things were clear to us. First, management couldn't seem to run the business for cash. Second, the outside equity investors were plainly not in accord, a situation that might grow into a stalemate with disastrous consequences for all. Unless we [EAB] took a more proactive role, the company seemed doomed. So, in late November, we managed to persuade everyone that the firm was to be managed for cash generation, rather than for earnings growth, and found Henry Hounslow, who agreed to step in as finance director and run the business solidly for cash. In addition, we began spending our time with potential receivers in Scotland, to prepare for possible liquidation. We hired Hogarth Hobbes Partners [specialists in media investments] to place a value on the company. They opined that in a breakup asset sale, Caledonian Newspapers was worth between £1.0 and £1.5 million. They said the company's receivables were worth 70 percent of book value, or about £700,000, and they believed that the titles were worth £800,000. The total value placed our loan under water by £1.0 to £1.5 million.

---

[3]Sir Max Ealing, age 67, was a leading figure in newspaper publishing in the United Kingdom. Starting from his origins as an orphan foundling in Battersea, he accumulated a personal net worth in excess of £20 million through the purchase and management of local and regional newspaper-publishing companies. Following a near failure of one of his publishing companies in the 1950s, he disavowed the use of debt financing as the basis for building his business interests; his personal and corporate balance sheets, thus, were virtually debt free. He was known to be an extremely shrewd negotiator and a tough controller of costs. In the present recession, none of his newspaper titles had folded, nor had any of his companies gone bankrupt. Also a leading figure in the Conservative Party, he was a personal friend of prime ministers and numerous cabinet ministers.

In November 1990, EAB downgraded the loan to Caledonian to a risk rating indicating serious doubt of complete repayment and wrote off £1.25 million of the loan.

THE PUBLISHING INDUSTRY

Advertising revenue growth in the regional newspaper industry in real terms was 15 percent in 1988, 4 percent in 1989, and negative 2 percent in 1990. Many industry analysts expected that the real growth rate for 1991 would be negative 2 percent again, but that the monthly rate of change would turn positive by the end of the year. One financial commentator had this to say for the industry:

> Publishing shares have had a rough time in 1990, with the more sluggish economy causing advertising cutbacks in many areas. . . . It is difficult to see, too, when the upturn will come; magazine publisher EMAP has suggested that it won't be before next spring. A pick-up in the housing market would obviously help, with estate agents' advertising important for regional weeklies . . . publishing should be among the first businesses to benefit when upturn comes. Even if that isn't going to happen soon, the big share price falls seen in 1990—taking the sector index to its lowest level since 1986—are making a lot of allowance for dull results. This, then, is a sector with some good recovery situations.[4]

A financial analyst for Emergent Ventures characterized the market's attitude toward the publishing industry as "short-term paranoia." He also noted that the general recession had slowed the pace of acquisitions in newspaper publishing. Exhibit 2 summarizes four recent newspaper acquisitions, and Exhibit 3 gives valuation information on comparable companies. This analyst also called three large publishing firms that were potential buyers for a company like Caledonian. The following is a sampling of the comments he received:

Firm A:

> Few deals are currently being done, and we perceive that prices have dropped dramatically in recent months. Many local papers are struggling; even we have had to close down some of our own titles. Caledonian's strategy of the free newspaper may be flawed; we've had, at best, mixed success with it. A more sensible strategy may be to tighten costs down as much as possible, play hard on the strengths of the core ("paid for") business, and market aggressively the overall readership size of the two daily titles. All things being equal, we wouldn't be looking to buy or sell a business at this point in time. You can't expect to receive more than seven-to-eight times earnings for a business like Caledonian.

Firm B:

> The advertising market is suffering and was particularly bad in July and August. Values have declined since then; there are several properties on the market at this time. A number of previously aggressive groups are not buying, and some publicly quoted companies like Adscene and Goodhead are in a mess. The current environment for a seller is not attractive.

---

[4]"Coping with Tougher Times," *Investors Chronicle*, November 9, 1990, p. 23.

Firm C:

I should say that I am not looking to buy anything and haven't for a year or so. I would not buy anything on a multiple of earnings now, particularly historic ones. Frankly, I would look at asset values at this moment. The industry is struggling. A strategic buy (that is, if it was a newspaper located in the middle of our area) would be different. Then I would look at potential profits and beyond the present economic cycle. Market leaders are very much stronger than those in second or third position. I wouldn't pay much for goodwill unless it was a strategic buy.

LIQUIDATION ALTERNATIVES

Stirling weighed the possibility of simply liquidating the business to recover as much of the bank's principal as possible. Two liquidation scenarios were possible. First, the assets of Caledonian could be sold piecemeal, fetching between £1.0 and £1.5 million. Second, Caledonian might be sold as a single entity, on a going-concern basis. Hogarth Hobbes Partners opined that, on this basis, the firm would fetch about £2 million (see Exhibit 4) or more, if the economy turned up. Unfortunately, virtually no buyers for newspaper companies could be found in the current market climate. To obtain a going-concern price for the company would require waiting.

EMERGENT VENTURES' RESTRUCTURING PROPOSAL

In mid-November, Emergent Ventures had proposed to EAB a choice between two possible loan-restructuring alternatives. The first was that EAB sell its entire £2.50 million debt (including any accrued interest) for a total fixed consideration of £0.75 million, to be received within the next three-month period.

The second alternative called for Eagle American to remain as a debt lender, and Emergent Ventures and Ealing would invest £325,000 in total in noninterest-bearing junior secured convertible debt. Emergent Ventures believed this amount would restore the company to financial health and see it through even an extended downturn in its business. EAB's existing debt would be restructured as follows:

- £1.25 million would remain as senior secured debt. Interest would be paid at LIBOR (the London Interbank Offering Rate) plus 2 percentage points, with the first payment due on June 30, 1991, and quarterly payments thereafter. The rate of principal repayment on the senior debt would need to be negotiated.
- £1.25 million would become junior secured convertible debt, ranking equally with the new Emergent Ventures money. Interest would accrue at LIBOR plus 3 percent until December 31, 1992 (and be payable quarterly in arrears thereafter). Repayment of all junior secured convertible debt, plus accrued interest, would be scheduled in 10 equal annual installments commencing December 31, 1992. On the sale of the company, senior secured debt would become immediately repayable, and junior secured debt would automatically convert into ordinary shares.

EAB's junior debt would convert at the rate of £1 per share into a 25 percent interest on a fully diluted basis. Meanwhile, Ealing and Emergent Ventures would be able to exchange their junior debt for shares at the rate of £0.25 per share. Exhibit 5 describes the capitalization of the company, pro forma the Emergent Ventures proposal.

MAX EALING'S RESTRUCTURING PROPOSAL

At first tentatively and then over the course of several long conversations with Stirling, Ealing sketched out a competing restructuring plan for Caledonian that would call for the current equity investors to subscribe for new common shares in the following proportions:

		Percentage of Shares	
	Cash Investment	*Primary Basis*	*Fully Diluted*
Eagle American Bank	0	0	32.0%
Max Ealing	£360,000	50.7%	34.5
Emergent Ventures	250,000	35.2	23.9
Management	100,000	14.1	9.6
Total new equity	£710,000	100.0%	100.0%

EAB's warrant would increase to 32 percent of the shares (fully diluted), to be exercised at a price equal to the subscription price of the other equity investors, which implied a total exercise price of £334,000. In essence, the former equity claims on the company would cease to exist; any former equity investor who did not subscribe would be wiped out.

Ealing initially proposed that EAB forgive half of its loan to the company. Then later he suggested, instead, that the loan outstanding remain at £2.5 million; but, if the company successfully met all of its interest payments and made the first principal payment in June 1992, EAB would formally forgive half the debt. At the date of forgiveness, the option on 32 percent of the common stock would become active. Until June 1992, Caledonian would have to make interest payments on only half of the loan (£1.25 million) at an interest rate of 12 percent. (EAB's cost of funding was 11 percent.) In effect, Ealing's proposal would decompose the Caledonian credit into a "bad" loan and a "good" loan. The "good" loan would be currently serviced; the "bad" loan would not be serviced; but—if things went well—would be converted into common stock.

Ealing was concerned that, if EAB exercised its large option on Caledonian's stock, he could lose majority control of the company. Therefore, he requested the right of first refusal on the sale of any shares by EAB. If Ealing refused to buy EAB's shares, the bank would have the right to find another buyer, and all other shareholders would be bound to sell their shares at the buyer's offering price or else pay that price to acquire Caledonian themselves.

STIRLING'S FINANCIAL FORECASTS IN DECEMBER 1990

Exhibit 6 presents Stirling's forecast of Caledonian's financial performance for the next 2.5 years until Caledonian's fiscal year end in June 1993. He believed that the fortunes of the company would either have turned sharply better by then or it would be in liquidation. If things turned out well, Emergent Ventures would probably seek to cash out quickly by a partial or complete sale of the company. In either case, a longer forecast horizon was not warranted.

Based on extensive conversations with Dumbarton and Ealing, Stirling came to believe that earnings before interest and taxes (EBIT) would turn positive and, thereafter, hover in the low £400,000 range. This outcome reflected modest increases in advertising and circulation revenues, roughly in line with inflation. Also, the new controller was proving to be quite capable in managing the cash costs of the business. More important, Stirling believed the now completed program of redundancies finally would show a significant effect in reducing production and editorial costs. In short, his EBIT forecast assumed no radical transformation of the business.

Exhibit 6 also shows the earnings and cash flow before debt amortization under three different financing scenarios: (1) the original loan remained outstanding (i.e., £2,500,000 at rates of 17, 18, and 19 percent); (2) Ealing's "good loan/bad loan" proposal went into effect (i.e., £1,250,000 at 12 percent); or (3) Emergent Ventures' senior/convertible subordinated loan proposal was accepted. Stirling noted that, under the current loan structure, both EBIT and cash-flow coverage of interest payments were less than 1.0 for the three-year forecast period, which confirmed his view that the current loan structure was untenable. The two restructuring proposals produced EBIT coverage ratios of greater than 1.0.

Unknown to the other providers of capital to Caledonian Newspapers, Eagle American Bank had funded its loan to Caledonian with an interest-rate swap that effectively locked in a cost of funding at 11 percent. Half of this swap had been unwound when EAB wrote off half the loan in November 1990. However, Stirling viewed the balance of his loan exposure as being funded at 11 percent for the duration of the forecast period in Exhibit 6.

CONCLUSION

Stirling's response to the restructuring proposals was guarded. First, he wondered whether an asset liquidation might not be the highest valued strategy. Every other course of action ran large risks. At the rate at which Caledonian was expected to consume cash, simply waiting for things to get better might be simply waiting for the asset values to deteriorate. (Exhibit 7 presents a summary of current capital-market conditions. The marginal corporate tax rate was 35 percent.) Emergent Ventures' proposal would partially impair EAB's seniority claim on Caledonian's assets. Ealing's proposal injected the unpalatable concept of loan forgiveness in EAB's dealings with Caledonian.

At present, Eagle American Bank was under pressure from U.S. government bank regulators to create reserves against nonperforming loans. The remainder of the loan to

Caledonian, £1.25 million, was currently on nonaccrual status; if it stayed there, the bank would be expected to set aside up to 80 percent of that amount as a provision against loan loss in its income statement. Stirling noted:

> *The bank wants to restructure troubled loans like this, to be proactive, rather than just passively let the mud hit the fan,[5] but our attitude is that any restructuring has to have a strong commercial rationale and not just be driven by accounting rules and banking regulations.*

Stirling believed that quick action was important because of Caledonian's weak cash position. Moreover, he was worried that the longer the restructuring negotiations continued, the more fractious and acrimonious they would become. Even though EAB had substantial power through its priority claim on the assets, using that claim would be a clumsy weapon. The highest valued solution from EAB's standpoint might require continued strong cooperation among the bank and equity investors.

---

[5]In late 1988, Sokol and Metla Garabedian, two well-known raiders, had bought 12 percent of Eagle American Bank's outstanding common shares at prices ranging between $14 and $19 per share. Now, in December 1990, EAB's shares were trading at around $5 per share, a reflection of depressed earnings in the U.S. banking industry stemming from the surprisingly high wave of loan losses being announced. EAB had had its share of these losses. The Garabedians were known to be extremely unhappy with the paper losses on their investment position.

EXHIBIT 1 Original Loan Terms

Facility amount:	£2.5 million revolver/term loan.
Purpose:	To finance acquisition of Caledonian and £750,000 of redundancy costs/working capital.
Maturity:	June 30, 1995 (Pre-payment allowed without penalty.)
Amortization:	Revolving during year 1, then amortising in line with the following repayment schedule (reduction to be scheduled half-yearly): year 2, £200,000; year 3, £400,000; year 4, £500,000; year 5, £500,000; year 6, £900,000; total, £2,500,000.
Pricing:	Year 1 fixed @ 16%
	Year 2 fixed @ 17%
	Year 3 fixed @ 18%
	Year 4 fixed @ 19%
	Year 5 fixed @ 20%
	Interest is payable quarterly in arrears. (Currently, EAB's cost of funding was 12.5%. However the swap reduced the cost of funding *this loan* to 11%.)
Facility fee:	1% payable at closing.
Security:	Fixed and floating charge over all assets of Caledonian.
Covenants:	A full range of covenants will be applied including, *inter alia*:

1. Quantitative tests:

		Minimum EBIT	Minimum EBIT/Interest
Months	1–6	£ 35,000	no minimum
Months	7–8	£ 15,000	no minimum
Months	9–12	£100,000	1.00
Months	13–18	no minimum	2.00
Months	19–24	no minimum	2.50
Year	3+	no minimum	3.00

2. Limitations on indebtedness, liens, guarantees, disposal of assets, investments, distributions, change of management.

3. Key-man insurance of £1 million on Dumbarton.

4. Assignment of property insurance.

Equity participation:	EAB to have a five-year option (exercisable at par value per share, aggregating to £22,000) to acquire 9% of Caledonian common stock.

Fully diluted ownership:	
Management	18.2%
Emergent Ventures	72.8%
EAB (via warrants)	9.0%
	100.0%

Policy issues:	This credit will initially qualify as a highly leveraged transaction, with debt/equity of 1.6:1.

Source: EAB memorandum, June 18, 1989.

EXHIBIT 2   Recent Newspaper Acquisitions (excerpted from an Emergent Ventures memorandum)

Trinity/Pennysaver

Date: February 1990
Target country: USA

Trinity acquired Pennysaver Publications, a Pennsylvania group that published a weekly advertisement-only publication, for £8.02 million. Profit before tax for the year to December 31, 1988, was £250,000, and the group
had net assets at completion of £760,000. The valuation represents a price of 32 times profit before tax.

Trinity/Richmond

Date: May 1990
Target country: Canada

Trinity acquired the *Richmond Review,* a tri-weekly paper with a Friday paid-for circulation of 17,000 and a free
mid-week and weekend edition (home delivered) of 40,000 circulation. Turnover was (Canadian) C$4 million
and the purchase price was C$6.9 million. Whether the business was profitable was not disclosed. The price
represents a multiple of 1.7 times revenue.

Guiton/Guernsey Press

Date: November 1989
Target country: Channel Islands

Guiton launched a hostile bid for its Channel Islands competitor, which failed. The bid value was £17 million.
Guernsey Press made pre-tax profits of £0.73 million on undisclosed turnover. This represents a multiple of
23 times profit before tax.

Southnews/Fulham Times

Date: September 1989
Target country: England

Southnews acquired Fulham Times, which published three free weekly papers, for an up-front consideration of
£240,000 plus a maximum earn out (to March 31, 1991) of £200,000. The Fulham Times group made a loss
of about £100,000 on sales of about £500,000 in the year to March 31, 1989. Thus, the up-front consideration represents 50% of sales and the maximum price might be 90% of sales.

EXHIBIT 3 Information on Comparable Companies

Company	Market Value of Equity	Annual Revenues	Historical Earnings (P/E)	Expected Earnings (P/E)	Equity Value to Revenues	Beta	Market-Value Debt-to-Equity Ratio	Sigma*
Adscene Group PLC	**£9 million**	**£21 million**	4.8×	9.5×	0.43×	1.06	0.242	0.42
Published a portfolio of weekly newspapers (70% of revenues) and provided contract printing services (30%). Historical multiple less than half the sector average because of a 50% decline in profits and a reported 33% decline in turnover for the first 6 months of the year.								
Bristol Evening Post PLC	**£41.8 million**	**£58 million**	12.3×	12.0×	0.72×	0.67	0.052	0.26
Published a number of regional newspapers and also operated a chain of regional newsagents and convenience stores. Publishing accounted for 60% of turnover. The group had been the subject of an offer from David Sullivan, proprietor of the *Sunday Sport*. The Monopolies and Mergers Commission recently blocked the offer; even so, the P/E was at a 10% premium to the market.								
Home Counties Newspapers PLC	**£15.8 million**	**£16.9 million**	5.7×	N.Av.	0.94×	0.79	0.133	0.41
Published a range of weekly newspapers in England. Since January, the company's share price had declined from 250p (pence) to its present level of 158p (a 2-year low). Recent statements from the company said that "it is well placed to withstand the effects of the current difficult economic climate."								
Independent Newspapers PLC	**£143.0 million**	**£138 million**	14.2×	N.Av.	1.04×	0.89	0.178	0.28
Printed and published a range of national and provincial newspapers in Ireland and the United Kingdom and owned a number of outdoor-advertising businesses around the world. Publishing represented 75% of turnover. The group had recently made a number of small acquisitions.								

725

EXHIBIT 3 *(concluded)*

Company	Market Value of Equity	Annual Revenues	Historical Earnings (P/E)	Expected Earnings (P/E)	Equity Value to Revenues	Beta	Market-Value Debt-to-Equity Ratio	Sigma*
Johnston Press PLC	**£40.6 million**	**£41.7 million**	10.8×	N.Av.	0.097×	0.73	0.255	0.21

Printed and published a portfolio of weekly newspapers, both paid for and free. Chairman said he remained "cautiously optimistic" for the current year. Publishing was 75% of turnover.

Company	Market Value of Equity	Annual Revenues	Historical Earnings (P/E)	Expected Earnings (P/E)	Equity Value to Revenues	Beta	Market-Value Debt-to-Equity Ratio	Sigma*
Portsmouth & Sunderland Newspapers PLC	**£32.4 million**	**£71.7 million**	8.7×	8.9×	0.45×	0.58	0.088	0.26

Published daily and weekly paid-for and free titles in England. Also had a retailing division (newsagents) and small film and video interests. Chairman in his latest statement said that the outlook for the publishing business was uncertain and remarked on the slowdown in advertising revenue as "significant" and that vigorous action was being taken to control costs. The company was trading at its 12-month low. Publishing was 70% of turnover.

Company	Market Value of Equity	Annual Revenues	Historical Earnings (P/E)	Expected Earnings (P/E)	Equity Value to Revenues	Beta	Market-Value Debt-to-Equity Ratio	Sigma*
Southnews PLC	**£13.2 million**	**£19 million**	10.7×	N.Av.	0.70×	0.99	0.089	0.37

Published a portfolio of paid-for and free local newspapers in England. Made a number of small acquisitions over the last 18 months. In his most recent statement, the chairman said that, despite the severity of the decline in advertising revenues suffered in England, the board remained confident of the company's future potential.

Company	Market Value of Equity	Annual Revenues	Historical Earnings (P/E)	Expected Earnings (P/E)	Equity Value to Revenues	Beta	Market-Value Debt-to-Equity Ratio	Sigma*
Trinity International Holdings PLC	**£100.8 million**	**£119 million**	8.8×	N.Av.	0.85×	0.96	0.333	0.36

Published newspapers in the United Kingdom, United States, and Canada and also was engaged in the manufacture of papermaking and packaging products in the United Kingdom. Had recently been consolidating its overseas portfolio through acquisition and stated that it was considering a number of further acquisitions at home and abroad. Publishing was 63% of turnover.

*Sigma is the annualized volatility of returns on a company's stock and is a measure of risk used in the valuation of options.

Sources: Internal EAB memorandum, *Risk Measurement Services*, December 1990, and casewriter's estimates.

EXHIBIT 4   Report of Hogarth Hobbes Partners

November 30, 1990

Dear Ian:

Re: Caledonian Newspapers

You asked for an immediate opinion on the strategy to pursue with your debtor; in addition you asked us to consider the price that Caledonian Newspapers might achieve in the event of an orderly sale of the company as a 'going concern' during the course of the next six months. Our responses are as follows:

(1) It is crucial in this assessment exercise to maintain a clear analysis of trends. On acquisition, Caledonian appeared to be breaking even including its frees with a turnover of £6.9 million. In fact, it was losing about £250,000 on a turnover of £6.5 million in 1989. Profit was therefore disappearing because the Sunday paper was being hit extremely hard by recently increased competition. It is not difficult to see these facts, covered up during the sale, as good reasons for the long-standing owners seeking to sell. Alas, the launch of the free has in itself generated a loss of some £400,000 in its first year of operation. Consequently the Group in the first year post acquisition made a loss of around £500,000, against an anticipated profit of towards £900,000. In summary, therefore, we apportion this £1.4 million shortfall approximately evenly between the deterioration of the Sunday paper and the slower take-off in the new free paper.

(2) We would advise you to proceed most cautiously. There is a distinct downturn in newspaper advertising revenue creeping North-West from the South-East. It has not yet hit Liverpool or Yorkshire or Scotland; we expect it is yet to reach Glasgow.

(3) The market for newspaper companies is very quiet at present. Almost all deals announced over the last six months are consolidation deals—outposts being relinquished to stronger local players. The Monopolies and Mergers Commission is not keen on giving you that option! The number of capable and willing purchasers and the price they might offer are reduced by: *(a)* low market ratings; *(b)* diminished profits; *(c)* lack of confidence; *(d)* high interest rates; *(e)* a feeling "cash is king"; *(f)* that the bottom has not yet been hit; *(g)* that it is a buyer's market. . . .

(4) The investors' buy-in plans were, frankly, astonishingly bold. The price was not unreasonable, but it was later in the cycle. . . . The plan was to destroy hard-won circulation revenue and high advertising yields by the launch of a daily free in the hope of a much bigger share of the market. . . . It is a fundamental of publishing that paid-for circulation can achieve higher advertising yields than free; mixing them, as here, dilutes the strength. . . .

(5) The first year, financially, has gone exceptionally badly. . . .

EXHIBIT 4   *(concluded)*

(7) Assume you carry on. Even if budget is met, a further £1 million cash is needed for 1990/91 before, in the following year, interest payments can be resumed. In 24 months, the paper is projecting £600k and £7.2m. Its likely value would be 0.5 to £5m assuming lower interest rates and a moderate upturn in buyer's interest. The upside is not greater—and that assumes the budget will be met. We instinctively feel it is likely the budget would be missed by up to £500k.

(8) At some point, some of the other interested parties . . . could well lose confidence in their investment. While you are covered first, if they throw in the towel, you lose also. . . .

(9) How saleable is Caledonian anyway? . . . it is a fundamentally unattractive place . . . the paper is far from dominant in its market . . . in a spatially isolated market [with] relatively little natural expansion possible . . . why did no other established group come forward in 1989 when the market, while cooling, was more active than today?

(10) In summary, a sale in 2–3 years at £10 or even £5m—the odds, for all these reasons, seem very much against it. We, therefore, see very little light at the end of that tunnel.

(11) The standard guideline for the valuation of publishing businesses at the present time is 5 times actual operating profits for the period shortly about to end (i.e., calendar year 1990). By and large, publishers are assuming that 1991 will be around the same as 1990, and that 1990 in most cases will be about the same as 1989. Add backs and other development costs, which used to be treated benevolently by purchasers in assessing value, are now treated with much greater scepticism. Higher promotional expenditure, stated as exceptional, is being considered unexceptional. On this very simple basis, there is not significant rushing in to buy papers at break-even or loss.

Based on our analysis, we feel it may be possible to construct an orderly sale for the company built around the profitability of the *News Clarion* at up to £2 million. . . . In our opinion the value attaching to the *News Clarion* masthead is a relatively enduring value. . . . As far as the rest of the group is concerned, we feel the case for the continued publication of the Sunday and the daily free remains unproven. The daily free may simply not be a viable publishing product. . . . The battle ahead for the Sunday paper appears to be exceptionally tough. . . . If the recession bites hard, and lingers, the sale value will fall sharply. . . . However, it will rise if turnover moves towards £5 million and margins improve towards and beyond 10 percent. A value then of around £5 million could not be ruled out. If we owned the papers, we would not accept an offer of less than £2 million for the Newsletter goodwill.

(12) Our advice has to be to protect your downside vigorously and immediately. . . .

In conclusion, we strongly recommend against going further in . . . you need to bang the drum for immediate profit, even if it reverses management strategy, because that is the best chance of recovering your £2.5m.

We await your further instructions.

Yours faithfully,

(signed)

Michael Blimpson, Partner

EXHIBIT 5 Pro Forma Capitalization: Restructuring Proposal by Emergent Ventures

	Par Value Currently[1] (£ 000s)	Changes (£ 000s)	Par Value Pro Forma the Restructuring (£ 000s)	Par Value After Exercise of Debt And Options (£ 000s)	Number of Shares (000s)
Senior debt	2,500	(1,250)	1,250	1,250	
Convertible debt (mgt.)	100	(100)	0	0	
Junior convertible debt:					
Eagle American	0	1,250	1,250	0	
Emergent Ventures (EV)		200	200	0	
Ealing		125	125	0	
Management		100	100	0	
Cv. pfd. stock (EV & Mgt.)	1,200	0	1,200	0	
Common stock:					
Eagle American	14	0	14	1,264	1,264 (25.1%)
Emergent Ventures	305	0	305	1,665[2]	2,265 (44.9%)
Ealing	188[3]	0	188	313[4]	688 (13.6%)
Management	385	0	385	525	825 (16.4%)
Total capital	£4,692	£325	£5,017	£5,017	5,042 (100.0%)

[1] The capitalization and ownership of shares outstanding at the end of November 1990 could be broken down as follows:

	Number of Ordinary Shares	Number of Convertible Preference Shares	Par Value Originally Invested
Emergent Ventures	305,000	1,160,250	£1,465,250
Management	385,000	39,750	424,750
Eagle American	14,000	0	14,000
Ealing	188,375	0	350,000
Totals	892,375	1,200,000	£2,254,000

In addition to its share ownership, the management group had contributed £100,000 of loans in May 1990; these loans were still outstanding. Finally, completing the long-term capitalization of the company were Eagle American's loans totaling £2,500,000. Note that EV's investment in convertible preference shares rose from 900,000 shares to 1,160,250 in the third-round financing.

[2] The conversion price on Emergent Ventures' junior debt investment was £0.25 per share. Therefore, £200,000 par value of convertible debt amounted to 800,000 shares. In combination with the 305,000 initial shares, plus convertible preference stock with an exercise price of £1.00 per share, the total resulting shares for Emergent were 2,265,250.

[3] Max Ealing bought shares in the summer of 1990 at a premium. Of the total invested amount of £350,000, par value was £188,375 and premium or surplus was £161,625. The losses of the company through November 1990 had completely depleted the amount of the paid-in surplus.

[4] Ealing's junior debt investment converted to shares at the rate of £0.25 per share. Thus, £125,000 converted to 500,000 shares. When combined with the initial 188,000 shares, Ealing's new total was 688,000.

EXHIBIT 6   Financial Forecast (fiscal years ending June 30)

	Estimate 1990/91	Forecast 1991/92	Forecast 1992/93
Revenues:			
Advertising	£3,600,490	£3,823,322	£4,041,920
Circulation	2,294,462	2,428,102	2,523,284
Sundry	121,212	119,615	126,000
Total	6,016,164	6,371,039	6,691,204
Costs:			
Production	2,007,719	1,730,230	1,804,536
Editorial	1,413,762	1,250,174	1,287,000
Advertising	691,822	721,558	760,185
Vehicles	80,877	136,527	145,600
Plant	355,491	338,603	496,961
Distribution	647,406	648,320	667,731
Publicity	54,453	39,987	45,500
Administration	1,014,388	871,441	857,624
Depreciation	147,916	200,889	200,888
Total	6,413,834	5,937,729	6,266,025
EBIT (earnings before interest and taxes)	£(397,670)	£433,310	£425,179

Earnings and Cash Flow: Assuming the Original Loan Remained Outstanding

Interest expense	£(425,000)	£(450,000)	£(475,000)
Other expenses:			
Goodwill amortization	(122,668)	(116,079)	(116,077)
Redundancy	(304,955)	0	0
Pension-fund reversion	0	100,000	0
Profit before tax	(1,250,293)	(32,769)	(165,898)
Tax	0	0	0
Net earnings	(1,250,293)	(32,769)	(165,898)
Cash-flow adjustments:			
+ Depreciation	147,916	200,889	200,888
+ Goodwill amortization	122,668	116,079	116,077
− Cap. expends.	(10,000)	(25,000)	(25,000)
− Addns. to net working capital	0	0	0
Cash flow before debt amortization	£(989,709)	£259,199	£126,067
Ratios:			
EBIT/sales	−6.6%	6.8%	6.4%
EBIT/interest	N.M.F.	0.96×	0.90×
Free cash flow/interest	N.M.F.	1.58×	1.27×

EXHIBIT 6   *(concluded)*

	Estimate 1990/91	Forecast 1991/92	Forecast 1992/93
Earnings and Cash Flow Assuming Ealing's Proposal			
Interest expense	£(287,500)	£(150,000)	£(150,000)
Net earnings	(1,112,793)	267,231	159,102
Cash flow before debt amortization	£(852,209)	£559,199	£451,067
Ratios:			
EBIT/interest	N.M.F.	2.89×	2.83×
Cash flow/interest	N.M.F.	4.73×	4.01×
Earnings and Cash Flow Assuming Emergent Ventures' Proposal			
Interest expense	£(250,000)	£(181,250)	£(316,875)*
Net earnings	(1,075,293)	235,981	60,575
Cash flow before debt amortization	£(814,709)	£527,949	£352,540
Ratios:			
EBIT/interest	N.M.F.	2.39×	1.34×
Free cash flow/ interest	N.M.F.	3.91×	1.90×

*Interest expense for 1992/93 under the Emergent Ventures proposal was estimated as follows:

$$
\begin{array}{rr}
\text{Current interest on senior debt} = & \pounds181,250 \\
\text{Current interest on junior debt} = & 96,875 \text{ (half year only)} \\
\text{One tenth of accrued interest on junior debt} = & \underline{38,750} \\
& \overline{\pounds316,875}
\end{array}
$$

Source: Ian Stirling's notes.

EXHIBIT 7   Information on Current Capital-Market Conditions, December 7, 1990

London Money Rates

LIBOR (£) (offer rates):

One month	14.188%
Six months	13.000
One year	12.500
Bank base rate	14.000

U.K. gilts: (Treasury securities)

6 months	11.875
1 year	11.582
5 years	11.082
10 years	10.655
20 years	10.255

Equity Market

	June 1989	*December 1991*
Average P/E ratio, equity market	11.2×	10.46×
Average dividend yield	4.13%	5.43%
Share price index, (1985 = 100)	180	161

Financial Outlook

	1991	*1992*	*1993*	*1994*	*1995*	*1996*
Inflation rate (consumer prices)	5.8%	4.4%	4.6%	4.5%	4.2%	4.0%
Bank prime rate (yearly average)	12.8%	11.7%	13.2%	12.0%	10.0%	9.8%

Sources: *Financial Times*, December 7, 1990; OECD, *Economic Outlook*, January 1991; *Economist*'s Intelligence Unit, *Global Forecasting Service*.

Euro Disneyland S.C.A.: The Project Financing

Anyone who has had builders in knows that the first law of building is that the estimate is a figure approximating to half the eventual cost of a project. The second law of building is that the customer always pays. The third law of building is not to assume that just because the figures have a row of naughts on the end that the costing is any more accurate than that which is employed to build your conservatory. Time will tell. Meanwhile we ought also perhaps to take a sanguine look at the projections for the number of people who are going to visit the site. . . . What I find difficult to square, if this is such a cast iron certainty, is why [Disney] has not kept the whole project for itself, and why it is so keen to use other people's money. Disney may have made Cinderella, but the rest of us should not believe in good fairies.[1]

In the spring of 1989, The Walt Disney Company (Disney, or WDC) set in motion a complex series of transactions that would have several effects on its Euro Disneyland project, the largest metropolitan development project in Western Europe. These effects would include the following:

- The reduction of The Walt Disney Company's equity interest from 100 to 49 percent.
- The repayment to Disney of FF2.8 billion in project-development costs.
- A massive increase in leverage; FF12.3 billion in debts and lease obligations.

---

[1]"Fact and Fantasy in Disneyland," *Evening Standard*, October 10, 1989.

This case was prepared from public information by Professors Robert F. Bruner of Darden Graduate Business School and Herwig Langohr of INSEAD with the assistance of Anne Campbell, Research Associate. The authors thank S. G. Warburg Securities for its cooperation with the research. Neither The Walt Disney Company nor Euro Disneyland S.C.A. has been involved in the preparation of this case, and neither company takes any responsibility for its contents.

Copyright © 1992 jointly by INSEAD, Fontainebleau, France, and the University of Virginia Darden School Foundation, Charlottesville, Virginia. Revised February 1993.

- One of the largest European initial public offerings of common stock, by a company that had no revenues or earnings.
- The creation of a bewildering ownership and governance structure for the project.
- The generation of a cascade of French government subsidies, investments, and tax breaks.

Some analysts viewed these developments with alarm, voicing suspicions about Disney's partial removal from the project. Others welcomed the opportunity to invest alongside the world's most successful theme park operator. Virtually everyone struggled to understand the implications for Disney and other stakeholders in Euro Disneyland.

THE EURO DISNEYLAND PROJECT

Disney planned to build the park on approximately 1,945 hectares[2] (4,800 acres) 32 kilometers due east of Paris. Disney chose this site on the basis of availability, communications, and proximity to a potential audience after considering 200 possible sites in France and Spain. About half of the developable land, 857 hectares, would be devoted to entertainment and resort facilities; another 808 hectares would be set aside for retail, commercial, industrial, and residential purposes. Regional and primary infrastructure, such as roads and railway tracks, would constitute the balance of 280 hectares.

The heart of the entertainment area would feature two separate theme parks: (1) the Magic Kingdom, modeled after similar parks operating in the United States and Japan, and (2) a park based on Disney's MGM Studio theme park in Florida. The Magic Kingdom's five themed "lands"—Main Street, Frontierland, Adventureland, Fantasyland, and Discoveryland—would occupy 160 hectares and were expected to cost FF8.6 billion. The Disney MGM Studio theme park, which would offer visits to studio film sets and presentations on Hollywood film making, was expected to cost FF5.9 billion.

Disney planned to make hotels the linchpin of a comprehensive resort facility. Six hotels (with 5,200 rooms) were to be ready by 1992; by 2011, these facilities would increase to more than 20 hotels with 18,200 rooms. Future entertainment facilities would include two golf courses, a water-recreation area, campgrounds providing 2,100 sites, and a 60,000m[2] retail/entertainment complex.

Euro Disneyland's commercial development would lie just beyond the ring road that would surround the entertainment core on the southern part of the site. Facilities would consist of single and multifamily residences, time-share apartments, 700,000m[2] of office space, 750,000m[2] of industrial space, and 95,000m[2] of retail space.

Visitors would access Euro Disneyland using an interchange from a high-speed multilane highway, an extension of the suburban railroad system serving Paris, or the high-speed *train à grande vitesse* (TGV) railroad train system serving travelers from more distant regions of France and neighboring countries.

Disney planned to open the Magic Kingdom theme park in April 1992. A total cost

---

[2]A hectare is a measure of area equal to 10,000 square meters, or 2.471 acres.

of FF14 billion was budgeted for "Phase IA," the initial capital investment in the Magic Kingdom; the Magic Kingdom Hotel; and peripheral development, organization, interest, and preopening expenses. About FF4.9 billion of this amount would be spent by the end of September 1989.

PROJECT OWNERSHIP AND GOVERNANCE

Euro Disneyland would be organized as a *société en commandité par actions* (S.C.A.), a type of French company that had certain features similar to those of a limited partnership. Exhibit 1 summarizes the ownership structure and percentages of investment in the Euro Disneyland project. There were four primary participants in this structure:

1. Euro Disney S.A., a *gérant* or management company and a wholly-owned subsidiary of The Walt Disney Company, would manage and direct the project. The *gérant*'s responsibility would be to manage Euro Disneyland S.C.A. in the company's best interests. The *gérant*'s compensation would consist of a base fee and a management incentive fee.[3]

2. The shareholders, or *associés commanditaires,* could elect the supervisory board and approve the annual accounts and dividend payments. Shareholders would have no liability for the debts of the company. By agreement with the French government, The Walt Disney Company would use its best efforts to ensure that, until opening day, investors living in the European Community would hold 51 percent of the shares that Disney did not own. Shares would be listed for public trading in Paris, London, and Brussels. EDL Holding Company S.A., a French *société anonyme* and a wholly-owned subsidiary of The Walt Disney Company, would hold the other 49 percent of the shares.

3. The role of the supervisory board, or *conseil de surveillance,* would be to monitor the general affairs and management of Euro Disneyland S.C.A., to report on the performance of the *gérant,* to approve contracts between the *gérant* or its affiliates and Euro Disneyland S.C.A., and to prepare an annual report. This board could not, however, remove the *gérant* or require the *gérant* to take any action.

4. The *associé commandité,* or general partner, had unlimited liability for all debts and liabilities of the company. The general partner would be EDL Participations S.A., which was wholly owned by Disney through EDL Holding Company S.A. It would receive a distribution each year of 0.5 percent of Euro Disneyland S.C.A.'s net after-tax

---

[3]The base fee in any year would equal 3 percent of Euro Disneyland S.C.A.'s total revenues in that year, less 0.5 percent of the S.C.A.'s net after-tax profits, until the later of (1) the expiration of five financial years of Magic Kingdom operations or (2) the end of the financial year in which the company satisfied certain financial tests under the bank-loan agreement. Thereafter, the base fee would be 6 percent per year less 0.5 percent of the S.C.A.'s net after-tax profits. The base fee was reflected in the operating expenses of the theme parks. The incentive fee would be equal to 35 percent of any pre-tax gains on sales of hotels, plus a percentage of the S.C.A.'s pre-tax cash flow. This percentage would range from zero if the cash flow was below 10 percent of the actual cost of Phase IA; 30 percent if the cash flow was between 10 and 15 percent of the cost of Phase IA; 40 percent if the cash flow was between 15 and 20 percent of the cost of Phase IA; and 50 percent if the cash flow was above 20 percent of the cost of Phase IA. These thresholds would increase proportionately if inflation were more than 5 percent per year, or decrease proportionately if inflation were less than 4 percent per year.

profits. EDL Participations could not be removed as general partner without its consent. On the other hand, it could not dispose of its interest as general partner without a majority vote of the shareholders of Euro Disneyland S.C.A.

As part of the general financing plan for the project, one other entity would be established:

A. Euro Disneyland S.N.C., *société en nom collectif,* or "financing company," would serve as a vehicle to finance the construction of the Magic Kingdom through the use of a tax-leveraged financing lease. Euro Disneyland S.C.A. would build the Magic Kingdom and sell it to the financing company for the cost of the land and construction.[4] The financing company would lease the Magic Kingdom back to Euro Disneyland S.C.A. for 20 years, with lease payments essentially matching the debt service and incidental costs of the financing company. Upon complete amortization of its liabilities, the financing company would sell the Magic Kingdom back to Euro Disneyland S.C.A. for a nominal value, whereupon the S.N.C. would be dissolved. Euro Disneyland Participations S.A., a wholly-owned subsidiary of The Walt Disney Company, would provide 17 percent of the partners' equity capital in Euro Disneyland S.N.C. During the construction and early years following completion of the Magic Kingdom, interest expenses and depreciation of assets over a 10-year period were expected to produce tax losses for the S.N.C. The structure of the financing company would permit the partners to take these losses directly into their accounts for tax purposes.[5]

In addition to its 49 percent interest in S.C.A., and its 17 percent interest in S.N.C., The Walt Disney Company would receive royalties[6] in return for granting a 30-year intellectual and industrial-property-rights license to Euro Disneyland S.C.A.

---

[4]Of the total Phase IA budgeted cost of FF14 billion, S.N.C. would effectively finance FF10.3 billion, leaving S.C.A. to finance the balance, FF3.7 billion. These investments would be financed as follows:

	S.N.C.	S.C.A.	Total
Market debt	4,300	200	4,500
Government loans ...	3,000	1,800	4,800
S.N.C. equity	2,000	—	2,000
S.C.A. equity	1,000*	1,700	2,700
Total	10,300	3,700	14,000

* This amount is invested by the S.C.A. in the S.N.C.

---

[5]Although the partners were legally liable for the financing company's debt, Euro Disneyland S.C.A. waived any right of recourse against the partners in the event of the financing company's default. Moreover, Euro Disneyland S.C.A., Euro Disneyland Participations S.A., and The Walt Disney Company agreed to indemnify the partners for any liabilities they might incur.

[6]The royalties would be equal to 10 percent of the gross revenues at theme parks, plus 5 percent of gross revenues from merchandise, food, and beverage sales, plus 10 percent of fees due from participants who invested money toward the construction of specific rides, plus 5 percent of gross revenues of theme hotels.

THE MASTER AGREEMENT WITH THE FRENCH GOVERNMENT

Although it did not appear in a listing of investors, the French government would be an influential participant in Euro Disneyland's development. The Walt Disney Company and the French government signed a master agreement in February 1988 that committed each party to certain obligations. France agreed to:

1. Provide 1,665 hectares for theme-park resort, commercial, and residential development at a fixed price; the price was set at the 1971 cost of raw agricultural land, or approximately FF140,000[7] per hectare. By comparison, raw land zoned for commercial uses in the Île-de-France region was listed for prices ranging from FF170,000 to FF210,000 per hectare. Euro Disneyland S.C.A. would have 20 years to complete the land purchases at the same price. The government explained that it wished to "damp down" property speculation in the area.[8]

2. Finance, construct and operate a 20km extension of the Paris suburban railroad to provide direct access from central Paris to the gates of the Magic Kingdom. This would entail building two railroad stations, a car park, and a bus station.

3. Finance and construct two junctions to link the A4 motorway with the Euro Disneyland site.

4. Contribute FF200 million toward the construction of secondary roads.

5. Provide up to FF4.8 billion in loans at an annual fixed rate of 7.85 percent—a rate less than the French government's own borrowing rate.[9] The loans would mature in 20 years and would amortize from years 6 through 20.

6. Apply the lowest VAT rate of 5.5 percent on all Euro Disneyland's consumer products (compared with 18.6 percent for consumer durables and cars and 33 percent for luxury goods).

In addition to the master agreement, the French government agreed to provide TGV train service to Euro Disneyland starting in June 1994. France also confirmed that the Magic Kingdom could depreciate assets over a 10-year period, rather than the usual 20-year period. One journalist estimated that the entire package of concessions would cost the French taxpayer $54,000 (about FF297,000) for each new job the park would create.[10] Other analysts estimated the value of the government concessions at up to FF6 billion.[11]

The master agreement required Euro Disneyland S.C.A. and Euro Disneyland S.N.C. to open the Magic Kingdom by April 1992 and complete Phase IA. In addition, Euro

---

[7]This is the casewriters' estimate. The master agreement actually cited a land cost of FF111,000 per hectare, but added to this cost would be direct and indirect infrastructure costs (not including roads and railroads), and certain overhead and financing expenses.

[8]George Sivell, "Mickey Mouse Weaves a Magic Deal," *The Times of London,* May 29, 1989.

[9]The 20-year French government bond was currently priced to yield 9.1 percent in the market.

[10]The journalist, Gilles Smadja, was quoted in "Presto! Let the Magic Begin," *Newsweek,* April 13, 1992, page 14. Euro Disneyland was projected to employ over 11,000 people, implying that the estimated value of the concessions was FF 3.267 billion ($594 million).

[11]"Disney President Pelted with Eggs at Stock Announcement," Associated Press article, October 5, 1989.

Disneyland had to guarantee a minimum amount of suburban rail system traffic,[12] pay FF45 million for utility and electrical networks, guarantee a minimum level of tax revenues to the Department of Seine-et-Marne,[13] encourage share ownership by EC nationals, use French and other EC contractors and suppliers (subject to their availability on a competitive basis), and include at least one attraction in the Magic Kingdom depicting French and European civilization.

The Walt Disney Company agreed to refrain from opening or licensing another theme park within 800km of Euro Disneyland for five years after opening the Magic Kingdom. Disney agreed to hold at least 17 percent of the shares of Euro Disneyland S.C.A. and Euro Disneyland S.N.C. until the fifth anniversary of opening day.

THE WALT DISNEY COMPANY

The Walt Disney Company, headquartered in Burbank, California, was the parent, or sponsor, of the Euro Disneyland project. Disney derived 60 percent of its revenues from the development and operation of theme parks. Observers generally acknowledged that The Walt Disney Company dominated the theme-park industry by virtue of its size, customer franchise, and product leadership. Fifty million visitors attended Disney's four theme parks annually, an average of more than 12 million a park. The next-largest competing park attracted 4.6 million. Disney achieved dominance in the theme-park industry through the nature and quality of its facilities,[14] its crowd-handling techniques, its use of entertainment culture, and its operational and marketing[15] skills.

---

[12]Euro Disneyland guaranteed a minimum of 9.13 million one-way journeys each year for a five-year period after oepning day. Failing that, Euro Disneyland would make payments varying from four to seven French francs (measured in 1986 francs) per journey to the extent that actual traffic would fall below 75 percent of the minimum agreed level.

[13]This aimed to reimburse the Department of Seine-et-Marne for the FF 200 million in expenditures for primary and secondary infrastructure. The aggregate taxes would have to reach FF200 million by 1999 (measured in 1986 francs). Any shortfall would be filled jointly by Euro Disneyland and the Republic of France.

[14]Disney designed all of its own rides and attractions, using an in-house "imagineering" department. This approach guaranteed uniqueness, consistency, and high product quality. Rides could be tailored to the unique needs of the theme area and of the entire park and designed especially for Disney's high-volume attendance. Finally, the in-house approach guaranteed Disney exclusive ownership of the numerous design innovations (many of which were patented).

[15]Disney aimed to maximize attendance at the parks and to achieve high occupancy at the Disney resort hotels. The company's main marketing tools were public relations, media promotions, participant campaigns, national advertising campaigns, and special events. Some attractions and services were co-marketed with "participants," such as Renault, Banque Nationale de Paris, and France Telecom, that had committed to sponsoring an attraction at Euro Disneyland. Special pricing and travel packages played a key role in maintaining demand throughout the year.

FINANCIAL FORECAST AND VALUATION

In a departure from usual practice, Disney intended to publish a detailed financial forecast for the project in advance of the initial public offering of shares. Exhibit 2 presents a forecast of the operating statement and dividends by year from 1992–96 and for each fifth year thereafter to 2016. This exhibit concludes with the total annual return to shareholders. Exhibit 3 presents the sources and applications of funds for the forecast period, evincing a substantial reliance on debt financing in the first few years followed by steady debt amortizaton. Exhibit 4 gives the debt/equity ratio by year for Euro Disneyland S.C.A.

Disney made the unusual assumption that certain revenue items would grow at a greater rate than inflation. Magic Kingdom ticket prices, hotel rates, campsite rates, and lease rates in the retail/entertainment center were projected to grow at 6.5 percent, versus 5.0 percent for inflation. Analysts wondered what might account for a 1.5 percent *real growth rate* over Disney's forecast period. By comparison, ticket prices at Disney theme parks in the United States had grown at a real rate of 2.6 percent per annum since 1972.

On the basis of a discounted cash flow analysis of this forecast, S. G. Warburg, the prospective lead underwriter for the initial public offering (IPO), concluded that shares in Euro Disneyland S.C.A. would be worth approximately FF70 each. Warburg's analysis used a 12 percent discount rate.[16] Warburg also conducted an extensive sensitivity analysis of the share values, the results of which are given in Exhibit 5.

FINANCIAL TRANSFORMATION

The Euro Disneyland project would be transformed in a two-stage process from an all-equity, wholly-owned unit of The Walt Disney Company into a lever-aged public firm, minority-owned by Disney. Exhibit 6 presents the balance sheet

---

[16]In estimating a discount rate for the project, S. G. Warburg acknowledged that "there are currently no quoted investment opportunities which are directly comparable to Euro Disneyland in the sense that they offer a direct and undiluted play on the theme park industry." The Walt Disney Company in the United States offered one comparison. Warburg identified two comparable companies in the French business community. The first was Club Mediteranée, the world leader in holiday villages which, like Euro Disneyland, provided the concept of a "total" destination resort. Club Med and Euro Disneyland differed in that Club Med offered a globally diversified portfolio of destination resorts, whereas Euro Disneyland offered only one. The countries where the Club Med resorts were located, however, experienced greater weather and political risks than Europe. Warburg also compared Euro Disneyland with Accor, the leading French hotel operator. Accor's assets were located primarily in France, and the properties were, on average, quite young. They, therefore, held the prospect of long lives and capital gains similar to Euro Disneyland. Warburg forecasted dividends and estimated an internal rate of return (IRR) for Disney, Accor, and Club Med. Against an estimated IRR of 9 percent for The Walt Disney Company, 11.3 percent for Accor, and 11.9 percent for Club Med, Warburg reasoned that the market would fix on a discount rate of 12 percent for Euro Disneyland's return to share investors after April 1993. Warburg suggested that during the development period (October 1989 to April 1992) investors would look for an implicit return of 20 percent on their investments. This higher rate would reflect the development risks prior to opening and the fact that Euro Disneyland was not a going concern at the initial public offering.

of Euro Disneyland S.C.A. and adjustments that resulted from the two-stage process.

Step 1: *Sale of ORAs, March 1989.*   To set in motion the complex project financing, the *Caisse des Depôts et Consignations* (the large pension-fund management company operated by the French government) required that Euro Disneyland prove its ability to sell shares of stock in the project. Accordingly, in March 1989, Euro Disneyland arranged for four investor banks to purchase 510,000 shares of stock at FF15 per share. These banks were Banque Indosuez, Banque Nationale de Paris, S. G. Warburg & Company, and Caisse Nationale de Crédit Agricole. At the same time, EDL Holding Company purchased 465,000 shares at FF10 per share.[17] The investor banks and EDL Holding Company also purchased debt securities of Euro Disneyland, called *Obligations Remboursables en Actions* (ORAs), which were to be repaid substantially from the proceeds of the forthcoming initial public offering.[18]

Step 2: *Initial Public Offering of Common Stock, Fall 1989.*   The sale of shares was expected to raise net proceeds of FF5.73 billion. The proceeds would be used to repay the ORAs that were issued by the company in March 1989 and to support the funding of Phase IA and subsequent phases. Following the IPO, The Walt Disney Company would own 49.0 percent of the shares, the investor banks would own about 0.5 percent, and the public would own about 50.5 percent. Immediately following the IPO, the issued share capital of S.C.A. would be FF1.7 billion, divided into 170 million shares of FF10 each.

Analysts noted that The Walt Disney Company would receive a substantial gain through this initial public offering. Disney's shares, carried at the purchase price of FF10 each, would be revalued at FF72 each. Disney responded that the resulting total value of its shares (FF5.997 billion) would be fair recognition of an already substantial investemnt of know-how, personnel resources, and cash expenditure, and an acknowledgment of Disney's role as the risk-bearing sponsor of the project. As of September 30, 1989, the

---

[17]In March 1989, shareholders approved an increase in capital: 510,000 shares were issued at FF15 per share to the investor banks (i.e., Banque Indosuez, Banque Nationale de Paris, S.G. Warburg & Co., and Caisse Nationale de Crédit Agricole). In addition, 465,000 shares were issued at par (FF 10) to EDL Holding Company. Prior to the IPO, shares were held as follows: EDL Holding Company (490,000), Banque Indosuez (204,000), Banque Nationale de Paris (153,000), S. G. Warburg & Company (102,000), and Caisse Nationale de Crédit Agricole (51,000); for a total of 1,000,000 shares. On June 30, 1989, the share capital would amount to FF 10 million, comprising 1 million fully paid FF10 ordinary voting shares. Shareholders' equity would increase by FF 5.73 billion from the net IPO proceeds, plus FF828.1 million from the conversion of Disney ORAs. In September 1989, 85,880,000 new shares would be issued in order to be subscribed in cash as part of the IPO. This would increase S.C.A.'s share capital by FF858,000,000 to a total of FF868,000,000.

[18]In March 1989, S.C.A. completed a private placement of ORAs and stock purchase warrants that raised FF2,129,950,000. EDL Holding Company subscribed for 828,100 noninterest-bearing ORAs at par with a nominal unit value of FF1,000. Upon completion of the public equity offering, these ORAs would convert into 82,810,000 shares of S.C.A. The investor banks subscribed *pro rata* for a total of 861,900 ORAs at par with a nominal unit value of FF1,500. These ORAs bear interest at 12.5 percent per year. Upon completion of the IPO, the ORAs held by the investor banks would be redeemed in cash at their par value plus accrued interest. On June 30, this amounted to FF13,469,000. The investor banks also received warrants to purchase between 310,000 and 3,260,000 additional shares, depending on the redemption date of their ORAs.

total assets of Euro Disneyland S.C.A. amounted to FF4.833 billion. Disney's projected net cash invested in the equity of Euro Disneyland S.C.A. would be approximately FF833 million.[19]

Analysts puzzled over various cash flows that composed the return to The Walt Disney Company from the Euro Disneyland project: (1) royalties, (2) incentive fees (see footnote 3), (3) dividends from the S.C.A., (4) depreciation tax shields from the S.N.C.,[20] (5) Disney's participation in net profits, and (6) the reimbursement of FF2.762 billion of development costs previously incurred by WDC. Exhibit 7 presents a forecast of these various cash flows to The Walt Disney Company based on the *pro forma* for the project financing. Because the extent of WDC's future tax burden was unclear, this exhibit presents the total cash flows to WDC under two scenarios: (1) WDC pays no taxes on its returns from Euro Disneyland and (2) WDC pays taxes at the maximum 35 percent rate on *all* returns from Euro Disneyland. To provide a basis of comparison for the project-financing results, Exhibit 8 gives a forecast assuming no project financing but holding the capital structure constant.

CONCLUSION

The transactions of 1989 would transform the Euro Disneyland project dramatically: from a private to a publicly-owned project; from a simple governance and ownership structure to a complex one; from one stakeholder to many; from internal financing to external financing; from an unlevered to a levered project. Analysts pondered the implications of this transformation. Most important, they asked why WDC brought many players into the project: why should banks, equity investors, and the French government participate so massively? Who stood to gain what?

---

[19]Disney's cash investment in equity consisted of outlays for the initial 25,000 shares at FF10 in 1985, another 465,000 shares at FF10 in March 1989, and FF828.1 million for the ORAs, also in March 1989.

[20]As stated earlier, because the lease payments received by the S.N.C. from the S.C.A. would just equal the S.N.C.'s financing expenses, the only source of income to the investors in the S.N.C. would come from the tax losses generated from depreciation of the Magic Kingdom theme park. This annual return would be a tax savings to the investors equal to the tax rate times annual depreciation.

EXHIBIT 1   Management and Control Structure of the Euro Disneyland Project

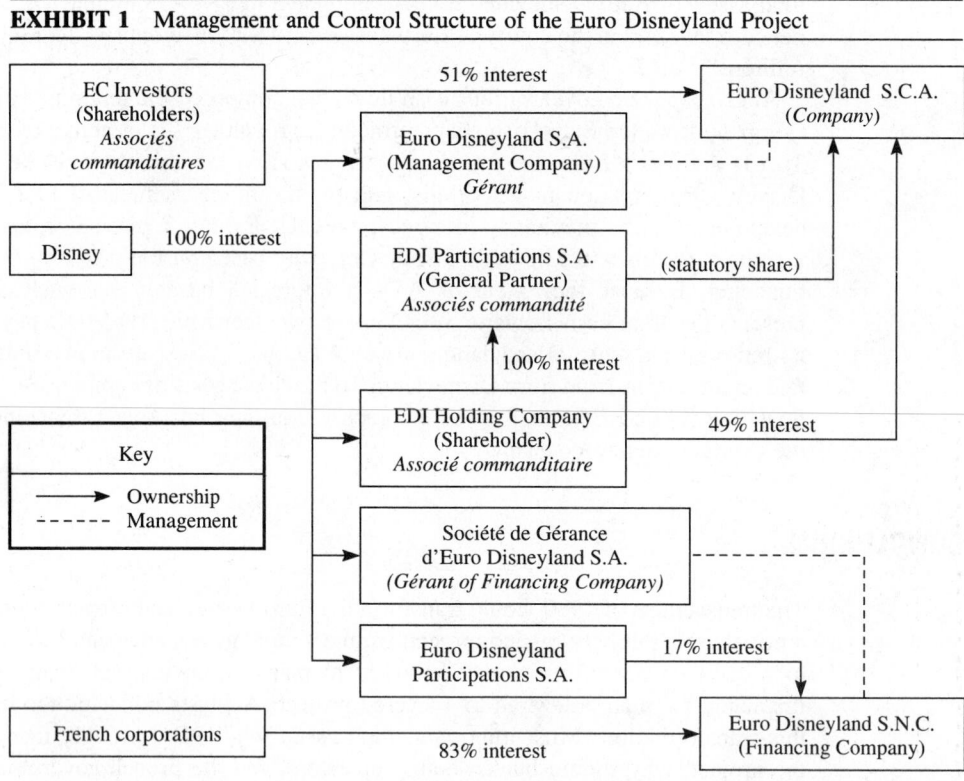

EXHIBIT 2 Profit Projections (in millions of French francs)

				Years Beginning April 1				
	1992	1993	1994	1995	1996	2001	2006	2011	2016
Revenues:									
Magic Kingdom*	4,246	4,657	5,384	5,853	6,415	9,730	13,055	18,181	24,118
Second theme park	0	0	0	0	3,128	4,565	6,656	9,313	12,954
Resort and property development	1,236	2,144	3,520	5,077	6,386	8,133	9,498	8,979	5,923
Total revenues	5,482	6,801	8,904	10,930	15,929	22,428	29,209	36,473	42,995
Operating expenses:									
Magic Kingdom*	2,643	2,836	3,161	3,370	3,641	5,504	7,384	10,175	13,097
Second theme park	0	0	0	0	1,794	2,644	3,695	5,020	6,830
Resort and property development	796	1,501	2,431	2,970	3,694	5,210	6,369	5,753	2,211
Total operating expenses	3,439	4,337	5,592	6,340	9,129	13,358	17,448	20,948	22,138
Operating income	2,043	2,464	3,312	4,590	6,800	9,070	11,761	15,525	20,857
Other expenses (income):									
Royalties	302	333	387	422	717	1,085	1,509	2,120	2,802
Pre-opening amortization	341	341	341	341	341	0	0	0	0
Depreciation	255	263	290	296	625	658	723	842	228
Interest expense	567	575	757	708	1,166	920	623	352	0
Interest and other income	(786)	(788)	(768)	(778)	(790)	(615)	(266)	0	0
Lease expense	958	950	958	962	975	1,242	882	83	0
Management incentive fees	55	171	477	963	1,820	2,747	3,916	5,590	7,876
Total other expenses (income)	1,692	1,845	2,492	2,914	4,854	6,037	7,387	8,987	10,906
Profit before taxation	351	620	870	1,676	1,945	3,034	4,375	6,539	9,951
Taxation	147	260	366	704	818	1,274	1,837	2,746	4,180
Net profit	204	360	504	972	1,127	1,760	2,538	3,793	5,771
Dividends payable†	275	425	625	900	1,100	1,750	2,524	3,379	5,719
Tax credit or payment (avoir fiscal)	0	138	213	313	450	536	865	1,908	2,373
Total return	275	563	838	1,213	1,550	2,286	3,389	5,287	8,092

*Includes Magic Kingdom Hotel.

† After transfers to legal reserve and deduction of a distributive share of 0.5 percent of net profits after tax payable to the *associé commandité*. In later years, dividends payable reflect the availability of cash. Dividends from 1992 through 1996 include distribution of profits carried forward from earlier years arising from interest income.

Source: Initial public offering circular, Euro Disneyland S.C.A., September 1989, p. 36.

EXHIBIT 3 Cash Flow Projections (in millions of French francs)

	Years Beginning April 1								
	1992	*1993*	*1994*	*1995*	*1996*	*2001*	*2006*	*2011*	*2016*
Source of funds:									
Profit before taxation	351	620	870	1,676	1,945	3,034	4,375	6,539	9,951
Depreciation and amortization	597	604	631	638	967	658	723	842	228
Issuance of long-term debt	990	693	2,950	2,950	0	779	1,146	0	0
Total	1,938	1,917	4,451	5,264	2,912	4,471	6,244	7,381	10,179
Application of funds:									
Capital expenditures:									
Magic Kingdom	310	326	293	313	334	335	471	658	114
Second theme park	0	0	2,950	2,950	102	101	134	178	196
Resort and property development	31	139	62	0	0	0	0	5	0
Acquisition of land	51	145	103	198	450	205	339	0	0
Repayment of long-term debt	0	24	540	781	1,600	1,872	1,584	440	0
Loan to financing company	0	(24)	(47)	(71)	(94)	(259)	0	0	0
Taxes paid	139	414	519	858	971	1,280	1,843	2,746	4,180
Dividends payable	275	425	625	900	1,100	1,750	2,524	3,379	5,719
Total	806	1,449	5,045	5,927	4,463	5,284	6,895	7,406	10,209
Movement in working capital*	(779)	(668)	516	997	1,548	683	100	45	57
Movement in net liquid funds	353	(200)	(78)	334	(3)	(130)	(551)	20	27

*The yearly movement in working capital may be analyzed as follows:

	1992	*1993*	*1994*	*1995*	*1996*	*2001*	*2006*	*2011*	*2016*
(Increase) decrease in resort and property-development inventories due to funding of projects and sales	(979)	(678)	507	785	1,527	656	65	0	0
Increase in current liabilities	200	10	9	212	21	27	35	45	57
Total	(779)	(668)	516	997	1,548	683	100	45	57

Source: Initial public offering circular, Euro Disneyland S.C.A., September 1989, p. 37.

744

EXHIBIT 4   Forecasted Debt/Equity Ratio (for Euro Disneyland S.C.A.)

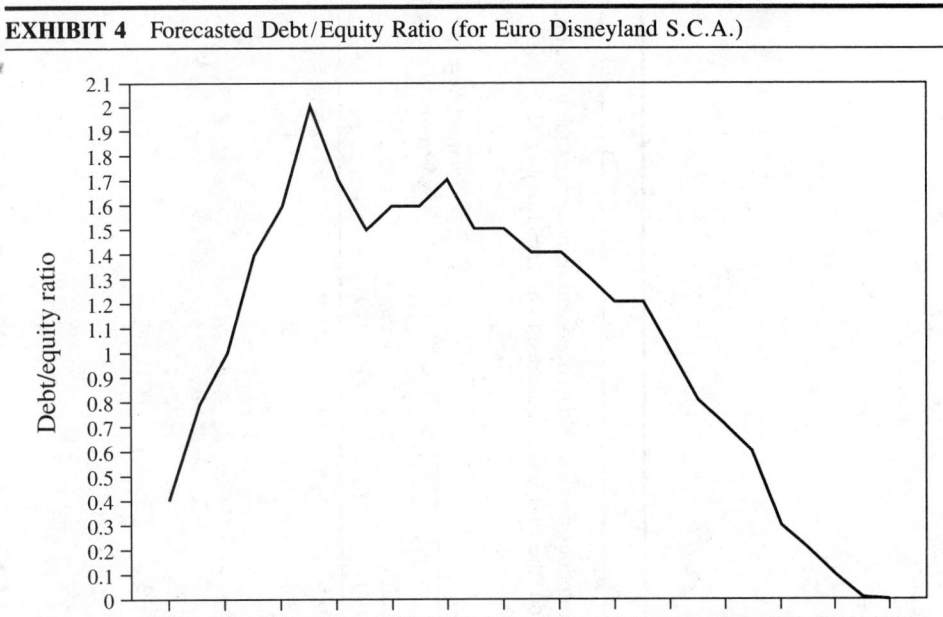

Source: Research report, S. G. Warburg, p. 106.

EXHIBIT 5 Returns to Investors and Sensitivity Analysis (in French francs)

The table below illustrates the projected returns to the investor based on the assumptions previously described and demonstrates the effect on these returns of variations in certain of the key assumptions. At the end of the period, the company is assumed to be capitalized at 12.5 times net profit available for distribution in the year ending March 31, 2017.

| | Net Dividend per Share | | | | | | Net Value in April 1993* | Internal Rate of Return over Period to 2017 | |
| | Years Beginning April 1 | | | | | | | | |
	1992	1995	2001	2006	2011	2016		Issue Price (FF72)	
Company's projections	1.6	5.3	10.3	14.8	19.9	33.6	131	13.3%	
Reduced attendance assuming 10 million visits in the first year of operations of the Magic Kingdom	1.6	5.3	9.4	13.8	18.4	31.7	119	12.7	
Increased attendance assuming 12 million visits in the first year of operations of the Magic Kingdom	1.6	5.3	11.1	15.9	21.3	35.6	141	13.8	
Reduced per capita spending assuming per capita spending at both theme parks is lower by 10 percent	1.6	4.8	8.9	12.9	17.4	30.3	112	12.3	

Increased per capita spending assuming per capita spending at both theme parks is higher by 10 percent	1.6	5.3	11.6	16.6	22.3	37.0	147	14.1
Delay assuming a six-month delay in the opening of the Magic Kingdom	1.6	4.5	9.7	12.6	21.8	33.6	122	12.8
Increased construction costs assuming costs of construction of Phase IA are higher by 10 percent	1.6	5.3	10.2	15.1	20.4	34.0	129	13.2
Reduced resort and property-development income assuming that income from all resort and property development is lower by 10 percent	1.6	5.3	9.8	14.3	19.3	33.0	126	13.0
Increased resort and property development income assuming that income from all resort and property development is higher by 10 percent	1.6	5.3	10.8	15.4	20.4	34.3	135	13.5%

* Net value in April 1993 reflects gross dividends per share and assumed residual value in 2017 discounted at an illustrative rate of 12 percent.

Source: Initial public offering circular, Euro Disneyland S.C.A., September 1989, pp. 38–39.

EXHIBIT 6 Pro Forma Balance Sheet of Euro Disneyland S.C.A. (in thousands of French francs)

	Actual (Dec. 31, 1988)	Project Devel. Activities	Sale of ORAs and Shares	Expected (Sept. 30, 1989)	Repay. and Conversion of ORAs	Exercise of Warrants	IPO	Pro Forma (Sept. 30, 1989)
Fixed Assets								
Intangible assets	0	8,644		8,644				8,644
Tangible assets	0	475,630		475,630				475,630
Deposits	0	4,232		4,232				4,232
Total fixed assets	0			488,506				488,506
Construction in progress	0	1,748,653		1,748,653				1,748,653
Current assets:								
Accounts receivable	0	761,994		761,994				761,994
Cash and investments	251	(1,010,518)	2,133,250	1,122,983	(1,292,850)		5,730,000	5,560,133
Total current assets	251			1,884,977				6,322,127
Deferred charges	0	710,460		710,460				710,460
Total assets	**251**	**2,699,095**	**2,133,250**	**4,832,596**	**(1,292,850)**	**0**	**5,730,000**	**9,269,746**
Shareholders' Equity								
Share capital	250		9,750	10,000	828,100	3,100	858,800	1,700,000
Share premium	25		2,550	2,575		1,550	4,866,550	4,870,675
Accumulated losses	(24)			(24)				(24)
Current period net income	0	7,333		7,333				7,333
Subtotal	251			19,884				6,577,984
ORAs and warrants	0		2,120,950	2,120,950	(2,120,950)			0
Deferred taxes	0	4,688		4,688				4,688
Current liabilities								
Payable to Euro Disneyland S.A.	0	1,908,567		1,908,567				1,908,567
Other accounts payable	0	537,124		537,124				537,124
Total current liabilities	0			2,445,691				2,445,691
Deferred revenues	0	241,383		241,383				241,383
Total equity and liabilities	**251**	**2,699,095**	**2,133,250**	**4,832,596**	**(1,292,850)**	**4,650**	**5,725,350**	**9,269,746**

EXHIBIT 7 Projected Cash Flows to The Walt Disney Company—Assuming Euro Disneyland is Financed as Proposed (in millions of French francs)

EDL ?

	Base Fees	Incentive Fees	Royalties	Profit Particip.	Dividends	S.N.C. Return	Reimb. Payments	Invest. Outlay	Cash Flow to The Walt Disney Company	
									(Untaxed)	(Maximum Tax*)
1989						(340.0)		(833.0)	(833.0)	(833.0)
1990							1,909.0		1,569.0	900.0
1991							360.0		360.0	234.0
1992	197.4	55.0	302.0	1.0	137.0	61.3	493.0		1,246.6	810.3
1993	244.8	171.0	333.0	1.9	281.0	61.3			1,093.0	710.5
1994	320.5	477.0	387.0	2.5	419.0	61.3			1,667.3	1,083.8
1995	393.5	963.0	422.0	4.8	606.0	61.3			2,450.6	1,592.9
1996	573.4	1,820.0	717.0	5.6	775.0	61.3			3,952.3	2,569.0
1997	614.1	1,976.2	778.9	6.1	850.1	61.3			4,286.7	2,786.4
1998	657.6	2,145.8	846.2	6.7	932.6	61.3			4,650.1	3,022.6
1999	704.1	2,329.9	919.3	7.3	1,023.0	61.3			5,045.0	3,279.3
2000	754.0	2,529.9	998.7	8.0	1,122.2	61.3			5,474.1	3,558.2
2001	807.4	2,747.0	1,085.0	8.8	1,231.0				5,940.5	3,861.3
2002	851.2	2,948.9	1,159.0	9.6	1,306.9				6,275.5	4,079.1
2003	897.4	3,165.6	1,238.0	10.4	1,387.4				6,698.8	4,354.2
2004	946.1	3,398.2	1,322.5	11.4	1,472.9				7,151.0	4,648.2
2005	997.4	3,647.9	1,412.7	12.4	1,563.6				7,634.0	4,962.1
2006	1,051.5	3,916.0	1,509.0	13.5	1,660.0				8,150.0	5,297.5
2007	1,099.3	4,204.9	1,615.2	14.5	1,843.6				8,777.4	5,705.3
2008	1,149.2	4,515.1	1,728.8	15.5	2,047.6				9,456.2	6,146.5
2009	1,201.4	4,848.2	1,850.4	16.6	2,274.1				10,190.7	6,624.0
2010	1,256.0	5,205.9	1,980.6	17.7	2,525.6				10,985.9	7,140.8
2011	1,313.0	5,590.0	2,120.0	19.0	2,805.0				11,847.0	7,700.6
2012	1,356.9	5,986.7	2,241.6	20.7	2,989.8				12,595.8	8,187.3
2013	1,402.3	6,411.6	2,370.2	22.5	3,186.8				13,393.5	8,705.8
2014	1,449.2	6,866.7	2,506.2	24.5	3,396.7				14,243.3	9,258.2
2015	1,497.7	7,354.1	2,650.0	26.6	3,620.5				15,148.9	9,846.8
2016	1,547.8	7,876.0	2,802.0	29.0	3,859.0			107,425.5†	123,539.3	67,749.5

* This takes into account the fullest possible tax burden, imposed on *all* cash inflows at the rate of 35 percent per year.

† The terminal value was estimated by capitalizing the sum of base fees, incentive fees, royalties, profit participation, and dividends at a rate of 12 percent. S. G. Warburg's estimate of a discount rate appropriate for this project. Estimated this way, the terminal value assumes no growth after the investment horizon.

Sources: Offering circular, Euro Disneyland S.C.A., September 1989, and casewriters' analysis.

749

EXHIBIT 8 Projected Cash Flows to The Walt Disney Company—Assuming Euro Disneyland is a Fully Integrated Internal Project (in millions of French francs)

	Oper. Income	Amort. and Deprec.	Net Interest Expense	Taxes*	Capital Expend.	+/− Debt	Terminal Value	Cash Flow to WDC
1989					3,800.0	2,767.5		(1,032.5)
1990					5,100.0	2,767.5		(2,332.5)
1991					5,100.0	2,767.5		(2,332.5)
1992	2,043.0	700.0	(219.0)	546.7	392.0	990.0		2,313.3
1993	2,464.0	684.6	(213.0)	697.3	610.0	669.0		2,038.7
1994	3,312.0	680.9	(11.0)	924.7	3,408.0	2,410.0		1,400.3
1995	4,590.0	817.2	(70.0)	1,345.0	3,461.0	2,169.0		2,023.0
1996	6,800.0	949.4	376.0	1,916.1	886.0	(1,600.0)		2,021.9
1997	7,203.3	946.2	360.6	2,063.7	830.5	(1,498.6)		2,449.9
1998	7,630.4	940.5	345.8	2,220.5	778.4	(1,397.2)		2,888.6
1999	8,082.9	932.4	331.6	2,386.6	729.6	(1,295.8)		3,339.3
2000	8,562.2	922.2	318.0	2,562.7	683.9	(1,194.4)		3,803.2
2001	9,070.0	910.3	305.0	2,749.1	641.0	(1,093.0)		4,281.9
2002	9,553.8	896.8	314.8	2,919.8	692.6	(962.0)		4,664.7
2003	10,063.3	886.6	324.8	3,098.2	748.3	(831.0)		5,061.0
2004	10,600.1	879.7	335.2	3,284.8	808.6	(700.0)		5,471.5
2005	11,165.5	876.2	345.9	3,480.2	873.7	(569.0)		5,896.7
2006	11,761.0	876.0	357.0	3,684.8	944.0	(438.0)		6,337.2
2007	12,432.6	879.4	356.0	3,919.0	922.4	(438.4)		6,796.8
2008	13,142.5	881.6	355.0	4,167.1	901.4	(438.8)		7,280.3
2009	13,893.0	882.6	354.0	4,429.8	880.8	(439.2)		7,789.3
2010	14,686.4	882.5	353.0	4,707.8	860.7	(439.6)		8,325.3
2011	15,525.0	881.4	352.0	5,002.1	841.0	(440.0)		8,889.9
2012	16,469.3	879.4	43.4	5,441.3	688.8	(352.0)		9,943.8
2013	17,471.1	869.8	5.3	5,808.6	564.2	(264.0)		10,829.0
2014	18,533.8	854.6	0.7	6,187.5	462.1	(176.0)		11,707.5
2015	19,661.1	834.9	0.1	6,589.1	378.5	(88.0)		12,605.4
2016	20,857.0	812.1	0.0	7,015.7	310.0	0.0	90,208.5†	103,739.8

2016 cash flow + terminal value → 90,208.5†

* Pre-tax income is taxed at 35 percent per year.

† The terminal value was estimated by capitalizing the free cash flow of the project at 12 percent, S. G. Warburg's estimate of a discount rate appropriate for this project. Estimated this way, the terminal value assumes no growth after the investment horizon.

Source: Pro forma adjustment of projections contained in the offering circular, Euro Disneyland S.C.A., September 1989.

Joint-Venture Negotiating Committee: Slavagrad, Government of Euroslavia

Late one afternoon in April 1992, Anna Krzykowiak (kri-KO-vi-ak), special assistant to the finance minister of Euroslavia, called together a special committee to prepare for negotiations with the large American automobile producer, General Motors. Earlier that month, General Motors had concluded a Memorandum of Understanding with the Euroslav government, committing both parties to work toward a final agreement under which GM would form a joint venture with the Euroslav state automobile manufacturer, AUTA,[1] to produce and sell Opel automobiles in Euroslavia. (See Exhibit 1 for a journalist's account of this agreement.) The Memorandum of Understanding nominally required GM to make an initial $113 million investment in interim assembly capacity, to be followed by a $400 million investment in a major, integrated (i.e., greenfield) auto assembly plant. A final round of negotiations was needed to hammer out a detailed series of commitments for both parties. To conduct the negotiations with GM, the minister of finance had appointed Krzykowiak the new chief negotiator, aided by a committee of assistants and consulting advisors.

---

[1]AUTA stood for AUTofabryka Azzotiazion and was the name of Euroslavia's second-largest automobile manufacturer.

The "GM–Euroslavia Joint Venture Investment Simulation" cases were prepared by Professor Robert F. Bruner with the assistance of Jane Sommers-Kelly from field interviews and public information. The cooperation of General Motors–Europe is gratefully acknowledged, as is the financial support of the Citicorp Global Scholars Program. All financial data and some market data have been disguised. Protagonists are disguised or fictional. Some license has been taken in describing the business situation in order to heighten the differences in points of view.

The Memorandum of Understanding had created the expectation that General Motors would make a major and long-term investment in Euroslavia. However, Euroslavia had experienced yet another change in government (the fourth in 18 months), which might create fears about political stability. The tightening of Euroslavia's anti-inflation policy had prolonged its current recession. Disturbing news was coming to light about the depth and severity of Euroslavia's recession that might discourage foreign investors. Finally, GM itself had experienced what some newspapers had called a management "coup." For these reasons, Krzykowiak believed the scope of the forthcoming negotiations was wide open and might result in one of these three outcomes:

- GM would first invest $75 million in a temporary plant and then $400 million in a greenfield plant and joint venture with AUTA. This alternative was embedded in the Memorandum of Understanding.
- GM would invest in a complete "knock-down" plant and joint venture with AUTA. For a $75 million outlay, GM would construct a movable plant that would assemble automobiles from kits manufactured by Adam Opel, Inc., in Germany.
- GM would supply the Euroslav auto market with imports from its Adam Opel subsidiary, thus maintaining the status quo.

An assessment of GM's possible proposals and negotiations was urgently needed, because the talks were about to begin. To delay the timetable of the talks would not be possible. The potential stakes were huge: Euroslavia desperately needed inflows of hard (i.e., Western) currencies with which to finance the growth of its economy. GM's investment represented a huge potential source of new capital, know-how, technology, and credibility for Euroslavia's market reforms.

GENERAL MOTORS CORPORATION

General Motors was the world's largest industrial company in terms of sales (US$125 billion in 1990). It employed over 761,000 people worldwide and held 19 percent of the world market (7.5 million GM vehicles sold in 1990). To maintain this share, the firm had to sell about 30,000 vehicles every day. General Motors' investment of over US$25 billion worldwide between 1986 and 1989 reflected the firm's significant market positions in Europe, Asia and the Pacific region, and Latin America.

Once identified not only as a mainstay of American prosperity but also one of the nation's prime beneficiaries, GM was now reeling from a series of competitive setbacks and financial losses. In 1991, the company lost more money (US$6 billion) than both of its two U.S. rivals *combined*. GM's U.S. market share dropped from 47 percent in the early 1980s to 35 percent by 1992. Falling consumer demand for new cars caused low use of capacity; high fixed costs resulted in a high break-even level and losses. By December 1991, GM's stock price was at a four-year low point. Moody's downgraded GM's senior debt rating from A1 to A2 in January 1992 because of poor financial performance in 1991. Newspapers speculated that General Motors' debt rating might be reduced below investment grade; this action would dramatically raise GM's cost of funds.

Robert Stempel became chairman and chief executive officer of General Motors upon the regular retirement of Roger Smith in early 1990. In a crisis atmosphere 20 months later, the board of directors became frustrated with management's slow response to the deteriorating performance of the firm. The board took action in an unprecedented coup in April 1992: Stempel's board position was restricted and his handpicked chief operating officer and chief financial officer were replaced. A major cash conservation program was initiated to stem losses. GM successfully sold $2.5 billion in new common shares to reduce its debt-to-capital ratio, which was at an unprecedented 70 percent (almost twice the historic 40 percent). Most important, the board appointed Jack Smith, the highly successful president of GM–Europe, as president and COO. *Value Line,* perhaps reflecting the optimism in the investment community, was cautiously bullish about GM's investment outlook (see Exhibit 2).

GENERAL MOTORS–EUROPE

GM's long-standing corporate policy was to establish local production and employment in its major markets whenever economic conditions permitted. In 1923, GM opened its first assembly operation outside North America in Copenhagen, Denmark. A second manufacturing plant was established in Antwerp, Belgium, in 1924. The firm acquired Vauxhall Motors in England in 1925; four years later, it acquired Adam Opel A.G. in Germany. More recent acquisitions included Group Lotus, the U.K.-based performance-car manufacturing firm, in 1986, and 50 percent of Saab Automobile AB, based in Sweden, in 1989.

General Motors' most extensive activities outside North America were in Europe and included facilities and sales companies in 20 European countries. The main car-related manufacturing operations were located in Germany (Rüsselsheim, Bochum, Kaiserslautern, Eisenach), the United Kingdom (Ellesmere Port, Luton), Belgium (Antwerp), Spain (Zaragoza), Austria (Vienna-Aspern), and Portugal (Azambuja). GM's more than 30 automotive-component plants employed about 124,000 people.

GM–Europe's Opel and Vauxhall brands had the highest growth rates among all volume-car manufacturers in Europe. With an all-time high 1.545 million passenger cars sold, 1990 marked the sixth consecutive year of new-car sales records. Opel/Vauxhall's market penetration rose from 9.0 percent in 1986 to 11.6 percent in 1990, placing the company fourth among all car makers in Europe. In 12 European countries, GM ranked among the top three sellers, and some industry observers had recently characterized Adam Opel A.G. as "the most profitable car company in the world" and "the engine of profitability for GM."

GM IN EASTERN EUROPE

As early as 1979, GM had established a joint venture, Industrial Delova Automobilia, in Belgrade, Yugoslavia. Since the political thaw that began in 1988, GM had successfully penetrated other Eastern European countries:

Former East Germany.   In early 1990, Adam Opel A.G. established a joint venture company with the state-owned Automobile Werke Eisenach (the former producer of Ladas and Trabants) to produce parts and assemble vehicles. The assembly of mid-size Vectras at an initial rate of 10,000 units per annum started on October 5, 1990, just two days after German reunification. A (deutsche mark) DM1 billion greenfield assembly plant, slated to open at Eisenach in July 1992, would produce 150,000 units annually.

Hungary.   In 1988, GM signed a joint venture agreement with RABA, the state-owned automobile company, to produce up to 200,000 1.6-liter engines at a greenfield plant to be opened in 1992. Over 90 percent of the engines would be exported to Germany for Kadett/Astra production. In addition, a smaller plant would assemble 15,000 Astras annually. The GM engine-and-transmission plant in Aspern, Austria, would serve as a "sister plant" to facilitate training and technology transfer. GM's total investment in Hungary was $200 million (DM320 million), of which Opel was the conduit for $125 million (DM200 million).

Other initiatives in Eastern Europe included:

Former USSR.   GM was negotiating to set up a joint venture to manufacture catalytic converters.

Czechoslovakia.   GM had begun negotiations in February 1990 to invest in a joint venture with BAZ, the state-owned automobile manufacturer. GM needed production capacity for automoible transmissions and wanted this capacity on-stream by March 1992, when it would complement other new productive capacity elsewhere in Europe. Disagreements between the Czech and Slovak negotiators had led to 12 months of delays. GM concluded that it would not be feasible to start up a transmission facility in Czechoslovakia within the time required and shifted the new capacity to Austria. No further discussions with the Czech government had occurred since then.

GM Europe continued to encourage GM's divisions to investigate East European investment opportunities. Several divisions were investigating possible future involvements.

COMPETITORS IN EASTERN EUROPE

GM's efforts to penetrate East European markets occurred against the background of a general thrust by European, American, and Asian automobile manufacturers into these markets. As one automobile executive noted:

We could just about hold an industry conference at any of the international-class hotels in Warsaw, Budapest, or Prague right now. One day I saw my counterparts from Ford and Volkswagen at the Metropole in Budapest. The next day, I saw my counterparts from Fiat and Peugeot at the

Marriott in Warsaw. These people weren't just sightseeing. It's a frenzy of deal-doing. You have to understand: North America and Western Europe are mature markets and the Japanese dominate Asia. Eastern Europe represents the only major remaining growth opportunity. No executive wants to be the one who missed the train. . . and the train is starting to leave the station.

The pattern of investment in Eastern Europe suggested that Western firms were more willing to invest in Eastern Europe if a competitor had already done so. In recent years several automobile companies had moved into Eastern Europe:

Volkswagen.   In 1991, Volkswagen acquired a majority interest in the Skoda automobile company in Czechoslovakia for an initial DM1.2 billion ($750 million) and was committed to investing an additional DM9 billion ($8.6 billion) by 1998. In addition, VW had committed $3 billion for the conversion of the East German Trabant assembly plant by 1992. In June 1992, VW announced its intention to pursue a business venture with Euroslavia's smallest automobile manufacturer. This venture might entail an investment of DM130 million ($81 million), although no specific agreement had been struck.

Eurauto.   In May 1992, Eurauto expanded its investment in a joint venture with BIS, the largest Euroslav automobile manufacturer, into a majority ownership for a total of DM3.2 billion ($2.0 billion).[2]

Ford.   In 1991, Ford announced its intention to build a components factory in Hungary for $83 million.

Suzuki.   In 1991, Suzuki committed $265 million to assemble automobiles in a joint venture with Hungary's Autokoncern. The joint venture would construct a new assembly plant.

Mercedes-Benz.   In 1991, Mercedes-Benz invested DM1.3 billion ($840 million) in the Liaz-Avia bus-manufacturing plant in Czechoslovakia.

Renault.   Renault had been actively pursuing an East European partner and location but had failed to win a bid or close a transaction. The company complained that East European governments unfairly taxed imports and chose their partners on subjective, not economic, grounds. Nonetheless, Renault's bid for Skoda was only half of Volkswagen's successful bid of $6.2 billion.

Notably absent from the list of major investors in Eastern Europe were Japanese automobile manufacturers. Some analysts believed the Japanese were taking a wait-and-

---

[2]By July 1992, BIS workers were striking for higher wages and job guarantees in advance of Eurauto's assumption of control.

see attitude about the future of East European automobile markets. Others suspected a policy of exclusion by the East European governments in an attempt to hasten integration of their countries with Western Europe.

THE EUROSLAV AUTOMOBILE MARKET

With a population of 40 million people, Euroslavia constituted one of the largest national markets in Eastern Europe—about the same population and area as Spain. It was also one of the youngest in terms of the demographic distribution of its population. Analysts believed that Euroslavia would have the largest number of new-car sales by the end of the decade, and even then would have the lowest vehicle density in terms of cars per 1,000 people. In Eastern Europe there were only 11 cars per 100 persons, compared with 35 in Western Europe and 60 in the United States. On average, Czech cars were 9.1 years old; East German cars were 12.0 years old. Although Euroslavia's purchasing power was below that of East Germany and Hungary, it was expected to improve. All in all, Euroslavia was extremely attractive in terms of size, geographical position, and potential growth in demand. By the year 2000, Euroslavia was expected to have the largest annual unit demand of any country in Eastern Europe.

No major automobile manufacturer could stay in the Euroslav market without a joint venture with the government. The import duties to be paid would either price cars out of the market or severely limit the volume sold to 3,000–5,000 cars per year. Under joint venture agreements, the government promised joint venturers with AUTA, BIS, and BUZ[3] duty-free imports of 30,000 cars per year (to raise 5 percent each year) and granted each partner one third of this quota.[4]

Demand for GM's products would be determined significantly by per-capita income, and demand for *new* Western cars. With real wages at 75 percent of their prior levels, household budgets were increasingly strained. On average, individuals had a purchasing power equivalent to US$3,900 per year, a standard of living 75 percent lower than of the United States. Demand also would be limited by steeply rising import prices and weakening exchange rates. One positive factor was that growth in private-sector activity would support increased spending on cars. Another important positive factor was cash payments from family members in Western Europe and the United States to their families in Euroslavia—these transfer payments represented a significant source of funds in the Euroslav private sector.

The composition of Euroslav automobile demand could be broken down into low-priced vehicles costing US$5,000–7,000 (DM8,000–11,000) and high-priced, new Western cars costing US$12,000–16,000 (DM19,000–25,000). The following table compares sales in Euroslavia of Opel cars and Euroslav new and used cars:

---

[3]BUZ was the third-largest of the three Euroslav automobile companies.

[4]The proposed allocation of the duty-free import quota was contentious. Several manufacturers who had no plant capacity in Euroslavia complained to the government and to the European Community. This situation might prove to be an embarrassment and could force the government to share the quotas more broadly.

Segment	Marque	Price (DM)	1991 Unit Sales
Small cars	Opel Corsa	14,000	2,150
	FSM-Eurauto Pina	7,500	(new)
	AUTA Slavi	10,000	40,000
Used cars*	0–3 years	11–13,000	37,000
	3–6 years	7–9,000	40,000
	6+ years	3–5,000	78,000
Compact	Opel Astra	21,000	600
Mid-size	Opel Vectra	25,300	1,300
Upper-medium	Opel Omega	33,000	200
Luxury	Opel Senator	52,900	30
Sports coupe	Opel Calibra	41,000	75

*The used-car totals include compact cars as well as small cars.

The low-priced segment made up 90 percent of the market, largely because the average Euroslav worker could not afford a new car: it took a worker 7.5 years to earn the price of a new GM Astra. Although new Western cars had only captured 11 percent[5] of the total market, they were expected to make up 25 percent of the total market within five years. Some industry forecasts expected this market share to remain relatively constant through 1995, when incomes were expected to rise.

Total car demand was the key figure. Projections ranged from 200,000 to 230,000 units in 1993 to between 300,000 and 350,000 in the year 2000. This scenario gave all Western new-car manufacturers and their joint ventures roughly 22,000–25,000 potential annual sales in the short term and 75,000–87,500 by 2000.

The car-supply picture was changing rapidly. All local manufacturers would most likely have Western joint venture backing and engineering capability by 2000. Cars of purely East European design already had fallen from half to a third of all new-car registrations, with Western imports and joint ventures making up the other two thirds. The flood of used Western cars competing with the cheap Eastern models created tough price competition.

GM executives perceived that Euroslav automobile manufacturing techniques were not competitive with those of Western European manufacturers. Jacques Schmidt, the leader of the GM negotiating team, told Anna Krzykowiak:

We used statistics on manufacturing hours per car to indicate to the Euroslavs where Skoda in Czechoslovakia and AUTA are relative to the other manufacturers in Europe. We said, "If you are intent on keeping these car companies alive, the hours per car must go way down. If the

---

[5]Anna Krzykowiak noted that all estimates of the size of the Euroslav car market included the sales of used Western cars, which at the time were flooding into Euroslavia. When one focused only on *new* cars, and on cars in the GM price range, the resulting Western new-car market share of the total car market was relatively small.

hours per car go way down, please reset your expectations about employment at these plants. You take 9,000 people to produce 60,000 cars per year. We build 500,000 cars with the same number of people."

Krzykowiak believed that the Euroslav negotiating team would need to reconsider its objectives for large, guaranteed employment.

ECONOMIC AND POLITICAL CONDITIONS IN EUROSLAVIA

Although the roots of many of Euroslavia's economic problems went back decades, any recent discussion of economic and political conditions in Euroslavia usually started with the watershed year, 1989, when the non-Communist trade union, Democracy, gained participation in the government. Shortly thereafter, the Communist party leader, Bulban Militar, declared the first free elections in Euroslavia since World War II. Jan Svoboda, the charismatic leader of Democracy, was elected president of Euroslavia in 1990.

The Euroslav economy receded seriously from 1989 to 1992. Euroslavia's gross domestic product (GDP) fell 9 percent in 1991, following a 1990 decline of 11 percent. Industrial production was down 24 percent in 1990, 12 percent in 1991, and a further 14 percent decline was expected for 1992. Certain sectors were particularly hard hit, with transportation equipment output falling a numbing 36 percent. Unemployment stood at 19 percent in 1992. Some analysts expected real wages to fall 5 percent in 1992 on top of a 22 percent decline in 1991. This economic deterioration was due to the combination of the collapse of Euroslavia's East European export markets and a sharp fall in domestic wages. On the positive side, the recession was considered a necessary transitional stage. The manufacturing sector needed to "clean house": eliminate unnecessary production facilities and begin producing on demand instead of via central planning. The government was trying to reequilibrate the economy away from the unprofitable heavy-industry sector and toward the service sector.

The economic outlook for 1993–95 was cautiously positive. GDP was expected to grow 1 percent in 1993 and 2 percent in 1994. The austerity program had brought consumer price increases down from 685 percent in 1990 to under 45 percent in 1992. Government public bonds were beginning to be sold, but only in 26-week maturities; they offered nominal interest rates of 53 percent.

The foreign-exchange rates for the bunt[6] were believed to reflect the underlying inflation differentials between Euroslavia and other countries. A 17 percent increase in exports had eliminated the trade deficit and brought in Western "hard currencies." The State Bank's reserves totaled $3.6 billion, three times more than in the pre-1989 years.

Liberalization of ownership of state enterprises had been a key focus of economic reform. As a result, a million new jobs were created by private businesses alone in 1990–91. Newly privatized companies were listing themselves on the stock market, although less than 15 were quoted in June 1992. The regulatory environment for foreign direct investment (FDI) had been liberalized; the ministry of finance hoped FDIs would average

---

[6]The Euroslav currency was the bunt, which traded at approximately 14,000 to the U.S. dollar in 1992.

US$1.2 billion per year from 1992–95. The government's restructuring programs—the most radical undertaken by any East European government—were considered successful by Western observers.

Political and economic risks remained for foreign investors in Euroslavia. The political uncertainty in Euroslavia had a strong bearing on economic performance. Unable to forge a coalition, four prime ministers had come and gone in three years. The most important economic tenet, fiscal discipline, required a government strong enough to withstand the resulting social unrest. In 1992, the lower house of parliament temporarily turned from its anti-inflation policies to an anti-recession spending program. Observers worried that this stop-and-go macroeconomic policy making could undermine the gains made to date.

JOINT VENTURE INVESTMENT ALTERNATIVES IN EUROSLAVIA

The Euroslav negotiating team had considered a range of potential joint venture strategies with GM and, by a process of elimination, had boiled them down to three main alternatives:

1. Complete knock-down (CKD) plant operated in a joint venture with AUTA. A CKD plant would consist of the tools and equipment necessary to assemble up to 30,000 Opel Astras a year from kits imported from Adam Opel A.G. in Germany. AUTA workers would assemble the cars and possibly add a few components of local origin. The output of the CKD plant would be sold in Euroslavia, although, in theory, the cars could be exported to other markets in Europe. The greatest value added already would be in the Opel kits; only marginal local value would be added by AUTA. In GM's experience—given the extra shipping and handling and the absence of economies of scale—cars produced in CKD plants were 20 percent more expensive than cars produced in high-volume integrated facilities. The cost of this plant was estimated at $113 million. As a *quid pro quo* for investing in Euroslavia, GM might receive a one-third allocation of the quota of 30,000 duty-free cars, which would permit it to bring in other cars in the Opel product line.

2. Greenfield assembly plant operated in a joint venture with AUTA. Funds would be allocated now; construction would begin in six months. The greenfield plant would be fully operational in 1996 and yield 200,000 Opel Astras per year. In the meantime, a CKD plant would be constructed rapidly to begin production before year-end 1992 and would yield up to 30,000 Opel Astras per year. The cost of the greenfield plant would be $400 million (DM640 million). The CKD plant would employ 9,000 of AUTA's 19,000 workers at least through 1996.

3. Status quo. At the time, GM manufactured units in Germany and exported them to the Euroslav market. Despite the Memorandum of Understanding, GM might consider developing its dealer networks, building its distribution chain, and postponing an investment decision, with its attendant risk. GM would have to continue paying duties on its cars shipped to Euroslavia, but the forgone import concessions would be balanced by the saved investment capital. Krzykowiak's team concluded that this strategy would sacrifice any hope of a joint venture with AUTA, because the Euroslav government would not wait to marry its major automobile manufacturer to a Western car company—indeed, it would deliver AUTA to one of GM's European competitors.

Krzykowiak's staff prepared a financial analysis of the three alternatives (the summary memorandum and quantitative tables are contained in Exhibit 3).

EUROSLAV NEGOTIATING TEAM

The negotiating team owed its allegiance to at least four interest groups within the Euroslav government:

Ministry of Finance.   Jerzy Katowicz, the minister of finance, was closest to the prime minister and was bearing the brunt of pressures on the government to do something about the country's economic crisis. His first priority was balancing the government's budget (several IMF loans depended on that); fighting inflation was No. 2; and spurring economic growth was third. He believed that the people and government of Euroslavia would accept a period of austerity necessary to achieve these goals. He genuinely believed that the austerity program would work, but that any retreat from the austerity program, while granting short-term relief, would have disastrous consequences in the long run. Unfortunately, austerity, the rate of inflation, and the recession had snowballed, and a political backlash was forming in the lower house of parliament. Minister Katowicz had to show tangible progress, *fast*.

The announcement of the Memorandum of Understanding with GM had been a ray of sunshine for the government. Katowicz wanted no retreat from the major investment program outlined in the memorandum, because major hard-currency investments were crucially important to Euroslavia's economic growth, as were the export businesses those investments would create. Moreover, the government's budget could not afford any bunt contribution to the joint venture. Katowicz wanted a detailed agreement soon. In pursuit of these goals, he personally intervened with the prime minister to have his own special assistant, Anna Krzykowiak,[7] appointed president of the committee that would negotiate with GM. She had proved to have outstanding qualities in recent crisis negotiations and

---

[7]Krzykowiak had been leader of the Euroslav team that had successfully concluded debt-rescheduling negotiations with the International Monetary Fund. In reporting on those negotiations, the *Financial Times* described her as "brilliant, tough, shrewd, and articulate." *Paris Match* profiled her as one of the 10 most promising European professional women for the 1990s:

After fleeing Euroslavia with her parents in 1976, she studied physics at the Max Planck Institute in Munich, and then earned a doctorate in economics from the London School of Economics. Abandoning a brilliant academic career at Stanford University, she returned to Euroslavia in 1988 to serve as an economic adviser to the Democracy movement and Jan Svoboda, its leader. She proved her negotiating skills in 1991 when she persuaded a group of striking machinists to end their occupation of a nuclear power plant. Friends say she is an idealist with no personal political ambitions. However, political observers suggest that she will be prime minister or president before the decade is over.

In addition to the IMF negotiations, she also had led the negotiations with Euroauto over its $2.3 billion investment in BIS, the other major Euroslav automobile manufacturer.

was an effective advocate of the free-market principles to which Minister Katowicz was committed.

Ministry of Industry and Trade.   Leczak Stepanski, the minister of industry and trade, viewed the negotiations with GM as one more opportunity to fashion the structure of Euroslavia's automotive industry for the long term. A fervent believer in the benefits of a national industrial policy, he wanted the negotiations to reinvigorate AUTA with modern plant and equipment, worker training, and new-product designs. AUTA's survival as an entity was important to Stepanski for symbolic and political reasons. In return, he was prepared to accept reductions in employees, to offer high import tariffs as a protection against GM's competitors, and to allow GM 10,000 duty-free car imports per year. He would worry later about problems such an agreement might create for Euroslavia's association with the European Community.[8]

Ministry of Ownership Transformation (formerly, ministry of privatization). Bogdan Lobachoff[9] would represent the ministry of ownership transformation, which was responsible for selling or arranging joint ventures with state-owned enterprises. AUTA was a particularly important focus of Lobachoff's attention: because of its size and market position, any action (or inaction) on the disposition of AUTA would affect his personal standing in the government. He was a realist who knew that AUTA's operations were essentially worthless when compared with those of Western manufacturers. Thus, a deal that attributed *any* value to AUTA's assets and its Slavi brand would be a victory. However, political opponents in the parliament had charged that the ministry was giving Euroslavia's industrial "crown jewels" to greedy foreign investors for "next to nothing." Lobachoff's goal, therefore, was to achieve a deal attributing as much value as possible to AUTA. He believed AUTA provided both a distribution network and an organized pool of automotive workers that were worth *something*. Ultimately, he had one goal in mind: to eliminate further state support for AUTA, which he viewed as an ailing behemoth.

Autofabryka Azzotiazion.   Janucz Lewandewski,[10] the general director of AUTA itself, would participate on the negotiating committee. The signing of the Memorandum of Understanding had been an important victory, for it seemed to guarantee the survival of

---

[8]Euroslavia was at the time negotiating the agreement by which it would become an "associate" of the European Community (EC). Ordinarily, countries assumed associate status for a few years before becoming full members. The statutes of the EC prohibited import tariffs of the kind designed to protect domestic manufacturers. The European Commission gave special scrutiny to the automotive industry, which had become something of a lightning rod for EC investigators. The EC had requested the phasing out of the protective tariffs and had demanded equal apportionment of the duty-free import quotas across all companies selling cars in Euroslavia, whether manufacturing in Euroslavia or not. The Euroslav committee had promised a 30 percent share of the quota to GM, but to ignore the EC requests might jeopardize the progress of the association talks.

[9]Lobachoff (LOB-a-choff) was a career civil servant.

[10]Janucz Lewandewski (YAN-ush lev-an-DEV-ski) had worked for AUTA his entire carreer. Raised in Slavagrad as the son of the local Communist party chairman, he joined the party at the age of 15. Trained as a mechanical engineer at the Moscow Institute for Heavy Machinery, his first job was as a production planner for AUTA. By 1992 he had been general director of AUTA for seven years.

AUTA and provide the opportunity for his management team to participate in the new joint venture. The memorandum's statement that GM would own 70 percent of the venture held implications for daily control of the operation that would need to be hammered out: What role would Lewandewski and his management team have in this new venture? How much operational flexibility would they have to run the plant? What budget oversight? What salaries?[11]

Lewandewski's managers openly expressed concern about interference from "the Germans" at Opel. Euroslavs widely admired the quality and workmanship of German products. However, as Lewandewski noted:

> There is an ancient difference between Slavs and Germanics that is deeper than can be explained by World War II. Euroslavs resent German methods and culture: too rigid, exacting, serious, domineering. But you have these kinds of differences between neighbors all over the world: Mexicans feel this way toward the Americans, Egyptians toward the Israelis, Vietnamese toward the Chinese, and so on. And so it is in Europe. I hope I won't have to take orders from a German.

In addition to these representatives on the negotiating committee, the ministry of ownership transformation had retained various consultants to advise the committee:

- Credit Suisse First Boston would prepare financial and valuation analyses.
- Arthur Andersen would prepare a final audit of AUTA and advise on financial accounting questions that might arise.
- Skadden, Arps, Slate, Meagher & Flom, a prominent New York-based law firm specializing in mergers and acquisitions, would draft the agreement on the Euroslav side and advise on the design of terms.

Reflecting on the makeup of the committee representing the Euroslav government in negotiations with GM, Anna Krzykowiak commented:

> To outsiders, we look monolithic. But the truth is that this committee has some potentially serious political divisions. In cutting the final deal with GM, we will have to make internal trade-offs. We must be careful that this doesn't trigger infighting between the various ministries and AUTA. To satisfy everyone on the committee, we must extract more of everything from GM: more invested deutsche marks, more guaranteed employment, and a faster timetable—while giving up less ourselves in the way of income tax revenues, import duties, and control. Unfortunately, our bargaining strength is weakening as the economy stalls and as we spin through prime ministers. If I can simply hold GM to the broad outline of the Memorandum of Understanding (i.e., with an initial $75 million investment in a temporary plant, followed by a $400 million investment

---

[11]Shortly after the announcement of Eurauto's joint venture with BIS, the workers and *managers* went on strike for employment guarantees and higher pay. The standard aspiration of workers in a privatized company was for a 50 percent increase in hourly wages. For managers, the aspiration was for a *tenfold* increase (the typical take-home pay of an industrial manager of a state-owned enterprise in Euroslavia was on the order of US$200 per month).

in a greenfield plant), the negotiations will be a success. The big question is, What will we have to give up to hold to the agreement? I am prepared to make deep concessions on:

- Number of jobs guaranteed in the joint venture.
- Wages and salaries.
- Local content of cars.

If forced to, I will give some ground on:

- Depreciation rate on plant and equipment.
- Percentage ownership of the Euroslav government in the joint venture.
- Import duties (larger duty-free quota for GM and higher tariff on nonduty-free cars).

I will be very reluctant to give ground on terms that affect overall hard-currency investment in Euroslavia, and which affect the government deficit:

- Total investment by GM into Euroslavia.
- Export allowances.
- Corporate tax rate.

Under no circumstances will I agree to terms that require my government to contribute cash to the joint venture. We are under tremendous pressure from the IMF to curb government spending. We have no means to make a hard investment. I am prepared to give up some opportunity inflows in return.

I have communicated these priorities to my colleagues on the negotiating committee, but they have not as yet expressed agreement with my views. My committee members disagree with me vehemently on some of these items. I have to fight with my adversaries and my own "friends" at the same time.

GM NEGOTIATING TEAM

GM was scheduled to send a negotiating team consisting of representatives from the manufacturing, marketing, and finance functions of the firm:

The planning and marketing views: Jacques Schmidt, vice president of planning, GM–Europe, Zürich.   Schmidt had been the chief architect of the trailblazing 1988 joint venture agreement with the government of Hungary, which industry observers had termed a bold stroke into a receptive market and an illustration of ingenious integration of manufacturing resources between Eastern and Western Europe. Schmidt had negotiated the Memorandum of Understanding with the Euroslav government and was unquestionably the "champion" for significant investment in Euroslavia.

The treasury view: James Sterling, manager of corporate finance, GM–Europe Regional Treasury Center, Brussels.   Sterling brought to the GM negotiating committee the financial point of view. In general, the Treasury Group, somewhat removed from the dominant car culture inside General Motors, was known for a tradition of independence and skepticism. The group thought of itself as a rigorous analytical shop and routinely scrutinized management's project proposals to make sure that risk-adjusted returns were sufficient. The treasury staff believed that 15 percent was an appropriate discount rate for deutsche mark cash flows associated with the automobile joint venture in Euroslavia.

The manufacturing view: Helmut Kunst, vice president of manufacturing, Adam Opel A.G., Rüsselsheim, Germany. An engineer by training and a lifelong manufacturing manager, Kunst would bring to the GM team an assessment of the operational feasibility of any joint venture proposals. He also would represent the interests of Adam Opel A.G. Based on preliminary discussions with him, the Euroslav negotiating team had concluded that Kunst was especially worried about work-force training and quality, potential logistical problems, condition of the facilities, and lack of management depth at AUTA.

CONCLUSION

Anna Krzykowiak anticipated hard work ahead for her negotiating team. Only that morning an analysis from the ministry of finance had described depressing developments in the Euroslav automobile market (see Exhibit 4). A second report also had just arrived that described AUTA's uncertain—possibly unhealthy—financial condition and a potentially worrisome environmental liability (see Exhibit 5).

Any final deal would have to be approved by the GM–Europe strategy board. Then the proposal would be presented to GM president Jack Smith and, ultimately, the board of directors. The Euroslavs also had an approval process that would culminate in review by the council of ministers and parliament.

EXHIBIT 1

"GM and AUTA Jump-Start Stalled Talks" *

U.S. motor manufacturer General Motors Corp. (GM) has signed a memorandum of understanding to invest $75 million in a joint venture with Autofabryka Azzotiazion (AUTA), Euroslavia's largest car maker. For almost a decade, the country has been seeking a western partner for AUTA. This agreement brings an end to many months of ebbing negotiations and wild speculations.

The memorandum was signed by Euroslav industry minister Leczak Stepanski as well as directors of GM Europe and AUTA. It creates a new company, as yet unnamed, in which GM will hold a 70 percent stake.

The two sides have announced plans to build a new factory on the present AUTA site to assemble GM's Opel cars. This alone will cost $75 million.

Sources say GM has pledged to invest a further $400 million by 1996 in a separate joint venture to make an Opel-designed car for which Euroslavia will have exclusive production rights. Rollo Meyer, a spokesman for GM Europe in Zürich, concedes that "the $75 million is only an initial investment figure."

The new venture should be ready to assemble as many as 35,000 Astra and Vectra mod-

EXHIBIT 1   *(concluded)*

els by mid-1993. Meanwhile, it will oversee the replacement of AUTA's outdated Slavi car with a new model. GM will also sign a separate agreement with AUTA to modernize its Eurauto-derived Slavi.

GM's desire to establish a strong East European network is firmly underscored by plans for an extensive supplier development programme that will bring together AUTA and its Euroslav component manufacturers with leading Western suppliers to the GM group. In support of this programme, GM's own European components arm has signed a memorandum with FA Krosno to pursue a joint suspension manufacturing project.

Negotiations are still taking place, but a conclusion satisfactory to both sides will help offset the obstacles and delays of the past year. "Talks broke down twice officially and a few more times unofficially. Virtually every time, the Euroslav side refused to grant the incentives sought by the Western side. These included the right to import cars into Euroslavia free of duty, which would save a considerable sum, and guidelines on government incentives," says Peter Hennessy, head of the Credit Suisse First Boston team, representing the Euroslav ministry of privatisation.

For this deal, Euroslavia was advised by a consortium coordinated by CSFB, which also included U.S. law firm Skadden, Arps, Slate Meagher & Flom and accountants Arthur Andersen. GM brought no external financial advisers to the table.

A number of Western car manufacturers have been linked with AUTA, and talks with various parties ran aground many times. There was a major deadlock in October 1991, when AUTA and the Euroslav government rejected offers to form a venture from both GM and Citroën of France, and asked both to amend certain financial aspects of their proposals before returning to the table. Neither GM nor Citroën had accepted previous Euroslav government invitations to buy a stake in AUTA.

Another source close to the GM deal process comments: "One main problem was that the Euroslav side wasn't really unified in knowing what it wanted from this— which is understandable for a country that is still learning."

But Meyer at GM is more neutral about the reasons why it turned into one of Eastern Europe's most protracted set of talks: "At first, the Euroslavs concluded from their calculations that our terms were not good. That is a matter of interpretation. It is difficult to pinpoint the problems along the way, but the constant arrival and departure of Euroslav officials did not help. We were almost at the point of signing this in December. Then, the next day, the government changed."

He insists that the deal in its present form is attractive enough without sweeteners to lure GM into Euroslavia and there are no unorthodox investment terms attached to the agreement, because Western motor companies are "all treated the same way in Euroslavia." But he admits that there is rough terrain ahead: "It is impossible to judge how long it will take to work. At the moment, we are not selling that many cars in Euroslavia. The market there is big but not very active."

This long-awaited deal is a setback for Citroën, a unit of French carmaker Peugeot, which bid against GM until the very end. However, French newspapers report that AUTA and Citroën are still in talks over another, smaller deal. French car manufacturers have had some bad luck in Eastern Europe, losing out on a number of major deals.

Renault lost a battle against Volkswagen to partner Czech plant Skoda in 1991, then lost out to Mercedes in a bid to link up with Czech truck makers Avia and Liaz, leaving it to pair off finally with bus maker Karosa Vysoke.

The other major deal to have been struck between the Euroslav car industry and a Western investor will see Eurauto take a majority stake in a joint venture with BIS (no connection with AUTA). The two signed a memorandum in October after a smooth but intense set of negotiations.

---

*Central European, Euromoney Publications, April 1992, page 6. Some persons and companies have been disguised. The article incorrectly states that AUTA was Euroslavia's largest car maker. Actually, AUTA was approximately half the size of BIS, the largest Euroslav car maker.

EXHIBIT 2　Value Line Investment Survey Report

GENERAL MOTORS NYSE-GM | RECENT PRICE **44** | P/E RATIO **NMF** (Trailing: NMF Median: 7.5) | RELATIVE P/E RATIO **NMF** | DIV'D YLD **3.6%** | VALUE LINE **105**

TIMELINESS **3** Average (Relative Price Performance Next 12 Mos.)
SAFETY **2** Above Average (Scale: 1 Highest to 5 Lowest)
BETA 1.05 (1.00 = Market)

1995-97 PROJECTIONS

	Price	Gain	Ann'l Total Return
High	85	(+95%)	22%
Low	60	(+35%)	13%

BUSINESS: General Motors is the world's largest auto manufacturer. 1991 sales were 16.8% of worldwide total. Automotive products account for 85% of sales. Makes Chevrolet and GMC trucks, GM diesel locomotives, and engines. Operates plants in 17 foreign countries, principally in Western Europe, which make Vauxhall, Opel, and Holden cars and trucks. Acquired EDS in '84, Hughes Aircraft in '86. Foreign business accounts for 16%, labor costs, 24% of sales. '91 depreciation rate: 10.3%. Estimated plant age: 10 years. The company has 756,300 employees, 2 mil. stockholders. Insiders own 1% of stock. Chairman: Robert C. Stempel. Incorporated: Delaware. Address: 3044 West Grand Boulevard, Detroit, Michigan 48202-3091. Telephone: 313-556-5000.

General Motors managed to earn a small profit in the March period. The news gave the share price a boost, and helped the company get a sympathetic hearing from investors when it recently offered $2.2 billion in new common stock intended to shore up its balance sheet and its underfunded pension plans. Still, GM's difficulties are hardly past. Such a major makeover of the company as is now under way will almost certainly take longer and cost more than anticipated, and labor peace (see below) cannot be assumed. Accordingly, we expect GM's return to profitability to be slower than that of its crosstown rivals. Assuming roughly 10% dilution from the new share issue, we now look for GM to earn its preferred dividend requirement in 1992; pent-up demand should drive a partial profit recovery in 1993, thus helping to keep the reduced common payout intact.

The changes being made at GM are real, and not everyone is going to like them. A recent example: In an effort to make its North American plants function more like its highly lucrative European operations, GM's new purchasing head has decreed that virtually all contracts with suppliers would be opened to new bids, and that the company's internal parts-making divisions would be given no preference in the coming competitions to supply GM world wide. This attempt to overhaul the way the company spends $50 billion annually on parts and raw materials is sure to cause bitter battles among suppliers and to alarm the United Auto Workers, 80,000 of whose members work in GM's sprawling parts operations fabricating 70% of the components that go into GM vehicles. Investors should note that several times in the past two years, the UAW has called strikes at key GM parts factories to protest similar decisions to "outsource" materials.

There's no urgent reason to commit to GM stock at this juncture, particularly after the recent share-price runup. For the 3- to 5-year term, we think that GM's resources (human and material) are larger than its problems by a wide margin. Still, dilution from the recent share issue has reduced the stock's attractiveness as a longer-term holding.

Mark Leach　　　*June 19, 1992*

(A) Primary earnings. Excludes nonrecurring gain: '91, $1.16; '92, 88¢. Next earnings report due early Aug. (B) Next dividend meeting about Aug. 4. Goes ex about Aug. 14. Approximate dividend payment dates: 10th of March, June, Sept., Dec. ■ Dividend reinvestment plan available. In '84, plus .05 shs. "E" stock. (C) In millions, adjusted for stock split. (D) Includes GMAC from 1988. (E) Excludes GMAC from 1988. (F) Includes intangibles. In '91: $10.2 billion, $16.12/sh.

Company's Financial Strength	A
Stock's Price Stability	80
Price Growth Persistence	25
Earnings Predictability	10

Factual material is obtained from sources believed to be reliable, but the publisher is not responsible for any errors or omissions contained herein. For the confidential use of subscribers. Reprinting, copying, and distribution by permission only. Copyright 1992 by Value Line Publishing, Inc. ® Reg. TM—Value, Inc.

Source: *Value Line Investment Survey,* June 19, 1992, p. 105. © 1992, Value Line Publishing, Inc. Reprinted by permission.

EXHIBIT 3 Financial Analysis of Euroslav Market-Entry Strategies: Memorandum and Spreadsheet Model

To: Anna Krzykowiak
        President, Negotiating Team
From: Alexandre Chopin
Re: Financial Analysis of Euroslav Market-Entry Strategies

We have completed the financial modeling of the three market-entry strategies for Euroslavia and can report the following results for the base case of macroeconomic and operating assumptions:

	Status Quo	*CKD Plant*	*CKD/Greenfield Plant*
Base Case			
Net present value	DM1,646 million	DM1,155 million	DM3,754 million
IRR	Infinite	65%	56%
Profitability index*	Infinite	7×	8.51×
Payback	0 years	2 years	4 years
Net hard-currency flow	DM(2,809) million	DM(1,425) million	DM4,473 million
Jobs created by 1996	0	850	1,600
PV tax revenues:			
Import/export duties	DM21 million	DM22 million	DM59 million
Income taxes	DM85 million	DM117 million	DM207 million
Pessimistic Case			
Net present value			
IRR			
Profitability index			
Payback			
Net hard-currency flow			
Jobs created by 1996			
PV tax revenues:			
Import/export duties			
Income taxes			
Optimistic Case			
Net present value			
IRR			
Profitability index			
Payback			
Net hard-currency flow			
Jobs created by 1996			
PV tax revenues:			
Import/export duties			
Income taxes			

*The profitability index is computed as the ratio of the present value of future cash flows to the value of the initial-year investment outlay.

EXHIBIT 3 (continued)

Of course, these are just the basic results. When you think it is appropriate, we will exercise the model to complete the grid in this table, and to identify key value drivers or break-even assumptions for critical variables.

Also, we have undertaken no work yet to test the sensitivity of these results to variations in points to be negotiated with General Motors:

- Percentage ownership by GM in the joint venture.
- DM total investment by GM into Euroslavia.
- Duties on imported cars.
- Depreciation rate on facilities.
- Number of workers for whom we guarantee employment.
- Local-content percentage of each car.
- Income-tax rate for the joint venture.

The computer-spreadsheet model is described in more detail as follows:

Description of Financial Model
of Entry Strategies for Euroslavia

The Lotus spreadsheet model permits rapid sensitivity analysis of financial results and is intended to support the preparation of the GM Treasury staff team for the Euroslavia Steering Committee meeting and, ultimately, for the negotiations with the Euroslav government.

The entire spreadsheet is summarized in the northwest corner, where a single screen of data lists 13 key assumptions, and 8 results for the three alternative strategies. One can conduct sensitivity analyses by varying assumptions and pressing "F9," the recalculation button on the computer. (Alternatively, one could construct data tables of results in an unused region of the spreadsheet.) Immediately below the summary screen on the spreadsheet is a summary of key macroeconomic assumptions underlying the financial forecasts. Farther down are the Free Cash Flow (FCF) forecasts for the three strategies, each of which consists of two pages of calculations working from units produced and sold toward FCF. Projections extend for eight years (1993–2000) and are denominated in deutsche marks (DM).

The input variables are broken down into two groupings: assumptions about marketing and operations, and assumptions about the ultimate "deal" to be struck with the Euroslav government.

Assumptions about Marketing and Operations

1. Percentage of total market held by new Western-made cars.
2. Opel's percentage share of the new Western-made-car demand.
3. Percent growth rate of car prices.
4. Production strategy, where the value "1" indicates the plant is run at full capacity with the surplus production available for export to other countries; or "0," which indicates that the plant produces only for Euroslav demand.
5. Real growth rate of demand after year 2000 (to be used in the terminal-value calculation).

Assumptions about Ultimate "Deal" with the Euroslav Government

6. Percentage ownership of joint venture by GM and Euroslavia.
7. Total investment by GM into Euroslavia.
8. Duties on imported cars.
9. Depreciation rate on plant and equipment.
10. Number of Euroslav workers guaranteed employment.
11. Local content of cars.
12. Corporate tax rate.

The results section of the summary screen presents 9 calculated results for each of the three entry strategies:

- Net present value of the joint venture.
- Internal rate of return.
- Profitability index (ratio of PV inflows to PV outflows).
- Payback.
- Number of jobs.
- Effect on Euroslav balance of payments.
- PV of tax revenues to Euroslavia (duties and income taxes).

The tabulated spreadsheet-model data follow.

EXHIBIT 3 *(continued)*

Summary Screen of Lotus Model

Key Value Drivers

	1993–1995	1996–1999	2000
1. New "Western" car mkt. share	14%	25%	49%
2. Opel mkt. share/new Western mkt.	36%	25%	18%
3. Price real growth rate (%)	2%	3%	5%
4. Euroslav government's % ownership of JV	30%		
5. Import duties	35%	35%	20%
6. Export duties	2%	2%	2%
7. Production strategy	1		
8. Straight-line depreciation years	8		
9. Terminal value growth rate	7.0%		
DM inflation from yr. 2000	4.0%		
Real growth in unit sales from yr 2000	3.0%		
10. Duty-free quota for GM	10,000		
	CKD	Greenfield	Status quo
11. Local content %	15%	100%	0%

Key Results

	CKD	Greenfield	Status Quo
1. NPV of free cash flows (DM MM)	425	1,460	330
2. Internal rate of return (FCFs)	35%	36%	Infinite
3. Profitability index	3.10	3.63	Infinite
4. Payback (years)	5	6	0
5. Net hard-currency inflow (PV)	(1,425,224)	4,472,608	(2,809,493)
6. Jobs created by 1996	850	1,600	0
7. PV tax revenues to Euroslav government:			
Import/export duties	22,400	58,528	21,277
Income taxes	492,862	206,886	84,881

EXHIBIT 3 *(continued)* Macroeconomic Assumptions Underlying Treasury Staff Analysis

	1993	1994	1995	1996	1997	1998	1999	2000
Macroeconomic Assumptions								
1. Euroslav car registrations (000)	200	210	220	230	240	250	265	280
2. Euroslav inflation	30%	30%	30%	20%	10%	10%	10%	10%
Compounded bunts (BTs)	130%	169%	220%	264%	290%	319%	351%	386%
DM inflation	6%	5%	4%	4%	4%	4%	4%	4%
Compounded DM	106%	111%	115%	120%	125%	130%	135%	140%
U.S. inflation	4%	4%	4%	4%	4%	4%	4%	4%
Compounded U.S.	104%	108%	112%	117%	122%	127%	132%	137%
3. Forward exchange rates:								
Bunts/DM	14,787	18,307	22,884	26,405	27,928	29,539	31,244	33,046
DM/$	1.62	1.64	1.64	1.64	1.64	1.64	1.64	1.64
Bts/US$	17,500	21,875	27,344	31,550	33,371	35,296	37,332	39,486
4. Euroslav corporate tax rate	40%							
5. German corporate tax rate	55%							
6. DM Discount rate	15%							
7. Retail price new Opels in Euroslavia—1993	19,000							
8. Opel Costs and Transfer pricing:								
Opel var. cost/completed car	13,500							
Opel var. cost. kit	11,000							
Opel bid/offer price/completed car	13,000							
Price to dealer compl. car in West	17,000							
Opel transfer price/kit	12,000							
Opel incremental fixed costs/CKD '93–95	10,000,000							
Opel incremental fixed costs/gfield '96–98	50,000,000							
Opel incremental fixed costs/st.Quo	0							

	CKD	Greenfield	Status Quo
9. Cost of each alternative (DM mm)	180	640	0
($ MM @ 1.6 DM/$)	113	400	0
10. Value of AUTA investment (DM mm)	54	54	

EXHIBIT 3 *(continued)* Forecast and Analysis of Joint Venture, Assuming CKD Plant Only (A)

JV–CKD cash flow

This section calculates the JV's cash flow with a CKD plant.

Layout = Market demand, units assembled, imported, and/or exported from/to Opel. Unit prices, total revenue, unit costs, total costs, and operating income. Cash flow in and out, NPV, and payback. GM-Opel pays for 100% of plant investment, JV realizes the depreciation.

(DM 000)	/unit	1993	1994	1995	1996	1997	1998	1999	2000
					Fiscal Year, Ending December 31				
Total Euroslav market purchases		200,000	210,000	220,000	230,000	240,000	250,000	265,000	280,000
New Western car mkt.sh. %		14%	14%	14%	25%	25%	25%	25%	49%
New Western car demand—units		28,000	29,400	30,800	57,500	60,000	62,500	66,250	137,200
Opel % of new Western demand		36%	36%	36%	25%	25%	25%	25%	18%
Opel units demanded		10,080	10,584	11,088	14,375	15,000	15,625	16,563	24,696
Production:									
Units assembled in Euroslavia		30,000	30,000	30,000	30,000	30,000	30,000	30,000	30,000
Units necessary to import from Opel		0	0	0	0	0	0	0	0
Surplus units for export		19,920	19,416	18,912	15,625	15,000	14,375	13,438	5,304
Revenue:									
Price/unit	DM/unit								
(1)/Unit sold to Euroslav dealer	14,961	16,083	17,208	18,241	19,335	20,496	21,725	23,029	24,411
Plus dealer margin and VAT tax	27%	4,342	4,646	4,925	5,221	5,534	5,866	6,218	6,591

= Retail price paid by consumer	19,000	20,425	21,855	23,166	24,556	26,029	27,591	29,247	31,001
(2)/Surplus unit exported to Opel	13,000	13,715	14,401	14,977	15,576	16,199	16,847	17,521	18,222
Revenue from Euroslav sales (DM 000)		162,113	182,134	202,256	277,947	307,433	339,458	381,415	602,843
Revenue from export sales (DM 000)		273,203	279,605	283,241	243,373	242,983	242,173	235,435	96,647
Total revenue		435,316	461,739	485,497	521,319	550,417	581,631	616,849	699,490
Costs:									
1. Opel transfer price/unit	DM/unit								
Completed car transfer price	13,000	13,715	14,401	14,977	15,576	16,199	16,847	17,521	18,222
Kit cost/unit (-local input)	12,000	10,761	11,299	11,751	12,221	12,710	13,218	13,747	14,297
2. Material local content for assembly:									
Material % of local content		15%	15%	15%	15%	15%	15%	15%	15%
Material cost/unit for assembly	12,000	1,899	1,994	2,074	2,157	2,243	2,333	2,426	2,523
3. Wages	per month								
Salary per month (Bt 000)	3,859	5,017	6,522	8,478	10,174	11,191	12,310	13,541	14,896
Social Sec./unempl. fund	4,200	5,460	7,098	9,227	11,073	12,180	13,398	14,738	16,212
Monthly cost/employee	8,059	10,477	13,620	17,706	21,247	23,371	25,709	28,279	31,107
No. of Euroslav employees	850	850	850	850	850	850	850	850	850
Wage cost/month (Bt MM)	6,850	8,905	11,577	15,050	18,060	19,866	21,852	24,038	26,441
Wage costs/month (DM 000)	463	602	632	658	684	711	740	769	800
Tot. annual wage costs (DM000)	5,559	7,227	7,588	7,892	8,207	8,536	8,877	9,232	9,602

EXHIBIT 3 *(continued)* Forecast and Analysis of Joint Venture, Assuming CKD Plant Only (B)

(DM 000)	/unit	1993	1994	1995	1996	1997	1998	1999	2000
					Fiscal Year, Ending December 31				
Variable costs incurred:									
1. Paid to Opel:									
Paid to Opel for completed car imports		0	0	0	0	0	0	0	0
Paid to Opel for kits		322,830	338,972	352,530	366,632	381,297	396,549	412,411	428,907
Total paid to Opel		322,830	338,972	352,530	366,632	381,297	396,549	412,411	428,907
2. Material local content		19,142	21,104	22,993	31,002	33,644	36,447	40,180	62,308
3. Annual wage costs		7,227	7,588	7,892	8,207	8,536	8,877	9,232	9,602
4. Export duties to ESL. govt.		5,464	5,592	5,665	4,867	4,860	4,843	4,709	1,933
5. Import duties to ESL. govt.		0	0	0	0	0	0	0	0
Total variable costs		354,663	373,256	389,080	410,708	428,336	446,717	466,531	502,749
Fixed costs:									
Sales, gen., & admin.		8,706	9,235	9,710	10,426	11,008	11,633	12,337	13,990
P&E maintenance		907	953	991	1,030	1,072	1,114	1,159	1,205
Depreciation, straight-line		29,250	29,481	29,723	29,975	30,237	30,510	30,793	31,088
less tech. transfer/training		10,550	11,078	11,521	0	0	0	0	0
Total fixed costs		49,414	50,746	51,944	41,432	42,317	43,257	44,289	46,283
Total costs		404,077	424,002	441,025	452,140	470,653	489,974	510,821	549,032
Operating income (DM 000)		31,240	37,738	44,472	69,179	79,763	91,657	106,029	150,457
Less Euroslav taxes	40%	12,496	15,095	17,789	27,672	31,905	36,663	42,411	60,183
After-tax (Euroslav) net income (DM 000)		18,744	22,643	26,683	41,508	47,858	54,994	63,617	90,274
Free cash flow calculations:									
Plus depreciation		29,250	29,481	29,723	29,975	30,237	30,510	30,793	31,088
Less capital expenditures		(1,846)	(1,939)	(2,016)	(2,097)	(2,181)	(2,268)	(2,359)	(2,453)
Less NWC requirement		(13,059)	(13,852)	(14,565)	(15,640)	(16,512)	(17,449)	(18,505)	(20,985)
Less GM CKD plant investment	(180,000)								
Less AUTA asset valuation	(54,000)								
Plus terminal value									1,309,744
Free cash flows	(234,000)	33,088	36,333	39,825	53,746	59,402	65,787	73,546	1,407,669
PV free cash flows	424,954								
IRR free cash flows	35.3%								
Payback (years)	5								
Profitability index	3.10								

774

EXHIBIT 3 *(continued)* Forecast and Analysis of Joint Venture, Assuming CKD Plant and Greenfield Plant

JV–Greenfield by 1996

This section calculates the JV's cash flow with a CKD built immediately and followed by a greenfield assembly plant built by 1996.

Layout = Market demand, units assembled, imported, and/or exported from/to Opel. Unit prices, total revenue, unit costs, total costs, and operating income. Cash flow in and out, NPV, and payback.

GM-Opel pays for 100% of plant investment, JV realizes the depreciation.

					Fiscal Year, Ending December 31				
(DM 000)	*/unit*	*1993*	*1994*	*1995*	*1996*	*1997*	*1998*	*1999*	*2000*
Total market		200,000	210,000	220,000	230,000	240,000	250,000	265,000	280,000
New Western car mkt. sh. %		14%	14%	14%	25%	25%	25%	25%	49%
New Western car demand—units		28,000	29,400	30,800	57,500	60,000	62,500	66,250	137,200
Opel expected % of new Western		36%	36%	36%	25%	25%	25%	25%	18%
Opel unit actual demand		10,080	10,584	11,088	19,375	25,000	25,625	26,563	34,696
Production:									
Units assembled in Euroslavia		30,000	30,000	30,000					
Units manufactured in Euroslavia					50,000	100,000	100,000	100,000	100,000
Surplus units for export		19,920	19,416	18,912	30,625	75,000	74,375	73,438	65,304
Units imported from Opel		0	0	0	0	0	0	0	0
Revenue:									
Price/unit:	/unit								
(1)/Unit sold to Euroslav dealer	14,961	16,083	17,208	18,241	19,335	20,496	21,725	23,029	24,411
Plus dealer margin and VAT tax	27%	4,342	4,646	4,925	5,221	5,534	5,866	6,218	6,591
= Retail price paid by consumer	19,000	20,425	21,855	23,166	24,556	26,029	27,591	29,247	31,001
(2)/Surplus cars' transfer price to Opel	13,000	13,715	14,401	14,977	15,576	16,199	16,847	17,521	18,222
Sales revenue (DM 000)									
On Euroslav sales		162,113	182,134	202,256	374,624	512,389	556,711	611,703	846,948
On export sales		273,203	279,605	283,241	477,010	1,214,916	1,252,894	1,286,677	1,189,940
Total revenue		435,316	461,739	485,497	851,634	1,727,305	1,809,694	1,898,380	2,036,888

EXHIBIT 3 *(continued)*

(DM 000)	/unit	Fiscal Year, Ending December 31							
		1993	1994	1995	1996	1997	1998	1999	2000
Costs:									
Unit costs:	DM/unit								
1. Opel transfer price/unit									
Completed car cost/unit	13,000	13,715	14,401	14,977	15,576	16,199	16,847	17,521	18,222
Kit cost/unit (– local input)	12,000	10,761	11,299	11,751	0	0	0	0	0
2. Local value added:									
Material % for assembly		15%	15%	15%	100%	100%	100%	100%	100%
Material cost/unit for assembly	12,000	1,899	1,994	2,074	0	0	0	0	0
Material cost/unit for manufacturing	10,200				12,221	12,710	13,218	13,747	14,297
3. Annual wage costs:									
Wage/employee/m (Bt)	3,859	5,017	6,522	8,478	10,174	11,191	12,310	13,541	14,896
Social Sec./unempl. fund/m (Bt)	4,200	5,460	7,098	9,227	11,073	12,180	13,398	14,738	16,212
Monthly cost/employee (Bt)	8,059	10,477	13,620	17,706	21,247	23,371	25,709	28,279	31,107
No. of Euroslav employees	850	850	850	850	1,600	1,600	1,600	1,600	1,600
Wage cost/month (Bt MM)	6,850	8,905	11,577	15,050	33,995	37,394	41,134	45,247	49,772
Wage costs (DM 000)	463	602	632	658	1287	1339	1392	1448	1506
Tot. annual wage costs (DM000)	5,559	4,227	7,588	7,892	15,449	16,067	16,710	17,378	18,074
Variable costs incurred:									
1. Paid to Opel for kits		322,830	338,972	352,530	0	0	0	0	0
2. Material costs		8,545	8,973	9,332	611,053	1,270,989	1,321,829	1,374,702	1,429,690
3. Wage costs		7,227	7,588	7,892	15,449	16,067	16,710	17,378	18,074
4. Export duties paid		5,464	5,592	5,665	9,540	24,298	25,060	25,734	23,799
5. Import duties paid		0	0	0	0	0	0	0	0
Total variable costs		344,066	361,125	375,419	636,042	1,311,355	1,363,599	1,417,814	1,471,563

Fixed costs:

SG&A costs		13,059	13,852	16,129	16,774	17,445	18,143	18,868	19,623
P&E Maintenance		500	900	900	1,800	1,800	2,300	2,300	2,300
Depreciation		69,250	69,481	69,723	109,975	110,237	110,772	111,055	111,350
Technology transfer fees		10,550	11,078	11,521	59,907	62,303	64,796		
Total fixed costs		93,359	95,310	98,273	188,456	191,786	196,010	132,224	133,273
Total costs		437,426	456,435	473,691	824,498	1,503,141	1,559,609	1,550,038	1,604,836
Operating income (DM 000): 40%		(2,110)	5,304	11,806	27,136	224,165	250,085	348,342	432,052
Less Euroslav taxes		(844)	2,122	4,722	10,854	89,666	100,034	139,337	172,821
After tax (Euroslav) NI		(1,266)	3,183	7,083	16,282	134,499	150,051	209,005	259,231
Free cash flow calculations:									
Plus depreciation		69,250	69,481	69,723	109,975	110,237	110,772	111,055	111,350
Less capital expenditures		(1,846)	(1,939)	(2,016)	(2,097)	(2,181)	(2,268)	(2,359)	(2,453)
Less NWC requirement		(21,766)	(1,321)	(1,188)	(18,307)	(43,784)	(4,119)	(4,434)	(6,925)
Less GM plant investment	(500,000)			(320,000)					
Less AUTA asset valuation	(54,000)								
Plus terminal value									4,831,088
Free cash flows	(554,000)	44,372	69,404	(246,398)	105,853	198,772	254,436	313,268	5,192,291

PV free cash flows 1,459,538
Internal rate of return 36.4%
Profitability index 4
Payback (years) 6

EXHIBIT 3 *(concluded)* Forecast and Analysis of Joint Venture, Assuming Status Quo Operations

Euroslavia—Status Quo Cash Flow

This section calculates cash flows in Euroslavia with no plant.

Layout = Market demand, units imported from Opel AG, unit prices to dealers, total revenue, unit costs, total costs, and operating income.

Cash flow in and out, PV. JV pays duties.

JV–Status Quo Cash Flow

(DM 000)	/unit	1993	1994	1995	1996	1997	1998	1999	2000
						Fiscal Year, Ending December 31			
Total Euroslav market purchases		200,000	210,000	220,000	230,000	240,000	250,000	265,000	280,000
New Western car mkt.sh. %		14%	14%	14%	25%	25%	25%	25%	49%
New Western car demand—units		28,000	29,400	30,800	57,500	60,000	62,500	66,250	137,200
Opel % of new Western		36%	36%	36%	25%	25%	25%	25%	18%
Opel units demanded		10,080	10,584	11,088	14,375	15,000	15,625	16,563	24,696
Sales via dealers (capped)		10,080	10,584	11,088	14,375	15,000	15,625	16,563	24,696
Unsatisfied demand		0	0	0	0	0	0	0	0
Production:									
Production in Euroslavia		0	0	0	0	0	0	0	0
Imports from Opel AG		10,080	10,584	11,088	14,375	15,000	15,625	16,563	24,696
Revenue:									
Price/unit:	/unit								
(1)/Unit sold to Euroslav dealer plus dealer margin and VAT	14,961	16,083	17,208	18,241	19,518	20,884	22,346	23,910	20,970
tax	27%	4,342	4,646	4,925	5,270	5,639	6,033	6,456	5,662
= Retail price paid by consumer	19,000	20,425	21,855	23,166	24,788	26,523	28,379	30,366	33,099
Sales revenue:									
On Euroslav sales		162,113	182,134	202,256	280,569	313,261	349,156	396,013	517,867
On export sales		0	0	0	0	0	0	0	0
Total revenue		162,113	182,134	202,256	280,569	313,261	349,156	396,013	517,867

Costs:									
1. Opel completed car transfer price	13,000	13,715	14,401	14,977	15,576	16,199	16,847	17,521	18,222
2. Local value added									
Material %									
(1) Material DM		0	0	0	0	0	0	0	0
(2) Wages		0	0	0	0	0	0	0	0
Variable costs incurred:									
1. Paid to Opel for completed car imports		138,247	152,418	166,063	223,903	242,983	263,232	290,187	449,999
2. Material local content		0	0	0	0	0	0	0	0
3. Annual wage costs		0	0	0	0	0	0	0	0
4. Export duty		0	0	0	0	0	0	0	0
5. Import duty to gov't on comp. cars	35%	3,528	3,704	3,881	5,031	5,250	5,469	5,797	8,644
Total variable costs		141,775	156,122	169,943	228,934	248,233	268,701	295,984	458,643
Fixed costs:									
Sales, gen., & admin.		0	0	0	0	0	0	0	0
P&E maintenance		0	0	0	0	0	0	0	0
Depreciation		0	0	0	0	0	0	0	0
Total fixed costs		0	0	0	0	0	0	0	0
Total costs		141,775	156,122	169,943	228,934	248,233	268,701	295,984	458,643
Operating income (DM000)		20,338	26,012	32,313	51,635	65,028	80,455	100,029	59,224
Less Euroslav taxes	40%	8,135	10,405	12,925	20,654	26,011	32,182	40,012	23,690
After tax (Euroslav) op. inc.,		12,203	15,607	19,388	30,981	39,017	48,273	60,017	35,535
plus terminal value									621,440
Free cash flow		12,203	15,607	19,388	30,981	39,017	48,273	60,017	656,975
Present value, FCF	330,471								
Internal rate of return	Infinite								
Payback	0								
Profitability index	Infinite								

EXHIBIT 4   Update on Euroslav Car Market

To: Anna Krzykowiak
        President, Negotiating Team

From: Jerzy Lobotonski
        Economics Research Staff
        Ministry of Finance

Re: Developments in Euroslav Car Market

The Economics Research Staff of the Ministry of Finance has just finished a lengthy analysis of the Euroslav car market. Their new conclusions can be summarized as follows:

- Automobile demand is forecast to be 350,000 units in Euroslavia by the year 2000. It may take longer than expected to recover from the current deep recession. The standard of living is lower in Euroslavia than previously believed, and the long-term GDP growth rate we had previously used (3.5 percent) may be optimistic.
- The trade accord with the European Community is projected to reduce tariffs on cars gradually over the next 10 years. A reduction of the tariff on new cars imported from the EC to 25 percent by 1996 effectively eliminates the advantage of a CKD plant and leaves a relative short window in which to make the project fully profitable.
- Of the 61,000 imports sold in Euroslavia in 1991, about two thirds were either small or low-priced cars. The mix will shift toward larger cars by the end of the decade.

To summarize:

- Previous forecasts of demand for cars in Euroslavia could be optimistic.
- The dual market could persist, depressing growth in demand for new Western cars and resulting in a severe cost penalty for CKD units.
- Unit growth, if it comes, could be concentrated in the small, rather than compact, and larger car segments, further jeopardizing the viability of a joint venture.

EXHIBIT 5   Assessment of AUTA Facilities, Operations, and Financial Condition

To: AUTA Negotiating Team

From: Ministry of Ownership Transformation

Subject: Summary of Audit and Physical Inspection of AUTA Facilities, performed by General Motors

Date: December 11, 1991

Following is a summary of audit and inspection findings from a visit to AUTA by a General Motors' team on December 9, 1991:

- The poor condition of AUTA's financial accounting systems prevented detailed audits of AUTA's financial condition. A moderate portion of the accounting system is computerized.
- Cash on hand and in various bank accounts on 30 November 1991 was 72,369,421.15 bunts (about US$5,169,244).
- Accounts receivable seem to be minimal (AUTA built only to order), although there have been irregularities in accounting for certain bad debts. The GM team was unable to make a final judgment on the magnitude of receivables.
- Raw material and work-in-process inventories appear to have been significantly understated in some vital commodities (e.g., glass and sheet steel) by as much as 25 percent. Exact quantities in stock currently are difficult to determine. However, on the basis of limited sampling, we estimate that market values of all inventories are 495,894,229 bunts (US$35,421,016), or approximately 18 percent *more* than reported in the financial statements (i.e., 89,260,961.22 bunts).
- Of the seven buildings at the AUTA complex, three were built in 1951, two in 1963, and two in 1969. All appear to be in fair repair. They have been completely depreciated. The environmental auditors, Enviro-audit of Fairfax, Virginia, report significant traces of gasoline, benzene, naphtha, lead, and other heavy metals at depths to eight meters in more than 15 locations on the property.
- The machinery and tools have been fully depreciated but are in excellent repair. Approximately 80 percent of the machines are of Czech and Euroslav origin and were acquired in the 1960s and 1970s. Five percent are of unknown age and origin. Fifteen percent are of Western origin and appear to have been acquired between 1980 and 1986. The vast majority of these machines would require special fittings and retooling to permit integration into a GM assembly operation. Given the age of the machinery and the cost of refitting, the production audit team from Opel doubts that the investment return on refitting would be satisfactory.
- AUTA currently has an order backlog of 14,289 cars, of which only 1,321 would be for vehicles similar to the Opel Astra.
- The AUTA dealer network consists of 39 local "agents," most of whom operate private garages. All primary, secondary, and tertiary communities are covered by these agents.

Part IX

Setting Corporate Financial Strategy

Case 51

The Home Depot, Inc.

The fastest growing major area of retailing today is that of do-it-yourself/home improvement. The most dynamic company in the business is Home Depot.

M. Gilliam, *securities analyst, First Boston*[1]

Trying to wed two conflicting strategies—low-cost structure with broad assortment and a high level of customer service—is arguably one of the most difficult retail concepts to pull off. Home Depot is further along the learning curve than anyone else.

David Bolotsky, *securities analyst, Goldman Sachs*[2]

Right now, when Home Depot goes into an area, they just cut up and spit out the independents.

Walter Stoeppelwerth, *consultant*[3]

We love a fight, a fair fight.

Bernard Marcus, *chief executive officer, The Home Depot*[4]

In March 1991, Bernard Marcus, chief executive officer and chairman of The Home Depot (HD), reaffirmed that the firm's annual, targeted growth rate in store space would be 25 percent for 1991 and beyond. The firm's sales had grown rapidly, from $22 million in 1980 to $3.8 billion in 1990. Return on average equity had exceeded 20 percent in

[1]M. Gilliam, "The Customer Is Always Right," First Boston Corporation, May 19, 1986, p. 6.

[2]M. J. McCarthy, "Home Depot's Do-It-Yourself Powerhouse," *The Wall Street Journal*, July 17, 1990, p. B1.

[3]Ibid.

[4]H. Gilgoff, "Home Center Ad Campaigns Heat Up with Latest Arrival," *Newsday*, November 28, 1989, Sec. B, p. 33.

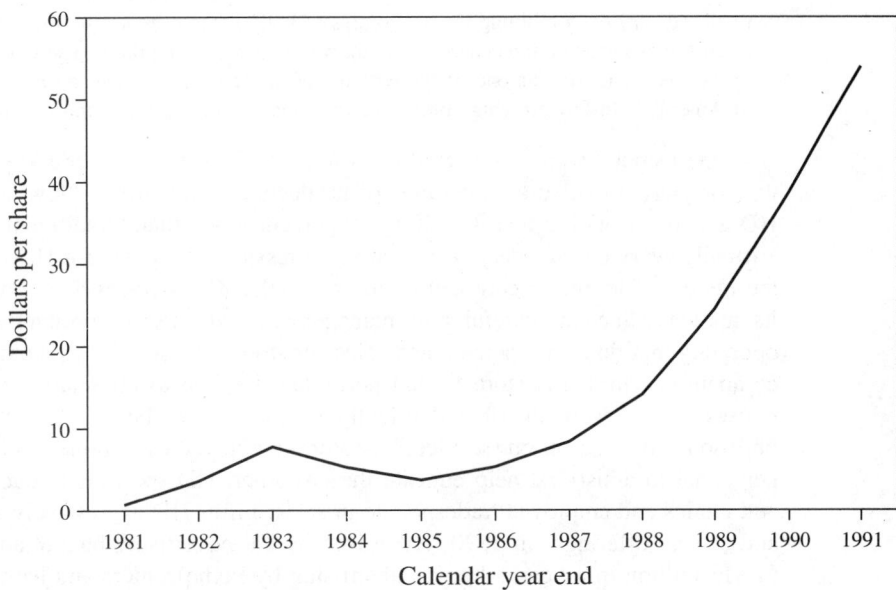

each of the previous five years. As Figure 1 shows, over the same period the stock price had risen from $0.75 per share to close recently at $54.00 per share, a 53 percent annual compound rate of growth. The stock was currently priced at 40 times trailing earnings per share, over 12 times book value. Securities analysts explained the firm's phenomenal stock-price performance in terms of the firm's aggressive growth strategy.

The company's aggressive expansion strategy suggested that HD would need $1.4 billion in external financing over the next four years, which raised questions about the firm's capital financing policies. Was the firm's historical financing strategy appropriate? Were there better financing strategies that would enhance shareholder value, competitive position, or managerial flexibility? What action should management take now to obtain the capital needed to open 35 new stores in 1991 and 43 stores in 1992?

THE COMPANY

In its 1991 annual report, The Home Depot described itself this way:

Founded in 1978 in Atlanta, Georgia, The Home Depot is now America's largest home-center retailer and is one of the fastest-growing retailers in the United States. At the close of fiscal 1990, the Company was operating 145 warehouse-style stores in 12 states. The average Home Depot store is approximately 92,000 square feet, with an additional 10,000 to 20,000 square feet of outside selling area. The stores stock approximately 30,000 different kinds of building materials, home improvement supplies, and lawn and garden products, a large proportion of which are sold to do-it-yourselfers as well as to home-remodeling and building-maintenance professionals. The Company has been credited with being a leading innovator in the home-center retail industry by combining the economies of scale inherent in a warehouse format with a level of customer service unprecedented among warehouse-style retailers. The Home Depot is ranked by *Fortune* magazine as one of the nation's 50 largest retailers and by *Business Month* as one of America's fastest-growing companies in terms of sales, profits, and return on investment.

Home Depot's warehouse-retailing concept was based on several key elements. First, the company provided a wide range of products at competitive, "low, everyday" prices. HD aimed for pricing that was 20 to 30 percent lower than "traditional home centers."[5] Virtually every day in every community, professional shoppers for HD checked prices at the outlets of its major competitors to ensure that HD's prices were competitive within its markets. Second, careful cost management and superior productivity provided an operating margin of 6.7 percent and sales per store at least twice as large as HD's nearest competitor. Third, the store format permitted the firm to eliminate intermediary warehouses: goods were distributed directly to each store. Fourth, in accordance with a philosophy of "one-on-one service," the stores employed well-trained and service-oriented personnel to assist and help educate the customer. HD sponsored educational seminars and clinics and employed tradespeople in sales. Fifth, HD aggressively advertised prices and special offerings. In 1990, HD raised its TV advertising budget almost nine times, to $15 million in a year, whereas advertising by home centers and hardware stores rose only 6 percent: the clustering of stores permitted the firm to exploit economies of scale in advertising. Compared with its competitors, however, HD's advertising budget was not large.

Implementation of this retailing concept required an unusual culture oriented to innovation, cost control, and customer service. The company innovated relentlessly with new concepts and merchandise and invited customers and employees to contribute their ideas. Out of this innovation process grew decorator centers, delivery services, bulk packaging for commodities, and The Home Depot Television Network, which broadcast and produced training programs. Home Depot's 1991 annual report stated: "We have never subscribed to the idea that if it's not broken, you don't need to fix it. To stay on the leading edge of our industry means fixing things before they break." The emphasis on cost control and service was reinforced by a rigid, promote-from-within, management-development policy and by quarterly question-and-answer rallies, beamed live by satellite, between senior management and the firm's 20,000 employees.

High-volume sales gave HD bargaining power on price and product quality in the company's negotiations with its suppliers. For instance, it pressured manufacturers to rewrite instructions deemed incomprehensible and to put bar codes on bulky items like wood to speed up checkout.

Central to the company's strategy was its commitment to growth. Management's publicly stated growth goals were to expand the number of stores at not more than 25 percent per year and to become the largest home-repair chain in the United States, with $10 billion in sales from more than 350 stores by the end of 1994.[6] The total investment per

---

[5]H. Jordan, "Competition Is Heating Up for Do-It-Yourself Dollars," *New Hampshire Business Review,* September 7, 1990.

[6]C. Hawkins, "Will Home Depot Be The Wal-Mart of the '90s?" *Business Week,* March 19, 1990, pp. 124, 126.

new store would be approximately $10.65 million.[7] Exhibit 1 summarizes the history of the firm's store expansion and shows the geographical distribution of the stores.[8]

The trend of expansion took two directions. The first was a conscious strategy of "cannibalization" (i.e., opening stores near existing HD stores). HD reasoned that this would relieve congestion and personnel shortages in existing stores. The second direction was an expansion into new territory, out of the Sunbelt of the United States and into the middle Atlantic and Northeast regions. The move northward began in January 1989, when HD opened a store in East Hanover, New Jersey. The company subsequently opened stores in New Jersey, Connecticut, and New York, and it hoped to open as many as 75 stores in the northeastern United States within five years.[9] Regarding the expansion into the Northeast, Bernard Marcus said:

> It costs more there, but the volume per store is incredible. And people can't believe the service. We opened one store in Connecticut and they asked us if we were a religious cult, some sort of love group. They are so used to prepackaged hardware and blank stares or rudeness if they ever ask a question.[10]

HD showed pugnacity in choosing store locations. For instance, HD entered Baltimore in 1990 with one store and announced that three others would be opened by 1993, despite the fact that Baltimore was dominated by 13 Hechinger home centers and was the location of Hechinger's corporate headquarters. Regarding the entry into Baltimore, the *Washington Post* reported:

> Hechinger executives had no comment about the arrival of Home Depot so close to the company's home territory, where Hechinger reigns as undisputed champion of the do-it-yourself retailers and virtually overwhelms area competitors like Builder's Square and Channel. But Bernard Marcus, Home Depot's chairman and chief executive officer, said he was looking forward to the imminent face-off. "We think the market is underserved and expect to do well there," said Marcus. "We think of Hechinger as a fine operation . . . but competition is healthy for everybody and, with us coming, Hechinger will be a better business and the consumer will be the winner."[11]

In 1990, HD also entered Long Island, the home base of Grossman's, a competitor, and began an aggressive campaign of price-comparison advertising. In response, Grossman's filed a complaint with the state fair-trade commission.

HD's senior management showed little inclination to expand by acquisition. On December 11, 1984, HD bought nine stores in the Dallas, Texas, area that were previously owned by the Bowater home-improvement chain. The total payment was $40 million:

---

[7]This estimate reflected pre-opening expenses ($550,000), fixtures ($900,000), land ($3.5 million), store construction ($3.9 million), and inventory ($3.5 million) net of vendor financing ($1.7 million).

[8]Of 146 stores in operation in March 1991, 86 were leased and 60 were owned (land and buildings). The leases were long term, expiring between 2007 and 2067. HD preferred, however, to buy rather than lease.

[9]*Value Line Investment Survey,* April 27, 1990, p. 898.

[10]A. Thurber, "Firing Launched Success; 125 Home Depots Is Proof," *Arizona Republic,* May 23, 1990, sec. C, p. 1.

[11]K. Swisher, "Home Depot Plans Entry into the Baltimore Area," *Washington Post,* December 20, 1990, sec. E, p. 1.

$26 million in cash and $14 million in 9 percent convertible notes. While the purchase gave HD critical mass in the Texas market, the move proved to be a disaster. The Bowater workers who were retained could not adapt to the HD culture, and the subsequent recession in Texas worsened the performance of HD's Dallas stores. As a result, the whole company's financial performance suffered badly in 1985: earnings per share fell to $0.10 from $0.17 a year earlier; average return on equity fell to 9.7 percent from 19.3 percent; and gross margin fell to 25.9 percent. Bernard Marcus commented that "he had seriously disadvantaged the shareholders and that it would not happen again."[12]

MANAGEMENT

The Home Depot was founded in 1978 by Bernard Marcus, Arthur Blank, and Kenneth Langone. Langone, who was now the chief executive officer of Invemed Associates, was a director of HD and was not engaged in its daily management; Invemed was a small securities dealer, however, and had co-managed several of HD's securities offerings.

Bernard Marcus, age 62, had received a bachelor of science degree from Rutgers University in 1954 and had begun his career as a registered pharmacist. He entered discount retailing when he was asked to run the pharmacy and cosmetics department of a discount chain in New Jersey. Gradually, he rose to the position of chairman and chief executive officer of Handy Dan, a subsidiary of the Daylin Division of W. R. Grace. Handy Dan was a home-improvement chain that had a standard hardware-store retailing strategy. When Marcus and the president of Handy Dan, Arthur Blank,[13] experimented with price discounting, they were fired. Marcus and Blank found financial backing with the assistance of Kenneth Langone and opened their first Home Depot store in Georgia in 1979; the first 16 warehouse stores were concentrated in Georgia, Florida, and Louisiana; the next five were in Arizona, which was a test region for going even farther west into California. Home Depot's expansion into California contributed to the demise of the Handy Dan chain: "'Handy Dan is gone now,' said Marcus with a smile."[14]

At the end of 1990, Bernard Marcus held about 5 percent of HD's common shares outstanding. Officers and directors held a total of 9 percent. Exhibit 2 summarizes the equity ownership of Home Depot and reveals that institutional investors held about 74 percent of the firm's common stock. A leveraged employee stock ownership plan (ESOP) was organized in 1988; by early 1991, the ESOP owned about 2 percent of outstanding shares. Marcus's salary and bonus for 1990 was $1,585,982; Arthur Blank's compensation was $1,362,965. The next most senior executives (including the chief financial officer) received $369,492.

---

[12]A. Zipser, "Down-Home Attitude," *Barron's,* October 1, 1990, p. 44.
[13]In March 1991, Arthur Blank was 47 years old.
[14]A. Thurber, ibid.

THE HOME-IMPROVEMENT RETAILING INDUSTRY

The industry in which Home Depot competed had aggregated sales of $100 billion per year,[15] which implied that HD had approximately 4 percent share of market. Competition was highly fragmented and localized. In 1989, the 10 largest retailers accounted for 1,704 stores and 15 percent of the total market sales. Taking local and regional firms into account, about 350 home-center retailers operated 5,479 stores by 1991.[16] Nevertheless, the trend in the previous 10 years had been toward larger establishments of 50,000 square feet or more in space that offered service or competitive prices. These establishments accounted for most of the industry's sales growth over the past 10 years, and they were gradually displacing local hardware stores.

Two merchandising strategies had emerged out of the rivalry among the largest competitors. The "home center" strategy used large stores, offered competitive (not discount) prices, and catered to both the professional tradesperson and the do-it-yourselfer. Examples of the home-center retailers were Lowe's, Grossman's, Pergament, Channel Home Centers, Rickles, and True Value.

The "warehouse" strategy, by contrast, also used large stores but displayed merchandise on pallets, offered discount prices, and catered to the do-it-yourselfer. The Home Depot introduced this strategy to the home-improvement retailing industry (it previously had been used among other specialty retailers in food, home furnishings, and office supplies). HD was referred to as a "category killer"[17] or "power retailer,"[18] a retailer that offered enormous selection in one particular specialty and did it extremely well, as opposed to the general merchandiser's one-stop shopping theme.

The emergence of the warehouse strategy was part of a larger trend of competition in retailing. *Fortune* magazine summarized the fundamental trends this way:

> Home Depot, Inc., The Limited, Toys R Us, Wal-Mart, Dillard, the Gap, J.C. Penney, and Nordstrom are emerging as the new champions of retailing. They are succeeding by developing exciting merchandising programs, finding innovative uses for technology, and expanding smartly and aggressively. . . . They have not forgotten the lesson of staying faithfully focused on their businesses. Respect for the downside of debt has given these companies some of the healthiest balance sheets in retailing. Once the champion retailers have customers sold on attractive merchandise and great-looking stores, they fortify their operations with technological might.[19]

The importance of Home Depot's innovation was not lost on its competitors.

• *Hechinger Company,* with sales of $1.39 billion, operated a chain of 116 specialty-retail, do-it-yourself, home-center stores in the middle Atlantic region of the United States. The firm pursued a strategy of "clustering" store locations in an effort to build

---

[15]M. McCarthy, "Home Depot's Do-It-Yourself Powerhouse," *The Wall Street Journal,* July 17, 1990, sec. B, p. 1, quoting results of analysis by the Home Improvement Research Institute.

[16]"Home Improvement Retailers," *Investext Report,* 1990, p. 45.

[17]H. Jordan, "Will Granite Staters Take to Warehouse Style Shopping?" *New Hampshire Business Review,* January 11, 1991, p. 2.

[18]P. Demery, "Power Retailers Move to Center Aisle," *LI Business News,* December 24, 1990, p. 19.

[19]S. Caminiti, "The New Champs of Retailing," *Fortune,* September 24, 1990, p. 85.

market share. Most of Hechinger's stores were in the older "home center" format, although the firm had recently purchased Home Quarters and Triangle Building Centers, retailers with a format identical to HD's, and the company had announced plans for aggressive growth into the Northeast. The company openly acknowledged that its Home Quarters subsidiary would be its main growth vehicle. In early 1991, Hechinger had 27 stores in the warehouse segment and aimed to increase to 36 stores by the end of 1991. The firm stated that its "major expansion thrust will be the Boston market," where plans called for 15 stores.[20] Hechinger also announced that it would convert all its stores in North Carolina to the warehouse format. Finally, in March 1991, the company announced that it would convert five Baltimore home-center stores to the new warehouse format: observers connected this to Home Depot's aggressive entry into the Baltimore market. In the fiscal year ended February 1991, the company reported a 35 percent decrease in net income—the second year in a row of a large earnings decline.

- *Kmart Corporation,* with sales of $32.1 billion, was the second-largest multifaceted retailer in the United States. It offered general merchandise stores as well as discount department stores, variety stores, and limited-line stores. The company had several warehouse-format retailing operations, including PACE Membership Warehouse (general merchandise), Sports Giant (sporting goods), Office Square (office supplies), American Fare (food), and Builders Square (home improvement). Builders Square had 145 units and aimed to open 15–20 units annually through 1995, for a total of 225 stores. Kmart had overall U.S. advertising expenditures of $561.4 million in 1989.

- *Lowe's Companies, Incorporated,* operated 306 stores located primarily in the southeastern United States. Its sales in 1990 were $2.8 billion. Since the mid-1980s, the firm had devoted itself to expanding the "warehouse" format. Analysts expected that, by the end of 1991, over half of Lowe's projected 9 million square feet of store space would consist of 45 warehouse outlets.

- *Waban, Incorporated,* operated 59 warehouse "Home Club" home-improvement stores in 10 western and southeastern states. It also operated 23 BJ's Wholesale Club stores, which offered food and general merchandise in a warehouse format. Waban's sales for the previous 12 months had been approximately $2.4 billion. Waban had expanded aggressively, and the company reported sales increases of 24, 32, and 38 percent for each of the last three fiscal years.

- *Wolohan Lumber Company* operated 51 building-supply centers in the upper Midwest region and was expected to add 5 stores in 1991. Its 1990 sales were $296 million.

- *Grossman's, Incorporated,* operated 158 home-center improvement stores, mainly in the northeastern region of the United States. The firm's sales in 1989 were $1.05 billion. In 1990, declining financial performance prompted a group of dissident shareholders to initiate a proxy contest, which ultimately failed. The chief executive officer resigned, however, and McKinsey & Company was retained to help develop a plan for building stockholder value.

---

[20]Annual report, Hechinger Company, February 1990.

Observers agreed that HD's competitors would not stand still while HD grew. Kmart, Hechinger, and Lowe's plainly were copying HD's warehouse format in their subsidiaries. Lowe's also was pursuing sales to small contractors, an important clientele. Smaller chains were adopting a convenience-store orientation. Still other chains were offering installation services. Virtually all major chains were expanding rapidly. Exhibit 3 compares operating and financial information about HD's principal competitors. Exhibit 4 presents excerpts from Standard & Poor's credit bulletins on HD, Lowe's, Hechinger, and Kmart and gives a summary of financial ratios associated with each rating category.

The total size of the future market in do-it-yourself, home-improvement, warehouse-format retailing was difficult to forecast, but one analyst estimated that the United States could support 600 warehouse-style home centers with sales of up to $15 billion (in constant dollars).[21] In early 1991, HD accounted for 146 of the 336 warehouse-style home centers in operation. HD had demonstrated the ability to garner up to 30 percent of the local do-it-yourself market in its more mature locations.

FINANCING

Exhibits 5, 6, and 7 present HD's financial statements and associated analytical ratios for the previous three years. The historical statements reveal a rising though still-moderate use of debt, large and rising returns on equity, and modest but rising dividends. The company had made little use of senior bank debt or long-term debt; rather, its pattern was to issue convertible subordinated debentures (see Exhibit 8 for a history of HD's securities issuance). The exact features of securities currently outstanding are detailed in Exhibit 9. The company had a $300 million revolving credit line, which it had not used.

In early 1991, management indicated that it would call its 6.75 percent convertible debentures on May 31, 1991. This security was deep "in the money" against its exercise price of $21.78 and would likely add 12 million shares to the company's outstanding stock.

Exhibits 5, 6, and 7 also forecast HD's financial performance based on management's target of 25 percent rate of store growth, maintenance of its traditional gross margins, and continuation of other average levels of performance. In general, the forecast assumptions listed in Exhibit 7 are consistent with reports issued on Home Depot in early 1991 by various securities analysts. Important assumptions in the model are: **gross margin** (line 1) at 27.5 percent; **operating expense to sales** (line 2) at 21 percent; and **days inventory outstanding** (line 14) at 67.5 days. These three assumptions are consistent with recent performance of the firm.

Other key forecast assumptions were the subject of debate among analysts in 1991: **number of new stores opened each year** (line 26) was consistent with management's 25 percent growth-rate target; **average square feet per store** (line 30) showed a rising trend from 94,000 to 100,000, consistent with an increase in store size in the warehouse segment of the industry; **sales per square feet** (line 31) also showed a gradual increase

---

[21]S. Helm, William Blair & Company, November 20, 1990.

reflecting a 4 percent rate of inflation; and **land and fixtures per store** (line 35) increased as a result of management's continuing process of store upgrading.

The forecast indicates that the firm would require cumulative external financing of about $1.4 billion over the subsequent four years. Earnings per share (EPS) would rise steadily at a 26 percent rate or greater, except for 1992, when it was assumed that dilution from converting the 6.75 percent convertible debentures would slow EPS growth.

VALUATION

An issue related to The Home Depot's financing plans was the appropriateness of its current stock price of $54 per share. Any analysis on this point would influence management's appetite for issuing stock, convertible securities, debt, or other securities. Several analysts had evaluated Home Depot's stock; their opinions are summarized in Exhibit 10.

Exhibit 11 presents a graph of the weekly closing prices of The Home Depot, Hechinger, and Kmart common shares for the 52 weeks up to the end of March 1991. The graph attests to the high volatility of HD's share prices and their buoyancy relative to the two other retailers' share prices. The prices of all three stocks had been hit hard when Iraq invaded Kuwait on August 6, 1990; prices then lifted at the onset of the air war on January 15, 1991, and at the termination of the war in February. Bernard Marcus expressed puzzlement at the sensitivity of his firm's shares to these events: he argued that, in recessions and times of national crisis, the purchase of new homes might decline, although home repair and do-it-yourself projects should increase. The actual financial earnings results for the fiscal year ended February 3, 1991, seemed to support his arguments.

CONCLUSION

HD management's distinctively aggressive expansion strategy created a large external-financing requirement over the medium term. Was this need best filled by using the firm's traditional financing approach? What were the weaknesses, if any, of the traditional approach? Was there a better approach? Exhibit 12 presents information on capital-market conditions in late March 1991.

EXHIBIT 1 Store Openings by Home Depot by State and Year

Fiscal Year	State												Stores Opened
	TN	GA	FL	AZ	LA	TX	AL	CA	NJ	NY	CT	SC	
Before 1981	4												4
1981			4										4
1982		2											2
1983		1	4	3	2								10
1984			1	2	1	6	1						11
1985		1	6	1		5		6					19
1986		1	2		1	1		5					10
1987		2	5		1	1		6					15
1988		4	4	1		1	1	9	1				21
1989		1	4	2		2		7		2	2	2	22
1990	1	4	5	1		1		8	3	3	1		27
Jan.–March 1991								1					1
Total	5	16	35	10	5	17	2	42	4	5	3	2	146

793

EXHIBIT 2 Equity Ownership Profile for Selected Major Home-Improvement Retailers

	Home Depot	Kmart	Hechinger's	Lowe's	Waban	Wolohan
Total shares outstanding (000s)	117,002	199,828	21,939	36,528	28,604	6,476
Where listed	NYSE	NYSE	OTC	NYSE	NYSE	OTC
Average value of holdings	$707,184	$117,178	$33,086	$124,620	$61,978	$43,245
Number of stockholders	4,900	69,917	4,500	6,360	NAv	1,350
Percent insider ownership	9% directors and management 2% ESOP	<1%	See "Special equity positions" below	24.5%	NAv	56%
Percent institutional ownership	74%	84%	56%	55%	46%	36%
Institutional holdings:						
Mutual funds	7.7%	8.4%	12.8%	9.3%	3.7%	4.0%
Advisors	45.8%	54.8%	28.3%	29.0%	33.4%	25.9%
Comm'l. banks	13.0%	17.8%	13.2%	9.3%	7.8%	5.7%
Insurance co's.	4.5%	3.8%	0.9%	7.4%	1.4%	0.3%
Number of institutional holders	372	486	82	157	84	43
Significant equity positions	Bkrs Tr (1.9m), Citicorp (1.8m), CREF (1.2m), Equitbl (1.1m).	Mellon (8.6m), FMR Corp (7.0m), Barrow (3.6m), Wells F (3.6m).	Templtn (1.6m), Morgan (1.8m), Nicholas (0.7m), Fidelity (0.6m).	Mellon (1.2m), CREF (1.1m), Ohio (1.0m), FMR (0.9m).	Forstmn (1.98m), FMR (1.89m), Chase (1.77m), Wells F (0.63m).	Sunamer (0.29m), Nicholas (0.20m), Ohio (0.27m), Wells F (0.17m).
Special equity positions			Equity shares are classified into 'A' and 'B' shares. 'A' shares trade publicly and carry one vote each. 'B' shares are held by Hechinger and England families and carry 10 votes each. 'B' shares account for 71 percent of total votes.			

Sources: O'Neill Database and *Value Line Investment Survey.*

EXHIBIT 3 Comparative Operating and Financial Information on Major Home-Improvement Retailers

	Home Depot	Lowe's	Builders Square	Hechinger	Home Club	Grossman's
Unit growth, 1988–89	23%	3%	7%	16%	26%	−36%
1989 sales per store ($ mm)	23	9	13	11	18	5
Average store size (sq.ft.)	88,000	20,324	80,000	60,000	100,000	31,900
Sales per square foot	$266	$426	$158	$192	$185	$160
Stock-keeping units	30,000	18,500	15,000	40,000	25,000	18,000
Stock-keeping units per square foot	0.34	0.91	0.33	0.67	0.25	0.56
Parent	none	none	Kmart	none	Waban	none
1991 standing:						
Beta	1.40	1.35	1.15	1.00	2.72	1.40
P/E ratio	43	12.9	10.4	9.2	10	8
Dividend yield	0.4%	2.2%	5.1%	2.3%	0	0
1989 results:						
Gross margin	28.6%	24.4%	27.9%	27.6%		28.2%
Net margin	4.1%	2.4%	2.5%	2.5%		1.3%
Return on equity	21.9%	11.6%	15%	7.8%		11.6%
Dividend payout	7.0%	24%	42%	10%		0
Long-term debt to net worth	0.59	0.259	0.744	0.421		0.744
Expected annual growth rates to 1993–95:						
Sales	23.0%	9.0%	8.5%	14.5%		0
Earnings	23.5%	11.0%	9.0%	2.5%		2.5%
Dividends	31.5%	11.0%	10.5%	7.5		0
Expected results, 1993–95:						
Gross margin	28.5%	24.5%	28.0%	27.5%		28.0%
Net margin	4.1%	2.9%	2.7%	2.0%		1.4%
Return on equity	17.5%	12.0%	16.0%	8.0%		9.0%
Dividend payout	10.0%	21.0%	41.0%	19.0%		0
Long-term debt to net worth	0.28	0.244	0.40	0.576		0.394

Sources: Investext and *Value Line Investment Survey*.

EXHIBIT 4   Excerpts of Ratings Comments on Major Warehouse Retailers

---

Home Depot (Rating of convertible, subordinated debt: BBB)

". . . Home Depot's effectiveness, largely due to its wide selection of competitively priced merchandise and highly trained sales force, has forced more traditional competitors to modify their merchandising practices. However, an ambitious expansion program, adding stores at the rate of 25% a year, continues to pose some risks. Also, financial leverage is aggressive, largely due to lease financing for new stores, with adjusted debt to capital at about 65%. Upgrade potential will demand a continuation of present operating trends and conversion of the outstanding convertible debentures. *Outlook: Positive.*"[1]

Lowe's Companies, Inc. (Rating of senior debt: A)

". . . The [A] rating reflects Lowe's solid business position and exceptional financial conservatism. The largest specialty retailer of building materials and products for the do-it-yourself and home-construction markets, Lowe's is experiencing a sharp and apparently sustainable recovery from its mediocre 1987 performance. . . . Lease-adjusted debt leverage presently is below 30%, and no material change in Lowe's conservative capital structure is expected. *Outlook: Stable*"[2]

". . . Despite a solid operating record, management has acknowledged a threat to its future growth posed by do-it-yourself retailers operating warehouse formats . . . Lowe's will need to sustain the greater profitability of the larger stores to maintain its competitive position, though business risk associated with this growth is mitigated by confining expansion to existing markets. *Outlook: Stable*"[3]

Hechinger Company (Rating of senior debt: A −. Rating of subordinated debt: BBB)

". . . risks associated with the company's aggressive growth. . . . Leverage adjusted for capitalization of operating leases, remains in the mid-50% historical range . . . sustained weakness in the business environment or in Hechinger's operating performance, particularly as Hechinger enters new markets, could erode credit quality, resulting in a downgrade in the next couple of years. *Outlook: Negative.*"[4]

Kmart Corporation (Rating of senior debt: A)

". . . strong competitive position . . . solid business profile. . . . The current rating anticipates continuation of Kmart's somewhat conservative financial policy along with an improvement in operating performance resulting from the refurbishing program. *Outlook: Stable*"[5]

[1] "Credit Bulletins," *CreditWeek,* Standard & Poor's Corporation, June 25, 1990, p. 67.
[2] "Credit Bulletins," *CreditWeek,* Standard & Poor's Corporation, February 26, 1990, p. 25.
[3] "Credit Bulletins," *CreditWeek,* Standard & Poor's Corporation, July 2, 1990, p. 65.
[4] "Credit Analyses," *CreditWeek,* Standard & Poor's Corporation, February 26, 1990, p. 23.
[5] "Credit Analyses," *CreditWeek,* Standard & Poor's Corporation, August 6, 1990, p. 30.

EXHIBIT 4   *(concluded)*

Key Industrial Median Financial Ratios (1987–89)

"These ratios are among those employed by S&P analysts in their quantitative analysis of credit strength. . . . Ratio medians do not reflect the many analytical adjustments that S&P common makes in calculating the ratios used in the rating process. For example, they do not incorporate operating lease adjustments or S&P's captive finance company rating methodology. As a proxy for the operating lease adjustment, ratio medians are given for interest coverage, including rents and total debt to capital, including eight times rents as debt . . ."[6]

	AAA	*AA*	*A*	*BBB*	*BB*	*B*	*CCC*
Pretax interest coverage (x)	12.02	9.13	5.54	3.62	2.29	0.99	0.75
Pretax interest coverage incl. rents (x)	4.79	5.04	3.30	2.22	1.76	1.01	0.73
Pretax funds flow interest coverage (x)	14.85	11.36	7.72	5.26	3.42	1.70	1.66
Funds from operations/total debt (%) .	89.1	79.2	48.7	35.7	18.6	6.4	5.2
Free operating cash flow/total debt (%)	26.1	16.7	9.1	3.9	(1.8)	(2.5)	(2.8)
Pretax return on permanent capital employed (%)	26.2	21.0	17.5	14.9	12.8	8.8	5.1
Operating income/sales (%)	21.3	16.2	13.4	12.1	13.2	9.5	9.7
Long-term debt/capitalization (%)	15.6	19.2	30.4	37.2	53.0	76.6	74.9
Total debt/capitalization incl. short-term debt (%)	23.3	28.0	35.2	40.8	54.5	77.8	77.6
Total debt/capitalization incl. short-term debt (incl. 8 times rents)(%) ..	35.3	39.1	48.7	55.5	65.5	81.5	81.0

[6] "Credit Analyses," *CreditWeek*, Standard & Poor's Corporation, November 19, 1990, pp. 30–31.

EXHIBIT 5 Home Depot's Historical and Projected Income Statements (000s)

	Jan. 29, 1989 (actual)	Jan. 28, 1990 (actual)	Feb. 3, 1991 (actual)	Jan. 1992 (proj'd)	Jan. 1993 (proj'd)	Jan. 1994 (proj'd)	Jan. 1995 (proj'd)	Jan. 1996 (proj'd)
1. Net sales	$1,999,514	$2,758,535	$3,815,356	$5,056,338	$6,653,424	$8,841,445	$11,694,730	$15,452,237
2. Cost of mdse. sold	1,459,862	1,991,777	2,751,085	3,665,845	4,823,732	6,410,048	8,478,679	11,202,872
3. Gross profit	539,652	766,758	1,064,271	1,390,493	1,829,692	2,431,397	3,216,051	4,249,365
Operating expenses:								
4. Selling and store op'g.	356,831	504,363	693,657	—	—	—	—	—
5. Pre-opening	7,552	9,845	13,315	—	—	—	—	—
6. General and administrative	48,485	67,901	91,664	—	—	—	—	—
7. Total operating expenses	412,868	582,109	798,636	1,061,831	1,397,219	1,856,704	2,455,893	3,244,970
8. Operating income	126,784	184,649	265,635	328,662	432,473	574,694	760,157	1,004,395
9. Interest income	751	13,320	17,579	12,388	16,301	21,662	28,652	37,858
10. Interest expense	(1,702)	(15,954)	(23,386)	(45,203)	(73,542)	(108,243)	(150,636)	(154,967)
11. Net interest expense	(951)	(2,634)	(5,807)	(32,814)	(57,241)	(86,582)	(121,984)	(117,109)
12. Earnings before taxes	125,833	182,015	259,828	295,847	375,231	488,112	638,173	887,287
13. Income taxes	49,080	70,061	96,400	110,943	140,712	183,042	239,315	332,732
14. Net earnings	$ 76,753	$ 111,954	$ 163,428	$ 184,905	$ 234,520	$ 305,070	$ 398,858	$ 554,554
15. Common shares and equivalents	115,325	118,470	120,835	132,835	132,835	132,835	132,835	132,835
16. E.P.S. (fully diluted)	$ 0.67	$ 0.95	$ 1.35	$ 1.39	$ 1.77	$ 2.30	$ 3.00	$ 4.17
17. E.P.S. (primary)	N.A.	$ 0.97	$ 1.38	$ 1.42	$ 1.80	$ 2.35	$ 3.07	$ 4.26
18. Primary no. shares	N.A.	115,176	118,066	130,066	130,066	130,066	130,066	130,066
19. Dividends per share	$ 0.05	$ 0.07	$ 0.11	$ 0.11	$ 0.14	$ 0.19	$ 0.25	$ 0.34

Fiscal Year Ended

Sources: Company annual reports and casewriter's analysis.

EXHIBIT 6 Home Depot's Historical and Projected Balance Sheets (000s)

	Jan. 29, 1989 (actual)	Jan. 28, 1990 (actual)	Feb. 3, 1991 (actual)	Fiscal Year Ended Jan. 1992 (proj'd)	Jan. 1993 (proj'd)	Jan. 1994 (proj'd)	Jan. 1995 (proj'd)	Jan. 1996 (proj'd)
1. Cash	$ 15,853	$ 69,525	$ 107,895	$ 176,972	$ 232,870	$ 309,451	$ 409,316	$ 540,828
2. Short-term investments	0	65,856	29,401	—	—	—	—	—
3. Accounts receivable	17,614	38,933	49,325	65,109	85,674	113,849	150,590	198,974
4. Merchandise inventories	294,274	381,452	509,022	677,930	892,060	1,185,420	1,567,975	2,071,764
5. Other current assets	9,201	10,474	17,931	25,661	33,766	44,870	59,351	78,420
6. Total current assets	336,942	556,240	713,574	945,672	1,244,370	1,653,589	2,187,231	2,889,986
7. Land	85,303	128,265	262,560	—	—	—	—	—
8. Buildings	111,350	171,323	272,095	—	—	—	—	—
9. Furniture, fixtures, and equipment	82,373	125,044	186,025	—	—	—	—	—
10. Leasehold improvements	58,707	94,641	160,760	—	—	—	—	—
11. Land, buildings, and improvements				1,220,201	1,589,744	2,052,649	2,637,258	3,349,872
12. Construction in progress	30,043	49,417	82,179	122,463	197,530	280,902	378,274	0
13. Gross property and equipment	367,776	568,690	963,619	1,342,664	1,787,274	2,333,551	3,015,532	3,349,872
14. Accumulated depreciation	35,360	54,250	84,889	127,854	185,047	259,721	356,218	463,414
15. Net property and equipment	332,416	514,440	878,730	1,214,810	1,602,227	2,073,830	2,659,314	2,886,459
16. Goodwill	22,664	22,032	21,400	20,000	19,000	18,000	17,000	16,000
17. Other assets	7,157	14,822	25,799	32,993	43,414	57,690	76,308	100,826
18. Total assets	$699,179	$1,117,534	$1,639,503	$2,213,475	$2,909,011	$3803,110	$4,939,853	$5,893,271
19. Accounts payable	$126,431	$ 172,876	$ 235,267	$ 311,346	$ 409,687	$ 544,415	$ 720,107	$ 951,477
20. Accrued salaries	22,027	46,253	63,547	—	—	—	—	—
21. Sales taxes payable	0	17,507	26,806	—	—	—	—	—

EXHIBIT 6 (concluded)

	Jan. 29, 1989 (actual)	Jan. 28, 1990 (actual)	Feb. 3, 1991 (actual)	Fiscal Year Ended Jan. 1992 (proj'd)	Jan. 1993 (proj'd)	Jan. 1994 (proj'd)	Jan. 1995 (proj'd)	Jan. 1996 (proj'd)
22. Other accrued expenses	43,378	54,306	76,381	—	—	—	—	—
23. Income taxes payable	2,067	0	8,800	—	—	—	—	—
24. Accruals and other payables	—	—	—	227,535	299,404	397,865	526,263	695,351
25. Current portion, long-term debt	233	1,447	1,906	—	—	—	—	—
26. Total current liabilities	194,136	292,389	412,707	538,881	709,091	942,280	1,246,370	1,646,827
27. New external financing required	—	—	—	229,476	544,359	929,918	1,400,936	1,449,021
28. Long-term debt	107,508	302,901	530,774	272,774	272,774	272,774	272,774	272,774
29. Other long-term liabilities	637	601	4,415	5,000	5,000	5,000	5,000	5,000
30. Deferred income taxes	13,960	9,512	8,205	8,000	8,000	8,000	8,000	8,000
31. Common stock	3,767	5,759	5,903	6,503	6,503	6,503	6,503	6,503
32. Paid-in capital	213,562	231,538	264,301	521,701	521,701	521,701	521,701	521,701
33. Retained earnings	185,609	289,177	439,770	609,882	825,640	1,106,305	1,473,255	1,983,444
34. Less: Notes receivable from ESOP	20,000	14,345	26,572	21,258	15,943	10,629	5,314	0
35. Total stockholders' equity	382,938	512,129	683,402	1,159,344	1,369,787	1,645,138	2,006,773	2,511,648
36. Total liabilities and stockholders' equity	$699,179	$1,117,534	$1,639,503	$2,213,475	$2,909,011	$3,803,110	$4,939,853	$5,893,271
Memo:								
37. Dividends	—	$ 8,062	$ 12,987	$ 14,792	$ 18,762	$ 24,406	$ 31,909	$ 44,364
38. Capital expenditures	—	200,914	394,929	379,045	444,610	546,276	681,981	334,340
39. Depreciation expense	—	18,890	30,639	42,965	57,193	74,674	96,497	107,196
40. Additions to net working capital	—	$131,045	$ 27,016	105,924	128,488	176,030	229,552	302,298
41. Incr. new external financing	—	—	—	$ 229,476	$ 314,883	$ 385,560	$ 471,018	$ 48,085

Sources: Company annual reports and casewriter's analysis.

EXHIBIT 7 Ratio Analyses of Home Depot's Historical and Projected Financial Statements

				Fiscal Year Ended				
	Jan. 29, 1989 (actual)	Jan. 28, 1990 (actual)	Feb. 3, 1991 (actual)	Jan. 1992 (proj'd)	Jan. 1993 (proj'd)	Jan. 1994 (proj'd)	Jan. 1995 (proj'd)	Jan. 1996 (proj'd)
1. Gross margin (%)	27.0	27.8	27.9	27.5	27.5	27.5	27.5	27.5
2. Operating expenses to sales (%)	20.6	21.1	20.9	21.0	21.0	21.0	21.0	21.0
3. Operating profit margin (%)	6.3	6.7	7.0	6.5	6.5	6.5	6.5	6.5
4. Average tax rate (%)	39.0	38.5	37.1	37.5	37.5	37.5	37.5	37.5
5. Return on sales (%)	3.8	4.1	4.3	3.7	3.5	3.5	3.4	3.6
6. Return on equity (%)	20.0	21.9	23.9	15.9	17.1	18.5	19.9	22.1
7. Return on assets (%)	11.0	10.0	10.0	8.4	8.1	8.0	8.1	9.4
8. Debt/equity ratio (%)	28.1	59.1	77.7	43.3	59.7	73.1	83.4	68.6
9. Debt/total capital (%)	21.9	37.2	43.7	30.2	37.4	42.2	45.5	40.7
10. EBIT/interest (×)	133.3	70.1	45.7	10.0	7.6	6.6	6.2	8.6
11. Cash and investment to sales (%)	0.8	4.9	3.6	3.5	3.5	3.5	3.5	3.5
12. Days in receivables	3.2	5.2	4.7	4.7	4.7	4.7	4.7	4.7
13. Days in payables	31.6	31.7	31.2	31.0	31.0	31.0	31.0	31.0
14. Days in inventory	73.6	69.9	67.5	67.5	67.5	67.5	67.5	67.5
15. Other current assets/sales (%)	0.6	0.5	0.7	0.7	0.7	0.7	0.7	0.7
16. Other current liabilities/sales (%)	3.4	4.3	4.6	4.5	4.5	4.5	4.5	4.5
17. Other assets/sales (%)	0.5	0.7	0.9	0.9	0.9	0.9	0.9	0.9
18. Quick ratio	0.17	0.60	0.45	0.45	0.45	0.45	0.45	0.45

EXHIBIT 7 *(concluded)*

	Jan. 29, 1989 (actual)	Jan. 28, 1990 (actual)	Feb. 3, 1991 (actual)	Jan. 1992 (proj'd)	Jan. 1993 (proj'd)	Jan. 1994 (proj'd)	Jan. 1995 (proj'd)	Jan. 1996 (proj'd)
				Fiscal Year Ended				
19. Current ratio	1.74	1.94	1.73	1.75	1.75	1.75	1.75	1.75
20. Primary earnings per share	N.A.	$ 0.97	$ 1.38	$ 1.42	$ 1.80	$ 2.35	$ 3.07	$ 4.26
21. Change in E.P.S. (%)	34.0	41.8	42.1	3.1	26.8	30.1	30.7	39.0
22. Dividends per share	$0.05	$0.07	$0.11	$0.11	$0.14	$0.19	$0.25	$0.34
23. Dividends to net income (%)	—	7.2	7.9	8.0	8.0	8.0	8.0	8.0
24. Sales growth rate (%)	37.6	38.0	38.3	32.5	31.6	32.9	32.3	32.1
25. Ending number of stores	96	118	145	180	223	282	355	442
26. New stores added	21	22	27	35	43	59	73	87
27. Unit growth (%)	28.0	23.0	23.0	24.1	23.9	26.5	25.9	24.5
28. Ending square footage (000)	8,216	10,424	13,278	16,920	21,408	27,354	34,790	44,200
29. Change in square footage (%)	33.4	26.9	27.4	27.4	26.5	27.8	27.2	27.0
30. Average square feet/store (000)	86	88	92	94	96	97	98	100
31. Average sales per square foot	$ 243	$ 265	$ 287	$ 299	$ 311	$ 323	$ 336	$ 350
32. Average sales per store ($ mil.)	20.8	23.4	26	28.1	29.8	31.4	32.9	35.0
33. Same store sales increase (%)	13.4	12.9	10.0	8.0	6.2	5.1	5.1	6.1
34. Advertising expense/sales (%)	1.5	1.1	0.9	N.A.	N.A.	N.A.	N.A.	N.A.
35. Land, buildings, and fixtures/store	$3,518	$4,401	$6,079	$6,779	$7,129	$7,279	$7,429	$7,579
36. Construction/next new stores	$1,366	$1,830	$2,348	$2,848	$3,348	$3,848	$4,348	$4,848
37. Annual depreciation/gross P/E (%)	—	3.3	3.2	3.2	3.2	3.2	3.2	3.2

Sources: Company annual reports and casewriter's analysis.

EXHIBIT 8   Pattern of Financings (in millions of dollars)

	1990	1989	1988	1987	1986	1985	1984
Senior bank debt		(71)	36	(53)	88		
Unsecured debt:							
7.95% note due 1995 (ESOP)			20				
Industrial revenue bonds 6.49% due 2011					5.8		4.2
Convertible subordinated debt:							
9s due 1999					(14)	14	
8.50s due 2009					(75)	75	
6.75s due 2014		258					
6s due 1997	230						
Common stock:							
Conversions of bonds					89		
New sales of shares				44.2			
Sale of shares to ESOP			20				

Sources: Company annual reports and Moody's *Industrial Manual.*

EXHIBIT 9   Terms of Securities Outstanding

1. Bank notes payable
   - Outstandings: 0
   - Agreements: ....   Revolving line of credit agreement for a maximum of $300 million through September 1994 with annual options to expend beyond 1994. Annual facility fee of 0.125%.
   - Covenants: ....   (a) Minimum tangible net worth of $270 million plus 65% of consolidated net earnings for periods beginning after January 29, 1989; (b) ratio of earnings before income taxes, interest, operating lease expense, and amortization of intangible assets to net interest expense of not less than 1.75 to 1; (c) ratio of debt to tangible net worth of no more than 2 to 1.
   - Agent bank: ....   Security Pacific

2. 7.95% unsecured note, due 1995 (incurred in connection with the establishment of a leveraged ESOP)
   - Issued: 1988
   - Outstandings: $20,000,000
   - Covenants: ....   Debt shall not exceed 66.66% of consolidated assets, net of goodwill and current liabilities.
   - Maturity: ....   September 1, 1995

EXHIBIT 9   *(concluded)*

---

3. 6.75% convertible subordinated debentures, due 2014

    Issued: ....   May 1, 1989

    Outstanding: $258,750,000

    Maturity date: ....   May 15, 2014

    Rated: A2

    Callability: ....   Yes

    Conversion terms: ....   Into common stock at $21.78 per share.

    Sinking fund: ....   Annually 1999–2013 sufficient to redeem 66.6% of bonds prior to
        maturity.

    Listing: ....   New York Stock Exchange

    Lead manager of offering: .   First Boston and Invemed Associates

    Bond trustee: ....   First National Bank of Atlanta

4. 6.00% convertible subordinated debentures, due 1997

    Issued: ....   June 15, 1990

    Outstanding: $230,000,000

    Maturity date: ....   June 15, 1997

    Rated: A2

    Callability: ....   Yes

    Conversion terms: ....   Into common stock at $48.17 per share.

    Sinking fund: ....   none

    Listing: ....   none

    Lead manager of offering: First Boston and Invemed Associates

    Bond trustee: ....   First National Bank of Atlanta

5. Leases (mainly operating leases on retail facilities)

    Future minimum payments: 1991, $74.8m; 1992, $86.8m; 1993, $85.7m; 1994, $81m; 1995, $80m.

    Total undiscounted future
      payments: $1,372,195,000

6. Common stock

    Issued: ....   September 22, 1981 (600,000 shares at $0.75)
        October 16, 1986 (2,600,000 shares at $4)

    Outstanding: ....   118,066,000 shares

    Listing: ....   New York Stock Exchange

    Lead manager of offering: .   1981, Bear Stearns
        1986, Merrill Lynch

    Dividends: ....   Stock dividends: January 1982 (50%)
                    April 1982 (25%)
                    December 1982 (100%)
                    June 1983 (100%)

        Cash dividends: paid continuously since 1987.

    Stock splits: ....   Split 3-for-2 September 1987 and again June 1989.

Sources: Company annual reports and Moody's *Industrial Manual*.

EXHIBIT 10   Analysts' Opinions of The Home Depot's Stock

Analyst	*Valuation*	*Analysis Based on*	*Home Depot Stock Price*	*S&P 500 Index*
W.N. Smith, Smith, Barney, March 12, 1991	$66 per share is target price over next 12–18 months.	P/E multiples	$52.00	370
K.K. Walin, Shearson, Lehman, February 26, 1991	"Selling at a discount. . . . Prospects remain out-standing."	P/E multiples	$49.00	363
W. Haad, Prudential-Bache, February 1, 1991	$46 per share over next 12 months.	P/E multiples	$43.25	343
B. Sharav, Value Line Invest-ment, January 25, 1991	$40–56 price range during 1993–95. "The high P/E makes us view the stock with some cau-tion."	Cash flow	$39.00	336
D. Wewer, Robinson-Humphrey, November 28, 1990	"Unusually attractive buy-ing opportunity at $43."	P/E multiples	$36.00	318
S. Helm, William Blair, November 20, 1990	HD is "widening its lead" over competitors. It can achieve 25% annual earnings growth over next 3–5 years.	P/E multiples	$35.875	315
J.G. Dennis, J.C. Bradford & Co., November 15, 1990	"This was one of the most successful public offer-ings of the 1980s. The party has not ended yet."	E.P.S.	$34.50	317

EXHIBIT 11   Comparative Stock Prices, Leading Warehouse Retailers

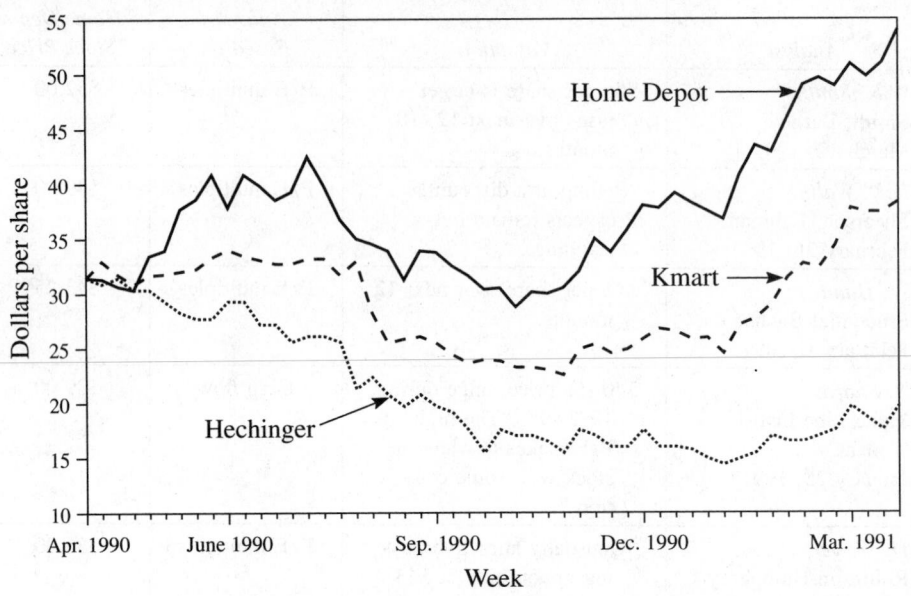

Source of data: Standard and Poor's Investor's Stock Laboratory
Note: Share prices of Kmart and Hechinger have been indexed to The Home Depot at April 1, 1990.

EXHIBIT 12   Current Capital-Market Rates and Indexes, March 31, 1991

U.S. Treasury Securities		*Other Interest Rates*	
1 month	5.89%	Prime	8.75–9.00%
2 months	5.82	Federal funds	6.125
3 months	5.73	Commercial paper:	
6 months	6.12	1 month	6.2
1 year	6.49	3 months	6.1
2 years	7.01	LIBOR:	
3 years	7.28	3 months	6.375
4 years	7.60	12 months	7.0
5 years	7.80	Eurodollars	6.35
10 years	8.08		
30 years	8.23		

Corporate Bonds	
Rating	*Yield*
AAA	8.95%
AA	9.25
A	9.70
BBB	10.33
BB	11.98
B	16.44

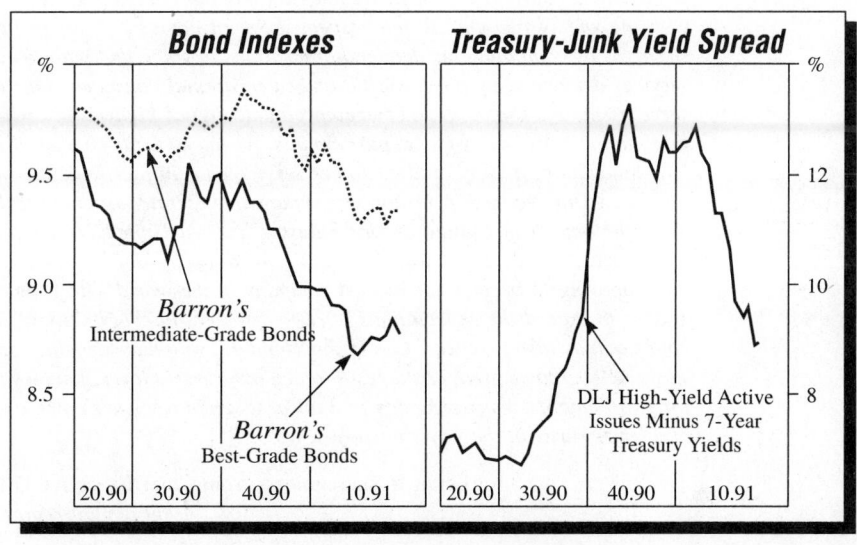

Sources: Standard & Poor's *CreditWeek*. Graphs are reproduced by permission of *Barron's*, © 1991 Dow Jones & Company, Inc. All rights reserved worldwide.

Case 52

United Telecommunications, Inc.

The year 1989 was . . . when we linked the human and technological capabilities of the corporation to become a significant force in the domestic and international communications industries. Our mission is straightforward—to be the best telecommunications company in the world—to rise above the competition and become the standard against which all others in the industry are measured. . . . Reflecting the importance of US Sprint to the success of our company, we will ask shareholders to approve changing our name from United Telecom to Sprint Corporation when we exercise our option to purchase the remaining 19.9 percent interest in US Sprint from GTE. We believe all of our companies will benefit from association with the widely recognized and respected Sprint name. . . . We're further leveraging our strengths by combining our leadership positions in voice and data to create a wide array of services demanded by the domestic and international consumer. Our domestic fiber routes serve as the backbone of an emerging global, digital highway. . . . We don't intend to be just another one of many global participants. We intend to play a leading role in demonstrating how innovation, quality, and customer service can, in fact, redefine the basis for competition. . . . Our leadership in applying innovative, service-oriented technologies will accelerate the impact of change on our industry. . . . At United Telecom, quality is more than just words. It's a way of working, a way of doing business, a way of life. Quite simply, we're moving to become the easiest company in the world with which to do business. Our goal is to exceed the expectations of our customers in everything we do. . . . United Telecom's quality also is reflected in its shareholders, who have demonstrated patience and trust as we've overcome great obstacles to reach our current level of achievement. We're grateful for your support. Your company and all of its employees are committed to producing even greater rewards in the years ahead.

Letter to shareholders from Chief Executive Officer William Esrey,
1989 annual report, issued Spring 1990

This case was prepared by Professor Robert F. Bruner.
Copyright © 1991 by the University of Virginia Darden School Foundation, Charlottesville, Virginia. Revised July 1993.

In November 1990, the senior managers of United Telecommunications, Inc. (UT), faced a serious test of commitment to their corporate vision as expressed in the annual report the previous spring. Only six months earlier, the firm's stock had traded at up to $46 per share. Quarterly performance, however, had lagged expectations in July 1990, triggering a 50 percent drop in stock price from the 1990 peak. Now, in an uncertain capital-market environment, UT's senior managers had to reconsider the financing plans necessary to support the corporate vision. They were uncertain to what extent the firm could generate funds internally to finance the purchase of the minority interest in Sprint, selected acquisitions, strategic alliances and joint ventures, and a new headquarters complex in Kansas City, Missouri.

Were the firm's financing policies appropriate? If not, what action should management take? What would be the impact of those actions both on symptomatic problems in the short run and on deeper challenges in the long run? Analysts estimated that the firm would have to raise $1.6 billion in new external capital in the next two years. How should this be done?

THE COMPANY

United Telecommunications was founded in 1938 as United Utilities, a holding company for gas-transmission and telephone public utilities. It sold its gas-transmission properties in the 1960s and began a program to acquire local, independent telephone companies: 2 acquisitions in 1965, 7 in 1966, 11 in 1967, 9 in 1968, and 2 in 1969. Fourteen local telephone companies were acquired in the 1970s, and two large local telephone interests were acquired in the 1980s (most notably a 9.8 percent equity interest in Southern New England Telephone in 1984). Fourteen computer-timesharing or -software firms were acquired between 1970 and 1985. Virtually all acquisitions had been consummated with an exchange of shares, rather than payment in cash. Through start-ups and small acquisitions in the 1980s, UT entered a range of complementary businesses, such as directory publishing, telephone equipment manufacturing, telemarketing, long-distance telephone service, and business data bases. For UT, the most significant event in recent years had been the formation of the US Sprint Communications Company joint venture in July 1986 between UT and GTE Corporation. In August 1989, Sprint acquired, for $295 million, Private Transatlantic Telecommunications Systems, Inc., which owned a 50 percent interest in PTAT[1] (Cable and Wireless, a U.K. firm, owned the other 50 percent). In October 1989, Sprint acquired Long Distance/USA for $271 million; it provided long-distance communications services with an emphasis on the hospitality industry. Both acquisitions were accounted for as purchases. Exhibits 1 and 2 present historical income statements and balance sheets for UT.

By the fall of 1990, UT was the *only* major player in *both* local and long-distance telephone service: it was the second-largest independent, local telephone system after

---

[1]PTAT was the world's first privately-owned, transatlantic, fiber-optic undersea-cable system. Alone, this cable could carry more volume than all other transatlantic cables combined.

GTE (the ninth-largest relative to the "Baby Bells" or regional Bell operating companies) and the third-largest long-distance company after AT&T and MCI by virtue of its 80 percent equity interest in US Sprint. UT also engaged in various complementary businesses, such as directory publishing and the manufacture of telecommunications equipment. Of the three elements in UT's business portfolio, Sprint dominated the reported performance of the company and had driven the firm's stock price in recent years. Exhibit 3 lists certain financial ratios for UT and its competitors in both the local and long-distance segments. The changes in UT's asset portfolio over the last few years are indicated in the following table.

(all amounts in $ millions)	1989	1988	1987	1986	1985
Consolidated results:					
Revenues	$7,549.0	$6,493.0	$2,935.1	$3,012.7	$3,083.8
Operating income	910.0	252.8	679.3	588.4	157.5
Intercompany revenues	(173.7)	(120.7)	(81.8)	(66.7)	(18.0)
Long-distance communications:					
Revenues	4,323.6	3,405.4	(Sprint not	212.4	342.6
Operating income	266.6	(386.1)	reported)	(109.8)	(494.9)
Local communications:					
Revenues	2,637.0	2,509.7	2,388.9	2,311.4	2,302.3
Operating income	636.6	596.8	636.6	667.8	642.4
Complementary businesses:					
Revenues	762.1	698.6	628.0	555.6	456.9
Operating income	47.7	42.1	42.7	30.4	10.0

The business challenges in UT's two telecommunications segments differed dramatically. The local telephone companies were nearly monopolies, were low-growth businesses, and were steady cash generators. In contrast, the long-distance business was fiercely competitive, growing rapidly, and extremely price sensitive.

UT's LOCAL TELEPHONE COMPANIES

Exhibit 4 presents a map indicating the market coverage of UT's local telephone operations; they consisted of 16 regulated telephone companies in 17 states, and boasted 3.8 million access lines (1 million in Florida alone). Operations in three states, Florida, Ohio, and North Carolina, accounted for 58 percent of the segment revenues. Revenue growth rates hovered between 4.0 and 4.5 percent, at or just above the industry average. The operations ranked among the most efficient and profitable in the industry.

One of UT's goals for this segment was to consolidate the operations in 10 to 12 states to exploit operating efficiencies—a widely dispersed set of local companies required great expense for monitoring and control and prevented implementation of operating economies. Another goal was to exploit both technological change and potential deregulation to enter new local markets, such as cable transmission. UT had dabbled in cellular telecommunications at one time and was considering reentering this segment by the mid-1990s.[2]

UT's COMPLIMENTARY BUSINESSES

Through DirectoriesAmerica, UT published nearly 270 telephone directories in 21 states. The subsidiary North Supply Company not only distributed telecommunications products from more than 700 manufacturers but also supplied alarm equipment to the security industry.

US SPRINT

As the third-largest long-distance telecommunications company, Sprint commanded a 9 percent share of market and revenues of $4.6 billion. Sprint had the only nationwide, 100 percent digital, fiber-optic network, which gave it both quality and efficiency advantages over its larger rivals—indeed, quality differentiation was the key element in UT's strategy to increase market share. Sprint was a so-called full-line provider of long-distance services: voice, video, private line, 800, 900, international, and so on.

When Sprint was formed in July 1986 as a joint venture between UT and GTE Corporation, UT already had been at work since 1984 building an all-digital, all-fiber network. Because the capital requirements were so much bigger than anticipated, UT concluded that a joint venture would be a more appropriate basis for building the network. At formation of the venture, both firms held an equal share. In 1988, UT assumed management control of US Sprint. In its early years Sprint sustained massive losses because of foul-ups in its computerized billing system[3] and in construction-related problems in its high-tech fiber network. In January 1989, UT purchased a 30.1 additional percent interest in Sprint from GTE for $585 million in cash, raising its total equity interest to 80.1 percent and leaving GTE with 19.9 percent. UT also held an option to purchase the

---

[2]In October 1988, UT sold its cellular-telephone and paging-services subsidiary for approximately $775 million, recording a gain of $367 million.

[3]When GTE and UT merged their long-distance operations in 1986, they had to combine different management-information systems, which proved challenging and resulted in widespread double billing (and/or lack of billing) of customers. These difficulties coincided with the addition of 2 million new customers in the first six months of operation.

remaining GTE interest at net book value (currently about $550 million) at any time up to December 31, 1995. Conversely, GTE held a put option allowing it to require UT to purchase the remaining interest any time between December 31, 1991, and December 31, 1995, at the net book value of the interest.

In the meantime, UT would determine whether and to what extent additional capital contributions from the two partners would be required: GTE would be required to contribute its proportionate share, subject to a cumulative upper limit of $300 million; at the end of 1989, GTE had contributed $65 million under the agreement. As recently as June 1990, William Esrey, UT's chief executive officer, had said that UT would purchase GTE's remaining interest in Sprint in 1990; but with the onset of adverse conditions, Esrey stated in the fall that the purchase would be deferred until 1991. In exercising its option early, UT's goal was to simplify the management structure and control of Sprint.

UT's strategic objectives with Sprint were to expand internationally via joint ventures,[4] add niche acquisitions (such as Long Distance/USA), lower its cost basis, and increase market share. The marketing plan called for service enhancement (e.g., an improved billing system), a fully competitive, high-quality product offering, and retention of a pricing advantage versus AT&T and MCI. With UT's nationwide network largely complete, its goal was to utilize capacity more fully.

COMPETITION IN THE LONG-DISTANCE TELEPHONE INDUSTRY

The long-distance segment was dominated by AT&T, which held a 68 percent share of market and fielded considerable financial and operational clout—in short, it was a multitier industry. The second tier consisted of MCI, with 14 percent of the market, and Sprint, with 9 percent. The industry included several other tiers, many of which were tiny players and resellers of services. Unlike other regulated industries, the competitors in the long-distance telephone industry did not compete like a stable oligopoly. Given the capital intensity in the industry, its resulting high operating leverage, and growing excess capacity, fierce competition was to be expected.

The competition for market share was based on several factors. Although price had been the most significant factor, quality of service (e.g., fiber-optic cables) and service customization (e.g., special packages for small businesses) were increasingly important factors in building customer loyalty. Spending on technological improvements was crucial, as was the advertising necessary to broadcast those improvements. Analysts estimated AT&T's advertising budget for 1990 at over $450 million, compared with $125 million for all other long-distance companies *combined*.

Two major technological advances were revolutionizing the telecommunications industry: fiber-optic cables and digital switching, both of which significantly increased the

---

[4]UT's 1989 annual report stated: "We don't intend to be just *a* player in making the world a smaller place. In the most creative respects, we can be *the* player."

carrying capacity of telecommunications networks.[5] The rapid rate of technological change often rendered obsolete equipment that otherwise was viable, as UT discovered in 1987 when it wrote off $260 million for its analog-microwave network, made redundant by the earlier-than-expected transition of traffic to its new fiber-optic network.

In 1990, revenues in the long-distance telephone industry aggregated about $50 billion and were expected to grow faster than the economy for at least five years, reflecting the expected quality improvements and price reductions that would increase demand. *Value Line* predicted that composite industry revenues (i.e., both local and long-distance segments) would grow at 6 percent per year for the next five years. The composite forecast, however, masked widely differing projected growth rates for individual firms: UT's revenues were expected to grow at 12 percent per year, compared with 15 percent for MCI and 3.5 percent for AT&T. Exhibit 5 presents comparative expected financial-performance figures for the major players in the industry.

The key trends in the industry were consolidation (purchase of small companies by large companies), stable or declining unit prices in the face of rising competition, and product/service proliferation. The three major players faced the prospects of rising marketing costs, entry by local telephone companies, revenue erosion from price competition, and the uncertainty attending the Federal Communications Commission's regulation of AT&T (price changes, entries permitted, and so on).

Many observers believed that the survivors in the industry would be large, offering geographical reach and a full product line, would be especially effective marketers and cost controllers, and would exploit a range of strategic alliances from joint ventures to partial and full acquisitions. Given its size, capital resources, and name recognition, AT&T already showed these characteristics. MCI had effectively segmented the market and established a reputation for service among price-sensitive customers. Sprint had the most advantageous pricing of the three as well as a technological lead; and its state-of-the-art billing system was expected to appeal to customers, such as businesses and government agencies, with specialized information requirements.

WILLIAM ESREY

Gradually, a new breed of senior manager was taking charge in the telecommunications industry. Before federal judge Harold Greene approved the breakup of AT&T into one long-distance and several regional companies in 1983, senior managers of telecommunications companies typically had come up through the ranks on the operational side, as engineers. This tendency reflected the focus on operating economies dictated by tight regulation of monopolies. After the breakup, however, a new emphasis was clearly

---

[5]Quite simply, a fiber-optic cable transmitted signals in the form of light, rather than electric pulses, enabling a single cable to carry much more volume than an ordinary copper cable. Digital switching enabled the cable to be packed even fuller: under the old analog technology, the sine-wave signal left considerable unused capacity in the cable, whereas the digital technology packed the cable virtually full.

required: marketers, strategic planners, and financial officers gained more influence in the executive suites.

William Esrey joined United Telecommunications in 1980 as executive vice president of corporate planning and was named chief financial officer in January 1984. He became president and chief executive officer in April 1985. Prior to joining UT, Esrey was managing director of Dillon, Reed and Company from 1970 to 1979; earlier, he had held management positions with AT&T, New York Telephone Company, and Empire City Subway Company, Ltd. He had earned a bachelor's degree in economics from Denison University and a master's degree from Harvard Business School.

Esrey's vision of the future of the telecommunications industry was summarized in the concept *infonics,* his term for the technological infrastructure he believed would "probably reshape the world." A UT press release noted:

> Esrey may be best known as an architect. His own building blocks are fiber-optic cable and digital switches. His most acclaimed structure is arguably the most advanced long-distance network in the United States. . . . He is now leading the company's strategic thrust into world-wide markets, where he sees advancements in the telecommunications industry giving consumers unprecedented opportunities to demand new services from their long-distance carriers.[6]

FINANCING REQUIREMENTS

UT's most prominent investment was its planned purchase of GTE's minority interest in Sprint for approximately $550 million, which would complete and simplify UT's control of Sprint. Although UT initially had intended to purchase the remaining interest in mid-1990, the adverse quarterly performance reported in July had forced the company to delay the purchase until 1991. The effect of any delay would be to share pro rata any ongoing profits or losses in Sprint. GTE had the right to put its interest to UT from December 31, 1991, to December 31, 1995.

UT's internal capital expenditures for 1990 would approximate $1 billion.[7] Observers believed that much of the internal spending was related to installation of digital switches and fiber-optic cable in the local telephone companies, and that internal capital expenditures would amount to $1.3 billion[8] in 1991 and a minimum of $1 billion[9] annually thereafter for the foreseeable future. These amounts compared with historical expenditures in the long-distance segment of $705 million in 1989 and $735 million in 1988, both of which were substantially driven by construction costs for the domestic fiber-optic network.

---

[6]"United Telecom/US Sprint Chairman Esrey Cites Fundamental Changes in Global Communications," September 4, 1990.

[7]UT's 1989 annual report stated that capital expenditures for 1990 would approximate $1.6 billion, which included the purchase of GTE's interest in Sprint. Netting that out would leave internal expenditures of about $1 billion.

[8]Jack R. Grubman, "United Telecom—Company Report," PaineWebber, September 17, 1990.

[9]Edward Greenberg of Morgan Stanley believed that UT's capital expenditures would exceed $1 billion annually at least through 1995. Specifically, he forecasted the following expenditure rates from 1991 through 1996 (in $ billions): 1.73, 1.18, 1.20, 1.33, 1.47, and 1.58.

The local-telephone segment required capital expenditures of $659 million and $676 million in 1989 and 1988, respectively. The relatively high rate of capital expenditures at the local level reflected the growth of access lines (i.e., customers) and the conversion from analog to digital switching. The diffusion of digital technology to UT's local operations was slow but steady—62 percent of local switching capacity was digital at the end of 1987, compared with 81 percent at the end of 1989.

A third major capital expenditure was the planned construction of a new office complex, adding 2.6 million square feet of space in a campus of 21 modular office buildings, ranging from 4 to 15 stories and connected by walkways.[10] The complex would consolidate the headquarters staff, currently spread over 24 buildings in the Kansas City area. A rough estimate of the expenditure for the new complex was $500 million[11] and did not include $50 million already spent to purchase the land. The timing of the expenditure was open to question: construction had been expected to begin early in 1990; but with the adverse quarterly report, the ground-breaking had been delayed. Now, in November 1990, analysts expected construction to be deferred at least through 1991.

Financing also might be required in future years to support acquisitions by UT. Observers believed UT would reenter the cellular-telephone market by the mid-1990s, a move that might require between $500 million and $1 billion.[12] Other strategic acquisitions might be made in complementary businesses, international telecommunications, and small domestic long-distance telephone companies. Observers generally agreed that being able to provide a full product line was essential to survival in the industry.

A final imponderable was the extra spending necessary to build the Sprint brand name and maintain it in the face of opposing efforts by AT&T and MCI. In the fall of 1990, AT&T initiated a massive telemarketing campaign in which it would telephone *every one* of MCI's and Sprint's customers to persuade them to switch to AT&T. One analyst said, "This is going to be a long drawn-out war. . . . Sprint may be the biggest casualty of a protracted marketing battle . . . and . . . may not be able to afford the escalating marketing wars."[13]

Another observer noted:

> The big trouble is spelled AT&T. After years of letting its share of the long-distance market slip, American Telephone & Telegraph has been fighting back with a vengeance, using tough ads and a telephone marketing campaign that includes ringing up an estimated six million of rivals' customers a month, asking them to switch . . . the slug-out is costly.[14]

---

[10]The company total would rise to 3.3 million square feet of space. UT currently had 2.63 million square feet of space in the metropolitan area. Of that footage, 1.5 million was leased and the rest was owned by United Telecom or Sprint. (Steven Wolcott, "United Telecom Imparting Mixed Signals about Move," *Kansas City Business Journal,* May 7, 1990.)

[11]Casewriter's estimate, based on an assumed cost per square foot of about $200.

[12]Casewriter's estimate, based on the sale price of UT's own cellular operation, US TeleSpectrum, in 1988 for $775 million.

[13]Jack R. Grubman (PaineWebber), "AT&T's Long-Distance Marketing Blitz Has MCI, Sprint Scrambling to Keep Up," *The Wall Street Journal,* November 19, 1990.

[14]John R. Dorfman, "MCI Shares Are Being Shed by Big Institutions, Which Fret over Heated Battle with AT&T," *The Wall Street Journal,* December 3, 1990.

FORECAST OF FINANCING REQUIREMENTS

Exhibits 6, 7, and 8 present forecasted financial statements for UT on a consolidated basis. The forecasts assume no major acquisitions (other than the minority interest in Sprint in 1991) and no sustained price war or adverse competitive developments for Sprint. The headquarters-construction expense is not reflected in the forecasts. The large additions to gross property, plant, and equipment over the forecast period assume expenditures to sustain the firm only at its present scope.

The apparent *incremental* external financing need (Exhibit 7, line 23) is about $600 million in 1990, $1 billion in 1991, and $70 million in 1992—all compared with $750 million of borrowing capacity available under the firm's most restrictive debt covenants.[15] Thereafter, incremental external needs are negative, because, under this forecast, Sprint would begin to throw off a large flow of cash beginning in 1992. The large external financing need has been driven mainly by UT's huge internal capital expenditures and by its high rate of debt refinancing. The future could differ dramatically from this forecast with relatively minor changes in operating assumptions for Sprint.

CORPORATE FINANCING[16]

Exhibit 9 presents a graph of leverage and capitalization ratios for UT over time. Dividend payout peaked at over 100 percent of earnings in 1986 and 1987. Although dividends per share held steady at $0.96 from 1985 to 1988, earnings per share dropped precipitously as the firm absorbed large losses from its fledgling US Sprint joint venture. The decline in dividend payout since 1988 resulted from slow dividend increases relative to earnings. Debt as a percentage of capital varied between 50 and 65 percent, with the last few periods at the high end of that range. UT incurred debt at the parent and subsidiary levels, as indicated in the following table:

Financing Entity and Debt	Dollar Volume of Debt ($ millions)	Percentage of Debt	Ratings
UTI (parent)			
Short term	194	10.0	A2/P2
Senior long-term	1,427	73.4	BBB/Baa3
Subordinated long-term	324	16.6	BBB−/Ba1
Total	1,945	100.0	

(continued)

---

[15]This estimate, drawn from UT's 10-Q statement of June 1990, contrasts with the $631 million in unused revolving bank-credit facilities indicated in its 1989 annual report and in Exhibit 13 of this case. For analytic purposes, one should work with the more recent figure of $750 million.

[16]The comments presented in this section refer to UT's *consolidated* statements.

Financing Entity and Debt	Dollar Volume of Debt ($ millions)	Percentage of Debt	Ratings
Local Communications Services			
Short term	11	0.7	A1/P1
Mortgage bonds	1,144	81.5	AA,A/A
Debentures/other	249	17.8	A/A
Total	1,404	100.0	
Long-Distance Communications Services			
Vendor finance	405	66.6	Not rated
GTE advances*	187	30.8	
Other	16	2.6	
Total	608	100.0	

*Advances by UT and other funding for Sprint are included at the parent level.

Definitions of Standard & Poor's rating categories are given in Exhibit 10. Exhibit 11 presents S&P's rationale for UT's debt ratings and a summary of the financial-ratio benchmarks UT used in rating securities.

Exhibit 12 gives further detail on UT's debt structure, and Exhibit 13 describes the securities in more detail. In addition to the items listed, UT used up to $300 million of receivables financing from Citibank and had $750 million of unused borrowing capacity available under the most restrictive debt covenants. On April 27, 1990, UT shelf-registered an issue of $500 million in debt securities; S&P rated the registration BBB. Exhibit 14 presents the long-term pattern of debt additions. A schedule of forthcoming debt maturities and payments under operating leases is given in Exhibit 15. Finally, Exhibit 16 summarizes public information concerning the ownership of UT's common stock and that of AT&T and MCI.

CAPITAL-MARKET CONDITIONS

Exhibit 17 gives the current term structure of interest rates in U.S. Treasuries as well as current yields to maturity on corporate bonds. Although observers believed the U.S. economy was slipping into a recession (one prominent economist declared the economy had gone into a "free fall"),[17] they also believed it would be short-lived and that the economy would start to rebound in mid-1991. One commentator expected the federal-funds rate to fall from 7.75 percent to 6.75 percent by mid-1991, because she expected the Federal Reserve Board to ease interest rates in support of the economy; the 30-year

---

[17]H. Erich Heinemann, "Free Fall," *CreditWeek,* Standard & Poor's Corporation, November 26, 1990.

Treasury bond yield was expected to fall from 8.750 to 8.375 percent by midyear, but then rise as the economy rebounded.[18] Exhibit 18 presents forecasts of interest and exchange rates through 1991.

STOCK PRICE

Some of the pressure that management felt in November 1990 was attributable to UT's sagging stock price. The price had reached $46 per share the preceding spring, but then, on July 17, it dropped 10 points in response to an unexpectedly poor earnings report. Exhibit 19 illustrates that the dramatic change in market valuation was not directly attributable to general marketwide movements, although the trend in the broad market indexes was negative from early August. Both MCI and AT&T experienced a slump in stock price of about a third over the same period, which suggested that industry factors were driving the downward revaluation of stock prices.

Exhibit 20 provides a detailed profile of the stock market and pricing of UT stock in mid-November 1990. At a trading price of $22.50 per share, the stock had a P/E (price/earnings) ratio of 14 times, about equivalent to that of AT&T (13×) and the broader market indexes. Only MCI, with a P/E ratio of 20 times, stood out. UT's dividend yield of 4.7 percent slightly exceeded the telecommunications industry average of 4.3 percent.

Analysts were divided on whether UT's stock was fairly valued in the low $20s. The following table summarizes recent assessments of UT's stock price by prominent securities analysts.

Analyst	Recommendation	Value of Local Telephone Operations	Value of Sprint	Value of UT
Edward Greenberg, Morgan Stanley, August 8, 1990	Buy	$18–24	$21–23	$39–47
Joel Gross, Donaldson, Lufkin & Jenrette, October 15, 1990	Buy	N.A.	$10+	$35–45 (Min. $32)
Jack Grubman, Paine Webber, September 17, 1990	"Attractive"	$20	$15	$35

---

[18]Evelina Tainer, "Economic Outlook," *First Forecasts,* The First National Bank of Chicago, November 15, 1990.

Analyst	Recommendation	Value of Local Telephone Operations	Value of Sprint	Value of UT
C.W. Shelke, Smith, Barney, July 24, 1990	Buy	$23	$ 7	$30
R.L. Altman, Altman, Brenner & Wasserman, August 30, 1990	Sell	N.Av.	N.Av.	Max. $23
K.M. Leon, Bear Stearns, July 20, 1990	Drops "Buy" recommenda-tion	N.Av.	N.Av.	N.Av.

Some analysts believed a stock price in the low $20s was virtually the value of the local-telephone segment *alone* and gave no regard to any value in Sprint. One analyst observed that, at a stock price in the low $20s, Sprint was valued at 17 percent of sales, 1.4 times cash flow, and 40 percent of book value or 4 times earnings.[19] Whatever the view, UT seemed to be a focus for strong feeling, as suggested by the following comments:

> The intense emotion surrounding United Telecom has driven the stock price down to levels bearing no relationship to underlying value—regardless of the perceived quality of management.[20]

> . . . we believe that the stock selling at current levels represents an excellent opportunity to raise cash. Given present macro- and microeconomic factors, the probabilities of US Sprint turning around . . . are very small, and US Sprint must work for United Telecommunications to be attractive. The question which remains now is whether US Sprint will ever be financially viable.[21]

Sprint was indeed the focus of both optimism and disdain, as illustrated in the following table that summarizes Edward Greenberg's discounted-cash-flow analysis of the Sprint and non-Sprint segments of UT.[22]

---

[19]Jack Grubman, "United Telecom: Doing the Right Things—Finally," *Company Report,* PaineWebber, Inc., September 17, 1990.

[20]Edward M. Greenberg, "United Telecom: Resisting Emotion," *Morgan Stanley Investment Research,* August 8, 1990.

[21]R.L. Altman, "United Telecommunications—Company Report," Altman, Brenner & Wasserman, Inc., August 30, 1990.

[22] Greenberg's results are reproduced as published in his report, "United Telecom: Resisting Emotion," *Morgan Stanley Investment Research,* August 8, 1990. The exact conclusions of his analysis cannot be reproduced with a handheld calculator, although the qualitative conclusions remain the same. Greenberg probably omitted presenting other assumptions that affect the exact results.

	US Sprint	Non-Sprint Businesses
Discount rate	15.08%	14%
Perpetual growth rate	7.0%	5%
Cash flow ($ millions):		
1990E	$ 113	$ 208
1991E	302	311
1992E	434	385
1993E	561	444
1994E	592	497
1995E	583	531
1996E	611	573
Terminal value ($ millions)	$7,132.8	$7,593.6
Present value of equity ($ millions)	$4,690.3	$5,028.7
DCF value per share	$ 21.92	$ 23.51

As apparent in Greenberg's analysis, the key driver of value was the growth rate of Sprint's cash flows over the 1990–96 period: while the non-Sprint cash flows were projected to grow 2.75 times, the Sprint cash flows were projected to grow *5.4 times*. Analyses such as Greenberg's rapidly focused investors' eyes on the determinants of Sprint's future cash-flow growth: not only the aggressiveness of capital spending but, more important, the ability to build volume throughput in what was a largely completed network. Because of the economics of high operating leverage, small increases in volume would create proportionally large increases in operating profits. In short, any assessment of Sprint's value was a bet on UT's ability to seize and defend market share.

CONCLUSION

The financing issues facing UT's senior management in November 1990 could be summarized in: To what extent was UT's corporate financing policy an *instrument* of its corporate vision and competitive strategy? If financing difficulties were allowed to constrain investment or operations, the company might not survive the growing competitive battle. All observers noted that Esrey's vision for UT was expansive: he was not a caretaker.

Did a financing policy exist that would assist the creation of both shareholder wealth and competitive advantage? What changes, if any, were required in the current policy? In considering alternative policies, where were the key trade-offs? What actions taken today would create or foreclose financing options in the future? On what timetable should any policy changes and financing tactics be implemented? Specifically, how should the firm externally raise $1.6 billion in new capital in the next 18 months?

EXHIBIT 1   Consolidated Statements of Income ($ millions)

	1989	1988
Net operating revenues:		
Long-distance communications	$4,323.6	$3,405.4
Local communications	2,637.0	2,509.7
Complementary businesses	762.1	698.6
Intercompany revenues	(173.7)	(120.7)
Total net operating revenues	7,549.0	6,493.0
Operating expenses:		
Long-distance	4,097.0	3,791.5
Local	2,001.3	1.912.9
Complementary	714.4	656.5
Intercompany	(173.7)	(120.7)
Total operating expenses	6,639.0	6,240.2
Operating income	910.0	252.8
Other (income) expense, net	(11.5)	7.1
Interest charges, net of capitalization	359.8	320.4
Minority interest in Sprint	33.4	(223.4)
Income (loss) from continuing operations before income taxes	528.3	148.7
Income tax provision (benefit)	165.4	6.9
Discontinued operations	0.0	367.1
Net income (loss)	362.9	508.9
Preferred stock dividends	3.0	3.3
Earnings applicable to common stock	$ 359.9	$ 505.6
Earnings (loss) per share:		
From continuing operations	$ 1.72	$ 0.68
From discontinued operations		1.80
Total	$ 1.72	$ 2.48
Weighted-average number of common shares outstanding	209.1	204.4

Source: UT's 1989 annual report.

EXHIBIT 2   Consolidated Balance Sheets ($ millions)

	1989	*1988*
Assets		
Cash and temporary investments	$ 114.8	$ 617.1
Accounts receivable	998.7	850.3
Notes receivable	84.4	330.6
Inventories	124.7	131.3
Deferred income taxes	33.5	44.7
Prepayments	153.1	151.0
Total current assets	1,509.2	2,125.0
Property, plant, and equipment:		
Long-distance communications services	4,281.4	3,493.0
Local communications services	7,213.9	6,900.8
Complementary and other	259.6	275.4
Less: accumulated depreciation	(3,870.0)	(3,339.4)
Net property, plant, and equipment	7,884.9	7,329.8
Intangible assets, net of amortization	122.4	124.3
Other assets	304.8	237.8
Total assets	$9,821.3	$9,816.9
Liabilities and Shareholders' Equity		
Current maturities of long-term debt	$ 384.3	$ 148.5
Accounts payable	738.7	716.9
Accrued local interconnection and leases	318.5	292.1
Advance billings	67.5	63.3
Accrued taxes	237.9	313.2
Accrued interest	107.0	100.8
Other	424.9	514.1
Total current liabilities	2,278.8	2,148.9
Long-term debt	3,747.0	3,674.8
Deferred income taxes	934.2	792.1
Deferred investment tax credits	156.7	188.8
Deferred other credits	126.0	137.3
Minority interest in Sprint	464.8	958.9
Redeemable preferred stock	36.9	38.9
Common stock (250 million shares auth'd)	517.8	256.6
Employees' stock purchase installment	22.3	7.3
Nonredeemable convertible preferred stock	4.0	2.4
Capital in excess of par value	650.0	882.5
Retained earnings	882.8	728.4
Total shareholders' equity	2,076.9	1,877.2
Total liabilities and shareholders' equity	$9,821.3	$9,816.9

Source: UT's 1989 annual report.

EXHIBIT 3 Comparative Financial Information, 1989

Firm	Net Profit Margin	P/E	Dividend Payout	Beta	Debt Rating	Long-term Debt to Capital	ROE
United Telecom.	**4.8%**	**17.2×**	**56.4%**	**0.95***	**A2/P3** **BBB/Baa3** **(Parent)** **A1/P1** **AA,A/A** **(Locals)**	**62.0%**	**17.5%**
Long-distance competitors:							
AT&T	7.6%	12.7×	48.0%	0.90	A1/P1 AA/A	39.0%	21.2%
MCI	9.7%	14.0×	4.0%	1.15	A2/P2 BBB/Baa2	52.9%	26.5%
Local telephone companies:							
Ameritech	12.1%	13.29×	69%	0.90		39.7%	16.0%
Bell Atlantic	11.5	16.87	65	0.90		47.3	15.3
Bell South	11.9	14.21	71	1.00		35.0	12.7
Nynex	8.6	17.89	74	0.90		40.8	12.1
Pacific Telesis	12.9	15.10	61	0.95		40.1	15.7
Southwestern Bell	12.5	14.61	71	0.95		39.5	13.1
US West	11.5	11.85	61	0.95		47.3	13.8
Cincinnati Bell	10.5	13.75	43	0.95		38.6	17.4
GTE	8.1	12.44	66	0.95		52.8	17.3
Rochester	9.2	14.31	71	0.80		44.8	12.7
Southern New England	10.2%	10.81×	58%	0.85		42.2%	14.1%
Average	10.8%	14.10×	65%	0.92		42.6%	14.5%

* UT's sigma (i.e., annualized standard deviation of common-stock returns) was 0.40.

Sources: *Value Line Investment Survey* and *Standard & Poor's Bond Guide.*

EXHIBIT 4   Map Indicating Market Presence of UT Local Communications Services

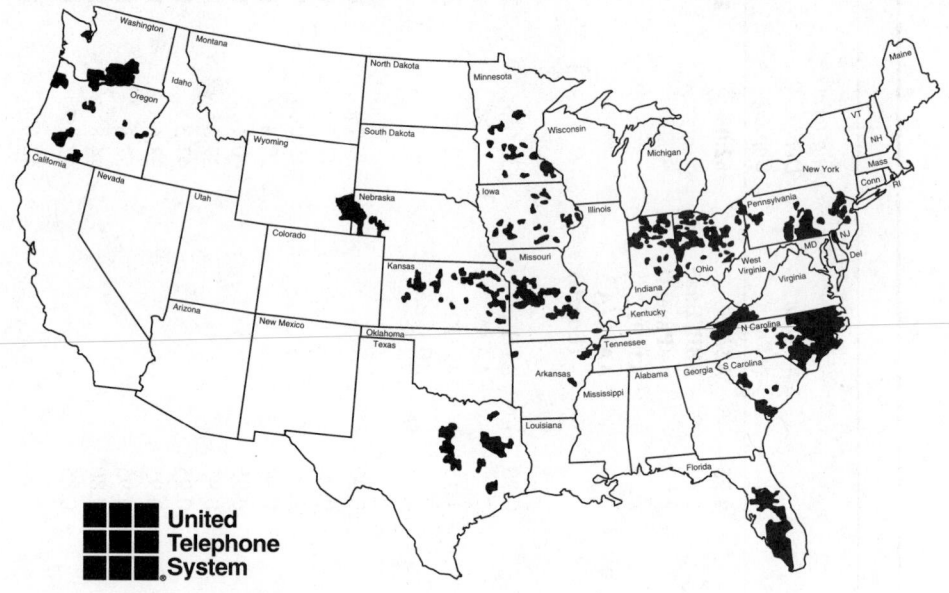

Source: *Moody's Public Utilities Manual*, 1990.

EXHIBIT 5   Comparative Projected Financial Ratios in Long-Distance Telecommunications
Industry (projected through 1995)

	AT&T	MCI	UT
Projected annual growth rates:			
Revenues	3.5%	15.0%	12.0%
"Cash flow"	5.5	17.5	12.5
Earnings	10.0	21.5	27.0
Dividends	7.0	N.M.F.	9.0
Book value	9.0	30.0	11.5
Expected dividend-payout ratio	47.0%	8.0%	40.0%
Projected LT debt to capital	29.5%	21.8%	52.0%
Projected return on total capital	14.5%	15.0%	22.5%
Projected net profit margin	9.5%	9.0%	7.2%
Projected price/earnings ratio (in 1995)	14×	15×	15×

Source: *Value Line Investment Survey*.

EXHIBIT 6 Projected Income Statements ($ millions)

Line		1988	1989	1990e	1991e	1992e	1993e	1994e
1	Revenue: long distance	$3,405.0	$4,324.0	$4,989.9	$5,553.8	$6,325.7	$7,110.1	$7,927.8
2	Revenue: local Telcos	2,510.0	2,637.0	2,755.7	2,879.7	3,009.3	3,144.7	3,286.2
3	Revenue: complementary	699.0	762.0	857.3	964.4	1,085.0	1,220.6	1,373.1
4	Total revenue	6,614.0	7,723.0	8,602.8	9,397.8	10,419.9	11,475.4	12,587.1
	(Revenues w/o intercompany)							
5	Op. expense: long distance	3,792.0	4,097.0	4,740.4	5,109.5	5,762.7	6,434.7	7,182.6
6	Op. expense: local Telcos	1,912.0	2,001.0	2,066.7	2,159.8	2,256.9	2,358.5	2,464.6
7	Op. expense: complementary	657.0	714.0	801.5	901.7	1,014.4	1,141.2	1,283.9
8	Operating expense	6,361.0	6,812.0	7,608.7	8,170.9	9,034.1	9,934.4	10,931.1
	(Op. exp. w/o intercompany)							
9	Gross profit	253.0	911.0	994.1	1,226.9	1,385.8	1,541.0	1,656.0
10	Interest income	(7.0)	11.0	0.0	0.0	0.0	0.0	0.0
11	Total short-term int. exp.	0.0	0.0	42.3	45.3	48.2	44.6	36.6
12	Total int. on sched. debt.	320.4	359.8	315.0	283.3	237.6	195.3	160.6
13	Interest expense: "plug" debt	0.0	0.0	30.8	104.6	154.0	154.0	131.5
14	Total interest expense	327.4	348.8	388.1	433.1	439.7	393.8	328.6
15	Minority interest	(223.0)	34.0	(53.0)	0.0	0.0	0.0	0.0
16	One-time charge (Sprint)	0.0	0.0	72.0	0.0	0.0	0.0	0.0
17	Earnings before taxes	148.6	528.2	587.0	793.8	946.1	1,147.1	1,327.4
18	Provision for income taxes	7.0	165.0	176.2	261.9	312.2	378.5	438.0
19	Earnings from discont'd op.	367.1						
20	Income after taxes	286.0	397.0	357.8	531.8	633.9	768.6	889.3
21	Net income	508.7	363.2	410.8	531.8	633.9	768.6	889.3
22	Dividends	201.0	203.0	213.0	223.0	233.0	243.0	253.0

Source: Independent analysis, consistent with assumptions drawn from leading securities analysts and historical company performance.

EXHIBIT 7 Projected Balance Sheets ($ millions)

Line		1988	1989	1990e	1991e	1992e	1993e	1994e
	Assets							
1	Cash	$ 100.0	$ 115.0	$ 100.0	$ 100.0	$ 100.0	$ 100.0	$ 100.0
2	Marketable securities	517.0	0.0	0.0	0.0	0.0	0.0	0.0
3	Accounts receivable	850.0	999.0	1,104.6	1,200.0	1,322.6	1,449.3	1,582.7
4	Inventories	131.0	125.0	138.2	150.1	165.5	181.3	198.0
5	Notes receivable	331.0	84.0	52.0	52.0	52.0	52.0	52.0
6	Other current assets	196.0	186.0	217.0	248.0	277.0	311.0	349.0
7	Total current assets	2,125.0	1,509.0	1,611.8	1,750.1	1,917.1	2,093.6	2,281.7
8	Gross prop., plant, and equip.	10,669.0	11,755.0	13,255.0	14,755.0	16,105.0	17,455.0	18,805.0
9	Accum. depreciation	3,339.0	3,870.0	4,928.0	6,129.9	7,466.9	8,925.3	10,505.3
10	Net property, plant, and equip.	7,330.0	7,885.0	8,327.0	8,625.1	8,638.1	8,529.7	8,299.7
11	Other intangibles	124.0	122.0	119.0	116.0	113.0	110.0	107.0
12	Other assets	238.0	305.0	317.0	331.0	346.0	362.0	378.0
13	Total assets	$ 9,817.0	$ 9,821.0	$10,374.8	$10,822.2	$11,014.2	$11,095.3	$11,066.4
	Liabilities and shareholders' equity							
14	Accounts payable	$ 717.0	$ 738.0	$ 777.6	$ 813.4	$ 859.4	$ 906.9	$ 956.9
15	Current portion long-term debt	149.0	385.0	478.0	446.0	537.0	373.0	373.0
16	Income taxes payable	313.0	238.0	44.1	65.5	78.1	94.6	109.5
17	Accrued interconnect charges	292.0	318.0	424.1	472.1	537.7	604.4	673.9
18	Advanced billings	63.0	68.0	68.9	72.0	75.2	78.6	82.2
19	Accrued interest	101.0	107.0	118.8	128.1	142.9	145.1	130.0
20	Other current liabilities	514.0	425.0	450.0	475.0	500.0	525.0	525.0
21	Total current liabilities	2,149.0	2,279.0	2,361.5	2,472.0	2,730.3	2,727.6	2,850.4
22	Long-term debt: scheduled	3,675.0	3,747.0	3,269.0	2,823.0	2,286.0	1,913.0	1,540.0
23	**Financing need**	**0.0**	**0.0**	**628.5**	**1,620.6**	**1,690.4**	**1,621.6**	**1,206.6**
24	Total long-term debt	3,675.0	3,747.0	3,897.5	4,443.6	3,976.4	3,534.6	2,746.6
25	Other deferrals	326.0	282.0	282.0	282.0	282.0	282.0	282.0
26	Deferred income taxes	792.0	934.0	934.0	934.0	934.0	934.0	934.0
27	Minority interest	959.0	465.0	518.0	0.0	0.0	0.0	0.0
28	Total liabilities	7,901.0	7,707.0	7,993.0	8,131.6	7,922.7	7,478.2	6,812.9
29	Common stock and paid-in capital	1,186.0	1,231.0	1,301.0	1,301.0	1,301.0	1,301.0	1,301.0
30	Retained earnings	730.0	883.0	1,080.8	1,389.6	1,790.5	2,316.1	2,952.5
31	Common equity	1,916.0	2,114.0	2,381.8	2,690.6	3,091.5	3,617.1	4,253.5
32	Total liabilities and equity	$ 9,817.0	$ 9,821.0	$10,374.8	$10,822.2	$11,014.2	$11,095.3	$11,066.4

Source: Independent analysis, consistent with assumptions drawn from leading securities analysts and historical company performance.

EXHIBIT 8 Historical and Projected Financial Ratios

Line		1988	1989	1990e	1991e	1992e	1993e	1994e
1	Oper. profit margin (P) (%)	3.83	11.80	11.56	13.06	13.30	13.43	13.16
2	Return on sales (%)	7.70	4.70	4.78	5.66	6.08	6.70	7.07
3	Return on equity (%)	26.57	17.17	17.25	19.77	20.50	21.25	20.91
4	Return on assets or inv. (%)	5.06	6.50	5.92	7.56	8.39	9.27	10.00
5	Return on net assets (%)	6.48	8.46	7.66	9.79	11.16	12.29	13.46
6	Debt/Equity ratio (%)	199.58	195.46	183.71	181.73	145.99	108.03	73.34
7	Debt/Total capital (%)	66.62	66.15	64.75	64.50	59.35	51.93	42.31
8	Equity ratio (%)	19.52	21.53	22.96	24.86	28.07	32.60	38.44
9	Times interest earned (×)	1.92	2.56	2.38	2.83	3.15	3.91	5.04
10	Op. earnings cash int. cvg.	N.Av.	N.Av.	2.56	2.83	3.15	3.91	5.04
11	Op. cash flow cash int. cvg.	N.Av.	N.Av.	4.14	4.67	5.14	6.28	7.98
12	Days in receivables (avg.)	N.Av.	43.69	44.63	44.75	44.18	44.08	43.96
13	Days in payables (avg.)	N.Av.	38.98	36.35	35.53	33.79	32.45	31.12
14	Inventory turnover (avg.)	N.Av.	53.22	57.82	56.68	57.25	57.30	57.65
15	Fixed asset turnover	N.Av.	0.98	1.03	1.09	1.21	1.35	1.52
16	Total asset turnover	N.Av.	0.79	0.83	0.87	0.95	1.03	1.14
17	Days in receivables	46.91	47.21	46.86	46.61	46.33	46.10	45.89
18	Days in payables	41.14	39.54	37.30	36.33	34.72	33.32	31.95
19	Inventory turnover	48.56	54.50	55.06	54.43	54.60	54.80	55.22
20	Quick ratio	0.68	0.49	0.51	0.53	0.52	0.57	0.59
21	Current ratio	0.99	0.66	0.68	0.71	0.70	0.77	0.80
22	Primary earnings per share	4.99	1.72	1.97	2.55	3.05	3.70	4.28
23	Dividends per share	1.95	0.96	1.01	1.06	1.11	1.16	1.21
24	Cash flow per share	N.Av.	0.81	0.53	2.55	4.42	5.43	6.15
25	Book value per share	18.67	10.21	11.51	13.00	14.94	17.47	20.55
26	Change in EPS (%)	N.Av.	(65.45)	14.38	29.67	19.30	21.34	15.78
27	Sales growth rate (G) (%)	N.Av.	16.77	11.39	9.24	10.88	10.13	9.69
28	Inc. fixed cap. inv. (F) (%)	N.Av.	92.97	50.24	37.49	1.28	(10.28)	(20.68)
29	Inc. work. cap. inv. (W) (%)	N.Av.	0.63	12.88	(0.52)	(0.03)	1.44	5.87
30	Cash income tax rate (Tc) (%)	N.Av.	15.17	33.46	33.35	33.32	33.26	33.20

Source: Independent analysis, consistent with assumptions drawn from leading securities analysts and historical company performance.

EXHIBIT 9   Capitalization and Payout Ratios over Time

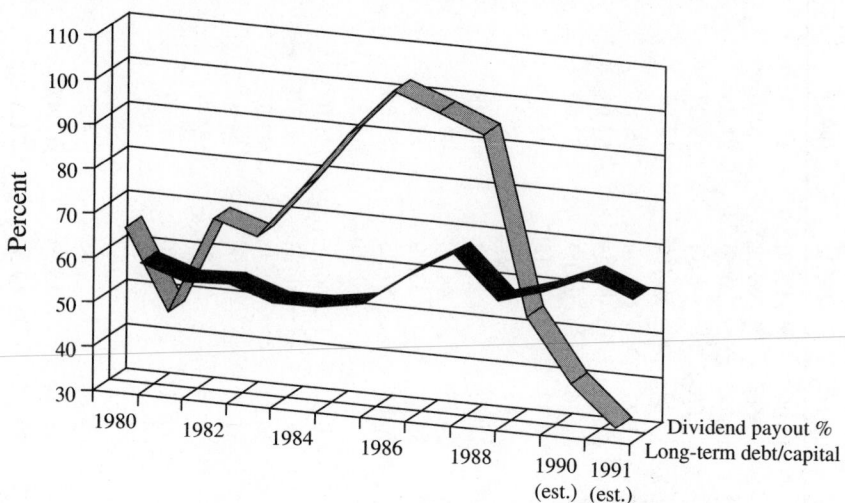

Source: *Value Line Investment Survey.*

EXHIBIT 10   Rating Definitions, Standard & Poor's Corporation

A Standard & Poor's corporate or municipal debt rating is a current assessment of the creditworthiness of an obligor with respect to a specific obligation. This assessment may take into consideration obligors such as guarantors, insurers, or lessees.

The debt rating is not a recommendation to purchase, sell, or hold a security, inasmuch as it does not comment as to market price or suitability for particular investor.

The ratings are based on current information furnished by the issuer or obtained by S&P from other sources it considers reliable. S&P does not perform an audit in connection with any rating and may, on occasion, rely on unaudited financial information. The ratings may be changed, suspended, or withdrawn as a result of changes in, or unavailability of, such information, or for other circumstances.

The ratings are based, in varying degrees, on the following considerations:

1. Likelihood of default—capacity and willingness of the obligor as to the timely payment of interest and repayment of principal in accordance with the terms of the obligation;
2. Nature of and provisions of the obligation;
3. Protection afforded by, and relative position of, the obligation in the event of bankruptcy, reorganization, or other arrangement under the laws of bankruptcy and other laws affecting creditors' rights.

Investment grade

AAA   Debt rated 'AAA' has the highest rating assigned by Standard & Poor's. Capacity to pay interest and repay principal is extremely strong.

AA   Debt rated 'AA' has a very strong capacity to pay interest and repay principal and differs from the highest rated issues only in small degree.

A   Debt rated 'A' has a strong capacity to pay interest and repay principal although it is somewhat more susceptible to the adverse effects of changes in circumstances and economic conditions than debt in higher rated categories.

BBB   Debt rated 'BBB' is regarded as having an adequate capacity to pay interest and repay principal. Whereas it normally exhibits adequate protection parameters, adverse economic conditions or changing circumstances are more likely to lead to a weakened capacity to pay interest and repay principal for debt in this category than in higher rated categories.

Speculative grade

Debt rated 'BB', 'B', 'CCC', 'CC', and 'C' is regarded as having predominantly speculative characteristics with respect to capacity to pay interest and repay principal. 'BB' indicates the least degree of speculation and 'C' the highest. While such debt will likely have some quality and protective characteristics, these are outweighed by large uncertainties or major exposures to adverse conditions.

BB   Debt rated 'BB' has less near-term vulnerability to default than other speculative issues. However, it faces major ongoing uncertainties or exposure to adverse business, financial, or economic conditions which could lead to inadequate capacity to meet timely interest and principal payments. The 'BB' rating category is also used for debt subordinated to senior debt that is assigned an actual implied 'BBB −' rating.

B   Debt rated 'B' has a greater vulnerability to default but currently has the capacity to meet interest payments and principal repayments. Adverse business, financial, or economic conditions will likely impair capacity or willingness to pay interest and repay principal. The 'B' rating category is also used for debt subordinated to senior debt that is assigned an actual or implied 'BB' or 'BB −' rating.

CCC   Debt rated 'CCC' has a currently identifiable vulnerability to default, and is dependent upon favorable business, financial, and economic conditions to meet timely payment of interest and repayment of principal. In the event of adverse business, financial, or economic conditions, it is not likely to have the capacity to pay interest and repay principal. The 'CCC' rating category is also used for debt subordinated to senior debt that is assigned an actual or implied 'B' or 'B −' rating.

CC   The rating 'CC' typically is applied to debt subordinated to senior debt that is assigned an actual or implied 'CCC' rating.

C   The rating 'C' typically is applied to debt subordinated to senior debt which is assigned an actual or implied 'CCC −' debt rating. The 'C' rating may be used to cover a situation where a bankruptcy petition has been filed, but debt service payments are continued.

C1   The rating 'C1' is reserved for income bonds on which no interest is being paid.

EXHIBIT 10 *(concluded)*

D Debt rated 'D' is in payment default. The 'D' rating category is used when interest payments or principal payments are not made on the date due even if the applicable grace period has not expired, unless S&P believes that such payments will be made during such grace period. The 'D' rating also will be used upon the filing of a bankruptcy petition if debt service payments are jeopardized.

Plus (+) or minus (−): The ratings from 'AA' to 'CCC' may be modified by the addition of a plus or minus sign to show relative standing within the major rating categories.

c The letter 'c' indicates that the holder's option to tender the security for purchase may be canceled under certain prestated conditions enumerated in the tender options documents.

L The letter 'L' indicates the rating pertains to the principal amount of those bonds to the extent that the underlying deposit collateral is federally insured and interest is adequately collateralized. In the case of certificates of deposit, the letter 'L' indicates that the deposit, combined with other deposits being held in the same right and capacity, will be honored for principal and accrued pre-default interest up to the federal insurance limits within 30 days after closing of the insured institution or, in the event that the deposit is assumed by a successor insured institution, upon maturity.

p The letter 'p' indicates that the rating is provisional. A provisional rating assumes the successful completion of the project being financed by the debt being rated and indicates that payment of debt service requirements is largely or entirely dependent upon the successful and timely completion of the project. This rating, however, while addressing credit quality subsequent to completion of the project, makes no comment on the likelihood of, or the risk of default upon failure of, such completion. The investor should exercise his own judgment with respect to such likelihood and risk.

* Continuance of the rating is contingent upon S&P's receipt of an executed copy of the escrow agreement or closing documentation confirming investments and cash flows.

N.R. Not rated.

Debt Obligations of Issuers outside the U.S. and its territories are rated on the same basis as domestic corporate and municipal issues. The ratings measure the creditworthiness of the obligor but do not take into account currency exchange and related uncertainties.

Bond Investment Quality Standards: Under present commercial bank regulations issued by the Comptroller of the Currency, bonds rated in the top four categories ('AAA', 'AA', 'A', 'BBB', commonly known as "investment grade" ratings) generally are regarded as eligible for bank investment. Also, the laws of various states governing legal investments impose certain rating or other standards for obligations eligible for investment by savings banks, trust companies, insurance companies, and fiduciaries generally.

Source: Standard & Poor's *CreditWeek*.

EXHIBIT 11   S&P Rating of United Telecommunications and Rating Benchmarks

United Telecommunications, Inc.
Current ratings:

		Senior debt history:	
Implied senior debt	—	1989	BBB
Senior secured debt	—	1988	BBB
Senior unsecured debt	BBB	1987	BBB
Subordinated debt ...	BBB −	1986	BBB
Preferred stock	BBB	1985	BBB
Preference stock	—	1984	BBB +
Commercial paper ..	A-2	1983	BBB +

Rationale: Credit quality of United Telecommunications Inc. is derived from its very strong and relatively low risk local telephone operations, which make up some 45% of assets, offset by a growing investment in the much riskier long distance carrier US Spring which amounts to 35% of assets. Outstanding securities total $3.8 billion. Expansion of its share of US Sprint to 80% from 50% in early 1989, and the likelihood that it will ultimately own 100% of the firm, sharply raises business risk. The debt-funded investment results in a weak consolidated financial position. Debt leverage exceeds 60% and pretax interest coverage is in the low to mid-2 times range. Telephone units serve some 3.7 million access lines in 17 states. The mainly rural and suburban properties enjoy strong growth with little bypass risk. They upstream nearly all of the cash necessary to meet United Telecom's interest on $2.5 billion of non-telephone debt and dividend needs that total about $500 million a year. While US Sprint's results seem on the mend, additional external capital may be required in the short run. Ratings anticipate that sufficient cash flow will be generated from US Spring in nearby years to begin meaningful repayment of the huge debt burden incurred by United Telecom. Ratings may be lowered if US Spring is not successful in increasing cash flow to levels sufficient to allow meaningful and significant reduction in United Telecom's huge debt load.
Outlook: Negative.

United Telecommunications, Inc., financial statistics
Year Ended Dec. 31

	1989	1988	1987	1986	1985
Total capital (bill. $) ...	6.72	6.71	4.74	4.58	3.85
Short-term debt (%) ...	5.7	2.2	2.6	1.9	3.4
Long-term debt (%)	55.7	54.8	64.3	58.6	50.6
Preferred stock (%)	0.8	0.8	0.9	1.5	1.9
Common equity (%) ...	37.8	42.2	32.2	37.9	44.2
Pretax interest coverage (×)	2.33	1.32	1.61	2.24	2.34
Preferred div coverage (×)	2.30	1.30	1.58	2.12	2.19
Income tax rate (%) ...	31.3	(5.1)	68.6	21.6	167.1
Ret on avg. equity (%)	12.6	5.2	N.M.	13.0	10.8
Common div payout (%)	55.6	140.8	N.M.	101.7	798.1
Net cash flow (NCF) (bill. %)	1.26	0.91	0.25	0.67	0.65
Capital expenditures (Capex) (bill. $)	1.39	1.44	0.70	0.95	1.06
Capex/avg. capital (%)	20.7	25.1	14.9	22.4	27.9
NCF/Capex (%)	91.0	63.4	36.6	70.4	61.3
NCF/avg. capital (%) ..	18.8	15.9	5.5	15.8	17.1
NCF/long-term debt (%)	34.0	27.1	8.9	28.8	34.3

N.M. = Not meaningful.

EXHIBIT 11   *(concluded)*

Financial Benchmarks

Financial benchmarks are guidelines to be used in conjunction with business risk assessments when evaluating credit quality. Local exchange telephone companies are classified as either "low" or "high" risk companies based on S&P's perception of their business risk *(see below)*

	"Low" risk	*"High" risk*
Total debt/total capital (%)		
AA	Under 47	Under 42
A	45–57	40–52
BBB	55–65	50–62
Pretax interest coverage (×)		
AA	Above 4.0	Above 4.5
A	3.0–4.5	3.5–5.5
BBB	2.3–3.4	2.7–4.0
Net cash flow/average long-term debt (%)		
AA	Above 25	Above 30
A	20–30	25–35
BBB	15–25	20–30

Financial ratios defined

Total debt/total capital—The sum of notes payable and other short-term obligations (including current maturities of long-term debt and capital lease obligations), plus long-term debt (including capital lease obligations), divided by the sum of total capital. Total capital is the sum of all short-term debt, long-term debt, preferred stock (including subsidiary preferred), minority interest, and common equity.

Pretax interest coverage—Income from continuing operations adjusted for nonrecurring items (before taxes), plus minority interest, income taxes, and interest expense, all divided by interest incurred. Capitalized interest is excluded from interest expense but included in interest incurred.

Net cash flow/average long-term debt—Funds from operations (cash flow from operations before working capital changes) less preferred and common dividends paid, divided by average long-term debt.

Source: Standard & Poor's *CreditWeek,* June 4, 1990.

EXHIBIT 12 Long-term Debt as of December 31, 1989

		Maturing	Balance ($ millions)
Corporate:			
Senior notes	7.50%	1990	$ 200.0
	8.42 to 9.50%	1991	225.0
	8.10 to 8.25%	1992	215.0
	9.75%	1993	100.0
	8.60 to 9.71%	1994	225.0
	9.40 to 10.45%	1995 to 1997	410.0
Debentures	9.40 to 11.00%	1999 to 2000	52.3
Subordinated debs.	5.00%	1993	2.3
	9.75%	2010	104.9
Subordinated notes	8.90%	1993	200.0
Commercial paper and bank notes	8.33 to 9.13%	1993	193.5
Other	6.13 to 14.63%	1990 to 2007	17.0
Long-distance communications services:			
Vendor financing	8.00 to 10.18%	1990 to 2001	405.2
Advances	N.Av.	N.Av.	186.8
Other debt	6.41 to 15.00%	1990 to 1993	15.9
Local communications services:			
First mortgage bonds			
	4.50 to 7.25%	1990 to 1994	58.6
	2.00 to 11.00%	1995 to 1999	192.0
	5.63 to 12.75%	2000 to 2004	303.0
	4.00 to 10.38%	2005 to 2009	244.0
	7.50 to 13.75%	2010 to 2014	48.7
	8.00 to 14.45%	2015 to 2019	297.6
Debentures	4.35 to 12.00%	1990 to 2016	232.4
Commercial paper and bank notes	9.01 to 10.00%	1993	11.3
Other debt	2.00 to 13.88%	1990 to 2016	17.2
Complementary businesses:			
Senior note	11.70%	2000	40.0
Vendor financing	10.18%	2001	116.9
Other debt	6.20% to 10.70%	1991 to 1993	16.7
Total			**4,131.3**
Less current maturities			384.3
Total long-term debt, excluding maturities			3,747.0

Source: UT's 1989 annual report.

EXHIBIT 13   Details Regarding Securities Issues Currently Outstanding

---

1. Bank notes payable and commercial paper

Outstanding:	$204,800,000 ($10.9 million of bank notes at 9.62% interest, 42.1 million of master-trust notes at 9.32% interest, and $151.8 million of commercial paper at 9.34% interest)
Agreements:	Master Trust Note Agreement: an agreement with the trust division of a bank to borrow funds on demand. The borrowings' rate was set to yield interest equivalent to the most favorable discount rate paid on 180-day commercial paper.
	Agreement in support of commercial paper: two banks provided an $80 million letter of credit and long-term revolving-credit agreement to support commercial paper issued by UT. The agreement was due to expire July 31, 1992.
	Bank commitments: at the end of 1989, UT and its subsidiaries had a total of $984 million of credit available. This included the agreement in support of commercial paper and a $700 million revolving-credit agreement. Total unused lines of credit were $823 million, of which $631 million was available on a long-term basis under the revolver. The 10-Q statement of June 1990 reported that the firm had $750 million of unused borrowing capacity under the most restrictive of its debt covenants.
Key covenants:	UT had to maintain a consolidated tangible net worth of $1.55 billion. At December 31, 1989, $610 million of United's retained earnings was restricted from payment of dividends. Subsidiary financing agreements restricted the payment of dividends to UT (parent): at December 31, 1989, $709 million of the related subsidiaries' $1.4 billion total retained earnings was restricted. The flow of cash, in the form of advances between UT and its subsidiaries, was not restricted.
Agent bank:	Chase Manhattan N.A.

2. United Telecommunications, Inc., sinking-fund debenture 9.40% notes due 1999

Outstanding:	$24,839,000
Rated:	Baa3
Issue date:	April 15, 1974
Maturity date:	April 15, 1999
Callability:	Yes, at various premia (102% in 1991 falling to 100% in 1994).
Sinking fund:	Yes, between $5 and $2.5 million annually. Designed to retire 90 percent of the issue before maturity.
Security:	Not secured.
Key covenants:	Limits asset dispositions and dividends.
Listed:	New York Stock Exchange.
Lead manager of offering:	Kidder Peabody.
Trustee:	Irving Trust Co.

3. United Telecommunications, Inc., sinking-fund debenture 11% notes due 2000

Outstanding:	$22,500,000
Rated:	Baa3
Issue date:	April 15, 1975
Maturity date:	April 15, 2000
Callability:	Yes, at various premia (2.75% in 1991 falling to 100% in 1995).

EXHIBIT 13   *(continued)*

Sinking fund:	Yes, between $5 and 2.5 million annually. Designed to retire 95 percent of the issue before maturity.
Key covenants:	Certain limitation on creation of additional debt.
Listed:	New York Stock Exchange.
Lead manager of offering:	Kidder Peabody.
Trustee:	Irving Trust Co.

4. United Telecommunications, Inc., 8.25% notes due 1992

Outstanding:	$200,000,000
Rated:	Baa3
Issue date:	April 1, 1986
Maturity date:	August 15, 1992
Callability:	Not callable.
Security:	Not secured.
Sinking fund:	None.
Lead manager of offering:	Kidder Peabody.

5. United Telecommunications, Inc., 9.75% notes due 2000

Outstanding:	$250,000,000
Rated:	Baa3
Issue date:	April 1, 1990
Maturity date:	April 1, 2000
Callability:	Not callable.
Security:	Not secured.
Sinking fund:	None.
Lead managers of offering:	Dillon Read, Goldman Sachs, and Smith Barney.

6. United Telecommunications, Inc., convertible subordinated debenture 5% notes due 1993

Outstanding:	$2,242,000
Issue date:	April 1, 1968 ($50 million offered)
Maturity date:	April 1, 1993
Rated:	Ba1
Callability:	Yes.
Convertibility:	Yes. Into 162,854 shares at $14 per share.
Sinking fund:	Yes, $2.5 million per year. Designed to retire 70 percent of the issue before maturity.
Listed:	New York Stock Exchange.
Lead manager of offering:	Kidder Peabody.

7. United Telecommunications, Inc., subordinated exchangeable debenture 9.75% notes due 2010

Outstanding:	$104,880,000
Issue date:	September 1, 1985
Maturity date:	September 1, 2010
Rated:	Ba1
Callability:	Yes, at premia ranging from 104.9% in 1991 to 100% in 1995.
Sinking fund:	Yes, $7 million per year. Designed to retire 70 percent of the issue before maturity.

EXHIBIT 13   *(concluded)*

Exchange rights:	Exchangeable at the option of UT for 4,248,330 common shares of Southern New England Telephone Company (SNET), acquired at a cost of $63 million (market value of $191 million at Dec. 31, 1989).* UT may, at its option, pay cash in an amount equal to the market value of the SNET common stock in lieu of exchanging the SNET stock.
Listed:	New York Stock Exchange.
Lead managers of offering:	Dillon Read and Kidder Peabody.

8. United Telecommunications, Inc., other debt unspecified

Parent company debt outstanding:	$1,191,602,000
Subsidiary long-term debt outstanding:	$2,200,937,000 (consisting mainly of mortgages and leases)

9. United Telecommunications, Inc., convertible preferred stock (two series)

Outstanding:	625 thousand shares
Issue date:	1968, 1969
Maturity date:	Perpetual.
Callability:	None.
Sinking fund:	None.
Listed:	New York Stock Exchange.
Dividend:	$1.50 per share, first series. $1.25 per share, second series.
Conversion:	Each share first series convertible into 3 shares of common stock. Each share second series convertible into 2 shares of common stock.

10. United Telecommunications, Inc., 7.75% redeemable preferred stock

Outstanding:	25.6 thousand shares
Maturity:	2007
Callability:	Yes, at premia from 103.33% in 1991, declining to 100% in 2003.
Sinking fund:	Yes, to redeem 12,000 shares annually, or $1.2 million per year.

11. United Telecommunications, Inc., common stock

Outstanding:	207,100,810 shares
Issue date:	Offerings in 1967, 1969, 1970, 1971, 1974, 1975, and 1985.
Listed:	New York Stock Exchange and Midwest and Pacific Exchanges.
Lead managers of offering:	Kidder Peabody sole-managed all issues except in 1985, when it co-managed the issue with First Boston and Shearson, Lehman.
Dividends:	Paid continuously since 1939.
Shares under option:	2,882,934 at exercise prices ranging from $8.00 to $39.31. Aggregate exercise amount under these options is $48.3 million.
Poison pill:	Yes, new plan adopted September 8, 1989, due to expire September 8, 1999, on preferred-stock purchase right granted per common share. The right would be exercisable upon the occurrence of certain takeover events and would entitle shareholders to buy participating preferred stock or common stock.

* SNET's stock price in late 1990 varied between $28 and $30 per share. Total shares outstanding were 61,965,025 in late 1990. For the years 1993 to 1995, *Value Line* forecasted a target price range for SNET shares between $35 and $40 per share. SNET's beta was 0.85 and its sigma (i.e., annualized standard deviation of returns) was 0.40.

Source: *Moody's Public Utilities Manual*, 1990.

EXHIBIT 14   Significant Changes in Long-Term Debt Outstandings by Year ($ millions)

	1989	1988	1987	1986
Corporate debt:				
Commercial paper and bank notes				
Classified as long term				
Debt 8.33–9.13%	$141.9	$(138.6)	$123.9	$109.0
9.75% senior notes due 1993		100.0		
8.54% senior notes			375.0	
7.5% senior notes due 1990				200.0
8.25% senior notes due 1992				200.0
Other senior notes				150.0
Subordinated notes due 1993				200.0
Long-distance communications services:				
Vendor financing agreements 8–10.18%*	83.9	321.3		286.0
Minority interest advances†	16.3	170.5		
Other debt		13.1		126.5
Local communications services:				
First mortgage bonds	164.9	(23.0)	(27.0)	(17.0)
Commercial paper	(19.2)	(32.2)	17.6	45.0
Carolina Tel. & Tel. 9% due 2016				50.0
United Tel. of Fla. 9.25% due 2016				60.0
United Tel. of Fla. 9.875% due 2017			65.0	

* GTE had guaranteed $144 million of US Sprint's borrowings at December 31, 1989.
† Advances by GTE to US Sprint under the joint venture agreement. The remaining portion of these advances is due to be repaid in 1999. The average interest rates on advances from GTE were 9.1 and 8.9 percent for 1989 and 1988.

Source: UT's 1990 annual report.

EXHIBIT 15   Maturities of Long-Term Debt and Minimum Payments under Operating Leases ($ millions)

Year	Debt Maturities	Payments for Operating Leases
1990	384.3	213.3
1991	478.3	164.9
1992	445.9	111.4
1993	537.2	52.7
1994	373.3	38.9
Thereafter		114.4

Source: UT's 1989 annual report.

EXHIBIT 16   Profile of Equity Ownership as of September 30, 1990

	UT	AT&T	MCI
Institutional ownership (percent of total shares outstanding):			
Mutual funds	8%	1%	10%
Investment advisors	35	12	43
Commercial banks	17	8	12
Insurance companies	6	2	4
Total	66%	23%	69%
Number of institutional holders:			
Mutual funds	109	105	167
Investment advisors	210	291	231
Commercial banks	133	211	119
Insurance companies	22	38	22
Total	474	645	539
Percent insider equity ownership	insignificant	insignificant	2%
Average dollar amount owned by an investor ...	$ 66,346	$ 12,810	$ 83,944
Number of stockholders ...	74,700	2,600,000	61,250
Total shares outstanding (000's) (September 30, 1990)	214,328	$1,089,111	$252,878
Other significant equity positions (shares held)	Lehman (5.5m), Prudential (4.5m), Eagle (3.5m), Wells Fargo (3.3m), CREF (3m), JP Morgan (3m).	Wells Fargo (16.4m), CREF (11.3m), NYState (8.3), CalPERs (6.9m), U of Cal (6.2m), Barrow (5.5m).	Wells Fargo (4.4m), Bankers Trust (4.1m), Michigan State (3.4m), Loo, Inc. (3.2m), NY State (2.9m), Miller (2.9m).
Special equity positions ...			IBM owns 100% of the outstanding preferred stock and controls 9.8% of votes.

Source: O'Neill Database.

EXHIBIT 17   Current Capital-Market Rates and Yields, November 19, 1990

U.S. Treasury Securities		Corporate Bond Yields		
		Rating Category	Industrials	Utilities
1 month	6.46%			
2 months	6.59			
3 months	6.98	AAA ...	9.35%	—
6 months	7.27	AA	9.68	9.70%
1 year	7.30	A	10.11	9.88
2 years	7.56	BBB ...	11.36	10.14%
3 years	7.97	BB	13.51	—
4 years	8.08	B	19.85%	—
5 years	8.18			
10 years	8.39			
20 years	8.62			
30 years	8.44			

Other Interest Rates

Commercial paper:	
30–89 days	7.75%
90–119 days	7.67
120–270 days	7.45
LIBOR:	
3 months	8.125
6 months	8.0
12 months	8.0
Bank prime rates:	
United States	10.0
Germany	10.5
Japan	8.0
Switzerland	10.5
United Kingdom	14.0

Source: *The Wall Street Journal*, November 19, 1990.

EXHIBIT 18 Forecasts of Interest Rates and Foreign Exchange Rates

Year Quarter	1990 IV	1991 I	1991 II	1991 III	1991 IV
Economic forecast (% change in data):					
Real gross national product	−0.7%	−0.9%	1.3%	3.2%	2.7%
Consumer price index	10.0	9.0	−1.6	2.4	4.1
After-tax profits (annualized)	18.5	10.6	−3.3	−16.2	−18.1
Interest rate forecast:					
Federal funds	7.75%	6.875%	6.75%	6.75%	6.875%
90–day Treasury bill	6.875	6.125	5.875	5.875	6.25
30–year Treasury bond	8.875	8.75	8.375	8.50	8.75
Corporate base rate	9.75	8.875	8.625	8.50	8.875
Foreign exchange rate forecast:					
Yen/dollar	127.00	123.00	122.00	125.00	127.00
DM/dollar	1.51	1.47	1.45	1.49	1.51

Source: *First Forecasts,* The First National Bank of Chicago, November 15, 1990.

EXHIBIT 19 Stock Prices, April through September 1990, of Major Telecommunications Firms

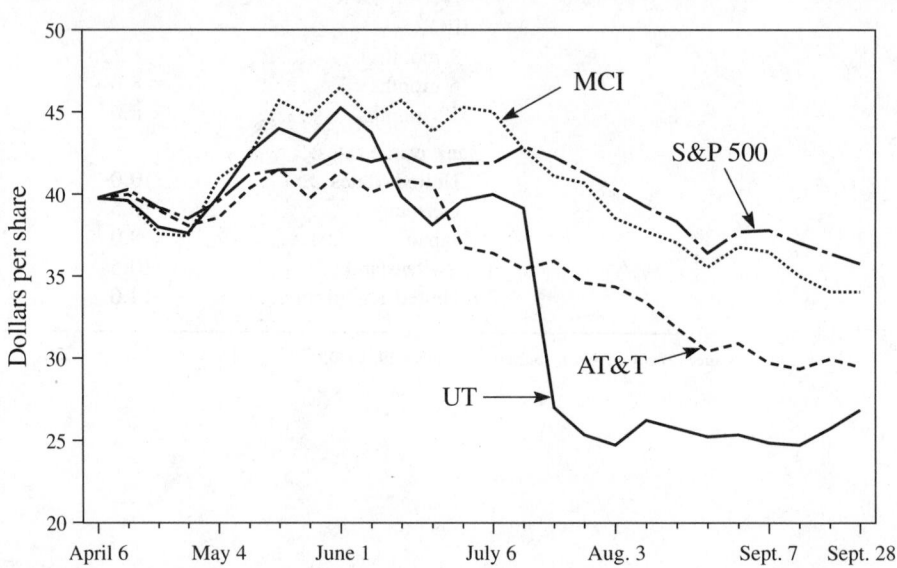

Note: Prices for AT&T, MCI, and the S&P 500 Index have been indexed to the price of UT's stock on April 6, 1990. The UT time series reflects the actual prices for UT stock.

EXHIBIT 20   Stock Prices and Indexes as of November 19, 1990

	Price	P/E	Dividend Yield	Earnings Yield	Market-to-Book
United Telecommunications	**$22.500**	**14.0×**	**4.70%**		
MCI Communications	22.625	20.0	0.50		
AT&T	32.000	13.0	4.80		
Dow Jones Industrial Average		13.1	4.01	7.51%	199.83%
Dow Jones Utilities Average		13.9	6.82	7.17	134.63
S&P 500 Index		14.6	3.88	6.84	215.35

Case 53

Rhône-Poulenc S.A.

Rhône-Poulenc is strategically committed to ranking, in each of its businesses, among the world's five leading chemical groups and the 10 largest pharmaceutical companies. By implementing this strategy, the Group is pursuing three key business objectives: achieve an operating margin of 15 percent, generate a 15 percent return on invested capital, and ensure average per share earnings growth of 15 percent per year.

Rhône-Poulenc, *annual report, 1990*

[These objectives will be achieved] *by globalizing a strategically related base of high value-added businesses with little cyclical exposure. . . . In recent years, these goals have led Rhône-Poulenc to acquire a number of companies and operations to reach critical mass and strengthen its positions in the global marketplace. At the same time, it has refocused on its mainstream businesses and divested underperforming or nonstrategic assets in ways that achieved optimum results for the people and businesses involved.*

Rhône-Poulenc, *press release, 1990*

The globalization of competition has gradually whittled down the number of market contenders in each of our business areas. Worldwide critical mass is thus indispensable to amortize the rising R&D costs, increasing capital expenditures, and higher marketing outlays required by accelerated technological developments and tougher standards in quality, safety, and environmental protection.

Chairman Jean-René Fourtou, *1989 annual report*

In September 1991, Rhône-Poulenc's corporate vision of high performance and growth to world-class standing faced its stiffest test. Year-to-date performance of the firm had

This case study was prepared by Robert F. Bruner from public information as the basis for classroom discussion while the author was a visiting professor at INSEAD, Fontainebleau, France.

fallen to a third of the firm's peak performance in 1989. Investment opinion was divided on the appropriateness of the firm's current share price of (French francs) FF427; some believed the price was low and that shares should be bought aggressively; others were cautious. The pace of technological innovation and industry consolidation commanded rising amounts of capital. One independent estimate suggested that the firm would need as much as FF38 billion of new external funds over the next five years, but where this capital was to be obtained was unclear. The firm was more heavily indebted than its competitors and apparently had saturated investor demand for its nonvoting equity. In addition, the French government, owner of all the firm's voting common stock, was fighting a large budget deficit and would not provide the needed capital; in fact, many analysts believed Rhône-Poulenc would be privatized within the next three years.

Were the firm's strategic and financial policies appropriate? If not, what action should management take? What would be the impact of those actions on both symptomatic problems in the short run and on deeper challenges in the long run? How should the firm's large requirement for external capital be met?

THE CHEMICALS INDUSTRY

Rhône-Poulenc's historical field of competition, the worldwide chemicals industry, was highly competitive and dominated by several large multinational companies. The following table lists the 14 largest firms, ranked on the basis of 1990 revenues (U.S. dollars):

Company	Country (headquarters)	Revenues ($ millions)	Profits ($ millions)	Number of Employees (thousands)
Du Pont	U.S.	$40,047	$2,310	143.9
BASF Group	Ger.	28,856	685	134.1
Hoechst Group	Ger.	27,766	927	172.9
Bayer Group	Ger.	25,773	1,164	171.0
ICI	U.K.	23,034	1,101	132.1
Dow Chemicals	U.S.	19,773	1,384	62.1
Rhône-Poulenc	**France**	**14,473**	**356**	**91.6**
Ciba-Geigy	Switz.	14,183	744	94.1
Montedison	Italy	13,971	207	44.6
Akzo	Holl.	9,491	364	70.5
Ashai Chemicals	Japan	9,202	302	25.9
Monsanto	U.S.	8,995	490	41.1
Solvay Group	Belg.	7,638	501	45.7
Union Carbide	U.S.	7,621	314	37.8

This industry had several distinctive characteristics: (1) pervasiveness in Western economies; (2) high level of international trade and production; (3) the use of capital-intensive, continuous production processes; (4) an oligopolistic competitive structure that tended toward cartels; and (5) high government involvement, because of the economic importance of the industry and because of its health and environmental side-effects. Although this industry accounted for no more than 3 or 4 percent of gross national product (GNP) in the typical Western country, it had a strategic impact on as much as 40 percent of the economies of those countries. Many macroeconomic and industry-specific forces influenced the financial performance of the worldwide chemicals industry: volatility in upstream commodities prices (especially oil), GNP growth, inflation, technological innovation, merger and consolidation among competitors;[1] and changing attitudes toward safety and pollution.

Observers characterized the industry as having two main segments: commodity chemicals (having relatively low margins and highly cyclical demand) and specialty chemicals (with higher margins, and less cyclical demand). Over the past 10 years, almost all the major competitors in this industry had dramatically restructured their commodity chemicals segments in pursuit of higher margins and had emphasized investment in the specialty chemicals segment. Ironically, in the late 1980s, the commodity segment actually performed better for most of these firms, because of the restructuring, than did the specialty sector. Even more ironic was the fact that the specialty sector, which was supposed to be the relatively less cyclical, suffered as badly in the recession of 1990–91 as did the commodity-chemicals sector.

THE COMPANY

At the beginning of 1991, Rhône-Poulenc ("the Group" or RP) was probably the seventh-largest competitor in the worldwide chemicals industry, with 1990 sales of FF78 billion (about US$15 billion). It had attained this scale through an aggressive program of acquisition and restructuring and now contained five major sectors: health products (e.g., human and animal pharmaceuticals), agrochemicals (e.g., insecticides and herbicides), organic and inorganic intermediates (i.e., chemicals used in the production of other products), fibers and polymers (e.g., nylon yarn), and specialty chemicals (e.g., surfactants). Exhibit 1 presents a breakdown of sales, operating margin, assets, and capital spending by sector.

In 1991, analysts expected about half the firm's sales and profits to come from health products, because of rapid internal growth and acquisition in pharmaceuticals and because of a severe slump in the firm's four other chemicals-related business sectors. The pharmaceuticals sector had optimistic prospects for growth and profits; the large uncertainty in the firm's future stemmed from its chemicals components.

---

[1]The industry leaders were not immune to hostile takeover threats. In May 1991, Hanson Trust, a well-known corporate raider, announced that it had acquired 2.8 percent of the shares of Imperial Chemicals of the United Kingdom. By September, ICI had undertaken a restructuring in an effort to evade Hanson, but, as of the time of this case, Hanson had not withdrawn.

Senior Management

Outside analysts characterized the senior management of Rhône-Poulenc as relatively young, ambitious, and bright. None of the top seven executives was older than 53. The presidents of the chemicals and agro sectors had doctorates in chemical engineering. Two other sector presidents (specialty chemicals and health) had master's degrees in business and economics. Most of the sector presidents had served with the company for the bulk of their careers.

Jean-René Fourtou, chairman of the Group, was 51 years old. After graduating from École Polytechnique,[2] he began his career as a consultant in 1963 with Groupe Bossard, a leading French general-management consulting firm. Nine years later, he rose to *directeur-général* and, during 1979–86, was *président* and *directeur-général* of Bossard. Exhibit 2 gives a summary of Fourtou's business approach written by him when he was president of Bossard. In 1986, Fourtou was appointed *président* and *directeur-général* of Rhône-Poulenc, at a time when that company had sustained a decline in both its earnings and sales. As of September 1991, he served on the boards of directors of IBM France and Société Générale, the third-largest bank in France. Fourtou cited his membership in the Racing Club de France as his major pastime.

RP's chief financial officer was Jean-Pierre Tirouflet, age 41. After studying economics and politics in college and graduate school,[3] he worked for the French government for eight years. By 1991, he had served with Rhône-Poulenc for nine years. Outside observers regarded Tirouflet's corporate finance group to be one of the sharpest and most innovative in Europe. The group had pioneered the design of several varieties of nonvoting equity securities and of unusual acquisition terms.

Strategy

Management pursued RP's goals (see quotations at the beginning of this case) with a five-point strategy calling for "rigorous management," competitive research and development, a high level of capital expenditures (at 9 percent of sales), the use of acquisitions to seize shares of market, and improvements in the qualifications and teamwork of employees. In early 1991, management declared its intention of reducing the firm's debt/equity ratio from $0.9\times$ at the end of 1990 to $0.5\times$ by the end of 1993, selling about FF8 billion of nonstrategic assets by the end of 1992, and laying the groundwork for partial privatization by 1994.[4]

Management's concern over cyclicality had spurred a heavy investment in life sciences, a sector that was less capital intensive and less cyclical than basic chemicals, or even than the French and U.S. economies. The company maintained:

---

[2]École Polytechnique, widely regarded as the élite institution of higher education in France, dominated in the ranks of corporate and government leaders in France.

[3]Tirouflet's degrees included the Diplôme de L'Institut d'Études Politiques de Paris and the Diplôme d'Études Supérieurs de Sciences Economiques.

[4]S. Bridges, "Rhône-Poulenc Company Report," Merrill Lynch Capital Markets, July 10, 1991.

When [the Life Sciences sector is] combined with the Group's other strategic family—composed of the organic and inorganic intermediates, the high value-added specialty chemicals, and the fibers and polymers sectors—they create a closely related group of highly integrated industrial companies, capable of weathering the cyclical fluctuations in a particular area.[5]

The strategy also sought to broaden the geographical base. Before 1982, the company was highly dependent on operations in two countries, France and Brazil. Because of recent acquisitions, the Group in 1991 generated nearly 25 percent of its revenue from the United States and had strengthened its presence in Europe and Asia, thereby reducing the influence of Brazil. Exhibit 3 summarizes the firm's financial performance by region.

The assessment by outside analysts of management's unfolding strategy was at best mixed. One journalist described Fourtou's program as trying to "turn a perennial loser into a global giant."[6] One securities analyst opined that the sales and market-share goals of the company seemed inconsistent with programs of asset sales and debt reduction; in all likelihood, the goals would be gained only by continued aggressive acquisition.[7]

GOVERNMENT OWNERSHIP AND POLICY TOWARD RHÔNE-POULENC

The French government controlled 100 percent of the shareholder voting rights in the Group. Capital stock was divided into common stock class A (held entirely by the French government) and class B, which was divided into nonvoting investment certificates (CIPs) and voting certificates; the French government also held the voting certificates. The general public held the CIPs and could trade them on the Paris Bourse and the New York Stock Exchange (NYSE). On December 31, 1990, the book value of capital stock consisted of the following:

Common shares, class A		79.4%
French government	56.9%	
Crédit Lyonnais (state owned)	9.4%	
Assurances Générales de France (state owned)	6.8%	
Other, state owned	6.3%	
Preferred investment certificates (CIPs) class B		20.6%

The French government nationalized Rhône-Poulenc (along with other large firms) on February 11, 1982, and, in doing so, snatched the firm nearly from the jaws of bankruptcy. François Mitterrand had been elected president of France, and the Socialist Party swept into power in May 1981 after 23 years of dominance of national politics by the political Right. Between 1981 and 1985, the combined losses of the French state-owned enterprises

---

[5]1990 annual report, Rhône-Poulenc, p. 7.
[6]S. Siwolop, "Rhône-Poulenc: Gallic Grandeur," *Financial World*, July 24, 1990, pp. 23–25.
[7]Bridges, "Rhône-Poulenc Company Report."

grew by FF90.8 billion. These enterprises badly needed restructuring, but the national budget could not afford the heavy investment. The election of an opposition majority (the Right) to the National Assembly in 1986 prompted legislation providing for the privatization of 60 state-owned enterprises. Public stock offerings privatized a number of prominent firms, but the stock market crash in 1987 and the return to power of the Socialists in 1988 arrested the privatization program.

The French government had intervened directly and indirectly in the French chemicals industry since the 1920s in pursuit of, often conflicting, goals to: (1) achieve national self-sufficiency in chemicals, (2) strengthen French firms' abilities to compete in world markets (i.e., create "national champions"), (3) (re)industrialize France, (4) control the internationalization of the French economy, (5) reduce unemployment, and (6) diversify the industrial base of the country. The Socialist Party program contained an explicit industrial policy that divided all chemicals production among three major enterprises: Altochem in base chemicals and plastics, CdF Chimie in petrochemicals and fertilizers, and Rhône-Poulenc in specialty areas, such as pharmaceuticals, agro-chemicals, fine chemicals, and synthetic fibers.

The government's ninth five-year plan (1984–88) specifically identified fine chemicals and pharmaceuticals as strategic focuses for investment and expansion. It also identified the need to convert production away from basic chemicals, in which competition was intense.

In pursuit of national policies, French state-owned enterprises had been active buyers of foreign businesses since the late-1980s. One journalist commented:

> France's state-owned industry today bears a passing resemblance to a large drifting jellyfish. It constantly changes shape in response to the currents around it, sometimes shedding bits of itself and sometimes stretching out a tentacle to scoop up a tasty corporate morsel that drifts by.[8]

From 1988 to 1990, Rhône-Poulenc had made eight major acquisitions and many small ones and had executed major programs to divest operations in the media and textiles sectors. The most notable acquisition was the purchase of Rorer Group, Inc., in 1990, because of both its size and its novel terms. The acquisition dramatically increased the scale of RP's pharmaceuticals business, raising sector 1989 sales by 34 percent to US$3.1 billion. Part of the acquisition terms called for Rhône-Poulenc to make up any shortfall in Rhône-Poulenc Rorer's (R-P Rorer) stock price should it fall below a specified level by 1993. The Group estimated that, at the end of 1990, the maximum liability under these contingent value rights (CVRs) was FF4.96 billion. Exhibit 4 gives details on the CVRs. Fourtou said that this acquisition would be Rhône-Poulenc's last big one for some time, and that the company planned more than a dozen sales of assets to pay the acquisition costs.

On September 11, 1991, Mitterrand announced that he had authorized the government to sell off minority stakes in state-owned companies, but he insisted that the state would remain the majority shareholder (with 50.1 percent of voting rights) wherever it held a majority. He justified this change in policy on the grounds that many state firms needed fresh capital to cut their crippling levels of debt, that other sources of finance for na-

---

[8]William Dawkins, "Breakdown of the Old Frontiers," *Financial Times,* July 23, 1991.

tionalized companies were drying up, and that the move would improve relationships with the European Commission in Brussels, which opposed state aid to industry. Many observers cited Rhône-Poulenc as a likely candidate for partial privatization. The timing and amount of privatization were, however, uncertain. Analysts speculated that full privatization was likely after the next French legislative elections in 1993, when the Socialist Party could lose its legislative majority. If the French government were to privatize the company, the government would sell off both its own (voting) shares and voting rights to accompany the nonvoting common stock.

Because of competing budgetary demands, the French government was unwilling to make additional cash investments in the common stock of the company, but indirectly, the government supported the company's need for equity infusions. First, in 1989 the government exchanged a 35 percent interest in a diversified pharmaceuticals company, Roussel-UCLAF,[9] in return for new shares of Rhône-Poulenc common stock. This move increased the company's equity base and permitted additional borrowings.

Second, the government encouraged the company to innovate in issuing quasi-equity securities (i.e., securities that would represent pecuniary equity interests in the company but would not dilute the government's voting control). These exotic securities had the qualities of both debt and equity, a characteristic pioneered by Rhône-Poulenc. Examples included participating preferred stock, called *titres participatifs* (for which the dividend varied in relation to the firm's performance), warrants on the participating preferred stock, issuance of the participating preferred to American investors as American Depositary Shares, and issuance of subordinated perpetual debt. Exhibit 4 describes these various securities in detail.

A challenge facing Rhône-Poulenc management in the 1991 capital-market environment was that investor demand for these kinds of securities was low. To stimulate interest in such securities would require a high dividend. One commentator also noted, "RP's nationalized status has been a handicap to its access to funding."[10]

FINANCIAL PERFORMANCE

Exhibit 5 contains a summary of key RP financial measures for recent years and reveals that performance in 1990 punctured a string of steady annual improvements. Exhibit 6 gives a comparison of Rhône-Poulenc's financial results with a sample of competitors. Exhibit 7 provides forecasts of financial performance by industry sector.

One analyst opined that 1990 "was a disastrous year for the group with nothing going in its favor . . . the year's results [are] dreadful."[11] Although sales rose from FF73 billion to FF78 billion, net profits fell by 54 percent, from FF4.1 to FF1.9 billion. If one were

---

[9]Roussel-UCLAF had 1990 sales of FF13.05 billion derived from human pharmaceuticals, nutrition products, and veterinary pharmaceuticals. The German chemicals company Hoechst owned a majority interest in Roussel's shares.

[10]D. Hunter and D. Jackson, "Rhône-Poulenc: Hey Big Spender," *Chemical Week*, March 14, 1990, p. 42.

[11]P. Tattersall, "Rhône-Poulenc—Net Loss in 90Q3, but This Should Represent Bottom," *Barclays de Zoete Wedd*, December 4, 1990.

to strip out capital gains and restructuring provisions from the analysis, profits would have slipped 66 percent. Accordingly, in January 1991, the Group's board of directors cut the firm's dividend on its preferred stock by 39 percent.

The slump of 1990 resulted largely from (1) increased interest expense associated with funds raised to finance the acquisition of Rorer, (2) unfavorable currency movements, (3) continued deepening of the Brazilian recession, (4) a drop in capital gains from asset sales, (5) a full-blown recession in Europe and the United States, (6) growing overcapacity in many product lines, leading to intensified price competition, and (7) a weakening export market to the Far East, where massive investments by Western chemical companies were starting to meet that region's demand. The dilution resulting from Rhône-Poulenc's swap of shares for the French government's interest in Roussel-UCLAF worsened the decline in performance on a per-share basis.

In the first half of 1991, Rhône-Poulenc's performance was even worse than the year before. Profits were 54 percent lower, because of the same factors that drove the slump in 1990. Management insisted, however, that the second half of 1991 would show a marked improvement as the chemical industry began a cyclical rebound.

STOCK MARKET RESPONSE

Exhibit 8 presents two graphs regarding the Group's performance in the capital markets. The first graph gives the share price of Rhône-Poulenc's publicly traded CIPs since 1985 and reveals that the CIPs were a much more volatile investment than the CAC-General, a large index of shares listed on the Paris Bourse. The first graph also reveals that the CIP price underperformed the market over the five years.

The second graph in Exhibit 8 plots the cumulative excess returns[12] on the Group's stock to both private investors and the French government. By August 1991, the cumulative excess return on the CIPs was +6 percent; for the French government, it was −11 percent. The difference in returns between these two equity groups arose from a 5-FF higher dividend received by the private investors and from special tax benefits on those dividends.

Over the past year, analysts had been divided on the appropriateness of the firm's share price.[13] The following table presents highlights of analysts' opinions:

---

[12]The excess return is the difference between Rhône-Poulenc's actual monthly investment return (reflecting stock-price changes and dividends) and a hypothetical *expected* return estimated by multiplying a beta of 1.30 times the return on the CAC index. The beta was derived from relevering the average asset beta of other chemicals companies. The return on the French government shares assumes that, if these shares had been traded in a competitive capital market, they would have been priced identically with the CIPs.

[13]Rhône-Poulenc's CIPs were traded on the NYSE as American depositary shares (ADS). One ADS had a claim to 0.50 of a CIP. The ADS was increasingly used by non-American corporations as a way of accessing the U.S. equity markets without having to comply completely with the stringent American financial-disclosure requirements. A trust owned the underlying Rhône-Poulenc CIPs and, in turn, issued claims against its securities portfolio, in the form of ADSs. The company's preferred participating A shares (PSSA) were also traded in the United States as ADSs, where one ADS would have a claim to 0.25 of a PSSA share.

Analyst and Date	Share Price	Stock Market Index	Comment
M. Glen, Lehman Brothers, August 13, 1990	CIP = FF310 ADS = $14.65 US$1 = FF5.28	CAC = 474.95 S&P 500 = 339	The bad news outweighs the potential good news at the moment for the stock.
P. Tattersall Barclays de Zoete Wedd, March 1, 1991	CIP = FF295.4	CAC = 465	. . the outlook for the chemicals activities continues to be somewhat clouded as a result of the economic implications of the gulf crisis . . . [but] sharp appreciation of the £ or a sharp fall in interest rates would lead to a substantial upwards revision of this forecast. We believe that the recent outperformance by the shares has more than discounted the likely good news in the shorter term.
J. Wilbur, Smith Barney, April 12, 1991	CIP = FF365 ADS = US$17 US$1 = FF5.65	CAC = 488 S&P 500 = 379	BUY: Annual growth of 25 percent at Rhône-Poulenc Rorer will cause Rhône-Poulenc itself to grow at rates above 15%. . . . Undervalued stock based on highly valued pharmaceutical subsidiary. . . . The chemical part of R-P, representing sales of $11 billion, is valued in the market at negative $12 per share. . . . There is considerable appreciation potential . . . trends to lower interest rates in France will stimulate that market, resulting in an upward P/E adjustment. On the negative side, the major ownership position of the French government in Rhône-Poulenc makes it likely that the stock will trade at a lower P/E than if it were a completely public company.
S. Bridges, Merrill Lynch July 10, 1991	CIP = FF332.9 ADS = US$14.50 US$1 = FF6.15	CAC = 463 S&P 500 = 377	Speculative Investment/Long-Term Buy: Considering the potential for earnings recovery [the shares] are speculatively attractive.
Allan Campbell, Value Line, September 6, 1991	CIP = 406.8 ADS = $16.00 US$1 = FF5.91	CAC = 492 S&P 500 = 389	Recent bottom-line results don't give a true indication of Rhône-Poulenc's earnings power. Last year, earnings per share . . . would have fallen to near break-even had it not been for gains on asset sales. This year, reported earnings are likely to slip lower, primarily because gains on divestitures will be down and interest expense up. . . . Next year we look for operating results to be up across the board as economic growth accelerates again in Europe. . . . Rhône's strengths are in pharmaceuticals and agrochemicals. . . . The company has a relatively small exposure to commodity chemicals. Nonetheless, Rhône's chemical earnings are down sharply in the current industry downturn as demand and prices have fallen for specialty, as well as for commodity, chemicals. The dividend could be cut again in 1992, if our earnings estimate is on target.

Since January 1991, Rhône-Poulenc's shares had outperformed the market, rising by over 50 percent. Trading volume also was up: the daily float was about 0.5 percent, more than double the preceding year. In September 1991, the median P/E ratio on the Paris Bourse was about $11 \times$.

FINANCIAL FORECAST

Exhibits 9–12 provide a forecast of financial performance. This forecast assumes no financial effects from possible privatization after 1993 and no payment under the contingent value rights (CVR) in 1994. Analysts focused on two key drivers of financial performance: sales growth and operating margin as a percentage of sales. Recognizing that Rhône-Poulenc consisted of two main businesses, the model breaks out the growth and margin assumptions for the life-sciences business (pharmaceuticals, which were dominated by Rorer) and the chemical businesses. Exhibit 9 summarizes specific assumptions used in the forecast. These assumptions are consistent with forecasts presented by leading securities analysts.

The forecasted balance sheet in Exhibit 11 reveals that Rhône-Poulenc would require almost FF19 billion in new external funds within the next 18 months; the cumulative external need would rise to about FF30 billion by 1995. Capital spending net of depreciation, additions to net working capital, and refinancing of maturing debt cause the need. Exhibit 13 contains information summarizing current capital-market conditions.

CONCLUSION

The strategic and financing issues facing RP's senior management in September 1991 could be summarized in a few questions. First, how appropriate were management's goals for enlarging the firm? Second, were these growth goals consistent with other goals for profitability and payment of dividends? Third, were these goals attainable, and were they consistent with past performance? If not, why would a departure from past experience be justified? Fourth, whose interests did the goals and strategy serve: management, the French government, public investors, the company in general? Fifth, did a better strategy and financing policy exist that would *(a)* sustain management's vision for the company, *(b)* create competitive advantage for the company, and *(c)* create shareholder wealth? What were the key trade-offs in considering any alternative policies? Sixth, when should changes in policy and financing tactics be implemented? Seventh, was the company fairly valued at the present CIP price of FF427? What constraints or opportunities did this price level imply? Finally, how should the firm raise the FF38 billion in new capital externally over the next five years?

EXHIBIT 1 Financial Performance by Business Segment (FF millions)

	Basic Chemicals (organic and inorganic intermediates)	Specialty Chemicals	Fibers and Polymers	Health	Agro	Others	Inter-group Adjustment	Total
1987								
Net sales	26,892	Combined	8,877	14,243	8,574	1,817	(4,244)	56,159
Depreciation	(1,446)	with	(661)	(587)	(316)	(154)	—	(3,164)
Operating margin	2,909	Basic	(305)	1,324	477	(826)	(33)	3,546
Identifiable assets	21,908	Chemicals	7,247	12,991	8,881	5,329	(252)	56,104
Capital expenditures	2,184		768	2,184	433	56	—	4,991
1988								
Net sales	18,861	8,009	13,957	15,671	9,733	2,016	(2,733)	65,334
Depreciation	(1,050)	(467)	(1,124)	(669)	(357)	(151)	—	(3,818)
Operating margin	2,767	384	1,115	1,567	779	(714)	(18)	5,880
Identifiable assets	15,039	7,030	12,017	15,787	9,570	6,063	(475)	65,031
Capital expenditures	1,894	860	1,164	1,259	512	212	—	5,901
1989								
Net sales	19,673	10,167	15,857	17,766	10,527	1,761	(2,683)	73,068
Depreciation	(1,259)	(626)	(1,161)	(781)	(399)	(139)	—	(4,365)
Operating margin	2,862	512	1,174	1,874	1,202	(526)	(35)	7,063
Identifiable assets	16,771	12,548	12,351	21,030	9,263	7,037	(468)	78,532
Capital expenditures	1,845	1,884	1,191	1,262	560	274	—	7,016
1990								
Net sales	18,040	14,086	14,132	23,869	10,168	1,383	(2,868)	78,810
Depreciation	(1,367)	(870)	(1,111)	(1,014)	(435)	(136)	—	(4,933)
Operating margin	1,573	(63)	340	2,465	1,321	(235)	17	5,418
Identifiable assets	16,551	17,020	12,103	37,181	9,943	11,088	(66)	103,820
Capital expenditures	2,214	1,394	1,206	1,908	567	249	—	7,538

Source: Company annual reports.

EXHIBIT 2 Summary of Jean-René Fourtou's Business Approach

Opening up to outside markets, reconverting a business, inventing new structures, discovering new ways of boosting productivity, gearing society to computerization, letting the people take charge of their own affairs, ensuring job satisfaction by making work relevant to people's cultural background and social outlook. . . . This is change, and we are all agreed as to the vital need of controlling and adapting ourselves to it.

First-hand experience of the workings of administrative bodies and large companies indicates, more often than not, the urgent need for change, for it is evident that the scope of freedom is becoming progressively restricted, while stagnation prevails.

As may be seen, there is no lack of studies, ideas, new directions, even ready-made solutions; however, the adoption and enforcement of decisions is constantly thwarted by the increasing complexity of systems, and by the inherent resistance to change in each structure and in the struggles for influence and power.

Bringing about change is, clearly, a subtle art, the success of which is governed by three cardinal principles:

- Clear-cut policy decisions (i.e., management's unshakable determination to follow its action through to the end).
- Accurate assessment of the time factor: at the project development stage, this means having ambitious concepts tempered by reason, and at the implementation stage it implies maintaining a fine balance between the company's capacity for absorption and the work tempo which will, nevertheless, be dictated by any action undertaken.
- Involvement of the full energies of a specialist task force, which remains as independent as possible from the issues of daily management, while maintaining constant and direct contact with the decisionmakers.

For effective change to be made, the appropriate methods must be used, in conjunction with the skills and abilities of qualified experts.

These principles and methods are well known to consultants, and particularly to organization consultants. Their professional know-how derives from their broad and varied experience of changes they have been called upon to introduce in highly different situations and companies . . .

J.-R. Fourtou

Source: "Brossard Consultants," a pamphlet about the firm published in 1985.

EXHIBIT 3 Financial Performance by Geographical Area (FF millions)

	France	Other Countries in Europe	United States and Canada	Brazil	Others	Eliminations	Consolidated
1987							
Net sales	36,450	19,802	5,582	5,015	1,662	(12,352)	56,159
Operating margin	2,290	564	453	295	161	(217)	3,546
Identifiable assets	30,154	12,464	4,495	8,164	1,188	(361)	56,104
1988							
Net sales	39,336	22,555	8,484	6,481	2,240	(13,762)	65,334
Operating margin	3,343	1,029	714	789	84	(79)	5,880
Identifiable assets	34,839	13,617	10,972	4,708	1,334	(439)	65,031
1989							
Net sales	42,569	25,016	10,498	7,854	2,627	(15,496)	73,068
Operating margin	4,322	1,001	936	650	98	56	7,063
Identifiable assets	36,339	17,319	14,275	4,894	6,087	(382)	78,532
1990							
Net sales	41,053	27,714	16,697	4,953	3,598	(15,205)	78,810
Operating margin	2,342	1,682	1,472	(229)	90	61	5,418
Identifiable assets	42,272	20,019	34,231	5,116	2,052	(320)	103,820

Source: Company annual reports.

EXHIBIT 4   Description of Securities

---

1. Long-term debt

Outstanding: FF6,962 mm bank debentures.
FF13,374 mm bank borrowings.
FF 20,336 mm total.
Unused multicurrency lines of credit totaled FF5.991 billion.

Currency: French francs 54%, U.S. dollars 29%, deutsche marks (DM) 6%, British pounds 4%, Dutch guilders 3%, other 4%.

Lease financing: Included in bank borrowings were capitalized lease obligations.

Repayment:

	Debentures	Borrowings	Leases	Total
1992	1,243	718	232	2,193
1993	882	1,128	193	2,203
1994	1,804	1,554	168	3,526
1995	1,465	1,697	128	3,290
1996 +	1,568	7,161	395	9,124
Total	6,962	12,258	1,374	20,336

Rate: Weighted-average interest rate on December 31, 1990, was 9.9% per year.

Options: Debentures included an amount of FF1,000 million carrying subscription rights to participating shares. This specific issue included 500,000 debentures issued at 2,000 francs nominal value and repayable at par in 1994.

Exotica: Debentures included a US$50 million Eurobond issue whose reimbursement value was tied to the $/DM parity.

Swaps: Total interest-rate swaps and foreign-exchange swaps covered notional amounts of FF1.552 billion. Debt balances reflect the effect of these swaps.

2. Participating loans

Description: These loans receive both a fixed rate of interest and a supplemental payment. The exact formula for the supplemental payment varies with each loan and lender. For instance, in the case of the Caisse des Dépôts et Consignations, the supplement is based on dividends distributed by Rhône-Poulenc.

Rate: After giving effect to supplemental payments, the weighted-average rate of interest on all participating loans was 14.4%.

Maturity: The participating loans are due as follows:

Lender	Issued	Due	Amount
Pool of banks	1982	1997	FF200mm
Pool of banks	1983	1998	147
Crédit National	1983	1991–98	390
Caisse des Dépôts	1983	1991–2013	93
Total outstanding			FF830mm

EXHIBIT 4 *(continued)*

3. Amortizable preferred securities

Currency:	U.S. dollars.
Outstanding:	$1,200 million (nominal amount). Rhône-Poulenc actually received only US$891.3 million after issuance costs of US$17.9 million.
Rate:	9.19%. For the first 15 years, periodic payments to vary at a slight premium to LIBOR (London Interbank Borrowing Rate). Thereafter, payments to be at a nominal rate into perpetuity.
Pay-in-kind provision:	If the payment of cash interest would imperil the Group's financial condition, the company could pay the interest with similar securities, also having no due date, but with a higher rate of interest.
Subordination:	Subordinated to the complete payment of creditors.
Date of issue:	July 13, 1988 (private placement).
Date of maturity:	No stated due date or maturity. Rhône-Poulenc had no obligation to redeem the securities except that, if a dividend was paid to any other shareholder of the group, but not to holders of these securities, the entire issue would become due and payable.
Trust and option:	Upon issuance of these securities, an independent trust was established by the investment banker. This trust, which was legally protected from invasion by the Group, invested in U.S. Treasury zero-coupon notes. At the end of 15 years, the holders of the securities had the option of exchanging their securities for the assets in the trust. The Group had the right, but not the obligation, to purchase these securities from the trust at their then fair market value.
Amortization:	The company amortized the par value of these securities against the gain in the underlying zero-coupon notes. As the value of the underlying notes accreted, the principal amount of the preferred was, in essence, repaid. The notes accreted, and the preferred amortized, as follows (French francs): 1991, 187 mm; 1992, 216 mm; 1993, 233 mm; 1994, 251 mm; 1995, 270 mm; after 1995, 3,082 mm.
Company comment:	*The Group has determined that these securities are in substance equivalent to equity instruments. However, in accordance with the SEC rules requiring presentation of temporary equity apart from stockholders' equity, the Group has classified the proceeds of the issue outside stockholders' equity under the caption "Amortizable Preferred Securities."*

4. Contingent value rights

Amount:	20,900,663 contingent value rights.
Investors:	Minority shareholders in Rorer Group, Inc.
Issuance:	In connection with the August 1990 acquisition of a majority interest in Rorer Group, Inc.
Description:	Entitled the holder to the right in 1993 (or 1994 at the option of Rhône-Poulenc) to a cash payment equal to US $49.13 (or US$53.06 if payment was in 1994), less the higher of the value of the Rhône-Poulenc Rorer share at that date and US$26.00. If the value of the Rhône-Poulenc Rorer share was equal to or greater than $49.13 (or $53.06), no payment would be made.
Listing:	American Stock Exchange in New York.
Liability:	At date of issuance, the market value of the rights was FF1,306 million, and the Group's maximum liability was FF5,165 million. At the end of 1990, the market value of the rights was FF844 million, and the Group's maximum liability was FF4,960 million. The foreign-exchange risk of the maximum liability was hedged.

EXHIBIT 4   *(continued)*

5. *Participating shares* (Titres participatifs)

Outstanding:	781,308 shares, par value FF782 million.
Rate:	Minimum of 10% consisting of 7% fixed component and 3% variable component indexed to consolidated sales. Paid on October 1 of each year. Rate paid in 1990 was 11.4%.
Redemption:	Not mandatorily redeemable, except in the case of liquidation.
Call provision:	The Group had the option of redeeming the shares between 1995 and 2003 at prices varying between FF3,000 per share (1995) to FF5,000 (2003).
Issuance:	620,000 shares in 1983. In October 1988, some debenture holders exercised an option for 161,308 shares.
Listing:	Paris Bourse.

6. *Capital equity notes*

Outstanding:	US$300 million (FF1,997 million).
Issued:	December 16, 1986. On the Eurodollar market.
Rate:	Semiannual payments at a rate slightly higher than LIBOR. Last payment in 1990 was at the annual rate of 8.1875%.
Pay-in-kind provision:	If cash interest payment would imperil the Group's financial condition, the Group could satisfy the obligation with similar securities, but paying a higher interest rate.
Maturity:	No fixed due date.
Subordination:	Subordinated in payment to the Group's creditors and to payments on participating shares.

7. *Preferred participating nonvoting share series A (PSSA)*

Outstanding:	4,025,000 shares.
Issued:	November 1989, at a price of FF465, in an international offering. Total amount was US$300 million. Simultaneous offerings in the United States, Europe, and Japan.
Warrants:	Issued in units with detachable warrants to purchase an additional 16,100,000 shares. Four warrants permitted the purchase of one PSSA at an exercise price of FF535. The warrants would expire on the earlier of December 31, 1992, and the date the company ceased to be a "public sector company." The warrants were listed for trading on the SEAQ International market in London.
Maturity:	No fixed maturity date.
Dividend:	Paid annually on August 15. Equal to the sum of a fixed portion (FF7.50 per PSSA) plus a variable portion equal to 150% of the greater of:

1. the dividend approved on ordinary A shares or
2. $A \times B/C \times D/E$, where:

A = 0.5484% of the FF465 par value of the PSSA,
B = latest year's net income,
C = net income for 1988,
D = sales for 1988, and
E = sales for latest year.

The dividend could not reduce the net income available to common shareholders to below FF1 million. The fixed portion of the annual payment was cumulative. The variable portion was not.

Listed:	SEAQ International (London, where it was traded as International Depositary Shares) and NYSE (traded in the form of American Depositary Shares where 1 ADS = 0.25 PSSA).

EXHIBIT 4   *(concluded)*

---

8. Common stock and preferred investment certificates (CIPs)

Description:	Capital stock was divided into common stock ordinary shares A and preferred stock class B. Preferred shares B were split into nonvoting preferred shares (preferred investment certificates B) and voting certificates. The voting certificates had no par value, and no compensation was paid to the Group upon their issuance. The French state held 77.52% of the voting rights; nationalized financial institutions held 22.48% of the voting rights.
Outstanding:	Common stock: 45,183,250 shares (FF100 par). CIPs: 11,720,676 shares (FF100 par).
CIP yield:	A fixed dividend of 5% of their par value (5 francs), plus a variable dividend of an amount equal to the dividend on ordinary shares A. The fixed dividend was paid if the net income of the Group was positive, and it was not cumulative.
CIP listing:	Paris Bourse since 1989; MONEP (Marché des Options Négotiables) since 1989; NASDAQ, New York, since 1987 (quoted as American Depositary Shares, where 1 ADS = 0.5 CIP); NYSE since 1989. Rhône-Poulenc was the first French company to be quoted on the NYSE.
CIP issuance:	5,671,658 CIPs issued in March 1987 in France and the United States. International units offered in November 1989. One unit = 1 ADS + 1 warrant to buy 1 ADS.
Lead underwriters:	Société Générale, Merrill Lynch, Shearson Lehman Hutton (international offering); Merrill Lynch, Drexel Burnham Lambert, Sogen Securities (American offering).
Transfer agents:	SICOVAM (France), Bank of New York (United States).
Custodian:	Banque Worms (for ADS).

Sources: Company 1990 annual report, Standard & Poor's *NYSE Stock Reports,* and Standard & Poor's *Standard Corporation Record.*

EXHIBIT 5 RP's Historical Financial Performance

	1983	1984	1985	1986	1987	1988	1989	1990
Net sales (FF millions)	43,115	51,207	54,712	51,642	56,159	65,334	73,068	78,810
Income before priority dividend	98	1,820	2,127	2,008	2,360	3,457	4,112	1,942
Preferred remunerations	(30)	(65)	(69)	(96)	(167)	(579)	(1,076)	(845)
Net income available to common	68	1,755	2,058	1,912	2,193	2,878	3,036	1,097
Total assets	39,009	43,312	45,288	53,726	60,069	67,688	83,182	109,147
Common equity	4,601	6,444	8,712	12,358	16,108	18,807	21,272	21,047
Contingent value rights	—	—	—	—	—	—	—	4,960
Preferred securities	—	—	—	—	—	5,400	4,974	4,239
Preferred equity in subsidiaries	—	—	—	968	801	909	868	769
Minority interests	—	960	968	1,086	1,448	1,331	2,624	6,021
Equity plus other funds	4,601	7,404	9,680	14,412	18,357	26,447	29,738	37,036
Nonvoting preferred shares	—	541,667	610,000	3,660,000	10,041,368	11,720,675	11,720,675	11,720,675
Voting common shares	34,643,378	34,643,378	34,643,378	36,643,378	36,643,378	36,643,378	36,643,378	40,169,310
Return on net assets*	8.5%	11.4%	10.2%	5.0%	4.9%	8.0%	8.4%	5.1%
Return on total capital†	9.8%	13.1%	16.2%	7.7%	6.8%	11.8%	12.1%	8.1%
Growth of sales (%)	—	7.6%	40.8%	10.5%	27.7%	2.2%	17.3%	22.4%

* Net assets are defined as total assets less current liabilities.
† Total capital is defined as long-term debt plus all preferred stock plus common equity.

859

EXHIBIT 5 *(concluded)*

	1983	1984	1985	1986	1987	1988	1989	1990
New long-term (LT) borrowings	3,630	3,443	3,234	4,809	1,615	1,967	4,111	7,930
Repayment of LT borrowings	(1,623)	(3,673)	(2,827)	(2,679)	(2,237)	(1,626)	(2,144)	(6,854)
Increase (decr.) in short-term (ST) borrowing	—	—		(585)	1,380	(2,177)	5,523	6,458
Issuance of ordinary A shares	—	—	—	—	2,439	—	—	4,685
Issuance of participating shares	1,000	300	1,135	193	132	279	1,712	—
Issuance of capital equity notes	—	—	—	1,984	—	—	—	—
Issuance (amortization) of preferred shares	—	—	—	968	—	5,419	700	(187)
Dividends paid:								
Class A	0	(88)	(470)	(470)	(408)	(614)	(787)	(905)
Preferred remunerations paid	(30)	(65)	(69)	(88)	(270)	(300)	(933)	(916)
Total financing activities	2,977	(83)	1,003	4,132	2,651	2,948	8,182	10,211
French government LT bond yield	13.63%	12.54%	10.94%	8.44%	9.43%	9.06%	8.79%	9.34%
French corporate lending rate	18.95%	18.85%	17.77%	16.28%	15.82%	15.65%	16.01%	13.00%
Net profits/sales	0.2%	3.6%	3.9%	3.9%	4.2%	5.3%	5.6%	2.5%
Sales/assets	1.11	1.18	1.21	0.96	0.93	0.97	0.88	0.72
Assets/common equity	8.48	6.72	5.20	4.35	3.73	3.60	3.91	5.19
Return on common equity	1.9%	28.6%	24.5%	16.3%	14.6%	18.4%	19.3%	9.2%

Sources: Company annual reports; International Monetary Fund; *Value Line Investment Survey.*

EXHIBIT 6 Comparative Financial Data for Selected Diversified Chemicals Companies, 1990 Results

	Rhône-Poulenc (France)	Akzo (Holland)	Imperial Chemicals (U.K.)	Montedison (Italy)	Dow (U.S.)	Du Pont (U.S.)	Monsanto (U.S.)
1990 sales (US$ billions)	14.47	9.47	23.1	13.97	19.8	40.0	8.99
Operating margin (w/o deprec.; %)							
1985–90 average	13.7	12.4	13.3	13.3	22.9	18.7	18.2
1991 estimate	14.0	12.5	11.0	12.0	19.0	18.5	20.5
1992 estimate	15.5	13.5	12.5	12.5	20.0	19.0	21.5
1994–96 estimate	17.0	14.0	15.0	13.0	21.0	21.0	20.0
Net margin (%)							
1985–90 average	4.0	4.6	6.0	2.8	9.3	5.8	5.6
1991 estimate	2.1	3.9	4.5	0.2	5.0	5.6	7.0
1992 estimate	3.2	4.8	5.7	1.3	5.2	6.3	7.8
1994–96 estimate	4.7	6.2	7.1	2.5	6.4	6.6	7.1
Return on capital (%)							
1985–90 average	9.3	11.5	13.0	7.6	15.1	11.1	9.6
1991 estimate	6.0	8.0	8.5	3.0	8.0	10.5	13.0
1992 estimate	8.0	9.5	10.0	4.5	8.5	11.0	15.0
1994–96 estimate	11.0	12.0	11.0	7.0	11.5	12.5	16.0
Dividend payout (%)							
1985–90 average	39	33	42	32	42	48	53
1991 estimate	84	45	69	N.M.F.	75	52	39
1992 estimate	62	31	55	67	66	48	36
1994–96 estimate	65	31	47	35	54	50	37
Sales growth rate (%)							
Past 10 years	N.A.	1.0	5.0	N.A.	7.5	6.5	5.0
Past 5 years	8.0	9.0	9.5	N.A.	12.5	2.5	9.5
1988–96 estimate	3.0	3.0	2.0	5.5	7.0	6.0	10.0
Capitalization (%)							
Debt	45	19	25	52	35	27	29
Preferred stock	17	0	0	8	1	1	0
Common stock	38	81	75	40	64	72	71
Average tax rate (%), 1991 estimate	28	34	35	N.M.F.	35	45	33
Statutory tax rate (%)	37	35	35	36	34	34	34
Beta	N.Av.	0.95	0.90	0.75	1.25	1.10	1.15

Sources: *Value Line Investment Survey,* 1991; *Country Profiles,* 1991, *The Economist* Intelligence Unit.

EXHIBIT 7 Forecasted Financial Performance for Selected Industries

	Change in Operating Margin (%)	Average Annual Sales Growth Rate (%)	Return on Total Capital (%)	Dividend Payout Ratio (%)
Basic chemicals				
1991 estimate	−0.5%	−3.0%	10.0%	59%
1992 estimate	+1.0	+5.0	11.5	53
1994–96 estimate	+1.5	+7.0	13.5	47
Specialty chemicals				
1991 estimate	+0.2	+1.0	12.0	34
1992 estimate	+0.5	+10.0	12.5	34
1994–96 estimate	+0.5	+11.5	13.0	33
Diversified chemicals				
1991 estimate	−0.6	−0.5	10.5	55
1992 estimate	−0.5	+5.0	10.5	46
1994–96 estimate	+1.5	+8.4	13.0	40
Pharmaceuticals				
1991 estimate	+0.6	+10.4	+30.0	+49
1992 estimate	+1.0	+8.7	+26.5	+48
1994–96 estimate	−0.5	+28.3	+28.0	+47

Source: *Value Line Investment Survey*, 1991.

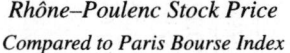

Rhône–Poulenc Stock Price
Compared to Paris Bourse Index

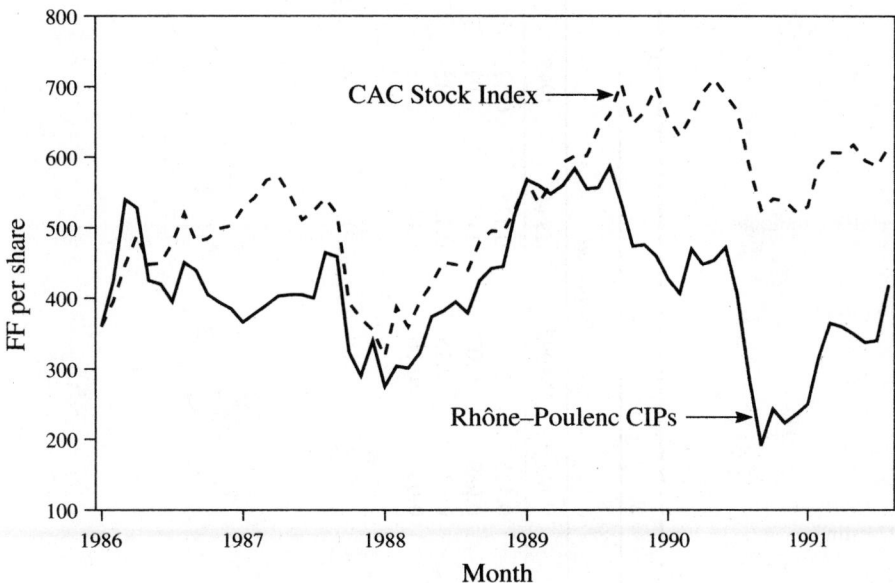

Cumulative Excess Returns
On Rhône–Poulenc Equity

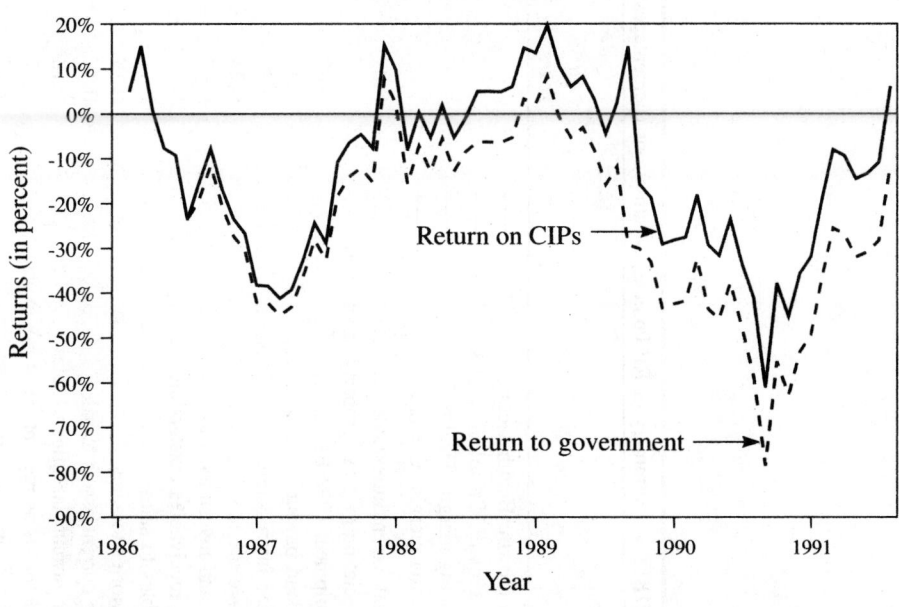

Source of underlying data: Datastream, Inc.

EXHIBIT 9 Summary of RP Forecast Assumptions (percentages)

	All Years	Projected					
		1991	1992	1993	1994	1995	1996
Sales growth: Health sector	→	0.17	0.125	0.125	0.125	0.125	0.125
Sales growth: Chemical sectors	→	0.001	0.089	0.07	0.07	0.07	0.07
Operating margin: Health	→	0.14	0.13	0.15	0.15	0.15	0.15
Operating margin: Chemicals	→	0.05	0.06	0.06	0.06	0.06	0.06
Capital expenditures/sales	0.09						
Depreciation to gross property, plant, and equipment (PP&E)	0.073						
Dividend payout	0.3						
Melded interest rate	0.1						
Average tax rate	0.24						
Cash and investments to sales	0.07						
Days receivables outstanding	50.0						
Payables to sales	0.11						
Inventories to sales	0.19						
Other current assets to sales	0.1						
Other current liabilities to sales	0.18						
Tax deferrals as percentage of tax expense	0.37						
Market/book value, asset sales	1.25						

Source: Casewriter's estimates drawing on assumptions of securities analysts.

EXHIBIT 10 RP Forecasted Income Statements (FF millions, fiscal year ended December 31)

	Actual					Projected			
	1988	1989	1990	1991	1992	1993	1994	1995	1996
1 Sales: R-P Rorer	—	—	17,269	20,204	22,730	25,571	28,767	32,363	36,409
2 Sales: RP other	—	—	61,541	61,603	67,086	71,782	76,806	82,183	87,935
3 Net sales	65,334	73,068	78,810	81,807	89,815	97,353	105,574	114,546	124,344
Operating expenses:									
4 Production costs and exp.	42,634	46,621	49,900						
5 Admin. and selling exp.	12,385	14,521	17,605						
6 Depreciation	3,818	4,365	4,933						
7 Restruc. provision	617	498	954						
8 Total operating exp.	(59,454)	(66,005)	(73,392)						
9 Operating margin	5,880	7,063	5,418	5,909	6,980	8,143	8,923	9,785	10,737
Other income (expenses):									
10 Interest expense	(1,557)	(2,125)	(3,488)	(3,500)	(3,637)	(3,915)	(4,329)	(4,609)	(4,881)
11 Gains on asset sales	51	122	1,840	1,500	500	0	0	0	0
12 Amort. of intang. assets	(204)	(422)	(719)	(854)	(854)	(854)	(854)	(854)	(854)
13 Other income (expenses)	(65)	505	543	500	500	500	500	500	500
14 Affiliates' earnings	471	306	164	350	410	410	410	410	410
15 Earnings before taxes	4,576	5,449	3,758	3,905	3,899	4,284	4,651	5,233	5,913
16 Income taxes	(686)	(1,052)	(1,010)	(937)	(936)	(1,028)	(1,116)	(1,256)	(1,419)
17 Minority interests	(239)	(285)	(806)	(1,600)	(1,700)	(1,800)	(1,900)	(2,000)	(2,100)
18 Change in accounting	(194)	0	0	0	0	0	0	0	0
19 Net earnings	3,457	4,112	1,942	1,368	1,263	1,456	1,635	1,977	2,394

EXHIBIT 10 (concluded)

	Actual					Projected			
	1988	1989	1990	1991	1992	1993	1994	1995	1996
Dividends on:									
20 Pfd. equity in subs.	(55)	(73)	(54)	(50)	(60)	(70)	(75)	(75)	(75)
21 Amortizable pfd.	(254)	(561)	(428)	(496)	(496)	(496)	(496)	(496)	(496)
22 Participating shares	(95)	(110)	(115)	(123)	(135)	(146)	(158)	(172)	(187)
23 Capital equity notes	(175)	(196)	(154)	(154)	(154)	(154)	(154)	(154)	(154)
24 Pfd. particip. ser. A	—	(136)	(94)	(46)	(41)	(47)	(53)	(64)	(77)
25 Total pfd. stock divs.	(579)	(1,076)	(845)	(869)	(886)	(913)	(936)	(961)	(989)
26 Earnings to common	2,878	3,016	1,097	499	377	542	698	1,016	1,405
27 Divs. to class A shares	(550)	(641)	(422)	(102)	(74)	(112)	(149)	(222)	(313)
28 Dividends to CIP shares	(234)	(264)	(182)	(88)	(80)	(91)	(102)	(123)	(150)
29 Dividends to all common	(784)	(905)	(603)	(191)	(154)	(204)	(251)	(346)	(462)
30 Retentions of earnings	2,094	2,111	494	308	223	339	448	670	942
31 Number of A shares	36.643	36.643	40.169	40.169	40.169	40.169	40.169	40.169	40.169
32 Number of CIP shares	11.721	11.721	11.721	11.721	11.721	11.721	11.721	11.721	11.721
Results per share of common stock:									
33 Earnings per share (EPS), class A	58.29	61.15	20.15	8.49	6.14	9.32	13.46	19.58	27.07
34 EPS, CIP	63.29	66.15	25.15	13.49	11.14	14.32	18.46	24.58	32.07
35 Dividends per class A share	15.00	17.50	10.50	2.55	1.84	2.80	3.70	5.54	7.78
36 Dividends per CIP share	20.00	22.50	15.50	7.55	6.84	7.80	8.70	10.54	12.78

Source: Casewriter's estimates drawing on assumptions of securities analysts.

866

EXHIBIT 11 RP Historical and Projected Balance Sheets (FF millions; fiscal year ended December 31)

	Actual				Projected				
	1988	1989	1990	1991	1992	1993	1994	1995	1996
Assets:									
1 Cash	851	1,298	909	5,727	6,287	6,815	7,390	8,018	8,704
2 ST investments	1,806	3,352	4,418	—	—	—	—	—	—
3 Accounts receivable	11,719	9,980	11,156	11,206	12,303	13,336	14,462	15,691	17,033
4 Inventories	11,802	13,938	15,801	15,543	17,065	18,497	20,059	21,764	23,625
5 Other current assets	4,242	7,271	8,826	8,181	8,982	9,735	10,557	11,455	12,434
6 Total current assets	30,420	35,839	41,110	40,657	44,637	48,383	52,469	56,928	61,797
7 Investments and other	5,400	6,456	11,000	11,000	11,000	11,000	11,000	11,000	11,000
8 Gross PP&E	53,148	59,690	67,161	69,724	76,207	84,969	94,470	104,780	115,971
9 Accum. depreciation	(26,578)	(29,505)	(33,099)	(38,189)	(43,752)	(49,955)	(56,851)	(64,500)	(72,966)
10 Net PP&E	26,570	30,185	34,062	31,535	32,455	35,014	37,619	40,280	43,005
11 Intang. assets, gross	5,998	11,495	24,394	24,394	24,394	24,394	24,394	24,394	24,394
12 Accum. amortization	(700)	(793)	(1,419)	(2,273)	(3,127)	(3,980)	(4,834)	(5,688)	(6,542)
13 Intangible assets, net	5,298	10,702	22,975	22,121	21,267	20,414	19,560	18,706	17,852
14 Total assets	67,688	83,182	109,147	105,313	109,360	114,811	120,648	126,914	133,654
15 Bank overdrafts	1,826	2,987	2,647	2,647	2,647	2,647	2,647	2,647	2,647
16 Accounts payable	7,340	7,771	7,864	8,999	9,880	10,709	11,613	12,600	13,678
17 Currently due LT debt	1,051	1,077	2,447	2,071	2,011	2,060	3,408	3,212	3,050
18 Short-term borrowings	1,373	5,737	13,056	—	—	—	—	—	—
19 Restruct. provision	768	0	0	—	—	—	—	—	—
20 Other current liabs.	9,312	12,777	15,847	14,725	16,167	17,523	19,003	20,618	22,382
21 Total current liabs.	21,670	30,349	41,861	28,443	30,705	32,940	36,672	39,078	41,757

EXHIBIT 11 *(concluded)*

	Actual					Projected			
	1988	1989	1990	1991	1992	1993	1994	1995	1996
22 New external financing:	**0**	**0**	**0**	**11,128**	**14,619**	**20,758**	**26,762**	**32,304**	**38,239**
23 LT debt: Debentures	6,044	6,403	6,962	5,719	4,837	3,033	1,568	768	268
24 LT debt: Banks	5,658	8,179	13,374	12,656	11,528	9,974	8,277	6,580	4,080
25 Participating loans	1,003	911	830	780	729	679	628	578	527
26 Deferred income taxes	1,364	1,694	2,080	2,427	2,773	3,153	3,566	4,031	4,556
27 Pensions and restruc.	5,502	5,908	7,004	7,004	7,004	7,004	7,004	7,004	7,004
28 Minority ints. in subs.	1,331	2,624	6,021	6,021	6,021	6,021	6,021	6,021	6,021
29 Pfd. equity in subs.	909	868	769	769	769	769	769	769	769
30 Amortizable pfd. secur.	5,400	4,974	4,239	4,052	3,836	3,603	3,352	3,082	2,792
31 CVRs	0	0	4,960	4,960	4,960	4,960	0	0	0
Stockholders' equity:									
32 Participating shares	994	994	994	994	994	994	994	994	994
33 Capital equity notes	1,997	1,997	1,997	1,997	1,997	1,997	1,997	1,997	1,997
34 Particip. shs., ser. A	0	1,815	1,815	1,815	1,815	1,815	1,815	1,815	1,815
35 Pfd. inv. certif. B	1,172	1,172	1,172	1,172	1,172	1,172	1,172	1,172	1,172
36 Common stock class A	3,664	3,664	4,518	4,518	4,518	4,518	4,518	4,518	4,518
37 Paid-in capital	5,051	4,948	8,838	8,838	8,838	8,838	8,838	8,838	8,838
38 CVRs' valuation adjust.	0	0	(3,664)	(3,664)	(3,664)	(3,664)	0	0	0
39 Retained earnings	5,194	7,420	7,910	8,218	8,441	8,780	9,228	9,898	10,840
40 Translation reserve	735	(738)	(2,533)	(2,533)	(2,533)	(2,533)	(2,533)	(2,533)	(2,533)
41 Total stockholders' equity	18,807	21,272	21,047	21,355	21,578	21,917	26,029	26,699	27,641
42 Liabs. and equity	67,688	83,182	109,147	105,313	109,360	114,811	120,648	126,914	133,654
Memo:									
43 Dividends to all common shs.	784	905	603	191	154	204	251	346	462
44 Invest. in PP&E	(5,901)	(7,016)	(7,538)	(7,363)	(8,083)	(8,762)	(9,502)	(10,309)	(11,191)
45 Other cap. expends.	(1,636)	(2,708)	(5,022)	—	—	—	—	—	—
46 Purchase of companies	(2,048)	(9,270)	(9,562)	6,000	0	0	0	0	0
47 Asset sales	694	648	4,541	6,000	2,000	0	0	0	0
48 Depreciation expense	3,818	4,365	4,933	5,090	5,563	6,203	6,896	7,649	8,466
49 Addns. to net wkg. cap.	8,744	(3,260)	(6,241)	12,966	1,718	1,511	354	2,053	2,190
50 Incr. new external fin.	—	—	—	11,128	3,491	6,139	6,004	5,542	5,935

Source: Casewriter's estimates drawing on assumptions of securities analysts.

EXHIBIT 12 RP Ratio Analyses of Historical and Projected Financial Statements (fiscal year ended December 31)

	Actual					Projected			
	1988	1989	1990	1991	1992	1993	1994	1995	1996
Measures of profitability (%):									
1 Operating profit margin	9.0	9.7	6.9	7.2	7.8	8.4	8.5	8.5	8.6
2 Average tax rate	15.0	19.3	26.9	24.0	24.0	24.0	24.0	24.0	24.0
3 Taxes defd./tax exp.	81.0	31.4	38.2	37.0	37.0	37.0	37.0	37.0	37.0
4 Return on sales	5.3	5.6	2.5	1.7	1.4	1.5	1.5	1.7	1.9
5 Return on equity*	18.4	19.3	9.2	6.4	5.9	6.6	6.3	7.4	8.7
6 Return on total capital	11.8	12.1	8.1	7.2	8.3	1	8.9	9.2	9.6
7 Return on net assets	8.0	8.4	5.1	4.8	5.6		6.7	7.0	7.4
8 Return on assets	5.1	4.9	1.8	1.3	1.2		1.4	1.6	1.8
Measures of financial leverage:									
9 Debt/equity ratio	70.0	96.4	155.5	137.8	143.1	.+	147.3	154.8	160.4
10 Debt/total capital	41.2	49.1	60.9	57.9	58.9	60.5	59.6	60.7	61.6
11 EBIT/interest (×)†	3.8	3.3	1.6	1.7	1.9	2.1	2.1	2.1	2.2
Measures of asset utilization:									
12 Sales/assets	0.97	0.88	0.72	0.78	0.82	0.85	0.88	0.90	0.93
13 Sales growth rate	16.3	11.8	7.9	3.8	9.8	8.4	8.4	8.5	8.6
14 Assets growth rate	12.7	22.9	31.2	−3.5	3.8	5.0	5.1	5.2	5.3
15 Cash and invest./sales	4.1	6.4	6.8	7.0	7.0	7.0	7.0	7.0	7.0

EXHIBIT 12 *(concluded)*

	Actual					Projected			
	1988	1989	1990	1991	1992	1993	1994	1995	1996
16 Days in receivables	65.5	49.9	51.7	50.0	50.0	50.0	50.0	50.0	50.0
17 Payables to sales (%)	11.2	10.6	10.0	11.0	11.0%	11.0	11.0	11.0	11.0
18 Inventories to sales (%)	18.1	19.1	20.0	19.0	19.0%	19.0	19.0	19.0	19.0
19 Other curr. assets/sales (%)	6.5	10.0	11.2	10.0	10.0%	10.0	10.0	10.0	10.0
20 Other curr. liabs./sales (%)	14.3	17.5	20.1	18.0	18.0%	18.0	18.0	18.0	18.0
21 Annual deprec./gross PP&E (%)	7.2	7.3	7.3	7.3	7.3%	7.3	7.3	7.3	7.3
22 Amort./gross intangibles (%)	3.4	3.7	2.9	3.5	3.5%	3.5	3.5	3.5	3.5
23 Changes in PP&E to sales (%)	13.2	9.0	9.5	3.1	7.2%	9.0	9.0	9.0	9.0
Measures of liquidity:									
24 Quick ratio	0.66	0.48	0.39	0.60	0.61	0.61	0.60	0.61	0.62
25 Current ratio	1.40	1.18	0.98	1.43	1.45	1.47	1.43	1.46	1.48
Miscellaneous performance measures:									
26 EPS growth A shares (%)	28.7	4.9	−67.0	−57.9	−27.7	51.9%	44.4	45.5	38.2
27 EPS growth B shares (%)	2.8	4.5	−62.0	−46.4	−17.5	28.6%	28.9	33.2	30.4
28 Dividends/net income (%)	27.2	30.0	55.0	38.2	40.9	37.6%	35.9	34.0	32.9

* In this calculation, "equity" includes participating shares, capital equity notes, participating preferred shares A, the CIPs, and the common A shares.
† EBIT = Earnings before interest and taxes.

Source: Casewriter's analyses of Exhibits 10 and 11.

EXHIBIT 13   Current Capital-Markets Information (as of September 18, 1991)

	Six-Month Interbank	One-Year Eurocurrency	Bank Prime
Short-term funds (less than 1 year):			
France	9.375%	9.25%	10.0%
United Kingdom	10.125	10.125	11.0
Germany	9.35	9.3	10.5
United States	—	—	8.0

	Domestic	Eurocurrency
Intermediate-term bonds:		
German (DM)	8.59%	8.99%
United States ($)	7.30	7.95
French (FF)	8.88	8.65
European currency unit	—	8.98
Long-term government bonds:		
Canada	9.66%	
Germany	8.47	
France	8.52	
United Kingdom	8.79	
United States	7.92	
Exchange rates:		
$1/Brazil cruzeiro	433.90	
$1/FF	5.69	
United States financial markets:		
Median price/earnings ratio of stocks (S&P 500)	21×	
91-day Treasury-bill rate	5.16%	
30-year Treasury-bond rate	7.92	
Moody's Aaa-rated corporate-bond yield	8.70	
Moody's A-rated corporate-bond yield	9.25	
Moody's A-rated preferred-stocks yield	9.00	
Geometric-mean equity risk premium	5.60	
Arithmetic-mean equity risk premium	8.40	

	1991	1992
Forecasted inflation rates:		
France	2.9%	3.1%
United States	4.0	3.6
All OECD*	4.4	3.8
European Community	5.0	4.5

* Organization for Economic Cooperation and Development.

Sources: *The Wall Street Journal Europe; Le Monde; Financial Times; OECD Economic Outlook*, July 1991; *1990 Yearbook*, Ibbottson Associates